Amerikanischer Postwagen

R. Weibezahl del.

An American stage coach such as was used between New York and Philadelphia about 1790. It followed the canvas covered "Flying Machines." 8vo. Lith. Col. Dutch.

A History of Travel in America

in

America

Being an Outline of the Development in Modes of Travel from Archaic
Vehicles of Colonial Times to the Completion of the First Trans-
continental Railroad: the Influence of the Indians on the Free
Movement and Territorial Unity of the White Race: the
Part Played by Travel Methods in the Economic Conquest
of the Continent: and those Related Human Experiences,
Changing Social Conditions and Governmental Atti-
tudes which Accompanied the Growth of a
National Travel System

BY

SEYMOUR DUNBAR

With two maps, twelve colored plates and four hundred illustrations

TUDOR PUBLISHING COMPANY

NEW YORK   1937

PRINTED IN THE UNITED STATES OF AMERICA
BY VAN REES PRESS, NEW YORK

To L. D.

PREFACE

A story of national growth does not simply recite the results of human endeavor: it is more deeply concerned with the character of the people discussed, and with the ideals, motives and methods underlying their acts.

Understanding of history is not gained through mere acquaintance with what was done. It is obtained by comprehension of the purpose and manner of the doing. Those individual figures and throngs of mankind who inhabit the pages of written history should not be manikins or mummies, but living men enacting their daily deeds, vitalized with the spirit that moved them while they were indeed here. We should be able to see them; to hear their cries of fear or delight; to smile at their revelry; feel anger at their evil and deceit, regret at their blunders, pride in their worthy accomplishments. Only by coming thus close to the past—by knowing it to be part of our own lives instead of looking upon it as a museum of curiosities—can we apply its value as a guide to ourselves.

Doubtless it is no longer possible to tell in words and pictorially portray, with reasonable completeness, the historical conditions considered in these volumes. That this should be so is cause for regret, since the story of those pioneer ideas, struggles and devices out of which grew a nation in the social and economic sense—rather than in a political sense—is the foundation history of the country.

We have now reached a period sufficiently removed

vii

from the pioneer constructive era to see it in its entirety, and, through our ability in that regard, to profit somewhat by the experiences of those earlier generations. They—just as we of to-day—displayed occasional wisdom in their joint undertakings; were often careless; sometimes quite blind; and at times permitted themselves to be swayed by desires whose indulgence wrought harm to them. But in one particular—during their upbuilding of a transportation system—they differed widely from present-day Americans. They sought to create facilities for movement and communication which should meet previous and desperate needs; they built for themselves and their own short day. We are beginning to do much more than that. We are looking ahead, both for the sake of ourselves and for those who are to come after us.

It therefore appears that the underlying thought and basic plan of the inexperienced pioneers, out of which grew the system they made and bequeathed to us—and which we are still using—is not altogether such a thought and economic plan as fits our later desire and determination. A conflict between old conditions and new ideas has resulted. Various methods and practises which developed out of the pioneer procedure have been outgrown, and no longer fit the age into which they have survived. We are now seeking to rid ourselves of the undesirable parts of our inheritance, with resolution so to do, and are likewise trying to avoid the making of similar mistakes while dealing with the same large subject.

It follows that a study of the pioneers, and of that work of theirs which has come to be of such importance to ourselves, may be of aid to us amid our present problems. If the following pages present some past conditions whose intimate relationship to the world of to-day could otherwise have been forgotten, and if they suggest the application of certain principles to our present and future affairs, then the work of preparing them will have been repaid. Nations—like individual men—must struggle over the road of the pilgrim's progress.

In preparing the accompanying volumes reliance has been placed, wherever possible, on original and contemporaneous material for text and illustration. Sources for the text have been files of early newspapers; various collections of manuscripts and documents in libraries, historical societies and elsewhere; diaries, letters and printed chronicles of pioneers; narratives in state and local histories; maps; state and governmental records; and information contained in earlier publications of a particular sort, the titles to some of which are given in an appended bibliography.

The illustrative material, with its attendant notes, is selected and arranged to form a flowing and connected story of its own, independent of the text. Yet at the same time the pictorial narrative is designed as a commentary on and explanation of the text. Technical description of the original prints and other material will be found in a proper place.

I wish to acknowledge my obligation to my friends Carl Burger, George Marriott, John Price Jones, Charles Fuess, Griffis Rhys Jenkyn, Franklin Harris, George Mather Richards, Frank P. O'Brien, Dexter Cook, Hillard H. Weer, Thomas Embly, Phanor Eder, Edward Broderick and Leslie Quirk for aid in connection with the preparation of this work.

My thanks are due to the American Antiquarian Society; to the British Museum; the Congressional Library; the State Libraries of Indiana, New Jersey, New

PREFACE

York and Ohio; the libraries of Boston, Cincinnati, Indianapolis, Newark, New York City and Providence; the Society Library of New York City; the University Libraries of Columbia, Harvard, Princeton, Wyoming and Yale; and the Historical Societies of Connecticut, Indiana, Long Island, New York, Ohio, Oregon, Pennsylvania and Wyoming, for information obtained from those institutions or the use of books and documents contained in their collections.

I wish also to acknowledge my obligation to the antiquarians Messrs. Robert Fridenberg, Emil Sauer, Charles Everitt, Edward Eberstadt, Edward Gottschalk, Joseph Sabin, P. Stammer, Oscar Wegelin and Henry O'Leary of New York City, Messrs. Rosenbach of Philadelphia and Messrs. Goodspeed of Boston, for their professional aid over an interval of years, in searching out and securing for me, in America and Europe, the historical illustrative material herein reproduced.

S. D.

New York City,
October, 1914.

x

CONTENTS BY CHAPTERS

CONTENTS BY CHAPTERS

CHAPTER V

CHAPTER VI

CHAPTER VII

CHAPTER VIII

CHAPTER IX

CONTENTS BY CHAPTERS

CHAPTER X

CHAPTER XI

CHAPTER XII

CHAPTER XIII

CONTENTS BY CHAPTERS

CHAPTER XIV

CHAPTER XV

CHAPTER XVI

CHAPTER XVII

CHAPTER XVIII

CONTENTS BY CHAPTERS

CHAPTER XIX

CHAPTER XX

CHAPTER XXI

CHAPTER XXII

CONTENTS BY CHAPTERS

CHAPTER XXIII

CHAPTER XXIV

CHAPTER XXV

CHAPTER XXVI

CONTENTS BY CHAPTERS

CONTENTS BY CHAPTERS

CONTENTS BY CHAPTERS

CHAPTER XXXIII

CHAPTER XXXIV

CHAPTER XXXV

CHAPTER XXXVI

CONTENTS BY CHAPTERS

CONTENTS BY CHAPTERS

CONTENTS BY CHAPTERS

CONTENTS BY CHAPTERS

CHAPTER XLVIII

CHAPTER XLIX

CHAPTER L

CONTENTS BY CHAPTERS

CHAPTER LI

CHAPTER LII

CHAPTER LIII

CHAPTER LIV

CONTENTS BY CHAPTERS

Key to Abbreviations

A list of the abbreviations used in the technical descriptions of the engraving, size, origin, date and other features of the original prints, drawings, manuscripts, documents, broadsides, maps, and similar material reproduced for illustrative purposes is here given. The technical description, in each case, follows the general description in the List of Colored Plates or List of Illustrations.

Sm. . . . . Small.
L. . . . . Large.
12mo. . . . . . . Duodecimo.
8vo. . . . . Octavo.
4to. . . . . Quarto.
F. . . . . Folio.
W. . . . . Engraved on wood.
S. . . . . Engraved on steel.
C. . . . . Engraved on copper.
A. . . . . Aquatint.
M. . . . . Mezzotint.
Lith. . . . . . . Lithograph.
Col. Lith. . . Lithograph printed in
        colors.

Lith. Col. . . Lithograph colored
        after printing.
C. Col. . . . . Copper-plate colored
        after printing.
O. . . . . Original.
Dr. . . . . Drawing.
D. . . . . Document.
Ms. . . . . Manuscript.
B. . . . . Broadside.
Adv. . . . . . . Advertisement.
T. . . . . Type.
c. . . . . About.
Proof . . . . . Unpublished.
Amer. . . . . . American.

Names of countries other than America are not abbreviated. If the engraving was originally published in Germany, France, England, Scotland, Holland, Sweden, or elsewhere, it is so stated.

In any case wherein the original engraving or drawing had a blank margin of considerable or unnecessary width, a part of the blank paper surrounding the drawing or engraved surface has been omitted in the photographic reproduction, as an economy of space.

In a few instances wherein only one detail of the original engraving or map required display, that feature alone has been reproduced and the irrelevant part of the original is not shown. Such cases are indicated in the technical descriptions by the words "Section of."

Save for the exceptions stated, the material used for illustration is shown in original form and existing condition.

List of Colored Plates

LIST OF ILLUSTRATIONS

LIST OF ILLUSTRATIONS

LIST OF ILLUSTRATIONS

LIST OF ILLUSTRATIONS

LIST OF ILLUSTRATIONS

LIST OF ILLUSTRATIONS

LIST OF ILLUSTRATIONS

xxxiv

LIST OF ILLUSTRATIONS

LIST OF ILLUSTRATIONS

LIST OF ILLUSTRATIONS

xxxvii

LIST OF ILLUSTRATIONS

LIST OF ILLUSTRATIONS

LIST OF ILLUSTRATIONS

LIST OF ILLUSTRATIONS

xli

LIST OF ILLUSTRATIONS

LIST OF ILLUSTRATIONS

xliii

LIST OF ILLUSTRATIONS

LIST OF ILLUSTRATIONS

xlv

LIST OF ILLUSTRATIONS

LIST OF ILLUSTRATIONS

LIST OF ILLUSTRATIONS

LIST OF ILLUSTRATIONS

LIST OF ILLUSTRATIONS

1

LIST OF MAPS

List of Maps

List of Maps

A HISTORY OF
TRAVEL IN AMERICA

A HISTORY OF
TRAVEL IN AMERICA

CHAPTER I

A SUMMARY OF THE GENERAL FEATURES OF THE SUBJECT
AND AN INDICATION OF THE METHODS AND PURPOSES
HEREAFTER FOLLOWED IN ITS DISCUSSION

THE story of the upbuilding of our present methods of
travel and transportation is not a record of the development of a system for the carrying of commodities.
It is a history of the devices originated by the people
primarily for their personal use and comfort in moving
from place to place. Only after the early population had
occupied some new region by means of the crude and
primitive travel methods then in use were there any commodities to move or men to move them, and not until then,
after each successive surge of population into fresh territory, were existing methods of human travel expanded,
or new ones brought into being, for the purpose of also
transporting the material wealth those pioneers had
created.

The pioneer, no matter of what date or locality, was
always a traveller before he was a producer or shipper of
goods, and the common experience of the people, gained
on their journeys, was — save in one instance — the basis
on which future permanent routes and methods of travel

1

were planned and created. The one exception to this manner of evolution lay in the memorable demonstration that steam could be successfully used for the propulsion of travel vehicles. It was an instance wherein genius and reason overshadowed experience and precedent.

America has witnessed the introduction and development of much that has been permanently adopted into the travel methods of the world. That this is so is not, in all probability, due chiefly to the genius or inventive ability of the nation as a first cause. Its underlying reason, rather, can be traced to the extent and configuration of the country, to the period during which its population assumed goodly size, to certain political events of its history, and to a universal restlessness and desire for haste which for a long time has been so characteristic of its people.

For nearly a hundred and fifty years from the establishment of the first permanent settlements along the Atlantic coast there were practically no improvements made in the manner of moving over the face of the land. Almost all progress, in that respect, was confined to improving Indian trails which led into the wilderness, joining a newly-established farm or settlement to its neighbors, or turning old pack-horse paths into crude wagon roads as the settlements gradually grew into towns. During all that time the trend of travel, generally speaking, was north and south. True, there were a few adventurous spirits who plunged into the unknown and sometimes came back, bringing tales of distances beyond comprehension, of never-ending woods, of unknown mountains, rivers or lakes. But that was not travel. That was adventure, hunting or sheer folly, and the population, clinging to its little strip of a hundred and fifty miles in width along the coast, never seriously considered giving battle to the vastness which brooded beside them.

Yet those early Americans were commencing the conquest, though they did not know it. Each new farm established a little farther on, each new child born, helped toward the far-distant victory; but their chief contribution to the contest in which nature was at last to be defeated by man's demand for movement in speed and comfort lay in a gradual change in the character of the people themselves. As generation after generation slipped by, the separation of related families and an increase in the petty business affairs of the population multiplied the small journeys between different settlements and colonies. The time of the individual man became more valuable. The restlessness and hurry of the modern American, his desire for speed and a short-cut to his destination, found its small beginning. Gradually, also, the attitude of the people toward the wilderness changed. It still remained—as do its present fragments—a thing of awe, but it was better comprehended and less feared.

Then was introduced into the problem a political element which had no visible relevancy at the time, but whose relationship to the subject, from this latter-day standpoint, is apparent. The revolution against England, the confederation of the colonies that followed its success, and the acquirement of the immense region known as the Louisiana Purchase gave to the people a lesson in the necessity of united action, a better understanding of the common welfare, and a gradual realization that they had, for a task, the subjugation of a continent.

The period during and immediately following these political incidents in America marked the beginning of a new social, intellectual and industrial era throughout the civilized world. All that had happened theretofore, for a long time, was practically the last chapter of the Middle Ages. Modern life as we know it, and the use of human creative energy in a way designed to transform

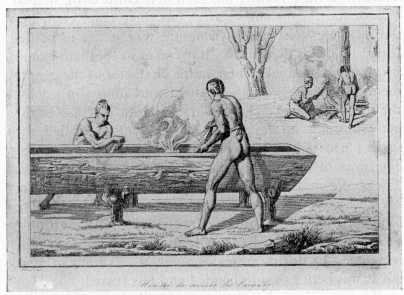

1.—Indians fashioning log canoes by means of fire and tools. Craft of this sort were the first vehicles used by English-speaking white colonists in America.

the circumstances of mankind, began then. It was the time of the great awakening; the birth of mechanical power; the beginning of an epoch whose unbelievable achievements would drive the mind to madness were they not, happily, so commonplace. We are scarcely human beings any more — merely spectators of a drama of development which has no visible end, and whose actors make up the plot as they go along.

From about 1785 until 1870 old methods and conditions went to the scrap heap, and the world, as we bump against it, was built all over again. And in no other one feature of man's affairs, perhaps, were greater or more extraordinary changes made than in his manner of travelling. In the revolution thus accomplished America, for obvious reasons, took a part that was very prominent. There were then but two continents — Europe and America — whose peoples found within themselves the necessity of change. Africa, Australia, South America and Asia were not ready. They were to escape the period of experiment and to install, at a later day, the tested and perfected systems brought to completion elsewhere. America had an advantage over Europe in that her problem was a larger one, and presented conditions more primitive and complex. Greater necessities resulted in bigger performances. To this may also be added the fact that Europe presented, to the impending evolution in travel, a multitude of comparatively small states whose size, peculiar geographical relationships and political quarrels definitely prevented the adoption of a uniform, continental system of communication development. America, on the contrary, offered in her compact mass and shape an ideal opportunity for the planning and methodical creation of such a system. But she did not see the chance, and threw it away. Twice — first when steamboats came into general use, and again in the early years of railroad building — those who had the shaping of public affairs failed to see the portent of what was taking place, and the petty jealousies of individual states were permitted to warp and disfigure the results of those vital years. Viewing the history of the whole American period under discussion — from about 1630 until 1870—it seems as though the clearest perception of the significance of events and of public necessity and intent was to be found most quickly, not in the minds of those whom history names as leaders of men, but in the collective understanding of the multitude. In their attitude toward the national need for travel facilities, during nearly all the big and important periods of the story, those famous ones have held aloof, remaining dull to opportunity and laggard in performance until the onrush of the nameless thousands swept them, like a torrent, into tardy action. Yet there were times when the multitude, as well as the head men of the country, could not understand its opportunities.

A somewhat comprehensive review is necessary—as far as the text of the record is concerned — to indicate the travel conditions existing during the first hundred and sixty years of the national history, together with the human experiences and social life which accompanied them. After those things have been considered the narrative need concern itself only with the comparatively short but important epoch between 1788-9 and 1868-9. During that interval of eighty years the transformation from archaic conditions to the vehicles we use to-day was brought about. Its chief features are better known than are those of the former era. The changes made within the last forty years have been, with few exceptions, refinements or better forms of what already existed; inevitable outgrowths of methods that preceded them. They do not call for extended comment. The pictorial part of the review must necessarily be devoted principally to the eighty years during which the revolution in methods of transportation occurred.

It is but reasonable to expect, in studying any epoch of human advancement, that certain things which took place during its continuance will stand out with prominence. That is true in this case, and we find in considering the development of travel in America and the relation of such development to the national progress that there were five events, or movements, within the years discussed, which occupy in its history positions very similar to those held by decisive battles in the story of a nation's political life. The five events were:

The governmental organization of the Ohio country and the Northwest Territory, and the beginning of a general migration to those regions, in 1787-1789;

A general public recognition of the value of steam as a means of propulsion, in 1807-1809;

The beginning of the railway building period, in 1828-1829;

Discovery of gold in the West and the general rush across the plains, in 1848-1849;

Completion of the first transcontinental railway, in 1869.

It is an interesting circumstance that these movements, each of which was largely due to the attitude and active participation of the whole population, followed one another at intervals of almost exactly twenty years. Whether or not they were merely a series of coincidences, or whether they had their source in some deeper condition that resulted in successive periodic eruptions of mental and physical energy affecting a whole people, may be left to experts in the psychology of a growing nation. However ably the phenomenon may be explained on the basis of chance, there will, perhaps, remain a lingering notion that it was not wholly due to accident.

The years that witnessed the slow transformation from primitive to modern conditions contained, of course, much more than is indicated by these five events. They are but later landmarks from which we may most easily take our

bearings from time to time. Nor should we fail to remember that progress, in the upbuilding of our present
system, did not take place with uniformity based on the
lapse of years. It often happened — almost always happened, in fact — that some one section of the country was
far ahead of the others in its travel facilities. This was
due either to earlier settlement, disparity of population,
inherited customs of the people or to the physical condition of the contrasted localities. The days of the stage-
coach, for instance, persisted in the West in full vigor

2.—A white traveller in a log canoe. Such a boat was propelled by the use of
a rude paddle or a pole.

for a generation after that vehicle had disappeared from
the eastern states. Only within the last few years have
conditions become substantially the same throughout
the whole three million square miles of continental area.

A HISTORY OF TRAVEL IN AMERICA

The story of our upward growth from the dugout canoe to the floating hotel of to-day, from the dog-sled and Conestoga wagon to the thunderbolts that we call express trains, wonderful as the progress has been, is not one which inspires us with pride alone. There are tragedies in it, blunders and blindness and mistakes innumerable. With few precedents to serve as guides, and sometimes with no precedents at all, the problem was not like the task of an architect who draws a plan and then builds his house accordingly. In this case there was no plan, for never at any stage of the task did there appear a man who was big enough both to picture the needs of the future and to compel the attention of the public mind to them. A few men, from time to time, had visions of those things that now exist in concrete form, and many others commanded the confidence of the people in matters of different nature, but it did not happen that those two qualities were ever combined in one early personality interested in the travel and transportation facilities of the nation.

The development of the system from its primitive conditions, as a consequence, was in large degree a history of feverish energy based upon incomplete experiment; the discarding of mistakes; shortsightedness; jealousy; and a lack of unity and coherence among the various parts of the system as they were at first created. When railroads came into use, for instance, the distance between New York and Washington was at first spanned by several companies, each of which adopted a track-width different from that of the others in order that the cars of one road could not run on the rails of its rivals. Some states would not permit railroads incorporated by them to cross their boundary lines into adjoining states.

Since this preliminary chapter is, in a sense, a series of suggestions designed as a glue to hold together all that comes after, it is desirable to refer to one other general aspect of the subject. Several times within the last hundred and twenty-five years the development of our travel system has been affected — usually to its serious disadvantage — by the operation of certain well recognized phases of American character. The traits that have had such an influence are the tendency of the public mind to concentrate all its attention on some one subject of spectacular or popular interest at the moment, to the exclusion of other matters often more deserving of thought; an intensity of public feeling which, when once aroused, fosters either a general optimism or corresponding pessimism; and the restlessness and desire for hurry at any cost that has been so prominent and so steadily increasing for about a century.

The exhibition of these traits has varied, and still does, in different periods, regions and cities. More than once it has happened that some circumstance or experience of easily recognized importance to the whole people has had a powerful effect, for a considerable time, in exciting one or more of those qualities. And whenever such an occurrence or condition of public affairs has coincided with a critical period in the history of our travel system the effect has always been noticeable, and often strange — from our present viewpoint. Sometimes the public mind has been made incapable of seeing an opportunity which, if realized and grasped, would have saved many years.

Again, when under the sway of an era of happy-go-lucky optimism, the people have tolerated or accepted much discomfort and danger in going from place to place, only to alter their attitude, suddenly manifest their dis-

10

3.—Large bark canoes were sometimes employed in bays and along the coast. Also showing a sailing vessel made by laying a deck on the transverse timbers which united two canoes. This principle was afterward used in small craft on interior rivers. See illustration No. 89.

pleasure at such undesirable conditions, and suggest the ending of them forthwith. That particular series of events is constantly recurring even until to-day. But the imposition, public awakening and compelling of drastic though necessary reform which is now occasionally apparent is attended with less of popular outcry than formerly accompanied such situations. We have become more self-contained, and, in addition, the transportation system in all its ramifications has learned that the comfort and safety of the traveller must be considered before all else.

The subject to which these pages are devoted is the foundation whereon the country, considered as a social and industrial organization, has been built. A few years ago — until as late a date as 1806 — the six or seven million people of America were contentedly visiting their friends, or moving about on business, in flatboats, dog-sleds, stage-coaches, strange wagons or canoes. Those were the only vehicles of travel and when they were not available, as was very often the case, the traveller walked or else rode upon a horse. To go from the Atlantic sea-coast to such remote regions as Cincinnati or St. Louis or Fort Dearborn — now Chicago — in those days meant a journey of many weary weeks, with possibly the loss of a scalp. Such a thing as a trip across the continent and back was not within the range of thought of the ordinary man. A vast undertaking like that, requiring years for its accomplishment, demanded the resources of the national government and an elaborate exploring expedition. When at last it was performed, the successful making of a transcontinental journey became the subject of a universal interest and acclaim. Books were written about it.

To-day we are annoyed if we are late for breakfast in

Chicago or Cincinnati after having left the Atlantic coast in the middle of the previous afternoon, and the railway apologizes, and returns part of our money. Also we are ninety millions instead of seven, and by the waters of the Pacific sit great cities but five days separated from their sisters of the East.

The stage-coach, canal-boat, canoe, dog-sled and prairie schooner, and the archaic steamboat and railway train also, have become fossils in the geology of modern life. But the tale of the part they played in the growth and development of the country still remains. It is the one story written by all Americans in collaboration.

In this present realm of four-day ocean steamships, of trains that dive beneath rivers or plunge through a thousand miles in twenty hours, of subways, motor-cars, submarine boats, and with the flying machine just beginning to dot the sky, we are privileged to remember, if we choose, that once upon a time the express boats on the canals maintained a speed of three miles an hour for day after day, and that the Pioneer Fast Line advertised it would rush its passengers through from Philadelphia to Pittsburgh in four days — and often nearly kept its word.

CHAPTER II

THE CONDITION AND APPEARANCE OF THE COUNTRY IN
EARLY DAYS — DIFFICULTY OF TRAVEL THROUGH THE
VAST FOREST — INDIAN TRAILS THE FIRST MEANS
AND BASIS OF LAND MOVEMENT BY THE WHITES —
TRAVEL BY WATER PREFERRED WHENEVER POSSIBLE —
HOW THE DIFFERENT TYPES OF CANOES WERE MADE
AND USED

ONE of the best records of the difficulties and methods
of American travel in the early days is contained in
a few words of a lately discovered document written in
1694.[1] In that year Benjamin Fletcher, Governor of His
Majesty's Province of New York, was planning an attack
on the French in Canada, and he called on his subordi-
nates for a report which should show the strength of the
enemy and by what route and method of travel he could
most easily reach them.

The answer to Governor Fletcher's demand, recently
brought to light, was written by William Pinhorne and
N. Bayard at New York, on July 25 of the year named,
and in it they said:

"It is Impossible to march with any party of men to
Canada by Land, either in winter or summer, but they
must passe a Considerable Part of ye way over ye Lake,[2]
ye Land on each side being extream steep and Rocky,

---

[1] Now in the New York Historical Society's collection.
[2] Lake Champlain.

14

mountains or els a meer morasse cumbred with underwood, where men cannot goe upright, but must creep throu Bushes for whole days' marches, and impossible for horses to goe at any time of ye year."

And in a letter written by Deputy Governor Hinckley of Plymouth Colony, about 1680, in which he appeals to the English officials in London for certain favors, he argues that the colony is entitled to what he asks because it was "the first that broke the ice, and underwent ye brunt, at our own charge, for the enlargement of his Majesties' dominions in this heretofore most howling wilderness, amidst wild men and wild beasts."

In these two quotations may be found the essential outlines of the conditions under which the people of America in those days, and for long afterward, lived and moved about the country. It was, indeed, a "most howling wilderness," so immense in its extent and unconquerable in its aspect that for more than a century and a half the white population sat, helpless and afraid, along a little strip of seacoast but a hundred and fifty miles in width. Yet the interior of North America is more easily accessible for travel, when approached and entered from the Atlantic seaboard, than is the corresponding region of any other continent.

There are few descriptions that were written in those very early days expressly to show the methods and hardships of travel. No doubt the lack of such narratives is due to the state of mind revealed by every people, in every period, toward those things that, to them, are commonplace and familiar. The Americans of two hundred and fifty years ago prepared many long and careful accounts of such things as they saw but once in a lifetime, but of records far more interesting to us, records illuminating the every-day conditions by which they were surrounded, they left but little that was set down with historical purpose. Most of our knowledge of the sort has been pieced together from fragments such as diaries and personal letters that have survived by accident.

The report to Governor Fletcher condenses into a few words certain conditions which dominated all travel in America from the time of its first permanent English oc-

4.—Indians building bark canoes in the forest. They were made from the bark of the birch, spruce or elm. The first white settlers at once adopted this conveyance, and used it in their westward advance for more than two centuries.

cupation until shortly before the Revolution. Those conditions were the use of water routes wherever possible; the uselessness of horses except near settlements or on beaten paths; the necessity of performing extended journeys on foot; and the extreme difficulty of progress through the woods. From the Atlantic Ocean to the Mississippi River — excepting some open country in the region now in part occupied by Indiana, Kentucky and Illinois — the land was covered by a continuous and almost unbroken forest. This wilderness was a thousand miles in extent from east to west, and about as long from north to south. Through it, in every direction, ran countless rivers and their tributaries.

Now this genuine primeval forest of America was very different in its character and appearance from any of the so-called primeval American woods of to-day. Centuries of alien human companionship affect the nature of forests in a marked degree. Those that still remain, even though covering areas never swept bare by the hand of man, have become, in a sense, civilized. The bulk of the wilderness, as it was until about 1790, was composed of trees that were from two to five feet in diameter. In those regions where the trees grew close together the girth gave way to height, and many reached a hundred and fifty feet into the air. Not until a tree was some six or eight feet in diameter was it considered a large one and those that attracted the attention of travellers, and were measured, were ten, twelve and sometimes even fifteen feet in thickness. There are numerous records of such monsters in the region east of the Mississippi now occupied by the Middle States.[1]

The earth beneath these huge growths was cumbered with fallen trees of all sizes and in all stages of decay. The hurricanes that now do occasional damage to towns and farms regularly wrought their havoc in the wilderness, and the confusion and tangle of the forest after the

[1] On Manhattan Island, New York City, there still survives one of those ancient monarchs. It is a tulip tree about ten feet in diameter at the ground, and six feet thick at the height of a man.

visit of such a storm can easily be pictured. Up from the earth made rich by ages of decayed vegetation sprang all manner of thickets and similar small growths that sometimes choked the lower spaces and were frequently bound together by a snarl of vines tough as wires or as big as a man's wrist. The rains or melting snows left such soil very slowly, and that is why there are frequent references, in olden records, to swamps or morasses which then occupied sections that have long since become dry and solid ground.

Such was the wilderness. It climbed the hills and mountains with its three hundred species of trees, and, stopping only for the passage of a river, resumed its sway upon the farther bank and still marched on. The little streams, completely covered, flowed under archways amid somber shadows.

The human habitants of this vast and gloomy region, in which the sun's rays in places never reached the ground, were two or three hundred thousand copper-colored natives,[1] whose numbers were too small to have made any impression on it, even had they been so inclined. But they were not so purposed. Instead, they were peculiarly in harmony and sympathy with their home, and desired that it should remain always as they knew it. The few agricultural clearings made by some of the Indians who lived north of the Ohio River, by the Iroquois in what is now central New York state, and elsewhere, were trivial gashes amid the universal woods. When the Indians travelled they moved by water if their purpose made it possible. For their land travel they created paths leading from one stream to another. In going across country they had a wonderful faculty for establishing routes that were,

[1] Early estimates of the number of the Indian population were much exaggerated.

18

in an economic sense, the best that could be chosen. An Indian overland trail always led the traveller to his destination in less time, or with fewer physical obstacles to overcome, than any other course that could be selected

5.—White men travelling through the wilderness by bark canoe. The craft is about to be unloaded and carried overland around the rapids.

between the two points which it connected. Practically the whole present-day system of travel and transportation in America east of the Mississippi River, including many turnpikes, is based upon, or follows, the system of forest paths established by the Indians hundreds of years ago.

These Indian trails — the corner-stone of land travel in America — were from twelve to eighteen inches in width, and sometimes, when they led through regions where the native travel was particularly heavy and long continued, were worn a foot deep by generations of soft

moccasins. Along such native highways the trained runners of the Indians are believed to have covered, on some
few occasions, almost a hundred miles between sunrise and
sunset.

Centuries after their paths were laid out a white man
named Nathaniel Hawthorne spoke of the use of them
made by his fellow white men of Massachusetts, and he
said: "The forest track trodden by the hob-nailed shoes
of these sturdy Englishmen has now a distinctness which
it never could have acquired from the light tread of a
hundred times as many moccasins. It goes onward from
one clearing to another, here plunging into a shadowy
strip of woods, there open to the sunshine, but everywhere
showing a decided line along which human interests[1] have
begun to hold their career . . . And the Indians
coming from their distant wigwams to view the white
man's settlement marvel at the deep track which he makes,
and perhaps are saddened by a flitting presentiment that
this heavy tread will find its way over all the land."

Hawthorne, had he not the mind of a poet, would
have put the idea more bluntly than he did, for it was no
mere flitting presentiment that the Indian of his day held.
It was a realization of the inevitable, acknowledged with
a despair that was felt, though unspoken. When Peter
Wilson, a Cayuga chief and very able Indian, visited New
York City in 1847 he delivered an address before the New
York Historical Society in which he referred to this same
subject. "The Empire State, as you love to call it," were
the words of the red chief, "was once laced by our trails
from Albany to Buffalo; trails that we have trod for centuries; trails worn so deep by the feet of the Iroquois that
they became your roads of travel, as your possessions grad-

[1] White men's interests is what he meant.

ually ate into those of my people. Your roads still traverse those same lines of communication which bound one part of the Long House[1] to the other."

The forest roads of the natives — first aids to such land travel as was attempted in early days by the white population of America — were not the only contribution made by the red men to the methods of the newcomers. From them, also, was taken the earliest form of water craft. The canoe, as used by the Indians and at once adopted by the whites, was of two very different forms. One was made from a log of suitable size, and the other from the bark of trees, especially the birch, spruce, or elm. The use of these two types, both by the Indians and afterward by white invaders, depended on the nature of the waters to be navigated, the desire for speed, and the frequent necessity of making portages from one stream to another. To some extent also the type was a geographical one, since the birch tree from the bark of which the best kind of bark canoe was made was not so plentiful in the South as in the North. For a heavy wooden canoe a fallen log was selected that, while still entirely sound, had become somewhat seasoned. Sometimes a standing tree was chosen by the Indians and felled by means of hatchets or fire. A section of the trunk from fifteen to thirty feet long and about three feet in diameter was then cut out and elevated from the ground, for convenience in carrying on the work. The log was shaped and hollowed by fire and cutting implements, and a very strong and serviceable, though rough and slow moving craft was obtained.[2] Such canoes were only adapted for lakes or single rivers. They were not taken overland from one water to another.

In fashioning the much more graceful, mobile and

[1] The Iroquois name for their Confederacy.
[2] Such a canoe became known by the colonists as a "pirogue," or "perogue."

21

6.—Building pinnaces, schooners and similar boats for travel along the coast. A scene in New Amsterdam during the Dutch occupancy, drawn from an early description and sketch.

useful birch-bark canoe the Indian selected his tree, made a straight vertical incision in the bark from near the base of the trunk to a spot at the height of his head, and then, with utmost care, peeled the bark from the tree by the aid of his knife. The framework of the craft was made of thin strips of cedar or spruce, and the birch-bark covering was attached to it by long, tough, slender, fibrous roots of the larch or balsam, which had previously been manipulated into extreme pliability. The various strips of birch-bark were also sewed together with the same sort of roots, and, before being fastened to the framework, were cut to the necessary pattern. The boat was then completed and given its final shape by the insertion of the many narrow and elastic ribs of spruce. All seams and cracks were covered with hot pitch from the balsam or spruce, and the canoe was water-tight and ready for use. Each tribe had

22

its own pattern or style for its canoes, and they varied in size from ten or twelve feet to fifty or sixty feet in length.

In this wonderful and famous boat, created by the woodcraft genius of the Indian from the materials immediately about him, he could travel for thousands of miles if need be. When he came to the head waters of a stream, where the current no longer afforded the few inches of depth necessary to carry him on his way, he could pick up his canoe and carry it for miles to another lake or river. In times of storm it served him as a snug shelter, and the forest was a factory where it could be repaired, or even replaced, at any time, with prompt delivery guaranteed.

> "Thus the Birch Canoe was builded
> In the valley, by the river,
> In the bosom of the forest;
> And it floated on the river
> Like a yellow leaf in Autumn,
> Like a yellow water lily."[1]

[1]Longfellow's lines, from "Hiawatha."

CHAPTER III

EARLY DEVELOPMENT GOVERNED BY THE NEEDS OF COMMUNITIES RATHER THAN BY KNOWLEDGE OR EXPLORATION — THE CENTERS FROM WHICH TRAVEL MOVEMENTS RADIATED — PRIMITIVE B R I D G E S — THE BUILDING OF SMALL BOATS BEGUN — A PHILANTHROPIC MISTAKE OF THE DUTCH — ORGANIZED MIGRATIONS OF LARGE COMPANIES OF PEOPLE AN IMPORTANT FEATURE OF THE FIRST CENTURY

THE many years of early exploration throughout the whole extent of the continent, carried on by brave individual adventurers and trappers chiefly from Spain and France before the year 1620 had almost no effect in shaping the after-history and development of America's travel system. The significance of any discovery in its relation to the subject, whether of route or method of travel, did not lie in the earliest information respecting that route or method, but in the popular impulse which was later — sometimes much later — to recognize its value and demand its use. It was necessity or comprehension, not knowledge; the needs or desires of the people rather than the exploits and achievements of individuals that always influenced the progress of the system and led on, little by little, to what now exists.

Hence it was that definite and visible progress in creating established methods of getting about the country did not begin until several English colonies had found firm foothold along the Atlantic coast. There were three motives that caused the first travel movements among the early population. One was the natural wish of a settlement to get into touch with its neighbors; another was need of betterment and growth; and the third was an occasional impulse, due to differences of one sort or another, which sometimes caused part of a colony to separate from the rest of it and go elsewhere to set up for itself.

The five principal localities from which radiated the first travel movements of the country were the Chesapeake Bay region; eastern Massachusetts; New York Bay and the Great River of the Mountains;[1] the Connecticut River valley and Long Island Sound; and Delaware Bay and the Delaware and Susquehanna Rivers. Three of these, the Chesapeake, New York and Delaware Bays, are important among those gateways already referred to through which the interior of the country is accessible from the Atlantic seaboard. But the two biggest entrances of all—the Mississippi River with its tributaries and the St. Lawrence River and the Great Lakes — were destined to play a much smaller part in the story than their importance warranted. For it so happened that the course of wars and politics in Europe produced conditions in America which deprived the Mississippi, the St. Lawrence River and the lakes of much of the influence they might otherwise have had in shaping the development of travel in America.

For generations five mutually jealous and conflicting groups were quarreling and fighting in an effort to get control of the continent. Each of three nations— France, Spain and England — was scheming to extend its own possessions and oust the others; the English colonies

[1] An early name for the Hudson River.

25

were trying to secure the administration of their own affairs; and the Indians were doing what they could to be rid of the lot or restrict their movements. The continuous control of the St. Lawrence by the French for nearly a hundred and fifty years after the arrival of the first English colonies, and the similar uninterrupted holding of the Mississippi by France and Spain until some time after the Revolution, long prevented the use of those two gateways as factors in any progress in which the English speaking inhabitants were interested. And the impulse

Penn's Pot Tavern; Landing; and Crossan's Academy.

7.—Vessels of considerable size were often built at a distance from the water and then drawn by oxen to the scene of their employment. While so moving they rested on trucks whose wheels were solid sections of hardwood trees. The scene here shown is in Philadelphia, where a large sailing boat is being finished at the side of a street.

which was finally to result in giving the Mississippi a place in the free and unobstructed travel system of the country came, not from its mouth, but from the upper valley of the stream, where a vigorous English speaking

26

population had become established and demanded the use of the river.

By about the year 1636, then, the movement of the population in and from all of the five regions named had

8.—The first sort of bridge used by white pioneers was a log thrown across a stream.

already begun and some action had been taken, both by the guiding minds of the colonies and by the people on their own impulse, to make such travel as easy and rapid as was possible under the conditions that surrounded them. On order of the authorities of Plymouth Colony all creeks and rivulets were bridged by felling trees across them, and canoe ferries were established for the passage of the larger streams. A few of the first canoes used by the people of Massachusetts Bay and Plymouth Colony were doubtless of the birch variety, bought from the Indians, but the prompt and unfortunate results of the unstable equilibrium of those canoes under the unpracticed guidance of the white pioneers quickly decided them to shift to the less graceful, but more calm and sedate type of craft such as was made by hollowing a log. It is not difficult to picture the inward emotion of an Indian as he sold a birch-bark canoe to a high hatted Pilgrim, and then, standing on the river bank, watched his customer step into the craft, only instantly to leave it from the other side and disappear head first into the water. Having fished out the white interloper the red man would buy back his canoe, enter it, and depart. After the adoption cf log canoes became general, and as population increased, trees especially suitable for canoe making were often marked by the authorities and protected by orders which forbade their use for any other purpose.

The difficulty of movement on the land, added to the location of the colonies on navigable waters and a growing desire to get into closer relationship with one another, led the colonists at an early date to the building of small sailing vessels suitable for navigating the many bays and short stretches of sea that separated them. These little boats were variously called pinks, pinnaces, ketches, schooners, lighters, shallops, sloops and periaguas, the names depending on differences in the rigging of the craft or the shape of the hull, or on local usage. The New England people were noticeably active in this boat making, and their first vessel, the *Blessing of the Bay,* was launched at Mystic in 1631. By 1635 six little ships had been built, and after the year 1640 the industry was well established at Boston, Gloucester, Plymouth, Salem, New Haven, New London, Dorchester, Scituate and Newport. During the forty-five years ending with 1676 no less than seven hundred and thirty vessels of some size had been created by Massachusetts colonists alone, and many hundred others by the men of Connecticut, Rhode Island and Maine. A considerable number of the first craft were devoted chiefly to fishing or to trade with England, the West Indies and the other colonies, but boats of some sort or another were kept by families living near water just as a modern farmer or business man keeps an automobile. They were used to travel in whenever circumstances permitted, and were not infrequently hired for that purpose.

It was not unusual for early boats to be constructed at a considerable distance from the water, since it was occasionally more economical of time and labor to move the completed vessel overland than slowly to carry heavy timbers to the water's edge. When a ship so built was finished the settlement gathered on an appointed day, placed her bodily in a stout, rude, cradle-like platform with wide wheels, propped her securely, and off she went on her first and only land voyage. Many oxen did the hard work of pulling, and in that way boats were at times hauled a mile or two before they reached a more easily navigated element.

By the year 1641 New England had a population of about twenty thousand, and even before that time the governing bodies of the various colonies and towns had recognized the need of improving the land routes between such settlements as were near together. The Massachusetts General Court, in 1639, declared there should be a road between Plymouth and Boston, and work on it was soon commenced. As yet there was no travel by land vehicles, and the few horses were used almost solely for farm purposes. The Indian trails, or traces as they were also called, still remained the best and established links of land communication. All such trails, however, were gradually being widened without official action and changed to roads by the increasing travel over them, and the governmental purpose was merely to hasten and improve a process that had already begun.

Probably the earliest important travel movement by a part of the population from one section of the country to another was that which resulted in the permanent establishment of English influence in what is now Connecticut. For this the Dutch at New Amsterdam were responsible, much to their later sorrow and regret. When the Dutch first planted themselves in the New World they chose, with canny foresight, three points of highest importance at that time, namely, Delaware Bay, the Hudson River valley and the Connecticut River valley. Having bought Manhattan Island for twenty-four dollars' worth of trifles that were sweet in the sight of the Indians, Governor Van Twiller indulged himself in a burst of generosity which was not thereafter repeated. He sent a party up to Plymouth to call on his English neighbors, and told the Pilgrims that the valley of the Connecticut, where the Dutch already had a sentiment or two, was very much nicer for farming than their bleak location, and recommended that they try it. This was in 1627. The Puritans of Massachusetts Bay Colony also heard favorable rumor about the Connecticut River region in 1631.

As a result of these reports a movement from the two Massachusetts colonies began in 1633, and by 1636 no less than a thousand men, women and children had undertaken the journey to their new homes. The *Blessing of the Bay* made a trip from Boston to the mouth of the Connecticut in the year first named, and at the same time a small party started overland to the river, penetrating as far as the present site of Springfield, in Massachusetts.

Later in the same year a company of people travelled by boat from Plymouth to the Connecticut coast, landed there, proceeded up the river, and started the settlement that became Windsor. Small parties followed at intervals, usually going in boats, but in November of 1635 a party numbering sixty persons succeeded in making the trip overland. This remarkable and hitherto unparalleled

9.—Bridges similar to this were the most elaborate that were required until wheeled vehicles came into use for journeys between separated settlements.

land journey of about one hundred miles was accomplished in two weeks. The household goods of the travellers were sent by water, but the live stock, consisting of numerous cattle and a few horses, marched through the forest with their owners. The speed of the caravan averaged a little more than a mile in an hour. All the men, women and sturdy children walked, and those who became ill or exhausted were placed on the broad backs

31

of the oxen, or on the horses. The men carried packs of food and small utensils on their backs, and were also armed, but suffered no molestation.

The climax of the migration came in 1636, when Pastor Thomas Hooker of the church in New Town led a memorable overland expedition from Massachusetts Bay colony into the Connecticut region. Although the number of those who made the journey was only about one hundred, yet the pilgrimage, with those that immediately followed it, seriously depleted the population of Dorchester, Watertown and New Town. Governor Winthrop refers to Hooker's famous exodus in his records by saying:

"June 30, 1636. Mr. Hooker, pastor of the church of New Town, and the most of his congregation went to Connecticut. His wife was carried in a horse-litter. And they drove an hundred and sixty cattle, and fed of their milk by the way."

This throng of early travellers, like their predecessors of the previous year, moved through the wilderness along the famous Indian trail afterward to become known as the Old Connecticut Path, and they established new homes on the present sites of Hartford, Windsor and Wethersfield. The trail after leaving New Town proceeded in a general western or southwestern direction, and, passing through the locations of the present towns of Marlborough, Grafton and Oxford, came at last to the future site of Springfield, on the river which was the travellers' goal. Hooker's expedition also spent two weeks in marching through the woods, and though its members were compelled to ford many streams and push their way through dense thickets and swamps under the burden of their packs, they experienced no extreme suffering. The Indians were friendly. It was simply a matter of resolution, perseverance and hard work.

While these things were going on the Dutch had sincerely repented their hearty recommendation of the region to the English and did all they could, short of the use of actual force, to prevent its occupation. But it was too late. The English refused to be frightened by the pointing of blunderbusses and the tooting of admonitory trumpets. They discovered to their surprise that Van Twiller had told them the truth; kept coming; and when they got there, remained. For a time the Dutch remained also, in a state of dignified indignation, and then went away.

Such was the manner of travel at that time. As years went by the movements of the population gradually increased in number, covered wider areas and extended over greater distances, especially in the North. There was one common aspect of them, natural to such a newly and thinly settled country, that persisted for about a century. The people travelled in groups or companies, just as they were later to do in the settlement of the Northwest Territory and still later in their progress across the plains of the far West. Individual travel did not exist save for short distances until close to the year 1700.

Many definitely organized migrations similar to the one from Massachusetts to Connecticut followed it in all parts of the colonies during the next hundred years. They were in fact a feature of the period. During the same year that witnessed the Hooker pilgrimage a small company went northward from Massachusetts to what is now Exeter, in New Hampshire, and still another Bay State party moved to the vicinity of Dover, New Hampshire, to find a new home. Roger Williams also made his winter journey of fourteen weeks through the wilderness in 1636,

33

and in his wanderings to the spot where the city of Providence now stands he was fed, sheltered and kindly treated by the Indians. Others soon followed him to the same locality. The number, extent and importance of the early journeys made by organized bodies of the popula-

SETTLERS OF CONNECTICUT

10.—Nearly all extensive travelling for a century and a half was undertaken by large parties moving together. Sometimes the women and children were carried in horse-litters. Many pedestrian caravans moved through the forest between such widely separated localities as New England and the Carolinas.

tion from one part of the country to another can best be shown, perhaps, in a chronological list, and a record of that sort, exclusive of those already mentioned and doubtless far from complete, is here given:

1638.—Several companies left Massachusetts and journeyed to Quinnipiac (now New Haven, Connecticut).

1639.—Milford and Guilford, in Connecticut, were similarly settled.

1639.—Parties of Dutch left New Amsterdam and occupied distant points along the Hudson River.

1640.—Settlers from New England proceeded to Long Island and established themselves at Southampton.

1642.—Emigrants from New Haven colony went to Delaware Bay, bought a tract of land at Burlington from the Indians and settled on the Delaware River. On their arrival they lived for a time in the cow houses of Swedes who had preceded them.

1642.—Another party from New Haven moved to the Delaware Bay region, bought lands from the natives on the Schuylkill River and began to establish themselves there.

1653.—A company went from Virginia into what is now North Carolina, stopped near the Chowan River and began the Albemarle settlement. Some Quakers were in this body of emigrants.

1655.—Jamaica, on Long Island, was established by people who travelled down from New England.

1656.—Many Dutch removed from New Amsterdam to the settlements on Delaware Bay.

1660.—A number of New England people went to North Carolina, bought lands of Indians on Cape Fear River and settled there. They did not like the location, however, and left.

1665.—A body of emigrants from New Hampshire journeyed to the Raritan River, in New Jersey.

1665.—From Milford, Guilford and Bramford, in New Haven colony, a considerable party set out and went to the present neighborhood of Newark, New Jersey.

1665.—A company of settlers from Newbury, in Massachusetts, established themselves on the Raritan River, in New Jersey. These three last named migrations were the result of a systematic campaign made by agents of New Jersey in New England, where they were sent to praise the country and get immigrants.

1671.—A group of Dutch from New York settled along the Ashley River, in the Carolinas.

1682 to 1690.—Large parties from Virginia, Maryland, New York, Massachusetts, Connecticut and other colonies travelled to the Delaware River region and settled in the new colony of Pennsylvania and the town of Philadelphia.

1732.—People living on the Potomac River, in Virginia, began to move over the mountains to the valley of the Shenandoah.

1737.—A party of a hundred Potomac families journeyed through this last named region and settled near the present towns of Winchester and Strasburg.

1725-1740.—A steady stream of emigration travelled from Virginia and Pennsylvania into North Carolina.

1735-1740.—Similar groups from Virginia and Pennsylvania moved into South Carolina.

These were not the trifling shifts for short distances, such as were also going on during the constant establishment of new farms and new settlements near older ones. They were long and pretentious travels, often for hundreds of miles, calling for careful and elaborate preparation, the breaking up of homes and the enduring of many trials. They were the first manifestations of the restless desire for movement and change, the somewhere-else feeling, that has ever since been a characteristic of the native born American. Through them and similar early migrations, accomplished on foot or by the aid of boats and a few horses, marked by hardships and sometimes ending in disaster or disappointment, a better knowledge of the condition and character of the country was gradually obtained by the population.

CHAPTER IV

POLE-BOATS AND THE MANNER OF THEIR NAVIGATION —
INCREDIBLE LABOR PERFORMED IN USING THEM —
THE INFLUENCE OF CONNECTICUT — BEGINNING THE
SYSTEMATIC TRANSFORMATION OF INDIAN TRAILS
INTO CRUDE ROADS — EARLY FERRIES AROUND BOSTON
AND NEW YORK — SEDAN CHAIRS — THE FIRST
HORSE VEHICLES AND THEIR TRIUMPH OVER PURI-
TAN PREJUDICE — LAWS AGAINST TRAVEL — THE
INTRODUCTION AND EQUIPMENT OF SLEDS — TRAVEL
IN WINTER — RESULT OF THE FOUNDING OF PHILA-
DELPHIA — THE EVOLUTION OF THE OLD INDIAN
TRAIL ACROSS NEW JERSEY — LONG HORSEBACK
JOURNEYS BECOME POSSIBLE — THE ADVENTURES OF
MISTRESS KNIGHT OF BOSTON

TWO of the earliest types of river boats that followed
the canoe, as the needs of the growing settlements
became greater, were probably first used by the pioneers
on the Connecticut River. Both sorts of craft with slight
modifications were widely adopted in various regions,
particularly where the streams were rapid or shallow, and
were common throughout the country until after the year
1800.

One was called a pole-boat, from the means by which
it was propelled up-stream. Usually made of planks
hewed from the pine, it was from twenty to thirty feet
long, three to five feet wide, some two or three feet deep,

pointed at both ends, and had a flat bottom. Even when heavily laden it was serviceable in less than a foot of water. Such a boat was navigated down a stream by means of oars or poles with almost no effort, but going back upstream, especially against a rapid current, was a far different matter. The crew — exclusive of steersman — consisted of four, six or eight men, according to the size of the craft, and each man was armed with a long, stout pole made of ash or hickory, with a heavy, wrought iron spike at one end. There were two methods of propulsion. With an equal number of men standing on each side of the boat, as near to the bow as possible and facing the stern, they would plant their spikes in the bottom of the stream at an angle, and with the upper end of each man's pole against his shoulder they would all walk as far

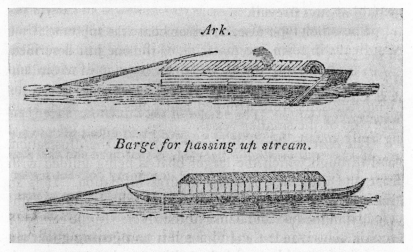

Ark.

Barge for passing up stream.

11.—Early types of river boats used by families on long journeys. They probably originated on the Connecticut and Delaware Rivers. The ark, or flatboat, varied somewhat in form, was built of heavy timbers, and was rarely navigated against the current. The barge, a lighter vessel with canoe-like lines, was pushed up-stream by poles. At first the barge was called a keelboat and had no covered shelter.

toward the stern as possible.[1] By so doing they pushed the boat out from under their feet in an up-stream direction and propelled it, with each repetition of the process, nearly a boat's length. Two men would then hold the distance gained until the others hurried back to the bow and planted their poles in the bottom again. The second method of advancing consisted in facing the bow of the boat with the workers in two stationary groups, one near the bow and the other near the stern. The groups would push on their poles alternately, with a helmsman to correct the zigzag impulse. The labor necessary for ascending a rapid river in either of these ways was so great as to be beyond exaggeration, yet it was constantly accomplished over long distances, and the method remained in wide fashion for very many years. Men took it for granted there was nothing else to do, and that the same conditions would always prevail.

The other type of early river boat was substantially a duplicate, in form and material, of the one just described. It was, however, about twice as long and wide, and equipped with a mast and sails. When going against the wind the sails were dropped and poles were used, as in the case of the smaller vessel.

The obstruction in the river shown in the illustration, and through which the larger boat is being guided with care and difficulty, is not a natural formation. It is an ancient fish-dam, built by the Indians with boulders gathered from the bed and banks of the river. In the center of such a contrivance the Indians left an opening about six or eight feet wide, and below this gap they constructed, with woven roots, willow branches and such material, a

[1] They moved back and forth on narrow wooden runways, about ten inches wide, that were built on each side of the boat for the purpose.

great basket-like enclosure that reached down-stream a dozen feet, and was tightly joined at each end to the dam. When food was needed a large number of the red men would enter the water and form in line across the stream

A View of the Boats & manner of navigating on the Mohawk River.

12.—Two keel-boats ascending a river. Those of large size carried masts, and used sails whenever possible. The curved obstruction in the stream, with an opening in the center, is not a natural formation but an Indian fish-dam built of boulders.

about half a mile above their trap and wade slowly down, kicking and beating the water with sticks as they moved. The frightened fish fleeing before them would finally encounter the dam and be converged by it to the opening, through which they would rush into the woven sack to be scooped out by thousands. In this way did the Indian often do his fishing, much to the embarrassment of future white navigators. Several of these early stone fish-dams still exist in the upper reaches of Tippecanoe River, in northern Indiana, just as they were built by the Potawatomi.

But Connecticut's most important contribution to the

progress of those primitive days did not lie so much in the devising of methods of travel as it did in the remarkable way in which her people wandered over the face of the land. They went everywhere, until at last their universal presence became a proverb in the mouths of the people. Any stranger, any new settler in a community, was dubbed a "Connecticut Yankee," and the chances were that the guess was a good one. From those few square miles there went forth a pioneer influence that was always strong, and sometimes decisive, in shaping the affairs of new regions. The Susquehanna River valley in Pennsylvania, eastern Long Island, western Massachusetts, northern New Jersey, western Vermont, central and western New York and at a later date the Western Reserve of Ohio all were swayed or powerfully affected, in their beginnings, by Connecticut migrations. There is a legend which says that at one time the natives of Connecticut and graduates of Yale College lacked but five of constituting an actual majority of the National Congress.[1]

By the year 1683 the towns of Boston and New York and the new settlement of Philadelphia had become so bustling and important that travel from one to another was a common thing, and necessity began to urge the making of such land highways between them as would permit of regular traffic. Indian trails and paths made by settlers already linked the three centers with a route passable over a part of its extent by horses, though most of the travel from any one of the towns to another was still accomplished by boat. In the cities some of the wealthy and governing classes had been using sedan chairs for a long time, and a few private coaches of various sorts had begun to appear. Boston and New York, because of the numer-

---

[1] The saying is sometimes attributed to Calhoun.

13.—A bill submitted to Massachusetts Bay Province by Ferryman John Knight of Boston, in 1709, asking payment for services rendered to the Sheraft, military officers and other officials during the preceding three years. He asked £6, 3s, and was allowed £3, 1s, 6d, or just half the amount requested.

ous smaller settlements situated on the waters all around them, had also grappled with the problem of ferry facilities for the primeval suburbanites who lived near by.

In Massachusetts Bay the business of ferrying was given into the hands of watermen who used big barge-like boats capable of carrying horses and goods as well as men. One of these ferry owners was a certain John Knight, and a bill rendered by him for work performed is herein reproduced. It indicates that he had allowed the account to run for more than two years, since the first entry, for ferrying "a Sheraft and 33 of his men" is dated in August of 1706, and the last, for transporting "John Bunker, 6 Indians and 1 horse" has the date of January, 1709. The total bill was but six pounds and three shillings, or about thirty dollars. Ferryman Knight duly presented his account to the authorities, and owing to the scarcity of paper the House of Representatives of the colony used the other side of the bill itself for the formal engrossment of its action thereon. The resolution, duly signed by the Speaker and Secretary of the House, shows

THE FERRY HOUSE, 1746.
(Fulton Street, Brooklyn.)

14.—The flatboat with a sail is one of the first city ferry boats, like those used in New York, Boston, Philadelphia, Baltimore and other coast towns until about 1800.

that Knight was allowed for his work the sum of "three pounds, one shilling and six pence," or exactly one-half of the amount called for by his bill.

The ferries in use on the waters around New York

44

City, or some of them at least, were similar barges, equipped with sails. Such was the ferry boat to Brooklyn. Owing to the strong tides and currents and the squalls of wind for which the bay has always been noted, many capsizings and other accidents in which men and beasts were sometimes drowned, attended the history of the early New York ferries.

The sedan chairs in which certain of the wealthy people and official classes were accustomed to travel about the towns were commonly carried by servants, though vehicles of a type resembling the one made for Pastor Hooker's wife, and borne by a single horse, were also in use. Such things as sedan chairs were distinctly an importation — in idea at least — from Europe, though they were used in America for a long time, chiefly in New York and Philadelphia. Benjamin Franklin rode in a sedan chair, on occasions, as late as the year 1789. One of the earliest of them in English America was that which belonged to Governor Winthrop, of Massachusetts Bay colony. It was a rich and magnificent specimen, originally made at the order of a viceroy of Mexico and intended for some dignitary in Spain. It was found on a Spanish galleon captured by the English and by them presented to Winthrop. He said, in speaking of the gift, that he "had no use for it."

There was more behind that remark of Winthrop's than appears on the surface. Doubtless he would have been glad to move about in comfort in the carved, silver-bedecked and silk-upholstered box, for he was a human being after all, but public opinion and the ruling spirits of the church in the Puritan colony would not have permitted such an action. Men and women of New England were banished, or had their ears cut off, or were hanged

45

in those days for offenses scarce more heinous than the use of such a devil's trap as a gaudy sedan chair. Even in 1687, nearly fifty years afterward, the first horse coaches which appeared in Boston were severely frowned upon as contrivances fit for this world only, and their brazen owners were subjected to scorn and derision. But the shameless proprietors of those first vehicles found in the possession of them a solace that was sufficient recompense even for social ostracism. And, sad to relate, others of sufficient wealth were also tempted and fell. The use of horses and coaches continued, and slowly increased. Satan was triumphant.

Outside the towns and their immediate neighborhoods the utility of the first coaches was very limited indeed. Roads were scarcely worthy of the name, and there were no bridges. When a coach came to a stream too deep to be forded it was stood upon its wheels in two parallel canoes, and thus conveyed across. The horses swam.

There were three types of the earliest American wheeled vehicles. One was patterned after the heavy and cumbrous two-horse family carriage that had just come into limited use in England. The others were better adapted to conditions in such new country, and each was drawn by one horse. The first of the Americanized types was called a chair, and the other a chaise. The chair was a two-wheeled vehicle with a seat for two, and sometimes with an additional small seat, almost over the shafts, for the driver. Of this carriage the Canadian caleche was a variety. The chaise was simply a chair with a covered top of leather. None of the earliest specimens had springs, but swung on stout braces of wood or leather that somewhat alleviated the constant jolting. All were made by local blacksmiths and wheelwrights, some of whom built up reputations by the excellence of their work and thus became the first carriage makers of the country. There was not much change in the three types of vehicles for a hun-

15.—The first wheeled vehicles to appear were a few private coaches, made in the large towns for town use only, late in the seventeenth century. The condition of the roads did not permit their employment elsewhere. A dozen or so vehicles like this existed in Boston, Philadelphia and New York before 1700. They had bodies either of wood or leather and were generally painted in bright colors.

dred years or more, except that they gradually became more ornate in their outward aspect. All through the colonies a tendency toward the use of brighter and still brighter colors, both for personal wear and for application to miscellaneous belongings was apparent for a long time. This trait of the people reached its climax shortly before the days of the Revolution. Its effect on vehicles was seen in their brightly-painted wheels, their bodies of red, yellow, blue or brown, with panels of different hues and trimmings to match. Especially was this craving for warmth of color observable in the middle and southern colonies. And it must have been a dazzling sight to see such equipages in a festal hour with the women in white satin gowns and filmy shoulder veils of purple or emerald green, beside men in lace ruffles, blue coats, yellow waistcoats, knee breeches of buff, scarlet stockings and silver buckles.

Philadelphia possessed about thirty carts and other wheeled vehicles in 1697, and New York also had a number, but the introduction of such things did not proceed with any uniformity throughout the country. In Connecticut, for instance, there were no carriages until about 1750 and few until after the Revolution. When Governor Trumbull of Connecticut visited the town of Norwich during the Revolution he travelled in a chaise, and the people of the village abandoned their affairs with one accord and flocked to behold such an extraordinary contraption. No vehicles were used, or any travelling performed on Sunday in some of the colonies until after the era of independence began. It was prohibited by law. Sunday, by the statutes, commenced at sunset of Saturday and continued until the same time on the Sabbath. On one occasion a man who was about to resume his horseback journey left his tavern on Sunday evening, stood beside the animal and patiently waited until the sun had retired, as he thought, for the night. Then he mounted and rode away. But a moment later one last brief gleam of sunlight broke for an instant from behind the clouds and was spied by a vigilant constable. The traveller was arrested and fined.

Much travelling by land was performed in the winter. During the spring, summer-time and autumn, particularly in the northern colonies, a large part of the population was busy in the work necessary to an agricultural, land-clearing and seafaring community. But winter was the time for recreation and visiting, and for making journeys to towns where markets could be found for the sale of such commodities as the farmer and his family had produced. In winter the roads of the middle and northern colonies were no longer seas of mud with archipelagos of stumps, but were made smooth and firm with a pavement spread upon them from the sky. The smaller streams and rivers, too, were turned to highways of ice and were often used. Sleighs of various crude and simple types appeared at an early date, and by the year 1700 were in general use. One of the commonest varieties of these vehicles for winter

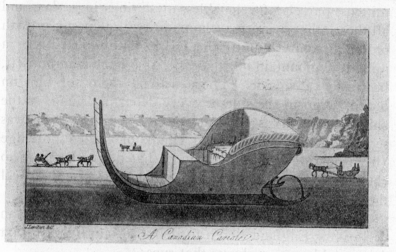

A Canadian Cariole

16.—American colonial sleds were generally called either pungs or pods, though the Canadian cariole was also used. The pungs and pods ordinarily had an open space between the bed of the sled and its runners. Each American type also had a shelf-like extension of the floor beyond its sides for its whole length. Horse-drawn sleds preferred to travel on the smooth surfaces of frozen streams when possible.

travel was an idea adopted[1] from Canada. The Canadians spoke of it as a cariole, but the people of New England, who have always preferred to use home-made names for

[1] With alterations.

things, called a sleigh either a pung or a pod, and found it just as serviceable. They were more concerned with features of utility than with melodious nomenclature. A pung was drawn by two horses; a pod by one. When loaded and equipped for a long journey over the snows a pung must have been an interesting spectacle. In the body of the vehicle sat the farmer's wife, with maybe a child or two, all of them bundled up with coats, blankets, hoods, mittens and mufflers against the sharp air. Around them were heaped the things they had prepared for sale — cheeses, dried herbs, bundles of knitted stockings and mittens, parcels of vegetables, mysterious jugs, flax, and all those other primitive commodities of domestic growth or manufacture — until the whole outfit looked like a miniature mountain on runners. As for the man himself, he trotted alongside. There was no room for him on board. And to the side of every departing pung, as the chiefest part of its equipment for a journey, there was securely tied a huge round chunk of frozen porridge (bean porridge, of course) and a hatchet with which to chop off a chunk of it when any of the travellers might feel the need of nourishment.

No doubt this curious commissary department of an early New England sleigh throws a certain light on that famous old nursery rhyme that runs:

"Bean porridge hot; bean porridge cold;
Bean porridge in the pot, nine days old."

Preliminary to every such trip, and a few days before it, the housewife would cook a big pot of porridge and then, setting it out-of-doors in the kettle, would allow it to ripen and freeze while awaiting the time for the journey to begin. There is no present way of finding out whether the epicures of that period considered nine days as the most appetizing age for winter bean porridge, but of one thing we may be sure; it was very, very cold.

For short winter trips, or whenever the snow was too soft or deep for horses, snow-shoes were used, and the traveller carried a staff at the bottom of which was fixed a

Great Snow in 1717

17.—Winter travel in the northern colonies was performed on foot, or in sleds drawn by dogs or horses. The New England winter pedestrian, in addition to his snow-shoes, was equipped with a pole having a large wooden disc at its bottom for extra support.

wide, flat piece of wood, usually round or oval in shape, as an additional support. Still another means of travel during the winter season was the dog-sled. This method of conveyance was copied from a similar usage of the Indians, who in times of hostility sometimes also employed sleds for transporting their baggage or feeble captives through the wilderness. The dog-sleds were small and simple affairs, consisting of a flat base of pine or spruce about two feet wide, upcurved in front, and with room for but one person to seat himself. From two to six

51

dogs constituted a team. Although the dog-sled never came into widespread use at any one time or in any given locality, except in the far North and Northwest, it nevertheless persisted in various forms as a vehicle of travel in America for perhaps two hundred years, and is still used in Alaska and Canada.

The establishment of the town of Philadelphia and its rapid growth had exerted a decided influence on the development of land travel in the colonies. By 1690 the place consisted of some six or eight hundred houses, people were journeying to it from all other parts of the country, and there was no longer any doubt that it was on its way toward an assured greatness. Three chief centers of social and commercial activity — New York, the Massachusetts towns and the settlements on the Delaware — then existed in the North, and it was inevitable that they should soon become linked by definite and continuous land routes of travel. The Dutch, who had previously held that part of New Jersey between Amboy on New York Bay and the Delaware River, abandoned the region about the year 1675. At that time it was still a wilderness traversed only by Indian paths and but seldom crossed by white men. The main trail of the aborigines extended through the territory from Elizabethport, near New York Bay, and proceeding by way of the future settlements of New Brunswick and Trenton, finally reached the Delaware River. Such, then, was the route by which the colonists travelled overland between New York and Philadelphia in 1675. They made the journey on foot if they went at all, and under ordinary circumstances were from three to five days on the road.

It was this path of the Indians which was adopted as the best line for a steam railroad across New Jersey a hundred and sixty years afterward, and it was exactly above the same old historic travel route, two hundred and thirty-five years afterward, that a flying-man made the first flight on schedule time ever performed. On that occasion an aeroplane was driven in an uninterrupted journey from New York to Philadelphia in an hour and fifty minutes as announced in advance, or five minutes faster than the running time of the swiftest regular railroad train between the two cities.[1] Such things, however, did not abide within the philosophy of the red men. To them belongs the credit of pointing out the best paths, but we use the information in our own peculiar way. They went beneath the trees. We can go above.

By about the year 1682 the people of the Delaware River towns were beginning to open short roads between their various settlements, and the roads were gradually followed by local vehicle traffic for small distances. The few wagons or carts were very crude and awkward, had immensely wide wheels, and were most used in going to previously arranged gatherings that were sure to be attended by considerable numbers of people. The inhabitants of Burlington, for example, held fairs at stated intervals, to which the inhabitants of other settlements travelled in order to buy or exchange commodities or to visit friends and relatives.

Little by little the roads in all settled parts of the colonies were extended by the coöperation of communities and through individual labor, until in a few years continuous horseback journeys between Boston and Philadelphia were possible with comparative ease. But since all intending travellers did not own horses it often happened that a party of four would set out for a common destina-

[1] Hamilton's flight of June 13, 1910.

tion with one horse. In such a case it was the practice for two to mount and ride a couple of miles, leaving the others to follow on foot. Then the riders would dismount, tie the horse by the roadside and continue on foot in their turn until the others, having reached the animal and mounted it, would overtake them. In that manner they proceeded, with considerable satisfaction to all concerned except the

INDIA DOG TRAIN.

18.—The dog-sled, or Indian dog train, was used when the snow was too deep or too soft to uphold horses. Such a sled was six or seven feet long, and its bottom was made of smooth planks. The title on the original engraving is a misprint.

fifth member of the party. Two travelling together also used the same system if but one horse was available. In the year 1702 a woman went on horseback from Boston to Philadelphia and carried a baby in her lap for the entire distance. That was a notable occurrence. When a man and his wife rode one horse the man, in a saddle, sat as usual, and the woman was perched behind him on a cushion called a pillion. The woman's pillion was strapped to the motive power of the expedition, and below it, on one side, was hung a narrow wooden platform for her feet.

A school-teacher — Mrs. Knight — who travelled from Boston to New York on horseback in the year 1704 wrote a little book describing her trip, and her narrative contains much interesting information regarding the character and manners of the people she met on the way, as well as a recital of the experiences which she encountered. It is related by her that on one occasion she came to an inn late at night, and desiring shelter, summoned the inmates. Finally the landlady appeared, but instead of immediately bustling about to make the guest comfortable, and postponing a manifestation of her interest in the arrival, she planted herself immovably on the solid rock of her feminine curiosity and began:

"Law for me! What in the world brings you here this time of night? I never saw a woman on the Rode so Dreadful late in all my versall life! Who are you? Where are you going?" And so on. But Mrs. Knight, being a schoolmistress, finally passed the examination and got to bed.

On the same trip she met a man and his daughter, riding on separate horses. The girl had only a bag for a saddle, and Mrs. Knight heard her plaintively say: "Lawful heart, father! This bare mare hurts me dingily. I'm dreadful sore, I vow." It was small wonder she was uncomfortable, for it developed that she and her father had been jogging along for thirty miles.

Mrs. Knight also gave her opinion of the canoe, whose erratic propensities as a vehicle filled her with misgivings. Coming to a stream she was compelled to embark in one of the craft for transportation to the other side, and she said of it: "The Cannoo was very small and shallow, which greatly terrify'd me and caused me to be very circumspect, sitting with my hands fast on each side, my eyes steady, not daring so much as to lodge my tongue a hair's breadth more on one side of my mouth than t'other. A very thought would have oversett our wherry."

It is the little incidents like these — little bits from the actual experiences of those distant times — which best reveal the travel conditions that then prevailed. But such records are, unfortunately, all too rare. It usually happens in searching through the narratives of early travellers, no matter in what form they may be found, that the record tells of leaving a certain place on a certain day and of reaching another place in the course of time, but nothing else. Of the adventures and conditions encountered, the expedients and methods used during the journey there are few details given, or none at all.

CHAPTER V

ANOTHER ELEMENT IN THE PROBLEM — EARLY CONDITIONS PROFOUNDLY INFLUENCED BY THE NATIVE INHABI- TANTS — THE STRATEGIC GEOGRAPHICAL POSITIONS HELD BY THE INDIANS — THEIR EARLY ATTITUDE TOWARD WHITE MEN — NATURE OF INDIAN PROPRIE- TORSHIP OVER LANDS — COVETOUSNESS OF THE WHITES — DEVELOPMENT OF NATIVE PREJUDICE TO- WARD ENGLISH TRAVEL MOVEMENT AND ITS CAUSES — TREATMENT OF EACH RACE BY THE OTHER — A CENTURY AND A HALF OF CONFLICT — BLOCKHOUSES — EFFECT OF EUROPEAN POLITICS AND INTERCOLO- NIAL JEALOUSIES — FIRST SYMPTOMS OF THE IM- PENDING WESTWARD MOVEMENT APPEAR — THE DOMINATION OF THE WHITE RACE INEVITABLE

THUS far, while tracing the earliest growth of a system of internal communications destined to develop from such crude beginnings into the most extensive and valuable series of public works ever con- structed by men, whose relation to the national life has finally become one of the principal social and indus- trial problems at present existing, it has only been neces- sary to consider the primitive needs of our forefathers and the first devices created or adapted to meet those necessities.

But the growth of the white man's travel system in America and his subjugation of the continent by its use

57

was, in its first stages, a matter of somewhat more complexity than has as yet been suggested. Progress in the early days did not depend solely on the creation and extension of thoroughfares and the successive introduction of new and better types of vehicles. There was yet another element in the problem, one that exerted a strong and at times decisive influence for generations. That factor was the Indian. And since no complete picture of the white man's aspiration for movement and of the travel conditions that existed until comparatively recent days can be drawn without introducing the native occupants and original owners of the territory involved, it is well to turn for a time from the primary question of routes and vehicles in order to observe why — and to what degree — the population movements of early times were influenced by the white man's copper-colored antagonist.

The Indians of the eastern part of the continent, when the first permanent white men's settlements were made in that region, had seemingly occupied the land, unaffected by any outside or visiting influence of importance, for several thousands of years. They had perhaps been here, slowly ascending from a very primitive level, since that period when mastodons were common, when Niagara Falls did not exist,[1] and possibly even since the time when Lakes Erie and Ontario, as one body of water, had their drainage westwardly through the Wabash River, thence into the Ohio and the Mississippi. Collectively these native Americans had held undisputed possession of the continent, and with the lapse of many centuries the various tribes into which the race had broken up had acquired, in a certain sense, recognized title to the territories they severally held.

[1] About seven thousand to ten thousand years ago.

Such titles were not the precise recorded legal instruments of white civilization, but were established or altered by occupation, treaties and strength of arms, and were maintained by coöperative action based on tribal government or by the still more powerful joint action of federations of tribes. Regions so held were sometimes roughly bounded by natural lines such as mountains, lakes, or conspicuous landmarks, and — howsoever delimited — the adjoining tribes, save in time of war, respected the territorial rights or pretensions of their neighbors. Sometimes a region was made neutral by the tacit or formal agreement of many tribes and used by them for a common purpose, such as hunting. The lands lying in the present state of Kentucky were an uninhabited territory, so rich in game that no tribe was allowed their exclusive control. In short, the use, dominion over and occupancy of land and favorable locations was a subject on which the Indians placed a high importance.

Themselves accustomed to great distances and long journeys, the Indians had, as has been suggested, an unerring appreciation of the importance of good lines of communication and the best and easiest travel routes. The strongest and most influential tribes and confederations lived on or near important rivers, bays or lakes, or in territory that offered the easiest means of subsistence and travel. The Indians were economic strategists. When the white men came they found the natives were established in those localities that seemed most desirable for white settlement. The red men had already seen the advantages of such locations as Delaware and Chesapeake Bays, the Delaware, Susquehanna and Potomac Rivers, New York harbor, the Hudson and Connecticut Rivers,

Massachusetts Bay,[1] and the easily traversed route, through what is now New York state, from the upper Hudson to the westward by way of the Great Lakes. This last mentioned region was occupied by the most powerful and best organized group of Indians in eastern North America, the League of the Iroquois, a confederation,

19.—A horse-barrow. Crude home-made barrows, carts and wagons slowly developed, outside the towns, wherever conditions made them useful. Thereafter they showed but slight improvement for more than a century. The wheels of many barrows and carts consisted of solid sections of tree trunks, and were from six to twelve inches in width. Original sketch by the early American artist, Joshua Shaw. One of eleven recently found drawings by the same artist, reproduced in these pages and depicting conditions of pioneer life and travel.

at that time, of five strong tribes whose common affairs were administered by a central council made up of delegates from each.

The first human quality which seriously affected intercourse between the natives and the white strangers was covetousness. The newcomers wanted—and determined to possess—those choice territorial tidbits which the

---

[1] Modern names for these localities are used, instead of those given by the natives or early explorers, in order that they may be more quickly identified. The native name for the Connecticut River, for instance, was "Quinni-tukq-ut," or "Quoneh-ta-cut," and the Dutch called it "De Versche Riviere."

Indians equally esteemed as desirable regions for habitation. At once began the long history of negotiation, treaty and purchase, inevitable as a phenomenon of human progress but too often defiled by the sordidness of power, by which the country passed piecemeal into the possession of the white race. It is true the newcomers acknowledged that ownership of the lands was vested in the native occupants, and that they usually paid for the territories, in a technical sense, under terms of formal purchase. But it was the white men who demanded to buy.[1] It was the white men who fixed the purchase price, and the red men who realized what refusal would mean. The occupation of continents and the sway of white skins over dark skins is determined by laws not passed by legislatures. The unfortunate effect upon the red men of the process by which they were stripped of their possessions was the speedy creation of a hostility — always existent thereafter in at least a passive sense and often fanned into warfare by imposition or pressure upon them — toward the movements of the white men. For the Indians soon saw that much white travel resulted in more demands to buy land, more purchases, permanent white occupation and a curtailment of their own territory and natural means of subsistence. The presence of white men meant the absence of game, and Indian poverty.

That conception of the red man which has been summed up in the ethnological proverb, "The only good Indian is a dead Indian," runs somewhat wide of the truth. It is not too much to say that in the early days of their association with the English speaking colonists, the native Americans compared rather favorably with the strangers in the exhibition of those human qualities

[1] Reference is made to the English speaking colonies and colonists.

that inspire confidence and serve to distinguish honor and fair dealing from duplicity. When an Indian and a white man were about to engage in a transaction involving something of value owned by the native and coveted by the Caucasian, it was for a long time a common custom to make the Indian drunk as a preliminary to the negotiation. Peter Kalm, in his *Voyage to North America,* refers to this practise, and says: "Many persons have assured me that the Indians are frequently cheated in disposing of their goods, especially when they are in liquor, and that sometimes they do not get one-half or one-tenth of the value of their goods. I have been witness to several transactions of this kind."[1]

When a white man had a just grievance against a native and the attention of the offending Indian's tribe was called to the matter, the chiefs of his clan compelled the culprit to make restitution and often visited upon him a severe penalty.[2] The Iroquois held deceit in such abhorrence that on some occasions they punished lying with the penalty of death. Among the early colonists the personal accountability code of the Indians was not looked upon with favor for use in dealing with offenders of the white race. As a consequence the estimation in which the newcomers were held by the natives was lowered. Under normal conditions, and in dealing with colonists who did not impose on them, the Indians as a race were hospitable and kind to the limit of their opportunities. In their sight, at first, a white man was pre-

[1] An Indian once said to Sir William Johnson (England's agent in dealing with the northern natives): "You English buy territory by the use of the bottle."
"With liquor as the bartering medium, nothing could save the Indian from wrong."—Winsor, in "The Westward Movement."
[2] This attitude of the natives gradually ceased. The authorities of the colonies got into the habit of disowning the white trouble-makers along the border, and of disavowing responsibility for their unfair or unlawful acts. Trespassers on Indian lands sometimes committed their outrages at such a distance from the hand of authority that it was impossible to catch the culprits even if the desire to do so existed. So the natives followed the example of the whites, and took the same position.

sumed to be a good man, kindly disposed. If he proved himself to be bad, that was another matter. There were bad men on both sides. But the Indian had to prove himself, against open prejudice, to be good. Occasionally and after long effort he was successful, but it was a hard matter at best, and from the chronicles that have come down from those times it is apparent that such attempts on his part, even when sincere and justified by the facts, failed more often than they succeeded.

One of the best records of the relative viewpoints from which each race regarded the other lies in the words spoken to Conrad Weiser, an early traveller, by Canassatego, the Onondaga chief who was his host. "If a white man in travelling through our country," said the savage to the civilized man, "enters one of our cabins, we treat him as I do you. We dry him, if he is wet; we warm him, if he is cold; and give him meat and drink that he may allay his hunger and thirst, and we spread soft furs for him to rest and sleep on. We demand nothing in return. But if I go into a white man's house and ask for victuals and drink, they say, 'Where is your money?' and if I have none they say, 'Get out, you Indian dog.'" Whatever value Canassatego's words may have as a possible illumination of Indian character does not lie in the manner of their utterance but in the philosophy that inspired them. Few Indians could have spoken thus, but there is much evidence to indicate that the Indians as a race felt as he did, until their character and attitude, in so far as relations with white men were concerned, were much changed by long brooding on imposition and the impending wreck of their birthright.

The things that resulted in enmity between the red men and the white are not hard to define. They were a failure by the bulk of the newcomers to understand the viewpoint of the natives with respect to the ownership of the country and the effect of white men's presence in it, and the display, on the part of the strangers, of motives and methods that antagonized both the philosophy and material interests of the original inhabitants. Whenever it happened, in the earlier days of their association, that a white man treated his Indian neighbors as decent fellow men, and not as dangerous creatures that should be removed from the face of nature, such a white man was esteemed as a friend. Accounts of the early troubles between the races, having all been prepared and handed down by one party to the controversies, can be depended on as reliable and conservative whenever they give praise to the opposition. And narratives of the sort, written by colonists, contain the record — sometimes by inference and sometimes frankly — of native traits such as are here outlined. In later years, unhappily, a white man was often considered to be an enemy simply because he was white, just as a colonist looked on an Indian as an enemy because he was an Indian.

Civilization in its final aspect is not demonstrated by the possession and operation of railroads, steamboats and flying machines. We may with safety say, despite a considerable lingering impression to the contrary, that further and greater progress can be made by the use of more intangible elements than these. The Indians had not progressed in mechanical ingenuity to the point that we have reached, nor could they, but in one sense their cultural state surpassed that of the race which was to overthrow them. Their age-long battle with and study of Nature had woven into their character a consideration of the common welfare, a man-to-man accountability for

The Yarmouth Coach.

20.—The Yarmouth Coach, which originated in England, was a very small, cart-like pleasure conveyance, with two broad-tired wheels. When similar vehicles were employed for more serious purposes in America the standing driver ceased to appear.

word and act, a disdain of petty evasion, an ability to discern motive, and a keenness in separating honesty from hypocrisy and friend from foe, that excelled the similar attributes possessed by the white-skinned men who appeared among them. The strangers from abroad, though they did not realize it, were under one disadvantage. Their methods of life — their civilization — had blunted in them those qualities in which the Indians were supreme. That was why the Indians as a race did not get along in their dealings with the white men as a race. There was no common footing, either of character or material interests, on which both could stand. The whites thought the Indians were children; heathen. But it was the Indians who were wise in their comprehension of the significance of events, and the strangers who were blind.

So the colonists came and settled down. Around them was the wilderness. That they could see, for it was tangible. It held them back, but it stood still when attacked and could be slowly demolished as occasion required. The other barrier which surrounded them was one they felt, rather than saw. From the most northern settlements in Maine to Virginia, the Carolinas and Georgia, an elastic and tightly drawn cordon of native influence stretched close around them and hampered them. From it came forth a ceaseless constriction, manifested in many ways, against their free and general progress about the country. The restraint irritated and angered them, and when the strain and bickering reached a certain point, as it often did, there came an open rupture and fighting.

Sometimes the restraint exerted by the Indians was due, in whatever form it took, to preconcerted action, but its underlying origin and motive—no matter whether it was the act of one or many, whether spontaneous or planned — was a general realization by the whole native population of the continental menace that confronted them. The natives looked into the future and saw, perhaps before the white men did, what was happening. Therefore it was not the individual traveller in whose path obstacles were laid. There was nothing immediate to fear from an individual. He would return whence he came. The two things that brought alarm and sadness to the souls of the Indians were bulk-movements of the white men and any manifestation of a desire to creep toward the West. Thus it was that the early extensive

66

travelling of the whites, as we have seen, was performed in parties sufficiently large to insure mutual support and safety in case of need. And all the influence of the natives — in which they were greatly aided for a time by the physical barrier of the Appalachian Mountains — was exerted in keeping the tide of travel movement confined to a north-and-south direction along the narrow coastal region some hundred and fifty miles in width. Had that native influence not been exerted, both by the display of strong and ceaseless objection and the use of their land titles as a barrier, a general travel toward the West must have taken place many years before it actually began. But so long as the colonies remained divided — although they several times tried to unite in a diplomatic sense to oppose the Indian policy — the native strategy prevailed. It was not until a more centralized government and a deeper feeling of American solidarity came into existence and devoted the joint energies of all the states to the effort, that the stubborn native opposition to widespread travel was finally broken down, and the westward movement became national in its character.

Unknown thousands died in those outbreaks of border warfare that lasted for a century and three-quarters, and at times certain regions were for a while swept clear of their Caucasian inhabitants. But the final result was always the same. The white race, in its contact with other men, has been a glacier whose implacable and grinding advance makes up the chief part of recorded history, and the moraines that mark its progress are forts and guns. There was no exception here in America. No matter how severe the setback was, other white men came in force enough to guarantee safety and reoccupy the devastated and deserted territory. They rebuilt the burned log dwellings and set up little fortifications which they called blockhouses, strongly made of huge hewn timbers, with loopholes for rifles and usually with a projecting upper story from which fighters could command the entrances below. In the course of time the outlying districts and main travel routes throughout all the region held by the whites were dotted with such blockhouses, into which the population could retire if it became necessary. Those structures, and the larger palisaded or smooth timber forts which were also built, were long an essential feature of American life and movement.

Many times it happened that a party of travellers journeying through the wilderness learned from some swift courier that hostilities had begun, and their leisurely advance changed upon the instant to wild flight toward the nearest blockhouse and safety. Usually they gained the refuge, there to be held in siege while the rifles without which no men went abroad were used against other and duskier men who claimed the territory they had invaded. At other times the travellers did not reach the little forts in season, and vanished into the forest as captives or else went forth upon a yet longer journey — from which there could be no return.

It seems probable that for a short period after their first coming the various colonies entertained a belief that they could go their own way without much relation with the Indians beyond such association as they themselves decreed, or as was necessary in exchanging trinkets for square miles; that they might consider the natives as part of the surrounding scenery. This hope — to whatever extent it existed — speedily disappeared, and the newcomers came to a realization that their contact with the original proprietors of the continent was the chief problem of their domestic affairs. Then began a prolonged period during which the power and territorial location of the Indians gradually became an element in the vast and complicated game of international politics wherein France, England and Spain were the contestants, and North America was the prize for which they struggled.

Wheedled by gifts, by crafty appeals to their tribal animosities, by the blandishment of honeyed words and promises not always meant to be fulfilled; in short, by all

21.—The first four-wheeled wagons were small, with flat beds and straight body lines. They were often covered, in whole or in part, with tops of home-made linsey-woolsey designed as a protection for women and children. The men walked.

those arts of civilization which white men can employ with such proficiency in like emergencies when dealing with aborigines, the Indians became catspaws for the contending forces that coveted their dominion and sought their undoing. To this state of affairs was added the constant demand, by the English speaking colonies, for "more land; more land."

The purpose of the Indians in thus taking sides with some white men against others — after realizing that all the strangers could not be got rid of — was clear. If a group of tribes decided as a result of conference that the French would be better permanent neighbors than the English, and had a chance to destroy the English, then they helped France. Often they decided the other way, and acted accordingly. And of all those native decisions none approached, in its importance and effect on American affairs, the determination of the League of the Iroquois to oppose the ambitions of the French and remain on a friendly footing with the English, if possible.[1] The geographical position of the native confederation has already been outlined. When, in addition, it is kept in mind that any travel by white men on Lakes George, Champlain, Ontario and Erie, the Hudson and Mohawk Rivers, the upper Susquehanna and Delaware Rivers, or through the entire territory stretching westward from Albany to the neighborhood of the present city of Cleveland, was for a long time dependent on their willingness and consent, the power of the Iroquois as a factor in the early mobility of the white men will be understood. So great was their influence, and so wide the recognition of it, that they came to be known as the Keepers of the Highway of America. The governors of Pennsylvania, Vir-

[1] It is not meant that the Iroquois wished to be on friendly footing with the English colonists, but with the English government. That confederation, and many other tribes as well, considered themselves to be—and in some few respects were—on a political equality with the white colonies in so far as relations with England were concerned. For a considerable time prior to the Revolution England dealt with the natives not through the colonies, but more or less directly. One of her chief embarrassments over American affairs was the constant conflict between the two races and the native demand for protection against the encroachments of the colonists. In the Revolution many Iroquois fought on the side of the English against the Americans.

ginia, New York, Maryland, and perhaps of other colonies came to treat with them — did not summon the Iroquois, but went in person to them.

The story of the beginning of the unfriendly attitude of the Iroquois toward the French is an interesting one, relevant to the subject under consideration. In the summer of 1609, while the explorer Champlain was on his way through the country in search of knowledge that might aid France in her plans for the control of America, he fell in with some Hurons who were going to fight the Iroquois. From the Hurons he learned of the lake that now bears his name, and also of Lake George, the Hudson and Mohawk Rivers, Lake Ontario, and the strategic travel route leading toward the West of which those waters were a part. The tribes that inhabited and controlled the important region in question, he was told, were the ones with which his native companions were at odds. Champlain and the Hurons continued to travel together, and one day they came upon a party of Iroquois. The French explorer and his fellow countrymen were of course provided with firearms, and though the Iroquois were not his enemies he fired upon them. It was quite safe to do so, and the act was an adventure that relieved the monotony of the march. The Iroquois fled. Before the terrible bang-stick of the white man the legs of two warriors standing afar off became as the stems of broken flowers, and they fell down dead. The Indians could not cope with a weapon like that, but the story of its existence and use went through the wilderness and the relationship between France and the Five Nations was fixed. For nearly a hundred and fifty years afterward the effect of that prejudice was still apparent, despite many later efforts of France to secure the Iroquois as allies.

It is useless to speculate on what might afterward have taken place had not that early antagonism of the Iroquois against the French been created by Champlain's act. History is a hen that sits upon the eggs of opportunity and chance, and the events she hatches are a strange brood. Had the French, from their position in Canada, secured the lasting coöperation of the Iroquois they could in that manner have held the region whose control was to determine the destiny of the continent.

One aspect of colonial affairs which for a long time played into the hands of the Indians was a sort of complex jealousy the colonies had of one another and that prevented them, save on unusual occasions, from acting in unison. Each colony feared that the schemes of consolidation from time to time proposed would deprive it of various privileges of self-government which it insisted on and held in high esteem. There were also numerous acute and long continued quarrels between some of the colonial governments, especially those of Virginia, Pennsylvania, New York and Connecticut, over boundary lines and the political future of the territory toward the West. But despite these matters the colonists did occasionally try to present a united front in their dealings with the natives. Six times within a period of sixty-seven years — in 1684, 1694, 1711, 1722, 1748 and 1751 — there were gatherings or congresses held to negotiate with the Keepers of the Highway. The population was growing; the developing spirit of nationality had already created a cleavage between the interests of England and America, and a restless tendency to move and spread out became more and more apparent.

As early as the year 1753 a dribble of white men began from Pennsylvania and Maryland into the region around the headwaters of the Ohio River, constituting a movement toward the West instead of in the old north-and-south groove. The French and Indian War and Pontiac's uprising delayed but did not prevent the white occupation. The Indians protested, and in 1768 there was another conclave at Fort Pitt between the Iroquois, Shawnees and Delawares, and the white men. The meeting was due to the alarm of the Indians over increasing encroachments on their territory and the killing of natives by invading whites. Among the subjects considered at the congress of the races were land titles, outrages committed against the natives and the privilege of unhampered travel. The white authorities apologized for previous murders and the Delaware chieftain — Beaver — finally grasped the wampum belt of peace and said: "Take hold of the end of this belt, which we may stretch along the road between us, in order that we may all travel it in peace and safety."

Thus another agreement was made by which the colonies promised to respect the territorial interests of the red men. The Indians, as they understood existing conditions, were well within their prerogatives in making protest at invasion, since the British government had recognized the rights of the Indians to undisturbed occupancy of all the lands west of the Alleghany Mountains, and by a proclamation issued in 1763 had fixed the western bounds of the white colonies at the natural line formed by the range in question. But the forces that were at work and the conditions that existed were too elemental to be controlled and directed by the routine methods of organized society. A king who lived across the seas could not be the stage manager of the drama whose preliminary scenes were being enacted here. Its development was dependent on things that had happened before ever there was an England; on processes which took place in that remote and geologic time when men of fair skins and gray eyes came out of savagery and found within themselves a desire to rule and the power to destroy their duskier fellows. Here was a virgin continent, rich beyond conjecture, and owned by a handful of lowlier men whose hue was the pronouncement of their doom. Beside them had become entrenched a horde of the restless and all-pervading race, smitten once more with the fever of conquest that surges in its blood and whose impatience at the limitations to its movement and dominion was swiftly reaching a stage at which transmutation into action would begin. Against such an impulse the ordinary machinery of political government and the decrees of kings could have no effect. As well might an effort be made to stop the sweep of an ocean's tide by aldermanic resolution.

Like pent-up waters that can no longer be contained in the reservoir designed to hold them, the white men overflowed the mountains. The little vanguard of a coming army was not content, as others had been, to find new homes within the coast region so long overrun by the whites, but with one long leap penetrated far into the wilderness. The founding of Pittsburgh furnishes an illustration of the distances to which those pioneers travelled through unknown country. There was as yet no outright breaking of the dam; no advance which resembled a human flood sweeping through the immense and gloomy forests. That was to come a little later. But the period of shoulder-to-shoulder life was passing away, and between the older regions along the Atlantic and those new and wilder lands where the first interior settle-

22.—A New England two-wheeled ox-cart. Used for nearly two centuries as a means of transport between farms and villages lying within a day's journey. The scene is in New Haven, with some buildings of Yale College in the background.

ments were planted there intervened a wilderness some two hundred miles in width that was without white habitation.

There were native protests, bloody reprisals, more conferences, and in 1768 an impoitant new treaty was signed at Fort Stanwix giving to the white men all the country south and east of a line which began on the Ohio River at the mouth of the Cherokee River,[1] that continued up the Ohio to Pittsburgh, thence up the Alleghany to Kittanning, thence overland to the most western branch of the Susquehanna (in New York), thence to Awandoe Creek and the upper Delaware, and finally up the Delaware to a point near Fort Stanwix. For their title to this territory, which included large parts of the present states of New York, Pennsylvania, West Virginia, Kentucky and Tennessee, the white men paid to the Indians about fifty thousand dollars and pledged themselves that no colonists should travel, for purposes of settlement, either north or west of the line which fixed its limits. All territory north and west of the line was confirmed to the Indians.

But friction still continued, and in 1774 the conflict known in history as Dunmore's[2] War broke out. The immediate event which aroused the Indians to a fury and caused them, under the leadership of the Shawnee war chief — Cornstalk — to fight one of the very few pitched battles in their history, was the murder by white frontiersmen of all the family and relatives of the Iroquois chief Logan. Logan was a friend of the white race. He was a native who possessed a sufficient loftiness of character to forgive the murder of some others of his kinsfolk by

[1] As the Tennessee River was then known.
[2] Lord Dunmore was the governor of Virginia at the time. The wrath of the Indians was directed toward the settlers of that province, and Virginia white men were the only colonists who fought.

settlers at an earlier day. His sense of honor, and his dignity, fairness, loyalty and kindness had won for him the admiration and respect of many prominent white men. One day in April of 1774 a party of nine Indians, including men, women and babies, and embracing all of Logan's family, left his village[1] and set out on a friendly visit to the trading camp of a white man named Greathouse with whom they were on good terms, and whom they often went to see. There the grown up natives were made drunk, and when they had become helpless and easy to despatch, Greathouse and two of his companions killed the whole lot, not omitting the children.

So began Dunmore's War. Indian runners sped through all the trails of the forest, leaving the news at every little village of native huts and rushing on again, while the warriors who listened to the tidings they brought were on the way to join Logan and Cornstalk almost before the messengers had vanished in the shadows that swallowed them. When Logan was told what had been done he became a madman. The color of a man's skin makes small difference when he hears a story like that.

Logan went to war in his turn.[2] His friendship for the whites was changed to hatred, and with the vision of his murdered kin before him he killed with ferocity and joy. While the madness lasted he revelled in blood. But the war ended, as usual, in the defeat of the red men before the rifles of the Virginians, and after the overthrow of the Indians in a pitched battle near the Ohio River a peace was concluded between Governor Dunmore and the natives. Logan refused to attend the treaty negotiations, saying that he was a warrior and not a diplomat

[1] At Yellow Creek on the upper Ohio River.
[2] In the eyes of Indians, and according to their immemorial practise, such an act was war.

whose only strength lay in his tongue. He sent to the conference, instead, the message known as Logan's Speech, a few brief words in explanation of his position that have from that day taken rank as perhaps the loftiest utterance made by a native American. So profound was the impression the message created at the conference that the white men who were there assembled — all of whom had known and esteemed Logan — sat up half the night beside their camp-fires in order to talk about it and commit it to memory.

By the terms of the treaty that ended Dunmore's War the white population of the colonies was granted permission to navigate the Ohio River without molestation by the natives, and one more step was thereby taken in the travel movement toward the West. So the white men's boats, cumbrous, uncouth of aspect, yet freighted with the restless energy and strength of a conquering people, floated out at last on the waters of the Beautiful River. It was also agreed in the treaty that no northern Indians were to go south of the Ohio, and that no white men should thereafter penetrate into the native territories north of that stream.

Such was the situation just previous to the Revolution, whose near approach was already apparent. With the outbreak of that struggle all lesser affairs, including the relations between colonies and Indians, and the questions bearing on safe and improved travel conditions throughout the country were swept aside, not again to be taken up until the outcome of the struggle for political independence should be determined.

The Indians as a rule took sides with England during the contest[1] and fought against the colonial forces. Their

---

[1] Some Indian nations remained neutral.

action in that respect was understandable in view of what had gone before, for whatever protection they had secured in their quarrels with the colonials had been due to action by the British government itself and its crown repre-

Calèche du Canada, ou marche donc.

23.—The Canadian caleche, which was used in northern New England, gradually evolved into one of the early colonial two-wheeled vehicles called the chair. When equipped with a linsey-woolsey or leather cover the chair became a chaise. See illustrations Nos. 59 and 156.

sentatives on this side of the water. The Continental Congress and its agents made efforts to secure Indians as allies for the colonies against the English, but with such small success that the attempt was soon given up as hopeless. The red men understood that overtures from the new American government were not prompted by friendliness, but by desperate need. And in addition to the native memory of past grievances an incident which happened early in the war made any such alliance out of the question, even if otherwise possible.

79

Among those Indian nations whose head men sought to keep out of the struggle between England and her revolting possessions were the Shawnees, of which Cornstalk was a leader. But the hot bloods among the Shawnees, eager for revenge against the colonists, were for fighting under the Cross of Saint George. In an effort to maintain peace between his people and the colonials Cornstalk went on a visit of friendliness to a fort of the American troops, taking with him Redhawk and another chief. To the Americans he explained the situation, saying that though many of the Shawnee fighting men wanted war, he and the other leaders were against a clash and hoped to prevent it. He also said, as any man in his position would do, that in case his best efforts were unsuccessful he would be in honor bound to fight at the head of his warriors. On those words the white Americans seized Cornstalk and the other two visitors and imprisoned them as hostages.[1]

Thereupon the Shawnees went to war against the colonists, and soon killed a soldier of the fort where Cornstalk was held prisoner. When a party of the other soldiers found their dead comrade they ran with one accord toward the fort and rushed in with a tumult. Cornstalk heard, and divined what it meant. Rising to his feet he bade his son[2] stand likewise, saying to him that it was good they should die together. As the white soldiers burst into the room Cornstalk turned and faced them and so perished.

The outcome of the Revolution placed both the new-born nation and the Indians in a difficult position. Eng-

[1] An act showing how little the Indian character was understood by its perpetrators. In addition to its uselessness as a factor for peace, such a deed was more apt to incite hostilities than to prevent them.
[2] Who had come to visit him.

land, by ceding to the American states all territory she had held south of the Great Lakes and east of the Mississippi had of necessity abandoned her red allies to the mercies of a country which they had just been fighting, and left them on lands the title to which had, in theoretical sense, passed to the confederated colonies. The Republic, on the other hand, could not rid itself of the native red population that had so recently been armed foes. It was brought face to face with a situation that demanded free and unimpeded travel through much of the outlying regions, while at the same time circumstances called for a recognition of the property right of the Indians to lands on which they might live and gain their sustenance. The necessity of more territory toward the west in which the nation might expand and meet the needs of a growing population, together with the attainment of safe travel toward the west were plain, and gradually became — aside from politics — the principal feature of the nation's internal affairs. In fact the conditions here stated, and which were first brought into prominence soon after the Revolution, continued to be the controlling influence in the development of the Republic from that day until the Atlantic and Pacific Oceans, and all that lay between, were linked together by an unbroken travel system eighty-six years afterward. There were times when the people seemed to pause for a while on the march, as a giant who sleeps, but they always went on again, ever demanding a little more room in which to move and a better way of getting where they wanted to go.

Beginning with the Congress of the Confederation, the newly created United States recognized the several groups of Indians as separate nations having sovereignty over and ownership of territory, and dealt with them on that basis.[1] Whenever it occurred — as it did many times — that the United States found need for regions owned and occupied by the Indians it acquired possession of such territories by the negotiation of formal treaties, just as it did in buying the Louisiana Territory from France and Florida from Spain.

In the early years of the Northwest Territory the armed troops of the confederated colonies sometimes used force in evicting settlers who had encroached on the Indians' lands in that region, and even burned the log cabins of such invaders. Yet at the same time the nation was demanding that the Indians allow white men to travel into and settle on the territory where the evictions were taking place. These things indicated a willingness — even a desire—on the part of the Caucasian officials to accomplish a predetermined purpose by methods quite correct from the civilized standpoint of orderly legislative and legal process. From the more primitive viewpoint of the natives the curious spectacle presented simply an unworthy quibble. To the Indians it mattered little what method was used in depriving them of their land. They didn't want to give it up at all. It was small consolation for them to discover that henceforth they were to lose

---

[1] Among the acts of the new American government in which the Indians were acknowledged to be people distinct from the citizens of the Republic, and in which their land proprietorship and qualities of separate nationality were stated may be cited the following:

Articles of confederation; adopted by the Continental Congress in 1777: Article 6.— "No state shall engage in any war without the consent of the United States in Congress assembled, unless such state be actually invaded by enemies, or shall have received certain advice of a resolution being formed by some nation of Indians to invade such state, and the danger is so imminent as not to admit of a delay, till the United States in Congress assembled can be consulted."

Constitution drawn up by the Congress of the Confederation and put into effect in 1789: Article 1. Section 8.—"Congress shall have power . . . to regulate commerce with foreign nations, and among the several States, and with the Indian Tribes."

Northwest Ordinance, adopted by the Congress of the Confederation in 1787. Section 8.—"The Governor . . . shall proceed, from time to time, as circumstances may require, to lay out the parts of the district on which the Indian titles shall have been extinguished, into counties and townships."

From the same instrument: Article III.—The utmost good faith shall always be observed toward the Indians; their lands and property shall never be taken from them without their consent; and in their property rights and liberty they shall never be invaded or disturbed, unless in just and lawful wars authorized by Congress."

it through reluctantly signed documents, portentous with ceremony and red seals, whose completion was always promptly followed by the appearance of soldiers, surveyors and more white travellers marching through the forest. Some chiefs at last refused to sign any papers, saying that every time they did so their people lost something.

From 1774 until the Treaty of Greenville in 1795, following Wayne's decisive victory over the confederated tribes at Fallen Timbers, there was no real peace along the northwestern border. Caucasian movement either by land or water was at all times unsafe, and many a traveller found a destination he was not seeking. But from 1795 until Tecumseh tried, sixteen years later, to organize the interior tribes into a confederacy opposed to further white advance, reasonable quiet reigned upon the frontier. Whatever other dangers and hardships the traveller might encounter he was in little peril that was due from Indian molestation of any sort.

CHAPTER VI

EARLY CONDITIONS IN THE SOUTH — RADICAL DIFFERENCES
BETWEEN ITS DEVELOPMENT AND THAT OF THE
NORTH — THE LIMITED MOVEMENT OF EARLY DAYS
— ORIGIN AND EFFECT OF THE PLANTATION SYSTEM
— SOCIAL CLEAVAGE — WASHINGTON AS A TYPE OF
ONE CLASS — THE TASK OF THE PEOPLE AND THE
MANNER IN WHICH THEY FOUND STRENGTH TO
PERFORM IT

DURING the early years of their history[1] the growth
of the southern colonies, with the exception of Virginia, did not proceed nearly so rapidly as that of the
regions which have already claimed attention. Nor did
important movements of the population develop so
promptly. As a whole the general settlement of the future
southern states along the Atlantic seaboard took place at a
decidedly later date than did the rise of the New England
and middle colonies. Other elements that helped to bring
about the condition stated were the nature of the southern
region itself, and the character, traditions, habits and necessities of the first white men who permanently occupied
it. That part of the South extending from the Atlantic to
the Mississippi and from the Ohio River to the Gulf of
Mexico had not been so favored as the North with a profusion of natural highways of travel in the shape of lakes
and rivers. It had, to be sure, the Chesapeake Bay and

[1] The period before 1770.

84

Potomac River as a gateway into the interior, the Cherokee and Cumberland Rivers flowing northward into the
Ohio, and a few coastal streams against whose currents
slow progress could be made by small boats or log canoes
for goodly distances into the wilderness. In an almost
literal sense the South of that early day was a solid block
of primeval woods that, apart from the actual coast itself,
demanded travel on land or none at all. It was further

24.—A very fine private coach of the late eighteenth century. Probably built
about 1790 by David Clark of Philadelphia, for Samuel Powell of that city.
Exhibited during the Civil War period, in museums and public fairs, as a
coach that had belonged to Washington.

true that rough and mountainous country made up a
larger proportion of the territory than was the case in the
early settled parts of New England and the middle sections. Virginia, Tennessee, Kentucky, the two Carolinas
and Georgia were notable for the obstacles they presented
to early and primitive land travel. Yet it was precisely
those difficulties that inspired their early inhabitants with

the indomitable spirit from which victory is born, and made the southern wilderness a scene of memorable deeds. That part of the continent was to witness the first westward march of a white population through the forest; the first organized display of the new travel impulse that afterward continued without interruption by flatboat, steamboat, canal-boat, stage-coach, prairie schooner and railway until there was no more land to cross, and the Pacific Ocean halted the long migration.

Among all phases of the varied history that deals with the occupation and economic conquest of the continent by the white race, that which relates to the South from the time of its first settlements until the War for Independence is perhaps least known. We possess the dates and stories of certain important events, and a few human figures stand out with the prominence of silhouettes against a background of mystery, legend and conjecture. But mere dates are no longer esteemed the chief elements of history. They are not even the skeleton of it, for chronological records alone do not enable us to reconstruct the whole symmetrical substance of a period. They do not portray its features, analyze its qualities of strength and weakness or transform its vanished people and activities into a living drama that can be exhibited like moving pictures thrown upon a screen. The southern generations of that early time lived afar off. They had a hard time of it at first — even harder in many ways than those to the north of them. They tried to be sufficient unto themselves as far as possible; were very busy in the struggle to establish themselves securely in a new country, and — doubtless because of their surroundings, isolation and labors — developed less of the recording instinct than appeared among other white pioneers of the country.

A HISTORY OF TRAVEL IN AMERICA

During the early years of the white invasion of Virginia and the shores of Chesapeake Bay practically all travel was carried on between the various little settlements and plantations by means of big log canoes and heavy, broad-beamed sailing boats. And because of their fear of the Indians it was the habit of the people to build shields along the sides of the craft as a protection against arrows, and to fasten small poles in the boats, with hats on top of them just high enough to be seen above the shields, in order to make the natives think the moving parties were stronger than they really were. No effort was made for a long time to extend white activity more than a few miles back from the coast, and from the very first the character of development in the South showed a marked divergence from the tendency that manifested itself in the northern colonies. In the North the people at once began to gather into compact little communities which speedily became towns and served as central points from which radiated the white influence. In the South this was not so. The main impulse that directed the method and progress of southern settlement in its earliest days lay in the control of men who, before coming to the new continent, had been accustomed to traditions and methods of life handed down from the feudal period of large landed estates which produced all that was needful for owner and retainer alike. Hence the establishment of the plantation system of the South, and the creation of conditions that profoundly affected its future history not only with regard to travel movement, but in respect of all those other social and economic conditions that are always based on the accessibility of population units to one another. It must not be understood there were no towns whatever in the South during its first century and a half, for there were such communities, but they were very few in number, very small, and exerted practically no influence in the life of the inhabitants.

By the year 1689 Virginia had some 50,000 or 60,000 people scattered in obedience to the plantation system, but keeping close to water. The few points where population was at all concentrated were little settlements called Henrico, Bermuda and West Shirley. Rude paths through the forest were increasing, and a few rough roads were in existence, but no travel by vehicle was yet possible. All land journeys of consequence were made on horseback, and three years before the date named the Burgesses had recognized the importance of quicker travel by passing a law for improving the breed of horses in the colony. The landed proprietors met this appeal of the government with enthusiasm and the result was the evolution of a splendid type of animal that, together with an equally famous breed developed about the same time in Rhode Island,[1] served through all the English colonies, for a long time, as the best means of getting from place to place.

The early conditions in Maryland were similar to those in Virginia. Plantations were established all along the bays and rivers, each with a water frontage, and boats were the standard vehicle for such little travel as took place. Until the time of the Revolution the colony — aside from plantation clearings on the waterways — was one unbroken forest. The old Baltimore was a trivial settlement that appeared on Bush River about 1683, but the new and present city was established on the Patapsco in 1730. Even as late as the year 1752 the town had but twenty-five houses. Twenty years after the founding of

[1] The Rhode Island horses were called the Narragansett breed. It is believed to have died out soon after 1800. Horses were expensive, and good animals for horseback riding were worth from £25 to £40.

the colony there were only about eight thousand people within its limits, and by 1689 the population had only grown to some thirty thousand. After that time the increase was more noticeable and by 1751 Maryland had 145,000 people. Road building was advancing in a few

25.—Method by which coach or carriage travellers were conveyed across a stream in the days when journeys in wheeled vehicles were first becoming possible. If the ferry boat was a small one, the horses were compelled to swim.

localities and the first wheeled vehicles and sedan chairs had appeared.

The early population of these two colonies differed from that which established itself in the North in as striking a degree as did the economic conditions of the two regions. From the first there existed in the South a sharper social cleavage in the population than was to be found in New England and the intermediate settlements. It practically divided the people of the South into two classes, one of which had brought to America and transplanted here all those qualities and customs that had

long distinguished the man of culture and landed proprietor of England. The other class, numerically the
greater but of infinitely less consequence in directing the
political and social affairs of the people during the first
century, was made up of small independent husband-
men from abroad or from the northern settlements, and
of agricultural employees and retainers of the rich. The
language of Lord Calvert in cataloguing his first party
of settlers as "twenty gentlemen and three hundred laborers" gives a fairly good idea of the distinction that long
existed between the two sorts of inhabitants. The body
of the population performed the labor necessary in trans-
forming a vast primeval forest into a civilization. Its
members felled and burned the huge trees, made potash
from their ashes, planted the soil, built the log cabins and
propelled the boats when journeys were made. Their lives
were dedicated to severe and unceasing toil, to eating,
sleeping and fighting. There is little need for wonder that
they left practically no annals of the years they lived in.
They spent their days in doing things; not in telling about
them. And in the performance of the tremendous task
that had fallen to their lot they were sustained by a
strength not appreciated by themselves. They and their
ancestors had never been on speaking terms with luxury
and they were not able, through personal knowledge and
understanding, to compare their situation with a less stern
necessity. It was well for America that this was so.

The other class organized and directed the activities
of the time, valiantly led their fellow men in battle when
need arose and sought, in the utmost degree permitted
by their surroundings, to perpetuate on the edge of an
immense wilderness all those refinements and light diversions of society without which their situation must have

been intolerable. They, much more than the bulk of their fellows, had need of other interests which could distract them for a time from the problem they had attacked. Even they did not behold their task as we do, for they were in actual contact with it, and so could not mentally grasp its full proportions. Only a distant view and a perspective like the one of to-day could do that. Such travel as they were able to enjoy was to England or to the northern colonies aboard little vessels bearing cargoes of their tobacco.

So the South slowly grew, and each plantation or settlement created its own little lost and forest-circled world, the uttermost limits of which included only the other humans within a radius of forty or fifty miles — a day's hard horseback journey. Usually the geographical distance within which neighborly intercourse was constantly maintained was decidedly less than that. The rare occasion which brought about a more general gathering of the population was a prearranged hunt for wild pigs[1] or a meeting at some common center for a carnival of horse racing or other sport. To events like these the landed proprietors and numbers of the less important figures of the population would often journey through the woods for a hundred miles or more. It was out of such early assemblages that later grew the fairs held at Norfolk and other towns, to which the populace travelled in still larger numbers. These meetings, and the experiences gained by them, had much to do with the establishment of permanent land routes of travel that gradually came into existence.

The type of landed gentlemen who from the first so indelibly impressed their character and traditions on

---

[1] Doubtless the ancestors of the "razor-backs" still found in some woods of the South.

the life of the South can be well portrayed by reference to a certain prominent and highly esteemed young soldier and pioneer named Colonel George Washington. He came somewhat late upon the scene, but in him were embodied not only the attributes that had ruled the region for generations, but other traits that presaged the American of the future. More than any other man of his era or of all the colonies up to that time, he seems to have penetrated the future with a prophet's half-veiled vision and beheld a little of the needs and restlessness of an unborn nation, and the approaching demand for means of swift and comfortable movement throughout the land. Yet in that respect he was not a miracle of omniscience, any more than he was the perfect, self-sacrificing, wholly immaculate, austere and almost godlike man into which later generations, moral precepts and millions of school-books have hopelessly transformed him.

He was a serious minded human being of extraordinary ability, self-control and justifiable self-confidence into whose character was woven the executive instinct, somewhat of selfish thrift, and an unusual power for commanding the best endeavor of other men. He had a keen appreciation of the value — in public affairs — of a large dignity and sobriety, and in private life showed a strongly developed fondness for the good things of this world. The respect in which Washington was great above his contemporaries did not lie in his abilities, for numerous men of his time were as able as he, but in a certain rare quality of the will by virtue of which he could effectively isolate and apply those abilities, each in its appropriate circumstance and time. Many men are equipped by nature as he was, and, despite opportunity, remain mediocre

92

in deeds accomplished, for they lack that one further thing without which the rest are valueless possessions — a self created and dogged determination to apply their powers

26.—Picturesque bridges, supported by huge logs or hewed timbers, began to appear as soon as wagons came into general use.

with utmost skill and effort to the tasks which confront them. That is a gift which nature does not bestow.

Like any other gentleman of the period he drank his half pint or pint of wine at dinner, together with additional punch and beer. He would ride ten miles to attend a dance and skip about for three hours without sitting down after he got there. He spent whole days over the card table and bought his cards by the dozen packs at a time. He raced his horses, bet his money on their chances to win, and delighted when they came home in front of all the rest. In a period of two months he had visitors from other plantations on twenty-nine days, and himself went away on seven other occasions.[1] He gathered about him, in the shadow of the wilderness, a library of the best books in history, literature and the arts,[2] and read them. Other men of his class did the like in all respects. It was their necessary way of life; an antidote for a sedentary and immobile existence and their endless battle with the rude conditions of a new country. But the other sort of people had no such diversions. The forest fell before the "greatest wielders of the ax the world has known;" the smell of burning wood hung always in the air; a haze of smoke drifted over the clearing.

Gradually, as the regions still farther to the southward were invaded by the white race there came increasing rumors back to the northward of their fertility and mildness of climate. Rumors at length changed to more or less authentic information, and then began a slow but constantly increasing stream of travel toward them from New England and the middle colonies. Some of the more important movements of the sort have already been mentioned. The Carolinas had been occupied by various driblets of immigration from other colonies during the period from 1653 to 1740,[3] and several parties from abroad had also arrived. The Ashley River region was peopled by the English in 1670, and two years later saw the site of Charleston occupied. Quite a number of Huguenot refugees also came to the country after the revocation of the edict of Nantes in 1685, and settled along Cooper River. By the year 1689 the territory now known as North Carolina and South Carolina held some five or six thousand inhabitants, and in 1693 the region was

---

[1] He tells of these various things in his "Journal."
[2] The large part of his books is now in the Athaneum in Boston.
[3] See list of early organized migrations in Chapter III. Some of those who journeyed into the Carolinas from Virginia did so in order to escape the harsh measures of government that followed an insurrection in the last named colony.

divided into two colonies. The population of the north-ernmost of the two at that time had been mainly secured through migrations from other American settlements,[1] and the principal points at which the newcomers had gathered were around the Albemarle section. It was to Albemarle that the New Englanders came and to which the Virginians fled after the uprising there. The southern colony, on the contrary, was more strongly influenced and peopled by settlers direct from England, Scotland and Ireland,[2] and their first important centers of activity were the Ashley River and Charleston. Gradually the coast settlements spread and threw off fragments that made their way into the interior.

Georgia did not appear on the map of American territory permanently occupied by the English speaking race until 1733. In the previous November Oglethorpe[3] had reached Charleston from England with thirty-five families[4] chosen to be the nucleus of a new invasion, and leaving them in the South Carolina town he set out to visit the unknown country that was his destination. Travelling by canoe he finally reached the spot destined to become Savannah, bought land from the Indians there, and his little company took up in its turn the conquest of the wilderness. The progress of Oglethorpe's colony was slow, despite the arrival of several parties of Italians, Salzburgers and Scotch during the next few years. In 1736 Oglethorpe brought over two hundred and two more colonists, among whom was John Wesley. Augusta, which was founded in 1734, had but forty-seven in-

[1] Though about the beginning of the eighteenth century a few Swiss and Germans settled at Newbern.
[2] Other elements that entered into the early population of South Carolina were parties of German Palatines that came over after 1720, and some Swiss that settled near the Savannah River about 1732.
[3] He had received a grant from the Crown.
[4] A hundred and thirty souls, all told.

habitants in 1741, exclusive of a small garrison of soldiers, and in 1752, when the colony's charter was surrendered to the crown of England it contained only about two thousand three hundred white people and a thousand slaves. They had made scarcely any impression on the forests that surrounded them, and moved about hardly at all.

But little more need be said concerning general conditions in the South as they were just before the commencement of the population movements that introduced a new era into the history of America. Florida was merely the shuttlecock of foreign wars, alternately held by Spain and England, and her affairs bore no relation to the greater events of permanent human progress. Alabama was an unknown country with a slight fringe of settlements along the coast. Mobile, the chief of them, was a little town hedged in by a stockade and held by the English from 1763. New Orleans, like Florida, was the shifting prize of European warfare. France owned the Louisiana province until 1762, when she ceded it to Spain, and England was scheming to possess it. New Orleans had already become a place of considerable importance and contained some eight hundred houses and about four thousand inhabitants. It was surrounded by the inevitable stockade, two and a half miles in diameter. Nearly six thousand other people lived in the neighborhood of the city, whose activities extended up the Mississippi to a little French settlement called St. Louis, far off in the interior of the continent. Boats sometimes went up the river to St. Louis, taking two or three months for the trip, but, as has already been said, the navigation of the Mississippi at that time, or during its control by European nations, was not a factor in the development of the American travel system.

CHAPTER VII

THE FIRST AMERICANS WHO MARCHED TO THE WEST —
THEIR ANCESTRY, QUALITIES, APPEARANCE AND MAN-
NER OF LIVING — LOG CABINS, THEIR CONSTRUCTION,
FURNISHINGS AND INDUSTRIES — NATURE OF THE
EDUCATION OF THE HILL PEOPLE OF THE SOUTH —
THEIR PECULIAR FITNESS FOR THEIR APPROACHING
TASK — THE REPUBLIC OF WAUTAGA

WE may now return to the region included at present in western and southwestern Virginia, western North Carolina and eastern Tennessee, and consider the people who were the first Americans to take up their march toward the West, together with the conditions that produced them and out of which their performance grew. Those men and women were Americans by birth and habit, and although the date of the exploits soon to be told was as early as the period between 1769 and 1779, the population that performed them could even then look back through several generations of ancestry which, like themselves, had grown up within the shadow of the woods and fought for life and substance with the same primitive conditions. They were the descendants of the bands of restless spirits that came down by overland marches from the more northern localities of Pennsylvania and New England during the north-and-south migrations of the period from 1735 onward, and who had brought with them into the South not only the traditional knowledge of

97

border existence but a lifetime of personal experience as well.

So — as a race — they had no new things to learn. The instinct of the pioneer was in them, and a cool caution, surprising alertness, bravery and entire self-reliance

27.—A backwoodsman and his dog. The cabin dwellers' clothing was all of home fabrication, and made of linsey-woolsey or deer skin. Original sketch by Joshua Shaw. This and the following fifteen illustrations, to No. 42 inclusive, constitute a series showing conditions of pioneer life and travel in the wilderness.

marked all their acts. They had no schools, but a boy's education nevertheless began as soon as he could walk. His lessons were not mere words for the brain to memorize and the tongue to repeat; they were the methods in which things were done and results accomplished by people older than himself, and it was his duty to observe those processes, comprehend their purpose and duplicate them with equal skill. He learned the lessons well, for he knew that many times his life would depend on his proficiency. At the age of twelve or fourteen his father handed him a rifle and he ceased to be a boy.[1] With that act he became a man, having his man's share of responsibilities in the community and his particular loophole to defend.

The education of the girl was a similar process. By the time her brother had received his rifle she had mastered all the duties of a housewife. When a boy went on an errand he did not go spinning over the country on a bicycle or clattering along the pavements on roller skates. He took down his rifle from its pegs on the wall, looked at the priming and started across the clearing with every sense alert, and with a mind so trained that the appearance and condition of all the objects about him, together with the action of beast or bird and each other detail on the face of earth, spoke its true meaning. Though he had received no schooling in the fashion of later days he had long been enrolled in nature's university — the forest. All its varied aspects and voices had been his teachers at an age when the boys of nowadays are still flying kites and playing marbles. He had received his degree in the difficult art of self-preservation, and was about to enter on a post-graduate course in rearing a family and increasing his stock of worldly goods. Many of those little men and women were married at the age of fifteen or sixteen, and the rigid training they had received in self-reliance and the serious concerns of life made them competent to assume such relationship and—measured by the standards of the time — to win success.

[1] Long before reaching the age indicated he had become an expert with the weapon. The presentation of a rifle at that period of life had somewhat the quality of a ceremonial, and was intended to impress upon him his standing among the elders.

In personal appearance the people reflected the conditions under which they lived. Their faces, brown from exposure to the elements, were singularly set in expression and carried a sort of grimness. Nothing surprised them. The happening of every event was discounted in advance. Its coming was calmly awaited, and whatever action it demanded from them was performed so quickly that it seemed rather to be by instinct than as the result of thought or reason. Their eyes were the distinguishing feature of their countenances. Clear, inscrutable and direct, the vision of man or woman saw everything. When talking with one another they spoke eye to eye. While about their work, in the open or the forest, a single glance had the gathering power of a fisherman's net and the analysis of a microscope. But the chief quality and value of such a look was its instant perception of the abnormal. Trained from babyhood to recognize the normal appearance of all things about him, the eye of the woodsman automatically ignored what was undisturbed and pounced on whatever was as it should not be. A footprint of any sort shrieked like a ten-inch shell, and a single leaf standing on edge when it should have been lying flat made him halt and ask the question, "Why?"

Those early Americans carried no superfluous flesh. Somewhat above the average height, as men and women go, they were lean and supple. Their ancestors had been dwellers in the hills before them, and, of choice, had come into a mountainous country to make their new homes. Much walking and incessant labor had given them great endurance. The strength of their rough hands could break bones. Those who were weak died early, and many of the rest lived until they were killed in one way or another. They walked with a soft and swinging stride, keep-

28.—Backwoodsmen at work in the forest. "Greatest wielders of the ax the world has known." Showing details of dress and the type of instrument by which the wilderness was swept away. Original sketch by Joshua Shaw.

ing themselves always well poised, for no man ever knew whether his next move would be a leap to the right or to the left, a dive behind a log, a dash ahead or a rush backward over the path he had come. Then again he might decide to climb a tree. He could never tell beforehand. Circumstances decided those things. They were a nervous people in a certain sense, yet they held themselves with such a grip that they seemed almost phlegmatic. Nerves — or at least any indulgence in the state of mental excitability which has become a modern disease—were not in harmony with the surroundings. When a man or woman aimed a rifle the body that upheld it was like a carved figure. And after the smoke floated away there was no exultation to be seen; only the same outward calmness. Every task, whatever its degree of importance, and no matter how swiftly it was to be performed, was undertaken with careful and methodical process. Each individual sought to save his strength by planning his acts beforehand, that no energy might be wasted by indecision or misdirected effort when the need for action came upon him.

Such were the qualities of the people and the methods by which they adapted themselves to the country their fathers had invaded. Perhaps no race has ever been more successful than they were in fitting themselves to the natural conditions around them and for the work they were destined to accomplish.

A glance at any map will reveal the character of the region in which they lived. It was a rough country whose chief natural feature was a confusion of hills and mountains that as a general rule extended in parallel ridges from northeast to southwest. Between the ranges were valleys through which ran many rapid and usually shallow rivers and lesser streams. In the valleys, but near to the hills, were set up the homes of this strong primitive population. When the original migrations took place the forest swept over the whole land, mountain and valley alike, in its untouched and forbidding aspect. During the years that had gone by since then a multitude of little clearings had been made by the mountaineers, whose numbers had rather rapidly increased. The number of people who lived in the hills of western North Carolina and western Virginia at the time their organized exodus began can not be accurately given, but perhaps it amounted to fifteen or twenty thousand souls.

All their efforts had made but small impression on the forest. The number of trees to be felled in such work was so incalculable and their individual size so great that they cumbered the ground. There was no way to move them and nowhere to have taken them if the moving had been possible. Nor was there any use to which they could be put. They had to be burned where they fell. The timber used for fuel, and in building cabins, making fences and fashioning household furniture was such an infinitesimal part of the whole mass as to be unworthy of mention.

So far as travel facilities and opportunities for getting about the country were concerned, the hill people of the South, from 1735 to the time of the Revolution, faced just the same situation that confronted the Pilgrims and Puritans in 1635. They were beginning all over again, in their part of the continent, a process of evolution that had elsewhere been in active operation for a century or more. They had a few Indian trails and some horses, but mainly depended on their own legs. The streams that were narrow were spanned by log bridges, and at various well-known points on the wider rivers, big flat-bottomed ferry

103

boats were built, and kept for the common use of the inhabitants. Canoes were also used, but not nearly to the extent that prevailed in the early days of New England. Most of them were made from logs, and were called dug-outs. The one big advantage possessed by the mountain-eers over the earlier inhabitants of the North was to be found in their habits and qualities rather than in any phase of their natural surroundings. In truth the country they lived in offered much less inducement to easy move-ment than that of the former Americans with whom they are here compared. But the southerners were an even bolder and more self-reliant people, as might have been expected of a race with three generations of wilderness experience as an inheritance. They were more easily adaptable to conditions.

No settlements that resembled towns were to be found in the hills. The cabins of the settlers — each with its clearing — showed a tendency to spring up beside some attractive stream along which they might be scattered, over a distance of a dozen miles, to the number of fifty or more. Each of these loosely connected communities, as soon as it was large enough, used its common effort in building at a convenient point a blockhouse and stockade for mutual defense. Later the people often put up a log church in whose pulpit of rough oaken slabs certain ones of the valley presided in turn, while the rest of the people sat on benches beneath them. On rare occasions a genuine ordained preacher of the gospel — a circuit rider on a salary of fifty or seventy-five dollars a year — sent word that he would visit one of the chapels. When such an event was to happen the tidings of it went through many valleys, and on the appointed Sabbath day there assem-bled a company drawn from all the country round. Every tree near the log structure was a hitching-post where weary horses stood, while the men and women who had ridden them crowded within to listen to a real sermon redolent of brimstone and filled with the deep, sincere and devout feeling that reflected the inward lives of the congregation. The hill men, for all their roughness, were an earnest and religious people who clung fast to an abiding belief that their affairs were swayed by a guidance higher than their own.

Though the region was far removed from effective legal control, crime was practically non-existent. Such a tie of common need and dependence as bound the population together, added to the labor of their existence, operated strongly to suppress any tendency toward internal disorder. It must be said, nevertheless, that the white men assumed an attitude toward the Indians that was not always in harmony with the recognition they gave to the rights of one another. In this respect they were far from being exceptional. Such regulation of their mutual affairs as seemed necessary was largely a matter of common consent, and in every district there were a few figures who, as always under like conditions, were looked upon as leaders of the rest.

The homes of the people were a faithful mirror of their character and surroundings. To those little cabins of the early centuries of American development a fascinating interest has always clung, and strong as that attraction has been it is destined to be greater still in the future, as more attention is paid by each succeeding generation to the formative period of national life. More and more it is coming to be realized that America has a history which underlies the catalogue of her wars and political wrangles; a history that, because of the conditions amid which it developed and the problems it solved, contains an interest to rival the story of any other nation. Nothing is better fitted to be a symbol of that narrative than the log cabin, for if but one such habitation and its contents had survived we could, with no other knowledge whatsoever of the period it represented, reconstruct from it and its furnishings the qualities, habits and methods of those early people with a striking approximation to the truth.

Log cabins were always, when possible, built by community effort. On an appointed day the neighbors of the man who needed a house appeared on the spot selected, inquired the intended dimensions of the cabin, and began chopping down seventy or eighty of the tallest and straightest small trees in the immediate neighborhood.[1] A common size for the house was about twenty feet long by sixteen feet wide, often with a low room, or upper floor, under the sloping roof. When the felled trees had been chopped into proper lengths the logs thus made were rolled to the site picked out. These preliminary processes required two or three days.

Two logs each sixteen feet long[2] and of greater thickness than the others were then put in position twenty feet apart, and at each end of each log a deep notch was cut on the upper surface extending through about one-third of its diameter. Two other logs, each twenty feet long and correspondingly thick were next fitted with notches at the ends, both above and below, and were laid on the first pair, into which their lower notches dovetailed. A foundation was thus obtained that lifted the body of the cabin some three feet above the ground. About a dozen slender logs

[1] The most common trees of the southern forest were the oak, cottonwood, mulberry, hickory, sycamore, persimmon, ash, locust, tulip, walnut, fir, birch, pine, chestnut, maple, beech and hemlock.
[2] If the cabin was to be of the dimensions named, as is supposed in this description.

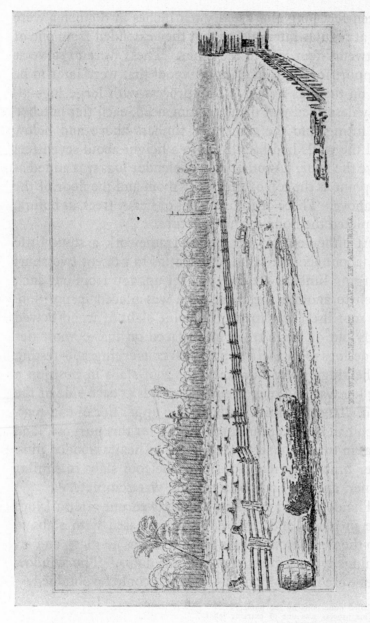

NEWLY CLEARED FARM IN AMERICA.

29.—After the ax had passed. The stumps were left to rot. Only a trifling fraction of the timber was needed for fences, fuel, cabins and home-made furniture. The fallen trees covered the ground and had to be burned where they fell.

sixteen feet long and usually ten inches in diameter were laid at regular intervals, so that they extended from one of the twenty-foot logs to the other. These were to serve as a support for the thin slabs of wood[1] that were later to be laid on them as a floor. The process with large logs already described was then recommenced, each tier notched and fitting into the transverse timbers above and below until the walls had been built to a height about seven feet above the floor. Another row of slender logs was added at this point as the top of the lower room and the floor of the one above. Three or four courses of heavy trees, as before, completed the body of the structure.

At either end of the upper framework a stout little tree, about six feet tall and so cut as to present two short diverging limbs at the top, was set up, and from one such crotch to another the ridge pole was placed in position. The roof itself was formed by wide slabs of wood hewed bodily out of large trees[2] and placed on the topmost tier of side-logs with their upper ends converging and resting on the ridge pole. To keep the roof slabs in position a long log was laid over their lower ends at each side of the cabin. Its extremities rested on the upper tier of end-logs, which had been kept unusually long for this purpose,[3] and it was in turn held secure by means of heavy wooden pins. Other timbers were placed over the roof slabs in similar manner, and the body of the cabin was complete.

The doors and windows were sawed out after all logs were in place, and their edges were cased with slabs to keep the walls from sagging. There was no glass, and all openings were protected by strong doors. The window panes were made of paper — when it could be obtained —

---

[1] Called puncheons by the pioneers.
[2] This process was one of extreme labor.
[3] See picture reproduced.

plentifully coated with hogs' lard or bear grease. The big fireplace was constructed of large flat stones, and the chimney was built of sticks laid in the same alternating manner as were the timbers of the house, with the chinks of the chimney structure filled and covered with clay that was soon hardened by the heat. All spaces between the logs were then stopped up with mud and moss and generally plastered over with clay in addition. Slabs were laid for the floors, a perpendicular ladder of five or six rounds served as a staircase, and the domicile was finished. The whole job ordinarily took about a week, but was often done in less time if six or eight men were busy in the work. Not a scrap of metal had entered into its construction. It was wholly a product made from materials found within a quarter of a mile of the spot where it stood ready for occupancy.

The furnishings of the cabin were as simple as the structure itself. Sometimes the chairs were short sections sawed from the trunk of a hickory tree,[1] but often they were more ornate and pretentious affairs, consisting of a slab of green wood stuck on top of three legs. One type of table was a similar contrivance, but with four legs, and movable. The other sort was built permanently against the wall at one side, with its other edge on sticks. The bed frame was usually held up at one side by supports driven into the wall. On it were laid the inevitable slabs, and then a bedtick filled with chaff, pine needles or dried moss. Up-stairs, if there was an up-stairs, were more beds, and smoked meat and dried herbs that hung from the roof. Pillow covers and sheets were almost unknown. Of blankets, though, there was usually an abundance. Beside the larded window through which the sunshine came with

---

[1] Such a chair was called a "block."

golden mellowness stood a home-made spinning-wheel, and on puncheon shelves around the walls were a few dishes, pots and kettles. Near the fireplace and doorway hung rifles and yellow powder horns, and somewhere, perhaps, there was a comb and bit of looking-glass. But there was a limit to extravagance. Forks and spoons were either whittled out of wood or made by a blacksmith, and the knives served for a large variety of other purposes that need not be discussed. One other feature of the cabin that deserves mention was a habit often displayed by the floor and furniture. Owing to the haste with which everything was built the flat slabs of wood that entered so largely into the construction of the home were usually put in place while still in a green state, and the heat from the big fireplace caused them to warp amazingly. A bed so made would soon undulate beneath its occupants like the waves of the sea; the dinner would all slide to the center of the table and the floor would curl up like a porcupine.

Each little settlement constituted an independent and self-supporting establishment[1] and the cabin itself was a veritable industrial institution. The man, or some neighbor more skilled than he in metal working, made his rifle, ax, hoe and sickle. Ploughs were usually brought into the wilderness from a coast town, though occasionally they were forged on the spot. The head of the family made all the house furnishings, his wife's loom and spinning-wheel, shaped dishes out of wood, and contrived a hand-mill for grinding corn. The hominy block was a piece of hickory tree trunk with a bowl-shaped depression burned into it at one end. The boys helped their father in all such things,

---

[1] A wilderness settlement produced all its own necessities of life excepting powder, lead, salt and iron. Salt was made at several places in the colonies where salt springs had been found, and from thence laboriously carried over the country, by boat as far as possible. Wild honey served for sugar.

30.—The home and clearing of a backwoodsman. It was a gash cut in the universal forest, with a cabin and farm buildings made of logs.

and dried the strips of venison over the fire[1] after the day's work in the open was done. As each new baby arrived its elder brothers made a cradle of bark for the little stranger. When the man wanted a new suit of clothes he tanned and worked deer and raccoon skins into pliability and turned them over to his wife, who cut them and sewed them together. Such a suit was considered to fit well if it did not hamper its owner's movements in any way.[2] His cap was of skin with the fur on, and his shoes were soft moccasins, as were the foot coverings of all the family.

Cloth was called linsey-woolsey, and was a mixture of flax and wool made by the wife by carding and spinning. From it she created her jacket, petticoat and poke bonnet. Once in a while she made coats and trousers for her husband or the boys out of the same home-made fabric. The girls helped their mother in her household manufacturing, knit their own heavy stockings and made similar socks for the men. They also cut and sewed the bedticks and filled them, collected pine knots to serve as lamps in the summer evenings, made the soap, learned how to distinguish such herbs as were used as remedies in time of sickness, and hung them up to dry.

Actual money was a thing of fable, having no place in such a community. If a man by some strange chance came into possession of those curious pieces of copper or silver he hastened to swap them for something of practical use, and kept to himself his opinion of the man who took them. All necessities of life had their accepted ratios of value to one another, and needed things were got by barter.

---

[1] It was then called "jerked meat," and was hung up under the roof for future use.
[2] A deerskin suit was often decorated with fringes at the bottom of the coat and down the sides of the trousers. They were of similar skin cut into narrow ribbons and were sometimes dyed red or blue. City-made boots, any kind of a hat and coats with buttons on them were esteemed sure evidence of snobbishness and were severely frowned upon.

Skins of all useful sorts came nearer to actual currency than anything else.

Powder, salt, iron, and lead for bullets were brought in from distant towns on the coast or to the northward, and were carried overland in as large quantities as the nature of the country would permit. Powder, in the cities, was worth about two dollars and a half a pound and lead about sixteen cents. When the hill people needed fresh stocks of such things they sent out bales of skins by some of their number,[1] and in that way got the few commodities they could not produce themselves.

There was an intimate relationship between all these conditions and the travel impulse that so suddenly sprang into existence from amid them. For the social organization here described was the only one that could successfully have conducted such a movement. It was as though some far-seeing power had long since planned a westward advance of the population, and, without disclosing its predetermined purpose, had trained the people for the part they were to play in history. No army of soldiers could have made the journey on which the cabin dwellers of the southern mountains were soon to set forth. It was a task far beyond the ability of military discipline merely, and the larger the force of trained automatons which had attempted it, the speedier and more complete would have been the disaster that must have followed. The westward advance through the wilderness was one of those few instances of record in which the attendant conquest was made, not primarily by the force of weapons, but by the adaptability of the invaders to their new surroundings and a resourcefulness as self-sustaining domestic arti-

[1] The pack-train method of travel by means of which this intercourse was carried on will be described in a later chapter.

113

sans rather than as warriors. Such conquests are always vital to the region affected. A military army scars the land that feels its presence, but after a time it either retreats, or, ceasing to be an army, is absorbed by the country it has reached, and its visit becomes a paragraph in text-books. But when in earlier times white men of Anglo-Saxon stock resolved on an expedition from which there could be no retreat, and to whose success there must be no alternative, they did not begin it with guns and food alone. Instead, they burdened themselves down with their women and children, dogs, pots, pans and cattle, and started into the unknown. The eras of such spectacles are past, and considering them from these later days it can be understood how needless were the fears with which more timid souls sometimes looked on such hegiras. The multitudinous details of human, inanimate, and four-legged baggage that paralyzed speed and seemed to presage failure were the elements that made success inevitable. Without them the men could have returned.

The first symptom of the permanent invasion of the region beyond the mountains was seen in 1771 and 1772, when a little stream of people drifted down toward the southwest from Pennsylvania and northern Virginia into the broad valley that is bounded on the west by the Cumberland Mountains and on the east by the Unaka or Great Smoky range.

Through it ran the various branches of the Clinch and Holston Rivers, that empty into the Tennessee.[1] The men travelled under the trees on foot, while the women and household goods were loaded on the horses, and the elder children drove the cows and pigs. It was a journey that,

[1] Heretofore referred to in these pages as the Cherokee River.

save in its greater length, was in many respects a repetition of the march of Pastor Hooker and his congregation through the wilds of Massachusetts a hundred and thirty-five years before. The political boundaries of the colonies were rather vague in those times, and the people of these little bands, knowing that the upper part of the valley was a part of Virginia, thought the region where they stopped to build their cabins and make clearings in the

Pioneer Life in the West.

31.—Usual type of a cabin dweller's home. The method of building such a house is described in this chapter. Habitations like this were the abodes of nearly all Americans, except town-people, for a century and a half.

forest was also in that colony. It was not, but was theoretically under the jurisdiction of North Carolina, and was later to become the extreme eastern part of the present state of Tennessee. They were so far removed from any other civilization, and so much out of the reach of any government that they soon proceeded with all deliberation to set up in their valley a little republic of their own. It was called Wautaga,[1] from a small stream that empties into the Holston River, and it had a formal written constitution,[2] which was the first instrument of the sort drawn up by Americans west of the mountains. The affairs of the state were administered by a legislature of thirteen men. Five of these were appointed to carry on the executive and judicial business of the republic. Courts were organized with stated sittings, and an instance of their authority and methods lies in the case of a horse thief who was arrested on a Monday, tried on Wednesday and hanged on Friday.

Wautaga negotiated formal treaties with surrounding nations of Indians, and for six years its machinery of government successfully administered all its affairs, while the people themselves built their cabins and blockhouses, felled the forest, raised crops and fought against the Indians whenever war with the natives occurred.[3]

On one occasion hostilities between the red men and Wautaga broke out with such suddenness that the settlers had to run pell-mell to a fort without thought of saving any of their possessions. When finally behind shelter with whole skins they began to consider what they had left in the cabins, and somebody cried out that they had forgotten the Bibles in the church. Forthwith a sally-party was organized and left the stockade to secure the volumes, while the rest of the population awaited in suspense the result of the attempt. Shots were heard at intervals, and at last

[1] Also spelled Watauga and Wataga.
[2] The phraseology of the document unfortunately has not survived.
[3] The principal Indians of the South were the five Appalachian confederacies called the Cherokees, Chickasaws, Choctaws, Creeks and Seminoles. They lived principally in permanent settlements, and were not nomadic in the sense that many other tribes were. Their number is believed to have reached about 70,000. The tribe with which the early white invaders of the South had the most trouble was the Cherokees, who lived in the mountains of Tennessee, the Carolinas, Alabama and Georgia. In all its essential features and underlying causes the border warfare in the South between the two races resembled the troubles in the North that have been described.

the men were seen to be on their way back with every appearance of triumph. A jubilation attended their return and the demonstration of joy was soon discovered to be justified. For the party had not only rescued the Bibles, but had stopped on the way back and scalped eleven Indians. This was in 1776. Two years afterward North Carolina took charge of things and the sovereignty of the little backwoods republic disappeared for all time.

Shortly before the incident of Wautaga there had entered into this history one of its two commanding human figures. His name was Daniel Boone, and in his personality and exploits were centered the beginning of the events with which we have now to deal.

CHAPTER VIII

POPULAR IGNORANCE OF THE COUNTRY BEYOND THE ALLE-
GHANIES — DANIEL BOONE COMES ON THE SCENE —
HOW HE GOT HIS LOVE OF FORESTS AND SOLITUDE —
EIGHT GO AWAY AND TWO COME BACK — THE RESOLVE
OF THE CABIN DWELLERS — BEGINNING OF THE
WESTWARD COURSE OF EMPIRE — A CARAVAN ON THE
MARCH — A TEMPORARY CHECK — THE SCHEME OF
THE TRANSYLVANIA COMPANY

THERE were three principal reasons that impelled
thirty thousand people of the South to turn their
backs on established homes within the space of a few years
and "wander through the wilderness of America in quest
of the country of Kentucke."[1]

One cause was the comparative congestion of the
population immediately to the eastward of the unseen
land; a second was strong popular protest against illegal
taxes and the display of luxury based on oppression;[2] the
third was an interest suddenly born of tales that described
the character of the West. A few other minor elements
contributed toward the impulse, but these three factors in
the life of the cabin dwellers, all coming simultaneously
into operation, started the travel through the forests.

It is hard to realize that an almost complete ignorance
of the region west of the Alleghany Mountains continued
among the English speaking population until such a little

---

[1] Boone's quaint description of the movement.
[2] For an extended understanding of the domestic troubles of the North Carolina people see "Historical Sketches of North Carolina," by John H. Wheeler.

32.—External appearance of an early blockhouse such as was built on the border as a place of refuge for the cabin dwellers during Indian troubles. It was usually erected on an elevation and the trees were cleared from the immediate vicinity.

while ago as 1767.[1] For nearly a hundred and fifty years
the colonists had bustled up and down the coast of the
continent; the wilderness had given way to cities, towns
and farms; Indian trails had grown into busy roads that
served as arteries for a rapidly growing travel and commerce. On the west of the narrow little strip so occupied
stood a few parallel ranges of low mountains and beyond
them — mystery. Speaking of that strange condition a
few years after it had ceased to exist, the state of affairs
which prevailed in 1767 was described by Chief Justice
John Marshall in the following words:

"The country beyond the Cumberland Mountain, still appeared to
the dusky view of the generality of the people of Virginia, almost as obscure and doubtful, as America itself to the people of Europe, before the
voyage of Columbus. A country there was — of this none could doubt,
who thought at all; but whether land or water, mountain or plain, fertility or barrenness, preponderated — whether inhabited by men or beasts,
or both, or neither, they knew not. If inhabited by men, they were supposed to be Indians — for such had always infested the frontiers. And
this had been a powerful reason for not exploring the region west of the
great Mountain, which concealed Kentucky from their sight."

If the cabin people of the South seem to have been un-
wittingly trained for the task they were now to accomplish,
so was Daniel Boone in like manner fitted by inheritance
and personal experience for his own individual work of
leading the march of a population through a wilderness.[2]

---

[1] In 1750 Doctor Thomas Walker, of Virginia, made a trip to the headwaters of the
Kentucky River and discovered Cumberland Gap. Christopher Gist visited the Scioto
River as early as 1751. In 1765 George Croghan descended the Ohio, and in 1766 James
Smith explored parts of Kentucky and Tennessee. But the general public knew little of
these expeditions.

[2] His grandfather before him—parent of nine sons and ten daughters—had left
England because that country seemed to be getting too crowded for him. He wanted
more room, so he came to America in 1717 with nine sons and two daughters, and bought
a tract of land in Pennsylvania near a frontier post in Bucks County. There Daniel's
father was married and lived, also with a wife and eleven children, until about the year
1752 or 1753, when he in turn felt the need of wider spaces and became one of those who
joined the previously mentioned migrations toward the South. Daniel — the date of
whose birth is uncertain, but which was possibly in 1732 or 1735 — was some eighteen or
twenty years old when this pilgrimage took place. His youth had been spent in the necessary manner of the time, and he had already shown somewhat of those qualities of leadership in the affairs of frontier life that were later to be so much more strikingly displayed. The march of the Boone family was through the forests of Maryland, Virginia
and North Carolina to the locality of its future home in the western part of the Old
North State near the South Yadkin, a branch of the larger river bearing the same name.
There Daniel was married and became the father of nine children.

To a well-defined hereditary instinct that demanded freedom of movement and wide areas for action had been added a youth spent on the frontier and the experience, gained at the most impressionable period of life, while his father's family was journeying through the woods. Besides all this he was fascinated by speculation regarding the country that lay beyond the mountains, to whose eastward base he often penetrated during his earlier years on the Yadkin. These qualities are believed to have resulted in a number of extensive trips toward the west for exploring and hunting purposes that may have begun as early as 1760,[1] some of which were made in company with other men and some alone. But of these half legendary expeditions nothing certain can be said. As of a large proportion of the events of the time, no contemporary evidence of them exist. Human life and action are lost behind the veil that hides those years like a thistledown that has floated away in the wind.

But with the year 1769 there begins in the pathmaker's career a period of known things. It beheld the commencement of a journey by Boone which was to arouse all the North Carolina and Virginia cabins and suggest to the dissatisfied population a means whereby they might, with one stroke, be rid of their troubles and solve the mystery of the West. In May of that year a party of six men, of whom Boone was leader, set out to penetrate far beyond the mountains into the country south of the Ohio

---

[1] On a beech tree that stood near the Wautaga River in the extreme eastern corner of Tennessee and west of the Great Smoky Mountains until as late as the early years of the nineteenth century, could be seen the following ancient inscription cut by the knife of a hunter:

D. Boon
Cill ED   A BAR   On
    ThE   Tree
  In yEAR
        1760

River.[1] For more than a month the woodsmen travelled steadily to the westward and on the seventh day of June, after several hours spent in ascending a low range of hills, they reached the top of an eminence and saw stretching away beneath them an immense and luxuriant country spread out like a map and watered by a pleasant river. Even as they looked upon the scene, and realized that their quest was done, they beheld innumerable bison and deer moving over the open spaces that lay like islands amid the sea of cane-brakes and woods. The spot from which they gazed down into the country of "Kentucke" is believed to be in Morgan County, of that state.

Here the wanderers made camp and lived and hunted for more than six months. They were in that neutral territory used by the Indians of both the North and the South as a hunting ground, and not permanently occupied by natives of any tribe. Though the red men must have known of their long journey and presence they were not molested until December, when Boone and Stuart, while on an excursion, were suddenly made prisoners. They were intruders in the sight of the Indians, who treated them with kindness and displayed no other design than to take them out of the country. On the seventh night of the captivity Boone contrived their escape without attacking the sleeping natives, and the two white men returned with caution to their camp. The other four were not there, nor from that day did any man have knowledge of them. Nevertheless the two persisted in remaining, and in the following month, while they were hunting in the woods, a younger brother of Boone[2] and another white man

---

[1] The other members of the expedition were John Finley (or Findley), James Moncey, Joseph Holden, William Cool and John Stuart. All were experienced frontiersmen, and, like Boone, had made previous trips in the same direction.
[2] He was Squire Boone, named after his father. The identity of the other man is unknown.

from the Yadkin calmly walked up to them. That meeting in the wilderness was an instance of the ability with which backwoodsmen came to practise the art of woodcraft. Squire Boone and his companion had come four hundred miles through unknown forests and found the objects of their search, of whose whereabouts they had no previous knowledge.[1] Soon after this incident Stuart was killed by Indians. That left three. Then Squire's unknown companion failed to come back one night, and of the eight who had left North Carolina there remained only Daniel Boone and his brother.

Still the survivors persisted in their sojourn, representatives of a race that was never afterward to relinquish the land. By May the ammunition of the brothers ran low and Squire spent three months in a trip to North Carolina to replenish their stock, rejoining Daniel in July. During those months Daniel Boone, solitary premonitor of white supremacy, not only evaded captivity or death by the exercise of a skill quite beyond present understanding, but actively explored central Kentucky. He gained an intimate acquaintance with the country in all its features. Of this period Boone afterward went so far as to say: "I confess I never before was under greater necessity of exercising philosophy and fortitude. A few days I passed uncomfortably." Such was his comment on a situation in which any ordinary man might have been killed in twenty-four hours or else have starved to death in a week.[2] In March of 1771, after an absence of almost two years in the wilderness, Boone suddenly appeared unscathed among his neighbors on the Yadkin.

[1] Boone's family had begun to be concerned about him, and had sent Squire to take more ammunition to the absent one.
[2] Though game existed in abundance, every shot made to secure food was a proclamation of his presence and whereabouts.

It can readily be imagined with what interest Boone was greeted on his return from such a journey. His neighbors were almost excited. The time was one in which acts of valor were performed by many men, but his exploit stood out alone. It lifted him to a very high place in the estimation of those who knew of him, for the people among whom he lived were keen in estimating the character and metal of their fellows. But the degree of bravery and ability that the man had displayed was overshadowed by another feature of the expedition which his tale presented. His elaborate description of the distant region into which he had penetrated was so inviting that its desirability as a place for white habitation was apparent, and at once took first place in the public consideration given to the exploit. Mere bravery had always been obtainable to any extent when wanted, but here was something much more rare — news of a fair country where men such as they could live free lives, uncrowded by conditions that irked them. The fact that but two had come back of the eight who had gone away was of little consequence. Such things were trifles with which the people had always been familiar. They knew that more children would come to take the places of men that vanished and so, in time, they would win. The perils of the forest they could endure, but to hardships imposed on them by other white men they would not submit. And as though to clinch the matter Boone declared his determination to take his family into the far country where he had wandered.

His example was soon followed by similar declarations, and as the narrative of the returned traveller made its slow way through the scattered population and its significance grew into the minds of the cabin dwellers,

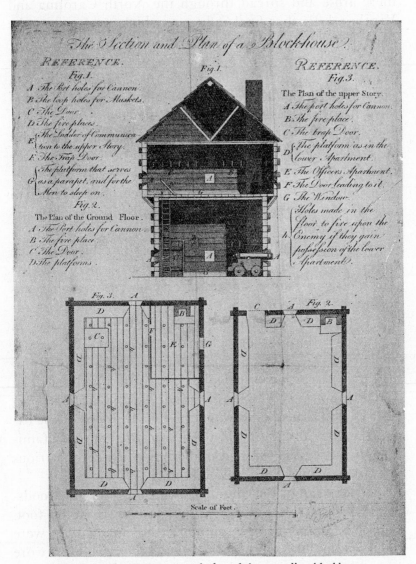

33.—Internal arrangement and plan of the preceding blockhouse.

The Section and Plan of a Blockhouse.

REFERENCE.
Fig. 1.
A The Port holes for Cannon.
B The loop holes for Muskets.
C The Door.
D The fire places.
E The Ladder of Communication to the upper Story.
F The Trap Door.
G The platform that serves as a parapet, and for the Men to sleep on.

Fig. 2.
The Plan of the Ground Floor.
A The Port holes for Cannon.
B The fire place.
C The Door.
D The platforms.

Fig. 1.

REFERENCE.
Fig. 3.
The Plan of the upper Story.
A The port holes for Cannon.
B The fire place.
C The trap Door.
D The platform as in the lower Apartment.
E The Officers Apartment.
F The Door leading to it.
G The Window.
h Holes made in the floor to fire upon the Enemy if they gain possession of the lower Apartment.

Scale of Feet.

there arose and spread through the North Carolina and Virginia hills that final influence which was to start the American people on their long westward march.

The next two years were spent in a discussion of the impending exodus and in preparation for it. Though many were anxious to get away from the conditions that burdened them, and eager to find new homes in the distant Kentucky region, the contemplated migration could not be commenced offhand. The cabin people owned tne little log huts and clearings where they lived, and their properties could not be altogether sacrificed. Such a radical and unparalleled shift demanded forethought and much preliminary arrangement, even on the part of a population so fertile in expedient and adaptibility as they were. At last seven families were ready, including the households of Daniel and Squire Boone, and after plans had been made by which the remaining five and a considerable number of other men were to join the Boones in a nearby valley, the day came for the start. It was on September 25, 1773,[1] that the course of empire began to take its westward way from the banks of the Yadkin. The Boones were joined by the remainder of the party according to arrangement, and when the two divisions of the expedition had united the cavalcade consisted of seven families, including women and numerous children of various ages, and about forty individual men.

At the head of the column marched a group of woodsmen, all, of course, bearing rifles. Some strode on foot, but many of them — perhaps the majority — were mounted on horses that walked slowly along. They wore loose hunting shirts and trousers of dressed deerskins,

---

[1] According to Speed, in "The Wilderness Road," and probably correct, though Hartley, in his "Life," puts the day exactly one year later.

gayly decorated with the colored fringes so widely affected as a backwoods fashion. Their feet were clad in moccasins and on their heads were many sorts of fantastic caps of skins, or of linsey-woolsey, each fashioned according to the whim of its owner. Every man was girt by a leather belt, from the right side of which hung a tomahawk to be used either as a hatchet or for some more violent purpose. On his left side he carried his hunting knife, a full powder horn, a leather pouch of home-made bullets and another larger leather pouch holding a quart or two of parched corn.[1] Each man's rifle lay with apparent carelessness within the crook of his elbow, but as he moved onward his glance swept ceaselessly — almost unknowingly — from side to side, pausing with each swing to dwell for an instant on the distance ahead. Behind this foreguard came the pack animals led by other similarly garbed men or boys, and bearing the women, small children, provisions and household goods. The women sat either on pillion saddles similar to those of the North or rode astride, as they pleased. The younger children swung in wicker baskets made from hickory withes, and two or three horses were thus loaded with the next generation, whose members had nothing to do but eat hoe-cake and count the trees.

Behind the pack animals came a small drove of pigs and several cattle — those ingredients of a domestic caravan that regulate its speed — and flanking the farm animals were still other men on horseback to keep them from straying from the proper path. A few rifle members of the expedition marched as a rear-guard behind all the rest. There was no iron-clad regularity about the progress of the group that thus made its way through the forest. Its

[1] Parched corn was an article of food always taken on forest expeditions.

127

individual members were constantly shifting as the men stopped to chat with the women, or as they argued with a reluctant pig, readjusted the ropes of bark that bound the burdens of the horses, or stole off into the woods to shoot a deer and bring back its carcass for the next meal. Dogs frisked about the legs of the horses, yelped with excitement as they found the scent of an animal in a nearby thicket, and distributed showers of spray after swimming some creek that the rest of the caravan had forded.

The distance covered by the marchers in the course of a day varied with the nature of the country. Perhaps the average was about ten miles of advancement. In mid-afternoon a part of the band increased its speed a little to find a camping-place, leaving the stock in care of others who brought it in an hour or so after the foremost had chosen a spot for the night's sojourn. Then each member of the expedition fell upon his appointed task. In an incredibly short time — so adept were they in such neces-sary duties — a snug shelter made from the limbs and foliage of trees was raised for the women and children; horses were relieved of their burdens and tethered; the stock was herded and put under guard; fires were kindled; water brought from a clear stream; huge slabs of venison were broiled on ramrods held over the hot coals; corn pones baked, and the day's labor was done. The feast was a royal one, few and simple though its ingredients were, for toil such as theirs and the air they breathed bred appetites whose mere possession was itself a luxury. People did not nibble at dainty luncheons and munch macaroons in those days; they devoured their food as a fireman throws coal into a furnace, and for the identical reason. What they ate was the fuel that carried them

A View of Fort Roterdeau, in Sinking-Spring Valley, State of Pennsylvania.

34.—A timber fort. Used for the same purpose as a blockhouse, but designed to accommodate a greater number of persons. Such a structure was generally made in the shape of a hollow square, with various small buildings and a watch-tower within. Showing the line of loopholes at shoulder height.

onward. Man himself was the engine at that stage of travel.

After the meal beside the camp-fire the petticoat and juvenile divisions of the wandering army disappeared beneath the lean-to. The leather-clad men stretched out their long legs around the blazing logs, lit their clay pipes and puffed big clouds of rank tobacco smoke up toward the stars until they fell asleep, while a few still figures, that almost blended with the shadows amid which they crouched, sat with rifles ready until another dawn separated the branches of the trees.

No direful happening befell Boone's people for two weeks, and their immunity from attack by Indians up to that time had gradually — perhaps to an extent imperceptible to themselves — resulted in a slackening of those methods by which danger of the sort was best to be avoided. At any rate, while they were approaching Cumberland Gap on October 6 the men who were driving the stock allowed themselves to fall behind the main body by five or six miles — which was too far — and while the two divisions of the party were so separated the rear body was surprised by a band of Cherokees, and six of its seven members were killed. Among those cut off was Boone's eldest boy, James, a fine young fellow of seventeen. The sound of the firing brought Boone and the rest back helter-skelter, but it was too late. This attack by the red men was significant of the attitude which the natives had long taken toward white movement along the whole border. They had previously allowed Boone and his small party of six to travel four hundred miles to the west, for on that occasion the whites were obviously hunters and did not, to the Indian mind, presage any general advance into or permanent occupancy of the terri-

130

tory so highly prized by the natives. But no sooner did the same white leader start into the forbidden region with women and children and every other plain proof of an intention to settle on the interior lands than the whites were attacked. The difference in the two groups was plain to the Indians. They looked on the white men as one tribe or allied tribes; white men's treaties and promises had often been broken, and now the proclamation of 1763 was in peril of violation also.[1] So the red men killed. It was their last resort against those strange, obstinate, grasping, palefaced people who seemed never content to stay where they once settled, but were always edging just a few miles farther in the wrong direction.[2]

Boone and the rest held a consultation after the attack and it was agreed to stop for a time in the most westward permanent white settlements, on the Clinch River in Virginia, and there await a better season and reinforcements before continuing the journey. This they did. There was no thought of abandoning the plan of proceeding to Kentucky.

The preparations being made by the people for their removal to the West had by this time come to the ears of those in authority in the two colonies affected by the agitation[3] and Governor Dunmore of Virginia, which state claimed all territory "West and Northwest" to the Mississippi River, promptly decided to find out whether the reports concerning the Kentucky region were true. So he organized for that purpose a party of frontiersmen

[1] The Cherokees who attacked Boone's column were the nation whose title to the land they held had been ignored by Johnson at the treaty of Fort Stanwix, despite his instructions.

[2] In the absence of native records it is, of course, possible to attribute the attitude of the Indians on this occasion to a different motive. Their attack may have been made merely for the pleasure of killing. A due consideration of conditions then existing, and of the past acts and character of both races must be our principal aid in determining which explanation is the more reasonable.

[3] Boone's presence in the Clinch River valley of Virginia after his temporary check spread still wider a knowledge of the western country.

and surveyors under the leadership of Captain Thomas Bullitt. Bullitt led his men over the trail to Pittsburgh, with which path through the wilderness he was familiar, and there the party built boats in which they went down the Ohio despite the dangers attending such a voyage at that time. Dunmore's expedition arrived safely in the neighborhood of the future Louisville, built the usual

35.—Pioneer ferryman navigating a small canoe by means of a setting-pole. A sketch by Joshua Shaw.

timber fort as a base of operations, explored a considerable territory and found that Boone's description of his discoveries was amply justified.

The men under Bullitt observed with amazement the migrations of the bison, which travelled through the cane-brakes and forests in columns containing tens of thousands. The wide roads thus made by the animals, who trampled veritable avenues through the wilderness, were at once adopted by the white men for their own use in journeying over the land and by them were called streets. From that time, and for many years afterward, buffalo streets were used as travel routes by settlers in that part of the country as they gradually pushed the herds westward. The paths created by armies of bison moving four or five abreast were driven so cleanly through the woods, and packed so firmly under the hoofs of the ponderous beasts that vegetation required years in which to reclaim them.

While Bullitt's men were still remote in the new country it became evident to Dunmore that widespread trouble with the natives was about to occur, and the governor found it necessary to send another party to warn them of the impending danger and if possible bring them back to civilization.[1] He therefore summoned Boone, and the pioneer was commissioned to attempt the task. Starting once more toward the West in June of 1774, Boone with one companion, reached the Bullitt party and conducted them safely back, making the round trip of over eight hundred miles in the remarkably short time of sixty-two days, an average of almost thirteen miles a day.[2] The expected hostilities soon began, and for a time no further important step in the impending exodus toward the West could be taken. Thus we get a glimpse of Dunmore's

[1] And a few other bold individuals who had ventured into the region on their own responsibility as a result of Boone's recital. Among the others were James Harrod and some companions who had located where Harrodsburg now stands. Their camp was at first known as Harrod's Town, or Old Town. The Harrod party held their ground for a time, though warned by Boone, and in July a party of them was attacked and dispersed. One man reached the Ohio River, hastily made a bark canoe, went down the Ohio and Mississippi in it and finally got back to Philadelphia by sea.
Still another party which was in Kentucky at the time was that of John Floyd and seven others, who had gone down the Kanawha and Ohio in canoes to the present neighborhood of Louisville, to explore and survey. The Floyd party had been sent out by Colonel George Washington and Patrick Henry. Floyd mentions a sycamore tree 37 feet in circumference. He and his men got back to the Clinch River safely in August.
[2] Boone nonchalantly speaks of having encountered "many difficulties" on the journey.

War as it affected affairs in the South. During the struggle Boone took an active part in the frontier military operations with the rank of captain. When peace had been made he went back to the settlement where his family was still waiting after the interrupted journey to Kentucky. From that point he was soon to start on the final enterprise that set in motion the general tide of westward travel.

Among those to whom Boone's exploits had most clearly revealed the future was a certain James Henderson, a judge and man of prominence in North Carolina, who as a result of the returned explorer's story had conceived the idea of acquiring and settling all the immense extent of country bounded by the Ohio, Kentucky and Cumberland Rivers.[1] For that purpose he, with eight others, organized an association known as the Transylvania Company, and got Boone to act as the representative of the company in dealing with the Indians for the desired tract. The coveted region, as distinguished from the neutral ground to the west and south of it, was claimed by the Cherokees, and to them Boone went. There is no story of what took place between him and the chiefs of the nation, but regarding several factors that led to the result of the meeting a reasonable certainty can be entertained. In the first place the red men had an admiration for Boone and respected him. He had conspicuously shown himself to be possessed of those attributes held by the natives in high esteem, whether possessed by friend or foe. It is also likely that the head men of the Cherokees read the signs of the times aright, and knew from past native experiences that if they did not then strike a bargain for the territory craved by the whites, and get

[1] Some have even suggested that Boone may have first gone beyond the mountains at the request of Henderson.

134

something for it, they would in the end lose their land anyway, without recompense. At all events they agreed to sell. No sooner had the pledge been given than Boone hastened away to take a certain decisive action the performance of which had depended on the result of the negotiations, meanwhile sending word to Henderson of his success. These things happened either late in February or in the earliest days of March, 1775. As soon as Henderson knew the way was clear for his company to proceed openly he hastened to Fort Wautaga, on a branch of the Holston River in North Carolina, and there on March 17, and in behalf of the Transylvania Company, he met twelve hundred natives in council and acquired the Indian title to the country just described.[1] For the land he paid a price that has been variously estimated as low as ten wagon loads of cheap goods and whisky,[2] and as high as the equivalent of ten thousand pounds sterling.

The work that Boone had hurried away to undertake was the making of the First Road through the wilderness.

[1] He had been very quiet in the preliminary work, and the extent of his plan was unrealized either by the government or people.
[2] The estimate of Dr. Smith, an English agent of Dunmore.

CHAPTER IX

THE party which Boone gathered to aid him in laying out through the wilderness a plain way that could be followed by the emigration now to begin numbered about forty men in all. He and his woodsmen started westward from Fort Wautaga as soon as the natives had pledged themselves to hold the treaty with Henderson, leaving the Indians to await that gentleman's arrival. Pack-horses[1] carried their necessary equipment and provisions, and a few negroes were included in the expedition to care for the animals and perform camp duties during the journey. The men carried axes.

As they proceeded Boone chose the line of march, and indicated it as he went along by cutting deep notches in prominent trees with a tomahawk.[2] Behind him came

---

[1] The pack-saddles used at the time were made from the forked branches of trees, and were bound to the animals by broad strips of deerskin. In order to fit a horse's back the forked branches had to be of a certain peculiar shape. It is related that on one occasion an early preacher, while exhorting his people in a grove, stopped abruptly in the middle of his appeal to call the attention of the congregation to such a suitable fork in a near-by tree.

[2] The marks so made were called "blazes," and the process of thus including a line of travel was called "blazing the way," or "blazing ahead."

136

axmen who chopped down the small trees it was desirable to remove, though all work of that sort was avoided when possible. A détour was always preferred by moving pioneers to the labor of hewing a swathe through the woods. The chief obstacles to be overcome were undergrowth in the forest itself, or dense thickets on lands that held no large timber. Such growths were swept aside

36.—A travelling family preparing a meal over the camp-fire. All its members are wearing moccasins. Sketch by Joshua Shaw.

by the tomahawk or short-ax with hardly a pause in the slow speed of the party, and at the end of each day's march the road they had followed lay open behind them. There was no thought in Boone's mind of creating a route which would be practicable for wagons, for no such things were then used in that part of the country.[1] His idea was to make a road that would be plain for the use of horsemen,

Though wagons of a certain crude type had appeared in near-by localities to the east.

footmen and drivers of live stock, even though the travellers upon it had never moved through the wilderness before. Carrying out the leader's plan as it went forward the party finally came to the Holston River at a point where a large island[1] lay, and there apparently it paused for a few days. During the first two weeks Boone had proceeded through a country more or less familiar to all who were with him, for it had often been traversed by hunting parties from settlements to the eastward. No definite path, however, had ever before been made through it by white men.

While encamped on the Holston, Boone was joined by eight other frontiersmen and a few more negroes. Two of the new white recruits were Felix Walker and Captain Twetty,[2] and in his later reference to the journey Walker described Boone as "our pilot and conductor through the wilderness to the promised land." Thus reinforced the party numbered some fifty souls, and on March 10th they again took up their progress through the woods, marking the trail with tomahawks and cutting down small timber on occasion. Still advancing in a general westwardly direction, through country he had seen on at least four previous trips, Boone and his men crossed the Clinch and Powell Rivers and came to Cumberland Gap, through which they passed.

Here Boone's route changed abruptly toward the north for a reason relating to a phase of early white travel already discussed. The Cherokees and other Indians of the South, and the Miamis and various native nations who lived north of the Ohio had for centuries made intermittent war on one another, and in times of peace had used

[1] Called "Long Island."
[2] Twetty was killed during the march and Walker badly wounded.

the land of "Kentucke" as a neutral hunting ground. In their age-long travel back and forth for those purposes the red men had made, from Cumberland Gap on the south to a point on the Ohio just opposite the present Portsmouth,[1] one of the largest and most frequented In-

37.—A loaded pack-mule. The animal's burden was conveyed in baskets made of woven willow or bark. Babies were also carried in such receptacles during journeys. Sketch by Joshua Shaw.

dian trails on the continent. From the time of its first discovery by Caucasians this travel route of the Indians was called the Warriors' Path.

Boone turned into the Warriors' Path, once again appropriating an Indian trail for white men's use. He did

[1] At the mouth of the Scioto, in Ohio.

more. He adopted that native path into the very highway along which soon swept a white horde to overwhelm the race which created it. Advancing northward on the Indian trace Boone followed it for about fifty miles through the region included in Knox and Clay counties, in the present state of Kentucky. Near where the town of Manchester stands he left the native route and again veered toward the west, abandoning the red man's trail for an equally well-defined street made by the bison. This wilderness avenue he used through the present Clay and Laurel counties until he came to Rockcastle River and then, still keeping on the bisons' street, he turned northward once more and passed over the country now embraced in Rockcastle and Madison counties until he came to the existing location of Boonesborough on the Kentucky River. There, on April 1st, he halted. The Indians had attacked his column twice, killing four of its members and wounding five others, but the work he had set out to do had been accomplished.[1] From the verge of the settlements in the East to the center of the unknown and long-sought land of "Kentucke" he had blazed a broad trail that any other man might follow, and the interior American wilderness had been penetrated for the first time according to a predetermined plan for its permanent white occupation. The work had not been one of unusual labor or hardship to the men who had performed it, for they were accustomed to such effort and danger, and Boone's adoption of existing Indian and bison routes for a considerable part of the distance had saved much time and trouble. But the significance of the newly created road in its relation to economic and political events that were soon to follow was great indeed.

[1] The road was at first known as "Boone's Trace."

A log fort was at once begun,[1] and on April 15th Boone sent a message to Judge Henderson telling the Transylvania Company of his success. In it he said: "My advice to you, sir, is to come or send as soon as possible. Your company is desired greatly, for the people are very uneasy, but are willing to stay and venture their lives with you; and now is the time to flusterate their [the Indians'] intentions, and keep the country whilst we are in it. If we give way to them now, it will ever be the case."

Henderson soon arrived, accompanied by nearly forty more men, many pack-horses and considerable equipment necessary for frontier life.[2] The reinforcement so delighted Boone that he hurried back to the Clinch River for his family and other settlers, convinced that the long awaited time for a general advance was at hand. He was right. The people of the settlements received his announcement of conditions in the "Kentucke" region with a satisfaction equal to his own, and in September or October he started westward again over the Wilderness Road that he had himself created, at the head of the first community caravan which was to make the march in uninterrupted security. His companions were twenty-six men, four women, half a dozen children in baskets and the usual live stock. At the head of this cavalcade, identical in its picturesque appearance with the one stopped by Indians on a previous occasion, he travelled safely through the forests, and at last the voices of white women, the laughter of children, the melancholy call of cattle and the squealing of pigs were heard in the promised land. By

---

[1] The fort was about 250 feet long by 150 feet in breadth. At each corner was a house about 20 feet square and two stories high, built of hewn logs. The four houses were connected by a continuous stockade of pointed timbers planted side by side. Along the interior of the stockade on all its sides were rows of cabins built of rough logs. The gates were thick slabs of timber hung on wooden hinges. The fort was finished on June 14th.

[2] He had started with a few wagons, but had to abandon them at the outset.

the end of the year several hundred people were established at Boonesborough, Harrod's Town and other settlements which at once sprang into being.

It is not to be imagined that Boone's Trace was in any respect an easy road to travel, in spite of the fact that families and their belongings began to move over it from the first days of its existence. It was easy only in comparison with the untouched and unexplored wilderness, through which one man alone could never have conveyed his household by his unaided strength. That was why so many people had to march together on the Wilderness Road, even after the element of danger from Indians had been eliminated from the journey. By proceeding in the old community method the mishap of one individual could be remedied by all the rest, and only in that way was organized travel possible over it. Fortunately for a modern conception of the difficulties with which a trip from the eastern settlements to "Kentucke" was made at the period in question, there exists an original diary in which the journey is described. It was written by William Calk, of Virginia, who started from Prince William county in that state on March 13, 1775, and reached Boone's fort on April 20th. Calk was one of those who went westward with Judge Henderson. No better way can be found of describing the travel conditions that then prevailed throughout the country — except on the few established highways of the Atlantic seaboard — than by quoting from Calk's record.[1] Some of his experiences were set down in the following manner:

1775, Mon. 13th — I set out from prince wm. to travel to Caintuck on tuesday Night our company all got together at Mr. Priges on

---

[1] Calk's original diary is still in possession of his Kentucky descendants. It was incorporated by Thomas Speed in his monograph on the Wilderness Road, published by the Filson Club, from which the extracts here quoted are taken.

38.—Backwoodsman putting his wife on a pack-horse in preparation for a journey. Sketch by Joshua Shaw.

rapadon which was Abraham hanks philip Drake Eanock Smith Robert Whitledge and my Self thear Abrams Dogs leg got broke by Drakes Dog.

Wednesday, 15th,—We started early from priges made a good Days travel and lodge this night at Mr. Cars on North fork James River.

Thursday, 16th—We started early it rained Chief part of the day Snowed in the Eavening very hard and was very Coald we traveled all day and got to Mr. Blocks at the foot of the Blue Ridge.

Friday 17th—We started early cross the Ridge the wind Blowsz very hard and cold and lodge at James loyls.

Monday 20th — We start early cross the ferry and lodge this night at Wm. Adamses on the head of Catauby.

Wedns 22nd —We start early and git to foart Chissel whear we git some good loaf Bread and good whiskey.

fryday 24th—we start early and turn out of the wagon Road to go across the mountains to go by Danil Smiths we loose Driver Come to a turable mountain that tired us all almost to death to git over it and we lodge this night on the Lawrel fork of holston under a granite mountain and Roast a fine fat turkey for our suppers and Eat it without aney Bread.

Satrd 25th —We start early over Some more very Bad mountains one that is called Clinch mountain and we git this night to Danil Smiths on Clinch and there we staid till thursday morning on tuesday night and wednesday morning it snowed Very hard and was very Coald and we hunted a good deal there while we staid in Rough mountains and kild three deer and one turkey Eanock Abram and I got lost tuesday night and it a snowing and Should a lain in the mountains had not I a had a pocket compas by which I got in a littel in the night and fired guns and they heard them and caim in By the Repoart.

thusd 30th — We set out again and went down to Elk gardin and there suplid our Selves With Seed Corn and irish tators then we went on a littel way I turned my hors to drive before me and he got scard ran away threw Down the Saddel Bags and broke three of our powder goards and Abrams beast Burst open a walet of corn and lost a good Deal and made a turrabel flustration amongst the Reast of the Horses Drakes mair run against a sapling and noct it down we cacht them all again and went on and lodged at John Duncans.

fryd 31st — We suplyed our Selves at Dunkans with a 103 pounds of Bacon and went on again to Brileys mill and suployed our Selves with meal[1] and lodged this night on Clinch By a large cainbraike and cuckt our Supper.

April Saturday 1st —This morning there is ice at our camp half inch thick we start early and travel this Day along a verey Bad hilley way cross one creek whear the horses almost got mired some fell in and all wet

---

[1] In the Clinch River valley. The travellers' last chance to supply themselves with provisions other than game.

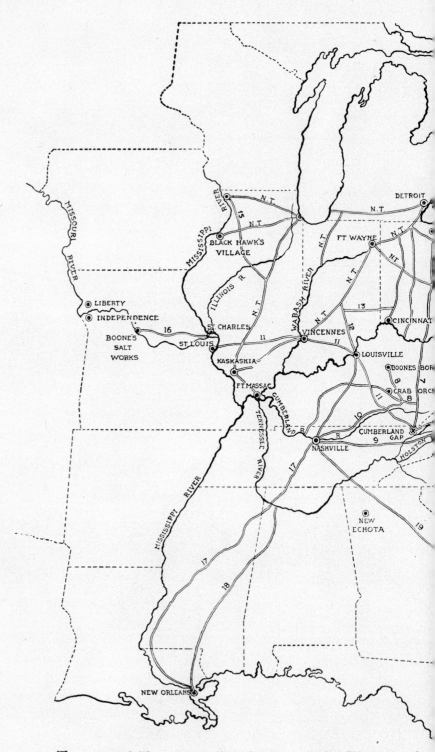

Travel and Transportation System of the Pioneers thr

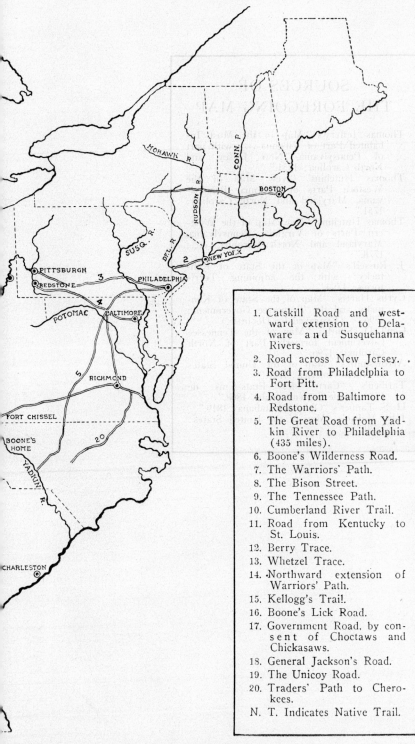

1. Catskill Road and westward extension to Delaware and Susquehanna Rivers.
2. Road across New Jersey.
3. Road from Philadelphia to Fort Pitt.
4. Road from Baltimore to Redstone.
5. The Great Road from Yadkin River to Philadelphia (435 miles).
6. Boone's Wilderness Road.
7. The Warriors' Path.
8. The Bison Street.
9. The Tennessee Path.
10. Cumberland River Trail.
11. Road from Kentucky to St. Louis.
12. Berry Trace.
13. Whetzel Trace.
14. Northward extension of Warriors' Path.
15. Kellogg's Trail.
16. Boone's Lick Road.
17. Government Road, by consent of Choctaws and Chickasaws.
18. General Jackson's Road.
19. The Unicoy Road.
20. Traders' Path to Cherokees.
N. T. Indicates Native Trail.

Wilderness between the Atlantic Coast and Missouri

SOURCES OF
THE FOREGOING MAP

Thomas Jeffery's "Map of the Most Inhabited Part of Virginia . . . with part
of Pennsylvania, New Jersey, and
North Carolina: 1751."

Thomas Hutchins' "New Map of the
Western Parts of Virginia, Pennsylvania, Maryland and North Carolina;
1751."

Thomas Hutchins' "New Map of the Western Parts of Virginia, Pennsylvania,
Maryland and North Carolina, etc.;
1778."

J. Russell's "Map of the State of Kentucky; with the adjoining Territories: 1794."

Cyrus Harris' "Map of the State of Kentucky and the Tennessee Government:
1796." (Engraved by Doolittle.)

Gen'l D. Smith's "Map of the Tennessee
Government formerly Part of North
Carolina: 1796."

Arrowsmith's "Map of the United States
of North America: 1796."

Tardieu's "Carte des Etats-Unis de
L'Amerique Septentrionale: 1808."

H. S. Tanner's "Ohio and Indiana: 1819."

John Melish's "Map of the United States:
1820."

their loads we cross Clinch River and travell till late in the Night and camp on Cove Creek having two men with us that wair pilates.[1]

mond 3rd — We start early travel Down the valey cross powels river go some through the woods without aney track[2] cross some Bad hills git in to hendersons Road[3] camp on a creek in powels valey.

Tuesday 4th — Raney we Start about 10 oclock and git down to Capt. martins in the valey where we over take Col. henderson and his Company Bound for Caintuck and there we camp this Night there they were Broiling and Eating Beef without Bread.

Wednesday 5th — Breaks away fair and we go down the valey and camp on indian Creek we had this creek to cross maney times and very bad banks Abrams saddel turned and the load all fell in we got out this Eavening and kill two Deer.

thursd 6th — this morning is a hard frost and we wait at Camp for Col. henderson and company to come up they come up about 12 oclock and we goin with them and camp there still this night waiting for some part of the company that had their horses ran away with their packs.

fryday 7th — this morning is a very bad snowey morning we still continue at Camp being in number about 40 men and some neagros this Eaven. Comes a letter from Capt. Boone[4] at caintuck of the indians doing mischief and some turns back.

Saturday 8th — We all pack up and started crost Cumberland gap about one oclock this Day Met a good many peopel turned back for fear of the indians but our Company goes on Still with good courage we came to a very ugly Creek with steep Banks and have to cross it several times on this Creek we camp this night.

tuesday 11th — this is a very loury morning and like for Rain but we all agree to start Early and we cross Cumberland River and travel Down it about 10 miles through some turrabel cainbrakes as we went down Abrams mair Ran into the River with her load and swam over he followed her and got on her and made her swim back agin it is a very raney Eavening we take up camp near Richland Creek they kill a beef Mr. Drake Bakes Bread without washing his hands we Keep Sentry this Night for fear of the indians.

Wednesday 12th — this is a Raney morning But we pack up and go on we come to Richland Creek it is high we tote our packs over on a tree and swim our horses over and there we meet another Companey going Back[5] they tell such News abram and Drake is afraid to go aney farther there we camp this night.

thursday 13th — this morning the weather seems to brake and Be

[1] Evidently none of the party had ever penetrated so far to the westward.
[2] In coming down from Virginia Calk did not hit on Boone's new route until the day this extract was written.
[3] Meaning the road Boone had just blazed for the Transylvania Company.
[4] This letter was sent by Boone before the one already quoted.
[5] Those who were returning to civilization were small parties made up of men alone. The movement of entire families in caravans did not begin until the autumn of the year.

'fair Abram and Drake turn Back[1] we go on and git to loral River we come to a creek Before wheare we are able to unload and to take our packs over on a log this day we meet about 20 more turning Back we are obliged to toat our packs over loral river and swim our horses one hors ran in with his pack and lost it in the river and they got it agin.

sunday 16th — cloudy and warm we start early and go on about 2 miles down the river and then turn up a creek that we crost about 50 times some very bad foards with a great Deal of very good land on it in the Eavening we git over to the waters of Caintuck and go a little down the creek and there we camp keep sentel the fore part of the night it Rains very har all night.

tuesday 18th — fair and cool and we go on about 10 oclock we meet 4 men from Boones camp that caim to conduck us on we camp this night just on the Beginning of the good land near the Blue lick they kill 2 bofelos this Eavening.

thursday 20th — this morning is clear and cool. We start early and git Down to caintuck to Boons foart about 12 o'clock where we stop they come out to meet us and welcome us in with a voley of guns.

fryday 21st — warm this Day they begin laying off lots in the town preparing for people to go to work to make corn.

Sunday 23rd — this morning the peopel meets and draws for chois of lots this is a very warm day.

monday 24th — We all view our lots and some Dont like them about 12 oclock the combses come to town and Next morning they make them a bark canew and set off down the river to meet their Companey.

wednesday 26th — We Begin Building us a house and a plaise of Defense to Keep the indians off this day we begin to live without bread.

Satterday 29th — We git our house kivered with Bark and move our things into it at Night and Begin housekeeping Eanock Smith Robert Whitledge and myself.

So ends the journal of William Calk. He and those others of whom he tells wrote chiefly in deeds, not language; with rifle and ax instead of pen and ink. By the light of camp-fires at night he traced a few words, but with his footsteps he traced the Path through the wilderness. To him more than to any other one man who made the journey over Boone's Road are later generations indebted for a picture of the conditions that accompanied the commencement of westward travel in America. Calk's narrative is short and fragmentary, but it tells more

___
[1] After all the trouble Abram had had with his "mair," and had overcome, it seems a pity to find that he gave up before reaching the goal.

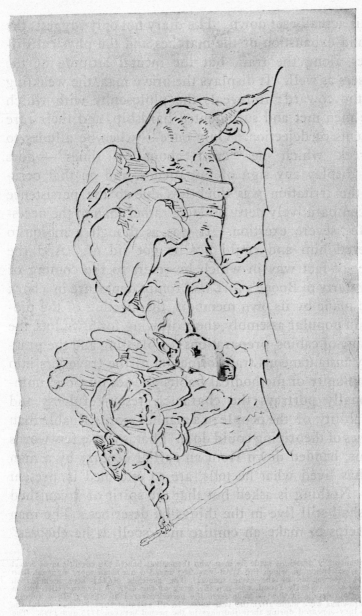

39.—Sketch showing a traveller and his pack-horse climbing a hill against a brisk wind. In this manner Kentucky and Tennessee were first reached and settled by caravans moving over Boone's Wilderness Road. Drawn by Joshua Shaw.

than is actually set down. His diary not only suggests the toil and exhaustion of the marches and the physical dif- culties along the trail, but the mental attitude of the pioneers as well. It displays the brave man, the weakling and the coward; it reveals the philosophy with which those men met and surmounted hardship, and their rare moments of dejection. Only once — when he alludes to a creek which he "crost about 50 times" — does Calk display any sign of impatience, and on that occa- sion the irritation was doubtless due to the persistence of a comparatively petty obstacle rather than to the neces- sity for severe exertion. It was as though a mosquito bothered him and could not be got rid of. And the matter-of-fact way in which he refers to the coming of a new party to Boone's fort, its prompt departure in a bark canoe made by its own members, the meeting of the pio- neers in popular assembly, their drawing for town lots, the building of cabins, preparations for planting and the prac- tically instantaneous transformation of the travellers into a community of methodical habits and set purpose, unin- tentionally portrays the character, resourcefulness and adaptability of the people in a manner more valuable than volumes of theorizing could do it. That is why a few words like his, handed down from an earlier century by a man who has lived what he tells, are so esteemed in present days. Nothing is asked but that the spirit of a vanished time shall still live in the things he describes. The man who helps to make an empire may spell as he chooses.[1]

[1] Contemporary drawings made by men who themselves beheld the conditions of travel during the generation in which the West was first invaded are even more unusual than manuscript descriptions of the same scenes. The sketches of the sort included in these pages were recently found, and are the work of the early American artist Joshua Shaw. Certain details in them — aside from the period covered by Shaw's life — indicate that the drawings were made after the year 1800. In all essential features they reveal the people as they appeared during their journeys in the period between 1775 and 1825. The lines of the artist's pencil show that he was making his sketches from knowledge gained by his own eyes.

Notwithstanding British and Indian hostilities, the Kentucky settlers, reinforced from time to time by new accessions, not only managed to hold their own but even to undertake aggressive measures against their enemies. In 1778-79 George Rogers Clark and his buckskin-clad warriors conquered the Illinois country. Their marches on that memorable expedition, particularly the one from Kaskaskia to Vincennes in midwinter across the flooded bottom lands of the Wabash, are among the most notable achievements in western history, but they are too well known to need description here. It is sufficient to say that American domination in Kentucky, Tennessee, and the region northwest of the Ohio was a direct result of the westward movement over the Wilderness Road.

Having followed the first cabin dwellers on their journey to Kentucky, it now remains to consider what they did when they got there. For this purpose the reference made by Calk to the assemblage of the immigrants in public meeting furnishes a starting point. It was believed by the pioneer arrivals at Boone's Fort and elsewhere that the Transylvania Company was founding a practically independent self-governing community. Separated as they were from all organized governmental processes by hundreds of miles of unoccupied wilderness the early white people of Kentucky were subject to no control except that of their own choosing, and the conditions which confronted them at once showed the necessity of joint action in regulating their affairs. The most important problem was that of insuring a supply of food sufficient to maintain them until a crop could be planted and harvested. When the first parties arrived they were almost wholly dependent on the country for sustenance, but fortunately found a seemingly inexhaustible abundance

149

of game. The bison, deer, bear and wild turkey existed in the forests and canebrakes in such astonishing numbers that the woodsmen, experienced- as they were, had no thought that the animal life about them would disappear. Yet within six weeks all the edible beasts and birds were gone and the settlements had to send hunting parties twenty miles into the woods in order to secure food. No sooner was the significance of this condition realized than the colonists formulated laws which protected the game except for food purposes, and "foreigners who came to hunt" were warned that their visits and activities were not wanted in that region. So the white men, as soon as they secured the country, adopted the policy of the Indians and by so doing justified the course previously pursued by the red men when they, as proprietors of the land, had similarly objected to the presence of alien people.

The belief of the settlers regarding the future of Henderson's project was soon altered. Both Virginia and North Carolina declared that the Transylvania Company's purchase of territory was void, and Virginia exercised proprietorship over the region until after the adoption of the Constitution.

CHAPTER X

THE NATIONAL TRANSPORTATION SYSTEM FROM 1775 TO
1800 — EXTENSION AND USE OF WILDERNESS ROADS
— A JUNCTION POINT IN THE FOREST — THE TRAVEL
ROUTE INTO TENNESSEE — RELATIONSHIP BETWEEN
FOREST TRAILS AND RIVERS — EARLY EFFORTS TO IM-
PROVE THE PATHS — DESCRIPTIONS OF MOVEMENTS
OVER THEM — PLACE OF WOMEN IN PIONEER LIFE
AND WORK — A CHART OF WESTWARD MARCHES

SEVERAL thousand people marched over the Wilderness Road each year during the Revolution period,[1] nearly all of them starting from North Carolina
and Virginia. On arriving in Kentucky every new family took up land, was presented with a log cabin by its
neighbors, cleared some ground and planted corn. In
the early years of the revolt against England the Kentucky settlements were often attacked by hostile red men,
but without permanent effect. Twice the whites were defeated with a loss of about sixty killed, but the tide of
white travel through the woods rose in such ever-
increasing volume that temporary reverses were soon forgotten. The pioneers never brooded over their dead. All
the attention and strength they could give were demanded
by those who still lived.

[1] Entire church congregations made the journey in a body, and on several occasions such a pilgrimage was led by the pastor, just as Hooker had conducted his people through the forests of Massachusetts long before. One of the religious organizations that travelled to Kentucky was the Baptist Church of Spottsylvania, Virginia, under the guidance of Pastor Lewis Craig. It proceeded across the country not only as a caravan of travellers but as an organized moving church.

151

A HISTORY OF TRAVEL IN AMERICA

The year 1784 found about thirty thousand people in the Kentucky region, and the immigration of that summer amounted to some twelve thousand men, women and children.[1] The overland movement still maintained a caravan character. By its increased use the Wilderness Road was being robbed of many of its difficulties, and to the one original path had been added various extensions and ramifications. A reference to the accompanying map will disclose with approximate completeness the several routes that at various times, and from different eastern localities, were used to reach the interior of the country. The relationship which these different roads bore to the general westward advance can be discussed with propriety at this point, though not all of them had become important highways of travel at quite so early a date as we have reached.

The origin and direction of Boone's Trace have already been given, and its course through the territory embraced in the map can be easily followed. Boone's actual work in marking the first road began at a point some distance to the northeast of Fort Chissel, and then proceeded to the Warriors' Path, as indicated. Within a few years the preferred route had veered from the Warriors' Path somewhat to the south of the point where Boone forsook that highway, and assumed a rather more direct line toward Boonesborough. The eastward end of the original trace marked by Boone was easily reached over rough roads, previously made, that extended westwardly from Richmond and eastern Virginia.

A route extending southwest through the valley between the Blue Ridge and Alleghany ranges was the one followed for a part of its way by Calk. He crossed

[1] Perkins' "Western Annals." Only approximate estimates can, of course, be given. It is certain that 1784 saw a great influx, and it has even been estimated that 30,000 souls went to Kentucky in that year.

over the Blue Ridge and reached Fort Chissel in nine days from the time his party started. Twelve days after leaving the fort he touched Boone's newly made path at the point where he joined Henderson's party, and continued on it thereafter. In following years a well-defined pack-horse road through the forests led all the way up through the valley to the southern boundary of Pennsylvania, where it swung to the eastward and finally reached Philadelphia. Over this, the longest of all land routes to the interior, came at a later time thousands of travellers from New York, Pennsylvania, New Jersey and Virginia. The distance from Philadelphia to Vincennes along this line of march was about eight hundred miles.

It will be seen that Fort Chissel[1] was an important junction point on all distinctively land paths made through the wilderness by white men. For many years all overland travellers, from whatever eastern community they came or wherever they were destined, converged at the little timber blockhouse for a brief pause before taking the plunge into far wilder regions beyond. East of that point the difficulty of westward progress, as well as the danger that attended it, was less in a marked degree than that encountered after it had been left behind. When at last the west-bound travel had grown to such proportions that parties passed along the various roads in almost continuous procession, the immediate neighborhood about the fort resembled the only port on a forbidding coast. Half a dozen caravans sometimes halted there in the course of a day, and the accumulation at one spot of hundreds of human pilgrims and more hundreds of horses, pigs, cows and dogs, all in the confusion of pitching camp

---

[1] The fort was a small blockhouse of the usual type built by the British in 1758, and intended as a protection against the Cherokees. At the time it was the extreme western outpost, though about 200 miles east of Cumberland Gap.

40.—Cumberland Gap, the gateway through the Alleghanies used during the overland migrations attending the first white invasion of the interior.

or of preparing for a fresh march, filled the forest with an uproar. Often there were a few Indians about, peaceable enough for the time being, and crouched somewhere on the outskirts of the brush to watch in silence the visible dissolution of their ancient heritage. They were no longer animated by a hope that the white flood could be turned back by any effort they could make.

A short distance to the southwest of Fort Chissel — as will be seen by a glance at the map — the early road into the wilderness became divided, and one part of it extended through northern Tennessee. The various Kentucky branches of the route merit prior examination. That part of the northernmost path extending to Boonesborough has been explained. The much longer trace, leading first to Crab Orchard, thence on through the

154

forest toward the present site of Louisville and across southern Indiana to Fort St. Vincent, soon came to be an even more important highway than the one over which Boone piloted his first party. Its creation was due to several causes, and covered a considerable period of time. The commencement of the trail in question came about in the following manner.

With Henderson's party of 1775 there travelled a certain Benjamin Logan, who had joined the head of the Transylvania Company on the Powell River. He and his small group of companions went along with Henderson until they all came to the Rockcastle region of Kentucky on the bison street, and there a dispute arose between the two men. As a result of the altercation Logan and a few others left Henderson and Boone's Trace near the Rockcastle hills and diverged to the westward along an Indian trail which Boone had followed when he journeyed to the Falls of the Ohio, at Dunmore's request, to bring back the surveyors. Logan kept on the trail thus selected until he reached a good country, and there established a station called Logan's Fort.[1] Other and later parties sometimes followed Logan's example; more little settlements sprang up along the route chosen by him, and so the road was pushed slowly toward the Ohio River. As boat travel increased on the Ohio the so-called falls, or rapids, which exist in that stream at Louisville became the natural stopping place of down-stream expeditions bound for the Kentucky region. There the boats were abandoned and the pioneers started inland toward the settlements established by Boone, Harrod, Logan and the rest. By the combined

[1] On one occasion, during the Revolution, Logan left his fort and companions in an effort to secure ammunition from settlements two hundred miles or more to the eastward. He got to the Holston River and back in ten days. This was one of the swiftest prolonged journeys ever made by a white man through the primeval American wilderness.

effect of those two movements a well-defined white man's path extending through the forest to the Ohio was created at an early day, and as time went on a still farther westward advance of the settlers prolonged the thoroughfare to Fort St. Vincent and St. Louis. The original Warriors' Path soon lost its native character and became a white man's road over which many immigrants passed northward through eastern Kentucky. A few of those who came down the Ohio also disembarked at the river end of the big Indian trail and marched south upon it to their destinations.

The road into Tennessee, as it appears on the map, was not the first route by which permanent white settlers penetrated into that district. In the very earliest years of the invasion the Tennessee people followed Boone's Trace to the point of Logan's divergence, then continued on Logan's path for a short distance and finally, leaving it also, swung through the woods until they came to a trail which followed in a general way the course of the Cumberland River. Then they kept on along the Cumberland until they found a locality that pleased them, and struck south into the present Tennessee. Many went in this manner as far as the site of Nashville.

But by the year 1783[1] a new and better method of getting into northern and middle Tennessee had been found, and this later route is shown on the map here given. Travellers to the Tennessee region followed existing roads from the East until well past Fort Chissel. There they left the old trail that led to Kentucky, and at the southern extremity of the Clinch range — or Clinch Mountain, as it was then called — proceeded in a line almost due west, through the country now included in Roane, Fentress,

[1] Speed's "Wilderness Road," pp. 63-4.

White, Jackson, Smith, Wilson, Sumner and Davidson counties until the site of Nashville was reached. Later this road was extended still farther west. The Tennessee path was a very popular line of march and was not only used by the future Tennesseeans, but by many who intended to take up land in southern Kentucky. Those on the road who were making for the Kentucky settlements left the Tennessee trail near the present Gallatin,[1] crossed the Cumberland River and turned north. In that fashion much of southern Kentucky received its first white population.

The Tennessee path lay through a territory less rough than that traversed by the original Wilderness Road, and became possible for wagon use within a short time after its adoption. It remained a great overland highway between the eastern seacoast and the interior until the introduction of steamboats on the western rivers destroyed its usefulness as a through line of travel. During its early years of importance the Cherokees, from their nearby mountain homes, gazed with resentment at the human traffic that moved back and forth upon it, but no longer fell with swift fury on the travellers to destroy them.[2] It was of this road that Senator Mason of Virginia spoke in the national Senate in 1802 when describing the western country and its travel facilities. "The pilgrim into those regions," said the Senator, "will have to pass through the country of the Cherokee Indian, nearly one hundred miles over the Cumberland Mountains, where he will be exposed to every inclemency of the weather without a shelter to retire to, for there is not a house nor a hut in the whole journey; a journey in which all travellers are obliged at

[1] In Sumner county, Tennessee.
[2] Although the worst element of the red nation did often rob white wayfarers.

all times and of unavoidable necessity to sleep one night
at least, and from the fall of rains and rise of water-
courses often many nights, without a roof to cover them
from the beating of the storm, and moreover where they

41.—Overland travellers pausing at the top of a hill during their march through
the wilderness.

are liable at every stop to be robbed by the Indians, as
I myself experienced passing through that wilderness."

One further glance at the map will reveal the relationship between the land and water routes that led into the
West. The earliest stages of the invasion of the interior
were characterized by mass movements of the population
overland, for in spite of the difficulties of such a journey
it was preferred to the greater dangers which for a time

attended a trip down the Ohio.[1] The slow moving flat-boats by means of which family or community migrations took place were so entirely at the mercy of the current, so exposed to wreck or so open to attack from Indians along the shores and in swift canoes, that a large majority of those who joined the westward hegira when it first began avoided the water and followed the footsteps of Boone, Calk, Henderson, Logan and the other land pioneers. Boats were chosen by a certain number of those who went to Kentucky in the first years of its occupation, but the extensive and finally predominant use of the Ohio system of rivers as highways of western travel was a somewhat later phase of the conquest.

But in the course of time the advance of the population along natural waterways did become the distinguishing feature of American travel, and on the accompanying map are to be found the several land routes by which the interior waters were reached from various eastern localities. In the northeast there existed a trail through Massachusetts[2] over which the New Englanders came to the Hudson River. Once having attained that stream they had a choice of many ways by which their migrations might be continued. They could float south on the river and with little difficulty join the throngs passing over the wilderness roads; they could go to the north and take a route to the lakes and the Northwest,[3] or an overland march through New York to the Susquehanna would bring them to the headwaters of the Delaware Bay region. Those who lived in New York, eastern Pennsylvania and New Jersey could do as the New England people did. Two lines of travel led out of Philadelphia.

[1] The experiences of those who travelled by water will be described in later chapters.
[2] Already mentioned.
[3] By way of the Mohawk and Oswego Rivers of New York.

Besides the one already mentioned, another, as shown on the map, extended directly west through the center of Pennsylvania to Pittsburgh and the headwaters of the Ohio. A similar trail that afterward like all the rest grew into a wagon road, connected Baltimore[1] with Redstone[2] on the Monongahela River. From Richmond a path led northwest through Virginia until it joined the trace from Baltimore just east of the Alleghany Mountains, and by that method the upper Ohio was gained from the Old Dominion. All these roads came into active use soon after the first penetration of the wilderness took place, and they, together with the waters which they touched, constituted the only extensive American travel routes during the generation which witnessed the eruption of population from the coast region into the interior. It was over such a transportation system that the people journeyed, amid difficulties and with a slowness no longer to be realized, as they began their conquest of the continent. A trip to Kentucky from the East, if expeditiously performed and free from accident, required from one month to two months for its accomplishment. The time spent on the road depended on the season of the year and point of departure.

There was one feature of the travels undertaken by the southern cabin dwellers in their exodus to the West that in principle furnishes a sharp contrast to later conditions. To-day all land transportation routes are laid out by scientists for the purpose of avoiding, if possible, every deviation from a horizontal level. Grades are abhorred, and if found to be inevitable, they are reduced to the

[1] The road from Baltimore passed for a part of its extent over the route taken by Braddock in his expedition. Fifty years later a section of it was incorporated in the National Turnpike, which was built by the government and in the heyday of stage-coach times formed an unbroken artery from the Atlantic to Indiana, Illinois and St. Louis.
[2] Now Brownsville, Pa.

lowest obtainable degree by every expedient of engineering. Water courses and valleys have therefore been looked upon with favor by the builders of modern man-created routes of travel. Not so with the pioneers who opened the overland way into the West. They shunned the continued proximity of rivers, crossed a stream or valley instead of following it, climbed mountains and

42.—A common incident of life in the Kentucky forest during the contest for racial supremacy there.

went stubbornly onward.[1] They moved like an army of ants, and fixing their eyes toward a distant land marched as directly as the country and their own powers would let them, surmounting each obstacle as it appeared until they reached the goal.

So many of the hill people of Virginia had started

[1] The increased use of tunnel and bridge construction by railroads in recent years is developing a tendency, on the part of modern travel systems, to return in a measure to the direct-line principle of the pioneers.

over the wilderness paths during the first four years of the exodus that the colonial legislature took official notice of the migration and recognized the need of a better means of travel to the western country. It passed an act in 1779 giving to certain officials the duty of laying out the most suitable line for a road, and of clearing it so that footmen and pack-horses could journey toward the west with least trouble. Provision was made for guarding the surveyors and laborers from hostile attack. Some work was done under this act and the original trace was thereby improved, but no horse-drawn, four-wheeled wagon was seen on it for sixteen years thereafter. In 1792 the Kentucky settlers themselves took up the matter of improving their communications with the East, and a considerable number of the most influential men among them subscribed a fund of several hundred pounds for bettering the first Wilderness Road. With the money so obtained a large force was put to work. The men were given two shillings and sixpence for a day's labor.[1]

Kentucky's first legislation in connection with the travel trails through the forest was an act passed in 1793. It related to guarding Boone's Trace by blockhouses, the enlistment of men for the purpose, and their pay. During 1794 the state provided for improving a part of the trace between Boonesborough and the neighborhood of Rockcastle River, where Logan's trail diverged from it, in order to provide an easier road between Boonesborough and the settlements in the vicinity of Crab Orchard. In 1795 the lawmakers passed a bill entitled "An act opening a Wagon Road to Cumberland Gap." This was the first legislation in the West dealing with the question of travel facilities. When it was placed on the statute books, far

[1] Speed's "Wilderness Road," pp. 47-50.

out in the interior forests, the present city of Buffalo was a trifling settlement less than a year old, and the white people of New York state had but recently established themselves west of the Susquehanna River.[1] Two thousand pounds were appropriated by the bill for the construction of the road, which was to extend from Cumberland Gap, along existing trails, to Crab Orchard. It was to be suitable for wagons and carriages. Other similar official action followed, and within a few years vehicles could make the entire trip over the path that Boone had marked with his hatchet as he pushed his way through the thickets and woods at the head of his little band of axmen.[2]

Travel by way of the wilderness roads continued to grow steadily, and when they became highways on which wagons could be used the extent of the traffic upon them was increased in an amazing degree.[3] Nor did the human tide flow over them in one direction only. The forest trails were but one of two ways of going to the West; for coming back with any degree of speed they were for a long time the only way. It was feasible to drop down the Ohio with the flow of the water, but a quick return to the East against the current of the river was out of the question. During the earliest years of the western invasion such a thing was not considered. All who were compelled to make the trip to the original colonies went back across the mountains and rivers.

The chief consideration of travellers in America up to about the last quarter of the eighteenth century had

[1] Binghamton and Elmira were settled in 1787, Ithaca in 1784, Auburn in 1793 and Buffalo in 1794. The Susquehanna was the limit of white settlements in New York until after the Revolution.
[2] Speed points out the tribute to Boone that lay in the after action of Kentucky. He says: "It required a mind of far more than ordinary calibre to locate through more than two hundred miles of mountain wilderness a way of travel which, for a hundred years, has remained practically unchanged, and upon which the state has stamped its approval by the expenditure of vast sums of money for its improvement." p. 29.
[3] By the year 1790 Kentucky had 73,000 white inhabitants and in 1800 the population was 220,000.

never been a desire to save time, but to proceed in safety and with as much comfort[1] as was possible. There were always some people who had legitimate cause for hurry, but they did not permit that state of affairs to make them careless. They preferred to pursue their way slowly and finish the journey intact, rather than to go a part of the distance lickety-split[2] and then fall off a mountain or run into an ambuscade. Ordinary conditions of existence were sufficiently enlivening without seeking further excitement through the medium of hasty and careless movement from place to place. The pioneers took a full measure of caution with them into the West, and so, when one of them foresaw the need of a journey back to the coast he made inquiry among the community to seek others of like mind. In that way parties for the return were slowly made up, and occasionally weeks went by before all were ready. Often a man would put a written statement of his intention on his cabin door and so secure companions. After newspapers were established their columns were employed to distribute such notices. One of the early Kentucky papers, the *Kentucky Gazette*,[3] contained many an announcement of the sort. A typical notice read: "A large company will start from the Crab Orchard on the 20th of Feb, in order to go through the Wilderness."

There were few tearful partings when the appointed day came. The women and children who were left behind in the care of their neighbors knew quite well what might happen — and often did happen — but the goodbys were usually spoken with more stolidity and matter-of-factness than prevail on similar occasions to-day. They

[1] Perhaps it would be better to say with as little discomfort.
[2] The pioneers used the phrase for indicating swift motion, and may have originated it.
[3] Published at Lexington in 1787.

43.—Town-people as they appeared in the eighteenth and early nineteenth century, during the period indicated by the preceding sixteen illustrations. Showing the more pretentious costumes of the cities. Backwoodsmen did not use buttons on their clothes as ornaments. The cabin dwellers deemed useless buttons, shoes and purchased hats to be signs of foppery and affectation. Sketch by Joshua Shaw.

were a people who of necessity, and by long habit and inherited custom, concealed their deeper emotions. For had they given way to the strain of their existence and allowed the uncertainty amid which they lived to overwhelm their thoughts and veto action they must have collapsed, as a social organization, utterly.[1]   A singular

[1] "An old lady who had been in the forts was describing to Dr. Brown the scenes she had witnessed in those times of peril and adventure; and, among other things, remarked that during the first two years of her residence in Kentucky, the most comely sight she beheld, was seeing a young man dying in his bed a natural death. She had been familiar with blood, and carnage and death, but in all those cases the sufferers were the victims of the Indian tomahawk and scalping knife; and that on an occasion when a young man was taken sick and died, after the usual manner of nature, she said the rest of the women sat up all night, gazing upon him as an object of beauty."—Bogart's "Daniel Boone."

Doubtless the playful roystering of the pioneers; their display of mirth and enjoyment over very trivial matters, and an insatiate seeking for such amusement and sport as their situation permitted, was an involuntary effort to strike a natural balance in the display of feeling.

restraint governed their outward recognition and acknowledgment of surrounding conditions. In the records they have left it is observed that gravest emergencies, and the expedients by which those events were met, are mentioned —if at all—in a brief and most commonplace way. Some things were not to be dwelt upon. They were well known. That was sufficient. So the partings were soon over, and the group of those who were going back for a time to the distant countries of the East disappeared in the forest. Months later some or all of them came back, dropped their packs on the cabin floors and went to work again.

One of the best and most dependable among the few connected narratives of the conditions that distinguished travel over the Wilderness Road is to be found in an address delivered by Chief Justice Robertson of Kentucky, in 1843. He was describing what had been told to him by his father and mother, who had made the journey in 1779. He said:

"This beneficent enactment [law under which settlers could acquire land] brought to the country during the fall and winter of that year an unexampled tide of emigrants, who, exchanging all the comforts of their native society and homes for settlements for themselves and their children here, came like pilgrims to a wilderness to be made secure by their arms and habitable by the toil of their lives. Through privations incredible and perils thick, thousands of men, women, and children came in successive caravans, forming continuous streams of human beings, horses, cattle and other domestic animals, all moving onward along a lonely and houseless path to a wild and cheerless land. Cast your eyes back on that long procession, . . . behold the men on foot with their trusty guns on their shoulders, driving stock and leading packhorses; and the women, some walking with pails on their heads, others riding with children in their laps, and other children swung in baskets on horses, fastened to the tails of others going before; see them encamped at night, expecting to be massacred by Indians; behold them in the month of December, in that ever-memorable season of unprecedented cold called the 'hard winter,' traveling two or three miles a day, frequently in danger of being frozen or killed by the falling of horses on the icy and almost impassable trace, and subsisting on stinted allowances of stale bread and meat; but now lastly look at them at the destined fort, perhaps on the eve of merry Christmas, when met by the hearty welcome of friends who had come before, and cheered by fresh buffalo meat and parched corn, they rejoice at their deliverance, and resolve to be contented with their lot."

But two more things remain to be said regarding the first extensive travels undertaken by the English speaking population in America. The journey of seventy thousand people through the wilderness to Kentucky, important as it was, can not fairly be called a general movement. It did not originate in an impulse that had swept over and affected the people of all the colonies. In its early and decisive stages the exodus was a local one, affecting only a comparatively small section of the country. For a number of years the Kentucky settlements and the white men's trail that led to them could be likened to a long, narrow peninsula of Caucasian civilization that jutted out for four hundred miles into unknown regions, and was surrounded by them on all sides save that from which the travelled road connected it with the East. Not until the Congress of the confederated colonies, in 1787, passed the Ordinance for the government of the Territory of the United States Northwest of the River Ohio[1] was there manifested such a general public interest in the western country as produced a migration to it from all parts of the new nation. With that governmental action, and the popular response which followed it, the sectional causes which had led to the first invasion of Kentucky were swallowed up in a general and national advance.

The remaining feature of the cabin dwellers' life

[1] The ordinance was applied to the territory south of the Ohio in 1790.

which must enlist attention in these pages concerns the fundamental character of their social structure—the basis on which was built the deeds they performed. Let us take our last view of them through the words of an early commentator.[1] He says:

"Could there be happiness or comfort in such dwellings

Clark's Inn &c. facing the State-House.

44.—A view showing the type of early houses in the towns, and the usual condition of their streets. The scene is in Philadelphia, opposite Independence Hall.

and such a state of society? To those who are accustomed to modern refinements,[2] the truth appears like fable. The early occupants of log-cabins were among the most happy of mankind. Exercise and excitement gave them health; they were practically equal; common danger made them

[1] The extract is one quoted by Ramsay in his "Annals of Tennessee." Ramsay does not give the author.
[2] The "refinements" of the early 19th century are meant.

mutually dependent; brilliant hopes of future wealth and distinction led them on; and as there was ample room for all, and as each newcomer increased individual and general security, there was little room for that envy, jealousy, and hatred which constitute a large portion of human misery in older societies. Never were the story, the joke, the song, and the laugh better enjoyed than upon the hewed blocks, or puncheon stools, around the roaring log fire of the early western settler. The lyre of Apollo was not hailed with more delight in primitive Greece than the advent of the first fiddler among the dwellers of the wilderness; and the polished daughters of the East never enjoyed themselves half so well, moving to the music of a full band, upon the elastic floor of their ornamental ballroom, as did the daughters of the emigrants, keeping time to a self-taught fiddler, on the bare earth or puncheon floor of the primitive log-cabin. . . . There we behold woman in her true glory; not a doll to carry silks and jewels; not a puppet to be dawdled by fops, an idol of profane adoration reverenced to-day, discarded to-morrow; admired but not respected. . . We see her as a wife, partaking of the cares, and guiding the labors of her husband, and by her domestic diligence spreading cheerfulness all round; . . . placing all her joy, all her happiness, in the merited approbation of the man she loves. As a mother, we find her the affectionate, the ardent instructress of the children she has reared from infancy, and trained up to thought and virtue, to meditation and benevolence; addressing them as rational beings, and preparing them to become men and women in their turn."

* * *

A HISTORY OF TRAVEL IN AMERICA

" Droop not, brother, as we go
Over the mountains, westward ho,
Under boughs of mistletoe
Log huts we'll rear,
While herds of deer and buffalo
Furnish the cheer;
File over the mountains, steady, boys;
For game afar
We have our rifles ready, boys,
Aha!

Cheer up, brothers, as we go
Over the mountains, westward ho,
When we've wood and prairie land
Won by our toil,
We'll reign like Kings in fairyland,
Lords of the soil,
Then westward ho in legions, boys,
For freedom's star
Points to her sunset regions, boys,
Aha!" [1]

[1] A chant for overland westward movers.

CHAPTER XI

UNIVERSAL TRANSPORTATION FACILITIES, RATHER THAN
POLITICS OR WARS, THE COMPELLING FORCE OF A REAL
NATIONAL UNITY — INTRODUCTION OF REGULARITY
AND PERIODICITY IN TRAVEL — ITS CAUSES AND CIR-
CUMSTANCES — UNHEEDED GROWTH OF THE PRIN-
CIPLE AND ITS FINAL EFFECT — REGULAR STAGE-
COACHES APPEAR — THE FOUR-WHEELED FLYING
MACHINE — TRAVEL CONDITIONS BETWEEN PHILA-
DELPHIA, NEW YORK, BOSTON AND BALTIMORE —
DESCRIPTIONS BY TRAVELLERS — THE "STEP-LIVELY"
ERA BEGINS

WHILE the activities just traced were prevailing in the South an altogether different state of affairs existed in the northern colonies. Three-quarters of a century had been required to produce the movement toward the interior from North Carolina and Virginia, and that phenomenon was destined to be the chief contribution of the South toward the development of a future national transportation system. All her energy and restlessness were gathered into one tremendous effort along a path of progress that the North could not tread. The surge of the southern white people across the mountains was a logical and perhaps inevitable outgrowth of the social and natural conditions that existed in the region whence it started. Those conditions, as has been noted, were in no way similar to the ones which had pre-

171

vailed from the first in the settled sections to the northward. The people of New England and the middle colonies had always showed a tendency to gather into or
near compact communities, instead of adopting the plantation and cabin system that chiefly distinguished the
lower commonwealths.[1] And just as the southern mode
of life found its expression in the exodus to the unknown
West, so also did the northern habits of living control the
methods by which its advancement toward better facilities of travel was made. The natures of the two sorts of
progress that distinguished the two sections were radically
variant. One was an outburst of supremely important
action founded on a deep-seated impulse that called for
wide, free, pioneer movement. The other — that of the
North—was a slow, long-continued, almost automatic
process which had for its purpose the improvement of
short paths from one spot to another spot near by. It,
in turn, was based on the highly developed gregarious
instinct that has always characterized the American
man of the North; a dependence on the mass rather
than on self; a craving for crowds and to be part of the
crowd, no matter what discomfort his desire inflicted on
him.[2]

There were two results of those northern habits of living in groups and constantly treading the same path,
and in time they came to shape the entire transportation system of the country and dictate every detail
of its operation. One effect was the speedy transformation of a few original primitive routes into
successively better arteries of travel as increasing popula-

[1] According to the census of 1910 more than forty per cent. of the population of the
northern states is concentrated in cities of 25,000 or more. In the South the corresponding
ratio is about twelve per cent. These figures fairly indicate the relative intensities of the
gregarious habit in the two sections during every period of their history.
[2] The quality in question is as pronounced to-day as it ever was, and its effect on
present travel conditions in congested localities is well known.

tion cried out for such improvement. The other result was the establishment of periodicity and regularity as the primary features of every sort of traffic that moves from one place to another throughout the continent. Those

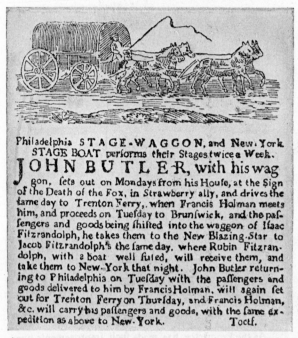

Philadelphia STAGE-WAGGON, and New-York STAGE BOAT performs their Stages twice a Week.

JOHN BUTLER, with his waggon, sets out on Mondays from his House, at the Sign of the Death of the Fox, in Strawberry ally, and drives the same day to Trenton Ferry, when Francis Holman meets him, and proceeds on Tuesday to Brunswick, and the passengers and goods being shifted into the waggon of Isaac Fitzrandolph, he takes them to the New Blazing-Star to Jacob Fitzrandolph's the same day, where Rubin Fitzrandolph, with a boat well fitted, will receive them, and take them to New-York that night. John Butler returning to Philadelphia on Tuesday with the passengers and goods delivered to him by Francis Holman, will again set out for Trenton Ferry on Thursday, and Francis Holman, &c. will carry his passengers and goods, with the same expedition as above to New-York.   Toctf.

45.—Advertisement of a stage wagon such as ran regularly between Philadelphia and New York about 1750. Both passengers and goods were carried. Periodicity in the movement of travel conveyances in America had been introduced in 1732, over the same route.

were the things that came to pass because the people of the North originally gathered together in towns and forever trotted back and forth over the same old trails. Such consequences, though slower of ultimate realization and unforeseen by those who brought them about, were to be no less important to the country's future than was the eruption that conquered the wilderness. Each section, in its own way, did the thing it could best do at a time when there was no coördination of action between them.

North and South had not yet united their conflicting and inharmonious methods and characters into one organ-

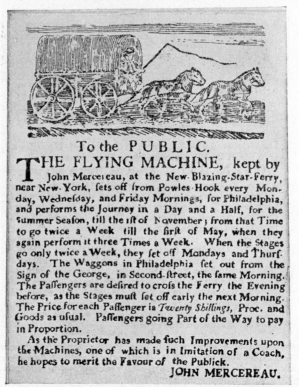

To the PUBLIC.

THE FLYING MACHINE, kept by John Mercereau, at the New-Blazing-Star-Ferry, near New-York, sets off from Powles-Hook every Monday, Wednesday, and Friday Mornings, for Philadelphia, and performs the Journey in a Day and a Half, for the Summer Season, till the 1st of November; from that Time to go twice a Week till the first of May, when they again perform it three Times a Week. When the Stages go only twice a Week, they set off Mondays and Thursdays. The Waggons in Philadelphia set out from the Sign of the George, in Second-street, the same Morning. The Passengers are desired to cross the Ferry the Evening before, as the Stages must set off early the next Morning. The Price for each Passenger is *Twenty Shillings*, Proc. and Goods as usual. Passengers going Part of the Way to pay in Proportion.

As the Proprietor has made such Improvements upon the Machines, one of which is in Imitation of a Coach, he hopes to merit the Favour of the Publick.

JOHN MERCEREAU.

46.—Mercereau's stage wagon, in 1771, reduced the time between Philadelphia and New York to a day and a half. In celebration of the achievement he advertised his conveyance as "The Flying Machine."

ism, and even when they did so the principal bond of national union, being at first political and arbitrary in character, lacked for a long time the elements that are necessary for the welding of a country into a nation. The day of a real unity in aspiration and action was only to be

reached through the creation of social and economic conditions which would bring to every American a realization that all other men between the oceans, no matter how
distant, were nevertheless his neighbors and friends. For
the accomplishment of such a result all the inhabitants
had to be brought so close together that they could become
acquainted with one another, and understand that in
fundamental things their best interests and common welfare were not dependent on sectional residence or affected
by distance. Those geographical considerations had to be
annihilated.

The importance of certain features of life in the northern colonies that finally—in the eighteenth century—
led to the establishment of periodic and regular movement
from place to place will thus be seen. The fabric of our
modern travel system acquired its vital characteristic at
that time. It was through the influence of transportation
methods and their improvement and expansion, rather
than by politics or wars, that a real national unity was at
last created. Some attention should therefore be given to
those conditions out of which grew the new phase of travel
history in America.

Previous to about the year 1725, the time at which a
traveller set forth on his journey was dependent on his
own desire, and the date of his arrival at his destination
was altogether a matter of chance. He was quite satisfied
to get there, and the usual delay of a day or a week in going a hundred miles or so did not seriously bother him.
The transaction of all the affairs of life was accompanied
by a certain elasticity and vagueness of arrangement whose
necessity, due to the uncertainties of communication, was
recognized. A man in New York, instead of telephoning
to his friend in Philadelphia, "I'll meet you in two hours

and talk it over," sent a letter which said, "I now expect to start one week from to-morrow, and hope to see you by the following Friday or Saturday." Perhaps he did; but if he didn't, no matter; he was reasonably sure to get there by Sunday or Monday, and that would do just as well. If he did not own a horse and could not hire one, he secured passage in one of the big, awkward wagons that had begun to appear on the road across New Jersey between Perth Amboy and Burlington soon after the year 1700. Those wagons were used both for the transportation of passengers and freight. They were drawn by four or six horses, often painted in gaudy colors, and were covered with canvas tops stretched on arched strips of wood. The wheels were big, and had tires from six to ten inches wide made of hard wood or thin iron.[1] The passenger made himself as comfortable as he could, and lodged in the tavern where his conveyance halted for the night. He finished the trip from Burlington to Philadelphia by sailboat, just as he had crossed New York Bay to reach Perth Amboy.

The owners of the wagons had no stated intervals for the trips, but made them whenever sufficient inducement was offered. In the year 1707 this road across New Jersey became the theater of the first American transportation monopoly of which there is any account. Governor Cornbury gave the exclusive right of conducting traffic to a few men acting together. The Assembly protested, and in answer to the complaint Cornbury said: "At present, everybody is sure, once a fortnight, to have an opportunity of sending any quantity of goods, great or small, at reasonable rates, without being in danger of imposition; and the sending of this wagon is so far from

[1] Many of the two-wheeled carts used through all the colonies at an early day had wheels that were sections sawed bodily from a round tree trunk.

being a grievance or a monopoly, that by this means, and no other, a trade has been carried on between Philadelphia, Burlington, Amboy and New York, which was never known before, and in all probability never would have been."[1] The monopoly lasted for only a few years, and the twice-a-month wagon between the two cities can hardly be called the introduction of the element of regularity into land transportation.[2] In truth the roads did not yet permit of the establishment of travel facilities as a business enterprise. During a considerable part of the year they were little else than mud-holes of a length equal to the distance between the two points they connected, and from ten to twenty feet wide. No important bridges had yet been built in the colonies, and few of any sort. No stream more than a few yards in width had been spanned by such a structure[3] and the

[1] The governor was short-sighted. To-day he could make five or six round trips between the two cities in twenty-four hours, using only regular public conveyances.

[2] One of the factors that no doubt contributed to the establishment of regular trips for stage wagons (the first periodic travel vehicles in America) was the early postal service, which did attain at times a slight semblance of regularity. The carriers travelled on horses. A summary of the development of the primitive post is here given:

1673.—First land conveyance of letters between New York and Boston. Time, three weeks.

1692.—Attempt to establish postal service in Virginia. Result a failure. Cause, "the dispersed condition of the inhabitants."

1717.—Mails carried from Boston to Virginia in one month during the summer; in winter the time was two months.

1720.—Regular mail from Philadelphia to New York once a week. Time of trip three days.

1729.—Regular mail each way between the same cities; once a week in the summer and twice a month in winter. Time of trip, two and a half days.

1754.—Franklin made Colonial Postmaster. He reduced the trip between New York and Philadelphia to about thirty-six hours and sent mails three times every week, except in winter, when two mails a week were despatched.

1755.—Franklin established a weekly mail between Philadelphia and Boston and announced with some pride that a letter might be sent from one city to the other, and an answer received, in three weeks. The time for such service was thus cut exactly in half.

1764.—Mails between Philadelphia and New York carried in twenty-four hours, by relay, and letters sent every other day.

1790.—Regular mails between Boston and New York. Time, five days. Sent three times a week.

The times given fairly indicate the swiftest travel between the towns named.

[3] The law passed by Pennsylvania colony in 1683 is an example of early bridge and highway legislation. In part it read as follows:

"Bridges shall be built over all small creeks and rivers that are difficult, or apt to be high by sudden Rain, in the King's highway, . . . which bridges shall be ten feet broad and a rail on each side; and that all trees stubbs, and stumps of trees, that lie in, and cross the said highway, and all passages [meaning fords] in and out of creeks and branches may be made safe and easy both for horse and cart, at the charge of the respective counties.

" . . . And such overseers shall summon in all their inhabitants of the respective limits, to come in and work at the making of all highways and bridges therein, upon penalty of five pounds . . . ."

traveller had to cross every river worthy of the name in a ferry boat or encamp on the bank until the subsidence of a freshet permitted him, in a few days, to proceed. None of the early laws relating to the establishment of ferries[1] and the rates of toll exacted for their use make

AMERICAN STAGE WAGGON

47.—A stage wagon such as was used in the East from about 1780 until 1800. It followed the Flying Machine variety of conveyance, and was an intermediate link between the canvas-covered wagon and the later stage-coach. Similar to the colored engraving reproduced as the frontispiece to Volume I.

mention of wheeled vehicles of any sort. The Pennsylvania ferry acts of 1683, 1690 and 1693 refer to packhorses, and to hogs, sheep and other farm animals, and fix a rate of "two pence a head for carrying over every

---

[1] The first ferries were single canoes, or two or more such craft lashed together. The second type was a wide, flat-bottomed plank boat moved by pole or oars. The third sort was a similar flatboat pulled across the stream by a rope or propelled by sails.

person, and with a horse, four pence." The New Jersey ferry legislation of 1716[1] only named toll rates for a "single person" or for "horse and man."

Then came a first inkling of what the future held in store. Road vehicles appeared and multiplied. The primitive two-wheeled cart and heavy, slow moving wagon, in neither of which could rivers be crossed or long journeys made, blossomed into land craft designed exclusively for travel purposes. The change took place during the years between 1716 and 1723, and, as might be expected, on the road between Philadelphia and New York. Pennsylvania colony established the ferry across the Schuylkill River between Philadelphia and the eastern shore of that stream in 1723, and in the law then enacted is to be found a recognition of the new conditions which had arisen. The ferry charges were: "For a coach or chariot,[2] one shilling. For a chaise[3] of four wheels, six pence. For a chaise of two wheels, four pence. For a cart or wagon, with their loading, one shilling; and without loading, six pence. For a sled, loaded or unloaded, one penny." Soon the highway between the two towns became busy with various types of equipages, more taverns sprang up along the route for the accommodation of wayfarers and the road itself, under the pressure of necessity, was made fit for the first stage wagons and the establishment of public conveyances as a distinct and separate commercial enterprise.

Periodicity and regularity as elements of travel in America seem to have appeared —so far as the records

---

[1] Dealing with the ferry over the Raritan, at New Brunswick, which had been established in 1696.

[2] A four-wheeled vehicle with the body entirely enclosed, and used exclusively for travel purposes.

[3] The chaise has been mentioned. It was a "chair" with a covered top. The two-wheeled chaise somewhat resembled a modern sulky with a leather rain shelter.

show—in the year 1732[1] and the men who first introduced those features into the transportation system of
the continent were Solomon Smith and James Moore, of
Burlington, New Jersey. The Philadelphia *Mercury,*
in March of that year, contained the following announcement:

> "This is to give notice unto gentlemen, merchants, tradesmen, trav-
> ellers and others, that Solomon Smith and James Moore, of Burlington,
> keepeth two stage wagons intending to go from Burlington to Amboy,
> and back from Amboy to Burlington again, once every week or oftener
> if that business presents. They have also a very good storehouse, very
> commodious for the storing of any sort of merchants' goods free from
> any charges, where good care will be taken of all sorts of goods."

From that advertisement and the little business
whose establishment it proclaims have grown all the
schedules, time tables, railway stations, freight depots and
the whole complex system of movement which has become
the chief and indispensable feature of modern American
life. Small thought did its originators give to the nature
of the enterprise whose seed they planted. Yet the principle of organizing and selling periodic transportation
was destined to creep unheeded over the land by such
slow and imperceptible degrees, and with so many alterations in its outward appearance and its relations to the
public need, that it had become the master of all men and
the arbiter of their affairs before the people awoke to
an understanding of its relation to them and the country.
At last they have realized what it means. Had they
appreciated at an early day the potencies which lay concealed within that principle there is little doubt that the
history of the last few generations would have been dif-
ferently written. The legacy bequeathed by Solomon

[1] The event may have occurred a little earlier without any prominent contemporary
record of it. If so, the first regular transportation of travellers no doubt took place in
the neighborhood of Boston.

High Street, Philadelphia, with an American stage wagon

48.—A stage wagon of 1798 passing through High Street, in Philadelphia. Similar to the preceding, but more heavily built. Even over good roads, coaches of this weight could only make five or six miles an hour when pulled by four horses.

Smith and James Moore has become one of the foremost problems of the present and future.

The passengers in the stage wagons of Solomon and James bounced over the road for about a week and in due course came to their destination. Other similar lines of regular public conveyances were soon established. Another road across New Jersey,[1] over which travellers between New York and Philadelphia went by way of New Brunswick and Bordentown, was made the route of rival stages in 1734. The proprietor guaranteed that his vehicle would make the trip "once a week if wind and weather permit." A line which was started in 1744 took people back and forth between Trenton and New Brunswick twice a week. Still another pioneer in the new business appealed to the public for patronage in 1750. He said he "had a stage boat well fitted for the purpose, which, wind and weather permitting, would leave New York every Wednesday for the ferry at Amboy on Thursday, where, on Friday, a stage wagon would be ready to proceed immediately to Bordentown, where they would take another stage boat to Philadelphia." This system of boats and wagons hurried travellers over the ninety miles in about five days, and the proprietor boasted that his conveyances reduced the previous time for the journey by about forty-eight hours. Within a twelve-month the growing demand of the public for convenience and comfort in travel was reflected in the announcement of a new company to the effect that its boat between New York and Amboy possessed a cabin, and was fitted with a table and other luxuries.

The year 1756 found a brisk competition for passenger traffic between the two cities, and the time consumed on

[1] It had existed for some time.

the way was still further reduced to three days. In an advertisement giving the itinerary by which this miracle was accomplished the proprietors of the wagons said: "It is hoped, that as these Stages are attended with a considerable Expense, for the better accommodating Passengers, that they will merit the Favours of the Publick; and whoever will be pleased to favour them with their Custom, shall be kindly used, and have due Attendance given them."

Besides the reduction in time of passage resulting from this competition, the contest between various proprietors of wagons produced the first public exhibition of jealousy, based on transportation rivalry, which appeared in the colonies. The proprietor of a new line was aggrieved at uncomplimentary criticisms of his enterprise scattered broadcast by opposing stage owners, and in reply he published the following advertisement:

Philadelphia, November 11, 1756.

Bordentown Stage Continued.

Joseph Borden's stage boat, Joseph Canida master, attends at the crooked-billet wharf every monday and tuesday, and his shallop, Daniel Harrison Master, at the same place every friday and saturday, stage waggons attends the said boats, the stageboat at Amboy commanded by Aaron Edwards. As to the owners of the Burlington stage boasting of their advantages being superior to mine, I shall not take the trouble to make reply too, because the publick by this time is the best judges of our stages and their advantages, only shall just note the last clause of their advertisement, that is, they say we are one tide more upon the water, than they are, which in fact, is saying we are always two tides upon one passage. Well done brother adventurers, that is a large one. All gentlemen and ladies, that please to favour me with their business, may depend upon the utmost care and dispatch, of their humble servant.

Joseph Borden.

Every hour clipped off the usual time of passage by the lumbering vehicles inspired a proud proclamation to the public. The suffering travellers, sitting on their benches during such a record trip, and bounced about in the springless wagons like corn in a popper, clutched one another in desperation while they gasped out their admiration and delight at the privilege of participating in the memorable event. If the trip was a slow one they held on just the same, and grumbled over the wretched accommodations and disgraceful delay. The cry was ever for more speed. The "step-lively" era had begun. By 1771 the public demand for hurry as a prime consideration of travel had become so marked that the trip from New York to Philadelphia was made in a day and a half, and the proprietor of the pre-Revolutionary express which sped over the distance in that amazing time was blessed with an inspiration. He named his wagon *The Flying Machine*.[1] In reality the advertised day and a half was nearly two days, for the west-bound wagon left Amboy at three o'clock in the morning, and an intending passenger had to depart from New York by sailboat on the previous evening in order to secure his seat. The fare between the two towns was twenty shillings, and additional expense of meals and lodging brought the total cost of the journey each way to about twenty-six shillings, or six dollars and a half.

As the owner of *The Flying Machine* says in his advertisement, one of his wagons was made in imitation of a coach. The old-fashioned vehicle which appeared soon after the year 1700, and that had remained in use with almost no alteration for nearly three quarters of a century, during the first part of which period it had carried both passengers and freight, was at last evolving into the first distinctive type of land craft exclusively used for human travel in America. The archaic wagon was distinguished by its straight sides and tunnel-shaped top

[1] See reproduction of the vehicle in Mercereau's advertisement.

184

made of linsey-woolsey or some similar heavy woven material. It contained three or four wooden benches with no backs, that extended from side to side of the vehicle. There were, of course, no springs. The first changes marking the transformation of such a wagon into the

WATERLOO INN,
the first Stage from Baltimore to Washington

49.—Another coach deviating still further from the archaic form and suggesting the football-shaped vehicle that was soon to appear.

earliest form of stage-coach were the flattening of its top and the adoption of side curtains made of leather or wool. The benches and their arrangement for a time remained the same, and a passenger had to climb over the foremost seats to reach those in the rear. Next, the benches were equipped with boards or strips of leather for backs, the body of the wagon was increased in height and built more substantially, and was still later increased slightly in its width. Finally the seats for passengers were set on wrought-iron springs, or held up by yielding leather straps. Such public equipages were still painted in bright colors, and were drawn by four horses which were changed every few miles.

A description of the trip from New York to Philadelphia in the *Flying Diligence* after the journey had been still further reduced to about sixteen hours of actual land travel is found in a record of that time.[1]

"Between three and four in the morning," the narrator says, "we set off in the stage, rode nine miles to Bergen Neck, and then crossed a ferry which brought us to Woodbridge. Just before we reached the second ferry we perceived the dawn of day, and, when we were two miles from it, the sun rose, so that we had ridden sixteen miles and crossed two ferries before sunrise, besides shifting horses twice. The third stage brought us to Brunswick, where we breakfasted. We crossed the Raritan in a scow, open at both ends to receive and discharge the carriage without unharnessing or dismounting, and the scow was pulled across the river by a rope. We passed through Princeton about noon, and got to Trenton for dinner; then passed the Delaware in another scow which was navigated only by setting poles; drove thirty miles over a plain, level country at a great rate, and arrived in Philadelphia at sunset."

Periodic and regular travel by means of similar stage wagons between Boston and other New England towns, and between Boston and New York, was speedily established. The Boston *Post* newspaper of 1767 contained an advertisement announcing the opening of a line between that city and Providence, in Rhode Island Plantations, and before the Revolution similar enterprises connected all the important places in Massachusetts, Connecticut and Rhode Island. Land travel to upper New England had always been exceedingly slow and difficult, and still remained so. When Franklin became postmaster of the Colonies, in 1754, the trip from Philadelphia to Portsmouth, in New Hampshire, required eighteen days, and a considerable part of the journey could only be per-

[1] Belknap's "History of New Hampshire."

186

formed on horseback.[1] The absence of numerous compact groups of population, coupled with the physical roughness of the country and the distances to be traversed, were conditions which necessarily postponed the introduction of travel periodicity in Maine, New Hampshire and Vermont.

The earliest stages that made through trips from Boston to New York were more than a week on the way.[2] Their introduction was delayed both by the condition of the roads and the greater physical comfort that attended a trip by water. Sailboats could be depended on to convey their passengers between the two cities as quickly as wagons, save under exceptional weather conditions.[3] One of the few early descriptions of a journey from Boston to New York in a primitive stage-coach is that of President Josiah Quincy, of Harvard College. He tells of it thus:

"I set out from Boston in the line of stages of an enterprising Yankee, Pease by name;[4] considered a method of transportation of wonderful expedition. The journey to New York took up a week. The carriages were old and shackling, and much of the harness of ropes. We reached our resting place for the night, if no accident intervened, at 10 o'clock, and, after a frugal supper, went to bed with a notice that we should be called at three which generally proved to be half-past two, and then, whether it snowed or rained, the traveller must rise and make ready, by the help of a horn lantern and a farthing candle, and proceed on his way over bad roads, sometimes getting out to help the coachman lift the coach out of a quagmire or rut, and arrived in New York after a week's hard travelling, wondering at the ease, as well as the expedition, with which our journey was effected." The fare was about two pounds and a half.

[1] When Daniel Webster came to Massachusetts to attend school in 1796 he made the trip from New Hampshire on horseback.
Webster, in speaking of travel conditions in New England in 1805, said: "Stages then no more ran into the center of New Hampshire than they ran to Baffins Bay."
[2] It took Washington twelve days to go from Philadelphia to Boston in 1775, on his way to assume command of the Continental army.
[3] The Boston and Providence newspapers published between 1780 and 1790 contained advertisements of passenger sailboats plying between those cities and New York. The fare on them was usually 20 or 24 shillings. Meals were 10 or 12 shillings extra.
[4] Pease was one of the prominent stage-coach proprietors of the time, and established numerous lines between many towns.

Those were the conditions under which a man was transported between the two cities in the early years of periodic travel. He spent nineteen hours a day either bouncing in or pushing his own conveyance, and was then allowed four hours in which to obtain sleep before setting forth again, without any breakfast, on another day of similar exertion. At the end of a week of like experiences the traveller "wondered at the ease as well as the expedition" with which he had reached his journey's end.

But things improved on that road, just as they did over the route to Philadelphia, and by 1793 the ordinary man could journey from Boston to New York in four days, along smoother highways, and at a cost of three pence (six cents) a mile. He could, in fact, do even better than that. The demand for speed had become so urgent that an express line existed for the accommodation of those whose business admitted of no delay, and which whirled the traveller to New York in three days and a half. An advertisement announcing the creation of these unusual facilities was printed in the *Columbian Sentinel* of April 24, and read:

Boston and New York Stages. The subscriber informs his friends and the public that he, in company with the other proprietors of the old line of stages, has established a new line from Boston to New York for the more rapid conveyance of the mails. The stage carriages of this new line will be small, genteel and easy, in which but four inside passengers will be admitted, with smart, good horses, and experienced and careful drivers. They will start from Boston and New York on the first Monday in May, and continue to run three times a week until the first of November, and will leave Boston every Monday, Wednesday and Friday at four oclock a. m. and arrive at New York in three days and a half from their departure. They will leave New York on the same days at one oclock P. M. . . . The proprietors have been at such great expense to erect this line, they hope their exertions will give satisfaction and receive the public patronage."

For this express service the fare was four pence (eight

Providence and Philadelphia Packets.

THE following vessels have commenced running as a line of Packets between the above ports :

Schr. Herald, Ahira Hall, master
   Messenger, Edward Hall, do
   Domestick, David Hall, do
   James Burrill, Abner Hall, do

All excellent vessels, and well commanded, one of which is expected to sail every week from this port. The captains have the privilege of acting as their own pilots. For freight or passage apply on board, or to   Royal Farnum.

May 23.   tf.

50.—Travel between widely separated towns on the Atlantic coast was undertaken by water when possible. The method was preferable to jolting over the bad roads. Regular lines of sailing packets were established to accommodate the business, and even after the general adoption of steamboats they successfully fought, for a time, the competition of the new mechanical vessels. Advertisement of a packet line in 1825.

cents) a mile, with fourteen pounds of baggage carried free.

Still another much travelled road on which periodic movement became important at an early day, and whereon an unusual condition prevailed, was that between Philadelphia and Baltimore. The early stage wagons along this route were the familiar vehicles with straight sides and tunnel-shaped canvas tops, and they made the journey in two days. One line between the two towns was called "The Philadelphia, Baltimore and Eastern Shore Line of Post-Coach Carriages," and in the Philadelphia *Independent Gazetteer* of 1788 its running schedule and rates of fare for passengers were thus stated:

> "From Philadelphia to Chester, 15 miles.......... £0. 5s. 0d.
> "From Chester to Queen of France, 7 miles........ £0. 2s. 6d.
> "Queen of France to Wilmington, 6 miles........ £0. 2s. 6d.
> "Wilmington to Christiana Bridge, 10 miles........ £0. 3s. 4d.
> "Christiana Bridge to Elk, 12 miles.............. £0. 4s. 2d.
> "Elk to Susquehanna, 16 miles................... £0. 7s. 6d.
> "Philadelphia to Susquehanna, 66 miles........... £1. 5s. 0d.
> "Susquehanna to Baltimore, 37 miles, gratis."

So the traveller paid about six dollars and twenty-five cents for his passage, and bought his meals and lodging besides. The uncommon feature revealed in the operation of these wagons lay in the fact that for a part of the distance they encountered the competition of sailboats and other passenger-carrying water craft, and for that part of their land journey they charged no fare whatever.

It should not be understood that any uniformity of travel conditions existed throughout the northern colonies during the two generations which witnessed the introduction and first slow growth of periodic movement as an element of progress. The contrary was true. Local circumstances, the weather, and the state of the roads still ruled traffic with almost arbitrary power. Between a few of the chief centers of population there took place, from year to year, a slight and steady improvement, but elsewhere the former conditions still prevailed without much alteration. It was a time of change, and of contrast and contradiction. The old order of things was giving way in places, and the need of betterment in methods of locomotion received a more general recognition. But over a large portion of the territory then firmly in the grasp of white men the physical obstacles to travel were still too great for any rapid progress to be made. The chronicles of the time show that occasionally there was even a lapse in the tendency toward better things, and a retrogression. In discussing traffic between Philadelphia and Baltimore at as late a date as 1797 a publication of the day[1] said:

"The roads from Philadelphia to Baltimore exhibit, for the greater part of the way, an aspect of savage desolation. Chasms to the depth of six, eight, or ten feet occur at numerous intervals. A stage-coach which left Philadelphia on the 5th of February, 1796, took five days to go to Baltimore. The weather for the first four days was good. The roads are in fearful condition. Coaches are overturned, passengers killed, and horses destroyed by the overwork put upon them. In winter sometimes no stage sets out for two weeks."

Such a state of affairs as here described portrays, in substance, the whole aspect of human movement from place to place during the later part of the eighteenth century. The traveller never knew what to expect or what adventure he might encounter. Yet on the whole advancement was apparent, and if the state of the country and the absence of any engineering knowledge held the people back, there had nevertheless been born within them an impatience that in time was to work the marvels then unconceived.

[1] "The American Annual Register" for 1797.

CHAPTER XII

THE ERA OF THE PACK-TRAIN — GENERAL USE OF THAT
METHOD OF TRAVEL AND TRANSPORTATION THROUGH-
OUT MUCH OF THE COUNTRY — OPPOSITION BY PACK-
HORSE MEN TO THE INTRODUCTION OF WHEELED
VEHICLES — CONDITIONS IN PENNSYLVANIA —
TWENTY DAYS TO PITTSBURGH — APPEARANCE OF
THE CONESTOGA WAGON — ITS LONG-CONTINUED
IMPORTANCE — WINTER TRAVEL MOST POPULAR

THE British authorities on one occasion reproved the
colonial legislature of Pennsylvania for not assembling with promptitude at critical times, when warfare
threatened, in order that it might take appropriate action
for the public welfare. In answer the Assembly pointed
out that the roads were often so bad they were impassable
even on horseback, and therefore the desired laws would
have to wait. What retort the English made is not of
record. It is enough to know that the explanation of
the Pennsylvanians was sufficient, if not satisfactory.

The incident is a typical one. It throws a light, with
official glare, on a problem which came home to every
early American. The introduction of carts and wagons
in some sections of the northern colonies during the early
part of the eighteenth century, and the later evolution of
the four-wheeled vehicles into stage wagons, acted as an
ever-increasing impetus toward the creation of better
highways. A pressing need for such thoroughfares was

192

51.—Interior of the cabin on a sailing packet having accommodations for about two dozen passengers. The dining-room by day and sleeping quarters at night. A contemporary pencil sketch. Probably about 1830.

more than plain. Nevertheless the roads did not improve. During any long-continued period of dry weather they became easily passable, only to be turned again, during wet seasons, into hopeless quagmires. No radical betterment was visible for more than fifty years after the stage wagons appeared.[1] This was due to several reasons. There was then no such thing as a knowledge of the proper way of road construction, nor was there any organized system put into effect for the carrying out of improvements. The mutual jealousies of the colonies occasionally cropped out over such a matter as the building of a travel highway, and now and then it happened that the proposed transformation of some primitive trail into a better road was actively fought by that part of the public whose ma-

[1] Nor was there any such development in road building, or the creation of permanent turnpikes with hard surfaces, until close to the year 1800.

terial interests would have suffered — at least for a time — by the suggested action.

There really were such people. They were the men who had built up the extensive business of pack-horse transportation. An overwhelming part of the land traffic of the country, except on highways connecting the principal cities, was carried on, between the years 1750 and 1790, by that means. It was an age of pack-horse travel. Pioneers in that sort of traffic were to be found in almost every town, especially toward the outskirts of the occupied regions,[1] and they controlled many thousands of horses and mules and employed large numbers of packers and caravan drivers. They regularly contracted to move parties of people over the country, together with their goods, and all the freight business of outlying settlements was carried on by them. The narrow land trails, called "tote-roads," "pack-roads," or "horse-ways" by the pioneers, over which frontier movement passed for a long time, were the foundation on which their enterprises were built, and they knew that so long as those paths remained unfit for vehicles their business would remain secure. Therefore they opposed the making of wagon roads.[2]

The pack-horse system of travel was more important and largely developed in Pennsylvania than in any other colony, and even at so late a date as 1783 the only way of carrying goods from Philadelphia to Pittsburgh, or of journeying between the two towns, was by that method. In Pittsburgh and other similarly inaccessible places salt was sold for five or ten dollars a bushel, and iron was worth from fifteen to twenty-five cents a pound.

[1] Philadelphia was one of the chief centers for them.
[2] In the history of the development of travel and transportation facilities, every improvement in method of movement has been opposed by those whose occupation depended on the maintenance of the system about to be abandoned.

A HISTORY OF TRAVEL IN AMERICA

A so-called wagon road, after it had developed from an Indian trace or white man's tote-path, was usually a narrow winding trail across the country, made of nothing but the natural soil. The first effort toward improvement of such a highway, as displayed in many localities, consisted in placing a multitude of small logs side by side across it. Over the logs was spread a layer of dirt two or three inches thick, and the improved thoroughfare was complete. It was then a corduroy road. There was no lack of timber for the purpose, but the work of cutting the trees and placing them side by side for many miles was so great that not much construction of the character was attempted. No vehicle could sink into the morass on a trail thus altered, but the dirt surface was promptly washed through the logs and the jolting soon shook a wagon to pieces. The economic advantage of the corduroy system, as it was at first applied, amounted to almost nothing. It was as unpleasant for a man to behold his wagon disintegrate as to abandon it in a sea of mud; worse, in truth, for in the latter case he could come back after a month or two and dig it out again. Gradually the people fell into a lethargy on the subject of road improvement—as far as outward action was concerned—and for a generation or more made no effort to move about on extensive trips except during favorable weather. They were also, during long periods, prevented by wars and poverty from making serious attempts through governmental means to improve their system of travel and communication. From the year 1755 to the close of the Revolution the country was in almost uninterrupted military turmoil. The struggle between England and France, Pontiac's War, the ceaseless embroilments along the frontiers and the contest with England collectively covered a period of nearly thirty years, within which time the only important progress in transportation was confined to a few highways between the half-dozen principal towns of the northern colonies.

Simultaneously with the general introduction of the first stage-coaches, however, two other important features of the early national travel system sprang into existence, and the Pennsylvania colony witnessed the birth of each. One of these was the cutting of Braddock's Road[1] through the wilderness, and the other was the appearance of a famous and indispensable pioneer conveyance known as the Conestoga wagon.

Braddock could not move his troops without wagons to carry supplies, and he could not use wagons without a road. At first he had neither. No path possible for vehicles existed along the western portion of his intended route, and at the order of the Pennsylvania Assembly a force of woodsmen was accordingly got together to widen the existing trail by chopping down enough of the forest to permit the passage of his transport train. Then Braddock called on Virginia and Maryland for wagons, but the two colonies collected only twenty-five.

In desperation he appealed to Franklin, and that official, by means of an elaborate printed address to the public, secured one hundred and fifty four-wheeled vehicles from Pennsylvania.[2] The brave but misguided general finally led his little army away over the new road, and on the disastrous field that bears his name compelled his veteran troops to stand shoulder to shoulder while the

[1] The highway is too well known to require more than brief mention. It followed an earlier Indian trail, and was cut through the woods to enable the British army under General Braddock to pass over the Alleghany Mountains and attack the French, whose chief stronghold in the Ohio valley was Fort Du Quesne.
[2] Franklin agreed that their owners should be paid if the wagons were not returned. They were all lost in the defeat, and Franklin was appalled at the prospect of his ruin until the British paid £20,000 for the destroyed equipment and horses.

52.—Many families who lived on the coast, or near bays or rivers, kept little covered boats for use in journey making, just as a farmer or business man of the twentieth century keeps a motor-car.

Indians, from behind their trees, enjoyed the human battue.

After the war between England and France Braddock's Road became one of the principal routes by which travellers from the northern and middle colonies advanced through central and western Pennsylvania to the Alleghany region, and the pack-horse train was the only method by which they moved themselves and their goods back and forth between the older towns and the frontier posts. Those immigrants who were making the trip toward the frontier for the first time journeyed in large groups, in the immemorial method, and also carried on their later intercourse with the coast region in a somewhat similar way. During the autumn of each year all the border inhabitants within a radius of ten, twenty or twenty-five miles contributed their joint efforts to the creation of a pack-train by which they sent furs and skins and whisky to the eastern towns in exchange for such necessities as they could not themselves produce. They had no money, and could obtain iron, salt and a few other commodities only in that manner.

In fact, the Whisky Rebellion of 1794 was a direct result of this transportation problem. To carry bulky grain and fruit to the eastern market was impracticable, so many of the settlers converted their surplus of such products into whisky and brandy. A horse could carry two kegs of eight gallons each, worth about fifty cents a gallon on the western and one dollar on the eastern side of the mountains, and he came back with a little iron and salt. The Federal excise tax of 1791 bore hard on the trans-Alleghany people, and those in western Pennsylvania rose in armed rebellion but were overawed by an army sent into the region by President Washington.

198

The organization and progress of a pack-train is thus described in the work of an early historian.[1]

"In the fall of the year, after seeding time, every family formed an association with some of their neighbors, for starting the little caravan. A master driver was to be selected from among them, who was to be assisted by one or more young men and sometimes a boy or two. The horses were fitted out with pack-saddles, to the latter part of which was fastened a pair of hobbles made of hickory withes,—a bell and collar[2] ornamented their necks. The bags provided for the conveyance of the salt were filled with feed for the horses; on the journey a part of this feed was left at convenient stages on the way down, to support the return of the caravan. Large wallets well filled with bread, jerk,[3] boiled ham, and cheese furnished a provision for the drivers. At night, after feeding, the horses, whether put in pasture or turned out into the woods, were hobbled and the bells were opened. The barter for salt and iron was made first at Baltimore; Frederick, Hagerstown, Oldtown, and Fort Cumberland, in succession, became the places of exchange. Each horse carried two bushels of alum salt, weighing eighty-four pounds to the bushel. This, to be sure, was not a heavy load for the horses, but it was enough, considering the scanty subsistence allowed them on the journey. The common price of a bushel of alum salt, at an early period was a good cow and a calf."

The appearance that such a cavalcade presented while on its march and the nature of the travel route over which it proceeded were told by another writer of earlier times,[4] who said:

"The whole amount of hide and peltries, ginseng, snake-root, and bears grease[5] were exchanged or bartered for salt, nails, and other articles of iron, and occasionally for a few pewter plates and dishes for the table. The bartering for the settlement being finished, the caravan was ready for its retrograde march. . . . The caravan route from the Ohio River to Frederick crossed the stupendous ranges of the Allegheny mountains as they rise, mountain behind mountain, in the distant prospect. . . . The path, scarcely two feet wide, and traveled by horses in single file, roamed over hill and dale, through mountain defile, over craggy steeps, beneath impending rocks, and around points of dizzy heights, where one false step might hurl horse and rider into the abyss below. To prevent such accidents, the bulky baggage was

[1] Doddridge's "Notes on the Settlements and Indian Wars": chap. 13.
[2] The horse collar was often made of woven corn husks.
[3] Smoked venison or bear meat.
[4] Monette: "History of the Valley of the Mississippi": Vol. ii, p. 14.
[5] An early family remedy highly esteemed.

199

removed in passing the dangerous defiles, to secure the horse from being thrown from his scanty foothold. This route, selected by experienced woodsmen, differed but little from that selected for turnpikes and railroads by professed engineers at a much later day. . . . The horses, with their packs, were marched along in single file, the foremost led by the leader of the caravan, while each successive horse was tethered to the pack-saddle of the horse before him. A driver followed behind, to keep an eye upon the proper adjustment of the packs, and to urge on any horse that was disposed to lag. In this way two men could manage a caravan of ten or fifteen horses. . . . When night came, a temporary camp and a camp-fire protected the weary travels."

Those who were going into the newly settled country for the first time joined an experienced caravan whenever possible. Twenty days or more, according to the state of the weather and trail, were required to pass over Braddock's Road by pack-train from the Atlantic coast to the head waters of the Ohio. The extent to which pack-trains were relied on as the one method of travel and transportation throughout many parts of the colonies as recently as the last quarter of the eighteenth century, and the causes that led professional pack-men to oppose the building of roads for wheeled vehicles, were referred to by a third writer who long ago discussed the period in question.[1] He wrote:

"Sixty or seventy years ago[2] five hundred pack-horses had been at one time in Carlisle, going thence to Shippensburg, Fort Loudon and further westward. . . . The pack-horses used to carry bars of iron on their backs; crooked over and around their bodies; barrels or kegs were hung on each side of these. Colonel Snyder, of Chambersburg, in a conversation with the writer in August. 1845, said that he cleared many a day from $6 to $8 in crooking or bending iron and shoeing horses for western carriers at the time he was carrying on a blacksmith shop in the town of Chambersburg. . . . When the bridle path passed along declivities or over hills, the path was in some places washed out so deep that the packs or burdens came in contact with the ground or other impending obstacles, and were frequently displaced. . . . When wagons were first introduced, the carriers considered that mode of

[1] Rupp: "The History and Topography of Dauphin . . . [and] Cumberland Counties [Pa.]": pp. 376-377.
[2] The words were written in 1848.

53.—A Conestoga wagon. The frigate of early overland travel and transportation in America. First appearing in Pennsylvania about the middle of the eighteenth century, it survived until the California rush a hundred years afterward.

transportation an invasion of their rights; their indignation was more excited and they manifested greater rancor than did the regular teamsters[1] when the line of single teams was started some thirty years ago."

So, while the roads leading out from Boston, Providence, New York, Philadelphia and Baltimore were witnessing the first introduction and early rivalries of the stage wagons and Flying Machines, the remainder of the northern and middle section was still dependent on the pole-boat, saddle-horse and pack-train.

The second important development witnessed in Pennsylvania about the middle of the eighteenth century — the first use of the Conestoga wagon — became noticeable during the decade between 1750 and 1760. The peculiar type of pioneer vehicle thus evolved remained in persistent use during all advance movements of the population for about a century. As the frontier inhabited by

[1] These teamsters were the drivers of four and six-horse Conestoga wagons, which had followed pack-trains, and that were in turn succeeded by the two-horse vehicles here mentioned, as the dirt roads were changed to turnpikes covered with gravel or broken stone.

white men was steadily pushed toward the west for generation after generation the Conestoga wagon was always in the van of travel progress, always years ahead of the stage-coach, the steamboat, canal and railroad. The ruts that were dug deep into the soil by its wide and ponderous wheels were the marks that guided all other vehicle movement by land. Its career as one of the agencies by which white men conquered the continent came to a fitting end in the period between 1848 and 1869, when by its use the final migration across the western plains was accomplished, and there was no longer any West to which it might continue.

The travel conditions which confronted the early inhabitants of Pennsylvania were in several respects different from those faced by the other colonists. There was no considerable seacoast that permitted movement from one part of the commonwealth to another by means of sailboats, the interior was not sprinkled by lakes or traversed by many rivers of the placid and navigable type found in other parts of the country, and much of the colony's extent was rough or mountainous. Necessity forced its people to resort to land travel for journeys of consequence, and to that circumstance was due the widespread use of the pack-train within its limits, and its early efforts to solve the problems of the roads. To necessity can also be attributed the creation of the Conestoga wagon, which, though at first evolved to fit conditions in the neighborhood of its origin, was speedily adopted, with slight modifications, for all long overland migrations and heavy traffic throughout the country.

The precise reason for the name of the vehicle is uncertain. A breed of very heavy horses had already been developed in the valley of the Conestoga, and had com-

Baltimore.

54.—An overland wagon of the Conestoga type approaching Baltimore. On busy roads such vehicles were frequently seen in trains half a mile or more in length.

manded wide notice. Probably the wagon was first built in the same region,[1] or else acquired its name from the type of horse with which it was no doubt associated in its earliest days. A Conestoga wagon was a huge affair, very heavily built, with a bed higher at each end than in the middle, and topped by a dull-white cloth cover which had a similar curve of still more pronounced degree. The wagon bed was constructed in concave shape in order that its contents might not spill out when it was going up or down hill. Still another distinguishing characteristic of the conveyance was its color. The underbody was always painted blue, and the upper woodwork was invariably bright red. This chromatic scheme was as inevitable

[1] Lancaster county.

for every Conestoga wagon as though it had been prescribed by law with a penalty for refusal so to decorate.[1]

No sooner was a road made fit for vehicles than the Conestoga wagon appeared upon it, sometimes in solitary grandeur as its owner and his family and household goods moved slowly over hill and valley toward a new home to the westward; sometimes in immense and brilliant caravans that stretched for miles along the highway. There was a majesty in their slow progress. The rumble of their enormous wheels as they lurched onward behind horses caparisoned with almost barbaric splendor, the creaking of harness and their swaying tops conveyed to the beholder a sense of power. They told of an advance that would know no retrogression. They were the frigates of the land. A description of such famous and distinctively American vehicles at the height of their popularity and usefulness,[2] as set forth by an authority on the subject, is given in the following passage:[3]

"The capacious wagons which the Conestoga farmers then had in use," said the narrator, "were the best means of land transportation which the times and circumstances of the country then afforded. These wagons and teams attracted attention and commanded admiration wherever they appeared; and hence the origin, as I conceive, of the horse and wagon to which the appellation of 'Conestoga' has been attached. . . . The harness was constructed of the best materials, with an eye to show as well as utility. In the harness and trimmings of these teams the owners frequently indulged in expenses that approached to extravagance. . . . It was, indeed, an animating sight to see five or six highly fed horses, half covered with heavy bear skins, or decorated with gaudily fringed housings, surmounted with a set of finely toned bells, their bridles adorned with loops of red trimming . . . as if half conscious of their superior appearance, and participating in the pride that swelled the bosom of their master."

In the course of time tens of thousands of Conestoga

[1] The gaudy painting of the Conestoga wagon was another manifestation of the tendency of the time toward bright color and vivid decoration.
[2] About 1800 to 1815.
[3] The quotation is from John Strohm's account in the United States Agricultural Report for 1863: p. 178.

wagons[1] rumbled over all the main roads of the country, serving the emigrant, the traveller whose time did not demand the express speed of a stage-coach, and conveying a large part of the freight that moved between cities not connected by water. The driver of a Conestoga rode on a wheel horse, and he and those with him carried their own bedding, which they spread out on the floor of the public room in the tavern where they halted for the night.

The slow progress that the country was making in its use of private travel vehicles during the early years of periodic transportation is illustrated by the fact that in the year 1761 there were but thirty-eight wheeled conveyances in Philadelphia. Their several types and numbers were: three coaches, fifteen chaises, eighteen chariots and two landaus. By 1772 the people of the town owned eighty-four vehicles, and in 1794 they had eight hundred and twenty-seven. There were twenty-two privately owned wheeled vehicles in Boston in 1768, and 145 like equipages in 1798. Similar figures for other communities do not appear, but the advancement of various important cities in the respect indicated was doubtless substantially parallel with the cases cited.

Throughout the eighteenth century, as well as in the seventeenth, the winter season continued to be a favorite time for travel. The scarcity of wheeled wagons of various sorts was not reflected in the use and popularity of sleds. Every family had one or more of them, and the discomforts due to cold weather and biting gales were much preferred to the troubles that attended a journey at any other time. In thickly settled parts of the country, during the frost months, a wayfarer in a sleigh was rarely

---

[1] Those that travelled between the East and Pittsburgh were often called "Pitt Teams," though they were identical with the Conestoga.

out of sight of equipages similar to his own. Many hundred horse-drawn sleds were to be seen in the streets of any town on a clear winter day,[1] and long-extended travel was undertaken in them.[2] A large proportion of the snow craft were home-made, box-like affairs, but like everything else of the period to which paint would cling they were highly seasoned with all the essences of the rainbow.

[1] Henry's "History of the Lehigh Valley" (Pa.) says five hundred sleds were either standing in the streets of Easton or passing through them at one time.
[2] Daniel Webster sometimes went between his New Hampshire home and Boston in a sleigh.

CHAPTER XIII

EARLY TAVERNS — THEIR RELATION TO TRAVEL AND PUBLIC
AFFAIRS — RATES FIXED BY LAW — CONSTABLES
WATCHED TRAVELLERS CLOSELY — HOW THE SLEEP-
ING PROBLEM WAS SOMETIMES SOLVED — A TAVERN
DINNER TABLE EQUIPPED TO SATISFY HUNGER RATHER
THAN FOR ARTISTIC DISPLAY — LAWS REGULATING
RETAIL CHARGES FOR FOOD — UNIVERSAL HOSPI-
TALITY OF THE SOUTH — FIRST TRAVEL TO INTERIOR
NEW YORK — EFFECT OF THE REVOLUTION ON THE
MENTAL CONDITION OF THE PEOPLE

THERE was one feature of primitive travel in America which, though not in itself a method of locomotion, was nevertheless so intimately related to the movements of travellers and to all public affairs as to require attention in a study of early conditions. That phase of the subject was the little tavern, or inn, destined at last to develop into a palace beneath whose roof the exacting demands of a thousand guests are supplied by an army of servants. The evolution of the public house has kept pace for nearly three hundred years with the changing system whereby the pilgrim has reached its doors, and in size, methods and conveniences it has consistently reflected the manner in which the traveller has pursued his actual journey.

By the middle of the eighteenth century the tavern had reached a position of consequence in the national life, and from that period until about the year 1830 its importance steadily increased both as a factor in the affairs of the people and as an essential element to be considered in the making of any journey. Conditions coming into being at that time gradually altered the status of the tavern in its relation to the public, and afterward, though increasing in bulk and magnificence, the inn lost much of its former influence. It has now come to be taken as a matter-of-fact incident; as an institution whose chief characteristics can be anticipated and depended on by those who have need of it. The modern hotel has been standardized and reduced to an automatic machine of entertainment. This was not true in the early times, for then the inn possessed nothing of system but revealed, instead, the character of its proprietor. If the host possessed a marked individuality, either congenial or unpleasant, so also did his hostelry. To-day there is no host, in the old sense; only a staff of trained experts in each of a dozen departments, who by invisible methods minister to the population that drifts through a maze of endless corridors and lofty halls. The early tavern has become a big department store for the sale of sleep, food and drink.

Public inns came into existence almost as soon as the English speaking race secured a permanent foothold in the northern colonies. The earliest known establishment of the kind was licensed by the General Court of Massachusetts in 1634,[1] and from that time they multiplied amazingly. By the year 1675 Cotton Mather declared that every other house in Boston was a tavern, though his assertion was of course an exaggeration. He objected to the smoking and drinking that prevailed in the houses of public entertainment.

[1] Drake's "Old Boston Taverns": p. 19.

All places of the sort were from the first regulated by strict laws passed for the purpose. Even the prices they might charge were named by the authorities. In 1634 the cost of a meal at a Boston inn was fixed at sixpence, and the Court declared that a patron must pay no more than one penny for a quart of beer.[1] Should an innkeeper demand more than the legal rate for food and drink he

FRAUNCE'S TAVERN, Cor of BROAD & PEARL STREETS.

55.—Fraunce's Tavern, a popular pre-Revolutionary inn of New York City. In the assembly room, occupying the second story, Washington took farewell of his generals. The building still remains. This and the following eight illustrations suggest the accommodations available to early travellers in the East.

was to be arrested and fined. Another Massachusetts law also provided that no private individual might take a stranger into his home without giving surety for the good conduct of the newcomer. The particular statute in ques-

[1] Similar regulations passed by the New York Common Council in 1675 fixed the price of tavern lodging at threepence, and the charge for a meal at eightpence.
A usual price for tavern accommodations throughout the colonies from 1700 until about the time of the Revolution was three shillings a day. For this sum the traveller got his lodgings, a fire, if necessary, three meals and beer between-times.

tion was passed in order that all travellers might be forced to sojourn at public taverns, where their actions could be kept more easily under the close gaze of town officials. A bailiff always watched the guests of an ordinary,[1] and if a stranger behaved in a way considered by the representative of the law to be unseemly, he was admonished. The constable even regulated the amount of liquor which the traveller might consume. If he thought the guest was passing proper bounds he would appear at the stranger's elbow and carefully pour out the libation himself.

Drinking, however, was not frowned upon.[2] Ale, beer and spiced cider were the principal potions, and almost every one consumed those beverages in quantities. A landlord was subject to penalty if he did not permit his guest to drink all that could legally be consumed on the premises, provided the man appeared able to take the amount without unpleasant consequences, and the bailiff had no objection. Excessive drinking was prevented or penalized by methods common to all times and countries, and by a few expedients peculiar to America only.[3]

Vastly different was the attitude of the authorities toward the use of tobacco, either in taverns or anywhere else. According to early New England laws smoking in public was an offense of grave character, and was forbidden.[4] One of the first Massachusetts pronouncements against smoking in taverns read: "Nor shall any take

[1] A public house was also called an ordinary.
[2] It was even customary for the people to drink as a part of the celebration attending the building of a church or the ordination of a clergyman.
[3] According to a law of 1676, whenever an Indian was found drunk in New York the tavern keeper responsible for his condition was fined. But if it could not be discovered in what house he drank his liquor, then every white man on the whole street was subject to fine.
[4] "Men are now living who have been asked to plead 'guilty' or 'not guilty' at the bar of a police court for smoking in the streets of Boston."—Drake's "Old Boston Taverns," p. 16.

56.—The Notch House, a noted tavern of the White Mountains, in New Hampshire. Typical of the good early hostelries of New England country regions. The washing pump is at the corner of the building and the dinner bell is mounted on the roof.

tobacco in any wine or common victual house, except in a private room there, so as the master of said house nor any guest there shall take offense thereat; which, if any do, then such person shall forbear upon pain of two shillings sixpence for every such offense." Nevertheless the men of New England continued to smoke with ever increasing vigor, and in the course of about a hundred and sixty years the legal warfare against tobacco was abandoned in the North.[1]

All early American inns for the accommodation of wayfarers were copied, in their usages and character, from the English institution of like nature, and, as in the parent country, they gradually became the chief centers of the life and news of the communities in which they were situated. They were also the most prominent landmarks of any journey, and it thus became the universal custom for travellers and business men to compute all distances from them, instead of from one town to another. In those days of few newspapers and fewer mails the arrival at a tavern of two or three strangers from some distant city was an event of real importance to the inhabitants. No sooner did the news of their presence get abroad than many of the principal men of the place gathered at the hostelry to welcome the pilgrims, ask questions of them, and listen to the tales they had brought from the outside world. Chiefly in that way did the doings of other regions sift through many parts of the country. From those gatherings at the taverns grew local clubs and societies that often took organized action in relation to business affairs, and eventually became the first

[1] Drake says that on one occasion, late in the eighteenth century, two travelling Dutchmen from New York who were walking about Boston in search for lodgings wandered into Harvard College by mistake. On getting inside they found the tobacco smoke so thick that one of them said, "This is certain a tavern." "Old Boston Taverns," p. 15.

A NEW-HAMPSHIRE TAVERN.

SOME years ago, his Rozinante striding
A gentleman was in New-Hampshire riding,
Far to the north—He'd travelled many a league,
One day; and now with hunger, thirst, fatigue,
Almost o'ercome, with most rejoicing eyes
A tavern sign he at a distance spies :
Approaching, on the sign these words appear :
"For man & beast best entertainment here."
Dismounting for the hostler now he calls,
But for the hostler all in vain he balls,
He opes the door : that sees with graces winning,
The landlady and daughter Bets a spinning
Humming away at most enormous rate,
This on the little wheel, that on the great,
' Where is the landlord ?'—' He is gone away
Clear down the lot with Joe, a mowing *hay*'
Grass, madam—have you oats ?—' No, none at all
My husband sold the whole last fall
To find the house in liquors'—Corn, ma'am pray ?'
' The last half bushel went to mill to day'
' Then you have meal ?'—' Not any ; you know, Bets,
All we've not baked has gone to pay our debts.
Let down them bars ; take out your bits, your horse
Will find as good feed, sir, as ever worz, (*was*.)
—This done, the trav'ller to the house returned,
And to allay his thirst impatient burned.
' I'll thank you madam, for a glass of gin
And water'—' Sir, there's not a drop within'
' Some brandy, then.'—' Sir, we have none at all ;
For here, for brandy people never call.'
' A glass then of West India.'—' sir we've none,'
' Well then New England.'—All our rum is gone.'
' Have you some cider, or some beer that's good !'
' Our cider's out—we have not lately brewed.'
' I'm very thirsty ; pray some water bring'—
' Bets take the gourd, and fetch some from the spring.'
Bets went—returned—' Mother, th' old sow, oh lud,
Has made the water all as thick as mud,
By wall'wing in the spring.'—The trav'ller now
Demands ; ' What keep you but yourselves and sow ?'
' Keep,' says the woman, feeling anger's spur
' What do we keep ? why we—keep *Tavern, Sir*.'

57.—A poem written by a traveller describing accommodations found by him
at a New Hampshire inn of less excellence. Published by A. Allen,
of Hartford, in his "New England Almanack for 1821."

merchants' exchanges and chambers of commerce in America. Many of the early merchants' exchanges, in fact, held their regular meetings in taverns, and in some instances the courts and legislatures did likewise. Whenever a mass meeting was to be held the public was directed to assemble in front of, or within, some prominent hostelry. Legal notices and governmental proclamations were fastened to the fronts of inns, and political caucuses assembled in those establishments,[1] where the leaders of public opinion always took up their headquarters during a time of unrest. Jefferson wrote the Declaration of Independence in a tavern[2] and discussed it there with his fellow revolutionists.

The main feature of any early tavern was a large public assembly room containing chairs and tables and with an immense open fireplace on one side. Opening from this apartment was the dining-room, and beyond it, the kitchen. The guest rooms were usually above. The stock of liquors was kept in barrels, jugs and bottles in the public room, behind a partition or counter. For nearly a century and a half the tavern stables contained no provision for the accommodation of vehicles. Only travellers on horseback or on foot were expected, and many of these carried their own blankets on their backs. When a wayfarer came to an inn and found the beds all in use his serenity of mind was quite undisturbed. The landlord considered it to be his duty to give shelter to all who opened his door, and did so. After the normal capacity

---

[1] During the political agitation that preceded the Revolution the "Green Dragon," in Boston, was the headquarters of the Whig, or American party. There Hancock, the Adamses, Warren, Revere, Putnam and others gathered to discuss the troubles of the colonies.

In the "Bunch of Grapes," another Boston inn, the Ohio Company was organized by Rufus Putnam and his friends, and in that way the tavern played a part in the movement toward the West that eventually led to the permanent settlement of Ohio.

Franklin and his cronies gathered nightly in the "Indian King" tavern of Philadelphia, to discuss public affairs.

[2] The "Indian Queen," in Philadelphia, where he was lodging at the time.

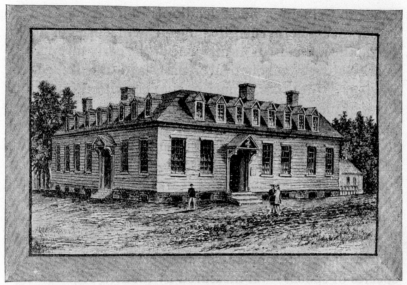

58.—The Raleigh Tavern. A southern inn of the best sort during the last half of the eighteenth century.

of the tavern was exhausted any additional arrivals were informed of the fact and knew what to do without further comment. At bed time they simply spread their blankets on the floor of the public room, lay down with their feet toward the fire and rolled themselves up like a row of human cocoons. Often the assembly room was so crowded with the forms of weary men that a very late comer had to explore by candle-light and careful steps in order to find space for himself. In the morning the guests unrolled, and arose full clad for another day upon the road. They made their ablutions, amid fearful splutterings, at the watering trough or a wooden tub outside, and passed the towel around with courtesy.

Then came the breakfast ceremonial. The host marched to the front door, lifted a cow's horn to his lips and sent forth the resounding blast that summoned all

215

hands to the table. Some landlords preferred a big bell rather than a horn, and filled the air with a clangor heard for a mile around. A meal at one of the early taverns was nearly always a bountiful repast, and usually ended, whether at breakfast, dinner or supper, with two or more kinds of pie. Everything was put on the big table at once, and everybody ate until he reluctantly made up his mind to stop. In those days a meal meant all a man wanted to eat. The price remained the same. A slice of bread was visible even when the edge of it was held toward the eye, the butter could be safely attributed to the cow, and a third cup of tea or glass of milk was as smilingly produced, if called for, as was the first. In short, the deplorable deficiency in varieties of knives and forks, and in different species of spoons — as measured by modern requirements — was made up by a plentitude of things that could be eaten instead of looked at. The tavern dinner-table of early days, when fully equipped for active service, was primarily designed for satisfying hunger rather than to tickle the eye of the gastronomical critic who would shudder to behold a slice of ham lifted to its doom on a sausage knife. The fundamental idea of the diner was to convey the food from the table to his teeth; the precise method of its conveyance thither being a matter of subsidiary concern. In his main purpose he was successful, and if the methods by which bread and meat are transported to their final destination have also improved with the lapse of years, it is well to remember that those earlier generations were sturdy men who fearlessly met whatever emergency confronted them, whether the problem was the conquest of the wilderness or the impalement of a distant potato.

Such were the essential features of the average early tavern of the frontier and its accommodations of bed and

board. City establishments were much more pretentious.[1]
Of course there were all sorts of public houses. A few
were poor establishments; many were excellent indeed. A
French traveller[2] who had large opportunity to judge
American inns of the late eighteenth century said of them,
as a class: "You meet with neatness, dignity and decency;
the chambers neat, the beds good, the sheets clean, supper
passable; cyder, tea, punch and all for fourteen pence a
head."[3] John Adams was commenting on an inn of high
quality when he wrote: "Oated and drank tea[4] at Pease's
— a smart house and landlord truly; well dressed with his
ruffles, etc., and upon inquiry I found he was the great
man of the town, their representative as well as tavern
keeper."

A careful comparison between early ordinaries and
the later establishments which had just begun to lose
their old influence and take on the character of modern
hotels has been left in the writings of an observant American scholar[5] who was familiar with national conditions
throughout a long period. "The best old-fashioned New
England inns," he averred, "were superior to any of the
modern ones. There was less bustle, less parade, less
appearance of doing a great deal to gratify your wishes,
than at the reputable modern inns;[6] but much more was
actually done, and there was greater comfort and enjoyment. In a word, you found in these inns the pleasures
of an excellent private house. If you were sick, you were
nursed and befriended as in your own family. To finish

[1] One of the greatest of the early taverns was the "Indian Queen" in Baltimore, which had no less than two hundred bed-chambers. Similarly large houses were to be found, by Revolutionary times, in Boston, New York and Philadelphia.
[2] Brissot de Warville.
[3] The price he names is too low to represent the average charge for equal enter-tainment.
[4] Meaning that the horse "oated" and he drank tea. Pease was the Yankee who also carried on so many stage-coach lines.
[5] Timothy Dwight.
[6] Those of about 1825.

the story, your bills were always equitable, calculated on what you ought to pay, and not upon the scheme of getting the most which extortion might think proper to demand."

One big basis of the small charges made by early taverns for the accommodations they offered was to be found in the prices of food during those times. Govern-

59.—A very large inn, with travellers arriving and departing. The vehicles are a two-horse private coach, a small two-horse stage-coach of oval lines, and three examples of the one-horse chaise.

mental regulation of commercial affairs—and even of retail trade and small transactions to which the ultimate consumer was a party—was a familiar feature of the period in some colonies, and no little care was taken that the people were not unduly charged for their foodstuffs. The business of supplying the public with those commodities commonly called necessities of life was not then the complex and artificially mysterious process it has since become. Neither the products of the soil nor essential manufactured articles were passed through many hands by a commercial mechanism devised for the purpose, and at constantly increasing valuations, before reaching the individuals who had actual use for them. The amount of money needed to produce a unit quantity of any ordinary kind of food and place it before the consumer in the market-place was a matter of common notoriety, or easily ascertainable if desired, and the legal prices of such commodities were based on that knowledge. Articles of food and other things requiring systematic labor for their production were cheap because they normally passed directly from the producer to the consumer, without the intervention of those devious commercial devices that have been, in part, brought into being by later structural changes in human society.

As an example of the retail value of foodstuffs in the second half of the eighteenth century, the lawful prices of certain commodities in the New York City markets in the year 1763 may be cited. They were:[1]

A hen turkey, two shillings and sixpence; a teal duck, sixpence; a quail, one and one-half penny; a wild goose, two shillings; a snipe, one penny; sea bass, two pence a pound; butter, ninepence per pound; lobsters, sixpence per pound; clams, ninepence a hundred; oysters, two shillings per bushel.

These were mostly luxuries. The prices of domestic meats and ordinary vegetables and fruits were in no especial need of regulation, for their values were too well known and trivial. Of some such things the consumer

[1] Watson's "Olden Time Researches and Remembrances of New York City." Phila., 1830. Contained in the first edition of the "Annals of Philadelphia."

could get all he required for whatever he wanted to pay. The vendor of them at times acted as if ashamed to take his customer's money, and added an extra peck or so to a bushel of vegetables as an apology for making a commercial transaction out of it. Thus, if the guest at a tavern was protected by law from overcharge, so also was the tavern keeper himself safeguarded in his purchases of provender that his own efforts did not produce.

The traveller in the South, in his search for food and shelter, encountered experiences radically different from those that came to him along the busier highways of the northern and central colonies. Very few taverns of any sort were to be found in southern regions until some time after the Revolution, and those that did exist were in Charleston, Richmond and two or three others of the infrequent towns. The man who found it necessary to make any extensive journey in the South could never expect to obtain provision for his needs at a public house established for the purpose. Yet in spite of such an apparent obstacle to endurable travel, the pilgrim in that part of the country found a reception even more cordial, and comforts often more elaborate, than those which greeted him in New England or the middle commonwealths.

From earliest times the people of the South displayed a personal hospitality to strangers unusual in its sincerity and universality, which has continued without interruption as a tradition and an existent reality. Massachusetts colony, as has been seen, had a law framed to make it difficult for a private person to entertain a traveller beneath his roof. Virginia, on the contrary, declared by an act of government that unless a wanderer within her boundaries himself stipulated that he was to pay for his entertainment no charge should fall upon him, no matter

Scene on the Susquehannah.

60.—An incident of pedestrian travel. Indicating the manner in which packs
of food, blankets or other necessities were carried between taverns. Two
of the men wear bootees, and the costumes of all indicate wealth. The
reptile is exaggerated. A rattlesnake nine feet long was a monster.

how long he remained, or where. There were almost no southern inns in the commercial sense, but every habitation, of whatsoever degree, was a sure refuge for the wayfarer at any time of night or day. So it was from the first. An early traveller in the region drew this picture of the extent to which the people of the South made it their duty to entertain the sojourner among them:

"The inhabitants," he said, "are very courteous to travellers, who need no other recommendation than being human creatures. A stranger has no more to do but to inquire upon the road where any gentleman or good housekeeper lives, and then he may depend upon being received with hospitality. This good-nature is so general among their people that the gentry, when they go abroad, order their principal servants to entertain all visitors with everything the plantation affords; and the poor planters who have but one bed will often sit up, or lie upon a form, or couch all night, to make room for a weary traveller to repose himself after his journey."[1]

The southern planters went even further than Berkeley said, for in the era when there were no public houses in that part of the country, planters along the most frequented roads sometimes kept slaves beside the highway whose duty it was to invite travellers to stop for the night and receive, as guests, whatever entertainment they required. The cabin dwellers of the South pursued the same policy, and few worse affronts could be given either to them or to the wealthier planters than to offer money in exchange for the hospitality they so freely extended.

But one other phase of travel movement remains to be mentioned as a salient feature of the conditions that existed until after the Revolution. It was the attention given to the Susquehanna River region of New York and Pennsylvania, and the first efforts made to reach and populate that part of the country. The struggle of the people of New England, New Jersey, eastern New York and

[1] Berkeley's "History of Virginia."

lower Pennsylvania to penetrate to the valley of the Susquehanna and establish themselves there, during the forty years from 1735 onward, emphasizes the trivial impression that had been made on the northern wilderness up to that time and illustrates the diversity of transportation methods which then prevailed. It has already been seen that the era was one in which desire for expansion and improvement first became apparent in any degree, and wherein, for the first time, striking contrasts in travel facilities were visible. Pedestrians and horsemen filled the roads between towns in more thickly settled regions; canoes and pole-boats were busy on the little coastal rivers of the North; long pack-trains wound through the Pennsylvania mountains; Conestoga wagons lumbered slowly across the country, and the feats of the newly established periodic *Flying Machine* made many believe that the millennium of locomotion was swiftly approaching. Progress was indeed a visible reality, but it was almost altogether confined to a few important highways and the neighborhood of half a dozen important cities. If the traveller in any part of the country left the beaten track, even but for a few miles, he found himself amid that "most howling wilderness" which appalled the earliest immigrants and presented such formidable obstacles to any advance through it. Those primeval barriers to progress were the ones encountered by men who fought their way toward the Susquehanna during the very years that the stage wagon and first stage-coaches were coming into use but a short distance away.

The importance of the Susquehanna River and valley as a travel route was recognized at an early time,[1] even

---

[1] That is to say, the route was an important one to a people who had no means of transport but small boats and horses.

when the geography of the region was but vaguely known. Perhaps the first prominent reference to it as a possible highway for white men was that made by Cadwallader Colden, in 1737, when he said that "goods may be carried[1] from this lake [Lake Otsego, in New York] in battoes or flat-bottomed vessels through Pennsylvania to Maryland and Virginia and . . . by either of these branches goods may be carried to the mountains, and I am told that the passage through the mountains to branches of the Mississippi (which issue on the west side of these mountains[2]) is neither long nor difficult, by which means inland navigation may be had to the Bay of Mexico."

The first general manifestation of public interest in the Susquehanna country became visible in New England about 1750, and was in part due to stories descriptive of the district brought back by missionaries who had penetrated into the western forest to convert the Indians.[3] These tales were spread through Connecticut and Massachusetts by word of mouth and the newspapers. A few adventurous spirits soon organized the regular little travel caravans and set forth to grope through the woods and establish new homes in the far-off land, two hundred miles away, that was known to them only by hearsay. They put their women on horses, loaded other animals with bedding and household goods, tied the babies in maple-syrup troughs for safe keeping, picked up their rifles, whistled to the dogs, and started.

Their way led them over the country to the Hudson River, which they crossed near the present town of Catskill. As the result of these first migrations a trail that

---

[1] On the Susquehanna.
[2] Colden, as well as other public men, knew of the head waters of the Ohio and dimly saw their possible future util'ty as an aid to progress through the interior.
[3] Elihu Spencer and John Sergeant were two of the missionaries whose narratives aided in producing this result.

THE

DOMESTIC MANNERS

OF THE

AMERICANS;

OR,

CHARACTERISTIC SKETCHES OF THE PEOPLE OF THE
UNITED STATES.

BY RECENT TRAVELLERS.

GLASGOW:

PUBLISHED BY RICHARD GRIFFIN & CO.

MDCCCXXXVI.

61.—Rough travellers carousing around the huge fireplace in the assembly room
of a large tavern at night. The floor is made either of puncheons
or slabs of flat stone. The liquor bar is shown.

promptly developed into a well-marked tote-road, and afterward into a highway fit for vehicles,[1] soon led from the settled districts of New England to the Hudson. Once that stream was passed the journey through the forest[2] became a more difficult one. The route still to be traversed before the upper waters of the Susquehanna were reached was a hundred miles long in a westwardly direction, and at first there was no serviceable path to be followed. The ground was a jumble of obstacles through which a caravan had to pick its way with infinite labor, at the rate of a few miles a day. One man who went over the trail in 1753[3] left a record of his experiences in the wilderness west of the Hudson in which he said the road was "obstructed by fallen trees, old logs, miry places, pointed rock and entangling roots. How bad the travelling is we cannot tell." The male members of the caravans made beds of pine boughs at night for their wives and babies, and themselves rolled up in blankets on the ground, where they got such sleep as the panthers and wolves permitted to them. On arriving at the Susquehanna the men of each pack-train built canoes in which to transport the goods, women and children of the party southward to a favorable location, and a few members led the tired horses overland along the banks of the river. When all had at last reunited and chosen a site for future homes they built log cabins and took up again the daily duties of their lives.

The other way of reaching the headwaters of the Sus-

[1] The road through Connecticut to the Hudson was made into a turnpike about the year 1800, and a flood of travel in Conestoga wagons and other vehicles then moved over it toward the new settlements in interior New York and northern Pennsylvania. Wagons, however, had reached the Hudson over the trail some time before it became a turnpike. A later reference will be made to the movement toward the Susquehanna as it developed after the Revolution.

[2] In 1871 a traveller between the Hudson and the Susquehanna measured a birch tree 26 feet in circumference.

[3] Gideon Hawley, who travelled from Massachusetts to the Susquehanna in that year.

quehanna was by means of big canoes, usually of the hollow log variety, that were propelled up the river by means of poles. Many of the people who first travelled into northern Pennsylvania and central New York from southern Pennsylvania and the Delaware Bay region in the second half of the eighteenth century made the trip in that manner. When laden with the members of his family and his worldly possessions, a man's canoe often weighed

62.—McCann's two-penny piece. A specimen of the metallic money issued by a few early American tavern keepers. Such pieces are among the uncommon examples of American coinage. Brass. Actual size. Revolutionary period. The punched hole, which corresponds to that made in some issues of early metallic stage-coach and railway tickets, suggests that tavern money was occasionally strung on wire, for convenience. See illustration No. 159.

a ton. In seasons of low water all the men and women got out, waded in the stream and pushed their craft along until another navigable stretch of the river was reached. Thus they journeyed, never at the rate of more than twenty-five miles a day and usually at about half that speed, until they gained their destination. Two or three weeks of hard work were required, under favorable conditions, to reach the interior of New York from either New England or the mouth of the Susquehanna.

Such were the methods by which the first travel of white people into upper Pennsylvania and central and southern New York was undertaken. The men who did such extraordinary things looked upon their experiences in a matter-of-fact way because they had no conception of other devices for human locomotion. They gave all their ingenuity to the problem of transporting themselves from place to place, and thought they succeeded admirably well. According to their notion the obvious troubles and discomforts were altogether due to natural conditions that would never be greatly different, and were in no degree due to the crudity of their own appliances, which, in their opinion, were nearly as good as could be fashioned.

All progress thus far made in land travel had been the result of patient effort, persistence and adaptability along one clearly defined but narrow line of development. No other element had entered into the attempted solution of the problem. There was manifest, as indicated, a certain quality of impatience that had brought about greater speed on highways, and which, when fully awakened, was to alter the face of the world and the affairs of humanity, but it was not an impatience born of knowledge that better things exist yet are unavailable for immediate use. Every small forward step in advance for a century and a half in using land and water vehicles — boats had hardly altered at all — had been due, either directly or indirectly, to physical labor either by man or beast, or both. Of those near impending miracles born of the brain and not of the hands, without which the task of continental conquest might not have been accomplished in a thousand years, there was no trace; no hint. The time was but lately passed when an exhibition of such things would have resulted in the execution of their originator as the master of infernal powers whose possession made him a danger to his fellow men. Then came the years of the Revolution as a climax to the incessant economic struggle, social disorder, political unrest and turmoil of warfare that had prevailed during all the history of the new civilization which was fighting for dominance on the edge of the continent. The close of the Revolution and the attainment of independence found the people of the new-born states in a curious condition of mind. In their consideration of, and attention to, the small affairs of their daily lives they behaved in a normal way, for the thought and action nec-

63.—Sample of the paper money issued by tavern keepers for the convenience of travellers and the neighboring population. Small silver was often scarce, and tavern money, in sums under one dollar, took its place. If the reputation of the inn-keeper was good, then the money was good. The paper was frequently printed from engraved plates, as in this case, as a precaution against counterfeiting.

essary to the carrying on of such matters was largely automatic. At least it did not require any departure from familiar precedent, any violent effort to adopt new customs and admit that former methods, as well as former years, were dead.

But apart from their daily routine the attention of the population was given to a consideration of political affairs and to the utterance, by voice or pen, of all the thoughts upon those subjects that germinated within their minds. There was a cyclone of discussion, a tumult of debate that was hushed only by the ocean on one side and the wilderness on the other. Let it be said, however, that in this strange period — as in all others of like nature in history — there were a few men whose thoughts were largely given to questions of material development and who tried hard, although in vain, to attract the attention of their brethren.

These conditions were not surprising when considered in connection with what had preceded them. They were, rather, natural and inevitable, and now require to be mentioned because of a phenomenon in which they were soon to result. For many years all that was strongest in the intellect of the colonies had been concentrated, with an intensity hard to exaggerate, on political affairs. For an equal time the people had lived a national life in which warfare and politics had been almost the only elements. The leaders of public thought and action had ceaselessly appealed to the country in utterances dealing with those things, and the mass of the people had done nothing but listen to the appeals, argue about them and fight in response to them.

And at last the end of the long tumult had come; the abstract political condition so long desired and struggled for had been gained. But the country could not at once put aside all memory of the period just ended, and turn with calm and unclouded thought to the more prosaic but equally important questions of domestic affairs and continental progress. Indeed, it is probable that such things were even further from the public mind immediately after the Revolution than before or during the struggle, since nations — like individuals — have youth, strength and senility, and their inhabitants collectively manifest in those periods many of the characteristics of the individual man. It was a very young, though vigorous and boisterous nation that had been born of the Revolution. It was old enough to realize its own existence, and was much interested in itself and its surroundings, but did not yet feel equal to the task of walking very far in any one direction. The colonies, though they had won their freedom, did not yet know what to do with it. Absorbed in a contemplation of past perils from which they had so recently emerged, the freemen suddenly found that independence, in itself, was not a complete solution of the problem created by their ambition. No sooner was the fighting ended than the chief figures of the land fell into another violent discussion over the next step to be taken, and the populace forthwith took sides and added to the clamor. During the years from 1783 to 1789 the country was a continuous political caucus, and no broad subject that did not in some way relate to state rights, Federal jurisdiction, term of office, taxation, the franchise, or such things, had much chance of winning the public ear. Even the significance that lay in the extension of the national territory to the Mississippi River failed to receive general attention. There was no way to get there. The national horizon, in the eyes of the mass of the people, still remained about two hundred miles wide from east to west.

CHAPTER XIV

JOHN FITCH CONCEIVES THE PLAN OF APPLYING STEAM TO
THE PURPOSES OF TRAVEL AND TRANSPORTATION —
HIS EARLY METHODS AND MODELS — THE IDEA PLACED
BEFORE MANY LEGISLATURES AND PUBLIC MEN — NO
ONE GRASPS ITS VALUE — HE SECURES RECOGNITION
AND MONOPOLISTIC PRIVILEGES — JEERS GREET THE
FIRST BOAT MOVED BY STEAM IN AMERICA — PER-
SISTENCE OF THE INVENTOR

IT was amid these conditions, in the year 1785, that a
man named John Fitch, born in Connecticut but then
living in Philadelphia, came forward with a plan for
revolutionizing the social and business affairs of mankind
by applying steam to the purposes of travel and transportation. He proposed to run boats on the Delaware River
by means of steam power, and proceeded to do it, while
the baby-among-nations looked on.

The complete record of Fitch's life and work is available,[1] and it is therefore only necessary, in these pages, to
preface the narrative of his invention of the steamboat in
America by saying that he was a gunsmith during the

[1] Whittelsey's "Sketch of the Life of John Fitch": Spark's "Amer. Biog.," Vol. VI.
Westcott's "Life of John Fitch":
Howe's "Historical Collections of Connecticut":
"Ohio Archæological and Historical Publications," Vol. VIII.
Lloyd's "Steamboat Directory":
O'Callahan's "Documentary History of New York":
Preble's "History of Steam Navigation":
Thornton's "Short Account of the Origin of Steamboats":
Watson's "Annals of Philadelphia":
U. S. Patent Office Report for 1850, Part I.
"New York Magazine," 1790; etc., etc., etc.

Revolution, a worker in metal, a maker and repairer of clocks and watches, and an explorer, map maker, surveyor and captive of the Indians in the western wilderness. Because of unhappy domestic relations he had left his family some sixteen years before the date mentioned, after long consideration of the consequences of that step on himself and his reputation. And in later years, when putting into words the manuscript record of his undertakings that was entrusted to the Philadelphia Library, to be opened thirty years after its deposit in that institution, he said: "I know of nothing so perplexing and vexatious to a man of feelings as a turbulant Wife and Steamboat building. I experienced the former, and quit in season, and had I been in my right sences, I should undoubtedly have treated the latter in the same manner."

Fitch's scanty education, of which proof is seen in the passage quoted, will be understood when it is said that his father, a close-fisted man, compelled him to quit his intermittent schooling at the age of ten despite the boy's protest. After that calamity he worked for himself during the hours in which his parent did not demand his services, raised a crop of potatoes which he sold for ten shillings, and bought a geography. He would have realized more from his labor had not his father demanded of him a quantity of the produce equal to that originally given to him to plant. The incident is an illustration of the qualities which later impelled the man to persevere, in the face of obstacles and derision, until he had turned his vision of a steamboat into a reality.

The idea of a steamboat came to him in the spring of 1785, and by August his first rough model was completed. On the 20th of that month, Doctor Ewing, Provost of the University of Pennsylvania, wrote a letter to William

Houston, a former member of Congress, in which he said: "I have examined Mr. Fitch's machine for rowing a boat. . . . It is certain that the extensive force of water, when converted into steam, is equal to any obstruction that can be laid in its way . . . and the application of this force to turn a wheel in the water, so as to answer the purpose of oars, seems easy and natural by the machine which he proposes, and of which he has shown me a rough model. . . ." With this as a basis Fitch started for New York City in an effort to interest Congress in his invention. He stopped on the way at Trenton, where Houston wrote a similar letter, and at Princeton, where Provost Smith of Princeton College gave him a third. Reaching the national capital, the inventor wrote a letter to Congress which read as follows:

"August 29, 1785.

"Sir:

"The subscriber begs leave to lay at the feet of Congress, an attempt he has made to facilitate the internal Navigation of the United States, adapted especially to the Waters of the Mississippi. The machine he has invented for the purpose, has been examined by several Gentlemen of Learning and Ingenuity, who have given it their approbation. Being thus encouraged, he is desirous to solicit the attention of Congress, to a rough model of it now with him, that, after examination into the principles upon which it operates, they may be enabled to judge whether it deserves encouragement. And he, as in duty bound, shall ever pray.

"John Fitch.

"His Excellency, The President of Congress."

This letter was referred to a committee of three members, who made no report as far as the records show. The minutes of Congress, at that time, contained no reference to any but matters considered to be of importance. Fitch's invention did not fall within that category. He returned to Pennsylvania filled with anger at the treatment he had received, and thereafter referred to the committee of Congress as "ignorant boys." But before departing from New

York he had approached the Spanish Minister with his boat. The diplomat was much interested, and desired that the invention should be the exclusive property of his master, the King of Spain. To this Fitch would not consent.

Fitch's first model is described by Provost Ewing of the University of Pennsylvania as having a wheel that turned in the water. The best description of it is by

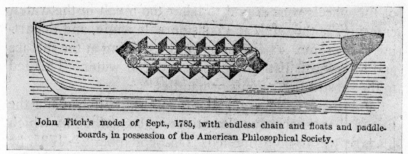

John Fitch's model of Sept., 1785, with endless chain and floats and paddle-boards, in possession of the American Philosophical Society.

64.—John Fitch conceives the idea that steam might be applied to the purposes of transportation, and invents a steamboat. His first steam-propelled craft, in 1785, was a skiff moved by little paddles (shown in black in the illustration) which were attached to an endless chain. The illustrations to No. 72, inclusive, also relate to Fitch's work.

Daniel Longstreth,[1] who says: "It was in this log shop [owned by Cobe Scout, a wheelwright of Bucks county, Pa.] that Fitch made his model steamboat, with paddle-wheels as they are now used. The model was tried on a small stream on Joseph Longstreth's meadow, about half a mile from Davisville, in Southampton township, and it realized every expectation. The machinery was made of brass, with the exception of the paddle-wheels, which were made of wood by Nathaniel B. Boileau,[2] whilst on a visit during vacation from Princeton College."

[1] The "D. L." of Watson's "Annals." Daniel Longstreth's father was an associate of Fitch while the inventor lived in Pennsylvania.
[2] Afterward Secretary of State of Pennsylvania.

Other accounts relating to Fitch's preliminary ideas are given by Doctor William Thornton, a member of Fitch's company, by Henry Voigt, also a member of the company and the inventor's principal assistant, and by Oliver Evans, an early engineer of America who himself built and ran a steamboat at Philadelphia in 1804. Probably because the wheels were too heavy for such a small model and weak engine they were almost at once discarded. On this point Whittlesey says: "The buckets of the wheels were found to labor too much in the water, entering, as they did, at a considerable angle, and departing at the same. They lost power by striking at the surface and afterwards lifting themselves out of water. This led to the substitution of oars or paddles."

For these reasons, in all probability, Fitch made the first of three successive alterations in the method by which his boat was to be propelled. On September 27, 1785, he attended the meeting of the American Philosophical Society at Philadelphia, and laid before that organization an amended drawing and model of his invention. The records of the Society on the subject read:

> "Tuesday, September 27, 1785.
> "The model, with a Drawing and Description, of a Machine for working a Boat against the stream by means of a steam-engine, was laid before the Society by Mr. John Fitch."
> "December 2nd, 1785.
> "A copy of the Drawing and Description of a machine for rowing a boat against the current, which sometime ago was laid before the Society by Mr. John Fitch, he this evening presented to them."

The model was preserved by the Society. By 1857, when Westcott investigated the subject and wrote his life of the inventor, all the drawings and descriptions were missing.

By reference to the illustration of Fitch's second

model it will be seen that he had substituted, in place of paddle-wheels, a series of upright paddles attached to endless chains, which passed over a roller toward the bow of the boat, entered the water, propelled the craft, and emerged to repeat the circuit. A section of the endless chain of paddles is also reproduced.

Fitch had worked himself into a mental frenzy. He believed he was on the right track, and was certain he could propel a boat by steam. No other thought possessed him. His days were given to alternate pleadings and arguments, or else to fits of rage, melancholy or exasperation because he was penniless and could not go ahead without help from others. But since aid was plainly necessary he set out to get it, armed with a determination to compel attention and secure the necessary money from some source either public or private. He began, therefore, a methodic visitation of legislatures and persons in high place that was as apparently endless as his system of paddles. His first effort was an attempt to enlist the interest of Benjamin Franklin, to whom he wrote a letter on October 12th. In urging the necessity of steamboats to Franklin he said: "It is a matter in his [Fitch's] opinion of the first Magnitude not only to the United States, but to every Maratime power in the World, as he is full in the belief that it will answer for sea Voiages, as well as for inland Navigation, in particular for Packets where there should be a great number of Pasengers." This letter Westcott found in possession of the American Philosophical Society of Philadelphia.

The next victim of the inventor's importunities was ex-Governor Thomas Johnson, of Maryland, who got rid of him by suggesting that he go to see General Washington. So Fitch posted forthwith to Mount Vernon, where

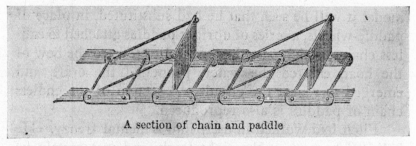

A section of chain and paddle

65.—Detail of the propulsion method of Fitch's first boat. The paddles were out of water as they moved forward, and after passing the front roller they entered the water and proceeded toward the stern, thus forcing the boat ahead.

the General, he says, received him with courtesy and listened to his plans. That was the usual thing. Everybody always received him, and everybody listened, or appeared to. His next stopping place was Richmond, in Virginia, where the legislature was in session. Legislatures at that time were Fitch's especial prey, and his memorial to the Virginia Assembly was presented by no less a person than James Madison. A committee was duly appointed — familiar procedure to the poverty-stricken man who was begging for the opportunity of enriching the world beyond computation — and its members spoke very favorably to the petitioner. But they made no report. He also saw Patrick Henry, then governor of the state, who said the plan was novel and interesting.

Returning to Fredericktown he again went to ex-Governor Johnson, who hastily subscribed to Fitch's map of the Northwest Territory as a means of being rid of him, and suggested that the legislature of Maryland was in session at Annapolis. So indeed it was, but Fitch was also aware that the Pennsylvania Assembly had gathered again in Philadelphia, and he went there first, presenting his usual petition. It was referred to a committee who made

238

a flattering oral report, but no action was taken. Finally, at Annapolis, and for the first time, Fitch's plan received formal notice. The Maryland legislature considered it for three days and then refused to endorse the invention. The committee said that although it was desirable "for liberal and enlightened Legislators to encourage useful arts," yet the state and condition of the state's finances did not permit such action in that instance. His next stopping place on the trip was at Dover, in Delaware. Fitch talked with the members of the legislature and doubtless finding the effort useless did not present his plan, but departed for Philadelphia. In February of 1786 he went to Trenton. On the defeat of his bill by the New Jersey legislature he returned to his home.

Fitch had then appealed to all the powerful men within his reach, to five states, and to the General Congress, without effect. Not one mind grasped the value of the idea. So he decided to begin all over again, and went once more to Doctor Franklin. That eminent man spoke in a calm and complimentary vein, declined to endorse the steamboat, and then, taking Fitch into another room, privately offered to give him several dollars in cash. The incensed inventor refused the money except as a subscription toward the building of the boat and withdrew in anger from the abode of philosophy.

Doubtless Benjamin Franklin had never before made such a mistake in his diagnosis of a fellow man, but doubtless, also, the same error would have been made by others as profound as he, if such there were. The tall, gaunt, shabby, excitable, almost incoherent enthusiast, pouring out words in a frantic effort to make others see the future as he saw it, already presented to many minds the spectacle of a madman babbling over a phantasy.

But the turning-point was almost at hand. After still another appeal to the Assembly of Pennsylvania which he left to its usual fate, he rushed away again to Trenton where he petitioned the New Jersey legislature for a special law giving to him the exclusive right to navigate the waters of that state by steam power. He had altered his tactics, and instead of trying to get money first he begged for legal privileges, hoping the necessary cash would be easier to secure if his claim as an inventor was recognized. This application was successful. On March 18, 1786, New Jersey granted to Fitch "The sole and exclusive right of constructing, making, using and employing, or navigating, all and every species or kinds of boats, or water craft, which might be urged or impelled by the force of fire or steam, in all the creeks, rivers, etc., within the territory or jurisdiction of this state." The right so given was to exist for fourteen years.

Whatever historical interest New Jersey's action of 1786 may have as a landmark in the evolution of travel facilities is overshadowed by its greater importance in another respect. The passage of Fitch's bill was the first step on a pathway of error along which the country stumbled for more than half a century, and some effects of the mistake are still visible throughout the whole modern system of American transportation. New Jersey's grant was a declaration of the principle that individuals or individual companies might hold exclusive privileges for the transporting of passengers and freight by certain methods within the limits of any state. Imitated, as it was, by other commonwealths, the idea thus established split the country into small fragments on the one feature of national development which, above all others, called for a policy continental in its scope.

The effect of the monopolistic privilege on Fitch's plans was highly favorable. Within five weeks he had organized a little company of nearly twenty men, and of the forty equal shares he was to have one-half for his invention and services. The others paid about twenty dollars each, and something over three hundred dollars was on hand with which to build the first American steamboat. At this time — April of 1786 — there were but three steam-engines in America. All were built on the old atmospheric plan, and the newest of them, that at the Schuyler mine, near Passaic, New Jersey, had been brought from England thirty years before. The other two were in New England, and still older. No one in the country had ever made anything like the engine that Fitch called for, nor was any man known to possess the skill necessary to do it. In the face of such conditions he started to create, out of nothing more tangible than the ideas of his brain, a vehicle that should navigate the water by means of power contained within its own fabric. The element of human invention had at last been applied to the problem of transportation.

While concerned over the proper construction of his engine Fitch fell in with an ingenious Philadelphia watchmaker named Henry Voight, and enlisted his services in the work. Together they built a small skiff and an engine with a three-inch cylinder, and about July 20, 1786, for the first time operated a steamboat on American waters. The miniature machinery and chain of paddles worked but poorly, and a little group who watched the boat from the shore jeered the two men and the wonder they had performed. Some local notoriety had attended the formation of the company and plan of the inventor, but all public comment was by word of mouth, accompanied by winks and jests. The newspapers made no mention of the matter. It was a joke, ill-fitted to the serious times and to those matters of consequence that engrossed popular attention.

A few days after this experiment Fitch conceived the idea of propelling the boat by a series of twelve upright

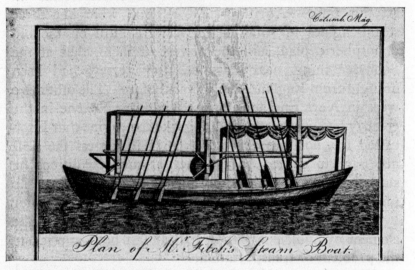

66.—Fitch's second boat. With his little experimental engine and upright oars it was operated on the Delaware River, at Philadelphia, in 1786. The contemporary engraving here reproduced is that printed in the *Columbian Magazine* for December, 1786. By an oversight the engraver of 1786 omitted to show the smoke-pipe.

paddles, like oars, arranged six on each side and operated by a system of cranks. The device was accordingly built and fitted to the skiff, and was found to move the craft with increased speed and power. It was nevertheless seen that additional money was needed for larger machinery and a bigger boat, in order to carry on a test under conditions more nearly approaching the practical commercial vehicle toward which the inventor was aiming.

Neither during his earlier efforts nor at any time did
Fitch falter in his certainty that he had hit upon a means
of transportation which would alter the affairs of mankind, or that he would succeed in producing, in concrete
form, the thing his brain had already constructed. It was
amid these days that he wrote a letter to Stacy Potts, a
member of the company, in which he said: "My expectations are daily increasing as to the success of our undertaking, and dout not but it will be a matter of the first magnitude to the World."[1] Two other letters written by the
inventor at the same time show an identical frame of mind.
One was a petition to the Pennsylvania Assembly asking
for a loan of £150,[2] in which he spoke of steam transportation as "a plan that would enrich America at least 3 times
as much as all that country N.W. [northwest] of the Ohio,
as it would make that country four times as valuable, beside the inconceivable advantages to the settled portion of
the continent." In the same communication he defined a
characteristic of the people by saying, "There is such a
strange infatuation in mankind that it seems they would
rather lay out their money in Beloons[3] and Fireworks, and
be a pest to Society than to lay it out in something that
would be of use to themselves and Country." The legislature refused to make the requested loan. The other
letter was a similar request addressed to General Thomas
Mifflin, of Pennsylvania, in which Fitch declared: "I am
of opinion, that a vessel may be carried six, seven or eight
miles per hour, by the force of steam, and the larger the
vessel, the better it will answer, and am strongly inclined

[1] This letter, quoted by Westcott in his biography of Fitch, has long been lost. It was
recently rediscovered by Émil Sauer, the antiquary, and presented to the New York Historical Society by S. V. Hoffman, Esq., the President of that Institution, together with
five other important Fitch documents found with it.
[2] It was the custom at that time for state legislatures to advance money to inventors
for the prosecution of enterprises useful to society. The Pennsylvania Assembly, a few
weeks before, had loaned another man £300 for the manufacture of bar iron.
[3] Balloons had lately been invented, and had been shown in America for the first time.

to believe that it will answer for sea Voiages as well as for inland Navigation. . . . Was it a thing of trifling consequence to my Country, I would not persue it with such assiduity."

All Fitch's efforts to obtain enough money in 1786 to enable him to continue the work were fruitless. In that year he deposited his plans and drawings with the American Philosophical Society, in Philadelphia, but like so much other material evidence of his invention, those things disappeared. When Westcott sought for them[1] they were not to be found. The models and drawings of Fitch's early boats were destroyed by the burning of the United States Patent Office in 1836. One contemporary evidence of what was done in 1786 remains. It is the picture of his second boat, engraved on copper and published in the *Columbian Magazine* for December of that year,[2] together with a brief reference to the mechanism then used which was soon afterward printed in the same periodical. The illustration in this work is photographed from the original printed in 1786. A part of the contemporary description of the mechanism of the second boat said:

"The piston is to move about three feet, and each vibration of the piston turns the axle tree about two-thirds round. They propose to make the piston to strike thirty strokes in a minute; which will give the axle-tree about forty revolutions. Each revolution of the axle-tree moves twelve oars five and a half feet. As six oars come out of the water six more enter the water; which makes a stroke of about eleven feet each revolution. The oars work perpendicularly, and make a stroke similar to the paddle of a canoe . . . and both the action and reaction of the piston operate to turn the axle-tree the same way."[3]

[1] About 1856.
[2] Through some odd oversight the engraver showed no smoke-stack.
[3] The thing that prevented early engineers up to about 1780 from developing the steam-engine, was the difficulty of converting the back-and-fourth motion of the piston into a rotary motion by means of a wheel moved by the piston. The mechanical princip'e thus sought had been in use for centuries on domestic spinning wheels, but no one thought of applying it to steam-engines until Pickard, in 1780, devised the crank attachment by which the dead point of the wheel was passed and a complete revolution obtained.

A

SHORT

TREATISE

ON THE APPLICATION OF

S T E A M,

WHEREBY IS CLEARLY SHEWN,

FROM

ACTUAL EXPERIMENTS,

THAT

S T E A M

MAY BE APPLIED TO PROPEL

BOATS OR VESSELS

OF ANY BURTHEN AGAINST RAPID CURRENTS WITH GREAT VELOCITY,

The same Principles are also introduced with Effect, by a Machine of a simple and cheap Construction, for the Purpose of raising Water sufficient for the working of

GRIST-MILLS, SAW-MILLS, &c.

AND *for* WATERING MEADOWS *and* OTHER PURPOSES OF AGRICULTURE.

By JAMES RUMSEY,

OF BERKELEY COUNTY, *Virginia.*

PHILADELPHIA,

PRINTED BY JOSEPH JAMES, CHESNUT-STREET,

M,DCC,LXXXVIII.

67.—Early literature relating to travel in America. Title page of Rumsey's pamphlet claiming precedence over Fitch as a steamboat inventor. Second edition of the first American book on steamboats. Printed in 1788.

Fitch was reduced to temporary inactivity through lack of money. Some members of his company had originally subscribed because of friendship for the inventor with no hope of return, while others, over-enthusiastic, had expected large and immediate results from their investments. Both sorts were disinclined to make further contributions, and in extremity Fitch turned again to the various legislatures in an effort to secure recognition of his rights as an inventor, and privileges in the use of the steamboat. His applications to some of those bodies were fought by various other men who had suggested improvements in the use of steam as applied to existing contrivances, but Fitch met such opposition boldly. In his statement to the Pennsylvania Assembly he said, among other things:

"I never pretended to be the first inventor of the steam engine, nor ever did Petition for an Exclusive right for them. I have never asked it in any other way than where it has never been applied, and I presume the World cannot produce a steam engine floating on the water. Neither do I conceive that all the Improvements that are yet to be made on steam are to be done on the water . . .

"I here produce seven different plans of applying the force of steam to a boat, and could produce four different models, if necessary . . .

"It is the force and power that I contend for. As to the thought of applying that force to vessels I claim priority, and not the mode of application. . . .

"It is an undoubted fact that I am the first inventor of the steamboat[1]; . . . I have set myself up as a mark of derision, and have suffered every insult that the contempt which the populace have for projectors could inflict. . . .

"The propelling of a boat with steam is as new as the rowing of a boat with angels, and I claim the first thought and invention of it."

Opposition collapsed before words like that, and the lawmakers recognized the inventor's claim. The state of Delaware, on February 3, 1787, gave to Fitch the exclu-

[1] He was the first in America, but not in the world. His work and devices show that he did not know of earlier similar inventions mentioned in a later chapter.

sive right to navigate all its waters by boats propelled in any way by steam for a period of fourteen years. New York passed a similar act on March 19 of the same year; Pennsylvania gave him identical privileges on March 28, and Virginia took like action on November 7. Each commonwealth bestowed on him a monopoly of steam navigation within its limits for a period of years, as New Jersey had previously done; but two of the states also took certain action that was, in the future, to have far reaching and long continued effect on the history of steam transportation in America. Virginia included in her law a proviso that Fitch must have "boats" — obviously meaning more than one — in operation on the waters of the state within a period of three years, and New York ordered that if any other man usurped the rights granted, such interloper was to forfeit £100 to Fitch and suffer the confiscation of his boat and engine by the original inventor. The stipulation made by Virginia was thought to be of especial value to the company, for as that state had long claimed sovereignty over much of the territory extending to the Mississippi River, a compliance with it meant, in the estimation of the company, that Fitch and his associates would enjoy a monopoly of steam transportation on the Ohio, upper Mississippi and other interior streams.

The action of Delaware and the other states elated the company and stirred it to renewed activity.[1] Success and wealth seemed assured. More money was subscribed, and Fitch and his assistant again began work in the production of a larger boat and an engine with a twelve-inch cylinder. Again they were balked in their efforts to produce a smooth-working mechanism. The task was a hard

---

[1] A new agreement was drawn up on February 9, 1787, which Westcott found in the American Philosophical Society archives when preparing his biography.

one. They were hampered by a lack of knowledge of the relationships and proportions which cylinder, condenser, boiler, pump and other parts of a steam-engine should bear to one another. They were building out of nothing, and could learn only by experience and repeated failure. No sooner did they have one part of the contrivance perfect than something else failed. In May of 1787 the whole engine was taken down and rebuilt at heavy cost, and once more the company became so discouraged that some of its members abandoned the enterprise altogether. But Fitch remained stubborn in his resolution to go on, wrote a long address to the public in which he elaborately reviewed his invention, reaffirmed his certainty in its value, pointed out its advantages in opening the country to white settlement, and used the words: "The Grand and Principle object must be on the Atlantick; which would soon overspread the wild forests of America with people, and make us the most oppulent Empire on Earth. . . . Pardon me, generous public, for suggesting ideas that cannot be dijested at this day."

CHAPTER XV

FITCH'S SECOND BOAT — CONTEMPORARY ACCOUNTS OF IT
— THE THIRD VESSEL — FIRST REGULARLY OPERATED
STEAMBOAT IN THE WORLD — IT IS RUN ON THE
DELAWARE FOR SEVERAL MONTHS — MORE CONTEM-
PORARY STATEMENTS — DISASTER — THE INVENTOR
IS CALLED A MADMAN — PERSISTS "FOR THE BENEFIT
OF OUR EMPIRE" — GOES TO FRANCE AND LEAVES HIS
PLANS THERE — RETIRES TO THE KENTUCKY WILDER-
NESS AND MAKES A STRANGE WHEELED ENGINE —
DESPAIR — DEATH

FITCH'S persistence once more had its way. His associates found additional funds, the second boat was completed, and on August 22, 1787, it was operated under its own power on the Delaware River in the presence of many people, including most of the members of the Constitutional Convention then sitting in Philadelphia. Still there was no general recognition of one of the most important events that had taken place since Columbus discovered the western world. The few current references to Fitch's work are short, and lacking in comprehension of the effect the invention was destined to have on man's progress. He himself seems to have been the only individual rightly to measure what he was doing. One of the contemporary mentions of the test of August 22nd occurs in a day-book kept by the Reverend Ezra

249

Stiles, of New Haven, who under date of August 27 made in his diary the following entry:

"Judge Ellsworth, a member of the Federal Convention, just returned from Philadelphia, visited me, and tells me the Convention will not rise under three weeks. He there saw a Steam-engine for rowing boats against the stream, invented by Mr. Fitch, of Windsor, in Connecticut. He was on board the boat, and saw the experiment succeed."

Another mention of the boat made at about the same time was contained in a written statement by David Rittenhouse, an early American scientist, who said under date of December 12, 1787:

"These may certify that the subscriber has frequently seen Mr. Fitch's steamboat, which with great labour and perseverance he has at length compleated, and has likewise been on board when the boat was worked against both wind and tide, with a very considerable degree of velocity by the force of steam only. Mr. Fitch's merit in constructing a good steam engine, and applying it to so useful a purpose, will no doubt meet with the encouragement he so justly deserves from the generousity of his countrymen; especially those who wish to promote every improvement of the useful arts in America."[1]

At about this time the inventor became involved in a controversy with James Rumsey, of Virginia, who had previously invented a boat in which the setting poles whereby it was propelled were to be operated through a system of mechanical cranks operated by wheels and hand power. Rumsey apparently found that such a device was not of value for he soon turned to the use of steam, and at first devised a boat based somewhat on a previous idea of Doctor Franklin, who had suggested that a forward movement might be obtained by forcibly ejecting a stream of water from the stern of the craft. Rumsey found many supporters among prominent men,[2] and an association

[1] Westcott's "Life of John Fitch."
[2] Fitch was an anti-Federalist, and his political, social and religious beliefs brought upon him the dislike of many who held contrary views. It was a time wherein personal idiosyncrasies were peculiarly potent in fixing the estimate in which a man was held by his fellow citizens. Men were often opposed in some projects because their opinions on irrelevant matters were not endorsed. Fitch encountered such opposition.

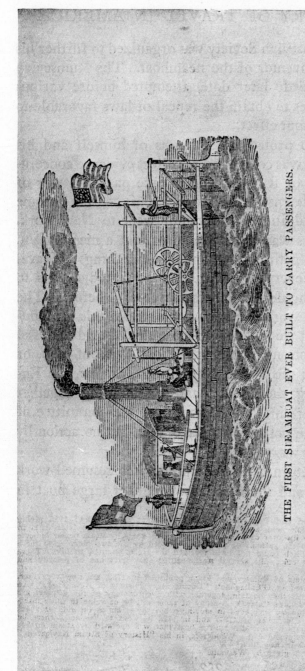

THE FIRST STEAMBOAT EVER BUILT TO CARRY PASSENGERS.

Constructed by John Fitch, and finished April 16th, 1798. Cylinder eighteen inches in diameter, speed eight miles per hour in smooth water. The following year this boat was run to Burlington regularly as a passenger boat.

68.—A later picture of Fitch's third boat. No contemporary illustration is known. First steamboat and first steam vehicle of any sort employed in the business of transportation. It made a trial trip of 20 miles in 1788, and in 1790 ran more than 1,000 miles on the Delaware River in accordance with advertisements printed in the Philadelphia newspapers. The date on the reproduced engraving is an error.

called the Rumseyian Society was organized to further his claims as the inventor of the steamboat. The Rumseyian Society, at a little later date, attempted before various state legislatures to obtain the repeal of laws favorable to Fitch, but without effect.

In order to protect the interests of himself and his company Fitch was compelled to collect evidence concerning the claims of Rumsey, and to take part in a war of pamphlets in defense of his work.[1] This consumed some time, and in addition the inventor went to New York, where Congress was in session, to present a memorial to that body. The petition[2] said among other things: "Haveing overcome every difficulty that ocationed doubts to arise, and having done what was never done before, (The world has been worrying against the stream this six thousand years) but we have exhibited to the World a Vessel going against strong winds and Tides, without sails, or men to labour; the Vessel carrying the Engine, the Engine propelling the Vessel, and all moveing together against the Currents." The report of the committee of Congress on the petition was favorable, but no action by the whole body was taken.

After his return to Philadelphia Fitch resumed work on the engine and the company bought a large boat in

[1] Virginia, Maryland and Pennsylvania had passed acts in 1784 and 1785 giving Rumsey rights in his pole boat, and the action of the same states, at a later date, in recognizing Fitch as the inventor of a method of propelling boats by steam power indicate there was no conflict in the systems of propulsion devised by the two men. Had there been such duplication Fitch could not have received the rights granted to him. There being no central patent office, the several states settled such questions of priority and privilege.

The original pamphlets of Rumsey and Fitch, published in 1788, are now very rare, but their text is reprinted in O'Callaghan's "Documentary History of New York." An analysis of the statements they contain, together with a chronology of the dispute, are also to be found in Westcott's "Life." A study of them will be of value to those interested in the subject. Rumsey succeeded in moving a boat by steam at the rate of about three miles an hour in December of 1787, and in 1788 he went to England, where he afterward died. His English associates built a boat that was operated by steam on the Thames in 1793, but was abandoned. Woodcroft, in his "History of Steam Navigation," refers to Rumsey's work in England.

[2] The complete text is given by Westcott.

which it was to be installed. This craft, destined to be the first steam vehicle of any sort in the world to make regularly scheduled and advertised trips for the carriage of passengers, was forty-five feet long and twelve feet wide. The company had desired to obtain a hull about sixty feet in length by eight feet beam, rightly believing such a model would obtain greater speed, but was unable to do so. It had also been the inventor's intention to use a cylinder of eighteen inches diameter in his engine, but after one of that size had been cast it was broken up by mistake. So the old twelve-inch cylinder was retained. At this time, also, Fitch made another change in his method of propulsion, substituting three or four broad upright paddles at the stern of the craft for the twelve side oars. The third boat with its essential features as here described was completed late in July of 1788, and — probably on one of the last days of that month — received its first important trial. It set out from Philadelphia bearing Fitch, Voight and a number of others, and steamed to Burlington, a distance of about twenty miles. When just off Burlington a leak developed in the boiler and the engine stopped. The crew dropped down the stream with the tide next day, and the steamboat was the object of scoffing from those in sailing craft on the river.

The mishap which had interrupted the first trip of the inventor's third boat almost at its conclusion was soon repaired, and several other round trips to Burlington were made during the following weeks. On October 12th, 1788, the steamboat took thirty passengers to Burlington in three hours and ten minutes, aided by a tide running about two miles an hour. Probably the speed developed by the vessel during 1788 was some four miles an hour in still water. Such a slow rate of movement did not satisfy Fitch, who, despite the personal destitution to which he had long since been reduced, insistently demanded more funds for the boat[1] and continued his labor in improving the machinery and in repeated tests of the vessel until the spring of 1790. At last he obtained a combination of mechanical parts that worked successfully, and on April 16th of 1790 made a trial which caused him to say exultantly: "We reigned Lord High Admirals of the Delaware; and no boat in the River could hold its way with us. . . . Thus has been effected, by little Johnny Fitch and Harry Voight, one of the greatest and most useful arts that has ever been introduced into the world; and although the world and my country does not thank me for it, yet it gives me heartfelt satisfaction."[2]

A number of other equally successful voyages soon followed, and for the first time public and newspaper attention was attracted to the invention. Governor Mifflin and numerous state and city officials were passengers on June 16th, and were so impressed that they had Fitch buy a set of flags at their expense. A cabin was built for passengers in the forward part of the craft, and at a formal test made by the aid of stop-watches the speed of the boat was found to be eight miles an hour.[3] Soon afterward it covered eighty miles in a day and was then put into commission as a regular passenger boat on the Delaware, making trips in accordance with advertisements previously printed in the local newspapers. The first of these advance notices of the steamboat's trips had ap-

[1] About $8,000 had been expended up to the winter of 1788.
[2] The spot on the river-front where Fitch had so long labored had come to be known as "Conjurer's Point."
[3] Thornton's "Short Account of the Origin of Steamboats": p. 5.

Mr. Cornell, sworn interpreter; to all which the Creeks gave an audible assent.

The President then signed the treaty—after which he presented a string of beads as a token of perpetual peace, and a paper of tobacco to smoke in remembrance of it; Mr. M'Gillivray rose, made a short reply to the President, and received the tokens.

This was succeeded by the shake of peace, every one of the Creeks passing this friendly salute with the President; a song of peace performed by the Creeks, concluded this highly interesting, solemn, and dignified transaction.

Aug. 16. Last Thursday evening the St. Andrew's Society of the state of New-York held their quarterly meeting at the City-Tavern. The Society, anxious of shewing their respect to the character of Col. M'Gillivray, availed themselves of his presence in this city, and unanimously elected him an honorary member of the Society, and immediately after a committee was appointed to conduct him to it.

Aug. 17. On Sunday embarked on board one of the Packets, on a visit to Rhode-Island, his Excellency the President of the United States, the Secretary of State, Gov. Clinton, Judge Blair, Col. Humphreys, Major Jackson, and Mr. Nelson.

Extract of a letter from Philadelphia, August 13.

"Fitch's steam boat really performs to a charm. It is a pleasure while one is on board her in a contrary wind to observe her superiority over the river shallops, sloops, ships, &c. who, to gain any thing, must make a zig-zag course, while this, our new invented vessel, proceeds in a direct line. On Sunday morning she sets off for Chester, and engages to return in the evening, the whole 40 miles. God willing, I mean to

be one of the passengers, were it only to encourage American ingenuity and the fine arts. Fitch is certainly one of the most ingenious creatures alive, and will certainly make his fortune. I am told he has now in contemplation to build a steam vessel on a larger scale, which may be capable of carrying freights and passengers to the West-Indies, and even to Europe. One great advantage I can foresee in these voyages, which is, that the steam ship can make progress in a calm when other vessels must lie motionless. How she would behave in a gale of wind must be left to experience to determine. Having no sails, masts or top-hamper, to lay too or scud under, it is probable she might at such time be in great jeopardy."

Aug. 20. On the 17th instant, the Trustees of the College of Philadelphia elected the Hon. Judge *Wilson* Professor of Law in that institution, and we hear that he intends to deliver a course of lectures in that important branch of education.

Quere *Whether there is not an impropriety both in electing a* Judge *to a Professorship, and in his accepting it?*

Aug. 21. His Excellency the President, with his suite, returned to this city from Rhode-Island.

On Thursday the 19th inst. embarked for St. Mary's river, in Georgia, in the sloop Betsey, and schooner Experiment, Col. Alexander M'Gillivray, and the several Indian Headmen and Warriors who have been in this city for some weeks past attending the treaty. Mr. Swan, we hear, has been chosen Secretary to Col. M'Gillivray, and has proceeded with that officer to reside in the Indian country.

Aug. 23. We are informed, via Boston, that on the 10th of June last the National Assembly of France decreed, " That the National Assembly wear mourning three days, in honour of the late Dr. *Franklin*; and that a letter of condolence be sent by

---

69.—Page 493 of the *New York Magazine* for 1790. The printed account of Fitch's steamboat, beginning at the bottom of the first column, relates to the vessel last shown.

peared in the *Pennsylvania Packet* of June 14, 1790, and read:

THE STEAMBOAT

is now ready to take passengers, and is intended to set off from Arch street Ferry, in Philadelphia, every Monday, Wednesday, and Friday, for Burlington, Bristol, Bordentown, & Trenton, to return on Tuesdays, Thursdays and Saturdays. Price for passengers 2/6 to Burlington and Bristol, 3/9 to Bordentown, 5 s. to Trenton.

tu.-th. s-tf.

During the summer and fall of 1790 the boat ran regularly back and forth between Philadelphia and various towns on the river. The *Pennsylvania Packet* and *Federal Gazette* newspapers issued between June 14th and September 10th of 1790 contained twenty-three advertisements similar to the one here quoted, announcing, altogether, thirty-one trips to different places. The aggregate of the advertised trips amounted to thirteen hundred and eighty miles. Fitch, in his manuscript journal, says the mishaps were few. "The axle-trees," he mentions, "broke twice; there was nothing but these accidents which could not be repaired in a single hour or two. . . . The boat run five hundred miles between these accidents."

Numerous accounts of the performances of 1790, either published at the time or written at a later day by men who had personally travelled on the boat or had seen it in operation during the year, are available. The artist Rembrandt Peale was one who was familiar with its work during the time in question, and his memoirs[1] describe its appearance and movement. General Joseph Bloomfield, of New Jersey, testified before a committee of the New York legislature in 1814 that he had frequently been a passenger on Fitch's boat on the Delaware.[2] Doc-

[1] Printed in the "Collections of the Historical Society of Pennsylvania," Vol. 1, No. 1.
[2] "New York Review," Vol. IV.

tor William Thornton's[1] pamphlet gives the recital of an eye-witness of and participant in the steamboat's activities. "Our boat," he said, "went at the rate of eight miles an hour in the presence of witnesses yet living."[2] The French author and traveller, Brissot de Warville, wrote a description of the third boat as it appeared when he saw it operated in 1788, while its speed was only about four miles an hour.[3] The most pretentious contemporary American notice of the vessel's successful operation in 1790 was published in the *New York Magazine*[4] for that year, and was an extract from a letter sent from Philadelphia. It ran:

"Fitch's steamboat really performs to a charm. It is a pleasure, while one is on board of her in a contrary wind, to observe her superiority over the river shallops, sloops, ships, etc., who, to gain anything, must make a zigzag course, while this, our new invented vessel, proceeds in a direct line. On Sunday morning she sets off for Chester,[5] and engages to return in the evening — 40 miles. God willing, I intend to be one of the passengers, were it only to encourage American ingenuity and the fine arts. Fitch is certainly one of the most ingenious creatures alive, and will certainly make his fortune. . . ."

The thing Fitch said he would do had been done. After five years of endeavor the steamboat existed, and moved briskly over the waters before the eyes of men. Steam had been harnessed and applied to the purposes of transportation and travel. A fourth boat,[6] similar to the one which had been running on the Delaware during the summer, was begun in order to comply with the Virginia law. Under its terms at least two steam vessels had to be in operation on the waters of the state by

[1] Thornton was a member of Fitch's company. His account, written in 1810 and published in 1818, is entitled "Short Account of the Or'gin of Steamboats."
[2] United States Patent Office Report for 1850; Part I, pp. 368-372.
[3] "A Recent Journey in the United States of North America, Made in 1788." Paris, 1791.
[4] Page 493. Photographically reproduced in this work.
[5] The regular Sunday trips of the boat throughout the summer of 1790 were to Chester or Burlington. They were somewhat in the nature of popular excursions.
[6] It was fittingly named the "Perseverance."

November 9th, 1790, and the time in which to comply with the requirement and secure a monopoly of steam transportation on all Virginia waters was short. Unforeseen disaster destroyed the plans of the company. The *Perseverance,* when nearly completed, was torn from her moorings by a violent storm and thrown at high tide on an island in the river from which it was impossible to remove her until too late to fulfill the conditions under which Virginia's privileges had been granted.

The loss of the Virginia monopoly came as a crushing blow to Fitch's associates, for upon it had been based their principal expectations of future profit. And so, at the very outset of success, the faint-hearted company finally crumbled to pieces. The inventor alone held up his courage. He at once petitioned the Commissioners of Patents to grant him exclusive rights in steam navigation for a limited time; originated a plan to put boats on the Mississippi under the patronage of Spain, and chided his former supporters in a letter in which he said:

"After the many thousands which you have expended to bring forward the most useful art that was ever introduced into the World, and even after you have perfected it, it seems that you are amazed at what you have done, and lost in contemplating, in thinking, how the world will gaze on the virtuous Few who have so nobly and liberally rendered such essential service to their Nation. . . .

"We had to explore an unbeaten path, and did not ascertain the true course until we had wandered into a thousand wrong Rodes. . . .

"I have given my country a most valuable discovery, on the 30 of August, 1785, for which I have received no compensation; and I doubt not but common justice will induce them to do something for me; especially when they can do it for the benefit of our Empire.

"Another inducement which urges me to persue this scheme is, to put it out of the power of future Generations to make excuses for the present one . . ."

In his long petition[1] to the national officials asking for

[1] Given in its entirety by Westcott.

the sole right to employ steamboats on all the waters of the country Fitch, "having," as he affirmed, "at length fully succeeded in his scheme, proof of which he is prepared to offer, he trusts he now comes forward, not as an imaginary projector, but as a man who, contrary to

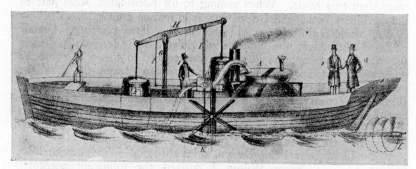

70.—Fitch's fifth boat. His fourth was wrecked by a storm when nearly completed. The fifth boat was a screw propeller, operated on Collect Pond, New York City, in 1796 or 1797. Its hull was a ship's yawl, and the craft was an experiment in the inventor's work for the better application of steam power. A model of one of Fitch's steamboats, later made by one of his assistants, is in the New York Historical Society's collections.

the popular expectation, has really accomplished a design which on examination will clearly evince the many and important advantages which must result therefrom to the United States. . . ."[1]

All active effort to carry on the work of building and running steamboats seems to have been abandoned in 1791. Biddle's *Philadelphia Directory* for the year mentioned, published in May, contained the following entry:

"Fitch, John, owner of the steamboat, 462 No. Second St."

A picture of the affairs of the company and of Fitch's destitution at that time was afterward written by Thomas

[1] Letters patent for the steamboat were granted by the government to Fitch on April 23, 1791, and formally issued to him in a signed document on August 26. Exclusive privileges were refused. Thomas Jefferson, whom Fitch had violently antagonized, was one of the Patent Commissioners.

P. Cope, of Philadelphia,[1] who lived in the city during the building of the steamboats.

"I often witnessed the performance of the boat in 1788, '89 and '90," reads the narrative. "It was propelled by paddles in the stern, and constantly getting out of order. I saw it when it was returning from a trip to Burlington, from whence it was said to have arrived in little more than two hours. When coming to off Kensington, some part of the machinery broke, and I never saw it in motion afterward. I believe it was his last effort. . . . Indeed, they [the company] already rendered themselves the subjects of ridicule and derision, for their temerity and presumption in giving countenance to this wild projector and visionary madman. The company thereupon gave up the ghost, the boat went to pieces, and Fitch became bankrupt and broken-hearted. Often have I seen him stalking about like a troubled spectre, with downcast eye and lowering countenance, his coarse soiled linen peeping through the elbows of a tattered garment. During the days of his aspiring hopes, two mechanics were of sufficient daring to work for him. . . . These were Peter Brown, shipsmith, and John Wilson, Boat builder. . . . From Wilson I derived the following anecdote: Fitch called to see him as usual — Brown happened to be present. Fitch mounted his hobby, and became unusually eloquent in the praise of steam, and of the benefits which mankind were destined to derive from its use in propelling boats . . . After indulging himself for some time in this never failing topic of deep excitement, he concluded with these memorable words: 'Well, gentlemen, although I shall not live to see the time, you will, when steamboats will be preferred to all other means of conveyance, and especially for passengers; and they will be particularly useful in the navigation of the River Mississippi.' He then retired; on which Brown, turning to Wilson, exclaimed, in a tone of deep sympathy, 'Poor fellow! What a pity he is crazy.'"

In 1793 Fitch went to France.[2] He had previously met in Philadelphia a man named Aaron Vail, the United States consul to L'Orient, France, who became interested in the steamboat and proposed, on his return to his official post, to secure patents and build such vessels under French laws. Fitch had bound himself to send over to Europe a man competent to construct the proposed craft,

[1] To be found in Hazard's "Register of Pennsylvania," Vol. vii, under the signature of "Epoc." [Cope].
[2] See Thornton's "Short Account"; William A. Duer's "A Reply to C. D. Colden's Vindication," 1819; Watson's "Annals of Philadelphia"; Whittelsey's "Life," etc.

and having no one to whom he might delegate the duty, went himself. He arrived during a time when all ordinary enterprises were at a standstill,[1] and finding it impossible to proceed with the contemplated design, left his steamboat drawings, plans and specifications in the hands of Vail, who was established as a merchant in L'Orient, and came back to America by way of England.

Little of Fitch's work remains to be told. He lived in Philadelphia and New York City until late in 1797 or early in 1798, and seems still to have been intent in perfecting the method of steam transportation. In 1851 John Hutchings, of New York, published a broadside[2] describing an experiment that Fitch made with a steamboat on Collect Pond, New York City,[3] either in 1796 or 1797, and in which Hutchings, then a youth, assisted him. The boat was a ship's yawl, and was moved by a steam-engine turning a screw propeller at the stern. It also had revolving paddles of the modern type at the sides.

At last Fitch ceased the hopeless struggle. In order that he might no longer hear the laughter of his fellow men he went out into the Kentucky wilderness, apart from bickering and jeers, and there, in a quiet and unobtrusive way made an end of his troubled life.[4] Yet even amid the primeval woods, during the few final months, his mind and fingers were busy with the work which had engrossed him. He built of brass a strange contrivance some three feet long that was found after his death, and is illustrated among these pages. Although it has a smokestack with an elbow at the top, apparently designed with

---

[1] The French Revolution was in progress.
[2] Reprinted in O'Callaghan's "Documentary History of New York."
[3] The pond was on the present site of the Tombs prison, Center Street.
[4] He saved many small narcotic pills, prescribed singly by a doctor for some trivial ailment. and swallowed them all at once. His death took place in June or July of 1798.

the idea of preventing a downward draught while moving at high speed against the wind,[1] and though the engine rested on a rectangular truck with four solid and flanged wheels,[2] this model of a steam-engine has always been discussed as one for a steamboat mechanism. A St. Louis newspaper[3] of 1854, while the original model was in that city, said:

"It was evidently thus arranged for the purpose of exhibiting the power of steam in propelling boats, and was constructed on a railway immersed in a trough of the proper depth for the paddles to strike the water, and when the motion was given, the wheels would guide it along the submerged railway."

The theory here expounded, and since accepted by those who have known of Fitch's last model or seen it, appears questionable when considered in connection with what had already been done by the man who designed and built it. Fitch had not found it necessary, in proving that steam could be used in moving a boat, to drag down the hull by a wheeled truck and keep the whole fabric on a submerged track along which it should move in a straight line. The added weight of truck and wheels, and the friction of wheels on submerged rails would retard the progress of the boat, if motive power was imparted to paddles alone. In practise the laying, maintaining and repairing of such a track would not be possible. River bottoms do not lend themselves to such a method of transportation. In deep water the wooden hull would either float the wheels off the track or else the wheeled underbody would pull the hull down, with unpleasant consequences to crew and passen-

---

[1] The same idea was suggested for railroad locomotives a half century afterward. When the early lithographer made the picture reproduced in this work he showed the smoke-stack elbow pointed forward! Doubtless the whole stack had been twisted around.
[2] With the wheels inside the truck, as some early railway engines and cars were first constructed.
[3] The "Democrat."

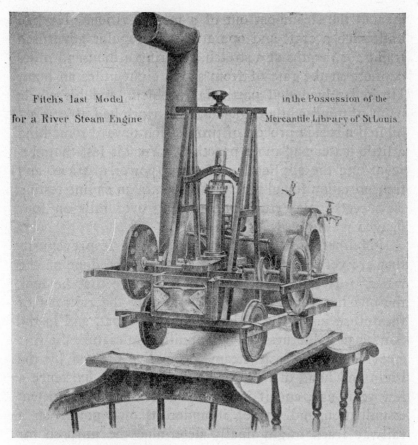

Fitch's last Model for a River Steam Engine in the Possession of the Mercantile Library of St Louis

71.—Last known handiwork of Fitch, made in Kentucky a short time before his death, in 1798. The model of a steam-engine is of brass and has a truck and flanged wheels to enable it to run on rails. If it operated successfully it was a miniature steam railway locomotive. When in possession of the St. Louis Mercantile Library, in 1854, the model was considered to be that of a steamboat engine.

gers. In short, the suggestion that the model under consideration was designed as a practical appliance to move a floating steamboat apparently reduces itself to an absurdity.

Fitch, by successive steps covering years of time, had

created the steamboat out of a mental vision. He had built such a craft and operated it in regular advertised traffic for months at a stretch, covering a thousand miles or more at the rate of from six to eight miles an hour. He had solved that particular problem, and his whole habit of mind while engaged in his work had always exhibited a steady process of progression toward something a little better and more practical. Yet his last thoughts regarding the application of steam power to travel and transportation found their expression in an engine resting on a rectangular truck and moving over rails on four flanged wheels. He had said:

"Neither do I conceive that all the Improvements that are yet to be made on steam are to be done on the water." It is perhaps possible to believe that he took the one last forward step; that he saw the railroad of the future just as he had seen the steamboat, and in the American wilderness, in 1798, built in miniature the first free moving, railway steam locomotive created by the brain and hand of man. The model was in existence a few years ago, and if it still remains intact a competent examination and test of it under its own power on a railway track might finally determine the purpose for which it was built.

The many letters and utterances of Fitch show he had a clear comprehension of the service he had performed, and that his chief impulse was the accomplishment of his task for "the benefit of our Empire." While his fellow men, still dazed at the discovery of their own independence, stood looking backward into the past like a boy who gazes awestruck into the chasm he has leaped, Fitch looked into the coming years and saw what they were yet to do. But his arguments, pleadings and

SHORT ACCOUNT

OF THE

ORIGIN

OF

STEAM BOATS,

WRITTEN IN 1810,

AND NOW COMMITTED TO THE PRESS

By W. THORNTON,

Of the City of Washington.

ALBANY:
PRINTED BY E. AND E. HOSFORD, STATE-STREET.

1818.

72.—Early literature relating to travel in America. Title page of Thornton's pamphlet in description of Fitch's boats. Thornton was a member of Fitch's company in Philadelphia, when the vessels were built and operated

demonstrations were necessarily without effect. The collective popular opinion of a newly created state resembles in many ways the mentality of an individual in the early period of self-consciousness. Some things are beyond its comprehension.

A knowledge of what Fitch did has been easy of access. The contemporary records, some of which are here reproduced, have been open for men to read. Yet it has been the custom to dismiss him, in discussing the development of steam travel in America, by saying he lived before his time. The expression is a familiar one, often adopted by a people for application to such a case in an effort to rid themselves of responsibility and place the blame where they wish it might belong — on the man who had presumption to do things his contemporaries did not appreciate. But the splendor of inspiration and original creation is not dimmed by such an artifice. No man is born before his time, for the days in which he lives belong to him, and are the ones that witness the performance of his labor. If what he offers is not accepted by his fellow men it is not because he is before his time, but because they refuse to walk beside him and accept the years of advancement that lie within his gift. The greater loss is theirs; not his. So it was in this case, and so passes the last individual figure of the story. Fitch was a genius cursed with a knowledge of the greatness of his own derided achievement. There can be no fate more sad than that.

It is idle to consider what would have happened if men of power had fought with one another for the privilege of aiding him and enriching themselves, as would be the case in like circumstance to-day. Had that thing happened the whole country east of the Mississippi would probably have been overrun by the aid of steam some

twenty or twenty-five years before it was conquered in that
way, with resultant consequences on all social and
economic progress, both in America and the world, which
forbid speculation. Fitch's method of travel was laughed
aside, but did not die. It slept.

CHAPTER XVI

THE AGE OF THE FLATBOAT, ARK AND KEEL-BOAT BEGINS —
EFFECT OF THE OPENING OF THE NORTHWEST TERRI-
TORY — A MILLION PEOPLE DRIFT THROUGH THE IN-
TERIOR — LIFE ON THE FLATBOATS — CONTRASTS OF
TRAGEDY AND REVEL — DESCRIPTIONS AND USES OF
THE VARIOUS CRAFT BY WHICH THE FIRST GENERAL
TRAVEL TO THE OHIO COUNTRY AND MIDDLE WEST
WAS ACCOMPLISHED

THE era of the flatboat, ark and keel-boat had already
begun. With the passage of the Northwest Ordinance by the Congress of the Confederation in 1787 the
territory now included in the states of Ohio, Indiana, Illinois, Michigan and Wisconsin was thrown open to settlement, and a general public interest in the immense region beyond the mountains and the Ohio River swept
through the original seacoast colonies. Hundreds of
thousands of the population, to which aggregate each
state contributed a share, decided to journey to the western country and set up new homes in the forest. Preparations for the migration affected every locality of the East.
That part of the interior toward which the eyes of the
coast inhabitants were now turned was unknown in its
details to the bulk of the people, though a knowledge of
its essential characteristics and the best ways of getting
there had been spread through the occupied areas by
means of tales brought back by numerous frontier travel-

THE KEEL-BOAT.

73.—River travel before the age of steamboats. The covered keel-boat, or barge, was for many years the principal river craft for quick journeys, especially up-stream. Barges often had sleeping bunks, but passengers carried their own bedding. The captain blew a horn at starting time. This and the illustrations to No. 90, inclusive, show the various types of drifting and man-propelled boats used from about 1788 until after the general introduction of steamboats, and indicate the manner in which hundreds of thousands floated down the Ohio and Mississippi to settle in the interior.

lers. The country was known to be densely wooded, and very fertile after the forest had been swept away. It could most easily be reached by the Ohio River, which traversed the border of the region for nearly a thousand miles and whose numerous tributaries furnished routes through the southern part of the inviting lands for considerable distances. The northern section of the territory affected by the Ordinance was all but unknown. It was not considered at the beginning of the first general westward rush of the people, because it could not be penetrated. The difficulties and dangers of such an attempt were too great to be wisely undertaken.

A journey to the head waters of the Ohio, at the time

the Confederation established an organized government for the so-called Northwest Territory, no longer presented peril to human life and could be made, in good weather, without extreme hardship. The wagon roads of settled sections in the East, together with the system of pack-train trails and wilderness roads leading toward the frontier from the domain of busier highways, constituted available paths to the upper Ohio region from every part of the Atlantic coast between Connecticut and Virginia. Things were getting easier. The one human quality essential in the successful performance of the trip from the seaboard to the Ohio was a physical capacity for enduring exposure and hard work during a period of from two to five weeks. All that was required after vehicular roads were left behind was the organization of a pack-train, and in due course of time the migrating bands — or such part of them as did not succumb to illness or accident on the way — climbed the last hill and caught a glimpse, in the distance, of the fabled and beautiful river thenceforward to bear them toward new lives and habitations.

Arriving at Redstone, Pittsburgh, or whatever other settlement was the goal of their overland travel, the westward movers established themselves in camp for a period of recuperation, and the men folk of the party set about the work of obtaining transportation facilities suitable for their future needs. The boats were sometimes bought ready built, but were more often constructed by the travellers themselves[1] from trees felled on the spot.

The curious craft destined to play a large part for a generation in the travel movement which populated the

[1] Especially in the early stages of the westward movement by water. After the first year or two many axmen and carpenters made a regular business of building boats and keeping them in stock at every river town.

Ohio and upper Mississippi valleys were of several types. Throughout thirty or forty years they were extensively used, and within that period probably a million people lived in them for weeks at a time, during journeys of from three hundred to two thousand miles. They were built by tens of thousands, yet not one of them remains as

74.—The flatboat, Ohio-boat or Kentucky-boat. Most common type of vehicle for river travel during the population movements that led to the permanent occupation of the Mississippi valley by the whites. It was entirely enclosed and was, in fact, a floating house. Such a boat was seldom pulled against a current.

a memorial of the vehicles which bore so important a share in the nation's expansion. Roman galleys and ships of the early Norsemen have been found for modern eyes to look upon, but there is small chance for future Americans ever to see an example of the quaint boats into which men, women, children, horses, pigs, chickens, cows, dogs, kegs of powder, dishes, furniture, boxes of provisions and farm implements were all loaded and jumbled together, to float down the rivers to somewhere. They resembled — those unwieldy vessels of such a short time ago — a mixture of log cabin, fort, floating barnyard and country grocery. At night, as they drifted on the dark waters, their loopholes often spurted jets of rifle fire, while women loaded the hot rifles of the men in the flickering light of pine knots held by silent children, and watched for the answering shots of red enemies through the mist that hid them. By day, on a more kindly voyage, some backwoods genius on the cabin roof would touch the resin to his fiddle-bow and send the wild strains of a hoe-down to the wooded shores and back again, while the family mule gave vent to his emotions in a loud heehaw, the pigs squealed, the children shouted and danced to the melody of the combined orchestra, and the women rolled up the bedding, milked the cow, hung out the wash and killed a few chickens for dinner.[1] Perhaps no other craft that ever moved on land or sea provided such episodes and contrasts, such diverse pictures of tragedy and revel, as did the flatboats in which the vast host of floating pilgrims travelled the interior rivers of America from about 1788 until as late a date as 1840.[2]

It is desirable at this point to refer to a certain feature of the narrative mentioned at its beginning — the chronological and geographical overlapping of periods of travel movement, and the duplication of vehicle epochs as new territory toward the west came under the sway of the

---

[1] A couple of the older boys would very likely be catching fish at the same time.

[2] Although a noticeable part of the westward migration to the Ohio and Mississippi valleys was carried on by means of flatboats until the last named date, that sort of travelling began to decline swiftly soon after the year 1830. The rapid multiplication of steamboats caused the change. Flatboats would have disappeared still earlier had not the flimsy character of western steamboats during the first twenty years of their history made the use of them so dangerous.

75.—A helmsman on a flatboat, shouting a warning to some one at the other end of the vessel, or to a near-by boat. Sketch by Joshua Shaw.

white race. In the conquest of a continent so large, requiring a period of nearly two and a half centuries for its completion, it was inevitable that the earlier stages of the process should be repeated in regions successively invaded. This was most noticeable during the generations before inventive genius and mechanical appliances made their appearance as predominant elements in the problem, and was to some extent true with regard to the use of large timber boats.

But every method of conveyance arose to its ascendency at one time or another, and each one—even if it played a minor part either before or after the period of its especial importance — must be chiefly considered with relation to the time and events of its greatest prominence. The long historical sequence of human endeavors that were consciously aimed toward better methods of progress over the land, and were unconsciously directed toward wider territorial dominion, new social conditions and national unity, resembled the march of an army. The temporary use of some means of locomotion outside of its normal place in the column of events was but the work of a scouting party, not to be unduly exalted in a chronicle of the main campaign. Previous generations could not see the whole process as we may, nor observe the relationships and effects of its various stages, for they were too close to it; they were themselves engaged in a work now completed.

Still another phase of the development of travel facilities that attracts attention in any consideration of their influence is the unusual manner by which, as a rule, they have advanced toward greater efficiency. Successive early improvements in transportation are not only classifiable by groups, but are perhaps unlike the corresponding steps of any other economic process because, in a sense, they have nearly always progressed backward. Broadly speaking, there have thus far been four general phases of travel history in America, to be roughly defined as follows:

First Period: During which all travel was performed,

76.—Travellers on top of a flatboat. During a long voyage, lasting for weeks or months, the principal diversions of the emigrants were story telling, singing, and dancing on the upper deck to the accompaniment of the universal fiddle. A ladder or flight of steps led down into the interior.

when possible, through the utilization of natural waterways and in the most primitive craft.

Second Period: Distinguished by the extensive use of prior overland routes—the Indian trails—and the creation of other land roads by white men.

Third Period: Characterized by the elaboration of earlier vehicles for both land and water travel; such conveyances being moved either by manual labor, animals, the wind, or natural water currents.

Fourth Period: In which both boats and land vehicles, of types already existing, were for the first time propelled by mechanical power generated within the conveyances themselves. During this cycle, which still prevails, the boats and land carriages have gradually been increased in size and altered in form.

No sharply defined lines emphasized these epochs, for there have been times when all of them have prevailed at once, though in widely separated parts of the land. Until very recent days it has almost always been the case that at least two of the periods existed simultaneously somewhere within the limits of the country, either in the same locality while earlier conditions were giving way to later ones, or in adjacent regions. But every section of the continent has witnessed the arrival and progress of all four eras in some degree at least, always in the procession here indicated and in orderly advancement from the East toward the West.

The conditions that have so often resulted in the betterment of travel facilities by means of a retrogressive method are due to a relation which has necessarily prevailed between vehicles themselves and the roadways on which they move. No means of travel can attain its utmost value unless the conveyance and its highway, of whatever sort, are mutually fitted for one another to the greatest possible degree. But since mankind cannot devise or perfect a path for what does not exist, or else has no inducement to do so, it has generally happened that a new transportation conveyance has appeared before there was a fit road for it.

A visible improvement has often waited, either in

actual disuse or limited utility, until the generation in which it appeared turned back and perfected some earlier feature of the existing transportation system, or else added another to it, in order to apply successfully and widely the new device to public need.[1]

The appearance of wheeled vehicles forced the transformation of tote-paths and pack-train routes into wagon roads, and as fast as dirt highways were built the wagons multiplied and compelled still farther extension of such avenues of travel. The early stage-coaches showed the necessity of abandoning dirt roads in favor of turnpikes with a permanent stone surface, and resulted in their creation. The general introduction of steamboats on the interior waterways forced governmental control and improvement of the rivers in order that their safe navigation, not previously possible, might be obtained. Railway locomotives were to be of limited value and slight use until proper road beds, after long experiment, could be made for them. And to-day the same sort of progress is being forced by motor-cars. They constitute an impulse compelling the tardy creation of improved highways worthy of the name, and which will be limited only by the nation's boundaries.

While the years from about 1788 to 1830 were the ones witnessing the ascendency of big, unwieldy timber boats as travel vehicles on the interior rivers of the country, it is nevertheless true that similar craft had for a long time been a familiar means of human transport on several widely separated streams in the old colonies.[2] It

---

[1] The canal building period was a confirmation of the common rule of progress rather than a contradiction of it. It is true that in the creation of a canal the track is made before the vehicle known as a canal boat appears, but the making of a canal is nothing but the construction of an artificial river in which the roadway is a safe, unobstructed track for conveyances — water craft — that already exist. And in its early form the canal boat was only a modified type of a certain kind of river vessel.

[2] Perhaps the earliest reference to such vessel is to be found in Thomas Budd's "Account" of Pennsylvania and New Jersey: 1685.

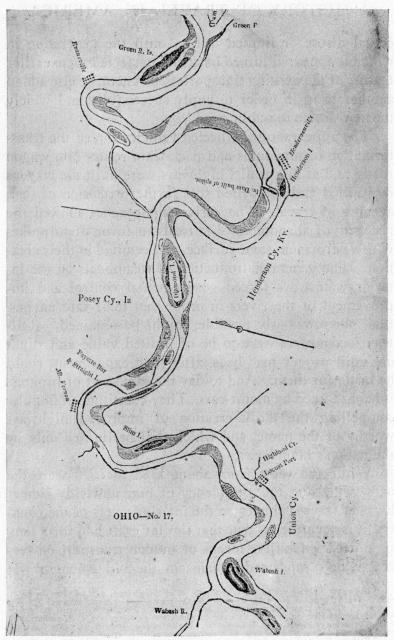

Green F.

Green R. Is.

Evansville

Hendersonville

Henderson I

Is. Dam built of spiles.

Henderson Cy., Ky.

Posey Cy., Ia

Diamond I.

Fayette Bar & Straight I.

Mt. Vernon

Slim I.

Highland Cr.

Locust Port.

Union Cy.

OHIO—No. 17.

Wabash I.

Wabash R.

77.—Sample page from one of the chart-books used by a flatboat family for
guidance while descending the Ohio or Mississippi. The continuous line
indicates the best course for a flatboat on the Ohio between Evansville,
Indiana, and the mouth of the Wabash. From Cummings' "Western Pilot."

therefore happened that when the general tide of westward travel began immediately after 1787, the various
sorts of existing eastern river vessels were extensively in-

Directions for Map No. 17.—Ohio River.		
Green River, left side. _ _ _ _ _ _ _ _ _ _ _ _ _ _ _ _ _	2	798
Channel near the opposite shore. At a middling stage of water keep wel to the right to avoid the rocks below its mouth.		
Green River Islands, (channel to the left.)		
In sight of Green river below. The large one is hardly visible; the chute to the left is nearly grown over with timber. The other lies in the middle of the river along side of the large one, and about a mile below its head. In low water you must run the point of the bar that makes up from the head of the island in the middle of the river, middling close to avoid a shore bar on the left, then keep down the left hand bend until near the point opposite Evansville, then keep near the middle until opposite the head of dry bar under the point on the left, then go in towards it, then turn and go over towards the steam mill, below the town.		
EVANSVILLE, right side. _ _ _ _ _ _ _ _ _ _ _ _ _	8½	806½
Pigeon Creek, right side. _ _ _ _ _ _ _ _ _ _ _ _ _	1	807½
When one an a half miles below Pigeon, at the point and rocks on the right, go over to the left, keep down near the left shore to the point on the left; then go into the middle of the river, keep it around the point and bear on the left to avoid some rocks and logs in the bend on the right, under water. When up with the right hand point make a long crossing to within 200 yards of the left shore opposite a house on your left and big bar on your right, then straighten down; don't go near the shore until you get 300 yards further down, then keep nearest that shore until you get to		
HENDERSONVILLE, left side. _ _ _ _ _ _ _ _ _	10	817½

78.—Text printed in Cummings' "Western Pilot" to accompany the particular
chart shown in the preceding illustration. Similarly explicit directions were
given, both by illustration and text, for navigating each mile of the river's
course.

troduced on the Mississippi system of waters, together
with certain modifications of them. A few new forms
better suited to the larger streams and greater dangers of

[1] Eastern emigrants to the West, on reaching the Ohio, at first built the sort of boats
with which they were most familiar.

western navigation also appeared. One result of the invasion of the interior by floating domestic establishments of the period was a confusion of the names by which such craft were known in different localities. This did not matter at the time, for everybody then understood the differences or similarities between a broadhorn, a keelboat, a Durham boat and an ark, as well as a twentieth century man knows what is meant by street-car, automobile, subway or aeroplane. But the early travellers who left accounts of the first overrunning of the West never wrote explanatory descriptions designed for the enlightenment of those who, in the future, might want to find out just how the people undertook their long journeys. When one of them had occasion for mentioning a boat he referred to it by a name common to one neighborhood or river, omitting to say that the same identical sort of craft, or a type very similar, was known elsewhere by a different name. Nor did they describe the floating homes of the moving population in careful detail. Only by the comparison of various narratives and the piecing together of numerous references can the extensive river travel of the early West, as carried on for about forty years, be seen in substance as it was. Any description of it must be a composite picture, a mosaic made of many fragments joined as best they may be, with many details gone.

A list of the several kinds of non-mechanical river boats used during the days when water travel by means of them was at its climax, together with a short description of each and mention of its origin and utility will illuminate the time and its habits. Such a catalogue may consequently be given.

The most simple of the boats still in use for river travel was the log canoe. It was employed by one or two men, particularly when the need of speed became urgent, and could be bought for three dollars or less.

A pirogue[1] was a very large canoe, often forty or fifty feet long and six or eight feet wide, capable of carrying a family and several tons of household goods. It was sometimes employed after danger from Indians had ceased, but vulnerability to attack made it unpopular for long trips on western streams in the early part of the white invasion. The pirogue cost from five to twenty dollars, according to size.

The skiff was a wide, flat-bottomed affair, made of planks, similar to the small pleasure boat bearing the same name to-day. It was occasionally used by parties of two or three on long trips, but was most commonly employed as an attendant on the big boats for use in carrying their occupants to shore when necessary. The value of a skiff was about five dollars.

A batteau was a very big skiff that bore to its smaller brother the same relation a pirogue held to a canoe. The batteau could carry a family, cost from twenty to fifty dollars, and was moved down-stream by several pairs of long oars called sweeps. Another sweep served as rudder. On up-stream trips it was propelled by poles.

The keel-boat[2] received its name because it had at the bottom, and extending for its whole length, a heavy timber about four inches wide and equally thick. The timber was so placed to take the shock of a collision with any submerged obstruction. Stout planks served in constructing the hull. It was usually from forty to seventy-five feet long, from seven to nine feet wide, and carried a mast and sails. One steersman and two men at the sweeps could

[1] Sometimes spelled peroque or perrogue. Likewise of Indian origin.
[2] It developed from the batteau. The early illustration of boats on the Mohawk River gives a good idea of the appearance of one type of keel-boat.

navigate the keel-boat down-stream, but its progress against the current was effected by the wind or the labor of men at setting-poles. The cost of such a craft was from $2.50 to $3.00 for each foot of its length. Keel-boats were extensively used on every navigable stream in the country. They originated in the East, probably by independent development in several localities, and gradually assumed certain standard sizes and shapes. Introduced on western waters at the outset of the great migration which began in 1788, they were long employed there both in their original form and with modifications to be related in connection with the barge and Ohio packet-boats.[1]

Mohawk boats were the sort of keel-boats used on that river, or any similarly shallow stream.

Schenectady boats were Mohawk keel-boats. Both were names used in New York.

The Durham boat was a keel-boat shaped much like an Indian bark canoe, and it acquired its name from a celebrated eastern builder of river vessels. He was Robert Durham, of Pennsylvania, who began turning out his product about the year 1750 for use on the Delaware River, where the craft became very popular. A description of them[2] reads:

"Durham boats were 60 feet long, 8 feet wide, and 2 feet deep, and when laden with 15 tons drew 20 inches of water. The stern and bow were sharp, on which were erected small decks, while a running board extended the whole length of the boat on each side.[3] They carried a mast with two sails, and were manned by a crew of five men, one steering, and four pushing forward with setting-poles, two being on each side."

The ark was a type of boat originating either on the Susquehanna or Delaware River. After Indian warfare

[1] The keel-boat was also the immediate ancestor of the canal boat.
[2] From Pearce's "Annals of Luzerne."
[3] Running boards were a necessary feature of all keel-boats. On these long, narrow platforms the pole-men walked while they pushed.

79.—Another group of travellers smoking and telling stories on a flat-boat. Showing the knee-breeches, hunting-shirt, moccasins, coon-skin cap and long clay pipes of the period; also, a small hatch leading down into the boat. Sketch by Joshua Shaw.

ceased in the West the ark was very popular on the Ohio, Mississippi and all other streams in that part of the country. It was usually from seventy-five to a hundred feet long, fifteen to twenty feet wide and from three to five feet deep. Heavy timbers and planks were necessary for its construction, and the lumber necessary in building one cost about a hundred dollars. The ark had vertical bulwarks all around, and both bow and stern ended in a broad V-shaped point. So huge and unwieldy was the vessel that it was much at the mercy of the current, and only a general guidance could be given to it by side sweeps and steering. The steering oar was a wide sweep about forty feet long, requiring the strength of two men for its manipulation. An ark could never go up-stream. On reaching its destination it was sold for what the timber would bring — ten to twenty-five dollars — or else broken up for metamorphosis into a cabin and furniture. On western waters the ark usually had a wooden house for the family near one end, and an enclosure at the other for the live stock. It was never roofed entirely over, and, because of its inability for defense, was not widely adopted until the country was tranquil and travelling was freed from the incidents of warfare.

A Susquehanna boat was an ark used on that stream.

The flatboat was the standard water vehicle for travelling families, and was a creation of the Ohio River valley. In size it varied greatly, each craft being originally built or bought in accordance with the needs of the party intending to occupy it. Due consideration was given, in its construction, to the nature of the stream or streams to be navigated, the length of the trip, the purpose to which the timber was to be put at the end of the voyage, and probability of attack by hostile natives. It was never

VIEW ON THE OHIO RIVER
at the Pa. & Ohio State Line

80.—The broadhorn was an Ohio or Mississippi family flatboat with three
steering oars, two of which stuck out, like huge horns, from the
sides of the structure. The flag was exceptional.

less than twenty feet long by ten feet in width, and sometimes developed into a huge floating domicile sixty feet
in length and eighteen or twenty feet wide. The hull of
such a boat was made of big square timbers of hard wood,
and it drew from a foot to two and a half feet of water
when full laden. Its timber hull rose, under like conditions, three or four feet above the surface of the river —
sometimes even more — thus making it an oaken fort
with sides often eight or ten inches thick and impervious
to rifle fire.

Upright timbers four feet high and four or five inches
thick were set on top of the hull, and the whole was then
enclosed, like a house, with heavy planks. A similar roof

285

completed the structure, which contained a barricaded entrance, loopholes; a window or two and a trap-door for upward egress. The flatboat floated at the mercy of the current, and was steered by a big sweep as long as the vessel itself. A small craft of the sort required the attention of three men. Its cost was about three or four dollars for each foot of length. The top was occasionally — but not often — built in a slightly arched form, and after the time of Indian hostilities had ceased the live stock was kept out-of-doors, in an open yard added to one end of the boat. The family wash was hung out to dry on the roof, and sometimes a fond parent would also fence in a space on the upper deck to serve as a playground for the children.

The Kentucky boat was a small or medium-sized water conveyance like the one just described. The name was given to such as were bound for the Kentucky region or lower Ohio.

New Orleans boats were big flatboats destined for the lower Mississippi.

A broadhorn was a similar craft whose movements were habitually regulated, as far as possible, by two big sweeps that projected like horns from each side of the boat. Vessels of the flatboat type rarely proceeded upstream.

The barge was built somewhat after the style of a ship's long-boat, and closely resembled the keel-boat previously discussed. It was from thirty to seventy feet long, seven to twelve feet in width, and carried a mast, sails and rudder. Its down-stream progress was accelerated either by the wind or by four of the crew who wielded long oars. When going up a river the motive power was supplied by numerous men who used the familiar iron-tipped poles.

Barges cost about five dollars for each foot of length, and — with keel-boats — were the most rapid of all conveyances for water travel. They were used by business men whose time was valuable, by land speculators and government officials. Under ordinary circumstances they could make from four to five miles an hour with the current, and when going in the contrary direction attained a speed of about two miles an hour.[1]

Barges had covered enclosures for passengers. Sometimes the protection thus given was in the shape of a house built in the center of the boat, supported by timbers at its four corners and surmounted by a gable roof. At other times[2] the vessel was almost completely covered by a flat-topped superstructure of bullet-proof construction containing loopholes and even embrasures for the firing of small cannon. During troublous times the barge was anchored at night and sentries were posted.[3]

The Ohio packet-boat was a magnified barge, or keel-boat. In size it ranged from seventy-five to a hundred feet long by fifteen or twenty feet wide, with the passenger cabin usually in the stern. The steersman stood on the cabin roof. It had a mast and sails, was equipped with many pole-men, and on occasion the crew even went ashore and towed the boat by means of a long rope. Such packets, carrying both passengers and freight, plied regularly between Pittsburgh, Cincinnati and Louisville before the beginning of the steamboat era in the West. By travelling on a swift packet-boat a man could go from Cincinnati to Pittsburgh and back again in a month, and even have a day or so to devote to business before starting on the return trip.

[1] Even more if the wind was from a favorable quarter.
[2] Especially during periods when trouble with the Indians was feared.
[3] All river craft carried anchors, and night navigation on western rivers was not usually attempted until about 1800.

CHAPTER XVII

A RIVER JOURNEY THAT ENDED IN TRAGEDY — MANY VOY-
AGERS IGNORANT OF WILDERNESS EXPEDIENTS — THE
WESTERN BOATMEN — THEIR APPEARANCE, HABITS
AND SPEECH — FURNISHINGS OF A FLATBOAT — DAN-
GERS OF NAVIGATION — HUMAN VULTURES — FIRST
PERIODIC BOAT TRAFFIC — OHIO PACKETS — THE
ADMIRAL OF A FLOATING DEPARTMENT STORE —
TIME CONSUMED ON TRIPS — END OF THE FLATBOAT
PERIOD

NO extensive accounts exist by which the amount of
flatboat travel on western rivers from about 1788
until its final disappearance can be approximately reckoned. It began at a still earlier date, when a journey of
the sort was folly and its consequences almost sure disaster.
One of the first important organized trips of the sort was
made by about two hundred and fifty people then living
on the upper waters of the Tennessee, who had decided to
remove to a locality on the Cumberland River in North
Carolina. They proceeded by water in order to avoid the
shorter but more laborious overland march, and started
in the winter of 1779-1780.

Thirty boats — probably keel-boats or batteaux —
were built to carry the people, and the voyagers did not
reach their destination until April 24th of 1780, after
enduring much hardship. Their new home was separated
from the nearest neighbors by more than two hundred

81.—A little flatboat, equipped with a sail, used for down-stream journeys on some small and shallow rivers of the East.

miles of wilderness, and so out of touch with the world did the self-exiled party find itself that its members organized a little republic, similar to the one of Wautaga, and also based on a written document. Disease, the Indians and social isolation proved fatal to the venture so bravely yet foolishly begun.[1] But twenty of the original party remained in the settlement in 1792, and of those twenty only one is credited by tradition with a natural death.

About three hundred Kentucky boats are believed to have passed down the Ohio during the year of 1780,[2] and

---

[1] Clannish migrations, limited to one party however large, have not generally been successful in any period or country, and have not had a lasting influence on the occupied territory. All permanently important migrations have originated in a widely distributed public interest prior to the movement itself, and the first travellers in such cases have carried with them a confidence or certainty that others were to follow. That feeling of support has often been more valuable than mere numbers in sustaining pioneers in a new country.

[2] Those who made the trip before 1788 were bound for Kentucky.

MOUTH OF RED RIVER.   MUNDUNG DES RED RIVER.

82.—An Orleans or Mississippi boat. Constructed on the lines of the covered Ohio boat, but larger and heavier. Used in descending the Mississippi, and often equipped with a sail. From a drawing by the American artist, Henry Lewis.

a small but increasing flow of travel continued westward on the river thereafter until 1788. Then came the onrush of a whole people; the first national surge of the tide destined to continue under many different aspects of movement, but always due to similar impulses and purposes, until the oceans were united. The people did not then, nor for long afterward, have the shores of the Pacific as their avowed objective. What they wanted was new homes, wealth, and soil over which they could become the individual proprietors. Impelled onward by those aspirations they made their periodic advances, using each time, as an aid to their westward progress, the transportation method best fitted for the journey immediately at hand. This time they built boats; floated with the currents of the rivers; pushed themselves along by poles; lifted sails to catch the breezes; pulled themselves onward by ropes. Any way served as long as they made visible progress over the waters bearing them into the new country. And as they moved they fought, sang, fished, swore dreadful oaths, quarrelled among themselves, aided one another when in peril or distress, brought new children into the world, and buried their dead in haste that they might not lose an hour of the precious daylight or a favoring wind.

By the later part of the year 1788 a human flood was upborne by the flood beneath. Flotillas of fantastic craft dotted the surface of the winding rivers. New settlements sprang up along the banks of the Ohio,[1] and all those scenes attendant on the evolution of a wilderness frontier into a region suffering its first acute attack of civilization were again in progress of repetition.[2]

Practically all the invaders who so suddenly poured over the mountains and launched themselves headlong into extensive voyages on the Ohio and Mississippi systems of rivers were lacking in knowledge of the country through which they were to journey. Those who came from cities and towns of the East were also ignorant of the many expedients by which wilderness life, especially on a river trip, could be made more safe and easy. As a consequence they sought advice and aid before embarking, and

[1] Cincinnati and Marietta were founded in 1788. Cincinnati, then called Losantiville, at once became the most important western outpost, and its big timber fortification was named Fort Washington. The town was afterward a headquarters for all the white men's campaigns against the Indians until the natives gave up their struggle.

[2] The line where primitive races and civilization meet in final contest for supremacy is distinguished for a time by a display of the worst qualities of both those states of society. The more highly cultured combatants lapse from the standard elsewhere slowly attained and, as a class, resort to many of the cruder methods which they are avowedly seeking to eliminate.

generally made arrangements by which several flatboats were to travel together as a little fleet. The head of the family or party would also, if possible, hire a frontiersman to go with the boat and take charge of its navigation. Through those conditions there was created a class of men known as western boatmen, who became familiar with all the vagaries of the rivers and fertile in every device that

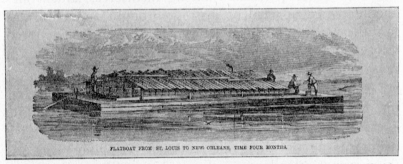

FLATBOAT FROM ST. LOUIS TO NEW ORLEANS, TIME FOUR MONTHS.

83.—Mississippi flatboat with superstructure of rough lumber. Craft of this sort were used by families which intended to use the lumber for house building after reaching their destinations.

might be helpful in an emergency. The professional boatman of the West spent years in travelling down the streams and back again, and became one of the most interesting figures of frontier life the needs of the country have ever produced.

He was of the restless type that in every period of American development has done the unusual and dangerous thing just for the love of doing it; who has never been satisfied unless each new day brought some unexpected event; who has only been happy when he could always keep moving. He was an epicure of excitement. Work no other man could do was his one luxury. In physical make-up the typical boatman was tall, thin and sinewy. His immobile face was tanned to a dark brown, and from above high cheek-bones and a long nose two dull gray eyes gazed blankly. In his normal state he was silently waiting for something to happen, knowing quite well it certainly would. When the bomb of circumstance exploded the human creature was on that dot of time transformed into a combination of rubber ball, wildcat and shrieking maniac, all controlled by instantaneous perception and exact calculation. After the tumult he subsided again into his listless lethargy of waiting, the monotony being endured by chewing tobacco and illustrating the marvelous accuracy with which he could propel a stream of its juice for any distance up to fifteen feet.[1]

The costume he wore was as picturesque as his personality, and in essential features was so widely adopted as to be almost a uniform. It consisted of a bright red flannel shirt covered by a loose blue coat — called a jerkin — that reached only to his hips, and coarse brown trousers of linsey-woolsey. His head covering was a cap of untanned skin, often with the fur side out; the universal moccasins clad his feet, and from a leather belt hung his hunting-knife and tobacco pouch.

Still a third distinguishing feature of the professional flatboatman was his iridescent vocabulary. As was the case with all Americans of the age he spoke in a ceaseless series of metaphors, similes and comparisons. Everything was described, whether the thing discussed was an inanimate object or human action, by likening it to something else. And, as was the fact through all classes of frontier people, he colored his discourse with references revealing his own occupation. In any miscellaneous backwoods assemblage of those years an expert in native speech could

[1] Boatmen, and many other men of the time, prided themselves on this accomplishment, and often made wagers on hitting a knot-hole or a fly.

have correctly told the kind of work done by most of the men in the gathering simply by listening to their talk for half an hour. When a boatman wanted to say that some act had been performed with celerity he declared it had happened "quicker nor a alligator can chaw a puppy." To be silent, in his phraseology, was to be "dumb as a dead nigger in a mud-hole." If he warned a companion to run he did it by shouting "Start yer trotters." In referring to strangulation, either legal or accidental, he said the victim "choked to death like a catfish on a sand-bank." A difficult thing to do was "harder nor climbin' a peeled saplin', heels uppard." To move very swiftly was to "travel like a nigger in a thunder-storm." And when the crisis for which he was ever waiting suddenly came he would scream "Hell's a-snortin'," and became a blur of arms, legs and profanity.

Guided and helped by men like these the emigrant families travelled down the rivers and absorbed useful knowledge on the way. The routine of daily life on a flatboat did not differ much, except in the actual work of navigation, from that of the cabins on land. At one end of the boat was a large space often called the parlor, or sitting-room, where the travellers ate their meals and the children romped between times. It was furnished with chairs, a table, a looking-glass, and such other articles as the women needed for their work. The kitchen was adjoining. A stove was set up there, and its pipe projected through the roof. A narrow passageway extended down the center of the boat for a considerable part of its length. In front the hall opened into the parlor, and on each side of it were several small bedrooms. At the rear of the boat was another large compartment for the storage of provisions, furniture and agricultural im-

84.—The ark was a big, cumbersome, wide flatboat, and as built in the East sometimes had V-shaped ends. It was extensively used on the Connecticut, Delaware and Susquehanna Rivers, and later introduced on the Ohio and other interior streams. It could not prevail against a current. Arks were not roofed over, but had little houses amidship. Showing Susquehanna arks that survived until the canal period.

plements, and still farther astern was the abode of the live stock. The rooms in those parts of the craft devoted to the use of the family were created, as a rule, by partitions of linsey-woolsey or chintz cloth that sometimes flared up from contact with a candle or pine knot and left no partitions at all. In more elaborate boats some rooms were divided by thin wooden walls. The enclosure for horses, pigs, chickens or other farm animals on board was separated from the rest of the space by a barrier of planks. Such were the general arrangements of a covered Kentucky boat.

The ark bore less resemblance to a land habitation in its internal arrangements. A wooden house was often built on it near one end,[1] the farmyard was fenced in at the other, and miscellaneous non-perishable goods, such as wagons, plows and furniture were distributed throughout the rest of the space in order to keep an even keel.

The navigation of the Ohio and "Massasip"— as the Mississippi was popularly called — presented a number of dangers to flatboats, only part of which could be avoided by intelligent precautions. From the others there was no escape except through good luck. First among the perils to which the cumbersome craft lay exposed were countless trunks of once floating trees that had become imbedded in the river bottoms, leaving their free ends pointed upward at an angle, like spikes, to stab whatever hit them. Menaces such as these were known by several names, dependent on their actions and position with relation to the surface of the water. A sunken tree moving slowly up and down with a periodic action under the influence of the current was called a "sawyer." The moving end might extend either up stream or down, and its successive brief liftings above the surface were usually separated by an interval of several minutes. But sometimes a log of the sort remained under water for twenty minutes before heaving upward again, and in that time a boat might easily have drifted into view of the place where it lay hid, and have reached the exact danger spot without any possible warning, only to be wrecked by running full tilt against the spear. There could be no predetermined avoidance of such a danger, and many a boat suffered catastrophe or grave damage by an accident of that nature. The vigilant boatman was always watching for the turbulent water which gave warning of a lift-

[1] Neither end of a big timber boat could properly be called the bow, for the current swung it around so that sometimes one extremity and sometimes the other would point down-stream.

ing sawyer just ahead, and a dozen times a day he saved the craft entrusted to his pilotage by desperately throwing his full weight against the sweep.

A sleeping sawyer was one periodically heaving upward, yet not appearing above the surface to give warning of its presence.

A planter was a log so solidly fixed that it never moved. With all three sorts of obstructions an up-stream inclination of the log was of course the most feared, but was decidedly the less usual.

Whenever a little flotilla of emigrant boats slowly drifted around a bend and discovered a strange boat

85.—An Ohio River ark, rectangular in shape. These were very large, and contained not only the travelling family, but its farm equipment, live stock and household goods. Arks were not safe travel vehicles until trouble with the Indians had ceased.

pinned on a planter or sawyer in the current below, the whole squadron would forthwith make for the nearest favorable spot alongshore and come to a halt. Then the men of the party tumbled into the skiffs, carrying axes, saws and other tools, and hurried out to the shipwreck. A few hours of hard work were enough in which to get the wounded boat loose and patch her up again if the damage was not severe, but it often was the case that two or three days were needed for the task. In many instances there was nothing to be done but leave the ark to its fate, and if that was the verdict of the aquatic jury its occupants and all their goods were apportioned among the rescuing armada and the lost boat would be left sticking on the fatal log like a big beetle on a needle.

Mutual help for those in distress was the iron rule of the road, except for the river pirates. They were a small class of white outlaws who roamed the waters to fatten on disaster, and a limping or crippled boat was juicy prey provided it did not contain enough men or firearms to fight them off. They even attacked a moving craft at night on occasion, especially if they had reason to believe its cargo was more than usually valuable. In order to get information respecting the contents of a likely boat, the probable time of its arrival near their headquarters and the number of its male inmates, some of the river pirate gangs kept scouts at important stopping places along the rivers. The spies would obtain all desired knowledge and then hasten on ahead to their comrades below, who were lying in wait for the expected arrival. Men of such stamp were rare, and they lived but briefly after they were taken.

The most notorious group of river outlaws was one with its headquarters at a point on the Ohio about twenty-five miles below old Shawneetown, in Illinois. The town itself consisted of a few log cabins originally built by the French, standing a hundred rods back from the river and inhabited by a rough population composed of French, Indians, Spaniards, half-breeds and Americans, some of

86.—Manual labor was frequently used, and even horses and oxen were at times employed, in pulling unwieldy craft toward their destinations at the rate of four or five miles a day.

whom were no doubt participants in the robber traffic. On the shore of the river at the point in question and in a little cave in a rock cliff overhanging the water, was the chief gathering place of the pirates when they were about to engage actively in the deeds of their profession. The place became known as Cave-in-Rock, and was long a spot approached with apprehension and passed with relief. It was the habit of the pirates of Cave-in-Rock to kill those on board a richly laden boat, provided an attack on it could safely be attempted, and then send the craft on to New Orleans or some other town on the lower Mississippi in charge of a crew picked from their own number, who would dispose of its contents and return with the proceeds. There were so many boats descending the river; so many emigrants changing their plans and voyaging to destinations other than they had at first announced; and the means of communication in the new country were so unreliable, that a boat and its occupants could easily vanish from the sight of those most interested in its welfare. When such a thing happened the disappearance was attributed to a disaster of travel, whereas it might have been due, and occasionally was procured, by a more sinister cause.[1]

Other occasional perils to the flatboats were due to falling banks, floating islands, and to stationary masses of trees and driftwood called wooden islands. The banks of the rivers — especially of the Mississippi — were constantly being undermined by the currents and falling into the water in large masses, and therefore no boat guided by experienced rivermen was ever tied up for the night on the side of a stream, below a bend, which felt the full force of a swerving current. Novices in navigation who came to rest at injudicious spots were at times overwhelmed by tons of earth and heavy trees slipping bodily upon them from above. Every river had its well-known danger spots that were to be widely avoided or passed

---

[1] The whole subject of brigandage on the rivers in early days is shrouded in much mystery. It did exist, but probably not to the degree that later legend has declared or even to such an extent as the travellers of the time themselves believed. Almost the only book dealing exclusively with the question is a fantastic tale entitled, "Mike Fink: A Legend of the Ohio," by Emerson Bennett. In many respects the atmosphere and manners of the time are portrayed by it without undue exaggeration, but the incidents of the story are fanciful.

FORT ARMSTRONG.

87.—A sailing barge of the Ohio and Mississippi Rivers. Swiftest means of water conveyance in the interior before the steamboat-era began. Used by business men, government officials, military officers and land speculators. After a drawing by the artist, Henry Lewis.

with unusual caution. They frequently received their names from accidents which had happened there, and the mention of such a place to an old boatman was sure to produce a reflective ejection of tobacco juice, followed by some unpleasant and harrowing narrative.[1]

Periodic navigation of rivers by boats did not first appear in the West. That development in the history of human transportation in America took place on the Delaware some time in the second half of the eighteenth century.[2] Keel-boats were the type of craft originally used as regular water conveyances for the public, and the ac-

[1] Names like "Sisters," "Hog Hole," "Sour Beer's Eddy" and "Old Cow" carried their own story.
[2] Probably in the interval between 1750 and 1755.

commodations they afforded were of very scanty extent. All they guaranteed to do was to float and move onward with whomsoever entrusted himself to that means of progress. The boats making regular trips usually started early in the morning like stage wagons, and when the time of departure was near at hand the patron[1] blew loudly on a horn to summon his intending passengers. A man who embarked for passage either carried his own blanket and rolled up in it at night[2] or else got off and

88.—The batteau was a big boat with the lines of a skiff. It was employed by those who were in a hurry, if a barge was not available. By the Philadelphia artist and wood engraver, Henry Robb.

slept in some tavern or neighboring farmhouse, resuming his voyage when the horn again tooted at early dawn. At a later day the Delaware River and other eastern passenger keel-boats were transformed into barges by the addition of house-like structures designed to furnish greater comfort and shelter. With these cabins there also appeared rude sleeping bunks, one above another, and thus developed the first germ of the future sleeping-car. But the traveller still carried his own bedding.

The packet-boats of the Ohio, which furnished the

[1] Captain.
[2] The very earliest regular passenger keel-boats had no covered shelter.

first periodic travel facilities in the interior of the continent, were keel-boats of twenty or thirty tons burden and came into use in the year 1794. They ran regularly thereafter between Cincinnati and Pittsburgh. At the time such packets were introduced the Indians were engaged in their last effort to prevent the westward progress of the white race,[1] and real danger to defenseless boats still existed. As a consequence the packets were stoutly built and heavily armed. An understanding of their character and accommodations can best be obtained through the advertisement printed in Cincinnati[2] to announce the inauguration of the service. It read:

OHIO PACKET BOATS.

"Two boats for the present will start from Cincinnati to Pittsburgh and return to Cincinnati in the following manner, viz.: First boat will leave Cincinnati this morning at eight o'clock, and return to Cincinnati so as to be ready to sail again in four weeks from this date. Second boat will leave Cincinnati on Saturday, the 30th inst., and return as above, and so regularly, each boat performing the voyage to and from Cincinnati to Pittsburgh once in every four weeks. The proprietor of these boats having maturely considered the many inconveniences and dangers incident to the common method hitherto adopted of navigating the Ohio, and being influenced by a love of philanthropy,[3] and a desire of being serviceable to the public, has taken great pains to render the accommodations on board the boat as agreeable and convenient as they could possibly be made. No danger need be apprehended from the enemy, as every person on board will be under cover made proof to rifle balls, and convenient port holes for firing out. Each of the boats is armed with six pieces, carrying a pound ball; also a good number of muskets, and amply supplied with ammunition, strongly manned with choice men, and the master of approved knowledge.

"A separate cabin from that designed for the men is partitioned off in each boat for accommodating the ladies on their passage. Conveniences are constructed on board each boat, so as to render landing unnecessary, as it might at times be attended with danger. Rules and regulations for maintaining order on board, and for the good management of the boats, and a table accurately calculated for the rates of

---

[1] In the Mississippi valley.
[2] In the "Centinel" newspaper of January 11, 1794.
[3] Quite an early appearance of that beneficent impulse as a motive for business enterprise.

freightage, for passengers, and carriage of letters to and from Cincinnati to Pittsburgh; also, a table of the exact time of the arrival and departure to and from the different places on the Ohio between Cincinnati and Pittsburgh may be seen on board each boat, and at the printing office in Cincinnati. Passengers will be supplied with provisions and liquors of all kinds, of the first quality, at the most reasonable rates possible. Persons desirous of working their passage will be admitted, on finding themselves subject, however, to the same order and directions from the master of the boats as the rest of the working hands of the boat's crew. An office of insurance will be kept at Cincinnati, Limestone, and Pittsburgh, where persons desirous of having their property insured may apply. The rates of insurance will be moderate."

The armed keel-boats took about twelve days to go from Cincinnati to Pittsburgh, stopping at Limestone, Marietta and a few other settlements on the way. They and the similar unarmed craft soon to follow were the best means of moving through the interior until the year 1811, and remained the only reliable up-stream conveyances on the rivers until 1817. But almost all water travel beyond the Alleghany Mountains was in the opposite direction — down-stream and toward the west. Few of the immense number of emigrants who floated to the new settlements in the Northwest Territory during the first generation of the influx ever returned to the East again. They took up government land for home sites and farms, and in less than twenty years the country had been overrun. The woods of Ohio and the groves and prairies of Indiana and Illinois were in their turn dotted with log cabins; territorial and state governments laid out roads between the principal towns; Conestoga wagons and stage-coaches appeared on land routes of travel and the Ohio valley had ceased to be a frontier. New arrivals still came drifting down the river in ever increasing numbers, but they found established communities and an organized society, although it was a rough and boisterous one.

A short time after western river towns sprang into existence the flatboat demonstrated its versatility in a new way. Having served as a travel vehicle, a domicile, a fort and a barnyard, it finally appeared as a retail business establishment stocked with dry-goods, crockery, bon-

ARTIST'S EN CAMPMENT.   DES KÜNSTLERS FELDLAGER.

89.—Boat used by the artist, Henry Lewis, during his trip down the Mississippi. The superstructure was erected on a platform which in turn rested on two large canoes. This type of boat combined cheapness, swiftness, safety, a considerable carrying capacity and a minimum of labor in its navigation. From a drawing by Lewis.

nets, paint, cutlery, real boots and shoes, ready-made clothing, big colored handkerchiefs, tinware and all those other notions, fabrics and household articles then to be found in the small dry-goods, hardware and general stores of the East. There was a lack of such useful things in the earliest days of the river settlements, and a shrewd trader who fitted up his flatboat in the semblance of a

305

rural dry-goods shop and filled it with appropriate merchandise received an enthusiastic welcome.

Formalities worthy of such an important event were observed in the approach of a trading boat to a newly established community. When within a short distance of his anchorage the Admiral of the department store mounted to the roof, and, striking a posture in which dignity and philanthropy were judiciously mingled, he announced his presence by repeated blasts on the familiar tin horn. It was a sound that by common agreement signified either the arrival of news or an important occurrence of some sort, and was sure to bring to the landing place a group that would scatter information of the arrival. Forthwith all the women folk of the little hamlet dropped their other affairs and hurried to the boat to enjoy again the almost forgotten delights of shopping, comparing patterns and buying the things they needed. A store-boat was fitted with shelves for the goods and counters for their display. The indefinable aroma of fresh, clean fabrics filled its creaking cabin, and the dignified Admiral of half an hour before, transformed into a smiling merchant with a huge pair of shears, snipped his calicoes, bargained with customers and told them the doings of the outside world. After he had accumulated all the money the population had on hand he once more assumed his nautical rank, blew a farewell blast and disappeared down the river. The floating merchant of the Northwest Territory tried to collect in his craft the standard articles ordinarily sold in half a dozen kinds of retail shops, and such an enterprise was the progenitor of to-day's universal emporium.

All long-distance travel on the interior streams was performed with almost incredible slowness until the gen-

BATON ROUGE (LOUISIANA)

90.—Sunken trees were the most serious natural menace to travel on interior
rivers during the flatboat age. Those hidden by the water were
most dangerous of all. From a sketch by Lewis.

eral introduction of steamboats.[1] The whole region lying
between Pittsburgh and Louisville was broadly known
as the Upper Country, and the big barges that regularly
moved from either of those towns or Cincinnati to the
Lower Country—which was the southern Mississippi
district — made one round trip a year. That was the
length of time it took to go from the Ohio towns to New
Orleans and back again in a barge which also carried
freight.[2] By swifter and smaller keel-boats the time
could be cut in half.[3] The down-stream journey was made
in six weeks, and four and a half months were sufficient

[1] Which did not take place until 1817 in that part of the country.
[2] According to the statement of Morgan Neville, an early writer familiar with river
travel, and many others. Neville's story of conditions in the pioneer days was written in
1829, and is to be found in "The West; Its Commerce and Navigation," by Hall: p. 130.
[3] Burnet's "Notes on the Settlement of the Northwest Territory."

in which to return. It required about a month to go from Louisville to Pittsburgh by keel-boat unless unusual effort was made.[1] A freight and passenger barge was three months on the same trip.[2] In the year 1817, just before the general introduction of steamboats, the whole passenger and freight traffic of the Ohio River was handled by twenty barges of a hundred tons each, and a hundred and fifty keel-boats of about thirty tons displacement.[3] These were the regular craft of the river. Their work had no relation to the travel tide of the emigrants, which proceeded as usual by means of the thousands of flatboats and arks that drifted down-stream every year.

The long reign of the clumsy timber boats did not abruptly end in western waters with the appearance of the steamboat there. It continued for some time even after steam was harnessed for river traffic, and did not entirely disappear until close to the year 1850. A few figures collected at St. Louis during the decade beginning with 1841 indicate the end of the period in which the many types of hand-power boats did so much toward peopling the Mississippi valley and in transporting its settlers and their goods. The statistics in question recorded the arrivals at St. Louis from the upper Mississippi, and showed the following facts:[4]

	Steamboats	Keel-boats
Arrivals in 1841............	143	108
Arrivals in 1842............	195	88
Arrivals in 1843............	244	55
Arrivals in 1845............	647	Not reported
Arrivals in 1846............	663	Not reported

Corresponding conditions would doubtless be revealed by similar tabulations made at other river towns if they

---

[1] Neville's narrative: "Hall"; p. 130.
[2] Ibid: p. 130.
[3] Ibid: p. 130.
[4] The figures are from Hall's "The West; Its Commerce and Navigation": p. 97.

were available. The day of the flatboat and keel-boat and ark was done. They were vehicles of an archaic time devised for a work which could not have been performed without them, and by their necessary aid hundreds of thousands of square miles came under the sway of the white race.[1] Although the conquest in which they played the vital part took place only a little while ago, the conditions of society that then prevailed — so swift has later development been — seem to be separated from modern life by an interval of a thousand years. If by a fortunate chance one of the old-time covered flatboats is ever exhumed in its completeness of form and furnishings from a river bed, no other relic of the period will command more interest than the floating cabin in which some backwoods American family of the eighteenth century made the water pilgrimage into the West.

[1] Among the states affected directly or indirectly by the river migrations, and that received much of their early population through journeys performed in whole or in part on the interior rivers are Arkansas, Illinois, Indiana, Iowa, Kansas, Kentucky, Louisiana, Michigan, Minnesota, Mississippi, Missouri, Ohio, Tennessee and Wisconsin.

CHAPTER XVIII

INTERIOR NEW YORK RE-OCCUPIED—HOW FENIMORE COOPER
ACQUIRED HIS LOVE OF THE WILDERNESS—TALLY-
RAND TELLS WHY HE LAUGHED—THE BALTIMORE
AND GENESSEE STEAM PACKET—A WATER ROUTE TO
THE WEST—ADVENTURES OF MICHAUX, CUMING AND
SCHULTZ—THE MAN FROM ST. LOUIS—A VIEW OF
TRAVEL CONDITIONS AS THEY EXISTED JUST BEFORE
THE EPOCH OF MECHANICAL VEHICLES

THE principal overland travel development in the
eastern states during the early years of the flatboat
era[1] in the West was one by which northern Pennsylvania
and the interior of New York were re-peopled by the
whites and permanently occupied. During the advance in
question the Susquehanna River—as will be understood
from what has already been said—played an important
part. The long struggle with England, together with the
frontier Indian warfare included in it, had driven all
white inhabitants out of the country, and the few roads
they had hewed through the woods with so much labor
were overgrown and disappeared.

There was no idea in the mind of the people when the
war with England ended but that all future conveniences
of travel and transportation through the country would
have to be created by the improvement of methods already known. The chief reliance of those who gave

[1] From 1787 to about 1805.

serious consideration to the question was placed in a greater usage of natural waterways and the building of roads or canals to connect them. And in mentally surveying the map of the country it was believed that the region so long controlled by the Iroquois was destined to

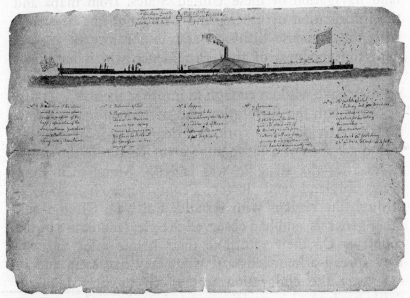

91.—More steamboats invented. A broadside view of the *Baltimore and Genessee Packet*. Like the two deck plans of the same vessel shown in colored plates, it is done in India ink and colors on a large folio sheet and reveals the lines of a trim-looking vessel. Original drawing of an unknown American inventor, about 1801-1803.

take an important position in the growth of future national communication facilities. General Washington was one of those to whom central New York presented opportunities of value, and in the year of 1783 he ascended the Mohawk River, from which stream he travelled overland to the head waters of the Susquehanna in order to study the problem himself, and to reflect in what manner the people might most easily move themselves and

311

their effects into the new lands soon to come under American control.

"Prompted by these actual observations," he said in a letter describing the journey,[1] "I could not help taking more comprehensive and extensive views of the vast inland navigation of these United States, from maps and the information of others, and could not but be struck with the immense diffusion and importance of it, and with the goodness of that Providence which has dealt her favors to us with so profuse a hand. Would to God we may have wisdom enough to improve them."[2]

Although the Revolution had postponed the overrunning of interior New York and Pennsylvania, it resulted in the advance of a large number of people to those districts after the struggle was ended. Many men from New England and lower Pennsylvania had moved through the regions with Arnold, Sullivan, Clinton and other generals, and had observed the pleasant nature of the country. On their return to their homes after the war they spread a knowledge of what they had seen, and in that way the emigration was given its new impetus. Settlers who had been driven out also prepared to return. The ensuing stampede assumed large proportions in the year of 1785, and grew steadily bigger for years thereafter. Those who moved into interior New York from the lower part of the state and from New Jersey made their way up the Hudson in sailing boats and thence pushed farther inland along the Mohawk River in batteaux, carrying their worldly possessions with them. Pennsylvania people destined for the same country or for the northern sections of their own state went up the

[1] Written to the Marquis de Chastelleux.
[2] Within two years from the writing of the wish so earnestly expressed in this letter, Fitch laid his plan for steam navigation before the General, who rejected it.

THE FIRST AMERICAN LOCOMOTIVE,
Or, Evans's "Eructor Amphibolis."

92.—Oliver Evans' steamboat of 1804, built at Philadelphia for use as a river dredge. It was not a land locomotive. He placed wheels under the hull and ran it through the streets to demonstrate that steam vehicles could be run on land as well as on water.

Susquehanna in the way others had done years before. New England emigrants marched overland along the existing trails and roads.

The condition of the present beautiful, fertile and densely populated interior of New York state, as it appeared in 1785, has been preserved in letters written by one of the earliest pioneers who journeyed into that lonesome part of the country after the years of warfare had ceased.[1] The writer says: "In 1785 I visited the rough and hilly country of Otsego, where there existed not an inhabitant nor any trace of a road. I was alone, 300 miles from home, without bread, meat, or food of any kind. Fire and fishing tackle were my only means of subsistence. I caught trout in the brook and roasted them in the ashes.

[1] William Cooper, father of the novelist, James Fenimore Cooper. His letters were gathered together in a little volume published in Dublin in 1810 under the title: "A Guide to the Wilderness: Letters to William Sampson."

313

My horse fed on the grass that grew by the edge of the waters. I laid me down to sleep in my watch-coat, nothing but the melancholy wilderness around me. In this way I explored the country, formed my plans of future settlement, and meditated upon the spot where a place of trade or a village should afterward be established."[1]

After his first trip, here mentioned, William Cooper returned home and organized a party to proceed to the district he had explored and settle there. Later letters describe the journey of the overland emigrants. "Not one in 20 had a horse," he declares. "The way lay through rapid streams, across swamps, or over bogs. They had neither provisions to take with them nor money to purchase them; nor if they had, were any to be found on the way." The travellers got their food in the country they traversed, as the narrator himself had done, by hunting and fishing. After the party had reached the selected spot they built themselves cabin homes and set about raising crops and opening the country. Cooper also tells of the people's trouble in establishing roads by which they might get into touch with the outside world. In the first year or two they found winter to be the best time for their journeys, and the writer goes on to say, "they travelled sometimes by partial roads in sleighs and sometimes over the ice. . . . I had not funds of my own sufficient for the opening of new roads, but I collected the people at convenient seasons, and by joint efforts we were able to throw bridges over the deep streams, and to make, in the cheapest manner, such roads as suited our then humble purposes." Similar pioneer work was going on during the same years along the shores of numer-

---

[1] William Cooper's letters reveal in what manner his more famous but perhaps not more gifted son acquired his love of the wilderness and the excellence with which he described its features.

ous other streams and lakes in New York state, and in that way the forest was gradually penetrated by many paths which in time connected the different settlements and linked them with the older communities toward the east and south.

Yet the process of creating easy and rapid communication throughout all the extensive region that lay between the Hudson and the Ohio, and extended from Philadelphia on the south to Lakes Erie and Ontario was a very slow one. Until about the year 1800 the only established and frequented travel routes in it were the Mohawk and Susquehanna Rivers, the road extending westward

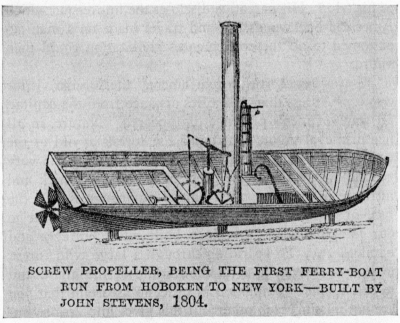

SCREW PROPELLER, BEING THE FIRST FERRY-BOAT RUN FROM HOBOKEN TO NEW YORK—BUILT BY JOHN STEVENS, 1804.

93.—John Stevens' screw propeller steamboat of 1804. Stevens had undertaken the building of steamboats as a result of Fitch's work. He and his friends used the craft in New York Bay and cn the Hudson River, but it was not intended as a public ferry. The machinery, in a reconstructed hull, is in possession of the Stevens Institute.

through the southern part of Pennsylvania to Pittsburgh, and the trail stretching from the Hudson at Catskill to the upper Susquehanna. At the commencement of the nineteenth century scarcely an impression had been made on the all-pervading woods in the territory here defined, nor had there been appreciable decrease in the difficulty with which a journey through them was accomplished. The people still moved about on horseback or their own legs, drifted with the currents of the rivers or pushed themselves up-stream in the same old way. Ten years after William Cooper first penetrated to Otsego Lake, the Genessee region of New York state was visited by the Frenchman Talleyrand,[1] who later penned a description of his trip.[2] His narrative discloses the impression which American backwoods life and travel made on a man accustomed to all the conveniences civilization could then afford.

"I was struck with astonishment," the foreign visitor wrote. "At less than 154 miles distance from the capital[3] all trace of men's presence disappeared. Nature, in all her primeval vigor, confronted us; forests as old as the world itself; decayed plants and trees covering the very ground where they once grew in luxuriance; thick and intricate bushes that often barred our progress. In the face of these immense solitudes we gave free vent to our imaginations; our minds built cities, villages and hamlets. . . . To be riding through a large wild forest, to lose one's way in it in the middle of the night, and to call to one's companion in order to ascertain that you are not missing each other; all this gives impressions im-

---

[1] Then residing in America because of inclement political conditions at home.
[2] In his "Memoirs." Talleyrand went northward from Philadelphia on horseback with a friend, and returned down the Susquehanna in a batteau.
[3] Philadelphia was then the capital.

possible to define. . . . When I cried, 'So-and-so, are you here,' and my companion replied, 'Unfortunately I am, my Lord,' I could not help laughing."

The trouble experienced by the people of interior New York in establishing an easy route to the outside world resulted in again bringing forward a plan for applying steam to river navigation. Though the inventor of the *Baltimore and Genessee Packet* is unknown, his plans and written proposal still remain, and serve to emphasize the many gaps to be filled before a complete chronicle of the earlier days is available.

The drawings of the nameless inventor are reproduced in this narrative. They show a paddle-wheel steamboat identical in its essential characteristics with the steam river vessels destined later to come into general use. Certain features of the drawings and of the written statements accompanying them fix the date of the invention sometime between the years 1801 and 1806, inclusive.[1]

The dimensions of the boat as given on one of the plans are "80 feet long 22 feet wide and 3½ deep or 4 feet." The paddles are stated to be "18 inches deep and 2½ [feet] broad—8 of them if possible." The rear part of the boat, says the inventor, is occupied by the stern sheets, "in which it is to be hoped many a passenger will be lodged and under these broad seats lockers where much cold provisions may be kept for the passengers for there must be no cooking on board." Immediately beneath the broadside view of the vessel are the words: "This being the first Steam packet,[2] we will call her the lady of the lake or Washington or the Genessee and Baltimore

---

[1] Probably between 1801 and 1803. The history and condition of the Genesee country between the same years is a further indication that this vessel was designed within the period named. No earlier plans of any steamboat can at present be traced, though it is possible that prior drawings exist. Fitch's drawings have disappeared.
[2] The inventor had seemingly never heard of Fitch's boat of 1788-90.

Packet." On the same drawing the inventor has written, "Passengers in abundance . . . all for Genessee," and in another part of the broadside view he refers to the forward flag as "a Packet signal of 13 stripes, the true good old standard of '76 the origin and foundation of all our happiness and independence—it is hoisted occasionally only and as a signal and lure for passengers."

On the sheet containing an amended deck plan the projector has written in pencil a plea in support of his steamboat in which he refers to it as "my discovery and contrivance,"[1] and discusses the purposes for which it is to be used. Enough of his statement is decipherable to show the craft was intended to ply from Baltimore to a point as far up the Susquehanna as it could reach, and that he was submitting the plans to a number of other men for their endorsement as a practical improvement in travel vehicles. The still readable parts of the written appeal are quoted.[2] Unidentified though the inventor

[1] Another indication that he had never heard of Fitch. Had he known of the extensive use of a steamboat on the Delaware, years before, it is not likely he would have claimed the invention of it for himself when laying these drawings before other men in an effort to secure approval of his proposition.

[2] Topmost inscription on Deck Plan No. 2. Line arrangement as in the original manuscript of the inventor. Undecipherable words indicated by dots, thus: . . . . Faint but apparent readings in parenthesis.

```
Line:
    1.—108
    2.—Set up end ways (in the)
    3.— . . . . . . . . . . . . . . . . . . . . .
    4.—I suppose 50 more might be
    5.—put length ways upon the
    6.—top of the others and in the
    7.—forcastle about 50 (more) end up
    8.—and about 30 lengthways but
    9.—there is no good (unless) . . . . .
   10.—untill she is loaded & then
   11.—we shall see how far she
   12.—sinks in the water . . . (and how)
   13.—deep the (water) . . . . (Generally) is
   14.—and those . . . . . . . . to . . . .
   15.—load largely (upon) . . . how . . .
   16.—lower that . . . . . .
   17.—(less) than a boat built
   18.—of this size by way of
   19.—experiment which
   20.—might be . . . . . . . . . (doubt)
   21.—& . . . . . . . . run as a packet up
   22.—(or) in (exploring) to Genesee . . . .
   23.—& on . . . . . . . . . . up the
   24.—small rivers branching
   25.—(into) the Susquehanna to
```

318

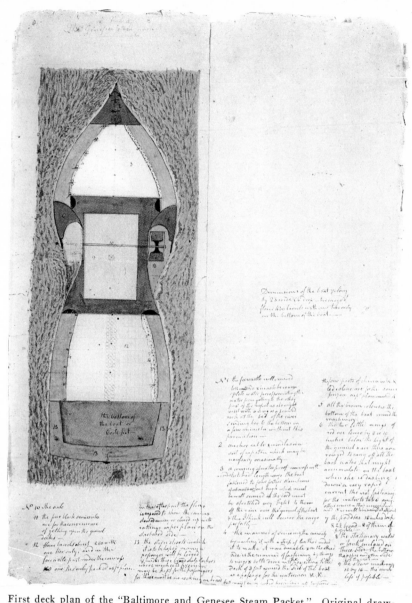

First deck plan of the "Baltimore and Genesee Steam Packet." Original drawing for an early American side-wheel steamboat designed to run from Baltimore up the Susquehanna river to the newly settled Genesee Country. The inventor is unknown. Date of sketch probably about 1801-1803. Drawing in India ink and colors on a large folio sheet, with specifications and description in marginal manuscript. Amer.

Second and revised deck-plan of the "Baltimore and Genesee Steam Packet."
The inventor has modified the lines of the forward part of the hull to get
greater speed. The indicated dimensions are 70 feet length, 23 feet width,
and 4½ feet depth of hold. Each paddle wheel to have eight blades. The
faint marginal notes on this plan, so far as decipherable, are quoted elsewhere. Drawing in India ink and colors on a large folio sheet. Date,
about 1801-1803. Amer.

of this steamboat is, his drawings and words reveal another of the early and forgotten efforts made to overcome an age-long handicap under which the people so laboriously struggled.

The state government of New York began to display some interest in the question of better highways about the year 1790, and took control of the road leading from the Hudson toward the Susquehanna. In 1792 a party of travellers passing over it from Connecticut required but eight days to cover the distance between the two rivers, although they were driving live stock with them. The highway was then twenty-five feet wide. In 1792 a weekly

26.— . . . . . (but what) such (boats)
27.—could do (& they)
28.— . . . . . certainly (go)

Another statement on Plan No. 2 reads:
Line:
    1.—in this plan I have lengthened the
    2.—forecastle part, taking in about a
    3.—third part of the whole into nearly
    4.—a triangle, believing that
    5.—such a form would more rapidly
    6.—force up stream against current . . . . downward
    7.—which is the great desideratum

Inscription in center of Deck Plan No. 2 at bottom of the sheet.
Line:
    1.—Cuts great economy both in time and money
    2.— . . . (I hope). . . make this trip . . . any other system & (there)
    3.— . . . very . . are . . . . . (of) Baltimore up into the upper part
    4.—(of Susquehanna) . . . . safely . . . . . is also worth
    5.— . . . . and safe against all . . .
    6.—(to land) . . . . the
    7.— . . . . I will be . . . .
    8.— . . . .

Inscription in lower right corner of Deck Plan No. 2.
Line:
    1.—(I) would be satisfied . . . . . . (up to a great)
    2.—deal (particularly) in carrying . . . .
    3.—of (every) kind . . . .
    4.— . . . and rapid (rivers) of that . . . . . a . . . . .
    5.—and easy conveyance . . . .
    6.—well Gentlemen this is all . . . . suppose
    7.—that my discovery and contrivance answers
    8.—all my . . . . (say it) suggests . . . .
    9.—(which possibly) may . . . .
    10.— . . . . (and when saved) . . . . (you)
    11.—most (sanguine &) enthusiastic . . . . .
    12.—(too often) . . . . only &
    13.—nothing else . . . . . it may be (sent)
    14.— . . . . . . (can with them) . . . .
    15.—However . . . . Gentlemen judge for your
    16.—selves . . . .
    17.— . . . . . . A great (mind) I should.

There is nothing known to show how the gentlemen judged. Three sheets of worn paper and some faintly written words are apparently all that remain of the eighth or ninth effort to introduce steamboats in America. A complete list of all early attempts of the sort will be found in a later chapter.

319

mail route was established over the thoroughfare, and from that time onward it constantly increased in importance. Later it was rebuilt with a surface of stone and gravel and became known as the Catskill Turnpike. The history of this road typified the last stages in the development of all similar highways by which they were

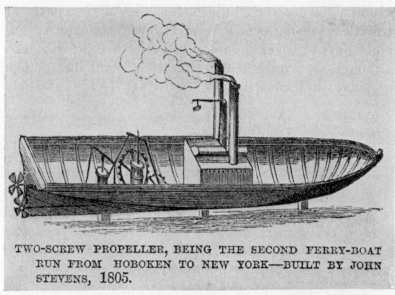

TWO-SCREW PROPELLER, BEING THE SECOND FERRY-BOAT RUN FROM HOBOKEN TO NEW YORK—BUILT BY JOHN STEVENS, 1805.

94.—Stevens' twin-screw propeller of 1805. Used by the builder as his former vessel had been. Both it and the 1804 boat attained speeds of from five to seven miles an hour. Machinery in possession of the Stevens Institute.

finally transformed from red men's trails into white men's routes of travel.

By the year 1800 a country-wide demand for good turnpikes was manifest. So many proposals for work of the character were introduced in every legislature that it became evident the states themselves could not undertake general highway construction. They were too poor, and yet were confronted by an urgent need of public utilities demanding an outlay of millions of dollars.[1] When the method of successful turnpike construction was found, the outcry redoubled. A new generation had grown up since the Revolution, and was fast assuming control of all those matters—except national politics—that concerned the mass of the people. Its members were anxious to improve their material welfare and the conditions under which they transacted their affairs of every sort. They lived in the present and future; not in the past. Looking backward had begun to go out of fashion. Whenever an improvement of any kind was proposed they considered it on its merits, no matter to what it related, and accepted or rejected it in accordance with their best opinion and limited experience. They believed their country was already the most wonderful nation on earth, and showed much irritation when they found any one who entertained doubt on the question. The new generation of Americans was alert of mind, quick to see opportunities, eager to move ahead toward wealth and power, and prompt to invest its substance in any enterprise offering advantage to the public and gain to itself.

Out of these new qualities of public thought came a suggestion that the task of turnpike building be turned over to private companies created for the purpose. The idea was adopted through all the country. Under its general operation many thousands of miles of improved roads were constructed, and within a few years it was possible to travel by stage-coach from the Atlantic Coast to the border of Indiana in about two weeks, at a cost of only forty-five or fifty dollars exclusive of board and

[1] Some states passed laws under which lotteries were organized, and the proceeds from the sale of tickets, after the prize money had been deducted, were devoted to the improvement of roads and the building of bridges.

lodging. But in order to make the journey in such quick time the traveller had to keep going sixteen hours of every twenty-four and escape accident on the way. His total expenses for the trip were usually about sixty-five dollars.[1]

The companies organized to build new roads or improve old ones were given authority by the states in which they operated to charge the public for use of the highways so made, and in that manner the toll system was established. Toll-gates sprang up like mushrooms, and the driver of any sort of vehicle was stopped every four or five miles—often more frequently—to pay for the privilege of going farther. The practise of laying out wagon roads by private enterprise and of maintaining them under corporate management remained in operation for a long period.[2]

The new public attitude toward questions relating to the advancement of the country was a most important feature of the time. Men commenced to fret at the obstacles to communication so long accepted as a necessary part of their surroundings. News came back from the western country of the immensity of the lately settled region and its possibilities as a home, a producing section and a market for many commodities. Little groups assembled to talk of such things. The mental horizon of the people expanded enormously, and the shadow of their future power fell upon them. It was prescience, more than vainglory, which impelled the people to

[1] No one stage-coach company or proprietor in the East ever had facilities to carry people any such distance. Usually a stage company ran its vehicles for a day's journey each way from its headquarters. Passengers were then transferred to the vehicles of another proprietor. Often there existed a sort of traffic arrangement whereby the coach of one owner awaited the arrival of another. West of Wheeling, in the earliest days, stage wagons were used before regular stage-coaches appeared. The average fare paid by a traveller on a journey to the West was about five cents a mile.

[2] Many of the toll road franchises have only lapsed in recent years, and a few are still effective. Maryland, and perhaps other states, yet possess toll-gates. Not until after the Civil War did the various commonwealths generally adopt a policy under which roadways were considered public works to be created and maintained by the people themselves and used without toll fees.

BRIDGE AND TURNPIKE LOTTERY.

Class No. V.

No.

THIS Ticket will entitle the Possessor to such PRIZE as shall be drawn to its Number, in LOTTERY (CLASS NO. V.) authorized by an act of the Legislature, if the same is demanded within six months after the conclusion of the drawing. Subject to a deduction of 15 per cent.

Commissioner.

Charleston, (S. C.) April, 1812.

95.—Soon after the year 1800 a general demand for better roads arose. Some of the states, instead of appropriating money or levying taxes directly for the purpose, fostered a widespread gambling mania by organizing and conducting "Bridge and Turnpike Lotteries" to secure the needed funds. Lotteries were very popular. Churches were occasionally erected by their aid.

proclaim so boastfully the might that did not yet exist.

As a consequence of political and social developments then taking place, it became the custom, soon after 1800, for many men of the old states to make extensive excursions through all the country east of the Mississippi in order to see for themselves the new conditions and judge in what manner the nation as a whole was likely to be affected by them. Numerous foreign visitors, similarly interested in the subject, came to study at first hand the situation created by the birth and expansion of a commonwealth so favorably endowed. On their return to the East or to Europe the investigators were overwhelmed by demands for precise information regarding what they had seen and how they had got about through the outlying territories. Such inquiries and the widespread interest revealed through them led to the writing of a number of books by men who had journeyed in the interior, and their narratives are the chief sources of present knowledge concerning American life and manners during the first decade of the last century. Among the individuals who undertook such explorations and whose stories of wanderings are highly esteemed were Fortesque Cuming,[1] Christopher Schultz[2] and F. A. Michaux.[3] A capitulation of some of the incidents told by those chroniclers[4] will reveal the travel conditions prevailing just before the beginning of the modern epoch of scientific, machine-driven vehicles.

Michaux comments on the new quality that had come so prominently into the national life with the generation after the Revolution. "There prevails in the United States," he declares, "a degree of public spirit which induces individuals to adopt any project that may tend to enrich the country by agriculture and commerce." He began his journey from Charleston, in South Carolina, and indicates that almost all travel between the South and North was then undertaken by way of the sea in sailing vessels "tastefully fitted up and conveniently arranged for the reception of passengers." The usual time consumed in the trip to New York was ten days, and the charge was forty or fifty dollars. From New York he went to Philadelphia in a stage-coach. A day or more was still required to move between the two cities, and a seat cost five dollars. At the inns he paid half a dollar for breakfast, a dollar for dinner and half a dollar for supper. The stage driver also got fifty cents from each passenger, the giving of which seemed to be customary.

Leaving Philadelphia the traveller set out for Pittsburgh, where he thought his voyage down the Ohio was

---

[1] Cuming was an Englishman of culture and wide experience in many countries. His book, "Sketches of a Tour to the Western Country," was printed in Pittsburgh in 1810. Cuming began his journey in 1807 and moved about for two years or more.

[2] Schultz' narrative is called "Travels on an Inland Voyage," and describes the country in 1807-8.

[3] Michaux was a French physician and scientist. His "Travels to the Westward of the Alleghany Mountains" was issued in Paris and republished in England in 1805. Michaux' trip was made in 1802.

[4] Like all travellers they made some mistakes, but they were observers without extreme bias and their descriptions of the country and statements of personal experiences are generally trustworthy. The principal errors in their narratives have to do with dates in antecedent American history. Cuming makes several mistakes of that nature.

to begin, and got as far as Shippensburg by regular lines of stage-coaches. The distance thus covered was a hundred and forty miles. "From Shippensburg to Pittsburgh," Michaux goes on to say, "the distance is 170 miles; and the stages not going farther, you are obliged to

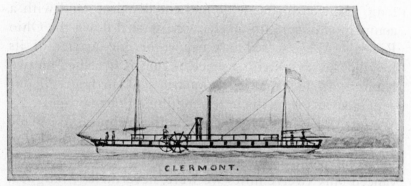

CLERMONT.

96.—Robert Fulton begins his building of steamboats in America. His first successful vessel, the *Clermont,* as she appeared in 1807. No authenticated contemporary picture of the craft is known. The one here shown is probably the most reliable, and was done from personal recollection by Richard Varick De Witt, in 1858. The original drawing, from which this is a photograph, belongs to the New York Historical Society. The next four illustrations are also of Fulton's work.

perform the rest of the journey on foot, or to purchase a horse, of which there are always many for sale; but the country people are such cheats that they always make you pay double the value for them; and on arriving at Pittsburgh you are obliged to dispose of them for half what they cost. I was inclined, from motives of economy, to travel the rest of the way on foot, but from some remarks which were made to me, I thought proper to join with an American officer who had travelled with me in the stage, and was likewise going to Pittsburgh; we therefore bought a horse between us, on which we rode thither by turns." He reached Pittsburgh nine days after leaving

Philadelphia, only three days of the interval having been spent in stages. His average speed over the whole distance was not quite thirty-five miles a day.

Michaux changed his plans on arriving at Pittsburgh and walked to Wheeling, in Virginia, a town of twenty-six houses. There he bought a log canoe twenty-four feet long, eighteen inches wide and equally deep, and with a companion picked up on the way, started down the Ohio River. "We covered our canoe for one-quarter of its length," he says, "with a piece of canvas stretched on two hoops.[1] In less than three-quarters of an hour all our arrangements were made for continuing our voyage. . . . We left Wheeling at six o'clock in the evening. We made twelve miles that evening, and stopped for the night on the right bank of the Ohio. . . . Although we had advanced only twelve miles we were, nevertheless, fatigued, less from paddling continually than from remaining constantly in a sitting posture, with extended legs. Our canoe, the bottom of which was very narrow, compelled us to keep that position: the slightest motion would have exposed us to upset. At the expiration of a few days custom caused these inconveniences to disappear, and we proceeded on our journey with comparative ease and comfort. . . . Our second day's progress was 30 miles; the third, 40. . . ."

The two men frequently fell in with all the various species of craft so numerous on the river, and Michaux's first vision of an emigrant flatboat is described in the following words:

"I could not conceive what such large square boxes could be, which seemed abandoned to the current, presenting alternately their ends, their sides, and even their

[1] As a protection against the sun. It was July, and very warm.

326

angles. As they[1] advanced I heard a confused noise, without distinguishing anything, on account of the height of the sides. On ascending the banks of the river I perceived in these boats several families, bringing with them their horses, cows, fowls, carts, ploughs, harness, beds, instruments of husbandry; in short, all the furniture requisite for house-keeping, agriculture, and the management of a farm. These people had thus abandoned themselves to the water for several hundred miles, probably without knowing where they might stop, to exercise their industry and to enjoy in peace the fruit of their labors."

Many references to the appearance of the country are contained in the relation of the trip. When about thirty-six miles above Marietta, as an example, the narrator measured a plane tree[2] forty-seven feet in circumference at a distance of four feet above the ground, and whose girth was maintained practically undiminished "to a height of fifteen or twenty feet." In commenting on the monster vegetable, Michaux goes on to say: "Our host informed us that if we would pass the day with him he would show us trees of equal size in other parts of the wood."

Thus the voyagers drifted along for ten days until they reached Limestone, in Kentucky. They had come only three hundred and forty-eight miles, "during which," Michaux says, "we were obliged to paddle incessantly." The slowness of his progress decided him to quit the river at Limestone, and leaving his companion to continue on alone, he struck off overland on the road to Lexington. The distance was sixty-five miles, and he got there in two days and a half. At Lexington he bought another horse

---

[1] It was apparently a fleet of five or six boats only partly roofed over; a combination of flatboat and ark.
[2] Platanus occidentalis.

without commenting on the transaction, and proceeded southward along the road to Nashville, in Tennessee, at the rate of nearly thirty miles a day. From Nashville, which settlement he left on September 5th, Michaux travelled eastward along an old wilderness road and

97.—The *Clermont* as she appeared in 1808, after being lengthened and having her paddle-wheels enclosed. From a photograph of the drawing by De Witt in the collections of the New York Historical Society.

reached Morgantown, in North Carolina—a distance of six hundred miles—in just one month. "I arrived in Charleston," he concluded, "on the 18th of October, 1802, three months and a half after my departure from Philadelphia, having gone through a space of nearly eighteen hundred miles." The visitor from abroad had found it either impossible or inconvenient to avail himself of stage-coaches for all but a hundred and forty miles of the distance. For almost the whole trip he went on horseback, on foot, or on the water.

In the same year of 1802 an unbroken communication by stage-coaches was opened from Boston to Savannah, in Georgia. The details of the through trip if then performed by land in the most expeditious time, were as here given:

	Time	Stage-coach fare
Boston to New York......	4 days	$10.00
New York to Philadelphia..	1½ days	5.00
Philadelphia to Charleston.	15 days	50.00
Charleston to Savannah....	2 days	5.00
Totals................	22½ days	$70.00

The distance traversed by the stage-coaches between Boston and Savannah was about one thousand two hundred miles, and the average speed maintained by the passenger was some fifty-three miles a day. In addition to the cost of transportation he spent at least twenty-five dollars for board and lodging.

Fortescue Cuming, like Michaux, first proceeded overland from Philadelphia to Pittsburgh.[1] He walked the entire distance and was twenty-seven days on the way. Thence he also went down the river, on which part of his journey we need not follow him except to notice two circumstances mentioned in his narrative. The first of them discloses—as did Michaux's reference to the big trees—the change wrought in the appearance of the country and in other related conditions since those days. He

[1] Starting in January of 1807.

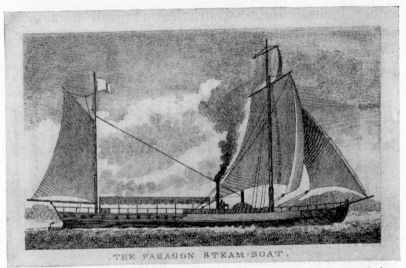

.THE PARAGON STEAM-BOAT.

98.—The *Paragon,* Fulton's fourth boat, built in 1811 for use on the Hudson River. She was 173 feet long, had two masts, and under steam power, without the aid of sails, developed a speed of about five or six miles an hour.

observed cotton growing as far north as Portsmouth, in Ohio, and saw vast numbers of bright plumaged paroquets in the same locality. The other incident was his encounter with a man who was paddling up the Ohio in a canoe. It developed that the up-stream voyager lived in St. Louis, and was on his way to visit his brother in Pittsburgh. He had been seven weeks on the water and expected to reach his destination in less than three weeks more.[1]

Cuming continued down the river to Kentucky, and after investigating the resources of the state[2] he turned northward into Ohio, which he crossed over the newly

[1] Fourteen or fifteen hours are now necessary for the same trip.
[2] In Lexington he found 39 two-wheeled gigs and chaises, 21 four-wheeled coaches and 4 billiard tables.
    The Golden Eagle tavern at Frankfort had a dining-room 72 feet long, and the flies were kept from the food by negro girls who waved green silk fans. The host presided in state at the head of the table. Beef was four cents a pound, and a quarter of lamb 25 cents. Vegetables, the writer says, were cheap. All the big Kentucky taverns had bells on their roofs which were rung at meal times to summon the guests.

improved post-road extending eastward through Chillicothe, Lancaster and Zanesville to Wheeling.[1] "I experienced amongst these honest and friendly farmers real
hospitality," he relates, "for they vied with each other
in lodging me at their houses and in giving me a hearty
and generous welcome."[2] In West Union he stopped for
breakfast at a tavern and partook of bread and butter,
eggs, and milk, for which he offered the customary quarter
of a dollar. But the landlord "would receive only the
half of that sum, saying even that was too much." Cuming was considerably impressed by the incident, for he
says "such instances of modest and just honesty rarely
occur." Proceeding blithely along the road with twelve
and a half cents more in his pocket than he had expected
to possess, the pedestrian was soon afterward overtaken
by a man on horseback with whom he struck acquaintance
in the manner of the highway. The stranger was going
from western North Carolina to Chillicothe, and had
traversed the five hundred miles in three weeks.

Encounters like that were constantly occurring
through all the expanses west of the Alleghanies. The
standard greeting was: "From what part of the world
did you come, stranger?" The roads were full of pilgrims from everywhere; some trudging alone; others
mounted; still others in the big canvas covered wagons.
"I found . . ." says Cuming, "a little old man. He
buckled on his knapsack, and we proceeded together. He
had travelled on foot from Tennessee River, through a

[1] His story of that part of the trip makes his narrative one of the most valuable of all
accounts descriptive of conditions prevailing along an early American land artery of
travel. The Ohio section of the road, before being taken over by the state—a few years
prior to Cuming's trip—was known as "Zane's Trace." It was laid out in part by
the pioneer Zane in 1796, and for a few years thereafter was not available for wheeled
vehicles. When Cuming went over it stage wagons were running regularly. The road
crossed into Kentucky at Maysville, and was the principal overland route southward
through Kentucky, Tennessee and all the lower Mississippi region to New Orleans.
[2] Cuming here refers to private farmhouses; not to inns.

part of the state of Tennessee, quite across Kentucky, and so far in Ohio in nine days, at the rate of thirty-six miles a day." The little old man had gone down the rivers from Wheeling as part of a flatboat crew and was returning home again. The companions came in the evening time to a log-cabin tavern, where they were received with hospitality in the shape of a concert organized by the host to entertain them. "Three of his sons play the violin by ear," remarks Cuming. "They had two shocking bad violins, one of which was of their own manufacture, on which they scraped away without mercy. I attempted to seem pleased, and I believe succeeded in making them think I was so."[1]

Near the little town of Cambridge, then a few months old and with but twelve log cabins, the Englishman met a travelling Massachusetts family. So admirable was the system its members pursued while on the march, and so many the comforts they enjoyed, that he speaks of the party and its methods with admiration. "They had a wagon with four horses," he explains, "and a saddle horse rode by one of the girls. On their stopping, the daughters began directly to prepare supper as though they were at home, baked bread enough to serve them that night and next day, and then they sat down to sewing as composedly as if they had been in their own house, and not on a journey; while the boys took care of the horses, and the old couple, though still active and healthy, sat at their ease, chatting and enjoying themselves."

Cuming had entered Ohio at a point opposite Maysville on August 6th of 1807, and he reached Pittsburgh on August 21st, having travelled by easy marches on

---

[1] Cuming himself was a musician and a performer on the instrument. He must have suffered more than he tells.

Sketch by J. Glennie Esq.

Hewitt Sc.

Catskill Mountains and the Steam Boats on the Hudson River.

99.—One of Fulton's boats, possibly the *Paragon*. Altered from an earlier engraving of the same scene in which the vessel was shown with sails. In this picture, Hewitt, the engraver, forgot to remove the shadows of the sails that no longer exist. From a sketch made by the early artist James Glennie.

foot, in the saddle and in the stage wagons, three of which passed each way during a week's time. He commented on the bad state of the roads as compared with those in his own country, and marvelled at the skill of stage drivers. "Though the European drivers far exceed the American in dexterity and speed on their fine roads," was his opinion, "in this country they would be good for nothing, and would pronounce it impossible to get a carriage through roads that the American driver dashes through without a thought."

Christopher Schultz began his journey into the West from New York City and went all the way by the water route. Upon reducing his narrative to a table showing the schedule of his movements between New York and Pittsburgh, the following result is obtained:

	Miles.	Method.	Days.
New York to Albany	160	Hudson river steam-boat	1½
Albany to Schenectady	15	turnpike	1½
Schenectady to Utica	104	5 ton keel-boat	5
Utica to Oswego	104	5 ton keel-boat	3
Oswego to Lewiston	172	lake sailing boat	3
Lewiston to Black Rock	17	mud road	1½
Black Rock to Presque Isle	90	lake sailing vessel	2
Presque Isle to Le Bœuf	14	turnpike	1
Le Bœuf to Pittsburgh	240	10 ton keel-boat	5
Totals	916		23½

His average daily rate of travel between the two towns was therefore a little less than forty-one miles.

The all-water route to the interior of the country

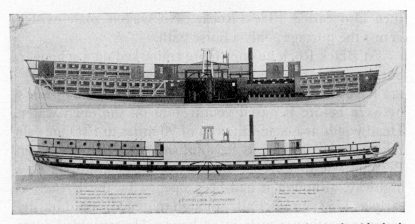

100.—The *Chancellor Livingston,* Fulton's last boat. Completed after his death in 1816. She was 156 feet long, and the fastest steamboat yet constructed. The cabin had 118 sleeping berths for passengers. Engraved from a drawing by the Swedish traveller Klinckowstrom.

had been in use ever since the end of the Revolution, and such part of it as lay between New York City and Lake Erie was a thoroughfare for many years before that time. Previous to the date of Schultz' excursion a traveller ascended the Hudson River to Albany in a sail-boat, and then, after a short overland jaunt of fifteen miles to Schenectady, embarked on the Mohawk and Oswego Rivers and so reached Lake Ontario. Schultz did the same in all respects save that he went up the Hudson in a boat propelled by steam power which had just been completed by an American artist and inventor named Robert Fulton. The craft that conveyed him on the first installment of his trip was the celebrated *Clermont.* At Oswego Schultz found passage on a lake schooner about to depart for Lewiston, a little New York town on the Niagara River, near its mouth, where he arrived in three days. Thence he pushed overland for seventeen miles to the site whereon Buffalo was to arise, a spot then also called Black Rock. No wagon road existed across the portage; only a horse path.

At Black Rock he once more embarked on a schooner, but the current in the lake moved so swiftly toward Niagara River that the boat had to be pulled for some distance by oxen before it dared venture out on the open water. Head winds arose, and the run of 90 miles to Presque Isle required two days for its accomplishment. The road from Presque Isle to Fort Le Bœuf[1] was a sad imitation of a highway, although it had been opened by the French as early as 1752; and Schultz, though mounted, could hardly cover more than a mile in an hour. He struggled from sunrise to darkness in a mud puddle fifteen miles long. So absurd was the road in question that wagons hauled by three pairs of oxen were sometimes three days in accomplishing the distance.

Coming at last to the little settlement where his embarkation as an inland navigator was to take place, the traveller found to his astonishment that French Creek would scarcely float a duck. It was normally but four inches deep, yet the stream was navigable for keel-boats of considerable size, and Schultz' experience was but an illustration of the expedients to which men of that period resorted. He simply waited for rain. The downpour came at last, and continued for six hours. With its beginning the whole town bustled into excitement, activity and confusion. Eight newly built keel-boats were hastily loaded, and all those who for any reason desired to go to Pittsburgh or the West made ready for departure. In twenty-four hours the creek was a muddy torrent two feet deep, and away floated another installment of the French Creek navy, never to come back again.

[1] Waterford, on the head waters of French Creek.

A rapid rise in a little stream was called a fresh, and by taking instant advantage of such a sudden temporary increase in water it was sometimes possible to use big boats for fifty or a hundred miles on trifling creeks otherwise but ankle deep in their upper reaches. Every brook in all the outlying regions was utilized in this way, and

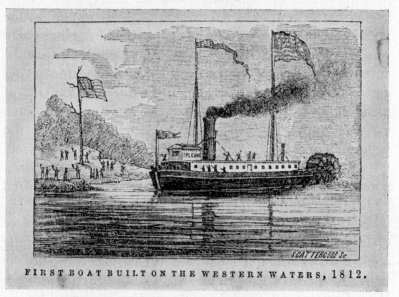

FIRST BOAT BUILT ON THE WESTERN WATERS, 1812.

101.—The *New Orleans*, first steamboat to navigate the Ohio and Mississippi. She was built at Pittsburgh by Nicholas Roosevelt in 1811, and under his guidance reached New Orleans early in the following year. Fulton and Livingston were the proprietors of the craft, which was constructed and sent south as part of the plan by which the owners were seeking to obtain a monopoly of steam transportation in America.

a fresh was then looked upon, by the inhabitants along the affected rivulet, very much as a special excursion train is now considered by a small railroad town. A transportation schedule arranged on that basis was somewhat irregular and uncertain, to be sure, but it was the best that could be provided in many localities.

Schultz thus descended French Creek for about a hundred miles. Whenever one of the boats ran aground, which was often, everybody in it jumped out and pushed. There could be no delay, for the craft had to be kept on the crest of the high water. After the party had reached the Alleghany River it was clear sailing. At night the passengers tied up the boats along the shore, built camp-fires, roasted venison on forked sticks for supper, rolled up in their blankets and went to sleep. Altogether there were forty-two individuals in the company, and they all reached Pittsburgh without serious mishap after a voyage of some two hundred and forty miles. The cost of the trip by water from Fort Le Bœuf was but two dollars, exclusive of food. Provender was either carried by the people themselves or furnished by the boatmen as desired.

At Pittsburgh, then a bustling town of five hundred houses, Schultz bought a big keel-boat for a hundred and thirty dollars and continued on down the Ohio. He gives the cost of a water trip from Pittsburgh to New Orleans as ten dollars, exclusive of board, though the charge was not a fixed one and varied according to the whim of the boat proprietor or his desire for passengers. Wheeling was a flourishing village of two hundred houses and a center of travel between the East and West. Two through stages arrived there each week from Philadelphia, and others continued onward to Lexington, Tennessee and the South over the road formerly called Zane's Trace. Cincinnati was a thriving city of three hundred houses and the center of Ohio valley activity. The favorite route across Ohio from south to north was by way of the Scioto River, which was sometimes navigable by keel-boats for about a hundred and ninety miles. At the head of northbound traffic on the Scioto the traveller walked across country to a branch of the Sandusky River and there took passage in another boat for conveyance to the shore of Lake Erie. The journey from the Ohio River to the lake only required a week or ten days.

Such were the routes and facilities for communication between the Atlantic coast and the middle states just after the nineteenth century began. The conditions described by Michaux, Cuming and Schultz prevailed until the general introduction of steamboats on the Ohio and Mississippi Rivers. It is well within the bounds of safety to say that a journey from New York, Boston or Philadelphia to the western settlements during the years in question demanded almost as much time, called for far more preparation and entailed many times the discomfort, hardship and danger now encountered in travelling around the world.

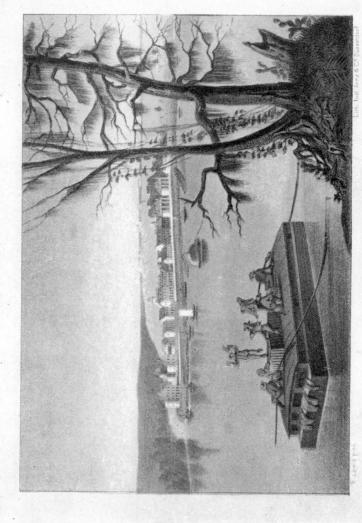

BAYON SACRA (LUISIANA).

A scene illustrating the principal dissipation on a Mississippi broadhorn. From a drawing by the American artist, Henry Lewis. Sm. F. Lith. Col. German.

A HISTORY OF
TRAVEL IN AMERICA

CHAPTER XIX

FULTON AND THE CLERMONT — PUBLIC ACCEPTANCE OF
THE PRINCIPLE THAT STEAM COULD BE USED IN
TRANSPORTATION — THE SIXTEEN AMERICAN STEAM-
BOATS OPERATED PRIOR TO THE CLERMONT — RELA-
TION OF EARLY STEAMBOATS TO THE CLERMONT AND
INCIDENTS CONNECTED WITH HER EVOLUTION

THE appearance of the steamboat *Clermont,* on which
Schultz proceeded from New York to Albany in
1807, marked the final acceptance, by the people, of the
principle that steam could be made of practical use in
travel and transportation. By that time the new generation
with its progressive ideas and enterprise was better able to
estimate the probable value of any innovation which
presaged greater material welfare to the country, and
perchance more eager to accept every device giving
promise of practical utility. The collective mind of the
Americans, emancipated at last from a belief that future
progress of every sort must be along existent and visible
lines of effort, was impatiently calling for the uninterrupted procession of wonders thenceforward to appear in
response to its demand. The generality of men did not
know what was to be done, or how, but they did realize
another age had begun and that the strange new problems

it presented would in some way be solved, and by themselves.

So when Robert Fulton turned his snub-nosed little steamboat out into the Hudson River and started her toward Albany, wheezing and coughing along at the rate of five miles an hour, the watching populace comprehended. A throng had gathered at the wharf and in its immediate neighborhood, drawn by a knowledge of what was to be attempted. There were some skeptics in it, and during the preliminary preparations and embarkation of the passengers an occasional jest and disparaging remark was heard. But the bulk of the crowd was of open mind. Its members did not believe travel was impossible in a boat propelled by steam simply because such a thing, so far as they knew, had never been seen or heard of before. Doubtless they wanted it to be possible; hoped it would be.

Then the machinery started and the *Clermont*[1] moved away from the dock under her own power. The uncertainty and hope of a moment before were changed to an instant appreciation of what it meant. Even before she had disappeared from their physical vision the minds of the spectators had gone on ahead of her, over all the rivers of the land, and peopled them with like contrivances. It was an actuality with a visible meaning; a meaning so plain that those who beheld the sight might have marvelled had they known of the similar drama enacted years before to the jeers of them that saw it. The boat moved slowly—but what of that. Improvements could be made. Everything could be improved, no matter what its use was. The thing had been done; that

[1] She was—as at first built—133 feet long, 18 feet wide and 7 feet in depth of hold, with two masts and sails.

View of the Port of Buffalo on Lake Erie
1815

102.—No steam vessel appeared on the Great Lakes until 1818. View of the harbor of Buffalo and lake shipping in 1815, during the embarkation of troops engaged in the war with Great Britain.

was the main point. A principle had been established. Therefore the citizens lifted up their voices in exultant hosanna, tossed their hats aloft, embraced one another with enthusiasm and unanimously admitted, once more, that they were indeed a very great people. They thought they were cheering Robert Fulton and his steamboat, whereas they were applauding a progress in popular judgment and the excellence of their own discrimination. This was no madman puttering at Conjurer's Point, but a benefactor of his race. So ran the verdict.

The *Clermont* steamed to Albany[1] on her first trip in thirty-two hours against a head wind that prevented the use of her sails, and came back to New York in thirty hours. She stopped at night, and four and a half days were consumed in making the entire experiment. A description of the appearance of the craft on the water and of the excitement she created along the shores of the river and among other shipping on the stream was later written by one who had, as a boy, beheld the boat.[2] The account says:

"It was in the early autumn of the year 1807 [3] that a knot of villagers was gathered on a high bluff just opposite Poughkeepsie, on the west bank of the Hudson, attracted by the appearance of a strange dark-looking craft which was slowly making its way up the river. Some imagined it to be a sea-monster, whilst others did not hesitate to express their belief that it was a sign of the approaching judgment. What seemed strange in the vessel was the substitution of lofty and straight smoke-pipes, rising from the deck, instead of the gracefully tapered masts that commonly stood on the vessels navigating the stream, and, in place of the spars and rigging, the curious play of the walking-beam and pistons, and the slow turning and splashing of the huge and naked paddle-wheels, met the astonished gaze. The dense clouds of smoke, as they rose wave upon wave, added still more to the wonderment of the rustics. This strange looking craft was the Clermont on her trial trip to Albany. . . .

[1] A distance of about 160 miles.
[2] The author of the narrative was H. Freeland. It was published by Reigart, one of the biographers of the "Clermont's" builder, in his "Life of Robert Fulton," Phila., 1856.
[3] The "Clermont" left New York at 1 p. m. on August 7, 1807.

"On her return trip the curiosity she excited was scarcely less intense—the whole country talked of nothing but the sea-monster, belching forth fire and smoke. The fishermen became terrified, and rowed homewards, and they saw nothing but destruction devastating their fishing grounds, whilst the wreaths of black vapor and rushing noise of the paddle wheels, foaming with the stirred-up waters, produced great excitement amongst the boatmen, until . . . the character of that curious boat and the nature of the enterprise which she was pioneering had been ascertained. From that time Robert Fulton, Esq., became known and respected as the author and builder of the first steam packet, from which we plainly see the rapid improvement in commerce and civilization. Who can doubt that Fulton's first packet boat has become the model steamer? Except in finer finish and greater size there is no difference between it and the splendid steamships now crossing the Atlantic. Who can doubt that Fulton saw the meeting of all nations upon his boats, gathering together in unity and harmony, that the 'freedom of the seas would be the happiness of the earth?' [1] Who can doubt that Fulton saw the world circumnavigated by steam, and that his invention was carrying the messages of freedom to every land that no man could tell all its benefits, or describe all its wonders? What a wonderful achievement! What a splendid triumph! Fulton was a man of unparalleled foresight and perseverance. His character and genius rise higher in our estimation, and still more grandly before our minds, the more we contemplate him. . . ."

Just as the pack-train drivers of a former time fought the introduction of wagons on the early roads of Pennsylvania, so did the sailing vessels of the Hudson uselessly seek to retard the general introduction of steamboats by working injury to the *Clermont*. The men who for years had earned their bread on the sloops which until then enjoyed a monopoly of river traffic recognized the significance of the steam craft.[2] In revolt at the new conditions it foretold they sought to disable the boat and to discredit her performances and make her an unpopular vehicle of travel. Several times she was run down and damaged in that manner, but no grave injury resulted. Occasionally she had a paddle wheel knocked off bodily.

[1] A favorite expression used by Fulton.
[2] Thurlow Weed was one who began his career as cabin-boy on a Hudson River sailing packet, and was so engaged when the "Clermont" appeared. But his mind was not of the caliber to resent such an innovation.

In commenting on the attacks one of the inventor's biographers[1] has said: "It is not important to notice these facts; they illustrate the character of Mr. Fulton. They show what embarrassments are to be expected by those

103.—The *Walk-in-the-Water,* first steamboat on the Great Lakes. Built near Buffalo in 1818, under license from the Fulton-Livingston Company. From a drawing made for use on the bills-of-lading printed for the boat, and reproduced in Hurlbut's monograph.

who introduce improvements in the arts which interfere with established interests or prejudices; and they evince the perseverance and resolution which were necessary to surmount the physical and moral difficulties which Mr. Fulton encountered. Sneered at by his own countrymen, called knave, fool and enthusiast, yet he bravely lived all opposition down."

[1] Reigart.

The *Clermont* prospered in spite of all jealousies.[1] During the remainder of the year 1807 she continued to be run as a passenger boat, always crowded with enthusiastic voyagers eager to avail themselves of the wonderful new system of conveyance, who paid scant heed to her slow speed and occasional breakdowns. In the winter of 1807-1808 the boat was rebuilt and in the succeeding spring resumed her popular career. Tales of her existence and exploits on the Hudson were published and commented upon in all the newspapers of the country, and the inhabitants of every section where navigable rivers were the chief arteries of travel displayed an anxiety to acquire a similar means of locomotion. Within a short time the recognized necessity of steam as an indispensable motive power in transportation assumed all the quality of an immemorial axiom. A clamor for steamboats arose, and the people could not understand how they had ever got along without them.

Nevertheless there was a delay of more than sixteen years before the use of steam propulsion became widely prevalent, and the underlying reason for that halt on the way toward further progress is to be found, most singularly, in the circumstances leading to the appearance of the *Clermont.*

Fulton's first boat, however suddenly and unexpectedly it seemed to the public to drop from the realms of unreality into the knowledge and use of men, was not the creation of a day or a year. It was, on the contrary— and perhaps to a greater degree than any other similarly epoch-opening device—the product of many minds and of a long series of strange and devious circumstances.

[1] After a number of attempts had been made to disable her the paddle-wheels were enclosed and protected by heavy timbers. The hostility shown toward the vessel by river boatmen was proof of the popular endorsement given to the craft, rather than otherwise.

104.—The first form of the bicycle, introduced from Europe, was contemporary with Fulton's steamboats in the East. The contrivance merely sustained the weight of the body, and progress was made by pushing the ground with the feet. It was variously called the Velocipede, Accelerator, Draisena, Hobby Horse and Dandy Carriage. Baltimore was the American center for its manufacture, and a specimen, made of wrought iron and hardwood, cost $30. By 1819 the use of the velocipede had spread as far west as Louisville.

At least sixteen steamboats had been built in America before the launching of the *Clermont,* fifteen of which had previously been operated under their own power by the eight different men who had designed them. Nor were Americans first in the field. A list in chronological order of some of the early experiments follows:

The first known contemporary evidence showing the application of steam power to water craft as a means of propulsion is to be found in connection with Denis Papin, a French scientist and engineer, who invented and built a steamboat while residing in the principality of Hesse, in Germany, in the year 1707. His demonstration of steam navigation having brought abuse upon him, he embarked on his vessel in an effort to proceed in it to London. With this object he started down the River Fulda, but at the town of Munden the boatmen of the river attacked him and destroyed his boat. He escaped with his life, and never, so far as is known, repeated his undertaking.

In 1736 an Englishman named Jonathan Hulls took out a patent for a stern-wheeled steamboat, and during the following year published in London a book describing the invention, the frontispiece of which is a picture of his steamboat engaged in towing a sailing vessel. An English investigator[1] of the subject affirms that Hulls' boat was built and used, but Preble[2] comes to a contrary conclusion.

M. de Jouffroy, of France, began experimenting in 1778, and in 1781 built a steamboat 140 feet long. In 1783 it ran under its own power with paddle-wheels, and a committee of the French Academy of Science made a favorable report regarding it. Jouffroy demanded a patent, but left France on the outbreak of the Revolution, and on his return found a patent for a similar boat had been awarded to another man.

1786.—John Fitch operated on the Delaware River, at Philadelphia, the first steamboat to move in American waters. It was propelled by an endless chain of paddles.

1787.—Fitch ran his second boat on the Delaware in August, with the system of upright paddles at the sides.

1787.—Rumsey, in December, moved a boat by drawing a stream of water in at the bow and ejecting it at the stern.

1788.—Fitch finished his third boat and in it made a

[1] Russell, in the "Encycloped'a Britannica."
[2] Rear-Admiral George Henry Preble, U. S. N., published in 1883 "A Chronological History of the Origin and Development of Steam Navigation."

349

twenty-mile voyage from Philadelphia to Burlington. This same boat afterward ran regularly as a passenger packet on the Delaware in 1790, covering a thousand miles or more. Its best speed was eight miles an hour.

In 1788 three Scotchmen named Patrick Millar, James

NORTH RIVER STEAMBOAT & SAFETY BARGE

105.—A Hudson River passenger barge of 1825. Owing to the numerous explosions due to carelessness on early steamboats many people hesitated to use them, and some companies resorted to the expedient of towing travellers on separate vessels, so they would be in less danger of death or injury if the boilers blew up. This and the illustrations to No. 114, inclusive, deal with steamboats and steamboat travel in the East.

Taylor and William Symington jointly built and operated a steamboat on the Lake of Dalswinton. It was moved by a paddle-wheel placed in the center of the boat, and ran at the rate of five miles an hour.

In 1789 the same men equipped a boat sixty feet long with an engine whose cylinders were of 18 inches diameter, and ran it on the Forth and Clyde Canal at the rate of about seven miles an hour. The contemporary Edinburgh newspapers contained information respecting it.

1790.—William Longstreet of New Jersey, then living in Georgia, built a boat that ran against the current of the Savannah River at the rate of five miles an hour.[1]

1792.—Elijah Ormsbee of Connecticut, then residing in Rhode Island, invented and constructed a steamboat propelled by side paddles moving back and forth like a duck's feet. In it he went from a point near Cranston to Providence; thence to Pawtucket and back to Providence again. Ormsbee's boat made from three to four miles an hour, and he used it for several weeks. No one being interested in it, the machinery was taken out of the boat and given to David Wilkinson, of Pawtucket, another mechanic who had made Ormsbee's castings for him.[2] Ormsbee constructed most of his own machinery and understood the principle of paddle-wheels. His use of side paddles was due to the cheapness of the mechanism for that means of propulsion and his lack of money.

1793 or 1794.—Samuel Morey of New Hampshire, then living in Connecticut, who began his experiments in the year 1790, built a paddle-wheel steamboat on the Connecticut River in 1794 and ran the vessel from Hartford to New York City at the rate of five miles an hour.[3] Morey placed his paddle-wheel at the stern of the boat, in the manner afterward adopted for many steamboats on western waters and some rivers of the East. Mann, in his account of Morey's work, indicates a lack of

[1] Preble's "Chronological History of Steam Navigation," p. 23.
[2] Dow's "History of Steam Navigation between Providence and New York."—Files of the Transactions of the Society for the Encouragement of Domestic Industry. Preble; p. 27.
[3] Preble: Mann's "Account of Morey's Steamboat" (1864).—The Patent Office records show that Morey took out several patents for steamboats.

knowledge of earlier inventors, for he says Morey's vessel was "so far as is known, the first steamboat ever seen on the waters of America."

The English Earl of Stanhope, in 1793, after three years of experiments, built a steamboat with side paddles like duck's feet on the same principle used by Ormsbee of Connecticut in 1792. Stanhope obtained for his vessel a speed of three miles an hour.

In the same year of 1793 John Smith, of England, ran a steamboat on the Bridgewater Canal from Runcorn to Manchester, at the rate of two miles an hour. The craft had side paddle-wheels.

Still another steamboat was operated on the Sankey Canal in Lancashire, England, in 1797. It was equipped with side oars like those used by Fitch in his second boat. The *Monthly Magazine,* an English periodical of the time, spoke of the boat in its issue for July of 1797, and said: "This ingenious discovery . . . may be ranked amongst the most useful of modern inventions, and in particular promises the highest benefits to inland navigation."

1796 or 1797.—Fitch built and ran his screw propeller boat on Collect Pond in New York City.

1797.—Morey built a side-wheel steamboat at Bordentown, near Philadelphia, on the Delaware River. He afterward ran the boat to Philadelphia and showed it there. In a letter written in the year 1818[1] Morey described this craft as follows: "In June, 1797, I went to Bordentown, on the Delaware, and there constructed a steamboat, and devised the plan of propelling by means of wheels, one on each side. The shafts ran across the

---

[1] To William A. Duer, who had a celebrated controversy with Cadwallader Colden over the question of early steamboats.

boat with a crank in the middle, worked from the beam of the engine with a shackle bar . . . I took out patents for my improvements. . . ."[1]

1798.—Robert R. Livingston, commonly known in history as Chancellor Livingston, built a boat on the Hudson River,[2] and by the legislature of New York was granted exclusive privileges "of navigating all boats that might be propelled by steam on all the waters within the territory, or jurisdiction, of the State for the term of twenty years, provided he should, within a twelvemonth, build such a boat, the mean of whose progress should not be less than four miles an hour." This grant was offered to Livingston in March of 1798, and was a transference of the right previously conferred on Fitch and now taken away because he had not availed himself of the monopoly given to him eleven years before. In October of 1798 Livingston's boat made a trip during which its speed was about three miles an hour. The Spanish Minister to the United States was on board at the time.[3] Since four miles an hour was not attained by the vessel before March of 1799, the State's proffer of exclusive privileges did not then become effective. Livingston's boat was variously moved on different trips by upright side paddles, endless chains of paddles, and by two stern wheels that were not upright, but apparently revolved horizontally on the same plane and in opposite directions. Probably each blade was hinged in order that it might fold up when returning toward the bow of the boat.

Hunter and Dickinson, of England, ran a steamboat on the Thames River in 1801. In discussing their boat

[1] Preble: p. 30.
[2] So many steamboats had by this time been operated in America that Jedediah Morse, the early geographer, took note of them and said in the edition of his "Gazetteer," published in 1797, that "it is probable steamboats will be found of infinite service in all our extensive river navigation."
[3] Spain seems to have kept a constant eye on early steamboats.

the *Monthly Magazine* spoke of its performance as "very creditable to them, and as exceeding everything before accomplished." It also said "the vessel was moved at the rate of three miles an hour through the water."

In 1802 William Symington, acting alone, built a steamboat on the Forth and Clyde Canal and ran it at

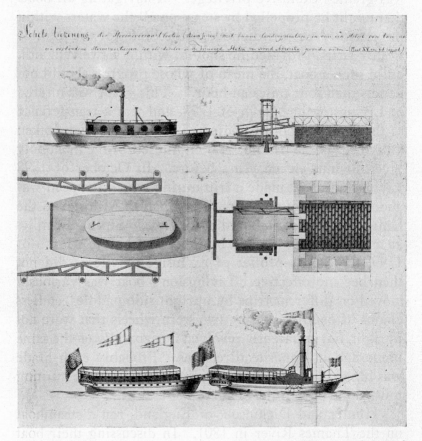

106.—New York steam ferry boat, ferry dock, Hudson River steamboat and passenger barge of 1825. A water-color sketch by the Dutch civil engineer Tromp, drawn to accompany an account of American transportation facilities written by him in 1825 as a result of his investigations during that year.

the rate of between three and four miles an hour while towing two other loaded boats, each of seventy tons burden. Without a tow the craft ran at six miles an hour. Symington's boat was the *Charlotte Dundas,* constructed at a cost of about $15,000. It was his intention to place her paddle-wheels at the sides, but for fear the wash of the water would injure the banks of the canal, the revolving paddles were put at the stern.

1802.—John Stevens, of Hoboken, New Jersey, who had been actively interested in the subject of steam navigation since 1791,[1] built a steamboat moved by a four-bladed screw propeller. He also used a high pressure multitubular boiler, and all his machinery was of his own design and manufacture. Stevens ran his boat in the waters around New York during the summer. Its speed was about four miles an hour.[2]

1803.—Stevens built a new engine of a different type, but also with a screw propeller, and ran his boat in the neighborhood of New York City as during the previous year.[3]

1804.—Oliver Evans, an early American inventor and engineer, built and operated a steamboat at Philadelphia. It was designed for use as a dredge, and was propelled by a paddle-wheel at the stern. In order to show that land vehicles as well as water craft could be moved by steam power Evans put wheels on his boat and ran it by steam through the city from Center Square to the Schuylkill River at Market Street. There, after its land wheels had been taken off and the paddle-wheel adjusted,

---

[1] Several of the early American inventors turned their attention to steam propulsion because of Fitch's boat and began their work in 1790 or 1791. Preble says of Stevens (p. 41, note): "In 1787 he became interested in steamboats, from seeing that of John Fitch."

[2] "Medical and Philosophical Journal," Jan., 1812.—Latrobe's "Lost Chapter."—Francis B. Stevens' "The First Steam Screw Propeller Boats to Navigate the Waters of any Country."—Preble.

[3] Ibid.

it entered the water, steamed down the Schuylkill to the Delaware and up the last named river to Philadelphia again, passing numerous other vessels on the way. It then entered on its work as a steamboat dredge.

107.—The *Champlaine,* finest steamboat up to 1835. Employed on the Hudson. After monopoly in steam transportation was overthrown by the Supreme Court various companies in the East built vessels of steadily increasing size and magnificence, the best of which appeared in the waters around New York, Boston, Providence and Philadelphia.

1804.—Stevens, of Hoboken, built and operated a small twin-screw steamboat. It was in use for some time between Hoboken and New York and had an ordinary speed of four miles an hour. For short distances it could attain about seven or eight miles an hour.[1] In 1844 the engine and propellers of this boat, as originally built, were placed in a similar hull and the craft was run on the Hudson River at eight miles an hour. The engine

[1] James Renwick, in the "Historical Magazine," Vol. II, No. 8. Renwick was a professor at Columbia College. New York, and saw the boat.—Preble.—Stevens' "First Steam Screw Propellers."—Stuart's "Anecdotes of the Steam Engine." London, 1829.

and propellers, together with the boilers, are still preserved in running order at the Stevens Institute in Hoboken, New Jersey.

1805.—Stevens built and ran a twin-screw steam propeller boat on the Hudson River. It was about fifty feet long, with a draft of four feet, and remained in use until some time in the year 1806.[1]

1806.—Stevens turned his attention to the side-wheel type of vessel and built the *Phoenix,* which was propelled in that manner. This boat was partly constructed when Fulton returned to America from England in 1806, prior to the commencement of the *Clermont.* Fulton's boat was first to take the water, being finished a few weeks ahead of the *Phoenix,* and Stevens' craft, debarred from New York state under a legislative monopoly granted to Livingston and Fulton, was run to Philadelphia and operated in that neighborhood.

Fulton had lived in Philadelphia from 1782 to 1786, during the last year or more of which time Fitch had been busy with his boat. There is nothing to indicate a knowledge of Fitch's work by Fulton until a later date. Fulton went to London in 1786, where he resided in the household of the American painter, Benjamin West, for several years, and devoted himself to a study of engineering. John Rumsey proceeded to England in May of 1788, and died in London on December 24, 1792.[2] Fulton knew of Rumsey's presence in England, went to see him there,[3] and discussed with him the subject of steamboats. It is not probable, in view of the controversy between Fitch and Rumsey, that Fulton could have talked about steam-

[1] Stevens' "First Steam Screw Propellers."—Preble.
[2] Bache's "General Advertiser," Philadelphia, March 5, 1793.
[3] "A gentleman not many years ago had in his possession letters written by Rumsey in London, which mentioned his receiving frequent visits there from a young American studying engineering, who showed a sympathetic and intelligent interest in Rumsey's labors. This young man was Robert Fulton. . . ."—Preble: p. 12.

108.—The *Swallow,* also a fine and swift Hudson River boat of the fourth decade, whose construction and appearance reveal further progress toward the modern type of eastern river craft. She was afterward wrecked by striking a rock in the river. From a drawing made by the Scotch civil engineer David Stevenson, in 1837.

boats in London with the last named of his fellow Americans without also becoming informed of what Fitch had done. Yet it may have happened so.

The future builder of the *Clermont* continued in England and France until 1801, during which year Chancellor Livingston was appointed American Minister to the Court of Napoleon. In Paris Livingston formed an acquaintance with Fulton, and the American diplomat, who had already built a steamboat, at once entered on close personal association with the young civil engineer, out of which the *Clermont* grew, and which was only to be broken by Fulton's death. Both men were interested in the use of steam for the purposes of transportation, and Livingston urged his young friend to pursue the matter. In the words of another biographer of Fulton,[1]

[1] Cadwallader D. Colden, in his "Life of Robert Fulton": pp. 148-149. Taken by Colden from a statement made by Livingston at a later date.

"he [Livingston] communicated to Mr. Fulton the importance of steamboats to their own country; informed him of what had been attempted in America, and of his resolution to resume the pursuit on his return. and advised him to turn his attention to the subject."

The advice was unnecessary. Fulton had been watching the work of other men in steam navigation for some eight or nine years and had displayed an intelligent interest in Rumsey's labors as far back, at least, as the year 1792. During the year of 1793 he had also been in correspondence with Lord Stanhope, of England, regarding the building of steamboats. About the year 1802 Fulton, in giving consideration to the question of propulsion, "thought of paddles and duck's feet, abandoning which, he took up the idea of using endless chains with resisting boards upon them as propellers, his calculations giving him a favorable opinion of the mode; at least, he was persuaded it was greatly preferable to any other method that had been previously tried."[1] While still in England, and in 1799, Fulton had also become acquainted with Cartwright, inventor of the power loom, and by him had been given the plan or model of a steamboat made by the Englishman about the year 1787.[2]

In reciting to Fulton what had been accomplished in America previous to the commencement of their acquaintance in Paris, Livingston might well have gone much further than merely to recount the list of steam-propelled boats above set forth. For in his own work of steamboat building the Chancellor had been associated with John Stevens, of Hoboken, and with Nicholas J. Roosevelt, of

[1] Colden's Biography of Fulton.
An endless chain of paddles was the first propelling system tried by Fitch and almost at once discarded. Stanhope had used the duck's-feet paddles.
[2] Fulton was afterward accused of selling, as his own, another invention of Cartwright's —a cordage-laying machine. The details of this controversy are contained in Thornton's "Short Account of the Origin of Steam Boats": pp. 17-18.

New York, and the three men had long been at courteous odds over the proposed details of their vessel. The Chancellor, though a very able man, was a bit stubborn in his opinions and somewhat intolerant of opposition. He preferred to have his own way. The trait in question had been shown in connection with the boat built by him and his two ·colleagues and operated in 1798 at a speed of about three miles an hour. Its speed not having been satisfactory, Roosevelt had proposed the use of side paddle-wheels, and on September 6th of the same year had written to Livingston as follows:

"I would recommend that we throw two wheels of

Group on Deck.

109.—Travellers on a Hudson River steamboat. As suggested by the attitude and apparel of the three men in the background, the costumes worn by the other group were becoming obsolete. The object on the bench is a traveller's bag called the "carpet-sack." It was made of carpet, and often showed a combination of colors such as red, green, brown, blue and yellow. From it the modern hand-bag and suit-case have been evolved.

wood over the sides, fastened to the axes of the flys with eight arms or paddles; that part which enters the water of sheet iron to shift according to the power they require either deeper in the water, or otherwise, and that we navigate the vessel with these . . . ."[1]

The Chancellor sent no reply to the suggestion for upright side paddle-wheels, so Roosevelt wrote to him again on the same subject under date of September 16th, saying: "I hope to hear your opinion of throwing wheels over the sides." To this Livingston made answer: "I say nothing on the subject of wheels over the sides, as I am perfectly convinced from a variety of experiments of the superiority of those we have adopted."[2]

On October 21st Roosevelt again returned to the subject, urging a trial of Livingston's wheels,[3] "contrasted with paddles on Mr. Stevens' plan, or with wheels over the sides, so as to ascertain the difference in the application of the power." The Chancellor finally laid down his ultimatum on October 28th, 1798, in a letter to Roosevelt characterizing Stevens' paddles as "too inconvenient and liable to accidents," and in which he also said, "as for vertical wheels, they are out of the question."[4]

Livingston's activity in keeping himself abreast of American steamboat building before he went to France is illustrated by his personal inspection of Morey's boat in 1793 or 1794, when he travelled on the craft from New York back to Greenwich.[5] John Stevens was also a passenger during the same trip. It is difficult to understand the Chancellor's later prejudice against paddle-wheels under the circumstances, for Morey's vessel had

[1] Latrobe's "Lost Chapter": pp. 18-19.
[2] Ibid: p. 19.
[3] Which revolved on a horizontal plane, instead of vertically.
[4] Latrobe's "Lost Chapter": pp. 19-20.
[5] Preble: p. 29.

been propelled by a stern wheel and had made five miles an hour. Nevertheless his influence on Fulton must have been strong, for Fulton, until as late a date as the fall of 1802, still clung to side oars as the best method of propulsion for a steamboat. On September 20th, 1802, the future builder of the *Clermont* wrote to a friend on the subject,[1] and in his letter he said: ". . . if the author of the model wishes to be assured of the merits of his invention before he goes to the expense of a patent I advise him to make a model of a boat, in which he can place a clock spring which will give about eight revolutions; he can then combine the movements so as to try oars, paddles, and the leaves [the duck's-feet system] which he proposes. . . . About eight years ago the Earl of Stanhope tried an experiment on similar leaves in Greenland Dock, London, but without success. I have also tried experiments on similar leaves, wheels, oars, paddles, and flyers similar to those of a smoke jack, and found oars to be the best."

Just as Fulton had known of Rumsey's presence in London, he was also aware that Fitch had proceeded to Paris in 1793 with the intention of building steamboats there in association with Aaron Vail, American consul at L'Orient. Possibly the incident was one of those things told to him by Minister Livingston as part of the narrative concerning what had been done in America. Livingston had visited Vail and had discussed Fitch's boat with him.[2] At any rate Fulton went to see Vail, and from him borrowed Fitch's plans and drawings, which he kept for several months.[3] The fact that Fitch's steamboat had

[1] See Preble, p. 35: the friend was Fulwar Skipwith, an American consul general in France.
[2] Duer's second letter to Colden, 1818.
[3] Preble; Thornton; Duer; etc., etc. For Vail's relation of the matter see Cutting's letter to Ferdinando Fairfax, printed in Thornton's "Short Account."

been the only one in extensive public use up to that time, and a knowledge of its propulsion by side oars and later by stern paddles, together with a study of the earlier inventor's own plans, may have been factors impelling Fulton toward oars as the best propelling power despite Roosevelt's advocacy of side wheels and Livingston's voyage on a paddle-wheel boat. But whatever the cause may have been, Fulton did not, until late in 1802 or early in 1803, devote serious attention to the revolving side paddles previously twice used in America by Morey, also urged by the Americans, Reed and Roosevelt, and used in Europe by the Frenchman Jouffroy, the Scotchmen Millar, Taylor and Symington, and the Englishman Smith.

In the year 1803 Fulton built a steamboat on the Seine at Paris. Owing to miscalculations in its construction the machinery overweighted the hull, broke through the bottom of it and sunk the vessel.[1] A new boat, sixty-six feet long and eight feet wide, was then constructed, but when tried in August of 1804 she moved too slowly to be of value. Fulton thereupon paid a visit to Symington of Scotland,[2] who had built the stern-wheel steamboat *Charlotte Dundas* and run her at six miles an hour. "In compliance with Mr. Fulton's earnest request," says Symington, "I caused the engine fire to be lighted up, and in a short time thereafter put the steamboat in motion, and carried him from Lock 16, where the boat then lay, four miles west in the canal, and returned to the place of starting, in one hour and twenty minutes, to the great

[1] "On the very day that this misfortune happened he commenced repairing it. He did not sit idly down to repine at misfortune which his manly exertions might remedy, or waste in fruitless lamentations a moment of that time in which the accident might be repaired. Without returning to his lodgings, he immediately began to labour with his own hands to raise the boat, and worked twenty-four hours incessantly, without allowing himself rest or taking refreshment—an imprudence which, as he always supposed, had a permanent bad effect on his constitution, and to which he imputed much of his subsequent bad health."—Reigart's "Life of Fulton."
[2] Woodcroft's "Progress of Steam Navigation." London, 1848.

110.—Going to bed in the men's cabin of a big eastern steamboat. The sleeping-bunk idea of the earlier river barges had been appropriated by all later water craft designed for passenger traffic. Ladders or other climbing aids were only required for the topmost tier of bunks.

astonishment of Mr. Fulton and several gentlemen, who at our outset chanced to come on board."[1] Fulton also took drawings of the machinery used to operate the *Charlotte Dundas*.[2]

After this actual ride on a steamboat Fulton was

[1] Preble: p. 36.
[2] Woodcroft.

greatly encouraged, and returned to his task with a personal knowledge that the work whereon he was then engaged could be brought to a successful conclusion. Previous to that time he had been compelled to depend on hearsay information from Livingston regarding what other men had done, coupled with his study of Fitch's drawings. Such information was now supplanted by a certainty born of personal experience. The occasional doubt or skepticism manifested by some of his fellow-countrymen after he had returned to New York and was busy in superintending the building of the hull of the *Clermont* was ignored by Fulton, for he knew steamboats could be constructed and operated.

The unfortunate experience of 1803, when his own engine had sunk a boat on the Seine, together with the failure of the same machinery in 1804 had, in the meantime, made him realize the necessity of securing competent help in constructing the essential parts of a steamboat. Under date of November 3, 1803, he had written a letter to Messrs. Boulton and Watt, the ablest machinery builders of England, indicating his desire to have them make him what he required.[1] In it he stated:

. . . "I have not confidence in any other engines, and hope you will be so good as to give me the necessary information on the boiler and other parts so as to produce the best effect. . . ."

He already desired to return to America and build a steamboat. But as England then forbade the exportation of machinery to any other country without express permission of the Privy Council in each instance, and as he could not build his own engine and had no confidence in any but such as were made by Boulton and Watt, he

[1] The original letter is now in the New York City Public Library, Department of Manuscripts.

THE LADIES' CABIN.

111.—Substantially similar arrangements prevailed in the women's cabin, which, however, commonly had but two rows of berths.

sought the aid of America's diplomatic representative in Great Britain. The United States Minister to the Court of St. James at the time was James Monroe, and to him Fulton wrote on November 6, 1803, as follows:[1]

"You have perhaps heard of the success of my experiment for navigating boats by steam engines and you will feel the importance of establishing such boats on the Mississippi and other rivers of the United States as soon as possible. With this View I have written to Messrs. Boulton Watt & Co. of Birmingham to forward me a Steam engine to America. . . .

[1] The original is in the New York City Library.

"Your desire to see useful improvements Introduced or created in our country is the strongest reason for your urging the permission and accepting of no refusal. The fact is I cannot establish the boat without the engine. The question then is Shall we or shall we not have such boats."

Reasons of diplomacy made Monroe unable to ask for an engine at the time, and he so informed his fellow American in Paris. In reply to the Minister's letter Fulton wrote again on March 4 ,1804:[1]

"I received your letter mentioning that particular reasons prevented your applying at present for permission to ship a Steam engine to New York. . . . As the Steam Engine is really designed for a Steam Boat and has no connexion with any of my other mechanical Experiments, and as the Establishment of Steam boats is of immense importance to our country the British Government must have little friendship or even civility toward America if they refuse such a request. . . .

"Independent of the private interest which I have in establishing steam boats, I consider them of such infinite use in America, and feel so sensible of the Activity and perseverance which is necessary to make the first establishment and secure success, that I should feel a culpable neglect toward my country if I relaxed for a moment in pursuing every necessary measure for carrying it into effect. I hope Sir you will be governed by equal patriotism and not accept a slight refusal. . . . The government has permitted engines to be sent to France and Holland before the war and do now permit them to go to Russia they surely then, can have no objection to let one go to a neutral and unoffending country like the United States. . . . I plead this not for myself alone but for our country. . . ."

Such were the preliminary links in the long chain of events that finally resulted in the general introduction of steam transportation. Fulton did not himself build either the machinery or hull of his first boat or devise the system used for its propulsion. After his mishap of 1803 he abandoned the effort to create the ingredients which differentiate a steam-propelled craft from a sailing vessel. Instead of persisting in the endeavor to solve the problem—with drawings of Fitch's eight-mile-an-

[1] Fulton's original is in the New York City Library.

hour engine and Symington's machinery to aid him—he turned to Boulton and Watt for the necessary information on the boiler and other parts so as to produce the best effect. His statement that patriotism was one motive for the undertaking was of course genuine, as Fitch's identical utterances of years before had been, but the activity and perseverance necessary to secure success, and his pursuance of every necessary measure consisted, after the attempt of 1803-1804, in asking a second person to secure from another government the work of a third person without which he said he could do nothing more to advance his project.

England finally permitted him to obtain the mechanical appliances he required, and they were shipped to New York. Fulton returned to America, where, after

STEAM CATAMARAN - H. W. LONGFELLOW.

112.—A few steamboats built on the catamaran principle were used in the East, but never with success. The old double-canoe idea did not prove useful when applied to steam navigation.

inspecting a model of Morey's steamboat and holding three interviews with its inventor,[1] he commenced the construction of the *Clermont*. The hull was built by Charles Brown, a ship builder of New York, under the supervision of Fulton himself, aided by a young mechanic named Stoudinger, who had been employed and trained by Nicholas Roosevelt, and who became Fulton's right-hand man. The Boulton and Watt machinery was duly put in place. It propelled the boat up the river on her first trip and during the remainder of her career.

Immediately after the first trip of his vessel to Albany, Fulton wrote several letters about the voyage. In one addressed to his friend, Joel Barlow, he said: "The power of propelling boats by steam is now fully proved. The morning I left New York there were not thirty persons who believed that the boat would ever move one mile an hour or be of the least utility; and while we were passing off from the wharf, which was crowded with spectators, I heard a number of sarcastic remarks. This is the way in which ignorant men compliment what they call philosophers and projectors. Although the prospect of personal emolument has been some inducement to me, yet I feel infinitely more pleasure in reflecting on the immense advantage my country will derive from the invention."[2]

The *Clermont*, as she appeared before being rebuilt, was somewhat ungainly of aspect. Her boiler was set in masonry and all the machinery was exposed to view. A very small distance at bow and stern was decked over. The smokestack was thirty feet high, and out of its top roared flames and sparks from the dry white pine used as fuel. The engine groaned in its labors, and a man with a

---

[1] Preble: p. 30. Whether Fulton examined a model of Morey's stern-wheeler or of his later side-wheel boat is uncertain.
[2] Colden's "Life of Fulton": p. 176.

pot of molten lead was constantly running about to stop up leaks from which steam escaped. The rudder had so little power as to be almost useless. During the winter following her first appearance the hull was lengthened, new steering apparatus installed, the deck was extended from stem to stern and two cabins were built below for the accommodation of passengers. Around the walls of the cabins were upper and lower sleeping berths, as in the keel boats of the previous generation. The whole extent of woodwork was then painted in various bright colors, and in her new guise the boat was quite the most imposing conveyance for public travel ever yet seen in the world.

CHAPTER XX

THE first trip of the *Clermont* was a memorable event in economic history. It was not invested with that quality by any radical difference between it and what had been done before, for there was no such difference, but by the popular comprehension of its significance. An awakened public at last admitted the relation of steam to the coming years. With that acknowledgment the old order of things passed, and the world of to-day was born.

We have traced the origin of the application of steam power to transportation in America, observed the attitude of the people toward steamboats during a period of about twenty-two years, and seen the close kinship borne by those early boats to one another. It is now appropriate to consider the delay which intervened between Fulton's

371

first undertaking and the general use of steamboats, together with the relationship between that delay and the long chain of circumstances resulting in the *Clermont's* creation. The connection was direct, and reveals the mental horizon of the generations that lived before modern conditions were imagined. If we of to-day feel astonishment because the leaders of a century ago were in large degree blind to mankind's impending development, it is only necessary to remember the laughter which, a few years since, greeted any prediction that men would soon arise from the earth and fly through the air with wings of their own manufacture.

A foresight of the future is possessed only by those who are indeed great—and by few of them. The average man gives thought to the relationship between his individual affairs and the approaching years, but under ordinary circumstances the distant necessities of human society are likely to be, in his estimation, a bugaboo. He does not sufficiently consider that the coming men must build on a foundation which he and his contemporaries are laying day by day, and that if his work is faulty then the structure it must uphold will be insecure or inadequate. Deliberate and intelligent national preparation for the economic needs of the future—especially in a country rich in natural resources—is a process not to be expected unless those chosen to administer its affairs are brave, wise, far-seeing and unselfish men uninfluenced by sectional jealousies, and possessed of a strength having its roots in the widespread confidence and support of their fellows and a slowly evolved popular appreciation of social duty.

When Fitch conceived the idea of carrying people by steam power he went to the central governing body of

VIEW OF THE CITY OF HARTFORD, CONN., FROM THE RIVER—SHOWING AN OLD-FASHIONED STEAMBOAT.

113.—The *Holyoke*, a primitive, stern-wheel steamboat of the Connecticut River, which survived into the days of the large, walking-beam, side-wheel vessels and the railway.

all the states and offered it to them. He saw its scope and effect, and suggested appropriate national action. No nation had before—or has since—been placed in a position to obtain a public utility of such importance for the untrammeled use of its inhabitants. Those results which would have followed if the government had acquired the inventor's system of transportation in behalf of the people may readily be imagined. It could have been obtained on whatever terms Congress might have chosen to make. Fitch asked nothing for himself. He said to the Congress of the Confederation in 1787: "I do not desire at this time to receive emoluments for my own private use, but to lay it out for the benefit of my country . . . . Congress might at a future day reward me further, according as they should see the utility of the scheme merited it . . . . I do not wish any premiums to make a monopoly to myself."[1]

Had Congress then acted, the chief aid to national economic progress would not have become a subject of monopoly and legal controversy for nearly forty years, as was destined to be the case. But the Federal legislature was then a body with scarcely a vestige of authority, reduced to that status by the conflicting desires, antagonisms and other like attitudes of the states represented in its membership. Each commonwealth, imbued with a greater or less degree of jealousy toward its neighbors and a feeling of separate sovereignty, was blinded to the interdependence and close relation destined to subsist between them. Even the framing of a common political programme was exceedingly difficult of accomplishment, and harmonious action for the best interests of all in those social and economic matters which are superior to state

[1] His second petition to Congress.

lines was still more so. In fact, the idea of an economic and social nationality was to all intents and purposes overwhelmed by political considerations. The real basis of lasting and beneficial union was at first subsidiary to its outward shell. A failure on the part of Congress to see the value of Fitch's plan was the first misfortune, and it was speedily followed by a second in the shape of the exclusive grants made by individual states.

New York's grant to Fitch, given in 1787, bestowed on him a monopoly of steam transportation on the waters of the state for fourteen years. In 1798, as has been seen, Fitch's privilege was cancelled by New York and transferred bodily to Livingston for twenty years, provided he ran a steamboat at four miles an hour within a twelvemonth. This he failed to do, and the grant of 1798 did not then become effective. But on April 5, 1803, the privilege of 1798 was revived by New York and again bestowed on Livingston for twenty years from the second passage of the law, provided a boat was run at four miles an hour within two years. Fulton was made a joint beneficiary under the act with Livingston. Nothing was done to secure the monopoly within the specified time, and the period allowed to them was extended until 1807. In that year the *Clermont* was completed and put in use.

The exclusive privilege held by Livingston and Fulton, then, was the act originally passed in Fitch's favor twenty years previously, and it was under the terms of the monopolistic grant that the *Clermont* was operated. The two men, just as Fitch had been, were given the power to seize any steamboat run by others without their license, and to collect a penalty for every trip so made. When the proposed legislation in Livingston's favor was introduced in the New York Assembly in 1798, its title was:

"An act repealing the act for granting and securing to John Fitch the sole right and advantage of making and employing the steamboat by him lately invented, and for other purposes." The other purposes were the transference of Fitch's privileges to the Chancellor.[1]

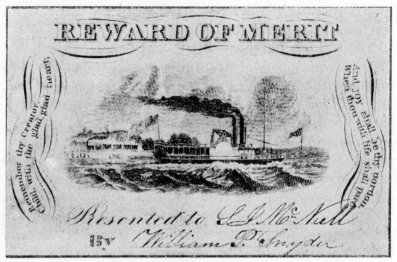

114.—In the pioneer days of mechanical transportation vehicles the "Rewards of Merit" bestowed on school children for diligence and good behavior were frequently embellished with pictures of steamboats and railroad trains, in order to give the pupils a better knowledge of the busy world outside. Their school books also showed such vehicles. See illustration No. 214.

Fulton's biographers, either through an ignorance of prior steamboat history or a tendency to magnify the work of the man whom they discussed, have omitted mention of various things relating to his connection with and study of steam vessels constructed by other men before he built the *Clermont.* They have phrased their accounts of his relation to the subject in such a way as to convey

[1] ". . . . the same privilege granted to Chancellor Livingston by the act of 1798 was granted in April, 1803, to Messrs. Livingston and Fulton."—Judge Yates' opinion in the case of Livingston against Van Ingen; 9 "Johnson's Reports": p. 558.

an impression that Fulton was the American inventor of steam propulsion, or at least of paddle-wheels. One of them,[1] in discussing New York's transfer of Fitch's monopoly to Livingston in 1798, says: "The Legislature, in March, 1798, passed an act vesting Mr. Livingston with the exclusive right and privilege of navigating all kinds of boats which might be propelled by the force of steam. . . ." He makes no mention of the main purpose of the law, to which the transfer was a sequel.[2] He also quotes the introducer of the bill[3] as saying: "The wags and the lawyers in the House were generally opposed to my bill. . . . One main ground of their objection was, that it was an idle and whimsical project, unworthy of legislative attention. . . ." The subject matter of the bill under discussion, as its title indicated, dealt with a law that had been on the statute books of the state for eleven years, and with a device publicly used eight years before the law was passed.

The same biographer quotes Chancellor Livingston as saying:[4] "After trying a variety of experiments on a small scale, on models of his[5] own invention, it was understood that he had developed the true principles upon which steamboats should be built, and for the want of knowing which all previous experiments had failed. But as these two gentlemen both knew that many things which were apparently perfect when tried on a small scale, failed when reduced to practice upon a large one, they determined to go to the expense of building an operating boat upon the Seine. This was done in the year 1803, at their

[1] Reigart.
[2] Nor does Colden, whose prior reference to the matter is contained in p. 145 of his "Life of Fulton." Reigart copied from Colden.
[3] Dr. Mitchell, of New York City, a friend of Livingston's.
[4] In Livingston's "Historical Account of the Application of Steam for the Propelling of Boats."
[5] Fulton's.

115.—The steamboat *Milwaukie,* one of the most pretentious vessels on the Great Lakes in 1838. Passing the lighthouse at Buffalo. Engraved by Bennett from a drawing by the artist J. C. Miller. This and the illustrations to No. 127, inclusive, relate to steamboats on western waters.

joint expense, under the direction of Mr. Fulton; and so fully evinced the justice of his principles that it was immediately determined to enrich their country by the valuable discovery as soon as they should meet there, and in the meantime to order an engine to be made in England. . . ."[1]

Chancellor Livingston did not clearly define the true principles and valuable discovery here mentioned. By some later commentators his language has been considered to refer to the use of paddle-wheels, but since both Livingston and Fulton had travelled on paddle-wheel steamboats several years before the *Clermont* was built, and since the Chancellor had considered Roosevelt's plan for

[1] This was written by Livingston after the "Clermont" was built. Quoted by Colden at pp. 149-150 of the "Life."

lature a fifth law in which their right to demand forfeiture of any usurping steamboat was reaffirmed in more specific terms. By the grant of 1811 Livingston and Fulton were given the same remedy for the seizure of a rival craft as they would have possessed if the opposition

Dampfboot auf dem Mississippi.

116.—The Ohio and Mississippi River steamboat *Belvidere*. A picture used for years in England, Germany and elsewhere in Europe to illustrate the flimsy and dangerous construction of many western river boats. The *Belvidere* was built at the town of Portsmouth, Ohio, in 1825, escaped all dangers incident to her duties, and survived to the venerable age of six years before being worn out. The average life of an early western steamboat was about three or four years.

boat had been wrongfully taken out of their possession. The law of 1811 further compelled the courts to grant an injunction forbidding the use of any competing steam vessel whenever Fulton should bring suit for forfeiture. And to cap the climax it made any rival owner liable to a fine of two thousand dollars and imprisonment for a year if he operated a steamboat without Fulton's license and permission.

Drastic as this law was, it still did not serve entirely to suppress competition in steam transportation. The legislature could not make the statute of 1811 retroactive in its operation and so its new provisions had no effect against the steamboats already built by the Albany company for use on the Hudson River, or against a boat called the *Vermont,* then running on Lake Champlain. Courts and legislature were doing all they could to restrict the new travel method, but the public took a decided stand against monopoly and gave the bulk of its patronage to the independent line. Advocates of the free and unrestricted use of steam travel asserted that Fulton had not invented steamboats and therefore had no legal or moral right to their exclusive employment, while the Livingston-Fulton company and its supporters denounced the intruders as rogues, rascals and law-breaking ingrates.[1] Cadwallader Colden describes the situation of 1811 and its effect in the following words:[2]

"The consequences which Messrs. Livingston and Fulton had anticipated from the establishment of the Albany boats were fully realized. There was a combination to break down Messrs. Livingston and Fulton, which it was obvious they could not resist. The owners of the Albany boats having their residence in this city, being intimately acquainted with all its inhabitants, and their influence extending to the remotest parts of the state, were enabled to divert almost all the passengers from the boats of Messrs. Livingston and Fulton. The Albany proprietors had not only their agents in every tavern in this city, but

---

[1] Livingston wrote two pamphlets at this time in support of the monopoly enjoyed by Fulton and himself, and discussing the relationship of national patents to state rights. Their titles are:

"An inquiry into the effect that a patent might have upon the exclusive privileges granted by the state to Messrs. Livingston and Fulton." New York; n.d.

"The right of a state to grant exclusive privileges in roads, bridges, canals, navigable waters, etc., vindicated by a candid examination of the grant from the state of New York to, and contract with Robert R. Livingston and Robert Fulton, for the exclusive navigation of vessels by steam or fire, for a limited time, on the waters of said state, and within the jurisdiction thereof." New York, 1811.

[2] See "A Vindication by Cadwallader D. Colden, of the Steam Boat Right granted by the State of New York," etc., Albany, 1818; pp. 147-8.

their emissaries on every road. These men made it their business, not only to seduce to the boats of their employers the persons who wanted a passage to New York, but to traduce Mr. Livingston and Mr. Fulton by the most wanton misrepresentations. Such an effect did this wicked industry produce, that the latter gentleman was looked upon by many who had hearkened to his calumniators as a vile impostor; and often have I listened with indignation to his calm and magnanimous recitals of the personal abuse and indignities he was daily accustomed to meet . . .

"I was once myself a witness of the effects of these measures. In the summer of 1811 I was a passenger on board the Paragon, then new and recently established, confessedly, in every respect, and particularly as to accommodation and speed, superior to the Albany boats. Chancellor Livingston was himself on board; and I recollect that Mr. Jacob Barker and his wife, and I think Mr. Walter Bowne, now a senator from the southern district, were also among the passengers, who in the whole were eighteen. We started a few minutes before one of the Albany boats. Something happened to our machinery before we had got far from the wharf, which stopped us, and enabled the Albany boat to go ahead. She must have had upwards of an hundred passengers on board: her decks were absolutely crowded. I wish you could at that moment have seen the Chancellor, and heard his reflections."

Livingston's attempt to enrich the country had taken a turn he and his colleague had not anticipated. A compromise was at last effected with the Albany line, and in that way the dispute was kept out of the national courts. The opposition boats continued to run.

During 1811 and 1812 Fulton built two vessels for Hudson River traffic[1] and a ferry boat to ply between New York and Jersey City. The demand for steam transportation continued to grow in other states, but though Fulton at first had no legal monopoly except in New York, and did not show inclination to prosecute under his United States patent, a fear of long and costly litigation served to retard the general introduction of vehicles so widely desired.

The adoption of steam power in transportation had

---

[1] They were the "Paragon," 331 feet long, and the "Firefly," of 118 feet length.

created new and unforeseen questions of relationship between individual states, as well as between them and the national government. The earlier giving of privileges to Fitch by various commonwealths was the basis of a widely entertained belief that persons or companies could properly hold franchises allowing them the exclusive right to supply steam-power transportation in states ·bestowing grants of that nature. Even the courts in many instances held a like view, though the rivers on which the new method of travel was to be used traversed more than one state or served as boundary lines. The whole matter was a complicated one, for it concerned not only the question of properly protecting inventive genius to whatever extent such protection was deserved, but also involved the harmony of Federal and state jurisdic-

117.—River types of 1825. From a drawing made by Captain Basil Hall of the British Navy during his trip through the United States. The man at the left is a steamboat pilot. Captain Hall describes the others as "backwoodsmen," but from their dress and demeanor it seems more probable they were men of some small town or settlement, belonging to that class which turned its hands, as need arose, to any one of a dozen tasks on land or water.

tions, and was seen to affect the country in a way not approached by any other phase of its internal affairs. Yet the chief men of the time displayed an inability to foresee in any appreciable degree the future growth of the nation or the inevitable elimination of state lines in all matters involving the social and industrial life of the republic. If there was any premonition of what the coming years held in store it lay in the minds of the multitude. The attitude of the people indicates that their perception was more trustworthy than the vision of their leaders. The darkness in which the chieftains groped can well be shown by quoting from the opinions of eminent judges who decided, in New York, that a state had power to halt or otherwise regulate all traffic at a state boundary line, no matter whence the traveller came or where he was going. In the case decided in Fulton's favor[1] respecting the right of New York to enjoin the operation of steamboats not licensed by him, Judge Yates said:

"It never could have been intended[2] that the navigable waters within the territory of the respective states should not be subject to their municipal regulations."

Chief Justice Kent declared in his opinion[3] that:

"Hudson river is the property of the people of this state, and the legislature have the same jurisdiction over it that they have over the land, or over any of our public highways, or over the waters of any of our rivers or lakes. They may, in their sound discretion, regulate and control, enlarge or abridge the use of its waters, and they are in the habitual exercise of that sovereign right . . . .

"It is said that a steamboat may become the vehicle of foreign commerce; and, it is asked, can then the entry of them into this state, or the use of them within it, be prohibited? I answer, yes, equally as we may prohibit the entry or use of slaves, or of pernicious animals, or an obscene

[1] Livingston against Van Ingen.
[2] By the Federal Constitution.
[3] Kent afterward became Chancellor. The opinion of the court was unanimous.

book, or infectious goods, or anything else that the legislature shall deem noxious or inconvenient."

Against such thunder-claps from the Sinai of the law did steam propelled vehicles struggle during the first years of public effort to procure their general introduction in America. The legal obstacles to the extensive use of steam transportation after the people had accepted it in principle were all traceable to the initial attitude of Congress in not securing the original invention from Fitch for free use, together with the theory of the various commonwealths that they could grant to him exclusive rights for the employment on navigable streams within their supposed jurisdiction, of a system of conveyance so profoundly affecting the whole country—a method of transportation destined to be the decisive instrument by which the continent should at last be conquered and all the states welded into one social unit.

Livingston and Fulton continued their effort to gain monopolistic control of steam propulsion throughout the United States, and in addition to building more boats and fighting competition in New York, they extended their activities in three other directions. They entered into negotiations with Louisiana in order to secure an exclusive foothold on the lower Mississippi, enlisted the services of Roosevelt[1] and sent him to the Ohio to study the adaptability of their enterprise to that stream, and began an advertising campaign in various cities offering to license steam craft on a percentage basis in localities to which they could not give personal attention. Their advertisement was published in numerous numbers of different newspapers,[2] and read:

[1] The Nicholas J. Roosevelt who had urged on Livingston the use of paddle-wheels in 1798, and whose assistant, Stoudinger, had become Fulton's chief aid in construction work.
[2] In New York it appeared in the "Evening Post," and in Philadelphia it was contained in the "General Advertiser."

STEAM BOATS

The undersigned patentees, anxious to extend the advantages of steam boats to every part of the United States where they may be useful and to prevent such of their fellow citizens as are not sufficiently acquainted with mechanics from being imposed upon by pretenders, who are ignorant of the principles, offer license to any respectable individual or company, who may be inclined to build Steam Boats, on any of the waters of the United States, the waters of New York, Mississippi and those already engaged, excepted—on the following conditions:

118.—The Ohio River steamer *Flora,* which was built at Pittsburgh in 1835. Her fate is unrecorded in Hall's list. The resemblance of the *Flora* to the *Belvidere* is noticeable. A contemporary pencil sketch.

The person or company taking a license and giving security for the performance of their contract, shall out of the gross receipts of each year, pay all the expenses which the Boat may incur within the year; and of the net profits, should there be sufficient, he or they shall take 10 percent for [of] the capital expended on the establishment.—But all profits exceeding 10 percent shall be equally divided, one half to the person or persons who built the boat, and one half to the undersigned patentees. Thus the year in which the boat clears 12 percent the owners will receive 11 and the patentees 1 percent and in like proportion for any greater sum. In the year that the boat clears 9¾, the patentees will have no dividend.

On these encouraging conditions, if any patriotic individuals wish to improve a navigation by establishing a Steam Boat, where the profits may not exceed 6 percent on the usual interest, such a laudable enterprise will not be checked by any claim of the patentees, the adventurers taking all profits until it exceeds 10 percent. In all cases, when required, the undersigned patentees will, whether for Passage, Merchandise or Ferry Boats, and at the expense of the adventurers, furnish correct drawings and rules for securing the most complete success to which this new art has arrived, and also have the engine and machinery made at their own works at New-York, and send their experienced engineers to put the work together and the boat in motion.

As success surpassing the most sanguine hope has attended the boats they have built, not one of them falling short, and several exceeding the calculations made on their speed and accommodations—as five years of practical experience may be considered to have given the undersigned more correct information on Steam Boats, than any other individuals possess—it is submitted to those who may wish to engage in such expensive operations, whether it will not be more prudent to proceed on grounds that are professed to be safe, than to travel an unbeaten path, or risque the penalties of the patent law, by intruding on the rights of the Inventors.

ROBERT R. LIVINGSTON.
ROBERT FULTON.

Little response was aroused by this offer. A few of the first steamboats of the East elsewhere than in New York were operated under license from Fulton, but public feeling against a monopoly of the sort claimed, together with a conviction that it could not long be upheld, and an aversion to the investment of money under the terms proposed, all served to defeat the aims of Livingston and his associate.

The effort to obtain exclusive privileges on the lower Mississippi was for a time more successful. Governor Claiborne of Louisiana met Fulton and Livingston in New York City in the autumn of 1810, and discussed with them the project of introducing steamboats on the Father of Waters. A summary of the negotiations there conducted was afterward made by Claiborne in a letter in which the governor said:[1]

"They entertained no doubt as to the ultimate success of the experiment; but spoke of the great expenditure and heavy advances with which it would be attended. These they were unwilling to encounter, unless previously assured of the protection of the legislature of the territory of Orleans. I enquired as to the nature of the protection desired, and was informed—'An exclusive privilege to navigate the waters of the Mississippi, passing through the territory of Orleans, with boats propelled by steam, was the only condition on which they would embark in this enterprise.' "

As a result of the discussion between the steamboat builders and the southern executive, a bill entitled, "An act granting to Robert R. Livingston and Robert Fulton the sole privilege of using steam-boats for a limited time in the territory," was passed on April 19th, 1811. Fulton had agreed that if the Mississippi monopoly was given to him he would send one or more boats to Louisiana as speedily as possible, and he proceeded to carry out his part of the bargain with expedition. As soon as news came that the legislature had passed the law demanded, he went with some workmen to Pittsburgh, and there,[2] in 1811, was built the *New Orleans,* the first steam craft to navigate any stream of the interior. The *New Orleans* was a small boat of a hundred tons burden, with a stern paddle-wheel and two masts.[3] She set out from Pittsburgh on her long voyage toward the South in October, and reached the city whose name she bore in the January following.

Not all the three months' interval was consumed by

[1] Written to J. Lynch, Esq., of New Orleans, on Jan. 25, 1817. Printed in full in Colden's "Vindication of the Steamboat Right;" Albany, 1818, pp. 168-70.

[2] During 1809, in behalf of Fulton and Livingston, Roosevelt had personally visited and studied the Ohio and Mississippi Rivers to discover whether steam navigation was practicable on them.
The "New Orleans" was built and launched under the direction of Roosevelt.

[3] Fulton still believed that the use of sails for auxiliary power would be necessary.

CHESTERVILLE
Ohio River Ky

119.—A small, stern-wheel, flat-bottomed boat of the Ohio River. It was this type of steam craft that pushed its way up the Muskingum, Hocking, Scioto, Licking, Miami, White, Wabash, and other Ohio tributaries before the days of the railroads. During the third decade such boats ascended the Wabash River to the town of Lafayette, in northern Indiana. Owing to the long disuse of those and other streams, some of them have come to be considered non-navigable, and their natural beds have been in part usurped by bridges and other building encroachments.

the voyage. The only persons on board were Roosevelt, his wife and family, a pilot, six members of the crew and some servants. Remarkably good speed was made from the starting-point to Louisville, and the progress of the boat down the Ohio to that city became a panorama of amazement and excitement over six hundred miles long. When she passed towns or settled communities all the people ran to the banks of the river and gazed awestruck at the spectacle, just as the Connecticut villagers had tumbled over one another to behold Governor Trumbull's chaise during the Revolution. They had heard of steamboats, knew such things existed in the East, and

390

had been told that one of them was being built at Pittsburgh. Yet no attempted mental picture of the much-
discussed contrivance could approach, in its overwhelming significance, a sight of the actuality. Imagination and
anticipation had aroused the interest of the people, but
the on-rushing truth brought a sense of stupefaction.
Long after the smoke from her iron chimney had vanished in the air, and for hours after the clanking of her
engine had become a whisper in the ears of memory, the
people stood at the edge of the waters they had fought
so long, looking blanking down the river. Something
had passed them, and yesterday was very far away.

Louisville was reached late at night, after all the town
was wrapped in peaceful slumber. On approaching the
shore the accumulated steam in the boilers was permitted
to escape through the exhaust pipe. Never before had
the resultant roar of that operation been heard on the
Ohio, and as the loud reverberating blast rolled through
the little city, sleep fled from its habitations and the
population with one accord sat upright in the darkness,
wondering why the crack of doom was so long drawn
out and how soon the angel Gabriel would follow it in
person. Alarm was general, but as the midnight cry
of a new power died away to a low muttering, and then
ceased altogether, assurance came again and news regarding the real cause of the disturbance soon spread through
the community.

Shallow water at the rapids detained the steamboat
for three weeks, during which time she made several trips
to Cincinnati and return, but during the last days of
November the southward voyage was again begun.

CHAPTER XXI

EARLY STEAMBOATS OF THE WEST — SHREVE AND HIS
CRAFT — THE NEW YORK COMPANY TRIES TO STOP
IT FROM RUNNING — SHREVE WINS AND THE DEVEL-
OPMENT OF THE WEST PROCEEDS — CAUSES OF DELAY
IN THE EAST — FULTON'S OFFER TO THORNTON —
NICHOLAS ROOSEVELT MAKES A FEW REMARKS —
THE WALK-IN-THE-WATER — WAR BETWEEN SAIL-
ING PACKETS AND STEAM CRAFT — NEW ENGLAND
STATES TRY TO KEEP NEW YORK STEAMBOATS OUT OF
THEIR WATERS — MONOPOLY FINALLY OVERTHROWN
— THE USE OF STEAM IN TRANSPORTATION MADE
FREE TO ALL AFTER NEARLY FORTY YEARS OF SPECIAL
PRIVILEGE

THE arrival of the vessel at New Orleans was an
occasion for a popular demonstration, and the boat
was at once employed in regular trips between the Louisiana metropolis and Natchez in Mississippi. But so abrupt
and uncanny was the contrast between the steamboat and
those craft she was intended to supplant that the public
held aloof from her in the bestowal of their patronage until several trips had been made. She seemed too much of
a miracle, at first, and many travellers and merchants
preferred to use the barges and flatboats with which they
were familiar until the new system of transportation had
somewhat demonstrated its reliability in practise. The
New Orleans, like all other early steamboats, was a flimsy

fabric laden with danger both from explosion and fire, and the careful business men of the South, though recognizing the value of steam propulsion, were not blind to those defects in its application which were later to result in catastrophes that appalled the country. The average up-stream speed of the *New Orleans* was about three miles an hour. She continued in service until wrecked by a snag in 1814.

The second steamboat in western waters was the *Comet*, built on the Ohio at Brownsville, Pennsylvania, in 1813, by Daniel French, who had obtained a patent in 1809. The *Comet* went to Louisville in 1813 and descended to New Orleans during the following year. After two voyages to Natchez she was dismantled and her engine was set up in a cotton factory.

The *Vesuvius*, built at Pittsburgh by Fulton's workmen in 1814, for his Louisiana company, was the third western boat, and she reached New Orleans in the early summer of that year. On her first north-bound voyage she ran on a sand-bar, where she reposed from July until December, and then returned to New Orleans. The *Vesuvius* plied intermittently between the southern city and Natchez in 1815 and 1816, was burned, raised, refitted, and finally fell to pieces in 1819, after a long career typical of the most venerable and fortunate boats of the time.

Number four of the early western steam craft was the *Enterprise*, built by French at Brownsville in 1814. After two trips to Louisville and return she proceeded to New Orleans and in the spring of 1815 went back to Louisville again, being the first boat to travel up-stream between the two cities by means of steam power. The trip was accomplished in twenty-five days, but was not accepted by the people of the interior as a final and de-

WESTERN WATER STEAM BOAT

Published by John Weale 59 High Holborn, 1838.
Stevenson's Sketch of the Civil Engineering of North America.

120.—First-class steamboat of the Ohio and Mississippi River trade in 1838. In boats of this sort the trip from Cincinnati to New Orleans required about seven or eight days. From a drawing by the Scotch engineer David Stevenson, in 1837.

cisive proof that steam craft were dependable for use against the river currents. She had ascended the Mississippi and Ohio during a flood, and avoided the opposing flow by travelling most of the way over inundated country covered by slack water. So the people still refused to give an unqualified verdict that the Mississippi had been conquered.

Such was the state of public opinion when Henry Shreve built the double-deck steamboat *Washington* at Wheeling, Virginia, in 1816, equipped his boat with high-pressure engines constructed by French, and embodied numerous technical improvements in the vessel and her machinery. The *Washington* was taken to New Orleans in the fall of 1816, and excited the admiration of the Louisiana city. While lying there the boat was inspected by Edward Livingston, brother and business representative of the Chancellor, who said to Shreve: "You deserve well of your country, young man, but we shall be compelled to beat you if we can."[1] On March 12, 1817, the *Washington* left Louisville for New Orleans on her second voyage, and accomplished the round trip in forty-one days. About twelve days were consumed in descending the rivers, and twenty-five in returning against the normal currents of the streams. From this upward passage may be dated the commencement of general steam navigation in the Mississippi valley. It dispelled the last doubt of the people that steam was the master of the mighty river, and Shreve was hailed as a hero. The population of the Mississippi valley was as excited over his accomplishment as it had been over Jackson's victory at New Orleans. Louisville greeted him on his return with a reception and a public dinner, and he made a speech in which he boldly predicted that the time would come when people could travel from New Orleans to Louisville in ten days. His hearers thought he was a trifle optimistic, but applauded him just the same.

No sooner had news of the *Washington's* performance spread through the Ohio valley than numerous steamboats were begun, but their appearance in large numbers was halted for two years more by the fear of legal proceedings against them. Robert Fulton had died in 1815, but his company was still active in its efforts to establish a monopoly in steam transportation, and did not confine itself to verbal warnings. Edward Livingston's threat was carried into effect. On the return of Shreve and his craft to New Orleans the *Washington* was seized by the sheriff at the instigation of the New York company and an action to prevent its further operation was begun in the courts of

---

[1] Meaning that the Livingston-Fulton company would try by legal means to prevent Shreve from running his boat.

Louisiana. The decision was in favor of Shreve, and the southern monopoly asserted by the Livingston-Fulton association was declared to be unconstitutional and void. In 1819 the claims of the New York men were abandoned as far as western waters were concerned, and steamboat building on the Ohio and Mississippi was resumed, without fear, by all who desired to engage in the enterprise. From that time the development of the interior continued with increased momentum. Cincinnati's first steamboat, the original *General Pike,* was put into commission in the year last named and marked the appearance of the pioneer steam transportation company of the West.[1] She conveyed her passengers to Louisville in thirty-one hours.[2]

For a dozen years or more after 1807 the use of steam transportation in the East spread even less rapidly than in the West. Two causes that contributed to delay in adopting the new vehicles—fear of lawsuits and dissatisfaction with the percentage terms offered by Livingston and Fulton—have been mentioned. Still other powerful agencies operating in the same way were the opposition of established travel systems such as stage-coach lines and sailing packets, the jealousies of the different states, and the actual taxation of travellers on steamboats. Yet none of these things, nor all of them put together, could prevail against the manifest advantages that lay in the use of steam power. Various small boats were now and then built in

---

[1] The United States Mail Line between Cincinnati, Louisville and St. Louis.

[2] The increase in the speed of travel throughout the interior between the days of the flatboat and the general introduction of railroads in that part of the country can be shown in a broad way by a table giving the time consumed in a steamboat trip from Louisville to New Orleans at various dates between 1815 and 1853. Such figures follow:

Year	Steamboat	Days	Hrs.	Min.	Year	Steamboat	Days	Hrs.	Min
1815	Enterprise	25	2	40	1840	Shippen	5	14	00
1817	Washington	25	0	00	1844	Sultana	5	12	00
1817	Shelby	20	4	20	1849	Bostona	5	8	00
1819	Paragon	18	10	00	1851	Belle Key	4	23	00
1828	Tecumseh	8	4	00	1852	Reindeer	4	20	45
1834	Tuscarora	7	16	00	1852	Eclipse	4	18	00
1837	Gen. Brown	6	22	00	1853	Shotwell	4	10	20
1837	Sultana	6	15	00	1853	Eclipse	4	9	30

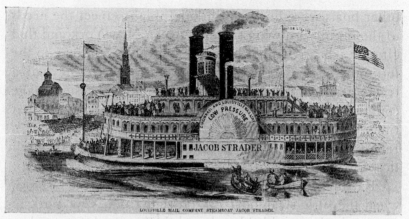

121.—The *Jacob Strader,* built in 1854 for service between Cincinnati and Louisville, was the finest boat yet seen on the Ohio. She cost $200,000, and developed a speed of 18 miles an hour. The words "low pressure" on the paddle-box were to reassure the public against the probability of explosions such as were then frequent on boats using high pressure boilers.

different localities, and they prospered when not opposed by narrow-sightedness or legal obstacles which they could not combat.

Philadelphia's first boat to be run for public patronage since Fitch's packet of 1788-1790 was the *Phoenix,* whose building by John Stevens, in 1807, has been related. For a time she was operated between New Jersey towns and New York City, but Fulton's opposition at last shut her out of New York state waters, and she was taken to Philadelphia, thus performing the first ocean voyage undertaken by a steam craft. After reaching the Delaware River, in 1809, the *Phoenix* ran between Philadelphia and Bordentown, carrying passengers who were moving to and fro across New Jersey from that town by stage-coach. She had thirty-seven sleeping berths. Warning of her impending departure on a trip was given by the captain, who stuck to the custom of the early keel-boats and blew on a long tin horn. During the next ten or twelve years several other boats were built at Philadelphia[1] to meet the needs of the rapidly growing travel between New York and that city. Each carried her passengers up the Delaware to the terminus of the stage-coach line with which she had a traffic arrangement. There were a number of such stage companies operating vehicles across New Jersey by that time, and so energetically did they seek patrons that a rate war occasionally broke out, and the price of a through ticket to New York dropped to a dollar.

Baltimore entered on the era of steam travel in 1813, when the little steamboat *Eagle* went from New York to operate in the neighborhood, and three years later another boat, the *New Jersey,* arrived at the Maryland city.

All five of Fulton's early boats on the Hudson and Jersey waters[2] remained rather slow of motion and somewhat awkward in operation. He recognized the desirability of obtaining greater speed if possible, and in 1811 wrote a letter on the subject to Dr. William Thornton,[3] in which he said:

"I shall be happy to have some conversation with you on your steam-boat inventions and experience. Although I do not see by what means a boat containing one hundred tons of merchandise can be driven six miles an hour in still water, yet when you assert perfect confidence in such success, there may be something more in your combinations than I am aware of. . . . If you succeed to run six miles an hour in still water with one hundred tons of merchandise, I will contract to reimburse the cost of the boat, and to give you one hundred and fifty thousand dollars for your patent; or, if you convince me of the success by drawings or demonstrations, I will join you in the expense and profits."[4]

By the year 1816 there were but eight boats on the Hudson, and the fare from New York to Albany was seven

---

[1] Some few of them were the "Philadelphia," the "Pennsylvania" and the "Aetna." The "Aetna" blew up in New York harbor in 1824, with loss of life.
[2] The "Clermont" (1807); "Raritan" (1807); "Car of Neptune" (1808); "Paragon" (1811); and "Firefly" (1812).
[3] Fitch's old business associate.
[4] Preble's "History," p. 64. Thornton, in speaking of this matter says: "I agreed to his proposal at once, but he declined to write the terms." Thornton's "Short Account," Albany, 1818, p. 9.

dollars. Passengers for way stations paid at the rate of about five cents a mile, but no ticket was sold for less than a dollar, no matter how short the distance its purchaser intended to go. Complicated legal controversies were still raging in Connecticut, New York and New Jersey over the subject of steamboat patents, and in the same year

PUBLIC LANDING, CINCINNATI.

122.—A view of the river front at Cincinnati during the period in which steamboat travel and traffic reached the height of their importance. Cincinnati was then the principal city of the interior, and, with Louisville and Pittsburgh, had been most affected by the adoption and spread of steam transportation. Along the levee at each city there constantly lay an unbroken line of steamboats about a mile in length.

of 1816 Nicholas Roosevelt came forward with a claim to the invention of paddle-wheels, which he had proposed to Livingston. He had taken out a patent in 1814, and now published in various newspapers the following advertisement:

STEAMBOAT NOTICE

"All persons are hereby informed that I claim the right of Inventor of Vertical Wheels, as now generally used for Steam Boats throughout the United States, having been first used, after my invention, in the North River Steam Boat, by Messrs. Livingston and Fulton.

"I have obtained a patent in due form of law, for my invention, which is dated the first day of Dec., 1814.

"No other person in the United States has any Patent, but myself, for the invention of Vertical Wheels. Having obtained a legal title to the sole use of steamboats with such wheels, I hereby forewarn all persons from using them hereafter without license from me. The patent and evidence of my right are in the hands of Wm. Griffith, Esq., of the City of Burlington, my Counsel-at-Law.

"On this subject, so very important to me (being the only real and efficient invention since Fitch's boat), I do not by this notice challenge controversy, but am prepared to meet it in any form. My object is to make known, that I am the Inventor, and have the Patent right. Individuals or companies who use such wheels without my license after this, will be prosecuted under the Law of Congress, for damages amounting to the profits of the boat. Licenses will be sold under me at moderate rates, and warranted.

"NICHOLAS J. ROOSEVELT.

"BURLINGTON, N. J., 4th March, 1816."[1]

After this public notice by Roosevelt, Fulton never urged his claim, but from that moment abandoned it.[2] It seems a justifiable inference, in view of the published statements made by Roosevelt and his manner of wording the advertisement, that there had been some sort of a falling out between him and the Livingston-Fulton organization during the time that had intervened since his activity in building boats at Pittsburgh for the company in 1811. At any rate Roosevelt's sudden appearance in the field as still another from whom permission must be obtained before steamboats could be built confused the public, instilled an additional fear into the minds of possible investors and thereby served further to retard the introduction of the new transportation device.

Of the ones who did take out licenses for the building of steamboats some dealt with the Livingston-Fulton company and others with the new claimant. Among those

---

[1] For a full account of the relationship between Roosevelt's patent and later developments in the legal fight over steamboats, see J. H. B. Latrobe's "Lost Chapter in the History of the Steamboat."

[2] Phraseology of Latrobe, p. 8. In 1826 the facts were submitted as a case-at-law, to William Wirt, for an opinion, and Wirt said: "On the above statement I am of opinion that the patent to Roosevelt is valid." Latrobe's "Lost Chapter," pp. 7-8.

Engraved expressly for the Progress at the Republic and entered according to Act of Congress

VIEW OF THE PUBLIC LANDING AT LOUISVILLE, KY.

123.—Similar aspect of Louisville's water front at the same epoch. Also showing two flatboats, which type of water vehicle had by that time almost disappeared.

who paid Roosevelt for the privilege of operating steam craft were Aaron Ogden, who established a vessel between Elizabethtown and New York, and the Shrewsbury and Jersey Stage Company, which ran a boat in connection with its land coaches. After Fulton's death the company organized by Chancellor Livingston and himself gave up

124.—A Mississippi steam packet with a cargo of cotton. In case of boiler explosion, collision, or other accident, the cotton bales sometimes served as rafts to which the people clung until they drifted ashore or were picked up.

the effort to secure half the profits on all earnings above ten per cent. under licenses granted by it. No public announcement respecting a modification of operating terms for steamboats appears to have been made, but such details were left to private negotiation. The company was trying as best it could to retain the semblance of monopoly still remaining, and made whatever arrangement was possible in each case. In 1821, for example, it entered into an agreement with several men living near Lake George, in

New York state, giving to them the exclusive right of steam navigation on that sheet of water, and exacting nothing from the owners of the boat until eighteen per cent. of all money invested had been taken in. After that amount had been cleared, half of any further profit was to go to the licensing company.[1]

Another pioneer steamboat whose origin and operation were somewhat related to the Fulton company was the *Walk-in-the-Water,* first steam vessel on Lake Erie. She was built near Buffalo in 1818, left Buffalo for the first time on August 23, 1818, arrived at Cleveland amid much popular excitement on the 25th, and reached Detroit, her destination, on the 28th. During her progress through Detroit River hundreds of Indians lined the shores of the strait and cried out in amazement. They had been told the white men would send among them a ship drawn through the water by sturgeons, and there, before their eyes, was proof of the incredible tale. Never more would they presume to oppose a race who could do such a thing —who could harness even the fish of the sea to do their bidding. The red men were soon disabused of their first belief, but an understanding that fire and machinery were used in propelling the boat produced an impression no less profound. "We are children," they said.

The builder of the *Walk-in-the-Water*[2] had paid the Livingston-Fulton company a sum now unknown for the privilege of operating the vessel, and all four men who at various times commanded her were brought from previous service on the Hudson River boats of the company. She cost about $50,000, had two masts, and paddle-wheels

[1] The contract here summarized was contained in a document in the collection of Dr. Romeyn Beek, of Albany, and later in possession of Mrs. Pierre Van Cortlandt. It was first published in the "Magazine of American History," Vol. xviii, No. 1 (July, 1887).
[2] Dr. J. B. Stewart of New York City. For a full history of the boat, see "Proceedings of the Buffalo Historical Society" for 1864; the "Detroit Gazette" of 1818-1821, and the "Michigan Pioneer Society Collections," Vol. 18.

403

sixteen feet in diameter. In still water she could make
nearly eight miles an hour, but owing to the strength of
the current at Buffalo she sometimes had to be hauled by
oxen at the end of a tow-line for a considerable distance,
when leaving port, before trusting to her own machinery.
As many as a hundred and fifty passengers were at times
aboard her. She continued to run between Buffalo, Cleveland, Sandusky, Detroit, and Mackinac until October of
1821, when she was wrecked in a gale near Buffalo. Her
usual time between Buffalo and Detroit was three days,
and the cost of a trip between those two cities was eighteen
dollars.[1]

In New England a number of unusual conditions and
circumstances marked the early days of steam travel. The
first steamboat of Boston[2] was a commercial failure. She
was built in 1817 to run between that city and Salem, and
on her initial trip—an excursion—something happened to
the machinery and her passengers had to be sent back to
their homes in stage-coaches. The accident was a severe
blow to her prestige, and the stage-coach lines thereafter
fought her by a campaign designed to shake public faith
in the new travel method. As a consequence the boat was
not patronized, and her owners decided to send her to
Charleston, South Carolina. On the trip toward that city
she was lost.

During the same year of 1817 Rhode Island beheld
the first steamboat to appear in that part of the world
since the days when Elijah Ormsbee built and operated
his little craft, back in 1792. In 1817 the Livingston-
Fulton company sent its boat, the *Firefly,* to run between
Newport and Providence. On her arrival at Pawtucket

---

[1] The spread of steam power on the Great Lakes was slow. In 1821 there was one
steamboat on those waters; in 1831, eleven; in 1836, forty-five; in 1847, ninety-three.
[2] Called the "Massachusetts." She ran about 8 miles an hour

from the Hudson she was greeted by the usual multitude eager to get its first sight of the new conveyance, and those of the younger generation marvelled as befitted the occasion. But among the throng were a few who said: "We have seen a boat moved by steam before." The *Fire-fly* was a slow and awkward little vessel, full of machinery, noisy in her operation, and she required twenty-eight hours to reach Newport from New York on her first trip.

At this time—1817—a large part of the travel between New England and the Middle States was carried on by regular lines of sailing packets. These were swift, beautifully modelled sloops of about a hundred tons burden, elaborately fitted with interior mahogany furnishings. Their hulls were painted in gay colors and sometimes even inlaid with designs made of polished hardwoods. The main cabin of a packet was about twelve feet square, and from it opened small but comfortable staterooms. Excellent meals were served, with wines and liquors at dinner and supper. The fare from Rhode Island ports to New York on a packet was ten dollars, and with favoring winds a passage was often made in eighteen hours. Similar vessels plied between all Atlantic coast ports. They usually ran once a week, and were deservedly popular.

When the *Firefly* appeared in Rhode Island and challenged the Newport and Providence packets for the passenger trade between those towns, the sailboats accepted the gauge of battle. Their agents stood on the very wharf used by the steamboat, crying aloud that the packets would take travellers from one city to the other for twenty-five cents, and refund the money if they did not land their passengers before the steamboat did. The sailing craft gained the victory. They were more than a match for the mechanical vessel in point of speed as well as in comfort, and the *Firefly* soon gave up the contest. No sooner did tidings of success reach the packet men than they assembled in convention, denounced the

Steamboat wooding at night

125.—Nearly every settler along the banks of the Mississippi chopped down trees and maintained a wood-pile, in order that he might sell fuel to passing steamboats. A boat signalled its need by whistling, and its crew carried the wood aboard while the owner of the fuel kept account of the amount taken. A vendor sometimes kept his reckoning by moving his hand down a series of notches cut in a long pole.

outrage so successfully foiled and adjourned to a tavern to celebrate their triumph over all innovations in general and despicable steam in particular. That was the last of steamboats in Rhode Island for four years.

Connecticut's reception of steamboats from New York

was even more hard-hearted than the greeting given to them by Rhode Island. The first steamer sent to Connecticut by the monopoly-holding company was the *Fulton*.[1] She was built in 1813-1814 for use on Long Island Sound, but was run on the Hudson until the second war with England was over. In 1815 she made a number of trips from New York to New Haven and New London with such small success that the service was discontinued. The people of the New England communities were angered by the law that excluded from New York waters the boats of any other state unless licensed by the monopoly, and they in turn refused to patronize any steam vessels from the neighboring inhospitable commonwealth. Two or three small independent steamboats were built and operated on the Connecticut River in the years immediately following 1815, and among them was the *Oliver Ellsworth*,[2] a craft in whose success the Connecticut public took a keen interest. The boiler of this boat exploded in 1818, killing a number of passengers. The state legislature happened to be in session at the time, and one excited man, eager to spread the deplorable intelligence, rushed from the street into the Assembly Chamber in the midst of a debate and screamed: "The *Eliver Ollsworth* has biled her buster!"

In 1821, the Livingston-Fulton company again made an attempt to capture the passenger traffic between New York City and New England, and began the renewed service with an excursion to Providence and Newport, using the *Fulton*. No steamboat had visited those cities from other localities since the *Firefly* had been beaten by the packet men in 1817. She entered the Rhode Island

---

[1] Dimensions, 134 feet long, 30 feet wide, 9 feet depth of hold. Her paddle-wheels were 15 feet in diameter and she carried a mast and sails.
[2] Named after the eminent Connecticut Justice.

harbors with a brass band blaring on her deck and her passengers shouting in response to the tumult ashore. The trip was a success, though for some reason no further voyages were made for nearly a year. Steam travel between New York and the Connecticut cities was resumed by the company in 1822,[1] and immediately met a violent popular hostility. Resentment at New York's attitude with respect to the use of steamboats had still further increased, and in retaliation the legislature passed an act forbidding the use of Connecticut waters to any vessel with a Livingston-Fulton license. By this law the boats of the monopoly were driven from New Haven and New London. Notice that steam travel between New York and Connecticut had ceased was published in the newspapers in June of 1822.

No sooner was the company ousted from Connecticut than it turned once more to Rhode Island, and the *Fulton* and *Connecticut* were again sent to Providence and Newport.[2] Neither boat had staterooms, and nearly all the space on board had to be filled with the enormous quantities of wood necessary to keep the fires going. The trip between New York and Newport required from eighteen to forty hours, according to the weather. With the resumption of steam service to Rhode Island the packet men rallied a second time in defense of their ancient privilege, and their influence caused the introduction of a bill in the state assembly imposing a tax of fifty cents on each steamboat traveller and restricting the landing, on Rhode Island territory, of steamboat passengers from another state. This bill passed the state senate but failed to receive the approval of the lower house. A majority of its members were of opinion that the pro-

[1] With the two boats "Fulton" and "Connecticut."
[2] The fare to Newport from New York was $9; to Providence, $10.

126.—A Mississippi wood-seller and his family in trouble during a season of high water. In those days the dwellers along the river had no advance knowledge concerning the time when the crest of the flood would pass, and not infrequently hesitated too long before seeking to escape.

posed law was unconstitutional. The steamboats therefore continued to run, and the days of the old packets were numbered. For a time, however—because of their comfort—sailing vessels still held a share of the public patronage in New England. The *Fulton* and *Connecticut* each contained almost as much machinery as a small factory, and made a most direful noise when in operation. The cog-wheel that turned the paddles of the *Fulton* had teeth five inches long, and so slow was her speed that she once consumed five hours in going from Providence to Newport. When she made a trip without using sails, her captain boasted of it.

Maine's first steamboat was the hull of an old, flat-bottomed sailboat in which Captain Seward Porter, of Portland, placed a little engine in the summer of 1822.[1] It ran to North Yarmouth and other near-by towns, and so strong was the effect of the innovation on popular imagination that even the local constable, Lewis Pease, burst into song at its creation and wrote a poem in honor of the advance in economic evolution. The stanza went thus:

> "A fig for all your clumsy craft,
> "Your pleasure boats and packets;
> "The steamboat lands you safe and soon
> "At Mansfield's, Trott's or Brackets'."

"For tickets," said the steamboat advertisement, "apply to Mr. A. W. Tinkham's store."

Porter's vessel was an emphatic success. Within two years he had a new boat with a speed of ten miles an hour,[2] and put her to work between Portland and Boston. She

---

[1] Its trips were advertised in the "Portland Argus" of that year.
[2] Built at New York.

TERRIBLE CONFLAGRATION AND DESTRUCTION OF THE STEAMBOAT "NEW JERSEY,"

On the Delaware River, above Smith's Island, on the Night of March 15th, between 8 and 9 o'clock, in which dreadful calamity over 50 Lives are supposed to have been lost.   F. Lith. Col. Amer.

From 1840 to 1858 pictures like this were hastily published after important steamboat disasters as a protest against them and a warning to travellers.

Names.		Where Built.	When Built.	Tonn.	Date of loss.	How destroyed.
Eliza	h	Cincinnati	1821	65		Worn out.
Emerald	h	Cumb'ld R.	1824	150	1830	Worn out.
Echo	h	Pittsburgh	1826	150		Worn out.
Erie	h	do.	1826	125		Worn out.　　　[Chain.
Essex	h	do.	1827	135	1829	Broke in two, on Great
Emigrant	h	Cincinnati	1829	76	1832	Sunk by ice.
Experiment	h	Browns'ille	1830	85		
Enterprise	k	Pittsburgh	1830	150		
Eagle	h	do.	1830	40		
Express	h	Cincinnati	1831	105		
Exchange	h	Louisville	1830	32		Abandoned.
Enterprise	h	Shoustown	1830	111	1832	Snagged.
Envoy	h	Cincinnati	1831	96		
Elk	h	Browns'ille	1829	60	1833	Abandoned.
Emigrant	h	Cincinnati	1832	90	1832	Lost by ice.
Erin		Covington	1833	100		
Erie	h	Browns'ille	1827	52		Worn out.
Eclipse	h	Marietta	1832	60		
El'n Douglass	h	N. Albany	1833	266		
Exchange		Cookstown	1835	68		[vieve.
Franklin		Pittsburgh	1817	150	1822	Snagged, near St. Gen-
Frankfort		Ky. River	1818	250	1822	Worn out.
Fayette	h	Louisville	1819	314		Worn out.
Fidelity	l	New York	1821	150		Destroyed.
Florence		Clarksville	1822	60		Destroyed.
Fire Fly		Louisville		19		Destroyed.
Florida	l	Pittsburgh	1826	278		Destroyed.
Fort Adams				125		Burnt.
Floridn	l	Cincinnati	1826	250		Burnt, on Mobile river.
Feliciana	h	Philadelpha	1820	408		Still running.
Favorite	h	Pittsburgh	1822	260		Worn out.
Florence	h	Silver Cr'k.	1822	60		Worn out.
Fanny	l	New York	1823	120	1827	Went back to N. York.
Friendship	h	Pittsburgh	1825	200		Worn out.
Fame	h	do.	1826	170	1830	Worn out.
Facility	l	Cincinnati	1827	117		Worn out.
Fairy	l	do.	1827	80	1831	Sunk.
Forrester	h	Browns'ille	1827	100	1833	Burnt, on Cumberland.
Farmer	l	Cincinnati	1831	277		
Freedom	h	Wheeling	1831	135		
Favorite	h	Nashville	1831	155	1832	Sunk, robbed & burnt.
Friend	h	Cincinnati	1831	118		
Falcon	h	do.	1832	91	1833	Sunk by S. B. Senator.
Fairy Queen	h	Brush Ck.	1832	66		
Friendship	h	Cincinnati	1833	100		
Free Trader	h	Pittsburgh	1832	109		

127.—Sample page from James Hall's "List of Western Steamboats," giving information regarding the age, size, length of use and fate of about seven hundred river vessels. From Hall's "The West: Its Commerce and Navigation."

was called the *Patent*,[1] cost $20,000, carried a mast and sails, and had a separate cabin for women.[2]

During the years and events just reviewed the monopoly in New York state continued to control traffic on the Hudson without serious opposition, and the attitude of that commonwealth with respect to the new travel method was made still more interesting by its imposition of a tax on people who patronized steam craft. In 1819 the comptroller of the state reported that the tax on steamboat passengers in 1817 and 1818 had amounted to $41,440. Only $3,819.82 had been required for its collection, leaving net profits to the state of $37,620.18. A steamboat traveller who made a trip of more than a hundred miles paid a tax of one dollar; to go any distance between thirty and a hundred miles cost him fifty cents. He could travel twenty-nine miles by steam power without paying any tax whatever.

But at last the long period of monopolies and exclusive grants for the use of steam power in water transportation was coming to a close, and a protracted triangular dispute between New York, New Jersey and the Federal government was the indirect means of bringing it to an end. New Jersey had early enacted a measure against New York steamboats in retaliation for the attitude of the larger state, and in 1814 Aaron Ogden, governor of New Jersey, again planned an invasion of the waters of New York Bay in an effort to upset the Fulton-Livingston claims. He had long been the proprietor of "an ancient and accustomed ferry" between Elizabethtown Point and New York City, and, in order still further to strengthen

---

[1] Doubtless indicating the payment of a license fee either to the Livingston-Fulton company or to Roosevelt.
[2] The "Boston Courier" of August 12, 1824, describes her first trip. In 1825 the steamboat fare from Boston to Portland, with meals, was $5; to Bath, $6; to Augusta, $7; to Eastport, $11.

his position, he also secured a coasting license from the United States and an assignment to himself, from Fitch's heirs, of the original patent granted to Fitch and all national and state rights of every sort in connection with it. Having so fortified his demand he presented to the New York legislature a statement asserting a right to run steam ferry boats over his route,[1] declaring that such service would tend to the public accommodation, and asking for action on his petition.

Ogden's memorial was considered by a committee of the New York legislature[2] which finally reported that the steamboat had been patented by Fitch, that Fitch or his assignee had all rights to the invention during the life of the patent, that the use of the contrivance afterward fell to the public, and that the exclusive legislation of New York in favor of Fulton and Livingston was unconstitutional and oppressive. This report was rejected by the New York senate, and Ogden was not granted the privilege he asked. Ogden then brought the matter before New Jersey's legislature, but there he was also defeated, and so powerful were the influences arrayed against him that New Jersey even repealed the former measure which excluded New York steamboats from its waters. A compromise between the Fulton-Livingston company and Ogden was then effected, the quarrel was kept out of the courts, and a decisive pronouncement on the question was once more avoided.

So the controversy hung for another ten years, with Federal jurisdiction over navigable waters still denied and fought by New York, until 1824. In that year it again arose in an acute form and was contested to a finish. A

---

[1] As above described.
[2] The chairman of the committee was William Duer, later president of Columbia College. Duer's active interest in the steamboat question, as a historical subject, dated from the events under consideration.

prominent business man and lawyer of Georgia, Thomas Gibbons by name, had settled in Elizabethtown, and there he invested some money in a steam ferry to New York in opposition to the one run by Ogden. Gibbons was convinced that New York's attitude could not be successfully maintained, and he resolved to embark in whatever course of litigation might be necessary to prove the soundness of his belief. In order to involve the general government in the contention he also obtained a coasting license from the Federal authorities. Ogden promptly obtained an injunction against Gibbons' ferry boat on the ground that his own rights had been invaded, and the Court of Errors sustained him because the case, in its opinion, presented no conflict between state and national laws and jurisdiction.

Gibbons appealed to the Supreme Court of the United States. He secured the services of Daniel Webster as counsel to aid the Attorney-General,[1] and Webster's argument at last placed before the country's highest tribunal a clear picture of the existing and intolerable conditions. Judgment, as pronounced by Chief Justice John Marshall, was rendered for Gibbons, and by that decision the navigable waters of the nation were at last opened to the free use of all men. State lines as a barrier to the movement of the people were swept away, steam vehicles were removed from classification with obscene books and contagious diseases, and the principle of unhampered interstate travel and transportation and commerce by mechanical methods was established.

[1] Wirt.

CHAPTER XXII

CONDITIONS JUST PRIOR TO THE FIRST APPEARANCE
OF A MODERN TRAVEL AND TRANSPORTATION SYS-
TEM — ORIGIN OF THE FEDERAL DOMAIN OF PUBLIC
LANDS — FINAL PHASE OF THE CONTEST BETWEEN
RED MEN AND WHITE — ATTITUDE OF THE GOVERN-
MENT TOWARD THE INDIANS BETWEEN 1795 AND
1830 — RECOGNITION OF INDIAN SOVEREIGNTY — CAU-
CASIAN SETTLEMENTS SEPARATED FROM EACH OTHER
BY NATIVE TERRITORIES — PERMISSION FOR WHITE
TRAVEL THROUGH INDIAN REGIONS OBTAINED BY
TREATY — HOW THE SCATTERED SECTIONS OF THE
NEW REPUBLIC WERE JOINED BY NATIVE CONSENT —
SOME RESULTS OF THE WHITE DIPLOMACY — GENERAL
HARRISON'S REPORT OF 1801

WHILE the people had thus been engaged in their
effort to secure an unhampered use of steam propelled vehicles on the natural water systems of the country
there had also been progressing a complex series of other
events destined to have powerful influence on the land
movement of the population and on all future phases of
their development. Those things had to do with the
acquirement of the Federal domain—or public lands—
the final phase of the conflict between red men and white,
and the acts of government[1] which accompanied a steadily
increasing realization that river transportation alone

[1] Both national and state.

415

could not meet the needs of the rapidly growing nation. The matters about to be discussed, in a word, reveal the methods by which all territory east of the Mississippi was unified under Caucasian influence, first united by overland highways, and finally brought into a situation which permitted the creation of a modern travel and transportation system in the shape of turnpikes, canals and railroads.

It is possible that the conditions now to be outlined, and certain described events, policies and acts which grew out of those conditions, have had a more intimate relation to the later affairs of the republic and the character of its inhabitants than is ordinarily accorded to them. The manner in which the American republic grew during the years now under review—from 1795 until about 1835 or 1840—and some of the methods by which its government obtained for its citizens the right to travel and spread over the face of the country, constitute a phase of history that has been somewhat neglected.[1] The generation and a half embraced within the years specified was a period of national character formation; a time during which the young eagle outgrew its pin-feathers, tested its wings and soared away toward an unknown destiny. We now seek to discover the direction of its first flight.

The military and political battles of the forty or forty-five years subsequent to 1795 are familiar, but they are not the basic annals of that epoch. Its real history, as is the case with respect to all periods of all nations, is a tale of the ambitions, aversions, high endeavor, selfishness and intrigues of men; not a record of the desperate struggles in which those human qualities reach brief but spectacular culmination. So for the purpose of these pages we need only concern ourselves with certain manifestations of the

[1] When compared with the attention and literature devoted to other epochs both before and after the one mentioned.

BY WILLIAM HENRY HARRISON,

GOVERNOR OF THE INDIANA TERRITORY, AND SUPERINTENDANT OF INDIAN AFFAIRS.

Whereas *Alexis Picard* of the county of *Knox* has made application for permiſſion to trade with the *Miami Potto* nation of Indians, and ha*s* given bond according to law, for the due obſervance of all the laws and regulations for the government of the trade with Indians that now are, or hereafter may be enacted and eſtabliſhed, licenſe is hereby granted to the ſaid *Alexis Picard* to trade with the ſaid *Miami Potto* nation, at their town *at near fort maple* and there to ſell, barter and exchange with the individuals of the ſaid nation, all manner of goods, wares and merchandizes, conformably to the laws and regulations aforeſaid; but under this expreſs condition and reſtriction, that the ſaid *Alexis Picard* ſhall not, by *himſelf his* ſervants, agents or factors, carry or cauſe to be carried to the hunting camps of the Indians of ſaid nation, any ſpecies of goods or merchandize whatſoever, and more eſpecially ſpirituous liquors of any kind; nor ſhall barter or exchange the ſame, or any of them, in any quantity whatever, on pain of forfeiture of this licenſe, and of the goods, wares and merchandize, and of the ſpirituous liquors which may have been carried to the ſaid camps, contrary to the true intent and meaning hereof, and of having *his* bond put in ſuit: and the Indians of the ſaid nation are at full liberty to ſeize and confiſcate the ſaid liquors ſo carried, and the owner or owners ſhall have no claim for the ſame, either upon the ſaid nation, or any individual thereof, nor upon the United States.

This licenſe to continue in force for one year, unleſs ſooner revoked.

GIVEN under my hand and ſeal, the *twenty third* day of *november*, in the year of our Lord one thousand eight hundred and *three*

William Henry Harrison

128.—The license of an Indian trader. These documents, giving white men the right to transact business with Indians, played a part of much importance in the Caucasian system for ousting the natives from their possessions. This and the succeeding twenty-two illustrations, to No. 150 inclusive, are designed to indicate the process by which the white race secured ownership of the Mississippi valley and much of the South. The subject is treated in Chapters XXII to XXIX.

popular feeling of the time, and with various acts of government that likewise reflected the underlying attitude of the English speaking race. A brief consideration of those things will make clear the strange embarrassments amid which the white men entangled themselves during the period wherein a need for increased methods of land travel and transport became acute. Such a survey will also reveal the way whereby the country finally solved the problems that its need created. The necessity faced by the whites was imperative if they were to march toward greater territorial dominion and economic development, but the tale of the means they took in accomplishing their purpose is not in all degrees a pleasant one.

The battle of Fallen Timbers, in the year 1794, indicated the end of the long era in which organized physical resistance was a chief method used by the Indians to retard Caucasian movement. With the Treaty of Greenville, following within a year as the result of the defeat of the confederated Indians at Fallen Timbers, began the second aspect of the contest between the two races. The final phase of that struggle continued until about 1840, and was marked, it is true, by occasional brief outbreaks of warfare,[1] but its most significant feature—on the Indian side—was a widespread and earnest effort by native tribes both of the North and South to adopt a new order of life and social customs patterned in many respects after the organized society of the white people around them. The distinguishing features of the Caucasian attitude, on the other hand, were a persistent effort to secure freedom of travel in Indian territory by negotiation, and an equally insistent attempt to obtain title to native territory by purchase through means of interna-

[1] Such as the campaign which ended at the Battle of the Thames in 1811, and Black Hawk's War in 1832.

tional treaties. Out of these conflicting aspirations finally grew a situation deplorable to the red inhabitants in its material results and perhaps equally unfortunate, in its moral consequences, to their victorious opponents. To the white participants in the struggle, however, came economic benefits of such enormous worth that the moral cost of their purchase was not then observed. The end of the contest found the Caucasians in undisputed ownership of all the territory east of the Mississippi River; with a right to move wheresoever they chose in that region without hindrance; and with a national treasure, in the shape of governmentally owned land, having value almost beyond comprehension. The course of events leading to the situation thus summed up bore a constantly intimate relation to the travel system that was expanding at the same time, and also to the government's position toward transportation facilities and their later growth.

It was admitted by the Federal government during the forty years from its organization in 1789 until about 1830, that purchase from European nations of political claims over additional territory, or the addition of more land to the national domain through the cessions made by states, did not carry with it a sovereignty over the Indians, or ownership of soil, or the unrestricted right to penetrate, for purposes of travel or trade, through the regions so obtained. Nothing could be further from the truth than the supposition that white Americans, after the adoption of the Constitution, were at liberty to travel wheresoever they pleased in what they called their own country. There were some districts in which they were not allowed at all; other immense tracts that they were only permitted to cross by the treaty consent of Indian governments and in which they had to proceed without pause by certain designated paths; and still others to which access could be rightfully and safely gained only by passport.

From the establishment of constitutional government the Republic conceded that the various nations and tribes of red natives were separate peoples vested with sovereignty over themselves and with rightful ownership and sovereignty over the areas they occupied. The only respect

129.—Indian traders and others who were confronted by the necessity of winter travel sometimes used sleds drawn by dogs while getting about the country now embraced in Ohio, Indiana and Illinois. Unless they employed dogs they had to go on snow-shoes. The "North West" meant by the engraver was the country north of the Ohio River.

in which the Indians' sovereignty over themselves may be said to have been questioned was in the matter of selling their lands, for they were always asked to refrain from disposing of their territory to any other foreign state except the United States of America. But since the United States always established friendly relations with Indian nations through formal treaties negotiated by plenipotentiaries or commissioners appointed by both sides for the purpose—as was the practise of the Republic in dealing with other independent countries—and since a clause was placed in each foundation treaty with an Indian nation to define the land selling agreement here alluded to, it follows that the United States thereby admitted the sovereign right of the Indians to sell lands to whomsoever they pleased in the absence of a treaty proviso to a contrary effect. Otherwise such a stipulation would have been unnecessary. The language of those treaties was written by the white men, and sometimes the red peoples were designated as "republics," "nations" or "confederations," and their executives as "kings," or "councils."[1] In short the situation created through the simultaneous occupation of the country by two radically different races was one—between 1789 and 1830—such as presaged the troubles that were later to arise. The rapidly growing Caucasian nation held a loose political power over half a continent, and yet acknowledged that it did not either rightfully occupy or own a large part of the soil over which its flag waved, and that its citizens could not move unrestrictedly about, either on river or land, of their own free will. To the north of the white confederacy, on its south and west as well, and even in its midst, dwelt other independent nations that had been there from time immemorial, that still owned the soil, and prescribed laws for the government of their own communities.

[1] The first treaty between the United States of America and any Indians was that of 1778 with the Delawares. It was a "Confederation entered into by the Delaware Nation and the United States." Article VI said: "Whereas the enemies of the United States have endeavored, by every artifice in their power, to possess the Indians in general with an opinion that it is the design of the States aforesaid to extirpate the Indians and take possession of their country; to obviate such false suggestion the United States do engage to guarantee to the aforesaid nation of Delawares, and their heirs, all their territorial rights in the fullest and most ample manner . . . And it is further agreed on between the contracting parties should it for the future be found conducive for the mutual interest of both parties to invite any other tribes who have been friends to the interest of the United States to join the present confederation and to form a state whereof the Delaware nation shall be the head, and have a representation in Congress; Provided, nothing contained in this article to be considered as conclusive until it meets with the approbation of Congress."—"Indian Affairs: Laws and Treaties. Compiled and edited by Charles J. Kappler, Wash., 1904. Senate Doc. 319: 58th congress, 2nd session."

Those dark-skinned peoples had formerly been opponents of the whites in either an active or passive sense, but had seen the uselessness of forcible opposition to them and were even adopting, in some localities, various methods of social and industrial life introduced by the invading millions. The newer Americans, on the other hand, knew they could finally exterminate the remaining red men by force of numbers if they chose to do so. But that policy would have required another generation or two of warfare and they were not inclined to follow such a plan. They believed they could acquire the country by using methods no less effective and more peaceable. So they abandoned advance by force of arms, admitted the sovereignty and soil ownership of the Indians, and set forth on a program of diplomacy under which the Indians were to be treated as ostensible friends and neighbors and through which the native possessions were to be secured by purchase and pressure as speedily as possible. Permission was also to be obtained for the establishment of white men's routes of travel over those numerous sections of Indian territory intervening between white communities.

Those two policies of the government—the systematic buying of native lands and the securing of public travel privileges across such extensive territories as could not at once be bought—were usually carried out simultaneously whenever possible, by means of the treaty method. The treaty of Greenville itself, in 1795, furnished one of the largest early opportunities[1] for pursuing the purposes in

---

[1] Though not the first. Title to some of the soil now embraced within the limits of the southern states east of the Mississippi had been previously gained through the following treaties, negotiated prior to 1795 by the Congress of the Confederation and the Constitutional government:

With the Cherokees on Nov. 28, 1785.	And soon after the Treaty of Greenville
With the Choctaws on Jan. 3, 1786.	still other fragments of the South were
With the Chicasaws on Jan. 10, 1786.	bought by the following treaties:
With the Creeks on Aug. 7, 1790.	With the Creeks on June 29, 1796.
With the Cherokees on July 2, 1791.	With the Cherokees on Oct. 2, 1798.
With the Cherokees on June 26, 1794.	With the Chickasaws on Oct. 24, 1801.

130.—Typical page from an account book kept by an Indian trader in the Indiana country. Date, 1801-1802. Showing the indebtedness of an Indian who had owed $76, of which $12 was for whisky, whose sale to natives was forbidden. The account and the bookkeeping method are mentioned in Chapter XXIV.

question. Its provisions gave the United States title to about two-thirds of the present state of Ohio,[1] and a considerable tract of country now embraced in Indiana.

But though the gaining of land ownership by the whites then seemed to be the most important feature of international negotiations with the red men, it is safe to say that the acquirement of travel privileges through Indian regions was no less essential to the future development of the new American union of states. Certain it is that the permission for white movement thus constantly requested and given reveals the dependence of the new nation on the tolerance of those older peoples it was seeking to displace. In a geographical sense, and with relation to methods of overland intercommunication, the settled districts of the white men found themselves but poorly bound together after constitutional government emerged from political chaos. Throughout all parts of the country, except in the sections along the Atlantic seaboard, there lay independently governed and alien-owned areas, sometimes extensive in size, that formed barriers between districts in which the white men possessed both soil and political sovereignty.

Travel into these independent foreign domains was not a right possessed by the white Americans. Yet without an unrestricted opportunity for white men to pass to and fro between all their own settlements there could be no broad development, no social and industrial progress of the whole Caucasian body of population according to its own methods. Hence the series of treaty provisos by which, from 1795 until 1830, the American government secured for its own citizens the establishment of white men's travel routes through Indian possessions. The

[1] Nearly 17,000,000 acres in that state.

diplomatic campaign in question brought about a constant intermingling of the two races east of the Mississippi; surrounded the sovereign nations of red men with ever larger white communities; progressively introduced among the natives those practises of Caucasian society which drained the Indians' strength and depleted their numbers; and finally rendered their further close contact with the whites, and its attendant ills, intolerable to them. Whenever that situation came about, as it unremittingly did in some locality or other, the natives were willing to sell their lands to the white government and go elsewhere. Indeed, it was more than willingness that then impelled them to such action; it was necessity; the instinct and need of self-preservation.

Those were some of the circumstances accompanying and following the plan by which, between 1789 and 1830, new travel routes were obtained to connect the possessions of the Caucasians. During the later years of the period in question, and as one means of inducing the Indians to grant desired privileges, the United States government by ambiguous treaty language sometimes led the natives to believe they were approaching citizenship in the white republic with a right to representation in its national legislature.

It is apparent, then—provided acts and events can be cited to sustain the suggestions here set forth—that the subjects: (1) of Caucasian purpose, (2) of native rights and aspirations, (3) of race conflict, (4) of land travel by white men, (5) of the Federal ownership of land, (6) of governmental attitude toward further traffic facilities, and (7) of the moral, social and economic development of the American nation were, during the era discussed, very intimately allied. In fact they were so inextricably interwoven that no important event could then occur or public policy be formulated in connection with any one of them which did not also affect all the others in greater or less degree. And since they were so connected it is perhaps wiser not to deal with every phase of the subject separately, but to review various incidents of the period somewhat in chronological order. Each narrated circumstance will fall into its proper place as the story unfolds. One thing, however, should be kept in view. The first and fundamental purposes of the new nation were acquirement of land and of permission for its citizens to travel in regions it could not immediately buy. Those later results of the government's methods and vacillation, including problems growing out of Federal ownership of territory and adoption by the people of certain moral, social and economic standards; and embarrassments which finally brought the country within sight of disturbances amounting to civil war, were natural and perhaps inevitable outgrowths of early acts in the general policy pursued.

Reference has been made to the battle of Fallen Timbers and the resultant treaty of Greenville[1] as jointly marking the commencement of the epoch now considered, and no better method of revealing the white man's attitude at that time can be chosen than by citing various passages from the compact which followed General Wayne's campaign.[2] That document, after transferring title in more than 26,000 square miles of Indian territory to the government, went on to say[3] " . . . . the United States re-

[1] The Indian nations subscribing to the treaty were the Wyandots, Delawares, Shawnees, Ottawas, Chippewas, Potawatomi, Miamis, Eel-rivers, Weas, Kickapoos, Piankashaws and Kaskaskias.
[2] Quotations from treaties between the United States and various Indians that are given in the text are taken from the Government's publication on that subject. The work is entitled "Indian Affairs, Laws and Treaties. Compiled and edited by Charles J. Kappler. Senate Document 319, 58th Congress, 2nd Session." The edition is that of 1904.
[3] In article IV.

linquish their claims to all other lands northwest of the river Ohio, eastward of the Mississippi and westward and southward of the Great Lakes and the waters uniting them . . ."[1] The jurisdiction of the natives over white men in Indian countries was recognized by the following statement:[2] "If any citizen of the United States, or any other white person or persons, shall presume to settle upon the lands now relinquished by the United States, such citizen or other person shall be out of the protection of the United States; and the Indian tribe on whose land the settlement shall be made may drive off the settler, or punish him in such manner as they shall think fit."[3] The United States was also granted the right to destroy illegal white settlements and to remove and punish the offenders, on the ground that such invasions of Indian territory would be injurious to the Caucasian nation as well as to the natives.

Now the negotiation of this treaty, in 1795, created a formidable barrier of alien-owned and independent territory between various long-established white communities and others of more recent origin. To the eastward of the described Indian domain lay a part of Ohio, Pennsylvania, and all the Atlantic coast region. South of it were the Ohio River, Kentucky, and Tennessee, already in the grasp of the Caucasians. Toward the north were Detroit and Lakes Erie and Michigan, with their obvious importance, and in the west were the Illinois towns won by Clark, and the upper Mississippi River. These possessions of the United States were all separated from one another, and part of them were cut off from the bulk of

[1] Certain small tracts excepted.
[2] In article VI.
[3] It is interesting in this relation to remember that only within comparatively recent times has the United States acknowledged that Japan possessed the right, through her own judicial processes, to deport or otherwise punish American citizens who might act contrary to the laws of that country or who might be undesirable sojourners therein.

white population in the East by a region that now includes about one-third of Ohio and practically all of Indiana and Illinois, yet access to them from the East and South, and constant communication between them, was vital to the white republic. There were as yet no roads in the country described, and the only travel routes by which such intercourse could be carried on were Indian trails and the rivers.

But these forest paths and streams were in acknowledged ownership of the red men, and could not be used without their permission. The white settlements in the then western and northwestern sections of the country were thus isolated from one another, and from the East, unless a concession for white travel was obtained from the natives. Consequently this favor was sought and granted, and a considerable part of the treaty of Greenville was devoted to a careful description of the precise routes through aboriginal territory over which the Indians consented that white men might journey. In the language of the compact[1] ". . . the said Indian tribes will allow to the people of the United States a free passage by land and by water, as one and the other shall be found convenient, through their country" (1) along the route from the Ohio River northward by way of the Great Miami, across the Ft. Wayne portage and thence down the Maumee[2] to Lake Erie; (2) from the portage at Loromie's Store[3] to the Auglaize River, and down the Auglaize to Fort Defiance; (3) from the same portage to the Sandusky River, down that river to Lake Erie, thence to the mouth of the Maumee and thence to Detroit; (4) from the mouth of the

---

[1] Article III. The long and detailed description of the five travel routes therein granted to white men is here condensed. A study of any map of the territory involved will disclose the importance of the travel-rights concession of 1795 in its relation to later Caucasian expansion and movement.
[2] Then called the "Miami of the Lakes."
[3] On a branch of the Great Miami.

Chikago[1] to the portage between that river and the Illinois, and thence over the portage and down the Illinois to the Mississippi; (5) from Ft. Wayne along the portage leading to the Wabash, and thence down the Wabash to the Ohio."

So it is seen that the pale-faced Americans—even after the final organization of their present political government and its theoretical extension to the Mississippi River—were far from having the right to go whithersoever they chose in the so-called United States. Other sovereignties lay scattered about between the Atlantic and the Father of Waters. If they were penetrated by a white man desirous of reaching some point beyond them, he had to follow a definitely prescribed path from which he could deviate only at his own peril. If he tarried on his way, and undertook to establish himself on forbidden soil he placed himself beyond the recognition or aid of his own government. Even his life was forfeit if the people whose rights he had invaded chose to take it. They could "punish him in such manner as they shall think fit"; he was "out of the protection of the United States."

These five travel routes, so obtained, linked together the white outposts of the Northwest and united them with the old communities to the eastward. Over them, for years thereafter, proceeded white movement in the region so penetrated, by canoe, flatboat, pack-train and moccasin-clad human feet until the forest trails at last became roads fit for vehicles, and little flat-bottomed steamboats puffed on the shallow rivers.

Some of the first results attending the acquirement of travel privileges through native territory, as has been said,

[1] The Chicago River.

Inland Settlers and Pioneers

131.—Following the traders into the interior came overland caravans of white settlers, while others floated down the rivers. The white settlers destroyed or drove away the game, making it impossible for the Indians to pay the traders by means of furs. A wagon caravan marching beside a small stream.

were an intermingling of the two races east of the Mississippi, the surrounding of red men by constantly growing white communities and the introduction, among the natives, of Caucasian practises harmful to Indian welfare. These consequences were more speedily visible and more widespread in the North than in the South, and may well be described by quoting from a document but lately discovered. The paper in question is a report dated at Fort St. Vincent,[1] July 15, 1801, and addressed by General William Henry Harrison to the Secretary of War.[2]

[1] Vincennes, Indiana.
[2] Hitherto unpublished, and now in possession of the Indiana State Library. The document is one of several thousand records, letters and manuscripts dealing with the early history of the Northwest Territory and states. They were the accumulation of General Hyacinthe Lasselle and his descendants, and, being but recently acquired by Indiana, had not been classified in 1913. General Harrison's report appears to be either a preliminary draft of the communication or else a copy made for purposes of office record. The War Department, referring to the document in question, says in a letter to the Indiana State Library under date of March 4, 1912: "An exhaustive search of the records on file in the War Department has resulted in failure to find the letter referred to or any record of it." Hence it is possible that General Harrison eventually decided not to send the document. If he did, then the copy received by the Government at Washington has been lost.

A HISTORY OF TRAVEL IN AMERICA

Perhaps no similar statement of the time, prepared by a man personally familiar with the matters discussed, presents in so clear a manner the condition of the frontier country and so dispassionately allots responsibility for it. The text of the document is as follows:[1]

FORT ST. VINCENT, July 15, 1801.

To the Secretary of War:—

For the last ten or twelve weeks I have been constantly engaged in receiving visits from the Chiefs of most of the Indian Nations which inhabit this part of the Territory. They all profess and I believe that most of them feel a friendship for the United States, but they make heavy complaints of ill treatment on the part of our Citizens. They say that their people have been killed, their lands settled on, their game wantonly destroyed, & their young men made drunk & cheated of the peltries which formerly procured them necessary articles of Cloathing, arms and amunition to hunt with.

Of the truth of all those charges I am well convinced. The Delaware Chiefs in their address to me mentioned the loss of six persons of their nation since the treaty of Greenville having been killed by the White people & I have found them correct as to number. In one instance however the White boy who killed the Indian was tried and acquitted as it was proved that it was done in self defense. In another instance the murderer was tried and acquitted by the Jury, altho it was very evident that it was a cruel and inprovoked murder. About twelve months ago a Delaware was killed in this Town by a Citizen of the Territory against whom a bill has been found by the grand jury. He has however escaped and it is reported that he has gone to Natchez or New Orleans.

But the case which seems to have affected the Indians more than any other is the murder of two men and one woman of this same nation about three years ago. This cruel deed was perpetrated on this side of the Ohio, forty or fifty miles below the falls & is said to have been attended with circumstances of such atrocity as almost to discredit the whole story were it not but too evident that a great many of the Inhabitants of the Fronteers consider the murdering of Indians in the highest degree meritorious. The story is this. About three years ago two Delaware men and a woman were quietly hunting in the neighborhood of the Ohio, I believe on the waters of Blue river. Their Camp was discovered by two men I think of the name[2] of * * * * brothers. And these * * * * mutually determined to murder them for the purpose of possessing themselves of about fifty dollars

[1] With the exception of three paragraphs at the close, dealing more with minor details than questions of broad policy.

[2] The name is given in the manuscript, but is here omitted.

431

worth of property and the trifling equipage belonging to the hunting camp of a Savage. They thought it too dangerous to attack them openly as one of the Indians well known to the white people by the name of Jim Galloway or Gilloway, was remarkable for his strength and bravery. They approached the camp as friends & as I am toled they have since confessed asked leave to stay at the Indians Camp and hunt for a few days. Their request was granted & they remained until a favorable opportunity offered to carry their design into effect & then the Indians were murdered. Although they were missed by their friends it was a long time before their fate was ascertained. The murderers thinking themselves safe from the length of time which had elapsed, now begin to talk of the affair, and one of them is said to have declared that he was very nearly overpowered by the Indian after he had wounded him, that he had closed in with him and the Indian was on the point of getting the better of him when his brother to whom the murder of the other Indian had been committed came to his assistance.

Although I am convinced that the facts above stated are all true, yet so difficult is it to get testimony in a case of this kind, that I have not as yet been able to get the necessary depositions on which to ground an application to the Executive of Kentucky for the delivery of these people to Justice.

Whenever I have ascertained that the Indian boundary line has been encroached on by the white people I have caused the Intruders to withdraw. But as the boundary line separating the Indian land from that to which the title has been extinguished has not been run, nor the manner in which it is to run precisely ascertained either at this place or in the country on the Mississippi called the Illinois, it is impossible to tell when encroachments are made on the Indians at those two places. As this is an object of considerable importance to the Citizens of the Territory I must beg you Sir to obtain the directions of the President to have it done as soon as possible. The people have been about petitioning Congress on this subject untill it was observed that the President was authorized by law to cause all the boundaries between the lands of the U. N. States & the Indian tribes to be ascertained and marked. Untill their boundaries are established it is almost impossible to punish in this quarter the persons who make a practice of Hunting on the lands of the Indians in violation of law and our treaty with that people.

This practice has grown into a monstrous abuse. Thousands of the wild animals from which the Indians derive their subsistence have been destroyed by the white people. They complain in their speeches to me that many parts of their Country which abounded with game when the general peace was made in 1795 now scarcely contains a sufficiency to give food to the few Indians who pass through there. The people of Kentucky living on the Ohio from the mouth of the Kentucky river down to the Mississippi make a constant practice of crossing over

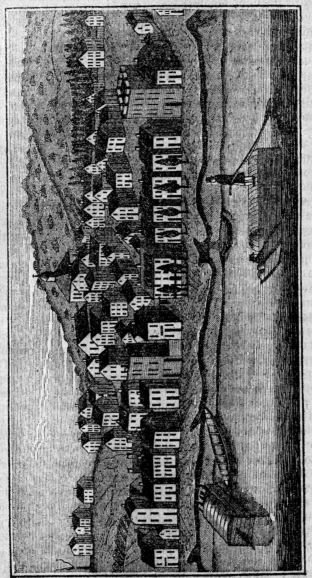

CINCINNATI IN 1810.

132.—The whites established permanent settlements along the rivers, on land bought from the natives through treaties or taken from them after outbreaks of border warfare.

on the Indian lands opposite to them every fall to kill deer, bear, and buffaloe, the latter from being in great abundance a few years ago is now scarcely to be met with in that whole extent. One white hunter will destroy more game than five of the common Indians, the latter generally contenting himself with a sufficiency for present subsistance, while the other, eager after game, hunt for the skin of the animal alone.

All these Injuries the Indians have hitherto borne with astonishing patience but altho they discover no disposition to make war upon the United States at present, I am convinced that most of the tribes would eagerly seize any favorable opportunity for that purpose & should the United States be at war with any of the European nations who are known to the Indians there would probably be a combination of nine-tenths of the Northern Tribes against us Unless some means are made use of to conciliate them. The British have been unremitted in their exertions to preserve their influence over the Indians resident within our Territory ever since the surrender of the Forts upon the Lakes & those exertions are still continued. Last year they delivered a greater quantity of goods to their Indians than they have been ever known to do, and I have been lately informed that talks are now circulating amongst them [1] which are intended to lessen the small influence we have over the Indians. I cannot vouch for the truth of this report, but I think it very probable that the British will redouble their efforts to keep the Indians in their Interest as a means of assisting them in any designs they may form against Louisiana,[2] which it is said will be shortly delivered up to the French.

I have had much difficulty with the small tribes in this immediate Neighborhood, viz, the Peankashaws, Weas & Eel river Indians. These three tribes form a body of the greatest Scoundrels in the world. They are dayly in this town in considerable numbers and are frequently intoxicated to the number of thirty or forty at once. They then commit the greatest disorders, drawing their knives and stabing every one they meet with, breaking open the Houses of the Citizens, killing their Hogs and cattle and breaking down their fences. But in all their frolicks they generally suffer most severely themselves. They kill each other without mercy. Some years ago as many as four were found dead in the morning & altho these murders are actually committed in the streets of the town yet no attempt to punish them has ever been made. This forbearance has made them astonishingly insolent & on a late occasion (within 8 weeks) when one of these rascals had killed without provocation two of the Citizens in one of the Traders Houses in this place, & it was found impossible to apprehend him alive, he was put to death. This piece of Justice so exasperated those of his tribe in the neighborhood that they actually assembled in the borders of the town with a

---

[1] Among the Indians. A "talk" was a message or communication, either verbal or written.

[2] Meaning the whole territory west of the Mississippi River.

design to seize some favorable opportunity of doing mischief. The Militia were ordered out and their resentment has subsided.[1]

Should you think proper to garrison Fort Knox with a small body of troops it will be the means of keeping the Indians under much better controle when they come here to trade & would enable the civil magistrates to punish those who violate the laws. Indeed I do not think that a military force is so necessary on any part of the fronteers as at this place. The inhabitants tho fully able to repulse them when aware of their designs are constantly in danger from their treachery. Five Hundred Warriors might introduce themselves into the settlement undiscovered by the White people & after doing all the mischief in their power might make their escape with as much facility. I do not indeed apprehend in the least that the neighbouring tribes have any inclination to make open war upon us. I fear only the effect of some sudden resentment arising from their constant intercourse with the people of this town. In this intercourse causes of irritation are constantly produced. Twice within a few months an appeal was made to arms by both parties, one occasioned by some drunken Indians attempting to force a House in which one was killed and another wounded, the other at the time when the two white men were killed as above mentioned. Luckily however no other mischief was done in either instance.

The Indian Chiefs complain heavily of the mischiefs produced by the enormous quantity of whiskey which the Traders introduce into their Country. I do not believe there are more than six Hundred Warriers upon this River [2] and yet the quantity of whiskey brought here annually for their use is said to amount to at least six thousand Gallons. This poisonous liquor not only incapasitates them from obtaining a living by Hunting but it leads to the most atrocious crimes. Killing each other has become so customary amongst them that it is no longer a crime to murder those whom they have been most accustomed to estem and regard. Their Chiefs and their nearest relations fall under the strokes of their Tomhawks & Knives. This has been so much the case with the three Tribes nearest us, The Peankashaws, Weas, & Eel River Miamis, that there is scarcely a Chief to be found amongst them.[3] The Little Beaver, a Wea Chief of note well known to me was not long since murdered by his own son. The Little Fox, another Chief who was always a friend to the white people, was murdered at mid day in the streets of his town by one of his own nation.

[1] In such cases, which were constantly occurring along the border, the tribes to which the involved Indians belonged generally asserted that the offending warrior had purposely been made drunk that the white trader might coax him into buying, on credit, goods which he would not have bought when sober, or else that he might be cheated in respect of prices. When the debts of the Indians had piled up to large proportions they had no way of paying except by selling more land to the Government and then turning all, or nearly all, of their cash proceeds over to the traders.

[2] The Wabash.

[3] Which probably accounts, in some measure, for the trouble due to those particular Indians, previously mentioned. The whisky resulted in affrays, the Chiefs lost their lives in trying to quell the drunken warriors, and the tribes lost the restraint exercised by the Chiefs.

All these Horrors are produced to these Unhappy people by their too frequent intercourse with the White people. This is so certain that I can at once tell by looking at an Indian whom I chance to meet whether he belong to a Neighbouring or a more distant Tribe. The latter is generally well Clothed, healthy and vigorous, the former half naked, filthy and enfeebled with Intoxication, and many of them without arms except a knife which they carry for the most vilanous purposes. The Chiefs of the Kickapoos, Sacks and Potawatimies, who lately visited me, are sensible of the progress of these measures and their Views amongst themselves, which they are convinced will lead to utter exterpation and earnestly desire that the introduction of such large quantities of whiskey amongst them may be prevented.

Whether some thing ought not to be done to prevent the reproach which will attach to the American Character by the exterpation of so many human beings, I beg leave most respectfully to submit to the Consideration of the President. That this exterpation will happen no one can doubt who knows the astonishing annual decrease of these unhappy beings.

The Delawares are now making an other attempt to become agriculturists. They are forming settlements upon the White river, a branch of the Wabash, under the conduct of two Missionaries of the Society of "The United Brethren for propagating the gospel amongst the Heathens" otherwise Meravians.[1] To assist them in this plan the Chiefs desire that one-half of their next annuity may be laid out in implements of agriculture and in the purchase of some domestic animals as Cows and Hogs. The Kaskaskias and Peankashaws request the same thing,[2] and the Patawatimies wish a few horse-hoes may be sent with their goods.

[1] General Harrison, of course, meant "Moravians."
[2] Yet the Piankashaws were one of the three tribes named by the General as giving him the most trouble because of their drunkenness. Evidently even they were willing to make a last effort for self-preservation.

CHAPTER XXIII

PURCHASE OF INDIANA AND ILLINOIS — THE GOVERNMENT
PREVENTS WHITE MEN FROM GIVING ADVICE TO
INDIANS — LAWS OF INDIANA TERRITORY ON THE
SUBJECT — FAILURE OF TECUMSEH'S PLAN TO
CHECK CAUCASIAN ADVANCE — HOW THE SANTE FÉ
TRAIL, THE MICHIGAN ROAD AND OTHER WHITE
TRAVEL ROUTES WERE OBTAINED THROUGH NATIVE
CONSENT — EXPERIENCES OF THE SHAWNEES OF
OHIO — THE STRANGE WYANDOT TREATY — ORIGIN
OF THE WAR OF 1832

THE process of acquiring title to the soil now embraced in the state of Indiana, which was begun
at Greenville in 1795, was resumed soon after Harrison's
report of 1801. In 1803 the Delawares sold a large extent
of Indiana territory through the treaty of Fort Wayne,
and in the following year the same native nation, in conjunction with other tribes, granted another extensive and
adjacent region to the United States. The Federal Congress, in 1804, also passed an act again acknowledging
Indian ownership of their lands.[1] This law marked the
first official step in the plan for ousting the Indians, in
bulk, from their eastern possessions to country west of
the Mississippi, and declared that "the President of the
United States is hereby authorized to stipulate with any

[1] In the law of March 26, by other sections of which a part of the Louisiana Purchase was erected into the "Territory of Orleans," to be governed by a legislature of thirteen members appointed by the President.

437

Indian tribe owning lands on the East side of the Mississippi, and residing thereon, for an exchange of lands the property of the United States, on the West side of the Mississippi, in case the said tribe shall remove and settle thereon."[1]

Almost the whole eastern portion of the present state of Illinois had been obtained by the treaty of Vincennes in 1803. That compact was negotiated with "the Kaskaskia tribe of Indians so called, but which tribe is the remains and rightfully represent all the tribes of the Illinois Indians."[2] The document said[3] ". . . Finding themselves unable to occupy the extensive tract of country which of right belongs to them and which was possessed by their ancestors for many generations, the chiefs and warriors of the said tribe . . . have, for the considerations hereinafter mentioned, relinquished and by these presents do relinquish and cede to the United States all the lands in the Illinois country . . . ."

The price paid for the eastern part of Illinois by the United States was:

1. Sixteen hundred and thirty acres of land within the territory ceded, which was to "remain to them [the Indians] forever";

2. A fence around one hundred acres of the land thus re-ceded to the Indians;

3. A house for the chief;

4. An annuity of $1,000 a year to the tribe;

5. A clergyman and teacher for seven years at a salary of $100 a year;

6. A church to cost $300;

[1] Section XV. For text of this and other laws quoted in this chapter, not otherwise identified, see "Laws of the Colonial and State Governments relating to Indians and Indian Affairs, from 1633 to 1831. . . . And the Laws of Congress from 1800 to 1830 on the same subject. Washington, 1832."
[2] Language of the treaty.
[3] Article I.

7.   Cash amounting to $580.

This aggregate payment, said the treaty, "is considered as a full and ample compensation for the relinquishments made to the United States."[1]

Various other treaties were negotiated with natives of the Northwest Territory and the interior during the next few years,[2] and in the meantime an ever increasing movement of white travel was visible over the communication routes already granted by the Indians.   Existing Caucasian settlements in the North were swiftly growing and new ones constantly appeared.   The leaders among the Indians began to realize that they were being outfought in the battle of wits, just as they had been beaten, during an earlier time, in physical strife.   So they sought advice from such white men as they trusted, and whose opinions, as they doubtless believed from long association, were disinterested.   In this way the red men hoped to obtain counsel which would guide them in their general course of action, and, especially, help them when negotiating

[1] Article III.
[2] Among them being treaties with the Sacs and Foxes in 1804; with the Osage in 1808 and the Chippewas during the same year.   The Ottawas, Potawatomi, Wyandots and Shawnees were also parties to the Chippewa treaty of 1808, and in it they jointly gave the United States permission to open a travel route between the white settlements of Ohio and Michigan.
   Article I said in part: "Whereas, by a treaty concluded at Detroit . . . in 1807 a tract of land lying to the west and north of the river Miami, of Lake Erie, and principally within the Territory of Michigan, was ceded by the Indian nations to the United States; and whereas the lands lying on the southeastern side of the said river Miami . . . still belong to the Indian nations, so that the United States cannot, of right, open and maintain a convenient road from the settlements in the State of Ohio to the Settlements in the Territory of Michigan, nor extend those settlements so as to connect them; in order therefore to promote this object, so desirable and evidently beneficial to the Indian nations as well as the United States, the parties have agreed to the following article, to wit:
   " 'In order to promote the object aforesaid, and in consideration of the friendship they have toward the United States for the liberality and benevolent policy which has been practised toward them by the government thereof, the said nation do hereby give, grant, and cede, unto the United States, a tract of land for a road, of one hundred and twenty feet in width, from the foot of the rapids of the Miami of Lake Erie to the western line of the Connecticut Reserve, and all the land within one mile of said road, on each side thereof, for the purpose of establishing settlements thereon.   Also, a tract of land for a road only, of one hundred and twenty feet in width, to run from lower Sandusky southwardly to the boundary line established by the treaty of Greenville. . . .' "
   In its language, meaning and effect this travel concession will be found to be similar to one negotiated with the Potawatomi of Indiana in 1826.   Those nations which agreed in 1808 to the compact here quoted gave permission for the creation of white highways designed to aid in destroying the native power.   By the language of the treaty the Indians were put on record as making the gift because of the liberality and benevolent policy of the United States toward them.

439

First Hotel at Zanesville.

133.—One of the first public structures in a wilderness settlement was a log
tavern for the accommodation of still more west-bound travellers. This
tavern, kept by Landlord McIntire of Zanesville, in Ohio, once had Louis
Phillipe of France as a guest.

with the United States for the disposal of their territories.
But the white men's government apparently did not wish
the Indians to receive aid of that sort, and seems to have
taken action in prevention of it. In the official records of
Indiana Territory is to be found the following law, passed
in 1810 and approved on December 15 of that year by
General Harrison, who was still the Governor. The law
reads:[1]

"Whereas, it appears probable from certain documents which have
been laid before the general assembly by the governor that the negotiations
between the United States and the Indian tribes are much interrupted
by the interference of mischievous individuals, and that the harmony and

[1] "Acts of the Assembly of the Indiana Territory Passed at the First Session of
the Third General Assembly of the Said Territory, etc. Printed by Authority. Vincennes, 1810." Chapter XXXIV.

440

good understanding between the United States and the said tribes are likely to be interrupted, and the peace which has so long and so happily subsisted jeopardized by such improper and unpatriotic conduct; and whereas this general assembly is desirous to shew its respect for the general government,[1] and to promote as far as possible its humane and benevolent policy of civilizing the Indians . . . and being desirous also to facilitate those extinguishments of Indian title which are at once so beneficial to the United States, their constituents, and the Indian tribes,[2] therefore . . . .

"5. Be it further enacted, That if any person or persons shall without the permission of the United States, or of this territory, directly or indirectly commence or carry on any verbal or written correspondence or intercourse with any Indian nation or tribe, or any chief, sachem or warrior of any Indian nation or tribe, with an intent to influence the measures or conduct of any Indian nation or tribe, or any chief, sachem or warrior of any Indian nation or tribe, in relation to any negotiations or treaties, disputes or controversies with the United States or this territory, or to defeat the measures of the government of the United States or this territory, or if any person or persons not duly authorized shall counsel or advise, aid or assist in any such correspondence with intent as aforesaid, he, she or they shall be deemed guilty of a high misdemeanor and on conviction thereof before any court having jurisdiction thereof shall be punished by a fine not exceeding three thousand dollars and not less than one thousand dollars."

It was during this time that Tecumseh was busily shaping his project for the organization of a new red confederacy which should again oppose, primarily through passive resistance but by arms if necessary, the Caucasian advance. The Shawnee saw the final result of influences then at work if they were permitted to go on unchecked.[3] He therefore urged the political union of all native nations from the Lakes to Florida, and advocated an agreement among them that no division of the proposed red federation should sell any of its lands to the United States without consent of all the allied groups. This was the first method by which he intended to combat the white repub-

[1] The language of this Indiana Territory law seemingly justifies the inference that the Federal government had requested its passage.
[2] Governmental plans for acquiring regions from the natives were usually put in similar language.
[3] What! Sell land!" he exclaimed on one occasion. "As well sell air and water. The Great Spirit gave them in common to all; the air to breathe, the water to drink, and the land to live upon."

lic's effective plan of dealing with the many tribes in detail. On his final embassy through the South, early in 1811, to secure coöperation of the Indians of those regions, he was promised the aid of the Muscogees, but his dramatic appeal to the powerful Choctaws and Chickasaws was barren of the result he so earnestly desired. In the memorable midnight debate at the Council on the Tombigbee the assembled nations were almost equally divided in opinion, and the eloquence of Apushamatahah[1] finally prevailed against endorsement of the project.

Tecumseh, as he spoke, stood alone near the huge council fire in an open space some thirty feet in width. Behind him on the ground were the members of his retinue. By the glare of the fire he looked out over hundreds of concentric rows of silent seated men, that stretched upward and backward into the darkness. While he spoke no other sound was heard. And at the end, when he called on those who believed with him to whirl their tomahawks upward as a token of agreement,[2] the air seemed filled with battle-axes as the light of the flames, for an instant, glinted from their polished blades. Apushamatahah followed the Shawnee, and again at the close of his address came that strange demonstration, impressive as before. There had been no overwhelming popular verdict, and the final decision was therefore left in the hands of a venerable councillor who at last advised against Tecumseh's plan and the general warfare which all believed would eventually grow out of its adoption.

[1] Or Pushamatahah. A Choctaw chieftain. For an extended account of the debate, see pages 303 to 319 of the "History of the Choctaw, Chickasaw and Natchez Indians. By H. B. Cushman. Greenville, Texas, 1899." The Tombigbee Council was possibly the largest in point of attendance, as it assuredly was one of the most important, in native history.

Apushamatahah fought beside General Jackson at New Orleans. He died while on a visit to Washington in 1824, and the Government fired minute guns during the progress of his funeral.

[2] A method sometimes used at Councils to show assent. The revolving tomahawks went but a few feet upward, and the skill with which they were handled prevented accidents on their descent, even in a throng.

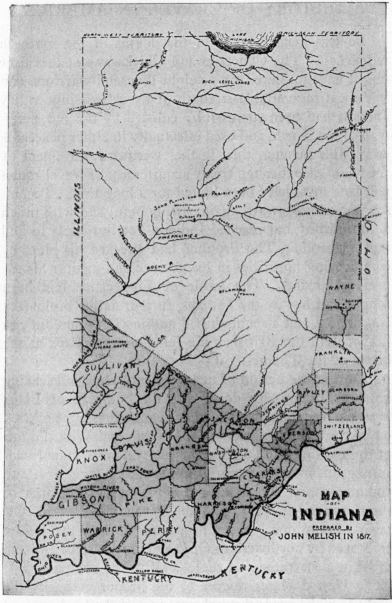

134.—Indiana in 1817, one year after its election into a state. First of a series of three maps showing the growth of a white commonwealth through gradual acquirement of Indian possessions. The dotted line roughly indicates the boundary between the territories then owned by natives and Caucasians. The white region belonged to the Potawatomi, Miami, Delaware and other tribes.

So was history made in the depths of the southern wilderness. The Choctaws and Chickasaws at that time might have mustered six or eight thousand warriors, and if the entire available strength of the Mississippi valley Indians had been successfully enlisted by the red statesman of the North, and used effectually in either peaceable or warlike manner, then farther westward movement by the white race through treaty acquirement of travel routes and land must have been halted for a long time. Tecumseh started northward again, still hopeful and with much accomplished, but reached Indiana Territory only to find that his brother, The Prophet, had wrecked his plans by commencing hostilities in his absence and against his express command. The battle of Tippecanoe had been fought and lost by the Indians, further native diplomacy was useless, and Tecumseh had nothing left to do but cast his lot with the British. He fell soon afterward at the battle of the Thames.

During the period of nearly twenty years intervening between Tecumseh's death and the outbreak of Black Hawk's War, numerous further negotiations were carried on between the two races in the North and West.[1] Four of the treaties made during the interval were notably advantageous in adding more links to the growing overland communication system of the white men. The first of these, ratified in 1817 with the Wyandots, Senecas, Ottawas, Potawatomi and Chippewas, opened the region embraced by northwestern Ohio and northeastern Indiana to white penetration. Article XIV of the compact said: "The United States reserve to the proper authority the right to make roads through any part of the land granted or reserved by this treaty; and also to the different agents

[1] A treaty with the Pawnees in 1818 designated that Indian government as "the said Pawnee Republic."

444

the rights of establishing taverns and ferries for the accommodation of travellers should the same be found necessary."

The next two treaties, by which native permission was asked for the use of an important travel route, dealt with the highway later destined to become famous under the name of the Sante Fé Trail. Congress, in 1825, passed an act[1] "to authorize the President of the United States to cause a road to be marked out from the western frontier of Missouri to the confines of New Mexico." Governmental commissioners were authorized to perform the work. But Congress, recognizing the rights of the Indians occupying regions through which the road was to run, also stipulated in the law that the commissioners "first obtain the consent of the intervening tribes of Indians, by treaty, to the marking of said road, and to the unmolested use thereof to the citizens of the United States."

The desired permission was obtained. A formal agreement was negotiated with the Great and Little Osages, in Article I of which was contained the following language: "The Chief and Head Men . . . for themselves and their nations, respectively, do consent and agree that the Commissioners of the United States shall and may survey and mark out a road, in such manner as they may think proper, through any of the territory owned or claimed by the said Great and Little Osage nations." For this permission the United States paid to the two contracting red nations $500 in money and merchandise valued at $300. A similar document was likewise drawn up in 1825 with the Kansa tribe, through whose territory a part of the road was to extend, and the Kansa were identically paid. Over the Santa Fé Trail,

[1] Approved March 3, 1825.

445

for many years thereafter, passed pack-trains, thousands of Conestoga wagon caravans and hundreds of thousands of westward bound emigrants until the completion of the transcontinental railroads.[1]

The last of the principal transactions—preceding Black Hawk's War—by which the whites added materially to their travel routes in the North and West through consent of the natives was that with the Potawatomi in 1826.

The Potawatomi still owned a broad strip of country extending directly across the northern part of the newly created state of Indiana,[2] and by reason of their possession the United States settlements of the lower Ohio valley were cut off from land communicaion with the white people of Michigan.[3] Congress therefore authorized a treaty whose terms, if the natives consented to it, should rid the country of such a condition, and the representatives of the two races met at the Potawatomi town of Mississinewa in October of 1826, to negotiate.[4] The Caucasians wrote the text of the agreement, as was the custom, and Article II reads as follows: "As evidence of the attachment which the Pottawattamie tribe feel toward the American people and particularly to the soil of Indiana, and with a view to demonstrate their liberality, and benefit themselves by creating facilities for travelling and increasing the value of their remaining country, the said tribe do hereby cede to the United States a strip of land commencing at Lake Michigan and running thence to the Wabash River, one hundred feet wide,

---

[1] A few white men from the United States had penetrated the region opened by the Santa Fé Trail between 1800 and the date of its creation. Their adventures are narrated in "The Old Santa Fé Trail" by Inman.

[2] The Indian territory in question reached from Lake Michigan southward to the Wabash River. See illustration No. 143.

[3] There was as yet no road for vehicles extending northward to any part of northern Indiana.

[4] The United States plenipotentiaries were Lewis Cass, John Tipton and James B. Ray.

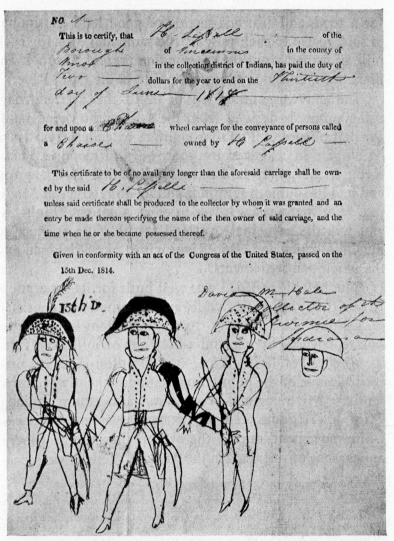

NO. 1

This is to certify, that *H. Lisselle* of the

Borough of *Vincennes* in the county of

Knox in the collection district of Indiana, has paid the duty of

Two dollars for the year to end on the *Thirtieth*

day of *June* 1818

for and upon a *Chaise* wheel carriage for the conveyance of persons called

a *Chaise* owned by *H. Lisselle*

This certificate to be of no avail any longer than the aforesaid carriage shall be own-

ed by the said *H. Lisselle*

unless said certificate shall be produced to the collector by whom it was granted and an

entry be made thereon specifying the name of the then owner of said carriage, and the

time when he or she became possessed thereof.

Given in conformity with an act of the Congress of the United States, passed on the

15th Dec. 1814.

135.—Roads were made through the forest and wheeled vehicles appeared.—A
license issued by Indiana in 1817 permitting a citizen to own and use a
chaise on payment of $2 a year. Sale of the chaise without notice forfeited
the permit. A contemporary hand has sketched the appearance of officers
of the Fifteenth Dragoons. Federal troops built and occupied military posts
to awe the natives.

for a road, and also one section of good land contiguous to said road for each mile of the same and also for each mile of a road from the termination thereof, through Indianapolis, to some convenient point on the Ohio River."[1]

Indiana was authorized to build the desired road, using proceeds derived from the sale of the ceded lands for that purpose. The thoroughfare extended from Lake Michigan in a generally southward direction, passed through the newly laid out capital called Indianapolis, and had its southern terminus on the Ohio River at Madison. For many years it was in effect a national highway, and was the principal overland travel route connecting the Ohio valley and Ohio River with Lake Michigan and the Michigan settlements.

The Michigan Road was well built for its generation. It was twenty-four feet wide, and in some parts consisted of seasoned oak timbers, twenty feet long and a foot square, covered by one-and-a-half feet of soil taken from the ditches beside it.[2] Over its 200 miles of length proceeded much of the population that permanently occupied southern Michigan and Wisconsin, and northern Indiana, Ohio and Illinois. In importance as a land artery of white movement, during the era previous to the general appearance of railroads in the Middle West, it was second

[1] In discussing the terms and phraseology of this treaty in his monograph "The First Thoroughfares of Indiana," Cottman says: "Why the Pottawattamie Indians should feel an especial attachment to the American people, who were gradually pushing them off the earth, and how they were to be benefitted by an inlet the sole purpose of which was to facilitate the oncoming of the usurpers, and how, by the light of previous land transfers, the value of their remaining country would be enhanced to them, make a series of queries that need not be discussed here."

For thus granting a travel route through their territory and land adjacent to it the Potawatomi were paid with apparent liberality. They received merchandise appraised at about $30,000, were promised $2,000 a year for twenty-two years, and $2,000 per year for Indian education as long as Congress might think proper. The value of their recompense, if the annuity was paid and the proposed education was maintained for twenty years, would have been some $114,000. More than $240,000 was obtained by Indiana through sale of the land they ceded, and the road was built and maintained until 1840 by money so taken in. See reports of the Indiana Auditor's office..

[2] "Reports and Estimates of the Michigan Road Survey," by Julian W. Adams, Engineer. (Indianapolis) December 29, 1837. Other sections were not so well constructed, and in rainy weather were at times—like other dirt roads—almost impassable.

only to the Cumberland Turnpike, or National Road. The red men did not find it to be of such advantage to them as the phraseology of the treaty of 1826 had led them to expect. The Michigan Road was one of the principal agencies of their undoing in the North, and that their assent to its creation should have been asked in such language as was prepared for their signatures by men who presumably understood the significance of the proposed work is, at least, unfortunate.[1]

The western part of what is now Illinois, embracing the country between the Illinois and Mississippi Rivers, had been sold to the United States by the Sacs and Foxes in 1804 and 1816.[2] In 1826 the Miamis of Indiana disposed of the remainder of their holdings in that state, lying north and west of the Wabash River. The Chippewas, Menomonies and Winnebagos, in 1827, ceded certain territories at present included in the limits of Michigan and Wisconsin, and in the same year the Potawatomi also sold a large part of their northern lands now in Michigan. The Shawnees of Ohio disposed of all their possessions in that state in 1831 and agreed to remove beyond the Mississippi. In the treaty of 1831 with the Shawnees the United States agreed, when speaking of

[1] The original manuscript survey of the Michigan Road has had a strange history, typical of the vicissitudes to which many similarly invaluable historical records in all parts of the country have been subjected. For years its whereabouts were unknown. Finally, in July of 1907, it was discovered in the cellars of the state capitol at Indianapolis, amid a mass of other early documentary material belonging to the state which had been stored there because of lack of room in the various administrative departments. Two invitations for its removal to intelligent custody were declined. The state librarian heard of the discovery, was unable to get possession of the manuscript for its proper safe keeping, and could only secure a traced copy, made by the man who had found it. Some time afterward a minor employee in the state capitol, whose duties lay chiefly in the cellars, sold as junk and old paper a part of the state's stored historical material which was estimated to the author, in 1912, as amounting in quantity to about ten tons. On Governor Marshall's accession to office he heard of the occurrence and sought to discover what had been sold, and who was responsible. But nobody knew what was gone. Since that time the Michigan Road survey has not been seen. It may still be in the cellar of the capitol. (Note: March 1914.—The original manuscript survey has again been found.—S. D.)

[2] For this territory, by the treaty of 1804, the Indians were given $2,000 in merchandise and promised an annuity of $2,000. Also included in the region sold by the same natives in 1804 was about one-third of the present state of Missouri. The total land area obtained by the whites in the transaction was some 50,000,000 acres.

the nation's new home in the West, "that said lands shall never be within the bounds of any state or territory, nor subject to the laws thereof."[1]

This agreement with the Shawnees, which is known as the Treaty of Wapakonetta, is one of the comparatively few compacts of the sort whose connected history has been preserved through white testimony independent of official records, and a brief review of the transaction and its results will be of interest.[2]

The representative of the government sent to negotiate with the Indians made an address to them in which he said that Ohio was about to extend its laws over them, that they would be taxed, killed if they resisted, and that their testimony in courts would be declared incompetent. He procured the native signatures to the instrument on his verbal declaration of its provisions, without reading or translating its text to the assembled chiefs. The white Indian traders who had dealt with the tribe, and who were creditors of the red men, "burnt up all their books"[3] as soon as the signatures had been obtained. On reading the consummated treaty the Shawnees found that it stipulated a monetary payment to them which was $115,000 less than that stated by the government's negotiator, and that the 100,000 acres embracing their new home in the West was included in a tract already owned by the nation through a prior treaty,[4] instead of being in addition, and adjacent to the land already owned, as explained to them. They also found that a promised clause binding the United States was not included in the document.

[1] Article X.
[2] The account here given is taken from the "History of the Shawnee Indians from the year 1681 to 1854, Inclusive. By Henry Harvey, Cincinnati, 1855." Harvey spent many years among the Shawnees, and was present and had personal knowledge of the events during and subsequent to the treaty discussed. A detailed account of the transaction, including various letters from governmental officials concerning its different phases, is contained in his "History."
[3] Harvey's language.
[4] That of 1825.

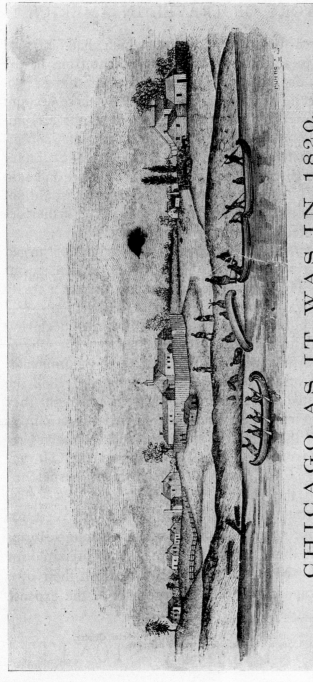

CHICAGO AS IT WAS IN 1820.

136.—Timber forts were erected by the whites in numerous localities considered to be of strategic value or future importance. Incoming settlers put up their cabins and houses in the neighborhood of the forts, and thus other little settlements came into existence.

The three principal features which had induced the natives to sign the treaty being absent from it, the nation sent a deputation to Washington as a means of procuring correction of the errors. Harvey, whose account is here followed, and whose knowledge of the circumstances was believed to be of value to the Indians, accompanied the party. On his arrival at the capital Secretary of War Cass discussed the matter with Harvey and said to him "that by ————' treaty the Shawnees would not realize one dollar for their land in Ohio."[1] Further details of the interview are given by Harvey.

"The Secretary," continues this narrative, "urged the President[2] to hear us on behalf of the Shawnees, but he refused. He [Cass] then proposed to make a treaty with the delegation now in attendance, and set ————' treaty aside; but in this he failed—the President declaring that the Shawnees should fare no better than the Cherokees did."[3] As the removal of the tribe at governmental expense had been promised for the spring of 1832 the Indians planted no crops on the lands they thought they were about to leave. So when the expected migration was not begun at that time the natives found themselves reduced to starvation. Finally, on appeal of Harvey to Secretary Cass[4] the War Department despatched provisions to the Indians and saved their lives. The overland journey of some 800 miles into the West was performed during the following winter, through storms and snow, and the Shawnees found no shelter prepared for their arrival. Many of them had to furnish their own teams and wagons and bear a large part of the expense

[1] Harvey's description of the interview.
[2] General Jackson.
[3] A reference whose meaning will become apparent in a later chapter.
[4] In a letter dated August 8. Text in Harvey's narrative.

of the journey.[1] Again they suffered from hunger. A bill was introduced in Congress by Mr. Vance of Ohio appropriating $5,000 for their immediate relief, but it failed of passage, and the tribe was kept through the remainder of the winter by charity.

WESTWARD HO

137.—Many men of the East, hearing tales of the western country, made extensive journeys through the interior on horseback, by boat, or on foot, in order to see the region for themselves or to pick out future homes for themselves and their families.

Among the improvements they had necessarily left in Ohio were their mills, which the government had promised to duplicate for them in their new home. Other mills were built in the West, but the government charged the

[1] Harvey's language. They travelled to what is now Kansas.

453

Shawnees $6,000 for them and took the amount from money due them. New blacksmith shops were erected on a similar basis. The Congress at length passed a bill acknowledging in some degree the circumstances here reviewed, and appropriating $30,000 additional compensation for the tribal lands in Ohio, to be paid in annual installments of $2,000. Four years elapsed without the annual payments thus provided for, the War Department taking the stand that the $30,000 was intended for use in canceling native debts to the white traders, but as the traders' claims had been found to be fraudulent, the appropriation was unnecessary. Harvey again took a hand in the dispute, and as a result of his protest the Indians received $8,000 of arrears.[1] Finally, at a still later date, the government reversed the action of the Indian Bureau regarding certain traders' claims for $8,000 which had been rejected as fraudulent after the burning of the account books, and paid them by diverting four subsequent installments of the additional $30,000 appropriated to the Shawnees for their Ohio lands.[2]

Another group of Indians, the Wyandots of Ohio, gave up in 1832 their effort to establish a new method of life as civilized agriculturists, and the treaty then negotiated with them is in one feature unique. It is the only instrument of that description wherein United States negotiators were parties to an official statement that the influence of white men, and association with white men, lowered the moral standard of the natives. The treaty begins:

[1] See Harvey's correspondence with the War Department, in his "History."
[2] Harvey's summary of the Shawnee character, and his measurement of them as compared with himself and other white men is interesting. He says:
"During the time I have spent with the Shawnees, on many occasions I have been looked up to for counsel by men vastly my superiors in years, in experience, in public affairs, in intellect and in power of speech, as well as in fine feelings; in fact, in everything except in a knowledge of letters and in the use of them. . . . They never ask for written evidences of the good character of a man, as we do. They only wish to see a man, to look him sternly in the face, and observe his manner for a few minutes; then it is no hard task to obtain from them their opinion of the man, and they are not often mistaken."

"Whereas, the said band of Wyandots have become fully convinced that whilst they remain in their present situation in the State of Ohio, in the vicinity of a white population which is continually increasing and crowding them, they cannot prosper and be happy, and the morals of many of their people will be daily becoming more and more vitiated . . ."

Words of similar purport were sometimes used by Caucasian officials in communications not primarily intended for the public eye, such as the Report of 1801 by General Harrison. But never before, nor never again, did national treaty makers of the United States join with red men in a written admission that the civilization which they represented did not uplift, but degraded, the moral nature of a people popularly considered to be lower in character than themselves, and that the presumed barbarians must go away to escape further contamination. So different is this Wyandot treaty language from the phraseology and pretentions customarily employed on like occasions, that a discovery of the circumstances under which it was introduced into the history of American diplomacy would be of interest. In all probability, however, the cause of the peculiar incident is now beyond research.

The last important resort to arms by the northern natives east of the Mississippi, in an attempt to keep possession of their lands and hold back the white advance, was the brief outbreak of 1832 known as Black Hawk's War. Its origin can be traced to the treaties of 1816 and 1804 by which the Sacs and Foxes[1] sold a part of their territories, but by the terms of which they were given the right to live and hunt on the ceded land as long

[1] Of which associated tribes Black Hawk was a member.

as it belonged to the United States.[1] The treaty of 1804
also guaranteed to the Sacs and Foxes immunity from
molestation by intruders or unlawful settlers. Its language on the points in question was as follows:

"Article 4.—The United States will never interrupt the said tribes
in the possession of the lands which they rightfully claim, but will on
the contrary protect them in the quiet enjoyment of the same against
their own citizens and against all other white persons who may intrude
upon them. . . .

"Article 6.—If any citizen of the United States or other white person should form a settlement upon lands which are the property of the
Sac and Fox tribes, upon complaint being made thereof . . . such
intruder forthwith be removed."

About the year 1818[2] an important stream of invading population from the eastward[3] had begun to enter
the Illinois country, coming down the Ohio River on flatboats and overland along the travel routes granted by the
Indians at Greenville and later treaties. By 1823 this
movement was in full swing, and had also somewhat
affected the region now embraced in southern Wisconsin.
The newly arrived whites objected to the continued use
of the ceded country by Indians for hunting purposes,
and also, as was always the case in similar advances, they
often settled down on lands to which title had not been
obtained. In truth the invading white people were il-

[1] "Black Hawk always alleged that the cause of his battle against the Americans was
the invalidity of the treaty of 1804 . . . but he also said when, at a subsequent treaty
(1816) he himself had 'touched the quill,' and by which treaty the same territory was
ceded, that he knew not what he was signing, and that he was therein deceived by the
agent and others, who did not correctly explain the nature of the grant. Doubtless the
indiscriminate and to a great extent the lawless spread of immigrating population over the
newly acquired country on Rock River, and the actual occupation of his own village by
the Illinois settlers, accompanied by the forcible ejection of his own family and others
of his band from their happy homes created a rankling wound which nothing less than
the shedding of blood of the whites could even cicatrize, much less effectively cure. Yet
he denied that he had gone to war willingly, and asserted that when his flag of truce was
fired upon by Stillman's men his intention had been to surrender; but as he was forced
into a combat, he said to his people: 'Since they will fight us, let us fight.'"—"The History of Wisconsin": By William R. Smith: vol. I, p. 285.
"That he was injured cannot be denied; and that he displayed the white flag, and
gave notice of his willingness to surrender, with his little band of warriors, on several
occasions, and was met and answered by the rifle, is also true."—"The History of Illinois":
By Carpenter and Arthur, Philadelphia, 1854, p. 211.
[2] When a state constitution was adopted by Illinois.
[3] The earliest movement of the sort had been into the southern part of the territory,
and had originated chiefly in Virginia, North Carolina and Kentucky.

legally on a part of the Sac territory from the year 1823. Although there was still a strip of unoccupied land some fifty miles wide lying to the eastward of the Sac region, the settlers from the East did not halt upon it, as they might properly have done, but advanced beyond it into the forbidden country. Once there they plowed up the Indian cornfields, whipped the native women, traded whisky to the men and again brought about, in an acute degree, those unfortunate conditions that often arose through the actions of a frontier population which refused to recognize the existence of native rights entitled to respect.

CHAPTER XXIV

THE CHARACTER OF THE CAMPAIGN AGAINST BLACK HAWK
AND THE SACS — ITS ENDING AT BAD AXE — SUCCESS
IN SIGHT IN THE NORTH FOR THE GOVERNMENT'S
PLAN TO RID THE EAST OF INDIANS — RELATION OF
THE INDIAN TRADER TO THE RACE DRAMA — THE
WILDERNESS ARITHMETIC TABLE — PROCESS AND
GENERAL RESULT OF MAKING THE RED MEN A DEBTOR
CLASS — NATIVE CHARACTERISTICS THAT MADE THE
OPERATION POSSIBLE — SPECIFIC EXAMPLES

AFTER the brief and bloody campaign of 1832 was
over the approval bestowed on its white participants by official decree and popular opinion speedily
obscured many of the circumstances that preceded and
were connected with it. But, though hidden in obscure
places, there still remains enough contemporary Caucasian
testimony to reveal what took place just before and during the last important clash of arms between red men and
white east of the Mississippi. The question of responsibility for the trouble was discussed by a historian of the
period soon after the war in the following words:[1]

"I could relate many anecdotes to show the friendly feelings entertained toward our government and people by the Sacs—feelings which,
whether of fear or of kindness, have rendered them wholly submissive,
and which nothing but the most unprovoked aggression on our side
could have kindled into hostility."[2]

[1] Judge James Hall, in the "Western Monthly Magazine," 1833. Hall was author of
"Statistics of the West at the Close of the Year 1836"; "The West: Its Commerce and
Navigation," and similar works dealing with the history of the Ohio valley.
[2] Among the incidents he thus narrates is the action of Sac chiefs in placing a guard
around an isolated home of white settlers to protect its occupants from possible annoyance by young Indians made drunk by other white men.

The outbreak of warfare in the early summer of 1832[1] followed the movement of Black Hawk and his band into Illinois from the western side of the Mississippi. He and the other natives said their intention was to raise a much needed crop of corn with the Winnebagoes. The presence of some two hundred women and children in the party, together with domestic and agricultural baggage, may be taken as sufficient indication that warfare was not the purpose of the Indians. Nevertheless a great excitement among the whites followed the arrival of the red men on the eastern shore of the river, and some militia and frontiersmen, together with a number of Federal troops were started in pursuit of them. The combined military force was under command of Brigadier General Atkinson of the United States Army. On May 14 a half hundred or more volunteer frontiersman attached to the white army were authorized, at their own request, to make a march of observation to a designated spot about fifteen miles from the encampment of the troops. These men disobeyed instructions and proceeded about twelve miles beyond the point named as their destination until— unknown to themselves—they reached the vicinity of Black Hawk's moving village. There, just before sundown, they saw coming toward them a little group of Indians.[2]

[1] Keokuk, principal chief of the Sacs, had finally ceded all tribal possessions east of the Mississippi to the government in 1830. Black Hawk protested against the sale of his village and Keokuk promised an effort to secure its retrocession. Black Hawk and his adherents then departed on the usual winter hunt, only to find on their return that white settlers were in possession of the village and that their own women and children were without shelter. Finally Black Hawk's community was ousted by Illinois militia, though United States General Gaines promised to provide its members with necessary food supplies equivalent to those abandoned, provided they remained west of the river. This aid was not given and the Indians were reduced in the autumn of 1831 to crossing the river for the purpose of stealing corn which they had planted before being driven from the Illinois village.

[2] Six or eight in number. Black Hawk's statement that they were on a peaceful mission and bore a white flag has been generally accepted. See the extracts from Smith's "History of Wisconsin" and Carpenter and Arthur's "History of Illinois," quoted in a previous foot-note. Stillman, commander of the frontiersmen, said the natives did not bear a white flag.

138.—On their return home, if favorably impressed, they organized or joined another caravan, loaded their possessions into wagons or boats, and swelled the increasing multitude of west-bound emigrants.

The whites fired on the natives, shot one or two, captured three and chased the others, who fled toward their own camp. Black Hawk on hearing of the affair said, "Since they will fight us, let us fight," and turned his men loose. Twelve of the frontiersmen were killed and the remainder fled. On the following day Governor Reynolds ordered three thousand militia under arms "to subdue the Indians and drive them out of the state."[1] War had begun, and some understanding of the sentiment toward the Sacs with which the whites entered the campaign can be gained by a letter written at the time by an officer of the white army, who said:

"General Atkinson will pursue them, and will give a good account

[1] An earlier petition of white settlers urging the use of armed force in driving the same Indians from Illinois recited a number of grievances against the natives. One item of complaint was Black Hawk's action in destroying a barrel of whisky which was being sold to the Sacs of his village.

of them, I hope, before he is done with them. Whether we are to have peace or war on this frontier is to be decided by the course taken with this band of murderers. They deserve nothing but death, and no quarters from us."[1]

In addition to the Federal and state troops called into the field the aid of the Sioux, hereditary enemies of the Sacs, was solicited by the government. The *Galenian* of July 11, 1832, printed an address delivered by General Street, a Federal Indian agent, at Prairie Du Chien on June 22 to a force of Sioux who had started to join Atkinson but had reconsidered their determination to take part in the campaign and had turned back. General Street was quoted as follows:

"Your Great Father has forborne to use force, until the Sacs and Foxes have dared to kill some of his white children. He will now forbear no longer. He has tried to reclaim them, and they grow worse. He is resolved to sweep them from the face of the earth. They shall no longer trouble his children. If they cannot be made good they must be killed. They are now separated from their friends and country, and he does not intend to let one return to trouble him again. And he directed me no longer to restrain you from war. And I said,[2] 'Go and be revenged of the murderers of your friends, if you wish it. If you desire revenge, you have permission to take it. I will furnish you arms, ammunition and provisions, and here is the man who is sent to conduct you to the enemy. . . .' You turn and come home without striking a blow. Why is this? To me your conduct is strange. I cannot comprehend it, and want you to explain the reasons that have influenced you to so disgraceful a course. . . . It was not that your Great Father wanted help from you that I told you to go to war. It was to give you an opportunity to revenge your slaughtered friends. Your Father has penned these Indians up, and he means to kill them all. . . . He does not ask you to help him; but if you want revenge, go and take it. This is what I said to you. And now I repeat it—if you want to kill the murderers of your friends and families, go now and do it; for your Great Father has devoted these Indians to death. He cannot reclaim them, and he will kill them."

The Sioux again refused, according to the *Galenian,* whereupon the governmental agent said:

[1] Written by Major Dodge to Dr. A. Philleo of Galena, Illinois, under date of June 25, 1832. Published in the "Galenian," of Galena, on June 27, 1832.
[2] The speaker evidently refers to a previous address made to the Sioux before they started. This speech was delivered after their first return.

"Go home to your squaws and hoe corn—you are not fit to go to war."

Further suggestion regarding the campaign was contained in a statement made by the Detroit *Journal* of July 18, 1832, which then said:

". . . We are confident in the expectation that if the Indians do not decamp before our troops and militia reach the ground where they are said to be stationed, few will be suffered to escape alive. A general massacre will be the inevitable consequence. General Atkinson could not prevent it if he would; and we doubt whether it be not a part of his orders that it should take place. Ordered or not, the blood of the whites is up, and nothing but blood will appease them."

The Sacs, fleeing northward into Wisconsin, and killing a number of settlers on the way, were overtaken August 2 on the east bank of the Mississippi, and there ensued what is called the Battle of Bad Axe. A sufficient insight into what then took place can best be given by quoting brief extracts from statements of white men who were present, or who through official position or investigation obtained knowledge of the circumstances of the affair. Such comments follow:

"The conflict resembled more a carnage than a regular battle." [1]
"It was a horrid sight to witness little children, wounded and suffering the most excruciating pain." [2]
"It is much to be regretted that very little discrimination appears to have been made in the slaughter, and that the dead were of both sexes, and, sadder still, of all ages."[3]
"When the Indians were driven to the bank of the Mississippi, some hundreds of men, women and children plunged into the river and hoped by diving, etc., to escape the bullets of our guns; very few, however, escaped our sharpshooters." [4]

A steamboat called the *Warrior* took part in the

---

[1] Reynolds' "My Own Times," 2nd Edition, Chicago, 1879.
[2] Wakefield's "History of the War." Jacksonville, Illinois. 1834.
[3] "The History of Illinois," by Carpenter and Arthur. Philadelphia, 1854, p. 207.
[4] The "St. Joseph Beacon and Indiana and Michigan Intelligencer" (of South Bend, Indiana), September 8, 1832. The same newspaper, in previously describing the condition of the Indians during their attempted flight from the white troops, had said of them: "They are in a deplorable condition for the want of food, making use of Bark, Roots, etc., almost entirely for subsistence." This was published on August 22, twenty days after the battle but before knowledge of it had reached the paper.

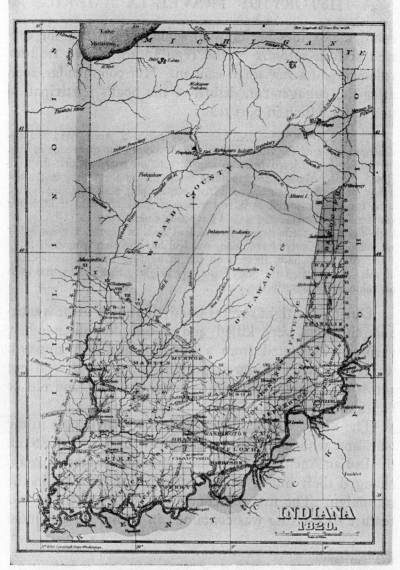

139.—Second map of the series showing the growth of a white state. Indiana when four years old. The incoming white settlers demanded more land, and previous settlers had driven away the Indian game. Meanwhile the traders had continued to sell goods to the natives on credit. These conditions created a situation which made it impossible for the Indians to pay their debts except by selling more land to the government and giving the proceeds to the traders. Showing the receding native boundaries after such transfers of territory.

conflict. Besides her crew of some twenty men she carried sixteen soldiers of the regular army, five frontier riflemen and a few small cannon. Her commander, soon after the engagement, described the boat's participation in a letter which in part read:

". . . As we neared them they raised a white flag, and endeavored to decoy us, but we were a little too old for them; for instead of landing we ordered them to send a boat on board, which they declined. After about fifteen minutes delay, giving them time to remove a few of their women and children, we let slip a six-pounder loaded with canister, followed by a severe fire of musketry; and if ever you saw straight blankets you would have seen them there. . . . This little fight cost them twenty-three killed and, of course, a great many wounded. We never lost a man, and had but one man wounded. . . . I tell you what, Sam, there is no fun in fighting Indians, particularly at this season, when the grass is so very bright. Every man, and even my cabin boy, fought well. . . ." [1]

During the fight several hundred Indian men, women and children were killed and a considerable number, variously estimated from a hundred and fifty upward, were drowned.[2] A large proportion of those who got across the Mississippi were women, children, and old or non-fighting men.

The Sioux who had been invited to participate in the war, and who had been reprimanded by General Street, the Indian Agent, for their vacillation in the matter, again changed their minds and did take an active part in the campaign. The first subsequent acknowledgment of this feature of the case was contained in an official statement

[1] Drake's "The Life and Adventures of Black Hawk." From the third (Philadelphia) edition of 1856, published by Rulison under the title of "The Great Indian Chief of the West": pp. 163-164.
John Throckmorton was captain of the "Warrior" and author of the letter. The Indians were without food, and desired to surrender. They could send no boat, for the two or three they had were across the river, whence some of the women and children had been ferried. The reference to the bright grass meant that it was no fun to shoot at targets which stood out so distinctly against such a background. Later in the battle the "Warrior" discharged canister into a partly submerged island where some swimming Indians had sought refuge.
[2] Reynolds says about 300 reached the west bank of the river and that fifty were taken prisoners. The total number of natives of both sexes and all ages was in the neighborhood of 1,000. The whites lost 17 killed and 12 wounded.

by General Scott[1] dated on board the *Warrior* on August 10 and addressed to Secretary of War Cass. In it General Scott said:

". . . A party of 100 Sioux was sent on the morning of the third inst. on the principal trail of the enemy to ascertain and report the direction of the enemy's retreat. No report has, as yet, been received from this party. . . ."

The result of thus sending the Sioux on the trail of the non-combatants west of the Mississippi is outlined by a communication published in the St. Louis *Times* of May 21, 1833, and signed "F." The letter read:

"I should like to know, for information's sake, who it was that employed a party of Sioux warriors to follow sixty or seventy poor unfortunate women and children of the Sac and Fox nations, who had crossed the Mississippi River above Prairie du Chien, and were traveling on their own land toward the Wabesepinnecon River—where some five or six hunters had gone forth to furnish some meat for the half starved and half dead women and children?

"Those unfortunate women and children were getting out of the way of danger, when the Sioux bands were let loose, and every soul perished by their tomahawks and scalping knives. The murder of these unfortunate women and children ought to be enquired into by the proper authorities, that is to say, by the Superintendent of Indian Affairs, and reported by him to the government; and let those who advised the Sioux Indians to commit these cruelties be punished."

Corroboration of this feature of the government's campaign was soon after supplied by an article in the *Military and Naval Magazine* for August of 1833, signed "By an Officer of Gen. Atkinson's Brigade."[2] It contained the following passage:

". . . After the action a body of one hundred Sioux warriors presented themselves, and asked leave to pursue on the trail of such of the enemy as had escaped. This was granted, and the Sioux, after two days pursuit, overtook and killed fifty or sixty, mostly, it is feared, women and children."

No governmental statement relating to the aid rendered by the Sioux was made, but it developed in 1859

[1] Who had reached the scene.
[2] Written by Captain Henry Smith, U. S. A.

that one of the pursuing chiefs, prior to setting forth after the Sacs, had been supplied by an Indian Agent and a "soldier father"[1] with a military uniform and a United States flag, under which the pursuing Indians conducted their later operations.[2]

After the conclusion of the war the following official reports regarding the campaign and battle of Bad Axe were made:

By General Atkinson to General Scott, dated August 5, 1832:— ". . . I cannot speak too highly of the brave conduct of the regular and volunteer forces engaged in the battle. . . ."

Secretary of War Cass to General Atkinson, on October 24, 1832:— ". . . The result was honorable to yourself, and to the officers and men acting under your orders."

Secretary Cass in his annual report, dated November 25, 1832:— ". . . The conduct of the officers and men was exemplary."

President Andrew Jackson in his annual message of December 4, 1832:—". . . The result has been creditable to the troops engaged in the service. Severe as is the lesson to the Indians, it was rendered necessary by their unprovoked aggressions, and it is to be hoped that its impression will be permanent and salutary. . . . Our fellow citizens upon the frontiers were ready, as they always are, in the tender of their services in the hour of danger." [3]

[1] An Indian term for a commanding officer or general.
[2] From a statement by Wah-Con-De-Cor-Ah, made by him to Charles E. Mix, Commissioner of Indian Affairs, while the Chief was on a visit to Washington in 1859. Published in the Washington "Constitution" of April 17, 1859.
[3] The following unpublished manuscript verses are copied from the original in the Lasselle Papers of the Indiana State Library. They illustrate the viewpoint held during Indian troubles by those frontier citizens here mentioned by President Jackson. As soon as hostilities commenced—even when first attack as well as provocation were due to themselves—the mass of the whites were genuinely unable to see but one side to the question and became possessed of a desire and determination to kill Indians which took on the appearance and proportions of an exalted patriotic frenzy.
These verses relate to the Black Hawk War, are dated "Logansport, June 3, 1832," and are signed "L." They read:

THE FRONTIER CALL

March! March! Hear ye the savage yell!
Far to the north where war whoops are sounding.
March! March! We'll onward to battle
Where Black Hawk and Warriors the helpless are slaying.

Onward! March onward where glory awaits thee!
Remember the deeds of your Spencer and White:
Remember their deeds! Their fame will inspire thee
When onward ye rush, the foremost in fight.

Bright is the laurel entwined for the brave,
Pure be the tears for the Hero who falls;
Honored forever the youth who will save
His country from foes, when to battle she calls.

There is a psychological interest in the impassioned appeal with which the white youth is exorted to save "his country" from its "foes." The white settlers had unlawfully entered the Sac town and lands nine years before. Black Hawk's village had been an established and permanent Sac community for at least a century and a half.

466

140.—The rich wilderness lands of the interior, into which the settlers were moving. A scene on Cut-off River, tributary to the Wabash. From a sketch by Carl Bodmer, the naturalist and artist. A log-canoe ferry is moored ready for use.

The treaty concluding the war transferred title to 30,000,000 more acres of land from the Indians to the United States. For this territory, equal in size to the state of New York, the natives were promised an annuity of $20,000.[1]

By this period the policy of the United States had proved so successful that, in the North, it was in command of the situation. The Caucasian population was multiplying so rapidly, and means of communication had been so increased by treaty, road building, canal construction and the use of steamboats that no further serious embarrassments were possible in carrying out the plan to push the natives across the Mississippi. A few more treaties were still to be negotiated before the remaining Indian territories in that part of the country fell under white ownership, but their speedy acquirement was seen to be assured.[2] Only one other feature of the time requires attention in completing a picture of the race relations as they then existed in the upper part of the Mississippi valley. That feature may have exerted a strong though regrettable after-influence on the moral fibre of the newer Americans, and was itself, in part, an outgrowth of methods and racial antagonism already noticed. It has been observed that the white people coveted the red men's land, brought pressure on the Indians to induce its sale, and gave money for it. It might be supposed that after a sale of that sort the Indians would then possess money but less territory. Such, however, was not necessarily the case. Very often they possessed neither. The transaction was not always completed

[1] Representing a lump payment of $333,333. or about ten cents an acre. The Sacs and Foxes gave up 26.000.000 acres and the Winnebagoes 4.000.000.
[2] For a detailed record of territorial purchases from the Indians to the date of its publication, see "Abstract of Indian treaties, whereby the United States acquired the title to lands in the States of Ohio, Indiana, Illinois. Missouri, Mississippi and Alabama, and in the Territories of Michigan and Arkansas. Washington, 1828."

to the satisfaction of a certain proportion of the whites until they had the land and money both.

But little has been purposely preserved by the history recording race regarding those details whereby the sums paid for native lands were got back, but in a general way the arrangements for the process can be pieced together. And again, for that purpose, we may with profit turn for a moment to General Harrison's report of 1801. He refers in that letter to the "Traders"; to a fatal affray in one of their establishments in Vincennes, and to the large quantities of whisky brought into the country by them for sale to the Indians. For a century before that document was composed, and for years thereafter, the white government through its various political organizations and agents had granted permits to white men authorizing them to sell merchandise to Indians. Those permits, or licenses, were sought by many white men as a rapid way to accumulate wealth, and the conditions under which such traffic was conducted did, in fact, often offer an opportunity for getting money in quantities that then represented riches. Several reasons combined to produce the result named. In the first place the Indians as a rule were honest in their dealings and presumed the honesty of other men. They were disinclined to question records of commercial transactions kept by white men, and kept none themselves. The goods bought by the white traders cost them[1] but a small fraction of the prices at which they were sold to the natives, and when the Indians paid for their purchases by means of furs or skins, then those skins[2] were, in turn, only accepted at a fraction of their value to the trader. And finally, the methods by

[1] Even after heavy transportation charges had been paid.
[2] Until the Indians began to obtain cash in large amounts for the sale of lands, furs and skins were specified by legal enactment as the only lawful medium of exchange when goods were sold to natives.

which a trader ordinarily kept the record of his accounts with native customers offered unexcelled chances for imposition.

Two examples of this manner of Indian traders' book-keeping are shown by photographic illustrations else-where. They are typical leaves from Indian traders' account books, the earliest dating from 1801-1802 and the second from 1829-1830. Both reveal dealings with natives of the Indiana or Illinois country at the periods stated. The first is an account showing that an Indian called Antoine had been indebted to the trader in the sum of about seventy-six dollars, of which fifty-two dollars had been paid. In order to arrive at a correct interpre-tation of the account it is necessary to know the chief factors of the wilderness arithmetic table on which, for generations, Indian trade was based.[1] It was as follows:

4 coon skins	=	1 "plus"
2 bear skins	=	1 "plus"
2 bear skins	=	3 "plus"
1 otter skin	=	2 "plus"
1 extra good otter skin	=	3 "plus"
Beaver skin, per pound	=	1 "plus"
Extra fine beaver skin, per pound	=	2 "plus"
1 "plus"	=	two dollars.

Antoine's account, then, showed that he had owed 38 "plus," or $76, which he might pay by any combination of skins acceptable to the trader for that amount. A "plus" was represented in the account book simply by a small

[1] The table of fur values as here given is copied from a manuscript found among the Lasselle Papers of the Indiana State Library.

vertical mark of the pen. An extra scratch or two and an Indian—by the face of the account—would owe \$2 or \$4 more, as the case might be. Antoine, it seems, bought \$12 worth of whisky at one time.

The other account, showing a transaction of about 1830, was kept in figures representing dollars. By that time the Indians were in occasional receipt of cash after selling lands, and paid debts either in furs or coin. In this case the Indian Chequa and his son maintained a joint account and had owed \$54.66. Credits by peltries are entered to the amount of \$31.33. As in the case of Antoine, there is a charge of \$12 for whisky, and still another of \$7.66 for the same commodity.

Without question there were honest men engaged in native trade, but the known practises of Indian traders as a class, together with the opportunity confronting them and the almost universal frontier Caucasian estimate of the Indian as a creature deserving but little more consideration than was accorded to an undesirable wild animal, indicate that the whites, in business transactions with red men, generally adopted toward them an attitude lacking in fairness or honesty.

The number of white men engaged in selling merchandise[1] to the natives by governmental permission was always large, especially in the region of an Indian frontier. General Harrison, as an example, issued forty Indian traders' licenses during the short interval between November 20, 1801, and January 7, 1802.[2] By that time, though only four months had elapsed since the preparation of his Report, he had apparently taken the law into his own hands with respect to the liquor traffic. Harri-

---

[1] The term "merchandise" at the beginning of the nineteenth century in the Mississippi valley, legally included whisky. That liquor was named in the printed licenses issued to retailers of goods.
[2] A manuscript list of these permits is contained in the Lasselle Papers.

son's printed traders' permits for the period read "the said
. . . shall not, by himself, his servants, agents or factors, carry or cause to be carried to the hunting camps
of the Indians any . . . spirituous liquors of any kind; nor
shall barter or exchange the same, or any of them, in any
quantity whatever, on pain of forfeiture of this license

141.—Type of a quickly built and temporary log cabin often set up by new
arrivals in the western forest. A cabin like this could be erected by several
men in three or four days, and sufficed until the construction of a more
pretentious log house. It then served as a storehouse or winter stable.

and of the goods, wares and merchandise, and of the
spirituous liquors which may have been carried to said
camps . . . and the Indians of the said nation are at
full liberty to seize and confiscate the said liquors so carried, and the owners shall have no claim for the
same . . . "

In March of 1802 the Federal Congress took notice

of the subject on which General Harrison had been so emphatic, and passed the following law.[1] "And be it further enacted, That the President of the United States be authorized to take such measures, from time to time, as to him may appear expedient, to prevent or restrain the vending or distributing of spirituous liquors among all or any of the said Indian tribes." But neither Governor Harrison's regulation nor the government's decree had visible effect, and it was not until 1822[2] that any more radical verbal action was taken. In that year power was given to various officials by virtue of which packages of goods designed by traders for Indian consumption might be opened and searched, "upon suspicion or information that ardent spirits are carried into the Indian countries by said traders . . . and if any ardent spirits shall be so found, all the goods of the said trader shall be forfeited."

These local and general laws were ignored by the traders, nor does there seem to have been either a genuine endeavor to enforce them on the part of the authorities, or fear of them by their violators.[3] Various means were used in concerted and widespread effort to make the red man a heavy monetary debtor, and the sale of whisky to him was the most powerful illicit method employed for that purpose. Such a transaction not only netted large profit in itself, but also—which was still more important—brought the Indian to a condition in which he further enmeshed himself in obligations. Then, when

---

[1] Section 21 of the general laws of March 30, in regulation of Indian affairs. This proviso, coming as it did about nine months after Harrison's plea, suggests that his Report may have been received and have been the basis of Congressional action.

[2] Act of May 6: section 2. Another law, approved on the same day, brought to an end the activity of the government itself as an Indian trader; the practise had continued since 1811.

[3] As shown by the reproduction of Chequa's account, set down in 1829 or 1830, the trader openly recorded his sales of whisky to the Indian, and in a total bill of $54.66 the sum of $19.66 was for that commodity. This is not an isolated or unusual case. It is typical.

the Indian was drunk and had bought what he did not want or did not need, the entries could be made in the trader's account book. It was but seldom that the individual native protested at records which afterward confronted him: the imposing army of straight pen marks or forbidding columns of figures. If he could not find the goods set down against him, then—so the trader might argue or he himself believe—he must have lost them.

These things had a vastly greater significance in Indian trade than they would have had in the similar case of a white purchaser. To the white customer it would have meant an individual obligation merely, or else bankruptcy and relief from debt through legal process.[1] But with the Indian this was not so. White traders encouraged the individual natives to buy and put no limit on the credit extended to them, even though they might be penniless and without peltry. That was one of the surest methods by which the pale-skinned race obtained more travel routes over the face of the land; more square miles of territory.

The explanation of this apparent mystery lies in the fact that, in the last analysis, an Indian's individual debts were tribal obligations. If a member of the tribe could not pay then his nation would pay, and did pay. His race-brothers would sell the far-spreading hunting grounds of the whole people; would sell their farms and the earth above the bones of their fathers, if necessary, rather than let it be said that any member of the tribe rested under an obligation which he could not requite. Therefore it was a practise of the whites to involve an

---

[1] Ordinary dealers in merchandise never extended to poor white men of a community a tithe of the credit that was habitually given to red men by Indian traders.

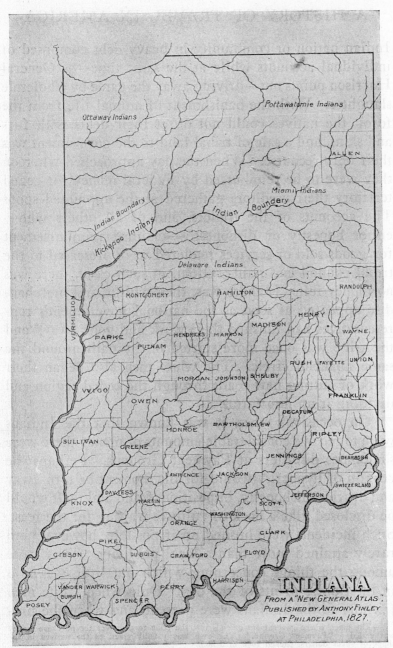

142.—Third in the series of maps. Indiana in 1827. Showing nearly all the lately purchased territory organized into white counties. The Potawatomi were then the largest proprietors of land north of the Wabash, and their country blocked intercourse between the white settlements of Michigan and Indiana.

Indian nation or community in heavy debt composed of individual accounts while at the same time—as General Harrison points out—driving away the game by wholesale slaughter. With the banishment of animal life from the forest the natives could not offset their debts with furs and skins, and a sale of tribal land to the government was their only recourse. When the day approached whereon they were to be reimbursed by Federal money for ceded territory their creditors gathered at the appointed spot.[1] The accounts of the traders, and of all others who—either honestly or dishonestly—claimed reimbursement for goods sold or services rendered were presented to the tribal council and paid. Often, in such cases, there was no money left. If there was, then whisky and merchandise appeared as soon as the national government's representatives had finished their work and gone away,[2] and the tribe was once more started on its path around the same financial circle. The white men also began their work of cutting new roads through the ceded region and dividing it up into farms.

On occasions when it was known that the Indians were to receive considerable amounts of money there were sometimes disorders at Payment Grounds. Perhaps the curtain of hypocrisy would for the moment be torn away and avarice, dishonesty, imposition, fraud and theft would be disclosed, like a flock of vultures waiting for the feast. Such incidents were hushed up if possible, however, and rarely attained more than a local publicity. They were among the things concerning which but little was said in the public prints of the day. Only when white men friendly to the Indians were present, and when the pro-

---

[1] The place where government officials met the tribe to pay over the purchase money was called a "Payment Ground." The cash was usually given to the natives in the shape of silver dollars, packed 1000 in a box.
[2] Which was usually very quickly.

ceedings excited the anger of such white men to a point
which overcame considerations of self-interest, was
clamor made. And even then it was necessary for the
friendly whites to voice the Indian protest, for the red
men, if left to their own initiative, generally decided to
endure in silence.

An event somewhat of this sort happened in connection with the payment of $63,000 to the Potawatomi
Indians of the Wabash, in 1836. These were the Indiana
Indians who, ten years before, had granted to the United
States and Indiana the right to build the Michigan Road,
and who had also parted with some of their land in order
that it might be constructed. The Wabash Potawatomi
had in 1836 sold the remainder of their heritage and
had gathered to receive their money. Part of the tribe,
as usually happened in transactions of the sort, was
strongly opposed to removal beyond the Mississippi, but
the treaty had been signed and further objections by the
disaffected ones, though bitter, were futile. A record of
what happened at the Payment Ground was made by a
white man friendly to one native faction, and from the
account therein contained—and also from what appears
between the lines of it—can be reconstructed the drama
which led up to and accompanied the disappearance of
the Potawatomi from their former home. That division of the nation which objected to the sale and removal
also had its white champion, and his views are indirectly
set forth by the chronicler. Both native factions were of
course willing to pay their just debts. The main contentions were concerning the methods by which the whites
had secured the treaty, and over the disposal of the money
received. The narrative is in the shape of an appeal to

the President by the treaty-signing faction, and reads as follows :[1]

To our Great Father,
   Andrew Jackson,
      President of the United States.

" . . . .Father, we have always listened well to your good advice and wise counsels, and we find them good. We know you are a great, brave and good man, that you will do as you promise. We come now with sore hearts and our minds filled with sorrow to speak with you and tell you true. We intended to speak to you through our Father whom you have placed here near us (Col. * * * *) [2] but he has gone away and can't hear us. Before we had signed treaties to him, Father, for all our Lands, he was always ready to hear us and to promise us the protection of your strong arm [3] but now he has our Treaties in his pocket for our entire Country, he has no time to hear us, nor to protect us. . . .

"We wish and intend to follow the advice and counsels of our Great Father and we look to him for support and protection. That protection has been promised us, and which was a strong inducement with us when we sold our Lands. . . Again we saw there were too many white people about our reserves for us to live on them in pease and we signed a general Treaty in September last, selling all our lands to our Great Father, and agreed to go West of the Mississippi, and accept of that home he had there provided for us.

"Father, so soon as this fact was known . . . being now assembled together near the Tippecanoe River where we were to receive our money a great excitement prevailed. Those Indians who opposed us held a Council of War and resolved that every one of us who had signed the Treaty should be killed, and they proceeded to appoint War Chiefs whose duty it should be, and now is, to see their decree put in execution. And on the next day, being the day on which we had received our annuity and Treaty money, the house we were in transacting business was surrounded by those Indians and their associates and advisers. . . . Alex Coquillard, a bad man who has always opposed our Great Father's policy, was among them. . . . He got upon a house and made a speech. . . . He told them we were not Chiefs, that we were boys and hog thieves, that the President of the United States was a bad man, a rascal, and that he had stolen the Indian Lands, that he was now robbing them of their money (because we were willing to pay our just debts) and that he would next send us away like dogs west of the Mississippi where we would be poor and unhappy. . . .

"Father, when the white people found we were willing to pay our

[1] Copied from the manuscript contained in the Lasselle Papers, in the Indiana State Library.
[2] Name stated in manuscript but omitted here. The Indian Agent.
[3] The "strong arm" of a President, or of the United States government, was an Indian figure of speech meaning the army, or soldiers.

honest debts and that we were willing to appropriate the most of our money[1] for this purpose they began to make papers [claims] and in this way and upon the Payment Ground, whilst we were transacting our own business and trying to do what was right and honest, claims and papers amounting to $200,000 were made and pushed in upon [us] for immediate payment. . . . Many large claims were urged by men from the River Raisin and from Detroit and from Post Vincennes of twenty-five and thirty years standing. Those we have no knowledge of, believe they are not just, and are not willing to pay any such claims. All the claims were paid by us in the treaties of 1826, 1828 and 1832, and some of them paid two or three times over. These claimants after getting drunk . . . rushed into the house in part and others began to tear it down, crying 'we will take the money by force,' and in this way a general mob took place. . . . We went to our Agent and reminded him of his promise that he would protect us and that we expected him to do so, that we had not done anything wrong as we were aware of. He spoke like a man to us, and said that the Great Father never broke his word and that he [the Agent] would protect us or would die, us to be quiet and keep still and leave the balance to him. This speech he made to us through our friend Ewing[2] and we believed it. . . .

"We then agreed, in order to satisfy the white people that we wanted to do what was right, that Colonel * * * * and Captain Simonton[3] might select five good white men more who should be entirely disinterested and they should be under our control, should help us pay out part of our money to our own people, and that then they should pay out such sums on the different claims against us as we should direct them to pay, after having first examined the claim and satisfied ourselves it was just. To do this it was thought best to remove the money from the payment ground to Judge Polk's about three miles distant. Accordingly five men were named by our Agent, but he did not select good or honest men, nor were they disinterested. . . .

"Our agent, after having told these men that they were to pay out that money as we should direct, and presuming we supposed that there would be no further trouble about it, left us and went into Logansport which we were very sorry for. He had promised and we think he should have staid with us until we had finished our business, for no sooner had he left than those five men took full possession of our money. We were not permitted to go into the house but were turned out and told that we had nothing to do with that money, that they were going to do as they pleased with it and truly they did so. . . . They never examined one single claim nor asked us whether we did or did not

[1] The amount received by the native nation on this occasion was "Sixty Three Boxes"; that is to say, $63,000. The accounts against members of the tribe which the Chiefs believed to be honest and were willing to pay amounted to the sum of $40,000.

[2] Ewing, who had lived among the Potawatomi for fifteen years, spoke their language. It was Ewing who prepared the manuscript letter here quoted.

[3] Whose only relation to the matter lay in the fact that he was the army officer who brought the money and paid it to the Indians.

owe certain claimants but gave it out thus arbitrarily or kept it themselves in part we know not how. Nor will they even give us a list of the names of the persons to whom they paid away our money.

"Father, is not this Robbery? And will you suffer us to be thus abused? We owed honest debts and were anxious to pay them, but we wanted the privilege of settling those debts ourselves . . . we poor, no money and those who have cheated us out of our money are

143.—Examples of roads built through Indian territory by native consent, in order that white men might travel between their disconnected settlements. Showing the Michigan Road (in the center) granted to the United States by the Potawatomi of Indiana by treaty in 1826. The Indians donated the land occupied by the highway and additional land whose sale procured enough money to pay for building the road, which extended to the Ohio River. From Mitchell's "Travellers' Guide Through the United States: 1835."

gone we know not where. . . . We wanted to talk to our Father, the Agent, but he left this morning.

"It is true we have no more lands to sell, but we hope our Great Father will not refuse to listen to his red children because they have no more land to sell. We have sold all our country to you, Father, because you told us you wished us to do so, and we are always willing to listen to your good counsels. . . .

"We want our Great Father to send a good talk to this frontier. Tell these bad Indians and the bad white people, too, that they must not do as they have done and that you will punish them for the injury they have already done. . . .

"Father what we have said comes through our hearts. It is true and we have nothing more to say."

A Federal investigation resulted in this instance, and its findings were printed in two obscure pamphlets during the following year.[1] Among other statements made by the Commissioner in his report was the following:

"The gentlemen who distributed the money in 1836 also preserved and delivered to me most of the claims presented to them, and the receipts then given for the money, which they paid. Those papers I also transmit herewith. They show several instances in which persons obtained money in 1836 to which they had no claim, and in direct violation of their full acquittances of the previous year. . . . ."[2]

The report also said:

"It is evident from all this that these Indians are fast sinking to the most abject poverty, and when to this is added the habits of intoxication which are produced by their vicinity to the white people, we must be aware that their entire destruction is close at hand. . . . They must be removed beyond the Mississippi, out of reach of the white men. . . . To remain among the white people must be certain destruction to them. . . . . A regulation rendering it impossible to collect of an Indian a debt of more than a year's standing would save them from a load of imposition. . . . They feel, as one of the Chiefs expressed it to me, 'These things make us blind; we cannot see; do you see for us.' "[3]

Reduced to figures the Commissioner reported the following financial situation of the tribe:

Total claims of alleged creditors.......$169,446.64
Obviously fraudulent and unsupported.. 83,883.50
Compelled to allow[4].................. 85,563.14
Paid out in cash to creditors.......... 62,802.10
Cash left to Indians out of $63,000......   197.90
Indians still in debt.................. 22,761.04

To which he adds that the nation had already paid in

[1] "Report of J. W. Edmonds, United States Commissioner upon the Disturbance at the Potawatomie Payment, September, 1836. New-York: 1837."
"Report of John W. Edmonds, United States Commissioner on the claims of creditors of the Potawatamie Indians of the Wabash; Presented under the Treaties made with them in 1836 and '37. New-York: 1837." Neither of these reports bears the United States government imprint.
[2] Report on the "Claims": p. 5.
[3] Report on the "Disturbance": p. 7.
[4] Though he says many here included were probably fraudulent. However, the account books of creditors were produced as proof of the debts.

cash to creditors $27,022.50 in 1835 and $41,150.00 in 1836.

Here, then, was a small and comparatively insignificant Indian tribe[1] which, in two years' time, had lost all its territorial possessions, had paid out $130,974.60 in money, and still owed $22,761.04. The case is one which illustrates what has been said, namely, that in transactions involving purchases of territory from the natives there was a part of the white race which did not consider the matter satisfactorily closed until it had the land and money both. Nor was the instance, in its general features, an isolated one either in the North or South. The methods illuminated by it had been in operation for many years. In 1830 the Miami nation of Indiana[2] had undertaken to build up a civilization resembling that of the surrounding white race, and even appropriated money out of the national fund for use in the education of its youth. Yet by 1840 the red community was overwhelmed by a traders' debt of $300,000.00, was forced to sell its territory, and its creditors had an influence sufficient to cause the insertion of a proviso in the arrangements which declared that the sum named must be applied at once "to the payment of the debts of the tribe."

No satisfactory estimate of the extent of the business carried on by traders with the Indians or set down in their books as a basis for future claims can ever be possible, but from the instances here mentioned, which affected only about two thousand red people in one end of one state, and which were embraced within a period of ten years, it is apparent that the similar aggregate dealings throughout the country were enormous. They were a part of the white man's procedure, privately conducted and gov-

[1] It numbered but about a thousand souls, all told.
[2] Neighbors of the Potawatomi.

ernmentally tolerated, which had for its design the weakening and ousting of the Indian in order that the newer race might spread over the land without physical conflict. The system of which such transactions were a part, and into which they fitted, was a masterpiece of economic, social and commercial diplomacy from every standpoint except that of the aborigine.

The original and most effective use, in America, of the principle of monopolistic combination and the suppression of competition as a means of acquiring wealth and economic power, lay in the policy pursued by the Federal government toward the Indians for the purpose of acquiring native territories. The white commonwealths acted as a combination; objected to combination by their opponents; denied advice to their adversaries; created conditions that weakened the opposition; refused to permit the opposing side to deal, in land transactions, with other customers than themselves; and fixed the prices that were paid. As a consequence the white monopoly was able to buy hundreds of millions of acres of Indian lands at an average cost of about three and a half cents an acre.

The later copying of this governmental example by groups of private individuals, and the application of identical practises to economic phases of national development conducted under private auspices, led to those commercial monopolies and business methods which the Federal government now characterizes as reprehensible and is seeking to abolish under conditions providing for restitution to the injured and punishment for the wrongdoers.

CHAPTER XXV

A STRANGE SITUATION IN THE SOUTH — PROBLEMS CREATED
BY THREE OVERLAPPING AND CONFLICTING SOVEREIGN-
TIES—OVERLAND COMMUNICATION BETWEEN NORTH
AND SOUTH BLOCKED ALONG A LINE OF SIX HUN-
DRED MILES — HEAVY PUNISHMENT FOR UNLAWFUL
TRAVEL — THE INDIANS GIVE ROADS THROUGH
GEORGIA, ALABAMA, MISSISSIPPI AND TENNESSEE TO
THE WHITES — FEDERAL GOVERNMENT DESIRES NA-
TIVES TO MAINTAIN TAVERNS AND FERRIES FOR
AUTHORIZED TRAVELLERS — THE CHEROKEE NATION
BECOMES PART OWNER OF A WHITE THOROUGHFARE
AND RECEIVES MONEY FOR PERMITTING UNITED
STATES CITIZENS TO JOURNEY BETWEEN GEORGIA AND
TENNESSEE — CAUSES OF THE STRENGTH AND DE-
VELOPMENT OF THE SOUTHERN RED NATIONS — THE
LAW OF 1802 AND THE GEORGIA COMPACT — ELE-
MENTS OF FUTURE TROUBLE

THE methods by which the white race secured in the
South a right to travel through and settle in that
region during the period previous to the introduction of
the railroad, and by which they also linked their southern
settlements with one another and with those of the North
by overland routes, closely resembled in some particulars
the processes just described. But in certain other of its
features, and also in some of the results which flowed from
them, the situation in that part of the country was quite

484

different from the one already outlined. Several factors contributed to this state of affairs. The white population, for one thing, was smaller than in the northern states and territories, and the native nations, though fewer in number, were larger and more powerful both in population and landed possessions. There was also for a considerable time, less close intermingling of the races. This resulted in the longer and more vigorous maintenance, among the southern Indians, of those native qualities of self-respect, dignity, sobriety, home-love and desire for self-government that were imperilled by intimate contact with Caucasians.

It is probable that shortly after the beginning of the nineteenth century the red commonwealths of the South[1] contained an aggregate population of a hundred thousand souls and that they owned not far from a hundred thousand square miles of territory, or an area considerably more than twice as large as that contained within the boundaries of the state of New York. These extensive holdings were of course divided into different tracts, some of which were entirely surrounded by possessions of the United States while others adjoined neighboring Indian territory on one or more sides.

At the time mentioned and for years afterward, the districts occupied by white men in Louisiana, in southern Mississippi, Alabama and Georgia, and also in Spain's territory of Florida, were almost entirely cut off from unimpeded overland intercourse with the North[2] by a chain of Indian nations that extended westward with scarcely a break from South Carolina to the farther side of Arkansas Territory, a distance of more than six hun-

---

[1] The principal native peoples of that part of the continent were then the Cherokees, Chickasaws, Choctaws and Creeks. The Seminoles occupied Spanish territory, in Florida.
[2] Except by consent of the natives.

485

dred miles.[1]   Along the southern boundaries of North
Carolina and Tennessee, and extending far south into
Georgia, Alabama and Mississippi, lay the rich countries
of the Cherokees, Creeks, Chickasaws and Choctaws.
These were then the most powerful red peoples within
the boundaries of the so-called United States east of the
Mississippi River.   Their land holdings were compact
and extensive; their population large, vigorous and intelligent.   The regions they owned were not only valuable,
but from the economic standpoint of the expanding white
race, extremely important.   Yet for a generation those
tribes clung with tenacity to their historical position;
secured in long established and undisputed rights; holding no official dealings with white men save through the
Federal government of the United States by treaties.[2]   They governed themselves, and their right so to do
was acknowledged.

These conditions in themselves presented an extraordinary and grave problem to the new white nation, and
one demanding, for its final settlement with mutual honor
and benefit, a high degree of statesmanship on both sides.
And there was still another element to the situation that
gave it an even greater complexity.   For the geographical
boundaries of the four most important Indian nations of
the South—as those limits had been defined and guaranteed by treaties with the national government of the
United States—included, in each case, parts of two or
more different states of the Federal Union.   The possessions of the Cherokees embraced undivided and continu-

---

[1] The southern territory within the present limits of the United States, not including
Florida, which was acknowledged by treaty to be within the ownership and jurisdic-
tion of Indian nations, originally exceeded in size the combined area of Maine, New
Hampshire, Vermont, Connecticut, Rhode Island, Massachusetts, New Jersey and
Delaware.

[2] Except in the technical case of a few hundred Indians in South Carolina who by
consent of the Federal government and natives, treated with the state directly.

144.—Map showing the overlapping of three white and red sovereignties in the
South. The Chickasaw nation, by treaty with the United States, extended
across the state line into Alabama, north of Marion county. The Choctaw
nation's southern boundary penetrated Alabama to the Tombeckbe River, at
a point north of Washington county. The map also shows The Old Natchez
Road, built through the two Indian nations by their consent; the Robinson
Road, General Jackson's Road, and other thoroughfares permitted to the
whites by the natives. From "Mitchell's Map of Louisiana, Mississippi and
Alabama, 1834."

ous lands extending across the boundary lines that separated Georgia, Alabama, North Carolina and Tennessee, and included territory in all those commonwealths. A like condition was true with respect to the Creek nation in Georgia and Alabama. Further to the west the Chickasaws and their southern neighbors the Choctaws owned about half of the state of Mississippi, and in each case their national possessions and authority extended eastward over contiguous and unseparated districts into Alabama.

Here, then, were three apparently overlapping and conflicting sovereignties occupying the same geographical limits. The separate white states acknowledged allegiance to their common Federal government. The national white union conducted the mutual affairs of the white states while at the same time it recognized the sovereignty of the red nations, and defined the territorial limits of those native peoples by treaties that admitted their ownership and control of lands which lay within and overlapped the theoretical boundaries of white political divisions. The Senate approving those treaties was composed of representatives of the affected Caucasian states.[1] The southern white states among which lay Indian nations acknowledged that their own jurisdiction did not cover the native possessions or peoples. And finally, the Indian commonwealths neither owed nor gave allegiance to local Caucasian laws, but conducted their relations with the white race through treaties with the United States and its accredited national representatives resident among them.

Such in effect was the situation in the South at the end of the long period during which the Indians had resorted

[1] For all the white states were intimately concerned in the question of Indian possessions and sovereignty.

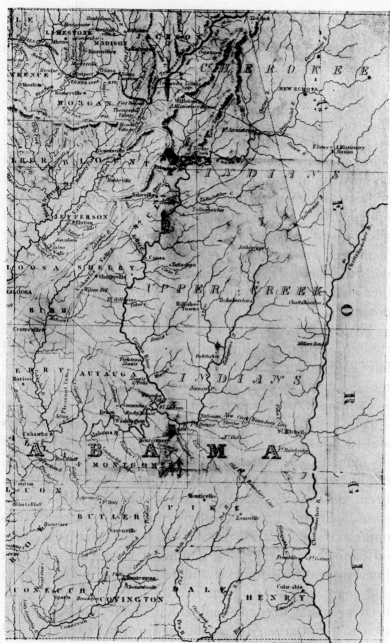

145.—Showing the Cherokee and Creek nations overlapping the boundary between Georgia and Alabama. All white roads came to an end when they reached the Creek country. The highway through the Cherokee nation from Etowee to the Tennessee River was the Unicoy Road, for the use of which, by whites, the Cherokees received monetary payments. From the same map as the preceding.

to warfare as their chief method of preventing Caucasian advance over the face of the land. The strong, ambitious, restless, arrogant and intolerant multitude of comparatively late arrivals had won their own independence and formed a far-spreading political organization. And at almost the outset of their national career they were confronted by the fact that their apparently close-knit union was not one in actuality, and that their intercourse and association with one another were in many localities impeded by the conditions here recited. The Federal government had taken a position concerning the standing of the red nations that was destined to interfere seriously with the methods, convenience, desires and ambitions of the individuals and communities of which it was composed.

That such a condition contained the elements of future trouble is apparent. The only way in which trouble could have been avoided under the circumstances was through the exercise by the master-people of those traits of friendliness, forbearance and good-will which were so obviously demanded by the situation and by their own acts and pledges. A sincere endeavor based on those motives of human action, rather than on hostility and greed, might have solved the problem. Had such an attempt been successfully made the white race in this country would perhaps for a time have remained somewhat less opulent in its material possessions, but it might also have offset the worldly loss by gaining a larger store of that inward wealth of honesty and fair dealing between man and man which was then overlooked, which has since been so much needed, and which in the end is a more secure foundation for national health, strength and wealth.

In view of the attitude long held toward the red men in all parts of the country it is not surprising that the event fell otherwise. Trouble did arise within a generation, and before the crisis was passed the country had been brought within measurable distance of disturbances which would have amounted to civil war.

The first important treaty negotiated by the United States with a southern Indian nation after the adoption of the Federal Constitution in 1789, was one made with the Cherokees in 1791. By that instrument the natives ceded a little land and granted two important travel concessions to the whites. Article V said:

"It is stipulated and agreed that the citizens and inhabitants of the United States shall have a free and unmolested use of a road from Washington district to Mero district,[1] and of the navigation of the Tennessee River."

This treaty was the outgrowth of a previous negotiation between the same parties in 1785, which had declared that a white intruder on Cherokee territory "shall forfeit the protection of the United States, and the Indians may punish him or not as they please." The violation of the compacts of 1785 and 1791 by whites was described by Secretary of War Knox as disgraceful.[2] When the treaty of 1791 was drawn it repeated the prohibition of white intrusion into Cherokee territory and contained a provision that no United States citizen might travel in the Cherokee sovereignty without a passport. Nevertheless white men continued to enter the forbidden region without permission, and after finding themselves unable to keep intruders out by means less severe the Indians punished invaders by death. Such methods were extreme, but the natives were within their treaty

[1] In Tennessee.
[2] And as due to the attempt of "white people to seize by fraud or force" the Indian land.

privilege. They could fix the punishment. Other white men retaliated by killing friendly Indians without provocation, and the red men, angered by the way in which their rights were ignored, committed similar crimes. They also demanded the protection of Congress. The Federal government attitude at the time, as put into words, can be shown by a communication from Jefferson to General Knox, in which he said:

"Government should firmly maintain this ground, that the Indians have a right to the occupation of their lands independent of the States within whose chartered lines they happen to be; that until they cede them by treaty, or other transaction equivalent to treaty, no act of a State can give a right to such lands. . . . The Government is determined to exert all its energy for the patronage and protection of the rights of the Indians." [1]

In actions, however, the national administrations of the period were not effective in abating the troubles complained of, and more or less friction was always existent on the Cherokee frontier. The next treaty with the Cherokees, in 1798, was distinguished by another travel concession to the white republic. Its seventh article read:

"The Cherokee nation agree that the Kentucky road, running between the Cumberland Mountain and the Cumberland River, where the same shall pass through the Indian land, shall be an open and free road for the use of the citizens of the United States in like manner as the road from Southwest Point to Cumberland River."

Tennessee and Kentucky were the most thickly populated and important outlying regions held by the whites, and the travel privileges already obtained from the Cherokees, and here referred to, had been for the purpose of gaining a freer movement between those interior parts and the East. It was also highly desirable that other

---

[1] Previously, and under the Confederation, the question of state rights in the matter of an Indian treaty had arisen in 1785, when North Carolina fruitlessly protested against the Cherokee compact as infringing the legislative rights of that state. After 1785, for more than forty years, no state took the position that such negotiations were not properly a function of the Federal Union.

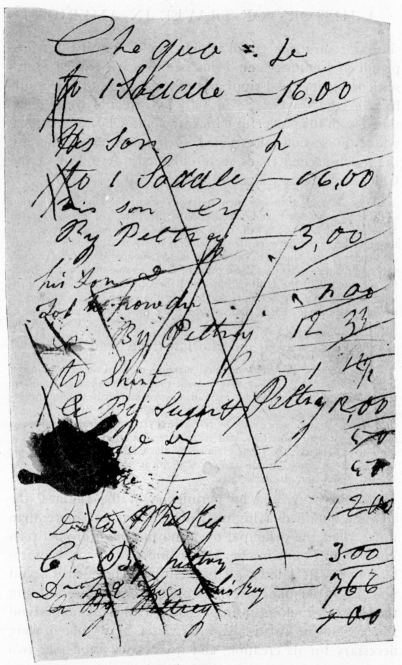

146.—Selling goods to the Indians on credit, under governmental authority, continued unabated. Page from an Indiana-Illinois trader's book in 1829-1830. Amounts set down in figures. The Indian was debited with $54.66, of which $19.66 was for whisky.

similar routes be secured which would permit the white people of Kentucky and Tennessee to reach United States settlements in Mississippi and other sections of the South by overland travel. So in 1801 two treaties were negotiated with the powerful Chickasaw and Choctaw nations, whose possessions obstructed such movement, whereby the much-needed roads were obtained. Article I of the Chickasaw treaty was as follows:

"The Mingco, principal men and warriors of the Chickasaw nation of Indians, give leave and permission to the President of the United States of America to lay out, open and make a convenient wagon road through their land between the settlements of Mero district in the State of Tennessee and those of Natchez in the Mississippi Territory, in such way and manner as he may deem proper; and the same shall be a highway for the citizens of the United States and the Chickasaw. . . . Provided always that the necessary ferries over the water courses crossed by the said road shall be held and deemed to be the property of the Chickasaw nation."

And article II of the Choctaw treaty read:

"The Mingos, principal men and warriors of the Choctaw nation of Indians do hereby give their free consent that a convenient and durable wagon road may be explored, marked, opened and made under the orders and instructions of the President of the United States, through their lands to commence at the northern extremity of the settlement of the Mississippi Territory, and to be extended from thence . . . until it shall strike the lands claimed by the Choctaw nation; and the same shall be and continue forever a highway for the citizens of the United States and the Choctaws."

In this way, and by permission of the Indians, the country obtained a highway which was for more than thirty years the principal overland thoroughfare between North and South in the Mississippi valley. It came to be universally known as the "Old Natchez Road," and was one of the main factors in populating and upbuilding the interior, ranking in importance with the Cumberland and Michigan Roads. Both treaties here quoted were necessary for its creation, and it extended for about two hundred miles through Indian sovereignties that could not have been crossed by white travel and commerce without it and the consent for its construction. Far indeed were the white Americans, during the period between 1800 and 1830, from right to go where they pleased in the United States without permission.

During the same year of 1801 the Cherokees were asked to cede more land and permit the construction of certain roads through a part of their territory for the greater convenience of white travel, but they declined to grant either request at that time. In the instructions given to the Federal commissioners who then visited them was contained the following language:

"It is of importance that the Indian nations generally should be convinced of the certainty in which they may at all times rely upon the friendship of the United States, and that the President will never abandon them or their children."

The year 1802 was marked by the passage of a Federal law entitled "an act to regulate trade and intercourse with the Indian tribes, and to preserve peace on the frontiers." This legislation contained various provisions recognizing the sovereignty of the still existing Indian nations, and two of its sections were afterward destined to play a profoundly important part in the final diplomatic contest between the races. One of its articles subjected United States citizens to fine and imprisonment if they entered the Indian nations south of the Ohio River without Federal passports. Another forbade any representative of an individual state to discuss the land question with natives except at a United States treaty conference, and in the presence and with the approbation of the Federal commissioner. A third section provided that if an Indian came into a white state and committed a crime, the state could not seize him except in its own jurisdiction. If he escaped back into native jurisdiction the state could not act, but an application for extradition of the criminal Indian must be made "under the direction or instruction of the President of the United States," and by a Federal official. The Indian nation then had a year to comply, and the United States guaranteed indemnity to the injured white person.

But the two parts of the law of 1802 which were later to have such deep effect on the affairs of the two races were sections V and XIX. The first of these read:

"That if any such citizen or other person shall make a settlement on any lands belonging, or secured, or granted, by treaty with the United States, to any Indian tribe, or shall survey, or attempt to survey, such lands . . . such offender shall forfeit a sum not exceeding one thousand dollars, and suffer imprisonment, not exceeding twelve months. And it shall, moreover, be lawful for the President of the United States to take such measures, and to employ such military force as he may judge necessary; to remove from lands, belonging, or secured by treaty, as aforesaid, to any Indian tribe, any such citizen, or other person, who has made, or shall hereafter make, or attempt to make, a settlement thereon."

And section XIX ran:

"That nothing in this act shall be construed to prevent any trade or intercourse with Indians living on lands surrounded by settlements of the citizens of the United States, and being within the ordinary jurisdiction of any of the individual states, or the unmolested use of a road from Washington district to Mero district, or to prevent the citizens of Tennessee from keeping in repair the said road, under the direction or orders of the governor of said state, and of the navigation of the Tennessee River, as reserved and secured by treaty; nor shall this act be construed to prevent any person or persons travelling from Knoxville to Price's settlement, or to the settlement on Obed's River (so-called), provided they shall travel in the trace or path which is usually travelled, and provided the Indians make no objection; but if the Indians object, the President of the United States is hereby authorized to issue a proclamation, prohibiting all travelling on said traces, or either of them, as the case may be, after which the penalties of this act shall be incurred by every person travelling or being found on said traces, or either of them, to which the prohibition may apply, within the Indian boundary, without a passport."

496

It would be difficult to show more clearly than by the significance of this language, the dependence of the United States on the red race at that time for the privilege of lawful travel in some parts of the country. The mere objection of the Indians to the use of certain paths by the whites was a sufficient cause for the President to

BATTLE OF BAD AXE.   SCHLACHT VON BAD AXE.

147.—The battle of Bad Axe, fought on the Mississippi at the mouth of Bad Axe River, in 1832. Culmination of race troubles brought about by the entry of white men into the Illinois country. A steamboat was used in the fight by the government troops. Many men, women and children of the moving Indian village, guided by Black Hawk, were killed. After a sketch by the American artist Henry Lewis.

issue a public proclamation to the whole people, informing them that if they ventured on designated roads without passports they would be liable to arrest, fine and imprisonment.

Interesting as is the revelation of travel conditions

thus made, however, the particular feature of section XIX, fated to become so vital at a later date, was the first portion of it, which discusses the law in its relations to "Indians living on lands surrounded by settlements of the citizens of the United States, and being within the ordinary jurisdiction of any of the individual states."

It is apparent that we are here dealing with a sharp and intentional distinction between two separate and widely differing conditions of Indian society. To one of them, and to the relations of the white race with it, the law applied; to the other it did not. If the difference in the two sorts of native life was sufficiently pronounced to render the same law applicable to one and yet unfitted for the other, then that distinction between them must have been radical indeed. The quesion arises: What is the meaning intended to be contained in the language of the law?

The only manner whereby that part of native society untouched by the law is defined, is its description as "Indians living on lands surrounded by settlements of the citizens of the United States, and being within the ordinary jurisdiction of any of the individual states." Now as a matter of fact — in one sense — all the Indians in the country east of the Mississippi lived on lands in some degree surrounded by United States citizens, since all the remaining Indian sovereignties were, geographically, scattered over the continental area like plums in a slice of pudding. Yet it is obvious that the distinct red nations still owning their own territories were not included, or intended to be included, in the exception named in the law to which the act did not apply, because regulation of intercourse between those native states and the whites was the purpose of the act. Those native sovereignties were still further removed from inclusion in the Indian society untouched by the law through the fact that they framed and lived under their own governmental regulations. In order that a group of Indians might be embraced in the section of red population which the Federal law of 1802 did not affect, it had to be both surrounded by white settlements and "within the ordinary jurisdiction of any of the several states."

Congress therefore meant to describe in its exception those numerous small communities of red people, here and there, which had lost all their national functions and vitality.[1] Such fragments of once strong tribes had in the slow lapse of time — and in nearly every case prior to the organization of Constitutional government — given up their native rights and customs, fitted themselves into their new surroundings and voluntarily placed themselves, little by little, under the statutes and protection of the white states in which they lived. By their relinquishment of ancient privileges and treaty relations with the national government they had thus finally come, as the law of 1802 described it, within the "ordinary" jurisdiction of the white people. And, also, such little groups lived within close and constant reach of established seats of justice and all the operating fabric of white government, to which they might resort upon desire, or which could extend a hand to seize them, if need be, without undue exertion or the creation of new machinery or jurisdiction for the purpose.

That, in short, seems to have been the Indian population which Congress intended should be unaffected by the operation of the law of 1802. The people were quite

---

[1] As the Shinnecocks of New York, Penobscots of Maine, Narragansetts of Rhode Island, Nanticokes of Maryland, Pamunkeys of Virginia, and many dozens of other tribal remnants.

familiar with those natives who had thus become virtually merged with white communities, just as they also knew the large, powerful red nations who still governed themselves, who still held immense territories and to whose courtesy they were often indebted for the privilege of travelling somewhere. So well known to every class of white society and to government were the two elements of red population and the radical differences between them, that their further identification by Congress was probably considered superfluous. Yet on the interpretation, by one man, of this short passage of forty-one words was later to hang the fate of a widespread, flourishing, peaceful Indian civilization, and the destiny of the red race.

Still another event of the year 1802 was ordained to figure with equal prominence in the eventual downfall of Indian effort to build up a modern social and economic system. Georgia, in that year, ceded to the United States "all the right, title and claim" which she had in the country lying immediately to the westward. Out of the region thus acquired by the Federal government were soon afterward erected the territories of Alabama and Mississippi. The United States paid to Georgia a cash consideration and also promised to extinguish Indian title to native possessions in Georgia "as early as the same can be peaceably obtained, on reasonable terms."[1]

More overland routes were constantly being asked of the southern red nations, and by 1805 the Cherokees were again in an obliging frame of mind. The treaty then negotiated with them at Tellico[2] contained this:

"The citizens of the United States shall have the free and unmolested use and enjoyment of the two following described roads, in

[1] Thus leaving with the Cherokees and Creeks a right to determine when, if ever, the extinguishment in question might take place.
[2] October 25, 1805. Article IV.

1. *A spirit of adventurous enterprise :* a willingness to go through any hardship or danger to accomplish an object. It was the spirit of enterprise which led to the settlement of that country. The western people think nothing of making a long journey, of encountering fatigue, and of enduring every species of hardship. The great highways of the West —its long rivers—are familiar to very many of them, who have been led by trade to visit remote parts of the Valley.

2. *Independence of thought and action.*—They have felt the influence of this principle from their childhood. Men who can endure any thing: that have lived almost without restraint, free as the mountain air, or as the deer and the buffalo of their forests—and who know that they are Americans all—will act out this principle during the whole of life. I do not mean that they have such an amount of it as to render them *really* regardless alike of the opinions and the feelings of every one else. But I have seen many who have the virtue of independence greatly perverted or degenerated, and who were not pleasant members of a society, which is a state requiring a compromising spirit of mutual co-operation in all, and a determination to bear and forbear.

3. *An apparent roughness,* which some would deem *rudeness of manners.*

These traits characterize, especially, the agricultural portions of the country, and also in some degree the new towns and villages. They are not so much the offspring of ignorance and barbarism, (as some would suppose), as the results of the circumstances of a people thrown together in a new country, often for a long time in thin settlements ; where, of course, acquaintances for many miles around are soon, of necessity, made and valued from few adventitious causes. Where there is perfect equality in a neighbourhood of people who know but little about each other's previous history or ancestry—but where each is lord of the soil which he cultivates. Where a log cabin is all that the best of families can expect to have for years, and of course can possess few of the external decorations which have so much influence in creating a diversity of rank in society. These circumstances, have laid the foundation for that equality of intercourse, simplicity of manners, want of deference, want of reserve, great readiness to make acquaintances, freedom of speech, indisposition to brook real or imaginary insults, which one witnesses among the people of the West.

The character and manners of the traders and merchants who inhabit the principal cities and towns of the West, do not differ greatly from those of the same class in the Atlantic states.

148.—Character and manners of the settlers of the interior. From Baird's "View of the Valley of the Mississippi, or the Emigrants' and Travellers' Guide to the West"; published in 1834: pp. 102-103.

addition to those which are at present established through their country, one to proceed from some convenient place near the head of Stone's River, and fall into the Georgia road at a suitable place toward the southern frontier of the Cherokees. The other to proceed from the neighborhood of Franklin, on Big Harpath, and crossing the Tennessee at or near the Muscle Shoals, to pursue the nearest and best way to the settlements on the Tombigbee."

The Cherokees, at almost the same time,[1] granted permission for the conveyance of the mails through their territory. The treaty language ran:

"And whereas the mail of the United States is ordered to be carried from Knoxville to New Orleans through the Cherokee, Creek a.id Choctaw countries; the Cherokees agree that the citizens of the United States shall have, so far as it goes through their country, the free and unmolested use of a road leading from Tellico to Tombigbee."

Creeks and Choctaws were equally accommodating in the matter, and the mails went through. Still later in the same year the Creeks donated a horse path to the white people. Their consent read:[2]

"It is hereby stipulated and agreed, on the part of the Creek nation, that the Government of the United States shall forever hereafter have a right to a horse path through the Creek country, from the Ocmulgee to the Mobile, in such direction as shall, by the President of the United States, be considered most convenient, and to clear out the same, and lay logs over the creeks; and the citizens of the United States shall, at all times, have a right to pass peaceably on said path, under such regulations and restrictions as the government of the United States shall, from time to time, direct; and the Creek chiefs will have boats kept at the several rivers for the conveyance of men and horses; and houses of entertainment established at suitable places on said path for the accommodation of travellers. . . . "[3]

The Choctaws, also in 1805, permitted the establishment of inns for travellers on some of the roads through

---

[1] By Article II of the treaty of October 27, 1805. Louisiana had been bought from the French and it was necessary to have communication between it and our northern possessions.

[2] Article II of the Treaty of Washington; November 14, 1805. The Creeks also, in the same treaty, gave permission to the whites to navigate the Ocmulgee River.

[3] A treaty of 1802, held to name the limits between "the United States of America and the Creek Nation of Indians," was defined as having been agreed to by "Commissioners Plenipotentiary of the United States, on the one part, and the Kings, Chiefs, head men and warriors of the Creek Nation."

their territory whose use was given to white men, and later confirmed their concession in treaty language as follows :[1]

"The lease granted for establishments on the roads leading through the Choctaw country is hereby confirmed in all its conditions."

These taverns built in Indian countries along roads whereon whites were allowed to travel by international agreement were always kept by business men among the natives themselves, except in occasional cases wherein the red men did not desire such proprietorship. The ferries, also, were exclusively owned and operated by the Indians of nations in which they existed, and stipulations to that effect were put into the treaties. Both inns and ferries were operated as elsewhere, and the charges for their service corresponded to similar rates throughout the country. The food at Indian taverns was usually excellent and bountiful.

During Jefferson's presidency, from 1801 to 1809, the southern red nations progressed noticeably in their effort to build up a society based on the best principles employed by the white race, and Jefferson actively encouraged them in so doing. In a communication to the Cherokees[2] he said, "I sincerely wish you may succeed in your laudable endeavors to save the remnant of your nation by adopting industrious occupations, and a government of regular law. In this you may always rely on the counsel and assistance of the United States." He recognized them, as his predecessors and the government had uniformly done for twenty years, as independent neighboring nations. He continued to hold treaties with them, conducted extradition proceedings with them under the law of 1802, and referred to them in his public papers

[1] Treaty of November 16, 1805. Article VI.
[2] January 9, 1809.

as foreign peoples. Extracts from his annual message to Congress in 1808, near the end of his last term, will illustrate the United States' attitude on these points as expressed by its Executive. In that document President Jefferson said:

"With our Indian neighbors the public peace has been steadily maintained. . . .

"Beyond the Mississippi the Ioways, the Sacs and the Alabamas have delivered up for trial and punishment individuals from among themselves accused of murdering citizens of the United States. On this side of the Mississippi the Creeks are exerting themselves to arrest offenders of the same kind. . . .

"Husbandry and household manufacture are advancing among them more rapidly with the southern than northern tribes, from circumstances of soil and climate,[1] and one of the two great divisions of the Cherokee Nation have now under consideration to solicit the citizenship of the United States, and to be identified with us in laws and government in such progressive manner as we shall think best. . . ."

Nevertheless he did not neglect opportunity to acquire more territory from the Indians when favorable occasion presented itself. One of his messages on the subject of buying lands from them also indicates that the southern natives were in some degree being subjected to the same commercial processes which afterward wrought the undoing of the Potawatomi and many other of the northern tribes. The message[2] states that:

". . . The Choctaws, being indebted to certain mercantile characters beyond what could be discharged by the ordinary proceeds of their huntings, and pressed for payment by those creditors, proposed at length to the United States to cede lands to the amount of their debts, and designated them in two different portions of their country. These designations not at all suiting us, their proposals were declined. . . . Still urged by their creditors, as well as by their own desire to be liberated from debt, they at length proposed to make a cession which should be to our convenience. . . . The cession is supposed to contain about 5,000,000 acres, of which the greater part is said to be fit for cultivation, and no inconsiderable proportion of the first qual-

[1] And also, as has been pointed out, because the southern nations were in a better position to prevent intimate and constant intercourse with large numbers of whites.
[2] To the Senate, on January 15, 1808.

VIEW

OF THE

VALLEY OF THE MISSISSIPPI,

OR THE

EMIGRANT'S AND TRAVELLER'S

GUIDE TO THE WEST.

CONTAINING

A GENERAL DESCRIPTION OF THAT ENTIRE COUNTRY;

AND ALSO

NOTICES OF THE SOIL, PRODUCTIONS, RIVERS,

AND OTHER CHANNELS OF INTERCOURSE AND TRADE:

AND LIKEWISE OF THE

CITIES AND TOWNS, PROGRESS OF EDUCATION, &C.

OF EACH STATE AND TERRITORY.

"Westward the star of empire takes its way."—BERKELEY.

SECOND EDITION.

Philadelphia:
PUBLISHED BY H. S. TANNER.
::::::::::::
1834.

149.—Title page of the volume in which is contained the text shown in the preceding. An example of the guide books published to acquaint the eastern people with conditions in the Mississippi valley after Black Hawk's War.

ity . . . and the Choctaws and the creditors are still anxious for the sale. I therefore now transmit the treaty. . . ."

The United States' attitude during Jefferson's administration, and the President's utterances concerning the social and industrial development of the Indians had a deep effect on the large southern nations. Coming as it did after a considerable interval almost equally favorable to their aspirations, it led them to believe that the end of their long troubles had been reached and passed. With the systematic and officially expressed encouragement of the white republic they had definitely abandoned their old order of life, had settled down permanently on rich possessions and were turning as rapidly as possible toward practical agriculture and the domestic arts and crafts in keeping with their neighbors.[1] They still continued their hunting in regions where some game was left, but each year showed more acres under cultivation, more manufacturing, more houses built, more live stock in the pastures and a better ordering of their internal affairs. Indeed, so rapidly were the southern natives advancing in civilization and settled habits in accordance with declared governmental desire of the United States that — as Jefferson stated in his annual message of 1808 — some of the Cherokees were already considering the question of abandoning their national identity provided they might merge themselves in the United States as citizens.

Several more years elapsed, unmarked by events of consequence save the steady development of the Indians. Then, in 1813, the states of Tennessee and Georgia felt pressing need for a thoroughfare over which travel and commerce might be carried on between them. There was

[1] The law of 1802 had also said (section XIII): "That in order to promote civilization among the friendly Indian tribes, and to secure the continuance of their friendship, it shall be lawful for the President of the United States to cause them to be furnished with useful domestic animals, and implements of husbandry, and with goods or money, as he shall think proper . . . ."

nothing to do but appeal to the Cherokees as usual, for that nation lay between the two commonwealths and commanded the situation. So the states appointed commissioners who met the red men by consent of the Federal government,[1] and an agreement was concluded[2] under whose terms the necessary road was brought into existence. But this time the Cherokees demonstrated their advancement by proposing a legally organized company in which they should have equal representation with the whites, with national emoluments for the concession, and so the agreement was perforce made that way. The official document is in other respects an unusual one. It declared:

"We, the undersigned, Chiefs and Councillors of the Cherokees, in full Council assembled, do hereby give, grant and make over unto Nicholas Byers and David Russell, who are agents in behalf of the states of Tennessee and Georgia, full power and authority to establish a turnpike company to be composed of them, the said Nicholas and David, Arthur Henly, John Lowry and one other person by them to be hereafter named in behalf of the state of Georgia; and the above named persons are authorized to nominate five proper and fit persons, natives of the Cherokees, who, together with the white men aforesaid, are to constitute the company, which said company, when thus established, are hereby fully authorized by us to lay out and open a road from the most suitable point on the Tennessee River, to be directed the nearest and best way to . . . the Tugolo River, which said road . . . shall continue and remain a free and public highway, unmolested by us . . . for the full term of twenty years yet to come after the road may be open and complete; after which time said road, with all its advantages, shall be surrendered up, and reverted in, the Cherokee Nation. . . . And the said Turnpike company do hereby agree to pay the sum of $160 yearly to the Cherokee Nation."

Thus was presented the spectacle of an independent Indian nation becoming part owners of an important link in the internal travel system of the country and receiving money for permitting United States citizens to go back and forth between Georgia and Tennessee. Further-

[1] Under the terms of the law of 1802.
[2] The grant of Highwassee Garrison, March 8, 1813.

more, if future events had not happened as they did the Cherokees would have become entire owners of the thoroughfare. This turnpike was the famous Unicoy Road, one of the chief routes through the South for a long time.

No pretentions were made by Georgia, at this period, that her state boundaries included the possessions of either the Cherokee or Creek nations, or that her jurisdiction extended over the Cherokee or Creek nations; or that she could deal with them other than through the United States according to the provisions of the law of 1802. As recently as 1811[1] she had, in fact, taken legislative action which disclosed her attitude on those points and contained her acknowledgment of established boundary lines between her sovereignty and that of the two red peoples. The 1811 resolution of Georgia's legislature read:

"Whereas disputes have frequently arisen between the frontier inhabitants of Jackson and Franklin counties and the Cherokee nation of Indians, which might in a great measure be prevented by having the Chatahuchee River made the line between this state and the said Cherokee nation of Indians, and there being good reason to believe that the said Indians on proper application being made would dispose of said lands.

"Be it therefore resolved, That his excellency the governor be, and he is hereby authorized and requested, to appoint not exceeding three persons as commissioners on the part of this state, to make application to the Cherokee nation of Indians through the agency of the United States, for the purpose of obtaining the consent of said Indians to a disposition of the land lying within the following boundary, viz.: beginning where the line between this state and the Creek nation of Indians leaves the Appalachee River; thence on the said line to where the same crosses the Chatahuchee River [here follows a further description of the boundaries of the country desired] or so much thereof as the said nation of Indians may be disposed to part with." [2]

[1] In the resolution of the state legislature approved November 30, 1811.
[2] Reference to a proper map will disclose the significance of this statement by Georgia. The Chatahuchee River runs entirely across the state in a southwestern direction, and Georgia's largest hope at the time in question was to have that stream substituted as the boundary line in place of the one then existing. A vertical tier of five counties, either in whole, or in part, lies directly north of the then frontier counties of Jackson and Franklin; and that part of the Cherokee sovereignty lying north of the Chatahuchee River in 1811 was, in 1838, represented by 14 Georgia counties and parts of three others.

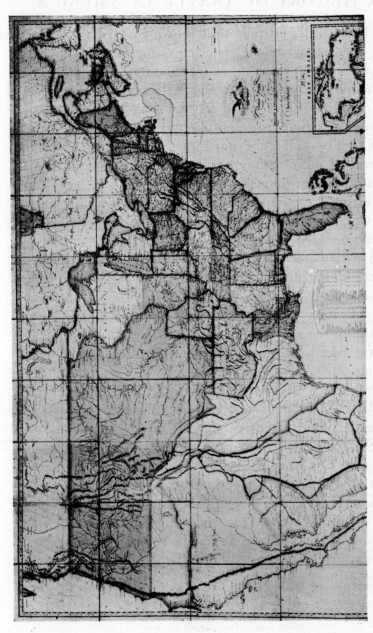

150.—Melish's fifty-sheet folio map of the United States in 1820. (Lower tier of sheets omitted for convenience in reproduction.) Showing extent to which the English speaking white race had advanced toward the West during two centuries. The furthest permanent white settlements were in Missouri. Indians still owned 115,000 square miles in Ohio, Michigan, Indiana, Illinois, Wisconsin, Georgia, Alabama, Tennessee, Mississippi and Missouri, and nearly all land west of the Mississippi. The white region on the map, northward to Oregon, belonged to Mexico.

The friendly attitude thus shown by Georgia still existed in 1814, when the state legislature passed a resolution[1] stating that many citizens of the state "have gone and frequently are going over and settling and cultivating" the Indian lands, by which action "considerable feuds are engendered between us and our friendly neighboring Indians." The Governor was requested to bring about the removal of such intruders and take proper steps "to prevent future aggressions."

With the close of the second war between the United States and Great Britain[2] the immigration from Europe became decidedly larger, and it was found necessary to place foreigners on the footing occupied by American citizens concerning restrictions of travel in native territories.[3] Accordingly, in 1816, Congress passed a law[4] supplementary to existing legislation and providing that no foreign subject without a passport might "go into any country which is allotted to or secured by treaty" to the Indians, on pain of fine not exceeding one thousand dollars or a year's imprisonment.

During the same year the Cherokees granted to the whites the most extensive travel privileges they had yet conceded. This action was indirectly due to the rapid filling up of Georgia, Alabama and Mississippi then in progress, and the Federal administration, under spur from the South, made an especially urgent and successful plea to the natives. The red ambassadors were brought to Washington for the negotiations, where they were treated with dignity and attention both by the official and private

---

[1] Approved November 19, 1814.

[2] During this war the United States, as was customary when she was in danger, sought and obtained the aid of Indians as allies. In 1814 the instructions of the War Department to General Jackson referred to the southern Indians as follows: "The friendly Indians must be fed and paid, and made to fight when and where their services may be required." Numerous Indians did fight under Jackson.

[3] The law of 1802 already regulated the passport question for United States citizens.

[4] Approved April 29, 1816.

life of the capital. Article II of the compact contained the valuable concession desired and was thus phrased:

"It is expressly agreed on the part of the Cherokee Nation that the United States shall have the right to lay off, open and have the free use of such road or roads, through any part of the Cherokee nation lying north of the boundary line now established, as may be deemed necessary for the free intercourse between the states of Tennessee and Georgia and the Mississippi Territory. And the citizens of the United States shall freely navigate, and use as a highway, all the rivers and waters within the Cherokee Nation. The Cherokee Nation further agree to establish and keep up, on the roads to be opened under the sanction of this article, such ferries and public houses as may be necessary for the accommodation of the citizens of the United States." [1]

In 1817 the national government succeeded in obtaining another small part of the Cherokee territory, but the Cherokees and Creeks, in company with the Chickasaws and Choctaws, had no thought of relinquishing all their possessions. The ceding of slices now and then, and the granting of travel permits were actions taken partly because of good will and in part because their holdings were greater than they needed.

Danger lay in these conditions unless the white republic based its future actions on loftier principles than had sometimes animated it in earlier phases of the long race controversy. If the white states of the South changed their attitude; challenged the validity of the position held by the red nations under Federal acknowledgment since the organization of constitutional government; placed their own immediate material profit above all else and looked at the complex situation solely from the white standpoint, then the consequences could not be foreseen.

A blunder had been made in 1814, through a treaty negotiated with the Creek nation. The Creeks in that year ceded a considerable section of their holdings

[1] In this same treaty South Carolina was authorized to arrange for buying the Cherokee lands overlapping the boundary of that state, and the United States became a surety to the natives for South Carolina's payment of $5,000 for the cession.

within the present limits of Alabama, and the action tended to move a part of the nation into the eastern section of their territory, at present embraced in Georgia. The United States thereupon guaranteed to them the integrity of their remaining possessions. This pledge was inconsistent with the 1802 compact with Georgia.

Still another similar promise by which the white re public agreed to the inviolability of a native nation's territory was that given to the Choctaws in 1820.[1] On that occasion the Choctaws ceded part of their country in exchange for a tract west of the Mississippi River, where such of them as wished to maintain the old hunter's life were willing to go. The remaining Choctaw possessions were guaranteed to the nation in Article IV as follows:

"The boundaries hereby established between the Choctaw Indians and the United States, on this side of the Mississippi River, shall remain without alteration until the period at which said nation shall become so civilized and enlightened as to be made citizens of the United States. . . ."

One of the Commissioners Plenipotentiary of the United States who in this manner indicated that the Choctaws were so advanced in their methods of life that their prospective status as citizens of the Union might with propriety be discussed in a treaty was General Andrew Jackson.[2]

It will thus be seen that the Federal government's policy toward the southern Indian nations was not a consistent one. While some of its manifestations effectively served to establish the natives as permanent and settled communities, and encouraged them in civilized endeavor, other of its acts had an opposite tendency. There was discord of purpose in urging and inducing the red men to adopt

[1] By the treaty of October 18.
[2] General Jackson had already acted in a similar capacity during treaty negotiations with the Cherokees in 1816 and 1817.

husbandry, manufacturing, permanent homes and self-government while at the same time gradually buying or trying to buy the regions thus transformed and improved by the natives. The only features wherein the white policy had remained unaltered for the twenty-nine years between 1789 and 1818 were in the recognition of sovereignty accorded to the large nations of the South, and in the acquirement of travel routes and territory from them. The first hints of a possible change in the attitude of the government appeared during the administration of Monroe, and can be discerned in certain of his public papers. They also seem to indicate, in some particulars, either a considerable misapprehension of existing conditions or the symptoms of a governmental purpose to foster, in the public mind, a misconception of those conditions.

President Monroe's annual message of 1817 did not suggest the new Caucasian position soon to be assumed. It is, however, valuable because of its revelation of the widespread extent to which the whites were still dependent on the consent of the red men for opportunity to connect their scattered settlements and move between them. A part of it reads:

". . . By these purchases the Indian title, with moderate reservations, has been extinguished as to the whole of the land within the limits of the State of Ohio, and to a part of that in the Michigan Territory and of the State of Indiana. From the Cherokee tribe a tract has been purchased in the State of Georgia and an arrangement made by which, in exchange for lands beyond the Mississippi, a great part, if not the whole, of the land belonging to that tribe eastward of that river in the States of North Carolina, Georgia and Tennessee, and in the Alabama Territory, will soon be acquired.[1]

"By these acquisitions, and others that may reasonably be expected soon to follow, we shall be enabled to extend our settlements from the inhabited parts of the State of Ohio along Lake Erie into the Michigan Territory, and to connect our settlements by degrees through the State

[1] A mistaken opinion. A few Cherokees removed to the West in 1817, and another group followed in 1819.

of Indiana and the Illinois Territory to that of Missouri. A similar and equally advantageous effect will soon be produced in the South through the whole extent of the states and territory which border on the waters emptying into the Mississippi and Mobile. . . .

". . . The difficulties attending early emigrations[1] will be dissipated even in the most remote parts."

Three further references to the subject by President Monroe, together covering a period of more than two years, are filled with significant statements and evidences of the misapprehension or new attitude alluded to. The first of these, contained in his annual message of 1818, declares:

"To civilize them, and even to prevent their extinction, it seems to be indispensable that their independence as communities should cease, and that the control of the United States over them should be complete and undisputed. The hunter state will then be more easily abandoned, and recourse will be had to the acquisition and culture of land and to other pursuits tending to dissolve the ties which connect them together as a savage community. . . ."

Aside from a recognition that the red nations still possessed independence, this summary of conditions and suggestion of future policy — particularly with relation to the southern natives — was unfortunately erroneous and even conflicted with similar public announcements by previous Presidents, such as that by Jefferson ten years before. The very Indian nations whose independence had been most frequently and elaborately recognized—those of the South—were the ones most flourishing and furthest advanced in civilization. In those nations the hunter state was already abandoned as a matter of definite future policy, and played a small and constantly decreasing part in the life of the population. Recourse to the culture of land and other pursuits had already taken place, though the Indians were much less concerned in the acquisition of more land than in the effort to keep what they already

---

[1] By this the President meant the travels of citizens throughout the country.

had. There were no indissoluble ties which connected the southern red nations together as savage communities, but many ties that bound them into rapidly advancing peoples. Among these the practises of husbandry, manufacturing and commerce were the most notable.

It was no longer possible accurately to discuss the Indian population of the whole continental extent under broad generalizations such as are here used by Monroe. Conditions among the natives were almost as diverse as among the whites. The Cherokees, Choctaws and Chickasaws were increasing in numbers and growing in wealth and civilization. They had successfully adopted a new culture. Many other tribes and nations, on the other hand, were unsuccessfully trying to accomplish the same result against odds that made their endeavor impossible, and still others were swiftly deteriorating in all the respects here named.

The statement of Monroe, above quoted, is the first official intimation of a coming change in the government's attitude toward the red peoples.

CHAPTER XXVI

FURTHER MISTAKES OF MONROE — FIRST OFFICIAL SUG-
GESTION THAT NATIONAL INDEPENDENCE OF INDIAN
PEOPLES IS NOT DESIRED BY THE UNITED STATES — THE
CAUCASIAN REPUBLIC STANDS AT THE RUBICON
OF POLICY — REFUSAL OF THE CHEROKEES TO SELL
MORE LAND AND PROCLAMATION OF THEIR FUTURE
PROGRAM — CALHOUN'S ADMISSION — M'KENNEY'S
REPORT ON CHEROKEE CIVILIZATION — FURTHER CON-
TEMPORARY TESTIMONY — J. Q. ADAMS PUTS A
STOP TO PREVIOUS METHODS OF TREATY MAK-
ING — GEORGIA INVADES INDIAN SOVEREIGNTY —
ADAMS' ACTION IN REPLY — GEORGIA THREATENS TO
SEIZE NATIVE TERRITORIES BY VIOLENCE — ADAMS
ADMITS THE MORASS OF DIFFICULTY IN WHICH THE
COUNTRY IS ENMIRED

THE second of Monroe's three statements heretofore alluded to was one contained in the President's message of November 14, 1820. It ran: ". . . Left to themselves their extirpation is inevitable. By a judicious regulation of our trade with them we supply their wants, administer to their comforts, and gradually, as the game retires, draw them to us."

The archives of the government contained a mass of reports, treaties and other evidences testifying to the contrary.[1] When left to themselves or when in

[1] The most recent of which was an elaborate review of the conditions of Indian society made by Jedediah Morse under commission by the President dated February 7, 1820. Extracts from Morse's statements respecting native civilization of the period are contained in an Appendix.

516

association with non-parasitical whites, the natives did well. It was when they were not left to themselves, but compelled against their desire closely and constantly to mingle with the unscrupulous white population which hovered about them like vultures, that they failed to do well. So excellently did they progress when able to pro-tect themselves from excessive spoliation that President Monroe's Commissioner Plenipotentiary, General An-drew Jackson, had anticipated United States citizenship for an entire red nation only twenty-seven days before the President made the foregoing statement.[1] The nature and deplorable results of the trade permitted with the natives have been discussed. It did not administer to their com-forts but added to their troubles. Judicious regulation of that trade was not a distinguishing characteristic of the government's attitude. Instead of being drawn closer to the whites as the game retired, the natives were as a rule despoiled to whatever extent was possible and thrust fur-ther away. The most notable exceptions to this rule, at the time, were to be found in the nations of the South, which still insisted on maintaining their independence unless their inhabitants were made citizens of the United States.

The third of the three statements by Monroe indicating a changing attitude on the part of the government was made in his second inaugural address, on March 5, 1821. It contained the first unequivocal declaration that national independence of Indian peoples was not desired by the United States. The utterance was:

"The care of the Indian tribes within our limits has long been an essential part of our system, but, unfortunately, it has not been exe-cuted in a manner to accomplish all the objects intended by it. We have treated them as independent nations, without their having any substantial pretentions to that rank. The distinction has flattered their

[1] The Choctaws. The treaty with them negotiated by Jackson was dated, as has been said, on October 18, 1820, and Monroe's message was dated November 14.

pride, retarded their improvement, and in many cases paved the way to their destruction. Their sovereignty over vast territories should cease."

The President did not state what were the objects intended to be accomplished by our dealings and relations with the natives. If those objects were, as often declared in words,[1] a genuine and unselfish desire to

151.—Development of the stage-coach from the Flying Machine and Stage Wagon. A New England coach of 1815-1820. Heaviest of all American vehicles of the sort, and built with especial thought for the comfort of passengers in cold weather. This and the twenty-seven illustrations to No. 178, inclusive, concern the evolution of the stage-coach and incidents of its use, between New England and the Mississippi River, from 1815 to about 1850.

aid the red population in attaining civilization and a manner of life similar to that of the Caucasians, then those purposes had thus far only failed when the government, by its discordant or lax methods, had neglected to protect the Indians from its own citizens and had indirectly interrupted their upward progress by buying their lands. Plentiful evidences existed that in

[1] As recently as March 3, 1819, President Monroe had approved an act of Congress authorizing the President to send among the Indians instructors in agriculture and the ordinary branches of education, as a means of "providing against the further decline" of the natives and of "introducing among them the habits and arts of civilization."

cases wherein those impediments to development did not unduly occur the native population responded to the impulse in question, no matter from what quarter it came. Consequently it was only necessary to eliminate those retarding conditions in order to achieve success, provided that was really the national object, left unexplained by President Monroe. The situation as then visible in the South—where the most conspicuous examples of the national white policy were existent—did not warrant a statement that the plan of treating the red peoples as independent nations had retarded their improvement or paved the way to their destruction. So if their impending destruction was in truth visible then its cause must also have been visible, and must have been discovered in some factor of the problem not inherent in the new red civilization itself.

But if the principal and underlying purpose of the Republic had been, and still was, the easy capture of the territorial possessions of the Indians, then it was true, as Monroe said, that the government's system had not been carried out in a manner to accomplish all the objects intended by it. The remaining important red nations were visibly entering into the realm of civic pride and a social state similar to that of the whites, and had announced a determination to sell no more land. Hence if the acquisition of their countries was the main object of the white nation, that desire had apparently been thwarted through a concrete realization by the Indians of the condition toward which they had been thoughtlessly encouraged. Such a theory would perhaps explain the altered position which the United States was obviously taking and whose symptoms first became visible during the Monroe presidency. Flattery, cajolery, small monetary payments and large promises no longer wrought their magic as of old. The red men of the South were becoming nations of settled farmers, merchants, inn-keepers and small manufacturers, with schools, councils, legislatures, laws and judges of their own, and had their eyes on Federal citizenship. The Caucasian republic stood at last beside a Rubicon of policy. It had either to prove the sincerity of its former protestations by endorsing the native progress and unselfishly perpetuating it, even at worldly expense and inconvenience to itself for a time, or else adopt some other course of action that would disclose another purpose.

It was at such a time that President Monroe said: "Their sovereignty over vast territories should cease." The inhabitants of the southern states had become restive as they gazed toward the rich countries of Cherokee, Creek, Chickasaw and Choctaw, and two years before, in 1819, Georgia had begun a series of protests addressed to the Union in relation to the still unfulfilled obligation incurred by the United States in the agreement of 1802. From that time on events moved steadily toward the final catastrophe.

Early in 1824[1] Monroe, being under a constantly increasing pressure from the South and especially from Georgia,[2] sent an urgent message to the Cherokee nation begging its people to sell their country and remove west of the Mississippi. The nation refused. Its answer contained these passages:

". . . We assert under the fullest authority that all the sentiments expressed in relation to the disposition and determination of the nation never to cede another foot of land are positively the product and voice of the nation. . . . They have unequivocally determined

[1] January 30th.
[2] Which state was now insistently calling for an extinguishment of Cherokee and Creek titles.

520

THE
AMERICAN TRAVELLER;

OR,

National Directory,

CONTAINING AN ACCOUNT OF

ALL THE GREAT POST ROADS,

AND

MOST IMPORTANT CROSS ROADS,

IN THE

United States,

LEADING FROM WASHINGTON CITY TO THE SEVERAL EXTREMITIES
OF THE UNION; AND FROM THE

LARGE CITIES AND STATE CAPITALS,

TO

TOWNS AND INTERESTING PLACES IN VARIOUS DIRECTIONS,

WITH

DESCRIPTIONS OF THE COUNTRY AND VARIOUS SCENERY WHICH
THOSE ROADS PASS THROUGH:

Some of the principal Lines of Stages, Steam-boats, and Packets;
Statements at large of *some* of the most Respectable Hotels,
Genteel Boarding Houses, Establishments, and Institutions, in
the large Cities, at the Springs, and Places of Fashionable
Resort.

A GEOGRAPHICAL AND STATISTICAL VIEW

OF THE

UNITED STATES;

WITH INFORMATION ON OTHER SUBJECTS INTERESTING
TO TRAVELLERS.

BY D. HEWETT, A. M.

Lecturer on Geography.

WASHINGTON:

PRINTED BY DAVIS & FORCE, (FRANKLIN'S HEAD),
PENNSYLVANIA AVENUE.

1825.

152.—Early literature relating to travel in America. Title page of Hewett's
Directory of Post Roads. First guide book of national scope issued for the
benefit of stage-coach travellers, and first comprehensive printed list of
United States roads.

never again to pursue the chase as heretofore, or to engage in wars, unless by the common call of the government to defend the common rights of the United States. . . .

"The Cherokees have turned their attention to the pursuits of the civilized man; agriculture, manufactures, and the mechanic arts and education are all in successful operation in the nation at this time; and while the Cherokees are peacefully endeavoring to enjoy the blessings of civilization and Christianity on the soil of their rightful inheritance, and while the exertions and labors of various religious societies of these United States are successfully engaged in promulgating to them the words of truth and life from the sacred volume of Holy Writ, and under the patronage of the general government, they are threatened with removal or extinction. . . .

"We appeal to the magnanimity of the American Congress for justice, and the protection of the rights and liberties of the Cherokee people. We claim it from the United States by the strongest obligation which imposes it on them—by treaties; and we expect it from them under that memorable declaration 'that all men are created equal; that they are endowed by their Creator with certain inalienable rights; that among these are life, liberty, and the pursuit of happiness.' "

The President, in a special message to Congress[1] informed that body of the result of his appeal, saying:

". . . By this it is manifest that at the present time and in their present temper they can be removed only by force. . . .

"I have no hesitation, however, to declare it as my opinion that the Indian title was not affected in the slightest circumstance by the compact with Georgia, and that there is no obligation on the United States to remove the Indians by force. The express stipulation of the compact that their title should be extinguished at the expense of the United States when it may be done peaceably and on reasonable conditions is a full proof that it was the clear and distinct understanding of both parties to it that the Indians had a right to the territory, in the disposal of which they were to be regarded as free agents."

Monroe nevertheless continued his diplomatic attempts to clear the southern country east of the Mississippi of the native races there established, and later in 1824 he called on John C. Calhoun, his then Secretary of War, for a report describing the condition of those peoples. In answer to this request Secretary Calhoun said to the President:[2]

". . . Almost all of the tribes proposed to be affected by the

[1] On March 30, 1824.
[2] In his report dated January 24, 1825.

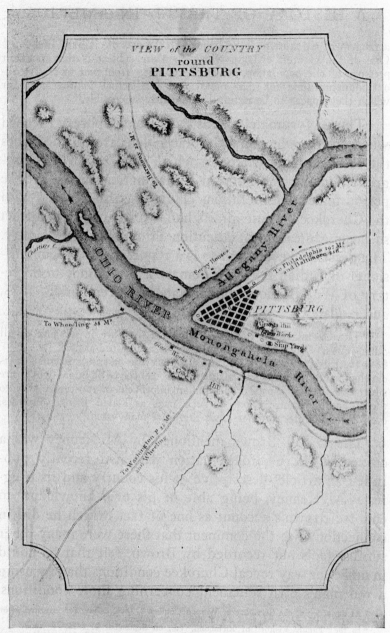

153.—Map of overland highways leading to Pittsburgh in 1812. The town could then be reached by one wagon road from the north, four from the east, two from the south and one from the west.

arrangement are more or less advanced in the arts of civilized life. . . . One of the greatest evils to which they are subject is that incessant pressure of our population, which forces them from seat to seat, without allowing time for that moral and intellectual improvement for which they appear to be naturally eminently susceptible."

There fortunately exists a contemporary record whereon dependence may be placed that carefully describes the most extreme extent to which civilization had progressed among the southern Indian nations at the precise period under consideration. Happily, also, it deals with the Cherokees, whose affairs had already begun to attract so large a measure of attention throughout the country. The description referred to is a report made by Commissioner of Indian Affairs Thomas L. McKenney to Secretary of War Barbour[1] under date of December 13, 1825, and reads:

"The Cherokees on this side the Mississippi are in advance of all other tribes. They may be considered as a civilized people. . . . It is truth we are in quest of, and facts are the best instruments for its development. Theory, and all previously conceived opinions which are adverse to Indian capacity and Indian improvement must give way to the stubborn demonstrations of such facts as David Brown discloses, even if there were no others; but there are many such."

The David Brown mentioned by McKenney was a citizen of the Cherokee nation who had recently published an article[2] descriptive of his country and its progress. McKenney, being able of his own knowledge[3] to endorse Brown's account as one of fact, which he did in connection with the comment that there were many other similar facts not recorded by Brown, felt that he could in no better way reveal Cherokee conditions than by using a red man's own statement concerning those conditions.

[1] At the order of the Secretary of War on October 3, 1825, calling for information on the effects "of the present system for civilizing the Indians."
[2] In the "Family Visitor" of Richmond, Va., on September 2, 1825.
[3] McKenney's studies of Indians extended over many years and were made at first hand among numerous tribes. He lived among them in their own manner. His works on the subject are well known.

This he accordingly did, incorporating into and making a part of his own report the following paragraphs by Brown:

". . . These plains furnish immense pasturage, and numberless herds of cattle are dispersed over them; horses are plenty, numerous flocks of sheep, goats and swine cover the valleys and the hills. On Tennessee, Ustanula and Canasagi rivers Cherokee commerce floats. The climate is delicious and healthy; the winters are mild; the spring clothes the ground with the richest scenery, flowers of exquisite beauty and variegated hues meet and fascinate the eye in every direction. In the plains and valleys the soil is generally rich, producing Indian corn, cotton, tobacco, wheat, oats, indigo, and sweet and Irish potatoes.

"The natives carry on considerable trade with the adjoining states; some of them export cotton in boats down the Tennessee to the Mississippi, and down that river to New Orleans. Apple and peach orchards are quite common, and gardens are cultivated, and much attention paid to them. Butter and cheese are seen on Cherokee tables. There are many public roads in the nation,[1] and houses of entertainment kept by natives. Numerous and flourishing villages are seen in every section of the country. Cotton and woolen cloths are manufactured; blankets of various dimensions, manufactured by Cherokee hands, are very common. Almost every family in the nation grows cotton for its own consumption.

"Industry and commercial enterprise are extending themselves in every part. Nearly all the merchants in the nation are native Cherokees. Agricultural pursuits engage the chief attention of the people. Different branches in mechanics are pursued. . . .

"White men in the nation enjoy all the immunities and privileges of the Cherokee people, except that they are not eligible to public offices. . . . The Christian religion is the religion of the nation. . . . The whole nation is penetrated with gratitude for the aid it has received from the United States Government. . . . Schools are increasing every year; learning is encouraged and rewarded; the young acquire the English, and those of mature age the Cherokee system of learning. . . . We are out of debt, and our public revenue is in a flourishing condition. Besides the amount arising from imports, perpetual annuity is due from the United States in consideration of lands ceded in former periods.

"Our system of Government, founded on republican principles by which justice is equally distributed, secures the respect of the people. New Town, pleasantly situated in the center of the Nation, . . . is the seat of government. The legislative power is vested in a national committee and council. . . . In New Town a printing press is soon to be established; also a national library and museum."

[1] Of their own as well as those on which whites were permitted to travel.

The printing establishment mentioned by McKenney was soon afterward set up. It was the property of the nation, and the work in connection with its operation was done in part by native editors, writers, translators, typesetters, printers, bookbinders and other craftsmen. From it issued hymn books, gospels and various other volumes in the native language, and a newspaper in both the Cherokee language and in English.[1] The Cherokee tongue had been reduced to a written and printed alphabet, also by a member of the nation,[2] as early as 1820, and the national Cherokee legislature had in 1823 conferred on him a medal for eminent public services. The affairs of the nation were carried on under a constitution shaped somewhat after that of the United States. Officials held office by popular election. A moderate system of taxation was in operation and the public funds were carefully administered. Crime was practically non-existent.

These demonstrations of native advancement, together with the conditions catalogued by McKenney, had appeared during the period of thirty-nine years following the adoption of constitutional government by the United States. The social and economic development shown in that interval by the Cherokees compared favorably with the progress accomplished by the earliest English settlers in New England during an even longer time. The first white colonists landed in Massachusetts in 1620, and seventy-two years later the communities they founded pos-

[1] It was a four-page weekly paper called the "Cherokee Phoenix," and was first published on February 21, 1828, continuing to appear at the Cherokee capital until May of 1834. Each issue contained several columns in each of the two languages. Partial files of this, the first Indian newspaper, are contained in the collections of the British Museum, the New York City Library and the Boston Atheneum. Occasional copies are also owned by Wilberforce Eames, Esq., of New York; by W. J. De Renne, Esq., of Atlanta, and perhaps by a few other collectors. The editor of the "Phoenix" was Elias Boudinot, an Indian, whose parents could not speak English.

The state papers of the Cherokees, and the editorial discussion of Indian affairs contained in the columns of the "Phoenix" from 1828 to 1834 are worthy of comparison with similar United States productions during the same period. An example of the native messages referred to is given in an Appendix.

[2] George Guess, whose native name was Sequoyah.

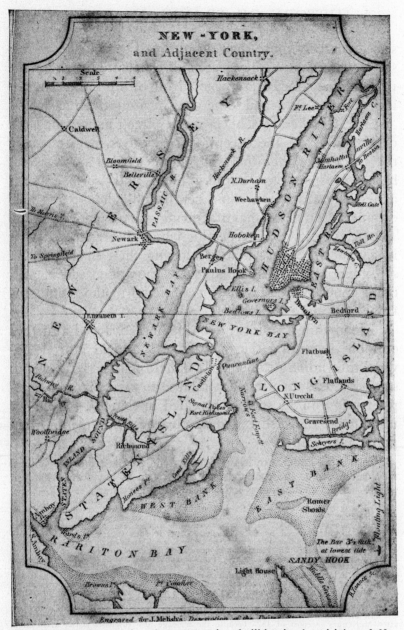

154.—Map of the travel and transportation facilities in the vicinity of New York City in 1826. The city and bay were touched by seventeen roads. From Melish's map, published in some copies of the second edition of Goodrich's *Northern Traveller:* 1826.

sessed scarcely more than an outward semblance of real self-government. They were still substantially under the rule of a theocracy that was torturing or mutilating the citizens of both sexes and sometimes burning them to death.[1]

The Chickasaw, Choctaw and Creek nations had not displayed all of the exceptional qualities manifested by the Cherokees, but their development had nevertheless been correspondingly rapid. They, likewise, had herds and cultivated acres, some comfortable houses, a little commerce, domestic manufacturing, schools and ambition. The principal matter respecting which they were less swift in advancement was that of altering their machinery of self-government. Their systems, though effective, still clung much more closely to traditional methods and suffrage was more restricted.

Meanwhile President Monroe had advanced a further opinion[2] regarding the question of national attitude toward the Indian problem. It upheld native rights, yet in some features manifested a relapse toward that non-comprehension of the subject revealed in some of his earlier utterances, and also failed of clearness on an important point. He said:

". . . Experience has shown that unless the tribes be civilized they can never be incorporated into our system in any form whatever, . . . Their civilization is indispensable to their safety. . . .

[1] In 1692 trials or executions for witchcraft had been taking place in New England for more than forty years. This comparison is in a certain respect, however, unfair to the white colonists, for they were not favored with a prior example in self-government analogous to that enjoyed by the Cherokees. But it does suggest that the red men possessed inherent qualities of character and mind which enabled them, under favorable conditions and in but little more than a generation radically to alter their method of living in a sane and thoughtful manner for the conscious purpose of race preservation and advancement, whereas the white colonists of Massachusetts and their descendants, at the end of a longer period, were further removed from normal community thought and life—as measured by present standards—than at the beginning of their experiment. The comparison perhaps emphasizes the "moral and intellectual improvement" for which Calhoun said the Indians "appeared to be naturally and eminently susceptible," and which McKenney characterized as "Indian capacity."

[2] In his annual message of December 7, 1824. Monroe's opinion is here reproduced after McKenney's report of 1825 because the message also discusses native civilization, and it was desirable to indicate what that civilization was before presenting Monroe's opinions. The difference between 1824 and 1825, in native advancement, was not enough to make the transposition unfair.

528

"Difficulties of the most serious character present themselves to the attainment of this very desirable result on the territory on which they now reside. To remove them from it by force, even with a view to their own security and happiness would be revolting to humanity and utterly unjustifiable. . . ."

Instead of civilization being a condition indispensable to the safety of the red peoples it was beginning to look as if their civilization, wherever attained, subjected them to a danger no less extreme than any they had previously undergone. The four biggest nations already revealed a state of society presenting more stability, quiet, thrift and wealth than might be shown by many frontier Caucasian communities. Two of them[1] had been discussing the question of American citizenship with the United States for years, and President Monroe had himself negotiated a treaty with one[2] guaranteeing the permanence of its existing possessions until the members of the nation were made citizens. Now, four years afterward, he found himself to be of opinion that difficulties of the most serious character interfered with the attainment of native civilization on the territory where they were then residing, even though that territory was their own. He overlooked the evidences that several of the red peoples had already substantially reached that state of society, and that they could assuredly proceed more easily toward the visible goal[3] in their long established homes than elsewhere, unless prevented by injurious outside influences from so doing. If the civilization of the Indians was really the main desire of the government in its relations with them, then no shifting of them could be of advantage, since that act would only be transferring the process to another and less favorable locality,

[1] The Cherokees and Choctaws.
[2] The Choctaws.
[3] The degree of development which the United States government was insisting on before awarding citizenship.

155.—Type of stage-coach most widely used throughout the country from 1815 to 1825. Its body, built of wood and sole-leather, was shaped somewhat like a football, and was swung on many thick strips of leather riveted together and called thorough-braces. Capacity, either six or nine passengers inside. Commonly drawn by four horses. From a drawing made by Captain Hall of the British Navy in 1825.

with loss of years and material gain as well as probable loss of native courage. The one decisive element to be dealt with in any honest and unselfish effort for Indian welfare had long since been seen to be the manner and purpose of Caucasian contact with the red people, and that element could not be dodged. Two centuries of experience had afforded ample demonstration of the point. Postponement of a problem does not accomplish its solution. The secret of a successful endeavor to protect and aid the natives lay then, as it had always done, in regulating that part of the white population which sought to prey upon them.

Monroe did not explain the nature of the serious difficulties whose existence he so unequivocally asserted. They did not abide in any quality or methods of the Indians, and soon became visible to all men.

President J. Q. Adams took office on March 4, 1825,[1] and his first encounter with the questions under review had to do with a treaty negotiated by the previous administration[2] with the Creek nation. By its terms the Creeks apparently ceded their territories embraced in the modern area of Georgia. In discussing this transaction in a special message to the Senate[3] President Adams used the following language:

"I do not deem it necessary to decide upon the propriety of the manner in which it was negotiated. Deeply regretting the criminations and recriminations to which these events have given rise, I believe the public interest will best be consulted by discarding them altogether from the discussion of the subject."

The delicacy of the Executive is forbidden here. It was sometimes a custom of white treaty makers, on occasions when other efforts had no effect, to resort to methods of persuasion, deception and bribery which should never have been employed. The Creek treaty of 1825 was obtained in such a way. It was incorrectly reported to the government as having been concluded with a large majority of the chiefs of the Creek nation and with a reasonable prospect of immediate acquiescence by the remainder. When the people of the Creek nation heard the terms of the treaty they uprose. Two of the native signers were put to death as traitors for an attempt to sell their country, and the others fled. After discovering the circumstances surrounding the transaction the Federal govern-

[1] On Adams' accession, in 1825, the number of Creeks living under their own rule and on their own lands in Georgia and Alabama totaled some 20,000 souls; the Choctaws in Mississippi and Alabama were about 21,000 in number and the Chickasaw nation, in Mississippi, had a population of about 3,600.

At the same date the Cherokees still owned 5,292,160 acres in the limits of modern Georgia, while the Creeks retained 4,245,760 acres in the same region. The aggregate holdings of the same two nations in Alabama were 5,995,200 acres, and the Cherokees also had 1,055,680 acres in Tennessee. The possessions of the Chickasaws and Choctaws in Alabama aggregated 1,277,376 acres, and in Mississippi the two tribes ruled over and owned no less than 15,705,000 acres. The total southern territory thus still in possession of the four red nations in the year named equalled 33,571,176 acres, or a region one and one-half times larger than the combined areas of New Hampshire, Vermont, Connecticut, Rhode Island and Massachusetts.

[2] The treaty of February 12, 1825.

[3] Dated January 31, 1826.

531

ment under Adams made no effort to enforce the treaty, and it was declared cancelled. A new agreement was made under whose terms a part of the Creek possessions were obtained on immediate payment of $217,600, a perpetual annuity of $20,000, and a cession of territory west of the Mississippi for such of the nation as decided to remove thither.[1]

The dissensions among the Creeks brought about by the methods employed by the United States during the last days of the Monroe administration weakened the native nation, and in the winter of 1826-7 Georgia entered its territory contrary to treaty rights of the Indians and the Federal law of 1802. Surveyors were instructed to plat a part of the Creek possessions, and the agents of the state were told they would be protected in their work by Georgia troops if necessary. The native nation appealed to President Adams, who, under the law of 1802, had power to halt Georgia's action either by civil process or use of the Federal army. Adams sent a special message to Congress[2] reciting the situation and stating his intentions in the following words:

". . . . In abstaining at this stage of the proceedings from the application of any military force I have been governed by considerations which will, I trust, meet the concurrence of the legislature. Among them one of paramount importance has been that these surveys have been attempted, and partly effected, under color of legal authority from the State of Georgia; that the surveyors are, therefore, not to be viewed in the light of individual and solitary transgressors, but as the agents of a sovereign state, acting in obedience to authority which they believed to be binding upon them. Intimations had been given that should they meet with interruption they would at all hazards be sustained by the military force of the State, in which event, if the military force of the Union should have been employed to enforce its violated law, a conflict must[3] have ensued which would itself have in-

[1] The Creeks who departed to the westward also received $100,000.
[2] On February 5, 1827.
[3] The word "must" is emphasized in the original.

flicted a wound upon the Union and have presented the aspect of one of these confederated states at war with the rest. . . .

"It ought not, however, to be disguised that the act of the legislature of Georgia, under the construction given to it by the governor of that state, and the surveys made or attempted by his authority beyond the boundary secured by the Treaty of Washington of April last to the Creek Indians, are in direct violation of the supreme law of this land,

MANSION-HOUSE,

BY P.F. HUBBARD.

MIDDLETOWN, CONN.

156.—Stage-coach similar to the preceding, entering a town. The driver is announcing his arrival by blowing his horn. A chair and a chaise are also shown.

set forth in a treaty which has received all the sanctions provided by the Constitution which we have sworn to support and maintain. . . .

"In the present instance it is my duty to say that if the legislative and executive authorities of the State of Georgia should persevere in acts of encroachment upon the territories secured by a solemn treaty to the Indians, and the laws of the Union remain unaltered, a super-added obligation even higher than that of human authority will compel the Executive of the United States to enforce the laws and fulfill the duties of the nation by all the force committed for that purpose to his charge. . . ."

533

Georgia soon took still more radical action. She passed a resolution which nullified Federal treaties with the Cherokees and Creeks, declared state ownership of such of their possessions as lay within her charter limits, and indicated an intention to seize those territories by force of arms if she could not obtain them in any other way. This resolution read:[1]

"A Resolution of the Legislature of Georgia, approved December 27, 1827.

"Resolved, That the United States in failing to procure the lands in controversy 'as early' as the same could be done upon 'practicable'[2] and 'reasonable terms' have palpably violated their contract with Georgia, and are now bound at all hazards, and without regard to terms, to procure said lands for the use of Georgia. . . .[3]

"Resolved, That all the lands appropriated and unappropriated, which lie within the conventional limits of Georgia, belong to her absolutely; that the title is in her; that the Indians are tenants at her will, and that she may at any time she pleases, determine that tenancy by taking possession of the premises—and that Georgia has the right to extend her authority and laws over her whole territory, and to coerce obedience to them from all descriptions of people, be they white, red, or black, who may reside within her limits.

"Resolved, That Georgia entertains for the general government so high a regard and is so solicitous to do no act that can disturb or tend to disturb the public tranquillity, that she will not attempt to improve her rights by violence until all other means of redress fail. . . .

"Resolved, That if such treaty be held, the President be respectfully requested to instruct the commissioners to lay a copy of this report before the Indians in convention, with such comments as may be considered just and proper, upon the nature and extent of the Georgia title to the lands in controversy, and the probable consequences which will result from a continued refusal upon the part of the Indians to part with those lands. . . .

"Resolved, That the late proceedings of the Cherokee Indians, in

---

[1] Three sections are here omitted. They are in the nature of emphasis and repetition, and do not affect the meaning of the resolution in any way not disclosed by the remainder as here quoted.

[2] An improper rendering of the compact of 1802. The word in the original was "peaceable," not "practicable."

[3] Up to 1824 the Federal government, in an endeavor to carry out its obligations under the compact of 1802, had bought lands for Georgia as follows:
From the Creeks, 14,748,690 acres;
From the Cherokees, 1,095,310 acres.
Between 1824 and 1830 the government further bought 4,083,200 acres from the Creeks for Georgia, making a total Federal purchase for Georgia under the 1802 act of 19,927,200 acres.

VIEW OF ST. PAUL'S CHURCH AND BROADWAY STAGES, N.Y. 1831.

157.—Stage-coaches like those used for city passenger traffic in large towns from about 1825. Scene at the corner of Broadway and Park Row, New York City, in 1831. Vehicles of this sort evolved into the omnibus, and still later (soon after 1850) into the horse-drawn street-car operated on a railed track.

framing a constitution for their nation, and preparing to establish a government independent of Georgia, is inconsistent with the rights of said State, and therefore not recognized by this government, and ought to be decidedly discountenanced by the general government."

The Cherokee National Council, sitting as a Constitutional Convention, had drawn up a written national constitution during the previous July. The Cherokees had not, however, lately proceeded to establish a government independent of Georgia for such an independent native government had existed since the organization of the Federal Union and had been recognized by it and by Georgia. Nor did the adoption of a constitution in 1827 mark the first occasion on which the Cherokees had altered their machinery of government in accordance with their development. They had begun to enact general laws by National Council in 1808. In 1819 they established a Commission government vested in a Standing Committee of 13 elected members. In 1820 the nation was divided into eight districts, each represented in the National Council by four salaried members chosen through popular election. Courts were established and judges appointed in the same year. Finally, in 1827, came the first written constitution and a legislative body composed of two houses.[1]

A contemporary account of the Cherokees and their republic, written and published in the same year that witnessed the foregoing action of Georgia, reads as follows:[2]

"Within the last twenty years the Cherokees have rapidly advanced towards civilization. They now live in comfortable houses, chiefly in

[1] The enactments of the Cherokees from 1808 to 1835, together with the Constitution of 1827, were collected and issued in 1852 by the Indians' governmental printing office, in a volume of 179 pages, under the title "Laws of the Cherokee Nation: Adopted by the Council at Various Periods. Printed for the Benefit of the Nation. Cherokee Advocate office, Tahlequah, C. N., 1852."

The second written constitution (that of 1839) and their legislative acts from 1839 to 1851 were similarly published at the same time in a volume of 248 pages entitled, "The Constitution and Laws of the Cherokee Nation. Passed at Tahlequah, Cherokee Nation, 1839-51. Tahlequah, Cherokee Nation, 1852."

Tahlequah was the native capital after the removal west of the Mississippi.

[2] From Sherwood's "Gazetteer of Georgia, 1827."

villages, and cultivate large farms. They raise large herds of cattle, which they sell for beef to the inhabitants of neighboring states. Many mechanical arts have been introduced among them. . . . The population, instead of decreasing, as is the case generally with tribes surrounded by the whites, increases very rapidly, ... increase in the last six years, 3,563. . . . Their government is republican, and power is vested in a Committee and Council, answering to our Senate and House of Representatives. The members are elected once in two years. . . . Their judges act with authority."

During the year 1828 the Georgia legislature passed two more acts dealing with the Indian question. The first of these was directed against the Creeks, and contained the following provisions:

"That from and after the passage of this act, it shall not be lawful for any Indian or descendant of an Indian, belonging to the Creek nation of Indians, to cross the river Chatahouchee, and enter upon the territory of said state, under any pretext whatever, except they have, and can shew a written permit from the United States agent . . . which permit shall not exceed ten days' duration. . . .

"And be it further enacted, That when any Indian or Indians shall be strolling over any country, on the frontier of said state, with such permit as aforesaid, and shall interfere with the private property, or interrupt the peace and tranquillity of any of the citizens aforesaid, it shall and may be lawful for them to be apprehended as aforesaid, on its being made appear to the satisfaction of the magistrate, to whom the warrant is made returnable, that said Indian or Indians were without lawful business, and disturbing the peace, or molesting the property of said citizens; for said magistrate to imprison said Indian or Indians not exceeding the term of time aforesaid. . . ."[1]

The remaining Georgia law of 1828 was directed toward both the Cherokee and Creek nations, and was entitled, "An act to add the territory lying within the limits of this state, and occupied by the Cherokee Indians, to the counties of Carroll, De Kalb, Gwinnett, Hall and Habersham; and to extend the laws of this state over the same, and for other purposes." The first five sections of the enactment defined the various geographical parts of the

[1] Ten days. Indians without permits were subject to similar imprisonment whether they interrupted the peace and tranquillity of the whites or not. It was more difficult for natives to travel safely in Caucasian territory than for whites to travel in native regions.

Cherokee territories placed within the counties named. Section six provided that all white persons in the affected districts fell under the operation of the statute immediately after its passage. Section eight read:

> "And be it further enacted, That all laws, usages, and customs made, established and in force, in the said territory, by the said Cherokee Indians be, and the same are hereby, on and after the first of June, 1830, declared null and void."

Sections 7 and 9 of the statute related to the jurisdiction set up by Georgia over the individual Indians of the Cherokee and Creek nations, and to the amenability of the Indians of those nations to laws passed by the Georgia legislature. Though separated in the original act by section 8 just quoted, the relationship of sections 7 and 9 is such that they require to be read together. The text of the two sections ran:

> "Sec. 7. And be it further enacted, That after the first of June, 1830, all Indians then and at that time residing in said territory, and within any one of the counties as aforesaid, shall be liable and subject to such laws and regulations as the legislature may hereafter prescribe."
> "Sec. 9. And be it further enacted, That no Indian, or descendant of Indian, residing within the Creek or Cherokee nations of Indians, shall be deemed a competent witness, or a party to any suit, in any court created by the constitution or laws of this state, to which a white man may be a party."

This state law spoke the approaching downfall of the Indian nations of the South, and both the date of its passage and part of its phraseology may have a significance which does not appear on the surface of the action. It was passed by Georgia's legislature on December 20, 1828, after it was known that Andrew Jackson was to succeed Adams as Chief Executive of the country.[1] Adams' attitude on the question of Indian rights under Federal law and treaties had been tested, and the law was

[1] Adams did not receive a vote in Georgia in 1828.

so worded that only white people in the annexed territories should be touched by it while Adams remained President. The application of the statute to the Cherokees and Creeks as individuals, and its destruction of Cherokee government, were to occur after the next Federal administration should be in office. Jackson had for some time declared "that if the states chose to

158.—Metallic ticket of a passenger stage line in New York City. Revealing a vehicle similar to some of those portrayed in the preceding illustration, but here called an "omnibus." Date, about 1830-1835. Brass; actual size.

extend their laws over them [the Indians] it would not be in the power of the Federal Government to prevent it."[1]

By the year 1828 the problem arising from the Indian situation in the South was attracting the attention of the country, and the predicament into which the white race had fallen was recognized. Government exerted its utmost legitimate effort to induce a migration of the four great red nations and the cession of their countries, but without avail. The natives refused either to sell or to go, stood on their treaty rights and demanded protection from invasion in order that they might develop in peace. President Adams' action in behalf of the Creeks prevented any further overt movement by a white state during the remainder of his term of office, but in the last year of his

[1] His own language in defining his position. Contained in a message to the Senate under date of February 22, 1831, in answer to the Senate's request for an explanation of his acts and policy toward the Indians. The alteration in Jackson's opinion must, however, have taken place since 1820, for in that year, as a Plenipotentiary of the United States, he had guaranteed the inviolability of the Choctaw possessions until the members of the nation became United States citizens.

administration it was seen that a crisis could not be far distant. One of Adams' efforts to secure the removal of the Cherokees consisted in negotiating a treaty[1] with them, non-compulsory in character as far as immediate general migration was concerned, but which, it was

159.—Metallic ticket of the Telegraph Line of passenger stages in New York City. Showing a further development of the former stages toward the omnibus type. All known examples are punched. Probably the driver carried his stock of tickets strung on a wire, to prevent loss. Brass; actual size. Date, about 1840-1845.

hoped, would offer guarantees for the future that might attract the bulk of the nation from the eastward. Never before had the United States used similar language in dealing with a native tribe. The tone of patronage and protestations of philanthropy that had so long distinguished Indian treaties did not appear. Conditions were serious at last. The pledges of the treaty are here given:

"Whereas it being the anxious desire of the Government of the United States to secure to the Cherokee nation of Indians . . . . a permanent[2] home, and which shall, under the most solemn guarantees of the United States, be, and remain, theirs forever—a home that shall never, in all future time, be embarrassed by having extended around it the lines, or placed over it the jurisdiction of a Territory or State, nor be pressed upon by the extension, in any way, of any of the limits of any existing Territory or State; . . . . the parties hereto do hereby conclude the following articles, viz.:

"Article 2. The United States agree to possess the Cherokees, and to guarantee it to them forever, and that guarantee is hereby solemnly pledged, of seven millions of acres of land, to be bounded as

[1] Dated May 6, 1828.
[2] "Permanent" is emphasized in official government texts.

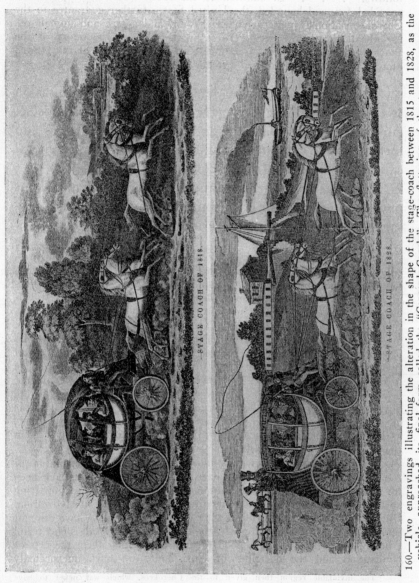

STAGE COACH OF 1818.

STAGE COACH OF 1828.

160.—Two engravings illustrating the alteration in the shape of the stage-coach between 1815 and 1828, as the vehicle approached its final form called the "Concord Coach." The flattening of the top gave more room inside, and, after railings were installed, permitted the carrying of baggage on the roof.

follows. . . . In addition to the seven millions of acres thus
provided for, and bounded, the United States further guarantee to the
Cherokee nation a perpetual outlet, West, and a free and unmolested
use of all the country lying West of the Western boundary of the
above described limits, and as far west as the sovereignty of the United
States, and their right of soil extend."

Those Cherokees who had removed to Arkansas in
1817 and 1819 thereupon gave up the Arkansas lands secured to them at that time and accepted the pledges and
territory above recited,[1] but there was then no general
exodus of the tribe from Georgia.

Near the close of his administration President Adams
gave his views on the race conflict in his last annual message,[2] and in the following terms:

"At the establishment of the Federal government under the present Constitution of the United States the principle was adopted of considering them as foreign and independent powers and also as proprietors
of lands. They were, moreover, considered as savages, whom it was
our policy and our duty to use our influence in converting to Christianity and in bringing within the pale of civilization.

"As independent powers, we negotiated with them by treaties; as
proprietors, we purchased of them all the lands which we could prevail
upon them to sell. . . . The ultimate design was to incorporate
in our own institutions that portion of them which could be converted
to the state of civilization. In the practice of European states, before
our Revolution, they had been considered as children to be governed;
as tenants at discretion, to be dispossessed as occasion might require;
as hunters to be indemnified by trifling concessions for removal from
the grounds from which their game was extirpated.

"In changing the system it would seem as if a full contemplation of
the consequences of the change had not been taken. We have been
far more successful in the acquisition of their lands than in imparting
to them the principles or inspiring them with the spirit of civilization.
But in appropriating to ourselves their hunting grounds we have brought
upon ourselves the obligation of providing them with subsistence; and
when we have had the rare good fortune of teaching them the arts of
civilization and the doctrines of Christianity we have unexpectedly

[1] The inviolable region then given to the Cherokees, which was never to have
extended around it the lines of any territory or state, lies south of Kansas, not far
from the present geographical center of the United States.
[2] December 2, 1828.

542

found them forming in the midst of ourselves communities claiming to be independent of ours and rivals of sovereignty [1] within the territories of the members of our Union. This state of things requires that a remedy [2] should be provided—a remedy which, while it shall do justice to those unfortunate children of nature, may secure to the members of our confederation their rights of sovereignty and of soil. . . ."

Three or four elements of President Adams' opinion require attention. One relates to his Executive declaration — the last one in history — to the effect that Indian nations were, in the eyes of the United States, "foreign and independent powers." With the expiration of Adams' term they had held that rank for forty years. Another phase of the retiring President's view has to do with the surprise voiced by him, and which suddenly swept over the white people when they at last realized that some of the red nations possessed qualities of manhood and civic pride which, under conditions even in a small degree favorable, made it possible for them to walk with their Caucasian fellows toward higher conditions of life — in the material sense. The mass of the newly arrived Americans had seemingly underrated the basic character of the red men, perhaps because they found it so easy to deceive them in matters which hung on the principle of honesty. They had hard work to comprehend a people who meant what they said; a people who—before the white men came—had apparently heard truth so long that they could not avoid the habit of believing, and who still tried to believe even when they knew they shouldn't. So the misconception got an early start and thereafter remained. Much of the civilizing process to which the natives had been subjected for nearly two centuries was

[1] A contradiction of the previous part of the message, wherein the President had already stated that the red people had long been officially recognized as foreign and independent powers.

[2] The remedy suggested by Adams was a colonization plan in the West, drawn up by the War Department and submitted with the message.

that which tended to drag them down[1] and make savages out of them. Civilizing a man does not necessarily make him morally better. It may make him worse.

Finally the red nations of the South got a chance, after the era of warfare ended, personally to select from the plane of human society called civilized life those elements of it which they desired, and to keep at arm's length for a time those other features of it which the white race had so lavishly bestowed on many natives. The result was immediate, and no doubt unexpected by the mass of the Caucasians. A feeling somewhat akin to indignation came over them. They acted as if they had been grossly deceived. They were angry at their own government, and blamed it for such a lamentable miscarriage of manifest destiny. Unfortunate children of nature, they felt, ought not experiment with patriotism and legislatures, and should either accept the particular variety of civilization offered to them by self-confessed benefactors or go without its blessing altogether.

President Adams said: "We have been far more successful in the acquisition of their lands than in imparting to them the principles or inspiring them with the spirit of civilization." There had apparently been no general desire by the white population to inspire the natives with the spirit of civilization in any fine significance of that expression, nor an unselfish and honest effort of the government toward the same end. The Cherokees and a few other red nations did believe until about 1825 that the republic's official interest in their welfare was unselfish, and they were grateful for it. But — for us of these later days — the sight of two consecutive Presidents trying for

[1] Reference is here made to the influence of the whites en masse; not to the splendid and helpful work of numerous individual white missionaries. The natives often asked such missionaries why they did not devote their effort to their own white brothers, who appeared to need it so much in matters of every-day living and mutual association.

161.—The Concord Coach. A stage of Beltzhoover and Company's Phoenix Line, running between Washington and Baltimore about 1830. Probably the largest and most pretentious American stage-coach print. Engraved by the artist Swett, after his own drawing.

a period of years to find a remedy for native civilization and its logical and beneficial results, casts a doubt on the sincerity of contrary governmental protestations. Congressional endorsement of Indian progress, and white legislative action designed to supply the southern native nations with materials of husbandry, ceased after unmistakable symptoms of their advancement became visible.

In giving concrete application to President Adams' remarks on the ratio existing between land acquired from Indians and civilization bestowed upon them, it will be found that the situation in the South was the contrary of his statement; nor had the United States brought upon itself any obligation to provide the southern nations with subsistence. They, instead, were exporting their surplus

545

crops to white communities. Again, their claim of independence and sovereignty to which the President refers as an unexpected phenomenon was but the inevitable corollary of the recognition accorded to them by the United States from the foundation of constitutional government. It could scarcely have been expected that their love of country would steadily dwindle, as they became more secure and prosperous in its possession, until finally they would be ready to abandon it. And every advancing step in their progress could not but be marked by an increase in the governmental machinery necessary to conduct the affairs of a more busy and complex society.

A sincere desire by one people, for any sort of civilization on the part of another people, must take thought of those elemental and essential features of civilization here mentioned, and expect them duly to appear. Indeed, a failure to anticipate them — by those capable of anticipation — is in some measure a suggestion that any advocacy of human advancement which fails to consider them is insincere. President Monroe had mentioned the lack of foresight used in dealing with the Indians, and now Adams — in commenting on the policy adopted toward them in 1789 — was to say: "It would seem as if a full contemplation of the consequences of the change had not been taken."

One other matter mentioned by Adams in his last message commands attention before the recital of historical events is resumed. It is a subject that at all times bore a more or less intimate relation to the misunderstanding between the races. President Adams mentioned that the red men had been looked on as savages, and that it had been considered both the duty and the policy of the whites to convert them to Christianity.

546

Now it so happened that the most deplorable tragedy enacted in the relations between light-skinned and dark-skinned peoples was due to the unfortunate and mistaken policy of Spain in her treatment of American Indians. A part of the persecutions to which the natives were subjected by early Spaniards took place in the near-by part of North America now occupied by Mexico, and their extent and long continuance caused a vague knowledge of them to spread slowly through a large part of the red population to the northward. Even after those cruelties abated the memory of them still persisted. Spain was a Christian nation and the native population, in some degree at least, came to link deception, avarice, injustice and oppression with Christianity as one of the phases or outcroppings of that religion. So when another light-skinned horde of invaders came, proclaimed Christianity as its religion and urged that belief upon the natives in place of their own, any endeavor to secure its general adoption by them was handicapped. The red men at once discovered, it is true, that there were many fine characters among the multiplying strangers; but certain traits, methods and practises which were exposed to view by the English speaking people as time went on often led the Indians to believe that though the Caucasian religion was — from their standpoint — a much milder and less dangerous kind of Christianity than that of which tradition told them, it was nevertheless not one which appealed strongly to them if men could believe in it and at the same time do various things which the white men did.

The sole standard of the natives for the measurement of human belief and action was their knowledge of themselves. Among the most advanced of them there was a considerable uniformity of basic ethical principles and a

similar uniformity in the manifestations of those fundamental beliefs through deeds. This was not so among the
white people, but the red men, applying their own standards of measure, long thought it was so, and therefore they
attributed to white men generally a willingness to commit

162.—A flat-topped coach, probably on the road from Philadelphia to Baltimore,
about 1832-1835. Engraved by the artist Tudor Horton.

the wrong acts which they saw individual white people
employ. Thus the natives in a measure misunderstood
those who had come among them.

The mass of English speaking people, on the other
hand, based their misconception of Indian character
and capacity on different, broader and characteristic
grounds. They simply took it for granted that no
primitive people — and especially one using bows and
arrows — could be their own equals in any respect either
of deed, thought or belief, and that consequently any
ethical or moral convictions which the Indians might by
chance possess could not be worthy of holding.

This attitude of the whites was no doubt one of the
gravest of their errors in dealing with the natives. It

prevented a possible meeting of the two races on a common plane of human sympathy and understanding that might perhaps have solved many of the difficulties of the situation without the unhappy events which did attend their solution. It was due to the mental arrogance of the Caucasians and to mistaken belief that human superiority, either among individuals or peoples, is chiefly demonstrated — if not invariably proved — by material possessions and physical power. The red men did not number more than a few hundred thousand souls, and the practical sense and clear, direct reasoning characteristic of their mental processes speedily showed them the advantage of harmonious relations and mutual good will. Had they been consistently met in the same spirit it is doubtful if the white Americans would in the end have lost anything they now possess, while both they themselves and the Indians would assuredly have preserved much that was lost.

As far as the ethical beliefs and resultant practises of the more advanced natives in their natural state were concerned they did, in fact, compare rather favorably with the strangers. Only a small number of competent white men gave serious study to those things until comparatively recent times, or had opportunity to do so, but the testimony they left is often valuable and enlightening. Three short examples of it are here given:[1]

"I fearlessly assert to the world, and I defy contradiction, that the North American Indian is everywhere in his native state a highly moral and religious being . . .

"I never saw any other people who spend so much of their lives in humbling themselves before and worshipping the Great Spirit as these tribes do, nor any whom I would not as soon suspect of insincerity and hypocrisy.

[1] The narratives of others who carefully studied the Indians while they were yet unaffected by intimate contact with the whites, and of travellers among them, will reveal similar opinions and statements.

"To each other I have found these people kind and honorable, and endowed with every feeling of parental, filial and conjugal affection that is met with in more enlightened communities." [1]

Another comment reads:

". . . Simply to call these people religious would convey but a faint idea of the deep hue of piety and devotion which pervades the whole of their conduct. Their honesty is immaculate; and their purity of purpose and their observance of the rites of their religion are most uniform and remarkable. They are certainly more like a nation of saints than a horde of savages." [2]

The third of these observations is a more detailed statement, and deals with the Sioux as they were in 1818. The later history of the West gives these comments an added significance: [3]

"The pagans on the River St. Peter have no knowledge of the Bible, but they believe in a Great Spirit who lives forever in a palace above all clouds—and that he made the sun, the moon, the stars, the earth, the lakes, rivers, trees, cattle, fishes, birds, and all things, and gave them to the Indians, who are like Him in shape, in benevolence, and in goodness; and they believe that if they are moral and pious they will be sent for by the Great Spirit to live with him in his palace forever, and want no good thing. Also they believe in the following revelation and laws, sent to their ancestors by the Great Spirit.

"1—Fear, love and praise the Great Spirit.
"2—Be honest.
"3—Love one another.
"4—Be charitable.
"5—Injure no man.
"6—Be merciful to animals.

"Thus live the Sioux Nations on the West side of the Mississippi to the Shining Mountains in perfect orthodoxy; no ways troubled about the opinions of fathers, councils, bishops, or churches, but contented with their short creed and divine rules.

"Since residing here amongst many pagan tribes, who are the most innocent, benevolent and moral part of the human race I ever saw, I have thought much. The moral perfection of these Indians and their creed have brought me to join with them in saying that their Articles are as good as the Articles of the multiformed churches of Christendom.

[1] "Letters and Notes on the Manners, Customs and Condition of the North American Indians." Second Edition: Vol. II, p. 243.
[2] "The Adventures of Captain Bonneville": chapter 9. Refers to the Nez Percés.
[3] This letter has apparently escaped notice in any history of the western Indians or of the regions concerned. It was written at Prairie du Chien, in May of 1818, and printed in the "Indiana Centinel" of May 29, 1819.

"These pagans have high prejudices against Christians, and believe the Spaniards are the only true Christians, whose cruelties, murders and robberies in South America of the Indians are well known by tradition among the Sioux tribes; and when any white traders cheat and deceive a Sioux Pagan they are called Spaniards and Christians. . . .

"If the Americans should ever attempt to introduce Christianity among the Sioux tribes, they must send honest traders, sensible and moral men, to deal with them, and make use of no severity. Mildness, benevolence and pious examples must be used among the Sioux Nations to induce them to adopt a life of civilization, and no use is to be made of the word Christian or Spaniard.

"Military compulsion will not be useful in civilizing Indians. The Sioux know they are the real and rightful owners of the land by virtue of the Great Spirit, by long possession and occupancy, and no white people have a right to build forts, houses, and cultivate their lands, until they obtain from the Indians a right by purchase, and consent of the owners and present possessors.

"This doctrine is not pleasing to military commanders, but must be attended to by our government, to prevent a war with the many tribes of Indians in this western territory. For two years past no crime has been committed among all these many Indian tribes."

The native beliefs of the red peoples, together with a discord which they observed between the spoken religion and numerous outward acts of the white men, were the causes contributing to the result mentioned by President Adams. Nevertheless some natives did embrace the religious beliefs so constantly offered to them by earnest and self-sacrificing missionaries in all parts of the country. In the case of the Cherokees practically the whole people became converts, built churches, and printed their own hymn books and other similar volumes in their own written language, from type set up in the government printing establishment in their capital, New Echota.

CHAPTER XXVII

MISSISSIPPI AND ALABAMA JOIN GEORGIA IN THE ATTACK
ON NATIVE INDEPENDENCE — DOWNFALL OF INDIAN
SELF-GOVERNMENT AND CIVILIZATION IN THE EAST
DRAWS NEARER — JACKSON ASSUMES THE PRESI-
DENCY AND CROSSES THE RUBICON — CHARACTER OF
HIS UTTERANCES ON THE INDIAN PROBLEM — AP-
PEAL OF THE CHEROKEE LEGISLATURE TO THE WHITE
PEOPLE — ACTION OF THE CHOCTAW NATIONAL
COUNCIL — PLEDGES OF THE CHOCTAW TREATY —
CONDITIONS OF CHOCTAW SOCIETY — DEMANDS OF
THE CHICKASAWS AND EXTENT OF THEIR ADVANCE-
MENT — JACKSON'S PERSONAL JOURNEY TO MEET
THE CHICKASAWS AND HIS SPEECH TO THEM — THE
UNITED STATES REAFFIRMS NATIVE INDEPENDENCE
AND RE-CREATES WEST OF THE MISSISSIPPI THE SAME
CONDITIONS WHICH IT IS TRYING TO DESTROY IN THE
EAST

THE states of Mississippi and Alabama joined with
Georgia in refusing longer to recognize the sov-
ereignty of the southern Indian nations immediately after
President Jackson assumed the duties of his office.
A year previous to that time, while Adams was still in
power, Mississippi had addressed a memorial to the
Federal Congress[1] recognizing that the United States
alone could treat with the Chickasaws and Choctaws

[1] On February 17, 1828.

552

within the modern bounds of the state. The document related existing conditions, announced that white men had gone into the native territories and said: "Your memorialists therefore respectfully suggest, that the removal of the aforesaid white persons by general government, and a judicious selection of commissioners to treat with these nations for their lands would obviate most of the difficulties which have heretofore opposed themselves to the acquirement of the Indian lands." The memorial also said: "A large portion of the most valuable territory within the chartered limits of this state is occupied by savage tribes."[1]

The Mississippi statute designed to cancel the sovereignty of the two red nations whose existence the state had decided thereafter to ignore despite Federal treaties was enacted on February 4, 1829,[2] some five weeks after Georgia's similar action. It was entitled "An act to extend legal process into that part of this state now occupied by the Chickasaw and Choctaw tribes of Indians." Following the law of 1829 Mississippi passed, in 1830, a statute reading:

"An act to extend the laws of the State of Mississippi over the persons and property of the Indians resident within its limits.

"Sec. 1. Be it enacted . . . That from and after the passage of this act, all the rights, privileges, immunities and franchises, held, claimed or enjoyed by those persons called Indians, and their descendants, and which are held by virtue of any form of policy, usage or custom existing among said persons, not particularly recognized and established by the common law or statutes of the state of Mississippi, be, and the same are hereby wholly abolished, and taken away."

Section two granted to the Indians "all the rights, privileges, immunities and franchises held and enjoyed by free white persons" of the said

---

[1] "Laws of the State of Mississippi passed at the Eleventh Session of the General Assembly, held in the Town of Jackson. Published by authority, Jackson, 1828": pp. 144-145.

[2] Winter travellers and news then required about two or three weeks to proceed from interior Mississippi to Washington, and information regarding the step taken would therefore have reached the capital in the final fortnight of Adams' term.

163.—A Concord coach on a road in the Catskill Mountains. About 1840.

state, "in as full and ample a manner as the same can be done by act of the General Assembly."

"Sec. 3. Be it further enacted, That all the laws, statutes and ordinances now in force in the said state of Mississippi, be and the same are hereby declared to have full force, power and operation over the persons and property of and within the territory now occupied by the said Indians. . . .

"Sec. 5. And be it further enacted, That any person or persons who shall assume on him or themselves, and exercise in any manner whatever the office of chief, mingo, head-man or other post of power established by the tribal statutes, ordinances or customs of the said Indians, and not particularly recognized by the laws of this state, shall, on conviction upon indictment, or presentment before a Court of competent jurisdiction, be fined in any sum not exceeding one thousand dollars, and be imprisoned any time not exceeding twelve months, at the discretion of the Court before whom conviction may be had." [1]

Alabama's enactment in nullification of Federal treaties, passed in 1829, was called "An act to extend the

[1] "Laws of the State of Mississippi. Thirteenth Session. Jackson, 1830": pp. 5-6. The parts here omitted—sections 4 and 6—do not alter the meaning of the remainder.

jurisdiction of the State of Alabama over the Creek nation." It contained no severe sections of individual application. Two articles read:

"Sec. 6. That nothing in this act shall be so construed as to impose taxation or military duty on the Indians, until the same shall be specially authorized by the state legislature."

"Sec. 8. That the Secretary of State be required forthwith to furnish the agent of the Creek Indians and each of our Senators in Congress, with a copy of this act."

President Jackson's first annual message[1] contained an elaborate review of the critical situation in the South and his attitude toward the problem presented by it. The Executive and governmental position, as expounded by him, was a reversal in almost every particular of the policy uniformly pursued by the nation from its constitutional organization up to that time. The Governor of Georgia had written to the Federal Secretary of War saying that if the President sustained the Indians, "the consequences are inevitable," and that if the Federal government opposed by force the occupation of the Cherokee region, then Georgia would be compelled to "war upon, and shed the blood of brothers and friends." Jackson said in his message:

". . . It has long been the policy of Government to introduce among them the arts of civilization, in the hope of gradually reclaiming them from a wandering life. This policy has, however, been coupled with another wholly incompatible with its success. Professing a desire to civilize and settle them, we have at the same time lost no opportunity to purchase their lands and thrust them farther into the wilderness. By this means they have not only been kept in a wandering state, but been led to look upon us as unjust and indifferent to their fate. Thus, though lavish in its expenditures upon the subject, Government has constantly defeated its own policy, and the Indians in general, receding farther and farther to the west, have retained their savage habits.[2] A portion, how-

[1] December 8, 1829.
[2] They were abandoning their earlier habits and adopting pastoral lives east of the Mississippi to the utmost extent compatible with their surroundings and the influence of the white race. Instances wherein this was not true were due to the fear, on their part, that it would be useless and that they would again be evicted.

ever, of the Southern tribes, having mingled much with the whites and made some progress in the arts of civilized life,[1] have lately attempted to erect an independent government within the limits of Georgia and Alabama.[2] These states, claiming to be the only sovereigns within their territories, extended their laws over the Indians, which induced the latter to call upon the United States for protection.

"Under these circumstances the question presented was whether the general Government had a right to sustain those people in their pretensions.[3] The Constitution declares that 'no new state shall be formed or erected within the jurisdiction of any other state' without the consent of its legislature.[4] If the general Government is not permitted to tolerate the erection of a confederate state within the territory of one of the members of this Union against her consent, much less could it allow a foreign and independent government to establish itself there . . .[5]

"Actuated by this view of the subject, I informed the Indians inhabiting parts of Georgia and Alabama that their attempt to establish an independent government[6] would not be countenanced by the Executive of the United States, and advised them to emigrate beyond the Mississippi or submit to the laws of those states.[7]

"Our conduct toward these people is deeply interesting to our national character. Their present condition, contrasted with what they once were, makes a most powerful appeal to our sympathies. Our ancestors found them the uncontrolled possessors of these vast regions. By persuasion and force they have been made to retire from river to river and from mountain to mountain, until some of the tribes have become extinct and others have left but remnants to preserve for awhile their once terrible names. Surrounded by the whites with their arts of civilization, which by destroying the resources of the savage doom him to weakness and decay, the fate of the Mohegan, the Narragansett, and the

---

[1] The progress made by the southern red nations was rather due to their refusal to mingle with the whites to the extent that occurred in the North. The southern tribes kept the bulk of the Caucasians at arm's length, thus becoming less contaminated by weakening vices and accepting only the useful teachings they could offer.

[2] The Cherokees' independent government here referred to, had been sixteen times recognized by the Federal Union and had been a matter of Congressional admission and Executive pronouncement for 40 years.

[3] Three years previously the general government, through its Executive, had declared its intention to sustain them, if necessary, by its military power.

[4] The United States had recognized the Cherokees as an independent state prior to the adoption of the Constitution, and had dealt with them by treaty in 1785. The recognition given to them was a continuing process whose origin antedated the Constitution.

[5] As already suggested, a foreign and independent government was already there in the case of the Cherokees, and it had held treaty relations with the Congress of the Confederacy before Georgia, Alabama, Tennessee and North Carolina had relations either with one another or with the Federal government under a Constitution; and before Alabama and Tennessee existed.

The points here advanced—in connection with Jackson's presentation of the matter —are examples of the difficulties and confusion, mentioned in an earlier chapter, in which the United States found itself involved at a time when the need of unimpeded communication between all parts of the country began to be keenly felt.

[6] Again the President phrases his address in a manner to make it appear that profession of native independence was a new thing.

[7] Thereby again wrecking "the policy of Government" by once more "thrusting them farther into the wilderness."

RAIL-ROAD LINE
Of Stages from North-Canaan to
New York. 184

PASSENGERS' NAMES.	No. OF SEATS.	WHERE FROM.	WHERE TO.	DOLLS.	CTS.	BY WHOM RECEIVED.
	1					
Mr. Burroughs	1	Kent	Connle B.	50		H. Benson

164.—Stage-coach way-bill, or manifest. The driver of a stage, or an agent at the starting point, kept a record of passengers on a printed form like this, and delivered the document to the owner of the line as an account of business transacted.

Delaware is fast overtaking the Choctaw, the Cherokee, and the Creek.[1] That this fate surely awaits them if they remain within the limits of the states does not admit of a doubt. Humanity and national honor demand that every effort should be made to avert so great a calamity. It is too late to inquire whether it was just in the United States to include them and their territory within the bounds of new states, whose limits they could control. That step can not be retraced.[2] A state can not be dismembered by Congress or restricted in the exercise of her constitutional power.[3] But the people of those states, and of every state, actuated by feelings of justice and a regard for our national honor, submit to you the interesting question whether something can not be done, consistently with the rights of the states, to preserve this much-injured race.

"As a means of effecting this end I suggest for your consideration the propriety of setting apart an ample district west of the Mississippi. . . . There the benevolent may endeavor to teach them the arts of civilization, and, by promoting union and harmony among them, to raise up an interesting commonwealth destined to perpetuate the race and to attest the humanity and justice of this Government.

"This emigration should be voluntary, for it would be as cruel as unjust to compel the aborigines to abandon the graves of their fathers[4]

[1] The southern Indians were no longer savages. Their man-created resources had never been more valuable, or their prosperity and advancement more marked.
[2] The question then remained whether or not the United States would abide by the consequences.
[3] The affected southern states had disclaimed ownership or jurisdiction of Indian territory until a short time before.
[4] While it is true that the southern nations, like other Indians, did have sentimental affection for their familiar territories, they were nevertheless more concerned about giving up their homes, flocks, farms, mills and the other material improvements of a generation.

557

and seek a home in a distant land. But they should be distinctly informed that if they remain within the limits of the states they must be subject to their laws. In return for their obedience as individuals they will without doubt be protected in the enjoyment of those possessions which they have improved by their industry.[1] But it seems to me visionary to suppose that in this state of things claims can be allowed on tracts of country on which they have neither dwelt nor made improvements, merely because they have seen them from the mountain or passed them in the chase.[2] Submitting to the laws of the states, and receiving, like other citizens, protection in their persons and property, they will ere long before merged in the mass of our population."[3]

Following the utterance of Jackson the position of the Indians of the South became more precarious than before. This was especially the case in Georgia, which state had assumed a somewhat more advanced attitude in hostility to them than had either Alabama or Mississippi. All four of the red nations were dismayed by the sudden alteration in the Republic's relation to them, but under the counsel of their leading men maintained a quiet demeanor and busied themselves with preparations for a decorous pleading of their cause in whatever quarter that method of defense appeared to offer best chance of success. Extreme care was taken by them to prevent clashes of violence, and, in consequence, very little disorder took place. White surveys of Indian lands were resumed in some quarters, but without resistance on the part of the natives. The United States for a time sent representatives to the South in an effort to prevail

[1] State laws already framed scarcely warranted the President's conclusion. In addition to those already quoted, Georgia had organized a lottery with Creek lands as prizes.

[2] The southern nations made no claims to territory that were not defined by treaty and acknowledged as valid by the white government. The United States, when it claimed from England all the region to the Mississippi River, in 1783, did more than President Jackson objected to on the part of the natives. It then claimed territories not even seen from the mountain, passed in the chase or otherwise known to them except by hearsay.

[3] In view of the easily accessible information possessed by governmental departments to which an Executive turned for accurate knowledge respecting the subjects discussed in official papers, and also in view of General Jackson's long personal acquaintance with the country's racial relations and problems, it is difficult to reconcile some of these assertions and opinions with a belief in the sincerity or ignorance of their author. It is easier, rather, reluctantly to believe that Jackson was influenced by a knowledge that individual states were in revolt against Federal authority, with civil war a probability unless he yielded, and that he chose a way out of the complicated dilemma which apparently benefited his fellow white men.

on the nations to sell their possessions and remove at once to the westward of the Mississippi. These agents received instructions to work on the principal men of the nations "in the line of their prejudices"; to "enlarge on the advantages of their condition in the West"; to "make offers to them of extreme reservations in fee simple, and other rewards, to obtain their acquiescence"; to "appeal to the Chiefs and other influential men, not together, but apart, at their own houses."

Considerable quantities of gold were found in the streams of the Cherokee country at the same time, and that discovery further excited the white population of the South and made it still more insistent upon the departure of the Indians. Many southern gold-seekers flocked to the wealth-bearing rivers and creeks in violation of existing treaty regulations.[1] The Cherokees sent a delegation to Washington to employ counsel and defend their interests, and John Ross, Chief Executive of the nation in 1830, convened the native Congress in extraordinary session.

Among the counsel before whom the matter of Indian independence was laid by the Cherokees for opinion was William Wirt, and his opinion read thus:

"On every ground of argument on which I have been enabled, by my own reflections or the suggestions of others, to consider this question, I am of the opinion:

"1. That the Cherokees are a sovereign nation: and that their having placed themselves under the protection of the United States does not at all impair their sovereignty and independence as a nation. 'One community may be bound to another by a very unequal alliance, and still be a sovereign state. Though a weak state, in order to provide for its safety, should place itself under the protection of a more powerful one, yet according to Vatell (B 1. Ch. 1. par. 5 and 6) if it reserves to itself the

[1] "We learn by a gentleman just from Georgia that there are about 5000 hands now digging gold in the Cherokee nation . . . The Indians and their agent begin to dispute with the Georgians about the soil and threaten to drive them off. The Georgians promise resistance and will not be easily removed." From the "Western Sun" (Vincennes, Ind.) of May 1, 1830.

MAIL-COACH CHANGING HORSES.

165.—Changing horses at a relay station. Fresh animals were attached to a stage at intervals of ten or fifteen miles. The new team stood awaiting the arrival of the coach, which was on its way again in one or two minutes.

right of governing its own body it ought to be considered as an independent state.'—20 Johnson's Reports 711-712. Goodell vs. Jackson.

"2. That the territory of the Cherokees is not within the jurisdiction of the state of Georgia, but within the sole and exclusive jurisdiction of the Cherokee nation.

"3. That consequently, the state of Georgia has no right to extend her laws over that territory.

"4. That the law of Georgia which has been placed before me is unconstitutional and void; (1) because it is repugnant to the treaties between the United States and the Cherokee nation, (2) because it is repugnant to a law of the U. States passed in 1802, entitled 'an act to regulate trade and intercourse with the Indian tribes and to preserve peace on the frontiers'; (3) because it is repugnant to the Constitution, inasmuch as it impairs the obligation of all the contracts arising under the treaties with the Cherokees: and affects moreover to regulate intercourse with an Indian tribe, a power which belongs exclusively to Congress.

"Baltimore, June 20, 1830.   WILLIAM WIRT."

The policy of the Jackson administration was explained and defended at this time by the Secretary of War, and extracts from his argument[1] are here given:

[1] Contained in a letter written by Secretary Eaton, on June 30, 1830, to Eli Baldwin, Corresponding Secretary of the Indian Board.

166.—Stage drivers were customarily accommodating in the matter of halting briefly for passengers who were near at hand, unless the vehicle was already full. Perhaps in this case there was not enough room left for another entire family. By the artist John Sartain.

"His [President Jackson's] fears are that strife, difficulty and dangers may be consequent upon a disposition on their part to remain where they are;[1] and these he has an anxious desire to avert, if within his power, through the exercise of any legitimate means."

"It is high time they were aroused to a sense of their actual and true condition."

"Every American would desire to preserve, not to oppress them. They will never be driven from their homes."

"It is not in his power to interfere with the exercise of the sovereign authority of a state, to prevent the extension of their laws within their own territorial limits."[2]

"Can he say to Georgia, you shall not consider an Indian a citizen and answerable to her civil and criminal jurisdiction?"[3]

". . . So far, then, as the government of the United States is concerned there is no course under action, or in anticipation, calculated to induce to any other than a voluntary departure."[4]

"If a desire to harass and ultimately to destroy was the governing motive, the argument to be adduced to them would be not to remove, but remain where they are."[5]

Congress in the meantime had passed a general law[6] providing for concentrating the Indians in a region west of the Mississippi. The national legislature did not make their migration obligatory, but the bill was originally drawn without reference to existing treaties with the natives. This defect was altered by an amendment reading: "Provided, that nothing in this act contained shall be construed as authorizing or directing the violation of any existing treaty between the United States and any of the Indian tribes." The law also said: "It shall and may be lawful for the President solemnly to assure the tribe or nation with which the exchange is made, that the United

[1] This way of stating the question tended to place responsibility on the natives for strife which would have come through the determination of the white race to dispossess them.

[2] The Secretary of War here assumes that the sovereignty of the affected states did extend over the Indian possessions, which was the principal and newly arisen point of dispute.

[3] Such, nevertheless, had been the position of both Georgia and of the United States for the thirty-eight years between 1789 and 1827.

[4] Scarcely an accurate statement. As soon as Georgia had officially notified Jackson of her claim to sovereignty over the Cherokee possessions he withdrew from the Cherokee boundary those Federal troops which had been previously stationed there to prevent white intrusion on Indian land. Lack of protection was what made departure compulsory.

[5] This was correct on the presumption that the United States would no longer carry out its treaty obligations, but leave the natives under the laws of the states.

[6] Approved May 28, 1830.

States will forever secure and guarantee to them and their heirs or successors, the country so exchanged with them."[1]

The passage of the law of 1830 by Congress was hailed with relief by the white population of the country, which had likewise looked with approval on the attitude of President Jackson.[2] For several years the Indian problem had been one of the matters chiefly engaging public attention, and it was realized that some definite settlement of it must speedily be made. The new law, it was hoped, gave promise of that result. It had also been generally admitted that civil strife was in sight if the South was not permitted to have its way. An example of the usual newspaper comment of the day will best indicate popular feeling:

"The great Indian question has been finally settled, leaving the red man the choice of remaining where he is, subject only to the laws of the state or territory in which he resides in common with the white inhabitants, or of removing to the west of the Mississippi under the bounty and protection of the general government, and receiving there in exchange for the land he quits a much wider territory, healthier climate and more abundant and profitable hunting grounds. This measure was projected under the former administrations, and its execution made necessary at this time to avoid the more serious alternative of civil war. Men the best acquainted with the subject in all its bearings consider the act equally the dictate of humanity as of necessity."[3]

When the Cherokee legislature had assembled in extraordinary session[4] to consider the course of the nation in the crisis that had arisen, Ross, the Executive, delivered to it the subjoined message:[5]

[1] A prediction concerning this pledge was made at the time by the Rev. Jeremiah Evarts, in a letter published in the "National Intelligencer" under the name of "William Penn." He said: "In a quarter of a century the pressure upon the Indians will be much greater from the boundless prairies, which must ultimately be subdued and inhabited, than it would ever have been from the borders of the present Cherokee country."
[2] Judging from the general tone of the newspaper press of the time. Even those newspapers which admitted the hardship bestowed on the natives by Jackson's reversal of the previous national policy took the position that their interests must be sacrificed in order to permit white progress.
[3] From the "Western Sun" of Vincennes, August 14, 1830. Reprinted by it from another and unnamed paper.
[4] At New Echota, the capital, July 11, 1830.
[5] From the "Western Sun," issue of August 7, 1830.

"To the Committee and Council, in General Council convened:

"Friends and Fellow Citizens:—The constituted authorities of Georgia having assumed the power to exercise sovereign jurisdiction over a large portion of our Territory, and our Political Father, the Chief Magistrate of the United States, having declared that he possesses no power to oppose or interfere with Georgia in this matter, our relations with the U. States are placed in a strange dilemma. The grave aspect of this picture calls for your calm and serious reflections. I have therefore deemed it my incumbent duty, on this extraordinary occasion, to convene the General Council of the Cherokee Nation.

"The prayers of our memorials before the Congress of the United States have not been answered. But it is edifying to know that numerous similar petitions from various sections of the United States have been presented in favor of our cause by a large portion of the most respectable class of the community, and that our rights have been ably vindicated in Congress by some of the most distinguished statesmen. But notwithstanding the unanswerable arguments which have been advanced under these appeals, there seems to have been a settled determination, by a small majority in Congress, to make further efforts to bring about a removal of all the Indians east of the Mississippi beyond that great river, by making the question a general one, and acting upon the principles of policy and expediency. The respective claims and rights of each tribe under existing treaties with the United States were viewed only as a secondary consideration. Consequently an act has been passed 'To provide for an exchange of lands with the Indians residing in any of the states or territories, and for their removal west of the river Mississippi.' The House of Representatives, however, by a very large majority, adopted this amendment, which has been accepted by the Senate, 'Provided that nothing in this act shall be construed as authorizing or directing the violation of any existing treaty between the United States and any of the Indian tribes.'

"It is much to be regretted that we find in the reports of some of the acting agents of the general government and other designing and interested individuals that our true motives, disposition and condition have been grossly perverted and misrepresented. This may in part be attributed to a want of correct and full information upon the points of which they pretend to speak, and in some respects to an inclination to deceive the public with the view of effecting certain political ends.

"The fee simple title to the soil has been vainly asserted to be in the people of Georgia; and that state has arrogated to herself the power to exercise sovereign jurisdiction over us, and by legislative enactments has declared all our laws, ordinances, orders, regulations and usages to be null and void, and peremptorily demands submission to her proscriptive and oppressive laws under the most degrading circumstances. She has pointed to her jails, penitentiary and gallows for practicing obedience to our own laws, and independent of all our treaties with the United States and the acts of Congress which have been passed for the protection of our individual and national rights, the Chief Magistrate of the Union has warned us against any hope of interference on his part with Georgia in the exercise of this power; yet he says that such power as the laws give him, for our protection shall be executed for our benefit, and this will not fail to be exercised in keeping out intruders; beyond this he cannot go. An officer commanding a detachment of U. States' troops,

Passengers are requested to get out and walk, one Gent particularly objects.

167.—A frequent experience. But the Gent always got out sooner or later.

who has been ordered into the nation, as it is said, for the purpose of removing intruders, has communicated to the Cherokees at the gold mines the following notice:

"'An arrangement has been entered into by which there will be mutual assistance between the U. States' troops and the civil authority of Georgia in all civil processes, the jurisdiction of Georgia having been extended over the chartered limits, and all the natives are hereby advised to return to their homes[1] and submit to the proclamation of the state authority.'

(Signed)   E. Trainer, Lieut. Com'g.

"'P. S. They cannot be supported any longer in anything inconsistent with the laws of the state.'

"Thus you will see that the rights and liberties of the Cherokee people are most grievously assailed.

"Our delegation[2] were authorized, if it should become necessary, to

[1] Many of the Indians were digging gold at the mines discovered in their territory.
[2] The national delegation sent to Washington.

consult and employ counsel to defend our cause before the Supreme Court of the United States, in which tribunal, as the conservatory of the Constitution, treaties and laws of the Union, we can yet hope for justice, and to which we should fearlessly and firmly appeal. I would, therefore, recommend the expediency of passing a law authorizing some person to assert the rights of the Cherokee nation in all the courts of law and equity in the United States; also to address the President of the United States frankly, openly and respectfully on the subject of our unhappy situation, and request his paternal interference in all points as far as the treaties and laws of the United States acknowledge and secure to us our rights; until the controversy at issue with Georgia be decided by the Supreme Court of the United States.

"I would further submit for your consideration the necessity of adopting some suitable and proper regulations for the observance of our citizens in working the gold mines of the nation and other valuable minerals, such as the public interest and peace and good order of society may seem to require.

"Confiding in the superintending care of a kind providence we should not despair, even should we for a season be plunged into the cells of Georgia's prisons. Means for our deliverance may yet be found. Let us not forget the circumstance related in Holy Writ, of the safe passage of the children of Israel through the crystal walls of the Red Sea and the fate of their wicked pursuers; let our faith in the unsearchable mysteries of an Omnipotent and all-wise Being be unshaken; for in the appearance of impossibilities there is still hope.

"NEW ECHOTA, C. N., July 11, 1830.   JOHN ROSS."

The official messages, protests and other papers of the Indians[1] at this time were occasionally characterized in Caucasian state documents as "tricks of vulgar cunning" or "insults from the polluted lips of outcasts and vagabonds." But such instances were fortunately rare. Their strength and sincerity made it impossible to deal lightly with them, however great might be the opposition to the arguments and claims they advanced.

Meanwhile the Choctaw National Council had also met[2] to take action due to Mississippi's claim of jurisdiction over the nation and Jackson's endorsement of Missis-

---

[1] Those of the Cherokees were printed in their newspaper, often in the English language. Some of the Cherokee state papers are also contained in the second edition of Armroyd's "Connected View of the Whole Internal Navigation of the United States. Philadelphia, 1830."
[2] On March 15, 1830.

168.—A stage-coach struck by a railway train and left on the roadside. Un-
signed water-color sketch, perhaps made by an unhurt traveller, while sitting on a stump, as a memento of his journey. Date, about 1845.

sippi's position. The proceedings of the Choctaws have
been preserved in a letter published in a number of newspapers at the time.[1] It reads:

"The National Council met on Monday the 15th day of March past,
to determine the future course in this great crisis of their national existence.

"On the evening of the first day of the Council the Captains re-
elected Greenwood Leflore Chief of the Western District without a dissenting voice. He was then carried in triumph through the Captains
of the other districts and a large assembly of Warriors, his officers singing a hymn in their native language; they then prostrated themselves
before the Eternal, when their Chief-elect closed the solemn scene by an
affecting prayer in behalf of his nation.

[1] Among them the Natchez (Miss.) "Galaxy" and Vincennes (Ind.) "Western Sun."
The text as here given is from the "Western Sun" of May 8, 1830.

"On the forenoon of the second day of the Council (the 16th) the Chiefs of the other two districts came forward with their Captains and Warriors, resigned their several offices, and unanimously elected Greenwood Leflore the Chief of the whole nation. Then followed a pleasant season of rejoicings, and the exercises of the forenoon closed by their Chief-elect in solemn prayer in which the whole assembly united as with the heart of one man.

"In the afternoon the National Council was organized, and the important object of its call introduced by the Chief.

"The Chief presented a concise view of the difficulties of their situation, and the alternatives which were before them, and the necessity of immediate choice. The address of the Chief was followed by one from an aged warrior who had fought under General Jackson, and another from a warrior still older who fought under General Wayne.[1] The discussion continued to a late hour, when the vote being taken was found in favor of emigration.

"On the 17th articles of a treaty were prepared,[2] and on that night signed by the Chief, the two late Chiefs, the Captains, and two or three hundred principal warriors. . . .

"The Chief directed all his Captains to execute faithfully the laws of the nation, not in opposition to Mississippi, but with belief that Mississippi would not interfere when she discovered the Choctaws were endeavoring to get out of her way.

"The Chief expressed a determination not to emigrate with a poor, penniless and ruined people.

"Throughout the whole proceeding the spirit of brotherly kindness and fervent piety were evinced, and the full faith that the Great Spirit would be with them in their removal and bless them in their new home."

The Choctaws numbered not far from 20,000 souls, and then owned nearly one-third of Mississippi and some one thousand four hundred square miles of territory in Alabama. They asked about one million dollars for their eastern possessions, in addition to unimproved lands in the West.

When Jackson submitted the Choctaw proposals to the Senate,[3] he said:

"It will be seen that the pecuniary stipulations are large; and in bringing this subject to the consideration of the Senate I may be allowed

[1] Some of the southern Indians fought with the United States under Wayne against the northern red confederation in the struggle that broke the Indian power of the Northwest Territory.
[2] Not the treaty itself, but the Choctaw terms for a treaty.
[3] In a special message on May 6, 1830.

to remark that the amount of money which may be secured to be paid should, in my judgment, be viewed as of minor importance. . . . The great desideratum is the removal of the Indians and the settlement of the perplexing question involved in their present location—a question in which several of the states of this Union have the deepest interest, and which, if left undecided much longer, may eventuate in serious injury to the Indians." [1]

A treaty with the Choctaws was concluded later in the same year[2] by whose terms the nation ceded to the United

TONTINE HOTEL, NEW HAVEN, Ct.

169.—Stages arriving and departing from a typical city tavern of the best sort. The large inns of the towns had begun to call themselves hotels.

States all their country east of the Mississippi. The United States, on its part, reaffirmed the nationality of the Choctaws which it had recently denied, acknowledged their civilized state and re-created, in the West, the same native conditions that had until then existed in the East.

[1] Jackson's fear or expectation of white violence is indicated.
[2] September 27, 1830. As sent to the Senate by the President it contained a statement saying he could not protect the Choctaws from Mississippi laws. This was stricken out by the Senate, possibly because of Adams' recent successful protection of the Creeks from Georgia laws.

The principal paragraphs by which this state of affairs was brought about were:

"Article IV. The Government and people of the United States are hereby obliged to secure to the Choctaw Nation of Red People the jurisdiction and government of all the persons and property that may be within their limits west, so that no territory or state shall ever have a right to pass laws for the government of the Choctaw Nation of Red People and their descendants; and that no part of the land granted to them shall ever be embraced in any Territory or State; but the United States shall forever secure such Choctaw Nation from, and against, all laws except such as from time to time may be enacted in their own National Councils, not inconsistent with the Constitution, Treaties and laws of the United States. . .

"Article V. . . . No war shall be undertaken or prosecuted by said Choctaw Nation but by declaration made in full Council, and to be approved by the United States unless it be in self defense against an open rebellion or against an enemy marching into their country, in which case they shall defend until the United States are advised thereof."[1]

"Article XXII. The Chiefs of the Choctaws have suggested that their people are in a state of rapid advancement in education and refinement, and have expressed a solicitude that they might have the privilege of a Delegate on the floor of the House of Representatives extended to them. The Commissioners do not feel that they can under a treaty stipulation accede to the request, but at their desire present it in the Treaty, that Congress may consider of, and decide the application."

The condition of Choctaw society at this time may be understood from further treaty provisos in which they insisted on three churches in their new country; the erection of a national Council House; public schoolhouses for their children; $50,000 for school teachers' salaries; blacksmiths; a millwright; one thousand carding machines; the same number of spinning wheels; four hundred looms; a thousand plows; quantities of other agricultural implements; three tons of iron and six hundred pounds of steel annually for sixteen years; and the educa-

---

[1] Treaty clauses like these do much to explain the later action of many of the transplanted Indians and tribes native to the West when the whites began their march across the plains toward the Pacific. The whites sometimes comported themselves as enemies or invaders during the western migrations, and the Indians believed, in view of such treaties, that they were defending themselves and their territories.

GREAT UNITED STATES MAIL LINES,

TO THE SOUTH & WEST,

VIA

BATIMORE & OHIO R. R. TO CUMBERLAND,

AND

NATIONAL ROAD TO WHEELING.

SIX DAILY LINES of Mail and Passenger Coaches leave Cumberland every Evening, after the arrival of the Cars at that place, for Pittsburg, Wheeling, Cincinnati,

Louisville, St. Louis and New Orleans. Through to Pittsburg or Wheeling in forty-four hours. Passengers taking this route will be out one night only. Leaves Philadelphia twice daily, Winter and Summer. For Seats and Through Tickets, or entire Coaches, apply at the General Rail Road and Stage Office, No. 45 South Third Street, or at the Rail Road Office Eleventh and Market Streets. For Stage Companies,

T. BLACKWELL, Agent.

N. B. The above named Offices are the only Offices that are authorized to receipt through to Wheeling or to Pittsburg, via Baltimore.   T. B.

170.—A route to the Middle West in 1852. Advertisement showing the coöperation of stage-coaches and railways. The Baltimore and Ohio road had been opened to Cumberland, and by taking a coach at that town a traveller from the East might reach Pittsburgh in 44 hours. Thence, by stage, he could continue to Cincinnati in about three days more, or to St. Louis in about seven days.

tion of forty selected Choctaw youths each year in Caucasian institutions.[1]

All efforts designed to persuade the Chickasaws into migration having failed, President Jackson journeyed in person to meet them and discuss the question. That nation had for some years suffered much annoyance from white intrusion and cheating, and being desirous of escape from those troubles had expressed a willingness, under certain stated conditions, to give up its possessions in Mississippi and Alabama. The terms under which it would consent to retire westward had been named in an address issued in 1827,[2] and the chief provisions therein contained were these:

"... As you have pointed us out a country on the north of the State of Missouri, ... and speak well of it, we agree, first and foremost, to go and look at it, and any other country that we may choose. When twelve of our people—three from each district—have examined it, assisted by a scientific doctor to see to our health, and by three good white men to be selected by ourselves, and three of your men of science from Washington or elsewhere—we say, when we have examined it; if we like it, if its soil is good and well wooded, if water is plenty and good, we will agree to exchange, acre for acre: provided you on your part will mark out the country and divide it into counties, and leave a place in the center for a seat of government, and then drive everybody off of it, and guaranty it to us for ever; and, as soon as may be, divide it for us into farms; ... and provided also, that in addition you examine our houses, and mills, and fences, and our work-shops here; also our orchards, and build and put up and plant as good there, at such places within the territory as we may choose; also, provided you count our stocks here, and put an equal number, and of each kind, within their respective owners' limits there; also, provided you establish schools in all the counties sufficient for the education of our children

[1] In the annual Executive message to the Cherokee National Council in 1828 it was stated that to each Cherokee citizen consenting to remove west of the Mississippi the United States had offered "a bounty consisting of a rifle gun, a blanket, a steel trap, a brass kettle and five pounds of tobacco." In commenting on this proposition the message said: "Such are the temptations offered to induce us to leave our friends, our relatives, our houses, our cultivated farms, our country, and everything endeared to us by the progress of civilization." The offer was described as a "burlesque." It was made about three years after the Cherokee civilization was reported to the Secretary of War by Commissioner McKenney.

[2] On October 9. The Chickasaw statement was incorporated by Armroyd in his "Connected View of the Whole Internal Navigation of the United States. Second Edition. Phila., 1830": pp. 516-8, from which the extracts here given are quoted.

D. TALLMADGE'S
MAIL STAGE LINES,

Between Zanesville, (Ohio,) & Maysville, (Kentucky.)

The Bainbridge and Cincinnati, Lancaster and Columbus Pilot line of four horse Post Coaches, leaves Zanesville every morning at 8 o'clock, running through Lancaster, Chillicothe and Bainbridge to Maysville, (Ken.) connecting at Bainbridge with his line to Cincinnati, through to Maysville in 36 hours, or to Cincinnati in 48 hours.

☞ *For seats in Zanesville, apply at the office of Neil, Moore & Co's General Stage Office, National House.*

☞ The subscriber informs the public, that he has the road stocked with the best horses, coaches and drivers, the country affords ; and there shall be nothing wanting on his part, to add to the comfort and convenience of all who may please to patronize him.

D. TALLMADGE.

Zanesville, Ohio.

171.—Stages were running through Ohio for twenty-five years before railroads crossed the state, and primitive stage wagons had appeared on the same roads as early as 1808. The line advertised by Tallmadge, in 1837, ran its vehicles over the road originally called Zane's Trace. According to the schedule here given the traveller was carried about two-thirds of the distance across Ohio in two days. One of the principal overland routes to Cincinnati and Louisville before the days of the locomotive.

and to teach our girls how to spin and manage household affairs; and provided, also, you send a sufficient force there to ensure our protection, and organize our people into companies like your militia; . . . and provided that you establish a government over us in all respects like one of your territories, Michigan, for example, and give the right of suffrage to our people as they shall be prepared, by education, to vote and act; and allow us after the territory is organized a delegate like your territories enjoy, in Congress: . . . give us the privileges of men . . . and we will treat for exchange upon the above basis.

"Should our offer not be accepted, then we are done. We hope to be let alone where we are, and that your people will be made to treat us like men and Christians, and not like dogs. We tell you, now, we want to make our children men and women, and to raise them as high as yours in privileges . . .

"Understand nothing is done unless the country we go to look at suits, and not then unless all we require is agreed to on your part. . ."

At the time the Chickasaws made the statement of their wishes and future hopes they were again on the up-grade with regard to numbers, having increased in population to the extent of about four hundred souls during the previous five or six years.[1] They lived in eight hundred houses of an average cost of a hundred and fifty dollars each, though some of their dwellings were worth from a thousand to two thousand dollars. Most of the native farm properties had barns, corn-cribs and other out-buildings. The nation also possessed ten mills, about fifty mechanical workshops of various sorts and a few orchards. Their live stock averaged two horses, two cows, five hogs and a flock of chickens to each householder. The total value of their stock, in that era of cheap prices, was about eighty-four thousand dollars. The value of the fences they had built around their farms was fifty thousand dollars.[2]

They maintained taverns and ferries along the roads

[1] As reported to Secretary of War Barbour by Indian Agent McKenney in his communication of October 10, 1827.

[2] This summary of Chickasaw affairs in 1827 is condensed from McKenney's reports. For further information dealing with the same nation's condition in 1830—the year of Jackson's visit to them—see "Report of John L. Allen, United States Sub-Agent among the Chickasaws. February 7, 1830."

granted by them for the privilege of white travel through their territories, and, like the Cherokees and Choctaws, exported a part of their agricultural produce and domestic manufactures to neighboring white states.

President Jackson went in person to see these men, and spoke thus to them:[1]

"Friends and Brothers: Your great father is rejoiced once more to meet, and to have it in his power to assure you of his continued friendship and good-will . . .

"By a communication from your elder brethren and neighbors, the Choctaws, during the last winter, your great father learned that in consequence of the laws of Mississippi being extended over them, they were in great alarm; and of their own free will, and without any application from him, they asked to leave their country and retire across the Mississippi river . . .

"By an act of Congress it was placed in his power to extend justice to the Indians . . . and to give them a grant for lands which should endure 'as long as the grass grows or water runs.' A determination was taken immediately to advise his red children of the means which were thus placed at his disposal to render them happy and preserve them as a nation. It was for this that he asked his Chickasaw and other friends to meet him here.[2] You have come, and your great father rejoices to tell you through his Commissioners the truth, and point you to a course which cannot fail to make you a happy and prosperous people. Hear and deliberate well on what he shall say, and under the exercise of your own reason and matured judgment, determine what may appear to you best to be done for the benefit of yourselves and your children.

Brothers: You have long dwelt upon the soil you occupy, and in early times before the white man kindled his fires too near to yours, and by settling around, narrowed down the limits of your chase, you were, though uninstructed, yet a happy people. Now your white brothers are around you. States have been erected within your ancient limits,[3] which claim a right to govern and control your people as they do their own citizens, and to make them answerable to their civil and criminal codes.

[1] At Franklin, Tennessee, where the Delegates of the nation met him on August 23, 1830. The speech is not contained in biographies of Jackson, in Cushman's "History of the Choctaw, Chickasaw and Natchez Indians," or in other works on the southern tribes. The text as here given is that contained in the "Western Sun" of September 25, 1830, by which it was reprinted from the "Nashville Republican."

[2] The Choctaws refused to attend the meeting because of differences over the question of emigrating.

[3] In addressing the white Congress, a few months before, he had spoken of new Indian states whose erection had been attempted in Caucasian commonwealths.

Your great father has not the power to prevent this state of things,[1] and he now asks if you are prepared and ready to submit yourselves to the laws of Mississippi, and make a surrender of your ancient laws and customs, and peaceably and quietly live under those of the white man?

"Brothers, listen—The laws to which you must be subjected are not oppressive, for they are those to which your white brothers conform and are happy. Under them you will not be permitted to seek private revenge, but in all cases where wrong may be done you are through them to seek redress. No taxes upon yourselves, except such as may be imposed upon a white brother, will be assessed against you. The courts will be open for the redress of wrongs; and bad men will be made answerable for whatever crimes or misdemeanors may be committed by any of your people, or our own.

"Brothers, listen—To these laws, where you are, you must submit— there is no preventive—no other alternative. Your great father cannot, nor can Congress, prevent it. The states alone can. Do you believe that you can live under those laws? That you can surrender all your ancient habits, and the forms by which you have been so long controlled? If so, your great father has nothing to say or advise. He has only to express a hope that you may find happiness in the determination you shall make, whatever it may be. His earnest desire is, that you may be perpetuated and preserved as a nation; and this he believes can only be done and secured by your consent to remove to a country beyond the Mississippi, which for the happiness of our red friends was laid out by the government a long time since, and to which it was expected ere this they would have gone. Where you are, it is not possible you could ever live contented and happy. Besides the laws of Mississippi which must operate upon you, and which your great father cannot prevent, white men continually intruding are with difficulty kept off your lands, and difficulties continue to increase around you.

"Brothers—The law of Congress usually called the 'Intercourse Act' has been resorted to to afford relief, but in many instances has failed of success. Our white population has so extended around in every direction that difficulties and troubles are to be expected. Cannot this state of things be prevented? Your firm determination can only do it.

"Brothers, listen—There is no unkindness in the offers made to you. No intention or wish is had to force you from your lands, but rather to intimate to you what is for your own interest. The attachment you feel for the soil which covers the bones of your ancestors is well known. Our forefathers had the same feelings when a long time ago, to obtain

---

[1] Since the previous May the President and his administration had been negotiating the Choctaw treaty above quoted (and which was signed thirty-five days after this speech), wherein the United States guaranteed to protect the Choctaws in future against the state of things complained of by the southern nations and here described to the Chickasaws as being beyond the power of government to prevent.

happiness, they left their lands beyond the great waters and sought a new and quiet home in distant and unexplored regions. If they had not done so, where would have been their children and the prosperity they enjoy? The old world would scarcely have afforded support for a people who, by the change their fathers made, have become prosperous and happy. In future time so will it be with your children. Old men! Arouse to energy and lead your children to a land of promise and of peace before the Great Spirit shall call you to die. Young chiefs! Forget the prejudices you feel for the soil of your birth, and go to a land where you can preserve your people and nation. Peace invites you there —annoyance will be left behind—within your limits no state or territorial authority will be permitted.[1] Intruders, traders, and above all, ardent spirits so destructive to health and morals will be kept from among you, only as the laws and ordinances of your nation[2] may sanction their admission. And that the weak may not be assailed by their stronger and more powerful neighbors, care shall be taken and stipulations made that the United States, by arms if necessary, will preserve and maintain peace amongst the tribes, and guard them from the assaults of enemies of every kind, whether white or red.[3]

"Brothers, listen—These things are for your serious consideration, and it behooves you well to think of them. The present is the time you are asked to do so. Reject the opportunity which is now offered to obtain comfortable homes, and the time may soon pass away, when such advantages as are now within your reach may not again be presented. If from the course you now pursue this shall be the case, then call not upon your great father hereafter to relieve you of your troubles, but make up your minds conclusively to remain upon the lands you now occupy, and be subject to the laws of the state where you now reside to the same extent that her own citizens are. In a few years becoming amalgamated with the whites, your national character will be lost, and then like other tribes who have gone before you, you must disappear and be forgotten.

"Brothers—If you are disposed to remove, say so, and state the terms you may consider just and equitable. Your great father is ready and has instructed his commissioners to admit such as shall be considered liberal, to the extent that he can calculate the Senate of the United

---

[1] Seemingly a contraction of his introductory statement that conflict between Indian independence and state authority could not be avoided. If it could not be prevented in the East, could it later be escaped in the West, as promised, where white settlements were already appearing beyond the Mississippi? In the East the states of Alabama and Mississippi had been erected to embrace part of the pre-existent Chickasaw sovereignty, and a similar process might not unreasonably be expected to occur in future beyond the great river.

[2] The nationality and right of self-government of the Chickasaws seems to be taken for granted.

[3] Existing treaties and laws—recently used with success by J. Q. Adams—already provided for the military protection of the red nations as here discussed by the President. Jackson had withdrawn Federal military protection from the southern red nations. In the case of the Cherokees this action had been taken at the request of the Governor of Georgia after that state had asserted jurisdiction over the Cherokee territories.

577

States will sanction. Terms of any other character it would be useless for you to insist upon, as without their consent and approval no arrangement to be made could prove effectual. Should you determine to remain where you are, candidly say so, and let us be done with the subject, no more to be talked of again. But if disposed to consult your true interests and to remove, then present the terms on which you are willing to do so to my friends, the Secretary of War and General John Coffee, who are authorized to confer with you, and who in the arrangements to be made will act candidly, fairly and liberally toward you."

CHAPTER XXVIII

THE CHICKASAWS YIELD — JACKSON'S GRATIFICATION AND
THE METHOD OF ITS EXPRESSION — NEW DANGERS
ARISE TO THREATEN THE PRESIDENT'S INDIAN POL-
ICY — GEORGIA DEFIES THE FEDERAL GOVERNMENT
AND JACKSON PERMITS THE NULLIFICATION—THE
CHEROKEES ATTEMPT TO CARRY THEIR CASE TO
THE SUPREME COURT AS A FOREIGN NATION—THE
COURT DECLARES IT HAS NO JURISDICTION—ITS REA-
SON FOR THE DECISION—UNEXPECTED EVENTS RESULT
IN A SECOND JUDGMENT WHICH GIVES THE CHEROKEE
REPUBLIC EQUAL RANK WITH OTHER NATIONS, PRO-
NOUNCES IT INDEPENDENT OF UNITED STATES LAW
AND CONDEMNS GEORGIA — JACKSON'S CONTRADIC-
TORY ATTITUDES AND THEIR SIGNIFICANCE

GENERAL JACKSON'S picture of future freedom
wrought its effect, and four days later the Chickasaw
nation decided to give up its country in exchange for the
promised liberty. Fear of civil war was considerably
reduced, and the unification of white territory east of the
Mississippi was apparently in sight. Jackson's relief at
the success of his plans was shown in his annual message
at the close of the year.[1] In that utterance he returned to
the former Caucasian attitude of self-laudation, and again
affirmed the philanthropy, benevolence and generosity of

[1] December 6, 1830.

579

the government. He also said that peril of civil conflict had existed as a consequence of conditions in the South, and drew attention to the consolidation of the national domain resulting from the success of the government's bloodless conquest. His argument in behalf of the Administration's action was put in the following terms:

"It gives me pleasure to announce to Congress that the benevolent policy of the Government, steadily pursued for nearly thirty years, in relation to the removal of the Indians beyond the white settlements is approaching to a happy consummation. Two important tribes have accepted the provision made for their removal at the last session of Congress, and it is believed that their example will induce the remaining tribes also to seek the same obvious advantages.

"The consequences of a speedy removal will be important to the United States, to individual States, and to the Indians themselves. The pecuniary advantages which it promises to the Government are the least of its recommendations. It puts an end to all possible danger of collision between the authorities of the General and State Governments on account of the Indians. It will place a dense and civilized population in large tracts of country now occupied by a few savage hunters. By opening the whole territory between Tennessee on the north and Louisiana on the south to the settlement of the whites it will incalculably strengthen the southwestern frontier. . . It will relieve the whole State of Mississippi and the western part of Alabama of Indian occupancy, and enable those States to advance rapidly in population, wealth and power. It will separate the Indians from immediate contact with settlements of whites; free them from the power of the States; enable them to pursue happiness in their own way and under their own rude institutions; will retard the progress of decay, which is lessening their numbers, and perhaps cause them gradually, under the protection of the Government and through the influence of good counsels, to cast off their savage habits and become an interesting, civilized and Christian community. . .

"Toward the aborigines of the country none can indulge a more friendly feeling than myself, or would go further in attempting to reclaim them from their wandering habits. . . . [1]

"With a full understanding of the subject, the Choctaw and Chickasaw tribes have with great unanimity determined to avail themselves of the liberal offers presented by the act of Congress, and have agreed to remove beyond the Mississippi river. . . In negotiating these treaties they were made to understand their true condition, and they have preferred maintaining their independence in the western forests to sub-

---

[1] In view of his recent effort to uproot the settled and prosperous Chickasaws, the declaration is little less than extraordinary.

580

FERRY.

The subscriber has prepared himself with a first rate

FERRY BOAT,

WITH APRONS AND BANNISTERS.

At his Ferry opposite Market street, Vincennes, immediately on the road to St. Louis, where, by his strict attention and care, he flatters himself all who may wish to cross the Wabash will be accommodated to their satisfaction.

JAMES NABB.

October 11th, 1823.

172.—Broadside issued by a ferry-boat owner on the mail stage road from Louisville to St. Louis, during the early years of periodic overland travel in the Mississippi valley. A line of stage wagons between the two cities named, and running through Vincennes, had been established in 1821. The stage-coach trip on this first periodic line of the interior required five days.

mitting to the laws of the States in which they now reside.[1] These treaties, being probably the last which will ever be made with them, are characterized by a great liberality on the part of the Government. If it be their real interest to maintain a separate existence, they will there be at liberty to do so without the inconvenience and vexations to which they would unavoidably have been subject in Alabama and Mississippi.

"Humanity has often wept over the fate of the aborigines of this country, and Philanthropy has been long busily employed in devising means to avert it, but its progress has never for a moment been arrested. . . But true philanthropy reconciles the mind to these vicis-

[1] The embarrassment of the government was such that a consistent statement was seemingly impossible.

581

situdes as it does to the extinction of one generation to make room for another. . . Nor is there anything in this which, upon a comprehensive view of the general interests of the human race, is to be regretted. Philanthropy could not wish to see this continent restored to the condition in which it was found by our forefathers. What good man would prefer a country covered with forests and ranged by a few thousand savages to our extensive Republic, studded with cities, towns and prosperous farms, embellished with all the improvements which art can devise or industry execute, occupied by more than 12,000,000 happy people, and filled with all the blessings of liberty, civilization and religion?

"The present policy of the Government is but a continuation of the same progressive change by a milder process. . . The waves of population and civilization are rolling to the westward, and we now propose to acquire the countries occupied by the red men of the South and West by a fair exchange. . . Doubtless it will be painful to leave the graves of their fathers; but what do they more than our ancestors did or than our children are now doing?[1] To better their condition in an unknown land our forefathers left all that was dear in earthly objects. . . Does Humanity weep at these painful separations from everything, animate and inanimate, with which the young heart has become entwined? Far from it. . . Can it be cruel in this Government when, by events which it cannot control, the Indian is made discontented in his ancient home? . . .

"And is it supposed that the wandering savage has a stronger attachment to his home than the settled, civilized Christian? Is it more afflicting to him to leave the graves of his fathers than it is to our brothers and children. Rightly considered, the policy of the General Government toward the red man is not only liberal, but generous. He is unwilling to submit to the laws of the States and mingle with their population. To save him from this alternative, or perhaps utter annihilation, the General Government kindly offers him a new home, and proposes to pay the whole expense of his removal and settlement. . .

"No act of the General Government has ever been deemed necessary to give the State jurisdiction over the person of the Indians. That they possess by virtue of their sovereign power within their own limits in as full a manner before as after the purchase of the Indians lands; nor can this Government add to or diminish it.

"May we not hope, therefore, that all good citizens, and none more jealously than those who think the Indians oppressed by subjection to the laws of the States, will unite in attempting to open the eyes of those children of the forest to their true condition, and by a speedy removal to relieve them from all the evils, real or imaginary, present or prospective, with which they may be supposed to be threatened."

[1] One group of humanity mentioned was willingly moving toward a wider dominion; the other unwillingly moving toward a lesser.

The use of such expressions as "wandering savages," "children of the forest" and "savage hunters," in describing the Indians east of the Mississippi—and especially the southern nations — during the period just discussed, was a habit of many whites in official position. Judging from an examination of governmental contemporary evidence set down by those who had knowledge derived from personal observation, examples of which have been presented, those terms did not fit the peoples to whom they were applied. Nor is it easy to believe that Presidents, Cabinet Ministers and other men in high place, with such evidence at their command, could have remained so uninformed of the condition and aspirations of the southern red nations as thus to characterize them with honest error. It seems more probable, in view of what was taking place, that the systematic use of such expressions was part of a method used to spread abroad a general misapprehension of the Indians in the minds of those who did not have personal knowledge of the facts, and so make it easier to overcome the natives by diplomacy without the necessity of combating any serious public sentiment opposed to the process in hand. The overwhelming preponderance of public opinion was then, as always before, against the natives, and it was obviously to the advantage of the administration that it should so continue. In his annual message just quoted, Jackson discussed the relationship of popular opinion to his actions in these words:

"I know of no tribunal to which a public man in this country, in a case of doubt or difficulty, can appeal with greater advantage or more propriety than the judgment of the people; and although I must necessarily in the discharge of my official duties be governed by the dictates of my own judgment, I have no desire to conceal my anxious wish to conform as far as I can to the views of those for whom I act."

Union Hall,

VINCENNES, I.I.

TEE subscriber respectfully in- forms the *travelling public*, and the citizens generally, that he has purcha- sed, and now occupies, that eligible & long established tavern stand, on Main street, where ladies & gentlemen who favor him with a call, shall be accom- modated in comfortable village style.

There is a *FERRY* attached to the premises, which shall be attended to in such a manner as to deserve public patronage.

WM. PRICE.

September, 1825.

173.—A broadside address to travellers circulated by a tavern keeper on the Louisville-St. Louis stage road in 1825.

These are laudable sentiments for an Executive pro- vided he does not mislead the people by distorting cir- cumstances at issue in accordance with his own desire and thus foster an erroneous popular judgment which will uphold him in his chosen course, and to which he can

Notice to
Travellers & Movers.

The subscriber having purchased the

FERRY,

crossing the Wabash from Market street, Vincennes, and the farm opposite, on the state road leading to St. Louis, formerly owned by Mr. Gibson—where

Corn, Hay & Oats

will be kept, and sold low for cash; a lot will be prepared for the accommodation of Drovers, Movers, &c.—new and substantial *BOATS* will be soon completed, one for the conveyance of heavy teams, one for carriages & light waggons, and the best skiffs. The ferry will be attended by experienced and trusty hands, and all damages that may result from the neglect or bad management of the hands will be paid for upon demand, by the proprietor, living at the Ferry landing, corner of Market & Water streets, Vincennes, where he has, connected with Mr. B. Olney, a general assortment of *Groceries, Liquors, Druggs, Patent Medicines, Salt, Tar,* &c.

WILLIAM MIEURE.

Vincennes, August 13, 1825.

174.—Another broadside circulated by a ferry owner on the same road, appeal-ing for the patronage of the travelling public. From the information con-tained in the hand-bill it is apparent that a considerable traffic, of diversified character, was moving over the highway.

then point as the mandate of those for whom he acts. Such a procedure was easier in those days than it now is, and was sometimes resorted to. Whether or not it was undertaken during the years under review, in connection with the grave crisis then attending the Indian question, is a matter of opinion and a debatable question. Certain it is, however, that Jackson's message of 1830 — in so far as it dealt with native character, conditions and progress — was a collection of sophistries, misleading suggestions and erroneous declarations in contradiction of official information gathered by the government during the period of ten years just preceding.

The foundation of Jackson's attitude toward the Indian question lay in the assumption — as voiced by him in the message of 1830 — that no act of the general government was necessary to give a state jurisdiction over the persons and territories of the Indians; that individual states possessed such power even before the acquisition of native lands; and that the general government could neither add to nor increase such power. He had made public utterance of his opinion in that respect before his election to the Presidency, and when vested with Executive duty he proceeded to act in accordance therewith, although he could scarcely have been unaware that his attitude was in conflict with both principle and practise as laid down and adopted by the executive, legislative and judicial departments of the government from its organization.

From two of those departments he had nothing to fear in carrying out his program. He himself was Chief Executive, and the Congress displayed general complaisance with the essential feature of his policy, which was to force Indian evacuation of the East through a denial of native independence.[1] The only visible snag on which his plan might founder was a possible attitude by the judiciary which would emphasize his constitutional duty to uphold native rights, in some specific case, against the newly advanced contention of the southern states and himself. Such a possibility had indeed been in sight for nearly a year, for the Cherokees had entered on a course of action having for its ultimate purpose a test of their position before the United States Supreme Court. And unequivocal as were Jackson's declarations regarding state jurisdiction over the Indians, his personal journey to Tennessee in company with the Minister of War, in an effort to persuade the Chickasaws and Choctaws to a policy of emigration in advance of any legal pronouncement on native sovereignty lends some weight to an inference that he was not altogether easy in mind concerning the outcome of the impending judgment, and wished to commit as many red nations as possible to his policy before an unappealable verdict was handed down.

But an unexpected event forced the President to reveal his ultimate attitude even before the case of the Cherokees was decided. In June of 1830 Georgia had asserted that she possessed title to all Indian lands within her newly claimed jurisdiction, and soon afterward she forbid the natives to mine the gold lately discovered in their territories. These acts were followed by another order to survey certain Indian lands. Some of the Indian improvements were seized, and arrangements were made to distribute Cherokee lands among

[1] This definition, however, does not precisely fit Jackson's attitude, which, in fact, is apparently impossible of exact definition. It has been seen that he refused to acknowledge native independence if the Indians remained in the East, while at the same time he acknowledged it and pledged its continuance in perpetuity if they removed to the West.

JOHNSON'S REPORTS,
IN THE CONGRESS OF THE UNITED STATES,
ON THE SUNDAY MAIL QUESTION.

"It should be kept in mind, that the proper object of government is, to protect all persons in their religious as well as civil rights, and not to determine for ANY WHETHER THEY SHALL ESTEEM ONE DAY ABOVE ANOTHER, OR ESTEEM ALL DAYS ALIKE HOLY."

"Congress acts under a constitution of limited powers. In vain do we look to that instrument for a delegation of power authorizing this body TO ENQUIRE AND DETERMINE WHAT PART OF TIME, OR WHETHER ANY, HAS BEEN SET APART BY THE ALMIGHTY for religious exercises.

175.—Many of the stages or stage wagons first operated in the interior bore resemblance to the vehicle here depicted. They constituted an intermediate form between the earlier stage wagon of the East and the Concord type that afterward replaced them. Title of the large broadside containing the Congressional committee reports which determined the Federal government's attitude toward Sunday travel. Issued in 1829.

the whites by lottery. In the midst of the disorders brought about by these procedures a Cherokee named Tassel, while resisting the execution of Georgia law in Cherokee territory, killed a man. Tassel was taken into custody by Georgia, convicted of murder by a state court[1] and sentenced to death. The Cherokee nation appeared before the Supreme Court of the United States in protest against these proceedings, and a writ of error issued from that tribunal commanding Georgia, in the person of its Governor, to appear and answer for having unlawfully arrested and condemned a Cherokee citizen.

On receipt of this mandate Governor Gilmer of Georgia sent a message[2] to the legislature saying he had received a document "purporting to be signed by the Chief Justice of the United States," and declaring that "orders received from the Supreme Court for the purpose of staying, or in any manner interfering with the decisions

[1] The Superior Court of Hall county.
[2] December 22, 1830.

MAIL STAGE RULES.

:·/////·◉·/////·:

I. THE names of passengers must be entered on the way bills, and stage fare paid before they enter.

II. Passengers will be permitted to carry fifteen pounds weight in the stage.

III. One hundred pounds weight will constitute a passenger, and be paid for accordingly; and a greater or less weight in proportion.

IV. No trunks nor baggage of any kind can be put in the stage at one office, to be paid for at another; but must be paid for where they are entered.

V. Stage officers will carefully examine way bills on the arrival of stages, to see that the entries agree with the passengers and trunks.

VI. When a stage officer adds up the amount of stage fare on a way bill, he will sign his name, and draw a line quite across the bill below his name.

VII. No stage driver will be allowed to receive stage fare, or sign his name to a way bill; but it shall be his duty to take in passengers on the way, and have them entered on the way bill at the first stage office or stand.

VIII. The mail bags must at all times be carried inside the stage, to avoid any injury from rain, or otherwise.

IX. The proprietors will not be responsible for any articles of baggage or trunks sent in the stage, in case of their being lost.

X. No person whatever is to go in the stage free, without written authority from the proprietor or agent.

XI. It shall be the duty of the stage driver to pay the most strict attention to the accommodation of passengers, and treat them with the utmost politeness.

XII. No driver shall at any time employ any other person to perform his duty, only in case of sickness; neither shall he absent himself from the line, without giving one month's notice, under the forfeiture of one month's wages.

XIII. All accounts against the mail stage for work, must be attested by the driver who had it done, or by some disinterested person.

XIV. Keepers of horses, post masters and stage officers, are respectfully requested to give the most early information in case of any improprieties, or neglect of duty they may discover on the line.

XV. It shall be the duty of the driver on approaching any town, village, post office or stand, to sound his trumpet, so as to give timely notice; also, in overtaking or meeting waggons or carts; and if any waggon or cart driver on having timely notice, refuse to give the road, so that the mail be detained on account thereof, the drivers are to report such waggoner or cart driver to the proprietors or their agent, but is specially forbidden, that any abrupt conduct be used on the part of the stage driver.

XVI. Stage officers are requested to keep these rules in some part of their houses most convenient for passengers and drivers to see.

XVII. No person must be left out, in consequence of trunks or baggage, that does not belong to passengers then in the stage.

EMISON & McCLURE.

176.—Broadside containing the rules of a stage-coach company operating on the Louisville-St. Louis road about 1825-1827. According to Rule No. III a passenger weighing two hundred pounds had to buy two tickets. Similar sets of rules were printed by all stage companies, and copies of the placards were displayed in the offices and given to passengers.

of the courts of the state, in the exercise of their constitutional jurisdiction, will be disregarded and any attempt to enforce such orders will be resisted with whatever force the laws have placed at my command."

The state legislature passed a resolution in which the Governor and all other officers of the state were enjoined "to disregard any and every mandate and process that has been or shall be served upon him or them, purporting to proceed from the Chief Justice or any Associate Justice of the Supreme Court of the United States," and the Governor was "authorized and required, with all the force and means placed at his command by the Constitution and laws of this state, to resist and repel any and every invasion from whatever quarter upon the administration of the criminal laws of this State."

Tassel was hanged, and the issue of nullification of supreme Federal authority by an individual state was thus unexpectedly confronted by Jackson. The President did nothing.[1]

Georgia was served by the Cherokee nation in December of 1830 with notice of a motion for an injunction restraining the state from enforcing its recent laws within the native possessions. The motion came before the Supreme Court on March 5, 1831, the plaintiff appearing under that section of the Constitution giving foreign and sovereign nations the right to make such an appeal. Chief Justice Marshall handed down the decision of the Court, and the essential substance of its majority finding is embraced in the following extracts from his opinion:[2]

" . . So much of the argument as was intended to prove the character of the Cherokees as a State, as a distinct political society, separated

---

[1] It is not unlikely that Georgia's successful nullification of 1830 was to some extent responsible for South Carolina's attempted nullification of national law in the more trivial matter of customs duties a short time afterward.

[2] Texts of all the opinions, assenting and dissenting, in 5 Peters, 1.

PILES' WAY BILL

FROM VINCENNES TO ST. LOUIS.

To Taylor's	8 Miles.
Lawranceville,	2
Clubb's	6
Delong's	11
Morehouse's	4
Dummetts', Fox R.	4
McCalley's, L. W.	12
May's	2
Elliott's	12
Fitch's	7
Joshua Piles'	12
Dumm's	8
Hicks'	8
Houston's	12
Carlisle	10
Shoal Creek	8
Webster's	9
Medley's	3
Lebanon	10
Hathaway's	10
Town	10
St. Louis	2

E. STOUT PR. *Vincennes.*

177.—A stage-coach way-bill, or manifest, used by another line running coaches between Vincennes and St. Louis at the same period. Distances were still commonly reckoned in miles intervening between taverns.

from others, capable of managing its own affairs and governing itself has, in the opinion of a majority of the judges been completely successful. They have been uniformly treated as a State, from the settlement of the country. . . . The acts of our Government plainly recognize the Cherokee nation as a State, and the courts are bound by those acts."

Having established in law the contention of the Cherokees respecting their separate and self-governing character as a state, the opinion went on to say:

". . . It may well be doubted whether those tribes which reside within the acknowledged boundaries of the United States can, with strict accuracy, be denominated foreign nations. They may, more correctly, perhaps, be denominated domestic dependent nations."

Thus the motion for an injunction and the merits of the case were not reached, on the declared grounds that the Cherokees were not a foreign nation; that the Court had no jurisdiction; and that the plaintiff could not apply to it for relief. One state is foreign to another if it is wholly under a different governmental jurisdiction, without regard to the relative geographical positions of the two sovereignties concerned. The political distinction embodied in the term "foreign" is in no sense related to or dependent upon geographical or territorial considerations. The decision was substantially equivalent to a pronouncement that an old, established and independent political state, if gradually surrounded by the territory of a newly created government, automatically loses its sovereignty and foreign quality to the younger nation by virtue of that process.

Justice Johnson, in assenting to the majority opinion[1] that the Court had no jurisdiction to give the Cherokees relief, stated that existing conditions in the South amounted to war and that the native nation's only appeal was to the sword. He said:

". . . Their present form of government . . . certainly must be classed among the most approved forms of civil government.

[1] Justices Thompson and Story dissented.

"What does this series of allegations exhibit but a state of war, and the fact of invasion? They allege themselves to be a sovereign independent state, and set out that another sovereign state has, by its laws, its functionaries, and its armed force, invaded their State and put down their authority. This is war, in fact; though not being declared with the usual solemnities it may perhaps be called war in disguise. And the contest is distinctly a contest for empire . . . not an appeal to laws, but to force. A case in which a sovereign undertakes to assert his right upon his sovereign responsibility; to right himself, and not appeal to any arbiter but the sword for the justice of his cause. . . In the exercise of sovereign right the sovereign is sole arbiter of his own justice. The penalty of wrong is war and subjugation."

Thus the Cherokees, having abandoned fighting for industry, appealed to the highest tribunal of their adversaries and were met with the information that the whites were making warfare on them in a contest for empire, and that their remedy was to seek their rights in battle and subjugate Georgia by the sword.

Neither of the two cases hitherto cited involved the lives, liberties or other rights of United States citizens in the dispute concerning the political status of the red nations. But an event soon occurred which did introduce those new elements into the controversy, with attendant results of importance. Georgia had passed an act[1] prohibiting white men from living among the Cherokees without permission from herself, and after the Supreme Court had denied its jurisdiction over the race quarrel, the commonwealth felt emboldened to adopt measures more extreme than those previously taken. Under the law mentioned she arrested a number of white men residing in the Cherokee nation with its permission, but without licenses from Georgia, and who had not taken oath to obey the laws of Georgia while they remained in native jurisdiction. One of these men was Samuel Worcester, a

---

[1] December 22, 1830, during the nullification of Federal authority in the Tassel case.

missionary and citizen of the state of Vermont.[1]
Worcester was tried under the law in question, found
guilty, sentenced to the penitentiary for a term of four
years at hard labor and there imprisoned. The Vermont
man took his case to the Supreme Court, which cited
Georgia to appear before it as in the Tassel matter, and
Georgia again ignored the summons. Argument was
heard in January of 1832, and the opinion of the Court,
as handed down by Chief Justice Marshall reviewed the
whole range of international relationship existing between
the white and red nations.[2] The Treaty of Holstein in
1791, said the Court, was one

"Explicitly recognizing the national character of the Cherokees, and
their right of self-government. . . All these acts [those of the United
States from the commencement of constitutional government] manifestly
consider the several Indian nations as distinct political communities, having territorial boundaries within which their authority is exclusive. . .

"The Indian nations had always been considered as distinct, independent, political communities, retaining their original natural rights. . .
The very term, 'nation,' so generally applied to them, means 'a people distinct from others'. . . The constitution . . admits their rank among
those powers who are capable of making treaties. . . The words 'treaty'
and 'nation' are words of our own language, selected in our diplomatic
and legislative proceedings by ourselves, having each a definite and well-
understood meaning. We have applied them to Indians, as we have
applied them to the other nations of the earth; they are applied to all
in the same sense.

". . . Georgia, herself, has furnished conclusive evidence that her
former opinion on this subject concurred with those entertained by her
sister states, and by the Government of the United States." The
acts of her legislature, the opinion continued, "proved her acquiescence in
the universal conviction that the Indian nations . . possessed rights
with which no state could interfere," and "that their territory was separated from that of any state." . . Her new series of laws, manifesting
her abandonment of these opinions, appears to have commenced in December, 1828. . .

"The Cherokee nation, then, is a distinct community, occupying its
own territory, with boundaries accurately described, in which the laws of

---

[1] Others were Elizur Butler, James Trott, Samuel Mays, Surry Eaton, Austin Cope-
land and Edward Losure.
[2] Judgment contained in 6 Peters, 515.

The following specification of the fare of the principal Stage
Routes, by which the traveller may reckon the cost of his
tour, will not be superfluous.

		Miles.	
From Philadelphia to Pittsburgh,		300	$15 00
Philadelphia	Baltimore,	128	3 00
Baltimore	Wheeling,	271	12 00
Pittsburgh	Wheeling	59	4 00
Wheeling	Columbus,	140	8 00
Columbus	Cleaveland,	177	10 50
Columbus	Chillicothe,	45	2 00
Chillicothe	Cincinnati,	94	5 50
Columbus	Cincinnati, direct,	110	6 50
Indianapolis	Madison,	86	4 00
Cincinnati	Lexington,	76	4 50
Lexington	Louisville,	75	4 50
Louisville	St. Louis, via Vincennes,	267	15 50
Louisville	Nashville,	180	12 00
Richmond Cincinnati, via Staunton, Lewisburg, Charleston on the Kanhaway and Guyandot, thence 155 miles by steamboat,		515	28 00
Richmond to Knoxville, via Lynchburgh, Abington, Kingsport, &c.,		444	28 50
Baltimore to Richmond, via Norfolk, by steamboat,		378	10 00
Knoxville to Nashville, via McMinville,		119	12 50
Nashville	Memphis,	224	15 00
Nashville	Florence,	110	8 25
Huntsville	Tuscaloosa,	155	10 00
Florence	Tuscaloosa,	146	9 00
Tuscaloosa	Montgomery,	119	8 00
Tuscaloosa	Mobile, by steamboat,	676	12 00
Augusta	Montgomery,	300	18 50
Montgomery Mobile		180	12 00
Mobile	New Orleans,	160	12 00
St. Augustine to New Orleans,		600	35 00
Boston and New York to New Orleans, by packet, cabin passage, fare inclusive, from			$40 to 50 00

178.—List showing the cost of various stage-coach trips in the East, South and
Mississippi valley in 1848. From Warner's "Immigrant's Guide," pub-
lished in the year named. The ticket for a journey from Louisville to St.
Louis then cost $15.50.

Georgia can have no force, and which the citizens of Georgia have no right to enter but with the assent of the Cherokees themselves. . .

"The act of the State of Georgia, under which the plaintiff in error was prosecuted is consequently void, and the judgment a nullity. . . The acts of Georgia are repugnant to the constitution, laws and treaties of the United States. . . ."

This judgment constituted a reversal of the Court's opinion in the case brought directly by the Cherokees themselves and placed them in the rank of foreign as well as independent nations. It stated that they had retained those original natural rights possessed by them before the United States territory had reached and encompassed them, and that, instead of being so-called "domestic dependent nations," the term "nation" as given by the United States to an Indian state was applied to it as to the other nations of the earth, and in the same sense. The violated rights of a white man had brought forth that unequivocal assertion of native sovereignty without which the United States citizen could not have been restored to freedom.

Worcester was not set free. A mandate issued from the Supreme Court ordering Georgia to liberate the prisoner, but it was not obeyed. Georgia maintained her attitude of nullification, the missionary was held in prison, and later released through the process of a state pardon.

Jackson again did nothing. Various efforts were made to procure Worcester's release not only before, but during and after the Supreme Court's consideration of the case, and among these endeavors was that of the American Board of Missions. That body laid a statement of the matter before Jackson and asked his aid. In reply the President addressed the following letter to the Board:[1]

"Gentlemen:—I have the honor to acknowledge the receipt of your

[1] Apparently not included in biographies of Jackson or other historical reviews of the events or times under discussion. Its text as here given is copied from "The St. Joseph Deacon" (South Bend, Indiana) of September 29, 1832.

memorial, stating that certain missionaries in the State of Georgia have been imprisoned for alleged offenses against the State, and requesting my interference in furthering their release.

"In reply I have to inform you that the power vested in me has been placed in my hands for the purpose of seeing the laws of the United States justly and impartially administered, and not for the purpose of abusing them, as I most assuredly should do were I to interpose my authority in the case brought before me in your memorial. The State of Georgia is governed by its own laws; and if injustice has been, or is committed, there are competent tribunals at which redress can be obtained. I do not wish to comment upon the causes of the imprisonment of the missionaries alluded to in the memorial; but I cannot refrain from observing that here, as in most other countries, they are, by their injudicious zeal (to give it no harsher name) too apt to make themselves obnoxious to those among whom they are located.

"ANDREW JACKSON."

During the same period wherein Georgia was declaring her nullification of national law with the purpose of ousting the Indians, South Carolina was threatening to take like action toward the Federal collection of tariff duties within her boundaries. Against South Carolina's attitude Jackson stood like adamant. In his dispute with that commonwealth he took the ground that nullification was inconceivable, and that as a matter of principle, in any form, was not to be tolerated. Among his utterances on the subject, made at the time, were the following:

". . . I fully concur with you in your views of nullification. It leads directly to civil war and bloodshed and deserves the execration of every friend of our country. . . The Union must be preserved and its laws duly executed by proper means. . . We must act as the instruments of the law, and if force is opposed to us in that capacity, then we shall repel it. . .[2]

Another letter said:

". . . In forty days I can have within the limits of So. Carolina fifty thousand men, and in forty days more another fifty thousand. . .

[1] Worcester and the other missionaries were located among the Cherokees at the desire of the nation. The President still clung to the assumption that they were located in Georgia.

[2] Manuscript letter from Jackson to Joel Poinsett of South Carolina, under date of December 2, 1832. Archives of the Pennsylvania Historical Society.

The Union will be preserved. The safety of the republic, the supreme law, which will be promptly obeyed by me. . . . "[1]

Jackson's public expression relating to state nullification of Federal law was embodied in his "Proclamation."[2] The document contained this passage:

"I consider the power to annul the law of the United States, assumed by one state, incompatible with the existence of the Union, contradicted expressly by the letter of the Constitution, unauthorized by its spirit, inconsistent with every principle on which it was founded, and destructive of the great object for which it was formed."

A third private message to Poinsett[3] ran:

". . . I can, if need be—which God forbear, march two hundred thousand men in forty days to quell any and every insurrection or rebellion that might arise to threaten our glorious confederacy and Union . . . Fear not, the Union will be preserved and treason and rebellion promptly put down, when and where it may show its monster head."

The letters to Poinsett and the Board of Missions were contemporaneous with the nullification crisis as it existed in two states, dealt with the same fundamental principle, and were substantially simultaneous utterances. The basic question in the two cases — defiance of Federal law by an individual state — was identical. Jackson's attitude in each was diametrically opposed to the position he concurrently assumed in the other. Public opinion upheld him in both. One state was subdued in a tariff argument; the other was permitted to have its own way in the larger matters of property, liberty and life. It was seemingly, then, not the principle of nullification which brought forth popular condemnation and Executive pronouncements threatening force for its suppression, but the particular sort of nullification which proposed to divide the white nation against itself. That other and graver nullification of Federal

[1] Ibid. Dated December 9, 1832.
[2] Issued on December 16, a week after the second letter to Poinsett.
[3] Manuscript letter in the Pennsylvania Historical Society. Date, January 24, 1833.

authority, which apparently tended to increase the future strength and unity of the white nation, was tolerated by the people and their official representatives.

Even after the Supreme Court, by its judgment in the Worcester case, swept away the Executive contentions and made Jackson the only competent tribunal to which an appeal might be made for the enforcement of law, he remained a passive spectator of the proceedings against the natives in the South.

CHAPTER XXIX

HOPES OF THE SOUTHERN NATIONS APPARENTLY DE-
STROYED BY THE SUPREME COURT'S FIRST DECISION —
CHICKASAWS, CREEKS AND SEMINOLES CEDE THEIR
DOMAINS EAST OF THE MISSISSIPPI — THE PROMISE
MADE TO THEM — IMPORTANCE OF THEIR CAPITULA-
TION — A TREATY FINALLY SIGNED WITH SOME OF
THE CHEROKEES — IT IS REPUDIATED BY THE RED
NATION — THE CHEROKEES REDUCED FROM PROSPER-
ITY TO DISTRESS — THEY ARE REMOVED TO THE WEST
BY A FEDERAL ARMY — OFFICIAL COMMENT ON THE
TRANSACTION — THE EAST AT LAST CLEARED OF
NATIVES AND A TRANSPORTATION SYSTEM ON UN-
BROKEN WHITE TERRITORY IS MADE POSSIBLE — CON-
CLUDING OBSERVATIONS ON THE RACE QUARREL

THE action of the Supreme Court in the case of the
Cherokee Nation vs. Georgia, whereby that body
declared it had no jurisdiction in a native appeal against
Caucasian invasion of Indian sovereignty, seemingly
killed the last hope of the southern red states. They saw
no help could be expected from the obstinate old warrior
who had been elevated to power by the whites; they were
shut off from the aid which might have been gained
through legal means, and could no longer endure the
methods employed to destroy their character as independent peoples in the East. Nothing was left for them

600

but to fight or to abandon the upward struggle begun a generation before at the urging of the Government and Jefferson.[1] So they capitulated. Jackson vigorously continued his efforts during the critical year of 1832, and before its end he had secured treaties under which the Chickasaws, Creeks and Seminoles ceded all their possessions east of the Mississippi in exchange for lands west of that river and the customary pledges.

Article XIV of the Creek treaty[2] said:

"The Creek country west of the Mississippi shall be solemnly guaranteed to the Creek Indians, nor shall any state or territory ever have a right to pass laws for the government of such Indians, but they shall be allowed to govern themselves, so far as may be compatible with the general jurisdiction which Congress may think proper to exercise over them." [3]

The preamble to the Chickasaw treaty[4] declared:

"The Chickasaw nation find themselves oppressed in their present situation, being made subject to the laws of the states in which they reside. Being ignorant of the language and laws of the white man they cannot understand or obey them. Rather than submit to this great evil they prefer to seek a home in the West, where they may live and be governed by their own laws. [5] . . ."

Had the Choctaws, Creeks, Chickasaws and Cherokees unitedly withstood the pressure on them until after the decision in the Worcester case then the treaties with them would not have been written as they were, for it overthrew the new white claim that those Indian nations lived in United States territory and were subject to its laws. That contention, jointly maintained during the crisis

[1] Associate Justice McLean, who concurred with Chief Justice Marshall in the case of Worcester vs. Georgia, also said in his opinion: "Would it not be a singular argument to admit that so long as the Indians governed by the rifle and tomahawk their government may be tolerated; but that it must be suppressed so soon as it shall be administered upon the enlightened principles of reason and justice?"

[2] Dated March 24, 1832.

[3] The proviso concerning Congressional jurisdiction was a result of the Supreme Court's definition of Indian states as "domestic dependent nations" in the case of the Cherokees against Georgia.

[4] Dated October 20, 1832.

[5] A later treaty guaranteed that the Chickasaw possessions in the West should be kept "without the limits of any State or Territory."

179.—The canal era. A packet, or swift canal boat, used exclusively for passenger traffic. It maintained a steady speed of three or four miles an hour, both day and night. The regular, or "line," boats carried freight as well as passengers, and only moved at the rate of about two miles an hour. Done by the artist Alexander Robb. The succeeding twenty-six illustrations, to No. 205 inclusive, concern the canal period and life while travelling on a canal boat.

by the Executive, the southern states and the Supreme Court, was the crucial consideration which induced the natives to cede their countries. Had they waited a little longer one of three situations must apparently have arisen. Either the red nations of the South would have been despoiled by organized force in defiance of law, or the white race would have engaged in civil war over the question, or else the Indian states would have been left to develop in peace, thus splitting the eastern half of the present white republic into two sections separated in part by foreign soil unless the Indians had afterward consented to a political amalgamation on their own terms. Viewed in any light the years here considered possess a relationship to the later development of the country exceeded in importance by but few other periods of its history.

The Cherokee nation was the only native commonwealth of the South[1] which had not committed itself to the sale of its territories and the westward emigration of its people when the decision in the Worcester case was announced. That decree encouraged them, for a time, to believe they might still maintain their position, but

[1] And the only important red state east of the Mississippi either North or South.

602

AN

HISTORICAL ACCOUNT

OF THE

RISE, PROGRESS AND PRESENT STATE

OF

The Canal Navigation in Pennſylvania.

WITH AN APPENDIX,

CONTAINING,

Abſtracts of the *Acts* of the *Legiſlature* ſince the Year 1790, and their Grants of Money for improving ROADS and NAVIGABLE WATERS throughout the State;

TO WHICH IS ANNEXED,

"AN EXPLANATORY MAP."

PUBLISHED BY DIRECTION OF THE PRESIDENT AND MANAGERS OF THE SCHUYLKILL AND SUSQUEHANNA, AND THE DELAWARE AND SCHUYLKILL NAVIGATION COMPANIES.

" Here ſmooth CANALS, acroſs th' extended plain
Stretch their long arms to join the diſtant *main*.
The Sons of Toil, with many a weary ſtroke,
Scoop the hard boſom of the ſolid rock;
Reſiſtleſs through the ſtiff, oppoſing c'ay.
With ſteady patience, work their gradual way;
Compel the Genius of th' unwilling flood,
Through the brown horrors of the aged wood;
Croſs the lone waſte the ſilver urn they pour,
And cheer the barren heath, or ſullen moor.
The traveller, with pleaſing wonder, ſees
The white ſail gleaming through the duſky trees;
And views the alter'd landſcape with ſurprize,
And doubts the magic ſcenes which round him riſe.
Now, like a flock of ſwans, above his head,
Their woven wings the flying veſſels ſpread;
Now, meeting ſtreams, in artful mazes, glide,
While each, unmingled, pours a ſeparate tide;
Now, through the hidden veins of earth they flow,
And viſit ſulphurous mines and caves below.
The ductile ſtreams obey the guiding hand,
And *ſocial Plenty* crowns the HAPPY LAND!"

PHILADELPHIA:

PRINTED BY ZACHARIAH POULSON, JUNIOR, NUMBER EIGHTY, CHESNUT-STREET,

M DCC XCV.

180.—Early literature relating to travel in America. First American printed book on the subject of canals. Although published in Philadelphia in 1795, five years after Fitch had operated his steamboat as a public conveyance on the Delaware River, the book contains no reference to the possible use of steam in connection with transportation.

the hope was short lived. An uninterrupted series of local harassments still pressed upon them, and in the face of these troubles a portion of the red farmers and artisans gradually lost some of their former spirit of resistance. The Federal white government, in addition, continued its pressure upon certain of the important natives in an effort to win their consent to a treaty. This endeavor was at last successful, and in 1835[1] about twenty officials of the nation signed a paper purporting to embody the consent of all the Cherokees, and which ceded to the United States the red nation's possessions east of the Mississippi in exchange for some seven millions of acres in the West. Some of the guarantees made by the United States in the agreement were as follows:

"Article V.—The United States hereby covenant and agree that the lands ceded to the Cherokee nation in the foregoing article shall, in no future time without their consent, be included within the territorial limits or jurisdiction of any State or Territory. But they shall secure to the Cherokee nation the right by their national councils to make and carry into effect all such laws as they may deem necessary for the government and protection of the persons and property within their own country belonging to their people or such persons as have connected themselves with them: provided always that they shall not be inconsistent with the Constitution of the United States and such acts of Congress as have been or may be passed regulating trade or intercourse with the Indians; and also, that they shall not be considered as extending to such citizens and army of the United States as may travel or reside in the Indian country by permission according to the laws and regulations established by the Government of the same." [2]

"Article VII.—The Cherokee nation having already made great progress in civilization and deeming it important that every proper and laudable inducement should be offered to their people to improve their condition as well as to guard and secure in the most effectual manner the rights guaranteed to them in this treaty, and with a view to illustrate the liberal and enlarged policy of the Government of the United States toward the Indians in their removal beyond the territorial limits of the States, it is stipulated that they shall be entitled to a delegate

[1] December 29th. The treaty of New Echota.
[2] The last clause is ambiguous and obscure. The Cherokees understood that the "permission," "laws" and "regulations' referred to were to be of their making, since their country was the last that had been previously mentioned in the clause.

in the House of Representatives of the United States whenever Congress shall make provision for the same."

In another article of the document the United States recognized the illegal despoilment of the natives during the previous seven years by agreeing to recompense them for "such improvements and ferries from which they have been dispossessed in a lawless manner or under any existing laws of the state where the same may be situated."

That this treaty sale of the native lands did not correctly represent the attitude of the Cherokee population was indicated by the assassination of several native signers of the document who were denounced as traitors, and by a general refusal of the Indians to abide by its terms.[1] To such an extreme degree did a large proportion of the nation carry repudiation of the transaction that, though gradually ousted from their homes and farms by invading whites and brought to poverty, they refused food, clothing or other aid from the Federal government for fear they would be considered, by that act, as acknowledging the validity of the treaty.[2] From a condition of prosperity and comfort they were reduced to hunger, and lived on roots and the sap of trees.[3] Early in 1837 the nation met in council at their settlement of Red Clay and denounced the compact of New Echota. Other features of the assemblage at Red Clay were religious services attended by several thousands of the Indians, and their united singing of hymns translated into the Cherokee language.[4] By this time the patience of President Jackson — never notable for its enduring qualities — had been exhausted, and finally realizing that he was dealing with an unusual

[1] Even after the two years within which the removal was to take place.
[2] One of its sections stated that the nation had been so beset that "their crops are insufficient to support their families, and great distress is likely to ensue," and provided for an advancement of Federal money to be used in the relief of suffering.
[3] "Thousands, I have been informed, had no other foods for weeks." General Wool's Report of 1837 to the War Department.
[4] "Early Indian Missions," by Walter N. Wyeth, p. 42.

181.—Building the first important artificial waterway. Scene during the digging of a deep cut on the Erie Canal in New York State. Published in 1825, just after the entire work was put in operation.

people who were in earnest he turned with reluctance to his one remaining method of persuasion — the bayonet. The United States possessed its signed copy of the compact of 1835 promising evacuation of their territories by the Cherokees, and they had to go. Treaties made by nations with one another must be kept. A Federal army was accordingly sent into the Cherokee country in the winter of 1838-1839 and General Scott, its commander, issued to the red nation the following proclamation in the spring of the last named year:

"Cherokees:—The President of the United States has sent me with a powerful army to cause you, in obedience to the treaty of 1835, to join that part of your people who are already established on the other side of the Mississippi. . . . The emigration must be commenced in haste, but I hope without disorder. I have no power, by granting a further delay, to correct the error that you have committed. The full moon of May is already on the wane, and before another shall have passed away every Cherokee man, woman and child in these States

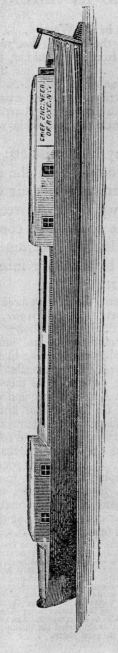

THE FIRST BOAT BUILT FOR THE ERIE CANAL.

The above is an accurate representation of the *Chief Engineer of Rome*, the first boat built for the Erie canal, and by which the trial and excursion trip was made, October 23, 1819, from Utica to Rome and return. Gov. De Witt Clinton, the canal commissioners, the chief and assistant engineers, other state officers and guests, with ladies and gentlemen of Utica, Whitesboro, Oriskany, and Rome, in all about sixty or seventy persons on board, composed the party. The boat was named in compliment to Benjamin Wright, then chief engineer of the Erie canal. The model, from which the cut was photographed, without the forward and middle cabins, was brought from England, in the early part of 1817, by Canvass White, then assistant engineer to Mr. Wright, and subsequently a distinguished civil engineer. The original model has been presented to the Buffalo Historical Society, by William C. Young, a resident member of the society—a rodman of the Erie canal surveys of 1816 and 1817, and a kinsman of the Whites, of Whitesboro, in which family the model has been kept for fifty years.

182.—The original canal-boat used on the Erie Canal. From a picture contained in Munsell's *Collections on the History of Albany.* Vol. II; 1867.

must be in motion to join their brethren in the West. . . . My
troops already occupy many positions in the country that you are to
abandon, and thousands are approaching from every quarter, to render
resistance and escape alike hopeless. . . . Spare me, I beseech
you, the horror of witnessing the destruction of the Cherokees. . . .
This is the address of a warrior to warriors. May its entreaties be
kindly received, and may the God of both prosper the Americans and
Cherokees, and preserve them long in peace and friendship with each
other."

The Cherokees offered no physical resistance. During the last days of May the troops began the task of
collecting them into camps preliminary to their exodus,
and the process continued for two or three weeks. A
highly colored description of the scenes and conditions
attending this final downfall of Indian government east
of the Mississippi was written by a white missionary
present at the time. It says in part:

"The Cherokees are nearly all prisoners. They have been dragged
from their houses and encamped at the forts and military posts all over
the Nation. In Georgia, especially, multitudes were allowed no time
to take anything with them except the clothes they had on. Well-
furnished houses were left a prey to plunderers, who, like hungry
wolves, follow in the train of the captors. These wretches rifle the
houses and strip the helpless, inoffending owners of all they have on
earth. Females who have been habituated to comforts and comparative affluence are driven on foot before the bayonets of brutal men.
Their feelings are mortified by vulgar and profane vociferations. It is
a painful sight. The property of many has been taken and sold before
their eyes for almost nothing—the sellers and buyers, in many cases,
being combined to cheat the poor Indians. . . . The poor captive,
in a state of distressing agitation, his weeping wife almost frantic with
terror, surrounded by a group of crying, terrified children, without a
friend to speak a consoling word, is in a poor condition to make a good
disposition of his property and is, in most cases, stripped of the whole
at one blow. And this is not a description of extreme cases. . . ."[1]

[1] From an account written by Evan Jones, of the Baptist Mission to the Cherokees,
and contained in Wyeth's "Early Indian Missions," (p. 43) previously mentioned. Possibly Jones' obvious desire to put the actions of the soldiers in the most unfortunate light
was to some extent due to the fact that he himself had been arrested and deported
from Cherokee territory in 1836. Yet it is apparent that the migration of the southern nations did result in heavy property losses to them, for the Cherokees and Creeks
alone were able to prove such damages as Jones described to the extent of about a million dollars. In 1838 the United States agreed by treaty to pay to the Creeks $400,000
for "property and improvements abandoned or lost" in their emigration. The Cherokees
were allotted $600,000 for expenses and losses incidental to their removal westward. Jones,
the missionary, together with a few other white men, accompanied the nation on its overland journey in an endeavor to keep its members in good cheer.

The total number of Cherokees to be moved was some eighteen thousand. The government planned to have about half of them make the journey of seven hundred miles on foot. Against this project the nation protested and asked the privilege of conveyance by wagons, estimating the cost at $65,000 for each thousand persons so transported and offering to let the expense be charged against themselves. Regarding this request the Commissioner of Indian Affairs reported: "As their own funds pay it, and it was insisted on by their own confidential agents, it was thought it could not be rejected." The officials of the nation also noted the omission of soap from the list of supplies to be furnished during the trip, and that article was also provided for the Indians.

It was at first intended by the government, as set forth in General Scott's manifesto, to conduct the movement during the hot months of summer, but such an earnest objection to this procedure was made by the Indians that after three thousand of them had been started away during June the remainder were held in camp until September. The road taken by the red emigrants was by way of Nashville, in Tennessee, and from three to five months was consumed on the pilgrimage by each of the fourteen detachments into which the whole body of natives was divided. From May 23d, when the enforced assemblage of the nation was begun by the troops until the last company reached its new home in the West, a period of ten months elapsed. The number of Cherokees who died on the way was more than four thousand — not far from twenty-two per cent. of those who started. After the terms of the treaty of 1835 had been fulfilled the Commissioner of Indian Affairs made a report on the movement in which he said:

"The case of the Cherokees is a striking example of the liberality of the Government in all its branches. . . . . A retrospect of the last eight months in reference to this numerous and more than ordinarily enlightened tribe cannot fail to be refreshing to well-constituted minds."

The Secretary of War said in his report:

"The generous and enlightened policy evinced in the measures adopted by Congress toward that people during the last session was ably and judiciously carried into effect by the General appointed. . . . Humanity no less than good policy dictated this course toward these children of the forest," [which course was adopted] "in the hope of preserving the Indians and of maintaining the peace and tranquillity of the whites."

The Commissioner of Indian Affairs further stated that

"If our acts have been generous, they have not been less wise and

183.—Invitation issued by New York City to its guests on the occasion of the formal opening of the Erie Canal. When the steamboat reached Sandy Hook, some water brought from Lake Erie was poured overboard to symbolize the union of the Great Lakes and the Ocean.

politic. A large mass of men have been conciliated; the hazard of an effusion of human blood has been put by; good feeling has been preserved, and we have quietly and gently transported eighteen thousand friends to the west bank of the Mississippi." [1]

The conditions and events outlined in the last few chapters indicate in a general way the relations of the two races between 1789 and 1838. Such were the methods used throughout the country, both North and South, in clearing the region east of the Mississippi for white movement and dominion, and that constituted the foundation on which the white race erected the unparalleled system of highways, canals and railroads by whose means the nation was finally bound into one homogeneous social unit. The crisis to the Indian question was reached during General Jackson's administration and was met by him in the manner described. Yet the small segment of Jackson's character and executive record here suggested cannot be taken as a picture of the whole man. He embodied, in extreme degree, nearly all the excellencies as well as many of the defects typical of the time in which he was such an overmastering figure. Superlative in vehemence, ignorance, obstinacy, contradiction and narrowness, he was also equally astonishing in chivalry, valor, power, perception and the courage of right purpose in many vital things. He was a product of the days that beheld him, and no understanding of his character in its entirety may be gathered without broad knowledge of the social crucible in which he was compounded. In discussing his relation to the Indian question his most ambitious early biographer said of him: [2]

"To this part of the policy of General Jackson praise little qualified

[1] By his expression "human blood" the Commissioner refers to the hazard of an effusion of white men's blood, due to the previous possibility of civil war over the Indian question. His error in the number of natives transported is due to using the number of Cherokees who started on the journey.

[2] Parton, in the "Life of Andrew Jackson": New York, 1860. Volume III, pp. 279-280.

can be justly awarded. The irrevocable logic of events first decreed and then justified the removal of the Indians. Nor need we, at this late day, revive the sad details of a measure which, hard and cruel as it was then thought, is now universally felt to have been as kind as it was necessary."

To-day we challenge the manner in which that opinion was set down. It is not the province of the student or historian to suppress those essential details — whatever their character may be — without which no appreciation of the relationships of past and present events can be obtained; it is not his function to award praise or condemnation without presenting the principal features of the case on which the verdict is based. He must tell what has happened, and how it happened, and leave the final verdict in other hands than his. Then, if he choose, he may express his own opinions and accept the risk which such a course entails.

In considering those governmental promises which finally brought about a trans-Mississippi migration of the Indians without warfare our chief present speculation must be: Were such words set down in duplicity, or were they a genuine manifestation of the stupidity which their honesty presupposes. The mind shrinks from adopting either theory, yet one or the other must seemingly be true. If the promises were honest pledges made in the light of what had taken place after similar negotiations for nearly two centuries, then the creation of a mental vacuity sufficient to produce them is, at least, a comforting evidence of the resources of Omnipotence.

Considered in all its aspects the subject is one that has not yet been treated with detail in written accounts of our formative period.[1] Chroniclers, in describing the era, have dwelt largely on the finer sentiments, valor, political

[1] In any one connected narrative. Nor is it so treated here.

quarrels and worthy accomplishments of its principal figures. So much attention has been paid to those phases of the time that the designs and deeds of the people as a mass, and related actions taken by public servants in accordance with popular desire have been skimped or omitted altogether. So commonly has this oversight occurred that it has sometimes seemed as though the particular phase of national development here discussed was looked upon somewhat as a skeleton-in-the-closet, and, if it were in truth such, that no good could come of throwing wide the door. By and by the bones would crumble and be forgotten. Or, if the ends attained by popular and governmental action from 1794 to 1839 were of necessity to be reviewed, then it has seemed that the immediate material value of those results was considered as the essential feature of the story demanding attention. The motives and methods used in obtaining the results, it appeared, need be but lightly touched. The things that happened were condoned as inevitable because the red men of the East were still popularly considered to be a race of savages. General Washington's opinion that a treaty with the Indians was a sop to quiet them was lamented as a thoughtless indiscretion, and the recompense therein contained was overlooked. For candor like that is surely a sufficient basis on which to build the legend that he never told a lie.

But there may be a value in the record of these somber years which is not yet utilized. The story of the civic and military glories of a nation's vanished heroes is not of necessity the wholesomest food on which to rear its later citizens. While men remain what they are, the tale of their deeds will not be one to inspire admiration only. Heroes make mistakes. A whole population can be carried away by an impulse that breeds ignoble things. The thought, attitude, practises and entire life of a nation, at any given time, is a product of the human qualities that have swayed its preceding generations.[1] Whatever is excellent in a nation's life, whether it be of old inheritance or sudden acquisition, is clearly to be seen and readily accounted for. Those other and dangerous traits, that at times steal like a poison through the character of a people until it is in peril of decay, are not so easily explained. Yet they too have their origin, and it is always to be sought in some widespread condition that presents to the people a choice between moral principles and material benefit at a time when the worldly profit can apparently be grasped without harm to themselves or to their country. If they then yield to temptation and resort to methods which win them earth-power at the expense of principle, they excuse themselves with the belief that only their increased opulence will descend to the future. They do not see that the chief inheritance they bequeath is a broad example of wrong committed and wealth unfairly gained without incurrence of risk or penalty. And the succeeding generation, thus corrupted before its birth by the worldly benefits awaiting its arrival as the result of such procedure, is not only forced into a defense of the sordid methods by which those riches were obtained, but is itself encouraged, in its turn, to continue the same policy of unfair acquisition from whatsoever class may appear to be its safest victim.

May it not be possible that in the treatment accorded to the red men by the American nation from its organization until 1839 is to be found an inciting cause of that insidious malady whereof fraud, corruption and violence

---

[1] "A Review of the Sinister Phases of American History: Their Causes, Relations and Later Effects on the Thought, Practises and Life of the People," is a needed book which has not yet been written.

184.—An example of the numerous private medals and advertisements issued
in celebration of the construction of the Erie Canal, and of similar early
public improvements. Brass. Actual size. Date, 1823.

are the outward symptoms, which has since persistently
spread and wrought such harm to the people? It was
during the years under discussion, and through association and dealings with the Indians, that a large class of
Americans first had the opportunity, yielded to the temptation, and applied on an extensive scale the corrupt art
of getting something of great value for little or nothing.
The practise, long existent in lesser degree, finally became
general wherever and whenever chance for its use was
possible, and was carried on by individual and government alike. Many of the methods used, together with the
success attending them, have been suggested. So widespread, safe, productive and long-continued was the
malign yet effective white system for self-enrichment at
the expense of the natives that it affected, either directly
or indirectly, a majority proportion of the population and
all classes of society. Many frontier communities existed
chiefly by virtue of the process. In distant cities, far
removed from direct contact with the operation, were
business men whose fortunes swelled through deeds or
conditions they did not personally see. The government
ceaselessly bought native territory at an average of a few
cents an acre[1] and sold it to settlers at two dollars an acre,
or else disposed of extensive tracts to speculators who

[1] Less than 3½ cents an acre up to 1825. See Appendix.

fattened without labor at the expense of other factors in the transaction.

The whole process was so simple and its immediate material profits so immense that the white race soon found itself gazing with complaisance on an almost national use of trickery, deceit, robbery and violence in the pursuit of gain. Those whites who were of contrary mind did indeed protest, but their objections were overruled by avarice and a predominant and perhaps partly genuine opinion — coming from exalted station as well as from the general public — that nothing but blessings to civilization could result from events and methods then in progress.

If an apportionment of responsibility for conditions then existing could now be made, it is probable that the chief burden would fall on those who, in high office, either yielded to the clamor of evil voices or themselves served as examples to the mass of the population. No people — when unmoved by the hysteria of warfare — has been more keen than this in estimating the essential qualities of its public men; none has been more quick to advance or halt in harmony with the will of real strength and leadership on the isolated occasions of their display. They have responded to the eloquence of honest purpose simply stated, and sensed the falseness of an unsound argument. When a President said he would use the power of the Federal Union to preserve to the Indians those rights guaranteed to them since the foundation of the government the country knew he meant it, and the destruction of the native commonwealths paused until a season more convenient for its accomplishment. During the years under review the people, as always, were balancing the words of public servants with their performances, and observing a general inconsistency between those manifestations of national policy, themselves proceeded along the indicated road of action rather than by the path of rhetoric. Thus the final tragedy was brought about.

Yet there was one bright side to the picture; bright, at least, in its ethical aspect. The Indians, in still forcing themselves to believe and to trust, reached in the consummation of their final defeat a height they could not have climbed by the aid of any alien civilization. It could only have been attained through the manifestation of their character as men. When they once again took up their western ways; without warfare, leaving behind their immemorial country fresh-covered by evidences of intelligence and thrift, and with courage set out to build anew in a distant land, they won a victory which need not fear comparison with the triumph of their conquerors.

At last they were alone and safe again. The ranks of their people were thinned and the new country was not as the one they had given up, but they were free of the ceaseless wrangle; free to grow. So they built their villages once more, planted their fields, re-established their affairs and clung to the words of the Great White Father; dreaming that some day they also might stand and speak in the vast stone Council House on the shore of the far Potomac.

When the native possessions east of the Mississippi had finally fallen into the hands of the white race, and the red men for a time had retired beyond easy access, the practises of which they had been the victims did not disappear. Their employment was shifted to a new quarter.[1] Instead of a substantially intact alignment of Caucasians against natives the white race became divided against itself, and the type that systematically seeks to gain wealth, power, or both, by fraud cloaked in outward respectability has since existed; not as a sporadic exhibit but as a large, recognizable, organized and material factor of society. Every basic method of the system first widely employed against the Indians has continued to flourish and has been deftly applied to new conditions as they arose. The general employment of violence against human life, together with popular indifference to the value of human life has also persisted. In governmental corruption, commercial immorality, crimes of violence and carelessness of human rights and welfare the United States has consistently held, since the era under discussion, a separate place among nations similarly advanced in the surface manifestations of civilization.[2]

The rise of such an abnormal condition predicates an inciting cause commensurate with its effect. If it be true that one origin of the grave dangers to popular welfare here enumerated is to be found in the methods employed by our predecessors in seeking wealth and aggrandizement at the expense of the Indian, then the nation has suffered memorable chastisement. And if these suggestions are sound, then it is not by adulation of earlier physical hero-

---

[1] A comparison of the inter-relations of the whites in commercial and allied affairs of life—as those relations existed prior to 1789—with the similar inter-relations of the whites from about 1835 onward, discloses a marked alteration in the general standards of action by which those affairs were usually conducted. A new element, unfortunate in its influence, had apparently entered into the moral character of the people as a whole.

[2] Several of the present standardized methods of commercial trickery, fraud and unfairness, such as are employed against individuals, each procure for their users a revenue of more than a hundred million dollars a year, obtained from those whose trust is invited. The extent of governmental corruption in American cities and states during the past two generations, together with its relation to national legislation, require no comment. The annual murders of the country are numbered in the tens of thousands; other crimes of violence are in proportion, and several hundred thousand human beings are yearly killed or gravely injured by industrial processes, nearly all of which economic loss is preventable. It is proper to say, however, that during very recent years, and more specially during the four years devoted to the writing of this book, numerous encouraging indications of a public awakening to the significance of these perilous conditions, and of a desire to combat the disease of which they are symptoms, have appeared.

ism or political patriotism that the needs of this and after times will be most surely satisfied. Only by searching into the darker pages of the national story; by analyzing motives; studying methods; observing results and gazing behind the panorama of superficial fame can we find inspiration to correct the present effects of mistakes already made and most surely fortify ourselves against the making of new ones. While we condone what should not have been done, so long will we tolerate eradicable consequences of former error and run the risk of more.

Whatever of blame may rest upon the people of America for certain methods it pursued in upbuilding and connecting the several parts of its present continental empire does not lie on scattered communities or states alone. The attitude of Georgia, Alabama and Mississippi toward Choctaw, Cherokee, Chickasaw and Creek was but motive-brother to the deeds committed by Ohio, Illinois and Indiana toward Wyandot, Sac, Shawnee and Potawatomi. If one region attained its end by intimidation and craft, so also did the other gain its purpose through the ruder but no less effective means of robbery, debauch and blood. And behind those commonwealths; behind official hypocrisy and governmental or individual wrong there could be heard the majority whisper of popular consent. An epoch is the picture of its people's morality. The stream of human events is a canal dug by human desire. The directness of its course and swiftness of its building is the measure of human agreement.

Without substantial accord of the Caucasian population the phase of the country's history here outlined could not have been written as it was. The most effective con-

spiracy is that which is without organized form. Each
of its myriad members can disavow. Together, they accomplish. All are responsible for what is done.

We do not too severely chide the boy for the cruelties
of unreasoning youth, no matter how wrong he may have
been, but when he has come to his full strength and
stature it is for him to look back and speak the truth
in a man's fashion.

CHAPTER XXX

THE PEOPLE, SOCIETY AND NATURAL CONDITIONS OF THE
MISSISSIPPI VALLEY AT THE COMMENCEMENT OF THE
MODERN ERA — THE TASK WHICH BEFELL THE LAST
PIONEER GENERATION OF AMERICANS — ISOLATION
AND MENTAL SELF-SUFFICIENCY OF THE POPULATION
—ITS CAUSES AND CONSEQUENCES — PECULIAR
GOVERNMENTAL CONDITIONS AND STRANGE LAWS —
RULE BY AN OLIGARCHY — REGULATION OF TAVERNS,
ROADS, FERRIES AND NAVIGATION — END OF THE
RIVER PIRATES — OVERLAND TRAVEL ROUTES OF THE
EXISTING FRONTIER

ONE of the subjects discussed by the convention which framed the Federal Constitution was the political and economic future of the region west of the Alleghany Mountains. It was proposed, among other things, that the country between the Alleghanies and the Mississippi River be kept subsidiary to the eastern states in order that the backwoodsmen might not obtain too much influence; that the future population of the interior be in some way controlled and restrained by the East, so that when—if ever—the Mississippi valley came to contain more people than the Atlantic coast states the rule of the wiser, wealthier and longer-established minority of the East might still prevail in giving shape to the destinies of the country.

In tracing the course of past events we have thus far

621

observed the life, methods and habits of mind of the eastern cabin dwellers as they conquered the wilderness and penetrated it by their caravans, pack-trains and cumbersome wagons; we have followed the men who toiled on the rivers in their keel-boats, flatboats, barges and batteaux; we have watched the building of the first crude highways and the appearance of the periodic stage-coach; we have beheld the creation and later adoption of the steamboat, and we have witnessed the eviction of the red men from their eastern possessions. The part played in some of these developments by the men of the Mississippi valley was a large one, and it is apparent they could never have been kept in subjection to the East even if a constitutional plan for that purpose had been adopted. They would probably have fought the East for their own independence even more quickly than the original thirteen colonies resorted to arms against Britain for a like purpose. The united strength of both East and interior was necessary for the task of continental conquest by means of traffic routes. After the direction of human movement shifted from its north-and-south groove to the westward trend it was the men of the trans-Alleghany country, indeed, who thenceforth exercised a controlling influence on the complex course of events under review.

The East had created the first highways and established periodic travel on them while yet the general movements of population ran north and south along the Atlantic coast, but it was the backwoods pioneers of the Carolinas and Virginia who altered the direction of those roads and extended them far into the wilderness. It was the backwoodsmen who adopted the timber boats of the East to the interior rivers and on them floated into distant and little known regions. While business men, legislatures

ENTRANCE OF THE CANAL INTO THE HUDSON AT ALBANY

185.—Lock leading from the Erie Canal to the waters of the Hudson River at Albany. Showing a loaded line boat and a passenger packet. Beginning a series of nine illustrations depicting the journey of a canal traveller from Albany to Lake Erie at Buffalo.

and courts of the East were seeking to restrict the use of steam and to convert steam-propelled vehicles into a licensed and country-wide monopoly it was men of the interior who first fought that purpose. And it was in the great central valley, and in the middle South, that the last scenes of the contest against independent Indian commonwealths were enacted.

The adoption and use of steam as a means of transportation on the rivers and the final struggle with the natives for possession of the land east of the Mississippi were two features of the story which moved side by side. Particularly was this true with relation to the years between 1810 and 1840. But those years contained other events calculated to make them even more important in the tale of national growth. They also witnessed the culminating point in the importance of stage-coach travel, the widespread but ill-timed resort to canals as arteries of commerce, and the sudden appearance of the railroad. The introduction of so many new factors into the ordinary life of the people within one generation produced an orgy of kaleidoscopic activity, a whirl of picturesque and confusing conditions, and a considerable alteration in the character and viewpoint of the people as a whole. It is, of course, true that the mental qualities of the population had been gradually altering with the slow passage of those blending and overlapping periods thus far discussed, but the change which came about during the era now mentioned was decidedly more sudden and radical. Within less than one short lifetime the people of the interior beheld a revolution in their surroundings, methods and material affairs that doubtless equalled—and perhaps surpassed in the extremes of contrast and visions of the future presented by it—any similar experience that has affected mankind in an equal interval. All those changes were due to their new devices for moving over the face of the country, and to the increased facility with which they met and communicated with one another.

The young men who penetrated to the interior on foot or by pack-train at the rate of ten or twenty miles a day were soon travelling in stage-coaches at a speed of seventy-five or a hundred miles a day. Families who floated down the rivers in flatboats, consuming weeks in their journeys, could in a few years embark on steamboats and be carried from Cincinnati to New Orleans in a week. Pioneers who once staggered through swamps to fight the Indians found themselves assembling, not long afterward, to discuss the building of a local railroad. Those incongruous conditions and situations, furthermore, often existed at the same time. The ark and steamboat lay side by side along the river banks; the east-bound stages still passed the west-bound pack-trains and Conestoga wagons; the last Indian fighting and the first railroad planning went on together. In his physical progress from place to place the average man of the period frequently started his journey on horseback, then resorted in turn to a steam-boat, to a stage-coach and to a canal packet, and finally finished his travels on a little railway at fifteen miles an hour. His mental processes were no less interesting. It was an era of readjustment in thought as well as in material surroundings; an epoch in which the old and the new ideas for a time waged warfare. There were some—as always—who could not see what was happening. Conservatism and progress were again at grips in their immemorial contest, but this time the issue was more clear cut than usual and the result of the battle did not long remain in doubt.

625

One human characteristic that speedily developed as a consequence of the new conditions in which the people found themselves during the years in question was an extreme spirit of self-sufficiency and self-importance, manifested to a degree never before nor since approached by them. That this was true is not a cause for wonder, nor

JUMP! JUMP!

186.—When a canal passenger failed to reach the starting place of a packet before its departure he was in no concern. He walked to the nearest bridge spanning the canal, waited the approach of the boat, and then leaped to its roof, some three or four feet below, as it passed under the bridge.

is it remarkable that the generation so affected should itself have denied the accusation. The white Americans were then somewhat in the position—with regard to the rest of the world—of a child of eight or ten without playmates, who, because of isolation, is growing into a savage boyhood possessed of the unfortunate and peculiar type of imagined wisdom which can only be attained through absence of association with others of its kind. They had no convenient standards for constant comparison and self-estimate; no near-by companions whom they might daily contemplate, and with whom they might mingle, play, and argue on occasion. They could only watch themselves and soliloquize. The life of a people is measured in millenniums, not in years, and this people was hardly out of its swaddling clothes. There is no cause for surprise that the infant nation was narrow-minded and self-centered, and that it gazed about with distorted vision, incapable for a time of seeing its relation to other and supposedly trivial details of the planet. It had begun to catch fantastic glimpses of its own destiny; it beheld the mirage of the Future.

In short, the situation was simply this: The white Americans—and especially those of pioneer location, spirit and action—having finally awakened to a realization that they had already accomplished numerous impossible things, and that they were in process of doing others of the same sort, were blinded to the still. existing crudities and ignorance of their own generation, and unconsciously assumed an attitude that discounted the unknown wonders which they knew were coming. In addition to the deeds of their own age they cloaked themselves in the greatness of their children, and believed themselves already the elect of the earth in all particulars. This state of mind was necessarily most manifest in the interior, where knowledge of other peoples and civilizations was vague and almost negligible in its effect, and relations even with the older eastern communities were limited by the difficulty of communication with them.

Thus there arose an interesting state of affairs possible

only among a people so isolated, with such a record of past endeavor, and in such a period of transition from old things to new. A generation exceedingly rough of manners and speech, familiar with hardships, living for the most part amid conditions immeasurably removed from those obtaining in older countries and with scant time for book knowledge or self-culture, had in one sense adopted an inner life which far outstripped its outward surroundings. Moreover that inward life and its attendant pride—based on the anticipation of excellencies dreamed but not attained—was apparently more real to its possessors and often more powerful in shaping their common acts and decisions than the hard material situation daily confronting them.[1]

So deeply did this attitude take root among the population, and especially among the western pioneers in the years soon after 1800, that widespread irritation—even anger—arose when foreign visitors, after journeys of investigation, wrote books about America in which more attention was given to frankly adverse criticism of the manners of the inhabitants and rawness of the country than to its unrealized destiny.[2]

Those Americans of the first four decades after 1800 —touchy, enthusiastic, rough, crude, practical, and yet

[1] The entrance of those qualities into the life of the people—the increased tendency to anticipate the future—was in a certain way illustrated by the contrasting receptions given by the public to the steamboats of Fitch and Fulton. The public many times saw Fitch's boat propelled at five miles an hour and was unable to grasp the future significance of the event. But the first time it beheld Fulton's boat do the same thing, about twenty years later, there was an immediate and general popular recognition of what it portended.

[2] Two such descriptions arousing the special ire of the American public were those of Captain Basil Hall, of the British Navy, and of Mrs. Trollope, the mother of Anthony Trollope. Mrs. Trollope's book really created a national furore. It was entitled "The Domestic Manners of the Americans." The three descriptions of America already mentioned in Chapter xviii—those of Cuming, Schultz and Michaux—avoided detailed discussions of the rough personal appearance, demeanor and habits that were intermingled with the numerous finer qualities of the western inhabitants, and, though honest in speaking of the difficulties of life in a new land, were therefore better liked. The Americans of the eastern cities, while appreciating the truth of some adverse published comment regarding the people of the interior, were nevertheless also angered by it because of their realization that crude conditions were for a time inevitable, and contained in themselves no valid indictment against the country.

swept on by dreams—were the ones who created modern conditions by building the National Road, the canals and the railroads. And it was to be their sons who in turn were to overwhelm the western half of the continent in one tremendous human surge and finally unite it to the east by bands of steel. It is due to them, therefore, that

187.—Packets rounding a curve on the Erie Canal. The big ditch followed the valleys of natural streams, and was also parallelled, in some localities, by country roads. Any individual or company choosing to do so could operate boats on payment of prescribed tolls, and scores of the craft were met or overtaken in the course of a day.

before proceeding to the final events of the story in which they played so large a part that we take a little glimpse at the actual men whose constructive work is about to concern us. We shall perhaps have a better understanding for the things they did if we first get a little closer to their character and personality. And to accomplish this purpose it is not necessary for us to linger in the older cities. They also had their necessary share in the approaching tasks, but cities in a new and growing country rarely originate the deeper purposes of its people or control their larger undertakings. The cities of a new land, rather, are mirrors reflecting those policies and instruments whereby certain details of the work are done. So it was in America. The impulse which put its stamp most indelibly on our history between 1800 and 1840 was the determination of the interior valley to bring itself into closer touch with the East by means of new communication facilities. The East likewise recognized the importance of such an undertaking, but was more self-contained and so had less requirement for the impending change. It looked at the subject from a more narrow and mercantile standpoint. But to the region beyond the Alleghanies the need was indeed vital in every respect. There could be no extensive growth, no broad progress, no economic and social unity of the two sections, without it.

Whatever method of movement was from time to time under discussion during that generation—whether it was a national turnpike, canals or railroads—the building impulse itself and the most insistent cry came from the West. The first great governmental work in response to the need and in aid of better communications was a turnpike to the West. The first great canals were planned to reach the West. The first real railroads ran toward the West. In each case the actual process of building began in the East, but the cities of the older regions were only complying with an irresistible demand that came to them from across the mountains. So if we would enter into the actual spirit of those times, and behold the men really responsible for what was about to happen we must throw aside the retrospective attitude, leave the older communities, their colleges, busy streets, pretentious hotels and settled habits of civilization, and live once more amid

630

the human figures who were out on the firing line of deeds and action.[1]

Some aspects of the social conditions prevailing in the Ohio valley at about the commencement of the nineteenth century have already been indicated in General Harrison's report of 1801. But that document dealt with matters connected with the race quarrel, and therefore failed to reveal innumerable other circumstances of life and human qualities which plead for attention in any consideration of the period and region involved.

At the time General Harrison prepared the document mentioned, and for a considerable interval both before and afterward, he and a few other men officially associated with him in the government of the Northwest Territory actually possessed, and sometimes exercised, an almost autocratic power. When the region now embraced in the states of Ohio, Indiana, Illinois, Michigan and Wisconsin was given a political organization it was so remote and inaccessible from the Federal government —as regards possibility of frequent communication—that the creation and enforcement of laws in the Territory was a matter of which the national administration knew little or nothing. It was inevitable that conditions of life in the vast and distant country north of the Ohio would produce situations requiring action by men having personal knowledge of them. Out of these things grew a state of affairs which—as far as civil government is concerned—was probably one of the most unusual that has ever developed in a land whose society was supposedly controlled by regulations having their source in popular

[1] Since the descriptions and comments of many foreign visitors during that period were then insistently denied, and are still the subjects of controversy, no information gained from such sources is used in this and the following chapter for purposes of picturing Americans and pioneer American conditions of the time. All material of the sort here used is derived from American writers, from official publications, original manuscripts of Americans and files of contemporary native newspapers.

VIEW OF THE JUNCTION OF THE NORTHERN AND WESTERN CANALS.

188.—The passengers, unless they were experienced voyagers familiar with the operation, always gathered on the roof of the packet to observe the process of lifting or lowering it to another level by means of the locks.

rule. For some eleven years the Northwest Territory did not possess a legislature, and the whole body of its local law had its origin in the pronouncements of three or four men whose arbitrary decrees could not, in the nature of things, be closely watched by the general government. The Federal authorities sent out individuals to act as governor and judges, and with that procedure their active participation in the affairs of the interior ceased. The result was an oligarchy. The little group of men out in the northern forest not only decreed the laws, but interpreted them and enforced them. They embodied all the functions of legislative, judicial and executive authority. Two circumstances gave a reasonable measure of success to this unrepublican form of government. Those in whose hands lay the despotic power exercised it in the main with good judgment—according to the light of their surroundings. The Caucasian population whose lives, liberty and property were under the control of the oligarchy recognized its necessity, and by their actions toward one another—even if not toward the native peoples —made the task of their rulers somewhat less difficult than it easily might have been.

During the fifteen or twenty years following 1800 there was not much change in the relations between the white and red races of the interior valley. Acute situations sometimes arose,[1] but the ordinary status was a strong dislike and distrust of each race for the other, manifested by an interminable series of misunderstandings, differences and downright quarrels for which each side was in greater or less degree to blame. Those troubles were always made worse by the unfortunate fact that an overwhelming bulk of the Caucasians despised the Indians and would neither try to comprehend their position nor cultivate the Indian languages to a degree necessary for better interchange of ideas. Even the necessary official intercourse between white and red men, at military posts and elsewhere, was often hampered by an inability on the part of each group to use the speech of the other. This difficulty was at times a matter of record, and one case of the sort is indicated in a letter written by W. W. Morrison, commanding officer at Turmonds Station, in Indiana Territory, to his superior at Fort Harrison,[2] under date of February 18, 1816. The letter said:

"Sir I hope you will See the nesesety of a person at this Station who Can Speak the Ingin Language & I am informed that you have in your Companey Severell Frenchmen that Can Speak ingin I hope you

[1] The most important of which was the outbreak led by The Prophet, connected with Tecumseh's aspirations for a native confederacy.
[2] The document was addressed to Lieutenant Lasselle, and the original is among the Lasselle Papers in the Indiana State Library.

will order one of them heir under my Command—the Ingins has Cald Severell time on mee I am at a Loss for a interpetor."

The social conditions—unrelated to race troubles—that prevailed among the English speaking people of the interior near the close of the eighteenth century and the commencement of the nineteenth can be well shown by citing some of the laws under which they lived. The first oligarchy in charge of the Northwest Territory was composed of Governor Arthur St. Clair, and Judges Samuel Holden Parsons, John Mitchell Varnum and John Cleves Symmes, who assumed their responsibilities in the summer of 1788. One of its first decrees[1] defined the punishments inflicted on lawbreakers of various sorts. A man found guilty of burning a house was put to death, as were also traitors and murderers. A burglar was fined and lashed with thirty-nine stripes on the bare back and could then be imprisoned for any length of time up to forty years. A perjurer, after being fined in an amount not exceeding sixty dollars, might be given thirty-nine lashes, placed in a pillory for two hours and disfranchised. Larceny was punished by fine or whipping at the discretion of the court. If the man found guilty of larceny could not pay his fine, then the decree empowered the court to sell the convicted man into slavery, for a period not exceeding seven years, to any citizen who would pay the fine.[2] Forgery was punishable by fine, disfranchisement and committal to the public pillory. A drunkard was punished by fine or by being placed in the stocks for an hour.

By 1792 the oligarchy governing the Territory contained only one of its original members, and then con-

---

[1] That of September 16, 1788.

[2] The judges of the court were themselves members of the oligarchy, and in their capacity as rulers they framed the law giving the power here described into their own hands.

189.—The poetry of travel by canal. Slipping through an Erie gorge on a moonlit summer night. Some of the skippers carried organs on board, and the passengers had concerts before turning in.

sisted of Winthrop Sargent,[1] John Cleves Symmes and Rufus Putnam. One of the decrees published in that year was designed to supply an important need of the pioneer society, namely, accommodations for travellers. It provided that:

"The commissioner for granting licenses shall have a power of establishing public inns and taverns." He was authorized to grant licenses "to such persons as the Justices of the General Quarter Sessions of the Peace in their wisdom may deem really necessary well qualified in person and character, well provided in accommodations for guests, and well situate in point of residence for the accommodations of travellers." The tax on such a license

[1] The Acting Governor.

was fixed at sixteen dollars a year, and the tavern keeper had to "set up in a proper manner on the front and outside of his house a board or sign with his or her name written thereon and some device expressive of his business as a tavern keeper. . . . on which board or sign shall also be written in large fair letters 'By Authority a Tavern.' " The act also provided that if the tavern keeper "neglect or refuse to do his or her duty therein as well in providing good and wholesome food for man and beast as in keeping ordinary liquors of a good and salutary quality and suitable lodgings and attendance for guests in a reasonable and proper manner according to the common usage and custom of well-kept taverns in an inland country," the said innkeeper's license lapsed and he became liable to the traveller for any damages sustained through failure to provide the liquor, lodgings or food aforesaid.[1] By later decree on the same subject, dated June 17, 1795, the penalty imposed on a tavern keeper for failure to provide for a guest was reduced to five dollars. The number of inns was curtailed, and no one could conduct such an establishment unless recommended by a judge on pain of a fine of one dollar a day. The pronouncement of 1795 also provided that an innkeeper could not get his license in the first place until he had given a bond of three hundred dollars for his good behavior.[2]

Nearly all the laws promulgated during succeeding years related to such matters as taxation, legal processes, court procedure, and offenses against public order. A curious decree of the last named sort, issued in May of 1798,[3] possesses unusual importance because of its revela-

[1] "Laws passed in the Territory of the United States North-West of the River Ohio, from July to December, 1792. Published by Authority. Philadelphia: MDCCXCIV."
[2] "Laws of the Territory of the United States North-West of the Ohio, Etc. By Authority. Cincinnati: MDCCXCVI."
[3] The oligarchy then consisted of Winthrop Sargent, John Cleves Symmes, Joseph Gilman and Return Jonathan Meigs, Jr.

tion regarding a certain savage custom of those days. It read thus:

"Whosoever . . . shall voluntarily, maliciously, and of purpose, pull or put out an eye while fighting or otherwise, every such offender, his or her aiders, abettors, and counselors, shall be sentenced to undergo a confinement in the jail of the county in which the offense is committed, for any time not less than one month nor more than six months, and shall also pay a fine not less than fifty dollars and not exceeding one thousand dollars—one-fourth of which shall be to the use of the territory, and three-fourths thereof to the use of the party grieved; and for want of the means of payment, the offender shall be sold to service by the court before which he is convicted for any time not exceeding five years, the purchaser finding him food and raiment during the term." And the decree concluded: "The foregoing is hereby declared to be a law of the Territory."[1]

This phraseology relates to the strange early frontier practise of gouging out a human eye with the thumb. Contemporary literature relating to conditions in America about the year 1800 contains few references to the barbarism in question, and those mentions of it have often been challenged.[2] According to tradition the practise was not altogether an uncommon one, and its employment in a fight was usually contingent upon a mutual agreement or understanding of the participants. When two men engaged in combat, and it was agreed that the mutilation was permissible, it became the purpose of each man to pin his adversary flat on his back. Then the successful fighter would insert the end of his thumb in an eye socket of his opponent and deliberately gouge out the eyeball. It was then the privilege of the prostrate man to

[1] "Laws of the Territory of the United States North-West of the River Ohio, etc., etc. By Authority. Cincinnati. Printed and Sold by Edmund Freeman: MDCCXCVIII."
[2] Probably the most widely known contemporary reference of the sort is that made by the English traveler, Charles William Janson, and contained in his "The Stranger in America." London: 1807. Similar comments, whether made by native writers or foreign visitors, were almost always based upon hearsay, and some later commentators on the period have expressed the opinion that contemporary writers who mentioned gouging from hearsay had been deceived by American frontiersmen who "pulled the long bow." But Janson says he was the spectator of an encounter between two men in which the deed in question was committed, and since he is possibly the only contemporary chronicler who makes such an assertion the dispute has been largely centered upon his statement.

indicate, if he chose, that he was defeated, and by such admission he saved his other eye.

The act of the rulers of the Northwest Territory in 1798, in framing the law above quoted, seems to be conclusive concerning the existence of such a practise as

GOING TO BED.

190.—Going to bed on an Erie packet. Three tiers of bunks were erected along each side of the main cabin after supper, and the passengers were usually permitted to select their berths according to the order of their arrival on board. The women's cabin was similarly arranged. If the number of men travellers exceeded the number of beds, then the late arrivals slept on the floor or the supper tables. The captain is calling the roll and alloting the bunks.

pulling out an eye. It also shows the extreme nature of the powers at times assumed by the oligarchy, for it provided that a man found guilty of the mutilation described might be sold into slavery unless he could pay the damages assessed against him. On this point the decree was not optional, but mandatory. It provided that the man "shall be sold to service." The law probably marked the last occasion whereon, in the United States, a white man might be reduced to the status of a slave by governmental process.

Another beam of light—though of a very different sort —is cast on the territorial affairs of the Northwest through a letter written by General Arthur St. Clair in 1796, in which he cautions a government surveyor about the devices often used by settlers in obtaining title to undue amounts of land. The communication[1] was addressed to Colonel Robert Buntin, who had been appointed a surveyor by St. Clair in October of 1795 and who, at the time of the incident here told, was in Vincennes. The epistle was dated "Cincinnati, September 19, 1796," and read in part:

> "Be pleased to observe it [the work done by settlers to obtain homesteads] must be actual improvement, not the marking or deadening a few Trees or throwing a few loggs together in form of a Cabbin, which are very commonly called improvements, in which way two or three Persons in one single week could cover a large tract of country."

But it was the brief postscript to this letter which after all gave to it its largest historical value. St. Clair said in his postscript to Buntin:

> "I am not certain whether it was you or not that was appointed Treasurer. If it was not you let me know who it was, for it seems I neglected to remember it."

At this late day we can only hope that Governor St. Clair discovered the identity of his treasurer, and that his mnemonic system of governmental records proved more efficient on other similar occasions.

By order of St. Clair the first popular elections in the Territory took place in December of 1798, and the legislature—which consisted of a lower house of nineteen elected members and an upper house of five members[2]—

---

[1] An unpublished letter among the Lasselle Papers in the Indiana State Library.
[2] Called the Legislative Council. Its members were appointed by the President from a list of ten names submitted by the lower house.

was finally organized in the autumn of 1799. Among the earliest laws passed by the assembly were three acts relating to the travel facilities of the region. The first of these was "an act to establish and regulate ferries." It provided that any citizen might establish a ferry after giving three months' public notice of his intention and securing a special act of authorization. The courts were empowered "to fix, from time to time, the rates which the ferry keeper shall hereafter demand for the transportation of passengers, wagons, carriages, horses, etc." A ferry owner was required to keep proper boats in operation during the daytime, and also at night unless night navigation was dangerous. For his services during the hours of darkness he was permitted to collect a double price, but if he overcharged at any time he was compelled to refund the ferriage and pay to the traveller two dollars in addition, as a penalty. This law made it an offense for any one but a public ferryman to transport "any person over any river or creek" within five miles of a public ferry, on penalty of a fine not exceeding twenty dollars.[1]

The second of the three laws mentioned dealt with conveyances commonly used in water travel and transportation. It provided that any one who found a "boat, flat, periague, canoe, or other small vessel" must give the authorities an exact description of it, which description was then officially posted on the court-house door. If the craft was claimed by its owner the finder was entitled to a reward of from fifty cents to a dollar, in accordance with the size and value of the boat. If it was not claimed within a year and was not worth more than five dollars,

[1] "Laws of the Territory of the United States, North-West of the River Ohio. Passed at the First Session of the General Assembly . . . at Cincinnati . . . 1799; Also, Certain laws enacted by the Governor and Judges of the Territory from the commencement of the Government to 1792. Etc., etc. Published by Authority. Cincinnati: MDCCC." The date of the act was November 15, 1799.

the boat belonged to the finder. If a craft worth more than five dollars remained unclaimed for a year it reverted to the Territory as public property.[1]

The third law provided for the construction of wagon roads on petition of the public, in case the requested roads

DEEP CUTTING LOCKPORT.

191.—View of a passenger boat going through the deep cut near Lockport, shown in illustration No. 181. The animals and their driver walked on a narrow shelf high up on the wall of masonry at the right.

were found to be desirable. The width of such thoroughfares was sixty-six feet.[2] The law also provided for a tax whose proceeds should be used in road building, ordered that male citizens contribute two days' labor during each year to such public work, and further directed that no citizen, while so working, might ask a traveller for either money or drink, on pain of a fine of one dollar.

Although the year 1799 witnessed the end of oligarchical government in the region now embraced by Ohio, the

[1] Ibid. Act of December 2, 1799.
[2] "Cart paths" 33 feet wide were also authorized.

same thing was not true in relation to the other parts of the Northwest Territory, of which the country now included in Illinois and Indiana was the only portion containing enough Caucasian population to justify attention.[1] "The Indiana Territory" was erected into a separate governmental jurisdiction in 1800,[2] and the oligarchy system was at once re-established there. The first three rulers were William Henry Harrison,[3] William Clarke and Henry VanderBurgh.[4] They met for the first time at Vincennes in January, 1801, and ordained ten laws, all but one of which related to methods of legal procedure and kindred subjects. The solitary act dealing with public improvements gave to the governor power to create public ferries by proclamation or otherwise.[5]

Almost no attention was given by the Indiana rulers to the subject of public improvements during the remaining four years in which all executive, legislative and judicial functions reposed in the hands of three or four men. During their fourth session,[6] however, steps were taken to minimize the danger connected with navigating the rapids of the Ohio, where many flatboats and other craft had been lost each year for a long time. The governor was authorized to appoint competent pilots who should receive two dollars for every boat taken past the dangerous spot. The decree also provided that any unauthorized person who acted as pilot at that place should be fined ten dollars, although the owner of a boat was

[1] Early in the summer of 1800 the civilized population of the Indiana Territory was estimated at 4,875. John B. Dillon's "Oddities of Colonial Legislation in America, etc., with Authentic Records of the Origin and Growth of Pioneer Settlements," p. 543.
[2] By Act of Congress approved May 7. It took effect on July 4.
[3] Who had been confirmed as Governor by the Federal Senate on May 13, 1800.
[4] Clarke and VanderBurgh were two of the three judges for the Territory. They, together with John Griffin, had been appointed by President Adams and confirmed by the Senate on May 14, but Griffin does not appear by name with the others in printed records reciting the acts of the territorial rulers.
[5] "Laws adopted by the Governor and Judges of the Indiana Territory at their First Sessions held at Saint Vincennes, January 12, 1801. Published by Authority. Frankfort, (K.) 1802."
[6] Held at Vincennes from September to November, in 1803.

permitted to conduct his own craft through the rapids if he so desired. The only other public improvements law issued in 1803 provided for the construction of bridges where necessary, although the provision for the building of bridges was made in connection with, and subsidiary to, the erection of "jails, pillories, stocks and whipping posts."[1]

One of the miscellaneous decrees ordained by the three men who ruled Indiana Territory in 1803 is especially illustrative of the sharp line drawn by the Caucasian pioneers between themselves and all other classes of society. The triumvirate during its fourth session prepared an elaborate code of civil and criminal laws which among other things provided that "no negro, mulatto or Indian shall be a witness except in the pleas of the United States against negroes, mulattoes or Indians, or in civil pleas where negroes, mulattoes or Indians alone shall be parties."[2]

General Harrison at the time in question—as he had been when he wrote his report of 1801—was Governor of the Territory. He was also the Indian Agent of the Federal government in the Territory, and, as now further appears, he was also one of three men who proclaimed all the conditions under which lived every individual of every race in the Territory. He interpreted the laws of which he was joint author; enforced those laws according to his own interpretation; and, with his two colleagues, had power over the life and liberty of his fellow men. Thus embracing within one personality an authority all but

[1] The two decrees last mentioned are to be found in "Laws Adopted by the Governor and Judges of the Indiana Territory at their Second and Third Sessions, begun and held at Saint Vincennes 30th January, 1802, & February 16, 1803. Published by Authority. Vincennes, (I. T.) 1804." This volume also contains the decrees resulting from the fourth session of the oligarchy, in whose membership Thomas T. Davis had taken the place of William Clarke.

[2] Paragraph twenty-first of the first act of the Session. Text contained in the volume last mentioned.

unique in modern times—especially in a state ostensibly under republican form of government—General Harrison promulgated the act here quoted and established, under the law, the racial cleavage created by it. By the terms of this decree no white man might be charged by an Indian with any crime or other wrong against native life, rights

192.—Four days and fourteen hours out from Albany, westward bound. Approaching the series of five locks at Lockport, thirty miles from Buffalo, by which boats were lifted for 62 feet to a higher level.

or property. In such a case Indian testimony was non-existent, irrespective of the character and reputation of the native or natives involved. When considered in connection with the official positions held by General Harrison, and especially when considered in contrast to the sentiments contained in the report written two years before, the law of 1803 has unusual interest and suggests

644

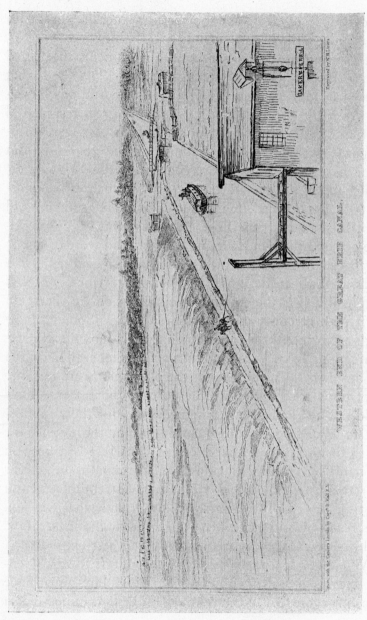

WESTERN END OF THE GREAT ERIE CANAL.

193.—At last, with a long stretch of excavation that ran straight as an arrow for miles, the canal reached the lake from which it took its name.

the existence of deep and powerful Caucasian desire in accordance with its provisions.

In setting up the oligarchical governments that ruled the Northwest Territory from 1788 to 1799, and that afterward administered the affairs of the Indiana Territory from 1801 to 1805, the Federal Congress reserved to itself the right to disapprove such laws as were promulgated for the control of those distant regions. But in the nature of things there could be little or no interference by the national legislature in such pronouncements as have been cited. The legislators from the old established states of the East could have but vague knowledge of conditions in the remote West, and were of necessity forced to leave the affairs of that far country in the hands of the men designated to administer them. It was not possible for the central administration to keep in touch with circumstances on the frontier. Sometimes as much as six months elapsed during which no official communications from Washington reached General Harrison at Vincennes. The decrees of the oligarchy were put into effect upon their utterance, or quickly thereafter. They could not await the long time necessary for their submission to Washington, their consideration there, and the return of an approval or veto. If Congress had been in the habit of vetoing such laws, many months or a year after their promulgation, the Northwest could never at any time have known what was lawful and what was not. The result would have been a region without any law. And besides, Congress was not always in session.

Whatever sentiment existed in Congress toward General Harrison and the Indiana Territory laws must have been favorable, for in the year 1804[1] all that immense part

[1] By act of March 26.

of the recently acquired territory of Louisiana lying west of the Mississippi River and north of the thirty-third degree of north latitude[1] was attached to Indiana Territory under the name of the "District of Louisiana," and placed under the control of General Harrison and his colleagues.[2] During the year in which this arrangement was continued[3] Governor Harrison and the two or three men associated with him had immediate jurisdiction and power over a region containing not far from one million square miles, and all the human beings who inhabited it. In October of 1804 they met at Vincennes and issued decrees for the enormous country under their administration. But in 1805[4] a segment of Indiana Territory was detached from it and erected into the separate Territory of Michigan, and the same year witnessed the creation of the first Indiana legislative assembly. With the advent of that elective body ended a period of seventeen years during which time a very large part of the interior and its people had almost constantly remained subject to the peculiar governmental system here described. With the appearance of a popularly elected assembly in Indiana Territory that district entered, after the usual pioneer fashion, upon a course of progress having to do with better communication facilities and convenience in using them.

Human overland movement in the West was then confined almost entirely to travel on horseback,[5] and as a consequence any offense against the one means of locomotion was punished with exceptional severity. During its first

[1] The boundary line of the modern state of Louisiana.
[2] The Governor and Judges of the territory were invested with authority to exercise over the District of Louisiana powers similar to those they were authorized to exercise for the maintenance of government in the Territory of Indiana.
[3] Louisiana District was detached from Indiana Territory by act of Congress on March 3, 1805. It had been attached to Indiana March 26 of 1804.
[4] By act of January 11, taking effect on June 30.
[5] In which feature the conditions there existing constituted a repetition of the era that had prevailed a century and a half before, in the Atlantic coast regions, only a few hundred miles to the eastward.

session the Indiana assembly passed a law providing that if a person stole "any Horse, Mare, Gelding, Mule or Ass," he should for the first offense pay to the owner the value of the animal, should be imprisoned until said value and costs were paid, and should receive from fifty to two hundred lashes on the bare back. The act provided that for a second offense the offender should "suffer the pains of death."

During the same session the assembly provided that all citizens should be compelled to work twelve days of each year in the creation of public roads, and made provision for the introduction of taverns. The law stipulated that tavern licenses could only be issued by courts, and the courts were in addition authorized to establish the rates to be charged against travellers by the tavern keepers. If an innkeeper presumed to collect any higher amount than that fixed by the court, his license was forfeited and he was compelled to pay twenty dollars to the complainant.[1]

The days that had intervened between Boone's journey and the close of the century had been marked, in the interior, by a hurly-burly of confusion and violence. But at last a systematic effort was on foot to bring about a more settled state of affairs. The inflowing horde of whites no longer remained close to the rivers and first settlements, but scattered rapidly over the country. The task of suppressing disorder, which had previously fallen in large measure directly on the people themselves, was more actively undertaken by state, territorial and local authorities. This endeavor was shown by the nature of certain laws here mentioned. New exertions were made to increase the security of travellers both by land and

[1] The early enactments of the First Indiana Territorial Assembly here mentioned are contained in "Laws Passed at the First Session of the General Assembly of the Indiana Territory, begun and held at the Borough of Vincennes, on Monday the twenty-ninth of July in the year 1805. By Authority. Vincennes: Printed by Elihu Stout. (1805.)"

LOOKING OUT OF THE WINDOWS.

194.—Some of the families whose men-folk spent their lives in canal work lived in boats that were furnished after the manner of houses. Even the family horse was kept on board.

water. The severity of punishment visited upon horse thieves represented in part a determination to insure safety and speed in movement from place to place.

Nor were the river pirates overlooked. Although they had long been a danger to travel on the Ohio and some of its tributaries, no official effort had as yet been made to destroy them and put an end to their operations. But this matter of safety on the Ohio was taken up by Kentucky soon after the opening of the century. It will be remembered that Cave-in-Rock was a favorite haunt of the river desperados, and at the time Kentucky began her fight to exterminate them the most active group of pirates was believed to contain about thirty members. Kentucky went to the extent of organizing a military expedition against the outlaws, and the militia met them in battle and came out of the fray victorious. A considerable number of the criminals were killed and the remainder were dispersed. Organized attacks on flatboats and other river craft never became popular afterward, and one danger of river travel disappeared. But the conflict that brought safety to river voyagers proved a curse to some of those emigrants who had occasion to journey overland through the South. The survivors of the pirate band, after their defeat, united under the leadership of three famous bandits named Mason, Corkendale, and Harpe, and for several years infested the region of southern Tennessee and northern Mississippi, where they killed and robbed travellers almost at will. Finally their operations became an intolerable scourge and the governor of Mississippi Territory offered a reward of five hundred dollars for the capture of Mason. The highwaymen heard of the offer, and two of them turned traitors to their chief and put an end to him. Then the two fell into a debate concerning the best method of proving their exploit and securing the promised money. This problem they solved by cutting off Mason's head and carrying it to Natchez, where, after a discussion with the authorities, and conferences between the authorities, the five hundred dollars was duly paid over to them. The two bandits were then arrested, tried, and executed, and as no heirs appeared to claim their estate—which consisted of the aforesaid five hundred dollars—the money duly reverted to the treasury of the commonwealth. The conferences of the territorial officials which preceded the payment of the reward may have had some connection with the final outcome of the case.

The pioneers who penetrated into the Indiana and Illinois country during the first fifteen or twenty years after 1800 encountered natural conditions that were substantially identical with those which had surrounded the New

Cave-in-Rock, the principal haunt of river pirates on the Ohio during the age of flat-boat travel. From a drawing by the American painter, Carl Bodmer, about 1835. F. C. Col. English.

England pioneers more than a century and a half before. The region north of the Ohio River, and extending westward from the Ohio boundary to the Mississippi River, was girdled by long-established Indian trails, and those were at first the only routes used by the newcomers. In Indiana the elaborate system of native paths seemed to converge at two points, from which they radiated somewhat like the spokes of a wheel. One of these junction spots of native travel lay on the White River, where it is joined by a small tributary now known as Fall Creek. To this spot extended a trail from Vincennes, another from the falls of the Ohio,[1] another from the White Water River,[2] and still others that reached down from the Potawatomi, Miami and Delaware towns in the north.

The other nucleus of native trails was the important Miami town called Ke-ki-on-ga, the present site of Fort Wayne. It was Ke-ki-on-ga, with its radiating system of various routes, which was described by Little Turtle, in his address to General Wayne at Greenville, as "that glorious gate . . . from the North to the South, and from the East to the West."

The first two distinctively Caucasian overland roads into the Indiana region were at first known as the "Berry Trace" and the "Whetzel Trace."[3] The Berry Trace was the principal path of white travel northward from the Ohio River into the interior of the territory, and for a considerable part of its distance it was merely an improvement on the pre-existing Indian trail extending northward from the falls of the Ohio to the White River. The

[1] At present followed by the tracks of a railway extending northward from Jeffersonville to Indianapolis. This trail was used by the Potawatomi, Miamis and Delawares of the upper Indiana country in their annual journeys to the neutral hunting grounds of Kentucky.
[2] This route is now occupied by the Pennsylvania Railroad.
[3] The first named was marked out by Captain John Berry, and the other by Jacob Whetzel, one of the members of a family that played a prominent part in the pioneer development and race wars of the interior.

THE LINE-BOAT CABIN.

195.—The living quarters on a boat of the sort shown in the preceding. It may be an interior view of the same room from whose window the woman is looking.

Whetzel Trace was the principal line of white travel into the interior of Indiana from the Ohio region and the East.[1] For a part of its extent it was really created by white men. Whetzel and his son Cyrus and four companions, all armed with axes, chopped their way westward through the forest for many miles during the year 1818, clearing a roadway sufficiently wide for the passage of a team— although there were then practically no teams to use it. The labor of Whetzel and his companions found an end only when they had penetrated to the interior of the state, where they at last reached the Berry Trace that led south-ward to the Ohio River.[2] The Whetzel Trace was used

[1] It began toward the eastern boundary of the territory, near the present town of Laurel in Franklin county, and extended in a generally westward direction to White River. A discussion of the first white traces of Indiana Territory, and of the preceding system of Indian trails, is to be found in Cottman's "The First Thoroughfares of Indiana."
[2] The junction point of the Whetzel and Berry Traces was in the central part of Johnson county, south of and not far from the site of Indianapolis.

by incoming white settlers from the East until about 1826.
They followed its course westward until they came to its
intersection with Berry's road, and then continued northward along that thoroughfare and the Indian trails leading still farther north toward Ft. Wayne. Numerous
lateral trails diverged to all parts of the territory from the
trunk lines of aboriginal travel already mentioned, and
in later years, after the new state had begun its own road
building, it adopted the routes followed by native paths in
many cases.[1]

The Illinois country also contained several local
points from which Indian highways radiated. Two such
places in the southern part of the state were Kaskaskia
and Fort Massac,[2] and similar situations in the north were
Black Hawk's village[3] and the present sites of Chicago
and Galena. An important native path extended across
Illinois from Galena to the neighborhood of Chicago,[4]
and a similar thoroughfare joined the Sac and Fox settlement on Rock River with the southern end of Lake Michigan. A third trail connected Kaskaskia and Fort Massac,
and still another forest trace united the northern and
southern parts of the territory. These native routes
through Illinois constituted the first roads used by white
settlers in their overland journeys through that region.
Not until 1827 did the white men have a road of their own
making in the northern part of Illinois. In that year a
path called "Kellog's Trail" was opened between the

[1] "When James Blake and William Conner viewed, as commissioners, the first road
between Indianapolis and Ft. Wayne, they found that after leaving White river they
could not improve upon the judgment of the Indians as shown in their old trails." Cottman's "The First Thoroughfares of Indians," p. 13.
   "One of the earliest wagon-ways out of Indianapolis, . . . which led to Wayne
county before the coming of the National Road, was laid out on the White Water
trail." Ibid, p. 14.
[2] An important frontier junction point on the Ohio River, nearly opposite the mouth
of the Tennessee.
[3] On Rock River, about three miles above its junction with the Mississippi.
[4] Later to be followed by a railroad.

settlement of Peoria, in the north-central part of the state, and Galena in the extreme northwest corner. Kellog's Trail made it possible for the people of southern and central Illinois to penetrate into its northern parts over a thoroughfare created by themselves.

The custom of blazing the trees along a wilderness road, which was brought into the interior by the pre-revolutionary pioneers, was continued in the Middle West during the period under discussion. But the later western men improved on the practise. Besides blazing the ways through the forest they adopted a method of showing the distances that had been traversed. At the end of each mile —as nearly as the distance could be determined—a prominent tree at the edge of the trail was selected, and on its trunk were carved large and deep numerals indicating the number of miles from the starting place to the point thus marked. The figures cut into the tree were then painted red in order that they might be still more noticeable.

The primitive communications system of Illinois was united to that of Indiana by the native trails on the north, by the Illinois and Wabash Rivers, and by the Ohio River on the south. The Indiana paths, in turn, were linked with those of Ohio by the Ohio River on the south and by the native highways extending eastward from Ke-ki-on-ga to Sandusky, to the western end of Lake Erie, and to Detroit. Three trails extended northward through the forests of central and western Ohio. The easternmost of these proceeded from a little settlement called Columbus to a line of forts called Morrow, Ferree, Seneca and Stephenson. Somewhat farther to the westward a second Ohio trace ran north from Springfield to military stations named Forts McArthur, Necessity, Finley and Meigs.

The third Ohio forest path reached from Dayton, on the south, to Forts Lorain, St. Mary, Amanda, Jennings, Brown and Defiance. All three of these Ohio wilderness highways were connected in the north by east-and-west traces, and at Fort Defiance the north-and-south trail of western Ohio joined the native highway proceeding eastward from Ke-ki-on-ga, in Indiana.[1]

The methods whereby travellers from the East reached the Ohio country before the introduction of periodic travel in that region have already been considered. On their arrival in Kentucky or in southern or western Ohio they were enabled, by means of the natural and native routes here outlined, to penetrate through nearly all the northern territory east of the Mississippi River.

[1] The early western system of overland travel communications, as above outlined, is well shown on the large folio map of "Ohio and Indiana," in the "American Atlas," published by H. S. Tanner in 1819.

CHAPTER XXXI

A MORE INTIMATE VIEW OF THE PERSONALITY, CHARACTER, THOUGHTS, HABITS, SPEECH AND MANNERS OF THE LAST PIONEER GENERATION, FROM ITS OWN CONTEMPORARY RECORDS — WHEELED VEHICLES APPEAR IN THE INTERIOR — TRAVEL ADVENTURES OF A POLITICAL CANDIDATE — A VISIT TO CHICAGO IN 1822 — ECONOMIC IMPORTANCE OF THE HORSE AND MATTERS GROWING THEREFROM — A NEW TRIAL DECLINED BY A HORSE THIEF — COURT SCENES, PROCEEDINGS AND TESTIMONY IN OTHER SORTS OF CASES — A WHITE MAN HANGED FOR THE MURDER OF AN INDIAN — THE INTRODUCTION OF THE NIGHTSHIRT INTO INDIANA TAVERNS — DAVY CROCKETT TELLS A STORY OF FLATBOAT LIFE — THE VALUE AND PURPOSE OF AN INQUIRY INTO THE CHARACTER OF THE LAST PIONEERS — A NEW WILDERNESS CONFRONTS THEM

SUCH were the social conditions and travel routes found in the interior during the first two decades of the nineteenth century by those restless multitudes who came from the East by means of their horses and boats, or on their own feet. On such a primitive foundation the settlers were destined to erect, in little more than a generation, the edifice of a new and modern society connected with the Atlantic coast by turnpikes, canals and railroads. Those are the people whose characters and habits— during the years while they still remained a compara-

656

tively isolated community—we are about to observe. The testimony here presented concerning them and their lives during the interval in question will consist of records left by themselves. And since one of those pioneers afterward preserved in written form a mass of unusual detail concerning the daily affairs of the people among whom he lived it is well to indicate, in his own words, the conditions found by him on his arrival amid the scenes in which his later life was to be passed.[1] In describing them, he said:

"At the time I came to the state [Indiana], in March, 1817, there was not a railroad in the United States, nor a canal west of the Alleghany Mountains . . . Fire was struck by the flint and steel; the falling spark was caught in punk taken from the knots of the hickory tree. There was not a foot of turnpike road in the State and plank roads had never been heard of; the girdled standing trees covered the cultivated fields; . . . not a bridge in the State; the traveling all done on horseback, the husband mounted before on the saddle, with from one to three of the youngest children in his arms—the wife, with a spread cover reaching to the tail of the horse, sitting behind, with the balance of the children unable to walk in her lap; not a carriage nor buggy in all the country."[2]

The pioneer chronicler made an error in the passage just quoted. He said there was "not a carriage nor buggy in all the country." He was living in the interior of Indiana, and did not know that a few vehicles such as he described had already appeared in the southern and more settled parts of the region. On another page is reproduced an official document issued by the infant commonwealth— then one year old—and showing that a resident of the town of Vincennes had paid a tax of two dollars for the privilege of owning and using for one year "a two-wheel carriage

[1] The individual to whom reference is here made was Oliver H. Smith, one of the prominent figures in the early group of Indiana pioneers. He was a circuit lawyer, a state lawmaker and United States Senator. His descriptions of the people among whom he lived are narratives of personal knowledge. His anecdotal history of the Middle West was published in Cincinnati in 1858 under the title, "Early Indiana Trials; and Sketches." Statements or stories quoted from his book are hereafter indicated by the foot-note "Smith."
[2] Smith, p. 116.

INCLINED PLANE ON THE MORRIS CANAL.

196.—Scene on the Morris Canal, in New Jersey. On this canal the boats
were lifted and lowered 1,334 feet to different levels by means of twenty-
three inclined plane railways. Only 223 feet were overcome by the lock
system. The boats were eight and a half feet wide and from sixty to
eighty feet long.

for the conveyance of persons called a chaise." So there
can be no doubt that travel vehicles of the sort described
had reached Indiana by the year named, although the
action of the state in putting a tax upon them indicated
that such things were regarded as luxuries—which they
undoubtedly were.

Other taxes imposed by the territory and state of

Indiana at about the same time shed further light on social conditions in the region. Between the years 1804 and 1807 a man who sold merchandise by retail was required to pay an annual sum of fifteen dollars. By 1817 this merchandising tax had been increased to twenty-five dollars, but the retailer was also permitted to sell wines and liquors as well as shoes, clothing, groceries and such things. A tavern keeper was required to pay an annual license fee of twelve dollars in 1813, and in 1816 the similar amount had been raised to twenty dollars, at which figure it remained at least until 1819. From earliest days the western people were imbued with a craving for playing the games known as billiards and pool, and the heavy tables required for that amusement were shipped into the interior on flatboats at large expense. The paraphernalia in question were always taxed, and in 1816 the proprietor of a billiard table was assessed no less than fifty dollars for the privilege of maintaining it in his establishment.[1]

In continuing his narrative of early western conditions Smith wrote:

"I stood . . . on the site of Indianapolis, the capital of our State, when there was scarcely a tree missing from the dense forest around it. I passed through the wilds of Marion [the name of the county] on my pony, upon the winding Indian path, when the bear, the deer and the wolf sprang up before me. . . . I recollect when the commerce of Marion and the infant capital was carried between Cincinnati and young Indianapolis by the semi-monthly six-ox train. . . . This was the second stage of commercial operations in Marion; the single horse and the pack saddle being then employed in carrying the mail, the letters and papers having become too bulky to be carried in the pockets of the mail boy."[2]

[1] There was a peculiar tax in vogue in Tennessee, at a little later period, the underlying reason for which is not very clear. For a time during the third decade a law of the state provided that travellers or other people who were moving up-stream on any of the rivers in the western district of Tennessee must pay a tax if they sold groceries, during such up-stream trips, to the inhabitants of the regions they penetrated. This law was not operative against people who were simultaneously moving down-stream on the same rivers. In 1829 the act was amended, and such up-stream travellers were relieved of the tax during the months of April, May, June, October and November, although it remained in effect during the other portions of the year.—"Acts passed at the Stated Session of the Eighteenth General Assembly of the State of Tennessee, 1829. Nashville; 1829."
[2] Smith, p. 287.

A HISTORY OF TRAVEL IN AMERICA

Although the population of the western country increased rapidly during the years immediately following Smith's arrival, the travel conditions encountered by the people did not alter in any material degree in much of the region north and west of Ohio until subsequent to the year 1830. Nine years after Smith had reached his new home he found himself a candidate for Congress, and in his memoirs he told of a campaign trip which he made between the towns of Indianapolis and Ft. Wayne in 1826. His description of the journey ran:

"There were no roads, nothing but Indian paths, to travel at that day through the wilderness. . . . The streams were high and the path for miles under water in places. . . . I rode in that campaign a small brown Indian pony, a good swimmer.[1] . . . The path wound around the ridges until the river [Wabash] came full in sight. . . . The moment we reached the river the Indian[2] jumped down and . . . was out of sight in a moment in the woods, and I saw nothing of him for an hour, when he returned with the bark of a hickory tree about 12 feet long and 3 feet in diameter. A fire was soon made. The bark was metamorphosed into a round-bottomed Indian canoe. . . . The canoe was launched; my saddle, saddle-bag and blanket placed in one end, and I got in the other. With my weight the edges were about an inch above water. I took the paddle, and, by using the current, landed safely on the other shore.[3] The Indian swam the horse over. . . . It was after twilight when I came to a large lake directly in my way. Fearing to go on, I turned the pony and rode out into the woods, to a beech tree that had been blown down some time before. Dismounting, I tied the pony to the brush of the tree, took off the saddle-bag and blanket, and laid down, without anything to eat, and very tired. In a few moments I heard the howling of wolves in every direction, sometimes close to me. The last thing I heard, as I fell asleep, was an old wolf barking some 20 feet from me. I slept soundly through the night, and when I waked the sun was full in my face. At dinner I was at the hotel table at Fort Wayne, with an excellent appetite, having eaten nothing from early breakfast the day before. I made a speech that day from

---

[1] All western horses used for travel at that time were thoroughly trained in the art of swimming.

[2] It was a usual thing for travellers through unknown districts to employ native guides.

[3] The incident is reminiscent of the experience related by Mistress Knight, of Boston, regarding her journey from Boston to New York about a century and a quarter before. One of the same travel methods employed with such trepidation by the New England schoolmistress was still commonly in use only a few hundred miles west of the spot where her canoe adventure took place.

the porch of the hotel. . . . I received just ten votes in the county to reward me for my perilous trip.[1]

During this same campaign of 1826 Smith one day borrowed a buggy which he intended to use on a road that permitted such an exploit. The vehicle had recently been brought from New England by a neighbor named Lovejoy, and had occasioned considerable talk. But after brief thought the candidate reconsidered his determination to move about the country on wheels, and he afterward gave his reason thus:

"I borrowed it to ride to Wayne County, but I gave up the buggy and took my horse, for fear the people would think me proud, and it would injure my election."[2]

On another occasion in the campaign of 1826 Smith and his adversary[3] engaged in a joint debate at the town of Allenville, and he later referred to the incident in his memoirs.

"The whole country was there," he said. "The judge was speaking, and for the first time introduced the new subject of railroads. He avowed himself in favor of them . . . and then, rising to the top of his voice: 'I tell you, fellow citizens, that in England they run the cars 30 miles an hour, and they will yet be run at a higher speed in America.' This was enough. The crowd set up a loud laugh at the expense of the judge. An old fellow standing by me bawled out: 'You are crazy, or do you think we are all fools; a man could not live a moment at that speed.' The day was mine."

At another meeting in joint debate the two candidates discussed the tariff. "The people knew but little about it," said Smith, "but what they had heard was decidedly against it. . . One old fellow said he had never seen one, but he believed it was hard on sheep."[4]

Despite the deplorable lack of appreciation displayed by Wayne county in giving him only ten votes Smith was

[1] Smith, pp. 81-2.
[2] Smith, p. 116.
[3] Judge John Test.
[4] Smith, p. 80.

elected, and he started from Indianapolis to Washington in November of 1827. He made the trip on horseback, and rode to the national capital in the short time of seventeen days. In commenting on the journey he afterward explained in his history that he could have availed himself of stage-coach accommodations for part of the distance,

197.—A Morris Canal boat was floated upon a massive wheeled cradle made of heavy timbers. There it was fastened, and the cradle was pulled up or let down the inclined plane by means of rope cables. On reaching the new level the cradle ran beneath the water on submerged tracks, and the boat was released and floated free again.

but preferred not to do so. "Stages were all the go," he declared, "and travelling on horseback fast going out of fashion."[1]

The conditions of overland travel in the Illinois country during the same years were identical with those just described. White men were wandering over the land in

[1] Smith, p. 88.

all directions; extreme interest was manifested by the public in reliable information regarding natural conditions, and the newspapers of the time sought in every way to satisfy the craving for such knowledge. They frequently printed letters written by men who had penetrated to out-of-the-way spots. A sample communication of the sort, written in 1822, is here quoted. It dealt principally with an almost unknown little settlement called Chicago, and read in part as follows:[1]

"After experiencing considerable privations and dangers in traveling by land from Green Bay to Chicago, a distance of about 230 miles, I was amply compensated by a view of the latter place, which presents so much for interesting observation. Nature has in store so many and so great advantages at this spot, which can be easily recognized [grasped] by unlocking them at a moderate expense, that any great length of time will not, according to the progress of improvement making in our country, continue before great attention is attracted to it. . . . Public attention will ere long be attracted to this important and interesting section of the country. The Indian title is getting fast extinguished, and is mostly done already, and the Indians are clearing out of it. . . . But few men of science and observation have yet visited the country, as the dwelling of a white man is not to be seen from Fort Clark to Chicago."

The extreme economic importance of the horse in the interior during the early part of the century constantly resulted in efforts to acquire beasts of burden by dishonest methods. A scheme sometimes used by plausible scoundrels who were engaged in horse stealing as a profession was to appear in a new community and set up in business as liverymen. This device was usually operated by two swindlers who worked together. After they had become established, and had been given custody of a quantity of horse-flesh they would disappear between two days, taking with them the valuable property entrusted to their care.

[1] Printed in the "Farmers and Mechanics Journal," of Vincennes, on June 12, 1823, and by that paper credited to the "Vandalia Intelligencer" of an unnamed earlier day. The letter was published under the title "Journal of a Traveller through the Great Western Lakes and down the Illinois River, in July, August and September, 1822."
A picture showing Chicago as it appeared about the same date is elsewhere reproduced.

The customary aftermath of such an incident—an indignant advertisement in the local newspaper—seldom produced the desired results. A typical public notice of such an incident began:[1]

"Eloped from Vincennes with one handsome roan Mare, two bay mares and one small flee-bitten grey." The advertisement, after describing the two swindlers, went on to say: "These rascals came to Vincennes some time ago, and got into business as Livery Stable Keepers, and by their fair speeches and apparent honesty and industrious habits, induced the subscribers to become their sureties in contracts to a large amount; and, after carrying on for some time, getting into debt as much as possible, and pocketing all the cash they could, they made their escape, leaving many people in the suds."[2]

Another popular way of acquiring horses through illegitimate means was the method of buying them by counterfeit money, of which a large amount was in circulation throughout the country. One Jesse Britton, also of Vincennes, was a victim of this practise during the same year of 1820. He sold a fine horse for a hundred dollars in counterfeit bills, and told his trouble to the public in an advertisement as usual.[3] Britton's notice in the newspaper was of no especial importance as a document affording new information on certain financial methods of the time, but it was noteworthy in a particular unrealized by its author. It contained what may well be one of the most vivid portrayals of the early type of American confidence-man or "sport" to be found in the literature of those years. Here is the description of the stranger:

"The rascal is rather stout built, 5 feet 8 or 9 inches high, white hair and whiskers, red flushed complexion, hairy and sunburnt about the neck, with long, yellow and disagreeable looking teeth. He wore an old white fur hat, green frock coat, the cuffs of which were edged with velvet—blue striped domestic overalls or trousers, short boots or bootees, which had been mended, and a seam across one of them."

[1] From the "Indiana Centinel" (Vincennes) of November 4, 1820.
[2] The expression of pioneer American slang which concludes this advertisement is probably the early form of a present-day expression which—measured by slang standards—is decidedly less dignified.
[3] In the "Indiana Centinel" of July 8.

Schuylkill

CANAL NAVIGATOR.

BY

S. ALSPACH.

—»•◉•«—

PHILADELPHIA:

PRINTED BY JOSEPH RAKESTRAW,

FOR THE AUTHOR.

1827.

198.—Early literature dealing with the subject of travel in America. Title page of a guide book written for those using the Schuylkill Canal. It gave the location of all stumps, rocks and similar dangers to navigation, with other information necessary for the avoidance of shipwreck.

The advertisement concluded with the information that whoever caught the scoundrel was to receive twenty dollars in genuine money. No immediate results seem to have been produced by the proclamation, for it continued to appear in the newspaper for several weeks.

The very striking masculine costume just described was characteristic of the period, and a somewhat similar array was worn by nearly every man who tried by means of his apparel to surround himself with an atmosphere of dignity, or the nearest approach to that quality which he could simulate. The imposingly tall and somewhat bell-crowned stovepipe hats of the time were either white, gray, brown or straw-colored, according to the taste of the wearer. The voluminous frock coat was blue, green, claret-colored, brown, dull red, or of any other color desired, and usually had a collar and cuffs made of velvet in some contrasting shade. The trousers were often equally spectacular in appearance, and the bootees reached about half-way between the ankle and the knee. The waistcoat—not mentioned in the above advertisement— was ordinarily of some color that would contrast with the big frock coat beneath which it was worn. Very little of the clothing used by men during the American pioneer period has survived to the present day, and such apparel is now exceedingly rare.[1]

Once in a while a few of the innumerable horse thieves who plied their trade throughout the West were captured and brought to jail. This usually happened after an epidemic of thievery, and a case of the sort that took place at Vincennes in the early days was described by Smith in

[1] Possibly the most comprehensive collection of the sort extant is that preserved in the little village of Geneseo, in New York state. It is in some respects unfortunate that the remarkable Geneseo collection of civilian and military apparel, personal belongings and household utensils of the pioneers is not located in a more accessible center where the significance and value of its treasures might be more widely recognized.

his reminiscences. Thirty-nine lashes on the bare back still remained the penalty inflicted on conviction for a first offense. The jail was for once full of horse thieves, and when the time arrived for their trial the judge before whom they were fated to appear was General Marston G. Clark, a cousin of George Rogers Clark. The judge was an unusually perfect and eye-filling specimen of the finest type of western pioneer, and Smith described his appearance as he presided over the backwoods tribunal.

"He was," said Smith, "about six feet in his stockings, of a very muscular appearance; wore a hunting shirt, leather pants, moccasins and a fox-skin cap, with a long queue down his back."[1]

When the first malefactor appeared before that awe-inspiring figure his lawyer made formal objection to the indictment on the ground that his client was improperly named in the instrument. Such was in truth the fact, for the defendant's middle initial had been omitted. The judge overruled the objection in the following language:

"That makes no difference; I know the man, and that is sufficient."

Objection number two: "There is no value put on the horse in the indictment."

Ruling: "I know an Indian pony is worth ten dollars."

Objection number three: "It is charged in the indictment to be a horse, when he is a gelding."

Ruling: "I shall consider that a gelding is a horse; motion overruled."

These preliminaries having been disposed of, the trial proceeded. Legal technicalities had already appeared in American judicial history, but had not yet acquired the commanding importance they afterward attained. Testimony was taken, the man was found guilty, and was

[1] One or more of the Justices of the United States Supreme Court still wore similar queues at as late a date as 1827.

sentenced to receive thirty-nine lashes. Whereupon the convicted man's lawyer interposed another objection.

"We move an arrest of judgment," he said, "on the ground that it is not charged in the indictment that the horse was stolen in the Territory of Indiana."

The figure on the bench remained for a moment silent. He sat as still as a graven image. "That I consider a more serious objection," he finally replied. "I will consider on it till morning."

Late in the evening Judge Clark held a brief consultation with the sheriff, and at midnight that official took the prisoner from the log jail, escorted him far into the forest, bound him to a tree with his face toward its trunk, stripped off his shirt, and laid thirty-nine fearful lashes on his bare back. In the morning the prisoner was again brought before the judge without having opportunity to communicate with his counsel, and the lawyer again arose and repeated his objection. Judge Clark announced that he had decided to grant the defendant a new trial.

Up sprang the prisoner. "No!" he screamed. "No! for heaven's sake! I discharge my attorney and withdraw the motion."[1]

Every other man in the jail got a like dose, and horse stealing was for several years a lost art in Indiana. What could technicalities avail against that ominous figure on the bench. Six feet of muscle in a hunting shirt, fox-skin cap, moccasins and leather pants. It was justice incarnate.[2]

In those days, even as in these, many of the beliefs and

[1] Smith, pp. 160-1.
[2] Immediately after the Republic of Texas came into existence, a few years afterward, the Congress of that nation passed a law ordaining that a horse thief should have the letter T branded on his flesh with a red-hot iron, "in such place as the court shall direct." That penalty was in addition to a fine not exceeding $1000, imprisonment up to one year, and 39 lashes on the bare back.—"Laws of the Republic of Texas, etc. Printed by Order of the Secretary of State. Houston, 1838," p. 189. The law was approved December 21, 1836.

practises of the people were reflected in their legal disputes, and the lost colloquial story of the early courts—could it have been preserved in its entirety—would have been an invaluable commentary on the life and society of the time. Smith told this incident: A case was presented to the grand jury against a man who had sold whisky at

WORCESTER FAIR.

TO accommodate those wish to attend the Worcester Cattle Show, from Providence, and the intermediate places, the packet boat Carrington will leave the Basin on Tuesday morning, October 6, at 6 o'clock for Worcester, going through on that day, returning, will leave Worcester on Thursday morning, and arrive in Providence the same evening.

Passengers who intend going in her, must be on board at the time above mentioned, as she will leave precisely at that hour.   sept 28

199.—Special excursion canal boats were run to accommodate the public on unusual occasions. Advertisement of such an excursion boat, which carried passengers from Providence, in Rhode Island, to the cattle show in Worcester, Massachusetts, in one day.

retail without license. The proof was positive. The question was put and the jurors unanimously voted that an indictment be drawn. Mr. Fletcher, the prosecuting attorney who was presenting the evidence to the grand jury, drew the bill, handed it to the foreman and asked him to sign it. The foreman replied: "I shall do no such thing, Mr. Fletcher; I sell whisky without license myself, and I shall not indict others for what I do." A deadlock thereupon ensued, and the two guardians of the public peace explained the situation to the judge in person, but that official was either unable or disinclined to suggest any practical solution to the dilemma. So the two men went back to the grand jury room again. Then Prosecuting Attorney Fletcher took off his coat, doubled up his fists, stepped up to the foreman and said, "The law requires the last step to be taken." The foreman signed the indictment.[1]

Another legal combat described by Smith shows the political feeling of those days and the personal animosity in which it sometimes resulted. The two political parties of the time were the Democratic-Republican, which was then in power, and the Federalist, whose influence was rapidly disappearing. Almost all the western people were Democrats, and according to the incident narrated a citizen named John Allen had called another man named Joshua Harlan "an old Federalist." Harlan brought suit against Allen for damages. His complaint declared that "by the publishing of which false, slanderous and defamatory libel the plaintiff has been brought into public disgrace, and his neighbors have since refused to have any intercourse with him."

The case came to trial and the first witness for the plaintiff was a man named Herndon, who had come to Indiana in very early days. He was asked the question:

"Do you consider it libelous and slanderous to call a man a Federalist?"

Answer: "I do."

Question: "Which would you rather a man would call you, a Federalist or a horse thief?"

Answer: "I would shoot him if he called me one or the other."

Twenty-nine more witnesses gave identical testimony

[1] Smith, pp. 57-8.

PROVIDENCE, R.I.

Published by Charles Magnus & Co. 12 Frankfort Street, New York

200.—View of Providence, showing the Basin mentioned in the preceding illustration. Canal boats started from the Basin, which, in canal-traffic days, served the purpose of a modern railway station.

for the plaintiff. The jury debated the subject all night and came back into court next morning with a verdict finding Allen guilty and fining him one thousand dollars. After the jury had announced the result of its deliberations the presiding judge said to its members: "The court are well satisfied with your verdict, gentlemen; you are discharged."[1]

The testimony of a defendant in a commonplace case wherein the charge was assault and battery was set down by Smith as follows:

"I told him he lied; he told me I lied. I spit in his face; he spit in my face. I slapped him in the face; he slapped me in the face. I kicked him; he kicked me. I tripped him up; he tripped me up. I struck him and knocked him down; he got up and knocked me down. I then got mad; he got mad, and we were just agoing to fight when the saloon keeper got between us. That is all."[2]

The plaintiff was fined one dollar; the defendant was fined one dollar.

But the case which was—in one way—the most important of all those recounted by Smith was a series of trials in which four white men were charged with the killing of nine Indians. The affair took place in 1824, at a time when the prejudice entertained by the mass of the whites against the natives was still occasionally in evidence, though not so extreme in its character as in former years. Two men of the Seneca nation, together with their wives and one other squaw, and four children between the ages of infancy and ten years, had established a hunting camp in the forest. Five white men came to the Indian camp one day saying they were travellers who had lost their horses in the woods. The Indian men dropped their own affairs, offered their help in recovering the animals,

[1] Smith, pp. 120-122.
[2] Smith, pp. 335-6.

and set forth with their visitors for that purpose. After the Senecas had been shot from behind the white men returned to the camp and killed the women and three of the children. The fourth child was only wounded, and was despatched by having its brains knocked out against the end of a log.

One of the whites concerned in the affair made his escape, but the other four were arrested. Although the old frontier doctrine that "the only good Indian is a dead Indian" still commanded supporters as a theoretical proposition, the crime inspired a general feeling of condemnation among the Caucasian population. The four prisoners were tried separately. The cases were considered to be of such importance, and public interest in them was so widespread, that a new and pretentious log court-house, containing two rooms, was built to serve as the theater of the legal drama. The court room itself was some twenty-five or thirty feet square, and the judges sat on a narrow platform about three feet high, built along one side of the room. Their seat was a long wooden bench. On the floor in front of the judges' platform was a similar bench for the lawyers, a little wooden pen for prisoners, a table for the clerk of the court, and still another bench for witnesses. A long pole separated the official section of the court from that part of its area devoted to the use of spectators, who stood up. The other room in the court-house was for the use of jurymen, and its dedication to such a purpose marked a decided advance in that element of pioneer court procedure. The grand jury which had indicted the four men had carried on its discussions while seated on a fallen log out in the woods.

An imposing array of counsel, including General Sampson Mason of Ohio, defended the first of the prisoners brought to account. General Mason discussed the scenes attending the trial in a letter that he sent back to Ohio, and which finally found publication in a newspaper there. One part of his description read: "As I entered the court room the Judge was sitting on a block paring his toenails, when the sheriff entered, out of breath, and informed the court that he had six jurors tied, and his deputies were running down the others." In discussing the passage here quoted from the letter of the eminent Ohio lawyer, Smith said: "General Mason, with all his candor, unquestionably drew upon his imagination in this case." It is a loss to the riches of historical integrity that Smith himself was not more specific in challenging the accuracy of his colleague. For if we analyze both General Mason's description and the precise terms of its impeachment, we find that Senator Smith might have based his contradiction on the point that the sheriff was not out of breath when he made his announcement.

The twelve men who sat in judgment were arrayed in the pioneer habiliments of the day, including moccasins and side-knives. The case was concluded for the prisoner "in able, eloquent and powerful speeches, appealing to the prejudice of the jury against the Indians; relating in glowing colors the early massacres of white men, women and children by the Indians; reading the principal incidents in the history of Daniel Boone and Simon Kenton . . . and not forgetting the defeat of Braddock, St. Clair and Harmar . . . Judge Wick charged the jury at some length . . . and distinctly impressing upon the jury . . . that the murder of an Indian was equally as criminal in law as the murder of a white man."

One of the defendants was found guilty of manslaughter and the other three were convicted of murder in the first degree. The sentence of one murderer was commuted, and the other two suffered the extreme penalty of the law. Of the final scene Smith remarked: "A Seneca Chief, with his warriors, stood on a hill that commanded a view of the gallows. 'We are satisfied,' the Chief said. Thus ended the only trials where convictions of murder were ever had, followed by the execution of white men, for killing Indians in the United States."[1]

Two other incidents contained in the printed annals of the time—one dealing with a tavern keeper and the other with an adventure of Davy Crockett—will be of aid in portraying the pioneer men whose lives, manners and characters are here discussed. The innkeeper in question was Captain John Berry,[2] who kept a tavern at Andersontown, in Indiana. Berry was inordinately proud of the cleanliness of his establishment, and his well-known feeling in that regard was on one occasion made the basis of a practical joke which came near to ending in unpleasant consequences. The date of the incident was about 1830, at which time it was the custom of probably a large majority of men—especially in the frontier regions—to retire for the night, no matter where they slept, without removing the shirts worn by them in the daytime. That useful garment known as the nightshirt, although well established and growing in popularity throughout the East, had not yet appeared in the West in sufficient quantities or with sufficient frequency to make it a familiar article of apparel. A man travelling in the interior went to bed in his shirt and never gave the matter a thought; nor did the tavern keeper at whose house he lodged.

[1] Smith, pp. 51-57 and p. 179.
[2] From whom the "Berry Trace" was named.

Now it so happened that there one day came to Berry's tavern in Andersontown a little group of prominent men among whom were the Smith mentioned in these pages, and another well-known lawyer named James Whitcomb.[1] Whitcomb possessed a nightshirt, and what is more he carried it about the country with him and used it. His companions of course knew of his idiosyncrasy, and on arrival at the Berry establishment they decided to play a joke on the proprietor which should have the Whitcomb nightgown as its foundation. So—giving the matter an aspect of unusual importance and secrecy—they went to Berry and told him that Whitcomb, on a previous visit, had acquired a poor opinion of the cleanliness of the sheets used on Berry's beds and that he had therefore brought with him a special shirt which he intended to wear when he went to sleep, in order that he might not soil his regular shirt.

Berry refused to believe the charge. He could not think so ill of his distinguished guest. But the conspirators insisted they were right, and told the landlord he might convince himself with his own eyes at the proper time. When Whitcomb retired to his room at night the landlord tiptoed silently behind him, still unconvinced, and gluing his eye to the keyhole he watched the procedure within. He saw Whitcomb actually take off his shirt and put on another one, as had been described. The substitute even seemed longer than the ordinary shirt, as though its wearer desired to protect himself to the last degree. The incredible story, then, was all too true. Berry burst open the door in a fury, rushed in, sprang upon Whitcomb and bore him down, preparatory to the infliction of condign punishment on a man who dared cast

[1] Who not long afterward became Governor of Indiana.

such unmerited odium on his establishment. The perpetrators of the hoax, hearing the struggle, hurried to the spot and declared it was all a joke, insisting that people in other parts of the country really wore such things also. Finally they convinced the landlord—or at least instilled a doubt into his mind—and peace was restored.[1]

It was this same Captain Berry who, while walking on Broadway one Sunday during his first journey to New York, paused in front of a pretentious building into which numerous people were entering. The edifice was a church, though the stranger from Indiana was not aware of the fact. He was cordially invited to enter by a man stationed outside for the purpose, and just at that moment the organ inside burst into the strains of a march. Whereupon Captain Berry hastily declined the invitation, saying that he "never danced."[2]

The Crockett adventure was written by himself, and was found among his personal papers in Tennessee after he fell at the Alamo. Though but a fragment describing an alleged incident of river life in the early days, it revealed the temper, customs and vernacular of a certain type of western men whose numbers were far from small. Crockett's narrative read:

"One day as I was sitting in the stern of my broad horn, the old Free and Easy, on the Mississippi, taking a horn of midshipman's grog, with a tin pot in each hand, first a draugh of whiskey, and then one of river water, who should float down past me but Joe Snag; he was in a snooze, as fast as a church, with his mouth wide open; he had been ramsquaddled with whiskey for a fortnight, and as it evaporated from his body it looked like the steam from a vent pipe. Knowing the feller would be darned hard to wake, with all this steam on, as he floated past me I hit him a crack over his knob with my big steering oar. He waked in a thundering rage. Says he, halloe stranger, who axed you to crack my lice? Says I, shut up your mouth, or your teeth will get sunburnt. Upon

[1] Smith, pp. 74-5.
[2] Smith, p. 75.

this he crooked up his neck and neighed like a stallion.[1] I clapped my arms and crowed like a cock.[2] Says he, if you are a game chicken I'll pick all the pin feathers off of you. For some time back I had been so wolfy about the head and shoulders that I was obliged to keep kivered up in a salt crib to keep from spiling, for I had not had a fight for as much as ten days. Says I, give us none of your chin music, but set your kickers on land, and I'll give you a severe licking. The fellow now jumped ashore, and he was so tall he could not tell when his feet were cold. He jumped up a rod. Says he, take care how I lite on you, and he gave me a real sockdologer that made my very liver and lites turn to jelly. But he found me a real scrouger. I brake three of his ribs, and he knocked out five of my teeth and one eye. He was the severest colt that ever I tried to break. I finally got a bite hold that he could not shake off. We were now parted by some boatmen, and we were so exorsted that it was more than a month before either could have a fight. It seemed to me like a little eternity. And although I didn't come out second best, I took care not to wake up a ring tailed roarer with an oar again."[3]

The conditions and incidents that have been related— glimpses at the people of the interior through records left by themselves—certainly do not constitute a complete picture of those times, nor is their present use intended to suggest such a canvas. But nevertheless they have their value to us in our desire to build up a better present understanding of the Americans of those days. For, somewhat as the comparative anatomist by the aid of five or six bones may reconstruct with marvellous exactitude an unknown animal of long ago, and discover its habits and methods of life, so also may we gain a little broader knowledge of

[1] A challenge to battle.
[2] Acceptance of the challenge.
[3] From Vol. 7, No. 4, of "Davy Crockett's Almanack of Wild Sports in the West, etc." Nashville, Tenn., 1838. The preface of this publication states that it is printed by the heirs of Colonel Crockett, and that in addition to those numbers already issued, five more are in process of publication. It further says that the anecdotes, reminiscences and stories contained in the series of almanacs are transcribed from written material left by him, and that many of the woodcuts with which the almanacs are embellished are copies from drawings made by Crockett after a manner employed in the wilderness. The preliminary statement then goes on to say: "His posthumous papers contain a great number of wild frolics and scrapes, together with adventurous exploits in the chase, both those in which he was engaged himself, and others that came within his knowledge. The engravings are mostly taken from his drawings, which are very spirited. He drew on birch bark with a burnt stick."
The "Davy Crockett's Almanack" seems to have been unknown to American bibliographers until 1912, when the copy above mentioned was found in the museum room of the Indiana State Capitol. Since that date a widespread inquiry by antiquarians has resulted in the discovery of a few other numbers and a complete file may eventually be available.

the generation in question by the study of such fragments as these. Each circumstance, law or story in itself
is a small thing, by no means dependable as a basis for
general conclusions concerning the period discussed. Yet
when all of them are considered together we feel that we

MERCHANTS' CANAL LINE.
STEAM TOW-BOAT COMPANY.
Between New-York and Philadelphia, via Delaware and Raritan Canal.
FOR THE CONVEYANCE OF MERCHANDIZE, SPECIE, BAGGAGE, &c. &c.; AND INSURANCE EFFECTED,
WHENEVER REQUIRED, ON ANY PACKAGE, TO ITS FULL AMOUNT OF VALUE.
THOMSON & NEILSON, West Street, opposite Pier 2 N. R., New York, Proprietors.
South Wharves, Philadelphia, Agent.

201—After railways had appeared in the East and had made the old horse-
drawn canal craft unprofitable, a few of the boat companies tried to keep
up the fight by using steam tow-boats. Billhead of the Merchants' Line
on the Delaware and Raritan Canal, between New York and Philadelphia,
in 1843.

possess more than a surmise respecting the years we are
striving to see.

The laws, events, conditions, sketches and anecdotes
given in this and the preceding chapter are selections from
hundreds of similar ones that might be cited from the
same and other contemporary native sources. It is a
principle of historical narrative that the one who
writes must not incorporate in his recital any unusual
condition of earlier times merely because it was unusual,
or an isolated circumstance of former days whose
character is apt to produce, in the mind of the reader, an
impression inconsistent with truth. To avoid the creation

of a false belief, and to paint, as far as is possible, a real and somewhat comprehensive picture of an epoch under consideration, it is necessary that a historian summon to his aid the laws, surroundings, habits, beliefs, speech and deeds of the men he discusses. And it is best for him to let them tell their own story, adding only such comment and interpretation as he hopes will make their self-told narrative more clear and connected.

Even then he often fears he will in some degree mislead, for his space is limited, and, if he is dealing with a period rich in interest, whose story has formerly been told in diverse ways, he can only present a fragment of the material at his command, and that he has weighed. More than ever, in such case, does he see the need of choosing records that are typical, rather than exceptional. His best assurance of safety lies in the discovery that the illustrative matter so chosen by him—from the laws, surroundings, habits, beliefs, speech and deeds of the men portrayed, and from original sources widely separated and independent of one another—is consistent and inter-corroborative.

It must not be understood, in visualizing the last pioneer generation of America, that all men of that time—from 1800 to about 1835—lived on the same plane of social development. Nothing could be further from the fact. There were then American men and women of culture limited only by world-progress up to that interval. Every city and nearly every town held them. One of the first activities of every new commonwealth was the organization of a school system and a state college. But that element of society did not then—any more than now—dominate the beliefs or acts, or swiftly alter the circumstances of their fellow men. We are dealing with society in bulk. It is not unsafe to say that if we misjudge the pioneer population here considered, there is more likelihood that we err in allotting to those men too great a degree of polish and advancement, rather than in considering them too uncouth and distant, as compared with the generation of to-day.

We feel that men who thus spoke and acted in their mutual association must have had attributes in keeping with the deeds and utterances disclosed—that a people wherein such qualities were revealed as matter-of-fact elements of social life must have been, at least, a more consistent generation than the one of which we, amid the complexities of present days, form a part. And if we are right, and those men were consistent in so far as their mental attitude and intercourse with one another were concerned, then we can draw with reasonable sureness the chief outlines of the social era in which they lived. We find ourselves, like the comparative anatomist, building up the dominant American traits of the period as those qualities existed in the regions where new national impulses found their birth.

In this process we are aided by our knowledge of much that had gone before. The Americans of the years which witnessed the critical rush into turnpike, canal and railway building had been moulded in the rough, before their birth, by earlier conditions that had shaped the fundamental features of their character. The lesser features of that national character—as manifested during the period in question—were shaped by those new needs in which the people found themselves for the first time involved, to whose solution they could only bring inherited beliefs and methods, reinforced by such small experience as might be gained day by day. So, in hereafter following

202.—Canal travel in the Middle West. A packet boat on the Miami Canal, in Ohio. The passengers are gathered under an awning that has been stretched to protect them from the sun during the voyage.

the story of their successes and failures as they entered upon the important activities about to be recited, we will be aided in comprehending their aspirations and methods by an appreciation of the human qualities out of which their desires, limitations and acts necessarily sprang.

Some of those qualities have at least been suggested. The Americans of the epoch between 1800 and 1835—during which time definite trend was given to present-day conditions of social and economic affairs throughout the country—were still a pioneer people in thought and manner of life. They had conquered a Wilderness of one sort, and had accumulated much learning of one sort in so doing. In other knowledge they were, as a people, unusually deficient. Their long, unrelaxing struggle had given them no time to delve into the study of matters not in some way related to visible and immediate needs. All their immense fund of experience was of specialized character, exquis-

NORTH BEND

203.—Canal and river scene at North Bend, on the Ohio River, a few miles west of Cincinnati. The house was the home of William Henry Harrison.

itely fitted to its purpose, and that purpose was ceasing to
exist. They had reached the Mississippi.[1] The eastern part
of the continent at the commencement of the century was a
country of widely scattered, inert and immobile population
groups, large and small, between which slowly trickled a
few insignificant streams of information, commerce and
human movement. Then, during about a decade of time
—from 1802 to 1815[2]—there was borne in upon the people
a comparatively sudden realization that the contest with
nature which had occupied them for nearly two centuries
was practically finished. From that time onward, for a
score of years, the necessity for better means of transportation between different sections was the new and principal
subject of discussion.

The Wilderness—as such—was gone. Much of it had
been swept bodily away; the part remaining was simply a
forest and an obstacle.[3] And then, behold! there loomed
still another Wilderness before the last generation of the
pioneers. It was not a wilderness of nature, but one of
men's own making, for they themselves had created it. It
was not a wilderness of material form, assailable by the
brute strength of the ax, but one that needed for its successful conquest the use of knowledge and much wisdom.
It was a wilderness composed of civilization's necessities
and the desire of men to mingle with one another. Its
possible pitfalls, darkness and labyrinths were the intangible but no less dangerous elements of human ignorance,
avarice, jealousy and mistaken judgment.

Possibly no other people were ever before confronted
with a common task demanding for its best performance

[1] Missouri was the only state west of the river until 1836.
[2] Three years of this period were occupied by the War of 1812, which temporarily
distracted popular thought from the subject of better transportation facilities.
[3] Our long national blindness to the value of forests as a national economic asset is
doubtless due to the fact that for many generations we were smothered in riches of that
sort.

a more wise conception of the future, and a more unselfish consideration of the general welfare, than were those Americans who first keenly realized the need of linking all parts of their vast dominion by new and better methods of communication. That problem was the second—and greatest—Wilderness which they faced in their work of continental conquest. Upon the foresight and methods employed in their new undertaking depended, for an indefinite time to come, the material conditions under which they and their descendants were to live and progress. Every phase of the nation's life was thereafter to be shaped, and all its future inhabitants were to be intimately affected by their procedure and the attitude of their chosen servants. It is needless to say that neither the people of that period nor their governmental representatives realized, as we now do, the truths here stated. While following the developments of the decisive years soon to be considered, wherein our modern transportation system had its beginnings and took definite shape, we find numerous occasions on which the future economic history of the nation hung in the balance or swerved from one course to another.[1] And at times we are almost tempted to wonder whether the trend of events was not affected by some determining influence now beyond tracing, but whose source lay in the selfish foresight of a few rather than in any honest lack of foresight by the many.

The principal thought that needs be borne in mind while following the creation of our modern transportation system through the instrumentality of the national government, the state governments and private activities, is that it was brought into being by a pioneer generation; that definite shape was assumed by the system—between 1802

---

[1] As is the case to-day.

ILLINOIS AND MICHIGAN CANAL PACKET BOATS.

Three Daily Lines between CHICAGO and LASALLE, as follows:

Two daily lines of Mail Passenger Packets leave Chicago and Lasalle at 8 A. M. and 5 P. M., through in 22 hours, distance 100 miles, fare $4 ; connecting at Chicago with the Michigan Central Railroad Line, and Lake line of steamers to Detroit and Buffalo ; at Lasalle with a daily line of Passenger Steam Packets for St. Louis and intermediate places. Time from Chicago to St. Louis, from two to three days. Also, one daily line of freight packets between Chicago and Lasalle, leaving Chicago at 2 P. M., and Lasalle at 7 P. M., for the transportation of passengers and light freight generally. EMIGRANTS, with their furniture, &c., fare $3.

CANAL PACKET ROUTE,
FROM CHICAGO TO LASALLE,
VIA ILLINOIS AND MICHIGAN CANAL.

STOPPING PLACES.	Miles from Chic'go	Fare.	STOPPING PLACES.	Miles from Lasalle	Fare.
CHICAGO . . .	0	$ cts.	LASALLE . . .	0	$ cts.
Bridgeport . . .	4		OTTAWA . . .	15	60
Summit . . .	12	50	Marsailles . . .	22	1 00
Desplaines . . .	21	85	MORRIS	39	1 60
Athens . . .	25	1 00	Aux Sable . . .	44	1 75
Lockport . . .	33	1 40	Dresden	46	1 85
JOLIET	37	1 50	Kankakee Feeder	49	2 00
Chunahon . . .	48	2 00	Chunahon . . .	52	2 00
Kankakee Feeder	51	2 00	JOLIET	63	2 50
Dresden . . .	54	2 25	Lockport	67	2 75
Aux Sable . .	56	2 25	Athens	75	3 00
MORRIS . . .	61	2 50	Desplaines . . .	79	3 20
Marsailles . .	78	3 25	Summit	88	3 50
OTTAWA . . .	85	3 50	Bridgeport . . .	96	3 85
LASALLE . . .	100	4 00	CHICAGO . . .	100	4 00

204.—Westernmost work of the canal-building era. The Illinois and Michigan Canal was a hundred miles long, had three boats a day in each direction, and carried passengers over the whole distance in 22 hours, at a cost of four dollars. From "Disturnell's American and European Railway and Steamship Guide: 1851."

and 1835—while the people were necessarily untrained in the creative and administrative work they were performing. The only weapons they possessed for use in attacking the most formidable and complex wilderness that man can encounter—the problem of his own social and economic well-being—were such desires, ideas and methods as they had applied to the conquest of the least formidable variety of wilderness and to their own lives while so occupied. It follows that their first attitude toward the new work on which they entered, and the things they did during the early stages of that work, were direct manifestations of the national character as it then existed. Therefore any addition to our knowledge of the men of those days—however small—is of advantage in understanding their purposes, earnestness, enthusiasm, disputes, shiftings, wisdom, blindness and methods of procedure during a time whose events were freighted with such significance for the future.

As the story proceeds, and as the governmental turnpikes and the canals and railroads appear upon the stage of progress, we will be able to discern significant occasions whereon certain attributes of the national character exercised a controlling power in the development of events either for good or ill. Some of the qualities of mind acquired by the people through their long battle with primitive conditions were useful in various phases of their new undertaking, and were applied to it with benefit. Still others occasionally wrought harm. The central government's determination to undertake important social and industrial tasks for all the people in common—first manifested,[1] as will be seen, in connection with the need for interstate communication facilities in 1802—no doubt had its birth in the human instinct that caused all members of a wilderness community to unite in erecting the cabin of a newcomer because he alone could not build it. And the opposition of individual states to federated governmental purpose — which opposition was later to become politically known as "The State's Rights Doctrine"— together with the mutual jealousies displayed by various states and communi-

[1] The carriage of mails was not an exception. Private companies and individuals competed with the government in that activity until after 1840.

687

ties in connection with transportation plans, may likewise have had its ultimate source in the pioneer American conviction that each man was his own sovereign. So he was in the natural forest, but not afterward. Those days had departed.

There were three prominent qualities of the national

THE RAGING CANAL

205.—Even travel by canal packet had its dangers in the eyes of the early cartoonist.

character, all being outgrowths of previous pioneer conditions, that were to become noticeable in the years witnessing the birth of interstate turnpikes, canals and railroads. Those qualities were inventiveness, cocksureness, and a desire for argument. The facility with which the American pioneer had long devised expedients

688

fitted for his need was to be again proved. Through the manifestation of his versatility in that respect the transportation system created by him at once assumed its own individuality and was characterized, from the first, by many devices that he originated.

The popular tendency to argument, so prominently displayed in connection with the newly realized travel and transportation needs of society, grew out of the long national isolation and tendency to soliloquize which have already been mentioned.

Those human qualities that had been necessary for doing what had already been done by the American people were hardihood, directness of purpose and dogged determination. The task hitherto performed — notwithstanding its immensity — had been one essentially simple in its character. The knowledge they had gained during the process had been so drilled into their lives that it had literally become a part of them. The things they did know they knew most marvellously well. They had been so long isolated with regard to other Caucasian peoples and exterior information that they had gradually arrived at a state of mind which virtually ignored the existence of other conditions than their own. They were extraordinarily wise through the small arc of their own experience, and equally ignorant and narrow-minded throughout the remainder of the circle of human life and work. But since the remainder of that circle was unknown to them, and since they did possess a conscious mastery of their own environment, they imagined that their wisdom might be applied with propriety and profit to all departments of human affairs. Hence the phenomenon of American cock-sureness, a national trait whose most acute symptoms are perceptibly subsiding under the soothing ministrations of time, and which, in days soon to come, will seemingly be brought so far under control as to warrant a firm hope of complete recovery.

They had not hitherto been constantly required to apply a knowledge already obtained to the solution of new and radically different conditions of existence. They were in a rut, so far as methods of community life were concerned, and had been long in that situation. They had not discovered that ability to grasp the vital principle governing any social or economic condition, coupled with moral and mental strength to sweep away outgrown processes connected with its former use and courage to apply the principle itself—divested of hampering customs—in an effort toward achieving a better condition, is one of the highest manifestations of a people's civilization.

For these reasons the members of the last pioneer generation of Americans did not possess the qualifications which would have enabled them to attack with undiluted success the new situation faced by them. Probably no people so situated, and with such a past, could have done it. The wonder is, rather, that they succeeded so well as they did. Blind in large measure to their own deficiencies, and upheld by a supreme self-confidence and energy, they set about the work which was theirs to do. The creation of modern turnpikes, canals and railroads began.

CHAPTER XXXII

ORIGIN OF THE NATIONAL ROAD — THE GOVERNMENT
ADOPTS THE POLICY OF BUILDING TRANSPORTATION
FACILITIES BY PUBLIC FUNDS — THE OHIO LAW OF
1802 — ITS SIGNIFICANCE — LATER CONGRESSIONAL
ACTS PROVIDING FOR PUBLIC ROADS THROUGH THE
INTERIOR — CONSENT OF THE STATES FOR THEIR
CONSTRUCTION NO LONGER ASKED — JEFFERSON AND
MADISON FAVOR THE WORK — TWENTY YEARS OF
UNIFORM FEDERAL ATTITUDE — MONROE'S VETO OF
1822 — ITS POSSIBLE RELATION TO GOVERNMENTAL
RAILROAD BUILDING — A CONTROVERSY ARISES OVER
THE CONSTITUTIONAL POWERS OF THE NATION —
HENRY CLAY'S VISION OF THE FUTURE — HIS TEM-
PORARY VICTORY — PRESIDENT JACKSON REVERSES
THE COUNTRY'S POLICY AND THE NATIONAL ROAD IS
DIVIDED AMONG THE STATES

IT was said in a previous chapter that the inspiration
for the building of the important governmental traffic
route — the old National Road — came from the West,
and that the work itself, though begun in the East,[1] was
commenced in response to the repeated and imperative demands of the western pioneers. It should be added here
that the realization of the western desire was long delayed
by two causes. The first of these was the slowness with
which that part of the highway east of the Ohio River
was completed, and the other was due to a political strug-

---

[1] As a westward extension of existing roads.

691

gle arising from a contention that the Constitution did not confer upon the central government the power to undertake public improvements of the kind in progress.

The National Road — or Cumberland Road, as it was at first called — was begun in Maryland in 1808 and did not reach the border of Ohio until nine years afterward, in 1817. The first congressional act looking toward its creation was passed in 1802, and the Federal decision to unite the Atlantic coast with the Mississippi River by an overland governmental highway was reached in 1806. But it was not until 1820 that the work of surveying and locating the exact position of the road was begun through Ohio, Indiana and Illinois, and not until 1825 — after a national political campaign fought largely over the constitutional question just mentioned — that heavy appropriations for its construction through the interior were made and the enterprise pushed forward in that part of the country.

The purpose of the government to build a continuous road from the East to the Mississippi — as that pioneer intent existed before structural operations began on any section of the route — is shown in the message with which President Jefferson submitted to Congress a statement of the course chosen for the road in the East. Under date of February 19, 1808, he said:

". . . I shall pay material regard to the interests and wishes of the populous parts of the State of Ohio, and to a future and convenient connection with the road which is to lead from the Indian boundary near Cincinnati, by Vincennes, to the Mississippi at St. Louis, under authority of the act of April 21, 1806. In this way we may accomplish a continuous and advantageous line of communication from the seat of the General Government to St. Louis, passing through several very interesting points, to the Western country."

The genesis of the movement which resulted in the

A NEW BERTH.

Candid Landlady. "THE FIRST FROM THE TOP, SIR, IS THE ONLY BED VACANT; BUT YOU HAVE GOT VERY NICE NEIGHBORS—ONE GENTLEMAN CHEWS, BUT THE OTHERS ONLY SMOKE!"

206.—Cartoon indicating the opinion entertained by travellers toward the sleeping-bunk system so long offered for their accommodation by barges, steamboats and canal boats. Boarding-house landladies did not equip their bedrooms in that manner, but the artist apparently intended to suggest that they also might decide to adopt the prevailing fashion.

building of this transportation route from the East to the interior by public funds, as an interstate Federal project for the benefit of the entire country, is to be found in a law of April 30, 1802, entitled "An Act to Enable the People of the Eastern Division of the Territory

693

Northwest of the River Ohio to form a Constitution and State Government, and for other Purposes." Section 7, Article III, of the Act read:

"That one-twentieth part of the net proceeds of the land lying within the said State [Ohio] sold by Congress, from and after the thirtieth of June next, after deducting all expenses incident to the same, shall be applied to the laying out and making public roads, leading from the navigable waters emptying into the Atlantic, to the Ohio, to the said State, and through the same, such roads to be laid out under the authority of Congress, with the consent of the several States through which the road shall pass."

Commonplace as this language appears, the paragraph just quoted contained potentialities hardly surpassed in importance by those of any other law enacted by Congress during its history. For although the purpose of the act was merely the making of a turnpike, it affirmed the government's acquirement of powers so broad in their character that the nation, under its operation and the operation of later laws of like nature and purpose, was afterward brought within close and measurable distance of building its own railroads as Federal enterprises. A consideration of the circumstances accompanying, and developing out of the act, will indicate its character.

The present constitutional government had been put in operation in 1789. Vermont had entered the "Union" in 1791, but the admission of that state, owing to her location, had not brought up the question of communication facilities between her and her sister commonwealths. Kentucky and Tennessee became states in 1792 and 1796 respectively, but, as has been seen, they were already united with the East by usable roads created through pioneer enterprise. With Ohio — destined to be fourth in the list of new states — the situation was different. The northern edge of her territory could be reached by way

694

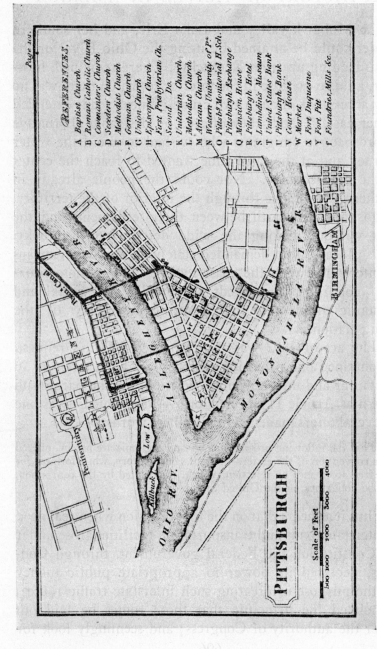

PITTSBURGH

Scale of Feet

500 1000 2000 3000 4000

207.—Pittsburgh, the most important gate to the Mississippi valley in the era of water travel. Map of the town during the steamboat and canal days, and before railways reached the city. From Baird's "View of the Valley of the Mississippi: 1834."

of the Mohawk valley and Lake Erie, and her southern border could be attained by using the Ohio River or the roads leading up from Kentucky. There remained, however, a large expanse in the interior to which there was no easy access, for, though two crude pioneer roads extended to her eastern lands they offered no desirable alternative to prospective emigrants who wished to avoid the water journey and at the same time wanted to reach the center of the new country. Nor could the people already in southern Ohio move through the interior of the territory, or go back and forth between their settlements and the East without making the wide détour into Kentucky. Thus placed, Ohio demanded statehood and better means of intercourse with the coast region. Her remote situation, condition and needs presented a new social and economic problem to the operating machinery of the young nation.

The act of 1802 was the response to Ohio's request. It contained one provision which placed the territory in a peculiar and unprecedented position, for the paragraph known as Article III of Section 7—just quoted—was one of several offers made to Ohio in these words:

"That the following propositions be, and the same are hereby, offered to the convention of the eastern State of said territory, when formed, for their free acceptance or rejection, which, if accepted by the convention, shall be obligatory on the United States."

Thus it appears that on the first occasion when real need of interstate roads and transportation facilities arose under the Constitution the Federal government, through Congress, declared its power to appropriate public money for the purpose of creating such interstate traffic routes; enunciated the principle that those routes be laid out under the authority of Congress; and seemingly took for granted the consent of any affected states. It went further, for it laid on Ohio the alternative of accepting or rejecting—as part of her basic law—the proposition that the central government had power to build a transportation route through her jurisdiction. Ohio could have become a state—under the phraseology of the enabling act—even though she had rejected the proposition. But she did not; she accepted it, and so entered the Union on the basis of an acknowledgment that the Federal administration had authority to build traffic routes in and through the state, and with knowledge that such action would be taken.

Ohio became a state under the act of 1802, and in due course of time a Congressional committee, to which the subject of the planned interstate road had been referred, made a report[1] recommending that the eastern section of the route extend from Cumberland, in Maryland, to Wheeling, in Virginia. In the report it was stated, among other things, that

"They [the committee] suppose that to take the proper measures for carrying into effect the section of the law respecting a road or roads to the State of Ohio, is a duty imposed upon Congress by the law itself, and that a sense of duty will always be sufficient to insure the passage of the bill now offered to the Senate. To enlarge upon the highly important considerations of cementing the union of our citizens located on the Western waters with those of the Atlantic states would be an indelicacy offered to the understanding of the body to whom this report is addressed, as it might seem to distrust them."

The bill providing for the building of a Federal interstate highway was passed by Congress, and approved by President Jefferson on March 29, 1806. The four states of Maryland, Virginia, Pennsylvania and Ohio, through which it was to extend, duly communicated to the gov-

[1] On December 19, 1805. Senate Document Number 195.—Ninth Congress; First Session.

ernment their consent[1] as suggested in the act of 1802, and work was begun.

Indiana was the next territory lying across the projected line of the government's road which sought statehood and better transportation connections with the East. The law admitting her to the Union was dated April 19, 1816, and Section 6, of Article III—after confronting her with the identical alternative faced by Ohio—read:

"That five per cent. of the net proceeds of lands lying within the said territory, and which shall be sold . . . from and after the first day of December next, after deducting all expenses incident to the same, shall be reserved for making public roads and canals, of which three-fifths shall be applied to those objects within the said State, under the direction of the Legislature thereof, and two-fifths[2] to the making of a road or roads leading to the said State under the direction of Congress."

It will be observed that this legislation differs from the law dealing with Ohio in an important respect which suggests that the power of the general government to construct interstate traffic facilities without regard to the attitude of the states had by that time ceased to be a questionable matter even to the extent fairly to be inferred from the act of 1802. For the Congress announces an intention to build a road or roads leading toward Indiana without reference to the consent of any states through which it or they might pass.

Two years afterward Illinois was authorized to erect a state government,[3] and again did Section 6 of Article III—after the usual alternative and land-sale preliminaries—read:

"Two-fifths to be disbursed, under the direction of Congress, in

[1] Virginia and Maryland consented later in 1806 and Pennsylvania in April of 1807. Ohio's consent was given in her acceptance of the act as the basis of her constitution.
[2] In 1803 a supplementary law in relation to Ohio had been passed apportioning the Ohio money in a similar ratio, so that three-fifths of it, or three per cent., should be devoted to building roads within the state, and two per cent. to the road or roads leading to the state.
[3] The date of the Act was April 18, 1818.

208.—View of Pittsburgh and the Ohio River below the city at the height of the water-travel period and before the coming of the railway.

making roads leading to the state; the residue to be appropriated, by the Legislature of the State, for the encouragement of learning. . . ."

By the terms of this law, a road leading to Illinois through Indiana could not come under the supervision of the Indiana legislature, but was placed "under the direction of Congress." This feature of the act, when considered in connection with the Indiana law of 1816, may indicate the existence of a distinction, at that time, between the interstate highway in process of creation and other roads local in character. Again was there no reference to the consent of such states as might be traversed by the roads which Congress announced would be built by the government toward Illinois. In 1820 Missouri's entrance to the Union was authorized,[1] and the familiar Section 6 of Article III in her case read:

"Five per cent. . . . shall be reserved for making public roads and canals, of which three-fifths shall be applied to those objects within the State, under the direction of the Legislature thereof; and the other two-fifths in defraying, under the direction of Congress, the expenses to be incurred in making a road or roads, canal or canals, leading to the said State."

Two months afterward[2] the national lawmakers made provision for surveying the route to be followed by the Cumberland Road in its future extension from Wheeling to the Mississippi River. By the year 1817 the thoroughfare was in use to Wheeling, and from 1802 until the date named fourteen governmental acts had been placed on the statute books in connection with its creation, after being formulated by ten Congresses and signed by three Presidents during five Presidential terms.

We see in these events, then, the birth, establishment and maintenance of a continuous Federal policy having

[1] The date of the Act was March 6, and it contained the same chance to accept or reject the road proposition.
[2] By Act of May 15, 1820.

for its object the building of a transportation route by public funds for the general welfare. At the inception of the plan, in 1802, the government seemingly took for granted the consent of some states to its operations within their limits and received their consent, meanwhile offering to a new state the chance to reject the large Federal power implied. After that time, during an interval of twenty years, the general government no longer directly requested state consent for its traffic-route enterprises but, as occasion arose, gave territories the choice that has been defined. The later acts of the series were weightier than the earlier ones in their suggestion of Federal power, since neither in providing for roads leading to Illinois, nor in allotting governmental funds for a road or roads to Missouri, was Illinois or its legislature mentioned.

Two other features contained in this series of laws call for attention. They indicate that Congress thought of the possibility of building more than one road if it so chose, and they show that the government did not consider itself limited to turnpikes as the only constituent parts of the Federal transportation system, but that it believed itself able to create other kinds of traffic routes, such as canals, if it saw fit to do so. By the year 1820 the government was apparently established in a position — based on public opinion and approved as indicated by the action of the people's legislative representatives and executives — that would have permitted it, without the alteration of its policy or of any other element in the situation, to build railways just as it was already building an interstate roadway or just as it proposed to build canals if it so decided.

Then befell an action by President Monroe the first effect of which was to precipitate a violent political and

701

economic controversy over the government's attitude toward interstate transportation facilities, and whose ultimate result was a reversal of the established Federal policy regarding that subject and an abandonment of the National Road as a national undertaking. On May 4, 1822, he vetoed an act "for the preservation and repair of the Cumberland Road," saying that he did so "under a conviction that Congress do not possess the power, under the Constitution, to pass such a law." His message went on to say:

"A power to establish turnpikes, with gates and tolls, and to enforce the collection of tolls by penalties, implies a power to adopt and execute a complete system of internal improvements. . . . A right to legislate for one of these purposes is a right to legislate for the others. It is a complete right of jurisdiction and sovereignty for all the purposes of internal improvement, and not merely the right of applying money under the power vested in Congress to make appropriations (under which power, with the consent of the States through which the road passes, the work was originally commenced, and has been so far executed). I am of opinion that Congress do not possess this power. . . ."

It is not likely that the President, when here speaking of the work "so far executed," referred to the manual labor then in progress as an outcome of the governmental mandates. He was discussing national prerogatives and policy. But if he did have in mind that phase of the undertaking when he said the work so far executed had been done "with the consent of the states through which the road passes," it is only needful to remember that, for the two years preceding, part of the human labor involved on the roadway had been performed in the jurisdictions of Ohio, Indiana and Illinois, in connection with surveying and laying out the thoroughfare. That work was being done under the direction of Congress, at the expense of the national treasury. When Monroe made his statement concerning the relationship of the states to the work so

702

GREAT CONFLAGRATION AT PITTSBURGH PA.
APRIL 10th '45 '45

209.—The Pittsburgh Fire of 1845, at the height of the city's importance as water gate to the West. Most important of the early pictorial "Catastrophe Broadsides." Steamboats, bridges and about 1,200 buildings were burned.

far executed, the Federal government had created by legislation a highway extending from Maryland to Missouri; had provided financial means for its progress throughout its length; had completed much of it, and was at public cost fixing its exact course through that part of its extent still unfinished. And the government had not, for sixteen years, directly asked the consent of any state crossed by the work or had its action in the matter challenged by any state concerned.[1] The congressional representatives of all the states had formulated the acts by which those things were done. Three laws providing for further road building on the highway between the Ohio and Mississippi Rivers, under the direction of Congress, had been passed during Monroe's administration and signed by him.

From that time the broad subject of Federal rights and duties in matters affecting the public irrespective of state boundaries became in much larger degree a shuttle-cock of politics in an era of increasingly violent partisanship. Party strategy and the possibility of personal or corporate advantage gradually became paramount to other considerations in determining the economic course of the country.

Monroe, indeed, was right in his definition of the significance contained in the attitude so long held by the nation. The series of related acts passed by the legislative branch of the government, beginning in 1802 and ending with the one vetoed by him twenty years later, did imply, as he said, "a power to adopt and execute a complete system of internal improvements."

Thus close did the country come to the building and

---

[1] The consents of Virginia, Maryland and Pennsylvania had not been embodied in their basic laws, and could have been withdrawn, though it is by no means certain that the rest of the country would have stopped the work in that event.

704

ownership of its railways from the beginning. Within three years after Monroe's veto of 1822 the first railway of the world designed as a public utility[1] was in operation; within four years thereafter the probable value of railroads as a method of travel and transportation was the principal subject of economic discussion in America; and one year afterward American state charters were being asked and granted for the construction of railways by private corporations. By that time the government would have found itself face to face with the question of building railroads as public enterprises, and — if the new transportation method proved advantageous — might have entered naturally and logically into their creation under the policy it had pursued since 1802. Only by that action could it have kept abreast of progress and the needs of the people in the one matter then of supremest importance to them. President Monroe's action challenged Federal right to compete with corporate enterprise in supplying the people with those public utilities most requisite for their general welfare and daily use. No other method than that could seemingly have diverted the country from its established policy to another and radically different position which permitted the country's most important interstate and national highways to become projects of corporate creation, financial speculation and eventual private fortune-building accomplished to an unknown degree by illegitimate inflation of capital and service charges fixed in accordance therewith.

The juxtaposition of Monroe's veto and the appearance of the first railroads was a fateful coincidence. The significance of the American government's attitude from 1802 to 1822; its later logical result if uninterrupted; the

[1] The Stockton and Darlington road, in England.

date of the appearance of railways; the clouding of American pioneer purpose by argument over the technical legality of that purpose; and the effect produced by diverting the government's activity from its previous channel, are matters possessing a close relationship. If the radical alteration in the national policy at a most critical time of American economic history was not brought about by any contemporaneous foresight of its enormous consequences, then the chain of events here outlined does indeed indicate how profoundly the affairs of men are sometimes affected by the whims of chance.

The only specific Constitutional authorization bearing upon the point at issue so strongly emphasized by Monroe was the clause which provides that Congress shall have the power "to establish Post Offices and Post Roads." "Strict constructionists" denied that this gave the general government a right to undertake such work as the building of interstate communication facilities. "Broad constructionists" of the Hamiltonian school met the argument with their doctrine of "implied powers," and pointing to the "general welfare" clause and that other "elastic clause" which confers upon Congress the right "to make all Laws which shall be necessary and proper for carrying into Execution the foregoing Powers," contended that the authority of the central government was ample for such internal improvements.

It should not be understood that the attitude of Congress toward the Cumberland Road was always uniform, even before Monroe's veto of 1822, or that the national legislature gave a continuous measure of unanimous approval to all other plans of internal improvement. That was not the case. Sometimes a Congress would be elected in which the preponderance of sentiment was so strongly in favor of such general welfare work that the bills in behalf of the government's road would be decisively passed as a matter of course. At other times a Congress would be returned whose membership was more equally divided with regard to the wisdom or constitutional propriety of the procedure on which the country had embarked, and then there would be long — often sharp and earnest — debates on the subject, and the interstate road bill would be temporarily beaten, or carried by a smaller majority than usual. But the general trend of thought was always in favor of the project, and — even after it had been made a subject of factional argument and a pawn in the struggle for political supremacy — the only substantial opposition to it was outwardly based on doubt respecting the constitutional power of the government to create such a thoroughfare as a national undertaking.

Monroe's predecessor — Madison — had been one of those who favored the creation of an interstate transportation system by Federal authority and the use of treasury funds, even though he was at times doubtful whether the Constitution contained provisions specific enough to warrant the performance. But his doubt on the point was evidently not sufficiently marked to influence him against the Cumberland Road project, for during his presidency he signed seven bills authorizing the expenditure of money for its building. His attitude toward governmental participation in highway and canal construction was shown in his annual message of December 5, 1815, when he discussed the subject in these words:

"Among the means of advancing the public interest, the occasion is a proper one for rousing the attention of Congress to the great importance of establishing throughout our country the roads and canals which can best be executed under the national authority. No objects within the circle of political economies so richly repay the expense bestowed upon them. There are none the utility of which is more universally ascertained and acknowledged; none that do more honor to the Government. . . . Nor is there any country which presents a field where nature invites more the art of man to complete her own work for their accommodation and benefit. The considerations are strengthened, moreover, by the political effect of these facilities for intercommunication and bringing and binding more closely together the various parts of our extended confederacy.

"Whilst the states, individually, with a laudable enterprise and emulation, avail themselves of their local advantages by new roads, by navigable canals and by improving the streams susceptible of navigation, the general government is the more urged to similar undertakings requiring a national jurisdiction and national means, by the prospect of thus systematically completing so inestimable a work. And it is a happy reflection that any defect of constitutional authority which may be encountered can be supplied in the mode which the Constitution itself has providentially pointed out."[1]

Jefferson had looked with favor on Federal participation in the making of a national transportation system, for he had approved the basic law of 1802 that provided for a road to Ohio. It was also during his presidency, and by his financial secretary, Gallatin, that the plan for the Cumberland Road was proposed as an administration measure. The construction work on it was begun by Jefferson after he had asked and received the consent of the first states involved.

On at least one occasion, namely in 1824, the national campaign for the presidency was fought largely on the issue of the government's constitutional right to build roads and canals. Despite the obvious benefit to the country of the construction of such an East and West interstate highway as a national road, the thoroughfare in question could only occupy a certain specific location,

[1] On the day before retiring from office he did veto one bill setting aside money received by the government from the second United States Bank and the proceeds of the bank shares held by the government, for the purpose of constructing roads and canals. In his veto message he said: "The power to regulate commerce among the several states cannot include a power to construct roads and canals, and to improve the navigation of water courses, in order to facilitate, promote, and secure such a commerce, without a latitude of construction departing from the ordinary import of the terms."

Those who advocated such work, however, did not base their support of it on the constitutional power to regulate commerce between the states.

708

and some of its benefits, in consequence, were naturally more apparent in the immediate vicinity of the highway than in regions remote from it. This inevitable condition aroused the jealousy of the states and districts it did not penetrate — or at least the jealousy of various political leaders in those localities. The people as a whole were in favor of the enterprise, whereas some public men both of large and petty importance were willing it should be discontinued—provided its further extension brought no personal benefit to them — rather than behold the country reap advantages from its existence. The use of political warfare over an economic policy which contained no element of partisanship or incentive thereto was but a further manifestation of a long existing condition. Again did the masses of the people have clearer vision than their ostensible leaders. In matters touching the economic and social well-being of a nation its citizens prefer to turn unheeding from any advice or plea to which suspicion of self-interest may attach, and decide the question in the light of experience gained by themselves or others, according to their best understanding. If instead they permit themselves to be inflamed by appeals to partisanship they lose in corresponding degree the faculty of judgment and more easily become the dupes of designing men. An error of popular judgment attributable to no other cause than lack of knowledge or careless thought is reasonably sure of speedy detection and correction, whereas the public error born of passion and nurtured by partisanship breeds still further passion and more error when its victims recognize their situation and seek to escape from its effects.

The popular champion of the westward extension of the Cumberland Road was Henry Clay. He advocated the measure as one national in its character, beneficial to all the country and not merely to the West. He pointed out that not one of the three states in which were contained the entire extent of the original Cumberland Road — nor all of them together — would of their own volition have created that highway; that two of them, in fact, afterward tried for a short time to place impediments in the way of its completion. During the campaign of 1824, as part of an address advocating the participation of the central government in the creation of improved transportation facilities, he thus gave utterance to his vision of the future:[1]

"The gentleman from Virginia sought to alarm us by the awful emphasis by which he stated the total extent of post road in the Union. 'Eighty thousand miles of post road!' exclaims the gentleman; 'and will you assert for the general government's jurisdiction and erect turnpikes at such an immense distance?' Not to-day, nor to-morrow, but this government is to last, I trust, forever; we may at least hope it will endure until the wave of population, cultivation, and intelligence shall have washed the Rocky Mountains and mingled with the Pacific. And may we not also hope that the day will arrive when the improvements and comforts to social life shall spread over the vast area of this continent? . . . It is a peculiar delight to me to look forward to the proud and happy period, distant as it may be, when circulation and association between the Atlantic and Pacific and the Mexican Gulf shall be as free and perfect as they are at this moment in England or in any other country of the globe."

Clay was at last temporarily victorious. Congress passed a law appropriating one hundred and fifty thousand dollars for further work on an extension of the road through Ohio, Indiana and Illinois, and directing the completion of the survey ordered by the act of May 15, 1820. This act was approved and signed by Monroe on March 3, 1825, as one of his last Presidential duties. It was the first piece of legislation in behalf of the Na-

[1] In his speech of January 31. Text from the "Western Censor" (Indianapolis, Ind.) of March 22, 1824.

MR. GORDON'S NEW STEAM CARRIAGE.

210.—Two ancestors of the twentieth-century motor-car. David Gordon's patent was dated 1824. He thought it was necessary to imitate the action of horses' feet, and his car was propelled by mechanical legs. The other carriage was made by Horace Gurney, about 1848, and had a speed of $8\frac{1}{2}$ miles an hour on common roads.

tional Road west of Wheeling that had been enacted since Monroe, in his veto of 1822, had brought forward in acute form the subject of the government's constitutional right to do the work. The building of the turnpike then went ahead, and during John Quincy Adams' administration— between 1825 and 1829— that Executive approved eight bills carrying appropriations aggregating nearly three-quarters of a million dollars for maintaining the highway and extending it westward.

But the question previously raised by Monroe — and especially his clear definition of the tremendous significance contained in the government's previous policy — was having its effect. By the time Jackson took office, in 1829, two conditions were clearly visible. Railroads were in actual process of construction, for one thing; and the doctrine that the central government had no power in or over a state except as specifically and unmistakably set forth by the Constitution was in the ascendency. These two factors in the national life— one economic and the other political—interacted on each other, and both influenced the government's attitude toward the National Road. Jackson himself was a "state's rights" man in the broad sense of the term, and his opinions on that subject were in harmony with those of the party which had placed him in power. He did not permit his belief to affect his financial support of the National Road, for during the eight years of his Presidency he approved ten laws appropriating nearly three and three-quarter millions of dollars for that enterprise, but he did oppose Federal ownership and control of the highway, and during his administration the several sections of the road were transferred to those states within whose borders they lay.

Thus, at the commencement of the railway era, the existing national policy which if continued could have resulted in Federal building of railroads was reversed, and it naturally followed that administrative endorsement for any proposals for governmental creation of the new metal highways was impossible while Jackson remained the chief executive. Those were the critical years during which the economic method of railroad building in America was decided.

Although Jackson's natural habit of mind was doubtless in harmony with the position he took toward the National Road, his attitude in that matter and kindred questions was very possibly strengthened by a certain situation encountered by him during the first part of his Presidency. The earlier governmental adoption of a policy that Federal resources might be constitutionally used in the creation of public thoroughfares had uncovered a rich stream of popular avarice. It had resulted in a widespread effort to obtain national assistance not only for important and necessary projects, but for a multitude of enterprises entirely local in character and which had no justifiable claim for the assistance of the central treasury. Instead of formulating a clear-cut, carefully planned and reasonable scheme for developmental work under the adopted policy, Congress had gradually become the theater of a mad scramble in which nearly all states and sections of states took part, in an endeavor to obtain public money for small, unimportant and nonnational enterprises. This tendency had become especially evident during the years from 1825 to 1829, in which period the need of improved transportation was a subject uppermost in public thought. Hundreds of these schemes were doubtless devised without expectation of their value

713

or permanent success as economic undertakings, but in the hope that the physical construction called for by them would bring rich profits to their projectors.

By the year 1830 bills had appeared in Congress for the proposed construction of isolated and disconnected turnpikes, canals, railroads and similar enterprises whose completion would have required more than two hundred and sixty millions of dollars. This state of affairs made it apparent that a rigid line must be drawn which would effectively exclude non-national public works from participation in national support, or else the Federal government would be compelled to abandon its position that the investment of treasury funds in such construction was warranted by the Constitution. The question thus presented became an important issue throughout the country, and in 1830 President Jackson took occasion, on the presentation to him of a bill which had been passed for the building of a small local turnpike,[1] to write a very strong veto message in which he pointed out that the government had no right to use its money for the creation of any enterprises confined wholly to individual states. His position was generally endorsed by the press and public, and the proposed raids on the treasury decreased from that time on.

At the time President Jackson vetoed the Maysville Road Bill not less than a hundred and eleven surveys, estimates and plans for canals, roads, railroads and river improvements were formally before Congress. These, it was calculated, would cost about sixty-three million dollars. Other similar projected improvements — not so far advanced in legislative consideration — would have cost two hundred million dollars more. At that period the

[1] The Maysville Road Bill. The project was a proposed turnpike sixty miles in length and lying wholly within the state of Kentucky.

714

total Federal receipts were only about twenty-four million dollars a year, of which sum ten per cent. was appropriated for decreasing the national debt, leaving less than twenty-two million dollars a year for paying all other operating expenses of the government. It was therefore obvious that embarkation in such an overwhelming amount of work as was contemplated by the mass of bills for public improvements — even though they had all been legitimately deserving of support under the policy adopted by the government — was out of the question.

President Jackson's action in calling a halt to the effort to use public money in local enterprises did not, however — as has been shown — apply to the National Road. Even Jackson, at the same time he wrote his elaborate message vetoing the Maysville Road Bill, approved another act which appropriated two hundred and fifteen thousand dollars[1] additional for the further extension and improvement of the government-built turnpike.

As originally planned, the Cumberland Road from Cumberland to Wheeling, a distance of practically one hundred and thirty miles, was to cost one and three-quarter millions of dollars. The further westward projection of the highway brought it to Columbus, Ohio, in 1833, and to Vandalia, Illinois, in 1852. More than thirty acts of Congress contained provisions for its building and maintenance between 1806 and 1838, and its total cost to the government was not far from seven millions of dollars.[2]

The roadway was made eighty feet wide, with a central section thirty feet in width covered with broken stone a foot deep and topped with a surface layer of gravel.

[1] Of which sum $115,000 was to be expended in Ohio, $60,000 in Indiana, and $40,000 in Illinois.
[2] Some estimates put the figure at about ten millions. The difficulty of analyzing and tracing early financial legislation makes it impossible to give the exact amount.

But this turnpike construction was not continued west of Indiana. Long before the road reached the town of Terre Haute, on the western edge of that state, it was realized by the people that the highway and its stage-coaches were not destined to be the chief means and method for all future communication with the East. Canals had come, only to be threatened in their turn by the westward creeping iron rails, and desire turned from the old ways to seek the new. So the turnpike lapsed into a dirt road across the prairies of Illinois and finally came to an end at Vandalia, whence another similar route led onward to St. Louis.

CHAPTER XXXIII

LIFE AND SCENES ON THE NATIONAL ROAD — THE TYPE OF
MEN WHO WORKED UPON IT — THREE CHARACTER-
ISTIC FEATURES OF ITS TRAFFIC — FURTHER EVOLU-
TION OF THE STAGE-COACH AND IMPOSING APPEARANCE
OF THE VEHICLE IN ITS FINAL FORM — SOME FAMOUS
DRIVERS — FEATS OF HOMER WESTOVER AND REDDING
BUNTING — CONESTOGA WAGON TRAINS AND THE
WAGONERS WHO PILOTED THEM — THE JOKE ON
GUSTY MITCHELL — HOG MUSIC — PROGRESS OF A
PRESIDENT'S MESSAGE — FATE OF TRAVELLERS WHO
JOURNEYED WITH THE DOCUMENT — SPECIAL
COACHES FOR THE PRESIDENTS THEMSELVES — VAN
BUREN'S ACCIDENT — INCENSE TO THE MEMORY OF
A VANISHED DAY

THE first stage-coach which rumbled over the entire
eastern section of the famous interstate highway between Cumberland and Wheeling reached the last-named
town on August 1, 1817. After that date the project—as
far as its value to the interior was concerned — remained
at a standstill for a number of years. But after its extension through the Mississippi valley, and from about
1827 until about 1850, the National Road became the
chief east-and-west artery of traffic from the Atlantic
seaboard to the middle states. Its activities not only intimately affected the growth of the interior, but throughout its entire length played an important part in the

regions which it traversed. Thousands of individuals were concerned, as a matter of business enterprise, in its maintenance and in the traffic which it bore. The tavern keepers, wagoners, packmen, stage drivers, hostlers, and all others who spent their lives in going back and forth upon it, or in ministering to the needs of travellers, were very largely the descendants of English emigrants, and their names furnish an interesting exhibit of one element which had colonized the country.[1]

The following is a list of some of the well-known characters of the National Road during the heyday of its importance:

Charles Allum	John Guttery	Samuel Riddlemoser
Davis Ashkettle	Robert Hogsett	Jeph Riggle
Samuel Breakbill	James Klink	Basil Sheets
Jacob Breakiron	John Livingood	Caldwell Slobworth
Redding Bunting	Michael Longstaff	Samuel Sidebottom
George Buttermore	Jeff Manypenny	Isaac Skiles
David Bonebraker	John Mauler	Philip Slipe
George Clum	Spencer Motherspaw	John Smasher
Caleb Crossland	Baptist Mullinix	Quill Smith
Joseph Doak	James Noggle	Nimrod Sopher
Hugh Drum	John Olivine	Michael Teeters
Paris Eaches	Abner Peirt	Thomas Thistle
Frank Earlocker	Peter Penner	Jacob Wagoner
George Gump	Elias Petticord	Adam Yeast

A knowledge of the methods used in constructing the highway can be obtained from newspapers of the time. When Congress had authorized its opening through Ohio and Indiana, the Indiana superintendents of the work published advertisements in the papers of the state in June, 1829, reciting the conditions required of the contractors. The road there, as elsewhere, was to be eighty feet wide, and for a width of thirty feet in the center —

[1] Nearly all these surnames have become practically extinct in modern American society.

according to the first specifications published — all stumps were to be grubbed up and removed entire. All hills were to be cut down and all valleys filled, so that no grade should exceed four degrees after the road was completed. On either side of the thirty feet all timber was to be cut and removed.

Investigation speedily brought to light the fact that such an amount of timber cutting and stump grubbing was not practicable. It would have exhausted the appropriations while building but a small part of the proposed thoroughfare. In August, therefore, the specifications for the road were amended and new ones were issued which read:

"The central part of thirty feet to be cut in the following manner, to wit:—All the trees of one foot in diameter (at one foot from the ground) and under to be cut level with the surface; all from one foot up to eighteen inches in diameter to be cut not exceeding nine inches from the surface of the ground; and all trees over eighteen inches diameter to be cut not exceeding fifteen inches from the surface; and all stumps within the said center of thirty feet must be rounded and trimmed in such a manner as to present no serious obstacles to carriages." The specifications further said that "of the remaining fifty feet all stumps must be left not exceeding one and a half feet in height."[1]

The careful manner in which is here described the extent to which stumps might be left in the most important overland traffic route then being built in the country, indicates the nature of the roads of the Middle West at that period and the difficulties which attended their use. It is evident that stumps one foot or more in width and from nine inches to fifteen inches in height were not then considered as serious obstacles to vehicular traffic. There still exists in Indiana a legend that many of the stage-coach drivers who piloted their craft over the path here described could tell on the darkest night

[1] From the "Western Sun," September 12, 1829.

whether they had strayed from the thirty feet of good road into the margin at the side.

But considering the handicaps which then beset road builders, much of the work was exceedingly well done; better in some aspects than is often the case when public works are in process of construction to-day.[1] The stumps obstructing the roadway through the three western states gradually disappeared, the surface of broken stone and gravel altered it to a turnpike in Ohio and many parts of Indiana, and for years it excellently served the purposes that inspired its creation.

That part of the National Road between Cumberland and Wheeling was much more substantially built than those portions of it lying between the Ohio River and its western terminus. Of the eastern section of the highway it has been said:

"Its numerous and stately stone bridges, with handsome, turned arches, its iron mile-posts, and its old iron gates, attest the skill of the workmen engaged on its construction, and to this day remain enduring monuments of its grandeur and solidity.[2] . . ."

The same authority just quoted gives this description of traffic on the road during the days of its greatest importance:

"As many as twenty four-horse coaches have been counted in line at one time on the road, and large, broad-wheeled wagons, covered with white canvas stretched over bows laden with merchandise and drawn by six Conestoga horses were visible all the day long at every point, and many times until late in the evening, besides innumerable caravans of horses, mules, cattle, hogs and sheep. It looked more like a leading avenue of a great city than a road through rural districts. . . .

[1] This was especially true of engineering details such as arches, stonework and bridges. An example of the conscientious methods and careful construction then in vogue is to be found in the history of the old National Road bridge at Indianapolis, Indiana. It was built of hewed yellow poplar timbers, stood without material deterioration for about sixty years, resisted many important floods of the White River unscathed, and finally had to be torn down. It was replaced by a costly modern structure of stone and concrete that was utterly demolished and swept away in 1913, after but a few years of service.

[2] Thomas B. Searight's "The Old Pike: A History of the National Road, etc." Uniontown, Pa., 1894: p. 16. Searight's book is the most important monograph dealing with the history of the Cumberland Road and the human activity along its course. The old iron gates here mentioned have disappeared.

A Reprefentation of a Coal Waggon.

211.—Development of the railway. An English coal wagon, about the year 1800. Most advanced application of the railed track principle, either in Great Britain or America, at that time. England had been running wagons on rails since about 1649, and had been making iron rails since 1738. The following one hundred and twenty-one illustrations, to No. 332 inclusive, depict the introduction of railroads into America, their improvement and effects, human experience in their use, and their westward advance toward the Mississippi River until the year 1857.

Excitement followed in the wake of the coaches all along the road. Their arrival in the towns was the leading event of each day, and they were so regular in transit that farmers along the road knew the exact hour of their coming without the aid of watch or clock. They ran night and day alike. Relays of fresh horses were placed at intervals of twelve miles as nearly as practicable. . . . Teams were changed almost in the twinkling of an eye. The coach was driven rapidly to the station, where a fresh team stood ready harnessed waiting on the roadside. The moment the team came to a halt the driver threw down the reins and almost instantly the incoming team was detached, a fresh one attached, the reins thrown back to the driver, who did not leave his seat, and away again went the coach at full speed." [1]

The three characteristic features of traffic over the National Road were the stage-coaches, the trains of Conestoga freight wagons, and pack-trains of either mules or horses — mules being usual. The stage-coaches were

[1] Searight: pp. 16 and 147.

ornate and spectacular apparitions, painted in bright colors and occasionally even gilded. Their panels were decorated with portraits of famous men, with allegorical designs or landscapes.[1] Their interiors were handsomely finished and painted, and lined with soft silk plush. The coaches were, indeed, vastly different from those elsewhere observed in the panorama of the early days. The slow and primitive canvas-covered "Stage Wagons" and "Flying Machines" of seventy-five years before had first developed into the more substantial type of vehicle such as was used throughout the East from 1780 to 1800. These, as indicated in contemporary pictures of them, had heavy wooden sides and tops. The next step in the evolution of the American stage-coach was its assumption of body lines that were slightly curved, and so pronounced did this ellipse-like tendency become that by 1820 the typical American coach was similar to the one drawn by Captain Hall of the British Navy, or the coach approaching the mansion house at Middletown, and the stage-coach of 1818. By this time the football shape was the distinguishing characteristic of the coach body. The top continued the curve of the under portion of the vehicle, and no baggage or other burden could be carried on the roof.

An ordinary stage-coach of 1820 and thereafter contained three transverse seats, and each seat accommodated three passengers. The three travellers who occupied the front seat sat with their backs toward the driver; the others faced the horses. A tenth passenger could be accommodated outside with the driver, and in fair weather

---

[1] "There was one mail coach that was especially imposing, and on its gilded sides appeared a picture of a post boy, with flying horses and horn, and beneath in gilt letters this awe-inspiring inscription:
"He comes, the herald of a noisy world,
News from all nations lumbering at his back.
"No boy who beheld that old coach will ever forget it."—Searight: p. 148.

European Magazine.

Drawn by J. Nixon Esq.

LORD PENRYN'S SLATE QUARRY,
near Bangor, N. Wales.

Published by J. Sewell at the Bible Crown & Constitution, Cornhill, November 1808.

Engraved by S. Rawle.

212.—A Welsh railroad in 1808. Several similar constructions, of which contemporary pictures are unknown, were in use in America from the year 1795. By 1812 the modern railway, in its essential features, had been described in prediction by American mechanical engineers.

this position was eagerly sought. Small luggage could be stowed away under the seats, and more bulky objects were deposited in a receptacle at the rear called a "boot." But one more noticeable change in the appearance of the stage-coach took place during the years of its widespread use. That was an abandonment of the oval roof for the comparatively flat surface on which baggage could be carried. This change also permitted a little additional space in the interior. Since those were the days before metal springs, the propriety of conveying passengers intact to their destinations — combined with a strong desire of the travelling public to be so delivered — had resulted in the creation of a device called thorough-braces. The contrivance was a pair of leather springs, or supports on which the body of the coach hung above the axles, and which transformed the old jolting of the Flying Machine into a series of oscillations that were almost equally violent, but decidedly less destructive to the occupants of the vehicle thus equipped. Thorough-braces were very long and wide, the pieces of tanned hide being either riveted or laced together, and each superimposed on another until a support equal in thickness to a dozen strips of heavy leather had been built up. On these two fore-and-aft supports the stage-coach body rested, and by their use a considerable part of the earlier discomfort of travel by stage was taken away.

The flat-topped coach — which probably first appeared about the middle of the third decade — came to be universally known as the Concord coach because its finest and most popular examples were the product of the little village of Concord, in New Hampshire. After the Concord coach appeared it soon superseded all other varieties of stage conveyances and spread through all parts

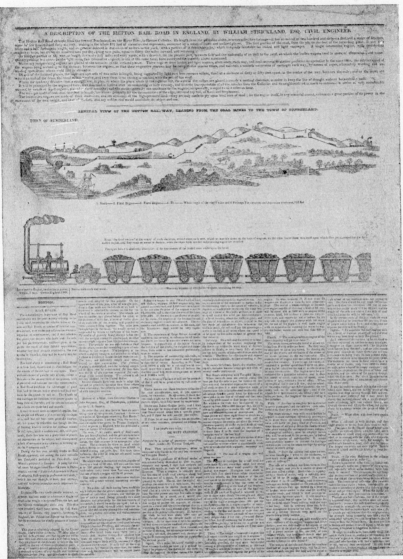

213.—The *American Traveller* Broadside issued in Boston in 1826. Probably the primary picture of an actual railway printed in the United States. Explaining the Hetton railway of England, and discussing the interest in railroads already acute in some parts of this country. First of six illustrations of early American literature on the subject.

of the country. It continued in active use in the West until as recent a date as 1880, and a few specimens are still employed in out-of-the-way localities.

Every coach on the National Road and its contemporary turnpikes had an individual name which was painted on each door. All the early heroes of the Republic as well as prominent personages of the times were immortalized by vehicles named in their honor. There was a *Washington* coach, a *Lafayette*, a *General Wayne*, a *General St. Clair*, a *General Harrison*, a *Rough and Ready*, a *Madison*, a *Monroe*, a *Henry Clay*, and even a *Columbus*, a *Pocahontas*, a *Santa Anna* and a *Queen Victoria*. Other coaches were named for the principal states and cities of the country and for foreign countries. There was also an *Erin Go Bragh*.

The two principal characteristics that exalted any particular stage-coach driver among his fellows of the craft were redoubtable feats of driving or personal peculiarities. Three of the most famous drivers of the National Road were Homer Westover, Redding Bunting and Montgomery Demming.

Westover was one of the most expert reinsmen of his time, and his feat of driving from Uniontown to Brownsville — a distance of twenty miles — in forty-five minutes long remained a record to be aimed at by his almost equally skilful competitors. This bit of work was performed as part of the task of distributing to the public printed copies of a special message addressed to Congress by Van Buren. The message was taken from Frederick to Wheeling — two hundred and twenty-two miles — in twenty-three and a half hours. A speed of almost ten miles an hour was thus maintained for a day and a night.

The famous Redding Bunting was notable for both

726

those reasons which made a driver conspicuous among his rivals. He was six feet and six inches tall without his boots, stood straight as a ramrod, had large, strong features, a red face, and a deep and powerful voice. When perched on top of the immense mail coach of the Stockton Line and guiding its splendid team of six matched horses, he assuredly cut an imposing figure. Many were his deeds of valor, but perhaps his most extraordinary accomplishment was on the occasion of the conveyance of the message in which President Polk notified the country that war with Mexico had begun. On that occasion he drove one hundred and thirty-one miles in twelve hours, or practically at the rate of eleven miles an hour. When his passengers recovered they said they would never forget him.

Montgomery Demming, while a good driver, owed his celebrity chiefly to his vast bulk. He slightly exceeded six feet in height and his average weight, when in good training, was four hundred and sixty-five pounds. But that was in the heyday of his busy career. As he grew older his size increased, and at his death he weighed six hundred and fifty pounds.

Another striking feature of daily life along the National Road was the Conestoga wagon traffic. The bottom of a Conestoga wagon curved upward both in front and rear, for a reason already stated, and all such vehicles were substantially identical in appearance. The ponderous wheels bore wrought iron tires from four to six inches in width. Six horses constituted the customary team, and the harness in which they marched was in keeping with the remainder of the massive outfit. The backbands were usually fifteen inches in width, the hip-straps were ten inches wide, and heavy black housing covered

7. But the most curious thing at Baltimore is the rail-road. I must tell you that there is a great trade between Baltimore and the states west of the Alleghany Mountains. The western people buy a great many goods at Baltimore, and send in return a great deal of western produce. There is, therefore, a vast deal of travelling back and forth, and hundreds of teams are constantly occupied in transporting goods and produce to and from market.

Rail-road Car.

8. Now, in order to carry on all this business more easily, the people are building what is called a rail-road. This consists of iron bars laid along the ground, and made fast, so that carriages with small wheels may run along upon them with facility. In this way, one horse will be able to draw as much as ten horses on a common road. A part of this rail-road is already done, and if you choose to take a ride upon it, you can do so. You will mount a car something like a stage, and then you will be drawn along by two horses, at the rate of twelve miles an hour.

214.—A description of the Baltimore and Ohio railroad in its earliest days, and picture of a horse-drawn car on it. From a schoolbook of the period.

the horses' shoulders down to the bottom of the hames. The traces by which a wagon was pulled were heavy iron chains made of short, thick links. The wagoner's saddle was a capacious seat covered with black leather and having long wide skirts. The bells used on the harness of the horses were not like the sleigh-bells of to-day. They were cone-shaped, almost as large as small dinner bells, and were fixed on wrought iron arches over the tops of the hames.

The men who had charge of these huge, gaudily colored wagons and heavily laden pack animals were a distinct class of the society of those days. They occupied, in the affairs and life of the National Road, a position very similar to that held on the rivers by the flatboat men. Their days were arduous, full of oaths, excitement and hard labor. In the early morning, after

728

hurried breakfasts, they deftly assembled their caravans amid a hurricane of loud cries and curses, and set off for the day's journey. They usually halted for an hour or two in the middle of the day at some well-known roadside hostelry where they could feed their animals, eat an enormous quantity of food themselves, and meet and argue with such acquaintances as might also have reached the same point while travelling in the opposite direction. Then, after copious drinking and boisterous farewells, they would again take up their appointed way. Many of the countrymen and settlers of the near-by districts could also be found at the taverns at such times, and on the occasion of the arrival of one or more large pack-trains and several stage-coaches laden with travellers, the scene before an inn was one of almost indescribable animation, noise and confusion.

Stage-coach travellers and freight traffic did not stop at the same taverns along the National Road.[1] When a wagoner reached his destination of the day he put his team in the wagon yard, where the horses remained until morning without regard to the state of the weather. During winter nights the animals were protected by blankets. They were fed from two feed troughs carried during the journey at the rear of the vehicle. When in use the feed troughs were attached to the wagon tongue, to which the horses were also tied, three on a side.

The wagoners carried their own bedding with them, and when they had finished their duties to the horses they took their blankets into the big assembly room of the tavern and threw them on the floor, where they themselves passed the night. Both white and negro wagoners slept at the same taverns, but the dark-skinned men ate at sep-

[1] Those taverns patronized by freight traffic were known as "wagon stands." The others were "stage houses."

arate tables. The cost of a meal at a wagon stand was twelve and a half cents; that of a drink of whisky was three cents. Two drinks ordered at the same time cost five cents.[1]

The assembly room of a wagon stand was at night the scene of many rude festivities. The wagoners drank, joked, sang and danced. They especially liked to dance, and all those establishments whose proprietors boasted a practical working acquaintance with the fiddle were sure of plentiful patronage. The spectacle presented by a hoe-down or a Virginia reel danced by thirty or forty boisterous, rollicking and roaring men, who sometimes diversified their enjoyment by resort to practical jokes and fisticuffs, must have somewhat resembled the similar antics that would have been displayed in like situation by a large den of good-natured grizzly bears. In those days the ethics and rules of practical joking were even more loose than those which now govern that branch of sport, as was attested by the experience that once befell a tavern character known as Gusty Mitchell. It was a habit of Mitchell to steal the wagoners' whisky, and one night in a spirit of playful remonstrance at his failing a group of his victims poured turpentine over him and set him on fire. Then — with some effort — they extinguished the flames before fatal injury had been inflicted on Mitchell, who abjured the company of wagoners from that hour.

The scenes in and around a wagon stand at the close of day have been thus described by one who beheld them:[2]

"I have stayed over night with William Cheets, on Nigger Mountain, when there were about thirty six-horse teams in the wagon yard, a hundred Kentucky mules in an adjoining lot, a thousand hogs in their

[1] At stage houses the cost of one drink of whisky was five cents.
[2] Searight: p. 142.

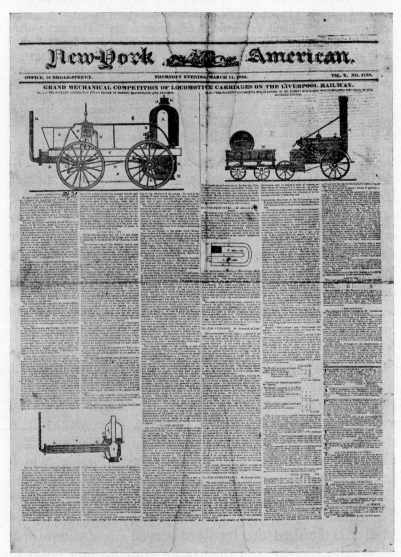

215.—The *New-York American* newspaper of March 11, 1830. Its first page was devoted to an account of the steam locomotive tests undertaken by the Liverpool and Manchester railway. The tests, thus treated as news, had taken place five months before, in October of 1829. Braithwaite's "Novelty" engine is shown on the left, and Stevenson's "Rocket" on the right.

enclosures, and as many fat cattle in adjoining fields. The music made by this large number of hogs in eating corn on a frosty night I shall never forget. After supper and attention to the teams, the wagoners would gather in the barroom and listen to the music on the violin furnished by one of their fellows, have a Virginia hoe-down, sing songs, tell anecdotes, and hear the experiences of drivers and drovers from all points of the road, and, when it was all over, unroll their beds, lay them down on the floor before the barroom fire side by side and sleep with their feet near the blaze as soundly as under the parental roof."

One of the wagoners on the National Road in its earliest days was a strong, swarthy young man named Tom Corwin. This youth afterward became a member of the lower house of Congress, and still later was Governor of Ohio and Federal Senator from that state. On an occasion while he and Henry Clay were travelling to Washington together, the two stopped one day at a stage house where Clay was well known but in which Corwin was a stranger. The landlord heard Clay address his companion as "Tom," and this incident — coupled with Corwin's dark complexion — caused the landlord to believe that Corwin was a servant of color in attendance upon the Kentucky statesman. Clay saw the opportunity for a joke on the tavern keeper, and assumed an attitude that served to confirm him in his error. Corwin, of course, fell in with the spirit of the occasion. When dinner was ready Corwin was given a place at the servants' table, which he took in a matter-of-fact way, and during the meal Clay called over to him, "How are you making out, Tom?" To which Corwin replied, "Very well, sir." After the meal was finished the landlord served his distinguished guest with a cigar, and then in an effort to find favor in the eyes of the famous Kentuckian he presented one to "Tom" also. When the stage was ready to resume its journey Clay formally introduced Corwin to the landlord, who was overwhelmed with mortification until the

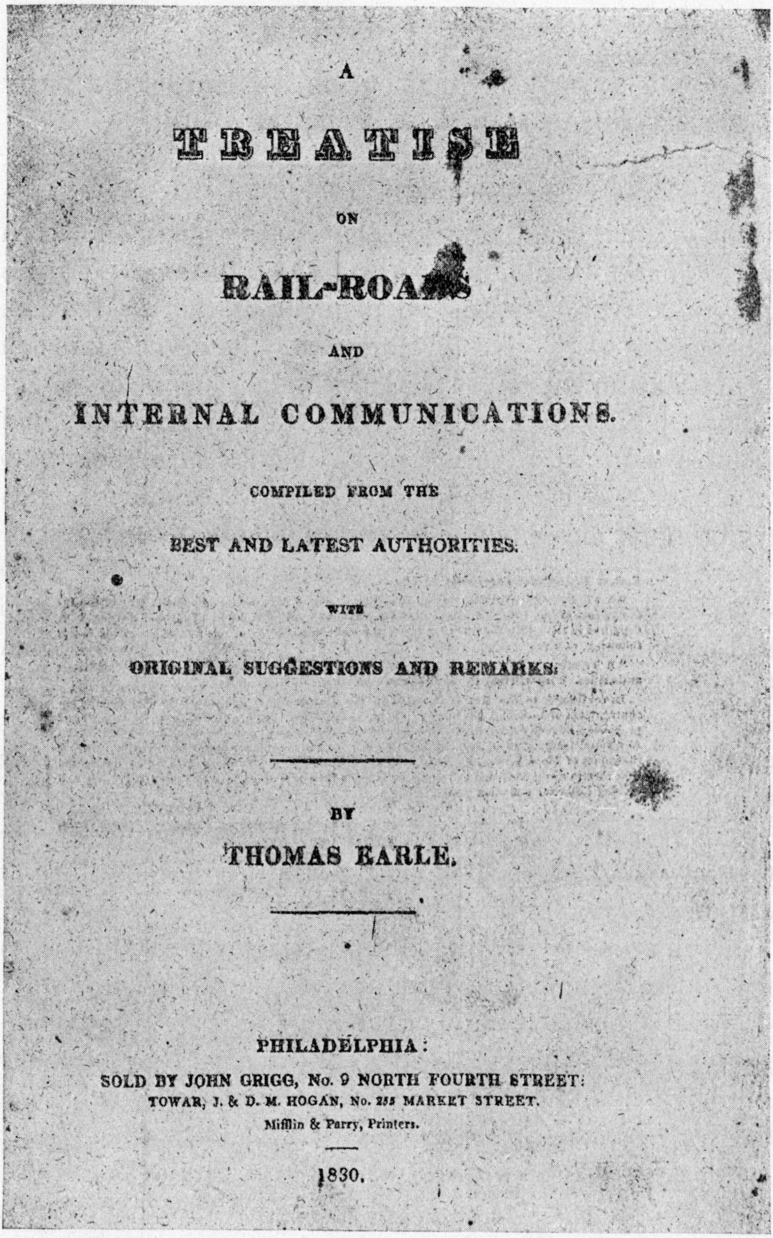

A

TREATISE

ON

RAIL-ROADS

AND

INTERNAL COMMUNICATIONS.

COMPILED FROM THE

BEST AND LATEST AUTHORITIES.

WITH

ORIGINAL SUGGESTIONS AND REMARKS.

BY

THOMAS EARLE.

PHILADELPHIA:

SOLD BY JOHN GRIGG, No. 9 NORTH FOURTH STREET;
TOWAR, J. & D. M. HOGAN, No. 255 MARKET STREET.
Mifflin & Parry, Printers.

1830.

216.—Title page of an American book on the subject of railways printed in
1830. Quotations from its opinions are given in Chapter XLII.

Ohio man pointed out that he himself had been a party to the deception.

There were still other phases of traffic over the road. There were emigrant families crawling slowly to the West in their smaller canvas-covered wagons, in which the women-folk rode by day and slept by night. Parties like these were usually independent of the taverns, yet whenever possible they encamped for the night near such an establishment in order that their members might mingle with the other travellers, listen to the news and acquire more information regarding the new regions to which they were moving. There were solitary men trudging afoot, often bearing packs upon their backs. These were sometimes advance scouts of families who were contemplating a removal to the interior and who had commissioned some member to go on ahead and gain knowledge that might aid the family in its final choice of a new home. Still others were similar investigators on horseback. And all of these, as well as all the other elements which composed the traffic that thronged the old National Road, met on a common footing at the taverns which were sprinkled along the thoroughfare at distances of two or three miles.

Numerous competing lines of stage-coaches plied on the old government turnpike as well as on all the other highways of that period. Among the stage-coach companies of the National Road were the *June Bug Line,* the *Pioneer Line,* the *National Line,* the *Good Intent Line,* the *Oyster Line* and the *Shake Gut Line.* The *Oyster Line,* as its name implied, made a specialty of transporting oysters, and was a freight enterprise rather than a travel service. The *Shake Gut Line* was largely employed in the swift conveyance of small and important parcels or perishable freight.[1] The *June Bug Line* received its name because of a prediction made at the time its service was begun that the enterprise would not survive until the appearance of the June bugs. The prediction was not fulfilled.

Although there was a keen competition for traffic among the various companies, it was usually the case that all competing stages were taxed to their capacity under ordinary circumstances. Travel over the road was always heavy. It often happened that a dozen or more coaches would leave Wheeling at the same time and in the same direction — either west-bound or east-bound — on the arrival of the passengers for whom they had been waiting. Then began a mad race toward the nearest relay station, where fresh horses were to be obtained. It was a subject for legitimate boasting when one stage outdistanced its competitors and excelled them in the speed with which the relay was accomplished. Coaches were often bereft of their exhausted animals and supplied with fresh ones within less than a minute of time. The one hundred and thirty miles of road between Cumberland and Wheeling were covered by the fastest coaches in twenty-four hours, or at a speed of about five and one-half miles an hour. Such was the regular schedule. It occasionally happened in stress of circumstances, when necessity arose, that the trip was made in twenty hours, though this was a severe strain not only on the passengers but on the equipment.

Those two events that always created the most excitement along the National Road, and that inevitably resulted in the performance of almost incredible exertions

[1]At first this was called the "Express Line." Its better known name was bestowed upon it because of its employment of Montgomery Demming, aforementioned, after that driver had ceased to pilot a "June Bug" coach.

on the part of the stage-coach companies were the annual transportation of the President's message to the West, and the trip of a President himself over the turnpike. One reason making the rapid carriage of the President's message a thing of consequence — aside from the public interest with which such documents were always awaited at the time — was the fact that much importance was placed by the Federal Post-office Department on the speed attained while transferring such a message in the mails. For occasions of this sort the most ambitious and expert stage drivers were selected, and as one of them sped madly across the country, urging on his six horses from the top of a heavy and careening vehicle, the population of all the region along the road gathered to watch and cheer him. In carrying an executive message the driver sometimes covered 150 or 200 miles at the rate of ten miles an hour. There was no profit to the companies in work of this sort however. The special relays of horses had to be provided at much more frequent intervals than was usual, and valuable animals were ruined by the exertions to which they were forced.

It was customarily the case — especially if the roads were bad — that the conveyance of the President's message by a stage-coach resulted in the avoidance of that particular vehicle by travellers who were not seriously pressed for time. They well knew the direful shaking they would receive if they became fellow passengers with the Presidential document. But if they were of necessity forced to travel with the annual address to Congress they made the best of it, and arrived finally at their destination, where the executive wisdom was enthusiastically received by the expectant multitude while they limped slowly and painfully to bed.

736

Whenever a President-elect travelled over the National Road to his inauguration at Washington, or when a President made a trip to the West over the same road, the company which he honored with his patronage either built a new coach for the occasion or else refitted the best one in its possession. The vehicle in that event was decorated with even greater vividness than usual. The coach itself was called *The President,* or the *General Jackson,* or *Old Tippecanoe* — as the case might be —

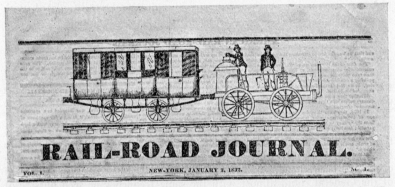

217.—Heading and Title to Volume I, Number 1 of the *Rail-road Journal.* The Journal was the second American periodical, in point of time, which was established to advocate the revolutionary method of transportation.

and the name was painted on the door panels in brilliant red or blue with all the skill of an artist engaged for the occasion. The dignity and consequence assumed and thereafter maintained by the driver of a President's coach need not be discussed. He was ever afterward looked upon as the possessor of an importance considerably surpassing in most respects that of his equally famous passenger.

President-elect Jackson declined the offer of free transportation in the new coach prepared to convey him to Washington in 1829, but permitted his family to occupy it. He himself paid his own way, in accordance with his rule to refuse gifts of value. When General Harrison went eastward over the road to his inauguration in 1841 he travelled in a fine new coach named *The President*. Polk and his immediate party occupied a similar vehicle. One of the incidents of the trip of General Taylor over the road in 1849 has thus been told:

"President Taylor and his party were, in 1849, conveyed over the road under the marshalship of that most indefatigable Whig, Thos. Schriver, who, with some other Cumberlanders, proceeded to the Ohio river and met the presidential party. . . . The Road was a perfect glare of ice and everything above ground was literally plated with sleety frost. The scenery was beautiful; to native mountaineers too common to be of much interest, but to a southerner like General Taylor, who had never seen the like,[1] it was a phenomenon. In coming down a spur of Meadow Mountain the presidential coach, with the others, danced and waltzed on the polished road first on one side and then on the other with every sign of an immediate capsize. But the coaches were manned with the most expert of the corps of drivers. Schriver was in the rear and in the greatest trepidation for the safety of the President. He seemed to feel himself responsible for the safety of the head of the nation. Down each hill and mountain his bare head could be seen protruding from the window of his coach to discover if the President's coach was still upon wheels. The iron gray head of the General could almost with the same frequency be seen outside of his window, not to see after anybody's safety but to look upon what seemed to him an Arctic panorama. After a ride of many miles the last long slope was passed and everything was safe. At twilight the Narrows were reached, two miles west of Cumberland, one of the boldest and most sublime views on the Atlantic slope. General Taylor assumed authority and ordered a halt, and he got out in the storm and snow and looked on the giddy heights of Will's Creek until he had taken in the grandeur of the scenery. He had beheld nothing like it before, even in his campaigns in Northern Mexico."

The mention of Presidential trips over the National Road would not be complete without reference to an incident that happened to Van Buren near the western end of the thoroughfare in 1844. Although not chief executive of the nation at that time, he was making an extended trip

[1] In reality, Taylor had seen too much of the world to be astonished by the mountains of Maryland, but he no doubt enjoyed them.

738

through the Middle West in the hope of securing the nomination soon to be made by his party, and in the course of his journey he reached the town of Indianapolis. A considerable feeling of hostility to Van Buren then existed in Indiana, partly as a result of his earlier action in vetoing a bill designed for the completion of the National Road through that state. So a number of his Hoosier Whig opponents sought out the stage driver who was to pilot him westward to St. Louis and had a secret conference with that individual. Van Buren resumed his trip the next day, and hardly was he out of sight of Indianapolis when the driver ran off the road and upset the coach. But owing to the discrimination with which the scene of the accident had been selected the ex-President entirely escaped any injuries save those consequent upon his precipitation into a large mud-hole. It is needless to say that both his temper and apparel were seriously damaged. Thus did the Whigs of Indiana glut themselves with revenge for a President's opposition to the building of an interstate thoroughfare.

The ordinary rates of passage paid by stage-coach travellers on the eastern section of the National Road and its Baltimore connection were as follows:

From Baltimore to Frederick	$2.00
From Frederick to Hagerstown[1]	2.00
From Hagerstown to Cumberland	5.00
From Cumberland to Uniontown	4.00
From Uniontown to Washington	2.25
From Washington to Wheeling	2.00
Through fare to the Ohio River	$17.25

There is an interesting tradition to the effect that the custom of granting free travel privileges to favored in-

[1]Hagerstown was not directly on the Road, but best reached by it, and so near that the town was always considered as a National Road "point."

dividuals originated on the National Road in connection with its use by government officials. The story goes that a well-known stage line proprietor named Reeside framed a cabalistic signature which he made with chalk on the hat of a man to whom he was granting free transportation. Reeside's agents were instructed to collect no money from passengers whose beavers bore the magic sign. The drivers soon came to say of such a favored traveller, "The old man has chalked his hat."[1]

One other peculiar and omnipresent feature of modern life for which the old National Road is responsible deserves notice. The drivers of the Conestoga wagons were inordinate users of tobacco, but owing to their small wages they protested loudly against paying the customary price for cigars. Some unknown genius thereupon devised a scheme for satisfying the wagoners. He invented an object, made of cheap tobacco and having the general size and shape of a lead pencil, which could be held between the teeth, and which would produce large quantities of strong smoke when manipulated according to the usage to which a cigar is customarily subjected. These nameless objects he placed on the market at four for one cent. They were adopted by the wagoners with enthusiasm, and were promptly dubbed "Conestoga cigars" by those who beheld them from a safe point of vantage. From this era of their history their transition to "Conestogys" and thence to "Stogies" was speedy and inevitable. "Stogies" they have since remained, and the smoke into which they disappear by the hundreds of millions is an incense — figuratively speaking — offered up to the memory of a vanished day.

---

[1] Possibly the still existing practise of railroad conductors, who often stick small pasteboard cards in passengers' hat-bands, is a survival of this early custom which made it necessary to look at a man's hat to discover if his fare had been collected.

Sample of wall paper printed in 1825 in celebration of the completion of the Erie Canal. Often used in making band-boxes of the period. Printed by a stencil process, endlessly repeated. L. F. Amer.

A HISTORY OF
TRAVEL IN AMERICA

CHAPTER XXXIV

IMPORTANCE OF STAGE-COACH TRAVEL BETWEEN 1800 AND
1840 — SPEED AND RATES OF FARE — COMPETITION
BETWEEN RIVAL NEW ENGLAND LINES — ITS EFFECT
ON A BOSTON DANCING MASTER — WHEELED VEHICLES
OF SMALL USE WEST OF THE ALLEGHANIES UNTIL
AFTER 1820 — CHICAGO IN 1833 — DEVELOPMENT OF
STAGE LINES IN THE MIDDLE WEST — THE STAGE
DRIVER — ACCIDENTS — ADVENTURE OF HENRY CLAY
— THE LOST SPEECH OF BLACK HAWK

IT is doubtful if any description written to-day
could adequately portray the importance — in its
relation to the affairs of the people — which stage-coach
traffic assumed during the period between 1800 and
1840. During the years in question it was the only means
by which a large part of the population could accomplish
overland journeys, and even in those instances wherein
rivers and canals were available for some portions of the
expeditions to be undertaken, travellers often had to resort
to the stage-coach for considerable parts of the distances
traversed. There was no general thought[1] of the future
possibility of more comfortable and rapid means of overland conveyance, and all those circumstances of progress

[1] Until about 1826.

741

by stage which now seem to us to be so archaic and remote were then esteemed as the height of travel luxury. It was seldom that complaints were made by the public about the uncomfortable and wearying conditions that inevitably attended stage-coach travel in those times. Whatever happened on a journey was accepted as a matter of course and endured with complaisance and fortitude. The foreign traveller Weld[1] gives an illuminating description of the spirit in which both passengers and stage-coach driver met, with mutual understanding, the difficulties of an expedition. He says: "The driver frequently had to call to the passengers in the stage to lean out of the carriage, first on one side, then on the other, to prevent it from oversetting in the deep ruts with which the road abounds. 'Now, gentlemen, to the right!' Upon which the passengers stretched their bodies half way out of the carriage to balance on that side. 'Now, gentlemen, to the left!' " and so on.

The speeds attained by the stage-coaches in those days were esteemed as little short of marvelous. Isaiah Thomas, Jr.,[2] had occasion in 1812 to travel from Washington to Baltimore. The trip required one and a half days for its completion in a coach drawn by three horses. He rode in a regular passenger conveyance. The much swifter mail coaches over the same route then left Washington at four o'clock in the morning and reached Baltimore, under favorable conditions, about an hour before midnight on the same day These rates of movement were typical of the speeds maintained throughout the East for many years. One of the best known stage-coach trips of the time was that between Provi-

---

[1] In his "Travels through the States of North America": Vol. i, pp. 37-38.
[2] The well-known Boston printer. His book is entitled "Reminiscences and Sketches."

dence and Boston. Travellers from New York to
Boston usually left their destination by a steamboat
which landed them in Providence in about twenty-
three hours, and they then immediately embarked in
stage-coaches to traverse the remaining forty miles to the
Massachusetts metropolis. No less than fifteen or twenty,
and sometimes twenty-five coaches a day plied between
the two cities. In a letter written in 1822 in description
of the trip, it was said: "We were rattled from Providence to Boston in four hours and fifty minutes. If any
one wants to go faster he may send to Kentucky and
charter a streak of lightning."

The fare for the Providence-Boston trip was ordinarily three dollars, but the price of a stage-coach ticket,
either for that journey or any other, was by no means
permanently fixed. Whenever a new stage line was established the older organizations whose field was thus invaded usually reduced their price of passage in the
hope that the new company would thereby find its business unprofitable and be compelled to abandon its
competition. If the new company met the lowered passenger tariff then the established lines would promptly
make another reduction. When all parties to one of these
rate-cutting controversies entered upon the struggle with
a grim determination to win, the results were sometimes
peculiar and also highly satisfactory to the travelling public. One of the most memorable of these fights for traffic
was begun by the action of a new Boston-Providence line
in reducing its charge to $2.50. The old lines retaliated
by a still further cut to $2.00. By this time the people of
the two cities became enthusiastic in their efforts to encourage the combatants, and so heartily did the warring
New England companies enter into the spirit of the fray

that the cost of tickets between the communities soon disappeared altogether, and every passenger by any of the competing lines was finally in receipt of a free dinner and a bottle of wine in payment for the privilege of transporting him over the road.

The people of the two towns — or as many of them as could possibly do so — arose to the occasion and for a brief interval the travel between the places assumed astonishing proportions. At this time one of the prominent dancing teachers of Boston was a man named Shaffer, very well known and famous for his wit. When the stage-coach lines had reached the point of carrying their patrons for nothing and giving them wine and food in addition, Shaffer could stand the strain no longer. He dismissed his classes; closed his academy; abandoned his profession; and spent his entire time for more than a week in being carried back and forth between Providence and his own home, pausing between trips to enjoy the hospitality of the company he had deigned to honor with his patronage. The inevitable truce between the competing proprietors, and its attendant restoration of rates, was the catastrophe which sent the dancing master and many other of his townsmen back to their ordinary vocations. It was Shaffer who responded one day when an extraordinarily fat man descended from the stage-coach in front of a tavern and inquired how much the establishment charged for its dinner. Shaffer walked slowly around the new arrival, then backed away a few steps in order to get a better view, cocked his head to one side and said: "For that size, four dollars."

Thurlow Weed,[1] in an account of a trip between Albany and Rochester, New York, in 1824, gives further

[1] In his "Autobiography"; vol. 1, pp. 139-140.

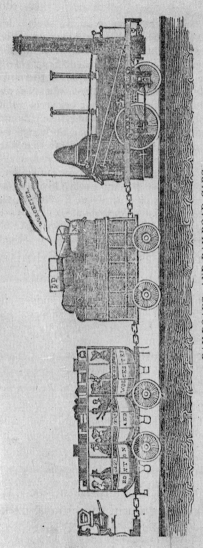

RAILROADS, AND RAILROAD CARS.

Here is a very good representation of the most common apparatus for travelling on railroads. First you see, on the right hand, the engine, as it is called—I mean the boiler—and place to put the fire and wood; and the pipe or large tube for the smoke to escape out. Fastened to the hind part of this, by a chain, is a car in which they put the passengers' baggage; and sometimes goods or merchandise. Attached to this last is a passenger car; and to that another, and another, and so on.

Sometimes they have six or eight passenger cars, or even more. In the present instance I have shown you only one, with a small part of another; just because I had not room enough for more.

What you see at the sides of the passenger cars, hanging down a little way, are steps or stirrups, much like those of coaches and chaises; to assist the passengers in ascending and descending. The wheels of the cars are low, but very strong.

218.—A contemporary explanation of the new apparatus for travelling. Page from a book of the period. The consequences of linking the cars of a train together by means of chains are discussed in Chapter XLIII, in an account of the first railway of New York State.

insight into conditions encountered by stage-coach travellers. He says in his narrative:

"We left Albany at seven o'clock in the evening, and traveled diligently for seven nights and six days. The road from Albany to Schenectady, with the exception of two or three miles, was in a horrible condition, and that west of Schenectady, until we reached Tribe's Hill, still worse. For a few miles in the vicinity of Palatine Church there was a gravelly road over which the driver could raise a trot, but this was a luxury experienced in but few localities and those far between. Passengers walked to ease the coach every day and each night. Although they did not literally carry rails on their shoulders to pry the coach out of the ruts, they were frequently called upon to use rails for that purpose. Such snail-paced movements and such discomforts in travel would be regarded as unendurable now; and yet passengers were patient and some of them even cheerful, under all those ills and annoyances. That, however, was an exceptional passage. It was only when we had horrid bad roads that the stages dragged their slow length along."

Josiah Quincy[1] also left his observations of a stage journey from Philadelphia to Washington in February of 1826. The record was made in his diary and reads:

"At three o'clock this morning the light of a candle under the door and the rousing knock told me that it was time to depart, and shortly after I left Philadelphia by the Lancaster stage, otherwise a vast, illimitable wagon, with seats without backs, capable of holding some sixteen passengers with decent comfort to themselves, and actually encumbered with some dozen more. After riding until eight o'clock we reached the breakfast house, where we partook of a good meal, and took on Messrs. Storm and Wheaton. We then proceeded through a most beautiful tract of country with good fences and stone barns which proved the excellence of the farming. The roads seemed actually lined with Conestoga wagons each drawn by six stalwart horses and laden with farm produce."

On this trip Quincy went from Boston to New York in four days, from New York to Philadelphia in one day, and from Philadelphia to Washington in three days, making his entire time for the journey between Boston and Washington eight days. It was in the following year of 1827 that the work of building the Baltimore and Ohio

---

[1] His description of a trip from Boston to New York appears in Chapter XI.

219.—The *Baltimore and Ohio Railroad March*. Its publication was inspired by the interest and excitement attending the commencement of the road and the ceremonies of July 4, 1828, on which day the piece of music was offered for sale in Baltimore.

Railroad was proposed, and Quincy's trip, therefore, furnishes a fair illustration of conditions attending stagecoach travel and of the time consumed by it just before the commencement of the railroad era.

Quincy also tells a story of a Massachusetts traveller who, at about the same period, was dashing through the town of Andover on a Sabbath day in his carriage, in defiance of the laws of the commonwealth, when he was halted and threatened with arrest by an indignant church deacon. But the wayfarer was equal to the emergency. Checking his horses and assuming an appearance of profound anxiety, he cried to the deacon, "Tell the good people of Andover that you permitted me to pass because my mother is lying dead in Boston"; and as the deacon recoiled a step from the news thus shouted to him, the traveller gave his horses their heads again and called back to the deacon, "You may add also, if you please, that she has been lying dead there for some twenty years." The carriage then disappeared in a cloud of dust.

Owing to the lack of bridges across the rivers, except in a few thickly settled districts and the immediate neighborhood of cities, any extended journey by coach or wagon necessitated frequent recourse to ferries. Many of these were nothing but rickety scows whose pertinacity in holding together was often the marvel of those voyagers who sought their use, although they sometimes did fulfil expectations by collapsing or sinking under a too onerous burden. Nearly every passage of a river by ferry — except on a busy highway — was an hour of anxiety. An experience of the sort was apparently too familiar to the Americans for comment or chronicle, but a few visitors from other lands did leave accounts of such navigations.

One of these[1] wrote the following description of the manner in which he got his equipage across a stream:

"The next job was to ferry the baggage over; and this effected, the horse was towed across by the nose, an operation of some delicacy both to actors and spectators. Lastly came the transportation of the wagon, and here all my seamanship served only to show the hazard incurred of losing the whole conveyance. If the rope . . . old and much worn, had given way, as I fully expected it would, when the wagon was half-channel over and nothing in sight but four or five inches of railing above the water, we must have bivouac'd where we were. . . . Fortunately we succeeded in dragging the carriage across, and when the four wheels fairly touched the bank I thought of course that all our difficulties were over. But the united strength of all aboard, males and females, young and old combined, could not budge it more than a foot out of the water. I don't know what we should have done had we not spied near the landing place a fathom or two of chain, one end of which our active little commanding officer soon tied to the carriage, and the horse being hitched to the other we drew it triumphantly to land, with a cheer that made the forest ring."

During the second, third and fourth decades after 1800 nearly all the principal cities as far west as Pittsburgh were connected by several lines of stage-coaches. Certain of these lines carried the United States mails and made the quickest trips between the communities they served. The other lines maintained slower schedules. This phase of the varying land travel accommodations obtainable at that time is well illustrated in a volume dealing with the development of Pennsylvania.[2] In its discussion of the service existing between Pittsburgh and Philadelphia in 1831, the book says:

"The announcement was made in the Pittsburg papers of May, 1831, that Reeside, Slaymaker & Company had, with their usual enterprise and public spirit, established four lines of stage coaches to run through to Philadelphia; the first in two and a half days; the second in four days, both of them daily; the third to start tri-weekly, and the fourth to run daily in four days . . . . This was considered at the time a great

[1] Captain Basil Hall of the British Navy, in "Travels in North America": Vol. i, pp. 270-271.
[2] W. H. Wilson's "Notes on the Internal Improvements of Pennsylvania."

advance upon the previous traveling facilities. The writer well recollects the advent of the fast mail line to run through in two and a half days. The coaches were built as light as possible consistent with strength and carried but six passengers each. The four-horse teams were carefully selected, and changed every ten miles. As the sound of the horn announced the approach of the stage to the changing station the fresh horses were brought out, each in charge of a groom, and the change was effected and the coach rolling away before the passengers hardly realized what was being done. The contrast to the old order of things was so marked as to excite a good deal of wonder and remark along the road."[1]

By the year 1832 the trip between Boston and New York — in which Quincy but six years before had consumed four days — had been reduced to one of forty-one hours. In the last-named case, however, the passengers were not permitted to stop during the night at a tavern even for four or five hours of sleep, but were carried forward both day and night without intermission. At that time the swift-moving passenger between the two cities ordinarily paid a fare of eleven dollars. During the previous forty years the general improvements of roads throughout the East, coupled with competition, had resulted in a considerable reduction in the cost of stage-coach transportation. Whereas in 1832 a man could be conveyed from Boston to New York for eleven dollars, in 1783 and for some time thereafter the stage patron had been compelled to pay ten dollars for his passage between Boston and Hartford. Perhaps in a general way the decrease to the public in the cost of stage-coach travel amounted to about fifty per cent. during the generation immediately following 1800.

In the winter time — except in those regions where snow was not a serious impediment to travel — the stage-coach lines sometimes placed their vehicles on sled bodies instead of wheels and succeeded in maintaining their

[1] Stage tickets from Philadelphia to Pittsburgh, during the heyday of stage-coach travel, cost from $15.00 to $20.00.

service with but a small decrease in speed. On occasions when the ordinary stage-coach body would have been too heavy to be dragged through the snow its use was temporarily abandoned in favor of small, open, box-like structures, in which the travellers were exposed to all the in-

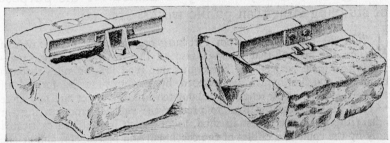

220.—Primitive American rails and tracks. The stone sleeper and rail at the left illustrate the track construction of the Portage railway, built by the state of Pennsylvania between Hollidaysburg and Johnstown in 1832. The block and rail at the right show the first track of the Camden and Amboy road, in 1831. From the National Museum's illustrations of its original specimens.

clemencies of the weather. The salient features of a winter trip to Philadelphia from New York in 1836 are thus stated:[1]

"On the fourteenth of February, 1836, I left Philadelphia at 5 p. m., and was fourteen hours going to New York with the Great Southern Mail, although the sleighing was good. We rode in an open sleigh or box on runners, and the passengers sat on the mail-bag. The fare from Philadelphia to New York was six dollars."

The conditions of land travel just previous to the introduction of the canal and railway were very far from being uniform throughout the whole extent of territory east of the Mississippi. It was only in the northern and eastern sections of the country, and as far west as Pittsburgh, Wheeling and Washington, that there existed so favorable a situation as has been described. Some of the

[1] S. W. Robert's "Address to the Pennsylvania Historical Society."

typical adventures to be expected by the man who journeyed west of Pittsburgh by stage, even at as late a day
as 1837, are suggested in an account of an overland trip
from Pittsburgh to the town of Erie, Pennsylvania, written
by a Scotch civil engineer[1] who travelled extensively
through the country in the year named for the purpose
of studying American public works. He said:

"On the road leading from Pittsburg on the Ohio to the town of
Erie, on the lake of that name, I saw all the varieties of forest road-
making in great perfection. Sometimes our road lay for miles through
extensive marshes, which we crossed by corduroy roads, formed of
trees. . . . cut in lengths of about ten or twelve feet and laid close
to each other across the road to prevent the vehicles from sinking; at
others the coach stuck fast in mud, from which it could be extricated
only by the combined efforts of the coachman and passengers; and at one
place we traveled for upward of a quarter of a mile through a forest
flooded with water which stood to the height of several feet on many
of the trees, and occasionally covered the naves of the coach-wheels.
The distance of the route from Pittsburg to Erie is one hundred and
twenty-eight miles, which was accomplished in forty-six hours, being
at the very slow rate of two miles and three-quarters an hour, although
the conveyance by which I traveled carried the mail, and stopped only
for breakfast, dinner and tea, but there was considerable delay caused
by the coach being once upset and several times mired."

In the South the roads suitable for vehicles were still
few and far between when compared with similar highways in the North, and much of the overland movement
of the people, except on north-and-south roads near the
coast, was still accomplished on horseback. During the
second war with Great Britain communication by sailing
packets between the north Atlantic states and the southern
seaboard was almost entirely cut off, and for commercial
purposes there remained no method of intercourse between those two sections of the country save that afforded
by the Conestoga wagons. Long trains of those land

[1] David Stevenson. The quotation here given is from his "Sketch of the Civil Engineering of North America, etc.," London: MDCCCXXXVIII, pp. 216-8.

frigates departed daily from the northern cities toward the South, laden with commodities desired by the people of that region. As a natural consequence of the time and expense incurred in making a journey by that means from the North to the South, the expense of conveying goods between the two regions was extraordinarily high. The freight rate by Conestoga wagon from Boston to Charleston was no less than forty cents a pound for goods of light weight, or eight hundred dollars a ton.

From ten to twenty overland wagons that had started from Baltimore, New Haven, New York, Philadelphia, Boston and Richmond arrived in Charleston every day during a considerable period of the War of 1812, so that if the various charges on the goods carried by them averaged but ten cents a pound, the aggregate freight costs for ten or twenty wagon loads of articles so transported from the North to that one city would have been between four thousand and eight thousand dollars a day. Not all this merchandise, of course, was destined for Charleston. Much of it went still farther south to other communities.

This long interruption of sea travel by means of the swift sailing packets that had hitherto united the northern and southern ports really proved a stimulus to the development of land movement between the two sections, for it forced the people to an increased use of stage-coaches and to the betterment of their roads. After the war the Atlantic sailing packets never wholly recovered their previous prestige as passenger carriers. Within a dozen years little steamboats appeared on the various bays and rivers, and in course of time those mechanical craft began running in close business connection with various southern stage lines. Thus was forming a new system that competed for and secured a large portion of the human traffic between North and South until railways supplanted the stage-coach part of the coalition.

Other conditions that retarded the development of travel facilities in the South between 1800 and 1830 have been outlined in those chapters dealing with the diplomatic conflict between the white and red races. Land travel from the South to the West — save on three or four roads leading through Virginia and North Carolina to Tennessee and Kentucky — was still a matter of considerable toil. Yet the communication facilities between the East and the Mississippi were showing a marked improvement when compared with the situation that had existed a few years before. An illustration of the progress made in bringing the East and the extreme West more closely together is that contained in the respective intervals of time which were required to carry the President's message from Washington to Little Rock, Arkansas, in 1819 and in 1829. The message of December 7, 1819, was seventy-eight days on its journey to Little Rock, and did not arrive in that town until February 22 of 1820. Jackson's annual message of December 8, 1829, in contrast, was hurried from Washington to Little Rock in the astonishing time of fourteen days. A local newspaper[1] commented on the prodigy in the following words: "Thus have the improvements which have been made in the expedition of our mails brought us, as it were, sixty-four days nearer the city of the General Government than we were ten years ago." Doubtless the editor who uttered this encomium on the progress of his day thought that the possibilities of development had about reached their limit.

The disabilities under which the people of the West

[1] "Little Rock Gazette," December 29.

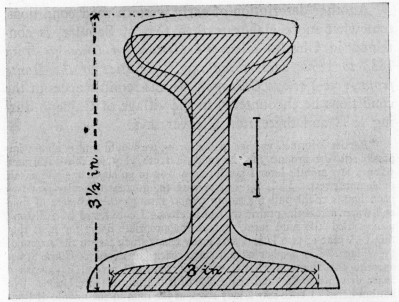

221.—The first T rail. Shaded section shows the design as originally whittled out of a pine stick by Stevens in 1830. Unshaded section shows rail as made in England for him in 1831. This is the Camden and Amboy rail depicted in the preceding. From the National Museum's illustration of its original specimen.

labored, from the beginning of the century until about 1825, are suggested by an observation of Christopher Schultz in his *Travels on an Inland Voyage*. Schultz remarks: "If the mud does not get quite over your boot tops when you sit in the saddle they call it a middling good road."

The observation here quoted is a humorous exaggeration, but it is nevertheless true that any human movement over the so-called roads of the Middle West was at certain times out of the question. In the rainy seasons, in fact, vehicle traffic was not even attempted throughout large districts of the country and travel was performed on horseback or not at all.

Another description of early western road conditions, somewhat more elaborate than that of Schultz, is contained in Charles Cleaver's *History of Chicago from 1833 to 1892; Describing the Difficulties of the Route from New York to Chicago.*[1] In his reminiscences of the conditions he encountered in the village of Chicago during 1833 and thereafter, Cleaver says:

"Parties informed us that in the spring we would find it almost impossible to get around for the mud—a truth very forcibly illustrated when a few months later I got into a wagon to go about one and a half miles northwest. . . . It was with the greatest difficulty that two good horses could pull the empty wagon through the two feet of mud and water across the prairie we had to cross. I once heard Mr. Elston's place called 'the mud farm,' not an inappropriate name for it at that time. A year or two later I saw many teams stuck fast in the streets of the village. I remember once a stage coach got mired in Clark Street opposite the Sherman House, where it remained several days with a board driven into the mud at the side of it bearing this inscription: 'No bottom here.' I once saw a lady stuck in the mud in the middle of Randolph Street at the crossing of La Salle. She was evidently in need of help, as every time she moved she sank deeper and deeper. An old gentleman from the country, seeing the situation, offered to help her, which had such an effect upon her modesty that with one desperate effort she drew her feet out minus her shoes, which were afterward found over a foot in the mire, and reached the sidewalk in her stockings."

At the time Henry Clay was making his appeal for a national highway between the East and the West, it usually required about three or four weeks to travel from New York or Washington to Cincinnati, Corydon,[2] or St. Louis. In a copy of the *Western Censor and Emigrant's Guide,* published in Indianapolis on January 19, 1824, appeared a little paragraph indicating that the latest news from the state capital was dated January tenth. Eight days, therefore, had been required to span the distance between Corydon and Indianapolis. In the same issue of the *Western Censor* appeared another item in-

---

[1] Page 50.
[2] Then the capital of Indiana; a small town in the southern part of the state.

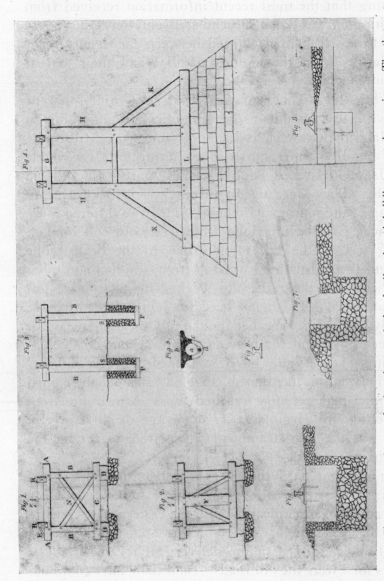

222.—Figures 1 to 4 show early American methods of railroad track building across low regions. The three lower figures show the track of the road built by Pennsylvania between Philadelphia and Columbia in 1832-4. Discussed in Chapter XLII. From Wood's "A Practical Treatise on Rail-Roads: Philadelphia, 1832."

dicating that the most recent information received from Washington was dated December twenty-seventh. More than three weeks had elapsed between the departure of the letters from the national capital and their arrival at Indianapolis.

The first number of the *Western Censor*—that of March 7, 1823—contains a communication describing an overland trip between Indianapolis and Fort Armstrong, four hundred miles north of St. Louis. It was made by Israel Mitchell and a small party of Indiana people. They were twenty-three days on the way. In telling of the journey Mitchell said: "We suffered more than can well be imagined from wet, cold and hunger, being wet to the knees and often to the neck. The streams through Illinois were all high, and had no timber on them to make rafts, and we had no alternative left but to swim. Had it not been for honey we must have nearly perished. We had not a full meal of meat for thirteen days, and for four days nothing but honey. . : . Fasting and fatigue have weakened us very much." Mitchell also mentioned that a steamboat named *Virginia* had recently reached Fort Armstrong from Wheeling, in Virginia, after a voyage of three weeks. This was the first steamboat to penetrate so far up the Mississippi River.

It was not until the year 1820 that the upper part of the Mississippi valley found itself in fairly reliable and regular communication with the eastern states. Even then the new era in overland rapid transit was at first mainly concerned with the delivery of the mails. The routes used were the old roads — and their later continuations — which extended westward through the mountains and into Tennessee and Kentucky. A St. Louis newspaper of 1820[1] mentions the revolution in the speed of the mails in the following paragraph:

"After the vexatious delays which we have been long subjected to in our mail communication with the Atlantic states it is a matter of agreeable satisfaction to find a line established on which dependence can be placed. On the Vincennes route we now have regular arrivals from the principal towns in Kentucky and Ohio in six days, from Washington to Baltimore in twenty, Philadelphia twenty-one, New York twenty-two, and Boston twenty-four."

From this it will be seen that by special effort a man might, at that date, proceed overland from New York to St. Louis in but little more than three weeks, and that only six days were required to go from Cincinnati or Louisville to the town on the western bank of the Mississippi. Passenger stage-coaches appeared on the western part of this route a few months later. An Indiana newspaper of 1820[2] announced certain new facilities for travel then impending in a paragraph which read:

"We are gratified in seeing it announced that a line of stages is established to run from Louisville through Vincennes to St. Louis. This will be an invaluable accommodation to travelers to the West, who have hitherto been obliged to resort to tedious and vexatious means of conveyance. We are glad also to see the progress of public improvement. Comfortable houses and good farms are creating on the St. Louis road, and a stage coach with passengers will soon be humming across those vast and cheerless prairies, where, but a short time since, the wolf and deer were the principal inhabitants, or men in savage attire, as ferocious and wild as they. The benefits of the enterprise of Mr. Foyles will be felt and acknowledged by many a grateful traveler, and we hope it will receive the particular attention of the Postmaster-General."

This overland movement to the West, aided by Mr. Foyles, followed the earlier Kentucky roads to Louisville. There the travellers crossed to the north side of the Ohio, and by means of the old Vincennes trail — recently widened and improved — they proceeded to the second

[1] "The Enquirer," Feb. 12.
[2] "The Indiana Centinel" of Sept. 2.

capital of Indiana territory and then swung westward across Illinois.[1] On this and some other of the early roads of the West the pioneer stage-coach companies adopted a rule which caused a considerable fluctuation in the rates of fare which passengers were charged for their transportation. A traveller was arbitrarily considered to weigh one hundred pounds. As the "Mail Stage

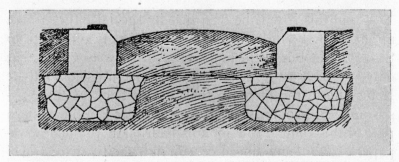

223.—The road-bed, stone foundations, stone stringers and flat iron rails used in laying part of the Baltimore and Ohio Railroad in 1833. Numerous experiments and methods in track-making were tried by the Baltimore and Ohio during the first years of its existence. From the National Museum's illustrations of its original rails and stone blocks.

Rules" of the Emison and McClure Company put it, "one hundred pounds weight will constitute a passenger, and to be paid for accordingly, and a greater or less weight in proportion."[2] So it will be seen that if a traveller had the misfortune to weigh one hundred and fifty pounds he would, according to the regulations, constitute a passenger and a half, and would be compelled to pay for himself on that basis; and if he tipped the scales at two hundred pounds he then represented two

[1] On another page will be found a photographic reproduction of a stage-coach "way bill" used by one of the stage companies which operated over this road shortly after 1820. It will be noticed that the distances along the road are reckoned in almost every instance in the number of miles between two taverns. Only four settlements are recorded on the way bill, in contrast to the names of sixteen taverns at which the coaches stopped for food or a change of horses. One of the taverns—that of Joshua Piles—was owned by the proprietor of the stage line.

[2] This is rule number three contained on the Emison and McClure broadside of stage-travel regulations, a photographic reproduction of which is shown elsewhere.

persons, as far as the price of his ticket was concerned. He was, however, allowed to carry fifteen pounds of excess weight in the stage, provided the said fifteen pounds was baggage and not a component part of his own person. Rule number nineteen of the Emison and McClure Company disclaimed responsibility for the loss of any trunks or other baggage carried by coach. Aside from these features of administration, which were doubtless common to all or nearly all the early stage companies of the interior, their rules indicated a real and business-like desire to satisfy their patrons. The employees of the companies were forbidden to indulge in language or conduct that was unseemly, and were instructed to treat passengers with "the utmost politeness."

Although by this time there were numerous stage routes in the eastern states on which travellers went forward toward their destinations both by day and night without intermission, the newer roads in the interior did not permit a like procedure, and the speed attained by the pioneer stage lines of the Middle West was but a fraction of that accomplished by the eastern lines of the same years. The schedules of the first coaches running over the road between Louisville and Vincennes were announced to the public by means of advertisements when the service was projected, and one of these announcements[1] read:

"The Vincennes stage to Louisville leaves Francis Cunningham's in Market Street, Vincennes, on Wednesday mornings at six o'clock, arrives in Louisville at three o'clock P. M. on the Friday following— leaves Louisville on Saturday morning at six o'clock and returns to Vincennes on the Monday following at three o'clock P. M.—distance to Louisville one hundred and twenty-six miles."

Including the two nights spent on the road between

[1] From the "Indiana Centinel and Public Advertiser" of May 13, 1820.

the cities named, it consequently appears that the traveller proceeded at an average rate of less than two and one-fourth miles an hour. The running schedule for that part of the journey between Vincennes and St. Louis[1] was as follows:

"The Union Line of stages, in conjunction with the Louisville Line, will commence on the fifth day of September, inst., to run regular from Vincennes, Ia., to St. Louis, Mo., to leave Vincennes every Tuesday at two o'clock P. M., arrive at St. Louis on Friday by two o'clock P. M. Leave St. Louis on every Saturday at half past four A. M. and arrive at Vincennes on Monday by six P. M."

Similar advertisements, published during the next few years in the same parts of the country, showed that an average rate of movement not exceeding three miles an hour was all that could be expected by stage-coach during any extended journey which required one or more nights on the road. A man journeying from Vincennes to St. Louis by the road and in the manner here outlined spent three days in crossing the state of Illinois.[2]

A considerable traffic soon appeared on this first of the "through routes" of the Middle West, and two other necessary conveniences of travel — in addition to the stage-coaches themselves — speedily multiplied. These were the taverns and the ferries. Innkeepers and ferry proprietors competed almost as actively for traffic as did the coach lines themselves, and their representatives always met the incoming stages, distributing to the passengers printed handbills which called to their attention

[1] As announced by Proprietor Foyle in the "Indiana Centinel" of September 2, 1820. Regular service between Vincennes and St. Louis was not established until some months after the coaches were put in operation between Louisville and Vincennes.

[2] After writing the above paragraphs relating to the beginning of periodic stage-coach travel in the Middle West, the author, in an endeavor to fix the precise date of this event, came upon an advertisement reading as follows: "SPECIAL NOTICE. The U. S. Mail Stage from Vincennes to Louisville will commence its regular running on the twentieth April. The St. Louis Union Line from Vincennes to St. Louis will also start at the same time. Travelers from Louisville to St. Louis by this conveyance will be but five days on the road. THE PROPRIETORS." From the "Western Sun," of Vincennes, April 7, 1821.

the excellencies or conveniences of the institutions whose interests they advocated.[1] Although it often happened that a stage-coach company owned, or had an interest in, several of the taverns along its route, and although the coaches of any given line always stopped at one particular inn, there was no obligation on the part of the travellers themselves to patronize taverns with which their convey-

224.—Sectional View and side view of the roadbed and track structure adopted by the Boston and Lowell road in 1834-1835. The rails rested on stone blocks, which in turn stood on deep foundations of broken stone. From Stevenson's "Sketches of the Civil Engineering of North America": 1838.

ances were affiliated, and constant efforts were made by rival landlords and ferrymen to secure patronage. A steady stream of westward-bound emigrants also moved through the country either in their own canvas-covered wagons or on horseback, and these were likewise the legitimate prey of all those who represented any feature of the new transportation facilities that were so rapidly coming into existence.

The position held by a stage-coach driver of the old days, in the estimation of his acquaintances and the general public, was very similar to that of the captain of a steamboat. Some famous drivers, indeed, stood on so lofty a plane in the eyes of the world that they can only be likened to the commanders of the ocean steamships of the present time. By virtue of their duties they came into constant contact with all the prominent political, social and

[1] A number of these early western handbills, issued in advertisement of hostelries and ferries along the Louisville-St. Louis road, are elsewhere shown.

763

commercial figures of the country. Their attention and favorable opinion were also always sought by that large — though less consequential — part of the public which was so deeply impressed by the measure of their responsibility and the majestic demeanor of their professional attitude. The high place occupied by a famous stage driver in the eyes of the youth of the country during the heyday of stage travel is suggested by the words of one who was familiar with the life of those days. He said:

"My earliest recollections are intimately associated with coaches, teams and drivers, and, like most boys raised in an old stage tavern, I longed to be a man, when I could aspire to the greatness and dignity of a professional stage driver. In my boyish eyes no position in life had so many attractions as that of driving a stage team. A Judge, a Congressman, even Henry Clay or President Jackson did not measure up to the character of John Mills or Charley Howell in my juvenile fancy." [1]

Nor was this estimate of the coach driver confined exclusively to people other than the driver himself. There is a record that one of the fraternity once remarked, "While I drive this coach I am the whole United States of America." Yet the ordinary wage of a driver was only twelve dollars a month, exclusive of his board and lodging. While on duty he took his meals at the taverns along the road in company with his passengers — though he did not sit at the head of the table — and he was always sure of a bed to himself, no matter how urgently and vainly some belated traveller might plead for a like accommodation.

It was a time in which the free use of intoxicating drinks — especially of brandy and whisky — was more common than it is to-day, and stage-coach drivers, like a large majority of other men, drank whenever they had the opportunity and the inclination, yet it should be said

[1] Searight's "The Old Pike": p. 182.

225.—Track of the Albany and Schenectady road, 1837. Foundations of broken stone, topped by timbers; cross-ties of timber; rails of timber, on the inner edges of which were fastened flat strips of iron. From a drawing in the National Museum.

to their credit that few of them permitted themselves to be reduced to the condition which made them incapable of performing their really important work in a safe and proper manner. They were so continually pestered with invitations to drink that they might easily have remained in a state of partial incapacity for months at a time, provided they were permitted to retain their official positions during such an interval.

But it occasionally happened that a driver was false to his duty and forgot the value of the lives entrusted to his care. In cases of that sort disastrous accidents sometimes resulted. One such accident, which occurred in Massachusetts[1] in 1835, received the following newspaper comment:

"The driver, on taking charge of the team at Groton, was observed to be not very well capable of managing his team, which was observed by several persons, one of whom remarked on his incapacity to drive. It is not pretended that he was drunk at the time, but laboring under the stupefying effects of intoxication. After the arrival of the stage at a place called Littleton he took his glass of grog. Mr. Bullard, proprietor of this line of stages, rode on the box with him and had occasion to

[1] The account here quoted is taken from the "Maine Farmer" of April 3, 1835.

765

arouse him from sleep twice after leaving Groton. Mr. Bullard was still on the box with the driver when they left Littleton. On arriving at the summit of the hill where the accident happened the driver was unable to control his team, four spirited horses, and they ran full speed down the hill, coming in contact with Mr. Powers' six-horse loaded wagon . . . which upset the coach. Mr. Bullard, holding on the railing of the coach as it turned over, swung round and under it upon his side. . . . Previous to expiring Mr. Bullard communicated to those in attendance the facts above stated."

In noting this fatality, which was due to the condition of the driver, the same journal declared: "There is hardly a class of men whose sobriety and habits of carefulness are of as great importance as that of stage drivers. So far as our circumscribed vision extends in regard to this matter, the public around us are happily provided for in this respect; but this is not the case in all places."

One phase of the incident here narrated seems to be worthy of elucidation. The newspaper said, "It is not pretended that he was drunk at the time," but that "he was laboring under the stupefying effects of intoxication." Obviously a distinction is here asserted which the lapse of years has obliterated, and it is, in consequence, necessary to explain that during the period under discussion a man was not pronounced "drunk" unless he was prostrate and unconscious. While he still manifested any glimmering of understanding, or was able to make a distinguishable physical movement, the opprobrium attached to the stronger description could not fairly be applied to him. Until that condition had arrived he was, as explained in connection with the above case, merely "under the stupefying effects of intoxication."

Minor accidents were constantly taking place in the operation of the stages, but it was seldom that a mishap resulted in such unfortunate consequences as those which accompanied the runaway near Groton. Usually a vehicle was overturned and its occupants received a bad shaking up and some bruises; occasionally some one suffered a broken limb. Nor were the elect of the land any more immune from such happenings than the most humble traveller. Even Henry Clay himself, to whose influence more than that of any other man the creation of the Na-

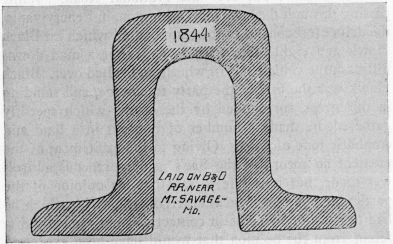

226.—The first rail rolled in the United States. Made in the first American rail mill, at Mount Savage, Maryland, in 1844. A few hundred tons were used on the Baltimore and Ohio road in that year. Weight, 42 pounds to the yard. From the National Museum's illustration of an original specimen. The picture is about three-fourths actual height.

tional Road was due, was involved on one occasion in an upset. He was on his way to Washington at the time, and the driver overturned the coach at Uniontown, in Pennsylvania. The Idol of the West was unhurt, and when he was dragged out of the vehicle he remarked that the Clay of Kentucky had been mixed with the limestone of Pennsylvania. The driver, jolted from his lofty perch by the concussion, alighted on his head and suffered a broken nose.[1]

[1] Searight's "The Old Pike": p. 16.

Another prominent stage-coach passenger who passed through a similar experience was the Indian, Black Hawk. After his capture he was taken to Washington, and journeyed eastward by steamboat on the Ohio River until Wheeling was reached. There he and the entire party of military men and Indians were transferred to coaches and set out over the National Road. While passing through the town of Washington, in Pennsylvania, the driver lost control of the team behind which sat Black Hawk and eight other natives, and after a mad downhill dash the vehicle left its wheels and rolled over. Black Hawk was the first of the party to emerge, and standing in the street, surrounded by the crowd which speedily gathered, he made a number of remarks in a loud and emphatic tone of voice. Owing to the excitement of the moment no record of the Sac's extemporaneous address was made, but it is safe to say that his opinion of the particular phase of Caucasian civilization with which he had thus suddenly come in contact was not radically different from the opinion that would have been expressed by a white man under similar conditions.

The coming of the railroad and the spread of that new method of movement throughout the East spelled the ultimate doom of stage-coach travel along the National Road and other roads in that part of the country. Various stage lines nevertheless fought hard and well to retain a vestige of their former glory, and some of them succeeded in maintaining a precarious existence until after 1850. But their day as a factor in the upbuilding of the country and in the movement of its population was practically done, and they were destined to survive only amid the sparsely settled regions of the almost limitless West. During the last two or three years in which the old National Road

768

still remained an essential factor in the traffic of the nation the voice of a driver along its way could sometimes be heard as he chanted this ditty in execration of the portentous change that had robbed him of his occupation:

"Now all you jolly wagoners, who have got good wives,
Go home to your farms and there spend your lives.
When your corn is all cribbed and your small grain is good,
You will have nothing to do but curse the railroad."

But long before the stage-coach and turnpike had ceased to be important factors in the national travel system, a new and radically different method of transportation — the artificial waterway, or canal — had appeared, which was destined for about a generation to play an interesting part in the country's development.

CHAPTER XXXV

AMERICA'S EARLY CANAL PERIOD — THE NATION HAS NOT
DEVELOPED BEYOND THE NEED OF CANALS BUT IS NOW
APPROACHING ITS REAL CANAL EPOCH — CAUSES
OF THE PHENOMENA APPEARING BETWEEN 1817 AND
1845 — FIRST AMERICAN ARTIFICIAL WATERWAYS —
ELKANAH WATSON'S IDEAS AND WORK — NEW YORK
STATE BUILDS THE ERIE CANAL — SCENES AT ITS
OPENING — PENNSYLVANIA'S ACTIVITY — HER EARLY
ERROR — A CHANGE IN POLICY RESULTS IN A RE-
MARKABLE ROUTE TO THE WEST — HOW A TRAVELLER
GOT FROM PHILADELPHIA TO PITTSBURGH

I N considering the subject of canals and canal traffic, in
so far as that method of travel and transportation is
related to the story pursued in these pages, one desirable
point to be kept in mind is that America has not developed
beyond the era of canals but is, on the contrary, apparently
still to enter upon it. The short period of canal construction which appeared in this country between 1817
and 1845 was largely the outgrowth of unusual circumstances, was begun and ended by conditions peculiar to
the country and period, and can best be described as a
sudden, sporadic, forced and exotic phenomenon instead
of the slow and natural outgrowth of broad necessity. It
is improbable that canals would have gained headway at
all had there been even a dim general realization of the
significance contained in the work performed with steam

by Fitch, Evans, Stevens, Fulton, and others from 1785 until about 1815. And, once a really valuable though premature canal system was in working order—as was the case by the fourth decade after 1800—it would not have been allowed to disintegrate in large part had there been a general or governmental appreciation of the future needs of the country, coupled with a popular sense of

227.—The earliest American railway passenger trains usually consisted of one car drawn by horses. The car was generally a stage-coach placed on special wheels, or else a two-story affair built on the lines of a stage-coach. That sort of vehicle was the best conveyance yet devised for land travel, and an effort to adapt it to the new transportation method was naturally made. From it the modern railway car slowly developed. Drawn and engraved by the artist Alexander Robb. Date, about 1830. A similar car then in use on the Baltimore and Ohio road was described in the *Baltimore American* of August 5, 1830. See Chapter XLV.

business morality sufficiently strong to resist those blandishments which finally resulted in the crippling or outright abandonment of important, costly and useful public improvements.

Perhaps the first definite idea regarding the building of a canal in America was that of joining the Susquehanna and Schuylkill Rivers in Pennsylvania. The possibility of doing such a thing attracted the attention of the earliest settlers in Philadelphia, and there was some small discussion of the subject even before the year 1700. But it was recognized by the pioneer inhabitants of Pennsylvania that even though the accomplishment of the task might be of benefit, its actual performance was beyond their physical power or financial capacity.

So the first theoretical argument was forgotten, and there was no further serious mention of such a plan for nearly three-quarters of a century. But about the year 1770 it appears that there was a revival of the idea, and two years later Benjamin Franklin—that extraordinary man who had something worth while to say concerning almost every matter of consequence to his country—wrote a letter from England to the mayor of Philadelphia,[1] in which he observed:

"I am glad my Canal Papers were agreeable to you. I fancy work of that kind is set on foot in America. I think it would be saving Money to engage by a handsome Salary an Engineer from here who has been accustomed to such business. . . . With regard to your question, whether it is possible to make the Schuylkill a part of the navigation to the back Country, or whether the Difficulty of that River, subject to inconveniences of floods, ice, etc., will not be greater than the expense of digging, locks, etc., I can only say that here they look on the constant practicability of the navigation, allowing Boats to pass and repass at all Times and Seasons, without hinderance, to be an event of the greatest importance, and therefore they seldom or ever use a River where it can be avoided. . . . Rivers are ungovernable things, especially in hilly countries. Canals are quiet and always manageable. . . . I warmly wish success to every Attempt For Improvement of our dear Country, and am with sincere esteem, yours most affectionately, B. Franklin."

Within a few years after Franklin had written this letter there was authorized the building of the first American canal of any consequence.[2] The action was taken by the Virginia legislature,[3] which formally provided that a canal be built between the towns of Richmond and Westham, a distance of some seven miles, in order that

[1] Mayor Rhoads. The letter was written in August of 1772.
[2] In 1750 there had been dug in Orange county, New York, by Lieutenant-Governor Holder of that province, a short and shallow dyke or ditch, which was used for moving stone loaded on small flatboats, and for other similar construction purposes. This little ditch was technically a canal, and it was probably the first work of such a character in the country.
[3] In 1785.

boats might thus be carried around the falls obstructing the navigation of the James River at that point. The canal was duly dug, and was in part maintained and enlarged through the use of state money. Other similar early American undertakings of the same sort[1] were:

The Dismal Swamp Canal, dug by authorization of Virginia and South Carolina. It was begun in 1787 and finished in 1794.

The Middlesex Canal, which was incorporated in 1789, begun in 1795 and completed in 1808. This canal was about thirty miles long, thirty feet wide at its top, twenty feet wide at the bottom, and three feet deep. It extended from the Merrimac to the Charles River, in Massachusetts. Twenty locks were built throughout its length, and the total cost of the enterprise was more than five hundred thousand dollars.

The small canal constructed around the Patopwick Falls in Massachusetts in 1797. The charter had been granted in 1792.

The Santee Canal, extending for twenty-two miles between the Santee River in South Carolina and the city of Charleston. It was thirty-two feet wide at the top, twenty feet wide at the bottom and four feet deep. This work was completed in 1802.

The Bow Canal in New Hampshire, a small artificial waterway three-quarters of a mile long, which was finished in 1812.

The Schuylkill navigation of Pennsylvania, commenced in 1815 and finished in 1826. Its total length from Fairmount to Mt. Carbon was one hundred and eight miles. The surface width of the canal was thirty-six feet, the bottom width twenty-two feet and the depth three

[1] Compiled from Tanner's "A Description of Canals and Railroads of the United States, Etc., Etc.," New York: 1840.

Exciting Trial of Speed between Mr. Peter Cooper's Locomotive, "Tom Thumb," and one of Stockton & Stokes's Horse-Cars.

The trial took place on the Baltimore and Ohio Railroad, on the 28th August, 1830. The sketch represents the moment the Engine overtook and passed the Horse-Car, the passengers filled with excitement.

(See Mr. Latrobe's description, page 119.)

228.—The Baltimore and Ohio Railway. Test of speed, in 1830, between a horse-drawn car and Peter Cooper's diminutive experimental locomotive known as the "Tom Thumb." Scene as the engine forged ahead. The horse finally won the race. From Brown's *History of the First Locomotives in America.*

and a half feet. The system contained one hundred and twenty-nine locks, and the cost of the project was about two and a half million dollars.

A survey was made in 1762 for a proposed canal between the Schuylkill River at Reading and the Susquehanna at Middleton. No work was performed on the enterprise until 1791 and about four miles were ready for use in 1794, when the undertaking was temporarily abandoned. Work on it was resumed in the year 1821, and in 1827 it was finished and called the Union Canal. Still later it was incorporated into the Pennsylvania Canal.

A canal between the Chesapeake Bay and the Delaware River was proposed in 1764, and the route for it was then surveyed. Actual work on this project was begun in 1804. It was abandoned soon afterward, again revived in 1822 and finished for thirteen miles in 1839.

The various small early canal enterprises here

mentioned were all substantially local in character, and none was planned as a travel and transportation route designed to open extensive new regions of the country or to facilitate movement or commerce between widely separated sections. It is a singular fact that the few artificial waterways created or projected in this country prior to the year 1803 were exciting more interest at that time in the minds of European observers than in the minds of the Americans themselves. In an important work published in London in 1803[1] there appeared the following paragraph:

"We may expect to see the interland parts of that large country so intersected as to bring the produce to market, or for exportation, which will interest Europe, and will make that country in a few years not inferior to the best cultivated and improved states in the old world. The immortal Washington was the original father and promoter of these canals and improvements and well did he deserve the admirable motto 'twice the savior of his country,'—after conducting her to liberty, he opened to her the way to posterity by new roads and canals. Those who wish any further information on these improvements in North-America, I beg leave to refer to the Journal of Mr. Elkanah Watson, a gentleman who has traveled much both in America and Europe."

It is apparent therefore that the two men here mentioned—General Washington and Elkanah Watson—demand attention in connection with the earliest phases of the canal-building period of the country.[2]

Elkanah Watson was a young American who, during the revolution against Great Britain, was sent by Congress to deliver despatches from that body to Benjamin Franklin, then in Paris on public business. Watson remained in Europe for five years—from 1779 until 1784—during which time he examined with attention the canals of Belgium, Holland and England. Soon after his return

[1] Philips' "General History of Canals." Fourth edition: p. 581.
[2] Washington's project was for a canal between the Potomac and Ohio Rivers. Its ultimate outgrowth was the Chesapeake and Ohio Canal, later described.

to America, and in the winter of 1785, he visited General Washington at Mount Vernon and at that time discussed with him the subject of river improvements and the project of connecting the waters of the Potomac by a canal with the Ohio or with the waters of the Great Lakes. His European observations and his conversations with Wash-

229.—Popular delight at the introduction of railways was at times manifested by the display of flags on cars and engines. A train of two or more cars was called a "brigade." The locomotive here shown is perhaps intended to represent the *Tom Thumb*. Drawn and engraved by Alexander Robb.

ington made a deep impression on him, and while undertaking extensive trips through many parts of the country during the next three years he found himself giving frequent consideration to the question of canal construction in various localities and to the possible advantages of such undertakings. During these expeditions Watson kept a record of his experiences and ideas, and at a later date the writings, originally brought into being under the conditions thus described, came to be known as the *Journal of Travels* by Elkanah Watson. It so happened that in September of the year 1788 Watson found himself in the interior of New York State, on the Mohawk River, and his thoughts regarding the future economic possibilities of that particular locality were thus set down by him:

"In contemplating the situation of Ft. Stanwix, at the head of Batteaux navigation on the Mohawk River, . . . I am led to think this station will in time become an emporium of commerce to Albany and the vast western world above. . . .

"Should the Little Falls ever be locked,—the obstructions in the Mohawk River removed and the canal between the said river and Wood Creek at this place, formed, so as to unite the waters running east with those running west; and other canals made, and obstructions removed to Fort Oswego,—who can reasonably doubt but that by such operations the state of New York have it within their power by a grand stroke of policy, to divert the full trade of lake Ontario, and the Great Lakes above, from Alexandria and Quebec to Albany and New York. . . .

"In view of escaping by locks from the Hudson into the Mohawk River, it appears to me that the obstacles at this place[1] would be much greater than to cut a canal through the pine plains into a basin back of Albany."[2]

In 1791 Watson began an active campaign of publicity having for its purpose the creation of a sentiment favorable to the making of public improvements and of canals in particular. The New York legislature passed such an act in 1792, and under its provisions Watson was named as one of the commission appointed to explore and lay out a possible route for a canal through the central and western part of the state which should connect the Hudson River with the Great Lakes system. The commission made its report in the autumn of 1792, and improvements in the navigation of the Mohawk River, together with the building of locks for the safe passage of boats at certain points on the stream were soon afterward authorized by the legislature and completed for use by the year 1796. During the next ten years the subject of connecting the Hudson with the Lakes system was brought forward on

[1] Watson here refers to the Cohoes Falls.
[2] The extracts from the Journals as here given are taken from the "History of the Rise, Progress and Existing Conditions of the Western Canals in the State of New York, from September, 1788, to the completion of the Middle Section of the Grand Canal in 1819, Etc., Etc." By Elkanah Watson, Albany: 1820, pp. 15-18.

different occasions by various public men of New York, but with no important or practical result. In the year 1810 the legislature caused a survey to be run which resulted in the recommendation that immediate efforts be put forth to induce the Federal government to adopt the plan as a national undertaking and itself perform the work. This suggestion was made by New York State and rejected by the national administration. New York then applied through her governor and legislature for the aid of Ohio and Indiana and again met with disappointment, although the interior commonwealths recognized and acknowledged the probable value of such a completed undertaking.

Being thus thrown upon her own resources, New York seemed rapidly approaching a decision to undertake the work on her own account, when the outbreak of the second war with Great Britain put an end for the time being to the maturing plans of the state. With the return of peace the subject was at once revived, and public meetings in advocacy of the enterprise were held in New York City and elsewhere. The legislature was memorialized; a new board of commissioners was appointed; and finally, in 1817, a law was passed providing for a system of canals and other internal improvements in New York State. Construction work was begun on the Fourth of July of that year[1] and a small section of the canal—about fifteen miles of waterway between the towns of Utica and Rome —was ready for traffic in October of 1819. The following contemporary letters give descriptions of the scenes attending the first canal boat trip in America:

"On the twenty-second of October, 1819, the first boat sailed on the Erie canal, from Rome to Utica. It was drag'd by a single horse, trot-

[1] In the historical neighborhood of Ft. Stanwix, Oneida county.

230.—The Charleston and Hamburg road. A sailing-car tried in 1829-1830.
Before a brisk breeze it carried fifteen passengers at the rate of twelve miles
an hour. On one trip the mast and sail, together with several passengers,
were carried overboard by the wind. A jury-mast was then rigged and the
journey was resumed. From Brown's *History*.

ting on the embankment, in the towpath. It was an elegant boat, constructed to carry passengers, called the Chief Engineer,—a compliment
to Benjamin Wright, Esq. The president, and the board of commissioners, attended by many respectable gentlemen and ladies, embarked
the ensuing day at Utica, with a band of music, to return to Rome. The
Scene was extremely interesting, and highly grateful. The embarka-

tion took place amid the ringing of bells, the roaring of cannon, and the loud acclamations of thousands of exhilarated spectators, male and female, who lined the banks of the new created river. The scene was truly sublime."

"Utica, October 22, 1819.

"The last two days have presented, in this village, a scene of the liveliest interest; and I consider it among the privileges of my life to have been present to witness it. On Friday afternoon I walked to the head of the grand canal, the eastern extremity of which reaches within a very short distance of the village, and from one of the slight and airy bridges which crossed it I had a sight that could not but exhilarate and elevate the mind. The waters were rushing in from the westward, and coming down their untried channel towards the sea. Their course, owing to the absorption of the new banks of the canal, and the distance they had to run from where the stream entered it, was much slower than I had anticipated; they continued gradually to steal along from bridge to bridge, and at first only spreading over the bed of the canal, imperceptibly rose and washed its sides with a gentle wave. It was dark before they reached the eastern extremity; but at sunrise next morning they were on a level, two feet and a half deep throughout the whole distance of thirteen miles. The interest manifested by the whole country, as this new internal river rolled its first waves through the state, can not be described. You might see the people running across the fields, climbing on trees and fences, and crowding the bank of the canal to gaze upon the welcome sight. A boat had been prepared at Rome, and as the waters came down the canal you might mark their progress by that of this new Argo, which floated triumphantly along the Hellespont of the west, accompanied by the shouts of the peasantry, and having on her deck a military band. At nine the next morning the bells began a merry peal, and the commissioners, in carriages, proceeded from Bagg's hotel to the place of embarkation.

"The governor, accompanied by Gen. Van Rensselaer, Rev. Mr. Stansbury of Albany, Rev. Dr. Blatchford of Lansingburgh, Judge Miller of Utica, Mr. Holly, Mr. Seymour, Judge Wright, Col. Lansing, Mr. Childs, Mr. Clark, Mr. Bunner, and a large company of their friends, embarked, at a quarter past nine, and were received with the roll of the drum and the shouts of a large multitude of spectators. The boat, which received them, is built for passengers;—is sixty-one feet in length and seven and a half feet in width;—having two rising cabins, of fourteen feet each, with a flat deck between them. In forty minutes the company reached Whitesborough, a distance of two miles and three-quarters; the boat being drawn by a single horse, which walked on the towing path, attached to a tow rope of about sixty feet long. The horse traveled, apparently, with the utmost ease. The boat, though literally loaded with passengers, drew but fourteen inches of water. A military band played patriotic airs.

"From bridge to bridge, from village to village, the procession was saluted with cannon, and every bell whose sound could reach the canal swung, as with instinctive life, as it passed by. At Whitesborough a number of ladies embarked, and heightened, by their smiles, a scene which wanted but this to make it complete."

The round trip of thirty miles was accomplished in twelve hours and twenty minutes, and the progress of the boat was heralded by the booming of cannon, the ringing of bells, the tooting of innumerable long tin horns, the cheering of the crowds and the music of every fife and drum corps and brass band of that part of the state. "A vast multitude of anxious people," said a local newspaper in its description of the event, "lined the sides of the canal, but everything succeeded according to the most sanguine expectations."

The opening of the successive sections of the Erie Canal formed the subject of description and comment by all the journals of the country. One newspaper[1] published the following correspondence regarding the departure of the first boat from Utica to Rochester on the occasion of the completion of that part of the work in 1823:

"Our village [Utica], on Friday, twenty-fifth inst., presented a scene of bustle and stir never before witnessed here. . . . On Saturday the Packet-Boat for Rochester left here with eighty-four passengers, on her first trip. A boat will leave this place every morning, Sundays excepted, during the season and continue through to the Genesee River. We think this a very judicious arrangement of the Company, as passengers are greatly incommoded by changing from one boat to another. The new boats which have been added to this line are built in the best manner and fitted up in a style of magnificence that could hardly be anticipated in the infancy of canal navigation in this country."[2]

[1] The "Farmers and Mechanics Journal," of Vincennes, Indiana, June 26, 1823. The letter was dated April 29th.
[2] This is a reference to certain early alterations in canal boats that are later discussed.

The same newspaper, on the same date, also printed another letter relating to the event, which read:[1]

"The packet-boat Bouck arrived at the basin on Friday evening last, and left this place yesterday morning crowded with passengers, and we understand that the line of packet-boats have commenced their regular trips. On Wednesday of last week a boat was launched from the yard of H. Goodman & Co., and though we may not announce the event in as lofty language as is used in city prints on like occasions, yet perhaps it was an occurrence equally interesting as the launching of the proudest ship from a seaport. To behold a vessel committed to the water four hundred miles inland, in a place which ten years since was a wilderness, and reflect that it was to navigate a stream erected by the hand of man, two hundred and fifty miles in length, to the naturally navigable waters, excites emotions of no uncommon kind, and must arouse a throb of conscious pride in the breast of everyone who belongs to the state whose enterprise could do and dare so much. Our village at this moment presents something of the bustle and business of a seaport, . . . and even something like ship-building is not wanting here in the forest, as there are several boats of from 20 to 40 tons now nearly ready to be launched which have been built in this place. This is the march of improvement."

Later in the same year of 1823 occurred the passage of the first canal boat from the waters of the canal into the waters of the Hudson River at Albany, and the event was made the occasion of an extraordinary celebration.[2] There was an imposing military display; the firing of innumerable salutes; the delivering of numerous long congratulatory speeches; the discharge of fireworks and the recitation of poems written especially for the occasion; a grand ball; a theatrical performance; and a large public banquet during whose progress those who sat at the tables were requested to drain their glasses to no less than thirteen formal toasts. And after the thirteen toasts had been drunk it appeared to be the consensus of opinion among those present that sufficient honor had not yet been paid to the happy occasion, so twenty-six additional toasts were

[1] This letter was dated at Rochester, New York, April 29, 1823.
[2] On the eighth of October. The festivities took place in Albany.

thereupon proposed and also drunk. The distinguished company finally left the banquet hall wholly convinced that nothing quite so important had ever before happened in the history of the country.

Two years later there was another celebration in honor of the completion of the entire enterprise to Lake Erie, and on that occasion the festivities began in Albany and did not end until a flotilla of western canal boats had finally reached New York City, where they were met by practically the whole population, and where a flask of water from Lake Erie was solemnly poured into the waters of New York Bay in token of their union.[1]

The Erie Canal as originally built was three hundred and sixty-three miles long, forty feet wide at its surface, twenty-eight feet wide at the bottom, and four feet deep. Its cost to the state, including its various branches or feeders, was $12,720,032.25.[2] The revenues of the Erie and Champlain canals of New York began to exceed the expenses of their maintenance in the year 1826, and by the year 1838 the net receipts of the public work in question had paid the interest on the debt created by its construction and had reduced the amount of the debt itself by nearly three and a half million dollars.[3]

In tracing the history of America's primitive canal epoch from the East toward the interior we find that the first important manifestation of Pennsylvania's revived interest in the subject of canals as a practical means of better travel and transportation facilities became visible

[1] A complete account of the celebrations attending the progress of the Erie Canal from 1819 until 1825 is to be found in Volume ii of the "History of Albany, from its Discovery to the Present Time, Etc., Etc." Albany: J. Munsell: 1867. The celebration of 1825 is also described in Colden's book on the subject, printed in 1825.

[2] Figures compiled from Tanner's "A Description of the Canals and Railroads of the United States."

[3] In 1835 work was begun on an enlargement of the prism of the Erie Canal. It is now being still further enlarged, and reconstructed into a ship and barge canal at a further cost of approximately one hundred million dollars.

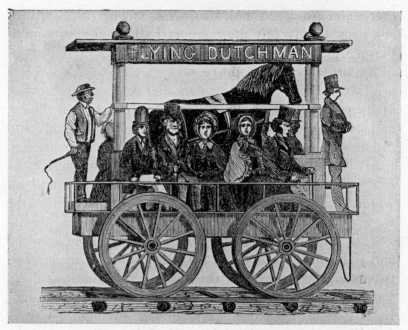

231.—A car propelled by a horse running on an endless platform was also tried by the Charleston and Hamburg road in 1829. Its inventor was awarded $500. This system carried twelve passengers at a speed of twelve miles an hour until the motive power stopped. From Brown's *History*.

in 1789. During that year was organized in Pennsylvania "The Society for Promoting the Improvement of Roads and Inland Navigation," and membership in the society soon increased to more than one hundred, embracing men in numerous sections of the commonwealth. The principal early activity of the association, as stated by a publication which appeared soon afterward,[1] consisted in meeting "on every Monday evening, during the session of the legislature, in order to suggest information, schemes and proposals, for promoting internal trade, manufactures and

[1] "An Historical Account of the Rise, Progress and Present State of the Canal Navigation in Pennsylvania. . . . Containing Abstracts of the Acts of the Legislature since the Year 1790, and Their Grants of Money for Improving Roads and Navigable Waters throughout the State; Etc., Etc." Philadelphia: MDCCXCV.

population, by facilitating every possible communication between the different parts of the state."

In the pursuance of its work the society prepared an elaborate memorial to the legislature in which were discussed the possibility and advantages of creating fourteen different routes of water communication designed to connect various parts of the state and also bring it into closer touch with New York, New Jersey, Maryland, Virginia and the Great Lake system. The memorial further advocated the building of various turnpikes designed for the same general purpose. This address to the representatives of the people was duly signed by its president, Robert Morris, on February 7th of 1791. It was presented to the legislature soon afterward and constituted the first systematic plan for the improvement of internal communications in Pennsylvania. The State Assembly, after some months of deliberation on the subject, decided on the adoption of a course described as follows:[1]

"That the legislators, although animated with the warmest zeal for the improvement of their country by means of roads and inland navigation, yet could not subject the finances of the state (even if adequate) to the burden of the whole; yet they would make liberal appropriations of public money for the improvement of such roads and navigable waters, as lying too remote from the more populous parts of the country, and the inhabitants, but newly settled, rendered it impracticable for them either to improve their own roads and waters by subscription or the usual county taxes; and the profits of the tolls would yet be too small to induce companies to undertake the work at their own expense; but that in the more settled parts of the country, especially near the metropolis, they would be ready to incorporate companies for the gradual and progressive improvement of roads and waters where the tolls would be sufficient to recompense the subscribers or stockholders, and the charge would fall according to justice upon those who were to be benefited in proportion to the use they might make of such roads and waters."

In accordance with the policy thus announced the state

[1] "An Historical Account, etc., etc.," p. 22.

legislature later in the same year passed an act[1] authorizing the incorporation of a company to build a canal
between the Schuylkill and Susquehanna Rivers, and
during the following year enacted another law[2] authorizing a similar waterway between the Delaware and
Schuylkill Rivers. During the two years following the
presentation of the memorial the state legislature, in accordance with its newly adopted policy, further appropriated various sums aggregating about $195,000 for use
in opening and building roads and for the improvement of
natural waterways. Active construction work both on
the enterprises undertaken by the state itself and on the
incorporated waterways began immediately, and Pennsylvania was thus the first state in point of time to adopt
and enter upon a pretentious plan for the improvement of
its communication facilities.[3]

But though Pennsylvania was indeed first in chronological order among those states which adopted a broad
governmental policy of river and canal improvement, she
unfortunately made a somewhat mistaken beginning. Her
first effort was largely devoted, not to the exclusive construction of artificial waterways, but to the attempted
taming of a number of her rapid, shallow and fluctuating
rivers. For about thirty years Pennsylvania clung to the
idea that she could create a practical and useful route to
the West by utilizing the natural channels of the Susquehanna, Juniata, Conemaugh and the Kiskiminitas. In
order successfully to perform such a feat and to build a
commercial highway possessing practical value for the
purposes of water transportation it would have been

---

[1] The act was approved on September 29, 1791.
[2] Act approved April 10, 1792.
[3] It was soon discovered that the original financial plans of these Pennsylvania canal companies were inadequate for the proposed work, and in 1795 the legislature authorized the two companies to raise $400,000 of additional capital by the selling of lottery tickets.

necessary not only to chain those streams but to surmount by their aid an altitude of almost two thousand and three hundred feet in a westward progress of about three hundred and twenty miles. New York, in joining the Hudson River and Lake Erie, was only confronted by the problem of surmounting an altitude of five hundred feet during a westward progress of about three hundred and sixty miles, and yet the accomplishment of her endeavor cost more than ten millions in money and about eight years of time. It is consequently only necessary to state the physical problem connected with Pennsylvania's first internal navigation scheme to indicate its impracticability as a dependable water transportation route.

It was at last perceived by the commonwealth that nothing practical could be accomplished until—through use of engineering skill—accurate knowledge was obtained regarding those problems of the mountainous district which in a westward route to the Ohio River would have to be encountered and conquered. Accordingly in 1824 the legislature of Pennsylvania authorized the creation of a commission to investigate and report upon the subject, and as one outcome of the explorations conducted by the commission it was discovered that the building of a distinctive lock canal was possible across the entire state from east to west except for a comparatively short distance which embraced the highest ridges of the Alleghany Mountains.[1] Early in 1826, in conse-

[1] The commission made its report in February of 1825, and then followed a period of excited public discussion between the advocates of canals and those others who believed that the newly discussed means of transportation called the "railroad" would, if adopted, prove more desirable for the purpose in hand than an artificial waterway. This and the following year were distinguished in Pennsylvania for the vehemence of the debate between the respective advocates of canal and railroad transportation, and one outgrowth of the altercation resulted—as will be seen in a later chapter devoted to railroads—in the action of certain men who sent a civil engineer to England for the purpose of studying railroad development in that country. So clamorous were the Pennsylvania advocates of railroads that on February 7, 1825—three days after the canal commissioners had made their report—the state senate granted their demand for the appointment of an additional commission to investigate the possibility of building a railroad from Philadelphia to Pittsburgh.

quence, the state legislature passed an act[1] definitely committing the commonwealth to the digging of a canal by the use of state funds. It was constructed in two sections, the eastern division of which found its western end at the town of Hollidaysburg at a height of nine hundred and ten feet above the sea level. The western portion of the

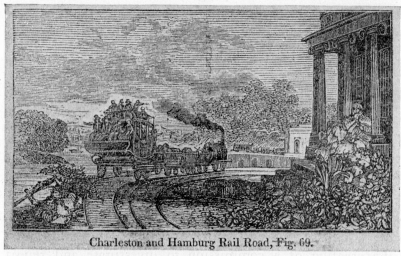

Charleston and Hamburg Rail Road, Fig. 69.

232.—Probably drawn before the road had a locomotive. The engine shown is somewhat similar to those used in England previous to the Rocket. A number of sketches of early American railroad trains were thus supplied with engines built by the imagination of the artists.

canal had a terminus at Pittsburgh on the Ohio River, and from there extended eastwardly to Johnstown at a height of eleven hundred and fifty-four feet above sea level. The short intervening distance of thirty-six miles between Hollidaysburg and Johnstown, within which the mountains rose to a height of twenty-two hundred and ninety-one feet, was at first crossed by travellers through the aid of stage-coaches, but was later spanned by a series of

[1] Approved by Governor Shulze on February 25.

mechanical devices which found no parallel in the annals of early American transportation.

There was no delay in commencing the construction work, and the great Pennsylvania Canal was begun at the town of Columbia, on the Susquehanna River, on the Fourth of July, 1826.[1]

The purpose of Pennsylvania in building her principal canal was to obtain for herself a travel and transportation route which should connect her seaport cities with the region west of the mountains, and thereby put herself in a position to compete with New York State for the traffic then largely monopolized by the lately finished Erie Canal. Pennsylvania succeeded in her pretentious effort to create such a highway, but the finished work by whose means the people were enabled to transport themselves and their goods back and forth between Philadelphia and the Ohio valley did not consist exclusively of canal construction. In its final form the line contained two small sections of railway, and since the description of a through trip from East to West over this very important route can only be given—and an understanding of its various physical features can only be obtained—by consideration of the whole work in its final form, it is necessary in this instance to slightly anticipate the occurrence of later historical events and to include at this point a picture of the two railroad links embraced in the Pennsylvania thoroughfare.

The first section of the trip from Philadelphia to Pittsburgh, as undertaken by a traveller after the work was finished, was made by a railroad that extended from Philadelphia to the little town of Columbia on the Susquehanna River. This road, as well as every other part of the route,

---

[1] The Fourth of July was in those days a pre-eminently popular date for the commencement of an important public work or for the celebration of its completion.

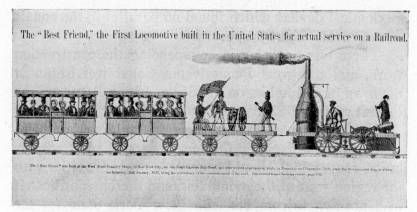

The "Best Friend," the First Locomotive built in the United States for actual service on a Railroad.

233.—First American-built locomotive designed for practical service. Made in New York City in 1830 for the Charleston and Hamburg line, and tried during the same year. During a formal trip in January of 1831, United States artillerymen and a cannon were carried on a flatcar to fire salutes in honor of the event. The *Best Friend* was also the first American engine to explode its boiler. A negro fireman was annoyed by the sound of the escaping steam, and stopped it by sitting on the lever which shut the escape valve. From Brown's *History*.

belonged to the state, and was also built by the commonwealth.[1] Twenty miles of the track were ready for use in September of 1832, and in October of 1834 the remaining sixty-one and a half miles of the road were opened for travel.[2]

It should here be explained that although the state built and owned all links of the traffic system to be described, and also installed and operated the motive power on the two railroads included in the system, none of the vehicles used on any part of the route either for the transportation of passengers or freight were owned by Pennsylvania. The railroad cars, stage-coaches and canal boats employed upon it were all owned and operated either by companies or private individuals engaged in transportation as a business enterprise. One of the principal com-

[1] The building of the Philadelphia-Columbia Railroad was authorized by act of legislature on March 24, 1828.
[2] The railroad was 81.6 miles long.

VIEW from the INCLINED PLANE, near Philadelphia

Lith of J T Bowen, Phila

A passenger train being pulled up a hill on the Columbia Railroad. Part of the Pioneer Fast Line from Philadelphia to Pittsburgh. Time, four days. F. Lith. Col. Amer.

panies thus organized for the purpose of carrying passengers and goods back and forth between Philadelphia and Pittsburgh was known as the "Pioneer Fast Line," and the experiences of a traveller here to be narrated may be considered such as were encountered after he had committed his person to the custody of that concern in his attempt to reach the western terminus of the route.

The traveller who set out toward Pittsburgh on the completion of the Columbia railroad made the first part of his trip by means of a horse-drawn railroad car.[1] These cars were of divers patterns, varying according to the ideas of their several owners. The earliest of those used somewhat resembled the stage-coaches of the same period. They were, however, mounted on small flanged wheels designed to run on the iron-topped wooden rails which constituted the track. By means of such a primitive railroad car the traveller was conveyed to a distance of about two miles beyond the city, where a considerable hill interrupted his progress in the vehicle in which he set forth. This acclivity was surmounted by an inclined plane two thousand eight hundred and five feet long, by which a height of one hundred and eighty-seven feet was overcome. Brigades of cars[2] were pulled up this inclined plane by an immense hawser nine inches in circumference, the cost of which was two thousand eight hundred dollars.[3]

The cars were pulled up the inclined plane by station-

[1] A contemporary picture of such a car, as it stood in the streets of Philadelphia before starting westward, is reproduced elsewhere.

[2] Trains of cars were at first called "brigades" of cars.

[3] The first hawser so installed was only six and three-quarter inches in circumference and proved inadequate to the work demanded of it. It lasted but a year, after which it was supplanted by the larger ropes mentioned. These hawsers considerably exceeded a mile in length. The total cost of the ropes used on the inclined planes on the Philadelphia-Pittsburgh route up to 1840 exceeded eleven thousand dollars.

ary engines of sixty horse-power. A contemporary colored lithograph, giving a view of this curious feature of an early American railway, is reproduced in its original colors elsewhere. After having reached the top of the hill near Philadelphia the traveller continued on his journey, and in the course of some eight or ten hours—if conditions were favorable—he finally reached the end of the railroad.[1]

The Columbia terminus was at first also distinguished by another inclined plane eighteen hundred feet long, built to surmount a height of ninety feet, but this plane was soon eliminated by the rebuilding of a section of the road for a distance of six miles. Some few miles of the track were laid with granite ties and wooden rails topped with flat bars of iron, but for most of the distance the track construction consisted of wooden ties and similar rails.[2]

The state derived its income from the road[3] through a system of charges here named:

Tolls for passengers, one cent a mile;

Tolls for passenger cars, one cent a mile for each pair of wheels;

Tolls for baggage cars, two cents a mile.

The three charges thus stated were exacted for the use

[1] From the autumn of 1832, when the first twenty miles of the road were opened for travel, until it was finished for its entire length in 1834, this part of the trip was made in horse-drawn cars. Steam locomotives then supplanted animals as a means of propulsion.

[2] About 1840 the primitive rails were discarded and replaced by rails of rolled iron, fifteen feet long and weighing about forty-one pounds to the yard. The total cost of the Philadelphia-Columbia road to 1840 was four million, two hundred and ninety-six thousand, seven hundred and ninety-six dollars.

The operating expenses of the road for the year ending October 31, 1838, were $177,854.13
Its receipts for the same time (composed of tolls paid by the companies and individuals using the road) were...................................$397,641.49
Its profits to the state for the same fiscal year were....................$219,787.36
The passengers using the road during the same fiscal year numbered..... 103,336
These figures are taken from Tanner's "A Description of the Canals and Railroads of the United States," p. 121.

[3] Exclusive of that obtained from the transit of merchandise.

The "West Point," the Second Locomotive built in the United States for actual service on a Railroad.

234.—The *West Point* was also created for the Charleston and Hamburg road in 1830-1831, and put in commission on March 5, 1831. A car loaded with cotton bales was hitched immediately behind the locomotive as a protection to the passengers in case the engine blew up. A further degree of safety was assured to the public by placing a negro brass band behind the cotton. No accident marred the occasion. From Brown's *History*.

of the tracks. After the introduction of state-owned locomotives on the road the state also collected additional fees for the use of its motive power, as follows:

One cent a mile for each passenger;

One cent a mile for each four-wheeled passenger car;

Two cents a mile for each eight-wheeled passenger car.

The owners of the cars paid all the above listed tolls to the state and collected three dollars and twenty-five cents from each passenger for conveying him from Philadelphia to Columbia. This was at a rate of four cents a mile.[1]

On arriving at Columbia the traveller at once embarked on a packet-boat and set forth for his voyage over the central division of the Pennsylvania Canal. That part of his journey was one hundred and seventy-two miles long and terminated at the little town of Hollidays-

[1] In Tanner's "A Description of the Canals and Railroads of the United States" (at pages 122-125) are presented tables designed to show that had the rolling stock of this road been owned and operated by the state it would have been a more profitable enterprise than any railroad operated elsewhere by a corporation at that time.

burg. The canal was forty feet wide at its top, twenty-eight feet wide at the bottom, four feet in depth, and the voyager passed through no less than one hundred and eight locks in advancing one hundred and seventy-two miles westward.

At Hollidaysburg he confronted the most unusual part of his journey, namely the thirty-six and a half miles intervening between that town on the east and Johnstown on the west. Between those two settlements the crest of the Alleghany Mountains attained a height of almost two thousand three hundred feet, and it had long been recognized that the lifting of canal-boats over such an obstacle by means of locks was commercially impracticable even if possible from an engineering standpoint. It had, therefore, been decided by the state legislature early in 1831 that the route should be carried over the mountains at this point by means of a railroad consisting of a series of inclined planes which should rise no less than one thousand three hundred and ninety-eight and seven-tenths feet in the first ten miles west of Hollidaysburg, and which should then drop one thousand one hundred and seventy-one and fifty-eight hundredths feet in the twenty-six and a half miles intervening between the highest point of the hills and Johnstown on the west. There was thus a total rise and fall of more than two thousand five hundred and seventy feet to be compassed by whatsoever vehicles moved over the thirty-six and a half miles constituting this part of the line. The difficulty was surmounted by building the inclined planes, as stated, and railroad cars were pulled from Hollidaysburg up the planes to the summit of the range by ropes and stationary engines similar to those employed near Philadelphia, and were then lowered down the slope to Johnstown.

This method of overcoming mountains was unique in the history of the early railroads of the country. Before actual track laying was begun it was necessary to cut a path through a dense forest for more than thirty miles, at a cost of thirty thousand dollars. An iron railroad was then laid in the shape of rails weighing about forty pounds to the yard[1] and resting on wooden cross-ties. Two stationary engines of thirty-five horse-power each[2] were installed at the top of every inclined plane, and the cars were pulled up by endless ropes.[3]

When the west-bound traveller reached Hollidaysburg—during the early days following the completion of the entire route—he left his canal boat, took a seat in one of the little cars designed to carry him over the mountains and in it was transported some thirty-six and a half miles farther along his westward way. These cars—like the canal boat he had just quitted—were private or corporation vehicles which paid Pennsylvania for the work of hauling them up and down hill.

The English story-writer, Charles Dickens, passed over the Pennsylvania route between Philadelphia and Pittsburgh during his first trip to this country, and in the book he afterward wrote describing his experiences while here[4] he gave this description of his journey over the Alleghany Mountains:

"On Sunday morning we arrived at the foot of the mountain which is crossed by railroad. There are ten inclined planes, five ascending and

---

[1] The rails used in building these inclined planes were eighteen feet long, and were imported from England. The total cost of building the thirty-six and a half miles of railroad across the mountains was $1,634,357. Locomotives were customarily used for pulling the cars along the comparatively few level places. Of the total rise and fall of more than two thousand, five hundred and seventy feet between Hollidaysburg and Johnstown two thousand and seven feet were encompassed by pulling and lowering the cars at the end of ropes.

[2] Only one was used at a time, the other being held in reserve in case of a breakdown or other emergency.

[3] Previous to March, 1834, when the railroad here described was completed, passengers were conveyed between Hollidaysburg and Johnstown in stage-coaches.

[4] "American Notes."

five descending; the carriages are dragged up the former, and let slowly down the latter by means of stationary engines; the comparatively level spaces between being traversed sometimes by horse and sometimes by engine power, as the case demands. Occasionally the rails are laid upon the extreme verge of a giddy precipice; and looking from the carriage window the traveler gazed sheer down without a stone or scrap of fence between, into the mountain depths below. The journey is very carefully made, however, only two carriages traveling together; and while proper precautions are taken is not to be dreaded for its dangers."

CHAPTER XXXVI

STILL ON THE ROAD TO PITTSBURGH — CANAL BOATS CAR-
RIED BODILY OVER THE MOUNTAINS ON THE SERIES OF
INCLINED PLANES — ORIGIN OF THE DEVICE — PAS-
SENGERS BY THE PIONEER LINE PROMISED A QUICK
TRIP OF FOUR DAYS — COST OF REACHING THE
INTERIOR CITIES BY THE PENNSYLVANIA ROUTE —
THE CHESAPEAKE AND OHIO CANAL — ITS EVOLUTION
FROM WASHINGTON'S "POTOMAC COMPANY"—
JEALOUSIES OF STATES INTERESTED IN THE PROJ-
ECT — THE FEDERAL GOVERNMENT BECOMES A
PARTNER IN THE WORK — MONROE APPROVES —
JOHN QUINCY ADAMS' SHOVEL STRIKES A ROOT —
FINAL COMPLETION OF THE CANAL AFTER MANY
DELAYS

B UT a still more remarkable scheme was soon put into
operation on this rugged part of the road. In order
that the traveller might not be subjected to the inconvenience entailed by so many shiftings from one vehicle to
another while making his trip, some of the transportation
companies built passenger canal boats that could be taken
apart into sections, placed on railroad cars constructed for
the purpose, and thus carried bodily over the mountains
while the people in each section of the dismembered
canal boat remained on board the water craft undisturbed.
After this plan was put in operation the traveller on his

797

arrival at Hollidaysburg did not disembark from the canal packet, but felt himself placed on wheels and lifted up over the hills.[1] Thus he came at last to Johnstown, and there he again slid into the water on the reassembled vessel and continued on his way along the artificial river toward Pittsburgh.

The custom of conveying canal boats over the mountains from Hollidaysburg on the east to Johnstown on the west by loading them on railroad cars had its origin in an incident happening in 1834. During that year a Pennsylvanian who lived on the Lackawanna River decided to remove with his family to the West and undertook to make the first part of his journey by boat. He accordingly built a suitable craft—somewhat on the plan of a western flatboat but considerably smaller in size— and embarked on it together with his family and household goods. He floated down the Lackawanna and Susquehanna and thence continued by canal to Hollidaysburg, where according to his original idea he had planned to sell his boat. But when he got to Hollidaysburg it was suggested to him that it might be possible to take the boat itself over the mountains by means of the inclined planes, in which case he could reëmbark in the canal at Johnstown, proceed to Pittsburgh on the canal and then enter the Ohio River for the remainder of his journey to Missouri.

The emigrant agreed that the attempt might be made, and so his floating house was taken out of the water, put on a specially prepared car and successfully transported over the series of inclined planes to Johnstown. There the boat entered once more into its proper element

---

[1] Despite all the ingenious methods used on this part of the Philadelphia-Pittsburgh route the physical difficulties encountered made its commercial success impossible after engineering science had become able to operate an all-rail route between the two cities.

and the migrating family set sail again for another thousand miles of the voyage to St. Louis.[1]

The length of the remaining canal from Johnstown to Pittsburgh was one hundred and four miles, within which distance sixty-six locks were encountered. The entire distance spanned by the traveller in advancing over the state-owned route from Philadelphia to Pittsburgh was three hundred and ninety-four miles, and, as earlier mentioned, the advertised time required for the journey was four days. But it can readily be understood that the complicated processes and many changes of vehicle and motive power involved in the trip made it impossible to maintain any regular schedule. In fact any such thing as a time schedule in the present-day sense of the word was not possible, since the railroad tracks and rolling stock were not under the same management, and the state was only called upon to furnish power and lockage facilities upon the arrival of some railroad car or canal boat.

A traveller's guide book published in 1836[2] had this to say concerning transportation over the highway here described, and its use in reaching the cities of the interior:

"The Pioneer Line on this route is exclusively for passengers, and professes to reach Pittsburg in four days—but is sometimes behind

[1] The American use of inclined planes for the purpose of conveying canal boats from one level to another, although more spectacularly shown on the Portage railroad in Pennsylvania, was not confined exclusively to that thoroughfare. A somewhat similar device was also employed on the Morris Canal across New Jersey between the Hudson River and the Delaware. The inclined planes of the Morris Canal were described soon after their installation by the Scotch engineer, Stevenson, who came to this country in 1837. He said:

"The boats are moved from different levels by means of inclined planes instead of locks. The whole rise and fall on the Morris Canal is 1557 feet, of which 223 feet are overcome by locks, and the remaining 1334 by means of 23 inclined planes. . . . The car . . . consists of strongly-made wooden crib or cradle, . . . on which the body rests, supported on two iron wagons running on four wheels. . . . The cars run on plate rails laid on the inclined planes, and are raised and lowered by means of machinery. . . . The railway on which the car runs extends along the bottom of the canal for a short distance from the lower extremity of the plane; when a boat is to be raised, the car is lowered into the water and the boat being floated over it, is made fast to the part of the framework which projects above the gunwale . . . the machinery is then put in motion; and the car bearing the boat drawn by a chain to the top of the inclined plane, at which there is a lock for its reception."

The above description is from David Stevenson's "Sketch of the Civil Engineering of North America." London: MDCCCXXXVIII, pp. 128-9.

[2] "A New Guide for Emigrants to the West." By J. M. Peck. Boston: 1836, pp. 369, 373-374.

several hours. Fare through, $10.00. Passengers pay for meals.

"Leach's line, called the 'Western Transportation Line,' takes both freight and passengers. The packet-boats advertise to go through to Pittsburg in five days for $7.00.

"Mid-ship and steerage passengers in the transportation line [meaning on a line-boat] in six and a half days; merchandise delivered in eight days. Generally, however, there is some delay. . . . The price of meals on the boat is about thirty-seven and a half cents.

"The whole expense of a single person from New York to St. Louis. via Philadelphia and Pittsburg, with cabin passage on the river, will range about $40 to $45. The time from 12 to 15 days.

"Taking the transportation lines on the Pennsylvania Canal, a deck passage will range between $20 and $25, supposing the person buys his meals at 25 cents and eats twice a day. If he carry his own provisions, the passage, etc., will be from $15 to $18.

"The following is from an advertisement of the Western Transportation, or Leach's Line, from Philadelphia:

	Miles	Days	
"Fare to Pittsburg	400	6½	$6.00
" " Cincinnati	900	8½	8.50
" " Louisville	1050	9½	9.00
" " Nashville	1650	13½	13.00
" " St. Louis	1750	14	13.00

"The above does not include meals.

"Packet-boats for cabin passengers same line:

	Miles	Days	
"Fare to Pittsburg	400	5	$7.00
" " Cincinnati	900	8	17.00
" " Louisville	1050	9	19.00
" " Nashville	1650	13	27.00
" " St. Louis	1750	13	27.00

"Emigrants and travelers will find it to their interest always to be a little sceptical relative to the statements of stage, steam and canal-boat agents, to make some allowance in their own calculations for delays, difficulties and expenses, and, above all, to feel perfectly patient and in good humor with themselves, the officers, company, and the world, even if they do not move quite as rapid, and fare quite as well as they desire."

· The first canal packet to reach the Ohio River from the East was the *Pittsburgh*. She was seventy-two feet long, eleven feet wide and eight feet high. The underbody of the boat was painted red and black, and the cabin

The First Steam Railroad Passenger Train in America.

235.—The Mohawk and Hudson Railroad train of 1831. First steam railway in New York State. Sketched just before the trip of August 9 by William Brown, a travelling silhouette artist of the time. The original silhouette made by Brown, from his drawing, is now in the collections of the Connecticut Historical Society. The picture here reproduced is accurate, but several of the printed statements on the lithograph are incorrect. It was not the first steam railroad passenger train in America; David Matthew of New York and not John Hampson of England was the engineer, and the locomotive was the American built *DeWitt Clinton* and not the English engine *John Bull*. The engine and cars of this train, on its first trip, were connected by short and heavy chains of three links each.

structure was a dazzling white. Along each side of the superstructure extended a row of twenty small windows with green shutters. She carried a crew of nine persons, and had accommodations for one hundred and fifty passengers.[1]

Although the early plans for joining the Schuylkill and Susquehanna Rivers were suffered to lapse they were revived in 1811 by an act of legislature providing for the incorporation of an enterprise known as "The Union Canal Company of Pennsylvania." This project was in substance a consolidation of the two old plans for joining the Delaware and Schuylkill Rivers to the Susquehanna,

[1] "Accommodations for passengers" on a canal packet did not have the same meaning possessed by that phrase to-day as applied to ocean steamships. It did not mean that the number of passengers "accommodated" could all be supplied with sleeping quarters. A canal packet frequently carried more than twice as many travellers as could be provided with berths. The surplus number slept on the floor or supper tables.

the early companies which had been organized for that purpose having failed and dissolved. Again did the War of 1812 interfere and cause a temporary abandonment of a transportation enterprise, but the Union Canal was aided by additional legislation in 1819 and 1821, when lotteries were authorized as a means of getting money whereby arrears of interest might be obtained for the holders of the stock authorized in 1811. Construction work was resumed in 1821 and the enterprise was completed in 1828, thirty-seven years after the first work on it was begun. The Union Canal was about eighty-two miles long and extended from Middletown on the Susquehanna to Reading on the Schuylkill. At Middletown it joined the Pennsylvania Canal, thus giving it a westward outlet to Pittsburgh, and at Reading it joined the Schuylkill Navigation project, by which it gained access to Philadelphia. The waterway never acquired unusual importance as a transportation route, and one of the principal causes of its failure in that respect was the inadequacy of the locking facilities throughout its length. Its locks were but seventeen feet wide.

By the year 1840 the state of Pennsylvania owned and operated six hundred and eight miles of canals and one hundred and eighteen miles of railways, the total length of the transportation system built by the state thus being seven hundred and twenty-six miles. The Union Canal was constructed and owned by a corporation, as was the Schuylkill Navigation scheme with one hundred and eight miles of navigable water; the Lehigh Navigation, whose length was eighty-four and a half miles; the Conestoga Canal, the Susquehanna Canal and various other minor waterways.

One other important canal begun in the East remains

to be noticed in a review of the early efforts that were made to join the East and the interior by means of artificial water communications. This was the Chesapeake and Ohio Canal, a work that had its inspiration in a plan promulgated by General Washington as early as the year 1784. Washington was an ardent advocate of better transportation facilities to the Ohio valley and the West, and as one means of acquiring a suitable route to the westward he favored the improvement of the Potomac River, together with the building of short canals around various obstructions to the navigation of that stream. The organization of a corporation known as "The Potomac Company" was largely due to his endeavors, and the company was incorporated by Virginia and Maryland in 1784-1785 with Washington himself as its president.

Although there had been as yet no really extensive movement of population toward the West—except for the local though highly important enterprises which followed Boone's exploits—it was dimly seen that the future of the new nation would be profoundly swayed by the relations later to exist between the original colonies and the vast region lying on the far side of the Alleghany Mountains. At that time the Spaniards still held the Mississippi River and it was feared—possibly with some reason—that if the future English speaking population of the interior was permitted to maintain close social and economic relations with them, without such opportunity to enjoy like associations with the East as would be afforded by better facilities for intercommunication, the result of that state of affairs might gradually produce a political effect injurious to the nation. Doubtless some such considerations as these were involved in all the early efforts to bring about a closer union of the seaboard and the interior by means of projects for better communications between the two regions, including the Potomac Company idea, although that enterprise was ostensibly a commercial one only.

After Washington's death the importance of the Potomac Company decreased rapidly, and at last became

RAIL ROAD SCENE.

236.—An engraving intended to depict a scene on the Mohawk and Hudson Railroad, in New York State. Published in Cincinnati about 1838. The locomotive shown is fictitious. It slightly resembles a primitive English type of which none was used in America. When the picture was printed there was but one locomotive in Ohio, and it was in the northern part of the state. Perhaps the western artist had never seen one, or even a good representation of such a machine.

virtually negligible. Yet the idea of creating a traffic route between the Potomac and the Ohio Rivers still maintained a spark of life, and the year 1816 witnessed its emphatic revival. In that year the Virginia Board of Public Works made the first new suggestion that a canal be built to join the waters of the Potomac and the

Ohio, and four years later, in 1820, Virginia began a survey to search into the practicability of such a plan. As an outcome of that survey the states of Virginia and Maryland engaged in a joint inquiry which resulted in the decision that the still existing Potomac Company was no longer useful and that its route ought to be supplanted by an artificial canal constructed by the two states in question. It was at once proposed to build such a canal westward along the Maryland shore of the Potomac from George-town on the east to the base of the Alleghany Mountains on the west,[1] and that the canal should be thirty feet in width and three feet in depth. The expense of such a work was originally estimated at about a million and a half dollars, but the final cost of the canal to Maryland was more than eleven million dollars, and other sums contributed to its construction by the Federal government and various cities brought the total to about fifteen million dollars.[2]

The first practical step which led to the building of what afterward became known as the Chesapeake and Ohio Canal was an act passed by Virginia in 1823 author-izing the incorporation of "The Potomac Canal Com-pany." Maryland, influenced by the interstate jealousies of the period, at first refused to give her legislative en-dorsement to the project, and her non-action inspired the numerous advocates of the plan to begin an aggressive fight in its behalf. Public meetings were held throughout Maryland, Virginia and Pennsylvania in 1823, and delegates were appointed by those assemblies to meet in a convention in the city of Washington in November of that year to consider the whole subject and take measures for its material advancement. When the convention duly

[1] With Cumberland as the western terminus.
[2] See "Report to the Stockholders on Completion of the Canal to Cumberland," 1850.

assembled its membership was composed of thirty-one delegates from Maryland, thirty-eight from Virginia, twenty-four from the District of Columbia, one from Pennsylvania and several self-appointed gentlemen from Ohio on whom were bestowed honorary memberships in recognition of their active interest in the undertaking. The reason for Pennsylvania's scanty representation in the convention is to be found in the fact that the state was already beginning to consider its own plans for a route to the West, for which reason its people were disinclined to participate actively in an enterprise that would no doubt compete with whatever plan they themselves might adopt. The convention[1] proceeded enthusiastically to the consideration of the subject it had assembled to discuss, and its opinion was ultimately embodied in a declaration which read:

"Whereas, The connection of the Atlantic and Western waters by a canal leading from the city of the National Government to the River Ohio, regarded as a local object, is one of the highest importance to the states immediately interested therein, and considered in a national view is of inestimable consequence to the future union, security and happiness of the United States,

"*Resolved,* That it is expedient to substitute for the present defective navigation of the Potomac River, above tide water, a navigable canal from Cumberland to the . . . eastern base of the Alleghany, and to extend such canal as soon thereafter as practicable to the highest constant steamboat navigation of the Monongahela or Ohio River."[2]

In the minds of many of the men who took part in the convention of 1823 the ultimate terminus of the proposed canal was Lake Erie, but they proposed to confine their first energies to the building of a section about two hundred miles long from tide water to the mountains. The existing Federal policy and public opinion in favor of using government funds in the construction of new trans-

[1] It sat in the Federal capitol.
[2] "Proceedings of the Chesapeake and Ohio Canal Convention." Washington, 1823.

Private Carriage. Carriage for Passengers. Car with Freight. Locomotive Engine.

RAIL-ROAD, ENGINE, AND CARRIAGES.

237.—Another picture probably containing as much imagination as actuality. The passenger car may have been a truthful delineation, but the engine is the English *Novelty*. The last car, which is a horse-equipage standing on a platform, is the first published intimation of the private car of the future.

portation routes—which policy was again destined to dominate Congress and to sweep the country as a political issue within the next two years—was also visible in the action of the convention, which proposed a scheme of ownership for the waterway that would distribute its capital shares according to the following plan:

The United States to own one million dollars' worth of stock; Virginia to own seven hundred and fifty thousand dollars' worth of stock; Maryland to own five hundred thousand dollars' worth of stock; the District of Columbia to own five hundred thousand dollars' worth of stock.[1]

It was also resolved that the United States should control and be responsible for all stock, and have a dominant voice in the management of the project. It was further decided to call the enterprise "The Chesapeake and Ohio Canal."

According to the ideas of the convention, therefore, the Federal government and certain of the states were to be partners in the undertaking, and the consent of all was necessary before it could be completed. The acquiescence of the national administration and of Virginia, Maryland and Pennsylvania was requisite before it could be begun. This condition of affairs resulted in a delay of not less than five years between the date of the convention and the day on which actual construction work was commenced. For a long time previous—and even during the period under immediate consideration—the individual states of the union had been and still were at odds on the subject of their interstate communications,[2] and jealousies born of

[1] At this time it was calculated that the cost of the enterprise from Georgetown to the mountains would be about $2,600,000.
[2] The action of the New York court in declaring that steamboats from another state could be prevented from entering New York, just as if they were infected goods dangerous to public health, will be recalled.

RAILROAD DEPOT AT PHILADELPHIA.

238.—Early Pennsylvania roads. Terminus and passenger car of the Philadelphia, Germantown and Norristown Railway in 1831 or 1832. First railroad in Philadelphia. The line did not then have a locomotive, and the artist supplied the deficiency by a good drawing of Stevenson's *Rocket*. The passenger car is the best contemporary portrayal of such an early American vehicle thus far found.

those relations had much to do with the postponement of the plan.

Virginia granted a charter to the company early in 1824, adding to her endorsement of it a declaration of her opinion on the constitutional question involved by the proposed use of government money in the enterprise. This she was compelled to do in order to maintain her established position respecting state's rights as opposed to broad Federal authority. Maryland refused for a time to pass a law permitting the organization of the proposed company, and Pennsylvania likewise declined to take any action. The attitude of both those commonwealths was in large part due to state jealousies and to a fear that the contemplated undertaking would bring more benefit to other communities than to themselves. Indeed, this apprehension was openly avowed during the next session of the Maryland legislature, and it was then believed by members of that body that the proposed canal would bring Washington and Georgetown into close touch with the West and thereby benefit those cities rather than Baltimore. Maryland finally did grant the desired charter, but only on condition that she might have the right to extend the canal in such manner as to bring the eastern end of it to her own metropolis.[1]

At this time, as has been shown by the history of the National Road, the Federal Congress believed that the country might constitutionally use its money in the building of travel and transportation routes, and a few weeks later that body passed a law confirming the action of Virginia and Maryland. President Monroe signed the act on his last day in office,[2] thus giving his endorsement to a

[1] See "Laws of Maryland: December Session 1824." Maryland's confirmation of the charter was under date of January 31, 1825.
[2] March 3, 1825. His approval of the extension of the Cumberland Road through Ohio, Indiana and Illinois was also recorded on the same day.

governmental policy which he himself had previously believed to be unconstitutional. So in 1825, practically two years after corporations began to apply for railroad charters, the nation was engaged in interstate turnpike and canal building in an effort to create a more efficient transportation system by public funds. The Pennsylvania legislature sanctioned the canal plan in 1826,[1] and for a short time everything seemed favorable for the commencement of actual work. But all the states involved discovered in the plan, as it then existed, certain conditions which they believed would operate against them individually, and numerous amendments to the canal charter were therefore passed by them. Some of these amendments required adoption by all parties to the enterprise, and not until 1830 were legal obstacles removed from the path of the desired highway.

Still another cause that entailed delay in beginning the canal lay in a hitherto unmentioned feature of the Federal policy toward the subject of constructing public improvements. Congress had passed a bill in 1824 appropriating funds to obtain "the necessary surveys and estimates on the subject of roads and canals," and President Monroe had given his executive signature to the act, which created a Federal "Board of Internal Improvements." This board had been directed to "make immediate reconnaissance of the country between the waters of the Potomac and the head of navigation on the Ohio, and between the Ohio and Lake Erie for the purpose of ascertaining the practicability of communications between these points, of discussing the most suitable route for the same and of forming plans and estimates in total of the

[1] February 9.

expense of erection."[1] In the spring of 1826 the Board of Public Improvements had reported that the eastern section of the proposed canal—that part lying between Georgetown and Cumberland—would cost over eight millions of dollars.

The announcement of this estimate was a serious blow to the advocates of the plan and gave corresponding encouragement to all those throughout the country who were turning toward railroads as the most desirable solution of the problem presented by the need for better physical communications between the East and the interior.

But sturdy believers in the Chesapeake and Ohio Canal refused to be overwhelmed. Another convention of its supporters assembled in Washington in December of 1826 and characterized the unfavorable financial estimate as excessive. A new survey of the proposed route between Georgetown and Cumberland was therefore made and a revised report was sent to Congress in March of 1828, in which it was stated that the work could be done for four and a half million dollars. The public began to subscribe for stock in the proposed company in the autumn of 1827, and within six weeks more than one million and a half dollars had been pledged. On May 24, 1828, Congress authorized the United States treasurer to subscribe to one million dollars' worth of stock and also guaranteed similar subscriptions made by the towns of Washington, Georgetown and Alexandria to the amount of one and a half million dollars. The United States therefore became a partner in the undertaking to the extent of two and a half million dollars.[2]

[1] Senate Document No. 32; 18th Congress, 2nd Session.
[2] The amounts subscribed by the three municipalities here named were paid by the Treasury to foreign stockholders who had bought the securities under the Congressional guarantee.

239.—A carefully drawn but crude print of *Old Ironsides,* first locomotive of the Philadelphia, Germantown and Norristown railroad, and the first engine made by Baldwin. Built and put in commission in 1832. The car, also sketched with obvious care, is seemingly the same vehicle shown in the preceding print.

The Chesapeake and Ohio Canal Company was finally organized in June, 1828, and ground was broken during the same summer—the date of course being July 4th. The usual procession, speeches and other ingredients of a public celebration characterized the occasion, and when all was ready for the climax of the day President John Quincy Adams stepped forward and dramatically thrust his shovel into the ground. It struck a root, and his effort to bring up a clod of earth was a failure. So he laid down his shovel, took off his coat and hat, picked up the shovel again and made a second and more vigorous effort in his temporary occupation of day laborer. This time he was successful, and the work was at last begun.[1]

[1] A description of the day's ceremonies was printed in Vol. 34 of "Niles' Register," p. 325.

The building details proceeded slowly amid many physical obstacles whose seriousness had not been properly appreciated, and the cost of going ahead assumed formidable proportions. There were times during the next two years when the question of continuing the project or abandoning it seemed to hang almost by a hair as a consequence of the extent to which the cost of progress exceeded the original estimates. One of these occasions developed in 1830, and is portrayed in a letter then written to President Mercer of the company by Richard Rush, one of its legal advisers. The letter ran:

"Private.

"Washington, April 17, 1830.

"My dear Sir: I have just returned from a short visit to Annapolis. I there learned that great pains have been taken to impress the Governor and Council with the belief that to complete the canal as far as Cumberland on the plan on which the work is now going on will require twelve or fifteen hundred thousand dollars more than the company now have, of all funds, including the Dutch loan; for it was so that I understood my informant. I was amazed, and stated my entire disbelief in the above representation, but had no facts in detail to repell it authoritatively.

"The Governor and Council have been vested with authority to vote the proxy of Maryland, and will endeavor by their votes to undo everything, I imagine, unless they get better information before the time arrives. I write you this letter confidentially. You, my dear sir, in conjunction with any of the Board to whom you may show it, will best know what to do on the occasion. It strikes me, however, that not one day should be lost in sending a proper person to Annapolis charged with materials for making known the facts as they truly are representing the cost, and in the most authentic way that the case will admit of.

"I remain as ever, my dear sir, sincerely yours,

"Mr. Mercer."   "Richard Rush."

This and other similar crises were successfully passed in one way or another, and by the summer of 1831 twenty miles of the canal at its eastern end had been finished. The company then found itself involved in a legal controversy with the Baltimore and Ohio Railroad over questions growing out of the physical location of the two enterprises.

By the year 1832 the canal company had disentangled itself from obstacles temporarily interposed against its extension, but in the meantime it had used up all its money and could make no further progress until it had found another source of financial help. The Federal government had decided that it would withdraw from active participation in the undertaking. Maryland had already expended more than half a million dollars, and could expect no returns on her investment unless she followed it with a much larger sum. Two years of debate ensued over the best policy to be pursued in these circumstances, and in 1834 the Maryland general assembly authorized the state to loan the company two million dollars. Pennsylvania and Ohio were already deeply engrossed in the construction of their own canal systems, and Virginia declined to do anything further unless those more western states could be relied on for a share of the support necessary to carry the enterprise ahead. So the whole burden fell upon Maryland, several million dollars more were supplied, and by the middle of 1837 the canal had been finished to a point a little more than one hundred miles west of Georgetown. The financial panic which swept over the country in 1837 brought still further trouble to the company, and in the following year the state was compelled to subscribe to its stock in the additional amount of one million, three hundred and seventy-five thousand dollars. Three years later, in 1841, the work was again brought to a halt through lack of funds and Maryland itself was involved in financial difficulty. About one hundred and fifty miles of canal were then in operation and bringing in some revenues, though its receipts were less than the outlay necessary for its maintenance. A final exertion by Maryland in 1844 resulted in bringing more help to the canal, and it was at last finished to Cumberland in the year 1850.[1]

At a considerably later day[2] the Federal government again displayed an interest in the original proposition of 1823, which was to complete the canal from Cumberland to Pittsburgh and the Ohio River. Surveys were then made in accordance with the plan, but it was never carried out.

It will thus be seen that no less than three important and extensive schemes for connecting the East and the West by artificial waterways characterized the early canal-building epoch of the country. Those of New York and Pennsylvania were pushed on to their intended destinations, and the southernmost of the three projected routes was carried almost two hundred miles into the interior. By the first of these three canals the waters of the Hudson were connected with Lake Erie and eventually also with the interior of the state of Ohio, with the Muskingum, Scioto and Miami Rivers, with the Ohio River, with the interior of Indiana, and with the Wabash River. By the Pennsylvania Canal and the two state-owned railroads operated in connection with it, the waters of the Delaware and Schuylkill Rivers were connected with the Ohio valley. The scheme out of which the Chesapeake and Ohio Canal grew was not carried to its intended conclusion, and so that important work did not become a thoroughfare comparable with those two which

---

[1] An elaborate history of the Chesapeake and Ohio Canal is contained in "The Early Development of the Chesapeake and Ohio Canal Project," by George Washington Ward. Baltimore: 1899, the same being Nos. 9, 10, 11 of Series XVII of the "Johns Hopkins University Studies in Historical and Political Science."
[2] 1870.

lay to the northward of it. But the two that finally did reach the Great Lakes and the head waters of the Ohio linked the eastern seaboard with the populous interior valley and formed practicable routes of transportation over which flowed for many years a constant stream of human and commercial traffic.

It is now desirable to trace the further development of the first American canal period, by which the public works just discussed were extended westward through the states of Ohio and Indiana, where extensive canal building by Federal and state aid finally came to an end, and was soon afterward overtaken and superseded by the use of steam and railed tracks.

CHAPTER XXXVII

THE CANAL SYSTEM OF THE MIDDLE WEST — OHIO TAKES
THE LEAD — INFLUENCE OF NEW YORK'S EXAMPLE
— TWO IMPORTANT WATERWAYS CREATED — THEY
UNITE THE OHIO RIVER WITH LAKE ERIE, THE ERIE
CANAL, THE HUDSON RIVER AND THE ATLANTIC —
INDIANA'S CANAL HISTORY — AID BY THE NATIONAL
GOVERNMENT — A FUNDAMENTAL ERROR OF JUDG-
MENT BY THE WESTERN PEOPLE — M'NAIRY'S DE-
CISIVE SPEECH — THE WABASH AND ERIE CANAL
ROUTE ENCOUNTERS AN INDIAN VILLAGE — RESULT
OF "LOG-ROLLING" LEGISLATION WHEN APPLIED TO
PUBLIC IMPROVEMENTS — TRAFFIC ON THE CANAL
— COLLAPSE OF INDIANA'S SCHEME — MOBS ATTACK
THE WATERWAY — ITS FINAL ABANDONMENT

THE history of the canal system of the Middle West
can best be outlined by dividing it into two sections.
Ohio first began the work of construction, and Indiana
carried it on. The later efforts of the two states to create
an artificial water route which should join them with the
East were so closely interwoven as to demand a simultaneous consideration, but the first attempt of the interior
to improve and expand a national transportation system
by the making of canals was centered in and confined to
Ohio. Ohio's pretentious undertaking during the early
days of actual canal building was closely connected with
the ambitious project of New York State that has already

been described, but a well-defined agitation for the creation of canals existed in Ohio even before New York built her waterway from the Hudson to Lake Erie. As early as the year 1807 a Federal senator from Ohio had urged in Congress that the national administration interest itself in the subject of canals and turnpikes.[1]

It has already been said that the Erie Canal Commission of New York made an attempt, soon after its organization in 1810, to secure Federal support for the proposed Hudson and Erie Canal. When that endeavor failed the New York Commission turned to Ohio for help, and the western state made a prompt and favorable reply to New York's appeal. The Ohio legislature passed a resolution[2] declaring its opinion that the digging of a waterway which should unite the Hudson River with the lake system was a matter of interstate and national importance, and that in its judgment the general government should itself undertake the work. The outbreak of the second war with Great Britain temporarily obscured the consequence of this and all similar internal concerns, however, and no action was taken by Congress. At the close of the war, after New York had finally abandoned her desire to secure Federal aid in building the Erie Canal, she again appealed to Ohio for assistance in carrying out her contemplated effort. Ohio's executive[3] laid before the legislature of his state in December of 1816 a letter written by De Witt Clinton in which that eminent advocate of canals asked Ohio to join in the creation of the New York waterway, and pointed out the advantages which would accrue to Ohio by such procedure.[4] But by

---

[1] A resolution to that effect was then introduced by Senator Worthington.
[2] On January fifteenth, 1812.
[3] Worthington, who as Senator had introduced the resolution of 1807.
[4] See "Ohio Senate Journal" for 1816, p. 68.

that time Ohio was beginning to discuss the building of canals within her own limits, and her legislature in consequence did not favor New York's appeal for financial help. During the next five years the question of canal construction in Ohio received the constantly increasing attention of the people of that state, and various plans for

240.—Another print of *Old Ironsides.* Showing the two types of passenger vehicles then most widely used. Drawn and engraved by Alexander Robb, who lived in Philadelphia at the time. Richard Imlay, the car-builder, who made for the Baltimore and Ohio road, in 1830, a car almost identical with the first one here portrayed, also had his shop in Philadelphia. Robb was therefore in position to see both locomotive and passenger coach. He duplicated the first of these cars in his engraving shown by illustration No. 227.

the suggested work were at all times before the assembly. Finally, in 1822, the legislature passed a bill providing that surveys and estimates be made for one or more canals which should extend across the state from north to south and join the waters of Lake Erie and the Ohio River. Again the mutual interests of Ohio and New York were disclosed, and the eastern state loaned to her western sister one of the few competent Americans[1] of that day who possessed sufficient engineering knowledge to perform the task which Ohio desired to begin.

Ohio's survey and further consideration of the contemplated ditch extended over the following three years, and early in 1825 her lawmakers entered on the

[1] James Geddes, who had been prominent in the construction of the Erie Canal up to that time. He made the Ohio survey.

policy of canal building.[1] By the terms of the act then passed the canals were to be undertaken wholly as a state enterprise and by means of borrowed funds, and a state tax system was devised by which it was expected that a sinking fund would be formed to meet the interest on the proposed loans and gradually retire the principal thereof until such period as the profits of the canals should be sufficient to meet those duties. At the time Ohio formulated her plan of canal digging it was estimated that the cost would be about $6,600,000. This estimate, as was usually the case in such matters, was much too low, and some $16,000,000 were ultimately expended before the state's system of artificial waterways was completed.[2]

Two canals were authorized by the Ohio act of 1825. One of these was to extend from Portsmouth on the Ohio River, following the course of the Scioto River in a generally northward direction to a point in Franklin county near the center of the state, from which it was to swing northeastward to Tuscarawas county, and thence proceed almost directly north until it terminated at the village of Cleveland on the shore of Lake Erie. The other route was to begin at Cincinnati and extend northward until it reached the valley of the Great Miami River, whence it was later to extend still farther northward until it entered the valley of the Maumee, and was thence to proceed along the Maumee until it joined the waters of Lake Erie at Toledo. Actual commencement of the work was set for July Fourth of 1825, and was attended by elaborate ceremonies and popular rejoicing. Governor Clinton of New

[1] By a law passed on February 4th entitled "An Act to Provide for the Internal Improvement of the State of Ohio by Navigable Canals."
[2] The profit produced by the operation of the canals did not suffice to pay the interest charges on the canal loans by the year 1837, as expected. The panic of 1837 and the financial and economic conditions produced by the introduction of railroads also exercised a powerful influence on Ohio canals and the monetary scheme originally devised for their creation. As a consequence the state debt incurred was not wiped out until a recent period.

York journeyed from Albany to be present on the occasion, and he lifted the first spadeful of earth that marked the beginning of the undertaking. Governor Morrow of Ohio dug the second shovelful, and as he and his colleague of the Empire State thus inaugurated the physical effort on which the commonwealth was embarked a mighty cheer arose from the thousands who had gathered to witness the scene.[1] Governor Clinton also took part in the festivities at Middletown, later in the same month, where the Miami and Erie Canal was begun.

After Governors Morrow and Clinton had laid aside their spades the further process of excavation was continued by thousands of laborers who were paid thirty cents a day and their subsistence for working from sunrise to sunset. For a few months those more capable though less celebrated diggers were also furnished with a daily allowance of whisky amounting to a quantity then termed a "jiggerful."[2]

Work on both canals went on without serious interruption, and the first completed section of the waterway between Portsmouth and Cleveland was opened to traffic exactly two years after the enterprise was begun. This part of the canal extended northward from Akron[3] to Cleveland, and was about thirty-seven miles long. The first packet passed along the waters of these thirty-seven miles on the Fourth of July, 1827, and an account of its triumphal progress was contained in the next annual message of the governor[4] in which he said of the boat: "She was cheered in her passage by thousands of our delighted

[1] This first digging took place at Licking Summit, in Licking county.
[2] Howe's "Historical Collections of Ohio," 1847. The precise amount of liquor contained in a "jiggerful" can not now be stated, and even at that time there may have been jiggers of varying capacities. But it is likely that even a small jigger held a substantial drink.
[3] The present city of Akron, in Ohio, had its beginning in a temporary encampment of laborers who were engaged in canal work between 1825 and 1827.
[4] Governor Trimble's message of December 4, 1827.

241.—Scene in Philadelphia showing a railway car of the "Pioneer Fast Line" to Pittsburgh. Passengers were transported between the two cities over a system of canals and railroads built and owned by Pennsylvania. The boats and cars were owned and operated by private companies, of which the Pioneer Line was one. Advertised time of passage, four days. Date, 1833-1834.

citizens who had assembled from the adjacent country at different points on the canal to witness the novel and interesting sight." A small division of the Miami Canal was also opened during the same year, to the accompaniment of similar popular enthusiasm. In an official account of the occasion it was said: "Three fine boats, crowded with citizens delighted with the event and interest of the occasion, left the basin six miles north of Cincinnati and proceeded to Middletown with the most perfect success. The progress of the boats was about three miles an hour, including locks and other detentions. The return trip was made with equal success."[1]

Additional parts of the Ohio system as originally planned were in succession opened for traffic, and the Miami Canal was practically finished before 1829. The channel between Portsmouth and Cleveland[2] was completed in 1833, and Ohio then owned more than four hundred miles of navigable canals. These additions to the transportation system of the state were never less than twenty-six feet wide at the bottom, forty feet wide at the surface and four feet deep. In many places the dimensions named were exceeded, for the state commissioners always caused the excavation of a larger channel than was called for by the law in regions where such a policy might be followed without materially increasing the estimated cost of the work. In consequence of this wise plan some portions of both canals were from fifty to one hundred and fifty feet wide, and from five to ten feet deep. So it came about that by the close of the year 1833, and through use of the Hudson River, the Erie Canal, Lake Erie, the Ohio and Erie Canal and the Ohio River, all cities and settle-

---

[1] "Sixth Annual Report of the Ohio Canal Commission," January 5, 1828. The trip described took place on November 28, 1827.
[2] Together with a number of short lateral canals connected with it.

ments along the Ohio River and many of the towns throughout the whole extent of the state of Ohio were connected by direct water communication with New York and the Atlantic coast.

At this point in the history of the canals of the interior it is desirable to introduce Indiana as a factor in the further extension of the system of artificial waterways built in the middle states.[1]

One of the considerations—in addition to those heretofore mentioned—which convinced both East and West that increased facilities of communication were necessary between the two sections, was the experience derived by the country from the War of 1812. It was recognized during and after the war that the existing wilderness roads extending out through Virginia and North Carolina to Tennessee and Kentucky, and the Ohio River, not only failed to furnish a sufficient means of transit for travel and commerce in time of peace, but that the lack of better

[1] The most important historical study of the Ohio Canal system is a monograph published by the Ohio State Archeological and Historical Society in 1905, under the title "History of the Ohio Canals: Their Construction, Cost, Use and Partial Abandonment." This is a careful work of one hundred and eighty-one pages, and was prepared by C. C. Huntington and C. P. McClelland, under the direction of Professor Haggerty of Ohio University. It not only deals with the history and construction of the canals of the state, but with their finances and economic value.

There have been two recent monographs dealing with the history of the Indiana canals. The earliest of these in point of date is Number Twelve of Cottman's historical pamphlets, entitled "Canals of Indiana." This is a twenty-four page pamphlet containing material previously published in Volume Three, Number Three of the "Indiana Magazine of History." The other recent item discussing the Indiana Canal System is Volume Five, Number Two of the publications of the Indiana Historical Society, its title being, "Internal Improvements in Early Indiana," by Logan Esarey, Indianapolis, 1912. Esarey's monograph is a book of one hundred and fifty-eight pages and constitutes the most elaborate historical review of Indiana's early road and canal system that has as yet appeared. Its narrative and facts were drawn from substantially the same sources as those used by the author of these volumes, namely the early official state records, and files of early newspapers in the collections of the Indiana State Library. It is proper to say in this connection that Mr. Esarey's investigation of the subject was made prior to that of the writer, although his monograph was not published until some months after material intended for use in these present volumes had been collected and put in form. When considered in relation to Indiana's early population and resources, that state's activity in an attempt to construct a system of public improvements was the most pretentious, as well as the most disastrous and significant in its lessons, of all similar pioneer efforts. The subject of such former state enterprises is receiving a constantly increasing attention, and the publication of Esarey's contribution to the social and economic history of the canal period, prior to the appearance of these volumes, has fortunately enabled the author of this history to abbreviate the space which he would otherwise have felt compelled to devote to Indiana's undertaking and the significance of its collapse. Esarey's work should be read in connection with Benton's "The Wabash Trade Route in the Development of the Old Northwest": Baltimore, The Johns Hopkins Press, 1903.

825

transportation facilities also left the interior almost defenseless against England in time of war. The conflict emphasized the need of continuing at once along the general lines of the national policy previously outlined by the road building provision in the Ohio Act of 1802 and the Cumberland Road Act of 1806.

Congress in 1816 passed a bill appropriating about one million and a half dollars, together with an annual sum of about four hundred thousand dollars thereafter, to be used for the construction of interstate roads and canals. The success of the bill in Congress was mainly due to the support it received from the interior commonwealths. They advocated the measure as an economic and social necessity rather than as a military expedient, but were not especially concerned over the reasons leading to its approval by the East so long as the object designed by the bill was attained.

President Madison vetoed the act, despite his previous approval of six laws in favor of the Cumberland Road. His decision on that occasion was perhaps the final determining influence that impelled the four states of New York, Pennsylvania, Ohio and Indiana to enter upon the creation of extensive canal systems as state undertakings. It was in 1817 that New York committed herself to the building of the Erie Canal. Pennsylvania, in the same year, passed a legislative resolution inviting Virginia, Kentucky, Ohio and Indiana to join with herself in a conference having for its purpose the improvement of communication facilities in the middle and western states. Clinton, of New York, also wrote to Governor Jennings of Indiana in 1817 in reference to the need of canals which should join the lake system of waters with the Ohio and Mississippi Rivers, and Indiana's governor discussed

Clinton's letter and its subject matter in his message to the state legislature later in the same year.[1] At this time the small population and limited wealth of Indiana[2] made it impossible for the young state to embark upon any such pretentious scheme of public works as was under way in the East, but public discussion of the subject continued to increase during the next three years.

The opening of the Erie Canal in New York, the commencement of work on the Ohio canal system in 1825, the rumors which came from England about a new method of transportation called the "railroad," Strickland's book on railroads published in 1826,[3] and numerous other similar events served still further to concentrate Indiana's attention upon the subject, and the active history of her early scheme of public improvements soon began.

During the preceding two or three years the state legislature had been petitioning Congress for a donation of public lands through whose sale she might secure funds for canal building. While one of these requests was before the national House of Representatives, in 1823, objection was made to the proposal on the ground that the land in question had been given to the Federal government by the state of Virginia with a proviso that it should not be used except for purposes of common benefit to all the states. The opponents of the suggested measure argued that the projected Indiana canal was a local work and of state importance only. Those legislators who opposed governmental aid to proposed internal improvements in the Ohio valley also pointed to Pennsylvania, where similar work was being done at that state's own expense.

[1] See "Journal of the Indiana House of Representatives" for 1817, p. 8.
[2] Even at as late a date as 1824 the yearly income of the state was only about forty thousand dollars.
[3] Strickland's work is discussed in a later chapter.

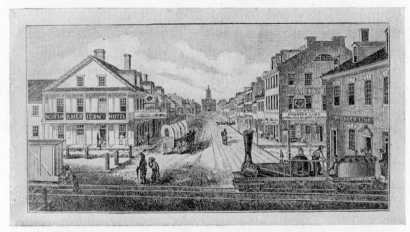

242.—A train of the Pioneer Fast Line passing through a Pennsylvania town at a considerably later period, when locomotives were common. Date, probably about 1842. The canals which constituted part of the system built by the state were sold to private companies between 1845 and 1858, and the main line of railway was sold in 1857.

But to this the western states retorted that Pennsylvania owned her own public lands, whereas in the West the public domain belonged to the general government and so could not be made the basis of state credit. It was finally decided that the proposed western artificial water-way was of national importance, and in 1827 the Federal government gave to the state a considerable amount of land in the neighborhood of the Fort Wayne portage on condition that Indiana create a canal connecting the navigable waters of the Maumee and Wabash Rivers. This donation was accepted in 1828, and the state thus stood committed to the building of the designated artificial traffic thoroughfare.

At this time the whole country, both East and West, was in a veritable frenzy of excitement over the subject of improving its travel and transportation routes. The National Road was being pushed westward through

Ohio; the Erie Canal was in successful operation throughout its entire length; Pennsylvania was spending large sums on her canals, some sections of which were in operation; parts of both the Ohio canals had already been opened to traffic; railroad cars pulled by horses were regularly travelling back and forth over a few miles of the new Baltimore and Ohio Railroad; South Carolina was preparing to build a long railroad from Charleston to Hamburg; the country was rapidly increasing in prosperity; thousands of its citizens in all the states were hastening to invest their savings in the stocks of projected railroads or canals; the subject of better travel and traffic facilities was the principal question occupying the attention of the newspaper press; and political parties achieved ascendency or encountered defeat in accordance with their attitude on the topic of universal public interest.

As soon as Indiana began her survey for the projected canal between the waters of the Wabash and the Maumee it was discovered that a part of the canal would necessarily have to lie in Ohio. This complication resulted in a conference at Cincinnati in 1829 between representatives of the two states, and it was agreed that Ohio should undertake that portion of the waterway within her own borders and accept some of the Federal land as recompense for her work. It was further agreed that each state should enjoy identical rights throughout the entire length of the canal. Indiana ratified the Cincinnati agreement, but Ohio refused to indorse it, and maintained her attitude of opposition for a number of years. Her position constituted another of those numerous instances of state jealousy or sectional narrow-mindedness which from time to time characterized the early history of the national transportation system. Ohio's attitude was due to the fact

829

that she was already digging two canals designed to unite Lake Erie and the towns along her southern border, and one of these[1] was to extend north and south throughout the length of the state and but a short distance to the eastward of the Indiana boundary. If the canal planned by Indiana and aided by the Federal government was created, and Lake Erie and the Maumee were by it joined to the Wabash and lower Ohio, it was obvious that a considerable amount of water travel and commercial business would thereby be diverted through Indiana as interstate traffic, instead of flowing southward to Cincinnati on a waterway controlled exclusively by Ohio. Nevertheless Ohio did finally consent, in 1836, to the physical union of her system with that of her western neighbor. Work on the Indiana part of the canal had already been begun near Fort Wayne early in the year 1832.

This was a critical era in the history of the transportation utilities of the Middle West. Scarcely a month went by that did not bring to the interior fresh news concerning the rapid advance of the railroad idea in the eastern states. To many minds it was already apparent that the railway was destined to spread over the land and ultimately revolutionize the conditions of its social and economic life. Those who entertained this belief were profoundly convinced that the adoption, in the comparatively sparsely settled interior, of a public policy committing the states to the immediate building of extensive canal systems would constitute a serious error. Though no less anxious than all other of their fellow citizens that facilities for movement and commerce should be increased, they felt it would be the part of caution, and better in the end, if they should wait yet a little while

---

[1] That between Cincinnati and Toledo.

longer in order to be sure of the wisdom of their course. And meanwhile an equal—or perhaps still larger—portion of the people of the West pointed to the established success of the Erie Canal and to the benefits it had brought to the commonwealth which had constructed it. And they

243.—A train on the West Chester railroad in Pennsylvania. The road was built in 1835 and was nine miles long. Horse-drawn cars were also employed on the West Chester line. Engraved in mezzotint by John Sartain from a drawing by the artist Thomas Ashton.

also advanced the argument that action of some sort was necessary if the West was to attain the place its undeveloped opportunities and potential strength entitled it to occupy. They failed to see that the Erie Canal—under the peculiar national economic conditions then existing—held a position which was not only unique in the communication system of the nation but one which could not elsewhere be duplicated until the interior itself possessed in substantially equal degree those circumstances of social development and industrial progress which then characterized the East. Amid conditions then prevailing the Erie Canal was not, and could not be, an artery through which might flow equal and reciprocal advantages for both sections. It was rather a broad estuary of trade movement into which rolled many smaller streams of traffic, and it became mighty in its effect in the region where it existed only because it resembled, in a sense, a natural river fed by innumerable tributaries.[1]

It was this error in estimating the economic relationship of a canal to a population that led the West to its early embarkation on the policy of canal construction. The people of the interior were carried away by their own desperate need, and failed to see that an extensive canal system is not a transportation device suited to a vast region of scanty population and undeveloped resources, but is preëminently a device suitable for such conditions as are gradually appearing throughout the whole region east of the Mississippi River, wherein the benefits of such a system might now be distributed with something like an approximate equality through all the districts connected and served by it.

So Indiana finally committed herself to the policy of canal building, but even after the legislature had formally acted on the question there still ensued a delay of several years, due in part to a continuation of the debate over the relative merits of canals and railroads. Nevertheless

[1] By the year 1847 the canal business concentrating at Albany was greater than that derived by New Orleans, in the same year, from the Mississippi River and its tributaries. In 1872 but one-twelfth of the tonnage reaching Albany by means of the Erie and Oswego Canals originated in New York State. The other eleven-twelfths came from outside states. The relative proportions here mentioned did not exhibit quite such a striking contrast in the early days of the Erie Canal, but the economic principle governing them existed from the first, and its effects were visible, though they were not taken into account by those of the interior who believed that Mississippi valley canals would at that time have corresponding value to the Middle West.

L. Crepon del.   Arch' of N. P. Osborn Bethlehem   P. S. Duval & Son's lith Phil.

M? PISGAH PLANE AT MAUCH CHUNK.
Length 2322 feet. Elevation 662 feet.

244.—Several of the early railways of Pennsylvania, the Mohawk and Hudson
line in New York, one in Indiana, and one or two roads in New England, at
first surmounted steep grades by means of inclined planes. The cars were
lifted and lowered by means of stationary engines and huge cables. But the
delay and cost of such practise, and accidents, resulted in the substitution of
détours and more gradual ascents.

the state eventually adhered to its decision, and one of the considerations impelling it to that course was the argument that all materials and labor for the making of a canal could be found in Indiana, and all the money expended in its construction would therefore remain in the state, whereas if a railroad was decided on, all the iron and many other materials for it would necessarily come from the East and the money representing their cost would leave the commonwealth.

When the day arrived whereon it had been agreed by the legislature to take a vote on the proposed measure the issue seemed to hang in the balance. The chamber of the House of Representatives was crowded with spectators and a powerful speech had just been made against the bill, when up rose Colonel John McNairy, a famous backwoods orator of the upper Wabash valley. Raising himself almost on tiptoe he secured recognition from the Chair, and then at the very highest pitch of his voice he shouted "Mr. Speaker, our population on the Wabash am great, but our resources for salt am slim. Salt! They cannot emigrate up the Wabash!" This speech settled the matter. No one asked for the floor to reply. The question was put from the Chair and the bill passed by a decisive majority. "The cannon were fired, the city was illuminated, and all was joy and hilarity at the capital for weeks thereafter."[1]

The Federal lands donated to the state had been put on sale in 1830, and Indiana permitted their purchase on a payment of one-seventh of the cost price in cash, the remainder to be paid in six equal annual installments.[2]

---

[1] This account of the incident and McNairy's address are taken from Smith's "Early Indiana Trials: And Sketches." Indiana's act was passed in January of 1832, and therein it was directed that work begin by March of the same year.

[2] Insufficient cash for the commencement of operations was obtained through this method, and the state was compelled to borrow $600,000 in addition to the sums thus received.—"Sessions Laws of Indiana" for 1831-2-4.

At the time work on the canal was begun at Fort Wayne, some of the country near that town was still owned and occupied by the Miami Indians, and the canal was built through their territory for part of its length. The natives had granted permission for the necessary work by treaty with the United States in language which read: "It is agreed that the State of Indiana may lay out a canal or road through any of these reservations."[1]

During the construction of the canal through the Indian village of White Raccoon[2] it was observed that a cabin belonging to Cha-pine, orator of the tribe, was situated precisely on the line chosen by the surveyors for the location of the waterway. Cha-pine's home was therefore taken down, moved and rebuilt at the expense of the canal fund of Indiana. The artificial river was dug literally through and among Indian villages and native farms.

The moving of the Miami orator's lodge by the consent of himself and his people carried a significance more important than the act itself. It typified the process by which America's modern transportation system came into being. In like manner were the Indians, group by group, set to one side in order that their habitations as a race might not interfere with the intercommunications of the white Americans.

The first section of the Wabash Canal, some thirty miles long and extending from Fort Wayne to the town of Huntington, was opened for business on the Fourth of July in 1835. During the same year the proposal was made that the state embark on the construction of an extensive system of canals, railroads and turnpikes whose

[1] Treaty of 1826 between the United States and the Miamis.
[2] White Raccoon was a chief of the tribe.

835

total cost was to be about six million dollars. The plan at once became the principal political issue before the people, and the elections held later in the same year were fought and decided upon it. When the legislature assembled for its next session public opinion was known to be in favor of the proposed law and it was overwhelmingly passed.[1] With the enactment of this legislation, which was without question based on the desire of the people and that contained some features of merit Indiana entered on a course of action destined to lead her for more than thirty years through a series of unhappy experiences and embarrassments. The main feature of the proposed system of internal improvements was to be the Wabash and Erie Canal, extending in a generally southwestward direction from the Ohio state line to the town of Terre Haute, near the Illinois boundary. About a dozen other canals, railroads and turnpikes were also provided for by the bill, all of which were to connect either with the main canal, the Ohio River or Lake Erie.

The principal weakness embodied in the elaborate scheme thus undertaken was the geographical distribution of the proposed new thoroughfares. Local and sectional jealousies played a dominant part in the final shaping of the plan, and various projects of undoubted value embraced in it were only enabled to obtain legislative support by the inclusion of other features introduced for the purpose of giving all parts of the state a share in the desired public work. As finally adopted the law was so drawn that only seven counties of the state were not included among those touched by the proposed improvements. The process of framing the legislation and adopting the policy to which it committed the state was sub-

[1] In January of 1836.

stantially identical with that which has long prevailed in the Federal congress in connection with the periodic passage of national laws providing for the improvement of rivers and harbors and for the erection of public buildings.[1] Under the operation of such a method important enterprises of undoubted general value can only secure support in legislative bodies by indefensible concessions permitting the expenditure of public money in needless and wasteful undertakings.

Another feature of the Indiana law was its establishment of a Board of Internal Improvements consisting of nine members, to each of whom was assigned supervision of certain portions of the construction work. The several members of this board made immediate haste to push the separate parts of the plan allotted to their individual jurisdictions, without giving attention to the big question of physical coöperation and connection between all the scattered units of the system or to public revenues that could only be derived from finished work.

During the years from 1836 to 1839 inclusive, Indiana borrowed $6,673,000 for the purpose of expanding her traffic routes, of which sum all but $400,000 was obtained for use on the new enterprises authorized by the law of 1836. The heavy loans thus negotiated in behalf of the general system seriously disturbed those financial arrangements planned for the obtaining of money to complete the previously authorized Wabash Canal, on which trunk line of the system the success of all its other parts to a large extent depended.[2] No plan for connecting adjoining sections of the whole scheme was followed. These oversights,

---

[1] In the national Congress the process came to be known as "You scratch my back and I'll scratch yours." The representatives of various states would combine to obstruct or defeat such a bill unless their commonwealths were included among those in which money was to be expended.
[2] The state also sold bonds on credit to eastern speculators and lost over three million dollars by those transactions.

together with the panic of 1837, the increased cost of labor and material, and heavy monetary losses due to lax methods employed in disposing of state bonds finally wrecked the whole pretentious enterprise. The almost complete collapse of Indiana's internal improvement policy was pictured by a newspaper of the state[1] in these words:

"The policy of constructing the work and parts of works simultaneously was so well pursued that no considerable portion of any work was completed or fit for use. . . . There lies the system still, its unfinished excavations, embankments, locks, culverts, aqueducts and bridges hastening to ruin."

The State Board of Public Improvements was unable to pay its bills by 1839 and ended its attempt to build the turnpikes, canals and railroads so auspiciously begun but three years before with the enthusiastic approval of the whole population. In 1841 the state offered to transfer nearly all the system to such private companies as might be willing to take its units, on condition that they be completed. Only the Wabash and Erie Canal was omitted from this offer and it remained the property of the state. Indiana's debt due to the work done on her improvements project then amounted to $9,500,000. To balance this expenditure she possessed only two hundred miles of canal in operation, from which she obtained about five thousand dollars a year in tolls; two little railroads whose similar receipts were $26,500; and various incomplete sections of smaller canals and turnpikes. A few of the unfinished transportation links were taken over by private companies and others were abandoned outright. Among those abandoned was a half-made turnpike between Jeffersonville and Crawfordsville on which $350,000 had been expended. The state-owned railroad between the towns of

[1] "The Tippecanoe Journal," Lafayette, Indiana, Dec. 1, 1841.

245.—The New York and Harlem Railroad. Original passenger car on the line, or one substantially identical with it. The road was formally opened by the use of two such horse-drawn vehicles, and the day was marked by the first American railway collision. Drawn and engraved by Alexander Robb, who pictured a similar car in his drawing shown by illustration No. 240. Date, about 1832.

Madison and Indianapolis was bought by a corporation after it had cost the commonwealth $1,600,000 and had yielded $63,000. Indiana continued the operation of that part of the Wabash and Erie Canal already opened, and undertook to complete it to Terre Haute.

Meantime the canal had reached the town of Peru in 1837, Logansport in 1838, and the Tippecanoe River in 1841. Ohio at last complied with her pledge to connect her own Miami Canal with Indiana's Wabash Canal, and that part of the work lying within the limits of Ohio was ready for use in 1843. Its opening gave Indiana a water outlet to the eastward. She was then enabled to reach Lake Erie at Maumee Bay over the northern part of Ohio's Miami Canal, and to reach the city of Cincinnati by using the southern section of the Miami Canal from the point where that waterway was tapped by the Wabash Canal. The length of the Wabash and Erie Canal at the time was two hundred and fifteen miles, of which the first seventy-one miles westward from Lake Erie lay in Ohio and the remainder, one hundred and forty-four miles, in Indiana. Internal communication by water was then possible by means of the Hudson River, Lake Erie, and the Wabash and Erie Canal to the town of Lafayette on the Wabash River in Indiana.[1] Through traffic began in both directions in 1843 and the tolls received by the Wabash and Erie Canal increased no less than six hundred per cent. Yet even then its income amounted to less than the costs of maintenance and operation.

During this period a number of states had found themselves involved in serious financial difficulties due in most instances to errors of judgment connected with their plans for internal improvements. Indiana's condition has been indicated. Pennsylvania postponed payments on a part of her debt. Ohio was compelled to establish a tax rate of seventy-five cents on each hundred dollars in order to pay the interest on her public debt. Michigan's plan for internal improvements had encountered grave difficulties similar in some respects to those experienced by Indiana, and for a time she could not pay the interest on her obligations.[2] The states of Illinois, Maryland and Mississippi were also unable to meet their interest charges.[3]

Illinois by her own foresight fortunately escaped a fate similar to that which befell Indiana. She, as well as her sister commonwealths to the eastward, had decided to embark on the enterprise of pretentious canal construction, but altered her plan and used most of the money derived from her grant of public lands for the building of railroads. Her principal railway[4] prospered, and Indiana's canal project failed.

The first interstate packet-boats began to ply on the

[1] Indiana's canal reached Lafayette in 1843.
[2] Michigan negotiated a loan for the purpose of making internal improvements. She also sold her securities to financial houses that failed before she had received but a fraction of the amount due to her.
[3] For a detailed statement regarding the situation in the several states as here outlined, see Scott's "Repudiation of State Debts."
[4] The Illinois Central. Another of the early Illinois railways, however—a state enterprise—was not successful and was sold.

Wabash and Erie Canal in 1843. At first they did not run according to any fixed schedule but started on their trips after a profitable number of passengers was assured. Neither was there any attempt during the earliest months of the service to make regular time along the way or to reach destinations on any given day. Sometimes the passengers got their meals at farmhouses along the line of the canal. The first schedule service was announced in 1844, when two enterprising men[1] of Dayton, Ohio, established a packet line connecting Cincinnati on the south with Toledo on the north, and another joining Toledo on the east with Lafayette in the west. These lines of packets continued in operation until the opening of the Toledo and Wabash Railroad in 1854. One of the boats was the packet *Indiana,* which is mentioned in the following pages in connection with some experiences encountered by a family travelling on it.[2] The *Indiana* was an especially popular vessel, and her arrival at Fort Wayne was always the signal for a public concert given at the wharf by two enthusiastic citizens of the town named Ed Parker and Bill Patchen. When the well-known sound of the captain's horn rang through the streets of the village, announcing the coming of the craft, each member of the orchestra abandoned whatever work might be occupying him at the moment. Ed seized his clarinet, Bill grabbed his fiddle, and together they raced to the landing place, there to entertain the disembarking passengers as a token of the town's hospitality.

The distance traversed by a packet-boat from Toledo

[1] Samuel Doyle and William Dickey.
[2] Other boats employed by the same lines on the Miami and the Wabash and Erie Canals were named for different states and were called the "Ohio," the "Illinois," the "Missouri" and the "Kentucky"; still others were known as the "Atlantic," the "Banner," the "Erie," the "Fashion," the "Tempest," the "Cataract" and the "Niagara." The "Niagara" was a steam-propelled canal boat costing ten thousand dollars. She was a financial failure.

to Lafayette was two hundred and forty-two miles, and after a regular schedule had been established the trip between the two towns was regularly made in two days and eight hours. The rates of passage and distances between the four principal cities joined by the Miami Canal of Ohio and the Wabash and Erie Canal of Indiana were as follows:[1]

Trip	Distance	Cost of Ticket
Cincinnati to Fort Wayne	221 miles	$6.75
Lafayette to Fort Wayne	138 "	3.75
Fort Wayne to Toledo	104 "	3.25

The Federal government was to some extent involved in the disaster attending Indiana's plan for public improvements, since it had donated a part of the public domain on condition that the state build a canal by means of money received through a disposal of the lands thus given. Hence the Congress was compelled to give its consent to those plans of the state which followed the collapse, and under which the work of pushing the canal southward from Terre Haute toward the Ohio River was begun. The town of Evansville was at last reached in the year 1853. The length of the Wabash and Erie Canal was then four hundred and fifty-eight miles, and it was the longest artificial waterway in the country. From 1847 to 1856 its business steadily grew, but the action of Indiana in granting charters permitting railroads to parallel the course of the canal[2] later resulted in a pronounced decrease in its traffic, and it fell into disuse. Indiana could not refuse to adopt a new means of transportation in order that she might cling to the slower method

[1] These figures are taken from an advertisement published in the "Fort Wayne Times and People's Press," of October 21, 1847.
[2] The Wabash Valley Railroad, extending westward from Toledo, was finished to Lafayette in 1856. Another railroad extending northward from Evansville through the region occupied by the canal was also authorized by the state.

already established. Yet it is true that the state's action, in availing herself of progress and a new traffic system, did work harm to those of her creditors who held securities based on the older means of communication whose utility and value were thus impaired.

The first packet reached the Indiana town of Terre Haute from Toledo over the Wabash and Erie Canal in 1849, and some idea of the passenger traffic carried on it during that year can be obtained from the following figures:

Total mileage of boats clearing from Fort Wayne in 1849.... 209,982
Total mileage travelled by passengers departing from or arriving at Fort Wayne in 1849...................... 519,336
Total mileage of boats clearing from Lafayette in 1849...... 162,297
Total mileage travelled by passengers departing from or arriving at Lafayette in 1849........................ 505,397

The number of miles travelled by the canal boats departing from or arriving at the four Indiana towns of Fort Wayne, Lafayette, Logansport and Covington during the year 1849 was 485,736. The number of miles travelled by passengers departing from or arriving at the same towns during the year 1849 was 1,294,701.[1]

The number of canal passengers arriving at Fort Wayne during 1850 was 3,419. In 1851 the number of people who reached the same town by canal was 3,083, and those departing numbered 3,108. During the year 1852 no less than 76,962 pounds of passengers' baggage and furniture reached Terre Haute in canal boats, and 291,489 pounds of similar baggage and furniture belonging to west-bound travellers arrived at Lafayette during the same year. The similar figures for Fort Wayne were

[1] The above statistics are compiled from the "Annual Report of the Trustees of the Wabash and Erie Canal": December, 1849. Although passengers could then proceed as far as Terre Haute, the similar figures for that town had not yet been prepared by the company.

still larger, being 455,236 pounds. In those later days of its active history the waterway was exerting an important influence in the settlement of the region through which it extended.

The concluding years of the Wabash and Erie Canal were characterized by active public hostility toward the

246.—A later variety of car on the New York and Harlem. The captain stood on a very small platform at the rear. Horses were employed on the road for several years.

enterprise in some parts of Indiana, and its usefulness was several times destroyed as a result of mob violence. In May of 1854 a mob cut the embankment of a reservoir whose waters were necessary for feeding the canal, thereby disabling that part of the work extending from Terre Haute southward toward Evansville. In May of the following year the water necessary for the operation of the canal was again drained from a reservoir by similar means. The damage was committed by armed men, who worked with blackened faces at mid-day. After this outbreak the

844

governor sent state troops to the spot while repairs were being made, but as soon as the reservoir walls were built up they were once more demolished. Numerous inhabitants of the disaffected region were arrested and charged with complicity in the destruction but were discharged by the local courts. During the same year of 1855 one of the aqueducts of the canal was set on fire by a mob and partially destroyed. The system was by this time falling into disrepair, and the toll receipts became insufficient for its maintenance. A long dispute then ensued between the state and holders of canal bonds, and gradually the whole pretentious work fell to pieces, ceased to exist as a practical transportation route, and was at last abandoned.

The ultimate extent of Ohio's artificial waterway system as it appeared in 1850, after the era of active construction had ended and before the period of partial abandonment began in that state, will be disclosed in the following table:

Length of the Miami and Erie Canal............... 301.49 miles
Length of the Ohio Canal .... 512.26 "
Length of the Pennsylvania and Ohio Canal.......... 76 "
Length of the Sandy and Beaver Canal............. 79 "
Length of the Whitewater Canal .... 32 "

Total ....1000.75 miles

In building these canals Ohio had expended about fifteen millions of dollars.

The material result of the canal-building era throughout the whole country has thus been summed up and discussed by the government:[1]

"Adding together the totals of operating and abandoned canals, we have a grand total of 4,468 miles of canals, costing approximately $214,-

[1] In its review of "Agencies of Transportation," in the United States Census Report for 1880.

041,802. Of these, 1,953 miles are now abandoned, and a large portion of the remaining 2,515 is not paying expenses. This is largely due to railroad competition. All the canals of the New England States are abandoned for commercial purposes. . . . In New York State, 356 miles of lateral canals, costing $10,235,314, have been abandoned; in Pennsylvania 477 miles are abandoned, costing $12,745,780; in Ohio, 205 miles, costing $3,000,000, have been abandoned. Indiana, with the aid of her creditors, constructed 379 miles of canals, costing $6,-325,262, all of which were abandoned upon the construction of railroads along the lines of the canals."

Just as the National Road—as a macadamized turn-pike—paused in its westward course when it had reached the western limits of Indiana, so also did extensive canal building under the direct control or indirect patronage of governmental enterprise finally halt after it had reached the same region. The extension of the Wabash and Erie Canal southward from Terre Haute to Evansville, and its operation to the last-named town for a comparatively brief interval, virtually marked the end of the early canal-building epoch.[1] By the use of the artificial water routes which had up to that time been made through the states of New York, New Jersey, Pennsylvania, Ohio and Indiana, and the further use in conjunction with them of the Great Lakes and the waters of the Ohio and Mississippi Rivers, an immense system of combined natural and artificial interior waterways had been created. Several hundred thousand square miles of territory between the Atlantic Ocean and the Mississippi River had been roughly linked together, and the resultant canal travel undertaken by large numbers of people was for some time a prominent feature of national life.

[1] Although one waterway of the sort—the Illinois and Michigan Canal—was built in Illinois. It extended from Chicago to Peru, and was one hundred miles long.

CHAPTER XXXVIII

TRAVEL ON THE CANALS — THE EARLY BOATS PATTERNED
AFTER KEEL-BOATS AND BARGES — CHANGES IN THEIR
FORM AND ARRANGEMENT — LINE-BOATS AND PACKET-
BOATS — GOING TO BED ON A CANAL PACKET —
THE SLEEPING BUNKS — WHY A TRAVELLER SOME-
TIMES HESITATED TO CHOOSE A LOWER BERTH —
CONDITIONS ON A CROWDED CRAFT — SLEEPING ON
THE FLOOR AND TABLES — THE CLOTHES-LINE — EX-
PERIENCES OF AN UPPER-BERTH PASSENGER IN AN
EFFORT TO GET OUT ON THE ROOF — DELIGHTS OF
CANAL TRAVEL — THE "FIVE CENTS A MILE" SCHEME
— ADVENTURES OF AN ENGLISHMAN AND OF HORACE
GREELEY

THE subject of American travel by means of artificial
waterways is one that has received small attention in
discussions of the canal-building epoch and its effect on
human movement and the settlement of the country.
Doubtless this has been because our canals—to an extent
greater than was involved in the history of any other early
means of transportation—were built more for the avowed
purpose of freight traffic than for any other reason. The
arguments in favor of a canal-building policy contained
little or nothing regarding their possible development as
important factors in public travel. Yet no sooner were
man-made water courses constructed toward the West
than they were seized upon by the people as a means of

moving themselves from place to place, and preëxisting plans for their operation underwent material alteration in consequence of the popular attitude.

The first canal line affording any extensive opportunity for human travel was the one by which New York State connected the waters of the Hudson River with those of Lake Erie. And, even before that immense undertaking was completed in its entirety, the finishing of intermediate sections of the work at once proved that the people looked upon canals not only as routes for commodities but also as useful means for their own journeyings.

While the canals themselves were the enterprises of the states within whose limits they lay, the boats that navigated their waters were the property either of individuals or of companies organized for the purpose of operating them. The conflicting methods of those who built the first boats for canal traffic disclosed a considerable diversity of opinion regarding the most desirable form for such a craft. In fact, though the career of the vehicle was more brief, its history conformed in a general way to the life-story which we have already observed in following the development of the stage-coach. It underwent various changes and alterations in size, appearance and arrangement, and by a process of evolution at last emerged into a standard type which thereafter prevailed throughout the country.

The first canal boats varied in their construction and plan in accordance with the ideas of their builders, but all of them were more or less patterned after the keel-boat and barge of venerable and worthy memory. Indeed, numerous keel-boats and barges were still in use on various rivers, and were employed thereon for the same purposes for which canal boats were likewise being constructed. It was therefore only natural that the first builders of canal boats should turn to the older craft when seeking models for the new means of conveyance. This they did, and so the earliest canal boats were usually from fifty to sixty-five feet long, rather sharp at both bow and stern, and with rounded bottoms. Not even in their width did they ma-

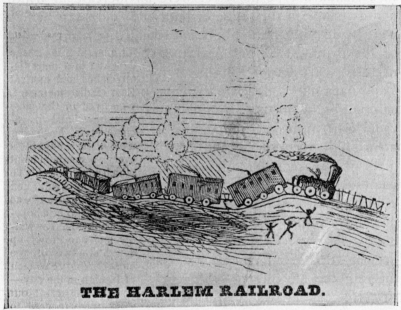

THE HARLEM RAILROAD.

247.—Cartoon suggesting that the roadbed of the Harlem Railway, which extended through the New York City streets, was too rough and undulatory for popular approval. The cars are apparently of the type shown in the preceding, and a locomotive has been substituted for animal power. Date, about 1840-1842.

terially differ from their narrow aquatic ancestors.[1] They also adopted from the barge those small superstructures, or cabins, which had been formerly added to the keel-boat as living places for the crew and passengers. They even

[1] A model of the first passenger canal boat which appeared on the Erie Canal in 1819 has been preserved by the Buffalo Historical Society, and it shows the similarity between the keel-boat and barge and their canal descendants. The canal packet of 1819 was but seven and a half feet wide and was sixty-five feet long.

took the sleeping bunks of the barge, and the berths were arranged in tiers along the sides of the canal-boat cabins in the immemorial fashion. A very scanty allowance of space was originally made for the important activities of the cook.

The first material alterations that were soon to result in a standard type of vessel were an increase in width and a change in the shape of both bow and stern, which were made much more blunt and rounded in form. Most of the primitive vehicles were designed either for the exclusive carriage of freight, or for the accommodation of perhaps half a dozen passengers in connection with a cargo of bulky goods. But the immediate adoption of the canal as a means of human travel—considerably to the surprise of the official and mercantile mind—speedily made it apparent that the original notions of the companies and builders were not altogether in harmony with popular ideas and the needs of the occasion. The people demanded transportation facilities for themselves to such an extent—especially as long stretches of water were opened—that arrangements obviously had to be made for meeting the unexpected emergency. The "step lively" principle, as far as it was applicable to progress by canal, also appeared, and the cry for speed was intensified whenever a route in process of construction opened for traffic a new extension which permitted farther penetration of the country by that means. As a consequence of these manifestations of public desire it soon developed that the shipment of both passengers and freight on the same vessel was poor policy, and so the building of boats designed exclusively for the use of travellers began.

At this point still another phase of the same general subject appeared. That part of the travelling public which desired to use the canals was evidently divided into two classes. One of these classes was composed of individuals or families who were removing permanently from their former homes to new locations in the West, and to whom time—measured in hours or days—was not of great importance. The other portion of the canal-patronizing public was made up of travellers who really had need to arrive at their destinations within the shortest possible period, and they demanded the swiftest progress that could be made. Persons such as these were willing to pay an increased price for quick transportation if necessary, while the first-named class wanted to move ahead at the cheapest possible cost. The same canal boat obviously was not an appropriate vehicle for carrying both these sorts of people, and so was brought about a division of passenger boats into two types, one of which came to be known as the line-boat and the other as the packet-boat. A line-boat somewhat resembled in its functions the modern second-class railroad car or railroad train. That is to say, it moved more slowly and was not equipped with such attention to the comfort of its occupants as were those boats designed for the other sort of patronage. Usually, though not invariably, a line-boat supplied its passengers with neither bedding nor food, and it advanced at about two or two and a half miles an hour. A canal packet[1] on the contrary was considerably more luxurious in its interior fittings and arrangements, was pulled by a better breed of live stock, charged one or two cents a mile more for its tickets, and progressed at the rate of three or three and a half miles an hour. If a line-boat and a packet-boat left a given point simultaneously, at the end

---

[1] The term "packet-boat," as given to canal craft so distinguished, was adopted from the term "packet" that had long been applied to the swifter sort of ocean sailing craft.

of twenty-four hours the lucky passengers on the packet-boat would find themselves about twenty-four miles ahead of their less fortunate fellow-travellers. After a week of steady travel they would probably be more than a hundred and fifty miles ahead.

Another feature wherein early canal boats at once began to deviate in external appearance from keel-boats and barges lay in the matter of their outward decoration. Scanty indeed had been the attention given to the esthetic inclinations of the floating public during the scores of years in which keel-boats, flatboats and barges had been the only means of water conveyance. During those times no fastidious sense of the voyager impelled him to refuse passage on a water craft because it was dingy or uninviting. All he then considered was the fact that it was going in the direction he desired to follow, and that with good luck it would convey him on his way. But the unknown man who first painted the sides of his Conestoga wagon in bright colors established a decorative principle in American travel conveyances which was speedily adopted thereafter by the owners of all other vehicles both on land and water. If a dozen line-boats or packet-boats were gathered together in one spot the chances were that most of them would be floating symphonies in either green, yellow, brown, red, white or blue, each being further embellished with panels and window frames done in other colors harmonizing with the general scheme.

In its internal arrangements the passenger canal boat also speedily assumed a standard pattern. In the bow was a small covered cabin containing five or six bunks for the crew, and this part of the vessel was separated from the rest of it by a partition. Nearly all the space aft of the crew's cabin was devoted to the accommodation of the

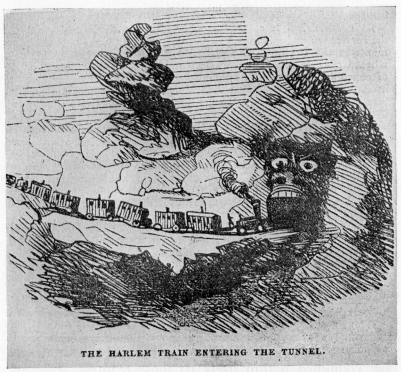

THE HARLEM TRAIN ENTERING THE TUNNEL.

248.—Another cartoon, published about the same time as the foregoing, and depicting a Harlem Railway train entering the tunnel through which it ran
from 34th Street to 42nd Street, New York City. The tunnel still exists and
is used by a street railway line.

public, and was divided into a number of compartments.
The first of these was usually a wash-room and dressing-
room for women, and following it was the women's cabin.
The largest compartment of all immediately adjoined the
women's quarters, and it was devoted to a variety of uses.
This large room, usually about forty-five feet in length,
served by day as a place of general assembly, and on
stormy passages was the spot in which men travellers
gathered for protection from the elements. Here they
might write their letters, and here also they could as-

semble to participate in those exciting games of checkers or backgammon that served to dissipate the tedium of the voyage. Here they would gather for their discussions regarding the political condition of the country or to sing their rollicking choruses. If the boat by chance possessed an organ—as a few of the most pretentious did—that musical instrument was located in the compartment here described. Nearly all the hand-baggage of the travellers likewise found its resting place in this big room.

Thrice each day, at morning, noon and evening, the captain and two other members of the crew[1] appeared and speedily converted the apartment into a dining-room. The process was effected by setting up a long table composed of wide boards placed on a system of trestle-work.[2] These necessary appurtenances of lumber, when not in use, were stowed away somewhere in a small storeroom. As soon as the meal was finished the tables were taken down and the main cabin again assumed its function of general gathering place. In short, this principal section of the boat combined within itself all those features of utility and comfort which are now to be found in the various lounging-rooms, restaurants, libraries, reading-rooms and smoking-rooms of a modern ocean steamship.

At night there came still another change and the big compartment[3]—through a metamorphosis likewise accomplished by the captain and two of his assistants—was converted into a floating dormitory. Small shelves of wood, about six feet long and three-and-a-half feet wide, were attached to the walls. These were held up at their

---

[1] The captain's two assistants on these occasions usually being the steersman and mule driver who were not at that time pursuing their regular duties.

[2] Many of the boats were equipped with tables of more solid contruction that remained permanently in the room.

[3] The entire superstructure of a canal passenger boat extended upward for some six feet or more above the sides of the hull proper, and the whole was covered by a nearly flat roof which served as a promenade and lounging place by day. The inner height of the main cabin was usually about nine feet.

outer edges by slender supports of wood or wrought iron,[1] and became the beds on which the men passengers were privileged to repose. Each shelf was equipped with a thin clump of clotted straw contained in a flat rectangular bag of blue canvas, the whole being commonly known as a mattress. A similar contrivance very much smaller in size, but closely allied to the mattress in species and called a pillow, was also placed on each shelf, and one blanket was likewise supplied. The beds were ranged in tiers, the lowest being within a few inches of the floor and the one immediately above being at a distance of about three feet from the bottommost bunk. A like interval of space separated the middle shelf from the upper one. The space between the top bunk and the cabin roof was usually not so great as that between the lower beds. There were thus three identical compartments in each tier, and a large packet generally had seven tiers of bunks along each side of the cabin. This arrangement permitted forty-two passengers to complete those preparations which are ordinarily followed by sleep. But as the cabin was practically devoid of ventilation, and as sundry other conditions that are about to be described entered into conflict with the ostensible purpose of sleeping berths on a canal boat, a comfortable night's rest under such circumstances was hardly to be expected. It should here be said that the night arrangements in the women's cabin were substantially identical with those just mentioned.

The usual method of allotting berths on a canal boat was to permit the passengers to choose their sleeping quarters in the order in which they embarked. Travellers customarily chose lower shelves as long as any still remained vacant, though a lower bunk had one undesirable

[1] Or sometimes by ropes.

855

feature in that there always existed the possibility of a collapse of those immediately above it. In such cases—especially when the catastrophe began by the giving way of the top shelf—the occupant of the bottom pigeon-hole generally found himself in the most awkward position of all the passengers involved. But accidents of that sort were rather uncommon on canal packets and could not be depended upon to occur with any degree of certainty. During periods of especially heavy travel it constantly happened that the number of people embarking on a canal boat far exceeded the number of sleeping berths with which it was equipped. At those times it was the necessary practise to permit late arrivals to sleep on the floor, and extra mattresses, blankets and pillows were carried for use in such emergencies. When the floor was full there still remained the dinner tables, which also were converted into beds when occasion required. Sometimes seventy-five or eighty or even a hundred men were thus closely packed into a room designed for the accommodation of forty-two. Few indeed were the canal-boat voyagers who dared to venture upon such preparations for a night's repose as were usual under home conditions. A man would take off his hat, collar, cravat, and his coat and waistcoat, and then climb into his allotted bunk. If unusually fastidious he would also divest himself of his trousers and shoes before retiring, but such passengers as went to the extreme here indicated were not uncommonly regarded as "fops" or "swells."

There remains still another condition which arose during the process of going to bed on a crowded canal boat. When the floor and tables were all occupied, as well as the shelves, it became necessary to erect a zigzag series of clothes-lines back and forth across the cabin on which the discarded garments of the passengers might be hung, and the scenic effect produced in the sleeping room when this process had been completed somewhat resembled that displayed by the back-yard of a modern tenement house on wash-day. Finally, after all the travellers were spread out upon their berths and on the tables and floor, and the light had been put out, the unhappy assemblage subsided into a restless but unseen throng in which the stillness was only broken by faint moanings, the creaking of the boat and an occasional stentorian snore. After suffering for several hours amid the conditions here outlined it was a common occurrence that some passenger abandoned his endeavor to obtain rest in an upper berth and decided to quit it for the better air and greater comfort to be found on the roof. He therefore cautiously lowered his feet in the direction of some table whose position as it stood when he went to bed was remembered by him. He would try to perform this operation of getting a foothold with utmost quietude, in order that he might not disturb his fellow-travellers. Hanging from his shelf by his elbows, and feeling in the darkness with his foot for the table he was seeking he might at last find it, only to step on the prostrate form of some belated passenger to whom it had been allotted. When that mischance occurred—and being anxious to comply with the sudden protest which it evoked —he would hastily try to shift the position of his feet, only to discover that he was astraddle of one of the clothes-lines. He then abandoned further hope of a peaceful solution of his difficulties and let go, without caring where he alighted, or how.

With the first indication of dawn the passengers emerged from their night's surroundings and sought the open air. The men's wash-room was so small as to be en-

249.—A still later picture of a train on the Harlem road. No enclosed cab or shelter had as yet been provided for locomotive engineers. The car shows a tendency toward improvement. All railways had abandoned the old stage-coach curves for passenger coaches, and had adopted the rectangular car bodies introduced by the South Carolina enterprise.

tirely inadequate for the use of any considerable number of persons, and members of the crew or some of the travellers themselves would in consequence lower buckets over the side of the boat and draw up water for their ablutions. Such of the group as were particular about their personal appearance afterward formed in line to secure use of the massive comb and brush that were always chained to the wall of the wash-room. While the passengers were thus resuming their daytime appearance the allotted members of the crew were busily dismantling the sleeping berths and converting the cabin into an eating room. The cook in his little cabin at the extreme after end of the boat had been busy since four o'clock at his work of preparing breakfast, and that meal was generally announced at six. Everything was put on the table at once, after the custom prevailing in the taverns of the day, and the man who ate most swiftly was most certain to secure a substantial meal, be its after effects what they might. From the very nature of things it was not possible to serve on a canal boat a meal of such variety or excellence as could be obtained on dry land. The food was limited in variety and, sad to say, often limited in quantity also. The breakfast in the women's cabin[1] was served at the same time to all the women and children on board, and after the meal was finished it again became the privilege of the two sexes to meet and spend the coming day together. Families were once more united.

Despite the slowness and apparent monotony of canal travel there was much to commend it to those who were starting upon extended journeys, especially if they had not previously visited the regions to be traversed. In the first place the method of movement was a safe one. It was true that a canal boat was occasionally halted by a sunken stump or rock, or reposed for an hour or two on a mud bank, but no accidents could occur on one similar to the almost countless collisions and explosions that daily wrought such appalling havoc on the river steamboats. Most of the big canals extended through interesting sections of the country, and parts of them penetrated districts wherein the scenery was attractive and often beautiful. Some canals skirted precipitous cliffs or ran between rugged and forest-covered hills. Certain of the routes contained deep cuttings that were almost tunnel-like, and in a situation of that sort the horses or mules were compelled to pick their way carefully along a narrow ledge built on the side of a wall far above the canal boat itself.

[1] The women's cabin was always called "Ladies' Cabin."

Such an unusual bit of canal scenery was displayed on the Erie Canal through New York State near the village of Lockport.[1] The process of passing a boat through a lock or series of locks was a never-ceasing matter of interest to the passengers, and whenever this operation was performed all but the most habitual canal travellers assembled on the roof to observe the work necessary for a transfer to a higher or lower level, and to comment critically on the manner and time in which it was accomplished. Numerous rivers and smaller streams were crossed by the voyagers on lofty aqueducts of wood or stone, and some few of the canals even had inclined planes on which the boats were placed and then pulled bodily up or lowered down to a different level of water.

No more delightful experience of travel could be obtained in all the country than that encountered by a canal-boat passenger while moving through a region of wooded hills during the hours of a moonlit summer night. Ahead he could see the plodding horses and their driver. The lights from the open windows gleamed on the towpath and the rugged hillsides, and each new turn of the waterway brought into vision some new scene of shadowy loveliness. From the cabins beneath came the sound of laughter and children's voices, and if by chance he was embarked upon a boat which boasted of an organ he heard the strains produced by its manipulation, accompanied by rollicking choruses from a score of voices in which he himself no doubt also joined. And even if there was no organ aboard it was a rare ship's company that did not possess among its membership some individuals accompanied by flutes, fiddles and accordions. Those universally en-

[1] The excavation of this deep cut, and a view of it after its completion, are elsewhere shown by reproduction of contemporary p.ctures.

countered instruments of melody were brought forth on every possible occasion and formed an orchestra whose harmonies, however vigorously produced, were often drowned by the terrific vocal outbursts they inspired.

The cost of passage on a line-boat which provided neither sleeping accommodations nor food for its patrons

On the Norwich & Worcester Rail Road.

250.—The road between Norwich and Worcester was built in 1840, and was 66 miles long. The wheels on the cars are shown to be outside of the car bodies, as was sometimes the practise in early construction.

was small; often but fifty cents a day. The cost of a ticket on a packet-boat, which also included the price of meals and sleeping bunk, usually amounted to about five cents for a mile of distance traversed. This price of five cents a mile for packet canal travel was early established and for a time formed the basis of an ingenious scheme that was frequently used by pedestrian travellers who were following the route of a canal. Such a man based his plan on the knowledge that a packet moved at the rate of about a mile in twenty minutes, and that the meals aboard the boats were served at certain regular times. As the hour for the canal-boat meal drew near he made himself prominent at a convenient spot on the bank of the waterway, and when the boat selected as the scene of his imposition approached he indicated by signal his desire to embark. The steersman would thereupon so divert the course of the craft as to enable the man to spring aboard, and as the repast was at that moment announced, he hastened to the table and consumed as much of the food before him as could be done in fifteen or twenty minutes. He then conscientiously paid the captain five cents and signified his desire to be put ashore. So generally was this petty trick practised for a number of years that at last it became necessary to issue rules which made it impossible, and thereafter a minimum sum of from fifteen to twenty-five cents was demanded from a passenger, no matter how short his trip might be.

The crew of a canal boat usually consisted of the captain, two steersmen, two drivers and the cook. The captain was on duty from dawn until after the passengers were in bed. The steersmen worked alternately throughout the twenty-four hours, and each guided the craft for a period of six hours before relinquishing the helm to his alternate; the two drivers worked in like manner with the steersmen. The cook worked all the time. The drivers were the most humble members of the crew, and if one of them displayed unusual care in performing his work he was eventually promoted to the position of helmsman: a helmsman in similar way sometimes became a captain, provided the boat was owned and operated by a company. In a case wherein the boat was the property of an individual the owner himself often acted as its captain. A captain ordinarily received fifty or sixty dollars a

251.—First train on the Erie Railroad, 1837. The eastern terminus of the road was on the west shore of the Hudson River, about 30 miles above New York City and just north of the New Jersey state line. New York would not then let the enterprise cross her boundary. But little work was done on the railway in 1837 and it is possible the first train was assembled for its legal value in relation to the franchise. Modern copy of an engraving printed in 1837 from a sketch made by the early American artist, A. C. Morton.

month, a steersman from thirty-five to fifty dollars a
month, and a driver about twenty dollars a month. All
members of the crew were also supplied with their food
and with such lodging as the boat provided.[1]

In addition to the freight boats and the two sorts of
passenger boats already mentioned there was also another
variety of canal boat whose uses formed a not inconsiderable feature of life along the early artificial water routes
of the country. This fourth species of craft was composed
of what may with some propriety be called family boats,
since they were both the homes and travelling conveyances
of entire families, and were used for no other purpose. In
fact they were closely analogous in their use and slightly
resembled in appearance the flatboats of the interior
rivers. They were considerably shorter and often a little
wider than the public canal boats and with relation to their
interior arrangements were fitted up in each instance in
accordance with the desires or interests of the families
who lived or travelled in them. They were domestic establishments in the literal sense of the word, and their various
apartments contained such furniture as might be found in
any ordinary unpretentious dwelling on the land. The
owner of such a boat even kept his own horses on board
when those animals were not engaged in pulling it along
the surface of the water. A few of these boats were built
for use in conveying families or other groups of people
to the West, and some of them made very extensive
journeys. They occasionally traversed the Erie Canal to
Lake Erie, thence proceeded slowly by means of towing
to one of the Ohio canals, and in that manner either
reached southern Ohio or continued on westward through

---

[1] James A. Garfield, later President of the United States, was for a short time, while
a youth, a driver on the Portsmouth and Erie Canal in Ohio.

Indiana by means of the Wabash and Erie Canal. Others of the same type did not migrate to such extreme distances from the place of their origin, but were employed as the homes of people whose lives were spent in canal work, or whose money was invested in canal enterprises.

On another page is reproduced a cartoon of the canal period, wherein an artist of the time has suggested that even such a staid and prosaic method of travel as that under discussion might have its accidents. This was perhaps true, though not to the extent that pilgrims on a canal packet might ever expect actual danger through the agency of tempest, wreck or collision. When a collision occurred—which was quite often—its only result was an unpleasant bump as the two heavy boats came together; and in the unimaginable emergency of a wreck the only resultant unpleasantness to the passenger would have been the necessity of wading ashore through three or four feet of mud and water. If a traveller happened to be standing at the edge of a boat when it came in collision with another and was overbalanced and thrown into the water by the shock, all he had to do was to clamber aboard again, change his clothes, and spend the rest of the day in expressing his opinion about the mules, the driver, the steersman, the captain and everybody else who had any part in the calamity.

But on numerous canals of the country, and especially on those parts of them which were in reality rivers used for canal purposes, there were many embarrassing obstacles to quick and comfortable travel.[1] This condition of affairs was so well recognized that two or three of the early canals of the country had guide books written about

[1] That is, to quick travel in the canal meaning of the term; namely, three or three and a half miles an hour.

252.—Pioneer American locomotives and locomotive building. The Rogers Machine Works, at Paterson, New Jersey, as they appeared in 1832. Outgrowth of a little machinery-making shop founded by Thomas Rogers in 1819. The initial railway work undertaken by the firm was the making of a hundred sets of wheels and axles for the Charleston and Hamburg road. Rogers, Ketchum and Grosvenor was the first name of the company.

them, in which the passengers and captains of the boats were warned of certain well-recognized obstacles to their safe navigation. In one such guide book[1] it was said in the preface:

"The Schuylkill Canal is considered very difficult without an experienced navigator, or proper directions; especially the lower section from Reading to Philadelphia, occasioned by points, rocks, and bars."

Certain of the directions contained in this guide book indicate some of the troubles which beset the Schuylkill voyager. A captain ascending the canal was cautioned in this manner:[2] "Tow the whole way to Manyunk—let the horse go at a slow walk—attend to the line—keep a look

[1] "The Schuylkill Canal Navigator," by S. Alspach. Philadelphia, 1827.
[2] Ibid., pp. 3-4.

out for stumps and rocks—keep out about 10 or 15 feet, according to the situation of the place, till you pass through the Little Canal, then keep out about 30 feet till you come to Young's Landing—then keep the tow-path channel at the Falls about 10 or 12 feet from shore, and so continue till you have passed the rocks; then you may keep farther from shore till you come to Manyunk Landing— tow the boat above the landing and take on the horse— make for the Locks by using the poles."[1]

Another urgent caution was directed by the same publication to canal-boat captains who were passing a point known as "Little Catfish Dam." Here, the publication read, "Keep out about 30 feet from shore, avoid stumps and rocks." At "Little Dam" the boatman was warned "to keep out about 30 feet; by going in much nearer to shore there is danger of sticking on the rocks," and of another section of the canal, twenty-two miles long, it was declared that "caution must be used to prevent running the boat aground in the short turns and narrow places; also in passing other boats, by running against them." Of that part of the canal between Reading and Mt. Carbon the navigating directions proudly stated:

"It is in such complete order that it may be passed without danger, only observing to keep out from the tow-path about 10 or 12 feet from the dams—by going farther out there is danger of sticking on rocks or stumps in the canal—keep in the middle."

But no records of canal disasters have come down to us, nor do the printed annals of those days—recent as they were—contain more than a few striking accounts of canal travel in any of its features. Most of the contemporary descriptions of packet trips are condensed into a para-

[1] Long iron-tipped poles were also carried by many canal boats for use in turning the craft, releasing it from rocks or sand-bars, or navigating it into a harbor or basin. These necessary poles were a survival of the earlier keel-boats, from which canal boats themselves had descended.

graph or two, as though the travellers preferred to forget their experiences as soon as possible rather than revive their memories through the process of telling them. One of the best relations of a canal voyage preserved in the words of former times is that written and published by an Englishman who, with his family, journeyed eastward from Terre Haute across Indiana and Ohio over the Wabash and Erie route. He travelled in the packet *Indiana,* previously mentioned, and the internal arrangements of the boat, according to the description set forth in his book,[1] were as follows: At the stern were the kitchen, steward's room and offices. In the center of the boat was the large salon—the sitting-room of all by day and the sleeping room of male passengers by night. Adjoining it toward the bow was the ladies' apartment, beyond which again was a small cabin. In this small cabin were a looking-glass, a hand basin, two towels, and a comb and a brush for the use of the ladies. It was a rule on all canal boats, said Beste, that no gentleman might go into the ladies' salon without express invitation from the ladies there present, even though one of them was his own wife.

When dusk began to descend the numerous young children of the Englishman's family, who had been exploring the mysteries of the boat with great interest, returned and asked their parents where they were to sleep. "The steward, however," Beste went on to say, "soon solved their doubts by hanging up some shelves to the wall, and laying mattresses and sheets[2] upon them. After tea[3] we all began a most murderous attack upon the mosquitoes that swarmed on the windows and inside our berths in expecta-

[1] "The Wabash, or Adventure of an English Gentleman's Family in the Interior of Indiana." By J. Richard Beste, London, 1855.

[2] The sheets were unusual, though the journey in question was made after 1850, and by that period such bedclothes may have become more common than formerly.

[3] Meaning the repast then known in America as "supper," which was served on canal boats about six o'clock in the evening.

tion of feasting upon us as soon as we should go to bed; but those on whom we made war were soon replaced by others, and the more we killed the more they seemed to come to be killed. . . . At last we gave up the task as hope-

253.—The Baldwin Locomotive Works in Philadelphia and types of engines they made. Baldwin's first locomotive was *Old Ironsides*. Engraved in mezzotint by John Sartain after a drawing by the artist William Mason.

less and resigned ourselves as well as we could to passing a sleepless night."

A description of the efforts of the travellers to enjoy repose in the berths hung on the wall was written at the time by Lucy Beste, a grown daughter of the family, and her statement of the conditions she encountered was incorporated by the author in the published story of his family's journey. Lucy Beste's remarks read:

"The berths were in tiers three rows high. I was put in the top one. . . . I lay awake, but still, for a long time. At last I heard every one turning and sighing with the heat, so I gave way to my own feelings and did so, too. But the shelves or tiers on which we lay were so short that I found my pillow constantly slipping down below my head; and if I put it lower down my feet hung out at the other end; so that, although I was not very tall I was obliged, at last, to curl myself up and be quite still, while the mosquitoes devoured and the heat melted me."

At last the night ended, and with the first gleam of sunlight the travellers left their beds and prepared for another day. In order to wash their hands and faces they were compelled to lower a pail overboard at the end of a rope, by which means they secured from the canal itself the water necessary for that purpose. Lucy Beste continued in her diary:

"Then came the breakfast. The bread was hot and very heavy, and the beefsteaks were dry, small, and much underdone. I do not know how papa managed. Captain Davis looked very black if any one asked to be helped a second time."

The Englishman after thus permitting his daughter to interject certain of her observations into his narrative, went on to describe the scenery through which the canal boat moved as it crawled toward the East. He said:

"We passed through scores and scores of miles of woodland that had never heard the axe; passed thousands of acres where trees were rotting in the steaming pools collected about them. . . . I never saw more magnificent timber than shaded the valleys. . . . Great sticks of black oak shot up straight from the bottoms without a knot or branch, until their heads spread out some scores of feet above, like the tufted summits of the Italian pine. At times partial clearings or little prairies offered vistas in the land beyond, and still the same noble timber everywhere arose. On the banks of the canal, as on mounds of higher earth, the spaces between the trees were filled with wild and untrodden copses. Shrubs with large, gorgeous leaves shot up amid creepers of various hues, and glistened in the sun."

At length the boat bearing the English family reached the eastern terminus of the Wabash Canal at a little place called Junction, and there its members trans-shipped to another packet, destined to carry them southward on the Miami Canal toward Cincinnati. In changing boats at Junction the passengers stepped directly from one to the other, as both lay side by side in the canal basin. The south-bound boat happened to be exceedingly crowded, and Beste described the conditions upon it in these words:

"I never saw people packed so close as they were that night in the men's saloon. I and my remaining son had our accustomed berths in a corner: every other one of the three tiers around the walls was occupied. Mattresses completely covered the floor, on which people lay as close as possible. The dinner table was covered with sleeping humanity more thickly than Captain Davis ever strewed it with beefsteaks; and those who lay under the table thought themselves favored, inasmuch as they could not be trodden upon."

A description of a trip between Albany and Buffalo, made on an Erie Canal line-boat by an American more famous than the Englishman Beste, well serves as an example of those narratives that suggest a desire to forget the conditions described. It reads:[1]

"I made the journey by way of the Erie Canal, on those line-boats whose 'cent and a half a mile, mile and a half an hour' so many yet remember.[2] Railroads, as yet, were not. The days passed slowly yet smoothly on those arks, being enlivened by various sedentary games. But the nights were tedious beyond any sleeping-car experience. At daybreak you were routed out of the shabby shelf-like berth, and driven on deck to swallow fog, while the cabin was cleared of its beds and made ready for breakfast. I say nothing about 'the good old times'; but if anyone would recall the good old line-boats, I object."

When Greeley made his western trip to Buffalo there were not, as he says, any such things as railroads. But when Beste moved slowly eastward on the *Indiana*, in 1854, the early American canal period had virtually reached its end. Already the locomotive had penetrated to the same region in its westward progress, and three years afterward the Mississippi River could be attained over iron rails extending continuously to the Atlantic Ocean. The railway age had come, bringing with it in a few years changes infinitely more important than had taken place during the two preceding centuries.

[1] From "Recollections of a Busy Life," by Horace Greeley: p. 64.
[2] These figures indicate a speed of 36 miles a day at a cost of 54 cents a day.

CHAPTER XXXIX

THE FOSSIL RAILWAYS OF AMERICA—GENERAL FEATURES
CONNECTED WITH THE FIRST APPEARANCE AND USE
OF THE RAIL HIGHWAY PRINCIPLE IN THIS COUNTRY
—OLIVER EVANS' PROPOSITION OF 1812—DESCRIPTION
OF THE RAILWAYS BUILT BEFORE 1827—JOHN
STEVENS, IN 1812, URGES ON CONGRESS THE IMPOR-
TANCE OF BUILDING RAILROADS AS A NATIONAL UN-
DERTAKING—CONGRESS CONSIDERS THE MATTER
UNIMPORTANT—OBJECT LESSON OF THE STEAMBOAT
IGNORED—THE NEW TRANSPORTATION METHOD IS
DESTINED TO DEVELOP UNDER THE GUIDANCE OF
PRIVATE ENTERPRISE

THE acceptance of railways by the United States as an
improvement over other methods of movement
already in use was a process that somewhat resembled,
both in slowness and its relationship to national conditions,
the previous introduction of steamboats.

In tracing the circumstances connected with America's
pioneer railroads and the endorsement finally given to
them, four general features of the period between 1807
and 1829 appeal for notice. First of all, the earliest and
exceedingly crude rail highways of this country were designed by their builders simply as mechanical improvements of existing turnpikes, and were intended to facilitate
the movement of wheeled vehicles usually drawn by horses.
Second, there were a few men with understanding of the

872

254.—The engine *York*. Named from the Pennsylvania town where it was made. Built by Phineas Davis, a watchmaker, in 1831-1832, to obtain a prize of $4,000 offered by the Baltimore and Ohio management. After some alterations it was accepted and used on that road for several years. It had a vertical boiler, ran on four wheels, weighted 3½ tons, and could pull a load of 15 tons at a speed of 15 miles an hour on a level track.

possibilities contained in the new idea, who put their beliefs on record and persistently—with ultimate success—strove to interest the public in the subject. Third, there was at first no widespread opinion that the principle of a rigid and permanent track, thus applied to land transportation, would soon be associated with steam as a motive power and alter almost every phase of man's affairs. Finally—though in no degree impeaching the value and primacy of George Stephenson's practical locomotive building in England and the world's obligation to him—it is more than probable that steam railways would soon have been developed on this side of the Atlantic even had Stephenson not built his *Rocket*[1] locomotive in 1829, or even if he had never lived at all.

The conditions prevailing in this country with respect to the projection and building of railroads prior to the era opened by the memorable trial of the *Rocket* go far toward justifying such a conclusion, and a brief account of the primitive railway ideas and actual enterprises of America is therefore desirable.

We find, then, that in 1786 a petition was presented to the legislature of Pennsylvania by Oliver Evans[2] of Philadelphia in which he asked for the sole right to use wagons propelled by steam on the highways of that state. In the same memorial he also requested a similar right in connection with a steam flour mill. The legislators listened with tolerance and some interest while the inventor explained the principles of his mill, but when he began to discuss a vehicle designed to move along roads by its own power and mechanism their patience came to an end, and a belief arose that Evans' mental capacity was becoming seriously impaired. His similar application, made shortly afterward to the lawmakers of Maryland, was more successful. They bestowed the privilege he asked on the ground that such action on their part could harm nobody.

[1] The "Rocket" was built in response to a proposal by the Liverpool and Manchester Railway, then under construction, and which offered a prize of £500 for a locomotive that would do certain specified work. Not one other civil or mechanical engineer in England believed moving engines would furnish high speed or satisfactory motive power for railroads. Most of them, except Stephenson, advocated the use of stationary engines. The "Rocket," in October of 1829, pulled a train weighing 13 tons at an average speed of 15 miles an hour and attained a maximum speed, when running alone, of 35 miles an hour. The engine itself weighed 4½ tons. It was the first machine of the sort to demonstrate the practicability of moving locomotives for railways. The performance of the "Rocket" was largely due to the use of the multitubular boiler, originally devised by John Fitch, improved by Voight, and patented by John Stevens in 1791 and 1803 (in America) and in 1805 (in England). Stevens used multitubular boilers in his screw propellers of 1804 and 1805.
[2] About a year after Fitch, his acquaintance, had invented boats propelled by steam.

Armed with Maryland's monopolistic grant Evans labored diligently among the moneyed men of the day in an effort to arouse interest in steam-propelled land vehicles, and to secure capital by which he might give the plan a practical test. Failure attended his efforts to enlist aid for the enterprise. Finally, when he built his little five-

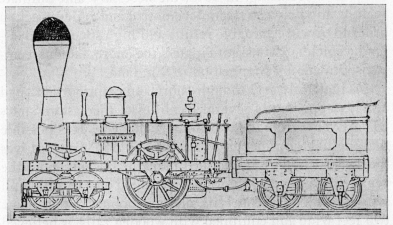

255.—The *Sandusky*, first engine made by Rogers, Ketchum and Grosvenor. It was finished in 1837, and was originally designed for a New Jersey line. Bought by the Mad River road of Ohio, where it arrived in November of 1837, before any track had been laid to receive it. The road was built to fit the engine, and its gauge of 4 feet 10 inches dictated the width of the pioneer rail highways of Ohio.

horse-power steamboat in 1804 he put wheels under it and ran it through the streets of Philadelphia as proof that his idea for operating land wagons by mechanical power was a sound one. Still he met nothing but skepticism. Those who did give attention to the demonstration argued that the speed attained by the clumsy boat during its trip across the city was too slow to be useful. "I silenced them," said Evans, "by answering that I would make a carriage, to be propelled by steam, for a bet of $3,000, to run upon a level road against the swiftest horse they would

875

produce. I was then as confident as I am now that such velocity could be given to carriages . . . I am still willing to make a steam carriage that will run fifteen miles an hour, on good, level railways, on condition that I have double price if it shall run with that velocity, and nothing for it if it shall not come up to that velocity."

By thus declaring, in 1812, the necessary and intimate relationship between steam locomotive and railed track in order to procure valuable results and high speed for overland vehicles, Evans anticipated the more famous comparison made by Stephenson of England.

Actual railways, though short and unimportant, had already appeared in several localities of the eastern states when Evans wrote the words above quoted. It is possible that the first application of the principle in America was the construction of an inclined plane in Boston, about the year 1795. A brick kiln in that city stood on a certain high spot known as Beacon Hill, and an inclined plane, some two feet wide and equipped with wooden rails, is believed to have been used in lowering the finished product of the kiln to a street below. The loaded cars ran down the track and were hauled up by a cable when emptied. Twelve years later, in 1807, a short railway was built in Boston by Silas Whitney near the location of the previous inclined plane. It was without such an abrupt grade, and was intended to facilitate the movement of horse-drawn wagons.[1]

Still another early American application of the railed-track principle was that of Thomas Leiper in 1809. Leiper owned a stone quarry in Delaware county, Pennsylvania, and he conceived the notion that parallel wooden rails such as had long been used for wagons in the coal

[1] Concerning these two Boston railroads but little is known.

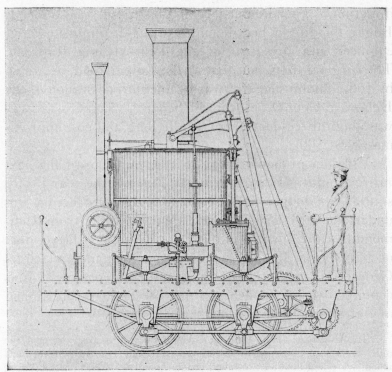

256.—A locomotive used on the Baltimore and Washington railway in 1837. Closely resembling the *York,* but weighing eight tons. Built by Gillingham and Winans, at Baltimore. From a drawing made by the Scotch engineer David Stevenson, in 1837.

mining regions of England and Wales could be introduced with advantage in his quarry. He accordingly hired a Scotchman familiar with such devices to lay an experimental track, and one was put down near the Bull's Head tavern, Philadelphia, in September of 1809. The little railroad near the tavern was about sixty yards long, and so satisfactory does it seem to have been[1] that Leiper at once began to make a similar track on his quarry property. The Delaware county railway was built under the

[1] As an experiment. It of course had no other value.

877

direction of a man named John Thompson, whose son, J. Edgar Thompson, became in his turn a distinguished civil engineer and president of the Pennsylvania Railroad. The original map and plan of the Leiper road, as drawn by John Thompson, afterward came into possession of the Delaware County Institute of Science. Leiper's railway was about three-quarters of a mile long and cost approximately $1,500[1].

Virginia probably witnessed the building of the next railroad on this side of the ocean, since in the year 1811 a similar but longer and more elaborate construction was undertaken at Falling's Creek, about ten miles from Richmond, for the purpose of more easily moving the product of a powder mill. This road was planned and erected by George Magers, and the most authentic record of it is contained in a statement written by Thomas McKibben of Baltimore. The account says:[2]

"It was about a mile long, and run between the magazine and the mill. . . . Cross ties or floor joists were laid, and the rails, of hard wood, were laid about an ordinary wagon gauge. One rail was grooved and the other tongued. The rails were cut out of the solid timber, and between them a flooring, securely fastened to the cross ties, was laid the entire length of the road. The country was very hilly, and at one point on its length it passed over a valley about a quarter of a mile wide. Across this valley the inventor erected an immense trestle some 75 feet high. . . . The wagon that ran upon it was very large, 18 or 20 feet long in the body, running upon low wooden wheels about two feet in diameter, composed of double plank of hard wood, cross-grained to each other, and securely fastened. The wheels one side were tongued, and the others grooved, to suit their respective rails, and there was a lever or brake to control the speed down to the magazine. When the car was unloaded it was hauled up again by a stout rope winding on a huge vertical drum, operated by the water wheels at the mill. . . . My uncle returned to Baltimore in 1823, and at that time the railway was still in use, but only as a curiosity, as the mill blew up in 1819.

[1] See "Minutes of the Proceedings of the Delaware County Institute of Science" for Feb. 1, 1873, for an account of Leiper's enterprise.
[2] Prepared from descriptions given to McKibben by a relative, and published in the "American Engineer" for 1886.

257.—The engine *Hackensack,* of the Hackensack and New York Railroad. Date, about 1846. Locomotives of the time were usually painted in bright red, blue, green and other colors and fitted with much ornamental brass-work. Cabs for the engineers were coming into general use. Built by Rogers.

The railway was not affected by the 'blow up,' and the people around the country used to visit it, the hands living in the neighborhood operating it for their own amusement, making excursions on the road."

The details of this Virginia railway show that in its general features it was not far removed from similar constructions then being used in England, and that in a few things it excelled them.[1]

No doubt there were numerous railed roads laid down in various places in America during the first years of the century, but their use was either unnoticed in the printed

[1] But not in the use of motive power or iron rails. Cast iron rails—three or four feet long—were made in England in 1767 and used on a road in Loughborough in that year, and Trevithick's first locomotive ran in 1804.

annals of the time or else told so obscurely that a list of all of them cannot now be made. Of several others, however, there are contemporary accounts, and they, like those already mentioned, were efforts to create a track which should be an improvement over existing highways and designed for the easier use of existing vehicles. There was a little railway built at Kiskiminetas Creek, Pennsylvania, in 1816, and one at Bear Creek, in the same state, in 1818. The last-named road was devised to move the iron made at a furnace. Its rails were also of wood. Another short railway was laid at Nashua, New Hampshire, in 1825.

One of the earliest American roads on which iron rails were used, if not the first, was constructed in Massachusetts in 1826. The Bunker Hill monument was then being put up, and Gridley Bryant, owner of the quarries from which stone for the monument was taken, built the railway in order to transport blocks of granite from his quarry to tide water at Neponset. Its foundation consisted of stone sills, or sleepers, placed eight feet apart. On top of the cross-ties ponderous wooden rails were laid. These were beams a foot high and six inches thick. Flat strips of iron three inches wide and one-fourth of an inch thick were then fastened by spikes to the top of the wooden rails and the construction was complete. The road was about three miles long, and the wagons which ran on it were drawn by horses.

During these first years of American railway building the plans and visions of a few men had sped far ahead of actual creation. Another early native engineer who realized the practical value of the new transportation idea was John Stevens of Hoboken, whose previous work in steamboat enterprises—from 1804 to 1809—has already been observed. In 1811 Stevens applied to the New Jersey legislature for a charter empowering him to construct a railroad,[1] but he almost immediately shifted to the opinion that all such extensions of the internal communications system should be created by, and belong to, either the national government or the several states. So when

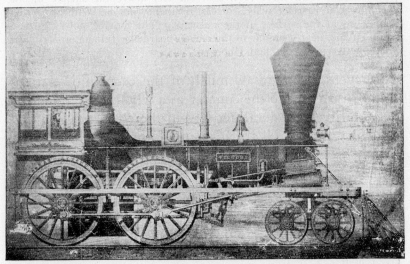

258.—The *Victory,* a type of railway engine used about 1848. Built by Rogers. For twenty-five years nearly every American-built locomotive was given a name.

New York's plan for digging the Erie Canal began to take shape a year later, he advocated the making of a railway instead of the contemplated water highway, as the most practical and best connecting link between the Hudson River and the Great Lakes. Stevens even went to the extent of writing a pamphlet[2] in advocacy of railroad building. In his arguments upholding the advantages of a rail-

[1] First application of the sort in America.
[2] "Documents Tending to Prove the Superior Advantages of Railways and Steam Carriages over Canal Navigation." New York. Published by T. and J. Swords, 1812. Doubtless the first American printed work on the subject.

881

road over the proposed canal then under discussion he said, among other things:

"Let a railway of timber be formed, by the nearest practicable route, between Lake Erie and Albany. The angle of elevation in no part to exceed one degree, or such an elevation, whatever it may be, as will admit of wheel carriages to remain stationary when no power is exerted to impel them forward. This railway, throughout its course, to be supported on pillars raised from three to five or six feet above the surface of the ground. The carriage wheels of cast-iron, the rims flat with projecting flanges, to fit the surface of the railways. The moving power to be a steam engine, nearly similar to the one on board the Juliana, a ferry boat plying between this city and Hoboken."

Stevens also foresaw much of the economic relationship of railroads to the country as a whole, and urged the desirability of Federal activity in their construction and control. In that regard his action, appeal, and unselfish motive were similar to the previous attitude of Fitch in connection with the steamboat. Stevens said:[1]

"I consider it [the building of railroads] in every point of view, so exclusively an object of national concern that I shall give no encouragement to private speculations until it is ascertained that Congress will not be disposed to pay any attention to it. Should it, however, be destined to remain unnoticed by the General Government, I must confess I shall feel much regret, not so much from personal as from public considerations. I am anxious and ambitious that my native country should have the honor of being the first to introduce an improvement of such immense importance to society at large, and should feel the utmost reluctance at being compelled to resort to foreigners in the first instance. As no doubt exists in my mind but that the value of the improvement would be duly appreciated and carried into immediate effect by transatlantic governments, I have been the more urgent in pressing the subject on the attention of Congress. Whatever then may be its fate, should this appeal be considered obtrusive and unimportant, or, from whatever other cause or motive, should it be suffered to remain unheeded, I still have the consolation of having performed what I conceive to be a public duty."

This was in 1812.

Congress considered the subject unimportant. Its

[1] Ibid.

members had before them the recent history of the steamboat from 1785 onward, and beheld the results that had
flowed from a failure to accept, on behalf of the people,
Fitch's offer in an identical case. The steamboat, instead
of being a national possession free for employment by
every man in every locality, had fallen into private hands
and its use had become subject to the whims of separate
states, to political influence, and to monopolistic grants
that forbade its general utilization on pain of fine and imprisonment. Here was another and even broader opportunity to seize and apply the same principle of steam transportation for the benefit of the country at large, and yet,
even with the parallel example and existing conditions before them, the sifted leaders of public thought and action
once again failed to grasp an opportunity. They even
refused to make a proposed test of the new method of locomotion whereby vehicles propelled by steam were to be
run on land tracks instead of on water.

No governmental action was taken, and the introduction and building of railways—most powerful of all instruments affecting the development of the nation—thereafter proceeded under private auspices, without systematic
experimentation, control, uniformity of construction, or
harmonious relationship as parts of one continental system
designed and operated as the chief mechanical servant of
the public. Instead—and for two generations or more—
the railways of the country were usually brought into being without sufficient regard for their need, coöperation
or location; were built with more thought of cheapness
than of efficiency and safety; sometimes became political
machines that ruled cities or dominated whole commonwealths; occasionally came into the hands of unscrupulous
men who systematically used them to filch money from

others; and at last the entire fabric—drunk with a fallacious belief in its own power—fell into such a state of moral collapse that its members conspired both with outsiders and among themselves, to injure communities, to destroy private enterprises, and to favor one man at the expense of another.

Within recent years these conditions, methods and acts have gradually been disappearing. The people have indicated a desire that they cease. A better, wiser, more far-seeing and competent species of guiding minds has slowly been coming into control of the vast system on which the progress, prosperity and happiness of the country so largely depend. This is not a proper occasion for analytical discussion regarding the desirability or undesirability of governmental ownership or regulation of transportation routes, nor is the discussion of that complex and important question here undertaken. It is, however, necessary to state the government's attitude at the beginning of the railroad era as a historical incident relevant to the matter in hand; to suggest the alternatives in development methods which then offered; and briefly to summarize certain other historical conditions that later prevailed. The relation between private ownership of transportation facilities and the physical and administrative excellencies and demerits of those existing facilities in America, together with comparisons between American conditions and similar systems governmentally controlled elsewhere, are already the subject of a large and accessible literature in which popular interest is increasingly manifested.

CHAPTER XL

THE MODERN RAILROAD ACCURATELY FORESEEN AND DE-
SCRIBED BY AMERICAN ENGINEERS BETWEEN 1813 AND
1819—STEVENS ABANDONS HOPE OF NATIONAL AC-
TION—DEARBORN MAKES ANOTHER APPEAL TO CON-
GRESS IN 1819—STEVENS BUILDS A LOCOMOTIVE AND
EXPERIMENTAL ROAD AT HOBOKEN—HIS TEST OF
1820 THE FIRST INCIDENT IN A SERIES OF EVENTS
THAT LED TO AMERICAN ADOPTION OF THE IDEA—
THE PENNSYLVANIA CHARTER OF 1823—PUBLIC
DISCUSSION—ATTITUDE OF THE MONEYED MEN—
ORGANIZATION OF THE PENNSYLVANIA INTERNAL
IMPROVEMENTS SOCIETY

I T was suggested in the first chapter of this narrative
that the development of our national transportation
system had on several occasions been affected—usually
to its disadvantage—by the occurrence, at critical periods,
of important or spectacular events that attracted the attention of the people and made it impossible for the public
mind to see opportunities which, had they been improved,
would have saved many years. Stevens' proposal of 1812,
urging Congress to consider railroad building as an object
of national concern and to take appropriate action in accord with such a policy, epitomized another critical period
of the sort referred to. But it so happened that an emergency in the political life of the country had to be faced at
the same time, and the needs of the future were, as always, hid by the imperative demands of the present. A

second war with England naturally absorbed all the government's energy and claimed public interest as well, and the new subject of railroads could command no thought.

Whether Congress' failure to embark on a systematic course of railroad investigation and development at that time operated to advantage or to disadvantage in the expansion and later history of our transportation facilities is a fair subject of debate. Whichever conclusion is reached by the individual man will largely depend on his prejudice against, or in favor of, governmental ownership and control of railways. It is not too much to assume, however, that if a tranquil condition of public affairs and sufficient publicity had induced the people and their representatives then to give serious consideration to the subject in some proportion to its importance, the existing and very striking object lesson of the steamboat would have had an effect, and the after-history of our railroad system would in some degree have differed from the form it was destined to take. And in the same connection it is desirable to bear in mind that during the ten years just preceding the Federal government had also adopted and maintained a policy which had for its purpose a further expansion of existing traffic routes by means of an interstate land highway built by treasury funds. Governmental adoption and use of the railroad idea at that time would have entailed no change in national policy.

Oliver Evans, in the same narrative of his early endeavors previously quoted,[1] also discussed the railway plan proposed by Stevens to the New York Canal Commission and then went on to say:

"When we reflect upon the obstinate opposition that has been made by a great majority to every step toward improvement; from bad roads

[1] The account published in "Niles' Register" in 1812.

886

LOCOMOTIVE COMING ALONG THE SUSQUEHANNAH STATION.

259.—An Erie engine of about 1850. The smokestacks on some locomotives of the period were enormous.

to turnpikes, from turnpikes to canal, from canal to railways for horse carriages, it is too much to expect the monstrous leap from bad roads to railways for steam carriages, at once. One step in a generation is all we can hope for. If the present shall adopt canals, the next may try the railways with horses, and the third generation use the steam carriage. . . . I do verily believe that the time will come when carriages propelled by steam will be in general use, as well for the transportation of passengers as goods, traveling at the rate of fifteen miles an hour, or 300 miles per day." [1]

Within a year Evans' conviction of the speed to be obtained by the use of steam railroads had still further strengthened, and he declared:

"The time will come when people will travel in stages moved by steam engines, from one city to another, almost as fast as birds fly, fifteen

[1] This was two years before George Stephenson built his first locomotive, in 1814. It made four miles an hour.

or twenty miles an hour. A carriage will set out from Washington in the morning, the passengers will breakfast at Baltimore, dine at Philadelphia, and sup at New York, the same day. To accomplish this two sets of rails[1] will be laid, so nearly level as not in any place to deviate more than two degrees from the horizontal line, made of wood or iron on smooth paths of broken stone or gravel, with a rail to guide the carriages, so that they may pass each other in different directions, and travel by night as well as by day; and the passengers will sleep in these stages as comfortably as they now do in steam boats."

The neglect shown to the subject by the national government and New York State caused Stevens to revive his plan for the securing of a charter from New Jersey, and his request received favorable consideration three years later, in 1815, when he was authorized to build a railway between Trenton and New Brunswick. He could not get the financial help necessary to construct the road. In 1819 he urged the Pennsylvania legislature to build a railroad from Philadelphia to Pittsburgh, and that effort likewise received no encouragement. A similar fate befell the proposal addressed to Congress in the same year by Benjamin Dearborn, of Boston, whose ideas and plans were expressed in part as follows:[2]

"The memorial of Benjamin Dearborn, of Boston, respectfully represents that he has devised in theory a mode of propelling wheel-carriages in a manner probably unknown in any country; and has perfectly satisfied his own mind of the practicability of conveying mails and passengers with such celerity as has never before been accomplished, and with complete security from robberies on the highway.

"For obtaining these results, he relies on carriages propelled by steam, on level railroads, and contemplates that they be furnished with accommodations for passengers to take their meals and their rest during the passage, as in packets; that they be sufficiently high for persons to walk in without stooping, and so capacious as to accommodate twenty, thirty, or more passengers, with their baggage . . . and he feels confident that whenever such an establishment shall be advanced to its most improved state, the carriages will move with a rapidity at least equal to a mile in three minutes.

[1] Meaning that a double track road would be laid.
[2] Brown's "History of the First Locomotives in America," pp. 72-73.

"Protection from the attacks of assailants will be insured; [1] not only by the celerity of the movement, but by weapons of defense belonging to the carriage, and always kept ready in it to be wielded by the number of passengers constantly travelling in this spacious vehicle, where they would have liberty to stand erect, and to exercise their arms in their own defense.

"The practicability of running steam-carriages on the common road was long since advocated in a publication by that ingenious and useful citizen, Oliver Evans; your memorialist, therefore, does not assume the merit of originating the idea of steam carriages, but only of modifying the system in such a manner as to produce the results here stated, which could not be effected on a common road.

"Relying upon the candor of the National Council, this memorial is laid before them with the desire that ingenious and scientific artists in the different sections of the country may be consulted, by direction of Congress, on the probability of accomplishing the purposes here anticipated; and that an experiment be made, if sanctioned by their favorable opinions; for if the design can be put into successful operation by the government, a great revenue would eventually be derived from the establishment, besides the advantages before enumerated."

Dearborn's proposal was referred to the Committee on Commerce and Manufactures, and nobody ever heard of it again.

By the year 1820 Stevens had become exasperated because other people did not see the value of railroads as quickly and clearly as he did, and he resolved to prove, out of his own pocket, that the travel method urged by him was not a nonsensical scheme. He had been laughed at, disputed and called a maniac long enough. During the year named, therefore, and on his own estate in Hoboken, New Jersey, Stevens built a little railway of narrow gauge and a small steam locomotive. The engine was his own handiwork. He put the locomotive on the track with cars behind it, and so ran it repeatedly with himself as a passenger, to the amazement of those before whom the demonstration was made. As far as is now known that was the first steam

[1] Reminiscent of the precautions taken on the Cincinnati packets of the Ohio River in the flatboat age, about 1790. In 1819 there was much robbing of stage-coaches by highwaymen.

railway locomotive to be built or to be run on a track in America.[1]

The practical test of 1820, though made on a small scale, had far-reaching results. From it can be traced a series of subsequent events that by degrees, and with an

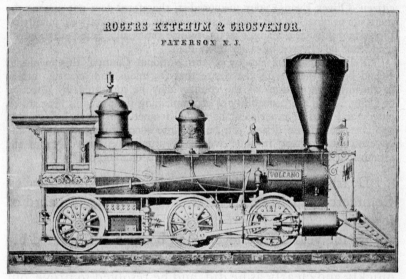

ROGERS KETCHUM & GROSVENOR.
PATERSON N. J.

VOLCANO

260.—The *Volcano.* Also a product of the Paterson builders. Date, about 1854. It, in conjunction with the three foregoing machines, shows a steady development toward the modern type of locomotive.

ever-increasing pressure, forced the public to give closer heed to the subject and, through popular discussion, at last brought money from its hiding place to take up the work demanded.

The various primitive railroad enterprises then in operation; the published discussions in newspapers and pamphlets; the arguments and predictions; the experiments; the appeals to legislatures and the petitions to

[1] Unless Fitch's last model—that of 1798—was designed as a railroad engine and run on rails by him before his death.

Congress heretofore recounted, were open to the knowledge of public men and far-seeing minds for about three years before President Monroe vetoed a National Road bill and stated that the work then being carried on by the government implied its power to create a complete interstate system of public improvements.

Stevens had abandoned hope that the Federal government would assume charge of national railroad construction, and no other path was left open to him but private enterprise authorized by separate states. He continued his campaign for support,[1] and by 1823 had enlisted some aid and secured a charter from Pennsylvania empowering him and his associates to build a railway from Philadelphia to Columbia. No work of the same nature had previously been undertaken on such a scale in this country, and the projectors could not, with sufficient accuracy, inform the lawmakers how much money they would expend or what amount of capital stock would be needed. As a consequence the financial provisions of the charter of 1823 were so framed as to make them of peculiar interest at this present time. Pennsylvania fixed the capital stock of the road at six hundred thousand dollars, but since it could not be foretold whether the actual cost of the work would be greater or less than the amount of money subscribed by the public, the following proviso was made by the legislature:

"That on the completion of said railroad the president and directors are hereby required to ascertain precisely the amount of the sum total of expenses incurred in the construction of the same, and said sum total shall constitute the existing capital of said railroad company."

Thus did an American commonwealth, in 1823, foresee that stock in such an enterprise might be issued without

[1] Though himself a well-to-do man for those days he could not, alone, bear the heavy burden necessary in building a railway.

equivalent value behind it, and thus did the state safeguard intending investors by providing against the possibility of such an action. Whether or not the sordid minds of the period also glimpsed the possibilities of gaining easy wealth by such unscrupulous financial methods, and whether or not the outcry which arose about that time in opposition to Federal building of traffic routes was due, in some measure, to their realization that governmental building of new national transportation facilities would destroy a large opportunity for acquiring ill-gained wealth, are questions perhaps impossible of answer at the present day.

Two other features of this early railroad charter deserve mention because of the archaic transportation viewpoints they reveal. One of them gave to Stevens—by inference at least—certain rights similar to those of a patentee, for it provided that all profits of the road, above twelve per cent., were to go to Stevens or his legal assignee. The other interesting feature of the charter dealt with remuneration which the road might exact for service rendered. It empowered the company to charge three and a half cents a mile on every ton of freight moving eastward, and seven cents a mile for a ton going west.[1]

No sooner had the legislature given permission to build and operate the road than a public discussion began over the mechanical possibility of doing such a thing. It was admitted that railways were practical for small distances, because a number of short highways of that description really did exist in various states, and vehicles were moved over them. But the proposed new road, of the stupendous length of seventy-three miles, was altogether

[1] Because westward movement was on an up grade.

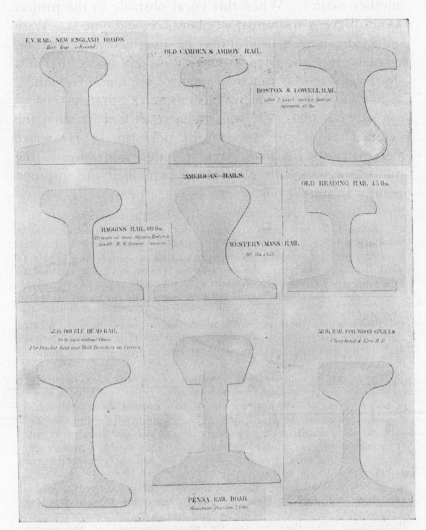

261.—Examples of the rails that supplanted timbers edged with flat iron bars. Many experiments were still tried, but a steady drift toward the T rail and a standard pattern was apparent. Some of the Boston and Lowell rails were laid upside down, and were used that way. Dates, from 1832 to 1852.

another matter. When this vocal obstacle to the project arose, Stevens promptly set about to overcome it. With outward calmness—and it may be imagined with what inward raging—he tried to make the skeptics see that if a short railway was practical then a long one, of identical construction and grade, was also practical; that the traversing of each new mile was but a repetition of what the vehicle had already successfully performed. He wrote and distributed a long circular letter, addressed to the public, in which he elaborately explained the disputed point. In part it ran:

"PHILADELPHIA, 1823.

"SIR:—It is now generally admitted that a railroad is not a mere visionary project but is actually practicable. An erroneous idea has, however, prevailed among its opponents, that it is only practicable to short distances, and that the contemplated extension of a railroad to a distance of 73 miles is ridiculous.

"As the railroad will, throughout its course, be, in its construction, exactly similar, it is only in its deviations from a horizontal line that any difference in the progressive motion of carriages thereon can take place. The charter contains a provision that the railroad in its progress shall in no part rise above an angle of two degrees with the plane of the horizon.

"Now let us suppose that a section of the intended railroad be constructed in the immediate vicinity of the city, of one mile in extent, in the progress of which elevations of two degrees do actually occur. Should it, however, be practicable, on such section of the intended railroad, to cause loaded carriages to move forward and backward, without encountering any impediment or difficulty, would it not be presumable that the effect would be precisely the same were a similar road to be extended ever so far?

". . . And when this great improvement in transportation shall have been extended to Pittsburgh, and thence into the heart of the extensive and fertile state of Ohio, and also to the great western lakes, Philadelphia may then become the great emporium of the western country."

Stevens' argument certainly sounded plausible, even if it did not produce the desired effect. The men who were both rich and honest could not refute his conclusions, nor did they try to. They simply held aloof and refused to embark their fortunes in enterprises such as he was urging.

One reason for their attitude was this: they could not at once bring themselves to believe that the old order was changing, and that the immemorial, undisputed sway of pack-horse, stage-coach, wagon train and water craft was seriously threatened. For two centuries the country had got along with those methods of travel and transportation. They themselves had come to manhood and won places of leadership without knowledge or thought of any other means of movement. Every act and circumstance of their affairs—the whole fabric of their lives—was bound up with, and based upon, the old ways. Now they were suddenly bedeviled by a lot of fanatics who bombarded them with strange and unanswerable questions; who proposed impossible, unheard-of, quixotic things; who waved countless diagrams, plans, surveys and calculations; and who demanded money for the immediate construction of fantastical rails and engines by means whereof the people might buzz about the country like bees in a clover patch.

It was too much. Never had it been necessary to perform a problem in trigonometry previous to the beginning of a stage-coach trip, nor even while waiting for the steamboat to slide off a sand-bar. What had science to do with going somewhere? If a man wanted to go to Pittsburgh or Ohio then let him begone, and have it over.

Yet there were a few things the big men were willing to admit. They conceded that these railroads concerning which they heard so much would very probably answer as improved portages between two natural or artificial waterways, and that short constructions of the kind might under certain conditions be otherwise useful. But the rivers were more reliable, the stage-coaches averaged six

PORTAGE BRIDGE.

OVER GENESEE RIVER AT PORTAGEVILLE.

262.—A common method of timber bridge construction. Some bridges were of massive masonry. Iron was rarely used.

or eight miles an hour on good turnpikes, numerous canals were already in operation and many others were either in process of building or under consideration. Canals promised to be profitable, and millions of money had been expended on them already. On the whole it was better to attend strictly to business and let well enough alone.

As an outcome of this attitude Stevens and his comrades failed to get the cash they needed.[1] But though his reasoning then failed to sway the men who could have aided him, the uproar, wrangle and debate produced by his seventy-three-mile railway proposition did arouse such

[1] And their charter was repealed in 1826.

a deep interest in the public mind that other and lasting effects soon appeared. The country—as far as the adoption of a new system of locomotion was concerned—stood literally at the parting of the ways. Canals and railroads both had their partisans, and the clash of opinion regarding the relative value of the two methods of communication speedily brought about a general hubbub and intensity of feeling such as had never before been aroused in this country by the discussion of any question unrelated to national politics or warfare.

This state of affairs was especially noticeable in Pennsylvania, and out of it grew the organization, late in 1824, of the Pennsylvania Society for the Promotion of Internal Improvements in the Commonwealth. Its members were business men, chiefly of Philadelphia, who had determined to take an active part in definitely settling the question then uppermost in the thoughts of the people.

CHAPTER XLI

ENGLAND, at that time, had enjoyed a more extensive experience both with canals and railroads
than had the United States, and the Pennsylvania association believed there was benefit to be derived from a study
of English methods used in the building and equipment
of the two systems of internal communication. It hoped
to utilize those foreign methods—as far as desirable—in
conjunction with some of the ambitious hopes already
discussed on this side of the water.

Swift action by the Pennsylvanians followed their conclusions. They at once employed an American civil engineer,[1] and sent him to England under secret instructions,[2]

---

[1] William Strickland.

[2] The injunction requiring Strickland to pursue his work as quietly as possible was
no doubt prompted by a natural desire on the part of the society to obtain the first
knowledge of his investigations, in order that its members might use the information
collected by him in business enterprises if they wished to do so.

263.—A "lookout pole." For about twenty years there was no way by which a railroad might discover the location or adventures of its trains after they had disappeared from sight. Nor could waiting travellers along the line be informed when the trains would reach them. So it became the custom of station agents, or of the roads themselves, to set up stout masts at stopping places, and shortly before a train was due the agent climbed his pole, sat himself in a little seat at its top, and watched the horizon for smoke. If successful, as was often the case, he shouted bulletins to those below. Otherwise there was nothing to do but wait.

enjoining him to prepare a report on the subject for which they were organized. The date of the society's confidential letter to its representative was March 25, 1825, and various essential parts of it read as follows:

"It is not a knowledge of abstract principles, nor an indefinite and general account of their application to the great works of Europe we desire to possess through your labors. . . . What we earnestly wish to obtain, is the means of executing all those works in the best manner, and with the greatest economy and certainty. . . .

"Of the utility of railways, and their importance as a means of transporting large burdens, we have full knowledge. Of the mode of constructing them, and of their cost, nothing is known with certainty. . . . You will bear in mind in your investigations of this subject that we have, as yet, no complete railway in Pennsylvania; and you will, therefore, so exhibit your facts, as that they may be understood by

899

reference to the drawings which you may make. . . . Locomotive machinery will command your attention and inquiry. This is entirely unknown in the United States, and we authorize you to procure a model of the most. improved locomotive machine, at the expense of the society."

It will be seen from the spirit and literal wording of these instructions[1] that the men responsible for them were in no uncertain state of mind regarding their own beliefs. They were not sending a man to England to find out whether railroads were of value or not. That point they already considered as settled. They wanted to find out how railroads were built, and how locomotives were built. No sooner had Strickland begun his work than clamor over the subject of internal improvements in America became louder than ever before, and increased popular interest in the question was reflected in a further instruction which was sent by the society to its representative on September 19th. The committee's letter to Strickland under that date said, in part:

"Canals and railways present the most important of all subjects for your attention. Upon every matter connected with both you will be expected to be well informed. . . . Much excitement prevails in this state upon the question whether railways are superior to canals, and the inquiries that are in progress in relation to them are in the hands of men of ingenuity and well disposed to the cause of internal improvement. It is, however, feared by many that the question between canals and railways will have an injurious influence in Pennsylvania, as it will divide the friends of the cause of improvement, and thus postpone, if not prevent, the commencement of the work. The importance of correct information in relation to them is thus greatly increased."

The society's representative brought back with him in 1826 a model of an English railroad locomotive of the inefficient type then in use[2] and during August of the same year his report was published by the society, together with many large reproductions of the drawings he had made

[1] The full text was put in type by the society at the time, in a confidential pamphlet of four printed pages.
[2] Which later came into possession of the Franklin Institute, of Philadelphia.

while abroad.[1] Strickland's elaborate and important volume produced an overwhelming impression; not so much
through the comparatively short text giving its author's
observations as by means of the engravings it contained.
An intelligent pictorial appeal to the understanding is
always effective, and when the matter illustrated happens

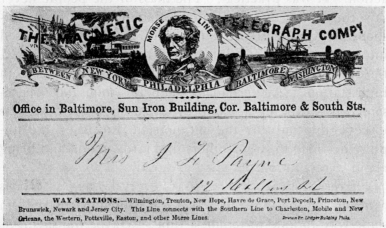

THE MAGNETIC *MORSE LINE* TELEGRAPH COMP'Y

BETWEEN NEW YORK PHILADELPHIA BALTIMORE WASHINGTON

Office in Baltimore, Sun Iron Building, Cor. Baltimore & South Sts.

WAY STATIONS.—Wilmington, Trenton, New Hope, Havre de Grace, Port Deposit, Princeton, New
Brunswick, Newark and Jersey City. This Line connects with the Southern Line to Charleston, Mobile and New
Orleans, the Western, Pottsville, Easton, and other Morse Lines.   *Drawn Pr. Ledger Building Phila.*

264.—A telegraphic message sent by the first Morse line. Design used on the
   delivery envelope. The telegraph was first used in connection with railway
   operation by the Erie road in 1851, and all other railroads immediately followed its example. The lookout pole then became extinct.

to be one concerning which the public is vitally interested
—as was true in the case mentioned—and regarding which
it has no other reliable information in similar form, then
such presentation of a subject has a power difficult to
exaggerate.

It should not be understood that the famous book in
question was a familiar object in every household, for
nothing could be further from the fact. Only a few

---

[1] Contained in a large folio atlas entitled, "Reports on Canals, Railways, Roads, and
Other Subjects, made to the Pennsylvania Society for the Promotion of Internal Improvement. By William Strickland, Architect and Engineer, while Engaged in the Service
of the Society." Strickland's drawings are reproduced in 72 very fine folio plates engraved
on copper, and include every detail of railway, canal and other public works construction
as then practised in England.

hundred copies of it were printed,[1] and its high cost[2] effectually removed it from the class to which popular novels belong. But it did show for the first time—not only in America, but in the world[3]—and in a manner easily comprehended, the whole process then employed in building and equipping a railroad. It furnished a basis for action. It was practical. The mass of the people never saw the book for which their clamor was directly responsible, yet the public felt its result at once, for it passed into the hands of, and influenced, those who had money, those who could do the work it described, and those in high station.[4] Again had the nameless thousands, represented this time by a group of citizens whose identity is discoverable only by the antiquarian, furnished the impulse destined to sweep others into tardy action and bring about a revolution.

There is a proverb which says every human act exerts a never-ending influence; that its consequences will in some way radiate to remotest time. Maybe the saying is true. Sometimes it surely is, and the deeds of men are strangely interwoven. The madman of Conjurer's Point dreamed a steamboat, and made one. From his work John Stevens of Hoboken gained inspiration for similar endeavor, and Stevens, in course of time, put wheels under his engine instead of a keel. A group of Pennsylvanians joined with Stevens in a plan to introduce those wheeled engines here, and out of the discussion attending that effort grew an organization which sent a man to England.

---

[1] The "List of Subscribers" indicates but 334 copies, and probably the whole issue did not exceed 500.

[2] The engravings it contains represent an expenditure of perhaps three thousand dollars, and it was sold for $10.00 a copy.

[3] For not even in England had any work been published which remotely approached Strickland's atlas in importance or value.

[4] Among the subscribers were the United States Post Office Department, the Navy Department, the War Department, the West Point Military School, and the national House of Representatives, which took 25 copies! The government was waking up.

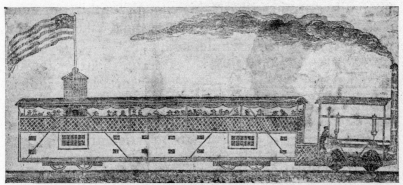

265.—Beginning a series of eleven illustrations showing the evolution of the passenger car after it assumed rectangular lines, and while a standard type was developing. In two-story cars of this sort the upper deck was most popular in fair weather as the lower floor was poorly lighted and ventilated. Such double-decked vehicles were not generally adopted. The cupola was very uncommon.

The man came back, his drawings were published, and America stepped over the threshold of a new age.

Forty years had elapsed since Oliver Evans asked Pennsylvania and Maryland for the right to use self-propelled steam carriages. Thirty-one years had gone by since the first application of the railway principle in America, at the Boston brick kiln. Fourteen years had passed from the day on which Evans offered to run a steam-engine on rails at the rate of fifteen miles an hour, while Stevens at the same time was urging the building of railroads by Congress as a national policy and advocating the construction of such a highway by New York State. Thirteen years had gone since Evans foretold a double-tracked, rock-ballasted railway over which men would journey between Baltimore and New York in one day, and in the cars of which they might sleep in comfort. Only seven years had slipped by since Stevens proposed a railroad from Philadelphia to Pittsburgh. The same period had passed since Dearborn placed before Congress his ideas

903

for a railway train with cars big enough for thirty or more passengers, in which they might eat and take their rest while moving at twenty miles an hour.

Those are the landmarks of America's journey toward the modern railroad. Their significance, as an indication that this country was already pursuing an independent line of thought and would speedily have reached a material realization of the new transportation principle, even without Stephenson's later demonstration with the *Rocket* in 1829, scarcely seems to require further emphasis. But if there be doubt concerning the point then there still remains a comparison between the American attitude as already outlined and that assumed toward the subject in England until the year 1829.

The three most important early English books relating to railways were those of Tredgold, Wood and Lardner. Tredgold said:[1]

"Locomotives must always be objectionable on a railroad for general use, where it is attempted to give them a considerable degree of speed. . . . That any general system of carrying passengers would answer, to go at a velocity exceeding ten miles an hour, or thereabouts, is extremely improbable."

Wood's comment on the same phase of the question read:[2]

"It is far from my wish to promulgate to the world that the ridiculous expectations, or rather professions, of the enthusiastic speculator will be realized, and that we shall see engines travelling at the rate of twelve, sixteen, eighteen, or twenty miles an hour. Nothing could do more harm toward their general adoption and improvement than the promulgation of such nonsense."

And Lardner asserted that:[3]

"Carriages could not go at anything like the contemplated speed; if driven to it, the wheels would merely spin on their axles, and the carriages would stand stock still."

[1] "A Practical Treatise on Railroads and Carriages," 2nd edition, London, 1825.
[2] "A Practical Treatise on Railroads and Internal Communication," London, 1825.
[3] "Lectures on the Steam Engine," London, 1827.

266.—Probably in some respects a fanciful sketch. Yet many of the early cars were very short, highly decorated, and occasionally of unequal heights. The engine and tender are not impossible in general outline, and the splint-brooms attached to the locomotive for the purpose of sweeping the rails are genuine. They were often used; once in Pennsylvania during a plague of grasshoppers.

The serious English periodicals of the time reflected public opinion in similar strain. A typical utterance of the sort[1] contained this passage:

"What can be more palpably absurd and ridiculous than the prospect held out of locomotives traveling twice as fast as stage coaches! We should as soon expect the people of Woolwich to suffer themselves to be fired off upon one of Congreve's ricochet rockets as trust themselves to the mercy of such a machine going at such a rate. . . . We trust that Parliament will, in all railways it may sanction, limit the speed to eight or nine miles an hour, which we entirely agree with Mr. Sylvester is as great as can be ventured on with safety."

When the proposed Liverpool and Manchester railway asked Parliament for a franchise, during the same year of 1825, George Stephenson was summoned by the Parliamentary committee to be questioned concerning the velocity of which a locomotive might be capable. As Stephenson was about to testify, William Brougham, the railroad's own lawyer, warned him that if he discussed the possibility of any unusual speed, such as twenty miles an hour, he would "inevitably damn the whole thing, and be himself regarded as a maniac fit for Bedlam."[2] Stephenson permitted himself to predict a speed of twelve miles an hour,[3] members of the committee whispered their doubts of his sanity, and the application for a charter was denied.

England had then been building railways for nearly two hundred years, had made iron rails since 1738 and steam locomotives since 1804. Yet in 1825 the combined use of all three devices had suggested nothing to her public men or civil engineers save what has been indicated in the utterances just quoted. Even after the Stockton and

[1] In the "Quarterly Review" for March, 1825.
[2] Smiles' "Life of George Stephenson."
[3] The maximum velocity attained by his best and latest engine, just completed for the Stockton and Darlington road. The average working speed of that locomotive was five miles an hour.

Darlington road was opened to traffic[1] the bulk of its motive power, for the moving of both passengers and freight, was furnished by horses. When one of its vehicles reached a down-grade section of the railway the horse would jump on a low platform built for the purpose at one end of the car, and so ride down to the bottom of the hill.

America, in considering the possibilities of the new locomotion system, stood on an equality with England as far as knowedge of the physical elements of the proposition were concerned. Neither possessed an overwhelming advantage. Each knew the railed track, the iron, and the steam-engine. If either can be said to have had a superior position from which to advance toward greater things—just before the general adoption and introduction of railways—then England was that one, for she had been aware of the railed-track device for a longer time and employed it more extensively. She had enjoyed a fuller opportunity to grasp its potentiality. Yet it was America which first saw—and demanded—the use of the whole value of the railroad idea. England, after nearly two centuries of railed tracks, eighty-seven years of iron rails and twenty-one years of locomotives, had progressed to the point illustrated by the Stockton and Darlington road and its methods. The possibility of further advance of consequence was unrealized in England; it was denied, after due consideration, by the men most competent to give judgment in such a matter.

America's less-experienced engineers were distinguished by one quality not possessed by their colleagues across the ocean. They had known of railed tracks for only thirty years, and had not employed iron rails or loco-

[1] England's first line for general business; opened in 1825.

motives at all. Yet to those three commonplace and material elements of mechanical construction, knowledge of
two of which was theirs by hearsay only, they added a
fourth and still more necessary component—imagination.
Men like Evans, Stevens and Dearborn were accurately
describing the railway and railway travel of the future
in written words, and were planning the construction and
equipment of railroads hundreds of miles in length, while
yet the English had no conception of the possibilities that
lay within the methods they had used so long.

Both countries were converging on the same historic
event—the creation of practical railroads—along path-
ways which, though very different in themselves, were
significant of the characters and processes of the nations
employing them. Each reached the goal by its own
method at substantially the same time as the other. Indeed, had it not been for the tremendous personality, remarkable mechanical ingenuity and persistence of the
unlettered pit-engineer George Stephenson, it is altogether likely that America would have outdistanced England in the race. For it was Stephenson's solitary work,
in opposition to which the influential body of his countrymen fought almost to the raving point, that pushed them,
against their will and frantic resistance, over the remaining distance that separated them from success. Conservative England had moved toward the modern railroad by
slow and almost imperceptible degrees for two hundred
years. America took one mental leap and stood beside
her.

It has been said the American contribution to the problem of railway creation was imagination. In reality it
was something which, though intangible, was much more
solid, substantial and valuable than that; it was the exer-

BOSTON.

*The above shows the appearance of Boston as seen from the south-west, near the intersection of the Providence and Worcester Rail Road.
the State-House, with its towering dome, and the Granary appear on the central part. Bunker-Hill Monument is seen on the extreme left.*

Drawn by J. W. Barber.

Engraved by A. Willard and J. Webster.

267.—Two railway trains on the outskirts of Boston. The wheels of the farther train are placed outside the trucks; those of the train in the foreground are inside. From a drawing by J. W. Barber. Date, about 1839-1840.

cise of an ability existing from the first as a national trait, and which had developed at last into the quickness of thought so characteristic of this western people. It was a supreme manifestation of the same elemental quality that enabled the American of 1630 to behold the shape of a finished canoe in the trunk of the untouched tree. For seven generations the pioneer population of the new continent had been drilled, by stern conditions, in the importance of foresight, in the need of anticipating future personal necessities and in the duty of claiming the ultimate particle of value from any object.[1] Long years passed, and by and by came the railed track and the steam-engine. The consequences of their appearance here were inevitable. The American mind, trained as it had been, looked upon them and beheld the railroad as it was to be—as it must be, if the last vestige of its usefulness was to be extracted from the idea. And that determination was axiomatic.

So automatic was the mental process in question that the unknown, unrealized railroad of the future, even to its double track and ballasted roadbed, and its dining and sleeping cars, were described by Americans in the period between 1813 and 1819 in a way that was almost matter-of-fact. Such things were certain. They already existed except in the unimportant feature of concrete form. Although knowledge of the manner of making them did not happen to be available at the moment, that was a trivial detail. Nothing further was necessary but to devise or find out a practical method of building the contrivances, and to get permission and money for their construction.

[1] Scarcely any article was thrown away, for fear that at some future time, in an unexpected way, it might "come handy." When its day of active usefulness was done it was taken up into that museum of American household archeology, the attic. So deeply was the trait in question implanted in those early generations that its effects are still clearly visible, and until to-day the destruction of useless home rubbish often constitutes an agony.

The men who saw all this—who created the railway in the American fashion of seeing first and then compelling their hands to catch up with their ideas—set about the job of getting permission and the money, and did not stop until they had succeeded. They were men who, though unknown and unpreferred among their fellows, had a broadness of vision that enabled them to perceive and proclaim the relationship between this new transportation method and the country's future. The universal practise of anticipating necessities was by them shifted from its personal basis to a national one. Their part of the work was not done with transit, plumb-line, pickax and shovel. Tens of thousands could use those implements. All they employed was brains. By their endeavors, extending through only a few years, America overstepped the age-long process by which England had advanced, and plunged headlong into an effort to produce in material form the elaborate vision that hung, like a rainbow of promise, before the eyes of their fancy.

That was the pathway along which America approached the creation of her first railways, and the one whereby, ever since the period in question, she has proceeded in her march toward industrial and economic progress. She has anticipated necessity, and welded the stuff of dreams into mechanisms that seem endowed with reason. But in one respect the nation, in an imaginative sense, has gone backward in the handling of its natural and man-created riches. We have become wasteful and careless. Nature's prodigality and the creative ability of the people have wrought an insidious harm. No longer do we seek to extract the last ounce of utility from the things we possess. Of each unit of energy or material or opportunity we cast aside one-third, and it is lost.

A HISTORY OF TRAVEL IN AMERICA

One other general feature connected with the creation of the early railways of the country is deserving of mention. It has been seen that the men who first built them in imagination, and furnished the impulse which resulted in their actual construction, dealt with the subject mainly in terms of speed, length, and the conveniences of human travel. The new highways were to connect regions separated by hundreds of miles, over which people were to be conveyed at fifteen or twenty miles an hour in cars wherein they might also eat and sleep. The men of money, without whose help no progress could be made, shook their heads at this and saw only the possibility of using railroads for the moving of freight over short distances between existing towns and cities. That was the big purpose, from a capitalistic standpoint, for which the first roads were begun.[1] They were simply to be improvements over previous highways, designed for the transportation of mercantile commodities created by established communities. But little provision, or none at all, was made for the accommodation of human beings. Yet when the railways were opened for traffic, and solitary rattletrap passenger cars were devised or stage-coaches put on proper wheels for the sake of experiment, the passenger vehicles were overwhelmed, as they have been ever since.

The foresight and understanding of the men who built in terms of fancy were clearer than that of the ones who used nothing but metal and stone and wood. Railroads were not wanted solely as carriers of goods between cities. They were children of the spirit of conquest and the demand for wider, swifter movement, even though the financial nurses who coddled them were blind to their parent-

[1] That is to say, it was the purpose of the capitalists. True of England as well as of America.

912

age.[1] The railways also in due course came to anticipate necessity, rather than simply try to catch up with it, and though their efforts in that regard were sometimes misdirected, yet on the whole such endeavors have been of value, and have done much in aiding the people to strike root in regions otherwise impossible of permanent and flourishing settlement.

[1] In two appendices will be found tabular statements showing the organization, first use, length, and source of income of ninety-five early American railways, together with the relationship between their capitalization and cost of construction. It was passenger traffic, and not the carriage of commercial commodities, that gave the railroads a great majority of their income, saved them, and encouraged their future building and extension up to 1850 or later.

CHAPTER XLII

THE DREAM-BUILDERS SUPPLANTED BY MEN DESTINED TO
PERFORM ACTUAL CONSTRUCTION WORK — EARLY
POPULAR IDEAS ABOUT RAILROADS — HOW THE PEOPLE
SHOWED THEIR INTEREST — CONTEMPORARY NEWS-
PAPER COMMENT AND PICTURES — THREE ASPECTS OF
THE SUBJECT — OPINIONS ON THE PHYSICAL CHAR-
ACTER OF THE NEW DEVICE — HOW TRACKS WERE
FIRST BUILT — MANY DIFFERENT GAUGES — A MIS-
TAKEN NOTION REGARDING THE USE OF RAILWAYS AS
HIGHWAYS — ITS RESULTS IN AMERICA — THE CEN-
TER-POST DEVICE — AN INDIANA PREDICTION OF 1830
— RAILROADS AS MORAL INFLUENCES — A MASSA-
CHUSETTS ROAD ASKS FOR SERMONS IN ITS BEHALF —
ONE OF THE RESPONSES

THE work of Evans, Dearborn, Stevens, the Pennsylvania Society and others had not been in vain.
Railroads had been discussed, advocated and described in
their future form by a few Americans during a period of
about fifteen years. Argument was now to be superseded
in part by action, and railroads themselves were to appear
and alter the character of the debate concerning them.

No sooner did it become apparent that actual physical
creation of the new transportation device was at hand
in this country than more interest in the subject which had
so suddenly usurped attention was manifested by all sorts
of odd methods. Crude representations of railroad loco-

914

motives and cars began to appear as decorative patterns on the dishes, china and glassware used by the people. Small metallic medals were struck in honor of the introduction of the railroad. The popular sheet-music of the period was occasionally embellished with pictures of steam-engines and cars. Even whisky bottles appeared bearing upon their sides crude designs and inscriptions commemorating the introduction of railed tracks. Nor was this manifestation of popular interest confined to the subject of railways alone. Pictures and all sorts of other representations of steamboats, stage-coaches and canal boats also multiplied at the same time, and hardly a household could be found either in the city or country whose possessions did not include various objects indicative of the feeling here suggested.[1]

This condition of the public mind was further shown by similar evidences appearing in the newspapers and books of the day. A picture of a railroad had been printed in a daily newspaper as early as March 7, 1826, when the *American Traveler,* of Boston, issued a full page broadside containing a view and description of the Hetton Railroad in England.[2] In the discussion of railroads contained in the broadside is the following:

"The acknowledged importance of Rail Road conveyance and the great anxiety existing in the public mind, respecting the relative value

[1] Examples of the wall-paper, medals, sheet-music and bottles here mentioned are reproduced elsewhere in these pages. The medal and wall-paper were issued about 1825 in celebration of the completion of the Erie Canal. The piece of sheet-music was engraved in celebration of the commencement of the Baltimore and Ohio Railroad, and was placed on sale in Baltimore on the 4th of July in 1828, when the building of the road was begun. The bottle which bears the inscription "Success to the Railroad" is also believed to have been made in the same year. It is "No. 1" in Barber's list of the eighty-six designs of historical American glassware thus far discovered. Of it Barber says: "Among the oldest forms of decorated glass bottles or flasks known to have been made in the United States is one which bears a relief design representing the first railroad. The device shows a horse drawing a four-wheeled car along a rail. . . . It is probable that this very interesting object was produced at the Kensington Glass Works, Philadelphia. . . . The character of the glass, the color, the shape and the peculiar mould markings point to such an origin." Barber's book is entitled "American Glassware Old and New." It was privately printed in Philadelphia in 1900.

[2] Reproduced on another page. It is, perhaps, the first picture of an actual railroad printed in America, and antedates the issuance of Strickland's book by about five months.

268.—Style of passenger car most frequently used during the decade from 1840 to 1850. The windows of this vehicle were not raised, but the entire panels were dropped bodily down into the sides of the car. Drawn and engraved by Alexander Robb.

of Canals and Rail Roads, as species of internal communication, must render any information concerning either of some interest; and if that information come from persons who have made the subject their particular study, and have given to the public the result of their faithful experiments, whether they tend towards establishing the one system or the other, they will be equally entitled to attention. . . .

"It may to many seem an object of surprise, that so simple and efficient a plan of moving carriages on a road has not been more generally employed; but it may be remarked, that though the idea of forming smooth surfaces for carriage wheels to roll upon, is not a modern one, still, until quite lately, there has been felt a great want of practical information on the subject, and consequently a lack of enterprise in our citizens, in entering upon the 'unbeaten path.'"

But very few other American newspapers of that date gauged the importance of the subject with such accuracy, or indicated by actions their appreciation of the public interest in it. Another newspaper of the East to print a similar railroad broadside was the *New York American,* whose page was issued on March 11, 1830. The *American's* broadside was devoted to an account of the locomotive competition held in England during the previous October[1] and was illustrated with pictures of two of the competing machines. Doubtless there were still other American papers that took occasion to comment on

[1] The entire first page of the paper was given to the matter, as news, though the event described had happened about five months before. Reproduced elsewhere.

269.—A train on the Hudson River Railroad, near the town of Hudson. Contemporary pencil sketch. Signature, Philip Doane. Date, about 1851.

railroads with equal prominence during the first three or four years after railway building on an extensive scale became assured in this country, but as a general thing the daily and weekly press — though in the aggregate giving a great deal of space to the subject — confined its activities to the printing of paragraphs and short articles.

Many of the books issued during those same years — especially such volumes as were devoted to description of the country — contained articles about railways, and sometimes the accounts were accompanied by illustrations.[1] A definition of railroads contained in an encyclopedia[2] of the period read:

"Railway.—A species of road or carriage way, in which the tracks of the carriage wheel being laid with bars or rails of wood, stone, or metal, the carriage runs with so much greater facility that one horse will perform the work of many. On some railways the wagons are moved by steam instead of horses. It is contemplated to make railways in various parts of the U. States. Many have been commenced, and several are already completed. Their utility and superiority over canals will, no doubt, cause general construction in most states in the U. States within a few years where the travelling is great."

While a majority of the people were thus thinking of railroads in their completed shape and were speculating about the future advantages they were so impatient to enjoy, the other and less numerous class of men then giving attention to the subject were concerned with problems relating to the physical character of railways and the best manner of their use after they had been built. Both in point of suddenness and of the revolutionary procedure which it entailed, the adoption of the railway idea to human movement and traffic no doubt constituted

[1] Two such articles from contemporary books are reproduced elsewhere. One of them is a description of the Baltimore and Ohio Railroad in its earliest days, accompanied by a wood engraving of a horse-drawn passenger car of that road. The other book illustration is a page that apparently shows a train on the Boston and Worcester road in Massachusetts, and the picture is accompanied by a printed description of the "most common apparatus for travelling on roads."
[2] "A Family Encyclopedia, or, an Explanation of Words and Things." By George Crabb, New York, 1831.

the most important alteration in established methods of performing certain work which mankind had yet undertaken. The last of the pioneers saw that here was an agency containing vast possibilities, while at the same time they admitted that the most desirable manner of employing the potentialities concealed in the new process must be discovered as they went along. Yet some sort of start had to be made, and much controversy arose regarding the proper things to do. Some thought one plan of building and use was best, and others considered a different method was preferable, but everybody, no matter what his opinion, was tolerably certain he was right. The old feeling of cock-sureness—developed by long contact with familiar economic problems whose well-known solutions had made such a mental attitude formerly excusable—was abundantly displayed.

During this widespread discussion of railroads all close consideration of the subject dealt principally with three phases of the newly arisen question: namely, the proper physical construction of railways; their precise character as highways; their social and economic influence. The debate naturally resulted in the appearance of a considerable literature devoted to the problem, and all the books about railroads published in America during the decade immediately following the commencement of railway building in the country contained numerous statements and arguments which—to our more modern thought—are curious and entertaining. The narration of some of these primitive methods of track building, and of contemporary ideas about them, will show the astonishing contrast that existed between the finished product of the former dream-builders and the actual plans that were adopted and applied by the men into whose hands were to fall the details of structural work. One of the earliest and least known of these American publications[1] began in the following words:

"The first thing to be determined in the formation of a Railroad is the kind of power that is to be employed on it, whether horses or steam engines. It is desirable not to use both kinds of power on the same road; . . . because the slow travelling of horses will present a serious obstruction to the free operations of locomotive steam engines, compelling them to frequently turn out and occasionally delay and inconvenience; . . . because the action of the horses' feet will throw dust and gravel on the rails, which it will be desirable to avoid on roads for engines. . . . A further reason is, that the dust thrown on the rails will be converted into mud in wet weather, and will materially diminish the adhesion of the wheels of the locomotive engine to the rails."[2]

The same authority advanced the argument that in creating a railroad designed for operation by horse-power it would be desirable so to build it as to secure a regular alternation of up-grades and down-grades. This expedient, he said, would enable the horses to jump aboard a car designed for their accommodation when the train was about to start down hill, thus saving the animals' strength and eliminating a waste of the motive power. In this connection he also remarked:

"A further advantage in travelling a gradually ascending and gradually descending road would be found in the carriage of passengers, and goods requiring speedy transportation. Travellers desire to go faster than a horse can travel with ease to himself, or profit to his owner, if the charges be moderate. By having the horses ride half the distance any admissible rate of speed for that portion of the distance might be had, so that the whole journey could be performed in less time."[3]

During his discussion of the proper method of laying a track the same authority declared:

"If the rails are not laid upon a foundation of sufficient firmness the supports soon settle unequally, so that the rails become undulating, re-

[1] "A Treatise on Rail-roads and Internal Communications. Compiled from the Latest and Best Authors. With Original Sketches and Remarks." By Thomas Earle, Philadelphia, 1830.
[2] Earle, p. 6.
[3] Earle, p. 17.

The "Baltimore and Ohio" whiskey bottle. Among all the many curious evidences of early popular interest in the subject of transportation the most strange, perhaps, was the designing of a whiskey bottle in celebration of the introduction of railways into America. Made of olive-green glass. Date, 1828-1830. American.

quiring a very irregular draught from the horses, and straining the wagons by the shocks they receive at the meeting ends of rails of different slope. . . . Where timber is scarce, and iron and stone abundant, it is considered advantageously to use rails entirely of iron, supported upon blocks of stone. Railways of this kind may perhaps be expensive, even in America, if steam engines are to be used. But where horses are to furnish the power it will generally be an important advantage to have a cheap work; and consequently wood, or wood and iron combined, will be preferred. . . . Locust or cedar wood is preferred for the sleepers as being slow to decay. . . . The wooden rails are of sawed timber. White oak is considered the best. They are of different dimensions according to the views of the proprietors, or the width of wagons to be used. Some are 3 inches wide by 5 in depth; some 4 by 6. . . .

"On some roads wooden rails without any covering of iron, except at crossing places and curves, are still used. Where the business of a road is small, and timber abundant, it may be expedient to save the expense of iron. In other cases iron plates should be used to protect the timber from wear, as well as to render the motion of the wagons somewhat easier. For this purpose plates of rolled iron are used, varying in dimensions from $\frac{1}{4}$ of an inch thick by $1\frac{1}{4}$ wide, to $\frac{1}{2}$ an inch thick by 2 inches wide."[1]

In speaking of the relative merits of single-tracked and double-tracked railroads the book written by Earle said:

"For the transportation of goods to a moderate amount, a single way will answer every purpose about as well as a double one. Engines can leave particular points at certain hours and arrive at other points at fixed hours.. . . . For instance, take the distance between one of our Atlantic cities and Pittsburgh, suppose a distance of 320 miles. If trains or wagons were to leave each city every morning, and travel the distance in 4 days, meeting places would be required every 40 miles. If wagons should leave each city at both morning and noon, and arrive at both noon and night, the places of meeting would be every 20 miles, at fixed hours. . . . Arrangements of this kind are inconsistent with the beau-ideal of travel. The imagination delights in freedom from obstructions, and from the restraints of fixed rules. But we are compelled to submit, in practical matters, to the curb of reason."[2]

And finally, in discussing the relative value and cost of railroads and canals, the work here quoted observed:

"The engines are supposed to travel but 80 miles a day, half the distance without loads. From the experience of the English there is

[1] Earle, pp. 19-22.
[2] Earle, pp. 34-35.

921

reason to believe this is 20 per cent., too unfavorable an estimate. The prices of locomotive engines are probably put too high. They were sold in England five years since, at £600 for an engine weighing 6½ tons, since which the price is reduced. . . . Railroads may be used at least 11 months in the year: canals, in a northern climate, not more than 8 months. . . . The celerity of transportation is a great object in many cases. This can be effected on rail-roads, but not on canals. Certainty is another important object. Canals are very liable to interruption from breaches in the banks, or giving way in aqueducts, &c. News was received in one day, this season, of the stoppage of three lines [of canals] in Pennsylvania, viz., the Schuylkill, the Susquehanna, and the Alleghany. But rail-ways will rarely be interrupted, as in case of any accident to one track the carriages can turn on to the other track and pass the imperfect place."[1]

In connection with these observations on the physical character of a railway, as that character was generally seen in 1830, it may be well to indicate in convenient form the systems used in laying the tracks of some of the various early railroads of this country. The following table will show such details, together with the widths of the tracks in a number of cases:[2]

ROAD	Date	Length in Miles	Gauge in Feet and Inches	Cross-ties; Size in Inches	Wooden Rails; Size in Inches	Iron Covering of Rails; Size in Inches
Mauch Chunk (Pa.)	1827	9	3.6	oak	4x6	⅜x1½
Schuylkill (Pa.)	1829	13	4.8½	oak, 12x12	4x7	½x1½
Mill Creek (Pa.)	1829	3	....	....	3x5	5-16x1¼
Schuylkill Valley (Pa.)	1829	10	3.4	....	3x5	none[3]
Mt. Carbon (Pa.)	1829	7¼	4.8½	....	6x4	⅜x2
Baltimore and Ohio (Md.)	1828	13	....	cedar,[4]	6x6	½x2
Quincy (Mass.)	1826	3	5	granite	...	......
Charleston-Hamburg (S. C.)	1829	6	5	wood	6x10	......
Albany and Hudson (N. Y.)	1830	17	4.9	wood, 7x7	...	9-16x2½
Delaware and Hudson (Pa.)	1829	5	....	hemlock	6x12	......
Western (Mass.)	1837	54	4.8½	wood, 7x12	iron	55 lbs.[5]
Long Island (N. Y.)	1835	12	4.8½	cedar, 6x6[7]	iron	38 lbs.[6]
Erie (N. Y.)	1836	10	6	wood	iron	......

[1] Earle, pp. 103-105.
[2] The table is constructed from information contained in "A Description of the Canals and Rail Roads of the United States, etc., etc." By H. S. Tanner, New York, 1840; in Earle's "Treatise," and in other similar publications of the decade between 1830 and 1840.
[3] Covered with flat iron bars after a few months of use. Size of iron bars, ⅜ by 1½.
[4] Some of the ties first laid down were stone slabs. Other sorts of wood were also used. A variety of experiments was tried in the construction of the roadbed.
[5] Per yard.
Per yard.
Ties of stone were also used for several miles on this road.

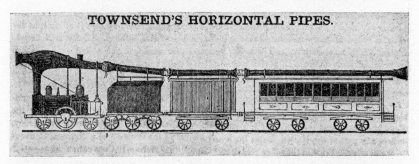

TOWNSEND'S HORIZONTAL PIPES.

270.—An American invention of 1847, designed to protect railroad passengers from the smoke and sparks of the locomotive. Nearly all the early engines used wood for fuel, and firebrands thrown out of the smokestack often burned the travellers' clothing. There is no record showing that Townsend's idea was put into practise. Published in the *Scientific American* of April 24, 1847.

It will be discovered from the preceding table that at least six different track-widths were used in building railroads during the first nine years following their introduction into America. The gauges so employed varied from three feet four inches to six feet, and there was not then, nor for more than thirty years after the commencement of the Erie road, any approach toward uniformity in the widths of this country's iron highways. For the first three or four decades of American railroad construction the distance between the rails of any track depended almost altogether on the whim of those in charge of its building. During all that time there was manifested no general appreciation of the relationship necessarily existing between uniformity of gauge and the utility of a continental railway system.

A number of pioneer American roads, embracing the earliest group laid down in Massachusetts and two or three in Pennsylvania and New York State, adopted the prevalent English gauge of four feet eight-and-a-half inches, together with the processes of track construction

then most common in that country, including the use of
stone rails and stone cross-ties, and eventually it happened
that the track-width in question was adopted throughout
the United States as a standard railroad gauge. But the
final choice of that gauge in this country was not due to
its employment by several of the pioneer lines of the
western hemisphere.

Those primitive American roads which closely copied
Stephenson's engineering practises naturally fell into the
habit of utilizing dimensions introduced by him, but
American railroad enterprises which were not begun or
carried out under the sway of English example did not
select the Stephenson gauge. They chose whatever track-
widths appealed to them as most suitable for their own
advantages. Often a gauge so adopted by American engineers approached very closely to the English standard;
at other times it showed a wide divergence therefrom.
Several of the pioneer roads of Pennsylvania were less
than four feet wide. The building of the first railway in
New York State—that between the towns of Albany and
Schenectady—was not controlled by English advice nor
did it obtain its first locomotive in England, and its gauge
was fixed at four feet and nine inches. New Jersey's first
pretentious railroad, the Camden and Amboy line, was
projected by American engineers and business men not
dominated by foreign opinion and it had a gauge of four
feet and ten inches. The decision of the Camden and
Amboy had so powerful an effect that a majority of the
other New Jersey railroads for more than a generation
adhered to the gauge last named. Those in charge of the
railroad between Charleston and Hamburg, in South
Carolina, decided on a width of five feet for their line,
and the precedent thus set by the first of all such southern

271.—Picture of a train made about the years 1850-1855. The locomotive, however, belongs to a period about ten or twelve years earlier. Although it possesses a lamp headlight, it has no engineer's cab. The cow-catcher is also of a style obsolete a number of years before the appearance of such cars as the engine is pulling.

projects resulted in the establishment and use of an identical gauge throughout almost the entire South until after the Civil War. The Erie Railroad was built with a space of six feet between its rails, and so popular did that gauge become that its use by various other roads eventually extended as far westward as the Mississippi River and also continued until after the Civil War.

A full-page contemporary engraving,[1] elsewhere reproduced, shows several of the principal devices employed in building the roadbeds of a number of early lines. The four upper figures in the engraving depict the manner in which trestlework was built wherever it was desired to avoid the expense of earthen embankments through flat or marshy regions. This system of roadbed construction was extensively used by the Charleston and Hamburg Railroad of South Carolina. The four figures under discussion show the tracks of a similarly built railroad—that extending from Carbondale to Honesdale, in Pennsylvania. The trestlework built by the Pennsylvania road was about eight feet in width and seven feet high, and rested on continuous parallel foundations of broken stone. The rails were six inches in width and twelve inches high, and the top of each rail was plated with flat iron bars two-and-a-fourth inches wide and half an inch thick. The gauge of this railroad was five feet. Figure No. 4 in the engraving indicates the manner whereby ravines were crossed on trestlework. In such cases the timber structures stood on pillars of masonry erected at intervals across the streams.

The three lower figures of the engraving portray track construction methods employed on the railroad built and owned by the state of Pennsylvania between Philadelphia

[1] From Nicholas Wood's "A Practical Treatise on Rail Roads, Etc." Philadelphia, 1832.

and the town of Columbia. The central one of these three diagrams shows a deep trench filled with closely packed broken stone, in which was imbedded a ponderous row of granite rails that were a foot square and from five to nine feet long. On the inner edges of these stone rails were laid flat iron bars fifteen feet long, two-and-a-half inches wide and five-eighths of an inch thick. The iron bars were attached to the granite rails by means of square wrought-iron spikes three-and-a-half inches long and about one-third of an inch in diameter. The spikes were encased in cedar plugs, and the plugs were driven into holes drilled in the granite at regular intervals of eighteen inches. Much trouble was experienced, by all early roads, in keeping flat iron bars attached to granite rails while that method of track building prevailed, and various devices were tried by different lines in the effort to hold the bars in place. Melted lead was sometimes used instead of wooden plugs as a means of preventing the spikes from becoming loose.[1]

Figures 6 and 8 of the same series of diagrams show other systems of roadbed construction employed on the Philadelphia and Columbia road. They depict tracks made of large wooden timbers surrounded by masses of broken stone, and topped by iron rails that bore some slight resemblance to the rails used to-day. In these two cases the rails were held in place by cast iron arrangements called "chairs" weighing fifteen pounds each and placed about a yard apart. The chairs were attached to the wooden rails by means of long bolts weighing ten ounces each.

When flat iron bars were laid on wooden rails—

---

[1] The melted lead method of fastening rail spikes was adopted by the Philadelphia, Germantown and Norristown Railroad. See Wood's "Treatise," p. 512.

especially if the bars were thin—it was found that the weight of the trains often pressed the iron into the wood beneath, and in order to prevent this defect some of the roads put sheets of zinc on the wooden rails at the places where the ends of the iron bars came together.[1]

The first rails of the Camden and Amboy road resembled the ones of to-day more closely than had those of any previous American line. They were made of iron three-and-a-half inches high, three-and-a-fourth inches wide at the bottom and two-and-an-eighth inches in width at the top, attached directly to stone cross-ties by means of long spikes encased in wooden plugs and driven into holes bored in the granite. Such construction was soon discovered to be too rigid, and so an effort was made to give greater elasticity to the track structure by inserting thin strips of wood between the rails and the stone work on which they rested. But the wooden strips speedily went to pieces under the strain imposed on them, and eventually the Camden and Amboy, like all other pioneer roads, ceased to use stone in track making.

The early customs of New England, both with respect to the building of railroads and the method of their use, were adopted in large degree from corresponding ideas then prevalent in England. A pamphlet published in Boston in 1829[2] and dealing with the subject of railway making discusses the matter in this fashion:

"The labor of the horse may be relieved by providing a platform, placed on small wheels, on the long distances, on which the horse himself may ride. . . . This expedient, singular as it may seem to persons unaccustomed to observe the ease of locomotion on a railroad, is adopted with success on the Darlington and Mauch Chunk. And the horses eat their provender while they are returning to where their labour is to

[1] This expedient was employed by the Little Schuylkill Railroad in Pennsylvania. See Wood's "Treatise," p. 514.
[2] "Practicability and Expediency of a Railroad from Boston to the Hudson River."

be resumed. . . . An easy and convenient rate of travelling, with perhaps an average of about three miles an hour, and the journey [from
Boston to Albany] may be accomplished in four days. . . .

"It will be found that an active horse may travel twelve or thirteen
miles a day at a rate of nine miles an hour. . . . This power will be
sufficient to draw, on a railroad of the description above supposed, a
weight of 2½ tons, or a carriage with 20 passengers, with their baggage.
On this assumption and estimate the cost of transporting 20 passengers
between Boston and Albany, if the road is provided with stationary
powers, [in the form of inclined planes to overcome hills] will be as
follows:

16 horses travelling 12 or 13 miles each day, 50c.....	$8.00
2 men and carriage.............................	3.00
	$11.00
Add 50 per cent...............................	5.50
For 20 passengers	16.50
For each passenger.............................	82½ cents

"Or, if without stationary powers it would require 22 horses and
cost per passenger $1.05, to which estimate add a toll tax of $2.00, and
it makes a cost of $2.82 or $3.05 for conveyance from Boston to Albany
in twenty-two hours."

One more example of the many ideas on railway building and utility entertained during the first years of the
new transportation method in America may be cited. It
was contained in a letter published in the *Maine Farmer*
newspaper of May 1, 1835. The communication—from
some constant reader or old subscriber—read:

"Railroads have been found useful means of communication, and they
are gaining favor rapidly with the community. They will be established,
I doubt not, far more generally over the country than is now expected
by most persons. This article is headed 'Rail Paths,' for I have in view
rail tracks not so massy, solid and expensive as the railroads usually make.
. . . Such solid and costly structures are not needed all over the country; and lighter and cheaper roads will be sufficient. . . .

"Such paths may be used by locomotives propelled by horses. . . .
Suppose that one of these machines, on proper wheels for a railroad,
weighs 1200 lbs. and the horse in it weighs 800 lbs.; then he could not
only move himself and his locomotive but a train of cars and their
loads weighing 28,000 lbs. or 14 tons. . . . It may, therefore, be easily
seen that a light rail road, sufficient to sustain at one point, or over a

272.—Two passenger trains of the same period. In this case the engines and cars are of contemporaneous creation, and represent the best existing equipment. Probably a scene on the Hudson River Railroad.

surface ten feet in length, 2000 lbs., will be adequate for all lines but the great routes of commerce and business.

"It is hoped that this subject will receive attention from those who are capable of studying the literary, religious and agricultural and commercial interests of the country. The writer has a conviction that not only may two great and distant centres of business be accommodated by rail roads, but that the system may be made to pervade our common towns, and extend its advantages even to the retired neighborhood."

Countless other books, pamphlets, arguments, and articles of similar character appeared in all the cities of the country, containing almost every conceivable speculation relating to the physical make-up and operation of a railway. Yet hardly one of these utterances was of appreciable value in shaping the after-history of the new transportation idea, and none of them suggested the future railroad half so accurately as those that had been made by Evans, Dearborn and Stevens years before. The so-called practical builders at first wandered far from the truth, and the initial railways of America bore little resemblance, either in their finished shape or usefulness, to the ideas of the men whose splendid visions they were designed to materialize.

Many of the first actual American railroad makers were also equally in error with regard to the economic character of the device after it was completed and ready for business. In considering the railed highway as a means of travel and transportation they adopted a mistaken idea originating in England, and in part established the American system on an erroneous economic basis. England at the outset considered that a railway was analogous in character to a "king's highway"; that is to say, the English thought that a line of rails suitable for the easy movement of vehicles was a public road which any man might use at will provided he built his wagon or car for that purpose. Before the introduction of railroads there had never appeared to the knowledge of men any method of general land transportation wherein the ownership and operation of the vehicles employed were vested in the same authority which owned and controlled the track on which those vehicles moved. So, since there was no precedent for the joint operation of both the road and wagons it was taken for granted in England—and for a few years in America—that the tracks of a railway and the wheeled cars moving over it had no very intimate relation with each other.

Several of the states entertained the notion that the new method of conveyance was to be merely a public highway over which any individual or company might run cars on payment of fixed charges or tolls. This was the plan first adopted by Pennsylvania. When that commonwealth built its state-owned railway from Philadelphia to Columbia there arose a public fear that the latest means of transportation might in some way fall into the hands of a monopoly, and so the state granted authority to no less than twenty different companies to run their

273.—Interior view of a passenger car of the best sort in 1852. Cars substantially identical with this composed the trains shown in the two foregoing illustrations.

horse-drawn cars over the road. There was no possibility of maintaining any schedule or regularity of traffic movement under such conditions, since the numerous wagons appeared on the tracks at any times suitable to the convenience of their owners. A kindred situation existed on other early lines.

The first ideas of Massachusetts were similar to those of Pennsylvania. In the early railroad charters granted by Massachusetts was included the following stipulation: "that a toll be and hereby is granted and established, for the sole benefit of said corporation, upon all passengers and property . . . which may be conveyed or transported upon said road, at such rates per mile as may be agreed upon and established from time to time by the directors of said corporation. The transportation of persons and property, the construction of wheels, the form of cars and carriages, the weight of loads, and all other matters and things in relation to the use of said road, shall be in conformity to such rules, regulations and provisions as the directors shall from time to time prescribe and direct, and said road may be used by any person who shall comply with such rules and regulations."

The attitude taken by those two states discloses the ideas probably entertained by a large part of the public during the first years when railroads were coming into existence on this side of the ocean. It was still supposed— by the majority—that they would be operated mainly by horse power, and that any one could run his wagons or cars on them if he did so in compliance with rules laid down by the company owning the road, or by the state if the new highway was a state enterprise. It required several years of actual experience, on railways at first used in that way, to bring about a realization that the vehicles of a railroad and the track itself were inseparable parts of one mechanism and could not be operated successfully under separate control. Those states and corporations which made an effort to conduct the business of their railroads in the manner indicated had no power over the owners or drivers of vehicles using the tracks, and were consequently unable to discipline them when they acted in a way that interfered with traffic.

Nearly all the first American roads were single-tracked affairs, and the only provision made by them for

THE CAR WINDOW.

274.—A glimpse of the past, seen through the window of a railway train. The early railroads, like the canals, followed the valleys of rivers when possible.

the passage of cars in opposite directions was the building of what were then called "turnouts." A turnout was a short strip of extra track a few yards or a few rods long, connected with the main line by switches at each end. Half-way between each turnout a large pole was set up near the rails, and this was called a "center-post." Whenever a car moving in its proper direction was met—before it reached a center-post—by another car travelling in the opposite direction, it was required to retreat to the last turnout it had passed in order to give right of way to the other vehicle. In the absence of any method of quick communication along the line, or between stations, this appeared to be the only practicable scheme for deciding which car should have preference over another, and numerous disputes and fights arose through its operation. A driver would hesitate to get very far from a turnout—

especially if the road was crooked and he could not see ahead for any distance—because he objected to returning in case he did not reach the center-post before meeting another vehicle. So he usually went very slowly until he got within sight of the timber goal and then whipped up his horses in a frantic effort to attain the coveted position before he encountered any opposition. If a driver who was coming the other way pursued the same tactics the two cars would be driven madly toward each other on the single track, each trying to get to the center-post first, and sometimes they met with a crash that disabled the horses or injured their drivers or the occupants. On a few occasions men were even killed by collisions brought about under the circumstances described. At other times there would be pitched battles between the drivers or the contrary-bound travellers, and considerable delays would necessarily ensue, much to the mental and physical anguish of the passengers who met defeat.

The foregoing conditions outline various popular ideas regarding the character of railroads as highways during the years of their introduction, and also suggest the experience of travellers who patronized such roads as were not equipped with locomotives from the first. There remains to be considered one other phase of the people's early attitude toward railways—their estimate of the social and commercial consequences destined to follow the adoption of the new contrivances.

Public opinion about that aspect of the subject was exceedingly diverse both in its scope and verbal manifestations. Most persons believed railroads would have a big effect on the social order and economic affairs; a few were of opposite mind. Doubtless, also, a majority of the people thought that whatever influence emanated from railways would be altogether excellent, but there were many who felt, and said, that the revolutionary system of movement in process of introduction would bring with it some results unfavorable to the country. There is always a considerable number of men who oppose important changes in established conditions of life. If that opposition is founded on an honest conviction that the proposed alteration is wrong in principle, or too extreme, or too rapid, then it is always useful to the permanent well-being of all the people, for such a belief tends to prevent unwise change and to retain an innovation within the realm of its greatest utility. But if such an opposition is not based on consideration of the comparative values of the old way and the new; if it is the expression of a fear that its possessor is about to be ousted from an unfairly won economic or social position, then the antagonism is either without effect or else works harm instead of good. For neither strength nor value can abide in such an attitude—either for or against change—unless its existence is founded on sincere belief untainted by greed. Whether or not the element of greed is present may sometimes be discovered by scrutiny of the worldly affairs of the objector, by studying the methods through which his existing position has been obtained, and by calculating the effect upon him of the condition he seeks to avoid.

The introduction of railroads did decidedly upset the previous methods of men in various ways and brought about radical alterations in their manner of doing numerous things. Many contemporary observers who foresaw the impending changes, and who awaited them with apprehension or delight, voiced their opinions at the time in letters to the newspapers, just as people do nowadays when the semi-weekly miracle is announced. One such

1.—GENERAL VIEW OF A NIGHT-CAR ON THE CENTRAL.

275.—A sketch published by *Harper's Weekly* in 1858. Although sleeping cars had appeared twenty years before, a large majority of the people who were compelled to travel by night did not look upon them as indispensable adjuncts to comfort.

communication of 1830, the apparent protest of a reader who "viewed with alarm," exclaimed:

"I see what will be the effect of it; that it will set the whole world a-gadding. Twenty miles an hour, sir!—Why, you will not be able to keep an apprentice boy at his work! Every Saturday evening he must have a trip to Ohio to spend a Sunday with his sweetheart. Grave plodding citizens will be flying about like comets. All local attachments will be at an end. It will encourage flightiness of intellect. Veracious people will turn into the most immeasurable liars. All conceptions will be exaggerated by the magnificent notions of distance.—Only a hundred miles off!—Tut, nonsense, I'll step across, madam, and bring your fan! . . . And then, sir, there will be barrels of pork, cargoes of flour, chaldrons of coal, and even lead and whiskey, and such like sober things that have always been used to slow travelling—whisking away like a sky rocket. It will upset all the gravity of the nation. . . . Upon the whole, sir, it is a pestilential, topsy-turvy, harum-scarum whirligig. Give me the old, solemn, straight forward, regular Dutch Canal—three miles an hour for expresses, and two rod jog-trot journeys—with a yoke of oxen for heavy loads. I go for beasts of burden. It is more formative and scriptural, and suits a moral and religious people better.—None of your hop skip and jump whimsies for me."[1]

But protests like this—even if they were genuine—could avail nothing when opposed to overwhelming popular desire. The step-lively microbe had slowly been multiplying until finally it was about to control and dictate the daily life of the people within whose thought it had long before found unsuspected lodgment. Only after the speed malady had run its destined course, generations afterward, was there to come a time when its dangers as well as its benefits demanded recognition; only after eighty years was it to be generally admitted that speed is not first among the advantages of movement; that safety, comfort and reliability of progress all take precedence over it in advancing the best interests of human society. The plodding citizens of those days did want to fly about

[1] From the "Western Sun," of Vincennes, Indiana, July 24, 1830. In view of the national temperament, and the manner in which this letter is phrased, it is easier to look upon the communication either as a joke or the product of a practised pen filched for the occasion than as the serious epistle it purports to be.

like comets. They did want to send their goods whisking away like sky-rockets. And they proceeded to gratify their desires, which grew as fast as they were satisfied.

It was believed by many, during the first days of railroads in America, that the new iron highways would exercise an appreciable and distinctive effect on the morals of the country. And over that question—just as in connection with their probable economic consequences—there existed a difference of opinion. A considerable number of men thought railroads would constitute an influence destined in some way to lower the prevailing standard of morality. That conviction was more noticeable in the East than elsewhere, and its existence in New England was visible for some time. The plea that railways were beneficial in a moral sense was sometimes employed in New England as a means of getting popular support for their creation, and the contrary opinion was advanced, on occasion, as an argument against them or their operating methods. Possibly the most conspicuous instance wherein a discussion of that sort took place was in connection with the building of the Western Railroad of Massachusetts.[1] The project was dragging a little in 1838 and the company, as one way of enlisting a larger public interest in it, appealed to the churches of the state and asked that sermons be preached on the moral effect of railways. This letter was sent out to the clergy of Massachusetts:[2]

"The Committee appointed by the Western Railroad Corporation, to assist the Directors in their application to the Legislature, for aid to finish the Road to the Western line of the State, have thought that the surest way to obtain their object would be to bring the importance of Rail-Roads before the whole people of our beloved Commonwealth. Its importance to our worldly prosperity we point out by an address circu-

[1] The Boston and Albany line. Chartered in 1833; begun in 1837; finished in 1841.
[2] In December of 1838.

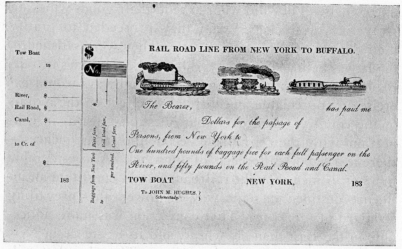

276.—Early railroad tickets and passes. Probably the first through ticket for railway travel used in America. Issued in 1831. It authorized the holder to journey from New York City to Albany by steamboat, thence over the Albany and Schenectady Railroad for seventeen miles to Schenectady, and then to Buffalo by canal boat. Printed in folio sheets containing three tickets to the sheet. Size of original, 9¾ by 5½ inches.

lated extensively throughout the State. But we are desirous to spread far and wide the Moral effect of Rail-Roads on our wide spread country. This, we think, can best be done from the pulpit. In this belief, we take leave, most respectfully, but earnestly, to ask you to take an early opportunity to deliver a Discourse before your Congregation on the Moral effect of Rail-Roads in our wide extended country.

"Trusting that the great importance of the subject to every inhabitant of this community will be a sufficient apology for asking your assistance in this great work, I have the honor to be, Reverend Sir,

"Respectfully your very ob't serv't,

"WILLIAM SAVAGE,

"Chairman of the Committee of Correspondence."

A number of sermons were delivered throughout the state in response to this request, and as a whole they indicated a pulpit belief that railways might become a beneficial moral factor in social affairs—or at least that nothing portentously bad need necessarily be expected of them. No doubt the committee was tolerably well satisfied with the result of its appeal. But the sermons were not unqualifiedly enthusiastic in their tone. There still existed in Massachusetts—and in other New England commonwealths as well—a considerable opposition to Sunday travel, and the prejudice in question cropped out in answer to the railroad's application for church approval. Much of the adverse criticism resulting from the letter was based on the proposed Sunday operation of railways, and in some of the addresses that feature of their policy was made the decisive issue which entitled them either to condemnation or endorsement. One of the sermons[1] which asserted that a railroad was either a good or a bad moral influence in accordance with its attitude toward Sunday observance said in part:

"The vision, however, is not one of unmixed brightness. . . . And among the causes for apprehension in the matter before us is the violation of the Sabbath, with which steam navigation and steam travel are connected, and judging from present appearances seem likely to be connected. The moral influence of Rail-Roads will be very much as it shall be made by the observation or violation of the law of the Sabbath. If this great method of locomotion, so distinguished that its introduction constitutes a new era in the history of the world, shall be so managed as to manifest due reverence for the God of the Universe and the institutions he has ordained, then its moral influence, it needs no prophet to foretell, will be good—eminently good. If, on the other hand, this distinguished improvement of the age shall be used in such a manner as to do dishonor to God and desecrate the institutions of religion which he has given to men, then its moral influence, as every one can easily see, must be evil—eminently evil.

"Livery stables not infrequently exhibit a scene of great desecration of the Sabbath. . . . No man who is worn down with worldly cares and labors may take the Sabbath for the purposes of recreation, and the mere recruiting of his physical energies to pursue the world again. . . . It would be much more reasonable that he should take a part of the week to recruit his energies for the Sabbath.

"It is the duty of the Stock-holder in any Company of the character mentioned, to raise the note of remonstrance against the desecration [of the Sabbath] which he deplores. . . . And as a last resort, when all

---

[1] That of the Rev. L. F. Dimmick, of Newburyport.

other means fail, or even before they fail, he can take the dividend which falls to him as the income of unrighteousness, and use it in the publication of Tracts and arguments for the correction of the very unrighteousness from which it flows.

"It may be proper here to remark that the lawmakers themselves are sometimes, perhaps, not sufficiently careful to observe their own statutes. Is it not the case that sometimes even they take the Sabbath to travel— and that to and from the very seat of legislation where the laws above recited are enacted? Do they consider the tendency of their proceeding? Will they themselves practice the very things which they prohibit in others as immoralities?

"Would not a Sabbath-keeping Rail-Road establishment be an honor to New England? . . . Sunday travellers are generally not happy men. It is deeply to be regretted that sometimes even professed Christians fall into this flagrant transgression.

"I have heard of an individual, sustaining some relation to the public conveyances of the day, and favorable to Sunday travelling, who professed to keep a list of all the Christians that went in his conveyances on the Sabbath, and threatened to publish them to the world. . . . Should not the Christian so live as to be free from the danger of exposure of this sort?"

So the controversies and discussions went on. Yet even while the impatient populace was thus arguing over the character of railroads, the best manner of their building and their probable influence, the new contrivance itself was taking visible shape before the eyes of the disputants.

CHAPTER XLIII

RAILWAY BUILDING BEGINS IN MARYLAND AND SOUTH
CAROLINA — CAN A RAILROAD TRACK SUCCESSFULLY
CROSS A GUTTER? — THE BALTIMORE EDITORS TRY A
HORSE LOCOMOTIVE — OBJECTIONS TO THE SINGLE-
MASTED METEOR — VON GERSTNER'S OBSERVATION
— A NEWSPAPER ANNOUNCEMENT OF AMERICA'S
FIRST PASSENGER TRAIN — THE TOM THUMB
VERSUS HORSE POWER — CHARLESTON CREATES THE
FIRST RAILWAY DESIGNED FOR STEAM — AMERICA'S
PIONEER HOME-MADE LOCOMOTIVE — ITS EXPLOSION
— LATER PRECAUTIONS OF THE DIRECTORS — THE
FIRST NEW YORK STATE RAILROAD — OPPORTUNE
PRESENCE OF MR. BROWN AT ALBANY — HE MAKES A
PICTURE — ALL ABOARD FOR SCHENECTADY — SOME
INCIDENTS THAT OCCURRED IN A TRIP OF SEVENTEEN
MILES

WITHIN a few months after the issue of Strickland's
book, in 1826, public meetings were called in
various states and cities for consideration of the railroad
question. Leadership in this popular movement was taken
by Baltimore in Maryland, and Charleston in South
Carolina.[1] The agitation in the two cities took place at
about the same time,[2] and each outburst of interest resulted
in the immediate commencement of a pretentious railroad. The work undertaken in South Carolina contained

[1] Both South Carolina and Maryland subscribed for several copies of Strickland's book.
[2] Early in 1827. The first citizens' meeting in Baltimore was held on February 12th.

943

some features of superior importance in their relation to the annals of American railway building and travel, but the more advanced ideas of the South Carolina enterprise resulted in a slightly later development of it. For that reason the events connected with the Baltimore project, and the primitive travel experiences of the people afforded by it, demand prior chronological consideration.

The public meetings in Baltimore found their con-

277.—First ticket of the New York and Harlem Railroad. Doubtless used for a short time only, on the first mile or two of track opened for traffic. The car is a representation of the original horse-drawn vehicles built for the road. Copper-bronze. Actual size. Die cut. Date, probably 1832. Circular pieces, made of silver-like alloy and bearing the same design, are also known. The round variety occasionally contains a punched hole, like some New York City stage-coach tickets of the same time.

sequence in the prompt appointment of committees, the preparation of charters, and the launching of the Baltimore and Ohio Railway by the Maryland legislature in March of 1827. A capital of one and a half million dollars was authorized for the road, which was eventually to be extended over the mountains to the Ohio River, and both the city and state were authorized to subscribe for its stock. "By this time," said one who had an active part in the work,[1] "public excitement had gone far beyond fever heat and reached the boiling point. . . . Parents subscribed in the names of their children. Before a survey had been made—before common sense had been consulted, even, the possession of stock in any quantity was regarded as a

[1] John H. B. Latrobe, in his pamphlet "The Baltimore and Ohio Railroad: Personal Recollections," p. 6. John Latrobe was counsel for the railway. His brother, Benjamin Latrobe, was an engineer in charge of construction.

provision for old age, and great was the scramble to obtain it. The excitement in Baltimore roused public attention elsewhere, and a railroad mania began to pervade the land."

The mania referred to by Latrobe was possibly a preliminary symptom of that approaching period of credit inflation and wide speculation which finally resulted in

278.—A later metallic ticket of the New York and Harlem Railroad. "Yorkville," on the reverse, indicates a northern district of the city to which the ticket holder was entitled to ride. The car here shown is probably identical with those portrayed in illustrations numbered 246, 247 and 248. Pewter. Actual size. Date, about 1840.

the panic of 1837. For several years after their introduction railroads were a chief subject of popular speculative interest, and an unbounded optimism led to the conviction that limitless riches were close at hand. That state of the public mind during the time in question ultimately operated to retard the widespread adoption of railways, for recovery from the resultant collapse of 1837 was slow, and not until about 1850 did railroad building begin to assume really extensive proportions.

Charles Carroll, the only surviving signer of the Declaration of Independence, laid the corner-stone of the Baltimore and Ohio Railroad on July 4, 1828, amid a most imposing civic demonstration and before one of the most enthusiastic multitudes that had assembled in the country up to that day. Every feature of the succeeding work was followed by the people with attention, and the various proposals of the engineers often aroused heated discussions and inspired long letters to the newspapers in approval or condemnation of the suggested plans. One of the most violent altercations of this sort arose from a proposition that the road be carried along Pratt Street, in Baltimore, which plan necessitated the crossing of numerous gutters at intersecting streets. A considerable faction of the public declared railroads must not try to pass such obstacles—that it was physically impossible for them to do so in safety. Finally one citizen wrote a letter suggesting that he saw but scanty prospect of building the road across the Alleghany Mountains if it could not be successfully carried over the gutters of Baltimore. Whereupon that particular dispute suddenly came to an end.

The first section of the railway to be finished extended from the city to Ellicott's Mills, a distance of some thirteen miles. In preparing one part of this roadbed two long parallel rows of holes were dug, each hole being two feet long and twenty inches wide. These were filled with broken stone, every individual piece of which was first passed through a small iron ring to test its size. Between each pair of stone-filled holes—and extending across the track—a narrow trench six inches in depth was excavated and similarly filled. Then cedar ties, or cross-pieces, were laid on top of the six-inch trenches. Near the ends of each tie, and just above the centers of the stone piers, notches were cut in which six-inch rails were laid, the rails themselves being pieces of yellow pine six inches square and from twelve to twenty-four feet long. These wooden rails were kept in place by wedges and spikes, and their outer edges were bevelled and covered with strips

946

of flat iron.[1] About seven miles of the track between Baltimore and Ellicott's Mills were laid in this way and the remainder of the line for the first thirteen miles was somewhat similarly built. In some places the cross-ties and rails were of huge stone slabs instead of wood. By the spring of 1830 the section of the railroad here described was ready for business.

In the meantime several experiments had been tried on the road in an effort to decide what motive power should be adopted for its operation,[2] and one of those trials was that of the second American locomotive, made by Peter Cooper. Between July 4, 1828—when actual work was begun—and the summer of 1829 the plans of those at the head of the enterprise were largely governed by English influence, and as a result its first section was built with nothing but the employment of horse power in mind.[3] During this first year of work on the Baltimore and Ohio road it was not believed by the business men in control of the matter that locomotives propelled by steam could furnish sufficient power for a successful operation of the new transportation device. Consequently they had prepared their roadbed and track in accordance with practise then obtaining in England in building horse-power roads.

But the general American public—notwithstanding the opinions of British experts and those on this side of the ocean who agreed with them—could not see any other motive force but steam as the agency of future railroad operation. There was in consequence a decided popular

[1] The strips of flat iron attached to the tops of the wooden rails in this case, and in some other early American railroad construction, were placed at the outer edges of the wooden rails because the flanges of the car wheels were at the outside of the wheels instead of the inside, as at present.

[2] "In the beginning, no one dreamed of steam upon the road." Latrobe's "Personal Recollections," p. 12.

[3] The competitive trial of locomotives by the Liverpool and Manchester road in England had not yet been held. That important event took place in October of 1829.

Pass Bearer over **WEST PHILADA. RAILWAY** from **Blue Bell (Paschalville) to Third and Market.**

Treasurer P. & D. R. R. Co.

M⁺FARLAND & THOMSON, PRS. 8II WALNUT STREET.

279.—Pass issued by an early Pennsylvania road. The West Philadelphia line was a connection of the State-owned Philadelphia and Columbia. The granting of free travel privileges was carried to extreme lengths in Pennsylvania. Original printed on cardboard. Date, 1835-1840.

dissatisfaction with the nature of the work being done. The situation then existing and the conviction of the people are indicated in the following letter afterward written by Cooper.[1]

"At that time an opinion had become prevalent that the road was ruined for steam locomotives, by reason of the short curves found necessary to get around the various points of rocks found in their course. Under these discouraging circumstances many of the principal stockholders were about to abandon the work, and were only prevented from forfeiting their stock by my persuading them that a locomotive could be so made as to pass successfully around the short curves then found in the road."[2]

Cooper accordingly, in the summer of 1829, brought from New York a little boiler—about as big as a hot-water boiler attached to a modern kitchen stove—and set it up together with a correspondingly diminutive steam-engine, on a small four-wheeled flat car. Anthracite coal was the fuel employed. Using this locomotive, which from its size has come to be known as the *Tom Thumb,* he made a few trips of several rods in length on the rails then in place, and though the result did not satisfy him it was apparently sufficient to avert the withdrawal of the dis-

[1] To William H. Brown, under date of May 18, 1869; printed in full in Brown's "History of the First Locomotives in America," p. 109.
[2] A part of Cooper's interest in the matter arose from his ownership of a tract of land whose future value was believed to depend largely on the road's success.

affected stockholders. Cooper then undertook some improvements in his little engine, and eventually made with it a more pretentious test to be later described.

Another locomotive tried on the Baltimore and Ohio line before its formal opening was operated by a horse. The animal trod on a moving platform, from which power was transmitted to the axles. The inventor of this contrivance—and other people also—was enthusiastic over its possibilities, and after a private preliminary trial he invited the editors of the Baltimore newspapers, together with other guests, to enjoy his system of railway propulsion. The excursionists took their seats on benches that surrounded the horse, the animal was started and all went well until a cow, doubtless dazed by the rapid progress of civilization in her vicinity, ran into the contrivance and upset it. After picking themselves up at the bottom of an embankment the passengers organized a mass meeting on the spot and adopted resolutions appropriate to the occasion. Then they started back home on foot, stopping at intervals to amend and amplify the sentiments previously expressed. The local newspapers displayed an editorial bias unfavorable to the suggested innovation, and thereafter it was eliminated from consideration.

Another proposed method for early American railway travel was a sailing car, built by a prominent citizen of Baltimore named Evan Thomas. This vehicle was called the *Meteor*. Its body was a large bowl-shaped receptacle made of basketry in which the passengers sat. One of the visitors who travelled in the *Meteor* during its first trip over the Baltimore and Ohio Railroad was Baron Krudener, then Russian Minister to Washington, who himself trimmed the sails and manipulated the halyards of the railroad car. The Baron expressed himself as much

pleased with the comfort and agreeable sensations connected with that manner of locomotion. As far as expense
of operation was concerned the plan was an ideal one, the
only apparent drawback being the unreasonable demeanor

280.—Season ticket sold by the Boston and Worcester Railroad. Used by suburban
dwellers in their daily trips to and from the city. The reference to "Express" business meant that the ticket holder must not carry parcels belonging to other people. Printed on blue glazed cardboard.

of the wind. In the course of a journey toward the west
the motive power might nullify all the skill of the train
crew and inexorably return the travellers to the spot
whence they had started. To put the matter in a nutshell,
it was found that the *Meteor* could only be depended
upon for east-bound traffic, and could only make such
trips when a stiff breeze came out of the northwest. And
since it was even then recognized that a practical, smooth-
working railway schedule providing for movements in
both directions could not be drawn up on those lines, the
inexpensive single-masted locomotive was abandoned.

As we look back from the pinnacle of to-day such ideas as these seem absurd, and the testing of them appears still more so, but the impulse behind them was not ridiculous. It was, on the contrary, invaluable. Such schemes illustrated the national method. They indicated an inventive spirit which at the outset of the railway era took a tremendous forward jump and thereafter resulted in the American creation of innumerable devices destined to universal adoption. America's predominant influence in shaping the outward form and enlarging the value of the new transportation instrumentality was recognized almost from the first by those whose practical experience and vision embraced the whole subject. When the Chevalier von Gerstner, a distinguished German engineer, was asked why he had come to America[1] to study railway development instead of remaining in England, he answered:

"That is the very thing I want to escape from—this system of England, where George Stephenson's thumb, impressed upon a plan, is an imprimatur which gives it currency and makes it authority throughout Great Britain; while here, in America, no one man's imprimatur is better than another's. Each is trying to surpass his neighbor. There is a rivalry here out of which grows improvement. In England it is imitation—in America it is invention."[2]

Von Gerstner's summary of the situation, expressed at such an early date, has since remained consistently true. Almost all America's railway methods have been of her own devising. Even at first she copied but little, and soon discarded nearly all the ideas so imported. Her rails, multi-tubular boiler, air brake, wheel trucks, locomotives, telegraph, dining cars, sleeping cars, and various other material features of her railroad system have been adopted by the rest of the world.[3] If America's contributions to

[1] While the railroad fever of the fourth decade was at its height.
[2] Latrobe's "Personal Recollections," p. 14. Von Gerstner made the utterance to Latrobe.
[3] The sleeping cars of some other countries, however, are superior to those of America. They are divided into compartments that afford a reasonable privacy to occupants.

the modern railway were subtracted from it, it would scarcely be considered as an indispensable feature of transportation.

By the summer of 1830 Cooper had made his contemplated changes in the *Tom Thumb,* and on August 28th of that year he ran it over the thirteen miles between Baltimore and Ellicott's Mills in an hour and fifteen minutes, or at an average speed of about six miles an hour. The return journey was made in sixty-one minutes, including a stop of four minutes for the taking in of water. On this occasion the little engine pushed in front of it a small car containing twenty-four passengers, who were thus the first representatives of the American public to be carried over rails by steam power. The trip had another aspect of importance at the time, for it also proved that steam could be used successfully on the road as constructed. This doubly momentous event in the early railroad history of the country was scarcely noticed by the newspapers of the day outside of the city near which it had taken place. One newspaper of New York City[1] mentioned it, nearly a month later, in the following paragraph:

"Railroad Cars.—The Baltimore Gazette mentions, that the first Rail Road Car, propelled by steam, proceeded the whole distance from Baltimore to Ellicott's Mills on Saturday last, and tested a most important principle, that curvatures of 400 feet radius offer no material impediment in the way of steam power on railroads, where the wheels are constructed with a cone, on the principles ascertained by Mr. Knight, Engineer of the Baltimore and Ohio Railroad Company, to be applicable to such curvatures. The Engineers in England have been so decidedly of opinion that locomotive steam engines could not be used on curved rails, that it was much doubted whether the many curvatures on the Baltimore and Ohio Road would not exclude the use of steam power."

This announcement of the first running of a steam passenger train in America was contained in fourteen

[1] The New York "Observer" of September 25, 1830.

lines of type placed at the bottom of the third column of the second page of the newspaper, and was printed without a head-line.

The achievement of Mr. Cooper, even if not fittingly received by the general public, did produce a striking effect in another quarter. It dismayed the stage-coach proprietors of the region, who beheld in it a menace to their own business and an ominous portent of the future. They could not with safety allow the people to gain an impression that this new travel method threatened the supremacy of stage-coaches, and one of the largest of the eastern firms of stage proprietors[1] therefore resolved to challenge the mechanical contrivance, and if possible demonstrate its inferiority as a vehicle of travel. So when Cooper took his engine and another load of passengers to the end of the road a few days afterward, a horse-drawn railroad car was also sent out to the same point on the second track[2] for the purpose of racing the locomotive back to the city. Cooper accepted the challenge, and when the word "go" was given both vehicles entered upon the competition, with the passengers of each hurling cries of defiance to those of the other. The big gray horse chosen to cast ridicule on the clattering mechanism sprang away on the instant and speedily obtained a lead of about a quarter of a mile. Finally the engine got up enough steam to move ahead, and thereafter gained slowly on its competitor until at last, after several miles, the passengers on the railroad car had the satisfaction of overhauling the wagon on the other track. The driver of the horse lashed his steed furiously, and responding with a still greater effort the fine animal for a time

[1] Stockton & Stokes.
[2] Two railroad tracks had been laid to Ellicott's Mills.

actually dragged his burden at a speed equally as great as that shown by the steam-engine. Then he slowly began to lag behind and victory seemed about to perch on the banner of progress. But the hope of those in the steam passenger car was destined to be blasted. Something went wrong with the locomotive, a leather band slipped from its wheel, and the engine lost its momentum. Cooper tried desperately to remedy the disaster, even injuring his hands in a foolhardy effort to replace the flapping band, but in vain. The horse recovered his lost ground, forged ahead for good, and finally won the race decisively.

Great was the exultation of those who planned to employ animal power on the railroad, and correspondingly deep was the depression of those who had pinned their faith to the strength of steam. Horse-drawn cars continued to be the only vehicles on the road until early in 1831. But by that time the success of locomotives elsewhere decided the company to adopt steam as a motive power, and on January 4th of the year named it published an advertisement in various newspapers offering four thousand dollars for the most efficient engine delivered for trial on the road by the first of the following June. A machine built by Phineas Davis of York, Pennsylvania, was the only one meeting the requirements of the company, which called for the pulling of fifteen tons of weight at the rate of fifteen miles an hour. This engine served as a model for those used on the road during several years thereafter.

The passenger cars built for the formal opening of the line[1] were large, open, wagon-like structures of cumbrous weight and uncouth appearance. They were equipped with roofs held up by stout timbers, and curtains

[1] May 24, 1830.

954

were provided which could be lowered for the protection of passengers in case of storm. These passenger vehicles were followed by others of decidedly more attractive appearance built on the general lines of the stage-coach, though considerably larger than stage-coaches and boast-

281.—A railway conductor's business card. Many conductors of long service and popularity became institutions on the roads they served. Rubber. Actual size.

ing an upper deck surrounded by a netting to keep people from falling off the top.

With the further construction of the road westward during ensuing years the locomotives and cars employed on it kept pace with improvements elsewhere throughout the country.

A little enterprise in Pennsylvania—through one incident that happened in 1829—had already acquired an importance in the history of early American railroads to which it was not otherwise entitled either by its size or general characteristics. This was the Carbondale and Honesdale Railroad,[1] extending for a distance of sixteen miles between the two towns named. It was chartered in 1826, begun in 1827 and finished in 1829. Its track ran for nine miles on trestlework, and also contained seven inclined planes. The line was built in connection

[1] The charter name of this road was the "Delaware and Hudson Canal and Railroad Company."

with some coal mines and was primarily intended to facilitate the transportation of their product. Immediately after its completion the road decided to make an experiment with steam power, and for that purpose obtained from England a locomotive named the *Stourbridge Lion,* which arrived in New York during early summer of the year named, and was soon afterward shipped to its destination and assembled by an American engineer named Horatio Allen. The *Stourbridge Lion,* operated by Allen, made a trial trip over the Carbondale and Honesdale Railroad on August 8, 1829, but was found to be so heavy that its employment on the trestles was unsafe, and it was never put into regular use. Nevertheless its trial trip constituted the first occasion on which a practical steam locomotive moved over a permanent railroad track on the American continent. After the *Stourbridge Lion* was discarded no further effort was made to use steam on the road, and the locomotive was offered for sale without avail. The engine was of nine horse-power and was calculated to haul a load of sixty tons at a rate of five miles an hour. It was about twelve feet long and weighed in the neighborhood of eight tons. The four wheels of the machine were made of oak surrounded by heavy wrought-iron tires, and on the front of the boiler was painted the head of a lion. After the engine was discarded it was placed in a little shanty beside the road from which it had been removed and there stood forsaken for more than a dozen years. It gradually disintegrated beneath the hands of curiosity seekers who carried away such parts of the mechanism as might be easily detached, and finally the remainder of the locomotive was sold for old iron.

Meanwhile a bill granting a charter for a railroad

SUMMER ARRANGEMENT

FOR MANAYUNK & NORRISTOWN

From April 19th to September 1st,
Leaves Philadelphia at 9, 3, and 5½.
Leaves Norristown at 7, 11, and 5½.

From May 15th to August 1st, the last train will leave Philadelphia and Norristown, at 6¼ instead of 5½.

On SUNDAYS the train at 11 from Norristown, and the last train from Philadelphia will be omitted.

SUMMER ARRANGEMENT

FOR GERMANTOWN,

From April 19th to September 1st,
Leaves Philadelphia at 9½, 2, 5 and 7.
Leaves Germantown at 7½, 10½ 4 and 6.
On Sundays, the trips at 4 and 5 will be omitted.

From May 15th to August 1st,
Leaves Philadelphia at 9½, 2, 4, 6 and 8,
Leaves Germantown at 7½, 10½, 3, 5 & 7
On Sundays the trips at 3, 4, 5 and 6 will be omitted.

☞ Omnibusses leave the Exchange for the Depot at 22 *Minutes* before the starting of the Cars, (Sundays Excepted)
WM. FOULKE, *Agt.*

April 19, 1847.

Autumnal Arrangement

FOR MANAYUNK & NORRISTOWN

From 1st of Sept. to 15th of Nov'r.
Leaves Philadelphia at 9, 3, and 5.
Leaves Norristown at 7, 11, and 5.
On SUNDAYS the train 11 o'clock, from Norristown, and the 5 o'clock train from Philadelphia will be omitted.

FOR GERMANTOWN,

From 1st of Sept. to 15th of Nov'r.
Leaves Philadelphia at 9½, 2, 4½ and 7.
Leaves Germantown at 8, 10½, 4 & 6.
On Sundays the trips at 3½ and 4½ will be omitted.

Winter Arrangement

For Manayunk & Norristown,

From 15th of Nov'r, to 1st of March,
Leaves Philadelphia at 10 and 4.
Leaves Norristown at 8 and 2.

FOR GERMANTOWN,

From 15th Nov'r to 1st of March,
Leaves Philadelphia at 9½, 2 and 5.
Leaves Germantown at 8½, 12 and 4.
☞ Omnibusses leave the Exchange for the Depot at 22 *Minutes* before the starting of the Cars, (Sundays Excepted)
WM FOULKE, *Agt*

Sept. 1st, 1847.

(TURN OVER.)

SPRING ARRANGEMENT

FOR MANAYUNK & NORRISTOWN.

From 1st March to 17th of April.
Leave Philadelphia at 9, 3, and 5.*
Leave Norristown at 7, 11,* and 5.

On Sunday's trips marked thus * omitted.

SPRING ARRANGEMENT

FOR GERMANTOWN.

From 1st March to 17th of April.
Leave Philadelphia at 9½, 2, 4,* 6, and 10½ *
Leave Germantown at 7½,* 8 35, 11. 3.* and 5.
On Sunday's trips marked thus * omitted.

Quarterly Tickets—Price Reduced.
Manayunk and Germantown, $10 } Children's $8.
Spring Mill, - - - 15 } Tickets. 12.
Norristown, - - - 20 } 16.

Omnibus Tickets included, $5 additional.
Omnibusses leave the Exchange for Depot at 22 minutes before the starting of the cars, Sunday's excepted.

March 1, 1848.

(TURN OVER.)

(TURN OVER.)

WINTER ARRANGEMENT

FOR MANAYUNK & NORRISTOWN.

1st Oct. to 1st April, ~~except as below~~
Leave Philadelphia at 9, 3. and 5.*
Leave Norristown

On Sundays, trips marked thus * omitted.

Quarterly Tickets—Price Reduced.
Manayunk, and Germantown, $10 } Children's $8.
Spring Mill, - - - 15 } Tickets. 12.
Norristown, - - - 20 } 15.

Omnibus Tickets included, $5 additional.
Omnibuses leave the Exchange for Depot at 22 minutes before the starting of the Cars, (Sundays excepted)
S. C. HENSZEY, Agent.

October 1, 1848,
Young, Pr.

(TURN OVER.)

282.—Railway schedules and time-tables. Four season time-tables of the Philadelphia, Germantown and Norristown Railroad. Showing commuters' erasures, by ink or paper strips, of trains in whose movements they were not interested. Actual size. Printed on white cardboard. 1847-1848.

between Charleston and Hamburg, in South Carolina, had become a law in December of 1827. Several citizens' meetings were held to discuss the subject immediately afterward; an amended bill in accordance with public desires was passed during the following month; and the final charter of the project was granted January 29, 1828. The company was organized on the 12th of the following May, and by January of 1830 some six miles of the road were ready. During the final weeks of 1829 and the first three months of 1830 it was the scene of experiments with horse locomotives and sailing cars similar to those on the Baltimore and Ohio line. The horse-power locomotive used once or twice on the South Carolina rails in 1829 moved at the rate of twelve miles an hour, carrying a load of twelve passengers. The employment of the sailing car took place before the road was open for regular traffic and appears to have been merely an impulse arising from impatience to travel on railroad tracks by any means whatsoever. One of the trips taken by such a vehicle was thus described in a local newspaper:[1]

"A sail was set on a car on our railroad yesterday afternoon, in the presence of a large concourse of spectators. Fifteen gentlemen got on board and flew off at the rate of twelve to fourteen miles an hour. . . . The preparations for sailing were very hastily got up, and of course were not of the best kind; but owing to this circumstance the experiment afforded high sport. . . . When going at the rate of twelve miles an hour and loaded with fifteen passengers, the mast went overboard with the sail and rigging attached, carrying with them several of the crew. The wreck was descried by several friendly shipmasters who kindly rendered assistance in rigging a jury mast and the car was again soon under way. . . . We understand it is intended by some of our seamen to rig a car properly and shortly to exhibit their skill in managing a vessel on land."

In September of 1829 Horatio Allen[2] was chosen to

[1] The Charleston "Courier" of March 20, 1830.
[2] The same civil and mechanical engineer who operated the "Stourbridge Lion" in Pennsylvania.

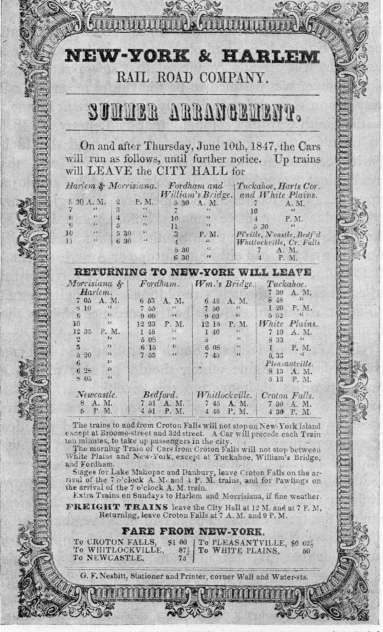

NEW-YORK & HARLEM
RAIL ROAD COMPANY.

SUMMER ARRANGEMENT.

On and after Thursday, June 10th, 1847, the Cars will run as follows, until further notice. Up trains will LEAVE the CITY HALL for

Harlem & Morrisiana.		Fordham and William's Bridge.	Tuckahoe, Harts Cor. and White Plains.
5 30 A. M.	2 P. M.	5 30 A. M.	7 A. M.
7 "	3 "	7 "	10 "
8 "	4 "	10 "	4 P. M.
9 "	5 "	11 "	5 30 "
10 "	5 30 "	3 P. M.	Pl'ville, N'castle, Bedf'd
11 "	6 30 "	4 "	Whitlockville, Cr. Falls
		5 30 "	7 A. M.
		6 30 "	4 P. M.

RETURNING TO NEW-YORK WILL LEAVE

Morrisiana & Harlem.	Fordham.	Wm.'s Bridge.	Tuckahoe.
			7 30 A. M.
7 05 A. M.	6 53 A. M.	6 45 A. M.	8 48 "
8 10 "	7 55 "	7 50 "	1 20 P. M.
9 "	9 09 "	9 03 "	5 52 "
10 "	12 23 P. M.	12 15 P. M.	White Plains.
12 35 P. M.	1 45 "	1 40 "	7 10 A. M.
2 "	5 08 "	5 "	8 33 "
3 "	6 15 "	6 08 "	1 P. M.
5 20 "	7 53 "	7 45 "	5 33 "
6 "			Pleasantville.
6 28 "			8 13 A. M.
8 05 "			5 13 P. M.

Newcastle.	Bedford.	Whitlockville.	Croton Falls.
8 A. M.	7 51 A. M.	7 45 A. M.	7 30 A. M.
5 P. M.	4 51 P. M.	4 45 P. M.	4 30 P. M.

The trains to and from Croton Falls will not stop on New-York Island except at Broome-street and 32d street. A Car will precede each Train ten minutes, to take up passengers in the city.

The morning Train of Cars from Croton Falls will not stop between White Plains and New-York, except at Tuckahoe, William's Bridge, and Fordham.

Stages for Lake Mahopac and Danbury, leave Croton Falls on the arrival of the 7 o'clock A. M. and 4 P. M. trains, and for Pawlings on the arrival of the 7 o'clock A. M. train.

Extra Trains on Sundays to Harlem and Morrisiana, if fine weather.

FREIGHT TRAINS leave the City Hall at 12 M. and at 7 P. M. Returning, leave Croton Falls at 7 A. M. and 9 P. M.

FARE FROM NEW-YORK.

To CROTON FALLS,	$1 00	To PLEASANTVILLE,	$0 62½
To WHITLOCKVILLE,	87½	To WHITE PLAINS,	50
To NEWCASTLE,	75		

G. F. Nesbitt, Stationer and Printer, corner Wall and Water-sts.

283.—Time-table of the New York and Harlem road, showing the train schedule for the summer of 1847. The southern terminus was at the City Hall. Extra trains on Sundays depended on the weather. Small broadside.

take charge of the construction work. Allen had recently been in England, and had observed the railroads there in use. He was already convinced that steam rather than horse-power was destined to be the future means of railway propulsion, and so insistently did he present his views to the South Carolina company that on January 14, 1830, its members unanimously decided their road should be built for the application of steam power and that mechanical propulsion exclusively should be employed upon it. The locomotive competition in England had taken place only three months before,[1] and it is accordingly probable that the South Carolina undertaking was the first railroad either in Europe or America formally to adopt the use of steam and pursue construction work in accordance with such a resolution. It is quite certain no other American railway had precedence of it in that respect.

By March of 1830 the South Carolina road had contracted for an engine which should be able to run at least ten miles an hour, and this machine, which was named the *Best Friend of Charleston,* was the first locomotive made in America for regular and practical use on a railway.[2] It was built in New York City, was shipped by ocean packet to Charleston in October of 1830,[3] and was placed on the road and operated in preliminary trials during the same year. The *Best Friend* ran off the track during a trial trip in November, but by the following month its performances had improved to such a degree that instead of moving at the speed de-

---

[1] It was concluded, and the prize awarded to the "Rocket," on October 14, 1829. That date was some months after Allen had left England, and after his opinion of steam power had been presented to the South Carolina company.

[2] A picture of the "Best Friend," together with a brigade of three cars propelled by it, is reproduced elsewhere.

[3] "The Charleston Courier" of October 23, 1830, contained the following paragraph: "Locomotive Steam Engine.—We understand that the steam engine intended for our road is aboard the ship Niagara which arrived in the offing last night."

THE UNITED STATES' MAIL LINE!

THE ONLY LINE
CARRYING THE GREAT MAIL!

DAILY TO THE SOUTH,

Via. Baltimore, Washington, Fredericksburg, Richmond, Petersburg, Weldon, Wilmington and Charleston, (S. C.) The Rail-Road from Weldon to Wilmington, (N. C.) being finished, and the whole Line in complete order, the Postmaster-General has ordered the following fast Schedule to take place from this date:

Leave Philadelphia, 1 A. M.—reach Baltimore 8 A. M.	- - -	96 Miles, in	7 Hours.
Leave Baltimore, 9 A. M.—reach Washington 12 M.	- - -	40 Miles, in	3 Hours.
Leave Washington, 12 M.—reach Fredericksburg 6½ P. M.	- - -	70 Miles, in	6½ Hours.
Leave Fredericksburg, 7 P. M.—reach Richmond 11½ P. M.	- - -	61 Miles, in	4½ Hours.
Leave Richmond, 12 P. M.—reach Petersburg 1½ A. M.	- - -	22 Miles, in	1¾ Hours.
Leave Petersburg, 2 A. M.—reach Weldon 6½ A. M.	- - -	60 Miles, in	4½ Hours.
Leave Weldon, 7 A. M.—reach Wilmington 6½ P. M.	- - -	161 Miles, in	11½ Hours.
Leave Wilmington, 7 P. M.—reach Charleston 10 next day,	-	170 Miles, in	15 Hours.

680 Miles, in 54 Hours.

Whole time, from Philadelphia to Charleston, (all Stoppages included,)

60 Hours, or nearly 12 Miles per Hour ! ! !

☞ This route now offers to Travellers, advantages SUPERIOR TO ALL OTHERS—it has been built up at an, **expense of Six Millions of Dollars!** between Baltimore and Charleston, which it is believed is a guarantee that the Companies composing it are sufficiently interested to make and keep up THE BEST LINE between the North and South. To Strangers, it will be found particularly attractive, as it passes through the Seat of General Government, and in sight of Mount Vernon by day-light,—and generally through the most important part of the Country. Rail-Road Travelling is now well known to be the safest, most certain, and expeditious mode of conveyance; and in the commodious Cars on this route, it will be found equally as pleasant and comfortable as any other.

☞ This is the ONLY DIRECT ROUTE to the interior of Virginia, North and South Carolina, and the ONLY ROUTE connecting with the Greenville and Roanoke and Raleigh and Gaston Rail-Roads now completed to Raleigh, N. C., a distance of 103 miles from the point of junction with the Petersburg Rail-Road. From the Raleigh and Gaston Rail-Road, several Stage Lines now branch off to the West and South-West, into Tennessee, the interior of South Carolina, Georgia and Alabama.

☞ PASSENGERS intending to take this Route must leave Philadelphia (in the Train,) at 1 A. M. if they wish to go through without delay. At Baltimore, they step immediately from the Philadelphia Cars into (the Cars of the) Baltimore and Washington Rail-Road Company. At Baltimore, they pay through to Garysburg, (North Carolina,) where they take the Wilmington Rail-Road Cars.

☞ PASSENGERS for the *Raleigh and Gaston Rail-Road* pay through to Petersburg, Va.

☞ For further information and Through Tickets, apply at the Office of

STOCKTON, FALLS & CO.,
Adjoining the Philadelphia Rail-Road Office, PRATT ST., *Baltimore.*

284.—Establishment of rail communication between North and South. Schedule of the journey from Philadelphia to Charleston in 1840, which was made possible by the completion of several short railways. There were no through cars, and in making this trip passengers were transferred at 6:30 P.M., 11:30 P.M., 1:30 A.M. and 6:30 A.M., or four times in 12 hours. The average speed of 12 miles an hour was announced with pride.

manded by the road when the order for construction was given, it made about thirty miles an hour when travelling alone, and pulled four cars containing forty or fifty passengers at a maximum velocity of twenty-one miles an hour for a short distance.[1] The first formal employment of the *Best Friend* took place in January of 1831, about a year after the building of the road had been begun. As was customary on such occasions the celebration was festive in character, and one of its features was decidedly unusual. A brigade of cars was attached to the locomotive for a trip over the road and on one of them was installed a cannon belonging to the United States government, together with a group of artillery-men detailed for the purpose. While the train moved proudly along the rails the soldiers loaded and fired their gun in honor of the day and its significance. A contemporary account of the trip[2] said:

"On Saturday last the first anniversary of the commencement of the railroad was celebrated. Notice having been previously given, inviting the stockholders, about one hundred and fifty assembled in the course of the morning at the company's building in Line Street, together with a number of invited guests. . . . The first trip was performed with two pleasure cars attached, and a small carriage, fitted for the occasion, upon which was a detachment of United States troops, and a field-piece which had been politely granted by Major Belton for the occasion. . . .

"At about one o'clock she again started with three cars attached, upon which were upward of one hundred passengers. . . . At four o'clock the company commenced returning and all were safely landed at Line Street about six. The number of passengers brought down, which was performed in two trips, was estimated at upward of two hundred. A band of music enlivened the scene and great hilarity and good humor prevailed throughout the day."

Besides being the first railroad designed for the use of steam power, and besides being the first such line in America to build and operate a steam locomotive, the

---

[1] Various paragraphs in the Charleston "Courier" published during November and December of 1830 mention the use of the engine.
[2] In the Charleston "Courier" of January 17, 1831.

road was also the scene of the first locomotive explosion on record. This incident took place on the 17th of June, 1831, and was due to the action of a negro fireman who was assisting the engineer. The fireman was annoyed by the incessant sound produced by the escape of steam from the safety valve, and at length the harsh roar caused by the operation in question became intolerable to him. In an effort to abate the disturbance he sat down on a lever controlling the safety valve, and finding his posture had the desired effect he there remained seated until the engine blew up. A current account of this first of all American railroad accidents was thus phrased:[1]

"The locomotive 'Best Friend' started yesterday morning to meet the lumber-cars at the Forks of the Road, and, while turning on the revolving platform, the steam was suffered to accumulate by the negligence of the fireman, a negro, who, pressing on the safety valve, prevented the surplus steam from escaping, by which means the boiler burst at the bottom, was forced inward, and injured Mr. Darrell, the engineer, and two negroes. . . . The boiler was thrown to the distance of twenty-five feet, None of the persons are dangerously injured except the negro, who had his thigh broken."

The explosion and a number of other minor accidents resulted in the preparation by the company of the first set of rules to govern railroad traffic and provide for the safety of travellers. The action of the company was expressed by the following resolution:

"That in future not over twenty-five passengers be allowed to go on each car. That the locomotive shall not travel at a greater speed when there is attached:

"One car and passengers at fifteen miles on hour;

"Two cars and passengers at twelve miles an hour;

"Three cars and passengers at ten miles an hour;

"And that directions be given to that effect."

The Charleston and Hamburg road ordered a second locomotive in 1830, and it arrived at Charleston in February of 1831 and was soon afterward put into regular

[1] In the Charleston "Courier" of June 18, 1831.

operation. This engine was the second to be built in America for practical work, and was named the *West Point*. The explosion of the *Best Friend* had created among the Charleston people a feeling of uneasiness about the behavior of locomotive engines, and so when the *West Point* was put on the line for a trial trip the officials of the road strove to allay the nervousness of the passengers by a novel and effective expedient. Instead of placing the first passenger car immediately behind the little platform carrying a hogshead of water and wood for the engine, that position in the brigade was filled by a car on which was built a pyramid made of cotton bales. The cotton bales were securely fastened down by means of ropes, and they arose upward in the air as high as did the roofs of the cars which followed. The whole arrangement constituted a rampart interposing between the passengers and the engine, and was designed to prevent the boiler of the machine from flying back among the travellers in case it followed the example of the *Best Friend's* boiler. But the precautions of the railway officials did not even pause at that point. They also put a car containing a negro brass band immediately behind the cotton pyramid, and so the first regular passenger coach was third in the brigade as it finally started, with the other passenger vehicles attached in due order. To cap the climax of solicitude the mechanism of the engine was so altered as to make it impossible for the fireman to emulate the example of his predecessor, should he be so disposed. The trial trip of the *West Point* fulfilled all favorable expectations and was thus described by the Charleston *Courier* of March 12, 1831:

"On Saturday afternoon, March 5, 1831, the locomotive 'West Point' underwent a trial of speed, with the barrier car and four cars

964

for passengers, on our railroad. There were one hundred and seventeen passengers, of which number fifty were ladies in the four cars and nine persons on the engine, with six bales of cotton on the barrier car, and the trip to the Five-mile House, two and three-fourths miles, was completed in eleven minutes. . . . The two and one-fourth miles to the forks of Dorchester road were completed in eight minutes. The safety has been insured by the introduction of the barrier-car and the improvements in the formation of the flange of the wheels. . . . The new locomotive worked admirably, and the safety valve being out of the reach of any person but the engineer, will contribute to the prevention of accidents in future. . . ."

Horse-drawn cars were never used in the regular traffic of the Charleston and Hamburg road, even in its earliest days. The success of its first two engines, despite the boiler explosion, was so emphatic that similar additional locomotives and cars were built for it as its rails gradually crept toward the West, and the experience of the road demonstrated at the outset the foresight of the man whose insistence had made it the first of all railways to be built and equipped for the use of steam.

While the events here related had been taking place in two of the southern states an almost equally important enterprise had been progressing in the interior of New York, amid a region memorable for a century and a half as the scene of significant steps in the history of American travel and traffic. As early as the year 1826 the New York legislature had granted a charter to the Mohawk and Hudson Railroad Company, and under its provisions work was begun in August, 1830, in laying out a road about seventeen miles long between the towns of Albany and Schenectady. Two inclined planes—similar to the one on the Pennsylvania state railroad near Philadelphia —distinguished the first New York railway, but these were of small length and the remainder of the distance traversed was over comparatively level ground. After a few miles of track had been laid two or three horse-drawn cars were operated on it, and these continued to run back and forth until the summer of 1831, at which time the entire seventeen miles of rails were in place. A knowledge of the success of the *Best Friend* in South Carolina had reached the men in charge of the Albany and Schenectady road, and so they decided to follow the course set by the Charleston undertaking. Early in April of 1831 they ordered a locomotive from the West Point foundry of New York—which had built the two South Carolina engines—and it was shipped up the Hudson River to Albany late in June of the same year. Their engine was named the *DeWitt Clinton*. After a number of preliminary trials without any burden the time finally arrived for a more pretentious demonstration, and August 9th was chosen as the date of the occasion. The trip made on that day by the *DeWitt Clinton* and its attached cars was, for several reasons, the most interesting journey ever undertaken by an early American railway train.

It so happened that on the appointed day there was temporarily sojourning in the town of Albany a man named William H. Brown. Mr. Brown was one of those itinerant silhouette artists who travelled about the country during bygone years, deftly cutting outline portraits of their customers from sheets of black paper. Brown was a master craftsman of his art, and in addition he was a man of intelligence and a close observer of the affairs of his time. Everybody in the city was discussing the approaching test on the railroad, and Brown heard the gossip. He had never seen a railroad or a railroad train, and putting aside his professional affairs—as he supposed—he joined the crowd that was trooping to the scene of the experiment. In company with many hundreds of others

DAILY
TO THE
SOUTH.
Via THE CHESAPEAKE BAY.

FOR NORFOLK, PORTSMOUTH,
AND CHARLESTON,
(Fare always the same as the Upper Route,)

IN THE SPLENDID STEAM BOATS,

ALABAMA, ... Captain SUTTON,
GEORGIA, ... Captain ROLLINS,
JEWESS, ... Captain HOLMES,

EVERY AFTERNOON,
From the lower end of SPEAR'S WHARF,—BALTIMORE.

FOR
PETERSBURG & RICHMOND,
EVERY DAY, SUNDAY EXCEPTED.
PASSAGE, Meals found, ... TEN DOLLARS.

THIS IS THE QUICKEST AND MOST COMFORTABLE ROUTE,
GOING SOUTH.

☞ PASSENGERS have A GOOD NIGHT'S REST in the Bay—there are no Changes from Steamboats, Stages and Cars *in the Night*, as on the Washington route. *N. B. The Boat never leaves until the Cars from Philadelphia arrive.*

☞ CAUTION !!!—Passengers are requested to give no faith to the statements made at the depot in Baltimore, The WASHINGTON RAIL ROAD COMPANY rufusing to admit ANY AGENT into *their Depot*, but such as are connected with the *Upper Route ! ! ! !*

285.—Issued by a steamboat company that ran in opposition to the railroad route advertised in the preceding. Date, 1840. When using this route the traveller went to Baltimore by rail and thence to Charleston by water. Agents for the rival lines sometimes engaged in pitched battles for the possession of south-bound passengers in Baltimore.

he committed himself to the inclined plane with which
the road began and was safely hauled to its top. There
he beheld a throng of spectators who were pressing closely
about the engine and brigade of cars as they stood ready
on the track. The locomotive was a little affair about
ten or twelve feet long whose principal features were its
large wheels, lofty smokestack and central dome. At its
rear was a platform built as a standing place for the engineer. Attached to the locomotive was a small flat car
on which stood a couple of barrels of water and a pile
of wood. Connection was made between the engine and
water barrels by a leather hose. Following the water-and-
fuel wagon were three passenger cars closely resembling
stage-coach bodies, and each containing interior seats for
six people. Additional seats at the outer ends of the cars
provided accommodations for several more passengers on
each vehicle. Five or six small flat cars were attached to
the rear of the three passenger coaches, and these were
equipped with plain wood benches. This was the appearance of the first steam railroad train assembled in New
York State, and about which a crowd had gathered on the
morning of that August day.

Brown alone, of all the multitude, had an appreciation of the historic importance of the thing he beheld.
He took off his big flat-topped beaver hat, held it crown
uppermost within the crook of his left arm, and made a
careful drawing of the train on the back of a letter which
he fortunately found in his pocket.[1] By the time this task
had been completed the train was preparing to get under
way and the passengers were taking their places. Brown
himself fortunately secured a seat. When all the cars

[1] It should not be understood that he made the drawing on the back of an envelope.
Envelopes had not yet come into use for mailing purposes. The sheet of paper commonly
used for writing was folded up and sealed with wax. When opened it was about as large
as a sheet of foolscap size.

were crowded to their utmost capacity the captain walked along the length of the train, collecting the fares of the travellers. Then he retraced his steps, climbed into a little seat attached to the rear of the water-and-fuel wagon and blew loud and long on the necessary tin horn. The train started.

It did not start all at once, but in sections. The tender was attached to the engine by a chain nearly three feet long made of three large links of wrought-iron; the first passenger coach was attached to the tender in a like manner; the second passenger coach was similarly connected to the first passenger coach; and so on down the train to the very last car. With the first forward jump of the engine the captain was nearly snapped backward out of his seat, but he seized a roof-support and luckily held on. The passengers in the first coach were unprepared for what was about to happen, and those sitting in the front and middle sections were projected backward and piled in a heap against the passengers at the rear. Those in the second car followed suit, and as the slack length of each chain was gathered up by the abrupt forward jerk the succeeding group of passengers was overturned. After the whole train was straightened out it rolled on in good order as far as smoothness of movement was concerned, but a new trouble then manifested itself.

The fuel of the engine, as has been suggested, was wood, and the smokestack soon began to belch forth big blazing sparks. These fell among the passengers. The damage done by them in the three covered coaches was not extreme, but the havoc they created on the crowded flat cars was sad indeed. Many of the travellers on the rear cars had carried their umbrellas, and those so equipped raised them for protection against the clouds of smoke and rain of fire. As a consequence all the umbrellas were soon in flames and were thrown overboard. Then the clothing of the passengers—a considerable number of whom were women—became ignited by the hot coals, and in a very little while the whole moving company resolved itself into a volunteer fire brigade, each member of which was belaboring the one next to him and trying to extinguish the conflagration in his neighbor's apparel. For a couple of miles, according to the stories of spectators along the track, the scene was one impossible of adequate description.

At this point of the interesting journey a further complication ensued. The train was approaching a spot where the locomotive's supply of water was to be replenished, and as it reached the tank the engineer threw a lever designed to apply the brakes and check the train's momentum. The mechanism worked to perfection. The water-wagon came up against the engine with a bump; the first passenger coach hit the tender with a crash; the second passenger coach flew against the first; and so on down the length of the train again, the resultant movements of the passengers being similar to those witnessed at starting, but in the opposite direction. As soon as the train was entirely stopped the travellers disembarked. The first thing they did was to put out the rest of the fires that still smouldered here and there in some coat or bonnet. The second thing they did was to tear down a farmer's fence, chop up the rails into appropriate lengths, and wedge them firmly between each two cars composing the brigade. This gave rigidity to the train, and after the engineer had taken on a fresh supply of water everybody resumed his place again with a heroism rarely duplicated, and the excursion moved on. The blazing sparks from

NEW SOUTHERN LINE,
ONE WEEK FROM NEW YORK TO NEW ORLEANS.
ONLY 36 HOURS STAGE TRAVELING!
WHOLE EXPENSE, $115.

BRUNSWICK & FLORIDA
LINE,

From Charleston to Mobile.

Via BRUNSWICK, TALLAHASSEE, PORT LEON, ST MARKS,
APPALACHICOLA, ST. JOSEPHS and PENSACOLA, viz.

From Charleston to Brunswick, Steamboat,   -   -   160 Miles.
   "   Brunswick to Tallahasse, Post Coach,   -   -   210 "
   "   Tallahassee to St. Marks, Rail-Road,   -   -   21   "
   "   St. Marks to Lake Wimico, S. boat, (innner passage,) 85 "
   "   St. Josephs to Mobile, Steamboat,   -   -   215 "

This line will commence operations during October, leaving Charleston every
alternate morning, and arriving in Mobile in three and a half days, and
In New Orleans in Four Days.

PASSAGE TO MOBILE, (including meals,) $65.

☞Seats may be secured in New York and Baltimore.

The Steam Packets are of superior order, for safety and comfort. The
Stage Road is unsurpassed by any in the Union for evenness and firmness.
The whole Line is well appointed, and will soon be seen to be on the best
possible route for Northern and Southern Traveling.
Due notice will be given of the days of running and of other particulars.

Brunswick, Geo., 1840.

286.—A third announcement showing the facilities for travelling southward in
1840. It indicates that by means of railroads, steamboats, and stage-coaches
a man might go from New York to New Orleans in a week, at a cost of
only $115 exclusive of meals on the land portions of the trip. The pro-
portion of stage-coach travel necessary in any long journey was steadily
decreasing.

the dry pitch pine fuel still rained down on the excursionists, but they had acquired increased dexterity in dodging or handling them and the effects were not so bad. Such clothing as still remained to the travellers was ruined anyway, so the further visitation of fire was accepted with comparative unconcern.

The remainder of the trip to Schenectady was practically without incident except for the behavior of the live stock encountered in the progress of the journey. Nearly all the farmers of the surrounding region had gathered in their wagons and chaises at all favorable localities along the turnpikes to watch the first trip of the steam-engine, and at numerous places the roads had the appearance they presented at circus time or during a county fair. The country people did not know just exactly what was coming, and their horses had even less information on the subject. The only thought animating the two-legged spectators was to get as close as possible to the railway tracks in order to enjoy the show. It is needless to say what happened as the bedlam-on-wheels whirled past, headed by a mechanical monster vomiting fire and smoke. The effect of the apparition on the assembled countryside was later described in these words by a passenger who was on the train: "As it approached the horses took fright and wheeled, upsetting buggies, carriages and wagons and leaving for parts unknown to the passengers, if not to their owners; and it is not now positively known if some of them have yet stopped."[1]

On its arrival at Schenectady the train was welcomed by a crowd of several thousand people who inspected it

[1] Extract from a letter written by Judge J. A. Gillis, of New York State. Contained in full in Brown's "A History of the First Locomotives in America," pp. 183-5. Judge Gillis also describes the crashing together of the cars, the burning of the passengers' clothing and umbrellas and the use of fence rails to give rigidity to the train.

and the passengers with utmost interest. After a short interval it started again on the return trip to Albany, during which the intervening landscape was entirely devoid of horse-drawn vehicles. The events of the day were somewhat inadequately described by a local newspaper[1] in the following words:

"Mohawk and Hudson Railroad.—On Monday, August 9, 1831, the 'DeWitt Clinton,' attached to a train of cars, passed over the road from plane to plane, to the delight of a large crowd assembled to witness the performance. The engine performed the entire route in less than one hour, including stoppages, and on a part of the road its speed was at the rate of thirty miles an hour."

After Mr. Brown had got safely back to Albany he went at once to his hotel and there prepared a long strip of black paper out of which he cut in silhouette fashion an outline picture of the *DeWitt Clinton,* the tender, and the first two passenger coaches it had pulled on the trip here described. The artist performed his work with such fidelity and minuteness of detail that even the pictures of the passengers in the two cars were recognizable portraits of the men who occupied the seats. After leaving Albany Brown exhibited this silhouette picture of the Albany and Schenectady train to thousands of people in other towns, charging a small admission fee for the privilege of beholding it. At a later date he presented the original silhouette to the Connecticut Historical Society, where it still remains as an invaluable possession of that institution. Brown's picture, as made under the circumstances mentioned, is the best authenticated portrayal of an early American railroad train that has been preserved. It has been many times reproduced.[2]

The annoying features of travel by the new method

[1] The Albany "Argus" of August 11, 1831.
[2] One of the early lithographic copies of the original silhouette is shown on another page.

that were disclosed on the trip of August 9th were gradually eliminated, and on September 24 the road ran between the two towns a train containing numerous state officials and other dignitaries. A newspaper account[1] said of it:

"On Saturday, September 24, a numerous company, at the request of the president and directors of the Mohawk and Hudson Railroad Company, enjoyed a very gratifying ride upon the road. . . The party . . . did not leave the head of Lydius Street until nearly twelve o'clock. They then started with a train of ten cars, three drawn by the American locomotive 'DeWitt Clinton,' and seven by a single horse each. The appearance of this fine cavalcade, if it may be so called, was highly imposing. The trip was performed by the locomotive in forty-six minutes, and by the cars drawn by horses in about an hour and a quarter. . . . After dinner the company repaired to the head of the plane, and resumed their seats for the return to Albany. It was an imposing spectacle. It was a practical illustration of the great preference of this mode of travel and conveyance. The American locomotive started with a train of five cars, containing nineteen or twenty persons each, besides the tender, and never did 'Brother Jonathan,' as it was familiarly called, perform the trip in more beautiful style. It came down with its train in thirty-eight minutes, being at the rate of nineteen miles an hour; the last six miles were performed in fourteen minutes. The cavalcade with horses came down in sixty-eight minutes."

The little seventeen mile railroad between Albany and Schenectady, whose early endeavors were so picturesque, was destined to be the first link in a series of five or six small roads built westwardly from town to town through interior New York State during the next few years. By them it was eventually made possible for travellers to move all the way from Albany to Buffalo in railroad cars. At first the companies operating these several short roads were independent enterprises and did not manifest any especial desire to coöperate with one another for the convenience of their many patrons. Passengers in the cars were compelled to disembark at the

[1] Contained in the Albany "Argus" of Sept. 26, 1831.

end of each road and take passage on the next link of the embryonic system whenever its train chose to start. Eventually the insistence of the travelling public and a growing realization of the fitness of things brought about physical connection between these independent enterprises, and at last they fell under one corporate management and became known as the New York Central Railroad.

CHAPTER XLIV

MORE EXPERIENCES ON EARLY AMERICAN RAILWAYS —
MANNER IN WHICH A PENNSYLVANIA ROAD ACQUIRED
A LOCOMOTIVE — ACCOUNT OF ONE OF ITS TRIPS BY
A PEDESTRIAN PARTICIPANT — NEW YORK CITY'S
FIRST LINE — APPREHENSIONS OF THE PUBLIC —
PRECAUTION TAKEN TO SOOTHE THEIR FEARS — THE
RESULT — THE CAMDEN AND AMBOY ROAD — ITS
MONOPOLY OF TRAFFIC ACROSS NEW JERSEY — HOW
ISAAC DRIPPS BUILT A LOCOMOTIVE TENDER — THREE
NEW ENGLAND ENTERPRISES — NO STEAM TRAVEL
THERE UNTIL 1834 — ONLY SIXTEEN HOURS BE-
TWEEN BOSTON AND NEW YORK — PROTEST OF AN
OLD-FASHIONED TRAVELLER

DURING the year 1832 several other of America's
pioneer roads were sufficiently advanced in construction over parts of their routes to permit travel upon them.
Three of these lines were the Philadelphia, Germantown
and Norristown Railroad, in Pennsylvania; the New
York and Harlem road, in New York State; and the
Camden and Amboy Railroad, in New Jersey. The first
of these to be ready for public business was the Philadelphia, Germantown and Norristown road, which was
opened for six miles between Philadelphia and Germantown on June 6, 1832.[1]

[1] It had been chartered on February 12, 1831. The tracks did not reach Norristown
until August 15, 1835.

The first few miles of the line were operated for a short time by means of horse-drawn cars built according to the patterns then in vogue, although a determination had been reached soon after the road was chartered to use steam on it if that method of locomotion should prove practicable. The manner whereby the road obtained its first locomotive is an odd story, aptly illustrative of the methods prevailing in America during those early years of progress and experiment in independent railroad building. The city of Philadelphia—as earlier events had shown—was one of those communities whose citizens were always actively interested in all phases of the general subject of improved travel and traffic facilities. So in the year 1830, when public interest in railroads had attained a high degree of intensity, Franklin Peale, the proprietor of the Philadelphia Museum, decided further to enlighten the inhabitants of the city regarding the matter then uppermost in popular thought, and incidentally to coin popular curiosity into profit for himself. He accordingly resolved to exhibit a genuine locomotive in one of the halls of his institution, and set about obtaining an example of the apparatus in question. In furtherance of his idea he turned to a local business man named Matthias Baldwin. Baldwin's first knowledge of mechanics in any form had been gained as a jeweler and repairer of watches some thirteen years before. In 1825 he had extended his understanding of the mechanical arts by undertaking the manufacture of bookbinders' tools and such machinery as was then used in the printing of calico. He had even built a steam-engine for use in his shop, and the fact that Baldwin had actually made a workable steam-engine was the circumstance impelling Peale to approach him with a proposition to build a locomotive. Baldwin did build

977

a small model locomotive, which was duly installed in the museum on the 25th of April, 1831, where it pulled two diminutive four-seated passenger cars around a circular track,[1] and the public was thereby enabled to gratify its highest ambition by riding in a railroad train—such as it was.

Of course the little locomotive in the museum became at once the talk of the town, and when the incorporators of the Philadelphia, Germantown and Norristown road decided that they wanted a steam railway engine, they, in turn, went to Baldwin and gave him an order for one of them. The Camden and Amboy Railroad was even then being built, and it had already imported from England an engine known as the *John Bull*. Although the *John Bull* had not yet been put together, Baldwin went and examined it carefully, and then came back home and set to work. The result of his effort was the engine known as *Old Ironsides,* first of all such contrivances to be operated in Pennsylvania. It could hardly be expected that a railway locomotive constructed—as *Old Ironsides* was—by a man who had never done such a thing before, could be a very successful mechanism, and in the early stages of its existence it was not.[2] The history, appearance and performance of *Old Ironsides* were afterwards described by an assistant of Baldwin's in the following account:[3]

"The first really effective locomotive in America, says Mr. Haskell, in the Coachmakers' Journal, was built in Philadelphia, from a draught by Rufus Tyler, brother-in-law of the late Matthias Baldwin, of Philadelphia. Messrs. Tyler and Baldwin had formed a co-partnership and entered into business at the corner of Sixth and Miner Streets, Philadelphia, where the plans and patterns were made and the building of the

[1] The track was made of upright pine boards, covered with hoop-iron.
[2] The same thing was true of all early American locomotives built by men without experience in such work. They required numerous alterations.
[3] In the Philadelphia "Public Ledger," January 18, 1869.

CENTRAL RAILROAD,

FROM SAVANNAH TO MACON, GA.,
190½ Miles.

Passenger Trains leave Savannah daily, at......8 00 A. M.
"   "   "   Macon daily at ....8 00 A. M.
"   "   arrive daily at Savannah at....6 15 P. M.
"   "   "   "   at Macon, at......6 45 P. M.

This Road in connection with the Macon and Western Road from Macon to Atlanta, and the Western and Atlantic Road from Atlanta to Dalton, now forms a continuous line of 391½ miles in length from Savannah to Dalton, Murray county, Ga., and with the Memphis Branch Rail Road, and stages, connect with the following places:

Tickets from Savannah to Jacksonville, Ala., ...$20.00
"   "   "   Huntsville,} Ala., ... 22.00
"   "   "   Decatur, }
"   "   "   Tuscumbia, Ala., ... 22.50
"   "   "   Columbus, Miss.,} 28.00
"   "   "   Holly Springs, }
"   "   "   Nashville, Tenn.,} 25.00
"   "   "   Murfreesboro' }
"   "   "   Memphis, Tenn., ... 30.00

An extra Passenger Train leaves Savannah on Saturdays, after the arrival of the steamships from New York, for Macon, and connects with the Macon and Western Rail Road; and on Tuesdays, after the arrival of the Macon and Western cars, an extra Passenger Train leaves Macon to connect with the steamships for New York.

Stages for Tallahasse and intermediate places connect with the road at Macon on Mondays, Wednesdays, and Fridays, and with Milledgeville at Gordon daily.

Passengers for Montgomery, Mobile, and New Orleans, take stage for Opelika from Barnesville through Columbus, a distance of 97 miles, or from Griffin through West Point, a distance of 93 miles.

Goods consigned to Thos. S. Wayne, Forwarding Agent, Savannah, will be forwarded free of commission.

WM. M. WADLEY, Sup't.

Savannah, Ga., 1852.

287.—Announcement of the Central Railroad of Georgia in 1852. Indicating the further growth of steam travel facilities in the South, the cost attendant on their use, the persistence of water travel to the North and the continued activity of the stage-coach.

iron horse commenced. . . . The wheels of the engine were made of wood, with broad rims and thick tires, the flange being bolted on the side. It was called 'Old Ironsides,' and was built in 1832. At eight o'clock in the morning she was first put in motion on the Germantown and Norristown Railroad at their depot, Ninth and Greene Streets. She ran a mile an hour, and was considered the wonder of the day. On trial it was ascertained that the wheels were too light to draw the tender, and to obviate this difficulty we had the tender placed in front of the engine, which kept the wheels on the track. Mr. Baldwin, the machinist, and myself pushed the engine ahead until we obtained some speed, when we all jumped on the engine, our weight keeping the wheels from slipping on the track. The boiler being too small for the engine, steam was only generated fast enough to keep the engine in motion a short time,[1] so that we were compelled to alternately push and ride until we arrived at Germantown depot, where we rested. . . .

"At four o'clock we started on our return to Philadelphia, alternating riding and pushing in the same manner that we had come. Upon arriving at a turn on the road, at the up-grade, the engine suddenly stopped, when, upon examination, it was found that the connecting pipe between the water-tank and the boiler had been frozen, and the steam was all out of the boiler. It was then about eight o'clock, and was growing each moment colder. 'Necessity knows no law,' and so, after a short consultation, we made a summary appropriation of sundry panels of a post-and-rail fence close to the track, and started a fire underneath the pipe to thaw it. In a short time thereafter we had steam up and resumed our journey toward Philadelphia, arriving at the depot about eleven o'clock. Several successive trials were made during the following year; after each Mr. Baldwin added improvements and made alterations in the machinery. In about a year it was found that the grease had saturated the hubs and loosened the spokes, and they finally went to pieces, and were replaced by new ones."

The above-mentioned occasion, described long afterward by a participant as that on which *Old Ironsides* was "first put in motion," does not appear to have been the first formal and public demonstration of the locomotive. Contemporary newspaper accounts of 1832 refer to a "first time" trial on November 23 that took place at a different time of day, and during which the engine went only halfway to Germantown and back again under decidedly different conditions. The account just quoted may refer

[1] The steam joints had been made by the use of canvas, covered with red-lead. This was an early English practise, which Baldwin had copied.

PENNSYLVANIA RAILROAD.

ARRANGEMENTS—1851.

FORTY-SIX HOURS TO PHILADELPHIA.
FORTY-FOUR HOURS TO BALTIMORE.

280 Miles Railroad—103 Miles Canal.

TWO DAILY LINES EXPRESS PACKET BOATS,

Exclusively for passengers.

TO PHILADELPHIA, BALTIMORE AND NEW YORK.

On the opening of Canal Navigation, two daily Lines, new Express Packet Boats, will leave for Johnstown, thence by Portage Railroad to

HOLLIDAYSBURGH,

There taking the NEW PENNSYLVANIA RAILROAD, two hundred and forty-five miles direct to

PHILADELPHIA.

☞ Time through, forty-six hours.

Fare to Philadelphia, $10.   Fare to Baltimore, $9.75.

☞ The cars on this route are new, and of the most approved construction for comfort and safety.

☞ Packets leave every morning *precisely* at eight o'clock, and every evening at the same hour.

PASSENGERS FOR BALTIMORE,

on arrival of Cars at Harrisburgh, take the York and Cumberland Railroad, (now finished,) direct to that city, (84 miles.) Time, four hours.

☞ *No charge for handling baggage on this route.*

The increased speed makes this the most comfortable, safe and desirable route now to the Eastern Cities.

For passage or information, apply to

J. P. HOLMES, Agent, Monongahela House, or to

D. LEECH & CO., Canal Basin, Penn-st., Pittsburgh.

N. B. On the 1st of July, the PENNSYLVANIA RAILROAD will be finished at Lockport, Pa., which will shorten the time through six hours.

288.—The journey between Pittsburgh and Philadelphia reduced to 46 hours. Advertisement of Leech's Line in 1851. It started two express canal boats eastward each day. On arrival at Johnstown the passengers still had to use the Portage railway across the mountains, but at Hollidaysburg they left the state-owned system and transferred to the newly built Pennsylvania Railroad, which company had been chartered in 1846, and whose line had been finished to Hollidaysburg in September of 1850. The state canal from that town to Philadelphia had been abandoned by passenger traffic.

to a preliminary test. One local newspaper[1] of November 24th said:

"A most gratifying experiment was made yesterday afternoon on the Philadelphia, Germantown and Norristown Railroad. The beautiful locomotive engine and tender, built by Mr. Baldwin, of this city, whose reputation as an ingenious machinist is well known, were for the first time placed on the road. The engine traveled about six miles, working with perfect accuracy and ease in all its parts, and with great velocity."

Another paper[2] gave a still more detailed statement as follows:

"It gives us pleasure to state that the locomotive engine built by our townsman, M. W. Baldwin, has proved highly successful. In the presence of several gentlemen of science and information on such subjects, the engine was yesterday placed upon the road for the first time. All her parts had been previously highly finished and fitted together in Mr. Baldwin's factory. She was taken apart on Tuesday and removed to the Company's depot, and yesterday morning she was completely together, ready for travel. After the regular passenger cars had arrived from Germantown in the afternoon, the tracks being clear, preparation was made for her starting. The placing fire in the furnace and raising steam occupied twenty minutes. The engine (with her tender) moved from the depot in beautiful style, working with great ease and uniformity. She proceeded about half a mile beyond the Union Tavern . . . and returned immediately, a distance of six miles, at a speed of about twenty-eight miles to the hour. . . . It is needless to say that the spectators were delighted. . . . We rejoice at the result of this experiment."

While Baldwin was adding improvements to his locomotive during the first months of its career the road of which it formed such an interesting part displayed a proper solicitude for its welfare. It advertised in the newspapers that the engine would haul the passenger cars of the railway at certain hours if the weather was good, but that if it rained the cars would be pulled by horses. Sometimes it rained. But eventually *Old Ironsides* was transformed by Baldwin into an extraordinarily effective piece of machinery for that day, and in 1833 it ac-

[1] "The United States Gazette."
[2] The "Chronicle" of November 24.

HUDSON RIVER RAILROAD.

REDUCTION OF FARES.

NEW-YORK TO AND FROM

ALBANY & TROY

THROUGH FARES ON ALL TRAINS

Between Albany and New-York, $1.50

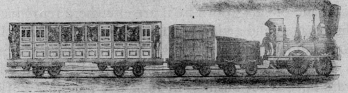

On and after Monday, July 12th, the Trains will run as follows:

GOING NORTH,

Leave New-York, from the office cor. Chambers Street and College Place, at

6 A.M. Express Train for Albany and Troy, connecting with Northern and Western Trains, stopping only at Peekskill, Fishkill, Po'keepsie, Rhinebeck, and Hudson. Through in 4 hours from 31st Street.

7 A.M. To Peekskill, stopping at all Way Stations.

8 A.M. Mail Train for Albany and Troy, stopping only at Manhattan, Dobbs' Ferry, Sing-Sing, Peekskill and all Mail Stations north.

9 A.M. To Peekskill, stopping at all Way Stations.

11½ A.M. Passengers and Freight to Po'keepsie, stopping at all Stations.

1 P.M. Way Train for Albany and Troy, stopping at Yonkers, Tarrytown, Peekskill, Cold Spring, Fishkill, New-Hamburgh, Poughkeepsie, Rhinebeck, Tivoli, Oakhill, Hudson and Stuyvesant, and connecting with the Express Train leaving Albany at 6.30 P.M. for Buffalo.

2 P.M. To Peekskill, stopping at all Way Stations.

4 P.M. Way Train to Albany and Troy, stopping at Yonkers, Dobbs' Ferry, Dearman, Tarrytown, Sing Sing, Peekskill, Garrisons, Cold Spring, Fishkill, New-Hamburgh, Po'keepsie, and all Stations north on signal.

4½ P.M. To Poughkeepsie, stopping at all Way Stations.

6 P.M. Express Train for Albany and Troy, stopping only at Peekskill, Fishkill, Po'keepsie, Hudson and Stuyvesant. Through in 4 hours from 31st Street, and connecting with Western Trains.

6¼ P.M. To Peekskill, stopping at all Way Stations.

7½ P.M. Emigrant and Freight Train for Albany and Troy, stopping at all Way Stations.

Leave Po'keepsie for Albany at

6¾ A.M. Stopping at all Way Stations.

GOING SOUTH,

Leave Troy Engine Station and Albany, viz:

Leave Troy	Leave Albany	
A.M. 5.45	**6 A.M.**	Way Mail Train for New-York, stopping at all stations where there are mails to be received and delivered.
A.M. 6.45	**7 A.M.**	Express Train for New-York, stopping only at Hudson, Rhinebeck, Poughkeepsie, Fishkill, Cold Spring and Peekskill. Through in 4 hours.
A.M. 10.45	**11 A.M.**	Way Train, stopping at Stuyvesant, Hudson, Oakhill, Tivoli, Barrytown, Rhinebeck, Hyde Park, Po'keepsie, Fishkill, Cold Spring, Peekskill, Cruger's, Sing-Sing and Dobb's Ferry.
P.M. 3.45	**4 P.M.**	Way Train, stopping at Stuyvesant, Hudson, Oakhill, Tivoli, Barrytown, Rhinebeck, Hyde Park, Po'keepsie, New-Hamburgh, Fishkill, Cold Spring, Garrison's, Peekskill, Cruger's, Sing-Sing, Tarrytown and Yonkers.
	4½ P.M.	For Poughkeepsie only, stopping at all Way Stations.
P.M. 6.	**6¼ P.M.**	Express Train, stopping only at Hudson, Rhinebeck, Po'keepsie, Fishkill and Peekskill. Through in 4 hours.
P.M. 8.30	**8¾ P.M.**	Night Mail Train, stopping at all stations on signal.

Leave Po'keepsie for New-York at

6¾ A.M. stopping at all stations above Peekskill, and at Cruger's, Sing-Sing, Tarrytown, Dearman, Dobbs' Ferry, Hastings, Yonkers and Manhattan.

8¾ P.M. Milk and Freight Train, stopping at all Way Stations.

Leave Peekskill for New-York at

5.50 & 6.30 A.M. Stopping at all Way Stations.

3½ & 6 P.M. Stopping at all Way stations.

Passengers will procure Tickets before entering the Cars. Tickets purchased in the Cars will be 5 cents extra.

New-York, July 10th, 1852.

GEO. STARK, Superintendent.

289.—Broadside train schedule issued by the Hudson River Railroad in 1852. There were twenty-six trains a day on the line. The picture of a locomotive shows a curious form of the lately introduced engineer's cab. A growing desire of all roads to have passengers buy tickets instead of paying cash on the cars is indicated by the request at the bottom. Printed on blue paper.

complished the astonishing performance of running a mile in fifty-eight seconds—without any cars behind it— and two and a quarter miles under similar conditions in three minutes and twenty-two seconds. This was indeed an achievement for a self-taught engine builder, and it is not surprising that out of the results here narrated and the American spirit responsible for them there slowly grew one of the principal locomotive building establishments of the world. Several contemporary pictures of *Old Ironsides* and of cars drawn by it are elsewhere reproduced in these pages, and a view of the station of the Philadelphia, Germantown and Norristown road is similarly shown.[1]

The second of the three roads already mentioned that were opened for business in 1832 was the New York and Harlem.[2] The work of building it had been begun during the previous year, and the first part of it to be finished was a short section of track about three-quarters of a mile in length extending southward from Fourteenth Street, in New York City.[3] Although this first division of the line was not dedicated to public travel until November 26th of 1832, it is evident that cars had been placed on the tracks a few days before the date named, since a local publication[4] mentioned the progress of the enterprise in these words on November 17:

"We were highly gratified on Wednesday last, as we were passing up

[1] As is likewise a picture of the Baldwin Works drawn by John Sartain about 1845, in connection with locomotives of the type then made by it and used in this country.
[2] Chartered on April 25, 1831.
[3] Additional sections were completed and used for travel as follows:
Between Fourteenth and 32nd Streets on June 10, 1833;
From 32nd Street to Yorkville, about 2¾ miles, May 9, 1834;
From Harlem to Williamsbridge, September 3, 1842;
From Williamsbridge to White Plains, December 1, 1844;
From White Plains to Croton Falls on June 1, 1847;
From Croton Falls to Dover Plains, December 31, 1848;
From Dover Plains to Chatham Four Corners, January 19, 1852;
The section extending southward from Prince Street to the City Hall was opened on May 4, 1839.
At Chatham Four Corners the road connected with the Albany and Westchester road.—Poore's "History of the Rail Roads and Canals of the United States of America, etc." New York, 1860. Vol. I (all published), pp. 287-288.
[4] "Railroad Journal." Vol. I, No. 47. New York, November 17, 1832, p. 737.

BEERS' TEMPERANCE HOTEL

THIRD STREET WEST,

North of Pennsylvania Avenue, and near the Railroad Depot,

WASHINGTON, D. C.

☞PRICES TO SUIT THE TIMES.☜

290.—Advertisement of a hostelry catering to railroad travellers and kept by a well-known temperance advocate of Washington. Date, 1851. Drunkenness was more common than at present, and travellers who objected to drinking and its attendant scenes preferred those few hotels where liquor was not sold.

the Bowery, with a view of the beautiful Cars of the Harlaem Railroad Company. We understand they were made by Miln Parker, coachmaker, of this city. They are spacious and convenient, being divided into three distinct apartments, each [apartment] amply large enough for eight, and can accommodate very conveniently ten persons—or twenty-four to thirty passengers inside; and, when we saw them, there were at least, we should think, an equal number upon, and hanging around the outside, the whole drawn by two fine horses abreast, at the rate of ten or twelve miles an hour. We admired their construction, and believe they are less liable to accident than most others we have seen, as the wheels are under the body. . . .

"We have now a specimen of Railroads in a busy, bustling street, and it will, we trust, satisfy those who have been apprehensive of danger from their introduction, that they are far more safe to the pedestrian than hacks and stages, as they pursue a direct, forward course, and usually at a uniform velocity.

"We consider this section of the Harlaem Railroad, now ready for use, the first link in a long line of railroad, which will, and at no distant period, connect this city with the far and fertile west, and we therefore wish to all who are concerned in it, success in the undertaking, a speedy completion of the work, and a liberal return for their investment."

In addition to the details of appearance mentioned by the article in the *Railroad Journal,* it may be said in description of the first cars on the New York and Harlem road that they possessed both springs and brakes. The springs were made of leather strips, riveted together in the manner used for making stage-coach thorough-braces. The brake was a friction-block, and was put in contact with the wheels by an arrangement which the driver operated with his feet. The driver himself sat on an elevated seat at the front of the car, just as the pilot of the stage-coach had done for many years.

During the building of the southern section of the road the location of a few miles of its track in one of the important streets caused apprehension in the public mind that numerous accidents would happen as the result of its operation. The officials of the road were naturally anxious to prove that any such alarm was groundless, and so they resolved that on the day appointed for the formal opening of the line they would give visible and conclusive proof that the heavy passenger coaches could be stopped almost instantly by the drivers, and that collisions between the cars and other vehicles need not be feared. The vice-president himself[1] took charge of affairs on the day of the opening and decided to run two cars along the tracks, one close behind the other, in order to produce a situation out of which a collision might result unless due care was exercised. But let it not be thought that it was his intention to have a mishap. He was arranging the stage and scenery, so to speak, for a dramatic proof that there need be no accident even under those conditions anticipated by the prospective travelling public. He chose for the driver of the first car one Lank O'Dell, a local character famed for his dexterity with the reins. The second car was entrusted to a hack driver. The passengers in the two vehicles were city dignitaries and other invited guests, of whom the mayor and members of the

[1] John Lozier.

city council rode behind O'Dell in the first car. Other municipal officials filled the second. At the appointed hour the streets were lined with enthusiastic citizens and away went the cavalcade.

O'Dell, in compliance with his instructions, urged his team into a sharp pace and the car containing the mayor and council bowled smoothly along, closely followed by its mate. Suddenly, at the appointed spot, O'Dell pressed heavily on the brake lever and brought his car to an abrupt stop. Vice-President Lozier instantly gave the agreed-upon signal which was to halt the second car also, but the hackman had become flustered over his temporary prominence as one of the central figures of the pageant, and instead of manipulating his brake he merely shouted "Whoa!" and pulled on the lines, just as he would have done if he had been sitting on his own hack. These precautions were insufficient to stop the heavy vehicle and the tongue of his car went smashing through the rear door of the one in front, while the mayor and council jumped off the front platform and climbed out of the windows. Nobody was hurt, and the procession was soon resumed.

New York City's first road was operated by horse power until about 1837, when locomotives were introduced on it and puffed their way through the streets of the town. The employment of steam on the road resulted in numerous accidents to pedestrians, and casualties of that sort soon came to be considered as inevitable. The somewhat callous sentiment of the time even looked upon such accidents as jokes, and the cartoonists made funny pictures showing the Bowery locomotives plowing their way unconcernedly through groups of men, women and children.

The New York and Harlem Railroad — because

some of its tracks lay in busy city streets — has often been considered as a street-railway in the modern understanding of that term. Such was not the fact. It was not built, and at no period in its history was it operated, as a railroad destined simply to carry city passenger traffic back and forth. As the *Railroad Journal* said in its article before quoted, the enterprise was considered "the first link in a long line of railroad, which will, and at no distant period, connect this city with the far and fertile West." It merely happened that the first of its trackage was laid in a city street, and it was no more a street-railway than were other similar early railroads in the highways of Philadelphia and other large communities, whether they were operated by horse power or by locomotives.

During the third and fourth decades no American city presented a problem of distinctively urban passenger movement that called for the creation of local railway facilities exclusively for its accommodation, although such a condition was slowly approaching. At that time all city passenger traffic along established routes was carried in stages and omnibuses.[1] The nature of the railroad tracks universally in use during the years under consideration made it impossible to build the sort of street railways ultimately destined for city traffic. The rails of those days — whether of wood or iron — stood up several inches above the surface of the ground, and the laying of such tracks throughout a city would have created serious barriers to all wheel traffic desiring to cross the thoroughfares so occupied. Street railways, as we understand them, could not exist until after the invention of

[1] Elsewhere is reproduced a scene in lower Broadway, New York City, showing the city stages which at that time occupied the place now held by street-cars. Examples of the metallic tickets used in connection with such city stage lines are also reproduced.

the low or sunken rail whose surface permit the use of

291.—Conditions in New York City. Aspect of lower Manhattan in 1850. Castle Garden was on an island reached by a bridge. The church at the left is Trinity. Windows of adjoining office buildings now look down upon its spire. Engraved by Poppel from a drawing by the artist Julius Kimmer.

the low or sunken rail whose surface permits the use of cars while offering little interference to other street movement.

The third of the railroads mentioned whose opening for traffic fell within the year 1832 was the Camden and Amboy, which was chartered in 1830 and finished for a distance of fourteen miles between Bordentown and Hightstown on December 22 of 1832.[1] The principal historical interest attaching to this early iron highway lies in its economic relation to the people who used it, rather than in any curious or picturesque phases of its operation. For many years it held an unparallelled place in the transportation system of the country, and the main features of that position can best be outlined by quoting certain words[2] which dealt with it at the comparatively late date of 1860. The statement ran:

"This road is probably the most productive work of the kind ever constructed. It has paid dividends averaging nearly 12 per cent. annually for twenty-seven years, accumulating in the meantime a very large surplus. Its extraordinary revenues are in a great measure due to the monopoly it enjoys of the right of way between the cities of New York and Philadelphia. This monopoly was not created in the act incorporating the Company, but was subsequently purchased by a grant to the State of stock in the road to the amount of $200,000, and by an agreement to pay certain transit duties on persons and property passing through its territory. The parties connected with this work were not long in perceiving the value of the exclusive right of way across the State, which may be regarded as the key to the great routes of commerce and travel for the whole country, with the power to levy exorbitant tolls. The State became a willing party to the scheme, under the idea that it could thereby draw the means for supporting its government from citizens of other States, thus relieving its own from the burdens of taxation. Such a result has been gained. The State now derives a revenue of over $200,000 annually from transit duties and dividends on the stock

[1] One part of the track between Bordentown and Hightstown was opened for travel late in 1831, and the English locomotive named "John Bull"—previously mentioned in connection with Baldwin's work—was then used in pulling a passenger train for a few miles. This was the first locomotive and train operated in New Jersey. The road was completed between the towns of South Amboy and Camden, a distance of 61 miles, in 1834.
[2] From "History of the Railroads and Canals of the United States of America, etc." By Henry D. Poore. Vol. I. New York, 1860, pp. 377-387.

presented to it. The effect, however, has been to build up within it a power, to which, in all matters touching real or fancied interest, the Legislature itself is the subordinate one—no act being allowed to pass that body against the wishes of the Company. Such a relationship, however, cannot exist without serious injury to the moral and material welfare of the people of the State. It is fortunate that this policy of imposing a tax for the privilege of passing through its territory is confined to two States—New Jersey and Maryland—otherwise the internal commerce of the country might be almost entirely destroyed, and our States converted into hostile communities, intent only in plundering each other. . . . Although there is no doubt that the State of New Jersey has suffered vastly more than she has gained by the monopoly, the prospective advantages of a liberal policy, necessary to a full development of the energies and resources of the State, weigh nothing against an absolute payment of more than $200,000 annually. The total amount received into the State Treasury from transit duties and dividends on its stock, . . . has been $3,870,250. This Company makes no reports, except the meagre ones to the Legislature. It has published no general statement for twenty years past, so that nothing can be known as to the conditions of its affairs. All inquiries for information, even to the amount of equipment on the road, were refused. . . . The Company is the paramount authority in the State, dictating the legislation upon all subjects in which it has a real or fancied interest."

The Camden and Amboy road closely followed one of the travel paths across New Jersey that had been in use for more than a century and a half. Its first history was that of a trail through the forest over which men made the journey between New Amsterdam and Philadelphia, either afoot or on horseback, in four or five days. Then came the introduction of the "Flying Machines" and those improved sailing vessels designed to carry travellers from Amboy across New York Bay to New York City. Following the Flying Machine wagons came the regular lines of real stage-coaches, which gradually decreased the time necessary in passing between the two cities, and finally a railed-track and mechanical contrivance in its turn supplanted the stage-coaches.

When the Camden and Amboy company was organized it chose for its president a man named Robert

L. Stevens, son of the John Stevens whose still earlier prominence in the building of steamboats and the advocacy of railroads has already been observed. Robert Stevens was sent to England soon after the company came into existence, and while there he ordered a locomotive for the New Jersey road. This was the *John Bull*. It reached Bordentown late in the year 1831, and its various parts were there assembled into working order — after Baldwin had studied them — by a young American machinist named Isaac Dripps, who had been chosen by Stevens to take charge of the mechanical details connected with the operation of the road. Young Dripps had never before seen a steam locomotive either in dismantled form or ready for use, but he nevertheless succeeded in putting the *John Bull* together and running it. No tender had been bought for the engine, and to rectify this oversight Dripps built a small flat car and attached to its platform an empty whisky cask bought from a grocery store. Then he found it necessary to connect his extemporized water tank with the engine, and to accomplish this purpose he hired a Bordentown shoemaker to make a hose out of leather. When the tender was further equipped with a box full of wood the engine was ready for service. The first passenger cars on the Camden and Amboy road were of the type resembling three stagecoach bodies united into one vehicle, with entrance at the sides.

When the road had been finished between Amboy on New York Bay and Bordentown on the Delaware River, the traveller between New York and Philadelphia could make his trip in this manner:

By steamboat from New York City to Amboy, a distance of twenty-three miles;

NEW-YORK & ALBANY RAIL-ROAD.

New-York, March 24, 1842.

Sir,—

Your attention to the subject of the following proceedings, is earnestly solicited, from the interest which it is presumed that you, in common with us, must feel in restoring and maintaining the prosperity of our City.

We believe that the immediate construction of a RAIL ROAD, between New-York and Albany, is absolutely necessary, to the Commercial and Landed interests of New-York,—and that such a ROAD can be constructed, as will not only secure to us the benefits of our heretofore unrivalled position, but will also produce a large income upon its cost to the Stockholders.

The enterprising citizens of Boston, have deemed it *their* interest, to expend upwards of nine millions of dollars, to effect a direct intercourse, over an almost impracticable country, between Boston and Albany, and thus compete with us, for the trade of the North and West. Less than one third of this sum, will construct a better ROAD between New-York and Albany: and only one million of dollars, towards this amount is required from this City. Can it be that New-York, with four times the population will not make the effort, to preserve the trade which our enterprising neighbors are seeking to divert,—and which if once diverted into new channels may never return to us.

292.—The Hudson River Railroad had been commenced in 1847 as a result of the agitation begun by this address, which was signed by thirteen prominent men of the city. It was finished and equipped in 1851, at a cost of $9,305,551, thereby connecting New York with the chain of little railways extending westward from Albany to Buffalo. All of these, whose capital stock amounted to $22,858,600, and the Hudson River line, were finally combined under one corporate ownership, and unbroken railroad trips from New York to Lake Erie became possible.

A HISTORY OF TRAVEL IN AMERICA

By railroad cars from Amboy to Bordentown, a distance of thirty-six miles;

By steamboat from Bordentown to Philadelphia, a distance of twenty-eight miles.

The road was soon afterward completed at its western end to Camden — opposite Philadelphia — and its eastern end was carried up to Jersey City, opposite New York, finally providing an all-rail method of conveyance across the entire width of New Jersey, after that path of travel had been consistently used by men in various ways for about one hundred and sixty years.

The following description outlines the conditions attending the use of this travel route after steam power had come into use over its whole extent:[1]

"The steam-boats depart from the piers in the Hudson River near the Battery, at six o'clock in the morning in summer, and at seven in the fall and in the cold season. . . .

"A busy scene ensues immediately after leaving the dock in New-York, from the crowding of passengers to the office window to pay the fare, $3.00, and to arrange for the seats in the rail cars; on this the comfort and pleasure much depend of a party of ladies or gentlemen, and this should, if possible, be attended to immediately, before or after starting, or even the day previous . . . . as the hurry and press is at times on this occasion disagreeable. . . .

"On arriving at South Amboy, the cars and locos will be found in readiness on the wharf; the ascent soon enters a line of deep cutting through the sand-hills, and continues in a barren and uninteresting region to Hubertsville, Hightstown, Spotswood, and Centreville, 36 miles to Bordentown, on the Delaware River. . . .

"The cars make a pause at the depot on the banks of the Delaware, and a change of conveyance takes place usually to the steam-boat, down the river to Philadelphia, although the rail-road is continued on the east side of the river, 28 miles, to Camden. The change in the mode of getting on from Bordentown, for the remaining distance by water of 30 miles, will be grateful, and will, like the part just traveled on the rails, occupy about two hours and a half very agreeably. . . .

"The entire and direct rail-road route that is now completed between New-York and Philadelphia . . . pursues very nearly the old-established

[1] From the "North American Tourist." New York, 1839, pp. 352-357.

revolutionary stage route, avoiding all water or steam-boat transfer from the land, and vice versa, but, in four or five hours quietly taking up the traveler in one of the principal cities referred to, at either end of the rail-road, and setting him down and transplanting him in all possible ease and luxury at the opposite extremity, a distance of 94 miles. . . . The first or six o'clock line of passengers from New-York will arrive at Philadelphia at three o'clock P. M. by the steam-boat.

"The second route from New-York to Philadelphia, leading by rail-road through Newark, Elizabethtown, and New Brunswick, . . . passes very nearly along the line of the old post-road, more in the interior of the State than the first route, and reaching Philadelphia at an early hour in the afternoon, fare $4.00."

The builders of the Camden and Amboy road were not content with the monopoly of railway travel between New York and Philadelphia obtained by them from New Jersey and already described. The road sought to further fortify its position by gaining control of a competing canal and some turnpike roads extending east and west in its vicinity. The canal,[1] in connection with the Delaware and Raritan Rivers and Staten Island Sound, formed a complete inland water communication between Philadelphia and New York. It was begun in 1831 by a joint stock company which in the same year was united with the Camden and Amboy Railroad company, and under this general management the waterway was continued and finally completed in 1838.

The connection between the railroad company and the Delaware and Raritan Canal, and between it and certain of the turnpikes in the neighborhood of the railway, was thus described in 1838:[2]

"The Company have also been allowed to take the stock authorized to be raised for cutting a canal from the Delaware to the Raritan river, and have purchased out all the turnpike companies from the one to the other, and thus secured to themselves the monopoly of the transit business of every kind during the continuance of their charter (50 years).

"It is proper, however, to add that the State has reserved one thou-

[1] Called the Delaware and Raritan Canal.
[2] In "The Traveller's Guide." Saratoga, 1838.

sand shares of the stock, amounting to $10,000 [$100,000], and has received from the Company a guaranty for the payment of $30,000 annually."

Another reference to this first of all American instances exhibiting the greed, political methods and mismanagement of privately owned railways reads:[1]

"By the terms of the charter which prohibits the construction of any other road within five miles of the one now in use, this company enjoys a complete monopoly in the conveyance of passengers and merchandise between Philadelphia and New York. The number of the former is immense, averaging during the travelling season about one thousand daily."

The three earliest railways of consequence in New England were all Massachusetts projects. They were the Boston and Lowell, the Boston and Providence and the Boston and Worcester roads. Massachusetts and the rest of New England had been a little slower than some other parts of the country in accepting the value of the new transportation system as a proved fact, and were likewise equally deliberate in the building of such enterprises after they had been determined upon. Although all the railroads heretofore mentioned — together with several others — had been created either in whole or in part, and were in operation either by steam or horse power, it was not until late in March of the year 1834 that a steam locomotive appeared in that part of the country where the travel impulse of the people had been born and whence it had spread until a third of the continent's width had finally been overrun and settled.

But when Massachusetts did decide to go ahead she undertook three important works at practically the same time, and advanced with their building at such a uniform gait that all three were finished in three years and

[1] Tanner's "Description," p. 90.

were opened for business throughout their entire extent within a period embraced by twenty-two days. The first of the Massachusetts roads to be chartered was the Boston and Lowell company, which was legally born on June 8, 1830. Both the other roads obtained legislative authori-

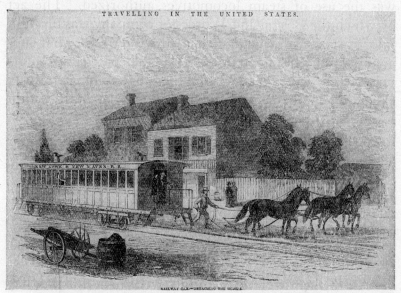

TRAVELLING IN THE UNITED STATES.

293.—Meanwhile the New York and New Haven Railroad had entered New York City and was using the tracks of the Harlem Railway. Permission for the physical junction had been given by New York State in 1846, and the necessary track laying was finished in 1848. Passenger cars of the New Haven line were pulled through the city streets by horses, and assembled into a train on Fourth Avenue, near the southern end of the tunnel shown in illustrations 248 and 295.

zation during the following year; the Boston and Providence being chartered on June 22, 1831, and the Boston and Worcester on the following day. As has before been said, the opinion of England that steam power would prove unreliable on railed tracks was reflected in New England for about a year after a contrary belief had been accepted in South Carolina and perhaps in one or

997

two other American states. The laws that created the Boston and Lowell and the Boston and Providence lines contained nothing indicative of the contemplated use of steam power upon them, and only in the charter granted to the Boston and Worcester road, on June 23, 1831, was the use of steam locomotives authorized. The act by which the Boston and Worcester company was brought into existence also contained a provision somewhat monopolistic in character in so far as that particular enterprise was concerned, for it provided that no other railway extending in the same direction should be built within five miles of the route allotted to it.

Construction work on the Boston and Lowell road was commenced November 28, 1831, and the building of the other two Massachusetts lines began in the latter part of 1832.[1] The lengths of these three railways as originally constructed were as follows:

The main line of the Boston and Lowell road .... 26.7 miles
The main line of the Boston and Providence road .... 43.50 miles
The main line of the Boston and Worcester road ..... 44.63 miles

All of them were exceedingly well made for that day and generation. Two of them, indeed, were altogether too well built, for the Boston and Lowell and Boston and Worcester enterprises used a great deal of stone as foundations for the rails, and the resultant structures were discovered to be entirely too rigid and inelastic for obtaining the best results in operation. The Boston and Providence company was fortunate enough to use wooden ties from the first, thereby escaping the necessity of much

[1] The first section of the Boston and Providence Road to be completed was that between Boston and Canton, fourteen miles, in 1834. The whole road was opened for public use on June 27, 1835.
    The first division of the Boston and Worcester Road to be finished was that between Boston and Newton, nine miles, on April 16, 1832. The road was completed to Needham, 13½ miles, on July 3; to Hopkinton (Ashland), 24 miles, on September 20; and to Westboro, 32 miles, on November 15, 1834. The public opening of the whole line to Worcester took place July 3, 1835.

roadbed reconstruction. This good fortune on its part was due to the shrewdness of an engineer who had been sent to England to study the newly built Manchester and Liverpool road. He detected the track rigidity produced by the use of stone in the foreign undertaking and avoided a repetition of the same blunder when he came back home to take charge of the work under his direction. The method of roadbed making employed by the Boston and Providence company furnished another instance wherein America declined to blindly follow English precedent and profited by the employment of its own ideas. In discussing the building of this and other early American railways a native student of the subject[1] afterward said:

"They were all well-built roads, especially that to Lowell, in the construction of which the Manchester & Liverpool precedents had been so closely followed that the serious error was committed of laying the rails on stone blocks instead of wooden ties. It is, indeed, matter of curious observation that almost uniformly those early railroad builders made grave blunders whenever they tried to do their work peculiarly well; they also invariably had afterwards to undo it."

All three of the early Massachusetts railways at first used horse-drawn cars on such sections of the roads as were opened for travel over short distances, but on March 24, 1834, the Boston *Advertiser* contained the following news announcement relating to the road in progress toward Worcester:

"The rails are laid from Boston to Newton, a distance of nine or ten miles, to which place it is proposed to run the passenger cars as soon as two locomotives shall be in readiness, so as to insure regularity. One locomotive, called the 'Meteor,' has been partially tried and will probably be in readiness in a few days; the second, called the 'Rocket,' is waiting the arrival of the builder for subjecting it to a trial, and the third, it is hoped, will be ready by the first of May."

[1] Charles Francis Adams, Jr., in his "Railroads: Their Origin and Problems," pp. 74-75.

SCENE IN CENTRE STREET, NEW YORK CITY, DURING THE LATE SNOW STORM.

294.—In winter time the process of making up a New England bound train in New York City was often attended with much difficulty. A scene in Centre Street, while a dozen or more horses were trying to haul a passenger car past the city prison called "The Tombs." Same period as the foregoing.

The first trip performed by steam between Boston and Newton was probably made on April 7th, on which occasion the directors of the company and more than fifty passengers enjoyed the journey. The same newspaper described the event in the following words:

"The party stopped several times for various purposes on the way out. They returned in thirty-nine minutes, including a stop of about six minutes for the purpose of attaching five cars loaded with earth. The engine travelled with ease at the rate of twenty miles an hour."

So elated were the officials over this successful test of their rolling stock that a still larger party was invited to repeat it on the following day. About one hundred and thirty passengers then crowded the cars, and they appear to have been overloaded, for the iron bars by which the cars were held together continually kept breaking, and the return was not finished until night. After this mishap several weeks were spent in improving the equipment, and on May 15th a very successful excursion took place in which six cars, containing about twenty passengers each, were pulled from Boston to Newton and back without accident. The return trip consumed less than half an hour. Two trains for the accommodation of the public were put into operation on the following day, and regular railroad passenger service in New England, therefore, began on May 16th. The advertisements published in the daily newspapers by the Boston and Worcester road at that time made the following announcements:

"The passenger cars will continue to run daily from the depot near Washington St., to Newton, at 6 o'clock and 10 o'clock A. M ., and at 3½ o'clock P. M., and

"Returning, leave Newton at 7, and a quarter past 11 A. M., and a quarter before 5 P. M.

"Tickets for the passage either way may be had at the Ticket Office, No. 617 Washington St., price thirty-seven and a half cents each; and for the return passage, of the Master of the Cars,[1] Newton."

Seven passenger cars, thronged by two hundred people and drawn by the locomotive *Yankee* were moved from Boston to Hopkinton on September 20, and on November 15 the opening of the road to Westborough was similarly celebrated. On that occasion it was arranged for trains to start from each end of the road as far as completed, and they were to meet and pass each other at the town of Needham, but a strong wind was blowing from the east that day and so one of the trains — drawn by the *Meteor* — found it hard work to fight the gale and was much delayed. The other train adhered to its schedule and had no trouble in reaching Needham on time. There

[1] It thus appears that the functionary now known as the conductor was at first sometimes called the "Master of the Cars."

CARS TAKING ENGINE FROM NEW YORK TO BOSTON.

295.—Eventually all the cars, containing passengers picked up along the way, reached the designated place of assembly. Then the horses were unhitched, the cars were coupled, the locomotive was attached, and the completed train started on its northward journey. In the course of time a large passenger station called the Grand Central Depot was built on 42nd Street, at the farther end of the tunnel here shown, and the Hudson River and New Haven trains thereafter departed from it. These two railways were for many years the only ones which had access to Manhattan Island. All other roads were halted by the surrounding waters, and conveyed their passengers to the city on ferry boats.

it waited for a while according to the plan agreed on, but at last grew impatient and continued along the single track. After running four miles farther it saw the *Meteor* coming from the opposite direction and was compelled to stop and go back to Needham again. As a consequence of these unforeseen complications the train from Boston to Westborough required three hours to finish its journey.

The first train to go over the whole road from Boston to Worcester consisted of a locomotive and one passenger car, and the trip was made on July 3rd, 1835. That date was chosen in order that the public opening of the road might occur on the national festival next day, and on the Fourth of July each of the four locomotives belonging to the company made two round trips between the two cities, pulling eleven passenger cars behind them. More than fifteen hundred travellers availed themselves of the service offered during the first day of the road's operation for its entire length. The civic festivities invariably accompanying the dedication of such a work took place two days afterward, when a train of twelve cars drawn by two engines was run from Boston to Worcester carrying a distinguished company of more than three hundred people. The following contemporary comment on the completion of the enterprise was printed by a newspaper already quoted:[1]

"The road was opened on the 4th of this month. It has a single iron track, laid upon cross sticks of chestnut, oak, etc., laid upon rubble, but is graded in most places for two. . . . The road is 44 miles in length, and the usual passage is performed in 2½ or 3 hours, including stoppages. The cars having to stop at several towns, tends to prolong the time of the passage, though a few years since, 14 miles an hour would have been considered rapid travelling. The cars now pass each way three times a day, and their rate of travelling is so well calculated as to cause but very little delay at the meeting place in Framingham. . . . The price charged for passengers from Boston to Worcester on the Rail Road is $1.50—formerly by the stages $2.

"So great are the advantages gained, that already one of the principal dealers here [Worcester] has offered to lay a side track from the road to his own storehouse and unload his goods himself, for his permission. In fact, so great and so numerous are the advantages of rail roads, that it only requires one to witness their beneficial effects wherever they are constructed, to become convinced of their utility. . . . A person in business here informed me that he left Worcester one day in the 12 o'clock car—arrived in Boston—had 1¼ hour to transact his business—that he returned by the 4 o'clock car, and arrived here at 7 o'clock in the evening—thus travelling 88 miles in 8¾ hours;—whereas it formerly required one day to go to Boston, a second day was consumed there, and a third employed in returning. . . .

"Some of the passenger cars on this road are very elegant, and will hold from twenty to thirty persons. . . . The motion of the cars upon

[1]The "Maine Farmer," July 18.

1003

the road is so easy that I saw a little child walking from seat to seat, as if in a parlor."

The first cars that traversed the Boston and Providence road from one end to the other moved over the line on June 2nd, 1835. It had been intended to make the trip by steam power, but the locomotive owned by the road could not be induced to run successfully and the two cars accordingly set forth behind horses. On the same day that witnessed the inauguration of railway travel between Boston and Providence there took place another important event in the annals of American travel.

THE JERSEY CITY FERRY BOAT, FROM NEW YORK.

296.—A New York ferry boat of the days when a majority of the people who entered the city were carried by such craft across the Hudson and East Rivers. The print suggests rashness on the part of numerous passengers, and small regard for their safety.

One of the purposes inspiring the building of the Boston and Providence road was a desire to lessen the time consumed in journeying from Boston to New York, and an arrangement had been made between that company and an enterprising steamboat proprietor named Cornelius Vanderbilt under the terms of which Vanderbilt was to run boats from Providence to New York in close connection with the service afforded by the new steam railroad. The steamboat man had fulfilled his share of the compact by the building of a new and splendid vessel called the *Lexington*,[1] and her first trip between Providence and New York was likewise made on June 2nd of 1835. Those Boston travellers who desired to catch the *Lexington* at Providence left Boston at two o'clock in the morning by stage-coach, embarked on the boat at Providence and arrived in New York at six o'clock, P.M. after a water trip of about twelve hours, having left Boston less than sixteen hours before. This was the swiftest passage ever made between the two cities up to that time.

As soon as the locomotive of the Boston and Providence line was put in good running order a schedule of traffic was adopted, and the hitherto extraordinary feat performed on June 2nd was in its turn eclipsed through the instrumentality of steam movement on land between the Massachusetts and Rhode Island cities. This method of journeying from New England to New York at once superseded the old manner of stage-coach conveyance and continued in use until Boston and New York were finally united by an all-rail route in December of 1848.

[1] The later destruction of this steamboat by fire on Long Island Sound, on January 12, 1840, was one of the most memorable American disasters of the sort up to that time. About 120 persons perished. In accordance with the custom of the period a lurid "Accident Broadside" of the calamity was at once prepared and issued for public sale. A copy of the "Lexington Broadside" is reproduced elsewhere.

That use of the new railroad was unpopular with some people, however, the following passage contained in the diary of a traveller[1] from Boston to Providence will show:

"July 22, 1835 . . . Five or six other cars were attached to the locomotive, and uglier boxes I do not wish to travel in. They were made to stow away some thirty human beings, who sit cheek by jowl as best they can. Two poor fellows, who were not much in the habit of making their toilet, squeezed me into a corner, while the hot sun drew from their garments a villainous compound of smells made up of salt fish, tar and molasses. By and by, just twelve—only twelve—bouncing factory girls were introduced, who were going on a party of pleasure to Newport. 'Make room for the ladies!' bawled out the superintendent. 'Come, gentlemen, jump up on the top; plenty of room there.' 'I'm afraid of the bridge knocking my brains out,' said a passenger. Some made one excuse and some another. For my part, I flatly told him . . . I had lost my gallantry, and did not intend to move. The whole twelve were, however, introduced, and soon made themselves at home, sucking lemons and eating green apples. . . . The rich and the poor, the educated and the ignorant, the polite and the vulgar, all herd together in this modern improvement in travelling. The consequence is a complete amalgamation. Master and servant sleep heads and points on the cabin floor of the steamer, feed at the same table, sit in each other's laps, as it were, in the cars; and all this for the sake of doing very uncomfortably in two days what would be done delightfully in eight or ten. . . . Talk of ladies on a steamboat or in a railroad car! There are none. I never feel like a gentleman there, and I cannot perceive a semblance of gentility in any one who makes part of the travelling mob. When I see women whom, in their drawing-rooms or elsewhere, I have been accustomed to respect and treat with every suitable deference,—when I see them, I say, elbowing their way through a crowd of dirty emigrants or low-bred homespun fellows in petticoats or breeches in our country, in order to reach a table spread for a hundred or more, I lose sight of their pretensions to gentility and view them as belonging to the plebeian herd. To restore herself to her caste, let a lady move in select company at five miles an hour, and take her meals in comfort at a good inn, where she may dine decently. . . . The old-fashioned way of five or six miles with liberty to . . . be master of one's movements, . . . is the mode to which I cling, and which will be adopted again by the generations of after times."

The opening of the first three Massachusetts roads completes in some of its features the picture of incidents

[1] "Recollections of Samuel Breck," pp. 275-277.

and experiences connected with travel by railway during the earliest years of that means of locomotion in America. It was inevitable that the employment of railroads in this country should first occur chiefly in those older and more thickly settled commonwealths that had also witnessed, in former days, the introduction of almost all methods of conveyance hitherto employed by the people in their movements. The first canoes, sailing-boats, dog-sleds and burden beasts had been employed along the Atlantic coast region two centuries before. Those vehicles had given way to the keel-boats, barges, pack-trains, arks, Conestoga wagons and Flying Machines, and by them the various scattered communities and their inhabitants had gradually been knit more closely together. Then came the periodic stage-coaches and the steamboats, and with their advent the people for a time believed the millennium of travel facilities had been attained. Up to that time only the covered flatboat of the interior rivers furnished a type of vehicle not beheld in active use in the East. Next came the canal and its packet-boats, destined to hold their sway but for a few years and in limited areas. Finally the steam railway had appeared, and with it a conviction in the public mind that the railed track and vehicles fitted for operation on it were destined to supplant all other methods of locomotion and transportation for a long time to come. Each previous vehicle-era had arisen in the East, reached its maturity there and gradually declined, only to be revived again in a region still farther to the westward during the years of its decay in the East. The railroad had come at last, and like its predecessors was fast fixing its grip on the older communities, whence it was in due course to follow the westward progress of all the devices it had dethroned.

CHAPTER XLV

AN UNEXPECTED DEMAND FOR TRAVEL FACILITIES — ITS EFFECT — FROM FENCE-RAIL TO AUTOMATIC COUPLER — EVOLUTION OF THE AMERICAN PASSENGER COACH — DESCRIPTIONS OF EARLY COACHES — CARS WITH UPPER DECKS, CUPOLAS, FLAGS AND BAR-ROOMS — A STANDARD PASSENGER VEHICLE FINALLY EVOLVED — CAPTAIN VERSUS ENGINEER — CAPTAIN AYRES INVENTS THE BELL-ROPE AND HAS A FIGHT — CONSEQUENCES OF THE COMBAT — EARLY SIGNAL SYSTEMS — STOPPING AN ENGINE — THE SIGNAL POLE — THE ORIGIN OF SOME RAILWAY EQUIPMENT AND PRACTISES

THE records say that when the first train on the Mohawk and Hudson Railroad was ready to begin its first public trip to Schenectady, carrying several car loads of passengers, the captain felt impelled to announce the impending departure by blowing a loud blast on a tin horn. From time immemorial that had been the proper way to start a passenger-carrying barge, a flatboat, a stage-coach or a packet canal boat. The mere fact that a new method of human transportation had come into use did not appear to constitute any valid reason for an alteration in those ceremonies that had always attended the commencement of a journey in a public vehicle.

The occasion in question, as the story of that peculiar day well indicates, formed one of the evolutionary links in

1008

a long and interesting chain of railway development. When railroads first began to appear in America their actual builders had no comprehension of the extent to which the new device would be used for the purpose of public travel. In that respect the history of the early days of railroads resembled the similar annals of the canal period, although the use of railroads for human movement—in proportion to the degree of its anticipation—was destined vastly to exceed the similar utilization of the canal boat. Before the iron highways came into existence the usual stream of human traffic between the cities of Baltimore and Washington was composed of less than fifty people a day, but no sooner was a railway completed between the two towns named than it found itself obliged to provide accommodations for two hundred and fifty people each day. A similar experience befell every new road as soon as it was ready for use.

Before the opening of the rail route between Charleston and Hamburg, in South Carolina, the demands of passenger traffic between those towns had been amply met by a two-seated stage-coach which departed three times a week each way. After the two places had been connected by a railroad, and during the six months ending December 16, 1835, no less than 15,959 passengers made the identical trip by rail, and the aggregate cost of their tickets amounted to $53,819.66.[1] This was an average of more than two thousand five hundred passengers a month, in comparison to a movement of perhaps fifty people each month before the railroad was built. The number of passengers carried by the Baltimore and Ohio Railroad during the year 1835 was no less than 97,786[2]; al-

---

[1] H. L. Barnam's "Reply to the President of the Ohio and Indianapolis Railroad Company." Jeffersonville, Ind., 1837.
[2] Ibid.

though its tracks were then only sixty or seventy miles long and had no western terminus of population importance. During the one month of August, in 1836, the receipts derived from passenger travel by the newly opened and short steam line between the towns of Schenec-

297.—The shape of New York City, combined with its size, had already made the daily movements of its population an important problem which pressed for solution. Tens of thousands hurried southward at the same hour in the morning, and all rushed northward together again in the evening. The stages and omnibuses could not carry the throngs, and as early as 1840 there began a discussion regarding the feasibility of building an elevated railway through the streets. This is a pictorial suggestion of such a plan, published about 1842.

tady and Utica, in New York State, amounted to $43,676.91.[1]

Every new eastern railroad as it was completed furnished similar evidence of the existence of a desire for travel to which its creation gave an outlet. This was afterwards as true of the first railways of the interior as

[1] Ibid.

it had been of the East. A like experience of the early
Indiana roads was thus described in 1852:

"The large and greatly increasing amount of travel upon the Indianapolis and Madison road is well understood by the public. In 1850
the number of passengers over that road was 64,986. In 1851 the number was 71,432. . . . The few weeks' experience on the Terre Haute
road affords abundant evidence of what is to be the result when all the
lines projected from Indianapolis are completed. Heretofore a nine-
passenger stage coach each way, daily, was sufficient to accommodate all
the travel between Terre Haute and Indianapolis; now the Rail Road
is carrying 100 passengers each way, per day."[1]

This sure proof of the people's craving for a means
of swifter travel was thus suddenly indicated with almost the violence of an explosion, and its influence upon
railroads and their equipment was immediately visible.
The crude tracks, engines and cars at first employed were
obviously inadequate, and American ingenuity was taxed
to meet the emergency.

None of the innumerable devices and conveniences
used to-day in connection with railroad travel, or that now
form component and indispensable parts of the cars and
trains with which we are familiar, sprang full fledged and
perfect into existence. Nearly all of them, on the contrary, had their origin in expedients devised by fertile
brains as a result of the necessities disclosed by accidents or other unforeseen occurrences. The trip of the
first train between Albany and Schenectady, for instance,
demonstrated two things conclusively. It proved that
railroad cars could not safely be connected by any method
which enabled one of them to move independently of the
others, even for a distance measured by inches. The
bumpings and car collisions which took place that day due
to the use of chains two or three feet long between the

[1] George H. Dunn's "Exhibit of the Lawrenceburg and Upper Mississippi Railroad
Company," n. d. (1837).

various vehicles, showed that a train of cars must be considered as one mechanism, and that when movement was imparted to it or taken from it, the motion should be applied or diminished in a practically instantaneous manner along the entire length of the train. This particular forward step in the practical business of railway construction was discovered by the travelling public before it was realized by the railway authorities themselves, and the method that was taken by passengers in remedying the defect has been described. From that date—as rapidly as suitable processes could be devised—railroad cars were attached to one another by means that made the entire train a moving unit. The result was at first accomplished through connecting the cars by iron bars. But the iron bars sometimes broke, as happened on the Boston and Worcester road when the train was overloaded with people, and they were gradually made of still greater strength and so continued in use until the single-link coupler and coupling pin were invented. That plan in turn prevailed until an automatic locking device was designed for coupling purposes.

The few cars that had been provided by the first railroads for such slight passenger traffic as was expected proved entirely unequal to the demands made upon them. The earliest coaches were small in size and sometimes consisted of stage-coach bodies transferred to appropriate wheels. Others were specially built affairs resembling stage-coaches but somewhat larger in size, and still others were rough vehicles made of heavy timbers and lumber, possessing wagon beds which bore some faint resemblance to the lower structure of the Conestoga wagon. The flat roofs of the last variety described were supported by vertical timbers rising from the sides of the wagon beds.

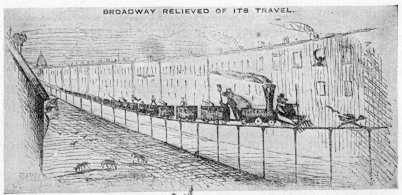

BROADWAY RELIEVED OF ITS TRAVEL.

298.—A cartoonist's idea of an elevated railroad in Broadway, printed about the same time as the foregoing.

The first passenger car on the Baltimore and Ohio Railroad was a three-seated stage-coach body mounted on special wheels, with leather thorough-braces for springs.[1] This vehicle was used for a short time early in 1830, but was discarded in favor of a vastly improved car described in one of the local newspapers[2] in these words:

"The body of the carriage will contain twelve persons, and the outside seats and both ends will receive six including the driver. On the top of the carriage is placed a double sofa running lengthwise, which will accommodate twelve more. A wire netting rises from two sides of the carriage to a height which renders the top seats perfectly secure. The whole is surmounted by an iron framework and an awning to protect from sun or rain. The carriage, which is named the 'Ohio,' is very handsomely finished."

Such a car, pulled by two horses, is shown on another page. The early woodcut from which the illustration is made was drawn and engraved by the Philadelphia artist, Alexander Robb. It displays a coach containing about twelve persons on the inside, with a double sofa extending along the roof, as well as the wire net, iron framework

[1] This does not take into consideration a car "not unlike a country market-wagon, without a top," which was used for experimental purposes when only one mile of track had been laid down.—See Latrobe's "Personal Recollections," pp. 12-20.
[2] Baltimore "American," August 5, 1830.

and awning mentioned in the newspaper account here quoted. Several other early American woodcuts, lithographs and copperplate engravings, of dates from about 1830 to 1835, and which are reproduced elsewhere, show a very similar type of early passenger car. It is quite possible that the coach thus used on the Baltimore and Ohio Railroad in 1830 was adopted or copied on some of the other lines opened for traffic between the years named.

It is apparent from official records of the Baltimore and Ohio road that neither the car here described nor those that followed it during the succeeding year were equipped with springs, since the report of the chief engineer of the road[1] for the year ending with September 30, 1831, contained this comment:

"It has been found absolutely necessary to the comfort of the passengers that carriages used for their conveyance should be mounted on springs or on some equivalent elastic fixtures. The jars and concussions that destroy the comfort of the passengers become increased with a load of stone, minerals or agriculture or with any other loading having a less elasticity than persons, and although the articles of traffic may not be damaged, yet the effects upon the carriage and road will be injurious. The chief disadvantage to be apprehended from springs is their cost. . . ."

Two or three years after the first section of the Baltimore and Ohio Railroad was opened for traffic there appeared on it a passenger car resting on eight wheels. This was a large, rectangular, box-like structure with the upper-deck arrangement previously described, and with a ladder at one of the rear corners for the use of passengers in reaching the seats on the roof. It is probable that the vehicle was the first eight-wheeled passenger car built in the country,[2] and in later years the question of its priority

[1] Jonathan Knight.
[2] It was designed and constructed by the civil engineer, Ross Winans.

Elevated Railway, Ninth Avenue.

299.—New York City's first elevated railway, as it appeared when built, many years afterward.

in the feature named formed the basis of an important legal dispute which was eventually decided against the originator of the Baltimore and Ohio conveyance. Evidence was produced at the trial indicating that four-wheel trucks had sometimes been put under the little flat cars devoted to the hauling of granite on the private Quincy railroad, in Massachusetts, during the years 1826-27. So the idea of employing eight wheels instead of four as a support for the body of a railroad car had been in use before it was applied on the Baltimore and Ohio, although not for passenger traffic.

An early vehicle placed on the New York and Harlem Railroad, in 1832, was thus described by its builder:[1]

"The car consisted of three separate compartments, each compartment holding ten persons, and being entered by separate doors, on the

[1] John Stephenson. From the construction of this car there afterward grew a private car building enterprise that was identified with American railroad history for many years.

side, from a guard-rail. Seats were provided on top of the car for thirty more persons. The car was very much like the English railway coach, though it was considerably lower. It was hauled by a team of horses, the conductor remaining outside on the rail, rain or shine. The company for which it was built was called the New York and Harlem Road, running from Prince Street, on the Bowery, along the line of the Bowery to Fourteenth Street, thence along the line of the present Fourth Avenue to Yorkville and Harlem."[1]

The primitive horse-drawn passenger cars employed on the Camden and Amboy Railroad were of the general type designed for the New York and Harlem enterprise, as were also the conveyances on several other of the railways opened for traffic between 1831 and 1835.

The original passenger cars on the Philadelphia, Germantown and Norristown Railroad are illustrated in a contemporaneous picture elsewhere reproduced. They were of the familiar stage-coach appearance—although not actually stage-coach bodies placed on trucks for railway use—and were pulled by horses, since the road did not possess a steam locomotive at the time they were first employed. The unknown artist who engraved the lithograph copied herein anticipated the future when he introduced an engine into his picture, and he also depicted an English railway locomotive very similar in appearance to Stephenson's *Rocket*. This was the road for which Baldwin built *Old Ironsides,* and two contemporary pictures of Baldwin's machine also show that passenger cars of the stage-coach pattern were still used by the Philadelphia, Germantown and Norristown line after steam power was introduced on it. The close resemblance between the Baltimore and Ohio passenger car described by the Baltimore *American* of August 5, 1830, and those

---

[1] A car resembling the description here given is shown on the small metallic ticket or medal of the New York and Harlem Railroad Company illustrated in these pages, and also in a woodcut drawn and engraved by the artist, Alexander Robb.
Stephenson's coach for the Harlem road was no doubt contemporary with the one described in the "Railroad Journal" of November 17, 1832, and mentioned in Chapter XLIV.

of similar type shown behind *Old Ironsides* two or three years afterward, suggests that perhaps the Pennsylvania road bought some of its cars from the same man who made the Baltimore and Ohio vehicle, or else copied it. There were only two or three builders of railroad cars in America

300.—Omnibuses and street-cars. The American omnibus was a modification of the previous stage-coach, and first vehicle used in connection with the periodic transportation of city populations. Adopted by many large towns during the period between 1835 and 1855. New York City's previous stages were doubtless the first omnibuses. The street-car, which appeared in the sixth decade, was a modified omnibus adapted to the railed track principle.

during the years in question, and the one used on the Baltimore and Ohio, and here mentioned, was constructed at the shops of Richard Imlay, in Philadelphia. It is likely that Imlay also built the first passenger cars used on the Philadelphia, Germantown and Norristown line, since his establishment was so near at hand.

As soon as it became apparent that the people wanted travel accommodations in excess of those first provided, the railroad companies set about the task of meeting the demands made upon them. They began to build bigger cars, though often they adhered to the original stage-coach idea therefor. This result was obtained by retaining the old lines of horse-vehicle construction and making the larger and longer vehicle appear as though it were composed of two or three stage-coach bodies joined together.[1] The seats for the passengers were sometimes situated as before, and extended across the vehicle from side to side. The trunks, hand-bags and other luggage of the travellers were still carried on the roof, which in most cases was surrounded by a wire netting or stout wooden lattice work erected to prevent such articles from being jolted overboard. Another feature of the stage-coach which was adopted by makers of the early cars was its gaudy decoration. The railroad vehicles were similarly painted in bright colors, and were endowed with individual names emblazoned on their doors or panels. All cars belonging to the same company were painted in a uniform color scheme, to distinguish them from the property of rival owners operating on the same road. A few were further embellished by the use of national flags which flapped over their upper decks, or by the erection of small wooden cupolas. Two of these practises—the naming of cars and the uniformity of painting and decoration—have survived until the present day, but the use of flags and cupolas never became general and soon died out.

The stage-coach sort of conveyance was supplanted on the Philadelphia, Germantown and Norristown road by a longer vehicle on eight wheels, with end doors, a central aisle, and benches extending along the sides. At each end of this new type of coach was a very small room about five

---

[1] The cars for the New York and Harlem, and for the Camden and Amboy, were examples of this type.

STREET RAILROAD CAR, NEW ORLEANS.

301.—One of the primitive American street-cars. Some of them were of strange and curious architecture. This was operated in New Orleans about the year 1856.

feet long. One compartment was for the use of such feminine passengers as might wish to make changes in their apparel under conditions of proper privacy, and the other was equipped as a bar-room for thirsty men travellers. The railroad built two cars of this description, one of which was named the *Victoria* in honor of the new sovereign of the British Empire, while the other was called the *President*. They were probably put into service in 1837. Doubtless they were also the first railway cars in the world that embodied any features—except seats—which were designed with the comfort and convenience of travellers in mind.

For about a decade the construction of passenger cars varied according to the notions of those who owned them. Then they began to assume a general resemblance and to approach more closely to a standard form and arrangement, just as had been the case with stage-coaches and canal boats. The curved lines reminiscent of stage-coach bodies disappeared because of the greater cost attending their presence, and were replaced by the straight and angular lines that have since distinguished railroad cars of all sorts. The use of the upper deck for passengers continued for a short while, and the top seats on cars so built were often more popular, except during inclement weather, than the accommodations within. Side entrances were altogether abandoned. After these changes had been brought about there were no further important alterations either in the outward appearance or principal interior arrangements of the vehicles designed for human use except those consequent upon their slowly increasing size.

The seats of some of the primeval passenger cars were even more uncomfortable than the seats of stage-coaches in use at the same time, and this circumstance, in connection with the fact that few of the new rail-carriages were equipped with springs, made riding in them very uncomfortable indeed. Some of the car seats were at first merely smooth wooden boards without any backs. Such things as cushions or seat-upholstery were then unheard of. With the change in the form of the coaches and their increased size, however, came a corresponding alteration in the method of placing the seats. They were no longer built entirely across the car from one side of the vehicle to the other, but were broken into two rows separated by a long aisle extending from door to door.

When passenger cars had assumed a somewhat standard form—about 1838 or 1840—they usually measured from thirty-five to forty feet in length and had a width of about eight feet. The central aisle was quite narrow, and the double seats on each side of the passageway were so short that two people of adult size could only squeeze into them with difficulty. The roof of such a car presented a slightly concave appearance when viewed by the passenger from below, and its interior surface was scarcely more than six and a half feet from the floor. The doors at either end were exceedingly small, and there was almost no ventilation. Some cars of the 1840 type contained a small ventilating hole eight or ten inches in diameter in the center of the roof, and as time went on the use of flues slowly increased and three or four were built in the top of each vehicle and covered with tin to keep the rain out. Even the numerous windows along the sides of a car were often so made that they could not be opened. In such cases some of the flimsy wooden panels between the windows were raised instead, provided they had not become warped and immovable. During hot weather a long trip in a train so constructed was an uncomfortable experience, even though no accident or other untoward event befell the traveller. In cold weather the only means of heating the car was a huge iron stove at one end of it, into which the captain or the passengers frequently threw big pieces of wood from a box across the aisle. Fortunate

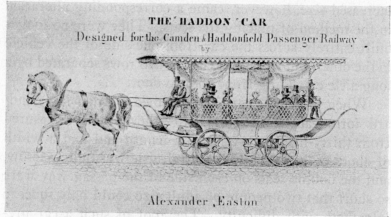

302.—A small, single horse street-car designed by Alexander Easton of Philadelphia.

was the man who on a day of freezing temperature succeeded in obtaining a seat near the stove. The fierce heat of the dry pine turned the iron to dull red, and the person who sat near it was bathed in sweat, while those in the center of the car and at its farther end were shivering with cold. But the passenger who had found an empty seat near the source of warmth was not fortunate in case the train met with disaster, for the construction of such a car with its big and red-hot stove were, in that event, the ingredients of danger not to be dwelt upon.

A night journey brought experiences equally poignant, although somewhat different in character. Both sexes had to make the best of their surroundings, and secure what rest they might while sitting erect in the narrow seats. A man hung his coat and waistcoat on one of the hooks along the wall, placed his feet on that part of the seat in front which was not occupied by the head of a fellow sufferer, reclined his own head on that part of his seat not occupied by the feet of the man behind him, and so awaited the coming of the morning. The womenfolk could not even do so much as this. They were limited to the removal of their bonnets and the closing of their eyes. During a night journey the cars were illuminated by two candles, one at each end. These were stuck in metal candlesticks fixed to the woodwork near the doors. After a number of years the roads discarded their candles in favor of a lamp of metal or glass that was suspended by means of chains or rods from the center of the roof.

About 1840—and on some roads shortly before that time—it became the practise to use iron to some extent in the framework of the seats, and to make them more comfortable by the employment of leather upholstery. Cars of this general description remained in universal use until the period of the Civil War, with almost no features of further improvement. Contemporary pictures of such railway equipment, showing both the outer and inner aspects of trains used about 1840 and thereafter, are reproduced in their appropriate places throughout the pictorial story.

The method of building the tracks of many early roads had a close relation to some of the incidents of travel which happened above them. It has been seen that for a time the rails on some lines were of wood, on which were placed thin strips of flat iron, and that the iron strips were fastened to the wooden rails by means of spikes. Now those spikes frequently became loose, thereby permitting the metal covering of the rails to get out of place. Often the loose iron strips would curl around the moving axles of a train overhead, or even penetrate bodily through the bottom of a passing car and bring it to a sudden stop even if none of the passengers within were injured by the intrusion. Accidents like this were not rare, and rather resembled in their character and effect the impalement of a flatboat on some western river by the sharp end of a sunken snag.

Every early brigade of cars employed on a road equipped with flat iron rails carried sledge hammers as part of its essential equipment, and whenever one of the rails worked loose and plunged through a car floor the big mauls were used to pound it back through the bottom of the car again. If this proved impracticable, then the part of the iron projecting into the car had to be laboriously filed off before the trip could continue. Whenever the engineer spied a loose rail on his own or an adjoining track he would stop the engine and the defect would be remedied before the journey was resumed.

For the first dozen years or more after the introduction of railroads there neither existed any way by which the position or safety of a train could be ascertained during its progress, nor any mechanical method whereby the captain could communicate with the engineer. It soon became evident that either or both of those things might frequently be urgently desirable, and so it came about that the men employed on the trains devised the first codes of railway signals. All systems of communication between the cars of a train and the engine were for a long time very crude. The cars on some early roads were equipped with ladders by which the captain might climb to the roof

1024

of his brigade and there shout at the engineer or throw something at him to attract his attention. If he did thus succeed in letting the engineer know he wanted to talk, the engineer would stop the train and find out what the trouble was. Many of the captains arranged signal codes requiring the use of their arms, hands and fingers. The waving of an arm in a certain way or the elevation

303.—Street-cars such as were first used in Boston. Except in their lesser length they closely resembled the steam railway cars of the time.
Date, about 1856.

of a hand or a particular finger had a specific meaning, and if the attention of the engineer could be attracted he would usually act in accordance with the information conveyed to him.[1] But for a number of years the official relationship between the captain of the train and the engineer was not definitely fixed. Many of the men in charge of locomotives considered that their authority exceeded the power possessed by the captains and acted in accordance with such belief.

The change by which the captain acquired his supremacy over the engineer and all other members of the train crew was perhaps rather gradual in some parts of

[1] This sign language called into being by early necessities is still used, and has developed into a rather elaborate code.

the country, and may have depended upon various circumstances and conditions. But there was one event, happening in the childhood years of the Erie Railroad, which because of its peculiar character and wide notoriety undoubtedly had much to do with finally establishing the authority of the modern train conductor.

At the time in question the Erie operated only one train a day, and it ran back and forth for a distance of forty-seven miles between the Hudson River and a little town called Turner's, then the western end of the road. This train, which ordinarily consisted both of passenger and freight cars, was in charge of an engineer named Hammil and a captain named Ayres. It happened on several occasions that Captain Ayres wanted very much to stop the train, yet had no means of doing so. Hammil, in addition, was a stubborn chap who did not take those frequent backward glances over his brigade that were customary to men performing similar duties. At last Ayres was inspired by an idea. He bought a big ball of strong twine, and by means of staples he carried the rope from the rear car along the roofs of all the intervening cars to the engine, where he caused it to hang down directly over the platform on which the engineer stood. To the engine end of the rope he then fastened a stick of wood such as was used in the locomotive furnace. All this was done in the absence of Hammil. When the engineer reported for duty, ready to start his train as soon as the steamboat arrived from New York with the passengers, Ayres explained the new system to him. He told Hammil that if he should wish the train to be stopped for any reason he would yank on the string, which would cause the stick of wood to be lifted from the platform of the engine and fall back on it with a thump, and that if

1026

Hammil at any time saw the stick jumping about he was to bring the train to a halt.

While the train was making its trip the captain decided to test his contrivance, but despite his repeated pullings on the cord there was no result. The brigade moved steadily on, and when it arrived at Turner's he found that Hammil had cut the string from off the stick. The engineer furthermore told the captain that he proposed to run the train without interference from any captain or anybody else. Next day Ayres tied a piece of wood on the string again and said to the engineer, "This thing has got to be settled one way or the other. If that stick of wood is not on the end of this cord when we get to Turner's you've got to lick me or I'll lick you." Ayres' signals during the journey produced no response, and as soon as the train came to a stop he ran forward and found the cord had been cut again. The captain thereupon took off his coat, climbed on the engine, knocked Hammil off the machine, jumped after him, and the desperate fight which then ensued settled once and for all the authority of a captain over an engineer on the Erie Railroad. After that combat the stick of wood remained in its place, and every time Hammil saw it hop from the floor of the engine and drop back again he stopped the train in accordance with the signal thus communicated to him. The story of this dispute spread among the other railways of the East, and within a few months all of them had installed signal cords on their trains. An iron weight supplanted the billet of wood on the engine, and at a still later date a bell was substituted for the piece of iron. Thus the bell rope came into use.[1]

An engineer, in his turn, often had need to commu-

---

[1] "How to Travel." By Thomas W. Knox. pp. 15-17.

nicate with the captain and other members of the train crew. Before the invention of the steam whistle he had tried different methods of accomplishing the purpose in view. One was the hoisting of a little flag on a pole set up on the engine, and the position of the flag would indicate the nature of the message. In case the engineer wished the crew to apply brakes to the train a great deal depended on the promptness with which the signal was detected, and a man was usually put on top of one of the cars during a trip in order that he might keep a constant eye on the engine. Another scheme available to the engineer for attracting the attention of the crew consisted in lifting the steam valve on the dome either with his hand or an iron rod. This action would permit the steam to rush out with a loud hiss, and the noise often served the purpose for which it was intended.

The first brakes on the cars were identical in principle with those that had long been used on stage-coaches. They consisted of stout blocks of hardwood, brought in contact with the wheels by means of levers operated by foot power. On the Newcastle and Frenchtown road, in Pennsylvania, the prompt halting of its first steam train was achieved in a manner still more archaic than this. When the locomotive was approaching a point at which a stop was necessary the engineer then shut off the power and sent a signal down the track by permitting steam to escape from the safety valve. Whereupon the negro roustabouts at the station would rush forward, seize hold of the engine and train with their hands, lean backward and dig their heels into the earth, and the station agent would thrust a fence rail between the spokes of a locomotive wheel. In that manner they could bring the train to a pause within a few yards.

Locomotives did not carry headlights for several years after the introduction of railroads in America. There were no such things. No night trips were at first undertaken, and the need for track illumination did not arise. The roads were so short that they could easily be traversed in a few hours, and the amount of traffic did not require their operation after daylight ceased. But when the

SCENE IN WINTER STREET, BOSTON, DURING THE LATE SNOW STORM.

304.—When heavy snow-falls made it impossible to maintain a service with the newly introduced street railways, the superseded omnibuses were brought forth again, placed on sled-runners instead of wheels, and pressed into use.

Charleston and Hamburg road had laid a hundred miles or more of track it became apparent that night travel would on some occasions be desirable. Horatio Allen, the civil engineer in charge of the line, realized that a man who was handling a locomotive in the darkness should be able to see the track ahead of him, and in order for him to do so it was obvious that a light must be shed upon the rails. Allen succeeded in solving the problem. He built a little square flat car, about five feet long, and arranged for attachment in front of the engine. On the car he spread a layer of sand several inches deep, and on top of the sand he built a fire of pine knots. The bonfire was so close to the front of the boiler that the flames were hidden from the eyes of the engineer, and their glare was thrown forward along the track. This headlight was put into use on the road, and required no further care for its operation except a frequent replenishment of fuel, which cost nothing.

Another circumstance that led to the use of railroads at night was the unexpected heavy passenger traffic which appeared as soon as the new travel method was brought into existence. The running of trains soon taxed the daylight resources of the roads to the utmost — because there were so few turnouts — and it was found desirable to conduct the freight traffic at night even on the short lines. The Charleston and Hamburg four-wheeled headlight was not generally adopted. It merely served as an incentive for further invention, and big lamps were soon attached to the front ends of night-running engines. Reflectors began to be placed behind the lamps about the year 1840, and with that device the locomotive headlight attained a form it was destined to keep for many years.

Locomotives, for a time, were made without cabs or other shelter for the engineer and fireman. Those appurtenances to the structure of a railroad engine did not come into use until about 1842, and were not adopted by all builders until several years after that date. Almost every early engine used wood in its furnace, and the fuel was carried on a little flat car immediately behind. It occasionally happened—on a long trip or because of some

1030

delay—that the supply of wood with which the trip was begun became exhausted. In such case the train came to a halt and the fireman and engineer, equipped with ax and saw carried for the purpose, dismounted and accumulated another stock of fuel from dead trees or fences in the immediate neighborhood. If wood was scarce in that vicinity and the delay threatened to be a long one, the passengers themselves joined in the work and aided in carrying the sticks back to the waiting engine.

The danger attending the issuance of sparks from locomotive smokestacks—so well illustrated during the first trip on the Albany and Schenectady road—was at once seen, though no means for abating it was discovered for several years. During seasons of dry weather innumerable fires were caused by sparks along the lines of various railroads, and it became necessary to hire many watchmen to patrol the tracks and extinguish incipient conflagrations in their neighborhood. Nearly all railway bridges were then built of wood, and a watchman was permanently installed on every structure of the sort, with several hogsheads of water convenient for his use. Finally an effort was made to prevent the emission of firebrands from the locomotives by covering the tops of the smoke stacks with wire screen, and this scheme, though it did not wholly remedy the trouble, proved so useful that it was generally adopted. A considerable number of small sparks and clouds of smoke still issued from the engine furnaces, however, and in 1848 an inventor named Townsend patented a method whereby the locomotive smokestack might be carried horizontally backward over the roofs of the cars, so that all smoke and sparks would issue at the rear of the train instead of at its front. The invention was illustrated in the *Scientific American* of that year and favorably noticed, but there does not appear to be any contemporaneous record of its adoption. Locomotives designed for burning coal instead of wood came into use a few years afterward, and the spark danger, in so far as it affected the travellers themselves, disappeared.

The origin of the sand-box on locomotives was due to a plague of grasshoppers in Pennsylvania in. 1836.

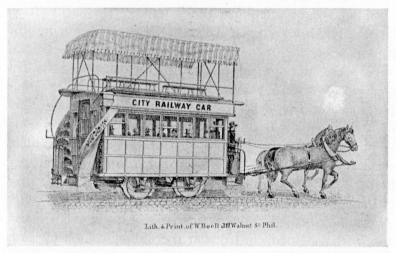

Lith. & Print of W.Boell 311 Walnut St Phil.

305.—Another pioneer street-car designed by Alexander Easton. Similar two-story vehicles appeared for a time in various cities, but the street-car, like the barge, flatboat, stage-coach, canal boat and steam railway car, gradually assumed a settled and general type, and peculiar forms disappeared.

They covered the ground in myriads, and seriously interfered with the running of trains on the railroads then in operation. For a week or two the roads employed men to walk back and forth along the tracks and sweep the insects off the rails with brooms, but this expedient was unavailing, for no sooner were they displaced from one point than the little pests jumped back again after the track

1032

sweepers had passed. Scrapers were then installed on some engines and small brooms on others, but these attempts to remedy the trouble also proved useless, since the brooms were worn out in a short time and the contact between scrapers and rails made it necessary to run the trains at a crawling gait. Finally some genius whose name has been forgotten hit upon the plan of attaching sand-boxes to the locomotives in such a way that streams of sand should be automatically deposited on the rails in front of the wheels. The scheme proved an unqualified success, was adopted by other existing roads and used thereafter by all new ones.

At first there were no such things as time schedules and inexorably fixed moments for the despatching of trains. No road ran more than two or three brigades of passenger cars in each direction every day, and the starting times for them were often governed by the arrival of stage-coaches or steamboats from other towns. If the stage-coach or steamboat was an hour or two late, then the railroad train chose to await its arrival rather than make a trip without any passengers, or with only half the number to be obtained by the delay.

The passenger on a train never knew beforehand when he might reach his destination, and a person who was waiting for a train at some station along the line never knew when it would get there. A brigade of cars often departed from its starting-point at some usual hour provided conditions were favorable, but after it disappeared in the distance nothing could be known of its adventures until it came back again the next day. The employees situated at other places along the line knew when the train was theoretically supposed to start from the end of the road, but made no rash predictions respecting its visits elsewhere. One of the first methods employed to discover approaching trains was the setting up of lookout masts at the various stations, and when the time arrived at which a train might perhaps be expected if nothing had befallen it, the station master at that point would climb to the top of his pole by means of ladder-like cleats, take his seat in a little chair fixed at the top of the pole, and then peer down the track through a spy-glass. He would so continue to gaze for half an hour, or an hour, or two hours, as the case might be, or until he got tired and came back down to earth again. If at last he did detect the smoke of the approaching engine he shouted the glad news to the waiting people below, and thus they knew the train would probably be there within the next five or ten or fifteen minutes. If by any chance—through a pedestrian or stage-coach—knowledge had reached the station that something had happened to the train, a flag of some particular color was attached to the signal pole. By previous arrangement the meaning of such a flag was understood by all the patrons of the line, and so the news was heralded abroad.

A railroad company often announced the hoped-for movements of its trains in the advertising columns of the newspapers, but all the inhabitants of any town which boasted of a railway understood the circumstance govern-ing its operation and knew when its trains expected to start as well as they knew any other fact of local con-sequence. About the year 1847, when business on a number of the principal roads had increased to such a point that a dozen trains a day were demanded in each direction, such roads began to issue regular printed schedules for the benefit of their patrons. Sometimes these printed an-nouncements were in the shape of small pieces of cardboard,[1] and others were on larger sheets of paper called "broadsides." When issued in broadside form the time-tables were displayed in the post-offices, hotel lobbies, theaters, court-houses, and other public buildings.[2]

[1] Like those adopted by the Philadelphia, Germantown and Norristown road of Pennsylvania. A series of the little cardboard schedules issued by this line is reproduced elsewhere in their original size.

[2] Several such "broadside" schedules, dated between the years 1847 and 1852, are shown in these volumes.

CHAPTER XLVI

EARLY RAILROAD TICKETS — THE "BOOKING" SYSTEM — ITS PRACTISE AT PHOENIXVILLE — THROUGH TICKETS PREVENTED BY THE JEALOUSIES OF ADJOINING ROADS — FREE PASSES APPEAR — ORIGIN OF THE MODERN RAIL — DRIPPS INVENTS THE COWCATCHER — THE FIRST PRIVATE CARS — SLEEPING CARS USED IN 1838 — THEIR CONSTRUCTION — THE TELEGRAPH EMPLOYED BY RAILWAYS — AMERICAN ROADS FREE FROM SERIOUS FATALITIES FOR TWELVE YEARS — REASONS FOR THE PHENOMENON — THE ACCIDENT PERIOD BEGINS — POPULAR OUTCRY — ATTITUDE OF THE PRESS — NEW YORK'S REGULATIONS OF 1856

THE early American practise concerning the collection of railroad fares and the issuance of tickets to passengers varied greatly. A few of the pioneer roads adopted the plan of printing tickets almost at once, while others preferred different methods for collecting the money paid by travellers who patronized them. Doubtless the first through ticket appearing in the country was one prepared in connection with the operation of the little seventeen-mile-long railroad from Albany to Schenectady in 1831.[1] This ticket entitled its owner to transportation from New York City to Buffalo, and was issued by the joint arrangement of a steamboat company on the Hudson River, the railway here mentioned, and a com-

[1] A reproduction of one of these tickets will be found on another page.

1036

pany operating packet-boats on the Erie Canal. The ticket was a sheet of paper about ten inches long by five and a half inches wide. Although it called for only seventeen miles of railroad travel, its purchase carried the right to accommodations during a trip of some four hundred miles. A few other railroads issued paper or cardboard tickets in the later years of the fourth decade, and probably three or four made use of small metallic discs. These were of all sizes varying from that of a silver ten-cent piece to that of a half dollar.[1]

Those roads which did not at once adopt tickets pursued the method used in England, which was known as "booking" the passengers. Under this system the traveller paid his money at the railway station, and his name was thereupon written in a book kept by the station agent for that purpose. The Reading Railroad is the possessor of such a volume, used at the town of Phoenixville, in Pennsylvania, from the summer of 1838 until 1840. The first booking recorded in it was under the date of July 17, 1838, and for about a year the names of the various persons embarking at that place were duly set down. But after a time the exactitude of the clerk suffered a serious lapse, and he no longer identified the patrons of the road in his previous formal fashion. Instead of writing their names in his book he described them more briefly as "stranger," "lady," "whiskers," "friend," or "boy."

The style and form of the early railroad tickets varied according to the notions of the issuing company. Some of them—such as that printed in 1831 for the trip between New York City and Buffalo—were awkwardly large

[1] Examples of early metallic passenger tickets issued by railroads and stage-coaches are included among the illustrations.

aper. The metal ones were made in the
wter, brass or copper coins. But the most
as a small oblong piece of cardboard
y the name of the company and the
between which the traveller was to be carried.
Very often it was glazed, and of some gaudy color such

Awful explosion on board the Helen Mc Gregor.

306.—Early American travel accidents and catastrophes. Explosion of the
steamboat *Helen McGregor* at the Memphis wharf in 1830. The number of
people who then lost their lives was never determined, but was variously
estimated as being between thirty and sixty. It was the worst accident of
the sort up to that time. From 1825, when numerous people refused to
travel on steamboats, until the period of railway disasters during the sixth
decade, the public sought, with no appreciable effect, to bring about a reduction of the danger which attended movements over the country in mechanical
vehicles.

as red, yellow or blue. The introduction of consecutively
numbered tickets—which were invented in Europe—did
not take place in this country until about the year 1855,
nor were they generally adopted until after the conclusion
of the Civil War. Only a few of the large cities possessed
pretentious passenger stations, and any intending traveller
could embark upon a train, if he chose to do so, without

buying or showing a ticket. In such a case he handed his fare to the captain. This condition of things resulted in a very large loss of revenues to the railroad companies through peculations, and soon after the year 1850 an effort was made by many roads to induce the purchase of tickets by passengers before they entered the cars. The method by which the roads sought to attain this end consisted in exacting a small amount in excess of the regular fare from those who paid in cash after the trains were in motion.[1] Several years after the Civil War the losses sustained by the railroads through the theft of cash paid to conductors became so serious that nearly all the principal lines of the country combined in the making of a secret investigation which disclosed the fact that an average of about two-thirds of all cash fares paid on the railroad trains never reached the coffers of the companies themselves. It was found that on some trips the conductors had received from twenty-five to seventy-five dollars in cash and turned in nothing at all. This revelation resulted in the establishment of the rule that no traveller could gain access to a train without first buying and displaying his ticket.

One reason that for a considerable time operated against the general adoption and use of through tickets lay in the jealousies of adjoining railroads and their refusal to coöperate with one another in the matters of uniform gauges and closely connecting schedules. Such was the situation over the route from Albany to Buffalo, in New York State, even after the entire distance between the two cities was spanned by railroad tracks. It was impossible to buy a railroad ticket from Albany to Buffalo

[1] The 1852 "broadside" schedule of the Hudson River Road, elsewhere shown, contains a request that passengers "procure tickets before entering the cars," and also states that "purchase on the car will be five cents extra."

CONVENT DU SACRAMENT.

307.—Explosion of the Mississippi River steamboat *Brilliant*, at Bayou Goula, in 1851. More than a hundred lost their lives. James Lloyd, in his *Steamboat Directory and Disasters on the Western Waters*, ascribes the *Brilliant* calamity to the common habit of using resin as fuel, in order to produce more steam and obtain greater speed. Four barrels of resin had been thrown into the boat's furnaces just before the explosion, and a fifth was about to follow them.

until the five or six railroads uniting those places fell under one control. The jurisdiction held by the captain of each train ceased when the end of his particular road had been reached. The progress of a train of cars beyond its own tracks and to the tracks of an adjoining road was for years virtually unknown, even though the thing was easily possible of physical accomplishment.

The habit of giving written or printed passes over railroads appeared about as promptly as the practise of issuing tickets. In Pennsylvania the distribution of free transportation had become widely prevalent at an early day, and the ownership of some railroads by that state resulted in the granting of free rides to every one in the common-wealth who had any semblance of reason on which he might base a request for such a favor and to a large number who did not. Of the pass-granting situation in Pennsylvania it has been said:

"The practice of giving train passes to politicians and other favored persons originated on the Philadelphia & Columbia Railroad and was carried to excesses never seen elsewhere. By the time the property went into the hands of the Pennsylvania Railroad Company every officeholder in Pennsylvania, from constable to Governor, held an annual pass on the 'State Railroad.' "[1]

Other distinctive features intimately connected with the operation of the modern railway and due to the American inventive spirit are rails of the type now in universal use, the cowcatcher, private cars, sleeping cars, and the telegraph. The modern rail, or "T-rail" as it is called, was designed by Robert L. Stevens in the year 1830. While Stevens was on his way to England, in the year named, to buy a locomotive for the Camden and Amboy road, he spent much of his time on shipboard in the Yankee habit of whittling, and since his thoughts were deeply engrossed in the subject of railroads his whittling operations followed the same trend. It occurred to him one day that a rail consisting of a line of flat iron bars was not necessarily the best track for locomotive wheels, and with his knife and a stick of pine wood he began to design possible substitutes for it. One of the models he thus shaped was the T-rail as it is now known, and on his urgent advice the Camden and Amboy company undertook to equip its road with rails of that description. At first the English iron mills avowed they could not possibly duplicate the wooden model which

[1] Sinclair's "Development of the Locomotive Engine," p. 109.

Stevens showed them, but he insisted that an effort be made to produce the desired pattern, and the task was eventually accomplished. Stevens' rails were laid by the New Jersey enterprise and proved so successful that other railways adopted them as the iron they had first used gradually wore out, until in course of time the rail pattern shaped by a Yankee jack-knife out of a pine stick superseded all others.

The cowcatcher device also first appeared on the Camden and Amboy road, and was an idea of the young machinist named Isaac Dripps — previously introduced. After Dripps had successfully assembled and put in operation the *John Bull,* which had been bought for the road in England by Stevens, he began to build locomotive engines himself, following the design of the *John Bull* in their general arrangement. During the first few weeks in which the Camden and Amboy line was operated it became apparent that wandering horses, cows and swine constituted a real menace to the safe movement of a railroad train, and Dripps devoted his ingenuity to the creation of an appliance that would enable an engine to sweep such an animal off the track. He built a low truck designed for attachment to the forward part of a locomotive, with its front end supported by two small wheels. Projecting about three feet ahead of the two wheels were several long, sharp pointed wrought-iron bars extending parallel with the track and about four or five inches above it. This formidable weapon, when pushed ahead of a locomotive, invariably impaled any animal that might be struck and prevented it from falling under the wheels of the engine. Such was the first cowcatcher, and its advantages were demonstrated a few days after its introduction. A big bull was hit

by an engine thus fortified, and so firmly was he held
by the metal prongs that the use of ropes and much force
was necessary to detach him. The incident indicated that
Dripps' cowcatcher as at first planned was even more
efficient than was necessary, so the prongs were taken
off and replaced by a heavy bar extending across the forward truck at a right angle to the rails. Subsequently

308.—Wreck of the Hudson River steamboat *Swallow*, whose appearance at
the height of her popularity is shown in illustration No. 108. She ran
on a rock, thirty miles below Albany, in 1845. Engraved from a sketch
made by the artist E. Whitefield. A "Catastrophe Broadside."

this second form of cowcatcher was amended and the
present variety came into existence.

Private cars were probably first used on the Massachusetts roads soon after their completion. They were of
two sorts, one being simply a flat platform on which a
domestic carriage or a stage-coach was securely fastened
for the exclusive use of a family or party which desired
to enjoy the sensation of a railroad ride without mingling
with the other travellers. The other kind of private car
was an ordinary railroad passenger coach chartered by

private individuals for the occasion. The usual price for exclusiveness of either description was from five to twenty-five dollars — in accordance with the length of the journey — besides the regular fares for the persons so transported.

The first railway sleeping cars were adopted by railroads from canal packets and did not materially vary, in construction or outer appearance, from the vehicles used for ordinary journeys. Some of them could only be transformed into sleeping cars on one side of the aisle. The seats on that side of the central passageway designed for sleeping purposes were so built that they might be readjusted to form a lower tier of bunks, while two other tiers were arranged immediately above. The middle row of sleeping shelves was composed of wooden boards that lay flat against the side of the car in daytime and were lowered into a horizontal position at night, when they were supported by chains, or by small iron or wooden posts. The topmost line of beds consisted of a similar series of wooden shelves. Most of the early sleeping cars were equipped with three rows of bunks one above another, after the manner of the canal packets, and those who patronized them were perhaps even more cramped in their quarters than were canal passengers on a similar occasion. Only after a number of years was this arrangement discarded in favor of one providing for but two berths where three had existed before. Fifty to seventy-five cents, according to the length of the journey, was the price of a berth.

Sleeping cars were probably first utilized between Baltimore and Philadelphia, and their impending introduction to the public was discussed in an article printed in the Baltimore *Chronicle* of October 21, 1838. The newspaper said:

"The cars intended for night traveling between this city and Philadelphia, and which afford berths for twenty-four persons in each, have been placed on the road and will be used for the first time tonight. One of these cars has been brought to this city and may be inspected by the public to-day. It is one of the completest things of the kind we have ever seen, and it is of beautiful construction. Night traveling on a railroad is, by the introduction of these cars, made as comfortable as that by day, and is relieved of all irksomeness. The enterprise which conceived and constructed the railroad between this city and Philadelphia cannot be too highly extolled, and the anxiety evinced by the officers who now have its control in watching over the comfort of the passengers, and the great expense incurred for that object, are worthy of praise. . . . A ride to Philadelphia now, even in the depth of winter, may be made without inconvenience, discomfort, or suffering from the weather. You can get into the cars at Pratt Street, where is a pleasant fire, and in six hours you are landed at the depot in Philadelphia. If you travel in the night you go to rest in a pleasant berth, sleep as soundly as in your own bed at home, and on awakening next morning find yourself at the end of your journey, and in time to take your passage to New York if you are bent there. Nothing now seems to be wanting to make railway traveling perfect and complete in every convenience, except the introduction of dining cars, and these we are sure will soon be introduced."

Although the first commercial line of electric telegraph[1] had been built and put into use in the year 1844, it was not until 1851 that the device was adopted by a railroad as an aid in the conduct of its traffic. In 1848 a telegraph line had been built[2] and operated between New York City and Lake Erie, following generally the track of the Erie Railroad,[3] and in 1851 that railway began to avail itself of the telegraph in transmitting orders to its employees.

At that time the men who directed trains on the road were their own operators, and no central authority

[1] That between Washington and Baltimore, for the erection of which the Federal government granted to Morse and his associates the sum of $30,000.
[2] By Ezra Cornell.
[3] "Historical Sketch of the Electric Telegraph: Including its Rise and Progress in the United States." By Alexander Jones. New York MDCCCLII, p. 79.

Fatal Conflagration of the Steam boat **LEXINGTON** In Long Island Sound on Monday Eve.ª Jan.ª 13ᵗʰ 1840. by which melancholy occurrence, over 100 PERSONS PERISHED.

309.—Burning of the steamboat *Lexington* on Long Island Sound in 1840. About 120 were lost. The fire occurred on a Monday evening, January 13, about sixty miles from New York. So primitive were the communication facilities of the country at that time, especially in winter, that the first rumors of the disaster did not reach the city until Wednesday. A relief boat started to the scene on Thursday, and on Saturday the newspapers were able to publish their "extras" with an account of the event. Another of the "Catastrophe Broadsides" that were hastily published after nearly every similar accident.

had knowledge of the whereabouts of all the rolling stock in active use. A telegraphic message coming over the wire for the information and guidance of a train conductor was received in the shape of dots and dashes printed on a narrow strip of paper. The translation of the message was a visual process. The symbols on the tape were read by the operator, who then wrote out the despatch and handed it to the man for whom it was intended. One day a conductor of the Erie line who was waiting at the little town of Addison for his train orders, noticed that the telegraph operator failed to look at

1046

the dots and dashes imprinted on the tape, but set down the words solely through his interpretation of the sounds made by the instrument. The conductor refused to accept or act upon orders acquired by him in such a manner. He further demanded that the instructions be copied from the printed symbols, in his presence, and reported the unprecedented conduct of the operator to the headquarters of the road. Fortunately the chief executive of the telegraph department recognized the importance of the discovery that electric tidings could be interpreted through their sound, and instead of being discharged, the unknown youth was promoted and became the first train despatcher in the world.[1] Within a few years thereafter all the railway lines of the country were equipped with telegraphic systems.

The acceptance of Morse's device[2] by Congress and the public, in the fifth decade of the century, illustrated the change — the awakening — that had taken place in the spirit of the people. Less than sixty years before the steamboat had been offered to the Federal government by Fitch without cost, for the common benefit. Only thirty years before Stevens and Dearborn had urged upon Congress the importance of railway building. But when Morse, in 1842, came forward with his instrument

[1] The operator who thus first read telegraph messages by sound was Charles W. Douglas, and the executive who recognized the value of the innovation was L. O. Tillotson.

[2] Morse's contribution to electric telegraphy did not lie in the discovery of scientific principles on which the process is based, but in the building of an improved mechanical contrivance for the employment of those principles. His relationship to the subject was defined by Professor Joseph Henry, of Princeton College, during the suit of Smith against Downing (Boston, 1850) in the following words:

"I am not aware that Mr. Morse has ever made a single original discovery in electricity, magnetism, or electro-magnetism, applicable to the invention of the telegraph. I have always considered his merit to consist in combining and applying the discoveries of others, in the invention of a particular instrument and process for telegraph purposes." (See "Evidence," p. 90.)

Smith, as a business associate of Morse, asked the court to enjoin Downing from conducting a rival telegraph line operating under patents issued to Royal E. House in 1848-9, on the ground that the House patents infringed on Morse's patents.

Morse's first caveat had been filed in 1837. The application for an injunction was denied. Much similar litigation was carried on for many years. In some cases Morse's requests for injunctions were granted.

Concussion of a passenger and lumber train of cars.

310.—Railroad collisions were at first called "concussions." This concussion occurred on the Portsmouth and Roanoke road in Virginia, in 1837, and the picture is one of the earliest published American illustrations of such a mishap. There was not, at that time, any method whereby a train captain could be informed concerning the whereabouts of other trains on the road.

to send human thoughts through space on a wire, over scores of miles in an instant of time, his reception was different from the one accorded to those other men. "To be sure," said the people; "why not? That's a useful contraption." The Federal lawmakers, though, were skeptical for a little while about the accuracy of the inventor's assertions and even had suspicions concerning his sanity. Senator Smith of Indiana, one of the members of Congress before whom Morse gave his demonstration in 1842, afterward wrote this statement about the attitude of himself and other Senators on the occasion in question:

"I watched his countenance closely, to see if he was not deranged. . . . and I was assured by other Senators after we left the room that they had no confidence in it."[1]

[1] "Early Indiana Trials: And Sketches," p. 413.

ACCIDENT ON THE BALTIMORE & OHIO RAILWAY.

311.—An English representation of an American railway accident of 1853 in the Alleghany Mountains. Frontispiece to Alfred Bunn's "Old England and New England." Published in London in 1853.

In a further comment on the same subject and the results flowing from it, Senator Smith said:

"The privilege is not allowed even to genius in this world to inspect its own elements, and read its own destiny, and it is perhaps well for mankind that it is so. Could we lift the curtain which hides our future lives, and glance hastily at the misfortunes, the vexations, and the disappointments which await us, we should be discouraged from attempting the performance even of such deeds as are destined eventually to crown us with honor."[1]

The skepticism of Congress, so manifest in connection with the steamboat and the railroad, soon vanished in the case of the telegraph. The government appropriated thirty thousand dollars for the building of a trial line, and another forward step in national development was the result.

The first fatal accident due to the operation of a steam passenger train took place in connection with the first trip made by a passenger train in England. When the Liverpool and Manchester road was formally opened, on September 15, 1830, eight train-loads of distinguished guests and other persons were conveyed from Liverpool to Manchester, and during a pause in the journey one of the throng,[2] who had dismounted from his car, was run over and fatally hurt by the locomotive *Rocket*. Lord Brougham was present on the occasion in question, and in commenting on the accident the next day he said: "I have come to Liverpool only to see a tragedy. Poor Huskisson is dead or must die before to-morrow. He has been killed by a steam carriage. The folly of seven hundred people going fifteen miles an hour, in six carriages, exceeds belief. But they have paid a dear price."

The second fatal accident attending the operation of steam railroad trains was the explosion of the *Best Friend*

---

[1] "Early Indiana Trials: And Sketches," p. 414.
[2] William Huskisson, a member of the British Parliament.

locomotive in Charleston, a few months thereafter. The negro fireman who brought about the explosion by sitting on the safety valve succumbed to his injuries. Another fatality took place in Massachusetts two or three years afterward. It happened on an inclined plane of the Little Quincy road, and was due to the breaking of the rope which drew the cars up the hill. The cars fell back to the bottom of the incline, and one of the passengers was mortally hurt. This incident occurred during the building of the first three Massachusetts roads, and was one of the causes operating to prevent the introduction of inclined planes in connection with the New England roads then under construction.

Several other minor accidents characterized the operation of American railways during the earliest years of their existence, and a small part of them were attended with serious or fatal consequences. But speaking in a broad sense it may be said that the first twelve years of the history of American railroads—covering the period from 1829 to 1841—were distinguished by a most remarkable absence of heavy calamities. This condition of affairs was due to several causes. In the first place the average speed of trains during those years was slow—usually from ten to eighteen miles an hour. Traffic over the roads was insignificant when compared with the proportions it afterward assumed, and the average length of a journey was very short. There was scarcely any travel at night, and when a passenger train was run during the hours of darkness it was usually preceded by a pilot engine intended to discover whether or not the track was in proper condition. If a defect in the road did exist then the pilot locomotive, instead of the train itself, suffered the penalty.

1051

Nearly all the accidents that did occur were due to one or another of four causes. They were either brought about by derailment, by the impalement of a car on a loose rail, by running into a stray animal, or by collision between two brigades of cars. Incidents like these were numerous and naturally resulted in much annoyance and delay to the travelling public, but it was seldom that an event such as described was attended by more serious effects. Even a collision between two trains running in opposite directions did not produce a memorable catastrophe during the first decade or more of railroad operation. A flimsy passenger coach of those years weighed less than one-tenth as much as a modern car, but the slow headway of the trains—though equipped with primitive brakes—made the operation known as "telescoping" practically impossible. Collisions in those days were called "concussions."

So the American public, for a period in excess of ten years, was gradually confirmed in the belief that really grave accidents were not to be expected in connection with railway travel. Perhaps in some degree this did not constitute an unmixed blessing. If an appalling railway calamity had occurred in America during the first decade of its railroad history it is reasonably certain that one consequence would have been a temporary check to the popular idea that iron highways were destined to supplant other methods of travel and transportation. But such a belief could only have been transitory in its effect and would gradually have worn away, whereas the unhappy event must assuredly have produced another thought whose consequences would have been more permanent and far-reaching. The occurrence of a great catastrophe during the first ten years of railway use would have emphasized, as no other circumstance could have done, the necessity of better standards in track building and rolling stock construction than those which then prevailed. No such disaster took place, and hence all American railroads, until well into the fifth decade, were so built and equipped that when the era of accidents did begin they were far

FALLING OF A RAILROAD BRIDGE, NEAR WATERFORD, N. Y.

312.—Inadequate or flimsy construction methods characterized much American railway building prior to the Civil War. In this case a trestlework track could not stand alone.

more lamentable in their results than would have been the case if the rolling stock had been more substantial in character. This long continued immunity from disastrous mishaps in the formative years of America's railroad system had a still further and even more enduring effect. The use of flimsy standards of all sorts had become so firmly established, by the time the accident epoch began, that the numerous roads then in existence had invested

1053

large sums in equipment and found themselves—because of the expense involved—unable or unwilling to discard their rolling stock in favor of more substantial cars and to rebuild their roadbeds accordingly. So the early type of passenger coaches was retained, with only immaterial improvements, until long after the Civil War, and for more than thirty years the railroad history of the country was mournfully distinguished by a long series of unnecessary calamities.[1]

During the fifth decade railway accidents gradually grew both in number and in seriousness, and soon after the year 1850 they became so common and so doleful as to produce an almost national outcry for their abatement. The causes for the conditions existing after the year 1850 are easily to be seen. By that time traffic over the roads had swollen to such an extent that many more trains were in operation, and their speed had been much augmented. The average rate of movement of a passenger train during the period in question was perhaps twenty-five miles an hour, and on numerous occasions the speed developed was as much as thirty or thirty-five miles an hour. The multiplication of trains and their velocity had taken place without corresponding improvement either in the cars themselves or the roadbeds over which they ran. In other words, an attempt was made to accommodate a new generation of speed and traffic by means of an old and practically outgrown generation of rolling stock and roadbed. It is true there had been gradual increase in the size and weight of rails, and that the old signal posts had been supplanted by the telegraph, but the

[1] Some passenger coaches built thirty or more years ago, substantially identical with the type here discussed except in their greater capacity and consequent greater danger, are still permitted in operation. Their employment is morally indefensible, though still technically legal so long as it is not forbidden by laws similar to those statutes everywhere directed against the human use of unsafe buildings.

ACCIDENT ON THE CAMDEN AND AMBOY RAIL ROAD,

NEAR BURLINGTON, N.J.

AUG. 29th 1855.

313.—The Camden and Amboy wreck at Burlington, New Jersey, on August 29, 1855. Twenty-one were killed and seventy-five injured. Illustrating the small progress in car construction during twenty-five years. One of the last of the "Accident Broadsides."

mechanical improvements in the actual transportation vehicles themselves had by no means kept pace with public needs.

Accidents of all sorts—many being attended with loss of life—became so common during the years after 1850 that the illustrated newspapers of the time were constantly filled with illustrations of such events and with articles in reference to them. Nor was the travelling public entirely dependent on illustrated newspapers for a revelation of conditions then existing. So important did the matter of travel conditions become as a subject of popular discussion that numerous enterprising publishers issued what were known as "accident broadsides" after many of the tragedies attending travel by water and rail, and these broadsides—often printed in lurid colors—found wide and ready sale. Several special pictures of the sort are copied elsewhere in these pages, and a study of the ones depicting railroad accidents will disclose the character of the cars then in use and the scenes attending disasters in which they were involved.

The statements printed in the influential press of the day were as outspoken as the illustrations. One characteristic article is here reproduced in part, as a means of disclosing popular feeling and opinion during the most dangerous period of travel in America.[1] It read:

"Nobody's murders.—The railroads are insatiable. It is not enough that the cars should be the most dusty, noisy and wearisome of carriages . . . that the companies should absorb so much of the savings of honest

---

[1] This article was printed in "Harper's Weekly" of July 31, 1858, p. 483. It relates to an accident that had lately taken place on the Erie road. But it must not be presumed that the railroad thus discussed in "Harper's Weekly" occupied an unenviable position among similar enterprises, or that it was distinguished by any unusual excess in the occurrence of such events. The contrary was seemingly the case, for the Erie road appears to have been among those most infrequently involved in like catastrophes. The language here used by "Harper's Weekly" could with equal propriety have been applied —and at various times and by all the newspapers of the country was applied—to all the other important railroads then operating throughout the nation. The article is chosen as a typical newspaper utterance of the period because of its character as a general review of the whole subject of the dangers of railroad travel.

laborers all over the land, and never return a doll
the mercantile morality of the community shou
from stock speculations, and apparently respectable ⊦
by their inability to resist the temptation to swindle
enough, but every man who leaves the city by a train must ⌄
ing look behind, in sober sadness, doubting whether the chances ⌄
arrival are not entirely against him.

"The recent disaster upon the Erie Railroad has received very propei
attention from the press; and it will very soon be time to organize vigilance committees for the protection of human life upon our railroads, by
securing the prompt punishment of the persons directly and indirectly
concerned. A train thunders along a down-grade around a curve above
a precipice at the rate of forty miles an hour—a rail snaps—two cars are
hurled off the track down the bank, and six or seven corpses and
a score or so of maimed victims are taken from the ruins—the President
or some other officer 'hurries to the scene of the disaster'—an inquest
is held—the officers of the road swear that it was in 'good enough' condition—that the rate of speed was not unusual; that the same thing had
been done a hundred times before safely; and as many other absurdities
as occur to them—and a jury return, of course, that nobody is to blame.
Nobody ever is. Boilers are bursting all over the country—railroad
bridges breaking[1] and rails snapping—human life is sadly and foolishly
squandered—but nobody is to blame. Boilers burst themselves. Rails
break themselves. And it may be questioned whether the consequent
slaughter of men, women and children is not really suicide.

"Take the Erie case, and look at it a moment.

"Suppose you can clearly free all the officers of the road from intentional guilt, and fix the fault upon the iron rail. There is no question that there was a flaw in the rail—that it was very poor iron. Now
the makers of the rail, and the purchasers, should employ competent
testers.[2] Considering the immense consequences, when rail iron is
proved defective, the name of the house from which it is purchased should
be widely advertised. In the present instance we learn that it was an
English house. Let the public know what house, that if it be dishonest
in its work it may be stigmatized; and if honest, that it may suffer the
consequences of an oversight or of incapable servants. The makers of
the rail are first to blame in this case, and then the buyers. . . .

"Why do the people submit to railroad accidents? Why not send
representatives who shall insist that no railroad charters shall be granted
except upon certain conditions of construction? Thus every road should

---

[1] An accident had taken place on the New York Central road a few weeks before, in
which a railroad bridge near Utica collapsed under the weight of two trains and pre-
cipitated them into the stream beneath. A picture of this accident, as printed immediately
afterward, is reproduced elsewhere.

[2] A noticeable increase in accidents due to imperfect or poor rails has taken place
during the last few years and has attracted widespread attention. The article of 1858,
here quoted, suggests that the problem in question has been calling for a solution for
more than half a century.

314.—In May of 1858 two trains on the New York Central road tried to pass each other on a double-tracked bridge near Utica. There was no collision, but the structure collapsed under the weight.

be carefully fenced along the whole route—where, upon high embankments, fences are impossible, there should be low walls, or the rate of speed diminished to an absolutely safe point—and after rails properly selected had been laid, the whole road should be garrisoned so amply that every inch should be inspected after the passage of every train by day and night.

"Of course it would be expensive—what of that? Fewer railroads might be built—what of that? Everybody knows that the first object of a projected railroad is not the advantage of any region of country, but of the stock-jobbers who originate the property and speculate in it. . . .

"The coroner's jury return that nobody is guilty of this last sad massacre. . . ."

The series of similar disasters happening throughout the country during the years after 1850 at last compelled a number of state governments to take official cognizance of existing conditions, and in several of the commonwealths an effort was made to form codes of operation under which railways might carry on their business with less danger to the public. One of the states so acting was New York, and in the year 1856 it drew up a series of rules for the purpose in question. The New York regulations exceeded two hundred and fifty in number, and as a whole they indicate the degree of care then demanded in the operation of American railway lines. They show that a train might expect to encounter an open drawbridge either by day or by night; that a difference of five minutes in time might without impropriety be recorded by the watches of conductors and engineers; that deviations from train schedules were only reported once a month; that recklessness on the part of engineers was to be presupposed; and that an engineer might run his train on the supposition that he would find another train out of its proper place at any point. Twenty paragraphs from New York's code of 1856 are here cited as examples of conditions still permitted at that day in the operation of the railroads of the country. They are as follows:[1]

1. "The Safety of Passengers is to be regarded as the highest and most important duty.

2. "All the operations of working, repairing or construction must be completely and entirely subordinate thereto.

3. "All rules, and the interpretation thereof and all contingencies where the rules do not apply, must be governed by the primary rule of safety to passengers.

38. "Flags are to be used . . . at drawbridges when open.

39. "Lamps are to be used for the same purpose after sundown.

75. "When on the road the train will be under the direction of the conductor.

98. "There shall be at least one Brakeman for every two passenger cars.

114. "No trains shall proceed towards a station where it expects to pass a train having a right to the road, unless it has ample time to arrive at that station strictly at or before the time, per time table, for the latter train to leave that station.

[1] From "Codification of Rules and Regulations for Running Trains on the Railroads of the State of New York." Albany, 1856.

118. "The five minutes, in this case, is intended to guard against a possible difference in watches.

122. "In no case shall a train leave the station unless its time shall be so arranged that it will not approach the forward train nearer than twenty minutes of the time of the forward train at any point between stations.

126. "Whenever a train is behind time, and a following train is liable to approach it nearer than twenty minutes, if between stations, a man with signals shall be left on the road.

135. "Trains that break down or have accidents between stations must immediately and always send out a man in each direction to a distance of not less than three miles, with signals.

138. "And the person in charge of a train under such circumstances must assume that there are trains approaching in both directions.

181—183. "Station masters must keep a record of the times of the passage of every train . . . and when any train is out of time, they must find out the cause of the irregularity and enter it on the record and make a monthly return of the same to the office of the Supt.

205. "It is the conductor's duty to check the enginemen when they run unsafely.

209. "Negligence or recklessness on the part of the engineman will be taken as a proof of the inefficiency of the conductor unless such conduct has been duly and distinctly reported on every occasion of its taking place.

229. "In case of accident the conductor 'may command the services of any freight, wood or gravel train, or hand-car on the road, either to forward his own passengers or to carry messages.'

238. "The engineman must invariably start with care, and see that he has the whole of his train before he gets beyond the limits of his station.

255. "He must always run on the supposition that at any station he may find a train out of place."

Shortly before the outbreak of the Civil War nearly all the illustrated weekly newspapers of the country suddenly abandoned their custom of printing pictures depicting fresh railroad accidents as they occurred, and to some extent they also modified the tone of their accounts of such accidents. Their articles became less severe in character. A somewhat similar phenomenon was also visible in the columns of the daily press, although many of the daily papers did not modify their previous position.

Whether this phenomenon was due to a desire that the public be not further alarmed regarding the dangers then attendant upon travel, or whether it was in part due to a desire or influence of the railroads themselves, must now be a matter of speculation. Perhaps the altered attitude of the press at that time was caused by a combination of all the possible motives here suggested. The number of accidents slightly abated during the following years, and some time after the close of the Civil War began an era characterized by heavier rolling stock and betterment of roadbeds, and also by the employment of new mechanical devices in the shape of improved brakes and car couplers. These improvements contributed to a decrease in the calamities that had so unfortunately marked the development of the national railroad system during the previous twenty-five or thirty years.

CHAPTER XLVII

APPEARANCE OF RAILWAYS IN THE MISSISSIPPI VALLEY —
OHIO'S PIONEER ROAD — BUILDING A TRACK TO FIT
AN ENGINE — INFLUENCE OF THE "SANDUSKY" ON
RAILROAD HISTORY — THE FIRST STEAM TRIP IN
KENTUCKY — PROTECTING A LOCOMOTIVE FROM
SNOWFLAKES — INDIANA CONTRACTS THE FEVER —
JOSEPH BRUEN'S MIGRATORY RAILWAY — HOW IN-
DIANA GOT HER FIRST REAL ENGINE IN 1838 — IL-
LINOIS BUILDS A ROAD — THE STRANGE TRAIL ON THE
PRAIRIE — CHICAGO'S ENTERPRISE — THE TOWN FOR-
BIDS A RAILWAY TO ENTER ITS LIMITS — EARLY ROADS
OF THE SOUTHERN STATES — WORK OF CINCINNATI
AND ST. LOUIS — THE MISSISSIPPI FINALLY REACHED
BY IRON TRACKS — THE CELEBRATIONS OF 1857

WHILE the people of the East were aflame with
excitement over the new device between the years
1827 and 1835, and while they were enjoying the experiences heretofore described, a very different state of affairs
existed in the interior. The men of the states beyond the
Alleghanies were keeping themselves informed about the
progress of railroad building in the eastern commonwealths, and were looking forward to the time when they
also might enjoy the benefits that railroads would bring to
them. They even built a few miles of iron track previous to 1840, but such roads as did come into existence
in the West before the year named had no general effect

in altering social and economic conditions in that part of the country. All human movement and commerce, except an insignificant fragment, went on as before. And no part of the constantly swelling human tide that swept into the interior was affected by railways for many years. While the people of Maryland, South Carolina, New York, New Jersey, Pennsylvania and Massachusetts were riding behind their steam horses, the westbound population was still floating down the Ohio in flatboats and steamboats, or crawling over the face of the land in their wagons, canals and stage-coaches. A description of travel conditions as they existed in the West and on the way thither, during the first years of railroad building along the Atlantic coast, was written by Timothy Flint, a historian of the time.[1] He thus related the conditions referred to:

"On account of the universality and cheapness of steamboat and canal passage and transport, more than half the whole number of immigrants now arrive in the West by water. . . . They thus escape much of the expense, slowness, inconvenience, and danger of the ancient, cumbrous, and tiresome journey in wagons. . . . Immigrants from Virginia, the two Carolinas, and Georgia still emigrate, after the ancient fashion, in the southern wagon. This is a vehicle almost unknown at the north; strong, comfortable, commodious, containing not only a movable kitchen, but provisions and beds. Drawn by four or six horses, it subserves all the various intentions of house, shelter, and transport, and is, in fact, the southern ship of the forests and prairies. The horses that convey the wagon are large and powerful animals, followed by servants, cattle, sheep, swine, dogs, the whole forming a primitive caravan. . . . The procession moves on with power in its dust, putting to shame and uncomfortable feeling of comparison the northern family with their slight wagon, jaded horse, and subdued though jealous countenances. Their vehicle stops; and they scan the staunch, strong southern hulk, with its chimes of bells, its fat black drivers, and its long train of concomitants, until they have swept by.

"Perhaps more than half the northern immigrants arrive at present by way of the New York canal and Lake Erie. If their destination be

[1] In his "History of the Mississippi Valley": pp. 188-190.

the upper waters of the Wabash, they debark at Sandusky, and continue their route without approaching the Ohio. The greater number make their way from the lake to the Ohio, either by the Erie and Ohio or the Dayton canal. From all points, except those west of the Guyandot route and the National Road, when they arrive at the Ohio or its navigable waters, the greater number of families 'take water.' Emigrants from Pennsylvania will henceforth reach the Ohio on the great Pennsylvania canal, and will 'take water' at Pittsburgh. If bound to Indiana, Illinois, or Missouri, they build or purchase a family boat. Many of these boats are comfortably fitted up, and are neither inconvenient nor unpleasant

THE BOWERY LOCOMOTIVE, OR THE PLEASURES OF A RAIL-ROAD.

315.—The new system of locomotion was a fruitful subject for cartoonists. Their drawings, for a time, seemed to reflect the idea that the mechanism probably had privileges superior to human rights and convenience; that it was the duty of the people to escape, rather than the duty of the railroad to be careful. This cartoon followed the introduction of the locomotive into the streets of New York City.

floating houses. Two or three families sometimes fit up a large boat in partnership, purchase an 'Ohio Pilot,' a book that professes to instruct them on the mysteries of navigating the Ohio; and if the Ohio be moderately high, and the weather pleasant, this voyage, unattended with either difficulty or danger, is ordinarily a trip of pleasure. A number of the wealthier emigrant families take passage in a steamboat."

In addition to the various purposes and methods of west-bound travel here described by Flint, it should also be said that business men of the epoch whose interests took them to the West travelled thence by stage-coach or by steamboat. The stages and mechanical river craft of the interior continued to grow in importance as vehicles of movement even until the year 1845, which was some time after all the important centers in the region east of the Alleghanies were linked together by railroads.

Ohio's first iron highway was the Mad River and Lake Erie Railway, which extended from Sandusky to Springfield. The road was begun September 7, 1835, in the town of Sandusky, and by the year 1840 it had attained a length of thirty miles.[1] The first locomotive on the Mad River line was called the *Sandusky*. It had been built in Paterson, New Jersey,[2] for a little New Jersey road, but was bought by the Ohio enterprise and taken to the scene of its future labors by way of the Erie Canal and Lake Erie. The *Sandusky* was the product of an American mechanic named Swinburne, an employee of the Paterson locomotive works. The firm had brought over an English workman to design and build its engines, but the Englishman had failed in his attempt, and Swinburne volunteered to undertake the task. He made the *Sandusky* a success. It was the first locomotive west of the Alleghany Mountains,[3] and its arrival in Ohio was destined to have a more profound effect on the future railway history of the interior than was imagined by the company that had become its possessor. No rails had been laid when the *Sandusky* reached the town after which it was named, and as the company therefore found itself in the possession of a locomotive, but no tracks, it built the tracks

[1] Tanner's "Description of the Canals and Rail Roads of the United States," p. 212.
[2] By Rogers, Ketchum and Grosvenor, a firm that afterward became the Rogers Locomotive Works.
[3] The first practical, working locomotive. A diminutive model machine, hereafter mentioned, had previously appeared in Indiana.

to fit the locomotive. The gauge of the engine was found
to be four feet and ten inches, and the gauge of the road
was established accordingly. Nor did the influence of the
Sandusky end at that point. Since the Mad River road
was the first structure of the sort in the state, and was being
still further extended, the legislature of Ohio passed a law

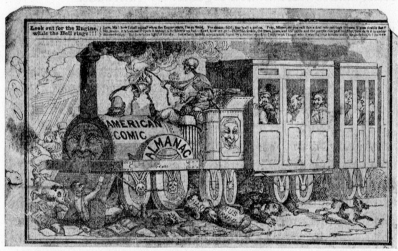

316.—Another cartoon of about 1840 dealing with the devastation caused by the
running of railway trains through streets occupied by other traffic. A
skeleton is in charge of the locomotive, and the engine bears grinning faces
that are laughing at the joke played on the victims. The passengers are
also unconcerned.

making the standard gauge of the state four feet and ten
inches, to conform with the track already in place. The
track-width introduced into Ohio in such a peculiar way
was later adopted by other roads in adjoining commonwealths, thus adding to the confusion of gauges which
afterward prevailed.

When the Mad River line was chartered in 1832 it
was authorized to extend between Lake Erie and the Ohio
River, and its course was specified in the law. The route

in question was one that had been adopted nearly two centuries before, by French fur-traders and trappers, as the northern portion of their trail between Canada and Louisiana. The charter law also reserved to the state a right to buy the railway after forty years. That option was never exercised. Small box-shaped passenger cars were used on the Mad River road, and the people of northwestern Ohio were exceedingly proud of their project, but it was necessarily without much importance, except for local travel, until with the lapse of years it was extended and became linked to other parts of the growing Ohio system.

Meanwhile an ambition to possess a railway had seized the little town of Frankfort, in Kentucky, and it was advancing with a similar scheme at the same time that Sandusky was building the first Ohio road. There was no particular reason why Frankfort, far out in the Kentucky woods, should have a railroad, except that it had heard other communities were building them. And as a railroad even at that early day had to extend somewhere, in order that it might possess two ends and a time-table, it was decided to build the track toward the neighboring town of Lexington. Or perhaps it was Lexington which decided to build the road and chose Frankfort as the other terminus.[1] At any rate the undertaking was decided upon and was begun in 1834.[2] It is probable that all the engineering work performed in connection with the construction and equipment of the road was done without enlisting outside aid. The track consisted of flat strips of iron two inches wide, laid on limestone slabs. These stone rails were of irregular lengths, being from eight to fifteen

---

[1] Lexington, the eastern terminus of the road, was only a few miles from Boonesboro, where many of those who came into the interior over the first Wilderness Road had halted.
[2] And finished in 1839.

feet long, in accordance with the luck attending their quarrying and transportation. The strips of iron were secured to the stone rails by spikes that fitted into holes drilled in the stone. Melted lead was then poured into the holes around the spikes to prevent them from shaking loose. All this hard labor was soon found to be worthless, since freezing and thawing split the limestone. The original rails were therefore taken up and replaced by timbers.

There was at first no freight hauled on the road, and the pioneer cars built by the company were designed exclusively for passenger traffic. They were double-decked affairs, the lower compartment being reserved for women and children and the upper deck for men. Only about a dozen passengers—half of them below and the rest of them above—could find comfortable accommodations in a coach. The motive power during the first few months after the opening of the line consisted of horses, each vehicle being pulled by two animals. No steam-engine was brought from the East for a considerable time, and the first locomotive used on the road was a small machine made by a mechanic of Lexington. The engine tender was similar to the one made by Isaac Dripps for the *John Bull,* and the water hogshead was replenished from wells near the track at which the locomotive stopped when its supply ran low. Two timbers stuck out in front of the boiler, and to each timber was attached a broom made of hickory splints adjusted to brush the dirt off the rails as the engine moved ahead. The inaugural trip of the first locomotive on the Frankfort and Lexington road was intended by the company to be a long-remembered occasion, and it was. A considerable number of invited guests took their places on a line of little flat cars built for the event, and the brigade moved off in good order, though at a very slow speed. But when the train was approaching Frankfort a snow-storm began, and the engineer could not be persuaded to continue the journey. He stopped the ma-

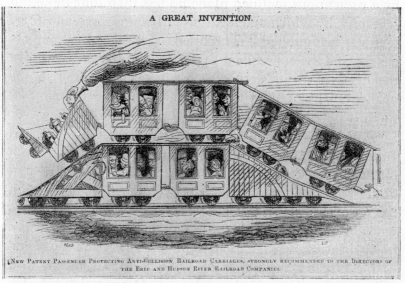

A GREAT INVENTION.

New Patent Passenger Protecting Anti-Collision Railroad Carriages, strongly recommended to the Directors of the Erie and Hudson River Railroad Companies.

317.—Gradually a new feeling became apparent in the pictorial comment on collisions and other accidents, and the cartoonists, instead of making fun of travellers or pedestrians who were killed, suggested that the railway companies find a way to lessen or prevent the growing number of accidents. That viewpoint was thereafter maintained. A cartoon of about 1850.

chine under a shed to protect it from the inclement weather, and those passengers who lived in Lexington had to go back home by some mode of conveyance to which a snow flurry did not constitute a menace. Although the first locomotive of the road could move by its own power and pull a number of cars behind it, it was not a success and was abandoned. Horses were again employed and continued in use until a more effective engine was obtained some time afterward. By the year 1840[1] this railway had

[1] According to Tanner's "Description," p. 193.

been extended in a northwestern direction to the Ohio River near Louisville, had attained a length of more than ninety-two miles, and had cost about a million dollars. The Frankfort end of the road was distinguished for a time by a pretentious inclined plane no less than four thousand feet long, by which an elevation of two hundred and forty feet was surmounted.[1] The breaking of a rope on one occasion, and the consequent drop of a number of cars down the declivity, with serious consequences, resulted in the abandonment of the inclined plane and the conquest of the hill by a more tortuous route.

Although Indiana's first railroad—the Madison and Indianapolis line—was not begun until 1836, and not opened for use over any considerable part of its extent until 1838, an agitation in favor of railroads had begun in the state about ten years before. Governor Ray had contended for railed tracks rather than canals in 1827. In his legislative message of 1830 he had suggested the union of the Great Lakes with the Ohio River by means of a railway extending southward from Detroit through Indianapolis to Louisville. A year later he again urged consideration of the subject upon the legislature, and a committee of that body spent some time in discussing the practicability of the new transportation device as compared with the value of canals. During this same year of 1831 many of the people of Indiana obtained their first sight of a locomotive. It was not a big and practical engine like the *Sandusky*—which weighed four or five tons —but a miniature locomotive then being carried about the country and exhibited by an enterprising Kentucky showman named Joseph Bruen. Bruen moved his little engine from place to place in a Conestoga wagon, together with

[1] Ibid. p. 193.

a diminutive passenger car and a few rods of portable track. When he reached a town of consequence he hired a man to help him take his railroad out of the wagon, and then he set it up and put it in operation, charging a small fee to such of the populace as desired to be moved by steam. Bruen's migratory railroad was a financial success, and his locomotive—although it really travelled much further in a wagon than on its own wheels—was the first machine of the sort in that part of the country.

No less than six railway charters were granted by the Indiana legislature in 1832, and about twenty-five more were bestowed before the first pretentious steam line was begun in the state. All these legal preliminaries, however, resulted in almost nothing. The private companies organized to carry out the many new enterprises could secure no capital for their proposed work. Only one of the roads chartered in 1832 succeeded in laying any tracks before 1836. The one exception was the Lawrenceburg and Indianapolis line, which was one-and-a-fourth miles long,[1] and was opened in 1834 with the usual Fourth of July celebration. The road had an embankment no less than ten feet high, another of five feet, and a cut five feet deep. It also boasted of two curves and two bridges. Its rolling stock consisted of one car, built at an expense of $222.12½, and a horse of value unknown. The total operating expenses incurred on the day of the opening were $12.62, and the net receipts were $60.00, which sum was immediately given in the shape of a dividend to the owners of the road, much to their gratification. As many as forty or fifty people crowded into the car for each of its trips, and the horse was found able to draw the load —for a very few yards—at the rate of nineteen miles

[1] The construction cost was about $1900.

1071

an hour. Doubtless the highly satisfactory gross receipts of the day would have been still larger had not the motive power succumbed to exhaustion. A barbecue also distinguished the occasion.[1]

More than four years intervened between the auspicious event just described and the opening of the Madison and Indianapolis road in 1838. The last-named enterprise was part of the ambitious but ill-fated scheme of public improvements upon which Indiana had entered in 1836.[2] The first part of the line to be built was a section of twenty-two miles between the towns of Madison and Vernon. Some idea of its physical characteristics and intended method of operation may be gained from the following contemporary statement:[3]

"The location & Plans of the road have all been adopted to the exclusive use of steam as the motive power. Of the propriety of this there can be no doubt. The cost of the horse path is thereby saved, the delay and confusion arising from the simultaneous use of both steam and horse power will be avoided, the character of the road elevated by the greater dispatch in the conveyance of passengers. . . . In the use of the rail roads constructed by the State it will probably be best for the State to furnish the motive power, leaving the cars for the conveyance of freight and passengers to be furnished by individuals or companies, from whom the State will exact the proper toll for the use of the road, and for the motive power."

The physical features of the roadbed were somewhat unusual. Two parallel trenches were dug, and in them were placed timbers about twelve inches wide and eight inches thick. Cross-ties were then laid on top of the two rows of timbers, at intervals of three feet. The cross-ties were eight inches wide and six inches thick. On top of the cross-ties were laid T-rails of the type first whittled by

---

[1] These features of the Lawrenceburg and Indianapolis road and of the formal opening thereof, were contained in a "Report" transmitted by the company to the legislature, dated December 5, 1834, and signed by James Blake, president pro tem.

[2] It was one of the roads chartered as a private corporation enterprise in 1832, but no work was done by the incorporating company and it became a part of the public improvement plan undertaken by the state.

[3] "Report of the Principal Engineer." December 5, 1837.

HOW TO INSURE AGAINST RAILWAY ACCIDENTS.
Tie a couple of Directors upon every Engine that starts with a Train.

318.—In course of time the new idea became more pronounced, and by the middle of the sixth decade the cartoonists, reflecting a slowly formed public opinion, were bluntly demanding that those in charge of the railways give heed to the duties resting upon them and administer the lines with more thought for safety and proper service, or else suffer the consequences of their negligence and greed. A cartoon of the last-described sort. Date, about 1858.

Stevens out of a pine stick. The rails were three-and-a-fourth inches high and came from England, where they were bought at a cost of eighty dollars a ton.

The locomotive of the road had been made in Philadelphia by Baldwin, and had been started to its destination on a sailing vessel by way of the Delaware River, Delaware Bay, the Atlantic Ocean, the Gulf of Mexico, and the Mississippi and Ohio Rivers. It never arrived. The ship bearing the important mechanism was lost at sea, and the time for the opening of the road drew near without anything to open it with. Confronted by this emergency the directors of the railway sought for another engine that might be brought to the scene in time, and discovered that the near-by Frankfort and Lexington line had a machine which it was willing to sell. It may possibly have been the one built by a Kentucky mechanic and brought to a halt under a shed to protect it from the snow-storm. At any rate the Madison and Indianapolis road bought the Kentucky locomotive, and it was somehow taken from Frankfort to Louisville. There it was loaded on a river ark, brought up the Ohio River behind a steamboat, unloaded on the shore of Indiana, hauled up a hill on the Michigan Road[1] by a multitude of oxen, and finally placed in triumph upon the awaiting rails. It was still able to move on its arrival, and in November of 1838 conveyed an excursion back and forth over the nine miles of track then finished. Among the guests of the occasion were the Governor of the state and many other officials. This event, rather than the much earlier Fourth of July celebration of 1834, is commonly reckoned as the commencement of Indiana's railroad history. Eighteen miles of track had been completed by April of 1839, and ten more miles were finished while the enterprise was still under state ownership. The twenty-eight miles built by Indiana cost $1,624,603. When disaster overtook the state's public improvement plan the road was for a time leased to a private company which operated it on a percentage basis, but the lessees were not pleased with their bargain and returned

---

[1] It is a strange incident of history that Indiana's first steam railway locomotive should have been dragged to the scene of its employment over a highway built by permission of the Indians.

the railway to the commonwealth. A second transfer to another company was effected, and finally by state aid the track was finished to Indianapolis in 1847. The road remained under joint ownership of Indiana and the operating company until 1852, when the state sold its interest and enacted a general railroad law under the terms of which competing lines might be built in opposition to any railroads then existing.[1]

The interest displayed by Ohio, Kentucky and Indiana, and the actual commencement of railroad construction in those states, had its inevitable effect on Illinois. At that time the revenues of the state were scarcely sufficient to meet the ordinary expenses of government, yet the people decided to begin railroad building on a rather extensive scale. The legislature of 1837 was the one that framed Illinois' prospective undertaking. Stephen A. Douglas was a member of the body, and he advocated state ownership of whatever new traffic routes were built. But his ideas regarding the extent to which the state should commit itself in the financing of such works were more conservative than the aspirations of his colleagues or the public. Douglas advocated merely the building of two railways and one canal, together with the improvement of the Illinois and Wabash Rivers. His plan was rejected, and in February of 1837 the legislature committed the state to the creation of more than one thousand three hundred miles of railroad, together with the improvement of various rivers and the laying out and improving of various turnpikes. The works thus proposed called for the expenditure of more than ten million dollars.[2] No

[1] Cottman's "Early Railroads of Indiana" gives much detail concerning the financial, political and economic history of the Madison and Indianapolis enterprise and other early roads of the state.
[2] Tanner, in his "Description," p. 197, gives the sum as $11,315,099 for the projected railroads alone.

319.—The railroads of the Mississippi valley and their effect. An early Kentucky railway train. Probably on the Lexington and Frankfort line, which was begun in 1834. Length of road, 28 miles. Date of engraving, 1837.

important canal system such as had been undertaken by New York, Pennsylvania, Ohio and Indiana was begun by Illinois.

Only one of the railroads authorized by the act of 1837 was actually finished by the state itself. This was the line from Meredosia to Springfield. Work on several of the others was commenced, but the financial panic made it necessary, almost at once, to call a halt in the plan that had been outlined. Track laying on the Meredosia and Springfield road was begun in May of 1837. The rails consisted of timbers to which thin flat strips of iron were fastened by spikes. A locomotive had been ordered by the state[1] immediately after the legislative act was passed, and it was shipped by water, being taken up the Mississippi and Illinois Rivers to Meredosia, which place it

[1] From Rogers, Ketchum and Grosvenor, of Paterson.

reached in September. It was put on the tracks and first operated on November 8th. The road was finally completed to Springfield, a distance of fifty-eight miles, in the spring of 1842.

Meantime a second locomotive, called the *Illinois,* had been obtained from the Baldwin works and was in operation. Trains were run from Meredosia to within a short distance of Springfield by March of 1842, and a Springfield newspaper[1] stated that "the cars ran from Jacksonville, 33½ miles, in two hours and eight minutes, including stoppages. It is believed that the distance can be passed over in an hour and a half." It is apparent, therefore, that the speed then obtained was about fifteen miles an hour. The schedule on this first railroad of Illinois provided for a train three times a week in each direction.

So scanty was the population served by the road that it could only be operated at a loss. Several annoying accidents, doubtless due to the archaic nature of the track, contributed to the misfortunes of the undertaking. The engine frequently jumped the rails, and so discouraging did the whole situation appear that one day, after an accident, the locomotive was left where it stood beside the track, and there it remained deserted for many months. Eventually it was bought by an enterprising individual who equipped the wheels with tires no less than two feet in width, and undertook to use it on the ordinary dirt roads of the neighborhood and across the prairie itself. The machine did make one overland trip between Alton and Springfield in its altered shape, but during most of the journey its deliberate movement was due to the persuasion of a yoke of oxen. The tracks it left excited the

[1] The "Journal," of March 18.

320.—The City of Louisville's certificate showing the municipality's ownership of 2,000 shares of stock in the Lexington and Ohio Railroad Company. Face value, $200,000. Several states owned railroads in the early days of railway building and numerous cities acquired a stock interest in the enterprises through subscription to them or in exchange for privileges granted. Date, 1835.

amazement of some travellers who came across them soon afterward, and so interested were they in the strange trail that they followed it to discover by what sort of creature it had been made. They found the locomotive where it had been abandoned by its latest owner. It was never again moved from the spot where it had been forsaken until it was dismantled for the metal it contained.

Even the schedule of three trains a week had been

1078

abandoned after the final mishap, and the road was no longer operated. The legislature authorized its sale in 1847, and it was then acquired by eastern capitalists who altered the course of the line at its western extremity and opened it again for traffic in 1849 under the name of the Sangamon and Morgan Railroad.[1]

Chicago's first railway was begun in 1848. In that year the town had a population of some eighteen or twenty thousand, and a number of business men of the place resolved on the building of a railroad which should cross the northern part of the state to Galena on the Mississippi River. Construction work was begun in June of 1848 on the western edge of the corporate limits of Chicago, since the municipal officials refused to permit the railroad to enter the city. The men behind the enterprise had intended to use T-rails of the Stevens sort for their road, but the comparatively slender financial resources of the small town at first proved more powerful in shaping the physical character of the roadbed than did the enthusiasm of its projectors. Despite every endeavor they were unable to obtain sufficient funds to satisfy their desire for an up-to-date track, and so they contented themselves with some old-fashioned and second-hand strap-rails that had formerly been used and discarded by a railroad in the East. The rails were shipped by the Erie Canal and the lakes to Chicago, and there put into place. Next came the problem of a locomotive, and again the company was hampered by lack of money. It could not afford to buy a new engine, so it secured one that had been built by Bald-

---

[1] According to "James' Rail Road and Route Book for the Western and Southern States," Cincinnati, 1853 (p. 55), the road then had its western terminus at the town of Naples, on the Illinois River, several miles south of Meredosia, and its length had been reduced to fifty-four miles by the change made in its course.

An article dealing with this early Illinois railway, embracing the incidents here given and other facts concerning it, appeared in "Potter's American Monthly," July, 1879. The author was A. A. Graham.

win in 1836 for the road between Schenectady and Utica, in New York State. After several years of use by its first owners this engine had been sold to a new Michigan railroad,[1] by which it was christened the *Alert*. The Galena and Chicago road in turn bought the *Alert* from the Michigan corporation, and it was shipped to the third scene of its diversified labors by lake. When it arrived at Chicago the company was confronted by another embarrassment. Since the local government refused to allow the road to enter the town, the company found itself in the possession of a track on one side of the municipality and a locomotive on the other, with no practical way of bringing them together. But the authorities modified their opposition to railways in some degree and finally permitted the laying of a temporary track from the terminal of the road to the Chicago River, and by that means the engine, which was renamed the *Pioneer,* arrived at its final home. The other original rolling stock of the Galena and Chicago line consisted of half a dozen second-hand freight cars that were also obtained from the Michigan road. With the equipment so obtained Chicago's first railway was opened for business, and it was successful from the start. The excellent showing made by the early operations resulted in obtaining enough funds to push the road westward to the town of Elgin, which was reached in 1850.

The quaint *Pioneer* was fortunately preserved after its period of usefulness was ended, and to-day it reposes safely in the Field Museum of Chicago where it receives the veneration of these later generations.[2]

Michigan's earliest active interest in railroads was dis-

[1] Destined later to become the Michigan Central.
[2] The "Pioneer" is one of the earliest American-built locomotives that has been preserved. Its history, as above outlined, was traced by Angus Sinclair, and told by him in his "Development of the Locomotive Engine," pp. 362-366.

321.—Picture of a railroad train used by the bank of Tecumseh, Michigan, on its bank notes in 1833. Engraved by Rawdon, Wright and Hatch, of New York. The engine has a sharp-pronged cow-catcher, running on little wheels. Such a device was employed by Isaac Dripps, of the Camden and Amboy road, in 1832, and the engravers appear to have seen or heard of it. The iron bonnet on the smokestack was intended to arrest blazing embers, and was one of the schemes tried on some locomotives as a result of the first trip of the *De Witt Clinton*.

played several years before a state government was organized. In 1832 the Legislative Council of the territory passed an act creating a corporation known as the Detroit and St. Joseph Railroad Company. It contained the following provisions:

"Said corporation, hereby created, shall have power to construct a single or double railroad, from the city of Detroit to the mouth of the St. Joseph river, commencing at Detroit, and passing through, or as near as practicable to the village of Ypsilanti and the county seats of Washtenaw, Jackson, Calhoun, and Kalamazoo, with power to transport, take and carry property and persons upon the same, by the power and force of steam, of animals, or of any mechanical, or other power, or of any combination of them."

The act also provided that the road should be completed within thirty years, and the state reserved to itself the right to purchase the railway at its first cost plus fourteen per cent. interest thereon. This road, which finally came to be known as the Michigan Central, was not begun for several years, but its construction was eventually undertaken, and by 1840 it was in operation to Ann Arbor, a distance of forty-four miles.[1] Its western terminus was later shifted from the point originally specified by the act of 1832 to a little settlement known as New Buffalo, located in the extreme southwestern part of the state. New Buffalo was for a time the western end of the road, and two steamboats departed thence each day to Chicago. By the use of these steamboats and the Michigan Central road in the West, and the chain of railroads through central New York State, it eventually became possible to travel from New York City to Chicago in about three-and-a-half days.

But the first Michigan road was not the one incorporated in 1832 and just mentioned. The first railway

[1] Tanner's "Description," p. 215. The road was finished in 1849.

operated in the state was a little road called the Erie and Kalamazoo, which was thirty-three miles long and extended from Toledo, in Ohio, to the town of Adrian in Michigan. A picture of an early—and perhaps the first— train on the Erie and Kalamazoo is given in these pages. It shows an engine named the *Adrian,* and one of the most peculiar passenger cars of which any graphic record has been preserved. In its panels, windows and façade the car conveys a slight suggestion of the ecclesiastical architecture of the Middle Ages, and indicates that the germs of art and originality had already appeared in the region where the vehicle was built.

The enterprises thus far enumerated tell of the first westward spread of the railway in the northern states during the fourth decade of the century. Wisconsin was still a sparsely settled territory, and its only internal improvements consisted of a few dirt roads and trails through the woods. The situation then existing in Wisconsin was described in 1840, by an authority already quoted, in the following words:[1] "With the exception of some surveys, authorized by Congress, nothing has been done in this section of the United States, in the way of canals or railroads." Numerous other small railways, and several having a length of a hundred miles or more, were built and opened during the fifth decade in the region north of the Ohio. Cincinnati, which was at that time the principal city of the Middle West, had its eastward outlet through a railroad extending northward to Sandusky, where the east-bound line of travel was reached.

The further spread of railways in the South remains to be considered. That part of the country, though not so restless as the North and more sparsely inhabited,

[1] Tanner's "Description," p. 220.

probably did a little more railroad building between 1829 and 1845—in proportion to its resources and population—than did the North. The early activities of South Carolina and Kentucky have been outlined. Virginia was another state displaying considerable enterprise during the fourth decade. One of the first iron highways of the Old Dominion was the Chesterfield Railroad, a line extending for about thirteen miles westward from Richmond.[1] This road was begun in January of 1830 and finished during the summer of 1831. It was primarily designed as an outlet for some coal mines, but also carried a little local passenger traffic. The Richmond, Fredericksburg and Potomac Railroad was thus described in 1840:[2]

"It is 61 miles long, and when extended to the Potomac . . . will be 75 miles long. . . . The superstructure is of the ordinary wooden rail, plated with iron, in general use in the south, and recommended on this and most other southern roads by the cheapness of timber and motives of economy. When the travel on this road, which is increasing very rapidly, shall have become larger, the company will probably find it to their advantage to lay down heavy iron rails the whole length of their road."

Among the further pioneer enterprises of Virginia described by Tanner were the Petersburg and Roanoke road, a plate-rail line fifty-nine miles long that had been built at a cost of eight hundred thousand dollars; the Greensville road, eighteen miles in length, and others that gave the state a railway system of more than three hundred and sixty miles by 1840.

North Carolina chartered the Wilmington and Raleigh[3] Railroad in 1833, and by 1840 it was in operation

---

[1] Its eastern terminus was really at the town of Manchester, across the James River from Richmond.
[2] In Tanner's "Description," pp. 162-163.
[3] Although by the original charter, this road was to extend from Wilmington to Raleigh, as its name indicated, an amendment to the act of incorporation in 1835 authorized it to change the location of its northern terminus. Hence its anomalous name, for as finally built it did not approach within fifty miles of Raleigh. It was begun in October of 1836 and finished on March 7, 1840.

for a hundred and sixty-one miles between Wilmington and the town of Weldon on the Roanoke River, where it connected with the Petersburg and Roanoke road of Virginia. Another of the early North Carolina roads was the Raleigh and Gaston, thirty-five miles of which had been finished by 1840. The Virginia and North Carolina roads were eventually connected on the south with the Charleston and Hamburg road previously described, and on the north with the railways of Maryland, Delaware and New Jersey, and thus a north-and-south route by rail along the Atlantic seaboard eventually came into operation.

Georgia had begun to build two pretentious lines before 1840. One of these—the Georgia Railroad—began at Augusta, at the head of navigation on the Savannah River. The town of Hamburg in South Carolina lay directly across the river from Augusta, and Georgia's early railroad system was thereby linked with that of South Carolina, since Hamburg was the western end of South Carolina's first road. The Georgia Railroad by 1845 had reached the northwestern corner of the state and connected with the early lines of Tennessee. Its first fifty-seven miles consisted of the familiar wooden rails topped by strips of flat iron, but throughout the remainder of its course the road was built, from the first, with improved T-rails having a weight of forty-six pounds to the yard. The other important early Georgia work was known as the Central Railroad. It began at Savannah and extended to Macon by a rather irregular route that followed the windings of the Great Ogeechee River. About eighty miles were finished by 1840, and its entire length of one hundred and ninety-three miles to Macon was in use a few years thereafter. Both passenger and

1085

322.—A train on the Erie and Kalamazoo Railway, Michigan, in 1836. The passenger car, which deviates in marked degree from prevailing lines and was doubtless made in the West, somewhat suggests a large hencoop whose design was affected by the Gothic influence.

freight trains were in successful operation for a short distance north of Savannah as early as 1838, and by the final months of 1839 its passenger traffic had assumed respectable proportions.[1]

No extensive railroad building could take place in Georgia, Alabama or Mississippi during the period in which Indian nations owned and occupied large parts of those states. Georgia was the first of the three commonwealths to undertake pretentious schemes of the sort after the Indians had departed into the West, and Alabama and Mississippi followed her example a few years afterwards, as did Louisiana also. Mobile and New

[1] Tanner's "Description" (p. 176) gives the number of passengers carried by the road during the three months ending with Oct. 31, 1839, as 2,310, whose aggregate fares amounted to $5,244.85. During the same period its freight receipts amounted to $20,232.25. On the early railroads of the South the passenger traffic during the first few years of their operation did not constitute so large a proportion of the total business as was the case on the northern roads.

Orleans took up the question of rail communication with the North at a comparatively early day, and were stimulated in their efforts by the enterprise of Charleston and Savannah. Those two communities became united by rail with Chattanooga in 1849. Mobile undertook a road northwestward through Mississippi soon after the departure of the Indians, and New Orleans, by means of a route through Mississippi that eventually penetrated Tennessee and Kentucky, finally became connected with the Ohio valley by an overland line. Mississippi's first roads, however, were on the west side of the state and extended eastward from the great river that forms the western boundary of the commonwealth. The most important of these were short railways that touched the river at the towns of Vicksburg, Natchez, St. Francisville and Port Hudson. Their importance as links in the slowly developing modern travel system of the country was almost negligible until the sixth decade, during which period the South became still more active in rail installation. In that decade the hitherto isolated roads of the South were gradually joined by intermediate constructions, just as the scattered roads of the North were being similarly connected. Nearly all the early southern railroads followed the example of the Charleston and Hamburg line in the matter of gauge, and were five feet in width.

There were no railways west of the Mississippi River in 1849, and it was not until the year 1857 that a traveller could be carried from the Atlantic coast to the Mississippi River by power supplied by steam locomotives. Cincinnati and St. Louis had observed with concern, for about ten years, the growing importance of the east-and-west path of rail communication that led from New York by way of the Mohawk valley to the south shore of Lake Erie, and thence through southern Michigan to Chicago. The two cities accordingly resolved to build a road from the Ohio metropolis to the growing Missouri town which should become a worthy rival of the more northern route when used in connection with the railways that were approaching Cincinnati from the East. A road had indeed been projected between Cincinnati and St. Louis as early as 1832, during which year a charter had been obtained and some money subscribed. But at that time the plan failed to command sufficient support and was soon abandoned. It was revived in 1848, however, through a charter granted by Indiana, and Ohio's legislature passed an act in its behalf during the following year. Illinois — the third state to be crossed by the road — gave its permission for the undertaking in 1851. The important link in the national communication system which grew out of these three enactments was the Ohio and Mississippi Railroad. Surveys were begun in 1848, ground was broken in 1852, and twenty-six miles of rails extending westward from Cincinnati were in use on April 2, 1854. Then followed a period of financial embarrassment, and it was not until three years later that the line approached completion throughout its whole length.[1]

In the meantime the Baltimore and Ohio Railway had been slowly progressing westward despite difficulties of various sorts. It had reached the town of Wheeling, in Virginia, in 1853. By its use a traveller could then go from Baltimore to Pittsburgh in forty-four hours, and could reach Cincinnati by stage-coach in about four days more. If he were on his way to St. Louis he then crossed Indiana by stage-coach to Vincennes, whence he pro-

[1] It had a gauge of six feet.

ceeded over the Vincennes-St. Louis stage route on which periodic overland travel in the interior was first established.

Virginia[1] had refused to allow the Baltimore and Ohio Railroad to enter her territory except on condition that

EMIGRANTS' LINE.
FROM BALTIMORE TO WHEELING & PITTSBURG,
IN FORTY-EIGHT HOURS!!!
BY THIS LINE, PASSENGERS LEAVE BALTIMORE EVERY

Morning and Evening.

☞ This Road is **91 MILES nearer to Wheeling, Cincinnati, Indianapolis, Cleveland, Columbus, Ohio, Kentucky, Michigan, Indiana, Illinois, and Missouri,**—pleasanter, quicker; and **$1 less than any other line**!!!

☞ A reasonable number of Pounds of BAGGAGE will be allowed—all *Extra Baggage* will be forwarded for $1 50 per 100 pounds, and a Receipt given for its delivery. Apply at the Office,

42 FELL STREET, FELL'S POINT,
To **ABRAHAM CUYK, Agent** for Stockton, Falls & Co., and Balt. and Ohio R. R. Co.

323.—Travel to the interior in 1850. An advertisement issued conjointly by the Baltimore and Ohio Railroad and a stage-coach company. The railway did not reach Wheeling until 1853, and previous to that time travellers transferred to the coaches of Stockton, Falls and Company when they came to the place where the rails stopped. Thence they continued in the stages. "Emigrants," in the advertisement, meant Americans moving to the West.

the town of Wheeling should be made its western terminus. But the Baltimore and Ohio wanted to build westward by a more direct path, and desired to reach the Ohio River at a point considerably to the south of Wheeling. Virginia eventually saw she had made a mistake, and so in 1851 she had authorized the building of a road from Parkersburg, on the Ohio, that should connect with the Baltimore and Ohio at the town of Grafton. Such a road[2] was begun in December of 1854 and was finished late in 1856. It was practically a direct western extension of the Baltimore and Ohio, and by mutual agreement[3]

[1] Which then, of course, also included the present state of West Virginia.
[2] It was at first known as the Northwest Virginia Road.
[3] Under date of December 27, 1856.

its operation was undertaken by the senior enterprise. Thus there came into existence a rail route from the Atlantic to the Ohio River at Parkersburg, while at the same time another road was being laid down between Cincinnati and St. Louis. Only an iron link across southern Ohio still remained necessary in the ambitious scheme of joining the eastern coast and the Mississippi River. The requisite link was supplied by the Marietta and Cincinnati Railway, which was also finished in 1856.

The almost simultaneous completion of these three connecting railroads attracted country-wide attention, and the three lines themselves decided to coöperate in an elaborate celebration designed to commemorate the conquest of the eastern part of the continent by steam power. It was resolved to run a series of trains from Baltimore to St. Louis, making the trip in four days, with pauses at the principal towns and cities along the way. All the well-known men of the country were invited to become the guests of the three railways during the journey, and many of them accepted the invitation. The letter sent out by the Baltimore and Ohio road to its invited guests read thus:

"Sir:—The Ohio and Mississippi Railroad, uniting Cincinnati and St. Louis, will be formally opened on Thursday, 4th of June next. The Marietta and Cincinnati Road, which connects Cincinnati with the Ohio River near the western terminus of the Northwestern Virginia Branch of this company's road, will also be opened on Tuesday, 2nd of June.

"It is proposed to celebrate at the same time the opening of the branch road of 104 miles in length,—which unites the Baltimore and Ohio line at Grafton (100 miles east of Wheeling) with Parkersburg on the Ohio (96 miles below Wheeling), and which forms an important link in the direct line between Baltimore and Cincinnati and St. Louis.

"You are respectfully invited to make one of the company on this occasion, and to participate in the joint incidents and ceremonies attendant upon the trip."

The other roads issued similar invitations, and the party which set forth upon the journey consisted of distinguished business men from all sections of the country, city officials, editors, governors, members of Congress, cabinet ministers, and diplomats accredited to the government at Washington. Elaborate festivities marked the arrival of the trains at Marietta, Chillicothe, Cincinnati and St. Louis. Governor Salmon P. Chase of Ohio met the excursionists at Marietta, and the address delivered by him on that occasion contained the following passages:[1]

"Three distinct periods seem to mark the progress of intercommunication between the eastern and western—western once, but western now no longer—sections of our country. Our fathers were glad to avail themselves of the Indian trails and buffalo paths on land, and of canoes and broadhorns upon the water. . . .

"But the days of canoes and broadhorns, of Indian trails and buffalo paths passed away; steamboats made their appearance on the rivers, canals furnished new channels of water communication, and turnpikes and macadamized roads facilitated intercourse by land. Over the Alleghanies and westward as far as Springfield, in Ohio, the National Road was built for the accommodation of the traveller and the emigrant, and to secure the means of prompt communication in times of peril. The traveller on this road may still see, standing by the wayside not far from the city of Wheeling, a simple monument which commemorates the services of Henry Clay in the creation of this then important bond and ligament of union between the Atlantic States and the interior. The monument will crumble, the road itself may be deserted and forgotten, but the name of Clay will live while patriotism is honored and genius finds a shrine in the hearts of men.

"Turnpikes and macadamized roads, rivers and canals still supply indispensable facilities of intercourse. But a third period has begun.— The railroad and the telegraph now assert their claims to pre-eminence as the most important means of rapid communication, and the most beneficial agencies of progress. . . .

"To-morrow you will be received by the Queen City of the great Central Valley. . . . There a greater wonder awaits you. The Ohio and Mississippi Railroad, forming still another link of the American Central Railway, stretches away still westward; and the iron horse,

[1] Governor Chase's words, as here quoted, are taken from the text of the speech in Smith's "Book of the Great Railway Celebrations of 1857," pp. 174-176.

impatient of delay, is eager to bear you on beyond the ancient limits of the Republic, where the memories of the Crusades and of French empire and of French civilization are perpetuated by the name of St. Louis.

"There you may pause; but the Railroad, the Locomotive and the Telegraph—iron, steam and lightning—the three mighty genii of modern civilization—still press on, and, I venture here to predict it, will know no lasting pause until the whole vast line of railway shall be complete from the Atlantic to the Pacific. . . ."

In response to the welcome of Governor Chase the Federal Secretary of State, Louis Cass, made answer.

"Fifty-one years ago," he said, "I represented this county in the legislature of the State. At that session Fulton and Livingston presented a petition asking for an exclusive right to navigate the waters of the State by steam, and offering as a consideration to employ boats which should be propelled up the Ohio at the rate of four miles an hour. To us, who had seen nothing descend the river but the unwieldy flat-bottomed boat, and nothing ascend it but the heavy barges, poled by almost naked men, and employing six months in a trip from New Orleans, the proposition seemed so impracticable as to approach the ridiculous, and unworthy of our consideration, and we wisely rejected it. And so you see that if the result had depended upon our action, the magnificent enterprise of steam-navigation would not now be startling us with its grand achievements.

"I have just passed over the railway traversing the mountains dividing the East from the West, a work which Rome never equalled even in her palmiest days, and during the whole passage my memory turned back to other days and scenes. I have traversed heretofore the whole distance from Washington to St. Louis by this route. I travelled on horseback, and it was a painful journey of many days." [1]

Cincinnati greeted the excursionists with congratulatory addresses, parades, banquets and a display by the fire department in Market Square.[2] Cincinnati was the first American city to employ steam fire engines, and several examples of the newly invented apparatus were assembled in the plaza to demonstrate their power by throwing torrents of water into the air for the edification of the strangers from the East. During the performance some firemen lost control of a hose, and the power-

[1] Smith's "Book of the Great Railway Celebrations of 1857," pp. 177-8.
[2] Now Fountain Square and Government Square.

ful stream was directed into a carriage containing Secretary of State Cass and Governor Chase. A contemporary picture of the celebration at Cincinnati is embraced in the pictorial story.

The arrival of the trains at St. Louis, about midnight of June 4, was greeted by the thunder of cannon,

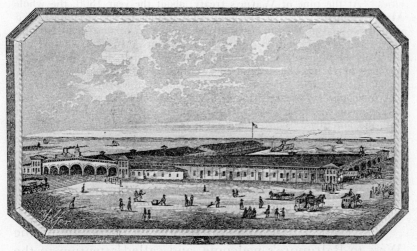

324.—Cleveland's railway station in 1854. The town then had about 37,000 people, an increase of some 36,000 since 1830. Six railroads, having an aggregate length of nearly 700 miles, already met there, and Cincinnati could be reached by an unbroken rail journey in nine hours. The trip to Philadelphia consumed but a day and a night.

the discharge of fireworks and the illumination of the city. The ceremonies on the banks of the Mississippi extended over a period of several days, and all the states and cities of the Middle West sent delegations to express their gratification at the completion of the work. During the following month official representatives of the interior states, and delegations from the principal cities and towns of the Mississippi valley made a return visit to the East, and were similarly entertained by the cities of Washington and Baltimore. On the arrival of the travellers from the West at Baltimore the mayor of that city[1] welcomed them by an address in which occurred the following passages:

"If we go back to the early explorations of Christopher Gist and Daniel Boone, not a century ago, we find the Indian watch fires burning upon the sites of what have since become prosperous and thriving cities. At the time of Wayne's treaty, about the year 1800, the whole Miami country with the exception of Cincinnati was an undisturbed wilderness, and at the same period the population of that great city did not exceed seven hundred and fifty inhabitants. In 1828, before the effect of her internal improvements began to be felt, her white population had barely reached a limit of twenty-five thousand souls.

"Until within the last quarter of a century the progressive energies of our people had scarcely found a vent in those efforts of power and development which have since resulted in so many stupendous works of skill and enterprise, which stand forth in every State as enduring characteristics of the age. Steam, gentlemen, is the active agent to which we are indebted for this new impetus which has been given to the march of improvement. . . . The voice of the locomotive is heard in the valleys and upon the hilltops; it has driven before it the redman of the forest; it has surmounted obstacles heretofore deemed to be impregnable, and has raised its shout of triumph amidst the repose of centuries."[2]

Governor Chase of Ohio responded on behalf of the West to Baltimore's welcome, and called attention to the historical relationship which existed between Maryland and the states of the former Northwest Territory. He said:

"The very existence of the State of Ohio and her sister States of the old Northwest, with their present dimensions and institutions, is due in no small degree to the persistent determination with which Maryland, during the Revolutionary struggle and at its close, insisted that the vast domain west of the Alleghanies was in fact, and of right ought to be, the common property of all the United States, and not the special property of any particular State. It was at Cumberland, in Maryland also, that the great National Road began; that first practical conquest of the Alleghanies, forever identified with the name and memory of the patriot statesman to whom his grateful countrymen are now rearing

[1] Thomas Swan.
[2] Smith's "Book of the Great Railway Celebrations of 1857." Part 2; pp. 62-63. The Baltimore celebration took place July 18th.

another monument amid the green fields of his beloved Ashland. And now you have made us your neighbors, and invited us into your midst by the great Railroad over which we have come hither. . . .

"No one, Mr. Mayor, who thinks at all of the westward progress already achieved by the railroads which form this American Central Line, can help anticipating the time when it shall reach the Pacific. How many years ago was it that Oliver Evans declared that the child was already born who would go from Baltimore to Boston in twenty-four hours? Many then thought him crazy. He only thought himself bold. But his anticipation lagged far behind the reality. As I was borne along, day before yesterday, from our State Capital to this city, in twenty-two hours, over great rivers and lofty mountains . . . I thought of Oliver Evans, and wondered how old is now the man who shall yet go from Baltimore to San Francisco in five days by rail. Perhaps it was a little presumptuous, but I did actually fancy myself hurled along, with shriek and puff and clatter, through the defiles of the Rocky Mountains, across the plains of the Great Basin, under or over the rugged summits of the Sierra Nevada, until the Bay of San Francisco flung back under my eye the glances of the sun. I hope, Mr. Mayor, I shall have the pleasure of meeting you at the celebration of the opening of the Atlantic and Pacific road, to which I trust the people of California will invite us all."

With the completion of the steam highway between Baltimore and St. Louis the Atlantic coast region and the Mississippi River were connected by rail. After the iron tracks had reached the great river of the interior valley, extensive railway construction toward the West paused for a time as though to gather strength for the final effort that was destined to carry it for the remainder of the distance across the continent. Active interest in a proposed railroad to the Pacific had been visible for more than a decade, but seven years were still to elapse before the plans for a trans-continental road were to assume concrete form and make its building an immediate certainty.

CHAPTER XLVIII

GENERAL VIEW OF TRAVEL CONDITIONS EAST OF THE MIS-
SISSIPPI JUST BEFORE THE GREAT OVERLAND RUSH TO
THE FAR WEST — A CONFUSING AND CHAOTIC HODGE-
PODGE OF STAGE-COACHES, STEAMBOATS, CANALS AND
LITTLE RAILWAYS — ONLY TWO WEEKS REQUIRED FOR
AN EXTENSIVE TRIP IN THE REGION — MORE SYMP-
TOMS OF IMPROPER RAILWAY PRACTISES APPEAR —
FRAUDS COMMITTED ON TRAVELLERS — COSTS OF
VARIOUS JOURNEYS AND THE TIME CONSUMED BY
THEM — CONDITIONS IN THE SOUTH AND MIDDLE
WEST — FROM BALTIMORE TO NEW ORLEANS IN
SEVEN DAYS, BY MEANS OF FIVE RAILROADS, TWO
STEAMBOATS AND TWO STAGE-COACHES, AT A COST OF
$62.50

BY the year 1848 about half of the continental width
had been overrun and permanently settled by the
white race. All that part of the country from the Great
Lakes to the Gulf of Mexico, and from the Atlantic coast
to the western part of Missouri was occupied by established communities and an active, restless, rapidly growing population. Nearly a hundred little railroads, from
five miles to a hundred and fifty miles long were scattered
over the eastern states and a score or more of similar roads
were likewise in actual operation in Ohio, Kentucky,
Indiana, Illinois, Michigan, and the interior commonwealths of the South. The navigable streams of the East

1096

were dotted with steamboats, and nearly six hundred such craft[1] were busy on the Ohio, Mississippi and other interior rivers. These were being blown up, burned, sunk by snags or otherwise destroyed at the rate of a hundred or more a year, and were being replaced just as rapidly. A thousand stage-coaches ceaselessly rolled over the turnpikes between the cities and towns. The nation's facilities for communication had so multiplied and increased in excellence that with good luck a traveller could make any ordinary long journey in a week's time, and but little more than two weeks were necessary, under favorable circumstances, in accomplishing the most extensive trip possible within the limits of the country just defined.

If a man wanted to wander from upper New England to the farthest edge of Missouri, for instance, he could get to New York, Philadelphia or Baltimore by stage-coach and sailing-boat in four or five days, and to Pittsburgh by rail, canal and stage-coach in three days more. He could then reach St. Louis on a steamboat in four days, and by the end of the second week be nearly at his destination, having perhaps made the trip across Missouri on horseback. Such an expedition was about the most protracted that could be undertaken at the time within the settled limits of the country. A traveller could go from Philadelphia to New Orleans over the eastern route by means of railway cars and stage-coaches in a week, at a cost of $94 exclusive of food and lodging, or by way of Pittsburgh and the rivers in nine or ten days, for $36. Land conveyances were popular, notwithstanding the cheapness of water transportation, because they were believed to

---

[1] According to the list embraced in James Hall's "The West; Its Commerce and Navigation": Cincinnati, 1848.

325.—The completion of each new railroad which extended a little farther toward the Mississippi was the occasion of a public celebration. Ticket to a reception given in Meadville, Pennsylvania, in honor of two foreign capitalists who had helped to build an American railway.

offer the traveller a considerably better chance of getting to the end of his trip without loss of life or limb. The countless accidents to river boats caused many people to avoid them altogether.

The effects of the disastrous panic of ten years before had disappeared, and the country was prosperous. Fifteen or sixteen years of experience with railways had been sufficient to prove their value, and money was preparing to venture bravely in the iron highways. An era of extensive railroad building was about to begin, and many enterprises of the sort were being organized in every occupied part of the republic. But there was no more financial delirium; no new "railroad craze" exciting the public as a mass. Though the results of the crash of 1837-1838 had vanished its memory still remained as a

1098

warning, and some of the new highways were planned and pushed forward in a more practical way than had characterized similar work in the former period of inflated credit and wild popular speculation. The bulk of the people not only saw the urgent need for better railway facilities, but also recognized the need of sanity in their creation.

At about this time, however, there likewise appeared the first outward symptoms of an unfortunate condition that was destined to become much more prominent as the years went on, and that has injuriously affected the railway system of the country since the period mentioned. Although the people as a whole had cast out their mania and viewed the subjects of railroad construction and administration with saner eyes, a small but influential portion of the population did not follow their example. Those avaricious men who represented, in the economic and political affairs of their day, the influences which these later times have come to define as "predatory wealth" and "special privilege," were beginning to recognize the opportunities that would lie within their grasp if they could control so vital a portion of the nation's industrial fabric as the railways were obviously destined to become. They caught glimpses of the power that would be theirs if they built, operated and manipulated railways as gigantic weapons, rather than as agencies of public benefit which would methodically aid in the creation of new wealth through the operation of those processes they were primarily designed to perform.

To characters so warped, and to able minds so inclined, the lure was irresistible and the result was sure. Thus began the extensive practise of building railways with the object of acquiring money through their construction rather than by their later efficient operation. One common method by which this purpose was attained was for the originators of the enterprise—acting as its directors—to award to themselves (separately organized as a construction company) a contract for the building of the line, paying to themselves for their work as contractors the amount obtained for the capital stock bought by the public. A considerable part of the sum so appropriated would then be diverted from its legitimate use, and inferior equipment bought with the remainder. Thus the road would not only start upon its career with a debt greater than the value of its assets, but would also be compelled to use part of its earnings each year indefinitely thereafter to pay interest on money never employed in its creation. In order to meet obligations thus dishonestly placed upon it, a road so built would be compelled to fix its rates for service at a higher point than should have been the case. Out of practises such as these there later grew the widespread railway habit of issuing large dividends of new capital stock for which the issuing roads received no recompense.[1] Such issues still further increased the debts of the companies, added more interest charges to their yearly burdens and resulted in additional advances in the rates they were compelled to charge as the price of their services.

Another external symptom of the deep-seated disease which attacked the railways of the country was the practise, long universally followed by their owners and manipulators, of granting secret concessions to favorites. This purpose was achieved through the bestowal of their service at a reduced price, or for no price at all. Those who were not so unfairly favored had to bear the burden.

[1] A process that eventually came to be called "cutting a melon."

·A third manifestation of the malady sometimes consisted in the dishonest manipulation of railways through their combination; a process designed to create one big and new company unit out of two or more small pre-existing units. Such an operation was often accompanied by intricate financial practises, obscure to the lay mind, but which usually had one common result. The new railroad company thus evolved nearly always found itself weighed down by a greater debt than the sum of all the previous debts of its constituent parts, and the amount represented by the discrepancy was the profit of the avaricious ones. The public did not object to the physical and operating amalgamation of such railroads as were involved in unifications of the sort, for such unions of previous separate, short and often hostile lines were exceedingly desirable and advantageous in so far as they contributed to more expeditious or safer transportation facilities. In that respect they improved railroad travel and traffic as much as the removal of a sand-bar and a thousand snags improved the navigation of a river. But the people did look askance at the mounting debts, unrepresented by a corresponding increase in assets, and at the greater annual interest obligations which they had to pay in the shape of correspondingly larger charges for service.

And, finally, a fourth symptom of the disease incurred by the railways through their contact with the special privilege of former days was their enforced and corrupt association with the political affairs of the republic, and of its states and cities.

The possibilities that lay in all these things were glimpsed at an early period, and tests made by the discoverers demonstrated the soundness of their judgment.

1101

A long continued carnival of wrong then began, and the result is familiar history. An unknown fictitious amount was added to the legal debt of the national transportation fabric,[1] colossal fortunes were built up by complicated swindle and theft,[2] the public service was corrupted, and private control, maintenance and operation of railways in the United States finally collapsed as a consequence of wrong-doing. The existing system of ownership and control did not contain within itself, or at least did not display, the elements essential to its moral rehabilitation and so the Federal government finally found it necessary to step in and undertake, with respect to the railroads of the country, those functions which ordinarily pertain to the ownership and administration of a legitimate, honestly conducted business enterprise.

Development of the modern traffic system, at the close of the fifth decade, was not going ahead in accordance with any comprehensive plan based on a view of the whole country and its requirements, but was still largely dictated by neighborhood considerations. The day was passing in which growth of that broader sort could be planned in all its features as a coherent, well balanced, continental undertaking and carried out, in all its ramifications, as the chief national work. Local impulse had been the original or controlling factor in a considerable part of such advancement up to that time.[3] Too much had been done hastily; too many standards of construction had been used; too much rivalry and jealousy had entered as governing motives into the various projects; too narrow horizons

---

[1] Some approximate idea of the sum may perhaps be obtained, about ten years hence, through the Governmental investigation lately begun into the financial history and present physical value of the railroads of the country.

[2] In which process the manipulation of the stock market was doubtless the principal factor.

[3] Although by no means in all of it. Such enterprises as the National Road and the Erie Canal had a broader foundation than mere local needs or desires.

326.—The Ohio and Mississippi Railroad was finished between Cincinnati and St. Louis in 1857, thus bringing the great central river and St. Louis into uninterrupted rail communication with the Atlantic coast cities. The event was attended by general popular rejoicing in the Middle West. In Cincinnati the city's fire department assembled in Market Square, as here shown, and threw water into the air. St. Louis held a big torch-light procession and fired one hundred guns. The first west-bound train was greeted with enormous enthusiasm along the way.

had influenced their creation and limited their usefulness. The needs of the various parts of the country were too divergent, or else altered too swiftly, to make it possible for all the new highways of movement to act in substantial harmony or be promptly welded into an economic machine purposely designed to furnish a maximum of accommodation to the public. The result of these conditions, under which the modern transportation system of the country came into being, and by which it was for a time so unfortunately though inevitably influenced, was a hodge-podge of facilities originally created with no thought of their common action for the people's benefit,

1103

and whose coöperation, when it did exist, was at first usually compelled by popular demand rather than foreseen and voluntarily undertaken. After a few years of mad scramble in all sorts of construction, and of piecemeal and unrelated work it had become too late to alter the conditions brought about by such methods, and the consequences of them were deeply stamped for a long time on the national life.

The fight by which railroads overwhelmed the canals and destroyed many of them, instead of recognizing the ultimate value of the two highways to each other, was one outcome of the jealousy and shortsightedness engendered by those conditions under which the modern era in transportation began. So, also, was the similar hostility manifested for a time by the railroads—though less openly—to the improvement of wagon roads and to river traffic. To-day many of the railways are systematically, and at large monetary cost, educating the people in the value of better wagon roads and are even beginning to suggest the resuscitation of the canal system and its extension, after the method used by France, in those parts of the United States to which that process is adaptable.

Nor did the virtual disappearance of the stage-coach, the curtailment of the canal system and substantial abandonment of the rivers, mark the end of a period of jealousy and hostility. After the railways had become dominant among the country's highways they began to fight among themselves, and for nearly two generations failed to rightly gauge their real relationship to one another and to the national life of which they formed so important a part. It was not altogether unnatural that this should have happened, for the railroads were born in a time of fierce controversy, were compelled to fight for their own existence, fell prey to an arrogance born of their victories, and grew up to maturity during a period when fraud and trickery in business affairs were looked upon with more complaisance than is lately the case. Thus they drifted into the practise of doing unfair and dishonest things to one another and to the people on whose good-will their corporate existence and self-control depended. Many of the errors that they made and the wrongs they did were, to a considerable extent, the result of a legacy left to them, and were committed by men who lived and worked and schemed according to the standards of a time now outgrown.

The travel conditions that prevailed throughout the eastern and middle states from about 1840 to 1850 were confusing and chaotic to anyone who had not purchased his knowledge at the cost of experience. There were so many different methods of making any contemplated journey of length, and so many possible conditions to be encountered during its progress that the prospective traveller was often bewildered—despite the advice he received and the innumerable guide books he read—with regard to the most desirable plan to pursue in reaching his intended destination. Of public conveyances fiercely competing for his patronage he sometimes had the choice of steamboats, stage-coaches, canal boats and railways in half a dozen combinations; and the advisability of using any particular combination often depended on matters or distant circumstances which it was impossible for him to know in advance. He was only certain of one thing, namely, that the representative of each line declared without qualification that his company's vehicles were pre-eminently the most desirable, comfortable, expeditious,

cheapest and safest. Furthermore, the extension of existing public travel routes of every sort was going ahead
with such rapidity that no source of advance information
to which an ordinary man might obtain access could safely
be depended upon as an accurate picture of the situations
which he would encounter on his proposed trip.

All those things combined to make possible the practise of deceptions and frauds on travellers, and the opportunities thus presented were in many cases seized by

327.—A revival of the old custom whereby taverns issued money. Sample of
the script printed by a Cincinnati hotel for the convenience of travellers
and the local population during the Civil War.

men who were in position to profit by such conduct.
Many of the guide books issued for the information of
travellers contained references to certain deceptions here
outlined and warnings against them, but perhaps none was
more outspoken concerning this phase of the travel conditions of the time than a little volume printed in Boston in
1851.[1] An extract from this book will give a glimpse at
some of those former elements of travel that sprang from
deceit and misrepresentation rather than from actual

[1] "The Irish Emigrant's Guide for the United States." By Rev. J. O'Hanlon.

DETROIT.

328.—Bird's-eye view of Detroit showing the water-front and a railway terminal after the railroad era had assumed importance in the Middle West. An example of the effect, upon an interior city's growth, of the introduction of steam transportation.

physical discomfort. In discussing the subject its author said:

"Frauds of boarding-house keepers, however, are cast in the shade by the impositions of forwarding houses and the persons in their employ. The nature of this business consists in a contract entered upon between . . . these firms and the owners of steamboats, stage coaches, canal boats and railroad cars, in which the forwarding houses agree to receive the tickets of these agents at a stated price, and to transport the holders and their luggage to places along their route. It will be the object of the forwarding agents to make as much on the tickets as the purchasers will agree to pay. This, however, would be the least objectionable feature in the business, if in all cases other engagements were fulfilled. But such is seldom the case. Sometimes tickets being [are] furnished to passengers in New York which profess to run them through to their destination without further charge; these tickets are protested[1] at the first stage of their route, and various objections made, either as to the mode of conveyance or the distance agreed on. The headquarters of these swindling concerns are established at important cities in the interior; as, for instance, those in the state of New York are principally located at Albany. Before the Emigrant starts from New York for a Northern or Western destination, he receives a ticket neatly printed and headed by engravings of a steamboat, railroad cars or canal boats, with three horses attached. He is given to understand that on the payment of an exorbitant or a low price, as the case may be, at New York, this ticket will carry him through Albany to a place mentioned; whereas the ticket itself only procures a passage to this latter city, where it has to be presented to some agent or company on which it is drawn. If the holder be supposed to possess plenty of money he is obliged to pay his fare over again, which he will frequently do, rather than delay or return to New York to prefer a useless complaint, no evidence being obtained to substantiate it. . . .

"Sometimes passengers are promised passage on packet boats on the canal, and are sent by line boats instead, when [where] they are crowded together in the hold without comfort or convenience. The following is the manner in which this deception is practiced in Albany. . . . The passenger with whom the false engagement is made is transported from Albany to Schenectady by railroad, a distance of 17 miles, and at a cost of 50 cents. Once there, the passenger cannot obtain redress, and is obliged to take up with any means of conveyance offered."[2]

The practise of defrauding travellers by means of misrepresentation and extortion grew so rapidly in New York

[1] By the transportation companies.
[2] The traveller who was proceeding to Buffalo and the West by canal embarked on his boat at Schenectady. O'Hanlon's "Guide," pp. 53-59.

CHICAGO—*By Railroad and Steamboat.*

NEW-YORK to	Distance.	Time.	Ex. Frt. pr. 100 lb.	FARE. Am. Cur.		FARE. En. Cur.	
		d. h.	cents.	$	c.	s.	d.
Albany,	145	12	18		50	2	1
Utica,	255	17	Free.	2	6	8	6
Syracuse,	316	1	Free.	2	92	12	6
Auburn,	365	1 2	Free.	3	36	14	0
Rochester,	415	1 2	Free.	4	61	19	4
Buffalo,	508	1 8	Free.	5	50	22	11
Erie,	600	2 12	39	7	50	31	3
Ashtabula,	650	2 12	39	7	50	31	3
Cleaveland,	700	3	39	8	00	33	4
Black River,	720	3	44	8	50	35	6
Huron,	740	3 6	44	8	50	35	6
Sandusky,	755	3 6	44	8	50	35	6
Maumee and Monroe,	780	3 12	44	8	50	35	
Detroit,	825	4	44	8	50	35	6
Sandwich, U. C.	820	4	44	8	50	35	6
Mackinaw and G. Bay,	1474	6	70	12	00	52	1
Milwaukee and Racine	1480	6 00	70	12	00	52	1
Chicago,	1520	6 12	70	12	50	52	1

By this route at least seven days are saved, as also the freight of baggage from Albany to Buffalo—100 pounds baggage free to Albany, and the same on the Lakes. Children under twelve years, half-price. Infants free. The above time can always be depended upon.

329.—Table giving the time occupied in travelling from New York by rail and steamboat, in 1848, to Cleveland, Detroit, Milwaukee and Chicago. Also the cost of tickets. From Warner's "Immigrant's Guide and Citizen's Manual: 1848."

during the decade beginning with the year 1841 that an investigation of the subject was finally undertaken by the legislature of the state in 1849. This investigation brought out the fact that all concerns called "forwarding houses"[1] employed men called "runners" whose business it was to induce prospective travellers to buy tickets over the lines they represented. The runner was either paid a stated salary or else was given any money that he could obtain in excess of the proper price which should have been paid by the traveller for his ticket. The effect of this system on the general public was exposed to the New York legislators by a witness who testified that the legitimate cost of a ticket from New York to Buffalo was two dollars and fifty cents; of which sum the river steamboat received fifty cents, the line canal boat one dollar and fifty cents, and the forwarding house fifty cents. He further stated that his "runners" represented the cost of the ticket at five dollars, and that for each ticket thus sold at double its proper value the runner himself received two dollars and fifty cents. "I pay the runners at the time the passenger pays his fare," the witness said. "The account stands thus: the passenger pays five dollars; from this deduct river fare, fifty cents; office in New York, fifty cents; canal fare, one dollar and fifty cents. The balance of two dollars and fifty cents goes to the runner."[2]

Another forwarding agent who testified during the New York investigation stated that he employed thirty-six runners whose salaries ranged from ten dollars to one hundred and sixty-five dollars a week.[3] His total payments to runners exceeded six hundred dollars a week,

---

[1] The name generally given to those establishments which made a business of seeking passengers for transportation lines, and which were paid on a commission basis for the passenger traffic they secured.
[2] O'Hanlon's "Guide," p. 55.
[3] Ibid., p. 55.

which amount, of course, represented the sum unduly obtained from travellers by his representatives. Early methods of this sort formed the foundation on which was later systematically erected the widespread plan of rate-making generally known as "charging all the traffic will bear."

The four principal travel conveyances of the time were described by O'Hanlon in his Guide as follows:

"First: Railroad cars.—The passengers that travel by the first-class carriages pay at least double or treble fares,[1] and are, in consequence, provided with more elegantly fitted cars, lined and cushioned; the higher grades of society take passage by them. The second-class carriages are further removed from the engine, but in other respects their accommodations are not so good, being unprovided with cushioned seats and exposed in summer to flying clouds of dust. . . . The railroad is a safe and most speedy mode of travel. . . . Sometimes danger is to be apprehended from a running off the track, which may be out of repair in places, but an accident seldom occurs through explosion.

"Second: Canal boats.—There are two classes of these, the packets and the line boats. The packets are elegantly furnished, and meals are served up on board by the owners, but the line boat is only used for transportation of freight and passengers who find themselves.

"If the latter desire dressed meals they will have to take on board a cooking stove and cooking utensils, as it will be found a matter of difficulty to procure use of the apparatus belonging to the boat. Most passengers, however, prefer the use of cold victuals, and are satisfied to put up with inconveniences for a few days. There are no berths or beds on the line boat, as on the packet, so that these necessaries have to be taken on board. Passengers sleep in the hold of the boat. Travelling by canal is the safest but slowest mode of conveyance in the United States; the packet boats, however, have a great advantage over the line boat in regard to speed. . . .

"Thirdly: Steamboats.—These have been termed 'flying palaces,' and many of them are fitted up in a style of great magnificence. But the comfort of travelling by them is confined to cabin passengers. Staterooms, accommodating two persons each, in separate berths, are appropriated for retirement by day and for rest at night; ladies and gentlemen have separate cabins, but dine at the same table, which is set out in the

---

[1] Hardly a proper way in which to state the proposition. The standard fare was the honest cost of a first class ticket; the cheaper tickets—often costing about half the standard rates—represented special ticket prices made to people who were departing from the East to settle in the interior, and which were only good for passage in cars or trains of inferior accommodation and quality.

'social hall,' and stocked with a variety of luxuries. . . . The deck passengers are immediately under the cabin, and in the hinder part of the boat. A few berths are fitted up for their reception without bedding. Provisions must be provided at their own expense, and also a mode of preparing them. Sometimes numbers are huddled together on board without having room to move, or stretch themselves out for rest; the inconveniences of this mode of travelling can hardly be appreciated without being experienced. It has been truly stated that more accidents by explosion, burning or sinking of steamboats occur annually in the United States, and more lives are [thus] lost, than in crossing the Atlantic. Travelling by steamboats is, therefore, not without its dangers.

"Fourthly: Stage coaches.—These are generally more expensive and incommodious means of conveyance, in proportion to distance travelled, than any other. . . . The roads over which they mostly run are so bad that accidents often occur by upsetting, and the passengers are continually jolted against each other. On some of the remote western routes they are nothing more than covered cabs, and afford little protection against cold in winter."[1]

By the middle of the fifth decade after 1800 the skeleton of the now existing railroad system of the East had come into existence, and railway journeys between most of the principal cities and towns could be performed. The following summary will sufficiently outline the principal features of railroad travel as they existed in the East at that time.

The traveller who left Washington on his way to Boston was limited to one train a day. It traversed the forty miles between the national capital and Baltimore in two-and-a-half hours, for which distance the price of a ticket was one dollar and sixty cents. Half an hour after arriving in Baltimore he was enabled to take passage in another train which carried him to Philadelphia, ninety-seven miles farther on his way, in six more hours. The fare between Baltimore and Philadelphia was three dollars. He was compelled to spend an hour and a half in Philadelphia, from which city he might secure a train that

[1] O'Hanlon's "Guide," pp. 72-74.

conveyed him to New York—eighty-eight miles—in five hours. His ticket for this part of the trip cost him four dollars. Arriving in New York at half past ten at night he was compelled to wait until the next day before resuming his journey, which began at eight o'clock in the morning, and he finally arrived in Boston at half past six o'clock on the second afternoon of his journey, after spending thirty-five and a half hours on the road. The total of his transportation expenses was eleven dollars and sixty cents.

The Baltimore and Ohio Railroad was in operation from Baltimore to Cumberland, which town, one hundred and seventy-eight miles distant, might be reached from Baltimore in nine and a half hours at a cost of seven dollars. One daily passenger train ran each way over the road, leaving in the morning and arriving at its destination in the evening. If a west-bound traveller was desirous of continuing onward from Cumberland he there found a stage-coach awaiting him in which he might proceed to Brownsville, Pennsylvania, a further distance of seventy-two miles. At Brownsville he transferred from his stage-coach to a steamboat and by it eventually reached Pittsburgh. He had then advanced two hundred and ninety miles westward from Baltimore at a cost of ten dollars, and the trip had taken him but thirty-four hours. So he had travelled by railroad, stage-coach and steamboat at the rate of almost nine miles an hour. If he took the National Road on arriving at Cumberland, and journeyed west by stage-coach he reached Wheeling thirty-six hours after leaving Baltimore, having paid eleven dollars for a ticket which had entitled him to travel three hundred and eight miles.

If the traveller desired merely to go from Baltimore to Philadelphia, and proceed no farther, he had the

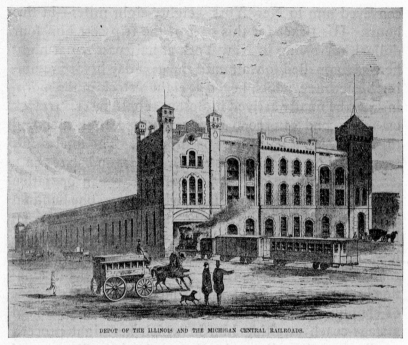

DEPOT OF THE ILLINOIS AND THE MICHIGAN CENTRAL RAILROADS.

330.—A train entering the Chicago railway station of the Illinois Central and Michigan Central roads. Date, 1857.

choice of two trains, one leaving at nine o'clock in the morning and the other at three o'clock in the afternoon. Either one would convey him to his destination in six hours. This was the daily service offered to the public by the Philadelphia, Wilmington and Baltimore Railroad, whose length was ninety-seven miles.

The journey from Philadelphia to Harrisburg, a distance of one hundred and seven miles, might be made in about seven hours at a cost of four dollars. To accomplish this trip the traveller used the Columbia and Philadelphia Railroad for seventy miles, and the Harrisburg and Lancaster Railroad for thirty-seven miles.

Passenger travel between New York City and the numerous near-by towns of New Jersey had increased to such an extent that several trains each day moved back and forth over the New Jersey routes. There were three daily trains between Jersey City and Paterson on the Paterson and Hudson Railroad, and the distance of seventeen miles between the two towns was frequently covered in less than one hour. A ticket cost fifty cents.

West-bound travellers leaving New York City for Newark, Elizabethtown, New Brunswick and Trenton had the choice of two daily trains, one departing at nine o'clock in the morning and the other at half past four in the afternoon. This rail route extended through to Philadelphia from Jersey City. It was composed of three lines, the first being the New Jersey Railroad, thirty miles long, between Jersey City and New Brunswick; the second being the New Brunswick and Trenton Railroad, twenty-nine miles in length; and the third being the Philadelphia and Trenton Railroad, which was twenty-eight miles long.

No less than eight passenger trains a day ran each way between New York and Newark, in New Jersey, and the price of a ticket between the two cities had been reduced to twenty-five cents. All those passengers between New York and the near-by New Jersey towns who bought their railroad tickets at the regular offices of the companies were presented, free of cost, with ferry tickets which entitled them to cross the Hudson River without extra charge.

The Erie Railroad, which still had to maintain its eastern terminus at a point on the Hudson River about twenty-four miles north of New York City, had been completed for seventy-seven miles of its length to the

1115

village of Middletown. A traveller desiring to use the Erie road embarked on a steamboat at New York, was conveyed to the eastern terminus of the road in an hour and three-quarters, and in three hours more he was in Middletown, a hundred miles from the big city where his journey had begun. His ticket had cost only one dollar and twenty-five cents.

If a traveller desired to journey northward from New York to Albany he had his choice of two stage-coach routes—one on each side of the Hudson River—or he could go up the river on a steamboat and reach Albany in about fourteen hours. He might then proceed still farther northward from Albany, by means of the Red Bird line of stage-coaches, which ran all the way to Montreal in Canada. The running time of the stage-coach between Albany and Montreal was forty hours, and the price of a ticket from New York to Montreal was sixteen dollars.

A through line of railroad no less than two hundred miles long[1] extended from Boston, in Massachusetts, to Albany, in New York, by means of which a man might be conveyed between the two cities in eleven or twelve hours, at a cost of five dollars. On this much travelled route two trains moved daily in each direction. One of them, however, stopped all night at Springfield, in Massachusetts, and passengers by it were about eight hours longer in making the trip than those who embarked on the cars that courageously refused to pause because of darkness.

The numerous little railroads which had been built with a generally east-and-west trend through central New

---

[1] Consisting of the Boston and Worcester Railroad, forty-four miles; the Western Railroad, one hundred and eighteen miles; and the Albany and West Stockbridge Railroad, thirty-eight miles.

331.—A bird's-eye view of Chicago just before extensive railway building began to alter a large town and favorable natural location into a world-center of population and economic consequence. The prediction of the unknown prophet of 1822 was in process of fulfillment within a generation.

York State had finally been physically united, and it was at last possible to go from Albany to Buffalo in railroad cars as well as by canal.

On the Erie Canal there were still two daily lines of packet-boats running between the same towns, on either of which a passenger might be carried the whole distance at a cost of five dollars and fifty cents. If he ate the meals furnished by the boat he paid two dollars in addition. The time between Albany and Buffalo by canal packet was about five days. On the Erie Canal line-boats the cost of travel was one cent, or a little more, a mile. But it should be borne in mind that when paying the cheaper of these two rates the traveller furnished his own provender and bedding.

A passenger on the Great Lakes was transported from Buffalo to Detroit for four dollars, and he was charged four dollars in addition for a cabin and his meals if he chose to avail himself of the bed and board furnished by the vessel. The lake boats made special rates to families, and five or six people moving as one party, together with all their domestic and household goods, could obtain passage from Buffalo to Detroit for twenty dollars.

On Ohio River steamboats—during favorable stages of water—the fare from Pittsburgh to Cincinnati was one dollar; to Louisville one dollar and a half; and to St. Louis, two dollars.

From Baltimore to Pittsburgh, by canal and railroad, the charge was about five dollars, with one hundred pounds of baggage free of cost. In journeying from Philadelphia to Pittsburgh the traveller paid from three to four cents a mile while on the canal and six cents a mile on the railroad.

The long trip from the eastern states to St. Louis by

1118

way of the Erie Canal and the lakes cost about fifty dollars, including meals and all other necessary expenses. If the same journey was undertaken by means of line-boats on the canal, and without either cabin or meals while on the steamboats, it could be performed for twenty or twenty-five dollars. The passage by river from New Orleans to St. Louis, a distance of more than eleven hundred miles, cost about eighteen dollars.

The succeeding table will show the length, the means of conveyance and the cost of typical journeys through the Middle West and the South during the same years:[1]

THE JOURNEY FROM	Means of Conveyance	Distance in Miles	Cost
Philadelphia to Pittsburgh	Stage-coach	300	$15.00
Philadelphia to Baltimore	Stage-coach	128	3.00
Baltimore to Wheeling	Stage-coach	271	12.00
Pittsburgh to Wheeling	Stage-coach	59	4.00
Wheeling to Columbus	Stage-coach	140	8.00
Columbus to Cleveland	Stage-coach	177	10.50
Columbus to Cincinnati	Stage-coach	110	6.50
Cincinnati to Lexington, Ky	Stage-coach	76	4.50
Indianapolis to Madison, Ind	Stage-coach	86	4.00
Lexington to Louisville	Stage-coach	75	4.20
Louisville to St. Louis (Via Vincennes)	Stage-coach	276	15.50
Louisville to Nashville, Tenn	Stage-coach	180	12.00
Richmond, Va., to Knoxville, Tenn	Stage-coach	444	28.50
Baltimore to Richmond, Va	Steamboat	378	10.00
Nashville to Memphis	Stage-coach	224	15.00
Augusta to Montgomery	Stage-coach	300	18.50
Tuscaloosa to Mobile	Steamboat	676	12.00
Montgomery to Mobile	Stage-coach	180	12.00
Mobile to New Orleans	Stage-coach	160	12.00
St. Augustine to New Orleans	Stage-coach	600	35.00
Boston or New York to New Orleans (including meals)	Sailing packet		40.00 to 50.00

By the year 1848 the building of railroads had gone ahead to such an extent that their use—whenever such use was possible—had resulted in a material decrease in the time required in journeying from the East to the interior. The following table will indicate the advantage, in point of speed, derived through avail of those

[1] The tables are compiled from information contained in "The Immigrant's Guide and Citizen's Manual." By I. W. Warner. New York: 1848.

railroads already extending toward the West or in operation there:

THE JOURNEY	Distance in Miles	Time by Steamboats and Canals	Time by Steamboats and Railroads	Cost by Steamboats and Canals	Cost by Steamboats and Railroads
New York to Utica............	255	2½ days	17 hours	$1.50	$2.06
New York to Buffalo	508	7¾ "	32 "	3.00	5.50
New York to Cleveland........	700	9 "	3 days	5.50	8.00
New York to Zanesville, O....	867	11¼ "	5½ "	7.62	9.75
New York to Portsmouth, O...1,010		13 "	7 "	8.75	11.50
New York to Detroit.........	825	10 "	4 "	5.75	8.50
New York to Milwaukee 1,480		14 "	6 "	9.00	12.00
New York to Chicago 1,520		14½ "	6½ "	9.00	12.50
New York to Pittsburgh	480	7½ "	6½ "	....	8.50
New York to Cincinnati	937	15 "	8½ "	8.25	12.00
New York to Louisville 1,068		....	9¼ "	....	13.00
New York to St. Louis 1,620		....	12½ "	....	14.50
New York to Dubuque, Ia....2,051		....	14¾ "	....	16.00

By means of steamboats, railroads and the Wabash and Erie Canal, the traveller could reach Toledo in four days from New York; Fort Wayne, Indiana, in five and a half days; and Lafayette, Indiana, in seven and a half days. The price of his ticket to Lafayette was twelve dollars and fifty cents. But if he went by way of the Erie Canal, then by steamboat from Buffalo to Toledo and continued thence on the Wabash and Erie Canal he had to pay only eight dollars and twenty-five cents, although he was fifteen days on the way.

In the South the revolution in travel facilities had not gone ahead quite so fast as in the North, but there was nevertheless a vast improvement visible over the circumstances which had confronted the pilgrim only ten or a dozen years before. Additional short railroads were springing into existence, the land roads were multiplying in number and improving in quality, the stagecoaches of the region were making better time than ever before and the steamboats on the rivers, though smaller in

THE GREAT THROUGH LINE
From New York via Baltimore

TO

St. Louis and the Southwest,

Is formed by the following

FIRST CLASS ROADS:

1.—New Jersey, and Camden & Amboy,
From NEW YORK to PHILADELPHIA—87 miles.

2.—Philadelphia, Wilmington & Baltimore,
From PHILADELPHIA to BALTIMORE—98 miles.

3.—The Baltimore & Ohio,
375 miles from BALTIMORE and 396 from WASHINGTON CITY to BENWOOD JUNCTION; (379 to Wheeling Terminus,) or 383 from BALTIMORE to PARKERSBURG, on the Ohio River, 96 miles below Wheeling.

4.—The Central Ohio,
From BELLAIRE (opposite Benwood Junction) to COLUMBUS—137 miles; or by *MARIETTA ROAD* from Marietta, (12 miles above Parkersburg,)—200 miles to CINCINNATI.

5.—The Little Miami,
From COLUMBUS to CINCINNATI—119 miles.

6.—Ohio & Mississippi, (Broad Guage,)
From CINCINNATI to ST. LOUIS—340 miles.

☞ In the following pages will be found the details of these several Roads, prepared by their officers respectively.

332.—The joint advertisement of six railways, in 1857, announcing that by their combined routes, over a distance of 1,156 miles, rail communication had finally been established between New York City and St. Louis.

size than many of those in the North, often rivalled them in the matter of their appointments.

The man who desired to journey from Baltimore to New Orleans[1] in the most expeditious manner went by rail to Richmond, in Virginia, which he reached in ten and a half hours at a cost of six dollars and sixty cents, after a trip of one hundred and sixty-eight miles. Thence he proceeded, also by a series of railroads, to Wilmington in North Carolina, where he arrived twenty-one hours after departing from Richmond, having left two hundred and fifty more miles behind him. The fare for this part of his expedition was eight dollars and forty cents. He next embarked on a steamboat on which he reached Charleston, in South Carolina, one hundred and seventy-five miles farther on his way, after sixteen additional hours of travel. His steamboat ticket had cost him six dollars. He travelled from Charleston to Augusta, in Georgia, by railroads, thus advancing one hundred and thirty-seven miles in eight hours, and at a further cost of six dollars. Another railroad trip conveyed him over the one hundred and seventy-two miles between Augusta and Atlanta, demanded six dollars and fifty cents more of his money, and twelve hours more of his time. At Atlanta he deserted the railroad for a stage-coach in which he finally attained the town of Chehaw, in Alabama. His fare in the stage-coach was twelve dollars and the time he spent in the same vehicle was twenty-four hours. On reaching Chehaw he shifted back to a railroad again and so came to Montgomery, in Alabama, after a short ride of about three hours, for which he paid two dollars. Again he was compelled to change his method of con-

[1] The information on which the itinerary here outlined is based is to be found in "A Guide between Washington, Baltimore, Philadelphia, New York and Boston, etc., etc." New York: Published by J. Disturnell; June, 1846.

veyance, since the long jaunt of two hundred miles between Montgomery and Mobile still had to be made by means of stage-coach travel. He arrived at Mobile in thirty-six hours, somewhat shaken in the matter of his bones, and ten dollars poorer in pocket. Here he escaped the overland bouncing of railroad car and stage, exchanging them for the possibility of steamboat explosion while he voyaged by water over the one hundred and seventy-five miles that still separated him from the big city on the Mississippi. He reached New Orleans at last after an additional outlay of five dollars, and sixteen hours spent on the boat.

The total distance he had traversed in going from Baltimore to New Orleans was some one thousand four hundred and sixty miles, and his expenditure in transportation charges was sixty-two dollars and fifty cents. The time which had elapsed since he left Baltimore was about seven days. A man who made the trip here outlined, during the year 1846, was compelled to use five railroads, two steamboats and two stage-coaches. His average rate of progress by means of all the nine conveyances required in carrying him to his destination, during the week he spent on the way, was about eight and three-quarter miles an hour.

By the year 1845 the states of the Middle West were rapidly becoming dotted with numerous little railroads, and by the first years after 1850 the facilities for railroad travel in that region closely resembled the similar opportunities that had existed in the eastern states some ten or fifteen years before. In other words it was then possible, in western Pennsylvania, Ohio, Indiana, Illinois, Michigan, Kentucky, Tennessee, and other near-by states, to move between some of the principal cities and towns by means of the new system of transportation. The following compilation[1] will somewhat indicate the degree of advancement which had been reached in the commonwealths mentioned with regard to the possibilities for railroad and other travel. These journeys could then be made at the costs of time and money indicated:

FROM	Distance in Miles	Approximate Time Consumed	Cost of Journey
Cincinnati to Cleveland[2]	254	11 hours	$7.00
Cincinnati to Chicago[3]	571	30 hours	11.00
Cincinnati to Indianapolis	177	9 hours	4.00
Cincinnati to Springfield, Ill.[4]	394	about 30 hours	14.00
Cincinnati to Charleston, S. C.[5]	919	5 or 6 days	35.20
Chicago to St. Louis	407	24 hours	7.00
Indianapolis to Cleveland	431	about 30 hours	11.00
Louisville to St. Louis	570	by steamboat	18.00
Louisville to Chicago	977	3 days	17.00
Nashville, Tenn., to Chicago	844	3½ days	17.00
Lafayette to Indianapolis	63	4 hours	3.85
Detroit to Chicago	277	12 hours	7.00
Atlanta to Chattanooga	140	10 hours	4.20
Macon, Ga., to Atlanta	101	8 hours	4.00
Savannah, Ga., to Macon	191	16 hours	5.75

Such—broadly speaking—were the facilities for human intercourse between separated communities east of the Mississippi just before the memorable days of 1848 and 1849. Pioneer life and crude national conditions in that part of the land were forever gone, to be there supplanted by another and no less absorbing phase of history having to do with the groping of its people through the pioneer experiences of a newer and more complex social life. And now we turn our gaze to observe those few final years—so crowded with cyclopean themes—wherein were encompassed the remaining events that completed the conquest of the continent.

[1] Based on information to be found in "James' Rail-Road and Route Book for the Western and Southern States." Compiled by J. Griswold. Cincinnati: 1853.
[2] By means of the Little Miami Railroad, length 64 miles; the Columbus and Xenia Railroad, length 55 miles; and the Columbus and Cleveland Railroad, length 135 miles.
[3] Price of ticket by way of the Lakes, $6.50.
[4] From Terre Haute, Ind., to Springfield, the traveller went by stage-coach.
[5] By river, stage-coach and railroad.

AWFUL ACCIDENT

on the North Pennsylvania Rail Road on Thursday July 17th 1856

PRINTED & FOR SALE by S. BOERUM North East Cor 4th & New Sts.

Railroad accidents due to carelessness were as common as steamboat disasters in the years from 1840 to 1858, and lurid illustrations of them were also printed and sold. F. Lith. Col. Amer.

A HISTORY OF
TRAVEL IN AMERICA

CHAPTER XLIX

THE OVERRUNNING OF THE WEST — LAST PHASE OF A TASK
COMMENCED MORE THAN TWO CENTURIES BEFORE —
AN OUTBURST OF HUMAN ENERGY AND AMBITION
— OUR TWO VIEWS OF THE MIGRATIONS — THEIR
WORLD IMPORTANCE — BOONE'S INFLUENCE STILL
ACTIVE — VALUE OF THE MISSOURI RIVER AS AN EARLY
ROUTE INTO THE WEST — ITS PIONEER CRAFT — FIRST
STEAMBOATS — AUDUBON AND THE WHISKY — CAP-
TAIN SIRE'S INSPIRATION

THE general invasion and overrunning of the immense region west of the Mississippi River by English speaking Americans may be said to have taken place within a period of about twenty years, between 1829 and 1850. No hard-and-fast date, to be sure, can be set for the commencement of the movement. Various things of importance in relation to it and numerous journeys through the country involved had already occurred before 1829, and they will necessarily be mentioned in this and succeeding chapters. But in the year named there took place an event that radically altered the conditions under which travel into considerable parts of the far West might be undertaken by those who wished to go there. That circumstance was the establishment of steam navigation on the Missouri

1125

River. The introduction of steamboats on the extensive stream seems to constitute, in a rough way, a dividing line between the previous era and that which came afterward. Their subsequent operation—infrequent as it was for a time—created a new and important link between the settled country and established periodic travel of the East, and the little known expanses to the westward. Caucasian civilization thereafter could—and did—reach out toward the Rocky Mountains without the compulsion of employing physical toil previously necessary in the process.

The contrast between the short interval here named and all that preceded it is amazing. More than two centuries had been required by the dominant people in their march from New England and Virginia to the Mississippi. During that lapse of time they had crept across and intrenched themselves in about one-third of the continental width and in considerably less than one-third of the continental area now embraced within the nation's limits. But even in that progress they had failed to absorb all the region between the Atlantic Ocean and the river, for, as has been seen, there still existed large territories east of the Mississippi into which they had no right to penetrate except by permission or passport, and across which, both in the North and the South, they could only lawfully travel by virtue of consent or highways obtained through treaty. So far, and with such incompleteness of eventual result, had the white Americans advanced.

Then, within a period of about twenty years—beginning with the simultaneous introduction of railways in the East and of steam navigation on the Missouri—they added to their domain and settled a quarter of a million square miles of territory known as the Oregon

333.—A view of the city of St. Louis during the period which embraced the climax of Missouri River traffic, the Oregon migrations, the Mormon exodus and the final rush to California. Published in Dusseldorf, Germany, from a drawing by the American artist, Henry Lewis. The following 66 illustrations, to No. 399 inclusive, relate to the Caucasian overrunning of the far West.

Country of the Northwest; took about six hundred thousand square miles of western and southwestern territory from Mexico;[1] established themselves along a thousand miles of the Pacific coast; and overran the whole of the intervening region between the Pacific and the Mississippi in an unparalleled series of overland migrations which had their origin in deep-seated impulses affecting the people as a mass. By the close of 1850 the extraordinary outburst—requiring so few words for its definition but which was so profound in its effect upon the world— was complete and irrevocable. The things that followed, including the continuation of the overland movement then in progress, were consequences of what had already happened. Not far from two million square miles of territory were penetrated and occupied as a direct or indirect result of the overland hegiras that took place in America between 1840 and 1850. Both the travel movement in question and the earth's area affected by it were, in respect of size, the most extensive and largest involved in any similar phenomenon within a like interval of recorded human history.

It is also possible that the economic and political history of the world has been, and is destined to be, more deeply influenced by these overland travel-surges that happened in America and are soon to engage our attention, than by any other similar movements which have taken place elsewhere.[2] They constituted the final effort whereby existing civilization girdled the earth with its

---

[1] Though no pride attaches either to this act or the manner of its doing.

[2] The one similar known movement comparable to that which took place in America is, of course, the early overrunning of a part of Europe by hordes from the eastward. Among existing conditions due in greater or less degree, and either directly or indirectly to the American people's sudden occupation of the region between the Mississippi and the Pacific, are a large addition to the world's stock of gold; the new importance of the Pacific Ocean and bordering countries in world affairs; the political expansion of the United States; the increase of immigration hither from all other lands; a swifter industrial and economic development of the nation; its evolution as a world power; the creation of the Panama Canal; and the far-reaching effects of those several things on the affairs of mankind.

daily influence. By their means was completed a long process whose place and time of beginning cannot now be defined, but as we stand on the Pacific shore and look still farther westward we behold the cradle out of which an infant race clambered to begin its wanderings. The chain of land dominion is complete, and to us was left the forging of the last link. The globe can be circled in less than forty days; every nation knows within a few hours what has happened to the other members of the earth family; the affairs of one have become the acknowledged concern of all, to be discussed and treated in a community way; a Parliament is coming whose presiding officer shall say: "Germany speaks"; "Nippon speaks"; "Switzerland speaks"; "Brazil speaks." And the nations will listen, and vote as their names are called.

The American men and women who set forth with their horses and oxen and wagons said they were starting to California or Oregon, and so they were. But beside them strode consequences which were going further still. And so as we read the story of their journeys; as we hear them tell of their toil through the desert sands; of eating the bodies of the dead who fell; of burning off their whiskers with hot grease at the camp-fire; of their concerts; of the mirage that taunted them; of hopes and struggles of every sort, we of this later day follow their narratives with a vision that does not stop at sight of yellow gold or the rolling tide of the Columbia. We behold them in two characters. In one sense we see them as men and women like ourselves, engaged in a long and hard journey undertaken for personal reasons of one kind or another, and hopeful of improving their condition. In the other and broader sense we do not look upon them as individuals, but as a strange and colossal spectacle moving in response to a world impulse which summoned them to play a mighty part in the deeds of men—and then left them ignorant of what they had done, just as most of us are ignorant of what we are collectively doing to-day. Our retrospective understanding still maintains its supremacy.

The westward overland movement from the Mississippi valley and eastern states was characterized by two phases. The first of these embraced nearly all of the interval previously mentioned, during which time the white men who advanced for considerable distances beyond the Mississippi without intention of return were comparatively few in number, and were animated principally by individual considerations or restlessness. Their westward journeying was not the result of any deep or widespread influence affecting the population as a whole. They may be likened to the far-flung spray of a ponderous wave that has been halted in its advance. The second phase of the movement was altogether different in character. It covered the two years of 1849 and 1850, and was the consequence of events and conditions affecting the entire people. It resembled the first onrush of a huge wave which has broken through a barrier, making way for the irresistible flood behind.

Those two aspects of the westward advance had one quality in common. Nearly all movement during both of them was a matter of individual exertion or clan effort. In such features the invasion and permanent occupation of the West, during the decisive years of that phenomenon, closely resembled the migrations throughout the Atlantic coast region in the latter part of the seventeenth century and the first part of the eighteenth century, during which time new districts were occupied

1130

MOUTH OF THE MISSOURI.   MÜNDUNG DES MISSOURI.

334.—The Missouri River. First travel route of white men to the Rocky Mountains. Mouth of the
stream, and craft engaged in its navigation at the height of its importance. From a drawing by Henry Lewis.

and new settlements were always made by means of the company-travel then necessary. But by 1851 the tide of overland travel across the plains had already become so large, and showed such certainty of still greater increase, that a new element was soon after introduced into the situation. Commercial management turned its interested gaze toward the hundreds of thousands who were struggling over the plains and mountains; lines of communication were projected on the basis of business enterprises; and the conveyance of passengers and information across the newly-occupied region in that manner was eventually brought about. All except a small part of the human tide still swept on for a dozen years as before, but individual initiative in providing means for the long journey, and personal effort in accomplishing the pilgrimage, no longer remained necessary. Organized methods grappled with the problem in ever increasing mastery until it was finally conquered.

But though the permanent penetration of the far West —by men who journeyed there without intention of immediate return—was accomplished substantially in the manner here outlined, there were nevertheless a few still earlier historical incidents so intimately connected with the region that they require to be here recalled. Three principal events of the sort were the explorationary trips of Lewis and Clark, of Zebulon Pike, and of Stephen H. Long.[1] At the time those three extensive expeditions were made, through country then unknown, the information acquired by means of them was of no value to the mass of the people in connection with any effort to occupy the territory explored. In later years, however, the journeys

[1] Still another was embraced by the early history of the Oregon country, which will be separately considered.

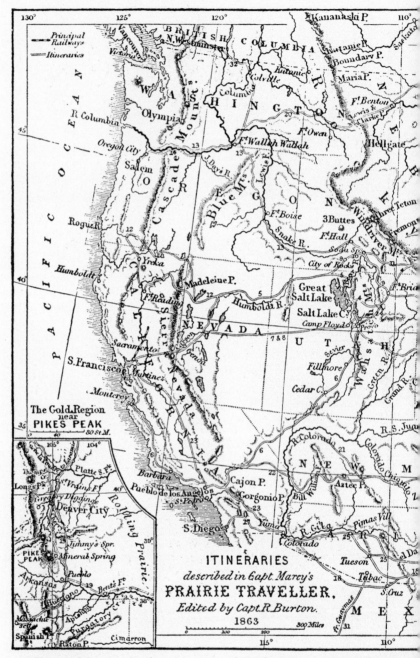

Ravenstein's map showing the system of overland roads between the Missis[sippi]
the period between 1843 and 1868. Roads are indicated by parallel lines and num[bers]
The territory thus penetrated is the largest continental area similarly overrun
movement by caravan.

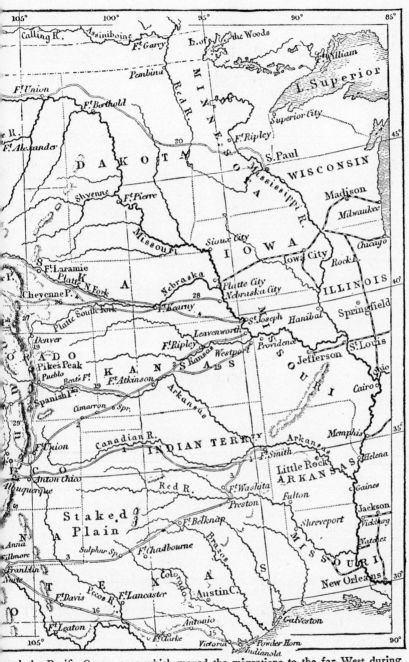

and the Pacific Ocean, over which moved the migrations to the far West during
ordance with Marcy's list of routes as arranged by Burton.
nently occupied by a civilized people during one short and uninterrupted travel

of those men were destined to bear rich fruit. They were among the first English speaking pathfinders, and the knowledge brought back by them served as a guide to the advance guard of the host which started to follow their almost forgotten footsteps.

Captains Lewis and Clark, of the United States army, in the years 1804-5-6, travelled up the Missouri River to its head waters, thence across the Rocky Mountains and down the Columbia River to the Pacific Ocean, and finally made their way back to civilization.[1]

Major Pike, also of the Federal army, journeyed from St. Louis to the head waters of the Platte, Arkansas and Rio Grande, and back again through the Southwest and northern Mexico, in 1805-6-7.

Major Long, who like his predecessors was an army officer, made a trip from Pittsburgh to the Rocky Mountains and return in the years 1819 and 1820. His expedition moved for some distance up the Missouri River by means of a little steamboat called the *Western Engineer,* which was built for the purpose at Pittsburgh, and was the first steam craft west of the Mississippi. The boat was seventy-five feet long, thirteen feet wide,

---

[1] President Jefferson did not—as is commonly stated—send Lewis and Clark to explore the region because it had been bought from France by the United States. His recommendation of the journey was made to Congress in a message dated January 18, 1803, and Congress had acted favorably and even appropriated money for the expedition before anyone in America knew we had bought the Louisiana Territory, or that we could buy it, or that our representatives in France had thought of such a thing. Jefferson had desired such an exploration since 1783. A detailed account of the genesis of the trip, and of Jefferson's ideas on the subject, may be found in Schafer's "A History of the Pacific Northwest" (pp. 53-68), although that authority, in discussing related national conditions of 1800, says (p. 61) that "the steamboat . . . was yet to be invented."

The results of Lewis and Clark's work were first made available in printed form in the "Message from the President of the United States, Communicating Discoveries made in Exploring the Missouri, Red River and Washita, by Captains Lewis and Clark, Doctor Sibley and Mr. Dunbar; with a Statistical Account of the Countries Adjacent. Read in Congress February 19, 1806. New York, 1806." The Lewis and Clark narrative was reprinted in Pittsburgh in 1807 as the "Journal of Lewis and Clark," and was also reprinted in London during the same year under the title "Travels in the Interior Parts of America, etc., etc." It was also reprinted in Philadelphia under the title "History of the Expedition under the Command of Captains Lewis and Clark, to the Sources of the Missouri, Thence across the Rocky Mountains and down the River Columbia to the Pacific Ocean. Performed During the Years 1804-5-6." Still another London reprint appeared in 1809 under the title "The Travels of Captains Lewis and Clark from St. Louis, by Way of the Missouri and Columbia Rivers, to the Pacific Ocean. Performed in the Years 1804, 1805, and 1806, by Order of the Government of the United States, etc., etc."

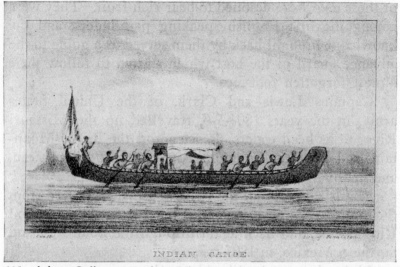

INDIAN CANOE.

335.—A large Indian canoe of the Missouri such as was used, on various occasions, by government expeditions toward the upper reaches of the river and its tributaries. Friendly natives sometimes navigated the boats.

and drew nineteen inches of water. For the purpose of mystifying and impressing the native peoples among whom it might pass, the bow of Long's steamboat was fashioned in imitation of the neck and head of a serpent from whose open mouth issued clouds of smoke. The propelling machinery was purposely hid from sight by a superstructure, as was the paddle-wheel at the stern, which violently agitated the water like the tail of some strange aquatic monster. The speed of the boat was about three miles an hour. It is needless to say that the effect produced among the Indians by the apparition was extreme.

These three notable journeys, though important because of the knowledge obtained for the government by them, were not an integral part of the permanent westward advance of the people.

A HISTORY OF TRAVEL IN AMERICA

The first drop of human spray thrown across the Mississippi by the advancing population wave was, in fact, the redoubtable explorer of Kentucky—Daniel Boone himself. It has often been said that man is a gregarious animal, and as a principle there can be no dispute with that conclusion. But the strange figure who now appears again for a brief instant in the story was one of the most noteworthy exceptions to the rule of whom history makes mention. Boone was not gregarious. Central Kentucky had become too crowded for him before the year 1800, and about the beginning of the century he took the radical step of leaving his own land altogether and settling in the foreign country beyond the great river. There he remained until his death in 1820, at the age of eighty-six. After his death a quoted expression of his long, unavailing quest for solitude was printed in the following words:[1]

"I first removed to the woods of Kentucky. I fought and repelled the savages, and hoped for repose. Game was abundant and our path was prosperous, but soon I was molested by interlopers from every quarter. Again I retreated to the region of the Mississippi; but again these speculators and settlers followed me. Once more I withdrew to the licks of Missouri—and here at length I hoped to find rest. But I was still pursued—for I had not been two years at the licks before a damned Yankee came and settled down within a hundred miles of me."[2]

In removing beyond the Mississippi, and later to a spot now embraced by central Missouri, Boone did not long remain an exile from his native land. Although the man himself thereafter remained stationary, the United States moved after him. On his arrival the King of Spain[3]—through the Lieutenant Governor of that country—appointed him to command of the district where he had taken up his abode and gave him eight

[1] In the "Farmers and Mechanics Journal" (Vincennes, Indiana) of June 12, 1823.
[2] The editor of the "Farmers and Mechanics Journal," in publishing Boone's statement, said that he printed it because of its interest, despite the fact that it was "incompatible with the dignity of history."
[3] Charles IV.

thousand five hundred acres of land on the Missouri River. France soon afterward came into ownership of the region, and in 1803 it passed into the possession of the United States through the purchase of the Louisiana Territory from Napoleon, bringing Boone once more under the jurisdiction of the country he had quitted, and creating those conditions which inspired the objurgated Yankees to follow him.

By 1804 Boone and two of his sons—Nathan and Daniel—were engaged in making salt at some salt springs that came to be known as "Boone's Lick."[1] They were then the only permanently settled white men who had established their abode west of the immediate vicinity of the Mississippi River. Their industrial product was obtained by boiling the saline spring water in kettles, and the salt thus obtained was periodically conveyed down the Missouri River in a curious species of craft designed for the purpose,[2] and sold to the inhabitants of the little French village called St. Louis. Within two or three years—as mentioned by the elder Boone in his indignant protest—another group of people from the East arrived and built cabins in the vicinity. A settlement called Franklin gradually came into existence, and with the presence of a growing population about one hundred and fifty miles west of the Mississippi the need of a road from the river to the interior soon became manifest. Such a pathway was begun about 1815, and the two younger Boones were leading spirits in the enterprise. The road was at first merely a wilderness path similar to countless hundreds of other forest highways, with log-canoe ferries stationed at the deeper streams which intersected its course. The trace

---

[1] A natural salt deposit in the West was called a "lick" because wild animals came to such a spot to obtain the mineral.
[2] To be later described.

extended from the town of St. Charles[1] westwardly to Franklin, and for many years was known as "Boone's Lick Road." Over it marched much of the early migration west of the Mississippi.[2]

The influx into the Missouri region over Boone's Lick Road was largely instrumental in bringing about the creation of the state of Missouri in 1821. Nor did the importance of the thoroughfare end at that time. During the years immediately thereafter it followed the movement of permanent white population from Franklin still farther west to Lexington, Bluffton and Liberty. And by about the year 1830 it constituted a road entirely across the state from east to west.[3]

It will be remembered that in 1825 Congress had passed an act "authorizing the President of the United States to cause a road to be marked out from the western frontier of Missouri to the confines of New Mexico," after obtaining the consent "of the intervening tribes of Indians, by treaty, to the marking of said road, and to the unmolested use thereof by the citizens of the United States." The road to the Southwest, obtained at that time and in the manner described, soon came into existence as a still further extension of the Boone's Lick Road across Missouri.[4] It is hence seen that the influence of Daniel Boone on the westward advance of his fellow-Americans did not cease in revolutionary times with the penetration

[1] On the Missouri River a short distance northwest of St. Louis.

[2] Although already of consequence as a wilderness highway, Boone's Lick Road was not indicated by John Melish on his "Map of the United States," which was published in Philadelphia in June of 1820. The fifty-sheet map in question, which was the most important cartographical delineation of the United States issued up to that time, shows two or three short roads in southeastern Missouri in the territory extending from Madrid to the town of Kaskaskia, in Illinois. The Melish map of 1820 displays the town of Franklin as the westernmost white settlement of any consequence at that time, and also bears the inscription, "Boon's Salt Works," a short distance to the westward of the location of Franklin. The map was issued during the year of Boone's death.

[3] The westward extension of Boone's Lick Road from Franklin to the three towns above named is shown on Mitchell's "Map of the United States," issued in 1832.

[4] The 1835 edition of "Mitchell's Map of the United States" shows the newly created town of Independence, in Missouri, and the Santa Fé trail extending onward from that point.

of Kentucky. His retirement into the wilds beyond the Mississippi had a close relation to the creation of the first state west of that river, and brought about the making of the first white man's road across Missouri and its farther extension for hundreds of miles into the Southwest to the

MODE OF CROSSING RIVERS BY THE FLATHEAD AND OTHER INDIANS.

336.—A peculiar variety of ferry boat devised by natives of the far West and used by parties moving overland when they wanted to cross unfordable streams. It was a big air cushion made of buffalo hides. After serving their purpose such boats were deflated and again loaded on a pack-horse. From a sketch by the artist Carl Sohon.

ancient Spanish city of Santa Fé. Boone's direct influence, therefore, in connection with westward white movement and the conquest of the continent, extended from North Carolina to the Rocky Mountains. Those who first penetrated into Missouri followed his footsteps and later traversed the road marked out by his sons. If they were marching still farther into the Southwest, it was by Boone's Lick Road that they finally reached the Santa Fé trail.

The last journey made by Boone was back toward the East, though it was not undertaken by any volition of his own; for he was dead. He had been buried near the spot where his last days were spent, but a number of years after his death, and as the result of official negotiations between the two states, Missouri gave him back to Kentucky, and a commission representing that commonwealth travelled up the Missouri River to the little town of Marthasville and returned with the remains of the pioneer. The trip of Kentucky's representatives was made by steamboat[1] and it was on such a vehicle—far removed in its character from those with which he had in life been familiar—that Boone went back eastward on his last journey to Kentucky.[2]

The Missouri River, whose lower course for a hundred and fifty miles above its mouth had been the scene of the first trans-Mississippi invasion undertaken by the whites, constituted the principal road by which early access to the far West was attained. The active employment of that stream as a travel path during the years of western penetration from 1804 until the creation of the first transcontinental railway, was another instance of pioneer resort to water routes of travel wherever possible. Even when progress was not made in water craft on the bosom of the river itself—as was to be the case in the later days of big wagon caravans—the moving men kept as close as possible, for many hundreds of miles, to the river and to its tributaries. Some of the man-power boats employed on the Missouri prior to the appearance of the steamboat on its waters merit brief description. They differed to a

[1] The name of the boat was the "Kansas."
[2] It is an odd coincidence that Fitch, the derided pioneer of the modern era, went out to Kentucky in bitterness of heart to seek solitude at almost the precise time when Boone, the pioneer of wilderness travel, left Kentucky for the same purpose.

considerable extent from those vessels used on the streams of the East and on the Ohio for similar purposes during the preceding one hundred and fifty years. The awkward and almost unmanageable ark, for instance, was entirely unsuited to Missouri River navigation, and never appeared on that stream. Neither did any type of the enclosed flatboat such as was variously known farther to the eastward as the Ohio boat, the Kentucky boat or the Mississippi boat.

The canoe, as usual, was the most common of all craft employed by pioneer travellers on the river. It was never made of bark, but always from the trunk of a tree, and it was most commonly constructed from a cottonwood log. The selection of the cottonwood as the raw material for a Missouri River canoe was due to three factors. It was exceedingly common, of large size, and of a texture which permitted its easy transformation into the desired form. A cottonwood canoe was of any size up to about thirty-five feet in length and four feet in width. The most familiar size was a length of about twenty feet combined with a beam of three feet. A desirable log was reduced to canoe form by manual labor with broad-ax and adz, and the hull had a thickness of some three or four inches along the bottom of the boat. The sides were left about two inches thick, but the entire interior of the log was not removed. Solid bulkheads of the natural wood were left untouched at intervals of five or six feet, thus giving an added element of strength to the completed vessel and preventing any perilous shift of cargo. The building of a large canoe of this type would occupy two men for at least a week. Sometimes a Missouri River log canoe was equipped with a low mast and small sail, but the ordinary propulsion was effected by paddles. Craft of this sort were often navigated all the way from the Mississippi River to the Rocky Mountains and back again. The ordinary crew consisted of two men at the paddles and one steersman. It was in small canoes of this general description that the Boones took their salt to St. Louis. They packed it between the natural bulkheads and covered it with skins above to protect it from water. Two other popular western pioneer commodities often transported on the Missouri and other interior rivers in the same way were bear's oil and honey. The distance that could be covered by a log canoe moving up stream on the Missouri varied from fifteen to thirty or forty miles a day, according to the force of the current, the course of the wind and other natural conditions.

The pirogue—as that name was applied on the Missouri—was a boat whose hull consisted of two log canoes about six feet apart, which were fastened together and covered with a rough wooden flooring. The propulsion of a pirogue up stream was much heavier work than the similar operation of a canoe, although a rather large sail could be used on such a boat, provided the wind was favorable, without any danger of an upset.

The keel-boat of the Missouri was quite similar to the identically named vessel already described, which was a familiar craft on the Ohio and other rivers still farther east. In fact, keel-boats were very rarely built on the Missouri, but were constructed at Louisville, Cincinnati or Pittsburgh, and navigated to the scene of their desired use. Missouri River keel-boats were from fifty to seventy-five feet in length and from twelve to twenty feet wide. Governmental explorers and military commanders, and all pretentious private up-river enterprises, before the days of the steamboat, used such vessels. The keel-boat of

337.—The expedition commanded by Long, and some subsequent exploring and
military parties sent up the Missouri by the government, were in part
transported on small steamboats. The fire-canoes of the white men made
a profound impression on Indians who beheld them for the first time.

the West was equipped with several means for expediting
its progress. In the first place it had a mast and sail. It
also carried long sweeps or oars for use in rowing, and a
set of poles to be employed upon occasion in the immemorial work of poles in American river navigation.
And finally it carried a heavy rope often more than a
thousand feet long, one end of which was fastened high
up on its mast. The other end of the cable extended to
the shore, where it was grasped by a considerable number
of men who pulled the boat ahead. It can easily be appreciated that under unfavorable conditions, or on a
stretch of river where walking facilities were poor, that
the up-stream progress of a keel-boat was very slow indeed, and that it entailed severe exertions on the part of
the men who were compelled to clamber along the shore

1142

and drag the burden at the other end of the line. The most expeditious long-distance trip recorded of the Missouri keel-boat was one made by a navigator named Manuel Lisa in 1811. On the occasion referred to his vessel traversed about eleven hundred miles in sixty-one days, thus attaining an average speed of eighteen miles a day.

The bull-boat of the Missouri and other western rivers was a type of craft unknown except on those streams. It resembled an enormous shallow oval basket, and in size it was ordinarily about twenty-five feet long and twelve or fifteen feet wide. Its sides stood two or three feet above the surface of the stream on which it was navigated, and when full laden it never drew more than a foot of water. The framework of the bull-boat consisted of long and pliable poles, some of which extended along the greater dimension of the craft, with the others lying at right angles to the first and securely fastened to them. All the poles were bent upward at the edge or circumference of the framework and secured in that position, thus producing the basket-like shape of the fabric. The frame was covered with dressed buffalo hides[1] which had been sewed together with sinews from the same animals and then soaked. After being placed on the poles in their soaked condition the hides soon shrank to a considerable degree and thus formed a very tight covering. The seams between the hides used in making a bull-boat were made water-tight by a mixture of melted buffalo fat and earth or ashes, and the final result was a craft of extreme lightness which floated on the water almost like a bubble. A large contrivance of this sort

---

[1] For this purpose the skins of bull buffaloes were used exclusively; hence the name "bull-boat."

could carry a burden of three tons in a stream whose depth did not exceed ten inches, and its propulsion by poles was a comparatively easy matter. The two principal objections to the bull-boat were the ease with which it was penetrated or reduced to a leaky condition by rubbing along a snag or rock, and its helplessness on a stretch of river wherein the water was too deep for the poles to be used. In a situation of that sort it was at the mercy of wind and current. Bull-boats were the favorite vehicles for down-stream transportation of furs.

The Missouri River substitute for the various types of flatboats used on the Ohio and the Mississippi was a peculiar vessel called the "mackinaw." The principal resemblance of the mackinaw to the Ohio flatboat lay in the fact that it was suitable only for down-stream navigation, and that its career—as a boat—was limited to one voyage. The mackinaw was a flat-bottomed affair, but instead of being rectangular in shape it was elliptical, and usually about four times as long as it was wide. A large boat of the sort was fifty or sixty feet long. From the edge of the raft-like structure which constituted the bottom of the mackinaw rose a gunwale several feet high, so that the hold of a large specimen was four or five feet deep. The oarsmen sat on benches near the forward end of the craft, and a seat eight or ten feet up in the air, reached by a ladder, was provided for the helmsman in the stern. From his elevated throne of authority the steersman kept watch for trouble ahead, manipulated his rudder and shouted his orders to the crew in the bow. The central section of the mackinaw was used for cargo purposes, and was separated from the rest of the boat, both fore and aft, by strong water-tight partitions. The cargo hold was also elevated a foot or two

THE CAMP OF THE UNITED STATES TROOPS.

338.—Camp of a large United States military expedition. Showing the type of covered keel-boat, or barge, that was employed on the Missouri, and the defensive formation of a wagon train. Thus arranged the wagons virtually constituted a fort in case of attack. From the Dusseldorf series, after Lewis's drawing.

above the actual bottom of the hull, so that an invasion of water might not damage whatever goods were stored there. The freight frequently rose high above the sides of the boat, and in all weathers was protected by a huge tarpaulin of skins made after the fashion in which the covering for a bull-boat was put together. Four men besides the steersman usually constituted the crew of a mackinaw. They worked from earliest dawn to night-fall, and sometimes moved more than a hundred miles a day, though the average speed of a mackinaw was four or five miles an hour. After such a boat reached St. Louis it was sold as lumber for a few dollars.

The first steamboat which appeared on the Missouri —that curious vessel used by Long in his expedition of 1819—got as far up the river as the present city of Council Bluffs, but it was not until ten years afterward that a regular steam packet made its appearance on the stream. In 1829 a steamboat began to ply between St. Louis and Fort Leavenworth, and three years afterward, in 1832, similar craft built and operated by the American Fur Company began to undertake the long voyage to the distant reaches of the upper river. One or two boats made the extensive trip each year. The first of these was the *Yellowstone,* a side-wheel steamer one hundred and thirty feet long, nineteen feet wide and drawing about five feet of water. She succeeded in passing the mouth of the Niobrara River,[1] near which she was stopped by low water. After some delay she went on, and at last reached the present location of Pierre, in South Dakota, which marked the limit of her first voyage. In the fol-lowing summer the same boat reached Fort Union, near the mouth of Yellowstone River. One of the passengers

[1] Northern Nebraska.

on the *Yellowstone* during her voyage of 1832 was the American artist George Catlin.[1]   A second boat—the *Assiniboine*—accompanied the *Yellowstone* on the voyage of 1833, and both reached Fort Union. As a matter of fact that *Assiniboine* went some distance farther, was caught by low water as a penalty of her rashness, and was compelled to remain amid the snow and ice of that distant country until the following spring.[2]

The most comprehensive account of early steamboat travel on the Missouri River is that embraced in the memoirs of Joseph La Barge, a pioneer boatman, navigator and Indian trader.[3] The historian of La Barge's adventures has said:[4]

"No craft on our Western waters, if upon any waters of the globe, displayed more majesty and beauty, or filled the mind with more interesting reflections, than these picturesque vessels of the early days in the boundless prairies of the West. The very surroundings lent a peculiar attraction to the scene. In every direction the broad and treeless plains extended without water enough anywhere in sight even to suggest a boat. Winding through these plains was a deep valley several miles broad, with a ribbon of verdure running through it along the sinuous course of the river. Everything was still as wild and unsettled as before the advent of the white man, and there was little or nothing to suggest the civilization of the outside world. In the midst of this virgin wildness a noble steamboat appears, its handsome form standing high above the water in fine outline against the verdure of the shore; its lofty chimneys pouring forth clouds of smoke in the atmosphere unused to such intrusion, and its progress against the impetuous current exhibiting an extraordinary display of power. Altogether it formed one of the most notable scenes ever witnessed upon the waters of America. Naturally enough the wild Indian viewed with feelings of awe this great 'fire canoe,' whose power to 'walk on the water' had

[1] Whose drawings constitute an important part of existing pictorial records showing the conditions and native inhabitants of the region as they were at that time.
[2] Among the passengers of 1833 was Maximilian, Prince of Wied, then on a journey of sight-seeing and exploration in this continent. As the result of his trip up the Missouri he afterward published a textual account of his adventures, accompanied by a separate folio atlas containing a collection of the largest, finest and most important engravings in revelation of early travel conditions in the region penetrated by him that were ever produced.
[3] Whose life and adventures constitute the basis of Chittenden's "History of Early Steamboat Navigation on the Missouri River," to which work the present author is indebted for a number of incidents relating to the subject.
[4] Chittenden, p. 110.

THE INDIAN CAMP.

339.—A large camp of Indians, adjoining the halting place of the troops pictured in the foregoing. Showing tépees and the ordinary sort of native canoe. Dusseldorf series, drawn by Lewis.

subdued the intractable current to its own will. It is said to have been the advent of the steamboat which finally turned the scale of the Indians' favor toward the Americans as against the British."

The experience of Long's boat, which halted at Council Bluffs, and of the *Yellowstone* and *Assiniboine,* which with their draught of five feet were stopped by low water, resulted in the altered construction of later Missouri River steamboats. They were afterward made with flat bottoms, so that a vessel two hundred feet long and thirty feet in width could be navigated successfully in two and a half feet of water. Later boats were also equipped with stern-wheels instead of side-wheels. One very unusual feature of a flat-bottomed Missouri River steamboat found its expression in the hold. The craft was there equipped with a little railway and tram-cars, which ran all around the circumference of the freight quarters for the purpose of lending greater facility to the handling of bulky articles. Although doubtless not so intended in the first place, those little railways of Missouri River packets sometimes played a peculiar part—later to be mentioned—in the commerce of the river, in social conditions along its course, and in the history of the extensive country through which the steamers found their long and winding course.

Steamboat navigation on the Missouri was even more difficult than on the Ohio, the Mississippi, or any other stream whereon steam had superseded the primitive craft of earlier years. Besides being filled with snags and sandbars, and being extraordinarily tortuous in its windings, the big river of the West was consistently erratic regarding its course through any given locality. Owing to the soil of the region, and to its freshets and other seasonal conditions, the bed of the stream was constantly shifting its position throughout nearly the whole of the twenty-six hundred miles with which its navigators were required by their business to be unremittingly familiar. The stream would often find itself flowing through a tract of country that lay miles away from the bed it had occupied during the preceding week. The almost hopeless task of maintaining an up-to-date knowledge of the river and its whims was once suggested by a western newspaper,[1] which said:

"Of all the variable things in creation the most uncertain are the action of a jury, the state of a woman's mind, and the condition of the Missouri River."

[1] The "Sioux City Register," of March 28, 1868.

If a steamboat was unfortunate enough to reach a spot where the river was at that moment in the process of altering its course the vessel found itself in real danger, for whirlpools and other violent agitations of the water were caused by the changing of the current. An incident of the sort has been thus described:

"The whirl of the water was so swift that the center of the eddy was nearly twelve feet below its circumference. The boat was trying to pull itself by with a line when it was caught by the eddy, swung out in the stream, whirled violently around and careened over until the river flowed right across the lower deck. Wood and all other movable material were swept off, and two men were drowned. Only the mate's presence of mind in slacking off the line saved the boat."[1]

The scenes marking the commencement of the long voyage up the Missouri during the early years of its navigation were thus told by La Barge:

"The departure from port [St. Louis] was always attended with more or less carousing and revelry, particularly in the keelboat and early steamboat days, when a trip up the river might mean years of absence. The kind of farewell that captured the fancy of the average voyageur was a general debauch, which often disqualified him from being ready when the hour of departure arrived. Sometimes these delinquents who failed to appear hied themselves across the country to St. Charles and joined the boat there. . . . As the boat swung out into the stream a running salute of musketry was kept up by the mountaineers and others until it was out of hearing. The roll was then called, and the engagés were given their parcels of clothing. Next began the work of putting the boat deck in order for the trip. The bales of goods, which were strewn about in disorderly heaps, were carefully stowed away, and before night the boat was reduced to the appearance which it would wear during the remainder of the trip. . . .

"The passengers composed an even more heterogeneous mixture than the cargo itself. There were, first, the regular boat crew, numbering from thirty to forty. Very likely there were several Indians returning home from St. Louis or even from Washington. Then there were recruits for the various trading companies, consisting of hunters, trappers, voyageurs and mountaineers, and possibly a company of soldiers for some military service. Nearly always there were passengers distinguished for wealth or scientific attainment, who were making the

[1] Chittenden, pp. 122-3. The steamboat involved was the "Miner," and the scene of her misadventure was near Sioux City, Iowa.

1150

Yanktonand, das Dampfschiff St. Ange erwartend (1851).
Nach der Natur aufgenommen von Fred. Kurz.

340.—A party of Yankton Sioux watching a steamboat ascending the Missouri.
Published in Stuttgart from a sketch made by the German artist and traveller, Frederick Kurz, in 1851. A regular annual steam packet service had
been established to the upper river in 1832.

journey for pleasure or research. Government exploring parties generally traveled by boat to the initial point of their expeditions. In all there were from one hundred to two hundred people on board, with sufficient variety to insure vivacity and interest, however monotonous the journey might otherwise be. . . .

"While the officers and crew were kept alert and active the live-long day in getting their boat up the troublesome stream, the passengers whiled away their time as best they could. Games of all practicable sorts were indulged in. It was a common pastime to stand on the forecastle or boiler deck and shoot at geese and ducks on the river. Now and then the sight of deer and other animals enlivened the moment, and occasionally the appearance of Indians on the bank caused a flutter of excitement. To relieve the tedium of the voyage it was a common thing, when there was no danger from the Indians, to land at the beginning of extensive bends and ramble across the country to the other side, rejoining the boat when it came along. . . .

"Among the important events of every voyage were the arrivals at the various trading posts. To the occupants of these remote stations, buried in the depths of the wilderness, shut out for months from any glimpse of the world outside, the coming of the annual boat was an event of even greater interest than to the passengers themselves.[1] Generally the persons in charge of the post, with some of the employees, would drop down the river two or three days' ride and meet the boat. When she drew near the post, salutes would be exchanged, the colors displayed, and the passengers would throng the deck to greet the crowds which lined the bank. The exigencies of navigation never left much time for celebration and conviviality. The exchange of cargo was carried on with the utmost dispatch, and the moment the business was completed the boat proceeded on her way. These are some of the typical features of steamboat life as it used to exist on the Missouri River."[2]

Two of the principal problems attending the long trip of a pioneer Missouri River steamboat were the question of securing fuel to keep the boat in motion, and the feeding of the one or two hundred people on board. Enormous quantities of wood were required for the furnaces, and its procurement was not always an easy matter. The cottonwood trees which grew in profusion along the shores furnished the principal source of supply,

---

[1] The "remote stations" and their inhabitants who were "shut out for months from any glimpse of the world outside," were the pioneer white inhabitants of the region now included in western Iowa, eastern Nebraska, and North and South Dakota.
[2] Chittenden, pp. 126-132.

but green cottonwood made poor fuel, and its combustion usually had to be stimulated by the use of resin. A big drift log, either on the shore or in the stream itself, was always a prize to the engineer. After a few years certain points of fuel supply called "wood yards" were established, but as the Indians owned the country they often objected to the free use of its products, and refused to let the white travellers cut wood without cost. In some localities they themselves supplied fuel to the boats on a business basis. In order to circumvent the natives and to reduce the danger attendant upon their opposition Captain La Barge on one occasion equipped one of his steamboats with a saw-mill, and in addition carried with him on deck a yoke of oxen. When he had need of more wood he swung out a heavy landing stage, drove the oxen ashore, hastily dragged a number of logs aboard by their aid and then sawed the trees in his mill as he kept on his way up the river.

The food furnished to passengers on the canoes, keel-boats, pirogues and other craft of the river before steamboats appeared, and even for a short time after the appearance of the mechanical vessels, was of monotonous simplicity. It consisted almost entirely of fat pork, beans, corn and coffee, with the occasional addition of flapjacks. Fare of this description had sufficed for the trappers and other hardy men who were the first to move regularly back and forth along the river. But as soon as scientists and other men of more diversified tastes and experience appeared in St. Louis and sought accommodations on boats about to start up stream, their presence was reflected in the larders of the craft on which they were about to embark. The prospect of subsisting for many months on salt pork did not appeal to them, and in order to satisfy their demand for fresh meat the steamboats employed on the river added new members to their regular crews in the shape of hunters, whose only duty it was to kill game for the table. The steamboat hunter was never required to perform physical labor of any sort. The vessel tied up for the night as soon as darkness fell, and about midnight the hunter was put ashore.[1] From that hour until the middle of the forenoon it was his duty, if possible, to kill enough deer, antelope, bears, bison or ducks to satisfy the company so largely dependent on his rifle. He scoured the country ahead of the boat—which was not due to start until about four o'clock in the morning—and whenever he shot any desired animal he hung it up in some conspicuous tree close to a bank of the river. When the boat finally started a sentry was placed on the upper deck whose sole responsibility was to keep a sharp lookout for suspended provender. So, from sunrise until nine or ten o'clock, the sentry in question might occasionally be heard to shout: "Buffalo quarter on the starboard bow"; "Deer on the starboard bow"; "Bunch of ducks on the port bow"; and so on, as the case might be. And whenever he spied any food thus left by the hunter a skiff would be put off from the boat and the trophies quickly brought aboard to be delivered into the hands of the cook. Finally the hunter himself would be observed and sent for, and he then had nothing more to do until the next night.

Allusion has been made to the little railways with which some of the Missouri River steamboats were equipped. The *Omega,* which was one of the boats that went up the river in 1843, had such a tramway in her hold, and one of her passengers was Audubon, the naturalist. The principal event of the trip that year was a little

---

[1] Or else paddled away himself, in a small canoe.

FORT BENTON: HEAD OF STEAM NAVIGATION ON THE MISSOURI RIVER.

341.—Farthest up-stream point reached during the days of Missouri River steamboat travel, and greatest distance from the sea attained by a steamboat on any water course. Fort Benton, in the present state of Montana, was 3,575 miles from the ocean by way of the rivers, and the boats at that spot rode nearly half a mile above sea level.

drama wherein the leading parts were played by the tramway and the distinguished traveller just named.[1]

The customary severe Federal laws forbidding the importation of liquor into the countries owned by the Indians were then on the statute books, but were, as ever, disregarded by those white men who traded in such places. It was into lands still owned by Indians that the *Omega* was running, and she had on board a considerable quantity of the unlawful commodity. The American Fur Company, which owned the vessel and was trying to smuggle the liquor to its trading posts up the river, had to get the contraband material past two places where river cargoes were subjected to Federal inspection. The salient features then characterizing the use of whisky in connection with the Indian trade of the West were thus explained by La Barge to Chittenden:[2]

"Liquor was the one article above all others that the traders considered indispensable to their business, and they never failed to smuggle it through in some way or other. In the earlier years there was only one place at which the cargoes going up the river were inspected, and that was Fort Leavenworth. Later, when an Indian agency was established at Bellevue that place also became a point of detention. At that particular time it [Bellevue] was the bête noire of the American Fur Company traders. The military authorities at Fort Leavenworth, from long experience in the country and intimate knowledge of conditions prevailing there, exercised their office as inspectors with reasonable judgment and discretion. They understood very well that the small competing traders would smuggle liquor past them in spite of all they could do, and that to deprive the only responsible company on the river of its means of maintaining itself was simply to debauch the trade with the Indians to a reckless and demoralizing rivalry among a horde of irresponsible traders. They were, therefore, very lenient in their inspections, and the company rarely had any difficulty in getting past them.

"Not so, however, with some of the newly-appointed Indian agents.

---

[1] The story about to be told is contained in Chittenden's "History of Early Steamboat Navigation on the Missouri River." La Barge was pilot of the "Omega" during the voyage, and his log book of the trip was used by Chittenden, to whom La Barge personally narrated the circumstances. Audubon's journal of his trip also furnishes some testimony regarding the matters here discussed.

[2] "History of Early Steamboat Navigation on the Missouri River," pp. 142-3.

It was about this time that the Indian Department tried the experiment of assigning clergymen to the agencies—an example of good intentions but bad judgment. These new agents showed more zeal than discretion in their work, and although they put the traders to a great deal of trouble, it is doubtful if they lessened by a single drop the amount of liquor carried into the country."[1]

When the *Omega* reached Bellevue the Indian agent was absent. Captain Sire,[2] delighted with his good luck, hastily despatched his business and continued up the river for several miles—in his anxiety to escape inspection— before tying up for the night at nine o'clock. But in the morning, just as the boat was getting under way again, rifle shots were fired across her bow and an army officer came on board with information that his captain would later arrive to inspect the vessel.

Audubon then entered the action of the frontier play.[3] He promptly set forth across the country, reached the army camp before the military officer had started to inspect the boat, and talked to the captain for about two hours. In the meantime Captain Sire and his crew had been busy. They loaded all the contraband whisky on the tram-cars which stood on the rails in the dark hold, and pushed them to that part of the boat farthest removed from the hatchway through which it was planned the captain should enter on his work of inspection. No accident spoiled the arrangements. La Barge said: "When Captain B—— arrived in Audubon's company, he was received most hospitably and treated to a luncheon in which was included, as a matter of course, a generous

---

[1] This statement by a man who was himself a prominent cog in the machinery of Indian trade, indicates that the system previously practised by white men in dealing with Indians east of the Mississippi had been transplanted to the West as soon as the Indians had been removed from their former eastern possessions. From La Barge's narrative it seems presumable that the Caucasian introduction of liquor into Indian relations had attained an importance even greater than before, for he describes liquor as "one article above all others that the [western] traders considered indispensable to their business."

[2] Commander of the boat.

[3] Audubon himself had a permit from the government allowing him to carry a quantity of liquor for the use of his party, and encountered no personal difficulty in the matter. To use his own words, he was "immediately settled comfortably."

portion from the provided store embraced in Audubon's 'credentials.' By this time the young captain was in most excellent temper and was quite disposed to forego the inspection altogether."[1] Captain Sire said: "I insisted, as it were, that he make the strictest possible search, but on the condition that he would do the same with other traders."[2]

Then the steamboat captain escorted his official guest down through the hatchway, and the inspection began under the illumination of a candle accommodatingly held by a member of the crew. Nothing suspicious was found. As the governmental officer and his escort slowly approached the farther end of the boat the cavalcade of incriminating tram-cars on the other side of the cargo was gently and noiselessly pushed in the opposite direction, and thus the procession completed the circumnavigation of the hold. The boat and her freight emerged virtuous from the ordeal, mutual assurances of esteem were exchanged between the scientist, the army officer and the steamboat captain, and the craft glided on her way up the river in peace.

The annual voyage of 1844 was made by the *Nimrod,* which was also navigated by the same captain and pilot. The *Nimrod* had an experience somewhat similar to that just described, and the incident was told by La Barge as follows:

"In passing the Indian agency at Bellevue this year it was necessary to indulge in some more sharp practice to get the annual cargo of alcohol past that point. The new Indian agent at Bellevue was an ex-Methodist minister of the name of Joseph Miller—as zealous in his new rôle of liquor inspector as he had ever been in the regular practice

---

[1] "History of Early Steamboat Navigation on the Missouri," p. 146.
[2] Sire's record of the matter was set down in his log under date of May 10th. The original transcription was in French, as follows: "Je force en quelque sorte l'officier à faire un recherche aussi stricte que possible, mais à la condition qu'il en sera de même avec les autres traiteurs."

of his profession. It was his boast that no liquor could pass his agency. He rummaged every boat from stem to stern, broke open the packages, overturned the piles of merchandise, and with a long, slender, pointed rod pierced the bales of blankets and clothing, lest kegs of alcohol might be rolled up within. The persistent clergyman put the experienced agents of the company to their wit's end, and it was with great difficulty that they succeeded in eluding his scrutiny."[1]

Captain Sire's solution of the perplexing problem on this occasion was an inspiration of genius. When he reached Bellevue he simply put the whisky ashore under the agent's nose, packed in barrels of flour. Paying no attention whatever to the freight already disembarked, the agent made his usual minute examination of the *Nimrod* and her cargo. He found nothing at all, which circumstance he could not understand, for he felt certain that the boat was trying to smuggle liquor as usual. After he had gone to bed the barrels of flour were put on board again, and the boat resumed her voyage.

Thus did the big steam canoes of the white men slowly creep farther and still farther westward into the immense and little known spaces which were then the last stronghold of the native races. In such manner were the new mechanical travel vehicles of the Caucasians employed in the work which had for its purpose the subjugation of the Indians and acquirement of their remaining territories. After the *Assiniboine* attained a point beyond the mouth of the Yellowstone in 1834 a period of nineteen years elapsed before her feat was surpassed by another steamboat. In 1853 a vessel named *El Paso* outdistanced the *Assiniboine's* record by about one hundred and twenty-five miles and passed the mouth of Milk River. Finally, in 1860, the *Chippewa* and the *Key West* arrived at the distant location of Fort Benton in the

[1] "History of Early Navigation on the Missouri," pp. 156-7.

present state of Montana, and in so doing they "reached a point further from the sea by a continuous water course than any other boat had ever been."[1] The vessels were then no less than 3,575 miles from the Gulf of Mexico, and in vertical height were almost half a mile above sea level.

Having observed pioneer conditions attending the use of a water route into the far West, we come now in due course to the five remaining features of importance connected with the Caucasian conquest of the West by overland travel. Those several phases of the subject are the relation of the Indians to white travel between the Mississippi valley and the Pacific Ocean; the movement to Oregon; the wanderings of the Mormons across the country to the present state of Utah; the various aspects of the exodus to California, and finally, the completion of the whole work through the building of a railway by which the oceans were joined and the continent was spanned by a modern transportation method.

[1] Chittenden's "Early Steamboat Navigation on the Missouri," p. 219.

CHAPTER L

THE RELATION OF THE INDIANS OF THE WEST TO TRANS-
CONTINENTAL TRAVEL — RED PEOPLES NATIVE TO THE
REGION BEYOND THE MISSISSIPPI STILL RETAINED
THEIR SELF-RULE AND OWNED MOST OF THE LAND
WHEN THE GREAT OVERLAND MIGRATIONS BEGAN —
INDIANS TRANSPLANTED FROM THEIR EASTERN
HOMES ALSO FORMED A BARRIER TO WHITE MOVEMENT
JUST WEST OF THE MISSISSIPPI — TREATY RELATIONS
BETWEEN THE GOVERNMENT AND THE WESTERN
TRIBES — THE NATIVES ARE PAID LARGE SUMS FOR
THEIR CONSENT TO WHITE TRAVEL TOWARD THE
PACIFIC AND FOR THE PRIVILEGE OF BUILDING RAIL-
ROADS

THE penetration, by the Caucasians, of that part of the
continent west of the Mississippi resulted in a long
series of race troubles somewhat similar to those which
had distinguished the earlier history of the East. The
native resentment manifested against fur-hunting expeditions in the upper Missouri valley just prior to 1825
may be considered as marking the commencement of such
difficulties, and they continued, in one form or another,
until after the completion of the first transcontinental
railway.

Just as had been the case in the East, the white government negotiated with the western tribes, nations and confederacies by treaty, recognizing their ownership of land

1161

and right of self-government. Some of the remote tribes conceded the sovereignty of the United States at an early day, while in other instances the treaties with them—by implication or otherwise—left that important question surrounded by uncertainty and doubt.

During the various migrations of English speaking Americans through the West—whose principal features are soon to be noticed—there constantly existed a very close relation between the Indian problem and white travel. Particularly was this true of the period beginning with the rush to California in 1849 and continuing until 1869. The Federal government of the United States, between those years, paid millions of dollars to the red nations beyond the Mississippi in return for the privilege of free and unmolested transit across native territories, and secured such rights by negotiations similar to the treaties which had led to their acquirement of many travel routes in the older sections of the country.[1]

The Indian nations native to the West were at no time so advanced in the arts and customs of civilized life as were their ethnological relatives of the East. Those of the far Southwest maintained many permanent towns, and some few tribes farther to the north carried on a little agricultural work in a small way, but the nature of the country and climate in which they lived dictated their manner of life. They were of necessity nomadic, or semi-nomadic, shaping their yearly routine in harmony with the habits of the living food and fur supply on which their existence so largely depended, and moving their villages, trapping camps and hunting parties periodically,

[1] For the purpose of these pages it has been considered more desirable to give an outline of this phase of western travel in one brief chapter, as a connected and chronological narrative, than to scatter the information through various subsequent chapters in disconnected form.

342.—A Blackfoot Indian. From a drawing by Carl Bodmer. Many natives of the plains and foothills were wonderful horsemen, and though they did not dare attack caravans of large size, even if so inclined, they frequently harassed the marching columns. Some of the tribes and bands carried away horses when possible, or else caused the animals to stampede at night. The feeling of the native Indians of the West, at sight of the immense Caucasian migrations, was probably a composite of anger, fear and despair.

in accord with the changes of the seasons. Many of the important native groups in that part of the continent ranged over areas vastly larger than the territories of the eastern red nations, and the boundaries of the countries occupied by them were never so definitely fixed.

Extensive dealings between the Federal government and the western Indians began in 1825. During the summer of that year—as a result of action previously taken in Monroe's administration and partly in consequence of the three battles with white fur-trappers—an embassy visited several tribes of the Missouri valley and adjacent regions[1] and negotiated important treaties with them. Certain provisions contained in the agreement signed with the Ogallala Sioux on July 25 will indicate the nature of the understanding then reached. In Article I the natives admitted "that they reside within the territorial limits of the United States." In Article II they agreed "to give safe conduct to all persons who may be legally authorized by the United States to pass through their country." Article III provided that any white man resident among the Indians, and who was wanted by the United States, would be extradited "on the requisition or demand of the President of the United States."

Similar stipulations, in substantially identical language, were contained in the other treaties of 1825. Those instruments laid the foundation for official regulation of Caucasian travel in the far West. The next treaty of consequence[2] was that with the confederated Pawnees living on the Platte and Loup Rivers. They ceded all their lands lying south of the Platte River, agreed to remove north of that stream, and "not to molest or injure the person or property of any white citizen of the United States, wherever found." For these cessions and pledges the Pawnees—in addition to cash—demanded and received agricultural instruments, schools, iron, blacksmiths' shops, mills, live stock and practical farm tuition. They acknowledged no jurisdiction of the whites over them or their remaining territories. Still another significant negotiation of the same period was that with the

[1] The Ogallala Sioux; Cheyenne; Teton, Yancton and Yanctonies Sioux; Hunkpapa Sioux; Arikara; Minitorees; Mandans; Crows and Pawnees.
[2] October 9, 1833.

Comanche and Wichita.[1] It was desired by the United States as a safeguard for the rapidly increasing travel and commerce over the Santa Fé trail, and provided[2] that "the citizens of the United States are freely permitted to pass and repass through their [the Indian] settlements or hunting ground without molestation or injury on their way to any of the provinces of the Republic of Mexico, or returning therefrom."

The Cherokee, Choctaw, Osage, Seneca and Quapaw nations were likewise native signatories to this agreement, and they, together with the Comanche and Wichita, were in return given free permission to hunt and trap "to the western limits of the United States." A decided international flavor was also imparted to the document by a proviso that the pledges made to the United States by the red nations should "in no respect interrupt their friendly relations with the Republic of Mexico." That such promises and understandings on the part of the whites were not the result of accident or vacillating impulse was indicated two years afterward, when[3] they asked a similar favor of the Kiowa and other prairie nations in behalf of traffic over the Santa Fé trail and in payment gave them similar rights of movement to the western limits of white sovereignty and recognized their friendly relations with Mexico. Those two instruments considerably increased the number of Indians who had acquired, by treaty, the right to journey, hunt and trap at will throughout the western possessions of the Caucasians.

The Kansa tribe, in January of 1846, ceded some two million acres of their lands to the white government and were paid about ten cents an acre therefor. A few months

[1] August 24, 1835.
[2] In Article III.
[3] May 26, 1837.

afterward—as a result of recent developments and impending political troubles in the Southwest—the Federal government induced a number of southwestern tribes[1] to place themselves under the protection of the United States. The natives involved, however, retained their lands and self-government.

343.—The bison. Principal source of such food supply as could be obtained during a transcontinental trip. An outpost bull on guard. From a drawing by the naturalist and artist, Carl Bodmer.

Up to the year 1846 the principal international dealings between the United States and the western Indians—save one—were those just recited. They had been an outgrowth of white movement along the Santa Fé trail and the Missouri River, and had not been accompanied, as a rule, either with threats or attempts to awe the red men by military force used as part of the diplomatic machinery. But by 1845 a new phase of the white inva-

[1] The Comanche, Aionia, Anadarko, Caddo, Lipan, Wichita, Waco and others.

sion had developed in the West. The migrations to Oregon were in progress, overland caravan travel by large parties had begun, and the Rocky Mountains and northwest coast on the Pacific were involved. As a result of this phenomenon the attitude of the natives was undergoing a change. Especially was this true in the region through which the Oregon immigrants were passing. The Indians saw they had underestimated the strength and numbers of the whites, and began to realize more clearly the menace contained in the white caravans. Then was adopted, also, the policy under which the white government thereafter systematically carried on its dealings with the natives of the far western country. A description of the peculiar ceremonies and other events, and of the statement made by the Federal commander on the occasion when that policy was first visibly manifested, was written and printed soon after it took place. The meeting in question was held at Fort Laramie, on the Oregon trail, in the summer of 1845, and the most detailed and interesting unofficial account of it is that embodied by two white travellers named Johnson and Winter, in a book which they published during the following year.[1] Their statement ran:

"The Sioux and Shians, [Cheyenne] who, next to the Black Feet, are the terror of the mountains, and the tribes which had been the cause of our greatest dread, were now [July, 1845] not so much to be feared. . . . They were beginning to have a much better idea of the strength of the whites. Formerly they had considered that they were weak, and that their numbers were very small. When the Emigration of 1843 passed through their country they told the traders at Fort Laramie that they believed it to be the white people's big village, and the last of the race. Under this belief they entertained serious notions of going back and taking possession of the country which they had abandoned. But an Emigration of twelve hundred the following year, and one of three

[1] "Route Across the Rocky Mountains, etc." Some further account of this little-known book, and references to it, are contained in a subsequent chapter dealing with the Oregon migrations.

thousand the present year, had an effect to open their eyes; and they began to respect their power. Col. Carney's visit this year, with two or three hundred dragoons, had even made them to fear a little, and would, we believed, have a tendency to promote our safety. He had not only passed through the whole extent of their country, as far as the South Pass, but had called together at Fort Laramie as great a number of those tribes as he could; among these were many of their Chiefs and braves, with whom he held a council; not only warning them of the punishment which they would receive if they continued to molest and kill the Americans, but operating on their superstition by a display of such things as, to them, were mysterious and supernatural.

"After he had had a long talk with the Chiefs, and told them what he wished them to do, and what not to do, in respect to the white people passing through their country, he obtained from them a promise that they would henceforth, in these respects, act according to his wishes and requests. Having obtained this promise, which without the addition of fear would have been violated as freely as it had been given, he determined to work a little, if possible, upon their superstitions. The dragoons, with all military show, were paraded, and a field piece rolled out upon the prairie. The Colonel then proclaimed to all the Chiefs and braves, and to all the Indians assembled, that he was about to inform the Great Spirit of their promise, and call him to witness the covenant they had made. He bade them look up and listen. A sky-rocket rose in the air, and darting away on its mission, had almost buried itself in the bosom of the sky when it burst, flashed in the heavens, reported to the Great Mysterious, resolved itself again into its airy form, and the errand was accomplished. Another, and another; three of the fiery messengers arose in succession into the presence of the Great Spirit and announced to him that the Sioux and Shians had entered into a solemn covenant with a Chief of the white people to be their friends, and to respect forever their lives and property.

"While they stood, with all the awe which ignorance and blind superstition could inspire, gazing into the heavens where just now they had been luminous with the mysterious display, a cannon was discharged; and while its deafening thunder shook the field, the ball, flying far away across the plain, bounding and rebounding, tore the earth and marked its dusty track with clouds.

" 'That,' said the Colonel, 'was to open your ears, that you might not be deaf to what I am about to say. Can you hear?'

" 'Yes,' replied the Chiefs, 'we can hear.'

"The second was discharged, roaring still louder than the first; and the ball again proved the power of the mighty engine that sent it. 'Can you hear, I say?' demanded the Colonel. 'Yes,' they replied a little submissively, 'we can hear well.' Again the cannon told, still louder. Three times it thundered in their ears. 'Can you hear?' reiterated the Colonel. 'I say, can you hear?' 'We are not deaf; we can hear well;

our ears are open. Speak. Let the great Chief of the white people speak whatever he wishes.'

"Colonel Carney addressed them. 'I am,' he said, 'very little. The Great Chief of the white people is afar: he is in the bosom of a mighty nation; and his warriors around him are like the grass upon the prairie, or the sands which cover the plains. He told me to go and talk to the Sioux and Shians, and I obeyed him. I am here. A thousand Chiefs who are mightier than I wait to do his commands. He loves his friends, and is kind to them, but to his enemies, to those who destroy the lives of his people, he is dreadful. As the storm when it walks upon the mountains and treads down the pines, so terrible are the warriors of the Great Chief when they come upon their foes. Beware then, lest ye make him angry. Think before you break the pipe which we have smoked together in friendship. Think well before you violate the covenant you have made with me and with my people, and to which we have called the Great Spirit to witness. Talk to your young men; counsel them that are foolish; tell them that we are mighty, and terrible in war. Bid them pause, and think, and tremble, before they spill again the blood of a white man. The past we will forget; it is buried. We will soon return to our homes with the tidings of peace: but when we hear that your hands have spilt one drop more of the blood of our countrymen, we will come again. We will come with war. We will revenge all the wrongs that we have ever received. Then your eyes shall not be dry from weeping over your fallen warriors, and the blood of your nations shall not cease to flow until we are weary from destroying. You say that you can hear. We will see. Be careful that your ears do not forget.'

"They all answered: 'It is good.'

"Such, we believe, is about the sense in which we understood Mr. Bisonette, describing the treaty made by Col. Carney with the Sioux and Shians. He is one of the principal partners in the neighboring trading establishment, Fort Platte, and we presume that it is mainly correct. He gave us as his opinion that for a time it would have a favorable influence over the conduct of the Indians; but that it would soon be forgotten and disregarded, and that nothing but a strong military post, located in their country, could keep them in awe and make the lives of Americans safe among them."[1]

Johnson and Winter, in addition, gave the following advice to overland travellers concerning their intercourse with the natives they met:

"The character of the Indians will be learned from our preceding remarks. The manner in which they are treated will, of course, make

[1] Johnson and Winter: pp. 121-124.

a great difference in their disposition towards those who chance to meet with them. They should never be trusted, nor should they, if it can be avoided, be allowed to have the advantage in any particular. And while everything that would be calculated to give them offense should be carefully avoided by those who wish to go in peace, they should at the same time be constantly held at a distance. The emigrant should refrain from all familiarity himself, and discourage it in them. In trading with them he should make use of few words; never attempt to deceive, and be prompt to the letter, in fulfilling every promise. Few presents should be given them, and those few should appear to be given, rather as an expression of friendship than to conciliate their favor. Under all circumstances, the least expression of fear should be sternly avoided. From the late difficulties with the Shoshonee Diggers, and with the Walawalas—to which we have referred—these tribes will not likely be well disposed towards emigrants."[1]

Following the Oregon migrations came the march of the Mormons to Utah, but that movement, large though it was, did not suffice to disturb—much less to disrupt—the entire native system then prevailing throughout the western half of the continent. The penetration and occupation of the last Indian territories, within a few years, could only have been brought about by an event such as took place almost immediately afterward, and the difficulties confronted by both races can be indicated by outlining the geographical positions and governmental relations of the opposing peoples just before the critical year of 1849.

A period of forty-four years elapsed between the transcontinental journey made by Lewis and Clark, and the discovery of gold by Marshall in 1848. During that interval eight or ten other governmental expeditions had spent either months or years in wandering through the areas between the Mississippi and the Pacific Ocean, and had returned to civilization with accounts of its native peoples, of the physical peculiarities of very narrow strips of the region, and natural conditions there

[1] Johnson and Winter: p. 145.

observed. A small though constant flow of Caucasian travel along the natural highway formed by the Missouri River had given to the eastern states a considerable amount of information regarding the country in the immediate vicinity of that stream. Another path of white travel

344.—West-bound white men had no right to halt and settle on the prairies beyond Missouri and Iowa until the lands had been acquired by the government from the Indians. As that right was gradually obtained a part of the immigrants from the East paused in Kansas and Nebraska, built cabins and tilled the soil.

penetrated to the Mexican—and former Mexican—possessions in the Southwest, in the shape of the Santa Fé trail over which white movement was carried on by permission of the Indians. And, in addition, a relatively small but spectacular overland migration to the Oregon country and to Utah had given two new footholds in the West to the rapidly expanding nation.

But in spite of these things the wide wastes between the central valley and the Pacific still remained almost wholly unoccupied by the white race and almost equally unknown to it. Until as recent a date as 1820 it was believed that a large river flowed almost directly westward from the main system of the Rocky Mountains of Colorado, and emptied into the Pacific Ocean through the Bay of San Francisco.[1] The only detailed knowledge of the region possessed by the government or available to the mass of people related to natural conditions existing in the neighborhood of the Missouri River and the Oregon and Santa Fé trails. Immense areas still remained concerning which no reliable information existed. A few military outposts had been established on the travelled routes, just as blockhouses had been built beyond the uttermost settlements of the eastern wilderness long before. But the real social frontier of the English speaking population stopped with the permanent settlements that had been established in Missouri, Arkansas and Iowa. Even Wisconsin—which had not been erected into a state from the last remnant of the old Northwest Territory until 1848—had its white population grouped along its eastern and southern edges, and along the Mississippi River on its western border. Nearly all the new state still remained a virgin forest unoccupied by white people.

To the westward of Iowa, Missouri and Arkansas there lay a solid phalanx of Indian tribes which extended in an unbroken line from central Texas to the British dominions far to the northward. The Comanches and Kiowas were in Texas. Immediately across the western boundary of Arkansas were the new countries given to the Chickasaws, Choctaws, Creeks and Seminoles when those tribes had been removed from their former posses-

[1] Melish's fifty-sheet map of 1820 indicates the general course of such a stream, with an accompanying inscription which says, "Supposed course of a river between the Buena Ventura and the Bay of San Francisco, which will probably be the communication from the Arkansas to the Pacific Ocean."

sions east of the Mississippi. The Cherokees were established west of Missouri, as were also the Potawatomi, Senecas, Shawnees, Delawares, Kickapoos and Iowas. To the westward of the lands occupied by those transplanted red peoples were the territories still owned and occupied by the Cheyennes, Arapahoes, Pawnees and the many tribes of the powerful and far-flung Siouxan stock. The Sioux were also strongly established in what is now the state of Minnesota, and from that region westward. Some of these nations, it will be remembered, held their new possessions under Federal guarantees that they should never again be included in or surrounded by Caucasian commonwealths; that they might henceforward have free access from their new homes to the Pacific Ocean; and that they should not again be subject to laws of white states.

This formidable rampart of native races had been in process of erection by the Federal government for nearly twenty years, and the circumstances under which it had been brought into existence, together with certain events that had taken place since its creation, had tended to give the transplanted tribes a considerable feeling of security. They were self-governed communities in accordance with immemorial custom or the stipulations of the treaties negotiated with them; the government had respected native rights connected with white travel through Indian territories, and on several occasions had restrained or ejected Caucasian individuals or groups of individuals who had sought to establish themselves on Indian lands. Some of the tribes native to the western part of the continent, and who still lived in localities they had occupied from time immemorial, had negotiated treaties with the United States government. Others had not; but all the

345.—A wagon train attacked by Indians. Whenever the number of wagons was sufficient, or there was time to perform the necessary manœuvre, the vehicles were formed into a circle or hollow square to resist an onslaught. From a drawing by Captain S. Eastman, U. S. A.

natives indigenous to the West still lived and carried on their pursuits in regions to which their rights had not been questioned. And although a part of the Indians native to the West were at times on terms of hostility to other tribes of the same sort, or to transplanted tribes, it may nevertheless be easily understood that knowledge of the Federal guarantees given to some of them during the fourth decade could have permeated all the aboriginal population then living to the westward of the most advanced permanent Caucasian settlements.

Although the red peoples of the West had been living for a short time under conditions which—to them—gave some promise of future permanence and security, they no doubt realized that if they again came into social conflict with the white race, or were menaced by another large advancing wave of the alien population, their situation would be desperate indeed.

That was the situation when the rush to California began, and from that time forth, for twenty years, the relations between the western Indians and the Federal government were shaped by the uncontrollable advance of the white men through lands which either belonged to the red men or over which the natives had been given treaty rights to move for their own domestic purposes. The national administration at Washington bought native territory as rapidly as possible in order that the people might find their way to the Pacific over routes not involved in or threatened by race troubles, but that process could not keep abreast of necessity, and, as before, permission for the overland travel in progress was sought and obtained by the previous treaty method. The Indians were continually involved in altercations with the marching hosts, whose members often gave scant heed to the rights of the peoples whose ancient homes they were overrunning. Probably only a very insignificant part of the white emigrants had any knowledge whatever of the endeavors made by their governmental servants to obtain for them, between 1849 and 1869, the right to move westward by wagon trains, stage-coaches and railways. They felt, and believed, that the ground they traversed was owned by them. A certain arrogance inevitably accompanied such a genuine conviction, and born of it—when it came into conflict with the anger and despair of the Indians—were the wars and other troubles that distinguished the final scenes of the long conquest.

The first of the native western red nations who, without qualification, acknowledged themselves to be under

1175

the jurisdiction of the United States as well as under its protection were the Navahos and the Utes.[1] Each tribe, by treaty, agreed that "the people of the United States of America shall have free and safe passage through the territory of the aforesaid Indians, under such rules and regulations as may be adopted by authority of the said states." The Utes, in addition, pledged themselves "to cease the roving and rambling habits which have hitherto marked them as a people . . . and to support themselves by their own industry, aided and directed as it may be by the wisdom, justice, and humanity of the American people."

By the year 1851 it had become imperatively necessary to reach an understanding with the powerful nations flanking and containing the overland routes then being used by white emigrants in the North, and so a treaty with them was negotiated.[2] In it they granted "the right of the United States government to establish roads, military and other posts, within their respective territories," and in return the Federal government bound itself "to protect the aforesaid Indian nations against the commission of all depredations by the people of the said United States." In the following year the Apache acknowledged themselves to be under the laws, jurisdiction and government of the whites, and declared that "the people of the United States of America shall have free and safe passage through the territory of the aforesaid Indians."[3] The Comanche, Kiowa and Apache, in 1853,[4] gave the United States the right "to lay off and mark out roads for highways" within their territories; promised to abstain from

[1] By treaties dated September 9, 1849, and December 3, 1849, respectively.
[2] On September 17. The native signatory peoples were the Sioux, Dacota, Cheyenne, Arapaho, Crows, Assiniboin, Grosventres, Mandan and Arikara.
[3] Treaty of July 1, 1852.
[4] Treaty dated July 27.

346.—Many who started across the continent, or to an intermediate destination, never finished the journey. After a few years every mile beyond Missouri was dotted with the whitening bones of beasts that had fallen, and with mounds that marked the graves of men. Comparatively few travellers were killed by natives, but many succumbed to accident and to natural illness aggravated by exposure and hardship.

levying contributions on, or molesting whites who were lawfully residing in or passing through their countries; agreed to render assistance to such travellers as needed relief, and to facilitate their safe passage. In consideration for the roads thus permitted, and for "the losses which they may sustain by reason of the travel of the people of the United States through their territories," and for other reasons, the white government agreed to pay $180,000 and to "protect and defend the Indian tribes, parties hereto, against the committal of any depredations upon them, and in their territories, by the people of the United States."

1177

It had already been realized that a transcontinental railroad was destined to be built in the near future, and governmental anticipation in that regard soon afterward became visible in the treaty stipulations providing for Caucasian travel through the West. Article XIV of an agreement with the Omaha, in 1854,[1] provided that necessary roads, highways and railroads which might be constructed on their lands "shall have a right of way through the reservations, a just compensation being paid therefor in money." The Shawnees gave a similar permission a few weeks later,[2] agreeing that all roads and highways laid out by authority of the law should have right of way through their lands, and that railroads might have like privileges, "on payment of a just compensation therefor in money." Still another tribe that made an identical concession during the same year was the Kickapoo, which gave railways a right of way through their "permanent home" as defined in the treaty.[3] The Choctaws and Chickasaws took identical action in behalf of future railroads at the urging of the United States in 1855,[4] and also conceded that telegraph lines might be built in their territories.

The year 1855 witnessed the drawing up of an important convention with the Blackfeet and Flathead nations of the Northwest. Article VIII said that "for the purpose of establishing thoroughfares through their country . . . the United States may, within the countries respectively occupied and claimed by them, construct roads of every description." For this and allied privileges the government agreed to pay $350,000. The

[1] Dated March 16.
[2] By the treaty of May 10, 1854.
[3] That of May 18, 1854. By this treaty the Kickapoo gave up a territory allotted to them as a permanent home in 1852.
[4] June 22.

FORT LARAMIE

347.—Fort Laramie. An important station on the Oregon trail, situated on the North Fork of the Platte River, in the eastern part of the present state of Wyoming.

Yankton Sioux, in 1858, also agreed that the whites might make roads across their country.

A treaty with the eastern Shoshoni, of Utah, re-established friendly relations between that tribe and the whites in 1863,[1] and much of its text related to the subject of the overland travel then in progress or in prospect. It said in Article II: "The several routes of travel through the Shoshonee country, now or hereafter used by white men, shall be and remain forever free and safe for the use of the government of the United States, and of all emigrants and travellers under its authority and protection . . . and the safety of all travellers passing peaceably over said routes is hereby guaranteed by said nation." The same article provided for the establishment of ferries and inns. Article III said: "The telegraph and overland stage lines having been established and operated through a part of the Shoshonee country, it is expressly agreed that the same may be continued without hindrance, molestation, or injury from the people of said nation; and that their property, and the lives of passengers in the stages, and of the employees of the respective companies, shall be protected by them." For these concessions the government paid $200,000, and an additional $10,000 for "the inconvenience resulting to the Indians in consequence of the driving away and destruction of game along the routes travelled by whites." Substantially identical treaties, for the same purpose, were negotiated during the same year with the Northwestern Shoshoni and the western Shoshoni.[2] The first named of these tribes was paid an annuity of $5,000 for its signatures, and the second received no less than $1,000,000, divided in twenty

[1] July 2.
[2] Dated July 30 and October 1, respectively.

installments of $50,000 each. The continued hostility of the Indians in question could have stopped a large part of the travel whose continuance they were thus induced to tolerate.

By this time the government had definitely committed itself to the building of a transcontinental railway, and in order to secure the good-will of the Shoshoni-Goship tribe to that undertaking a treaty was concluded[1] with the tribe in question which said: "It being understood that provision has been made by the Government of the United States for the construction of a railway from the plains west to the Pacific Ocean, it is stipulated by said bands that the said railway or its branches may be located, constructed, and operated, and without molestation from them, through any part of the country claimed or occupied by them." The Indians were paid $20,000 for their consent. Two years later, in 1865,[2] the Osage nation of Kansas gave a right of way to railroads, as well as to "all roads and highways" through "the remaining lands of said Indians."

At about this date the Federal government added another feature to the policy by which it was seeking to secure additional travel and traffic facilities to the Pacific, and the innovation may well be indicated by quoting Article IV of the treaty signed by the Miniconjou Sioux, of Dakota, on October 10, 1865. It read:

"The said band, represented in council, shall withdraw from the routes overland already established through their country; and in consideration thereof the Government of the United States agree to pay the said band the sum of ten thousand dollars annually for twenty

[1] October 12, 1863.
[2] Treaty of September 29.

1181

years. . . ." This plan of inducing the natives to remove from the neighborhood of overland travel routes, and of paying them large sums for so doing, was put into extensive operation in the north, and was attended with advantages.[1] The Comanche and Kiowa tribes signed another treaty in 1865[2] permitting the United States to build roads or highways in their countries and providing that the "injury sustained by reason thereof by the Indians" should be compensated.

When the United States, in 1866, approached the Choctaw and Chickasaw nations with desire to obtain the privilege of building railroads through their territories, those advanced and still independent commonwealths conceded the request,[3] but laid down certain conditions far more extreme than had previously been named by any other tribe. The treaty, in its finished form, provided that their own legislatures, as well as the United States, might charter railways. It also stated that the two red nations might subscribe to the stock of such roads built by the whites, which stock so owned by them should have the force and effect of a first mortgage bond on all that part of the roads and their equipment in the nations' limits, and be a perpetual lien on the enterprises. In this unusual treaty the United States also again acknowledged the self-government of the two native parties to it, for, in Article VII, it was declared that whatever legislation was enacted by the United States in relation to the Indian Territory, "shall not in any wise interfere with or annul their [the Choctaws' and Chickasaws'] present tribal organizations, or their respective legislatures or judiciaries, or the rights,

---

[1] Other Sioux tribes paid for like action, with the sums they received: Lower Brule, $120,000; Two Kettle, $120,000; Blackfeet, $140,000; Upper Yanktonai, $200,000; Ogalalla, $200,000.
[2] October 18.
[3] Treaty of April 28.

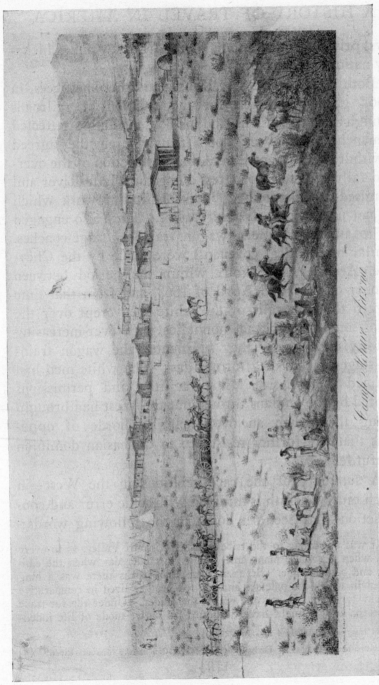

Camp Mohave Arizona

348.—Wagon train approaching Fort Mohave, Arizona. In the days of the westward migrations the government's forts were resting places for caravans, as Fort Chissel and other stations had been during the travel over the wilderness roads of the East. Engraved on stone by George H. Boker of San Francisco. Date, about 1855.

laws, privileges, or customs of the Choctaw and Chickasaw nations respectively."

Both the Delawares of Kansas and the Cherokees, in 1866,[1] gave permission for the creation of railroads through their possessions, and in 1867[2] the long-disaffected Comanche and Kiowa signed a treaty whereby they agreed to withdraw all opposition to the construction of the overland railway then in progress along the Platte River and promised no longer to oppose any similar work which did not pass over their reservations. They also engaged not to attack travellers, wagon trains or stage-coaches. Similar or identical covenants were made by the Cheyenne, Arapaho and Sioux within the period between October of 1867 and April of 1868, and from that time onward the iron rails of the white men crept over the plains and through the mountains with ever-increasing rapidity until finally they supplanted the wagon trains and stage-coaches of a former day. The white men had obtained their desire. The facilities and permissions granted by the Indians throughout the West had brought among them such an overwhelming horde of opponents that any further resistance to Caucasian dominion was futile.

A summary of the race relations in the West—in which much of truth is mingled with some error and contradiction—has been set down in the following words:[3]

"It was a sad day to the tribes of the Missouri Valley, as to every other, when the white man came, but a far sadder day when the emigrant and settler came. Between these two epochs there was a long interval in which the paleface and his red brother lived in comparative harmony together. It was the era of the trader. Under the fur-trade régime the Indian might have continued his native mode of life indefi-

[1] By treaties dated July 4 and July 19.
[2] October 21.
[3] Chittenden's "History of Early Steamboat Navigation on the Missouri River."

nitely. The trader never sought to change it. He introduced but few innovations; had no desire to introduce any; and looked with as jealous an eye as the Indian himself upon the approach of civilization. . . .

"All this was changed when the emigrant came. The traders were few in number and made no permanent settlements. The emigrants came by the thousand and spread themselves all over the country. They made roads, discovered rich mines, laid out cities, and declared their purpose to send the 'fire horse' across the plains, as they had sent the 'fire canoe' up the great river. Before this ever-increasing host the game wasted away. It was estimated that in the single year 1853 four hundred thousand buffalo were slain. As the buffalo was the very life of the plains tribes, its extermination meant inevitable starvation or hopeless dependence upon the government.

"All this the Indian foresaw with unerring vision, and it affected him just as it would any other independent people. A state of unrest ensued. Depredations and outrages occurred—for the Indian understood no other way of expressing his displeasure—and the government was forced to interfere. The era of the fur trade came to an end, and that of the treaty, the agent, and the annuity began—an era whose history will bring the blush of shame to its readers to the latest generations. And yet it would be wholly unjust to charge the flagrant wrongs which followed to this or that particular cause. History will exonerate the government from any but the purest motives in its dealings with the Indians. It may have been unwise in some of its measures; it was certainly weak in carrying its purposes into effect; but it always sought, with the light it possessed, the highest good of the Indian. The problem, unfortunately, was beyond human wisdom to solve. The ablest minds of this country and century have grappled with it in vain. It was the problem of how to commit a great wrong without doing any wrong —how to deprive the Indian of his birthright in such a way that he should feel that no injustice had been done him. It was the decree of destiny that the European should displace the native American upon his own soil. No earthly power could prevent it. This was the wrong; all else was purely incidental; and whatever consideration or generosity might attend the details of the change, nothing could alter the stern and fundamental fact.[1]

"With this impossible problem our law-givers wrestled for a century in vain. They sought to deal with the Indian on a basis of political equality, where such equality did not and could not exist. The treaty system was the outgrowth of this attempt. Perhaps it was impossible to deal with the Indians except by treaty, but it is difficult at this day

---

[1] [Chittenden.] "What consideration will induce you to give up war and remain at peace?" is the hypothetical question of a certain Indian agent to a tribe of the Sioux in 1867. And the hypothetical answer, based upon his many talks with them, was this: "Stop the white man from traveling across our lands; give us the country which is ours by right of conquest and inheritance, to live in and enjoy unmolested by his encroachments, and we will be at peace with all the world."

to see the wisdom of that method. It only deferred the inevitable. It made promises which, in the nature of things, could not be kept.[1] Made to be broken, they served no other purpose than to lull the natives into temporary quiet while the paleface was fastening his grip ever more tightly upon their country. It was throughout a policy of insincerity; the fostering of a spirit of independent sovereignty when in fact the tribes were only vassals. Like all insincerity, it bred endless wrong. The loss of his lands would not have been so bad to him if he had understood it from the start; but as it was, he had not only to bear this loss, but the ever-increasing evidence of the white man's bad faith; and he thus came to hate the whites and distrust their government.[2]

"This, if we were to venture a criticism, has been the government's one great mistake in dealing with the Indians. A firm attitude of authority toward the tribes, with an unqualified claim to sovereignty of the soil, and an assertion of the right to reduce it and them to a condition of ultimate civilization, would have eliminated the element of bad faith which has always characterized the treaty system. But instead of this the government continued to foster to the last the notion of tribal sovereignty over the lands of the West. Under the farce of obtaining these lands by treaty it saved itself from the charge of wresting them by force from the Indian. It was a distinction without a difference, and in its effort to save its honor in one direction, it hopelessly sacrificed it in another."

In the passages here quoted their author spoke of the white government's promises and treaties as "made to be broken," saying that "they served no other purpose than to lull the natives into temporary quiet while the paleface was fastening his grip ever more tightly upon their country. It was throughout a policy of insincerity." He also wrote: "History will exonerate the government from

---

[1] [Chittenden.] Gruff old General Harney had his own views upon this treaty business. When Commissioner Cummings came down the river from the council with the Blackfeet, and, having lost his mules at Fort Pierre, besought the General to give him some others to complete his journey with, the General replied: "Yes, Colonel, I have plenty of mules, but you can't have one; and I only regret that when the Indians got your mules they didn't get your scalp also. Here all summer I and my men have suffered and boiled to chastise these wretches, while you have been patching up another of your sham treaties to be broken to-morrow and give us more work."

"It is beyond question that such a system of treaty-making is, of all others, the most unpolitic, whether negotiated with savage or civilized peoples, and . . . . aside from its effect in encouraging and stimulating breaches of treaties of peace, is always attended with fraud upon the government and upon the Indian."—General John Pope, Report of August 3, 1864.

[2] [Chittenden.] "Send me one man who will tell the truth and I will talk with him," was the laconic reply of a celebrated chief who had been asked to meet a government commission in council.

any but the purest motives in its dealings with the Indians."

The subject is not one which so readily lends itself to the assumption of two contradictory attitudes concerning it. And it may also be said that though written history often possesses much power, nevertheless there are limits to the performances which should be asked of it.

CHAPTER LI

THE CAUCASIAN CONQUEST OF THE OREGON COUNTRY —
FLOYD AND BAILES, THE SEERS OF 1820 — TRACY IN-
VENTS THE IRRECLAIMABLE WESTERN DESERTS OF
SAND — RACE ANTAGONISM APPEARS BEYOND THE
MISSISSIPPI — WAGONS REACH THE ROCKY MOUN-
TAINS — INFLUENCES THAT DIRECTED PUBLIC AT-
TENTION TO THE NORTHWEST — WHITE WOMEN
FIRST CROSS THE CONTINENT — BONNEVILLE AND
WHITMAN TAKE WAGONS ACROSS THE ROCKIES —
NEW ENGLAND'S PART — ORIGIN AND ORGANIZATION
OF THE "GREAT MIGRATION" OF 1843 — A REVERSION
TO THE EARLY CLAN METHOD OF OVERLAND TRAVEL
— APPLEGATE'S STORY OF THE MARCH

THE first American settlement on the Pacific coast
was in some degree an outcome of the Lewis and
Clark expedition, and was made about five years after
that event. It was a fur-trading camp of the New York
merchant, John Jacob Astor, whose men paused at the
mouth of the Columbia River in the present state of
Oregon. The presence of the Astor party at that precise
spot, and just at that juncture of time, had much to do
with the later history of the Pacific coast and the Northwest. Great Britain had displayed some interest in the
locality for a considerable period,[1] but no British representative or settlement happened to be in the neighbor-

[1] Lieut. Broughton, of the British Navy, had taken possession of the Columbia River
valley in His Majesty's name, in 1792.

hood on the arrival of the Americans early in 1811.[1] In December of 1813, as part of the warfare then in progress between the United States and Great Britain, a British naval vessel entered the mouth of the Columbia and American influence for a time ceased to exist.

But as the treaty which marked the end of the war stipulated that each party thereto should occupy all positions held by it at the commencement of the struggle, and since Great Britain was compelled to admit that Americans had controlled the mouth of the river and adjacent coast at the outbreak of hostilities, she was constrained to restore the region to the United States in 1818. By a treaty framed in the same year, England and the United States agreed to a joint occupation of the mutually coveted territory during the following ten years, and the treaty also safeguarded whatever rights were possessed by Spain and Russia in that part of the continent. Spain sold her rights in the Oregon region to the United States at the same time she transferred Florida to the American flag in 1819, and Russia took like action in 1824. The later international controversy over the northwestern country, therefore, which came to be known as the "Oregon Question," was confined to England and America.

In spite of the exploit of Lewis and Clark, no noticeable interest in the far Northwest was displayed either by the public or by Congress until 1820. In that year a Virginia Congressman named John Floyd brought up the subject of future American settlements on the coast of the Pacific Ocean and the control of the Columbia River. Floyd was a seer. It has been said of him:[2]

"He evidently believed it would not be long before Americans would reach the Rockies, and stand ready to descend into the Oregon country.

[1] They reached the spot by a voyage around Cape Horn.
[2] Schafer's "History of the Pacific Northwest," pp. 130-1.

This was a new thought, just beginning to take hold of the American people, and as yet quite startling to most men who, in spite of what had already been done, found it difficult to conceive of the American population actually expanding till it should reach the Pacific. But he only hinted at these things, knowing very well that most members of Congress would regard predictions of this kind as the merest folly. . . . He tried to show that the Missouri and Columbia together would form a good highway for commerce across the continent, and that the entire distance between St. Louis and Astoria could be traversed with steamboat and wagon in the space of forty-four days."

Floyd's bill of 1821, providing a system by which settlers might take up land in the Oregon country, received no consideration. A similar measure introduced by him during the next year brought about the first Congressional debate on the subject. His principal ally in the national legislature was Mr. Bailes, of Massachusetts, who said:

"Some now within these walls. . . . in after times may cherish delightful recollections of this day, when America, almost shrinking from the 'shadows of coming events,' first placed her feet upon untrodden ground, scarcely daring to anticipate the greatness which awaited her."

Among the prominent opponents of the Floyd bill was Mr. Tracy of New York, who dismissed as fantastic the idea that a beneficial overland communication between the Mississippi valley and the Pacific coast was possible. He asserted that

"Nature has fixed limits for our nation; she has kindly interposed as cur western barrier mountains almost inaccessible, whose base she has skirted with irreclaimable deserts of sand."[1]

[1] Tracy's reference to the "irreclaimable deserts of sand" extending eastward from the Rocky Mountains was doubtless one of the first public utterances embodying a long-accepted belief that the region now occupied by Oklahoma, Kansas, Nebraska, the Dakotas, western Texas and nearly all the rest of the country eastward of the Rocky Mountains for a distance of several hundred miles was an arid and useless part of the earth, uninhabitable by white men. This part of the country eventually appeared on the maps of school geographies as the "Great American Desert." The extensive territory to which that mistaken name was first given gradually shrunk in size on the maps, but obstinately refused to entirely disappear until after the year 1870. A large part of the "deserts of sand" is now included in one of the principal natural granaries of the world.

INDEPENDENCE - COURTHOUSE
(MISSOURI)

349.—The town of Independence, in western Missouri. Most important "jump-off" for overland travellers on the Santa Fé, Oregon and California trails.

Mr. Tracy's opinions carried the day, and Floyd's bill was defeated by a vote of one hundred to sixty-one.

The town of St. Louis, by virtue of its geographical position, was in closer touch with the Missouri valley and the Oregon country than any other community, and in 1822 General William H. Ashley, of that city, organized a fur-trading company and an expedition designed to penetrate to the head waters of the Missouri. About ninety men in the Ashley party set forth early in 1823, but had trouble with the Indians—who objected to the destruction of their game—and in June nearly one-third of the white men were killed by the natives near the mouth of the Yellowstone River.[1]

When news of the affrays got back to civilization, some three months afterward, a force of United States troops was despatched to take the sort of action which later became known as "punishing the Indians." The unexpected outbreak, in the far West, of race antagonisms similar to those that had periodically characterized the history of the East for two centuries attracted wide attention and newspaper comment. A considerable proportion of the pioneer people of the Mississippi valley still retained and exhibited hostility to Indians as a matter of principle, and could not understand that the red races of those distant countries to the westward might possibly have valid reasons for their objection to the appearance and activity of white men among them. But some newspapers of the interior valley displayed a different attitude, and even went so far as to say that the red men might have justification for their opposition to the latest symptoms of

---

[1] Two other similar expeditions had like troubles in the same locality at almost the same time. They were Major Henry's expedition, and a party sent out by the Missouri Fur Company under the leadership of two of its men named Jones and Immels. The Missouri Fur Company had been organized in 1808, as a result of the knowledge brought back by Lewis and Clark.

KANSAS

350.—Kansas City as it appeared at the outset of the California rush. The settlement was one of the "jumping-off places." A "jump-off" was the last spot, on the route of a prairie schooner, where it might be replenished for the long journey ahead.

a further Caucasian advance. When word came of the three race encounters which had taken place in the upper Missouri valley in 1823, a western paper of the last described type made the following comment on the troubles and their possible causes:[1]

"Perhaps we do not exactly understand the conditions of the Indians, but it appears to us that the land yet unceded must be regarded as their own, and if so, we should suppose that a party of white persons cannot have any more right to enter upon it for the purpose of catching and killing the wild beasts of the forest than the Indians would have to enter our settlements and carry off whatever they pleased. The deer, buffalo and beaver are as needful to the subsistence and comfort of the Indians as horses, cattle and swine are to us; and it would appear that they may as lawfully prevent the destruction of their means of living as we ourselves can rightfully do."

Ashley abandoned his scheme in 1826, and one of the men to whom he sold his fur business was Jedediah S. Smith. Smith succeeded in making an overland trip from the Rocky Mountains to California immediately afterward, reaching the Mexican town of San Diego in October. Two years thereafter he successfully undertook another extensive overland journey from California northward to the Columbia River, but all except himself and three companions were killed by natives. His march from the Rocky Mountains to California was the first attempted or accomplished by a white American, and his later journey from California to the Oregon country was likewise the first overland trip between those two regions. He returned in safety to the United States in 1829, and in 1830 continued his exploits by organizing[2] the first train of loaded wagons from Missouri to the Rockies. The path of this vehicular trip lay along the courses of the Missouri, Platte and Sweetwater Rivers. Smith's wagons

[1] "Farmers and Mechanics Journal," of Vincennes, Indiana, Sept. 11, 1823.
[2] In conjunction with Sublette and Jackson, his partners in the purchase of Ashley's company.

could, indeed, have crossed the mountains by a route now known as the South Pass.[1]

The three principal factors which had so far been influential in directing some measure of public attention to the Oregon country had been growth of traffic and the recent introduction of steamboats on the Missouri River, the activities of fur traders, and the Congressional debate started by Floyd. Three other influences were now to appear and lend their aid in still further centering popular thought on the same matter.

The acute stage reached by the race conflict both in the South and North during the years immediately following 1830; the social advancement manifested by several of the southern native nations while still east of the Mississippi; the defiance of the Federal government by Georgia in the case of the Cherokees; and several other allied phases of the same broad subject, all tended to inspire curiosity or concern regarding those red men who had always lived west of the Mississippi, as well as solicitude for the native nations who were migrating thither. This speculation relative to the Indian tribes of the far West was still further augmented by an incident happening at the same time, which closely touched the affairs of those distant peoples. In 1831 or 1832,[2] one of the red tribes[3] living in the eastward portion of the Oregon country sent a delegation consisting of four of its prominent men to St. Louis in order to ask, as they phrased it, for "the white man's book of heaven." While in the town they were entertained by

---

[1] Schafer (pp. 141-2) credits the discovery of South Pass to the Ashley party. He says: "The discovery of this natural highway, so important in the history of the entire Pacific coast, must be credited to Ashley's trappers, some of whom first made use of it in 1823." Possibly the conclusion here quoted is open to discussion, since Melish's 50-sheet map of 1820 shows a pass, together with a travel-line through it, at long. 111° west from Greenwich, lat. 43° 50′ north, and the route so delineated is inscribed "Southern Pass." If Melish, in 1820, was seeking to define the near-by South Pass, then its discovery and first use must have antedated the Ashley expedition by several years.

[2] Schafer's "History of the Pacific Northwest," p. 147, says the date is in doubt.

[3] The Nez Percés.

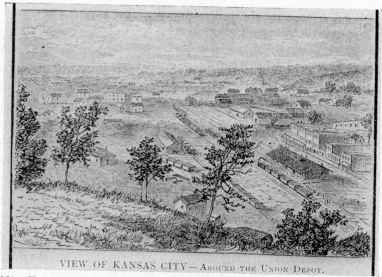

VIEW OF KANSAS CITY—Around the Union Depot.

351.—Kansas City in later years, after it had been reached by the railways.

General Clark, who, with Lewis, had visited their country a quarter of a century before. Two of the Indians died in St. Louis and still another on the long return expedition, so that of the four who had started out on a quest of nearly four thousand miles in the hope of improving the affairs of their people, only one reached his home again.

The facts attending this unusual plea slowly gained wide publicity. It may safely be presumed that the Nez Percés, in asking for the white man's book of heaven, made reference in a general way to a desire for those uplifting influences and better conditions—material as well as moral—which had attended the work of unselfish missionaries among the red race, and which had produced a noticeably beneficial effect on the principal Indian nations of the South. Of such things the Nez Percés must have heard encouraging reports, else they would not have taken

1196

the action they did take. Assuredly they did not send a delegation to the remote Caucasian country in search of disease, liquor, the vices of white society, avarice and the sword. This was the first occasion on which natives who lived near the Pacific coast had so signally expressed a desire for association with white men of any sort, or for more extensive acquaintance with white practises.

Up to the time mentioned such knowledge of the western native races as was possessed by the white people east of the Mississippi was scanty in amount, and had been obtained mainly from two sources of radically different character. One of those two sources lay in the casual impressions gathered by such explorers as Lewis, Clark, Pike and Long, who had travelled extensively through the western part of the continent, but whose knowledge of and acquaintance with the Indians of any given locality necessarily had been restricted to such observations as they might make in a few days, weeks or months. Impressions so obtained could scarcely be depended on with safety in any desire to penetrate deeply into the fundamentals of native character. Red men were slow to reveal themselves unreservedly to strangers. To one who came among them unaccompanied by any suspicion of ulterior motives their influential men showed a dignified courtesy and hospitality, but beyond that they did not go until a later time. But to such white men as had dwelt long among them in proved friendliness they exposed their thoughts and inward lives without hesitation. In the nature of things, few testimonies of the latter sort were available to the mass of the white people of the United States. One of them has heretofore been cited,[1] and others were later

---

[1] Reference is here made to the description of Sioux character and society which **was** published in the "Indiana Centinel" of May 20, 1819, and which is reproduced in Chapter XXVIII.

352.—On some stretches of the prairies, and in certain seasons of the year, light wagons were rigged to be driven by the wind. The device was of very limited use, however, and could not be adopted when loads had to be moved.

to be offered by men who had possessed somewhat similar opportunity for matured verdicts.[1] There was apparent contradiction between a few available early statements affirming the good qualities of the western Indians and those more recent reports which showed that the distant tribes were sometimes hostile to white visitors.

All these tales—whether favorable or unfavorable to the red men of the West—stimulated an interest in them, and, about the year 1833, led up to a period of missionary and educational activity which had the welfare of the natives of the far West as its incentive. One result of the conditions described was the departure of a little group of missionaries for the Oregon country and the establishment by them, in 1834, of an American colony and mission on the Willamette River. During the following year a missionary named Samuel Parker, accompanied by

[1] Two other statements regarding the character of the western Indians before they had been brought into close contact with white society have also been quoted in Chapter XXVIII.

a young physician named Marcus Whitman, set forth from the town of Liberty in western Missouri, and travelled overland to the Columbia River, in whose vicinity he spent some time. On his return home, in 1837, he published the results of his observation in a book[1] which still further directed public attention to the country described and of which several editions were sold during the next few years.

Whitman in the meantime had come back to the Atlantic coast more than a year in advance of Parker, and in 1836 he started from Liberty again with four more missionaries and teachers, two of whom were women.[2] The party travelled by pack-train, in company with some traders, but Whitman also took with him a wagon which he succeeded in piloting to a point beyond any hitherto reached by an overland wheeled vehicle. He drove the wagon to Fort Boise on Lewis River, a spot on the western border of the present state of Idaho, several hundred miles beyond the last trace of any previously travelled road then existing.

Whitman's second trip was also of interest in another particular relating to the annals of American travel. The two women in his party, who rode in the wagon most of the way, were the first English speaking white women to cross the North American continent.

By the year 1837 American missionary settlements were in existence on the Willamette, the Walla Walla and the Clearwater Rivers of the Oregon country, separated from one another in some instances by hundreds of miles, and located within the limits of the present states of Oregon, Washington and Idaho. The missionary

---

[1] "An Exploring Tour Beyond the Rocky Mountains."
[2] One being his wife. The other was the wife of H. H. Spalding, another member of the party.

settlement on the Clearwater River was in the country of the Nez Percés at a spot called by them Waiilatpu.[1]

The second circumstance of this period tending to stimulate eastern interest in the Pacific coast and the Columbia River country had its origin in President Jackson's ambition to buy a part of California in order that the United States might get possession of San Francisco Bay, whose value had been reported by American naval vessels.[2] In 1835 Jackson sent a governmental agent, W. A. Slacum, to the West, under instructions to visit all English speaking settlements in the neighborhood of the Columbia River, to make a census of all races, and to discover the opinions of those distant settlers on the subject of United States rights in the Oregon country. This was the first visit of a United States governmental official to Oregon. Slacum's report was laid before Congress late in 1837. It revived legislative interest in the matters under consideration, and that interest did not thereafter lapse until the United States had finally secured ownership of the great western river and the near-by extensive bay known as Puget Sound. Slacum was especially insistent that the United States should not accept the Columbia River as its northern boundary in the region inspected, in compliance with the desire of Great Britain since the signing of the joint treaty of occupation nearly twenty years before.

The third of the three influences at that time tending to direct public attention to the out-of-the-way wilderness of the Northwest was the organization in New England, in 1838, of a body called the "Oregon Provisional Emigra-

[1] It was at Waiilatpu that Whitman, his wife and twelve other whites were massacred in 1847 by the Cayuse.
[2] The relations existing between Texas and Mexico also contributed to the desirability of gaining as much knowledge as possible regarding conditions along the Pacific coast.

PRAIRIE ON FIRE.   PRAIRIE IM BRAND

353.—A fire sweeping across the prairie. The white men were often careless
about extinguishing their camp-fires, and wide stretches of country were
sometimes burned over as a result. Every event of that sort reduced the
supply of growing fodder on which the live stock of the caravans was compelled to subsist, and many horses, mules and cattle succumbed in consequence. By Henry Lewis.

tion Society." The purpose of the association was to assemble a party of several hundred American families and
move them overland to the Oregon country, where, in addition to creating a typical American white community
they might also give to the Indians an education both
secular and religious in character, and otherwise so train
them as to make them fitted—in Caucasian estimation—
for citizenship in a politically organized community. It
sent representatives through Ohio, Indiana, Illinois,
Michigan and Missouri to come into contact with the

1201

people and secure enlistments for such a party as it desired to bring together. The society failed to attain a concrete realization of its plan, but out of its work there nevertheless grew certain later results.

The seed sown by the New England society in the states of the Mississippi valley was slowly germinating. By the year 1840 the prospects offered by the Oregon country as a desirable location for American activities was a common subject of village argument throughout the middle states. Various accounts of the fertility of the soil and other advantages of the far Northwest were arriving and percolating through the population. Here and there a town meeting was held to discuss the Oregon Question and the relation of the United States to it. Petitions were addressed to the government recommending that diplomatic or legislative action be taken to definitely establish the rights of the United States in the territory considered. There was, it is well to say, nothing in any degree approaching the universal excitement and mania which developed a few years afterward in connection with another phase of affairs on the Pacific coast, but enough individuals were gradually brought to such a point of interest that by 1842 it became obvious that a movement of some considerable dimensions toward Oregon was about to take place.

The visible ingredients which had helped to create this state of mind have been outlined. But there was yet another, and not less important one. It was the stirring of that self-same, deep pioneer instinct which for more than two hundred years had ever filled its possessors with a vague restlessness and an uncontrollable desire to move into other and newer localities. This time the instinct in question — fanned into the flame of action by the means

354.—Method of taking a prairie schooner over a western river too deep to be forded. The ferry boats were occasionally owned by men who had seen the sure profits of the ferry business, and had halted to engage in it. Two dollars was a standard fee for wagon ferriage. At seasons of high water hundreds of vehicles were frequently assembled along the shore of a stream, awaiting the transfer.

here narrated — resulted in what is known as the "Great Oregon Migration."

During the winter of 1842-3 a bill was pending before Congress whose terms provided for the establishment of territorial government in the Oregon country, and for the granting of land to settlers there. The measure was adopted by the Senate in February, and that action was perhaps the final or immediate influence which led to the overland journey about to be described.[1] The "Great Migration" to Oregon in the spring of 1843, as eventually constituted, was made up of various small parties of men, women and children whose homes at that time were in Iowa, Missouri, Illinois, Indiana, Ohio, Kentucky and Tennessee. The exodus resembled those numerous and extensive migrations which took place in the Atlantic

[1] The proposed law was afterward rejected by the lower house of Congress.

1203

coast colonies during the late seventeenth and early eighteenth centuries, while the white population movement still extended in a north-and-south direction. It was, in fact, a comparatively modern return to the most primitive of all methods of American travel, and once again displayed that periodic recourse to former processes which had marked the whole story of national advance. It was another example of the chronological overlapping of travel periods. When the "Great Migration" of 1843 was organized there was an unbroken stretch of country from the Mississippi valley eastward to the Atlantic which was equipped with stage-coaches, canals and railroads. But none of those more modern agencies could be called into use for the journey about to be taken, and so the people who had determined to set forth into the West were compelled to do as their forefathers had done during the migrations from New England, New York and Pennsylvania down into the Virginias and the Carolinas.

The organization of each local group which finally became a component part of the migration was substantially similar to that of the others, and it is only needful to outline the incidents attending the formation of one or two parties. Iowa was a territory especially interested in the project, and for that reason the preparations made by some citizens of Iowa City and Bloomington are selected for description here. Those people of Iowa City who had decided to perform the journey assembled early in March, organized a company called the Oregon Migration Association, elected officers and adopted the following rules and regulations:

"It shall be the duty of the trustees to inquire into the character of all applicants who wish to join the company, and reject all intemperate and immoral characters. They shall also open books to receive subscriptions of stock, consisting of shares of fifty dollars each, to be paid in cash, materials or labor, as will best suit the subscribers, for the purpose of building a grist and saw mill for the company, also a schooner or sloop, if funds sufficient can be raised.

"That as soon as the company shall number twenty male members between the ages of eighteen and forty-five, they shall hold an election and elect one captain and five subordinate officers, whose duty it shall be to drill and command the company. After the above officers are elected the company shall meet once a month for the purpose of drilling said company.

"That before the company commences their march they shall elect a council of twelve persons who shall assemble in council with the officers of the company, who shall deliberate on and decide all matters pertaining to the company during their march.

"That there shall be hunting parties chosen who shall hunt for the company alternately while on their march.

"That each family and single person shall furnish a sufficient quantity of provisions and means of conveyance for those while on their march.

"That the male members of the company between the ages of eighteen and forty-five shall be disciplined, armed and equipt to act on the defensive if necessary."[1]

The members of the party met a few days afterward and established a system of government through four trustees and twelve councilmen to be elected by the male members of the society. The trustees and council were given power to impeach, try and remove the president or any other civil officer, and to "hear, try and determine all complaints against any member of the society for dishonest, immoral or improper conduct, and to dismiss any member from the Society who shall wilfully disobey or violate" any provisions of the by-laws. The executive authority of the intending marchers was vested in a president and two vice-presidents. The military authority was given into the hands of a captain, who had five subordinate officers. Every able-bodied male member of the band, while travelling, was made liable to discipline

[1] "Iowa Capital Reporter," Iowa City, March 11, 1843.

and military duty, excepting only the civil officers while actually on a march. But the civil authorities were also to be armed in order that they might protect the baggage train and the non-fighting membership in case of necessity. Every male member of the organization above the age of seventeen was given a vote.[1]

Another group of Iowa emigrants met at Bloomington on March 19 and adopted these resolutions:

"That the company here forming start from this place on the 10th day of May next, on their Journey to Oregon.

"That the route taken by the company shall be from here to Iowa City, from thence to Council Bluffs, and from thence to the most suitable point on the road from Independence to Oregon, from thence by way of the Independence road to Oregon.

"That the company leave or pass through Iowa City on the 12th day of May next, and invite other companies to join.

"That each and every individual as an outfit provide himself with 100 lbs. flour, 30 lbs. bacon, 1 peck salt, 3 lbs. powder in horns or canteens, 12 lbs. lead or shot, and one good tent cloth to cover six persons. Every man well armed and equipped with gun, tomahawk, knife, etc."[2]

All members intending to move by wagon were advised to use oxen or mules, rather than horses, and each unmarried man was urged to provide himself with a mule or pony.

During these days of preparation the newspapers also contained numerous communications giving advice to the travellers who were about to undertake the crossing of the continent. One such letter read:

"I have made every inquiry of those who have visited that region of country, and have read all, perhaps, that has been written of the character of the country, and have come to the conclusion that the distance from Burlington to the Council Bluffs is 350 miles—from the Bluffs west, on the north side of Big Platt River, by way of the Pawnee villages, to the foot of the Rocky Mountains at the old pass, where Captain Bonneville passed with his loaded wagons, is 500 miles—and no

[1] "Iowa Capital Reporter," Iowa City, March 23, 1843.
[2] "Iowa Standard," Iowa City, March 30, 1843.

stream to cross except the Loupe fork of Platt. The pass to which I allude is in about latitude 41° 30′ north. From thence take a west course, or nearly so, to the Wallamet River. The distance is about 500 miles, making in all about 1300 or 1400 miles travel. . . .

"My plan for outfit, etc., is as follows:—With oxen and mules you will travel with a caravan of say 100 persons, 15 miles per day, which, if you lose no time, you will accomplish the journey in 100 days, but make reasonable allowance for accident and delay, and say 150 days.

"100 men should be armed and equipped with a good rifle gun of large bore, carrying not less than 60 bullets to the pound;—4 pounds

355.—A wagon train on the march. It rolled over the hills for week after week, at an average rate of twelve or fifteen miles a day.

of powder, 12 of lead—(flint locks are to be preferred); caps and flints in proportion—and good knife and a small tomahawk. . . Percussion guns should have with them a spare tube in case of accident of one bursting; also canteens.

"As to provisions necessary for the journey, say 150 pounds of side bacon, 1 barrel of flour, a half bushel of beans, 10 pounds of rice, 20 pounds of coffee, 20 pounds of sugar, one year's stock of coarse and durable cloth, 2 blankets, and to every five men a tent. . . To every five men there should be a wagon and team sufficient to transport two thousand pounds, hauled by three or four yoke of oxen; they should be shod and spare shoes and nails taken along, and a water keg to contain

1207

at least ten gallons to each wagon. . . also in addition, each man ought to have a good poney or a mule to ride, (if he is able,) and that should be well equipped for packing and riding, a Spanish saddle and a picket line to tie your horse when feeding. . .

"It will be necessary in such a company that they should be completely organized like a company of regular soldiers; and I would advise that they agree (after choosing their officers) that they, while on their march thither, shall subject themselves to be governed by the rules and articles of war of the United States, so far as they shall apply to that service. I would recommend that to 100 men they elect one Captain, who should carry a spy glass, four Sergeants and four Corporals—and there ought to be a bugle to give the signals, and if one cannot be had, there should be a drum and fife. Guides and buffalo hunters will be required who will have to be paid a reasonable sum, as it will not do for every one to go hunting and shooting at pleasure. . . .

"Companies ought not to be less than fifty efficient fighting men, but 100 would be better; there are some Indians who are rather hostile, and they might attack a small party for plunder.

"One who intends to emigrate."[1]

All this discussion, organization, equipment, drilling, advice and preparation was in connection with a project to travel from the Mississippi valley to the Pacific coast at a period embraced within the lifetime of hundreds of thousands of Americans who are still living, and within the memory of many of them.

The existence of Boone's Lick Road, and its previous prominence for some twenty years as the main overland highway leading to the most advanced white settlements, naturally resulted in its use by the Oregon emigrants during the spring of 1843. Over it, for two months, straggled numerous bands of horsemen and many wagon trains, all moving toward the little town of Independence on the western border of Missouri. By the middle of May nearly a thousand people had gathered at the spot, and they then met in a body to perfect a general organization. Besides the thousand people the company also contained a hundred and twenty wagons of all sorts, and about five

[1] "Iowa Capital Reporter," March 25, 1843.

1208

thousand cattle, horses and other varieties of live stock. The pilgrims were divided for marching purposes into two groups. Each contained sixty wagons, and the foremost was composed of those whose owners were unencumbered with slow moving cattle. The second section, in addition to containing an equal number of wagons, also included the farm animals. Each division was under the command of a captain and his assistants, and in the form here outlined the "Great Migration" set forth on May 22, to traverse the two thousand miles which lay between it and its destination.

It so happened that the captain of the second division was a man named Jesse Applegate, destined thereafter to become a prominent figure of the far country to which he was leading so many of his countrymen. And in addition to his other qualities Applegate possessed— fortunately for our present desire—ability to describe the events in which he took part. He afterward wrote this description of the daily methods employed by the members of his camp during the overland trip:[1]

"It is four o'clock A. M.; the sentinels on duty have discharged their rifles—the signal that the hours of sleep are over—and every wagon and tent is pouring forth its night tenants, and slow kindling smokes begin largely to rise and float away in the morning air. Sixty men start from the corral, spreading as they make through the vast herd of cattle and horses that make a semicircle around the encampment, the most distant perhaps two miles away.

"The herders pass the extreme verge and carefully examine for trails beyond, to see that none of the animals have strayed or been stolen during the night. This morning no trails lead beyond the outside animals in sight, and by five o'clock the herders begin to contract the great moving circle, and the well-trained animals move slowly towards camp, clipping here and there a thistle or a tempting bunch of grass on the way. In about an hour five thousand animals are close up to the encampment, and the teamsters are busy selecting their teams and driving them inside

[1] In 1876, when he gave an account of the migration before the Oregon Pioneer Association. Applegate's narrative was printed by the Oregon Historical Society in its "Quarterly" of December, 1900.

356.—Month after month the wagons crawled through the lonely valleys.

the corral to be yoked. The corral is a circle one hundred yards deep, formed with wagons connected strongly with each other; the wagon in the rear being connected with the wagon in front by its tongue and ox chains. It is a strong barrier that the most vicious ox cannot break, and in case of attack from the Sioux would be no contemptible intrenchment.

"From six to seven o'clock is a busy time; breakfast is to be eaten, the tents struck, the wagons loaded and the teams yoked and brought up in readiness to be attached to their respective wagons. All know when, at seven o'clock, the signal to march sounds, that those not ready to take their places in the line of march must fall into the dusty rear for the day. There are sixty wagons. They have been divided into fifteen divisions or platoons of four wagons each, and each platoon is entitled to lead in its turn. The leading platoon to-day will be the rear one to-morrow, and will bring up the rear unless some teamster through indolence or negligence has lost his place in the line, and is condemned to that uncomfortable post. It is within ten minutes of seven; the corral but now a strong barricade is everywhere broken, the teams being attached to the wagons. The women and children have taken their places in them. The pilot (a borderer who has passed his life on the verge of civilization and has been chosen to his post of leader from his knowledge of the savage and his experience in travel through roadless wastes) stands ready, in the midst of his pioneers and aids, to mount and lead the way. Ten or fifteen young men, not to-day on duty, form another cluster. They are ready to start on a buffalo hunt, are well mounted and well armed, as they need to be, for the unfriendly

1210

Sioux have driven the buffalo out of the Platte,[1] and the hunters must ride fifteen or twenty miles to find them. The cow drivers are hastening, as they get ready, to the rear of their charge, to collect and prepare them for the day's march.

"It is on the stroke of seven; the rush to and fro, the cracking of whips, the loud command to oxen, and what seemed to be the inextricable confusion of the last ten minutes has ceased. Fortunately every one has been found and every teamster is at his post. The clear notes of a trumpet sound in the front; the pilot and his guards mount their horses; the leading divisions of the wagons move out of the encampment, and take up the line of march; the rest fall into their places with the precision of clockwork, until the spot so lately full of life sinks back into that solitude that seems to reign over the broad plain and rushing river as the caravan draws its lazy length towards the distant El Dorado. . . .

"The pilot, by measuring the ground and timing the speed of the horses, has determined the rate of each, so as to enable him to select the nooning place as nearly as the requisite grass and water can be had at the end of five hours' travel of the wagons. To-day, the ground being favorable, little time has been lost in preparing the road, so that he and his pioneers are at the nooning place an hour in advance of the wagons, which time is spent in preparing convenient watering places for the animals, and digging little wells near the bank of the Platte. As the teams are not unyoked, but simply turned loose from the wagons, a corral is not formed at noon, but the wagons are drawn up in columns, four abreast, the leading wagon of each platoon on the left, the platoons being formed with that in view. This brings friends together at noon as well as at night.

"To-day an extra session of the council is being held, to settle a dispute that does not admit of delay, between a proprietor and a young man who has undertaken to do a man's service on the journey for bed and board. Many such cases exist, and much interest is taken in the manner in which this high court, from which there is no appeal, will define the rights of each party in such engagements. The council was a high court in the most exalted sense. It was a senate composed of the ablest and most respected fathers of the emigration. It exercised both legislative and judicial powers, and its laws and decisions proved equal, and worthy of the high trust reposed in it. . . .

"It is now one o'clock, the bugle has sounded and the caravan has resumed its westward journey. It is in the same order, but the evening is far less animated than the morning march. A drowsiness has

---

[1] This widely adopted effort of the western Indians toward the conservation of their natural resources, under such circumstances, was considered by the whites as an unfriendly act. It was. The native western Indians, just like white men, naturally tried to make the penetration of their home by an invading force as difficult as possible, instead of making it easier by supplying food to the invaders. But the white men did not appreciate the philosophy of such an effort when it was applied in opposition to themselves.

fallen apparently on man and beast; teamsters drop asleep on their perches, and even when walking by their teams; and the words of command are now addressed to the slowly creeping oxen in the soft tenor of women or the piping treble of children, while the snores of the teamsters make a droning accompaniment. . . .

"The sun is now getting low in the west, and at length the painstaking pilot is standing ready to conduct the train in the circle which he has previously measured and marked out, which is to form the invariable fortification for the night. The leading wagons follow him so nearly around the circle that but a wagon length separates them. Each wagon follows in its track, the rear closing on the front, until its tongue and ox chains will perfectly reach from one to the other; and so accurate the measure and perfect the practice, that the hindmost wagon of the train always precisely closes the gateway. As each wagon is brought into position it is dropped from its team (the teams being inside the circle), the team is unyoked, and the yoke and chains are used to connect the wagon strongly with that in its front. Within ten minutes from the time the leading wagon halted, the barricade is formed, the teams unyoked and driven out to pasture. Every one is busy preparing fires. . . . to cook the evening meal, pitching tents and otherwise preparing for the night."

The marching company of 1843 was the first considerable body of organized travellers who crossed the American continent in an overland trip with the purpose of establishing homes on the Pacific coast, and the route it followed—that of the South Pass—was ever afterward to be an important factor in the development of the West. Discussion has long prevailed with regard to the discovery of the way through the mountains, with regard to certain incidents connected with the migration of 1843, and about the part played by one of its members[1] in the early history and political destiny of the Oregon country. Controversy concerning the last mentioned side of the subject has recently been brought to a definite end, but it is desirable that some attention be given to those matters associated with the pathway of the first overland pilgrims, their experiences, and the effect of their memorable journey.

[1] Marcus Whitman.

CHAPTER LII

THE SOUTH PASS ROUTE TO THE FAR WEST — A TRAPPER
WHO WAS ALSO A STATESMAN — EARLY RECORDS AND
HISTORY OF THE PASS—WHITMAN JOINS THE MIGRA-
TION OF 1843 — COMMENT OF AMERICA AND ENG-
LAND ON THE OVERLAND MOVEMENT — ITS IMPOS-
SIBILITY DEMONSTRATED IN PRINT WHILE IT IS BEING
PERFORMED — THE OREGON SETTLERS FORM A
GOVERNMENT — WHITMAN AND HIS COMPANIONS
KILLED — THE RESULT — DISCOVERY OF JOHNSON
AND WINTER'S LOST BOOK — THEIR ACCOUNT OF THE
BLOOD COUNCIL AT WAIILATPU — THE TWO TRAVEL-
LERS DESCRIBE THE RACE CONSEQUENCES OF WHITE
MOVEMENT INTO THE NORTHWEST AND RECORD
THEIR VISION OF THE FUTURE

THE path followed by the "Great Migration" of 1843
was afterward generally known as the Oregon
trail.[1] It extended along the banks of the Platte and its
northern branch—which had been surveyed during the
preceding year by Lieutenant Frémont—went through
the South Pass, and thence followed the valleys of Green
River and Bear River to Fort Hall,[2] on Lewis River.
From that point the overland travellers continued in
smaller parties to the valley of the Willamette, which they
reached in October, after a journey of more than two

[1] Until the extensive movement to California began in 1849. It was then, and thereafter, followed to the neighborhood of the Great Salt Lake by hundreds of thousands of
gold hunters, and came to be popularly called the California trail.
[2] Then an important station of the Hudson's Bay Company.

1213

BARE PEAK FROM MOUTH OF BARE PEAK CREEK.

357.—A wagon train in the Black Hills, Wyoming Territory. From a photo-graph taken by Lieutenant-Colonel Richard Dodge, U. S. A.

thousand miles accomplished in a period of some five months. In spite of the difficulties and privations necessarily attending such a movement, only seven members of the migration succumbed to accident or sickness on the way.

It will be borne in mind that Ashley's Fur Company had trouble with the Indians in 1823, but that its operations were carried on by others after his return, and that one or more of his employees had used the South Pass in 1823. General Jackson had begun to gather information in relation to the far West as soon as he entered the Presidency, and one of the sources to which his administration turned in seeking reliable knowledge regarding the subject was the fur company originally organized by Ashley, and at that time being carried on by Jedediah Smith, David Jackson and William Sublette.

From those men and some of their trappers the Federal government received, during 1830 and the early days of 1831, various letters descriptive of the Rocky Mountain region. This informatory material was submitted to Congress by President Jackson on June 24, 1831, accompanied by a brief message.[1]

One of the communications then sent by Jackson to Congress contained mention of the mountain gap now known as South Pass, and of its practicability as a route from the eastern to the western side of the mountains. The letter was undated, but its use by President Jackson on a known date removes any material loss in that regard. It was written by Joshua Pilcher, one of the employees of the fur company, and in discussing the mountains as a possible obstacle to overland movement Pilcher pointed out that

"Most erroneous ideas prevail upon this head. The Rocky Mountains are deemed by many to be impassable, and to present a barrier which will arrest the westward march of the American population. A man must know but little of the American people who supposes they can be stopped by anything in the shape of mountains, deserts, seas or rivers, and he can know nothing at all of the mountains in question to suppose that they are impassable. . . . Wagons and carriages may cross them in a state of nature without difficulty and with little delay on the day's journey. Some parts are very high, but the gradual rise of the country in the vast slope from the Mississippi to the foot of the mountains makes a considerable elevation without perceptible increase, and then the gaps or depressions let you through almost upon a level. This is particularly the case opposite the head of the Platte where I crossed in 1827. . . . It is, in fact, one of the best passes, and presents the best overland route from the valley of the Mississippi to the mouth of the Columbia."

Another of the letters from the fur company was written at St. Louis on October 29, 1830, and was addressed to Secretary of War Eaton. It said that the company, in the spring and summer of 1830, had taken ten

[1] "Sen. Ex. Doc. 39, 21st Cong. 2d Sess."

five-mule wagons and two other smaller wagons from St. Louis to the mountains, along the course of the Platte River. It further stated:

> "Here the wagons could easily have crossed the mountains, it being what is called the Southern Pass,[1] had it been desirable for them to do so."

On this trip the wagons moved at a rate of fifteen to twenty miles a day, and reached St. Louis again in October, having been gone six months.

These definite statements about South Pass having been made, their reliability was soon put to the test. During the year 1832 Captain Bonneville—who had obtained leave of absence from the army to carry on a fur enterprise—penetrated to the locality with a train of twenty loaded wagons which he successfully took through South Pass to the valley of the Green River on its western side.

Three years afterward, in 1835, the missionary Samuel Parker passed through the same district, and in his later printed account of his travels he went even beyond Pilcher's assertion regarding the gap, and affirmed that the spot offered no obstacles to the building of a steam railway.[2]

Marcus Whitman—the young doctor—went with Parker on his trip through South Pass in 1835, and even if he had been ignorant both of Pilcher's letter and Bonneville's previous wagon trip,[3] he could scarcely have gone through the pass in company with a man who was so far-seeing as to discuss its future utilization by a railroad, without an appreciation, on his own part, that no further

[1] The same phraseology used by Melish on his map of 1820.
[2] The text of Parker's observations of 1835 concerning South Pass as a railway route to the western side of the continent is hereafter reproduced in connection with the history of the first trans-continental railroad.
[3] It was then considered necessary by any prospective overland traveller to posess himself of all possible information about the country he intended to traverse.

COLDSPRING CAÑON, W.T. IN RED BEDS.

358.—Taking a wagon through Coldspring Cañon, Wyoming Territory. The gorge varies from about 200 feet to 50 feet in width, and the perpendicular walls are from 300 feet to 600 feet high.

proof of the value of the pass in connection with an over-land population movement to the westward was necessary.

For about thirty years, and until recently, it has been contended that Whitman's second trip through the pass—in 1836, on which occasion he took a wheeled vehicle to Fort Boise—was a turning point in the history of the Northwest because it demonstrated the existence of a practicable wagon route over which the head waters of the Columbia River could be reached from the head waters of the Missouri. The recorded history of the South Pass route from 1820 to the year 1835, as herein given, indicates that the relationship between the pass and the region west of it had already been substantially fixed, and that Whitman's trip of 1836, while interesting and important in so far as it did extend vehicular travel to the westward, was not in itself a big event in the westward movement. But in addition to these considerations there has lately been made public a letter written by Whitman himself at the time, in which he discussed the matter here under review. The communication was written in October of 1835, spoke of the trip with Parker, and said: "If Colonel Dodge could go to the Pacific and transport cannon as he did last year, we could cross the mountains with a wagon."[1] In other words, anybody could cross the mountains with a wagon, as Pilcher had affirmed as early as June of 1831, and as Bonneville had demonstrated.

Whitman was also a member of the "Great Migration" of 1843. For several years he had lived and worked

[1] The Whitman letter containing this statement was found by William L. Marshall and incorporated by him in his "Acquisition of Oregon and the Long Suppressed Evidence about Marcus Whitman," Vol. 1, p. 76. Marshall's book (published in 1912) contains a very elaborate analysis of his subject. He points out that Whitman's wagon of 1836 suffered a broken axle while six days east of Fort Hall—and also east of the point reached by Bonneville's twenty loaded wagons—and that westward from the scene of the broken axle, Whitman's wagon proceeded as a two-wheeled vehicle to Fort Boise.

in the isolated stations established by him and his missionary companions on the upper Columbia in 1836. But while the American settlements on the Willamette were flourishing those farther in the interior languished, and finally the missionary board in New England decided to discontinue its support of them. When Whitman heard of this intention, late in 1842, he at once set out for the Atlantic coast, which he reached in safety after the danger and labor of a winter journey. He arrived in New York still clad in his frontier costume of fur cap and leather clothes, paid a visit to Horace Greeley—who called him "the roughest man we have seen this many a day"[1]—and then pushed swiftly on to Boston where his report and pleading resulted in a revocation of the order that had brought him across the continent.[2] Then, hearing of the preparations for the "Great Migration," he hastened back to western Missouri and joined it. He had already made two trips over the route and through South Pass, and in consequence his advice and knowledge were of much help to the thousand people of the company.

The story of this overland march would remain incomplete if it did not show the attitude assumed by the outside world toward those who took part in the movement, toward the possibility of such a journey as they had undertaken, and toward the national significance contained in such a migration. More than twenty years had passed since Floyd introduced before Congress the subject of settling the Oregon country with American emigrants, and no action had as yet been taken by that body. Even the future ownership of the region was a

[1] New York "Tribune," March 29, 1843.
[2] The "Whitman Saved Oregon" story, during its life, was based principally on the contention that Whitman's trip to the United States in the winter of 1842-3 was for the purpose of arousing the Federal government to the importance of the Oregon country, and that he had much to do with originating the migration in whose company he returned to the West.

HORSE-LITTER.

359.—Whenever a man was hurt, or became too ill to go on, his companions or neighbors on the road put him in a wagon or else contrived a horse-litter in which to carry him. A litter was made of a buffalo skin or heavy blanket, and attached to two poles that were upheld by horses.

matter of uncertainty. A considerable part of the eastern population held the same opinion on the subject as did the Federal senator[1] who called on his colleagues to imagine, if they could, a state from which senators and representatives would require a year to travel to Washington and return home again.

At the very moment when the "Great Migration" was midway between its starting point and its destination the following utterance made its appearance in England regarding the impossibility of such an event:

"However the political questions between England and America, as to the ownership of Oregon, may be decided, Oregon will never be colonized overland from the United States. . . .

"The world must assume a new face before the American wagons may trace a road to the Columbia as they have done to the Ohio."[2]

A contemporary English work on the Oregon region,

[1] Senator McDuffie, of South Carolina.
[2] Edinburgh "Review," July 1, 1843.

which was published in London in 1844, but before news of the success of the migration reached that country, contained the following passages:

"Though several parties have penetrated into the Oregon territory from the United States, through the marshes and over the towering heights of the Rocky Mountains, yet it may be safely asserted, from the concurrent testimony of traders, trappers, and settlers, who have themselves passed those mighty barriers, that the difficulties are so numerous and formidable, and the time necessary for the passage so long, that there is no secure, expeditious, or continuous track, which can ever be used as a highway, so as to afford facilities for an influx of emigrants overland.

"Several routes have been tried of late, and each differs only from the other in the privations which the passengers undergo. None but the wild and fearless fur trapper can clamber over those precipices, and tread those deserts with security, and even these are quitting them as haunts, and using them only as unavoidable tracks. It is true, there have been published more favorable accounts within the last year or two, by parties who have made the journey safely, and who encourage others to make a similar experiment. But these accounts are in such a spirit of bravado, and accompanied with expressions of thankfulness of parties for their own success, that they are indirect evidence of the difficulty and danger of the undertaking, and of the utter hopelessness of such a route for general purposes."[1]

American authorities no less distinguished made similar declarations. In speaking of those who had joined the migration of 1843 Horace Greely said:

"For what do they brave the desert, the wilderness, the savage, the snowy precipices of the Rocky Mountains, the weary summer march, the storm-drenched bivouac and the gnawings of famine? . . . This migration of more than a thousand persons in one body to Oregon wears an aspect of insanity."[2]

There was to come a time when Greeley spoke in another vein. He was not one of the few men of his generation who saw these events with the inward vision of a prophet, and beheld the results that were to follow from them. But by and by, when the hardest of the

[1] Dunn's "History of the Oregon Territory, Etc." London, 1844: pp. 345-6.
[2] New York "Tribune," July 22, 1843.

pioneer work was finished, he himself went out to the Pacific coast in the footsteps of the men whose reason he had challenged, and looked with his physical eyes on the things they had accomplished. And born of his later journey was that utterance of his which will live longer than any other words he spoke. For he said, "Go West, young man."

But by that time the "young man" was already in the West. As it had been in the past, so it was once again. An obscure trapper named Pilcher had proved himself to be the statesman, and the nameless thousands had justified the wisdom of his estimate. They had completed their work, leaving only its ratification to be brought about by stage-coach and locomotive. Then it was that the mighty ones arose in the majesty of their abounding fame and advised the performance of what had already been done.

The party of Oregon emigrants which started from western Missouri in 1844 was even larger than that of 1843 and numbered about fourteen hundred souls. It was delayed on the way by inclement weather and encountered numerous hardships. In 1845 almost three thousand people similarly departed for the Northwest, although they did not move in one compact body as had been the case during the two preceding summers. They travelled in groups containing from fifty to one hundred and fifty wagons each. Some of these parties of 1845 combined at a point westward of Fort Boise, and unwisely sought to reach their destination by an untried route. They wandered in the wilderness for forty days, suffering much from hunger and thirst, and about seventy-five of the six or eight hundred involved perished.[1]

[1] According to Schafer, in his "History of the Pacific Northwest," p. 210.

U.S.P.R.R.EXP.&SURVEYS — 47ᵗʰ & 49ᵗʰ PARALLELS.   GENERAL REPORT — PLATE I.

Stanley. Del.

Sarony,Major & Knapp Lith. 449 Broadway,NY.

SAINT PAUL.

360.—St. Paul, as the settlement appeared before an overwhelming population movement invaded the upper Mississippi valley and the Minnesota and Dakota regions. During the first years of the filling-up process in the West nearly all the moving host swept onward to the Pacific coast.

By this time there were some six thousand Americans in the northwestern country, and a few of them had penetrated north of the Columbia River and settled in the Puget Sound district.[1] They already had a typical American government, although located more than two thousand miles from the nearest similar community that lay within close reach of the Federal power. Their first political organization had been effected in 1843, while the "Great Migration" was still on its march, a code of laws having been adopted by the people on July 5 of that year.[2] The declaration of the settlers began:

"We, the people of Oregon Territory, for purposes of mutual protection, and to secure peace and prosperity among ourselves, agree to adopt the following laws and regulations until such time as the United States of America extend their jurisdiction over us."

In taking this step the few hundred emigrants who so acted followed the example of the little Wautaga republic which was set up amid the forests of eastern Tennessee just before the first invasion of the Kentucky country by the hill people of the Carolinas and Virginia. Each of those groups of pioneers was temporarily lost in a wilderness, was out of touch with any source of higher authority, and wholly dependent upon itself for the creation of such regulations as would constitute an organic basis of society.

The arrival of the companies of 1844 and 1845 brought about a number of changes in the political organization of the northwestern pioneers, and the simultaneous action of the Hudson's Bay Company in placing itself under the jurisdiction of the provisional government established by

---

[1] This was in opposition to the desire and advice of the Hudson's Bay Fur Company, but the local officers of that powerful body did not go beyond the point of verbal remonstrance. They had treated American arrivals on the Columbia with consideration and had even given much needed aid to some of them.

[2] Known as the First Organic Law; quoted in full in Strong and Schafer's "Government of the American People," Oregon edition, Boston, 1901; Appendix.

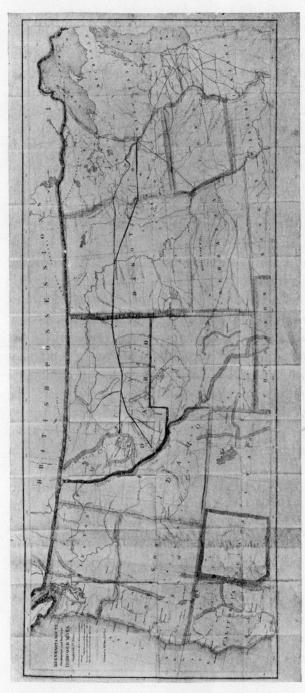

361.—The "Rubber Stamp" map of the Northwest. Published by D. D. Merrill, of St. Paul, in 1864, to show a new overland route from St. Paul, and the latest territorial lines and settlements in the northwestern country. When the map was being made Idaho embraced all the region between Nebraska and Dakota on the east, Colorado on the south and Oregon and Washington in the west, and was so defined on the printed sheet. But the map as printed was out of date before it was ready for sale. The boundary of the new-shaped Idaho was therefore drawn by hand with a brush, Montana was similarly corrected, and both territories had to be properly labeled by means of rubber stamps, while Wyoming was left as a blank space and the erroneous name "Idaho" had to remain as originally printed. Helena, Silverbow City and other towns were added by pen and ink, and the map was then offered to the public. It never caught up with shifting conditions.

the Americans resulted in making British interests in the disputed country subsidiary to those of the United States. The political destiny of the Oregon region was definitely settled by treaty with England during the following year, and the American Republic found itself in undisputed possession of the Pacific coast up to the forty-ninth parallel of north latitude. By means of the events here recited this country had come into possession of a province containing more than two hundred and fifty thousand square miles of territory, later to be erected into the commonwealths of Washington, Oregon and Idaho.[1]

But although in possession of the country from the standpoint of international law the United States still failed to exercise its authority, and did not bring about that closer union which would have been made possible through the organization of a territorial government by Congress. And again the cause of the delay in recognizing an accomplished fact was to be found in jealousy. When the Oregon pioneers established their first independent government they included in their constitution a provision that neither slavery nor involuntary servitude, except as punishment for crime, should exist in the region occupied and controlled by them. This decision on their part aroused the opposition of those far distant American commonwealths in which human slavery still existed, and the attitude of those states in the Federal Senate blocked the way to territorial government for the Northwest. Not until the occurrence of a tragedy which swept aside the elements of selfishness and appealed to profounder human impulses was it possible to consummate the work thus far carried forward. Marcus Whitman, his wife

[1] Thirteen thousand square miles of the original "Oregon" are also embraced in the northwestern part of the present state of Wyoming, and twenty-eight thousand square miles are in Montana.

and twelve other white men and women of the Oregon missions met death in terrible form at the hands of the Indians on November 29, 1847.

The causes leading to the native outbreak were multiple in number, rather complex in character, and of several years' growth.[1] But perhaps the immediate incentive to dreadful violence was a belief, entertained by the Indians, that the white physician was poisoning them. Immigrants from the East had brought measles to Whitman's settlement at Waiilatpu, and that familiar malady of civilization attacked the Indians and spread among them with virulence. Whitman, being a physician, ministered to both races with impartiality and to the utmost of his strength. Most of the whites who were attacked recovered quickly, but the natives persistently succumbed. The disease was one of those unfortunate gifts bestowed by the Caucasians on the red race with which the Indians were not previously acquainted, and of whose effects they strongly disapproved. When they beheld the consistent recovery of the whites and the death of their own people, it seemed in their eyes that the white doctor was unfair, and was saving the afflicted of his own race in preference to theirs. This attitude of mind even developed into a suspicion that the white man was poisoning the natives who were ill. They decided to carry out a long considered policy[2] by killing him, and did so, including in their supposed vengeance a number of his presumed co-conspirators. In addition to those who were

---

[1] Many of the natives resented the presence and increase of white men among them. As far back as 1842 they had been irritated by the effort of an Indian agent who tried to force certain Caucasian laws upon them; injudicious talk of white men, in 1842 and 1843, gave the natives an impression that Whitman had gone East for soldiers to fight them; a belief existed among many natives that the Americans wanted their land and wanted to kill them off in some manner; various Indians had been killed by white men without justification (though such crimes were frowned upon by the bulk of the white settlers); Whitman had entertained, in his home, other white men who had previously killed natives.

[2] Soon to be discussed in these pages.

Vereinigte Staaten Hundepost auf den nordamerikanischen Seen.
Nach der Natur aufgenommen von Fred. Kurz.

362.—Dog-sled of the far West. A favorite manner of winter travel. From a drawing done by Frederick Kurz in 1851.

murdered the natives imprisoned about fifty other white immigrants at the settlement. They, however, were saved by the exertions and influence of a Hudson's Bay Company official. Some of the natives who had done the killing were captured, sentenced to death after due trial, and so punished. As a result of the outbreak the settlers addressed another appeal to the distant government at Washington in which they said:

"If it be at all the intention of our honored parent to spread her guardian wings over her sons and daughters in Oregon, she surely will not refuse to do it now, when they are struggling with all the ills of a weak and temporary government, and when perils are daily thickening around them, and preparing to burst upon their heads. When the ensuing summer's sun shall have dispelled the snow from the mountains, we shall look with glowing hopes and restless anxiety for the coming of your laws and your arms."

Ten of the pioneers started eastward from the military camp of the colonists on March 4—which was as soon after the tragedy as travel conditions permitted—and reached St. Louis on May 17, in the short time of two months and thirteen days, bringing with them to civilization the tale of events that had happened nearly six months before. Congressional opposition to the establishment of Federal law on the western coast could not prevail against the nation-wide interest and sympathy inspired by such tidings, and Oregon was given territorial government in August of 1848. The first governor[1] started westward during the same month over the Santa Fé trail, and although he took ship at San Francisco for the last part of his journey, he did not reach Oregon until March of 1849.

We now come to the consideration of two or three matters associated with the early Caucasian movement to the Oregon country that—for an interesting reason—have not hitherto received attention. The dramatic and dreadful fate of Whitman and his colleagues led to the incorporation of the remote Northwest into the political fabric of the United States. Yet the proposed killing of Whitman, and the further strange fact that he and his associates had even debated that matter in formal council with the Indians, had been published in a printed book in the United States, and had received publicity in this country for a year or more before the tragedy took place.

Among the thousand members of the "Great Migra-

[1] General Joseph Lane.

tion" of 1843 were two men named Overton Johnson and William H. Winter, of whom but little is known. They returned to Indiana late in the summer of 1845,[1] jointly wrote a book in description of their experience while on the trip to the Pacific coast, and published their volume in the town of Lafayette during 1846, under the title: *Route Across the Rocky Mountains, with a Description of Oregon and California; Their Geographical Features, Their Resources, Soil, Climate, Productions, etc., etc. By Overton Johnson and Wm. H. Winter, of the Emigration of 1843.*[2]

The two travellers announced in their book the peculiar relations existing between Whitman and the white settlers on one side and the Indians on the other, and also included in it a statement concerning the treatment received by the emigrants of 1843 at the hands of the Hudson's Bay Company agent at Fort Hall, which second matter has long been a subject of debate.[3] On their journey homeward from Oregon they halted for some time near Whitman's missionary station, and there came in contact with events which they described in these words:

"While we were encamped in the neighborhood of the Mission,[4] a party of twenty or thirty Chiefs and braves, a deputation from the Walawala, Nez Pierce, and Kious Indians,[5] came, and met in council with Dr. Whitman, Mr. Spaulding, and other gentlemen connected

---

[1] While on their way back they encountered 3,000 members of the 1845 migration scattered along 500 miles of the trail.
[2] This work remained unknown to investigators of western history for sixty years. Marshall, who ransacked the country for material while preparing his "Acquisition of Oregon" (and who died in 1906) did not know of it. He said (Vol. 1, p. 97): "Unfortunately no contemporary book was published by any member of that [1843] migration." Shortly after Marshall's death the Oregon Historical Society discovered and announced the existence of the book, reprinted it in successive numbers of its Quarterly for 1906, and therein said that two copies were known, one in the University of California Library and another in the Congressional Library. The present author has located two more copies; one in the Indiana State Library, and another, privately owned, from which the extracts given in these pages are quoted.
[3] Johnson and Winter said (p. 118) that on their return trip in 1845 the agent— Captain Grant—gave them "every assistance, attention and respect," which attitude was "contrary to the treatment we formerly received from him, while on our way to Oregon."
[4] In May of 1845.
[5] The Walla Walla, Nez Percés and Cayuse.

with the Mission. They told the Missionaries that the hearts of some of their people were bad; and the object of the council proved to be a trial, to ascertain whether Dr. Whitman was not worthy of death. The charges brought against the Doctor were these:"

Then Johnson and Winter went on to relate the killing of several Indians by white men, one of the victims having been a native preacher and pupil of the Mission named Elijah, a son of Yellow Serpent, chief of the Walla Walla, who was present in person at the council to accuse the whites and demand an equal blood vengeance for the death of his son. The statement of the Indian attitude then continued:

"But their object, however, was not to punish; it was rather to have an equivalent. They only wished that the Americans should suffer a loss as great at their own. Dr. Whitman reasoned with them, and appealed to them, by every means which he thought would tend, in the least, to affect them in his favor; and so did all the others, but it was in vain. After a long consultation, by which they appeared to be not the least shaken in their opinions, they went away, saying that they themselves would not disturb the Missionaries; but that they could not help what their young men might do. After the council was ended, several of our party, who were present, expressed their opinions to the gentlemen of the Mission; saying that they considered it both imprudent and wrong in them to hazard their own lives, and the lives of their families, by remaining longer among these people. Dr. Whitman, who is naturally a man of excellent judgment, and especially so with matters relating to the Indians, and who is, moreover, not to be frightened where there is no cause to fear, replied that he also believed that prudence, and their safety, required that they should abandon the Mission for a time, at least. The same opinion was expressed by all the other gentlemen."[1]

Marshall, although unaware of the Johnson-Winter narrative here quoted, did discover and include in his *Acquisition of Oregon* a previously unpublished letter written by Whitman which corroborates their account of the extraordinary council. Whitman's communication was written on May 20, 1845,[2] and in part read:

"While most of the Indians have been for peace on their part, some

[1] Johnson-Winter, pp. 109-112.
[2] It was addressed to D. Greene, Secretary of the American Board of Commissioners for Foreign Missions.

have urged that as Elijah was educated and was a leader in religious worship and learning, and so in revenge one of the same grade must be killed of the Americans, and Mr. Spalding or myself were proposed as suitable victims. This subject is not yet settled. . . ."

The calm, apparently dispassionate council of Waii-latpu, in which red men and white men debated with one another concerning the moral propriety of killing one of the Caucasians who was participating in the discussion, was doubtless one of the strangest incidents connected with the long history of race misunderstanding and antagonism. And the council adjourned without having reached a definite decision, presumably to be convened again at the call of the proposed victim. As Whitman remarked in his routine report: "This subject is not yet settled."

Two thoughts spring into being when our minds first come in contact with the knowledge of this peculiar event. It brings to us, for one thing, a better understanding of the change wrought in our social affairs during very recent times. We realize, with somewhat of shock, that in the lifetime of men not yet considered old, white travellers in the western half of the present United States might be confronted with natural conditions and human standards that could involve them in such a situation as has just been described. And we are also impelled to wonder—profitless though the process may be—what different chain of events would have resulted had the published warning of Johnson and Winter inspired effective action, while there was yet time, to avert the tragedy. In that case the entrance of the Northwest into the American nation could still have been blocked by the dominant political influence of slavery, and it is inconsistent with our knowledge of pioneer character to suppose that those distant men—barred from this republic—

CONNECTIONS

OF THE

NORTHWESTERN STAGE CO.

◆◇◆

AT BOISE CITY

with Northwestern Stage Company's LINES OF STAGES for IDAHO CITY, SILVER CITY, PLACERVILLE, CENTREVILLE, PIONEER CITY, and CANYON CITY, Oregon.

AT BAKER CITY

with Northwestern Stage Company's LINES OF STAGES for ELDORADO, WILLOW CREEK and GEM CITY MINES.

AT WALLA WALLA

with Northwestern Stage Company's LINES OF STAGES for PIERCE CITY, LEWISTON and WALLULA.

AT UMATILLA

with Oregon Steam Navigation Company's STEAMERS for THE DALLES and PORTLAND, Oregon.

TIME, UMATILLA TO PORTLAND, 30 HOURS.

THE CONCORD COACHES

(DRAWN BY FOUR AND SIX HORSES)

RUN ON THIS ROUTE.

363.—After numerous towns had come into existence in Oregon, Idaho and Washington, Concord stage-coaches were introduced and the widely separated settlements of the Northwest were at first united by that method of transportation, as the villages and towns of the East had been similarly joined a century before.

would have done otherwise than set up a separate nation of their own within a short time.[1]

Johnson and Winter, in common with other observant travellers through unfamiliar lands, had much to say about the country they traversed, its native peoples and future possibilities. In some things they were right, and in others wrong, but always they were interesting. Of the continent between the Rockies and the Pacific they ventured to predict:

"With a very few exceptions in this whole vast scope of territory lying immediately beyond the Rocky Mountains, extending West several hundred miles and to an uncertain distance North and South, there can never locate any civilized society. Their inhabitants will be like those in the Deserts of Arabia, and in the Sahara of Africa."[2]

The two pilgrims from the United States naturally discussed those conditions due to Caucasian travel and settlement in the Northwest, and in the following fashion recommended a military occupation of the Oregon country:

"A good body of soldiers, garisoned in the Walawala Valley, would not only be of great benefit in protecting the emigrants, and whoever else might wish to pass through that country, but also to the Indians themselves. For such a garison would keep them in awe, and thereby prevent them from committing depredations, for which they would afterward have to be punished. They would, at the same time, protect the rights of the Indians, prevent feuds from arising between them and the white people, and establish a peace and friendship, which would be lasting, and beneficial to both; favorable to the civilization of the Indians, and to the promulgation and extension of Christian principles among them."[3]

The plan they recommended—so different in its character from the system advocated by the unknown philosopher whose letter of 1818 has previously been quoted[4]—was adopted. The wise man of 1818, out of the

[1] As, indeed, it was freely predicted in Congress and throughout the country that they would do if they were not made a part of this political union.
[2] Johnson and Winter, p. 87.
[3] Ibid, p. 112.
[4] The letter from Prairie du Chien, published in the "Indiana Centinel" of May 29, 1829.

riches of his experience, had said: "Military compulsion will not be useful in civilizing Indians." Never, in any age or continent of which the annals have been preserved, has a lasting, mutually beneficial peace and friendship between two peoples been established—as Johnson and Winter suggested—on a basis of guns held in the hands of one race for the purpose of keeping the other race in awe. Their expression of such a sentiment seems tinged with the mental reservations so characteristic of Caucasian thought on the subject at that time. But when the two travellers devoted themselves more to a review of conditions already brought about by race contact in the West, and to consideration of the future consequences of that social contact, they were on surer ground. Their discourse on that phase of the question ran:

"These Southern Valleys of Oregon, though in their present state of nature so lonely, so wild, and so secluded; though they now threaten the travelers who pass, at intervals of years, with dangers from the rugged mountain path, the swollen torrent and the savage arrow; though many a gloomy glen, and rocky gorge and dark and tangled wood which have been stained with conflict, or storied by some savage ambuscade, still stand to awaken terror in the passer by; yet these Valleys, notwithstanding their wildness and dangers, offer inducements (deadly to the fated native) for which, ere long, the stronger hand of the white man will beat back the present wild and implacable inhabitants, and make them the homes of civilization. . . . It is possible that this portion of Oregon will be acquired from the natives in the same manner that portions of the United States have already been acquired—by force. And should it be so acquired, and when judgment comes upon the conqueror for conquest, there will be none upon whom it will fall more lightly, for there are no people who deserve more justly, punishment for 'all manner of wickedness,' than the natives of the Rogue's River and Clamuth Valleys. . . .

"The Indians west of the Cascade Mountains are divided into numerous small bands, and many of them without any acknowledged head. There were once, on the waters of the Columbia, the Willammette, and along the shore of the Ocean, powerful tribes; but pestilence and disease, since the coming of the white man, have swept them rapidly away, until but a few, poor, wretched, degraded beings, beyond the reach of charity, remain. Once Chenamus, a proud, intelligent and influential Chief of the Chenooks held sway over all the tribes between the shores of the Pacific and the Cascades, and between the Umqua and Puget's Sound, and extended his influence beyond the Mountains. But after his death his place was never filled, and now the bones of his people are scattered upon the rocks and hills, and their dwelling places are their graves. The bones of hundreds, perhaps thousands, lay heaped up promiscuously, together. And every isolated rock that rises out of the Columbia is covered with the canoes of the dead. They are nearly all gone, and disease is still sweeping the miserable remnant away. . . .

"Perhaps no where on the great American Continent, on either side of the Isthmus of Panama, has their intercourse with the white man been more ruinous to them than it has here. It is, however, no less strange than true and deplorable, that wherever the white man has had intercourse with the Indian, almost without an exception it has tended both morally and physically to degrade, sink and destroy him."[1]

Last of all these delineations of the primitive Oregon which we may take from the pens of the two emigrants is their vision of the land as it was destined to become when transformed by men of the race they represented. In that effort they were more happy in prediction, and they said:

"Here may the imagination lift the veil which hides the future, and peer into the destinies of this fair land. As it runs over the wide prospect it peoples it with thousands and thousands of busy inhabitants, sees every plain checkered with fields, and even the steep and rugged mountain-side made to yield to the hand of the husbandman; everywhere houses, gardens, orchards and vineyards, scattered in countless multitudes over hill and valley; flocks and herds feeding on every hand; the broad highways coursing the valley or winding away over the hills, thronged with a busy concourse all moving hurriedly to and fro, engaged in the avocations of a civilized life; sees villages, towns and cities, with massive walls and glittering spires which have risen above the mouldering huts of a departed race. It looks forward to the time when . . . the powerful locomotive, with its heavy train, will fly along the rattling railway; when, instead of yon frail canoe, the proud steamer will dash along the majestic river; when that Ocean, now idly breaking on its cragged shores, shall be whitened with the sails of commerce."[2]

Here we may leave the Northwest, safely started on its way to the assured fulfillment of these dreams, and turn our gaze toward the unfolding of another panorama.

[1] Johnson-Winter, pp. 47-55.
[2] Johnson-Winter. pp. 67-68.

CHAPTER LIII

THE MORMON OVERLAND PILGRIMAGE OF 1846-1848 —
EVENTS THAT LED TO IT — EXPULSION OF THE
CHURCH OF LATTER DAY SAINTS FROM NAUVOO —
COMMENCEMENT OF THE MOST PRETENTIOUS GROUP-
MIGRATION IN AMERICAN HISTORY — LIFE IN THE
LOG HUTS, SOD HOVELS AND CAVES — ATTITUDE OF
THE INDIANS — A WINTER OF SUFFERING — MARCH
OF THE ADVANCE PARTY IN 1847 — DISCOVERY OF
THE GREAT SALT LAKE VALLEY — TAKING THE NEWS
BACK TO THE MISSOURI — ANOTHER WINTER IN THE
WILDERNESS — ARRIVAL OF THE WANDERING HOST
IN UTAH AFTER TWO AND A HALF YEARS ON THE
ROAD — UTAH SETTLED

DURING the same years that witnessed the migrations to Oregon and the establishment of American
government in that part of the continent there was also
taking place another series of events, very different in
character, which finally resulted in a still larger hegira
to the westward. These last mentioned happenings were
the events leading up to and attending the expulsion of
the Latter Day Saints, or Mormons, from their city east
of the Mississippi, and their movement to remote recesses
beyond the Rocky Mountains. About fifteen thousand
people began the long enforced journey in 1846, and the
larger part of that number reached their new home during the next two and a half years. But there was much

necessary halting by the way, and some did not arrive in Utah until as late a date as 1853.

A detailed account of the strange and interesting early history of the religious body popularly known as the Mormon Church—as that history developed in the states of New York, Ohio, Missouri and Illinois prior to the year 1845—does not belong in these pages.[1] It is sufficient to say that it was characterized by a gradually increasing distrust, bitterness of feeling and hostility manifested toward the Mormons by their neighbors in every locality where adherents of the new creed sought to establish themselves as permanent communities. That attitude was displayed through petty annoyances, and in some places by lawlessness which took the form of prolonged physical attacks against property and human life. Yet the animosity in question does not appear to have been founded on those aspects of the new sect which were peculiarly or exclusively religious in their nature. It was, rather, seemingly based on certain social and economic phases attending the religious movement, for some of which—both good and bad—the Mormons themselves were responsible, but others of which attached themselves to the organization like barnacles and brought upon the whole body of its membership severe tribulations they did not deserve. The popular thought and habits of the time, and a scantier regard for social order than now prevails, had much to do with the whole record of early Mormon troubles.

The first removal of the organization from the place of its birth in a New York state village[2] was not due to the enmity of a surrounding population, and is easily under-

[1] Few phases of the national history have excited more controversy. A detailed analysis of the subject may be found in Linn's "The Story of the Mormons."
[2] Fayette, Seneca county. It came into being on April 6, 1830.

NAUVOE, Illinois.

364.—March of the Mormons from Illinois to that part of Mexico now known as Utah. The Mormon city of Nauvoo, and starting point of the enforced exodus. Crowning the hill stood the Temple. From the Dusseldorf series of Mississippi River views, after Lewis.

standable. The church had its foundation in the statement of a young man named Joseph Smith to the effect that under guidance of a vision he had found, buried in the earth, a quantity of metallic tablets imprinted with strange characters which he had been given power to translate, and which he said proved to be the text of a religious book, or "bible," that had been deposited many centuries before in the place where he had discovered the plates.[1] He issued his translation in printed form in 1830, calling himself the proprietor of the work, and on it as a basis—aided by a few associates—established a new church and assumed the functions of priest and prophet. The speedy removal of Smith and his followers to the town of Kirtland, Ohio, in January of 1831, was principally due to the fact that the New York rural neighborhood where he had been known gave small attention to his new rôle in the community, and as a consequence the progress of the church was unsatisfactory.

Its growth in Ohio was much more rapid. In those days the population of the western country was peculiarly susceptible to all influences of the sort, and within a few years the Latter Day Saints constituted a considerable and growing community whose membership was industrious and land-acquiring. The cause probably contributing in largest extent to its collapse in Ohio was the failure of a financial plan of its leaders, who issued paper money which they were unable to redeem in specie on demand. Smith ultimately left Ohio in 1838 because of the resulting disfavor and went to western Missouri, where, at the town of Independence, Mormons had also organized a settlement in 1831. There the bulk of the Ohio church

[1] The "Book of Mormon," or Mormon Bible. As published by Smith it contained various chapters that were literal transcriptions of the King James Bible. The writing on the tablets, Smith said, was "reformed Egyptian."

soon followed him. But the rapid acquisition of land by the Mormons in Missouri, their growth in numbers, their manifestation of a clan spirit, and a fear on the part of surrounding settlers that they would soon dominate the region if permitted to remain, resulted in an outbreak of

365.—Ruins of the Mormon Temple at Nauvoo in 1853. Engraved from a sketch by the English artist, Frederick Piercy. Published in London by the Mormon Church in 1855, in company with Piercy's drawings of the Oregon trail and Mormon migrations.

virtual warfare against them. Much of their property was burned or otherwise destroyed, many members of the church were maltreated, Governor Boggs issued a proclamation saying they must be exterminated or driven forth, and in the winter of 1838-39 they were evicted from the state.

The last settlement made by the Mormons east of the Mississippi—following the events just narrated—was in a then insignificant village called Commerce, situated on the eastern shore of the Mississippi River in the state of Illinois, opposite the southeastern corner of the territory of Iowa. The town of Commerce contained perhaps three or four hundred people when the Mormons chose it because of its favorable natural location. By April of 1840 it had grown to be a town of two hundred and fifty houses, and its name was changed by the government to Nauvoo. Under the Mormon influence Nauvoo expanded so rapidly both in size and prosperity that by the year 1845 it had become the most important place in Illinois. It was bigger than Chicago or any other town, contained various growing industries, and was surrounded by an agricultural region that yielded good crops to the Mormon farmers. During the preceding three years its inhabitants had gradually become involved in the acrimonious political struggles of the time, as a result of efforts made both by Whigs and Democrats to secure the favor of its numerically influential population at elections. It also appears probable that jealousy of Mormon prosperity was growing in the minds of the surrounding white population, and it is certain that the neighbors of the Latter Day Saints objected to Nauvoo's reputation as a repository of stolen goods.[1] As a result of these and allied conditions a state of actual war against the Mormons developed in 1845, and by the autumn of that year it became apparent to the

[1] During the period under review an extensive adjacent district of Illinois was involved in a controversy regarding its land titles, and as a consequence lawless squatters had gathered on the affected territory. Horse thieves, counterfeiters and miscreants of all sorts swarmed through the near-by country. Many of them, discovering the habit of the Mormons to "stand together," had joined the Church of Latter Day Saints, ostensibly as a result of conversion, but in reality to secure the endorsement and aid of the Mormons in case they were accused of crime. That Nauvoo contained a population element of the sort, and that thieves brought their plunder there, was recognized by the church authorities in their official and printed statements. The surrounding victims of thievery came to look on the Mormon town as a menace, which—at least in the respect suggested—it was. And, besides, Illinois had granted to Nauvoo such extreme powers of self-government as to make the city almost independent of the rest of the state, and it was practically impossible to secure the punishment of the criminal element at the hands of its courts.

THE GREAT MISSISSIPPI STEAMBOAT RACE.

FROM NEW ORLEANS TO ST.LOUIS, JULY 1870.

Between the R.E.Lee, Capt. John W. Cannon. and Natchez Capt. Leathers.

WON BY THE R.E.LEE. TIME 3 DAYS 18 HOURS AND 30 MINUTES. DISTANCE 1210 MILES.

Most celebrated of all the innumerable speed duels between river steamboats. The whole country watched its progress, and vast sums were wagered on the result. F. Lith. Col. Amer.

governing men of the church that they could no longer maintain their position. They therefore announced an intention to vacate the city, and their declaration to that effect resulted in a partial though not complete cessation of hostilities. Having come to this decision the people worked with desperate energy through the winter of 1845-6 in preparation for their impending departure. The results of their exertions during the winter months were afterwards thus described:

"In the meantime, the Mormons made the most enormous efforts for removal; all the houses in Nauvoo, not even excepting the temple, having been converted into workshops, so that before spring more than 12,000 wagons were in readiness for removing their families and effects. By the middle of May about 16,000 Mormons had crossed the Mississippi on their march to California, leaving about a thousand of their number behind in Nauvoo, such as, having no money, or property which they could convert into money, were without the means of removing."[1]

The actual evacuation of the city was not a matter of a few hours, but began in February and was kept up for a number of months. Each daily cavalcade consisted of those families which were finally ready for the journey. The inhabitants of the town—it covered an area of several square miles and was surrounded by farms and orchards—had been selling their houses and lands since the autumn before and converting the proceeds into such things as were necessary for the coming march. Every household, if possible, provided itself with a big canvas-covered wagon, three or four yoke of oxen, a cow or two for milking, several cattle to be used as food, a number of sheep, a tent, farm tools, seeds, firearms, extra clothing, half a dozen barrels of flour and as much other portable food as might be obtained or carried. But this standard of equipment, if it may be so called, could not be followed

---

[1] Gerhard's "Illinois as It Is," p. 119. Gerhard's and also Ford's "History of Illinois" contain accounts of the lawlessness preceding and accompanying the Mormon evacuation of Nauvoo.

by all the people of Nauvoo. They had to dispose of their property for whatever it would command at forced sale. Even the most well-to-do were none too amply fortified against the experience about to befall them, and the poor —though aided as much as possible—were indeed in sorry state to begin an overland trip across half a continent. Some families had only the two-wheeled cart, drawn by a single animal, and a few had no vehicles at all.

Two dominant characteristics of the Mormons at this time deserve mention in order that their demeanor on their pilgrimage, and the attitude later to be displayed by them toward the nation whose bounds they left, may be better understood. They were, in the first place, a brave and resolute community undismayed by adversity and repeated disaster to their fortunes. And they were also filled with feelings of hostility and bitterness toward other Americans in general, as a consequence of the almost constant physical attacks to which they had been subjected in Missouri and Illinois for about ten years, in spite of their appeals to the Federal and state governments. These assaults had recently culminated in the destruction of much property on the outskirts of Nauvoo and in the murder of Joseph Smith—then mayor of the town—and his brother Hyrum. The two men, when killed, were confined in a jail at Carthage under the protection of state militia and the Governor's assurance of their safety.

Those composing the vanguard of the migration, after crossing the Mississippi in flatboats and skiffs, established a camp in Iowa and waited for the arrival of others before setting forth on the first stage of their expedition. The Mormons had asked Iowa for permission to march through its extent to Council Bluffs, a distance of about

1244

366.—On the Oregon trail. A group of Mormon wagons and a herd of live stock crossing the Missouri River at the Council Bluffs ferry. The trees are cottonwoods, chief reliance of the river traffic and overland caravans for canoes and fuel. From a drawing made by Piercy in 1853.

400 miles, and the territory had granted the request. Later in February the Mississippi became frozen, and many families crossed on the ice. Storms, snow, and a temperature of twenty degrees below zero distinguished the first encampment west of the river, and thus an initiation of suffering greeted the pilgrims at the outset of their movement. About two thousand men, women and children, and several thousand cattle and other farm animals assembled on Iowa soil before the end of the month, and the head of the long west-bound column was at last set in motion. One of the leading men of the Latter Day Saints afterward thus referred to the commencement of the pilgrimage:

"On the first of March, the ground covered with snow, we broke encampment about noon, and soon nearly four hundred wagons were moving to—we knew not where."

The astonishing assertion with which the above statement concludes was literally true. The Mormons did not know where they were going. They had no specific destination in view. They only knew they had failed to live in peace with their neighbors in the United States, and had to find a home elsewhere or disintegrate as a religious and economic body. So they turned their faces toward the West, hoping that somewhere in what was then northern Mexico, beyond the Rocky Mountains, they could discover a retreat where they might again live in their own fashion, free of the nation, flag and people at which they were angered. Those fifteen thousand human beings sold the city they had built and set forth into a virtually unknown country as avowed wanderers. Their head men told them that when they reached their future home they

1246

would immediately and intuitively know that the hegira had come to an end. And so it eventually happened. But, as in the case of Daniel Boone, the Mormons were in one matter doomed to disappointment. For hardly had the advance guard of the Saints reached the distant valley of the Great Salt Lake when it and all the surrounding territory passed into possession of the country from which they had desired to escape.

During the spring and summer of 1846 additional fragments of Nauvoo's population crossed the river and added themselves to the stream of emigrants that was slowly creeping westward over the Iowa prairies. A semi-military discipline was put into effect among the marchers. Companies were formed, each containing about fifty wagons, and the vehicles were assembled at night. Sentries were posted, and the live stock was entrusted to the care of guards. Each group of ten men was under control of a leader called a "captain of ten," and similar officers, of correspondingly higher rank, had charge of fifty men and of a hundred men.

Inclement weather followed the caravan until May. The ground had to be cleared of snow and ice before tents could be set up. There were no roads which might be followed by the wagons. After a heavy rain or snow the country was impassable for the baggage of such a host, and under those conditions long halts had to be made. Sometimes, at night, the wet clothing and bedding of the moving people would be frozen solid. Progress under such circumstances was very slow. The live stock suffered from exertion, exposure and lack of food, and began to die. A further glimpse at this part of the migration is afforded through the medium of a diary kept by

A HISTORY OF TRAVEL IN AMERICA

Orson Pratt, a prominent figure among the Mormons, which under the date of April 9, said:[1]

"With great exertion a part of the camp were enabled to get about six miles, while others were stuck fast in the deep mud. . . We were obliged to cut brush and limbs of trees, and throw them upon the ground in our tents, to keep our beds from sinking in the mud. Our animals were turned loose to look out for themselves; the bark and limbs of trees were their principal food."

In mid-April the leading detachment found it necessary to make a protracted halt for purposes of recuperation. A camp called "Garden Grove" was therefore established about a hundred and fifty miles west of Nauvoo, log houses were put up, wells were dug, land was ploughed, and seed was planted that crops might spring up for the benefit of those who were still to come. Again, in May, a similar camp named "Mount Pisgah" was created still farther west, and there several thousand acres were sown to grain and vegetables that later wayfarers might garner.

The whole course of the Mormon march across Iowa was dotted with like localities of temporary sojourn, and the American pioneer spirit was constantly manifested from the commencement of the exodus until its completion. Whenever a stop was made in Iowa many of those not wanted in the building of the camp—women as well as men—sold their services to adjacent permanent settlers and took their wages in much prized provisions for man and beast more needy than themselves. Still other men went on ahead to build rude roads and bridges. Flatboats were also put together as a means of getting the wagons across the larger streams. Skiffs for the women and children were carried by the Saints on specially made

[1] Printed in the "Millennial Star," Vol. XI, p. 370. The "Millennial Star," a newspaper published by the Latter Day Saints, was first issued in Liverpool, England, in 1840.

367.—On the Oregon trail. Mormon wagon train crossing the Loup Fork ferry. A rope was stretched over the river as an aid in pulling the floating wagons to the other shore. Huts built of cottonwood timber were erected at necessary halting places along the line of march. From a drawing made by Piercy in 1853.

boat-wagons until the Mississippi was reached. Nor was toil the only portion of these wanderers during the early days of their journey. They had their gayer hours as well. Partly because of the foresight of their leaders, and in perhaps still greater part due to the spirit of the people themselves, the nomads persistently clung to some of the amusements of that more civilized life which they had temporarily abandoned. No sooner had a camp been made—whether for a long stay or for but a single night —and its necessary work been done, than suitable spaces were cleared, a concert was given, the young folks danced and sang, and the older generation fell to gossip or consultation. It is safe to say that whatever else was abandoned at Nauvoo, no musical instrument of any variety was left behind when the city was deserted. All accompanied their owners, and they were daily tooted, scraped and twanged either in festal frolic, religious service, or dirge, from Illinois to the Salt Lake. The Mormons, while in their city, had maintained a really excellent band equipped with admirable instruments, and its organization was continued throughout the long expedition.

The head of the column reached the Mississippi River at Council Bluffs in June, and the bulk of the party which had set forth on March 1 attained the same point in July. It had been more than four months in traversing the four hundred miles. But let it not be understood that all the thousands involved in this movement travelled together, or in any order resembling one column. While the vanguard of the hegira had been traversing Iowa, and halting from time to time, still others had constantly been issuing from Nauvoo as they completed their preparations. By the month of August, then, there existed a line of exiled Mormon population which extended almost en-

ERECTED IN GREAT SALT LAKE CITY, LOOKING EAST

A. Kern. Lith. 379 Broadway N.Y.

368.—A view of Salt Lake City in its early days, soon after the wandering Mormons had found the valley of the Great Salt Lake, chosen it as their future abode and begun the creation of a new community.

tirely across Iowa territory. Some were encamped on the Mississippi and creating there a settlement in which to pass the approaching winter; others were sojourning in the several log-hut and agricultural camps already mentioned, where they proposed to spend the coming cold season; and still others were creaking over the prairies in their wagons, amid clouds of dust raised by the feet of their oxen and farm stock. Thus far the exodus had been more or less in touch with outlying settlers, and —save in the circumstances of its origin—had not been productive of features that were inconsistent with the migration of so large a population group under unfavorable conditions. There had been births, sickness, deaths, hunger, labor and laughter. The best equipped and earliest starters of fifteen thousand human beings and their herds had traversed four hundred miles, there pausing to prepare for a farther advance during the following year, and to permit those in the rear to catch up with them if possible.

Then began an interval of suffering and trouble that involved the entire host in greater or less degree, its effects extending from Nauvoo to the farthest westward outposts. And, unfortunately, the most connected and detailed contemporary narrative of subsequent events relating to the pilgrimage has been injured—with respect to its value as a dependable source of information—by the later attitude of the man who wrote it.

War with Mexico began while the Mormons were passing through Iowa. The Federal government, desirous of adding to its army, and knowing that Nauvoo had contained a large body of well-trained militia called the Nauvoo Legion, sent a representative to overtake the Saints and discover whether a battalion might not be ob-

tained by means of volunteer Mormon enlistments.[1] He
was accompanied by an American named Thomas Kane,
brother to the Arctic explorer Elisha Kane, and a man
of travel experience, education and ability. Kane paused
to inspect deserted Nauvoo, caught up with the main
body of exiles at the Missouri, took a decided liking to
them, was admired by them in return, remained with them
during their tribulations in the winter of 1846-7, and accompanied them on their farther westward advance.
After his return to the East he appeared before the
Pennsylvania Historical Society on March 26, 1850,
and delivered an address descriptive of the Mormon
migration, of which he himself had been a part.[2] Kane's
narrative was the first definite and extensive statement on
the subject to be obtained by the East; it was approved or
left substantially uncontradicted by non-Mormon investigators able to estimate its accuracy during the years
immediately following—in so far as it dealt with the
events of the migration—and has since, of necessity, remained an important source for inquirers into the subject. Among those who later commented on Kane's story,
after opportunity to estimate its value, was Lieutenant
Gunnison, of the United States Army, who in 1852 spoke
of its author as

"Their [the Mormons'] great and eloquent defender, whose historical oration on these dark periods of their fortunes does equal honor
to his charitable heart and intelligence—a sketch, however, of the epic
kind, replete with poetical ornament and fervor."[3]

In after years, and especially during the serious clashes
of authority which occurred between the Federal government and the Latter Day Saints in the administrations of

[1] The "Mormon Battalion" of the Mexican War was so obtained.
[2] Kane's address was immediately published under the title "The Mormons," and constitutes an octavo pamphlet of 84 pages.
[3] In "The Mormons, etc.," p. 133. Gunnison's history was published in 1852, after its
author had spent a year or more amid the people and scenes he discusses.

Presidents Fillmore and Buchanan, Kane performed political services in behalf of the Mormons whose nature can scarcely be reconciled with any reasonable hypothesis save that he was, at those times, a secret Mormon agent.[1] To what extent—if at all—he occupied a similar position when he delivered his address before the learned society of Pennsylvania is not now known. He apparently did try to create or to strengthen an impression that the indefensible attacks of which the Saints were victims had their origin in prejudice based on religious grounds, and he also assuredly strove to portray their fortitude and other good qualities in a manner well designed to win the public sympathy. Yet the last named endeavor was superfluous, because the undertaking that had been carried to success by the inhabitants of Nauvoo could not be recognized as other than a remarkable feat performed by a determined, courageous people.

So much must necessarily be said of Kane and his narrative if—as is designed—use is to be made of the recital. And it may be further suggested that those parts of his story relating to experiences of travel do not fall so readily under the suspicion of undue bias as those other sections more concerned with human motives and purposes. What he saw at Nauvoo, in Iowa, and beyond, was also seen by so many others that it was scarcely safe for him, even if he had wished, unduly to distort the truth regarding those matters. His account of the march itself is inherently credible; is corroborated in substance by various other early sources of information;[2] and, had Kane not afterward occupied the position he did in Mormon

[1] A review of Kane's activities during the periods mentioned may be found in Linn's "The Story of the Mormons."

[2] Lieutenant Gunnison; Illinois and Iowa contemporary newspapers; the diaries and statements of others who made the journey; the reports made to Governor Ford, of Illinois, by his representative, Brayman, published in the Warsaw (Illinois) "Signal" of December 24, 1845; Ferris's "Utah and the Mormons."

369.—When a caravan moved with tents, but without wagons, the tent poles were commonly dragged as here shown. Light baggage or tent canvas could then be lashed to the poles. This procedure was adopted from the Indians, who shifted their tépee villages in the manner described. The cone-shaped hill is Huerfano Butte, in New Mexico, about 650 miles from the Missouri border.

affairs it is doubtful if his story would have been seriously questioned.

Despite the continued evacuation of Nauvoo throughout the spring and summer of 1846, which process at last left only some seven hundred poverty-stricken inhabitants within its limits, the surrounding anti-Mormon population was dissatisfied with the slowness of the movement and early in the autumn attacked the town in force, assaulting it with musketry and a cannon. As a result of that affair the remaining Mormons, although unprepared, agreed to remove at once. So, "in the midst of the sickly season they were hurried in the boats and thrown upon the Iowa shore, without shelter or provisions; in consequence whereof, great numbers of them miserably perished."[1] Nauvoo was empty of Mormons at last.

It was at this time that Kane appeared on the scene, and his first view of the town was afterward thus described:

"I was descending the last hillside upon my journey, when a landscape in delightful contrast broke upon my view. Half encircled by a bend of the river, a beautiful city lay glittering in the fresh morning sun; its bright new dwellings, set in cool, green gardens, ranging up around a stately dome-shaped hill, which was crowned by a noble marble edifice whose tapering spire was radiant with white and gold. The city appeared to cover several miles; beyond it, in the background, there rolled off a fair country, chequered by the careful lines of fruitful husbandry. Unmistakable marks of industry, enterprise and educated wealth, everywhere, made the scene one of singular and most striking beauty.

"It was a natural impulse to visit this inviting region. I procured a skiff, and, rowing across the river, landed at the chief wharf of the city. No one met me there. I looked, and saw no one. I could hear no one move; though the quiet everywhere was such that I heard the flies buzz and the water-ripples break against the shallow of the beach. I walked through the solitary streets. The town lay as in a dream, under some deadening spell of loneliness from which I almost feared to wake it. For plainly it had not slept long. There was no grass

[1] Gerhard's "Illinois as It Is," p. 122.

growing up in the paved ways. Rains had not entirely washed away the prints of dusty footsteps.

"Yet I went about unchecked. I went into empty workshops, rope-walks and smithies. The spinner's wheel was idle; the carpenter had gone from his workbench and shavings, his unfinished sash and casing. . . . The blacksmith's shop was cold; but his coal heap and ladling pool and crooked water-horn were all there, as if he had just gone off for a holiday. . . I could have supposed the people hidden in the houses, but the doors were unfastened; and when at last I timidly entered them I found dead ashes white upon the hearth, and had to tread a tiptoe as if walking down the aisle of a country church, to avoid rousing irreverent echoes from the naked floors. . . Fields upon fields of heavy-headed, yellow grain lay rotting ungathered upon the ground. No one was at hand to take in their rich harvest. As far as the eye could reach they stretched away—they sleeping, too, in the hazy air of autumn."[1]

After having explored the city, and talked concerning recent events with an armed party of the anti-Mormons encountered by him, Kane retreated across the Mississippi and discovered the lately evicted rear-guard of the town's inhabitants. Of them he said:

"Here, among the dock and rushes, sheltered only by the darkness, without roof between them and the sky, I came upon a crowd of several hundred human creatures, whom my movements roused from uneasy slumber upon the ground.

"Passing these on my way to the light, I found it came from a tallow candle in a paper-funnel shade, such as is used by street venders of apples and peanuts, and which, flaring and guttering away in the bleak air off the water, shown flickeringly on the emaciated features of a man in the last stage of a bilious remittent fever.

"They had done their best for him. Over his head was something like a tent, made of a sheet or two, and he rested on a but partially ripped-open old straw mattress, with a hair sofa-cushion under his head for a pillow. His gaping jaw and glazing eye told how short a time he would monopolize these luxuries; though a seemingly bewildered and excited person, who might have been his wife, seemed to find hope in occasionally forcing him to swallow awkwardly measured sips of the tepid river water from a burned and battered, bitter-smelling tin coffeepot. Those who knew better had furnished the apothecary he needed—a toothless old bald-head, whose manner had the repulsive dullness of a familiar with death scenes. He, so long as I remained, mumbled in his patient's ear a monotonous and melancholy prayer, between

[1] Kane's "The Mormons."

the pauses of which I heard the hiccup and sobbing of two little girls who were sitting on a piece of driftwood outside. . .

"Cowed and cramped by cold and sunburn, alternating as each weary day and night dragged on, they were, almost all of them, the crippled victims of disease. They were there because they had no homes, nor hospital, nor poorhouse, nor friends to offer them any. They could not satisfy the feeble cravings of their sick: they had not bread to quiet the fractious hunger cries of their children. Mothers and babes, daughters and grandparents, all of them alike, were bivouacked in tatters, wanting even covering to comfort those whom the sick shiver of fever was searching to the marrow."

This final group of refugees, which had crossed the river on September 18, included all the infirm of the city whom it had previously been considered unwise to move. While its members lay on the western bank of the river their situation was deplorable, and their principal article of food was ground corn, adulterated with the bark of trees similarly treated. But tidings of their plight had been hurried westward to the main column, and in October they were rescued by a relief train of wagons sent back for that purpose and conveyed to the log-cabin camps ahead. Kane's description of such a settlement reads:

"A square was marked out; and the wagons as they arrived took their positions along its four sides in double rows, so as to leave a roomy street or passageway between them. The tents were disposed also in rows, at intervals between the wagons. The cattle were folded in high-fenced yards outside. The quadrangle inside was left vacant for the sake of ventilation, and the streets, covered in with leafy arbor work and kept scrupulously clean, formed a shaded cloister walk. This was a place of exercise for slowly recovering invalids, the day-home of the infants, and the evening promenade of all.

"From the first formation of the camp, all its inhabitants were constantly and laboriously occupied. Many of them were highly educated mechanics, and seemed only to need a day's anticipated rest to engage them at the forge, loom, or turning-lathe, upon some needed chore of work. . . I have seen a cobbler, after the halt of his party on the march, hunting along the river bank for a lap-stone, in the twilight, that he might finish a famous boot-sole by the campfire; and I have had a

370.—Prairie schooners halted near Red River. The wagons of the South, and those regularly engaged in the traffic of the Santa Fé trail, were larger and heavier than most of those which started to California from northern states during the gold rush. In some localities there had been a reduction in the size of the old Conestoga type.

piece of cloth the wool of which was sheared, and dyed, and spun, and woven during a progress of over three hundred miles.[1] . . .

"Inside the camp the chief labors were assigned to the women. From the moment when, after the halt, the lines had been laid, the spring wells dug out, and the ovens and fireplaces built, though the men still assumed to set the guards and enforce the regulations of police, the Empire of the Tented Town was with the better sex. . . And they were a nation of wonderful managers. They could hardly be called housewives in etymological strictness, but it was plain that they had once been such, and most distinguished ones. Their art availed them in their changed affairs. With almost their entire culinary material limited to the milk of their cows, some store of meal or flour, and a very few condiments, they brought their thousand and one receipts into play with a success that outdid for their families the miracle of the Hebrew widow's cruse. They learned to make butter on the march, by the dashing of the wagon, and so nicely to calculate the working of barm in the jolting heats that as soon after the halt as an oven could be dug in the hillside and heated, their well-kneaded loaf was ready for baking, and produced good leavened bread for supper."[2]

One other feature of the march through Iowa, as mentioned by Kane, deserves repetition. He thus referred to the frequent burials on the prairie:

"The general hopefulness of human—including Mormon—nature, was well illustrated by the fact that the most provident were found unfurnished with undertaker's articles; so that bereaved affection was driven to the most melancholy makeshifts.

"The best expedient generally was to cut down a log of some eight or nine feet long, and, slitting it longitudinally, strip off its dark bark in two half cylinders. These, placed around the body of the deceased and bound firmly together with withes made of the alburnum, formed a rough sort of tubular coffin, which surviving relatives and friends, with a little show of black crape, could follow with its enclosure to the hole or bit of ditch dug to receive it in the wet ground of the prairie. They grieved to lower it down so poorly clad, and in such an unheeded grave. It was hard—was it right—thus hurriedly to plunge it in one of the undistinguishable waves of the great land sea, and leave it behind them there, in the cold north rain, abandoned, to be forgotten? . . . So, when they had filled up the grave, and over it played the Miserere prayer, and tried to sing a hopeful psalm, their last office was to seek out landmarks, or call in the surveyor to help them determine the bearings of valley bends, headlands, or forks and angles of constant streams,

[1] Kane, pp. 35-36.
[2] Kane, pp. 45-46.

by which its position should in the future be remembered and recognized."[1]

The major part of the suffering endured by the Mormons befell them in their camps on the Missouri River bottom lands, near Council Bluffs, during the autumn of 1846 and the ensuing winter. There a majority of the moving host slowly assembled in August and September, and since all realized the impossibility of penetrating the mountain region while it was in the clutch of ice and snow, and while they were without adequate food, they made ready as best they might to wait until the following spring. A trading post of the American Fur Company was near by, and on the Iowa side of the river was a large settlement of Potawatomi Indians who had been placed there by the government a few years before. The western bank of the Missouri[2] was similarly occupied by the Omahas. Both tribes of red men received the unexpected concourse of white pilgrims in friendly spirit, and met the Mormon leaders in formal councils to arrange the relations that should exist between the two races while the travellers from the East remained in that vicinity. Big Elk, chief of the Omahas, announced that the Mormons might use what Indian timber they needed for their huts and fuel, and offered his men as guards for the herds of live stock. The whites, in return, agreed to aid the Omahas with their teams.

Pied Riche, the principal chief of the Potawatomi, made the following address at the meeting between his nation and the Saints:

"The Pottawatamie came, sad and tired, into this unhealthy Missouri Bottom not many years back, when he was taken from his beautiful country beyond the Mississippi, which had abundant game and timber

[1] Kane, pp. 13-14.
[2] In the neighborhood of the present town of Florence, Nebraska.

371.—A caravan from Missouri on the Santa Fé trail, arriving in sight of the town from which the road took its name. The successful ending of an overland trip excited much boisterous enthusiasm.

and clear water everywhere. Now you are driven away the same, from your lodges and lands there, and the graves of your people. So we have both suffered. We must help one another, and the Great Spirit will help us both. You are now free to cut and use all the wood you may wish. You can make all your improvements, and live on any part of our actual land not occupied by us. Because one suffers, and does not deserve it, is no reason he shall suffer always: I say. We may live to see all right yet. However, if we do not our children will."[1]

It was a singular situation. There lay two tribes; one red, one white, both despoiled and driven from their homes into the wilderness. There they met and mingled for a time; the white men and women, to the number of thousands, becoming guests of the red people and the beneficiaries of their bounty. The Potawatomi showed no trace of the rancor which might without unreason have been exhibited by them toward members of a race which

[1] Kane, p. 59. The attitude of the natives is also established by other means than Kane's narrative.

had treated them so ill. But they too knew what trouble was, and the principles of their philosophy did not permit them to refuse help to a homeless man who needed help, even though he wore an alien skin. So by the machinations of the fates it happened that the Caucasian occupation of the West, and the later resultant extension of Federal power amid the last territorial possessions of the American natives were materially aided through wholesale charity bestowed on wandering white men by their red adversaries. History—that sardonic old hen—had hatched another egg.

The conditions under which the main company of Mormons were compelled to live in the Missouri bottoms from August of 1846 to July of 1847 brought distress and illness upon them. Many had already been weakened by hardship and insufficient food throughout a period of several months, for the transition from their orderly life and abundance in Nauvoo to the status of under-fed nomads was an abrupt one. Malaria spread; the illnesses due to breaking virgin soil appeared; and symptoms similar to those of scurvy, caused no doubt by lack of a sufficient variety of food—there being little vegetable provender at hand—likewise developed. The people also were poorly sheltered. Log cabins were the best dwellings obtainable, and thousands of the multitude were compelled to live—or tried to live—in tents or shelters made of sod, or of tree branches and plastered mud. Some even dug holes in the hillsides and for a time existed in caves of their own making. The principal diet of many was cornmeal.

An unknown number died, both along the banks of the Missouri and back in the camps scattered through Iowa. Even those who did not succumb were weakened and re-

1263

duced. Kane thus described the situation of the people during this worst phase of their experience:

"The Mormons were scourged severely. The exceeding mortality among some of them was no doubt in the main attributable to the low state to which their systems had been brought by long-continued endurance of want and hardship. . . They let their cows go unmilked. They wanted for voices to raise the Psalm of Sundays. The few who were able to keep their feet went about among the tents and wagons with food and water, like nurses through the wards of an infirmary. Here at one time the digging got behind hand: burials were slow; and you might see women sit in the open tents keeping the flies off their dead children. . . I recollect overhearing a lamentation over some dear baby, that its mother no doubt thought the destroying angel should have been specially instructed to spare. I wish, too, for my own sake, I could forget how imperfectly one day I mourned the decease of a poor saint, who by clamor rendered his vicinity troublesome. He no doubt endured great pain, for he groaned shockingly until death came to his relief. He interfered with my own hard-gained slumbers,[1] and—I was glad when death did relieve him. . . I happen to recall, as I write, that I had some knowledge somewhere of one of our new-comers for whom the nightmare revived and repeated, without intermission, the torment of his trying journey. As he lay, feeding life with long-drawn breaths, he muttered: 'Where's next water? Team—give out! Hot, hot— God, it's hot; stop the wagon—stop the wagon—stop the wagon!' . . . In a half-dreamy way I remember, or I think I remember, a crowd of phantoms like these."[2]

One of the most ornate and comfortable dwellings characterizing this gloomy epoch of the hegira was that of Lorenzo Snow, a prominent figure in the church. As described by him[3] it was a log affair about thirty feet long and fifteen feet wide, with a roof of logs covered with dirt. The floor consisted of the earth, on which straw was scattered. Sheets covered the inner walls. The chimney was of sod. The lamps were hollow turnips, filled with oil or grease, from which protruded wicks. Yet in such habitations as these, or in the tents, brush shelters, wagons, sod hovels or caves, those who were able

[1] Kane himself being at that time in the grip of the disease for a month. It was before the winter set in.
[2] Kane, pp. 50-52.
[3] In his "Biography."

372.—A small government steamboat of the Colorado Exploring Expedition in Mohave Cañon. From a sketch by H. B. Mollhausen.

gathered in social conclave while not ministering to the sick or burying the dead, and cheered their own spirits by songs, simple games, stories, jokes or religious services.

So the weary winter passed, and eventually, in April of 1847, welcome activity came once more. A pioneer corps of one hundred and forty-three picked men, taking with them seventy-three wagons and a little field-piece on wheels, was sent out in advance to choose a farther route for the main body and to discover, if possible, a new home. The daily routine of this advance guard was simple. Its members were awakened by bugle at five o'clock. They prayed, ate, and were under way by seven. They marched all day, ate when they could no longer march, prayed again at half-past eight and were asleep by nine, in wagons drawn up in a circle with the live stock inside and guards on duty.

At Grand Island, on the Platte River, they halted briefly to consider whether they should adhere to the trail on the south side of the river used by Oregon emigrants, or, as a matter of pride, blaze a new path along the north bank of that stream. Pioneer pride won the debate, and the new road, so created, came to be known as the "Mormon Trail."[1] Poor forage was found, and the draught animals were kept going by feeding them part of the corn and wheat intended for the men. Guide posts were set up at intervals of ten miles, and written messages for the guidance of the ones to follow were fastened to them. On June 15 they met a party of ten white men and from them learned "that the Utah country was beautiful."[2] South Pass was reached on June 26, and Green River was crossed by rafts on June 30. At that time many of the party were

[1] Afterward followed by the Union Pacific Railway.
[2] From a Ms. "History of Brigham Young." Quoted by H. H. Bancroft in "History of Utah," p. 257.

ill with fever, and had been without bread for six weeks. Thence they pushed on through the rough country until July 14, when forty-four men, with 23 wagons, hurried still faster ahead. On July 19, after very hard work in making a road through a cañon, two of the party ascended a hill and from it looked down—somewhat as the searchers for Kentucke had done about three-quarters of a century before—into a promised land. They beheld the valley of the Great Salt Lake. One of the two men was Erastus Snow, and in after years[1] he described the moment in these words:

"The thicket down the narrows, at the mouth of the cañon, was so dense that one could not penetrate through it. I crawled for some distance on my hands and knees through this thicket, until I was compelled to return, admonished to by the rattle of a snake which lay coiled up under my nose, having almost put my hand on him; but as he gave me the friendly warning, I thanked him, and retreated. We raised on to a high point south of the narrows, where we got a view of the Great Salt Lake and this valley, and each of us, without saying a word to the other, instinctively, as if by inspiration, raised our hats from our heads, and then, swinging our hats, shouted. . . We could see the canes down in the valley, on what is now called Mill Creek, which looked like inviting grain, and thitherward we directed our course."

Next day they were sowing seed.

In the meantime a large body of the Saints, in obedience to instructions, had started from the Missouri on July 4 without waiting to learn the result of the pioneers' explorations. It was composed of about one thousand five hundred souls, with hundreds of wagons and a considerable amount of farm stock, and gained the Salt Lake valley late in September. The leaders of the migration, having found a new home, returned with the news to the camp on the Missouri, reaching there on the last day of October. The winter of 1847-8 was passed by the Mormons on the Missouri with much less hardship than

[1] In his "Address to the Pioneers," 1880.

had distinguished the first cold season and in June of 1848 another extensive company set forth for Utah, arriving in September. Two years and a half had elapsed since the pilgrimage began in March of 1846. By the year 1853 the former population of Nauvoo—or that part of it still living—was virtually reassembled in the Utah valley.

No sooner had the 1848 company attained its destination than its members, and the other Mormons already in Salt Lake City, heard of the discovery of gold in California. When that strange news came the head men of the Church of Latter Day Saints issued the following proclamation:

"The true use of gold is for paving streets, covering houses, and making culinary dishes; and, when the Saints shall have preached the gospel, raised grain, and built up cities enough, the Lord will open up the way for a supply of gold to the perfect satisfaction of His People. Until then, let them not be over-anxious, for the treasures of the earth are in the Lord's storehouse, and He will open the doors thereof when and where He pleases."

So the Mormons remained at home to raise grain and build up cities. In his Philadelphia lecture of 1850 Kane said of them, in conclusion:

"They mean to seek no other resting-place. . . They have at last come to their Promised Land, and, 'behold, it is a good land and large, and flowing with milk and honey': and here again for them, as at Nauvoo, the forge smokes and the anvil rings, and whirring wheels go round; again has returned the merry sport of childhood, and the evening quiet of old age, and again dear house-pet flowers bloom in garden plots round happy homes.

"It is these homes, in the heart of our American Alps . . . that hold out their welcome to the passing traveller. Some of you have probably seen in the St. Louis papers the repeated votes of thanks to them of companies of emigrants to California. These are often reduced to great straits after passing Fort Laramie, and turn aside to seek the Salt Lake Colony in pitiable plights of fatigue and destitution. The road, after leaving the Oregon trace, is one of increasing difficulty,[1] and when the last mountain has been crossed, passes along the bottom

[1] An interesting description of this part of the overland road will be found in extracts from the diary constituting James Abbey's "California: A Trip Across the Plains in 1850," embraced in chapter LV.

of a deep cañon, whose scenery is of an almost terrific gloom. . . . At every turn the overhanging cliffs threaten to break down upon the little torrent river that has worn its way at their base. Indeed, the narrow ravine is so serrated by this stream that the road crosses it from one side to the other, something like forty times in the last five miles. At the end of the ravine the emigrant comes abruptly out of the dark pass into the lighted valley on an even bench or terrace of its upper tableland. No wonder if he loses his self-control here. A ravishing panoramic landscape opens out before him, blue, and green, and gold, and pearl; a great sea with hilly islands, rivers, a lake, and broad sheets of grassy plain, all set as in a silver-chased cup, within mountains whose peaks of perpetual snow are burnished by a dazzling sun. It is less these, however, than the foreground of old-country farms, with their stacks and thatchings and stock, and the central city, smoking from its chimneys and swarming with working inhabitants, that tries the men of fatigue-broken nerves. The 'Califorrneys' scream; they sing; they give three cheers and do not count them; a few have prayed; more swear; some fall on their faces and cry outright." [1]

Thus ended, in a success greater than could reasonably have been anticipated, the Mormon migration. Though the Mormons of Utah, as Kane said in 1850, did for a time greet other overland travellers with hospitality, there came a day when they threatened to close the region and trails controlled by them to all such transcontinental movement. And the deplorable crime of the Mountain Meadow, of which overland travellers were the victims, took its place beside Gnadenhutten and other equal cruelties of eastern commonwealths in the category of acts for which Americans of these days can make no reparation. Yet, after all, no nation however splendid has been free of such wrongdoing. The process of eradicating cruelty from ourselves has been a long one, and still goes on. If it is sometimes necessary, in looking backward, to dwell for a moment on things we would rather forget, there is recompense in the discovery that we are progressing.

[1] Kane, pp. 75-76.

CHAPTER LIV

THE CRY OF "GOLD"— ITS EFFECT — CONDITIONS IN CALI-
FORNIA DURING 1846 — THE LAST GREAT RUSH OF
THE PEOPLE BEGINS — DARK SIDE OF OVERLAND
TRAVEL ILLUSTRATED BY THE ADVENTURES OF THE
DONNER PARTY — IT IS TRAPPED IN THE MOUNTAINS
BY SNOW — EFFORTS TO ESCAPE — MARCH OF THE
"FIFTEEN"— HUMAN FLESH AS FOOD — LIFE IN THE
BURIED CABINS — A CHRISTMAS FEAST — HALF THE
EMIGRANTS ULTIMATELY RESCUED — THE INDIAN
GUIDES

LATE in the summer of the year 1848 there spread
through the country east of the Mississippi a strange
and almost incredible tale from beyond the distant mountains that border the Pacific Ocean. It said gold had
been found there; gold in quantities beyond computation.

As men listened to the first versions of the persistent
story, a change came over them. A new restlessness began
to pervade the whole population. The eyes of the people
shifted from their every-day affairs and were directed
toward the vast, forbidding territory that stretched for
two thousand miles between them and the rumored El
Dorado. They gazed toward the unknown expanse just
as a runner concentrates his vision on a tremendous
obstacle that must be leaped.

And such, indeed, it was. The successive surges of
white pioneers had brought them at last to the farther

1270

side of the Mississippi River, where many settlements were springing up. During a period of about two hundred and twenty years the white race had advanced, as a compact body, some fifteen hundred miles into the interior of the continent, always bringing with them a power that knew no backward turning. Missouri and Iowa had become the frontier. But at that point the Caucasians had apparently paused, save for the comparatively small movements along the Missouri and toward Oregon and Utah. The bulwark of natives which lay just ahead of them, and popular ideas concerning the nature of the country extending to the Rocky Mountains and beyond, were acting somewhat as a brake to farther advance in bulk. A driblet of caravans—such as the one whose experiences are about to be described—had, it is true, been departing toward California for the last two years, but those expeditions had not been inspired by influences which affected the whole population.

Nor—until the tale of gold wrought its overwhelming effect—was there much probability that the white men would, for several generations, make serious inroads on the immense country between their western outposts and the shores of the Pacific. According to general opinion the distances to be overcome were too great, the lands of the plains were sterile in comparison with those of the East, and the endless tumult of mountains was a barrier impossible of profitable conquest.

Those beliefs and the orderly and reasonable processes of mankind, as such processes appeared to be unfolding in America, were swept away by one word within the space of a few weeks. "Gold!" came the cry. In it was contained the essence of all things craved, and mountains crumbled away. Though the distance and hardships still remained, they were seen but dimly. In one sense the west-bound emigrants moved as in a trance. To them the difficulties of the pilgrimage were phantasmagoria. Nothing was real but the mythical land that lay at the end of their wandering.

The newspapers published during the last half of the year 1848 reflect a curious state of widespread emotional excitement. They printed all obtainable stories of the extraordinary mineral discovery, and at the same time apparently strove to allay the furore they created. Many periodicals made efforts to simulate calmness and sobriety, and some belittled the news even after its substantial accuracy had been established. One eastern paper[1] quoted the words of the San Francisco alcalde, who had said: "The streams are paved with gold—the mountains swell in their golden girdle—it sparkles in the sands of the valley—it glitters in the coronets of the steep cliffs." And then the editor commented on the utterance as follows: "The author may have thought there was poetry in this, but he knew, as well as we do, that there was no truth in it." Finally, to cap the climax, the editor said there might be some truth in it, after all.

The nation believed, and so began a unique rush of thousands of miles undertaken by millions of Americans, which was possible only under the combination of conditions that brought it about. Those conditions were a goal of fabulous riches, the shock of its unexpected announcement, and a national hysteria affecting a nervous, restless people who had passed through eight successive generations of continuous pioneer exertion, conquest and excitement. The movement beginning on a large scale in 1849 was a final manifesta-

[1] The "Literary American," of New York; December 30, 1848.

THE

POCKET GUIDE TO CALIFORNIA;

A

SEA AND LAND ROUTE BOOK,

CONTAINING

A DESCRIPTION OF THE EL DORADO; ITS GEOGRAPHICAL POSITION;
PEOPLE, CLIMATE, SOIL, PRODUCTIONS, AGRICULTURAL
RESOURCES, COMMERCIAL ADVANTAGES,
AND MINERAL WEALTH;

WITH

A CHAPTER ON GOLD FORMATIONS;

ALSO THE

CONGRESSIONAL MAP,

AND

THE VARIOUS ROUTES AND DISTANCES TO THE GOLD REGIONS.

TO WHICH IS ADDED THE

Gold-Hunter's Memorandum and Pocket Directory.

BY J. E. SHERWOOD.

" Westward the course of Empire takes its way."—BERKELEY.

⸻ • ◆ • ⸻

NEW YORK:

J. E. SHERWOOD, PUBLISHER AND PROPRIETOR.
FOR SALE BY H. LONG & BROTHER, 46 ANN STREET; BERFORD & CO.,
ASTOR HOUSE; AND THE PRINCIPAL BOOKSELLERS THROUGHOUT
THE UNION.
CALIFORNIA: BERFORD & CO., AND C. W. HOLDEN, SAN FRANCISCO.
1849.

373.—Title page of a guide book such as was bought by those who sought information regarding the overland journey to California in 1849.

tion of a quality that ran in the blood of the country. In the extent to which it affected the population; in the demeanor of the emigrants, their stolid frenzy, quiet stubbornness, and persistence in the face of obstacles avoided by normal men, the last westward march across the continent presented in some aspects the appearance of an action due to hypnotic influence. Nor was this phase of the phenomenon confined to the actions of those who made the journey. There was not a community, however small, which did not contribute to the multitude of departing adventurers, and it is very possible that every stay-at-home was united either by blood relationship or personal acquaintance to one or more of the west-bound army. Those who remained in the East were, as a consequence, affected by the movement to a degree no less intense—though in a different way—than the gold seekers themselves, and displayed their relation to it through an attitude equally pronounced. All eastern thought and action were for a time ruled by the new situation in the West, and a number of years elapsed before the public slowly returned to a normal attitude in harmony with altered conditions.

The efforts of the men and women who took part in the final rush to the Pacific coast, and their experiences while on the way, constitute a drama in keeping with the theater that witnessed it. If the stage designed for the spectacle was vast and elemental, so were the human emotions there exhibited. If the scenery amid which the theme progressed was at once gloomy, tremendous, inspiring, beautiful and foreboding, so also were the man-qualities of the countless figures in the tragedy. For it was a tragedy, as all acts of the multitude always are when born in the frenzy of inflexible determination.

THE BROADWAY, ST. LOUIS.

374.—Scene in St. Louis during the migrations to California. Hundreds of canvas-covered wagons passed through the city every day. Some of them halted for a time, while their owners bought necessary provisions and equipment.

A HISTORY OF TRAVEL IN AMERICA

It so happens that the strangest events in the record of migrations from the Mississippi valley to California took place in 1846 and 1847, at the very outset of the movement and more than a year before gold was discovered. Those circumstances were embodied in the fate which overtook a wagon train of a hundred emigrants and resulted in the loss of forty-two of its members after trials seldom parallelled in the record of heroism and privation. The party was organized by George and Jacob Donner in Sangamon county, Illinois, and started from Springfield in April of 1846. It contained men, women and children from Ohio, Missouri, Iowa, Illinois and Tennessee.

But before turning to another phase of overland travel in a story of the Donner party's adventures it is desirable to summarize the conditions existing in California during the year of their occurrence.

In the spring of 1846 the population of California, exclusive of Indians, was about ten thousand, of whom some eight thousand were native Mexicans and the other two thousand foreigners, in part from the United States and lately arrived. Lieutenant-Colonel Frémont, of the United States Army Topographical Corps, was in the country at the head of a small exploring expedition. Frémont was at first received by the Mexican commander[1] of the territory in a friendly manner, but either because of the probability of war between the two countries or alarm over the number, character and demeanor of immigrants from the United States, the Mexican general suddenly changed his attitude and tried to expel all Americans from his military jurisdiction.

The undesired settlers united to resist expulsion, took

General Castro.

1276

Starvation Camp.—Stumps cut by the Donner Lake Party, 1846. For full description see page 160.
(From photograph by Thos. Houseworth & Co., San Francisco.)

375.—Scene of the tragedy at Donner Lake in 1846-1847. The Donner party, while on the trip across the continent by wagon train, was trapped in the mountains by the winter storms. Hastily built cabins were soon covered by snow to the depth of 15 or 20 feet. When the men ascended from the buried huts to get firewood, and plied their axes at the lowest visible parts of the tree trunks, they left stumps as here indicated by a photograph taken in later years. Forty-two of the ninety died after weeks of starvation, and, in some cases, the eating of flesh from those who succumbed. The others were saved by relief expeditions sent from California.

forcible possession of the town of Sonoma, organized a convention there, and named William B. Ide as their leader. Ide, on June 18, issued a proclamation calling on the immigrants from the United States to rise and proclaim their own sovereignty. On July 4, 1846, the Americans issued a so-called declaration of independence at Sonoma, elected Frémont as Governor of the country, and unfurled a banner known as the Bear Flag.[1] Commodore Sloat, of the American navy, hoisted the United States national ensign over Monterey at about the same time, and immediately thereafter the settlers from the

[1] It was a white banner with a red border and a grizzly bear in the center of the field.

East, together with Frémont and his men, offered their services to Commodore Stockton—who had succeeded Sloat—and the irregular and independent proceedings of Sonoma were submerged in the more formal warfare with Mexico which followed. From that time California remained in control of American forces, and eventually passed under the political sway of the United States.[1]

While these events—unknown to the people of the East—were transpiring on the Pacific coast, the small drift to California was already beginning, and the decidedly larger and more important exodus to the Oregon country was in full swing.

The Donner party followed in the wake of the Oregon caravan of 1846, and some weeks behind it. Independence, Missouri, was reached in May, and the Donners were there joined by a few individual emigrants such as always attached their vehicles to a large expedition for the sake of more safety. From that town the jump-off or real overland journey began, and when the party finally left Independence for California its two hundred wagons and thousand head of live stock stretched in a line two miles long over the prairie. Each canvas-covered prairie schooner was drawn, according to its size and load, by two, three or four pairs of oxen, yoked two abreast in the usual way, or by mules.

Nothing that threatened disaster or differed radically from the experiences of numerous similar groups of emigrants took place during the first three months. There

---

[1] For an account of the first days of American control in California, together with a history of the Bear Flag Party, see:

"Biographical Sketch of the Life of William B. Ide," by Simeon Ide; "Scraps of California History Never Before Published," by Simeon Ide; "A Sketch of the Life of Com. Robert F. Stockton"; "Message from the President of the United States Transmitting Information on the Subject of California and New Mexico" (being Executive document No. 17 of the 31st Congress, 1st session; Jan. 21, 1850); and Frémont's reports.

Simeon Ide's two little books (practically two editions of the same work) both contain William Ide's letter to Senator Wambaugh, giving his version of the Bear Flag campaign.

CROSSING THE PLAINS.

376.—A migratory family crossing the plains. Drawn by the English artist, Thomas Armstrong, in 1851. Armstrong was in California at the time, and his sketch was printed in the Sacramento *Placer Times and Transcript* for January 1, 1852.

were the usual quarrels between individuals, and Indians stole some cattle and caused occasional petty annoyance. Perhaps the most significant feature marking the first half of the journey was the development of a tendency on the part of the travellers to split into clannish groups. This resulted, to some extent, in a breakdown of that spirit of unity and common dependence so valuable to a little community engaged in a pilgrimage like theirs, isolated in an unknown wilderness and dependent on their own exertions for a successful termination of the enterprise. But though a day was to come when the instant coöperation of all the members of the party might possibly have saved it, yet the tendency mentioned—one quite natural in the assemblage of a group made up of families from different localities and common to most such expeditions—was not a cause of the final catastrophe.

Things went fairly well until the party reached the neighborhood just east of Great Salt Lake, where the broken nature of the mountain system and the presentation of alternative routes for farther progress resulted in a division of the caravan. The lake had to be passed by a détour either to the north or to the south. Thirteen members of the party took the northern line of march, by a trail leading from Fort Bridger northwest toward Fort Hall, and thence southwestward again. They reached their journey's end in California without serious trouble. The other eighty-seven, with whose fate we have now to deal, chose to move on by a supposedly practical route around the south shore of the lake. This was called "Hasting's Cut-off," and was reported to be shorter by three hundred miles than the northern path. For some days the party continued through the rough country and then fell into difficulties. Either they got off the trail

1280

ON EDGE BY CARTMAN

SUTTER'S FORT
1849

G. V. COOPER DEL.

377.—Conditions in California during the first years of the gold rush. Sutter's Fort. On Sutter's land, in 1848, gold was discovered by his associate, Marshall. From a sketch by the artist, G. V. Cooper.

—if, indeed, wagons had often passed that way before—
or else had been misinformed. At any rate they found
themselves in a position of exceeding difficulty. Sometimes they were compelled to lower their wagons bodily
over precipices by means of ropes, and at other times had
to use all the oxen of the caravan in pulling the prairie
schooners, one at a time, over bad places that stalled
them.

All this not only demanded extreme toil, but took up
much time and depleted the emigrants' stock of provisions. Twenty-eight days were consumed in moving
twenty-one miles. In those circumstances lay their danger. Every California-bound caravan shaped its speed
and plans to make certain the passage of the dreaded
Sierra Nevada Mountains before early winter set in on
that rugged and difficult range. The summer was now
almost gone, the Donner party was still far distant from
the Sierras, and its provender was dwindling fast. By
the end of October the snows would come on the mountains. Still the travellers pressed forward as best they
could, and sent one of their number ahead for help. On
October 19 he returned to the wagons again, accompanied
by two Indians and driving five mules loaded with provisions furnished by Captain Sutter, whose estate lay in
the Sacramento valley of California. From the 19th to
the 23d the party remained in camp near the present site
of Reno, Nevada, meanwhile sending two other men forward for additional food. Once more they resumed the
march, and in the high altitudes near Prosser creek,[1]
found six inches of snow. The weary animals attached
to the wagons were urged on and upward at all possible
speed, but it was too late. At the top of the mountains the

[1] About three miles from Trucker.

SACRAMENTO CITY

378.—Sacramento City as the town appeared in 1850.

marchers encountered from two to five feet of snow, and could go no farther. They were prisoners. The day was October 28.

Then was the time when agreement in council and common action in one supreme effort might have brought deliverance. The train had halted at Truckee Lake— called Donner Lake since the events here described—and was scattered over the neighborhood for several miles, each family or group living in or near its wagons. For several days the different sections of the caravan acted independently in various endeavors to proceed, but without success. Finally the uselessness of such isolated attempts was acknowledged, and all the emigrants were at last brought together for one determined struggle. Wagons were abandoned, since the folly of trying to move them through twenty or thirty miles of snow-covered mountains was obvious. A pack-train was formed, and in that shape the expedition started on its last march as an organized body. The effort failed. Men, women, children, oxen and mules floundered through the snow until the hopelessness of the action was plain,[1] and then gave it up and got back to the camps as best they could. On their return the people held a council in which it was decided to kill the animals, prepare their carcasses for food and try once more on foot.

This decision was never carried into effect. While they slept that night in their hastily built shelters a great snow came, and all knew what it meant. Most of the oxen and mules were covered up and never found. As soon as the downfall was ended some of the men cut poles and probed in the drifts for the buried animals, by which

[1] They got as far as the precipice where the tracks of the Central Pacific Railway now meet the wagon road.

C. V. COOPER DEL.

BROWN & SEVERIN LITH.

BETWEEN SACRAMENTO, AND THE MINES.

379.—Wagons and emigrants moving across the country from Sacramento to the gold-bearing streams. On arrival there they became miners. From a sketch by Cooper.

method a few of the frozen beasts were fortunately discovered. Other men set about the building of log cabins and the collection of wood for fuel. Storm followed storm; the little cabins were soon hidden from sight; and in a short time the emigrants were living beneath the snow. There was no outward sign of a human habitation in the dreary waste save an occasional hole, and icy steps that led downward.

On days when the weather permitted them to do so the men came up from below, chopped down trees, cut them into pieces and dropped them into the cabins for firewood. They could only hew off such parts of the trunks as projected above the snow. When the scene was visited in after days, and measurements taken, it was found that many of the stumps thus left standing were from fifteen to twenty-two feet high. Under a sky-avalanche of that depth the members of the slowly lessening band fought for existence. Sometimes they visited one another. The meat obtained from frozen animals found by probing in the drifts lasted about six weeks. After that the people boiled ox hides into a sort of paste and lived on it. Their drink was melted snow. When the ox hides were gone they boiled the bones. There were many children—some very young—in the party.

One of the emigrants kept a record of these and other things, and some of the circumstances he wrote down may be included in this narrative. Others may not be. Here are occasional entries from the diary of Patrick Breen:[1]

Dec. 17. Pleasant; William Murphy returned from the mountain party last evening; Baylis Williams died night before last; Milton and Noah started for Donner's eight days ago; not returned yet; think they are lost in the snow.

[1] His diary was published in full in the "Nashville Whig" of September 4, 1847.

Dec. 20. Clear and pleasant. Mrs. Reed here; no account from Milton yet. Charles Burger started for Donner's; turned back; unable to proceed; tough times, but not discouraged. Our hope is in God. Amen.

Dec. 21. Milton got back last night from Donner's camp. Sad news; Jacob Donner, Samuel Shoemaker, Rhinehart, and Smith are dead; the rest of them in a low situation; snowed all night, with a strong southwest wind.

Dec. 25. Began to snow yesterday, snowed all night, and snows yet rapidly; extremely difficult to find wood; uttered our prayers to God this Christmas morning; the prospect is appalling, but we trust in Him.

Jan. 1, 1847. . . . Dug up a hide from under the snow yesterday; have not commenced on it yet.

Jan. 15. Clear again to-day. Mrs. Murphy blind, Landrum not able to get wood; has but one axe between him and Keseberg. It looks like another storm. . . .

Jan. 17. Eliza Williams came here this morning; Landrum crazy last night; provisions scarce; hides our main subsistence. May the Almighty send us help.

Feb. 8. Fine, clear morning. Spitzer died last night, and we will bury him in the snow; Mrs. Eddy died on the night of the seventh.

Feb. 15. Morning cloudy until nine o'clock, then cleared off warm. Mrs. . . . refused to give Mrs. . . . any hides. Put Sutter's pack hides in her shanty, and would not let her have them.

Feb. 26. Hungry times in camp; . . . Mrs. Murphy said here yesterday that she thought she would commence on Milton and eat him. I do not think she has done so yet; it is distressing.

In the meantime, and on November 12, an unsuccessful effort to get over the mountains for help had been made by a small group of the emigrants. They got back to the camp alive. During the following month it was seen that all must perish if aid did not reach them. Many had already succumbed. So, in the middle of December, another party started out. It was composed of ten men and five women, and its members decided either to carry news of the situation to those who could bring relief, or else die in the endeavor. They knew there was no chance for them if their plan was not successful, and saw they might as well meet the end in one spot as another. Those who set out on December 16th to make their way through the mountains, over snow from ten to fifty feet deep, are known in western history as The Fifteen. Four miles were put behind them on the first day; six on the second; five on the third. The members of the Fifteen did not speak as they went forward. Some were made blind by the glare of the white wilderness, and these were led by the others. Such apology for food as the party had at starting was soon gone. It lasted for three days. At night they lay on the snow. The first to fall out of the group was a man who did not rise to his feet one morning when the others were ready to start. One of the women approached him and asked if he was coming. "Yes," he answered, "I am coming soon."

On the fourth day another of the men found in his clothing a fragment of frozen bear meat hidden there by his wife, wrapped in a scrap of paper on which were the words, "Your own dear Eleanor." She and her children at the camp were without food.

A storm began, and the little band sat down and waited. Somebody suggested that one of them die for the others, and they agreed. All drew lots—even the women. Patrick Dolan got the fatal slip, but the others could not decide who should kill him, so they rose up and staggered on. The snow turned to sleet. By great exertion they made fire, but it fell in and disappeared, and when they leaned over the hole through which it had fallen they heard, far below, the rush of a torrent. The storm became a tornado. At midnight the first one died —a man. Another, dying, pleaded with his wife, daughters and companions to eat him and thus save their own lives for the sake of those at the lake. Then he died. All lay down, covered themselves with their blankets, and

A MINER.

380.—At the mines. Realization of the hope that had sustained the pilgrims in
their marches. Sketch of a miner by the English artist, Armstrong, printed
by the *Placer Times and Transcript,* of Sacramento, on January 1, 1852.

were soon hidden by the falling snow. Dolan went crazy, escaped from shelter, was pursued, caught, fled again and again, was recaptured, and finally he died. Then morning came. It was Christmas Day. They had been away from the camp for nine days, without food for four days, and without fire for two and a half days. The matches were wet, but a woman took off one of her inner garments and by sparks from a flint they again got fire, roasted human flesh, ate it, and lived.

In this spot the party remained until December 29th. Those who survived divided into groups so that no family need eat its own dead. The heart of a boy was thrust through with a stick and broiled over the coals, and his sister beheld it. She endured it because she was fighting for her own life in order to save the lives of her own baby, mother, brothers and sisters back at the camp beside the lake. Unless she and the ones with her lived, those others and fifty more would die.

Accompanying the Fifteen, yet not included in its membership, were the two Indians who had come with the relief train from Sutter. They were the guides of the whites. No one else knew the country. The Indians would not eat. They went apart, built a fire of their own under a tree and sat there, not even watching. Finally the Fifteen—now become Eleven—ate their moccasins, and then the strings of their snow-shoes. Soon after this the Indians saw glances that made them fly in the darkness. For four days more the Eleven wandered, and then another died. His wife gave the body that the others might still keep up the fight.

On the morning of January 7, while stumbling ahead, the human skeletons found bloody tracks in the snow, and after a time came again upon the Indians. The two red men, still living but unable to move, were lying where they had last fallen. With their eyes they followed the halting progress of those who approached them. There were Seven in the group—two men and five women. Slowly the whites went past, and then, in turn, staggered and fell.

One of the two white men had with him a wife who had saved his life by cutting flesh from a dead man's body and feeding it to him. She, in turn, was starving. Lying near by was another woman whose husband he had killed by accident months before. Three other figures on the snow were women who had left children at the lake. The white man got up, and went back toward the dying Indians. The others heard two shots.

By and by the Seven went on once more, and in a few days they found other tracks—tracks that led to a little Indian camp. They had won the fight. So frightful was the appearance of the survivors that the Indian children fled in terror, and the squaws wailed. The Indians fed them with all the food they themselves possessed, which was bread made from pounded acorns. For seven days more the red natives guided the little group, and then, even in sight of the Sacramento valley, the emigrants fell down again. They could go no farther. So the Indians, themselves weak, lifted one white man and carried him over the last fifteen miles that he might tell his story, and got him to a ranch. Thirty-two days had elapsed since the start from Donner Lake, forty miles away. The other six emigrants were brought in, a courier crossed the flooded Bear River on two logs to take the news to Sutter's Fort, and the organization of a relief expedition was instantly begun.

1291

It is needless to recite some of the details at the camp during the march of the Fifteen. The glue made from hides gave out, and so did the bones of the animals. The children in one cabin cut up a piece of carpet, singed it in a fire and ate it. On Christmas Eve a few of the children got together in one of the buried cabins and told stories to one another of the Christmases of other days. They had a party, filling cups with snow that they sipped with spoons, pretending it was custard. They sang songs and played "hide-the-handkerchief."

One mother had saved a few beans and grains of rice, and had hid them, long before, for Christmas Day, together with a piece of bacon two inches square. Of these she made a thin soup, and when her children smelled the strange aroma they slowly rose, as in a dream, and crept toward the stove. Then their mother took the cover from the boiling pot and let them look. As a bean or grain of rice would pop up for an instant the children, watching, made inarticulate cries and clutched at one another.

At last those who still lived became too weak to chop down any more trees. Occasionally they climbed up from the huts to behold the daylight, and look about them. One evening—it was February 19, 1847—two women had thus ascended from one of the buried cabins. The daughter of one was dying. As they stood there they heard a distant shout—a sound that could not come from the lips of one who was starving. Others down below heard it also, for the cry carried far in the still air of the solitude, and soon there appeared at the tops of the tunnels a few faces over which the skin was very tightly drawn, and from which bright eyes peered strangely. Help had come at last. A small party, after tremendous effort, had reached the camp

A CALIFORNIA CABIN.

381.—Home of a party of California miners. But it is doubtful if firearms were
kept so far out of reach, unless the one attached to the roof
constituted a reserve.

from the Sacramento valley. When the rescuers were
asked if the Fifteen were safe, they lied.

Four expeditions in all were sent by the settlers already
in California to aid the wagon train trapped in the mountains, and by their help forty-five of the emigrants were
finally saved. Twenty-three started over the mountains
with the first relief party, which in turn was overwhelmed
by a storm and almost succumbed. Had it not been met
by the second expedition all its members, together with the
men, women and children in its care must have perished.
Some who went in charge of the first relief did die. Of
these one was a man too weak to keep on, and who was left
sitting beside a fire, smoking his pipe. He waved the

1293

others a good-by as they started on again without him.
He was a brave man, and more than that. For as he sat
there, alone, his near approach to the inevitable gave him
a strange, exalted power in his weakness, and he wrote a
few lines that were found, long afterward, beside his
frozen body. They read:

Ah, after many roving years
How sweet it is to come
Back to the dwelling place of youth,
Our first and dearest home;
To turn away our wearied eyes
From proud, ambitious towers
And wander in those summer fields,
The scene of boyhood's hours.

Ah, I am changed since last I gazed
Upon that tranquil scene,
And sat beneath the old witch-elm
That shades the village green,
And watched my boat upon the brook—
It was a regal galley—
And sighed not for a joy on earth
Beyond the happy valley.

So was a poet born, and lived for an hour, and died.

One Californian in the third relief, a man of herculean
strength[1] took charge of seven of the starved emigrants,
and often carried two of them on his back at once.

It has been seen that one of the leaders of the wagon
train—Jacob Donner—perished at the camp in December.
The fate of George Donner, and of George's wife, Tamsen,[2] remains to be told. As each rescue party reached the
buried cabins a choice had to be hastily made regarding
those who were to be carried out. In this way numerous
families were divided. Parents sent their children to
safety first, whenever possible. When the third group of

[1] John Stark. His father was a Virginia man who had made the trip through the
wilderness to Kentucky in Boone's time. The son inherited his father's spirit and
qualities.
[2] Tamsen Donner was a woman of exceptional qualities, abilities and education.

Californians had fought their way to the lake, about the middle of March, George Donner, as he himself knew, was slowly dying and could not be moved. The couple had two children. Donner told his wife to leave him and accompany them, since she also would face certain death if she remained. The hour came for the departure of the rescuers and those who were to go with them. Tamsen Donner took her children to the appointed spot. There she bade them good-by, turned, and started again toward the distant cabin where her husband lay. They watched her for a long time, but she never looked back. To do that was the one thing beyond her strength. Many days afterward, when the purpose for which she had remained had been fulfilled, Tamsen Donner started over the mountains,

382.—The Frémont Hotel in San Francisco. From a sketch by Frederick Kurz in 1851.

all alone and without any food. "I must see my children," she said. She went seven miles before lying down for the last time.

The story of the Donner party,[1] in its main details, shows but one aspect of an overland trip. It presents the extreme of hardship and suffering, both physical and mental. No other similar caravan, so far as known, had a like ordeal while trying to cross the western part of the country in the days when wagon trains were the reliance of the people during the long journey. That feature of its experience wherein it differs so woefully from all others —the eating of human flesh while in extremity—has given to the Donner expedition a separate place in the history of those days. The act in question has since been the basis of many discussions regarding the moral standard of the expedition's members. Every man can read the circumstances and decide the point for himself, though no man, by any exercise of the imagination, can put himself in the position of the Fifteen. Only one among those who were saved was ever looked upon with any aversion.[2] The Americans already in California—of all others best able to appreciate the facts—received the rescued emigrants with hospitality and delight, and did all for them that could be done.

These things happened in an attempt to cross America in 1846 and 1847. And yet, however freely we may concede to the white men and women a moral right to live under the conditions that surrounded them, by the only means they had, there persists a mental picture of the two

[1] For many years, and until quite recently, the history of this band of emigrants— and especially of certain phases of its suffering—have been distorted. A careful recital of the organization, adventures and fate of the expedition is available in "A History of the Donner Party," by C. F. McGlashan, Sacramento, 1877. McGlashan's work, based on statements of the remaining survivors, and on other authentic materials, tells the whole story. It is doubtless the most elaborate history of any individual overland expedition that has been prepared.

[2] And in that case perhaps unjustly. See McGlashan's "History."

Indian guides who went and sat under a tree. It is a strange circumstance that the white travellers who spanned the red man's continent at greater cost of suffering than any others, should have been guided at last by members of the vanquished race, and that they could only complete their journey through strength given to them by dead and living Indians.

CHAPTER LV

THE SUFFERING OF THE DONNER PARTY NOT TYPICAL OF
CARAVAN TRAVEL TO CALIFORNIA — THE ROAD BE-
COMES CROWDED — A LATER NARRATIVE, SHOWING
THE EXPERIENCES OF THE MARCHERS FROM 1849
ONWARD — DIARY OF JAMES ABBEY — HE AND HIS
COMPANIONS CROSS THE CONTINENT IN FOUR
MONTHS AND SIXTEEN DAYS — STAGE-COACHES AP-
PEAR — THEY START ONCE A MONTH FROM IN-
DEPENDENCE AND SALT LAKE CITY — ACTION OF
CONGRESS IN 1857 — ITS RESULT — THE OVERLAND
MAIL — FINAL CONDITIONS BEFORE THE COMING OF
THE RAILWAY

NO such tribulations as those experienced by the Donner party could befall an overland caravan in
1849 or afterward. By that time every practicable
path leading across the plains and over the mountains
was thronged with human beings, horses, mules, cattle
and wagons. The scenes along the way often resembled
those incident to a road in the neighborhood of a large
city. Sometimes hundreds of vehicles and thousands of
animals were in view at one time and the procession
of creaking wagons, foot-travellers and horsemen continued without interruption from dawn to nightfall. All
strove to press ahead as swiftly as possible, yet all, when
occasion required, were ready to lend aid to those
in any sort of trivial embarrassment or serious trouble.

There were innumerable circumstances wherein help was needed, and it was always forthcoming. In truth, those in the rear who gave their aid to others in an emergency were also frequently helping themselves, for if the mishap befell at a ferry, or in a gorge, or on a steep hill or mountain, those behind were likewise halted until the blockade was relieved.

Nor were any of the moving throng permitted to want for food or any other attention so long as provender and sympathy were within reach.

Those canvas-covered wagons, and the camps at night, were the scenes of births, christenings, marriages, sickness and deaths. Almost every aspect of pioneer life came again into view during the long journey, and every day was a day of toil.

Any present-day description of the scenes attending the long overland march which was made by hundreds of thousands[1] between 1849 and 1868, must necessarily fall short of the reality, nor should it be attempted. No man who had not himself passed through the experience could adequately tell it. Generalities are not enough to bring us face to face with the significant details of which it was composed, and without which no vivid and truthful picture of it can be obtained. So, just as we turned to the journal of William Calk for an invaluable story of the Wilderness Road to Kentucke, we have need again for a similar narrative which may bring to us a real understanding of the tribulations of the march to California. There are a number of such records, and among them there is one that perhaps stands forth preëminent for its value to these pages. It was written day by day, and

[1] In addition there were probably a million or more whose destinations and future homes lay at points east of the Rocky Mountains.

SAN FRANCISCO IN NOVEMBER, 1848.

SAN FRANCISCO IN NOVEMBER 1848.

383.—Two views of San Francisco. The topmost is engraved from a sketch
done by the artist, J. C. Ward, in November of 1848. The other is the
reproduction of a sketch made by Bayard Taylor a year afterward.

never suffered the later misfortune of being made into a pretentious book through the blighting process of re-writing. It was written in 1850, during the first surges of the human flood, when the road was choked with eager pilgrims. And finally, it was written by a buoyant, optimistic youth who gloated in work and who admitted he had found what he sought. Here begins the diary of James Abbey,[1] opulent in all those qualities for which, to-day, we often seek in vain. He departed from the town of New Albany, in Indiana, on April 3 of 1849, and left his jumping-off place on April 14th. Thence he proceeds:

April 14th.—After we had got all our cattle off the boat, and packed our goods in the wagon, we succeeded in getting over the river at St. Joseph last night, at 10 o'clock, in the Indian nation, where we camped on a dry sand bar.

April 18th.—The fatigues of a rainy night are over. I am seated again to note incidents as they pass. I endeavored to cook breakfast, but with wet wood and a horrid toothache I can assure you it is anything but a pleasant job. The boys are all seated round our camp-fire, patiently waiting for a hot cup of coffee. . . . Our camp consists of some 100 wagons. . . . After eating a hearty supper all hands volunteered and hauled up a big pile of logs for our camp-fire, around which all seated themselves to hear some music. Billy Reissinger was elected leader of the band. Our music consisted of cornet, ophicleide, trumpet, fiddle, guitar and a flute. They played "Home, Sweet Home" and "Life on the Ocean Wave."

April 21st.—Cold rainy day, with a hard wind. . . . I thought of home, my mother, sister and friends. Oh! how gloomy my thoughts ran.

April 26th. . . . All turned out by 4 o'clock and had breakfast, by five ready for a start. . . . We arrived at a small creek some eight miles from our morning's camp, when we found the banks steep and muddy, and where the ford had been filled up with brush to keep the cattle from sinking into the mud. . . . Duncan was the next to cross, so he drove into it and sunk into the mud up to his axles. There being about 80 wagons waiting to cross, all hands went to work to help

---

[1] "California. A Trip Across the Plains, in the Spring of 1850, Being a Daily Record of Incidents of the Trip Over the Plains, the Desert, and the Mountains, Sketches of the Country, Distances from Camp to Camp, etc., and containing Valuable Information to Emigrants, etc., etc." By James Abbey. New Albany, Ind.: 1850.

1301

out, some digging, some bringing saplings, some prying, etc., and, with the aid of eight extra yoke of cattle, finally fetched him out. After mending the road we all got over safe and sound. . . . Killed eight big rattlesnakes. . . . Made 20 miles to-day.

April 27th.—. . . At 8 o'clock we passed eight or ten graves of last year's emigrants. . . .

April 30th.—. . . The day is cold and the wind is blowing so hard that it is almost impossible to stand up, but the boys say we are bound for California and it will never do to stop for wind, so we toddled on. Travelled to-day 15 miles over a good road.

May 4th.—We met two mule teams from Fort Laramie, who report no grass this side of the Platte, and the emigrants ahead of us had set fire to all of last year's growth. . . . While grazing our stock at noon I counted 200 horse teams, 80 mule teams, and 60 ox teams pass by here.

May 9th.—. . . The road this morning is very good. A train of horse teams is passing us, a mile or more in length.

May 13th.—Eleven o'clock passed by Fort Kearney. . . . It is said that three thousand two hundred wagons had passed the fort before us, and three hundred more are now in the vicinity. We are now surrounded by several large trains in full view . . . cooked our supper with dry grass.

May 16th.—. . . We find many articles strewed along the road, such as log chains, ox yokes, horse collars, cooking stoves, etc., which the emigrants have been compelled to throw away to lighten their wagons. . . . compelled, for want of wood, to cook our suppers with buffalo chips. Made 17 miles to-day.

May 17th.—We had a meeting to organize our companies and to elect a captain. Mr. R. R. Stevens, of Louisville, was duly elected. It is a fine selection. . . . Our train consists of seven wagons.

May 18th.—We travelled some ten miles, came to a spring of pure cold water, which to a thirsty and weary traveller in this region nothing can be more luxurious, after travelling all day under the burning hot sun, with throats parched with heat and dust.

May 19th.—. . . We are still blessed with good health, mammoth appetites and getting on as finely as we could desire. . . . After breakfast I took a stroll some four miles from our camp. . . . I had rambled some distance from the roadside and came to a new-made grave. It was some poor fellow, and from appearances had not been made long. The wolves had been trying to dig it up. . . .

May 20th.—We started very early this morning, and before the sun had risen had left some 300 wagons behind us. . . . While at dinner to-day I went out and counted about 120 wagons in a quarter of a mile square; they were principally horse teams.

384.—By stage-coach to California. Each passenger was allowed 30 pounds of baggage besides his blankets and firearms. A hundred and eighty miles of the stage-coach trip was performed on muleback. Armed escort with every vehicle. Ticket, $200.

May 23rd.—Saw to-day large droves of buffaloes on the opposite side of the river. . . . Not a cloud to be seen in the heavens, nor a shrub or tree on the plains over which we have travelled to-day.

May 24th.—. . . We travelled some three hours when we arrived at the head of Ash Hollow. We descended into it down a steep precipice, some seventy-five feet, where our wagons had to be let down with ropes.

May 29th.—. . . Our oxen as well as ourselves suffer much from the effects of buffalo gnats, which are very numerous in this country.

May 31st.—I was put on guard last night, from 12 till 4, and had orders by our captain to turn all hands out by 2 o'clock to make an early start. By 3 o'clock we were on our way rejoicing, and before the sun had risen we had left some 80 teams in our rear. . . . Passed many wagons abandoned and destroyed. To-day's travel, 22 miles. . . . You must excuse all errors, as I write seated upon a bucket, with a board on my knees, a candle in a lantern, with the wind blowing and extremely cold.

June 4th.—Two months from home, sweet home, and all safe in camp, in fine health and spirits. . . . After partaking of a hearty breakfast we take our station in an ox train some three miles in length. . . . Still in view of the snow-capped peak of Laramie, which looks within five miles of you, but is in reality fifty. . . . Cooking our supper with sage brush.

June 6th.—. . . At 7 we stopped for breakfast on the banks of the Platte, about twenty-five miles from the upper ferry, where we learn there are nine hundred wagons waiting to cross.

June 7th.—. . . At 10 a.m. we reached the ferry and found about two hundred wagons ahead of us. . . . We waited till evening before it came to our turn. . . . There are three boats constantly running, which take nothing but the wagons, leaving the animals to swim the river. The fare for ferrying a wagon is four dollars.

June 8th.—. . . . The soil and water of the country through which we are now travelling are impregnated with alkali, salt and sulphur, rendering water dangerous and unfit for use. I saw to-day sixteen skeletons of cattle that had died last year from drinking this alkaline water, all within two steps of one another.

June 11th.—Troubled all last night with the jaw ache and this morning find my face swollen as big as a peck measure, but still able to do duty at breakfast. . . . It is astonishing how ox teams can travel. Their feet have been very sore, but travelling in the hot sand has greatly improved them.

June 12th.—We were up and on our way by 5 o'clock. . . . At 10 we arrived at the second crossing of the Sweet Water River, and, finding it too high to ford, we took our provisions out of our wagon and stretching a rope across the river we ferried our things across in

1304

a little less than no time. . . . After travelling about a mile up the bank of the river we came to another crossing, where we again had to ferry. Here we were compelled to carry all our things by hand a quarter of a mile over a cliff of rocks and through a pass barely large enough for one person to rub through. We took the running gears of our wagon all apart, and ferried them up the river on our bed [wagon bed] by means of a long rope stretching some distance up the river. . . . All of us pretty well tired out. . . . Travelled some five miles by moonlight to make up for lost time.

June 13th.—At 5 in the evening we came to the fifth crossing of Sweet Water, which we forded without difficulty, the water being up to our axles.

June 14th.—In a couple of hours we again struck the Sweet Water. . . . After having hitched up and travelling for about an hour we once more struck the Sweet Water, which seemed to haunt us as an evil genius. On leaving the river we travel over miserable, rough, rocky roads, very dangerous to wagons.

June 15th.—. . . We are now in about two miles of the summit of the dividing ridge between the waters of the Atlantic and Pacific oceans. It being a beautiful night, we concluded to go through the pass by moonlight.

June 17th.—Shoved out this morning at 5 o'clock, amid a violent snowstorm, travelled on till 10 o'clock, when we reached the forks of the two roads—the one to the right taking you to Sublete's Cutoff or Fort Hall, and that to the left to the Great Salt Lake. . . . We struck off on the Salt Lake road. From the appearance of the two roads, I should suppose that nine-tenths of the wagons had taken the Cutoff.

June 18th.—. . . The mirage has deceived us several times to-day. While worn with travel and thirsting for water, there might be seen, sometimes to the right, sometimes to the left, and then in front, representations of large rivers, lakes and streams of pure water; but as we would advance in the direction whence they would appear they would recede or fade away, leaving nothing to view but the barren desert.

June 21st.—The sun rose beautifully this morning, and we were off by 6 o'clock. An hour's journeying brought us to another tributary of Green River called Ham's fork, which we forded, the beds of our wagons having to be raised six inches on account of the depth of the water. We all got over safely, however.

June 22nd.—We travelled sixteen miles to-day under a broiling sun and over a dusty road without finding a drop of water for our cattle. . . .

June 23rd.—. . . For six hours we travelled over rough, rocky roads, and through narrow passes in the mountains, extremely dangerous for wagons.

June 24th.—. . . We reached Bear River and struck the ford

but finding the water too deep and rising fast we unpacked our wagons and ferried with the beds. . . . The water is clear and cold, and foaming and dashing over a bed of rough rocks, which makes it dangerous to the cattle in crossing. . . . The country through which we had been travelling the twenty-four hours before reaching Bear River presented a most woe-begone appearance. . . . To-day we only made 12 miles.

June 25th.—. . . Many persons are passing us on pack mules and horses. I have also seen a great number on foot with their packs on their backs. But in my opinion ox teams are the best. . . . Richey & Co.'s wagon upset and spilt out their "plunder," but doing no other damage.

June 26th.—. . . 3 o'clock brought us to the summit of a high ridge, the ascent to which is most beautiful. As we leave this summit the tug of war commences. We travel down sides of mountains which present the most gloomy aspect upon which a human being ever gazed. The road is an awful one, and many of the boys think we are in full view of the elephant [meaning the climax of difficulty]. Here the pass is so narrow and deep that the rays of the sun never penetrate to the bottom. The scene is one of grandeur, but, at the same time, one of solemnity and loneliness.

June 27th.—We have travelled six hours this forenoon over a road still more rugged than that of yesterday, and are still in a deep, narrow pass of the mountains. . . . This creek we are compelled to cross thirteen different times. The road here is difficult almost beyond conception . . . we encamped for the night in a deep ravine . . . the road being so thickly covered with dust that you cannot see the forward cattle more than half the time.

June 28th.—. . . We travelled six hours down a narrow ravine which leads to the valley of the Salt Lake over the most miserable road ever travelled by civilized man.

June 29th.—Left camp at 6 o'clock, and in an hour reached the Great City of the Salt Lake. . . . The houses of the city are principally built of logs. Some few, however, which serve as the dwellings of the aristocracy are built of sun-dried brick, covered with mud, and one story high. . . . Butter here is worth 75 cents pound; milk, 50 cents gallon; meat, 75 cents pound. A wagon such as can be purchased at home for $120 is here worth five hundred, and other articles in proportion.

June 30th.—It has been truly said that man was made to mourn, but still there are some bright spots in the pathway of human life. This morning, from some cause, I hardly know what, I felt happier than usual. . . . Whether it was such a feeling as this, or one of thankfulness that we had got thus far on our journey safely after so many hardships and difficulties, I know not, but certain it is my spirits were much

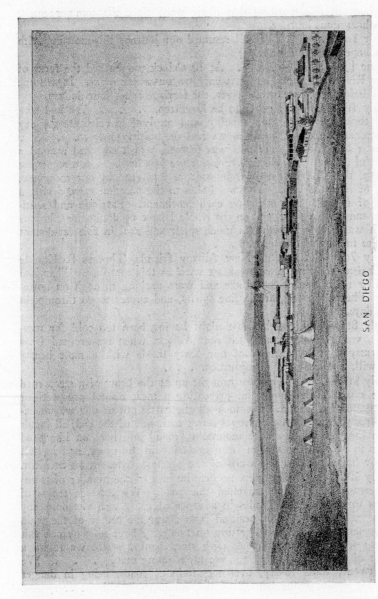

SAN DIEGO

385.—San Diego in 1849. Then an unimportant military post. In 1856 it had become the western terminus of the stage company whose advertisement is shown in the foregoing. Passengers for San Francisco continued northward from San Diego by boat.

more buoyant this morning than their wont since the commencement of this hazardous journey.

July 1st.—. . . We all resumed our journey this morning with bright hopes for the future.

June [July] 2nd.—. . . At 10 o'clock we reached the ferry of Weber River, and found about twenty wagons ahead of us. It was one o'clock before we got over the river, the ferriage being four dollars.

July 4th.—The day never to be forgotten. . . . We had consulted together the previous evening, and resolved to celebrate the day as customary at home, so far as we had the ability to do so. . . . At about 8 o'clock a procession was formed, which marched around a delightful grove of box elder, where a salute was fired. Upon returning to camp, the Declaration of Independence was read by our messmate, Frost, of Ky. . . . Toasts suitable to the occasion were drank, a salute of firearms accompanying each sentiment. Patriotic and sentimental songs were sung, and on the whole I have no doubt the Glorious Fourth was celebrated with as much spirit and zeal in this far-distant valley as in our own state. . . .

July 7th.—. . . Our New Albany friends, Thomas S. Kunkle and Christopher Fox, took breakfast with us this morning. They had left their teams at the Salt Lake and were packing through on horseback. They look well, are in fine spirits, and expect to go through in thirty days.

July 8th.—The weather last night having been too cold for mosquitoes, we all slept soundly till four o'clock, when we aroused from our grassy couches, partook of our hasty meals with a most hearty good will, and resumed our journey. . . .

July 9th.—. . . We were brought up at the brow of a steep road on the spurs of the mountain, presenting a most dismal prospect for the passage of a wagon. We took all the cattle out of our wagon except three yoke, and, putting ropes across each side of the bed, all hands got on the upper side of the mountain [road] and held on like good fellows to prevent the wagon from upsetting in the creek, and in half an hour had all scaled the walls of the precipice without an accident.

July 10th.—. . . I can fix no definite idea of the number of teams and persons which have travelled this road. We can see trains of wagons for a number of miles in advance of us. . . . We have any amount of company. Our position is in about the center of the train of emigrants, all apparently getting on finely. About nine o'clock this morning we arrived at a creek with steep banks, where we found a number of emigrants digging a grave for a young man. . . . We made twenty miles to-day, over mountainous roads, being in danger of sliding down to the bottom of the innumerable hills at every step of our progress.

July 11th.—. . . In the course of the day we passed seven dead

CHURCH MOUNTAIN VALLEY,
NEAR FORT CHADBOURNE,
Texas.

386.—Travelling through Texas by pack-train. One of the overland stage-coach companies, which carried its passengers eastward by way of the southern route through Texas, sold tickets on the understanding that its patrons would be compelled to ride on muleback for 180 miles.

horses, four mules, and three oxen, a fact which speaks plainly enough of the nature of the country through which we are passing.

July 12th.—I was aroused at two o'clock this morning to prepare breakfast. . . . The dust is so deep as to cover our boot-tops, and rises in such clouds as to prevent the driver from seeing his teams. At six o'clock we encamped for the night on the banks of a sloughy creek; here we found tolerable water after skimming the surface of frog slime to the depth of three inches.

July 13th.—The morning was disagreeably cold, the water in our buckets having frozen during the night to the thickness of a dime. . . . This has been the most fatiguing morning's march we have yet experienced. The road dusty and the sun pouring down upon us with such intense heat as to cause the perspiration to roll off my face in large drops. This contrast in the night and day—the one with the temperature of the frigid and the other of the torrid zone, and being exposed to both with scarcely any protection—makes it very trying on the constitution.

July 14.—. . . The mountains on our left are still covered with snow. We passed the grave of a poor fellow by the name of Robinson, from Rushville, Ill., who had just died of bilious fever. We also encountered on the way twenty dead horses, four mules and two oxen. To-day we made twenty miles.

July 16th.—. . . Used the last of our stock of sugar at breakfast. . . . Since travelling through this valley I have counted more than a hundred corpses of horses and mules which have mired and died in these swamps. Numerous Indians were seen prowling about to-day for the purpose of stealing. A train of horse and mule teams in advance of us had twelve horses and ten mules stolen from them in one night. The Indians caught the man who was on guard, gagged him, stripped him stark naked, and wounded him in several places with arrows. Another poor fellow, on a previous night, was shot in the back of the head, and died in less than twenty-four hours. . . . We have to keep strict guard at night. Twenty miles more of our long journey has been accomplished to-day.

July 17th.—Last night we put our shooting irons in good order for the Indians if they should feel disposed to trouble us. Before retiring to rest we fired a grand salute to show the redskins that we were about in case of necessity. . . .

July 18th.—The morning was clear and very cold, our blankets being covered with frost. . . . Pushed on through the cañon and over one of the roughest roads we have traveled since leaving home. . . .

July 19th.—. . . For the past few days grass has been very thin, and my opinion is that in less than two weeks from the present time it will be dried up. In which case, what will be the fate of the large crowd behind us?

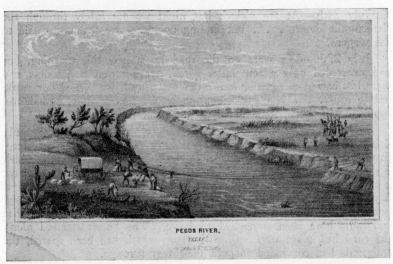

PECOS RIVER,
TEXAS.

387.—A Texas ferry. Ropes were used, as on many of the Oregon trail ferries. The hardest part of such work, especially in crossing a stream like the Pecos, lay in pulling the wagon up the steep bank.

July 21st.—. . . This is an awful looking place; no grass; nothing growing but wild sage and a few small patches of prickly pear. Distance to-day eighteen miles over a sandy plain.

July 22nd.—. . . Travelled twelve miles after night and found water but no grass. This is a gloomy looking place. We hope to be through in twenty days more. Made to-day eighteen miles.

July 24th.—. . . The prospect before us begins to look brown. No grass this side of the Sink, and what may be left by the emigrants in advance of us is parched up by the sun; so we are fearful that we shall not get our teams through. We have no fears for ourselves, as we are within 250 miles of the Gold Region, and could make that on foot; still we are in hopes of not being driven to that necessity. . . . The road has been awful—ascending and descending high sand bluffs, sinking in some places two feet deep. . . . Distance sixteen miles.

July 23rd.—. . . The boys complain that they are nearly worn out, having been compelled to swim the river last night to cut grass for the cattle, and then having to carry it on their backs for three-quarters of a mile through swamps and water up to their waists. But we are blessed with good health, are no ways dispirited, and the best of feeling prevails between all the members of our mess. . . . In the course of the afternoon we counted twenty dead cattle, forty horses, and sixteen mules; also some fifty wagons that had been destroyed or burnt by emigrants intending to pack through.

July 24th.—At ten o'clock last night we got safely through the sixteen-mile desert . . . but finding no grass, we tied our cattle to the wagons.

July 27th.—We were on the road by sunrise this morning, but had proceeded only a few miles when, hearing that a grassless and waterless barren of some sixteen miles was ahead, we turned our cattle out to graze. . . . There is said to be a large meadow, abundantly supplied with grass, some twenty miles in advance of us.

July 29th.—. . . We filled our kegs with water, being the only drinkable water we shall get till we have crossed a desert of sixty-five miles in advance. At one o'clock we reached the meadow of which I spoke . . . having traveled thirty-six miles without coming across a spear of grass. . . . We have concluded to remain here for several days. . . . In our day's travel I have counted near a hundred dead horses, thirty mules, and sixty oxen; also about twenty wagons that emigrants have been compelled to leave. The horses strewed along the road had given out, and, with those which had been spared, the emigrants had concluded to pack their way through.

July 30th.—All busy to-day making hay, and have now some six hundred pounds lying by our wagon, intended for use while crossing the desert. Had we not had the good fortune of coming across this grass our cattle would have been in poor plight for travelling. The labor of cutting it, however, is very great, and we have, besides, to carry it one mile on our backs and to wade through water three feet deep.

August 1st.—. . . The commencement of the sixty-five-mile desert. A drive of three hours brought us to another slough, where we took in our supply of water, and found two hundred wagons doing the same. Here we rested our cattle till the cool of the evening, when we took our place in a train about five miles in length. We soon struck a heavy, sandy road, and in the space of one mile I counted forty-six wagons that had been deserted, the horses not being able to drag them through. At one o'clock in the morning we brought to and halted till daylight.

August 2nd.—Started out by four o'clock this morning; at six stopped to cook our breakfast and lighten our wagons by throwing away the heavier portion of our clothing and such other articles as we can best spare. We pushed on to-day with as much speed as possible, determined, if possible, to get through the desert, but our cattle gave such evident signs of exhaustion that we were compelled to stop. Being completely out of water, myself, Rowley, and Woodfill bought two gallons from a trader (who had brought it along on speculation), for which we paid the very reasonable price of one dollar per gallon. The desert through which we are passing is strewed with dead cattle, mules, and horses. I counted in a distance of fifteen miles 350 dead

Overland California Stage Coach.

388.—A small, light, overland stage-wagon with a capacity for seven passengers, such as was used by some lines before 1858. Several companies engaged in the business, with varying degrees of success or failure, between 1851 and the completion of the first transcontinental railroad. The first route, extending through Salt Lake City, was found to be too far north. On two or three occasions a coach on that road was halted by snow in the autumn and detained until the following year before it could complete its trip.

horses, 280 oxen, and 120 mules;[1] and hundreds of others are left behind, being unable to keep up. Such is travelling through the desert. . . . A tan-yard or slaughterhouse is a flower garden in comparison. A train from Missouri have, to-day, shot twenty oxen. Vast amounts of valuable property have been abandoned and thrown away in this desert—leather trunks, clothing, wagons, etc., to the value of at least a hundred thousand dollars, in about twenty miles. I have counted in the last ten miles 362 wagons, which in the States cost about $120 each. The cause of so many wagons being abandoned is to endeavor to save the animals and reach the end of the journey as soon as possible by packing through; the loss of personal goods is a matter of small importance comparatively.

August 3rd.—We are now encamped in the desert, and a sweet place it is, too. . . . Our companion, Smith, returned from the river at one o'clock with five gallons of water—a most acceptable present.

August 4th.—. . . We remained in camp till six o'clock, P. M., when, having procured a light wagon,[2] we pushed out.

August 5th.—. . . Here we met several traders from Sacramento City, who had been out twelve days with provisions to sell to the

[1] An average of a dead animal for every 106 feet of the road.
[2] No doubt selected from the large stock displayed along the road.

emigrants. Flour is held at $1.50 per pound; sugar, $1.25 per pound; bacon-sides, $1.00 per pound, etc., etc.

August 6th.—This morning four of our companions started on ahead of the teams to pick out a suitable place at the mines for working. To-day we crossed a desert fourteen miles wide.

August 8th.—. . . We have now crossed the last desert. . . . Our only dread now is the Sierra Nevada Mountains. This night we encamped with some 200 wagons on Carson River, much worn down by night travelling.

August 9th.—. . . Ascended a mountain over a rough, rocky road. The snow-capped mountains are in view in every direction, and some of the boys say there is no way of escaping them, but I guess there is a way.

August 10th.—. . . Myself, Genung, and Woodfill remained be-hind with one of our oxen, which was sick. We watched the faithful animal and ministered to him all the remedies in our possession, but he died. It seemed like parting with an old friend. He had shared with us all the vicissitudes of this toilsome journey. . . . The loftiest mountains we have yet seen are now in full view; we suppose them to be the Sierra Nevada. . . . In the afternoon we came to a place called the Mormon Station, a perfect skinning post for emigrants. They have provisions of all kinds: Flour, $1.50 per pound; sugar, $1.75; bacon, $1.75.

August 11th.—. . . . The road which we are travelling defies all description. Of all the rough roads I have ever seen or even imagined, this beats them. Rocks from the size of a flour barrel to that of a meeting-house are strewed all along the road, and these we are com-pelled to clamber and squeeze our way through as best we can. The boys say they never saw a road a hundredth part as bad as this. . . . The mountains close in upon us on every side, and raise their lofty peaks high toward Heaven, which are covered with snow, glistening strangely in the sun.

August 12th.—Our cattle this morning look rough and fagged down by yesterday's jaunt. . . . We hitched seven yoke of oxen to our wagon. . . . This summit is covered with snow to the depth of eight feet, and the air is very cold. . . . Distance to-day twelve miles, over awful roads.

August 13th.—On consultation last night it was determined to throw one of our wagons away and double team. . . . Commenced ascending the second summit of the mountain; travelled about half a mile, in which distance we had gone up about a hundred feet, when the cattle gave out and refused to stir an inch. This was a pretty predicament; a number of teams were below, waiting for us to go ahead before they could move. Everything was thrown into confusion. Some were for packing the oxen; some for making a cart; some for

OVERLAND MAIL COMPANY,
VIA LOS ANGELES.

TIME OF DEPARTURE CHANGED

On and after the first day of December, 1858, the Coaches of THE OVER-
LAND MAIL COMPANY will leave the 'Office,

CORNER of WASHINGTON and KEARNY STS.

(PLAZA,) as follows:

THROUGH MAIL,

MONDAY AND FRIDAY, at 12 o'clock, M.

Fort Yuma and Intermediate Stations,

MONDAY, WEDNESDAY AND FRIDAY, '

At 12 o'clock, MERIDIAN, instead of 12 o'clock, Midnight, as heretofore.

FARE—FROM SAN FRANCISCO TO FORT SMITH, ARKAN-
SAS, OR TO TERMINUS OF THE PACIFIC RAILROAD,

☞ ONE HUNDRED DOLLARS! ☜

LOUIS McLANE, Agent Overland Mail Co.

389.—The Overland Mail. Most important stage-coach line to California. Its
vehicles ran twice a week in each direction and carried passengers between Arkansas and San Francisco for $100. Date, 1858. The line con-
tinued in operation for ten years more, until the advancing railway supplanted it.

one thing and some for another. It was finally concluded to pack
our oxen with what little provisions and clothing we had and throw
the wagon away. We went to work arranging things for packing;
at twelve o'clock, having everything ready, rolled out. . . . We had
travelled about an hour when our oxen became much wearied and badly
frightened; one young fellow that had our cooking utensils aboard,
such as dishes, knives and forks, cups, tin-pans, etc., etc., ran off down
the mountain with his pack hanging to him, throwing everything helter-
skelter in every direction. We finally overhauled him and gathered
up what scattered fragments we could find, changing his pack to an
older and more docile animal. At every tree we would pass, however,
the packs of some of the cattle would be dropping off; such was our
first experiment in "packing." About sunset . . . we stopped for
the night, having made six miles; tall travelling, that.

August 14th.—. . . About eight miles distant from our last encampment, over rough, rocky roads, and through banks of snow fourteen feet deep. . . .

August 15th.—. . . We recommenced our descent of the mountain, which in many places was very difficult. . . . Beautiful flowers, myrtles, etc., are frequently to be seen, exhibiting all the freshness of May. . . . We are now fifty miles from the gold diggings. . . . Distance to-day fifteen miles.

August 16th.—It appears to me that the miles in the mountains are twice as long as those in the valley. . . . Made twelve miles.

August 17th.—Last night was quite cold, and all the cover we had saved when our cattle refused to further pull our wagon, was not sufficient to keep us warm. . . .

August 18th.—. . . Drove on till about ten o'clock, when our cattle appeared so nearly exhausted that we stopped and cut down the limbs of some oak trees to feed them. For ourselves we had cherries, plums, raspberries, gooseberries, and filberts, which the boys gathered while in camp here. . . .

August 19th.—This morning we started at six o'clock, and in two hours struck the gold valley. . . . Travelled till ten o'clock, and, finding some grass and water in the valley, we unyoked our cattle and let them graze, while I prepared something for ourselves to eat; of which we were in great need. Here we cooked the last provisions we had on the route. We have been greatly blessed and favored by a kind Providence throughout this long and toilsome journey. Many have fallen by accident and disease, while we have been permitted to progress thus far smoothly and quietly, in fine spirits, and enjoying good health. At six o'clock we arrived in the city of Weaversville. . . . Its population is about one thousand; the dwellings are principally log cabins and shanties. Found the boys who had preceded us [the four who had started ahead on August 6th] all well, but in low spirits—provisions high, gold scarce, etc.

August 20th.—This forenoon was occupied in deliberation, and it was concluded to have a division of the mess; consequently we had an auction of a portion of our goods. I bought a sharp-pointed shovel for $13.00 and a pick for $4.50. The mess was then dissolved in "Friendship, Love, and Truth."

August 23rd.—. . . The most I have made in one day in digging here is four dollars,[1] and I have done some tall digging.

August 24th.—Our hole having given out, we rambled about for miles in search of a location, but every spot of ground appeared to be dug up or was occupied by miners.

August 26th.—. . . We washed out about fifty buckets of dirt, and got about a half ounce of gold, wet feet, and aching bones.

---

[1] The current market value of four soft-boiled eggs, or a gallon of molasses, or a seidlitz powder. Sugar was only 50 cents a pound in Weaversville, however, and bacon 75 cents a pound. Flour was cheap: 20 cents a pound.

August 27th.—Our hole having again given out, we prospected about several hours, and at length found a place which bid fair to yield tolerably well. So we set to work, and labored as hard as any poor fellow ever did, carrying our dirt about four hundred yards, over rocks, to the creek. It did not yield as well as we expected, and to our surprise soon gave out. Got half an ounce.

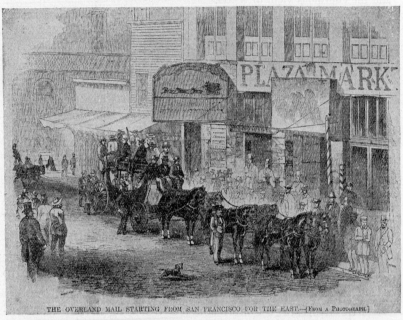

THE OVERLAND MAIL STARTING FROM SAN FRANCISCO FOR THE EAST.—[FROM A PHOTOGRAPH]

390.—A coach of the line advertised in the preceding illustration, as it appeared when about to leave San Francisco. Concord type of vehicle. Date, 1858.

August 28th.—. . . Moved our camp five miles further down the creek. . . . Worked till the sun got so hot that we were compelled to take to our tent.

August 29th.—The hard work yesterday caused me to pass a restless night. . . . By eight o'clock got down to a sufficient depth for washing; so we each shouldered a bag of dirt and started for the creek; and if carrying great bags of earth on one's back all day, in the hot sun and over rocks and deep ledges, is not hard work, then I am no judge of what hard work is.

August 30th.—. . . Our day's labor yielded about nine dollars.

August 31st.—. . . The proceeds of our day's labors amounted to nine dollars and some cents.

1317

September 1st.—Rowley is discouraged and thinks mining a poor business. My thoughts to-day [it was a Sunday] are more than a thousand miles distant—they are of home, mother, sister, and friends. . . .

September 2nd.—The result of my labor to-day is six dollars.

September 3rd.—The day's labor resulted in wet feet, aching bones, and the enormous yield of $5.60.

September 4th.—Passed the day in throwing up dirt in the ravine.

September 5th.—. . . $6.10.

September 6th.—. . . $5.70.

September 7th.—. . . Made some three dollars.

September 8th.—Spent the day in writing letters home. . . . Myself and Rowley go up to Sacramento City to-morrow to see if we cannot muster a letter or newspaper, neither of which we have seen for six months past.

Abbey's trip was a typical example of the overland journey as such an expedition was seen by a majority of the emigrants during the early years of wagon train progress to the Pacific. The western movement had already become so large, when he made the march just described, that stage-coach travel from western Missouri to Salt Lake City had already been established, and similar facilities between Salt Lake City and Sacramento came into existence soon afterward.

The first stage-coach service was begun between Independence and Salt Lake City in the summer of 1850, and was made possible by the action of the government in awarding a contract for the carriage of the mail between those places. A coach left Independence every month—except in winter—and at first traversed the twelve hundred miles in two or three weeks. Later, when stage stations and relays of live stock had been established along the road, the time consumed by the trip was materially reduced and a schedule of arriving and departing vehicles was established. The service between Salt Lake and Sacramento also consisted of a monthly coach, but its progress was very erratic. There was little use made of the transcontinental stages by the public during the first years of their precarious and irregular existence, but in 1857 Congress passed a bill authorizing the establishment of an overland California mail line, and as a result of that action there came into being the Overland Mail, whose Concord coaches moved between St. Louis and San Francisco on a roundabout route more than 2,700 miles long, in the short space of twenty-five days.

This enterprise, which was annually paid several hundred thousand dollars by the government for the transportation of letters, at once became a popular line of transcontinental travel and continued to hold that position until the completion of the first railway to the Pacific coast. At the hey-day of its career and prosperity the Overland Mail required for its use about a hundred coaches, seven or eight hundred drivers and other employees, and fifteen hundred horses and mules. The cost of a journey from the Mississippi to the Pacific in one of its vehicles was one hundred dollars.

After the establishment of the Overland Mail, and several other stage lines, no advance in methods of progress through the West was possible until the arrival of the iron rails.

CHAPTER LVI

THE IDEA OF A RAILROAD TO THE PACIFIC — ONE FINAL TASK NECESSARY IN THE LONG STRUGGLE FOR CONTINENTAL CONQUEST — BIRTH OF THE SCHEME — ITS EARLY ADVOCATES — PARKER'S WORDS — ASA WHITNEY APPEARS — HIS PROPOSAL AND THE WIDESPREAD SUPPORT IT RECEIVED — THE IDEAS OF CONGRESS — WHY WHITNEY'S PLAN COULD NOT SUCCEED — ITS RELATION TO THE OREGON MIGRATIONS — EFFECT OF THE EVENTS OF 1848 — THE RAILWAY CONVENTIONS — A CONTEST FOR ADVANTAGE — EASTERN JEALOUSIES DELAY THE PROJECT FOR A DOZEN YEARS

ONE last undertaking was still required in the long task of continental conquest after the establishment of stage-coach travel to California, and it consisted in building a still farther westward extension of the existing railway system that should supplant the primitive methods by which the Pacific coast was then reached from the Mississippi valley.

Perhaps the first clear and definite printed proposal for the construction of a railway that should connect the interior valley with the Pacific Ocean was made almost at the outset of America's railroad history. In a weekly newspaper called the *Emigrant,* published in the little town of Ann Arbor, in the territory of Michigan, on

February 6 of 1832, appeared an article from which the following is an extract:

"The distance between New York and the Oregon is about three thousand miles,—from New York we could pursue the most convenient route to the vicinity of Lake Erie, thence along the south shore of this lake and of Lake Michigan, cross the Mississippi between forty-one and forty-two of north latitude, cross the Missouri about the mouth of the Platte, and thence on by the most convenient route to the Rocky Mountains, near the source of the last named river, thence to the Oregon, by the valley of the south branch of that stream, called the southern branch of Lewis' River. We hope the United States will not object to conducting this national project. . . . But if the United States would not do this . . . Congress would not, we presume, object to the organization of a company and a grant of three millions of acres for this purpose."[1]

It will be noticed that this early proposal for a transcontinental iron road was published contemporaneously with the first outbreak of the railway fever in Michigan Territory, during the same year in which the territorial legislative council granted its first charter for a railroad designed to extend east and west through southern Michigan. Possibly the unknown author of the printed proposal found his inspiration in the local project then under consideration, which seems to have been included as a part of his much more ambitious vision.

The article in the Michigan newspaper attracted some attention in the East, and soon after its appearance a Massachusetts paper[2] published a letter written by Doctor Samuel Bancroft Barlow of the town of Granville, Massachusetts, in which he said: "An able writer in the *Emigrant* . . . in a series of numbers of which it has fallen to my lot to see only the first, is endeavoring to draw the attention of the public to the scheme of uniting New York

---

[1] The quotation from the "Emigrant," as here given, is taken from Davis's history, "The Union Pacific Railway," pp. 13-14. The original copy of the "Emigrant," in which Davis found the article, is contained in the collections of the Washtenaw County Pioneer Association, at Ann Arbor, Michigan.
[2] The "Intelligencer," of Westfield.

and the mouth of the Columbia River by railroad."
Barlow's article then went on to say: "I have a method
to propose by which this work can be accomplished by our
general government at the expense of the Union. . . . Let
preliminary measures be taken for three years to come,
such as making examinations, surveys, lines, estimates,
etc., etc., at the end of which time, the public debt being
paid, the national treasury overflowing (I presume also
that the present duties and taxes, indeed every source of
revenue, be continued at their present rates), then let the
work proceed with all possible and prudent speed and
vigor to a speedy and perfect completion, and let six,
eight, ten, twelve or fifteen millions of dollars of the
public money be appropriated to defray the expense annually until it is finished."[1]

The next mention of the scheme[2] was that made by
Samuel Parker, whose transcontinental trip between Buffalo and Oregon was made in the year 1835. His westward progress after leaving St. Louis was by way of the
Missouri and Platte Rivers, the Black Hills, and across
the high plains and the Rocky Mountains to the head
waters of the Columbia River, which he thence followed.
Parker began his journey on March 14, and on August

[1] The "Intelligencer" article is quoted in Smalley's "History of the Southern Pacific
Railway," pp. 52-56. Smalley is inclined to give precedence to Barlow as the originator of
the idea of a trans-continental road. He says: "Perhaps there were earlier advocates of a
Pacific railway than Doctor Barlow, but if so, the author of this volume has not been able
to identify them, and therefore accords to him the first place." But with this conclusion
Davis does not agree. Davis says ("The Union Pacific Railway," p. 15): "In the face of
Doctor Barlow's own acknowledgment, however, it is difficult to find a justification of Mr.
Smalley's statement. To this unwarranted conclusion by Mr. Smalley, attention was also
called by General Granville M. Dodge in a valuable paper on Transcontinental Railways,
read by him before the Society of the Army of the Tennessee at its Twenty-first Annual
Reunion at Toledo, Ohio, September 15, 1888." Davis has established the date of the
"Emigrant" article, and Smalley, in discussing (p. 52) the date of Doctor Barlow's letter,
says: "Evidently the [Barlow] article was written as early as 1834 and perhaps in 1833,
and the articles in a Michigan paper to which it refers are supposed to have been called
out by others previously written by him." Unless similar proposals of still earlier date
are hereafter discovered, the weight of evidence points to the author of the "Emigrant"
editorial as the first man who definitely and publicly advocated the joining of the oceans
by rail. Although the writer of the "Emigrant" article is unknown, Davis says: "It should
probably be accredited to Judge S. W. Dexter, the publisher and one of the editors of the
paper." (p. 13.)

[2] Thus far brought to light.

UNION PACIFIC RAIL ROAD
SURVEY OF 1864
MOUTH OF CAÑON OF SOUTH PLATTE.

391.—The first railway across the continent. A scene during the preliminary
work of the surveyors. Drawn by F. M. Case, one of the civil
engineers in charge.

10—having then reached the farther side of the Rocky
Mountains—he made the following observations in the
daily written record of his trip:

"The passage through these mountains is in a valley, so gradual in
the ascent and descent that I should not have known we were approaching them, had it not been that as we advanced the atmosphere gradually
became cooler, and at length we saw the perpetual snows upon our right
hand and upon our left, elevated many thousand feet above us. . . . .
This valley was not discovered until some years since . . . It varies
in width from two to fifteen miles; and following its course, the distance
through the mountains is about one hundred miles, or four days journey.
Though there are some elevations and depressions in this valley, yet comparatively speaking it is level; and the summit where the waters divide,
which flow into the Atlantic and Pacific, is about six thousand feet above
the level of the ocean. There would not be any difficulty in the way of
constructing a railroad from the Atlantic to the Pacific ocean. There is
no greater difficulty, in the whole distance, than has already been overcome in passing the Green mountains, between Boston and Albany; and
probably the time may not be far distant, when trips will be made across

1323

the continent, as they have been made to the Niagara Falls to see nature's wonders."[1]

The few men who had discussed the possibility or desirability of a transcontinental railway before Parker wrote the observations here given had considered the matter in an academic fashion, and from viewpoints far to the eastward. The importance of Parker's statement, therefore, lies in the fact that it was made by him after he had personally traversed the route which he described, and had discovered out of his own experience that the project of which he spoke was apparently a practical one.

Others who advocated a transcontinental line during the fourth decade were John Plumbe, of Dubuque, Iowa, who in 1836 proposed the building of a road from Lake Michigan to Oregon;[2] Louis Gaylord Clarke, who wrote[3] of a similar enterprise during the same year, and Hartwell Carver, of Rochester, New York, who in 1837 advocated[4] a railroad which should have its western terminus on the Columbia River. Lalburn Boggs, an early Governor of Missouri, prepared an article on the subject in 1843,[5] and an editorial contained in *Hunt's Merchants' Magazine* for January, 1845, predicted that "those persons are now living who will see a railroad connecting New York with the Pacific, and a steam communication from Oregon to China."

By this time similar arguments and suggestions had become rather frequent, although no inspired prophet or other personality with sufficient power to concentrate

---

[1] Parker's "Journal of an Exploring Tour Beyond the Rocky Mountains." Text quoted from pp. 76-77 of the fifth edition, 1846.
[2] A public meeting in promotion of Plumbe's project took place at Dubuque in March of 1838.
[3] In the "Knickerbocker Magazine."
[4] In the New York "Courier and Enquirer" (according to Davis, p. 17). H. H. Bancroft, in his "History of California" (Vol. VII, pp. 498-499), credits Carver with similar writings during the year 1832, but Bancroft's contention respecting Carver is rejected by Smalley (p. 52) and by Davis (p. 17).
[5] See Bancroft's "History of California," Vol. VII, p. 500, note.

public attention on the subject had as yet arisen. Two features characteristic of nearly all the early plans for an iron road to the Pacific are noticeable; namely, that the undertaking should be governmental in character, and that its western terminus be in the Oregon region.

At this point in the development of the idea the inspired prophet arose in the person of a New York merchant named Asa Whitney. Whitney was a man of foresight and wide travel throughout the world, and during two years spent in China between 1842 and 1844 he had elaborated a plan for building the highway that had been discussed in the manner indicated during the previous decade. He returned to America in 1844, and in the eight years immediately thereafter he expended his whole fortune and devoted all his time and energy to a ceaseless campaign having for its purpose the creation of a railroad from the interior valley to the Pacific coast. To him, more than to any other one man is due the credit for bringing the idea before the mass of his fellow countrymen. While his particular project was not realized in concrete form, and while—for reasons that will later appear—it could not be so realized, Whitney's work was nevertheless of extreme importance.

His first proposal to Congress in behalf of the plan he had formulated was made to the Senate on January 28, 1845.[1] The argument addressed by him to Congress read in part:

"Your memorialist begs respectfully to represent to your honorable body, that, by rivers, railroads, and canals, all the States east and north of the Potomac connect directly with the waters of the great lakes.

"That there is a chain of railroads in projection, and being built, from New York to the southern shore of Lake Michigan, which will produce commercial, political, and national results and benefits, which

[1] Its official publication is contained in "Senate Doc. 69; 28th Congress, 2d Session," from which the extracts here given are quoted.

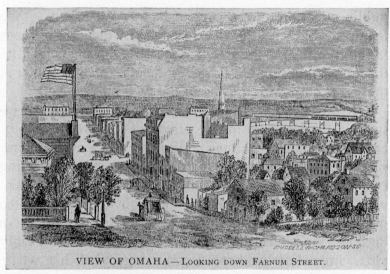

VIEW OF OMAHA — Looking down Farnum Street.

392.—Omaha, the eastern terminus of the first transcontinental iron road, was chosen because of its geographical location and because it was in a territory. Nebraska was not yet a state. Some members of Congress questioned the power of the government to build, or aid in building, a highway lying partly within state lines, but they gave no opposition to similar work in a territory. Thus Omaha became the first modern gate to the far West.

must be seen and felt through all our vast Confederacy. Your memorialist would further represent to your honorable body that he has devoted much time and attention to the subject of a railroad from Lake Michigan, through the Rocky mountains to the Pacific ocean, and that he finds such a route practicable, the results from which would be incalculable, far beyond the imagination of man to estimate. To the interior of our vast and widely spread country it would be as the heart is to the human body. It would, when completed, cross all the mighty rivers and streams, which wend their way to the ocean through our vast and rich valleys from Oregon to Maine, a distance of more than three thousand miles. The incalculable importance of such a chain of roads will readily be seen and appreciated by your honorable body. . . .

"Such easy and rapid communication would bring all our immensely wide spread population together as one vast city, the moral and social effects of which must harmonize all together as one family, with but one interest—the general good of all. . . ."

Whitney then went on to outline his plan for meeting the expense of the work, which he estimated at about $65,-

000,000. He asked Congress to give to him a tract of land sixty miles in width and extending from Lake Michigan to the Pacific. This land he proposed to sell at low prices to city dwellers, thereby to some extent relieving city congestion and poverty, using the proceeds in necessary construction processes. The road, when finished, was to belong to the nation, and any net profits resulting from its operation were to be devoted to public education. The final paragraphs of the proposal dealt with the future relations between the United States and Oregon, reading:

"Your memorialist believes that the time is not far distant when Oregon will become a State of such magnitude and importance as to compel the establishment of a separate Government—a separate nation, which will have cities, ports, and harbors, all free, inviting all the nations of the earth to a free trade with them; when they will control and monopolize the valuable fisheries of the Pacific; control the coast trade of Mexico and South America, of the Sandwich Islands, Japan, and all China, and [that the separate nation of Oregon and her cities will] be our most dangerous and successful rivals in the commerce of the world.

"But your memorialist believes that this road will unite them to us, enabling them to receive the protecting care of our Government, sharing in its blessings, benefits, and prosperity, and imparting to us our share of the great benefits from their local position, enterprise and industry."

The features of Whitney's proposal that made it appeal so strongly to the public are obvious. In the first place it provided for the long-discussed and important work, and furthermore outlined a plan by which the road might seemingly be carried to completion without becoming a direct financial burden on the country. It suggested a colonization of the West, and the creation of the railway by means of that colonization. Whitney's proposition was essentially an unselfish one. He asked for no part of the operating revenues of the undertaking, and for no financial benefit from land sales except in the improbable contingency that the proceeds of such sales exceeded the sum necessary for the faithful completion of the whole idea under the supervision of the government. The colonization and land-sale phases of the scheme—although they formed its basis—were, indeed, its fundamental weakness. Under the same rapidity at which public lands were then being sold in more thickly settled and desirable portions of the public domain it would have required almost a century to have obtained a sum sufficiently large to build the road according to Whitney's notion.

The national legislature took no action on the first memorial,[1] and during the same year of 1845 Whitney himself undertook an exploring expedition over that part of his projected route east of the Rocky Mountains. On his return to the domain of civilization, late in the year, he began a widespread campaign in advocacy of his proposal which soon produced astonishing results.

By correspondence with mercantile bodies in many cities, by articles printed in newspapers and magazines, and by addresses in all parts of the country east of the Mississippi, he succeeded in bringing the idea of a Pacific railroad before the whole people. He also kept his plan constantly before Congress through the medium of additional memorials, and by the year 1850 no less than fourteen states[2] had endorsed the scheme in legislative resolutions addressed to the Federal government. Innumerable cities and towns also took similar action as a result of public meetings.

The political developments of the period contributed materially in fixing public attention upon the subject. Texas was annexed in 1845; a settlement of the Oregon question was effected in 1846, and in the same year news

---

[1] It was presented during the final weeks of an expiring Congress.
[2] Kentucky, Indiana, Connecticut, Maine, Maryland, Michigan, New Hampshire, New Jersey, New York, Ohio, Pennsylvania, Rhode Island, Tennessee and Vermont.

reached the East that the American pioneers in Oregon had organized a provisional government. In fact all the interest displayed by the people in Oregon affairs up to that time, and the migrations thence, had a connection with Whitney's railroad plan which requires no comment here.

Congress showed itself to be favorably predisposed to such an undertaking. The members of the Federal legislature were in general agreement regarding the desirability of a steam road to the Pacific, and were principally concerned with the wisest economic method of its creation and its proposed route. The attitude of Congress toward the principle involved was indicated by a report on the subject made to the Senate in 1846 by the Committee on Public Lands. The document in question contained the following passages:[1]

"[The Committee report] that they have bestowed upon this proposition that consideration its importance demands, and which, but a few years since . . . a committee of this body would have been excused for treating as a visionary speculation. . . .

"The proposition is a startling one and of vast importance to our country and to the world. . . .

"Preliminary to the consideration of the proposition referred to the Committee, and before one of such vast magnitude and importance should be entertained, it is indispensably necessary that the way should be seen perfectly clear, and that no constitutional difficulty would be likely to present itself at the commencement of the undertaking, or obstruct its after progress.

"Fortunately, the task of showing the absence of difficulty on this point is a very easy one. The most scrupulous, in according to Congress power to construct roads and canals, have not doubted the propriety of exercising this power upon territory beyond the jurisdiction of a State sovereignty, as the constitution declares that 'the Congress shall have power to dispose of, and make all needful rules and regulations respecting, the territory or other property belonging to the United States.' . . . The sovereignty of the United States extends over the entire route contemplated for this road, and it only remains to extinguish the Indian title

[1] "Senate Doc. No. 466, 29th Congress, 1st Session; July 31, 1846," pp. 1-26. This report was made as the result of consideration of memorials submitted by Whitney, and by citizens endorsing the Whitney proposals.

to such portion of the territory as may be required for the site of the road and its appendages, and to be disposed of to obtain means for its construction.

"Thus far concerns the construction of roads beyond the jurisdiction of the States, but can Congress constitutionally exercise the power to make them within the States? It has been answered that, with the consent of the States on whose soil the roads are to be made, there can be no difficulty, provided the means be at the disposal of Congress. This principle was early admitted.[1] . . . A national road having thus been authorized and partially constructed, by the exercise of this power, from the Atlantic ocean to the seat of Government of Missouri, and within the jurisdiction of several States, it will not be expected that this committee should consider it necessary to argue the existence of still more ample powers to authorize the construction of a road through the public territory,[2] and beyond the jurisdiction of any existing State, to the shores of the Pacific ocean. . . ."

And in conclusion the committee recognized a prevailing fear that the Oregon country might organize itself into a separate nation if not joined to the United States by better means of travel. On that phase of the subject the report said:

"A well-grounded apprehension seems to exist, that, unless some means like the one proposed, of rapid communication with that region, be devised and completed, that country, soon to become a State of vast proportions and of immense political importance, by reason of its position, its own wants, unattended to by this Government, will be compelled to establish a separate government—a separate nation—with its cities, ports and harbors . . . and become our most dangerous rival in the commerce of the world. In the opinion of the committee, this road will bind these two great geographical sections indissolubly together, to their mutual advantage, and be the cement of a union, which time will but render more durable. . . ."

[1] It has been seen, in the discussion of the National Road, that more than this was early admitted. Federal power to appropriate money for building a National Road through states, and across state boundaries, was asserted without asking or obtaining the consent of states affected.

[2] The contradiction between these statements of a Congressional committee in 1846, and the actual situation as it then existed and afterwards prevailed for twenty-two years, will be observed by reference to the chapter devoted to the natives of the West and their relation to the development of white travel in those regions. The red peoples native to the West were still self-governing, and their ownership of soil was also undisputed. A few tribes in that part of the continent had in treaties previously acknowledged themselves to be under the protection of the United States, but no native nation of the West gave up its independence and acknowledged the jurisdiction of the United States until 1849, when the Navajos took those steps in a formal treaty. Despite the Congressional utterance here cited, the United States paid millions of dollars to western Indians during the following twenty years in return for permission to travel overland toward the Pacific and to build a railroad in that direction.

The 29th Congress—to the Senate of which the foregoing report was submitted—took no definite action. It
was not convinced that Whitney's plan was the wisest one
which could be formulated. Agitation in its behalf continued during the next two years, nevertheless, and the

First Construction Train passing the Palisades, C. P. R. R. (See page 133.)

393.—Laying the track. A construction train on the Central Pacific division
of the work, which was built from the Pacific coast eastward. The train
carried ties and rails, and slowly advanced above them as they were put
in place.

states and cities continued to record their endorsement
of the project. During the 30th Congress a Senate committee again submitted a favorable report,[1] but by the
close of the year 1848 there scarce remained possibility
that the Whitney idea might receive the sanction of a law
in its behalf. Although public thought was crystallizing
into realization that a railway to the far West would
become a certainty in the not distant future, new and
unexpected conditions were swiftly altering popular judg-

[1] July 7, 1848.

ment concerning the matter of its location. It was becoming apparent that a railroad toward Oregon, extending along the northern edge of the country, would not be the best solution of the problem.

Recent events had changed the entire aspect of the question. During preceding years all discussion of a railroad to the Pacific had been based on the belief that such a road must inevitably extend to Oregon, since the nation then owned no territory on the Pacific coast south of the present boundary of Oregon. But by the treaty of peace negotiated with Mexico the United States had come into possession of an immense region in the western part of the continent now occupied by the states of Arizona, California, Nevada, New Mexico, Texas, Utah, and parts of Colorado and Wyoming.[1] All this territory belonged to Mexico when the proposal for a railway to Oregon was first made. The people saw that its transfer to the United States extended the national possessions so far to the southward on the Pacific coast that a railroad to Oregon—if but one transcontinental road was to be built—would not serve the purposes for which such a route was intended. The acquirement of the new region also removed possibility that Oregon might later be erected into a separate sovereignty. Nor would a road to the West along the proposed Whitney line have been of much value as an aid to the penetration and development of the new lands taken from Mexico.

Still another circumstance intimately connected with the territorial aggrandizement of the nation; an event even more powerful in finally determining the path of the country's first transcontinental road, had taken place—

---

[1] Although Texas, of course, had previously arrived in the United States over the pathway of her own revolution and independence.

1332

though without the knowledge of the people of the East —a few days before the treaty of peace. On January 24, 1848, Marshall had found rich deposits of gold on the American River, in California. He told Sutter of the discovery, and the two men tried to keep the secret for their own advantage, but knowledge of it gradually spread through the neighborhood. During the following spring the news from California crept northward into Oregon, and by the late summer even the middle and Atlantic states were filled with rumors of a new El Dorado. The rumors were soon substantiated by definite reports whose immediate consequences were the mania in the East and the migrations growing from it. The acquirement of nearly a million square miles of additional territory toward the West and Southwest, coupled with the discovery of gold and the resultant overland rush by hundreds of thousands of people, made it apparent to the whole country that a Pacific railway had become a pressing necessity.

Such was the situation by 1850, and yet twelve years of economic and political jealousies were to elapse before the government finally gave its authorization to an enterprise whose need had so long been recognized. Before the territorial expansion and gold discovery of 1848 it had been taken for granted that the western terminus of any future ocean-joining railway line would be the Oregon region, and in the early days of debate over the Whitney idea no serious controversy had developed regarding the location of the eastern terminus of the road. But the two remarkable events of 1848 wrought a great change with regard to both those matters. It was promptly seen that the long coveted bay of San Francisco—centrally located on the newly-acquired Pacific coast boundary of the nation—was the logical western end of any transcontinental railway which might be created by governmental initiative or aid. And the obvious future importance of such a road gave the location of its eastern terminus a conse-

LAYING THE TRACK OF THE PACIFIC RAILROAD.

394.—The similar process as it was carried forward on the Union Pacific road from east to west. The two construction trains gradually approached one another for more than three years and seven months, until on the morning of May 10, 1869, the gap between them had been reduced to about one hundred feet.

quence which that matter had not previously possessed. Nearly all the states and important cities east of the Mississippi at once developed an extreme interest in the location of the eastern end of the proposed line and began a struggle to secure the benefits which would flow from the possession of that strategic point.

No less than four conventions assembled during 1849 to consider the subject of a transcontinental road. The meetings were held in Chicago, Boston, St. Louis and Memphis. Still another council of the same sort took place in Philadelphia in April of 1850. These gatherings showed the newly-awakened popular interest in the eastern terminus of the enterprise they had met to advocate. During the years of Whitney's agitation in behalf of a road to the Oregon country that plan had received much support in New England, New York, Pennsylvania and Maryland. It had then seemed likely that the railways already existing in those states, together with the similar roads extending westward along Lake Erie and through Michigan, would make Boston, New York, Philadelphia and Baltimore the logical eastern outlets of a Pacific road built in accordance with the Whitney suggestions, and the endorsement given to that enthusiast by the eastern cities here named was largely due to the opinion in question. Chicago and other lake towns were also energetic advocates of the Oregon route prior to 1850, and for the same reason.

But the radical alteration in the political map of the far western regions was immediately reflected east of the Mississippi, and the series of railway conventions was due in large measure to sectional jealousies and regional ambitions having their source in a desire to obtain the eastern end of the contemplated iron highway. St. Louis and all the upper Mississippi valley came forward with an argument in favor of a route considerably to the southward of Whitney's proposed line; Mississippi, South Carolina and Charleston entered the field in behalf of a route south of that favored by St. Louis; Memphis, backed by Tennessee and Arkansas, urged the building of a road extending westward from Independence in Missouri, with branches from that town to Memphis, St. Louis and Chicago. Even Texas entered the lists, and Sam Houston —then a Federal senator from the state—introduced a bill providing that a railroad to the Pacific coast might be constructed by a Texas railway company.[1]

The St. Louis convention was probably the most important of the various gatherings which assembled to promote better communication facilities with the far West. It met on October 15, 1849, and was attended by several hundred delegates, who represented no less than fifteen states.[2] Acrimonious debates characterized the gathering, which finally adopted the following resolutions offered by Richard W. Thompson, of Indiana.[3]

"Resolved, That in the opinion of this Convention it is the duty of the General Government to provide, at an early period, for the construction of a Central National Railroad from the Valley of the Mississippi to the Pacific Ocean.

"Resolved, That in the opinion of this Convention, a Grand Trunk Railroad, with branches to St. Louis, Memphis and Chicago, would be such a central and national one.

"Resolved, That a committee be appointed to communicate to the Convention to be held at Memphis the foregoing resolutions, and to request the concurrence of said Convention therein."

The Thompson resolutions were adopted by an almost unanimous vote, and the convention duly memoralized Congress in accordance therewith. From that time active agitation in favor of the route previously advocated by Whitney was no longer visible, although various bills in his behalf were presented to Congress until as late a date as 1852.[4]

[1] The Galveston and Red River Railway Company.

[2] Illinois, Indiana, Iowa, Kentucky, Louisiana, Maryland, Michigan, Missouri, New Jersey, New York, Ohio, Pennsylvania, Tennessee, Virginia and Wisconsin.

[3] "Proceedings of the National Railroad Convention, which assembled in the City of St. Louis, on the Fifteenth of October, 1849. Etc., etc." St. Louis: 1850, pp. 35-36.

[4] "Whitney's entire fortune is said to have been spent in an attempt to realize his dream of a Pacific Railway, and the 'Prince of Projectors' to have kept a dairy and sold milk in Washington for a livelihood in his declining years." Davis's "The Union Pacific Railway," p. 33.

CHAPTER LVII

ANOTHER CAUSE THAT HELD BACK THE FIRST TRANS-
CONTINENTAL RAILWAY — NORTH AND SOUTH COULD
NOT AGREE ON ITS LOCATION — THE REASON —
SENATOR IVERSON'S SPEECH — A LAW IS FINALLY
PASSED — THE QUESTION OF TRACK-WIDTH ARISES —
THE CONFUSION OF EXISTING GAUGES — LINCOLN'S
DECISION — CONGRESS REFUSES TO ACCEPT IT —
ACTUAL WORK BEGINS — HOW IT WAS PERFORMED —
A HISTORIC SCENE UP IN THE MOUNTAINS — THE
PEOPLE LISTEN IN THE STREETS — THE OCEANS
JOINED

THE political jealousies that contributed for twelve
years to the delay in building a Pacific railway were
intimately connected with those differences between the
North and South which eventually resulted in civil war.
Each of the two sections was striving to gain a pre-
ponderant power in shaping the political destiny of the
country, and between them stood a small group of men
who were trying by means of compromises to avert an
appeal to arms. The relationship borne to this condition
by the need of a modern transportation route through the
recently obtained West is easily to be seen. The acquisition of much territory from Mexico, the constantly increasing overland migrations to the westward, and the
visible necessity of creating new commonwealths in that
region during the near future, made the geographical

1337

location of a Pacific railroad a matter of unusual importance. The North was already resolved that slavery should not be established in new states admitted to the Union, and the South was equally insistent that its economic system should be perpetuated to the westward in at least a sufficient number of new states to maintain its relative importance in governmental affairs. The natural result of those divergent purposes was a deadlock, and although each side was willing to see the construction of such a transcontinental road as would benefit its own position, neither could muster sufficient strength to gain its object prior to the military conflict.

The contending regions did, however, agree on one thing essential to the contemplated highway. Congress passed a law in 1853 providing for an elaborate survey of the whole country between the Mississippi and the Pacific Ocean, in order to determine through what region a railroad could most easily be built.[1] It was made by civil engineers of the War Department, and the summary of the work laid before Congress by Jefferson Davis, the Secretary of War, showed the sectional feeling then so closely related to the subject under consideration. The War Secretary said: "The route of the 32nd parallel is of those surveyed the most practicable and economical for a railroad from the Mississippi River to the Pacific Ocean."[2]

During the following years there was always a congressional majority favorable to the proposed railway in principle, but the acute sectional differences of the time

[1] The result of the survey is contained in eleven elaborate volumes constituting a comprehensive report not only on the geography of the western country, but also on the Indian life and the natural history of the West.

[2] Sen. Ex. Doc. No. 78, 33rd Congress, 2d Session. "The surveys made under Secretary Davis's authority were critically discussed in DeBow's Review for December, 1856 (Vol. 21, p. 555), and even by that representative periodical of Southern industry the conclusions of the Secretary were not endorsed."—Davis's "The Union Pacific Railway," p. 60, note.

THE EAST AND THE WEST.

THE ORIENT AND THE OCCIDENT SHAKING HANDS AFTER DRIVING THE LAST SPIKE.

395.—The driving of the last spike and meeting of the engines on May 10, 1869, at Promontory Point, Utah. Culmination of a process that had required two centuries and a half. The continent was spanned.

made it impossible to concentrate that majority on any definite proposition. In 1856 the Democratic party and the new-born Republican party endorsed the plan in their national platforms, and President Buchanan, in his inaugural address, advocated the building of a Pacific road by governmental action or aid.[1] The fundamental reason underlying the inability of Congress to agree on any specific proposal for the road has been well stated by the principal historian of the undertaking.[2] He said:

"Statesmen had tried to persuade themselves that a Pacific railway, as a national project, was a possibility, had tried to persuade themselves that there was a nation, but all the time, in the undertow of thought and feeling, there was too keen an appreciation of a want of unity and nationality."

An open avowal of the condition just defined, and of the relationship borne by the proposal to the existing political situation, was finally made by a candid southern senator[3] in the following words:

"If one road is provided for and the route is left open to be selected by the company who shall undertake it, a northern route will be adopted . . . pouring all its vast travel and freight . . . into the northern states and cities of the Union. . . I believe that the time will come when the slave states will be compelled, in vindication of their rights, interests and honor, to separate from the free states, and erect an independent Confederacy; and I am not sure, Sir, that the time is not near at hand when that event will occur. . . It is because I believe that separation is not far distant; because the signs of the times point too plainly to the early triumph of the Abolitionists, and their complete possession and control of every department of the Federal Government; and because I firmly believe that when such an event occurs the Union will be dissolved, that I am unwilling to vote as much land and as much money as this bill proposes to build a road to the Pacific, which, in my judgment, will be created outside of a southern Confederacy, and will belong exclusively to the North. The public lands now held by the United States, as well as the public treasury, are the joint property of

---

[1] But Buchanan, like nearly all other public men of that period, weakly chose to advocate the enterprise as a useful military work rather than as a great, vital undertaking whose value lay in its economical and social relationship to the country.
[2] Davis, in "The Union Pacific Railway," p. 82.
[3] Iverson of Georgia, on January 6, 1859.

all the states and the people of this Union. They belong to the South as well as to the North; we are entitled, in the Union, to our just and equal share, and if the Union is divided, then we are no less entitled to a fair proportion of the common fund. What I demand, therefore, is that the South shall be put upon an equality with the North, whether the Union lasts or not; that in appropriating the public lands and money, the joint property of all, in connecting the Atlantic and Pacific Oceans by railroad, the South shall have an equal chance to secure the road within her borders, to inure to her benefit whilst the Union lasts, and to belong to her when, if ever, that Union is dissolved."

The outbreak of the Civil War witnessed the disappearance from the national legislature of the principal opponents of a transcontinental route built by governmental aid, and on July 4, of 1862, President Lincoln signed a bill providing for the commencement of the long-discussed thoroughfare.[1] But the capitalists of the country declined to coöperate with the government under the law of 1862, and in 1864[2] it was materially amended[3] and construction work began soon afterward.

The importance and significance of the decision to build the first transcontinental railroad by Federal aid and under Federal charter has long been recognized, and its relationship to the chain of events considered in these pages is obvious. The enactments through which the decision was expressed were written in obedience to popular will; they were virtually ordered by the people. The laws also constituted an important manifestation of a slowly reviving opinion on the part of the people that certain things affecting their common interests could best be done by their collective power and effort, exerted through the machinery of the general government. The public seemed to be returning to a belief that in dealing

[1] The act provided that the work should be performed by two corporations known as the Union Pacific Railroad Company and the Central Pacific Railroad Company of California.

[2] By the act of July 2nd.

[3] A discussion of the legislation of 1862 and 1864, together with a financial and corporate history of the road, is contained in Davis's monograph previously named.

with social problems of nation-wide scope the Federal administration was in closer touch with the population, and better able to serve human needs with beneficial results, than were the numerous separate—and often antagonistic—state governments. The states had always been more or less inclined to inject local considerations, based on state boundary lines, into the discussion or proposed solution of economic questions whose nature made such efforts impractical. Whenever such an attempt was made to solve a country-wide economic problem by state statutes—rarely uniform in their provisions—the result was either a halting of human progress or the creation of undesirable conditions which persisted until the commonwealth reversed its attitude or until the national government intervened.[1]

The Federal laws creating the first transcontinental railway were, to put it briefly, a partial return by the nation to that position assumed between 1802 and 1824, when Congress ordained and built the National Road. It has been said of the two more modern measures: "The significance of the Pacific railway legislation is that it marks the high-water level of the flood of national power; it is part of the drift . . . that was left at the highest point on the shore, when the flood of nationality receded."[2]

Exception, it seems, may fairly be taken to this characterization of the laws of 1862 and 1864. The acts under which the National Road was extended into

---

[1] A characteristic case of the sort was the action of New York, Connecticut and New Jersey toward the use of steam and steamboats as agencies of travel and transportation. And while such an early demeanor toward an economic matter must necessarily be called a "state" attitude, since it was expressed by form of law and by accredited officials, yet when such an attitude is traced to its origin, its source can often be found with reasonable certainty in the selfish desires of a small group of locally influential men whose political power or personal fortunes were maintained or enhanced by the "state" pronouncement which they were able to dictate. Such groups gave support to one another on various well-known historical occasions when the interests of some special group were in danger, and perhaps that process went on more often than surviving evidence can indicate.

[2] Davis, p. 133.

396.—An occasional experience of travellers on the first Pacific railroad after it was finished. They still had to get out and help, in one way or another, as they had done in the days of the keel-boat, *Flying Machine* and stage-coach.

Indiana, Illinois and Missouri provided for its building, by the general government, through states and across state boundaries under willingness of the commonwealths so penetrated by it. It was a national work,[1] undertaken for purposes identical with those which inspired the first railway across the continent. Both were highways of movement, designed to bring separated parts of the population into closer social and economic relations. The first was brought into being in a manner already described, and paid for by direct appropriations of government funds. The later enterprise was built by a less direct exercise of national authority, through corporate instrumentalities created by the nation for the purpose, and to which the government delegated powers which it had in the previous instance used in its own person.[2] Consequently it appears that the earlier case, rather than the later one, marked the high-water level of national power as that

[1] The first Pacific railroad has also been so defined by the Federal Supreme Court. See "The United States vs. The Union Pacific Railroad Company," 91 U. S. R. 79.
[2] Such as the right, given the corporations, to carry the railroad through the states of Nebraska, Kansas and California, and across their boundaries.

strength was formerly used in carrying out similar undertakings.

The employment, by the Federal government, of those attributes of sovereignty necessarily displayed by it in the direct construction of the National Road resulted in fears or jealousies that found voice in "state" protests, and the enterprise was eventually made over to the several states through which it passed. The people, in other words, for a time employed their general government as the machinery by which they created and maintained an interstate public utility. Then considerations based to some extent on partisan politics were introduced into the subject, and that method of doing such work was abandoned practically at its beginning. No doubt the shift was also due, in some degree not now measurable, to a popular feeling that such procedure involved danger because of inexperience and a national lack of the engineering and administrative ability requisite for the best guidance of like undertakings. Perhaps the members of the electorate doubted their own ability to choose efficient and honest servants from among themselves as the heads of publicly owned utilities. There had arisen a popular fallacy that was already working serious harm to national character and progress, and which was destined to exert an identical influence for many years thereafter. The error in question was embodied in a political saying which ran: "To the victors belong the spoils." The assertion itself is true enough; the fallacy lay in a perverted meaning given to it by the politicians of that day and applied to the result of an election. The electors of a real democracy are always the victors in a discussion and plebiscite conducted to regulate their affairs, for its result expresses their common judgment on the questions at issue. And the spoils which belong to them are the creation of conditions in accordance with the principles they have endorsed. But during the epoch in question "victors" meant only a part of the people, and those whose opinions had not been in accord with the result were "enemies." The "spoils" were not principles and improved conditions of society, but political office, to be bestowed exclusively on favored members of the "victorious" party with little or no consideration of their fitness for such enormous responsibility. Through the rise and widespread acceptance of this strange doctrine—so illustrative of the prevalent economic morality of the period—practically the whole purpose of government as an instrument designed by humanity for bettering its affairs was overthrown in the republic. Those excellencies of American character and condition which survived the era most acutely affected by the fallacy, endured in spite of rather than by the aid of the governmental system.

It was during this epoch that several states built and operated travel and traffic routes of various kinds whose existence was due, in part, to demands of party politics, and whose administrations as utilities were largely political in their nature. The failure of those that did fail was no doubt caused in some degree by faulty construction based on inadequate engineering skill, and partly by the destructive influence of the political idea just mentioned. During the same time, also, the corporation first became prominent in the business affairs of the country. It was an unfortunate age for the virtual birth and childhood of a commercial method so important, since the corporation was compelled to grow up in association with various political, business and economic ideas unfavorable to the strict maintenance of its own integrity. But the corporation grew apace, and was soon the principal factor—under state authorization—by which public utilities, including transportation routes, were built and operated. From that time until recent years the constantly growing corporation has naturally striven, with more than a modicum of success, to foster the early popular fear that the people themselves—through their government and chosen servants—could not successfully create and honestly administer those huge undertakings so necessary to modern society. It does not, however, necessarily follow that whatever inability was displayed by the people and their governmental machinery from sixty to ninety years ago—because of contemporary conditions and beliefs heretofore described—would be manifest to-day or in the future, should the people again decide to use their state or Federal governments as instruments for economic purposes. Whatever of failure or success they might now or hereafter attain in such enterprises would be determined by their education, experiences, desires and practises.[1]

The first transcontinental railroad was built by two corporations which were created by Congress with that object in view, and to them were loaned the credit and resources of the nation. The people, in that particular case, delegated their strength instead of using their powers in direct application to the work in hand and thus acquiring ownership of the finished product.

After the government had decided for the building of a road to the Pacific under a plan based on the use of national resources there still remained one essential detail of the project that demanded action by Federal authority

[1] The recent building of the Panama Canal by the United States, under the immediate direction of Federal engineers, suggests the present capacity of the national machinery in undertaking enterprises demanding a large degree of constructive, executive and administrative ability.

Since the foregoing text was written the government has also decided to build, equip, own and operate a railroad in Alaska.

before any construction work was possible. The gauge of the railway had to be fixed, and the effort to decide on a track-width resulted in a political and sectional dispute similar to those which had so often occurred during the preliminary discussions of the previous years.[1]

397.—Method of protecting trains from avalanches in the Sierra Nevada Mountains. Many miles of snow sheds had to be built.

The number of different gauges used by the railways of the country had so multiplied that during the seventh decade at least a dozen—and probably more—track-widths were employed in various sections, nearly every one of which was represented by several hundred or several thousand miles of line.[2] Many of the New England roads still adhered to the gauge of four feet eight and a half inches, and the series of roads through central New

[1] "Even the gauge of the track could not be determined without hours of debate, persistent lobbying, and a full measure of political chicanery." Davis, p. 113.
[2] A list of representative railroads in all parts of the country, showing the divergencies of gauge at the time, is contained in an appendix.

York State—previously assembled under one corporate control—together with connecting lines reaching westward along the shore of Lake Erie and through Michigan, were built in similar fashion. So were nearly all the roads in the neighborhood of Chicago and those extending westward to and through the state of Iowa. There were also various isolated roads in other parts of the country which had adopted the gauge here mentioned.

In some parts of New Jersey and Pennsylvania, in nearly all of Ohio, and in portions of Indiana and Illinois, a track-width of four feet and ten inches was in use. All the railways of the South were five feet wide, and that gauge had likewise been adopted in California by a state enactment. The Erie road in New York; the Atlantic and Great Western through New York, Pennsylvania and Ohio; the Ohio and Mississippi road through Ohio, Indiana and Illionis were all six feet wide, as were various other lines in New Jersey and elsewhere. Many of the roads in the Southwest and in Missouri were built with a gauge of five feet and a half.[1] All sorts of other and apparently inexplicable gauges[2] existed throughout the whole eastern region, making any approach to an effective national railway system an impossibility while such a condition continued. Up to and including the decade in question the multiplication of railways in America had not resulted in a simplification of the gauge problem, as might have been expected—or as assuredly would have been the case had the railroad building of the

[1] This group included the Missouri Pacific, extending westward from St. Louis, and a possible important factor in the transcontinental route to be created.

[2] Such as 4 feet 9½ inches; 4 feet 5½ inches; 4 feet 7 inches; 5 feet 4 inches; 4 feet 8 inches; 4 feet 9¼ inches and 4 feet 3 inches. In addition to all the different American gauges, an English parliamentary commission had recommended the establishment of a standard track-width of five feet and three inches, and Canada was building her railways with a gauge of five and a half feet. It is thus apparent that one of the most serious questions relating to the physical structure of railways was still a matter of dispute and widely divergent practise more than thirty years after the commencement of the railway epoch.

country been directed by a continental policy—but on the contrary the widespread divergencies in track-width had produced a confusion that was depriving the railroad system of the country of a large part—perhaps half—of its potential value. Some strong influence was imperatively needed to rectify the conditions described, and the creation of the transcontinental road was destined to become that influence.

Under the act of 1862 the President of the United States was authorized to fix the gauge of the Pacific road. When President Lincoln was informed of the responsibility placed upon him he said he would be pleased to comply with the law if he only knew what the best gauge was. Severe political pressure was brought to bear upon him in behalf of several of the gauges then in use. Missouri urged five and a half feet, Chicago and New York advocated four feet eight and a half inches, California demanded five feet, and so serious did the fight become that Lincoln actually called a cabinet meeting to consider the question. Finally he settled on the California gauge of five feet, and issued a proclamation in accordance with his decision. But the President's ruling—so urgently sought before he gave it—was not accepted. The quarrel was transferred to Congress, and at last, after eight months of contention, that body in March of 1863 passed a law naming four feet eight and a half inches as the gauge for the Pacific Railroad.

It is very likely that this action, more than any other one event in railroad history, was the determining factor in establishing the prevailing and so-called standard railroad gauge. All the roads of the country not built in accordance with that decision saw the necessity of track alteration if they were to participate directly in trans-

1349

continental traffic and enjoy its benefits. The necessary physical transformation began almost at once, and continued until the declared governmental standard became universal.

Work on the enterprise was begun at both its ends.

ACROSS THE CONTINENT.
THE SNOW SHEDS ON THE CENTRAL PACIFIC RAILROAD, IN THE SIERRA NEVADA MOUNTAINS.

398.—A transcontinental train cheered in its passage by the workmen who had built the road. From a sketch by the artist Joseph Becker.

The Central Pacific began to built eastward from Sacramento in 1864, and fifty-six miles of track had been laid down by the beginning of 1866. The Union Pacific began to build westward from Omaha, and by January, 1866, had completed its first forty miles of track. From that time on progress was rapid, although the actual builders labored under unusual difficulties. Those men who were advancing westward from Omaha were compelled to haul

all their building and commissary supplies overland from
Iowa, and the track layers who were marching toward
the East had to bring much of their material to the scene
of their work across the Isthmus of Panama or around
Cape Horn.[1] A description of the scenes and methods attending the advance of the railway was published in
pamphlet form by the Union Pacific road in the summer
of 1868, and read thus:[2]

"There is nothing connected with the Union Pacific Railroad that
is not wonderful. The possibility of constructing such a road at some
future day has long loomed up as one of the events of a grander future
which all believed was to come for the land. . . What the country
has dreamed about for many years is becoming a reality much faster
than the people know. One year ago but forty miles were finished.
To-night three additional miles of rail will mark the track of the day's
advance. . .

"The train, which was made up for the excursionists, consisted of
cars as elegant as any that can be found east of the Missouri. It was
very difficult to look at them and realize that before night they would
be roaring along over plains from which hostile Indians, deer and antelope have not yet been driven.[3] . . . The surface is almost perfectly
flat, though its regular ascent toward the west, of about ten feet to
the mile, gives ample drainage. The soil is very rich, and the mind fal-
ters in its attempt to estimate the future of such a valley, or its immense
capabilities. The grain fields of Europe are mere garden patches beside
the green oceans which roll from Colorado to Indiana. . . The hills
behind sink into the plain until the horizon there is perfect. Those
on either side grow fainter, till through the heated air they take on
the appearance of low islands seen across many miles of water.

"Much of the land at the mouth of the valley is under cultivation,
and the deep black of the freshly turned loam, the dark green of the
wheat, the lighter grass, the deeper shades, and the brown of that which
the fires of the autumn spared, make the wide expanse a mosaic which
nature alone could color, and the prairies only find room to display.
Further on, huge plows, drawn by eight oxen, labored slowly along,

[1] The bulk of the labor necessary in the building of the Central Pacific portion of
the line was performed by Chinese coolies. Most of the work on the Union Pacific was
done by Irish immigrants.
[2] From the "Union Pacific Railroad Company . . . Progress of Their Road," etc.,
etc., pp. 8-12. The description here quoted was written by a correspondent of the "Cincinnati Gazette," who inspected the progress of the undertaking in June of 1868. The correspondent's letter to his newspaper was incorporated by the railroad in its pamphlet, which
was issued a few weeks later.
[3] Popular opinion that Indians were interlopers with which America had become
infested, along with other species of desirable and undesirable fauna, was then so deeply
implanted as to forbid expectation of change.

each furrow being an added ripple to the tide which is sweeping up over all these rich regions—a tide whose ebb the youngest will never know.

"The common mileposts seem to measure insignificant distances upon the wide plains. Only each five miles are noted on this road, and when one has passed between two of these, the step taken hardly appears like an advance. But there is one point marked in a manner to suggest the distance which has been overcome, and the gigantic character of the work. At a point in the plain, which otherwise seems as indeterminate as the position of a floating log at sea, a wide, arched sign, between two strong-set posts, bears this inscription: '100th meridian.' . . .

"Within twenty miles of the end of the track a few of the party rode on the cow-catcher. It seemed marvelous to drive on at twenty miles an hour over rails that had only been down for ten days. . . Three hundred and twenty-five miles out, a construction train of eighty cars stood on a side track. It was loaded with iron, ties, spikes, and chains, in exactly such proportions as were needed. It looked the very embodiment of system, and was one key to the rapidity with which the work progresses. A little farther on stood a similar train, and next we stopped in rear of the one where the tracklayers resided.

"The road had been a constant wonder from the start. . . But all we saw was commonplace and natural beside the scene that awaited us where the track was being laid. If the rest had excited amazement, this new wonder took all the attributes of magic. Fictions of the East must be rewritten to match the realities of this West. . .

"The plain fact will reveal the magnitude of the work. The graders go first. There are 2,000 of them. Their advance is near the Black Hills, and their work is done to Julesburgh. Of the tie-getters and woodchoppers there are 1,500. Their axes are resounding in the Black Hills, over Laramie Plains, and in the passes of the Rocky Mountains. They have 100,000 ties in these hills awaiting safeguards [soldiers] for trains to haul them. Then follow the tie-layers, carefully performing their share of the work.

"Now go back twenty miles on the road, and look at the immense construction trains, loaded with ties and rails, and all things needed for the work. It is like the grand reserve of an army. Six miles back are other trains of like character. These are the second line. Next, near the terminus, and following it hour by hour, are the boarding cars and a construction train, which answer to the actual battle line. The one is the camp; the other is the ammunition used in the fight. The boarding cars are each eighty feet long. Some are fitted with berths; two are dining halls; one is a kitchen, store room and office.

"The boarding cars go in advance. They are pushed to the extremity of the track; a construction train then runs up, unloads its material and starts back to bring another from the second line. . . The trucks, each drawn by two horses, ply between the track-layers and their supplies. One of these trucks takes on a load of rails, about forty, with the proper proportion of spikes and chairs, making a load, when the horses are started off on a full gallop for the track-layers. On each side of these trucks are rollers to facilitate running off the iron.

"The rails within reach, parties of five men stand on either side. One in the rear throws a rail upon the rollers, three in advance seize it and run out with it to the proper distance. The chairs have, meantime, been set under the last rails placed. The two men in the rear, with a single swing, force the end of the rail into the chair, and the chief of the squad calls out 'Down,' in a tone that equals the 'Forward' to an army. Every thirty seconds there came that brave 'Down,' 'Down,' on either side the track. They were the pendulum beats of a mighty era. . .

"If it is asked, 'How does the work get on?' again let the facts answer. On the 9th of May, 1866, but forty miles of road were completed. In a hundred and eighty-two working days thereafter, two hundred and forty-five additional miles were laid. . . From one o'clock till four in the afternoon, a mile and two hundred feet were added to this while the party was looking on."

The Central Pacific Company laid down 689 miles of track eastward from Sacramento, and the Union Pacific corporation built 1,086 miles westward from Omaha. The people of all the states watched the progress of the undertaking with constantly increasing interest, and their enthusiasm and expectancy steadily grew as the two groups of builders gradually drew closer together. Early in the spring of 1869 it became apparent that the work would very soon be finished, and that the two sections of track would be connected amid the Rocky Mountains of Utah. By the first week in May only a few miles of the road remained uncompleted, and it was possible to select the precise spot where the lines of rails would meet, and the day on which the ceremonies attending that event might occur. A location known as Promontory Point was chosen as the meeting place, and the tenth of May was designated as the date.

Finally the morning of the appointed day arrived,

and between the rails that stretched to the Atlantic Ocean and those which extended to the Pacific there remained a gap of about one hundred feet. All the ties were in place save at the center of the gap, where the space designed for one wooden cross-piece still remained unoc-

GREAT RAILWAY STATION AT CHICAGO—DEPARTURE OF A TRAIN.

399.—The mingling of the people.. Drawn by the artist Thomas Hogan.

cupied. Then, simultaneously, the Orientals from the West and the Caucasians from the East advanced toward each other, placing the missing links of steel. At their heels followed the spectators, edging forward step by step. Some six hundred people composed the throng, which included white Americans, Irish workmen, Chinese in blue blouses, negroes, and Mexicans in tall sombreros. There was also a little group of Indians. The last tie—a piece of laurel-wood from California—was put in position, and the last two rails were laid. One was fastened down with its full complement of ten iron spikes and the other with seven.

Then Nevada presented a spike of silver which was driven home, and Arizona gave her like offering made of iron, silver and gold. But one more spike remained—the "last spike" of gold—and it was to be given by California.

All the country knew what was to happen that day in the western mountains. During twenty years the people had debated the possibility of spanning the continent by an iron highway, and for five more years they had watched the progress of the work. The task was almost done. It was no longer a matter of decades or years, but of hours —half an hour—five minutes—one minute. Unnumbered multitudes had everywhere gathered to await the appointed signal, for it had been arranged that the blows of the sledge on the last spike should be communicated afar by electricity, and that the impulse so sent should ring countless bells in distant cities. So, on that May morning, the streets of San Francisco, New York, Cincinnati, St. Louis, Chicago, New Orleans, Omaha, Detroit, Boston, Philadelphia, Washington, Sacramento and every other center of importance throughout the country were filled with silent, waiting throngs.

The six hundred spectators up in the mountains crowded more closely together, and the two engines crept nearer to each other. The men who were to wield the silver sledge took their places beside the rail. A caution sped over the wires saying: "To everybody. Keep quiet. When the last spike is driven at Promontory Point we will say 'Done.' Don't break the circuit, but watch for the signals of the blows of the hammer." Several other brusque communications followed at intervals of a minute or so. The first of them said:

"Almost ready. Hats off. Prayer is being offered."

Then this came from Promontory Point into the waiting world:

"We have got done praying. The spike is about to be presented."

And finally: "All ready now."

Down to the people in the streets came the sound of bells, slow and measured, and they knew the meaning of the cadence. To each note of the brazen clangor they responded with a fierce and exultant shout that was cut off abruptly so they might not dim the message for which they listened. It told them that the task begun nearly two centuries and a half before was finished. There was to be no more loneliness; no more sections. The oceans were joined, and all who dwelt between them might at last be neighbors and friends in a real sense. Never again could distance or isolation be decisive factors in the life, social conditions, culture or opportunities of the people. All might mingle with one another, get really acquainted, discover mutual needs, and work in better harmony for the common advancement. Such was the realization that swept over the multitudes as they lifted up their rhythmic shouts in answer to the bells. It was as though they were chanting the last, triumphant words in a long epic of human endeavor. And if those of future times should seek for a day on which the country at last became a nation, and for an event by virtue of which its inhabitants became one people, it may be that they will not select the verdict of some political campaign or battle-field but choose, instead, the hour when two engines—one from the East and the other from the West—met at Promontory.

VIEW OF SALT LAKE FROM AN OBSERVATION CAR.

An example of the observation cars used on the first trans-continental railroad in 1869. They resembled modern coal cars with seats. 12mo. Col. Lith. Amer.

CHAPTER LVIII

SUMMARY OF PRESENT CONDITIONS

THE opening of a modern travel highway across the continent marked the end of a work that began when English speaking white men landed on the shores of Virginia and Massachusetts. With its completion a destiny was realized, and the spirit in which the people saw the event showed that they divined its significance. The event itself, coming while the memory of the tremendous civil conflict remained undimmed, offered the first opportunity, since that struggle, to reveal a longing for real national solidarity.

The contrast between the new economic conquest and the recent war was a happy omen. One had been born of sectional differences, errors and misunderstanding whose origins reached far back into history. As a consequence of its outbreak the young nation had hung on the brink of dissolution, and its continuance spelled for a period the destruction of ties created by more than two hundred years of association in earlier times of need and trouble. The new conquest, on the other hand, was a common effort for the good of all. Its steady progress had been marked, not by disruption, devastation and sorrow, but by visions of closer intercourse, kindlier feeling and increased prosperity. Through it the desert places were to be made populous and fruitful. Its purpose was not to sever but to unite. By its aid all the communities of the land, however distant, were to become neighbors, and

1357

every city was to acquire a new relation to all the others and have its own larger duty to perform. There could be no more sections in the old and jealous sense, for in new days to come the mingling of the people was to bring upon them a fuller realization of their essential brotherhood. That was the prophecy borne by the ringing of bells and thunder of cannon loaded with powder only, and by the shrill exultant shout which sped from one ocean to the other within a moment of time. The inhabitants of America already aspired to an enduring unity, and their aspiration was transmuted into fact in the hour when comprehension of the one way to attain it swept over them.

Since that day the people have progressed somewhat in the path on which they then entered. At times they have strayed from it because of carelessness, and sometimes they have been beguiled from the safe road by the lure of ease or selfish gain, for the right way is hard, and must be cleared for every advance. But they have always come back to the new path, and to-day, more than ever before, there is appreciation that real union and the highest degree of general welfare is best sought by an intermingling of all the people, by their unselfish recognition of mutual needs and responsibilities, and courage to meet the obligations which time, new conditions and close associations have placed upon them.

Without that free and constant intercourse of the population brought about as a direct result of improved methods in continental travel and communication, the great invisible components of enduring nationality could hardly have been called into being. A region so immense, whose geographical and industrial conditions afford such contrasts and whose sectional needs and methods are so diverse, presents a very serious problem to the power of social coherence and to a desire for social advancement. It is quite likely that the political fabric of nationality would have become unwieldy and difficult of advantageous preservation had it not been enormously reinforced, throughout its whole extent, by a communication system which has created the saving sense of neighborliness to which reference has been made. Considered as a political structure the union is venerable of years, but as a people welded into one organism through the instrumentality of common purposes, desires and hopes, the nation is young indeed. These are still the days of its childhood. It is even now coming into a first realization of its own strength, and does not yet know how to use it. But if the mistakes and strange experiences of youth are not forgotten they will be of profit in the future, and wisdom will eventually invoke and guide the giant's power.

During the months immediately following the completion of the first transcontinental railroad a number of eastern cities showed their understanding of its meaning by sending delegations of their citizens on visits of neighborly friendship to San Francisco. Among the Atlantic communities which so acted was Boston, and in May of 1870 a hundred people from that city travelled to the Pacific coast in six days,[1] borne thence without change of cars. The journey then undertaken was at that time the longest yet made on any continent over continuous lines of rails. Those who took it were carried between the two oceans in less than half the interval Mistress Knight had required in going from Boston to New York. They moved across the country without effort of their own, in apartments

---

[1] Including halts in Chicago and elsewhere. Another delegation, composed of representatives of the civic and mercantile bodies of Cincinnati, also made a similar trip.

made beautiful by tapestries and carved woods. The sunlight did not come to them through paper coated with bear's grease, but through windows of plate glass. Their food was kept in refrigerators; they ate, with implements of silver, from fragile dishes that stood on rare mahogany. At night they did not lie down on warped puncheons, but in comfortable beds. They had a barber shop, baths, a music room, two libraries. They even had a printing establishment and a daily four-page newspaper that was written, put into type, printed and published every morning[1] in a section of their moving hotel. And in the eighth issue of their newspaper its editor mentioned the charming view they had enjoyed one evening, as they descended the mountains and looked down on a little sheet of water called Donner Lake. "It nestles," he said, "at the base of the mountain, and we gazed with pleasure on its clear, crystal surface, tinted with cerulean blue reflected from the cloudless vault of Heaven." Then the night fell, the brief glimpse at the beautiful lake was forgotten, and the travellers strolled in to dinner. Afterward, as was usual, they gathered for an hour or two with their books and their music.

Forty-four years have passed since America was crossed in six days by the Boston excursionists. The interval in question has been a period of extraordinary advancement in those matters pertaining to the subject here considered, but for perhaps half of that time—or until about 1890—it was not distinguished by the general adoption of any new or revolutionary methods of locomotion. Until recent years, rather, the period that has elapsed since the joining of the oceans has been charac-

---

[1] The first daily newspaper ever so created. It was called the "Trans-Continental." A complete file consists of twelve numbers, for it was also printed during the return trip of the party, on same train, in June.

erized mainly by the extension or improvement of those transportation methods which were then in active use. All the energy of the country was for some time devoted to a utilization and refinement of devices already known. Every nook and corner of the country had to be penetrated by the railways before the nation had at its disposal all the service they—as at present constituted—could render. And, in addition, the railway as an engineering and mechanical implement had to be perfected.

Only in name and elementary principles is the railroad of 1914 identical with the railway of 1870. The adoption of the air brake, block system, better roadbeds, the automatic coupler and enormously increased motive power, together with the introduction of heavy cars and a multitude of human conveniences has transformed the passenger-carrying service of our steel highways. Accidents are no longer looked upon as "acts of God," or unavoidable. Practically every occurrence of that sort is today considered by the people, the authorities, and by the railways themselves, as proof of prior human carelessness either in the construction process, administrative regulation, inspection or operation of the road on which it takes place. The existing attitude toward accidents is a sane one. Its adoption by the Federal government and by the present railway administrators of the country would doubtless have wrought a decrease in the calamities which for so many years have been a blot on the railroad system of the country had not the system as a whole been compelled to labor under a severe handicap imposed on it by lack of foresight, greed, and financial wrong.

The American people are no longer designedly unfair —except to themselves. Their habit is to be patient in the endurance of many kinds of imposition. They submit to counterfeit domination for periods longer than those during which other peoples tolerate similar unnecessary conditions; hoping each time, apparently, that the cause of irritation will be voluntarily removed by those responsible. When the situation becomes unbearable there arises a murmur of remonstrance the significance of which, despite many precedents, is rarely grasped by the ones toward whom it is directed. The will of this people—when determination to alter an existing economic condition has been reached—is not at once expressed in the phraseology of excitement or command, but in words of suggestion and entreaty. Opponents of a slowly formed popular judgment who disregard that apparent appeal and wait for further verbal outcry before giving compliance, await in vain. The next step of the public is quiet action. Threats are the weapons of the weak, and have no useful place in the relations between a people and those to whom the details of its well-being are entrusted. No man whose duties affect for good or evil the welfare of his fellow citizens; no institution whose conduct is similarly potent, is worthy of responsibility and power if amenable to threats and fear alone. Selfish standards have been cast aside and we are on the up-grade again. Our future motor of action is to be a sense of fairness geared to practicality. The schemer—whether personal or corporate—who seeks unfair advantage through devious ways will be stripped of his authority, while he who gives himself with open record and right purpose to any work whose legitimate functions contribute to the general good, will receive the trust of his fellow men.

It has been said there is no indication that the railways of the country would willingly revert to those days of their history so marred by unfair discrimination against individuals, cities and sections. Indeed, there are indications[1] that they rejoice, with the public, at their emancipation from such practises and regret that they were not able to bring the period of corruption to an end without assistance. But some of them are still confronted by another opportunity, equally large, wherein to display a newly acquired moral strength and thereby gain, in greater degree, the public confidence which is not yet wholly theirs. They can further improve their position by withdrawing from participation in political affairs and questionable financial transactions, and by confining themselves to the complex and increasingly important problem of transporting the people and commodities of the nation —the task for which they were primarily designed.

It is probable that the quality of service which can be given by American railways, as far as speed and luxury of travel are concerned, has reached the limit of excellence permitted by their present physical constitution. The brief age of steam is approaching its end, and the long age of electricity is near at hand. As a matter of fact the ability of electrical engineers to alter the conditions of travel and transportation is already somewhat in advance of opportunites presented for its exercise. For some years they have been prepared to build and operate electrically propelled trains at a speed of perhaps a hundred miles an hour[2] if there were roadbeds capable of bearing the shock represented by such a velocity. The existing American roadbeds were designed only to uphold steam travel at the rate of forty or fifty miles an hour, with about sixty miles as the limit of safety for regular

[1] Despite frequent revelation of discriminations and other improper acts practised by roads that are still burdened by evil administration.
[2] In the well-known German experiments a speed of about one hundred and thirty miles an hour was attained by electrical vehicles on a railed track for a short distance.

traffic on the best constructed tracks.[1] Even those speeds are much in excess of the average schedules for passenger service throughout the country, and it is not desirable that we acquire travel facilities swifter than those at present available until suitable roadbeds are established for the hundred-miles-an-hour electrical trains. The fact that we could even now move over the country at such a velocity, and yet do not do so, furnishes another instance of the "progress backward" method of evolution in land transportation. The hundred-miles-an-hour motor and vehicle are waiting, but the road for them is not yet built. Nor will it be constructed for a considerable period to come.

Instead of a further search for speed, another and more important need confronts the nation. The recent perfection and widespread adoption of mechanical vehicles designed for use on land highways—after experimentation lasting about a century—has made it necessary to rebuild a large proportion of all existing American land roads in order that the whole economic value of the revolutionary improvement may be made available. To this task the country is already turning, perhaps with a haste that may breed unnecessary waste and error. But enough experience has already been gained to show that permanent, scientifically constructed and hard-surfaced highways are essential for the purpose in view, and that public funds—from whatever treasury supplied—are wasted if devoted to the maintenance of existing dirt roads or others not created in accord with the modern practise of road laying. The work to be done is not one of repair or of improvement, but of original building by

---

[1] The recent American tendency has been to decrease the speed of express trains, rather than to increase it.

engineers from foundation upward. Its cost will be vast, and its benefits are destined to be still greater.

One factor of present-day American life that for some time has been exercising an influence in restraining both the speed and frequency of human movement is the omnipresence of the telegraph and telephone. Those devices have in some degree made physical travel unnecessary. Instead of going in person to conduct negotiations or to make visits we send our words or voices only, and keep our bodies at home. In the days of 1870 if an emergency called an eastern man to the Middle West he went in person, and was three or four days on the road. To-day, in similar case, he remains seated at his desk and in two minutes is talking with the other man in St. Louis, Chicago, Council Bluffs, Little Rock, Minneapolis or Denver. That also is travel, though of a species not imagined by the men who pushed pole-boats, guided pack-trains through the wilderness and drifted down the rivers on their arks. They could be in only one place at a time, and had hard work to get there. To-day we can be at both ends of a long pilgrimage in the same instant. When they were separated in the woods their halloos might carry for half a mile. We whisper and laugh at one another across distances that meant journeys of months to them. They fought their way on foot through forests and deserts and mountains. We can fly through the air from ocean to ocean and gaze down on the cities they founded.[1] Their log cabins are gone, and we sit amid wires, push-buttons and tubes by which we summon light, heat, water, food, drink, absent friends, messenger boys, motor-cars and music, as our fancy wills.

[1] Rodgers, an American aviator, flew from the Atlantic to the Pacific across the United States, in 1911. His actual flying time—he made many stops—was about three days and ten hours, and his average speed while flying was about fifty-one and a half miles an hour. He was the first human who crossed a continent through the air.

A HISTORY OF TRAVEL IN AMERICA

The recent accomplishment of human flight[1] is a feat
so tremendous that—even as we see the thing performed—
it still seems a figment of the fancy; an absurd hallucina-
tion. When the little speck has disappeared we look down
and observe the tracks made by the apparatus while it still
clung to earth. Then the tracks stop. The ton of machinery that was lately there has vanished. It is somewhere above, rushing forward at eighty or a hundred
miles an hour in a place where there are no tracks, yet
guided amid the clouds by human intellect.

A certain apparent popular indifference to man-flight
which is already visible—the seemingly matter-of-fact acceptance of such a deed—is perhaps not so real as it appears. The human race has been so mentally benumbed by
its own performances that this last wonder is not yet
grasped—and may never be. The limit of our comprehension had been reached before it came. We have entered, as
was said in the beginning, upon an era wherein the impossible has become commonplace, and the average man, in
instinctive self-protection of his sanity, no longer gives
deep consideration to those conditions with which he is
surrounded or to the powers harnessed by genius for his
benefit. The average mind already shrinks from effort to
assimilate what eyes behold and hands use, and so, hereafter, we must accept much of what is done for us without understanding, content to let a few work in regions not
for us, while we casually employ what they bestow.
Those who hereafter become benefactors of the race
through invention and discovery in the fields of physical
and mechanical science are destined to find their large
reward within their own thoughts.

[1] By the Americans, Wilbur Wright and Orville Wright. There are now (1914)
nearly eight thousand men in the world who can fly.

1366

400.—The old Indian trail of 1675 across New Jersey as it appeared on the morning of June 13, 1910. Hamilton, the aviator, on his flight from New York City to Philadelphia, overhauling a railroad train running at 50 miles an hour. First trip of an aeroplane made in accordance with a previously announced schedule.

A HISTORY OF TRAVEL IN AMERICA

Our only measure of a man's greatness—whatever his task may be—lies in our limited ability to appreciate what he has done and to comprehend the value of his work. If our understanding cannot grasp what he has accomplished, or follow him over the unfamiliar road along which he has moved to his victory, then our measure fails. We take what he gives and are pleased, or we cast it aside, but we do not see the man as he is. Thus it has always been, and much more often will it be so in the future. It is not because we are thoughtless, or ungrateful. It is because we have so many other things to think about, and to do.

It is perhaps not unfair to say that the mass of men constituting the last pioneer generations of America are in some respects more remote from us—through the broadening of our knowledge horizon and our increased power to do things—than they were from the men of the Glacial Epoch. So overwhelming has been man's accumulation of understanding and collective strength during the last three generations that, in respect of mastery over material conditions, we are giants in comparison with them. Yet in one regard their work was more splendid than ours has since been, for they—despite their relative ignorance and incapacity—advanced in the span of one lifetime from forest trails and flatboats to turnpikes, canals and railroads; whereas we, with our indescribably greater powers, have until now made no widespread improvement in our highways, have forgotten the rivers, have neglected many of the canals they created,[1] and have misused the railroads they introduced. But we are awakening, and soon we, too, shall be at our task with an awesome strength. It is needful.

[1] The extensive improvement of the Erie Canal, now in progress, is a noteworthy exception.

A HISTORY OF TRAVEL IN AMERICA

The pioneers have gone. Boone, Fitch, Evans, Tecumseh, Watson, Schultz, Clinton, Cuming, Shreve, Dearborn, Stevens, Strickland, Baldwin, Bruen, Pilcher, Roosevelt, Parker, Berry, Crockett, Floyd, La Barge, Smith, Bunting, Applegate, Whitney, Donner, Abbey—all the dreamers and the workers and wanderers have played their parts and disappeared. We are the custodians of their prodigious legacies, and we, in our turn, must pass them on—made better or worse by our use and stewardship.

In one respect we have failed to progress in like degree with the pioneers, and so our chiefest contribution to the swelling inheritance of the nation has not yet been made. We have not heretofore accompanied our new strength with a corresponding advance in those invisible standards by which it should be guided. The inward development has lagged behind, and so we live amid devices fashioned by us and theoretically subject to our direction, by whose better employment we might lift ourselves to a higher plane of common happiness and comfort, yet do not fully utilize them. We are not the masters of our environment and implements to the extent that the pioneers were. The complex economic machinery we have created has to some degree imperceptibly slipped from our common control into the hands of a few who have misapplied it and stolen its usefulness for their own enrichment. We have been wounded by the splendid tools that we ourselves have slowly fashioned for our own improvement. Not until we alter that condition, and regulate their future use by impulses and methods correspondingly fine will we reap the full benefits of the centuries and toil spent in their making.

The concrete machinery of our social organization—

1369

of which the existing transportation system is a part—is in principle competent for its task. So if it fails, or is ineffective, then the cause of its inefficiency must be sought in us and the methods of our manipulation, and not in it. We have been careless, have suffered spoliation in consequence, and are destined to pay still more. For some unfortunate effects of our laxity have probably penetrated too deeply into all our affairs to make their eradication possible without injuring the innocent more than the guilty. Those who have filched treasure from their brothers sit secure among their spoils, beyond reach of retribution save the verdict of self-contemplation and the calm judgment of their fellow men. Perhaps that will be sufficient.

As an atonement for the neglect of our affairs it now devolves on us to find within ourselves whatever degree of self-restraint may be required by present conditions, and, through the manifestation of statesmanship by all men, hereafter prove ourselves worthy to control our natural and created riches.

To one who has followed the story of progress and historical development that has been outlined in these pages must come the question: What do the approaching years contain? It is idle to speculate; rash to predict. Once more it is fitting to say that only those who are indeed great can see the future with certainty, and if there are any such amongst us they are silent. Perhaps they shrink from the laughter sure to greet their words if they did speak. Very likely we too would say of such a one: "Poor fellow; what a pity he is crazy." Human nature has in some particulars remained about the same. We prefer to prophesy a thing the day after we see it performed.

A HISTORY OF TRAVEL IN AMERICA

As we sit at meat in moving hotels which travel fifty miles an hour and look out upon the panorama that drops so swiftly away, or as we hear a strange sound above and gaze up into the sky we behold visions of the coming days that are not put into speech. We are afraid to whisper them. They may be dreams, or may not be. We prefer to wait and see. But of one thing we are sure, and can say it without fear. The preliminary work has been done. It has been a long, hard march from 1620 to 1914, but some of the results have been worth while. Almost every possible mistake has already been made, and so it only remains to correct their present effects wherever we can and avoid repetition of them hereafter. The present generation need not strike a pose on a pedestal of vainglory and mesmerize itself into a belief that ultimate perfection has been approximately reached. Such a thought would contain a prolific germ of error, nor is it likely to be entertained.

As we look back into the past we begin to see that the features of those times most important to us, and which have most deeply impressed their influence on these years, were not the wars waged by men but the influences and moral attributes—whether for good or evil—which impelled them to do what they did in the more ordinary affairs of life. Within and among ourselves we behold the complex result of former conflicting standards of belief and action. We see much to be regretted, and to be altered before we can reach the plane to which we aspire. May it not be well for us and for those who are to follow if we, as a people, henceforward study our past national life with more thought for the relationships which have always existed between our standards of conduct and our permanent and best material welfare.

1371

A HISTORY OF TRAVEL IN AMERICA

As we bustle back and forth we do not seek to build merely for an hour or a generation. There is also an ever present duty that can only be seen by standing in imagination among the unborn hosts and gazing back to now. Our lives are likewise to be told, and when they are recorded it will give us more worthy rank if it can be said of us, not that we were the first men to fly through the air, but that we were the first to recognize the highest value of history as a teacher and to prove it by our own deeds.

The wearying, slow, preparatory work has been performed. Behind us is an interesting record that, even with its tragedy and blunders, is an inspiration to the genius of men. Persistent effort is always an inspiration, even though its results are small. Much has been done, and various things remain to be undone. A new era is beginning whose chief characteristics in every field of endeavor are to be a finer wisdom, a smaller selfishness, and a more sincere thought for the comfort, safety, happiness and welfare of all the people. In the attainment of those things there lies a triumph worth more to the nation than that which will proceed from the discovery and use of forces and utilities yet unimagined. This epilogue is only the prologue of another, prouder and still more wonderful history that is surely destined to be written on some far day of the future. Our air-ships are the symbols of a new aspiration. Henceforth the travels of mankind are not to be across mountain and forest; but upward, through realms they have beheld but dimly from below.

APPENDICES

APPENDICES

CONTENTS OF APPENDICES

APPENDIX A

A STATISTICAL HISTORY OF NINETY-FIVE EARLY AMERICAN RAILWAYS IN TABULAR FORM — THEIR DATES OF CHARTER, DATES OF FIRST USE AND INDIVIDUAL LENGTHS — THE TOTAL RAILROAD MILEAGE IN EACH OF ELEVEN STATES AT ANNUAL INTERVALS — COST OF THAT MILEAGE AND EQUIPMENT AT CORRESPONDING PERIODS — THE YEARLY RECEIPTS OF THAT MILEAGE AS DERIVED FROM PASSENGER TRAFFIC AND FREIGHT TRAFFIC — THE SYSTEM SUSTAINED DURING ITS FIRST TWENTY YEARS BY INCOME OBTAINED FROM HUMAN TRAVEL — OTHER GENERAL AND PARTICULAR CONCLUSIONS DERIVED FROM THE FIGURES

APPENDIX B

TOTAL CONSTRUCTION AND EQUIPMENT COSTS OF THE SAME NINETY-FIVE EARLY ROADS COMPARED WITH THEIR TOTAL LIABILITIES OR CAPITAL FOR IDENTICAL YEARS — THE FIGURES PRACTICALLY CORRESPOND DURING THE FIRST THIRTY YEARS OF AMERICAN RAILWAY HISTORY — CERTAIN EXCEPTIONS AND THE REASONS THEREFOR — NET EARNINGS COMPARED WITH THE COSTS AND CAPITAL — THE MILEAGE AS COMPARED WITH THE COST OF ITS CONSTRUCTION AND THE CAPITAL INVOLVED

APPENDIX C

A LIST SHOWING THE CONFUSION OF GAUGES IN ALL PARTS OF THE COUNTRY UNTIL AS LATE A DATE AS 1866 — TWELVE DIFFERENT TRACK-WIDTHS IN USE — THEY RANGED FROM 4 FEET 3 INCHES TO 6 FEET — THIRTY RAILWAYS, FROM MAINE TO MISSOURI AND TEXAS, CITED AS EXAMPLES

APPENDIX D

GARFIELD'S ADDRESS ON THE RAILWAY PROBLEM, DELIVERED BEFORE HUDSON COLLEGE IN 1873—RELATION OF THE PROBLEM TO THE FUTURE OF THE REPUBLIC — WHAT THE LOCOMOTIVE IS LIKELY TO DO TO SOCIETY — HIS OPINION OF THE RESULT THAT MIGHT FOLLOW IF THE MECHANICAL MACHINE WAS COMBINED WITH THE LEGAL MACHINE KNOWN AS A CORPORATION — RELATION OF THE DARTMOUTH COLLEGE CASE TO THE QUESTION — POSSIBLE SOLUTIONS SUGGESTED—SERIOUSNESS OF THE SUBJECT—CONFIDENCE IN THE ULTIMATE DECISION OF THE PEOPLE

1375

APPENDIX E

A LIST OF THE FIFTY-THREE PRINCIPAL CANALS IN THE UNITED STATES IN 1850, AT THE CLOSE OF THE EARLY CANAL-BUILDING EPOCH — THEIR INDIVIDUAL LENGTHS AND TOTAL MILEAGE — THE CITIES JOINED BY THEM — SEVENTEEN STATES, FROM MAINE IN THE EAST TO LOUISIANA IN THE SOUTH AND ILLINOIS IN THE WEST, POSSESSED SUCH FACILITIES OF COMMUNICATION

APPENDIX F

SEWARD'S ADDRESS AT THE BEGINNING OF THE AUBURN AND OWASCO CANAL IN 1835 — INTERSECTIONAL JEALOUSIES INTERFERE WITH THE CREATION OF BETTER COMMUNICATION FACILITIES — PRETEXTS AND RESULTS OF THE FEELING — USE OF PUBLIC FUNDS ADVOCATED FOR ADVANCING LARGE ENTERPRISES — WEALTH NOT THE HIGHEST GOAL OF THE PEOPLE — MORAL, POLITICAL AND INDUSTRIAL EVIL CLOSELY ASSOCIATED — DANGERS INHERENT IN A REPUBLICAN. FORM OF GOVERNMENT — METHODS OF AVOIDING THEM — SOUND EDUCATION, UNDERSTANDING AND POPULAR RIGHTEOUSNESS MUST KEEP PACE WITH MATERIAL PROSPERITY — WEALTH WITHOUT WISDOM IS FATAL

APPENDIX G

FIGURES SHOWING THE EXTENT, METHOD OF ACQUIREMENT, COST AND USE OF THE PUBLIC DOMAIN IN 1826, AFTER HALF A CENTURY OF NATIONAL EXISTENCE — 214,000,000 ACRES OF LAND BOUGHT FROM THE NATIVES AT A COST OF ABOUT $3,400,000 — AVERAGE COST OF SUCH LAND ABOUT THREE CENTS AN ACRE — GOVERNMENTAL SALES OF LAND TO WHITE MEN HAD AMOUNTED TO LESS THAN 20,000,000 ACRES — RECEIPTS FROM THOSE SALES, $40,000,-000 — NUMBER OF INDIANS THEN IN ORGANIZED STATES AND TERRITORIES WITH AMOUNT OF LAND CLAIMED BY THEM — 750,000,000 ACRES IN THE WEST STILL REMAINED LARGELY UNDER NATIVE OWNERSHIP — OTHER ALLIED RECORDS

APPENDIX H

STATEMENTS MADE BY CAUCASIAN HISTORIANS BETWEEN 1643 AND 1847 REGARDING THE CHARACTER, DESIRES, CAPACITY AND ATTITUDE OF THE EASTERN AMERICAN NATIVES, THE ATTITUDE OF THE WHITES TOWARD THEM, AND THE PURPOSES, METHODS AND RESULTS OF THE WHITE POLICY

APPENDIX I

A CAUCASIAN ESTIMATE OF THE CHARACTER OF TECUMSEH, CONTAINED IN A LETTER PUBLISHED BY AN INDIANA NEWSPAPER IN 1820

APPENDIX J

AN INDIAN STATE DOCUMENT OF 1828 — MESSAGE OF THE DUAL EXEC-
UTIVES OF THE CHEROKEE NATION TO THE CHEROKEE GENERAL
COUNCIL — EXAMPLE OF THE MOST ADVANCED PROGRESS MADE BY
INDIANS UNDER THEIR OWN CONSTITUTIONAL GOVERNMENT AND
INDEPENDENCE — THE CLAIMS OF GEORGIA ANALYZED AND AN-
SWERED — VIEWS OF AN INDIAN REPUBLIC ON THE SUBJECTS OF
THE FRANCHISE, MORALITY, THE JUDICIARY, COURT PROCEDURE,
A FREE PRESS, FINANCE, EDUCATION, INTERNATIONAL RELATIONS
WITH THE UNITED STATES AND OTHER MATTERS OF GENERAL
PUBLIC INTEREST

APPENDIX K

THE WESTWARD MIGRATIONS OF 1849 — A STATEMENT, IN THE FORM
OF A CATECHISM, GIVING INFORMATION TO AN INTENDING EMI-
GRANT CONCERNING THE EQUIPMENT THEN NECESSARY IN TRAV-
ELLING FROM THE MISSISSIPPI VALLEY TO CALIFORNIA — ADVICE
ABOUT HIS WAGONS, HIS LIVE STOCK, HIS PROVISIONS, HIS WEAPONS
AND THE ROUTE TO BE FOLLOWED

APPENDIX L

A LIST OF THE PRINCIPAL OVERLAND TRAVEL ROUTES BETWEEN THE
MISSISSIPPI VALLEY AND THE PACIFIC COAST, AS USED BY CARAVAN
TRAVEL FROM ABOUT 1849 TO 1868

APPENDIX M

THE UNPUBLISHED MANUSCRIPT DIARY OF A MAN WHO TRAVELLED TO
CALIFORNIA IN 1849 — LIFE ON AND NEAR THE SANTA FÉ TRAIL —
INTIMATE REVELATIONS REGARDING THE DAILY AFFAIRS OF AN
OVERLAND CARAVAN — MEETINGS WITH TRANSPLANTED RED MEN
AND NATIVE WESTERN INDIANS — FUN AT THE EXPENSE OF NEW
YORK EMIGRANTS — BAD FEELING CROPS OUT AND FIGHTS OCCUR
— DIGGING CAVES TO ESCAPE HAILSTORMS — ARRIVAL AT SANTA
FÉ — LOST IN THE MOUNTAINS — CARRYING A WOUNDED MAN
ON A LITTER — SUFFERING FOR WANT OF WATER — GOLD AT LAST

APPENDIX A

A list of ninety-five of the early railways of the United States, together with certain information relating to their organization, first use by the public, length, cost, and source of income is here given.

In order that the value of such records might be extracted from them it was necessary to group the facts in tabular form, in the shape of statistics. For that reason they could not well be introduced into the body of these volumes. Yet the apparently prosaic figures of the following tables reveal several phases of the early railroad history of the country with a clearness not to be obtained in any other way.

The aggregate length of the ninety-five roads considered is three thousand nine hundred and thirteen miles. But two of them—the Baltimore and Ohio and the Erie—were enterprises born of broad vision. They were the only instances in which early American railways on the verge of construction were conceived and planned, from the first, as important arteries of general commerce designed to connect separated sections of the country. The average length of the ninety-five roads, including the Baltimore and Ohio and the Erie, was forty-one and one-fifth miles. Without those two railways the average length of the remaining ninety-three was less than thirty-four miles. In other words the first railroads of the country, as actually planned and constructed, were merely neighborhood conveniences built to join localities, towns or cities that lay close to one another—often only a short distance apart. In thirty-two of these cases the places connected were separated by a distance of less than twenty miles. The building of a railroad was sometimes the result of local pride. One town would decide to construct such a highway because a rival town had begun a like task. There was at first no coöperation among those who undertook the work. A railroad would begin somewhere, run a few miles and end somewhere else, with no prior plan or purpose to have it connect with a similar construction. Finally, after a number of small and disconnected railways had appeared in some region, the several links that would hitch them all together were laid down. And even then it often happened that the links were of different widths, or gauges, which of course

1379

made uninterrupted conveyance of people or goods an impossibility. It was eleven years after the introduction of railways in New York before the important chain of neighboring cities between Albany and Buffalo were finally connected by several iron roads that had all been built as separate pieces of work.

As has previously been said, both the early dreamers and the general public had considered the new subject of railways chiefly in terms of speed and human convenience. But the men with money, by whose coöperation only could railroad building be begun, refused to invest their funds for the purpose of facilitating public travel. Their habit of mind was to consider the making, movement and sale of commodities, and it was in connection with those purposes that they at last consented to give their support to the revolutionary transportation method. The records indicate they were in error, and that their action in investing money for the building of short railways between near-by towns in the belief that such highways would be profitable as carriers of goods was an exhibition of poor business judgment. But the investments were saved, in their early and critical stage, by the general desire for human travel to which so little attention had been given. From the very first days of their operation the main reliance of the new railroads lay in passenger traffic, and the records indicate that an overwhelming preponderance of railway income was for years obtained from that source. The facts show, as was said in the text, that America's railways were children of the spirit of conquest and the demand for wider, swifter movement, even though the financial nurses who coddled them were blind to their parentage.

Although the general situation as here stated is apparent from the appended tables, there were certain instances wherein the conditions under discussion were especially noticeable and easily traced, and one—in Pennsylvania—in which unique local conditions brought about a temporary exception to the prevailing rule. In Maryland, for instance, it will be seen that a little road of thirty miles in length, called the Washington Branch Railway, came into use in 1835. Its opening was the only new element of the year in the Maryland railroad situation. During the first twelve months following its use the freight receipts of all the iron highways of the state increased by about $8,400 and the annual income from human travel jumped $139,000. A similar incident is to be found in the Massachusetts conditions of 1840. The Western Railroad had begun business the year before, and while the freight income of all the Massachusetts railways showed a gain of about $51,000 for the year, the money derived from transporting passengers increased by some $148,000. Again, in New York, there was a striking example of the same state of affairs due to the opening of 89 miles of new road in 1835. The following twelvemonth showed a gain in New York's aggregate passenger income of more than $200,000, while freight brought only $8,000 more to the coffers of the railways than had been similarly derived during the previous year.

The first ten railways in the Pennsylvania list were built mainly for the transportation of iron and coal. But with the opening of the first general road in the state—the Philadelphia, Germantown and Norristown—in 1832, the effect of passenger traffic became at once apparent, and within six years the income derived by such roads from human travel exceeded the sums they received for carrying goods. In 1843, however, the freight income of Pennsylvania's railways again passed the mark set by receipts derived from passengers and that long established condition will, in Pennsylvania, no doubt prevail indefinitely because of well-known conditions peculiar to it or to any common-wealth in which is produced a large quantity of commodities necessary to modern social conditions. Certain communities and states have in course of time become chief points of origin for things all men must have, and the railways leading from them derive their principal revenue from the transporting of those goods.

Our first railroads were no exception to the general rule which governed the creation and adoption of each new method of movement. They were devices whose primary value lay in the increased facilities afforded by them for the personal use and comfort of the people in moving from place to place. Only after they were expanded did they assume a high importance as agencies for the transportation of material wealth. On railways, as on the preceding horses, sleds, boats and wagons, the American was a traveller before he was an extensive shipper of goods.

Under each state heading, in the appended tables, is a list of the early roads of that state, together with the dates of their charters, of their first use by the public (often before the lines were completed) and of their lengths as originally planned. In the chronological table under each state heading, the mileage and cost set down in connection with each year is the total mileage and total cost of all the railways of the state at the date mentioned. The passenger receipts and freight receipts are exclusively for the years named—not the accumulated totals of all previous years.

It should be stated that the figures here used in showing the cost, the passenger receipts and freight receipts of the early American rail-ways are taken from the important and exceedingly scarce "History of the Railroads and Canals of the United States of America," by Henry V. Poor, published in New York City in 1860. The author knows of no other equally authoritative, elaborate and early compilation of the sort. Poor's "History," considered as an assemblage of financial statistics relat-ing to the railroads of the country in their formative period, and as a bibliography of early American railway law, is a product of care, thoroughness and labor. The other statements and dates here used are gathered from various contemporary records and publications dealing with the subject.

The tables follow:

MAINE:	Chartered.	First use.	Length.
Bangor, Oldtown and Milford.......	1833	1836	11
Portland, Saco and Portsmouth.......	1837	1842	51¼
*Maine, New Hampshire and Mass....	1836		1¼
Calais and Baring.................	1837	1851	6

* Later consolidated, by legislative acts, with Boston and Maine and Portland, Saco and Portsmouth.

Year.	Mileage.	Cost.	Passenger Receipts.	Freight Receipts.
1837	11	$354,000	$11,040	$10,105
1838	11	354,000	11,596	9,955
1839	11	354,000	9,461	10,201
1840	11	354,000	10,220	6,104
1843	62	1,426,730	35,894	9,204
1845	62	1,615,286	116,113	26,938
1850	112	3,070,854	249,994	93,747
1851	284	8,404,778	365,746	190,288
1852	328	11,201,819	423,469	252,952

NEW HAMPSHIRE:	Chartered.	First use.	Length.
*Nashua and Lowell................	1835	1838	6¼
*Eastern	1836	1840	16½
*Boston and Maine.................	1835	1840	37¼
Concord Railroad Co.............	1835	1842	34½

*These were also early Massachusetts roads. The Concord road was the first New Hampshire railway entirely within the state limits.

Year.	Mileage.	Cost.	Passenger Receipts.	Freight Receipts.
1842-3	34½	$725,000	$48,035	$21,808
1843-4	34½	742,500	72,799	65,421
1844-5	34½	750,000	90,545	90,099
1845-6	34½	800,000	109,971	115,469
1846-7	103½	2,499,967	137,758	160,747
1847-8	151	5,244,500	238,907	199,602

VERMONT:	Chartered.	First use.	Length.
Vermont Central	1843	1848	119
Connecticut and Passumpic River.....	1835	1848	110
Rutland and Burlington............	1843	1849	119½
Western Vermont	1845	1851	54
Vermont Valley	1848	1851	23¾

Year.	Mileage.	Cost.	Passenger Receipts.	Freight Receipts.
1849	40	$800,000	$25,110	$32,211
1850	240¾	8,430,960	133,997	123,889
1851	378⅓	15,753,227	362,675	483,097

MASSACHUSETTS:	Chartered.	First use.	Length.
Boston and Lowell................	1830	1834	26¾
Boston and Providence.............	1831	1834	43½
Boston and Worcester..............	1831	1834	44½
Berkshire Railroad Co.............	1837	1842	21
Boston and Maine	1833	1836	35¾
Charlestown Branch Railroad.......	1836	1839	7¾
Eastern Railroad Co...............	1836	1838	44
Nashua and Lowell................	1836	1838	14½
*Old Colony Railroad..............	1838	1840	20
Taunton Branch Railroad..........	1835	1836	11
Western Railroad Co..............	1833	1839	117¾
West Stockbridge Railroad.........	1831	1838	2¾

*Between New Bedford and Taunton, to which its name was changed in 1839. Not to be confounded with the "Old Colony" road chartered in 1844.

Year.	Mileage.	Cost.	Passenger Receipts.	Freight Receipts.
1835	113½	$3,972,795	$224,874	$62,225
1836	127¾	4,495,570	369,601	129,334
1837	127¾	5,029,370	464,603	218,280
1838	176	6,818,956	522,926	260,753
1839	225¼	8,968,419	695,967	337,657
1840	318	11,775,595	844,045	388,572
1842	434½	19,066,671	1,273,257	721,074
1844	485½	21,135,726	1,586,468	1,017,983
1846	681¼	27,614,871	2,239,792	1,591,777
1848	947⅓	43,859,313	3,181,659	2,463,711
1850	1,125	51,644,808	3,616,516	2,692,425

RHODE ISLAND:	Chartered.	First use.	Length.
New York, Providence and Boston...	1832	1837	50
Providence and Worcester..........	1844	1847	43½
Providence, Warren and Bristol.....	1846	1855	13½

1383

Year.	Mileage.	Cost.	Passenger Receipts.	Freight Receipts.
1844	50	$1,950,000	$102,138	$39,762
1845	50	1,919,740	78,569	37,586
1846	50	1,902,140	86,049	41,796
1847	50	1,899,300	129,128	57,056
1848	50	1,886,650	117,908	56,469
1850	50	2,045,946	116,276	64,495
1852	50	1,893,000	134,410	63,802
1855	63½	2,363,860	167,692	108,878

These figures deal only with the first road named in this list. The Providence and Worcester railway was more properly a Massachusetts enterprise.

CONNECTICUT:

	Chartered.	First use.	Length.
Hartford and New Haven.........	1833	1838	61½
Boston, Norwich and New London...	1832	1840	59
Housatonic Railroad	1836	1841	74
New Haven and Northampton.......	1846	1848	46

Year.	Mileage.	Cost.	Passenger Receipts.	Freight Receipts.
1839	18	$ 729,606	*$20,000	*$10,000
1840	102¼	2,628,592	118,889	53,754
1841	102¼	3,023,373	154,334	82,594
1842	176¼	4,340,985	189,343	130,419
1843	176¼	4,380,215	190,856	159,105
1844	176¼	4,708,206	255,654	193,788
1845	201¾	5,268,591	286,201	237,665
1846	201¾	5,422,888	323,909	290,750
1847	201¾	5,928,418	404,415	369,229
1848	201¾	6,942,652	443,604	425,006
1849	288¾	8,834,070	502,849	470,685
1850	408½	13,720,451	1,023,068	624,786
1852	452½	16,962,696	1,299,927	774,763
1855	649	23,993,028	1,809,194	1,058,792

* An estimate. Probably somewhat under the actual figures.

NEW YORK:

	Chartered.	First use.	Length.
Mohawk and Hudson..............	1826	1831	17
Saratoga and Schenectady..........	1831	1832	21½
*New York and Harlem............	1831	1832	6¾
Buffalo and Black Rock...........	1833	1834	3¼

	Chartered.	First use.	Length.
Ithaca and Owego	1828	1834	28¼
Rensselaer and Saratoga	1832	1835	25¼
Brooklyn and Jamaica	1832	1836	11
Utica and Schenectady	1833	1836	78
Buffalo and Niagara Falls	1834	1837	22
Lewiston Railroad	1836	1837	6¼
New York and Erie	1832	1841	446
Long Island Railroad	1834	1837	84
Tonawanda Railroad	1832	1837	43½
Auburn and Syracuse	1834	1838	26
Hudson and Berkshire	1828	1838	31½
Syracuse and Utica	1836	1838	53
Auburn and Rochester	1836	1840	78
Blossburg and Corning	1839	1841	14¾
Albany and West Stockbridge	1836	1841	38¼
**Attica and Buffalo	1836	1842	32
Schenectady and Troy	1836	1842	20½

* Afterward slowly extended, as stated in the text.

** The last link in a completed line of railways from Albany to Buffalo.

Year.	Mileage.	Cost.	Passenger Receipts.	Freight Receipts.
1832	17	$795,303	$52,059	$.....
1833	39¼	1,328,725	94,319	8,708
1834	73¾	1,680,977	129,070	13,733
1835	99¾	2,682,429	175,305	38,987
1836	188¾	5,000,831	381,256	46,185
1837	259½	6,145,210	585,927	38,529
1838	278	7,200,462	623,197	43,696
1839	367¼	9,075,719	976,743	60,877
1840	394½	9,578,965	986,891	59,873
1841	414½	9,701,218	1,021,836	107,252
1842	573½	16,833,624	1,282,870	156,042
1845	722	21,269,126	1,575,241	301,593
1848	855½	33,252,324	2,553,633	915,313
1850	1,452½	63,631,538	3,749,674	1,518,998

NEW JERSEY:	Chartered.	First use.	Length.
Camden and Amboy	1830	1832	61¼
New Jersey Railroad	1832	1834	33¾
Paterson and Hudson	1832	1834	14
Morris and Essex	1835	1837	52½
Camden and Woodbury	1836	1839	9
Elizabeth and Somerville	1839	1839	25

Year.	Mileage.	Cost.	Passenger Receipts.	Freight Receipts.
1833	51½	$1,374,327	$307,021	$129,513
1834	61¼	2,337,630	351,955	157,838
1835	89½	3,613,917	502,319	236,623
1836	109	4,275,327	637,998	259,117
1837	132¼	5,122,301	624,137	279,132
1838	137¼	5,397,619	650,822	273,855
1839	194¼	6,160,857	661,317	272,197
1840	194¼	6,367,819	672,780	298,715
1845	197¼	7,731,212	892,305	375,097
1848	247¼	8,582,920	1,298,715	551,397
1850	254½	11,192,817	1,484,284	656,318

PENNSYLVANIA:	Chartered.	First use.	Length.
Lehigh Coal and Navigation	....	1827	9
Carbondale and Honesdale	....	1829	16½
Mill Creek and Mine Hill	1828	1829	4
Schuylkill Valley	1828	1830	9¼
Union Canal Co. Railroad	....	1830	3½
Mine Hill and Schuylkill	1828	1831	13½
Mount Carbon Railroad	1829	1831	7
Lykens Valley Railroad	1830	1833	15½
Room Run Railroad	....	1833	5
Little Schuylkill Railroad	1826	1832	28
Phila., Germantown and Norristown	1831	1832	17
Philadelphia and Trenton	1832	1833	28¼
Philadelphia and Columbia	Public work	1834	81
Alleghany Portage Railroad	Public work	1834	41
West Chester Railroad	1831	1832	9
Beaver Meadow Railroad	1830	1836	20½
Portsmouth, Mt. Joy and Lancaster	1832	1836	36
Cumberland Valley	1831	1837	52
Strasburg Railroad	1832	1837	4¼
Phila., Wilmington and Balto.	1831-2	1837	98
Franklin Railroad	1832	1838	22½
York and Maryland	1832	1838	22
Philadelphia and Reading	1833	1838	95
Williamsport and Elmira	1832	1839	25
Lehigh and Susquehanna	1837	1840	19¾
Lorberry Creek Railroad	1831	1840	5
Tioga Railroad	1828	1840	29½
Wrightsville, York and Gettysburg	1835	1840	13

1386

Year.	Mileage.	Cost.	Passenger Receipts.	Freight Receipts.
1830	9	$188,251	......	$22,317
1831	28¼	479,319	......	39,387
1832	49	1,197,318	......	61,342
1833	54	1,513,249	$22,606	101,727
1834	90½	2,941,708	51,709	113,514
1835	216¾	7,760,798	140,219	276,247
1836	228	8,391,527	205,109	392,967
1837	365	12,956,019	461,696	483,125
1838	377½	13,399,303	623,896	531,722
1839	383¾	13,928,196	738,938	617,940
1840	474½	18,452,642	850,410	777,895
1842	474½	21,861,905	799,516	768,716
1843	474½	22,476,905	806,744	881,314
1845	502¾	26,478,108	983,176	1,619,895
1849	521½	35,159,788	1,361,863	2,881,698

The table does not include figures relating to such roads as were built and exclusively used for the movement of coal and iron.

DELAWARE:	Chartered.	First use.	Length.
Newcastle and Frenchtown.........	1829	1832	16¼
Wilmington and Susquehanna.......	1832	1837	34

Year.	Mileage.	Cost.	Passenger Receipts.	Freight Receipts.
*1850	16¼	$908,927	$135,129	$1,976
*1851	16¼	908,927	135,231	1,913
*1852	16¼	908,927	89,978	1,899

*These figures are for the Newcastle and Frenchtown Railway only. Earlier statistics for the first two Delaware roads are not available.

MARYLAND:	Chartered.	First use.	Length.
Baltimore and Ohio	1827	1830	379
Baltimore and Susquehanna.........	1828	1831	36
Delaware and Maryland............	1832	1837	22
Washington Branch Railroad.........	1833	1835	30
Baltimore and Port Deposit..........	1834	1837	36
Annapolis and Elkridge	1837	1840	20½

Year.	Mileage.	Cost.	Passenger Receipts.	Freight Receipts.
1830	14	$1,178,165	$14,711	$ . . . . . .
1831	61	2,079,107	27,250	4,155
1832	69	2,279,841	67,910	69,027
1833	89	3,188,725	93,233	121,147
1834	101	3,619,222	104,182	131,255
1835	101	3,911,251	113,540	189,828
1836	131	5,761,196	253,126	198,186
1837	131	6,105,299	275,625	235,676
1838	131	6,251,333	326,694	288,539
1839	178½	8,113,794	430,182	283,260
1840	178½	8,722,917	431,940	334,349
1843	296	12,212,911	420,345	395,385
1845	296	12,534,410	546,010	494,530
1846	296	12,617,100	601,293	643,683
1848	296	13,890,479	667,487	958,379

The figures relating to the Delaware and Maryland Railway and to the Baltimore and Port Deposit road, are not included in this table. They were chiefly Pennsylvania enterprises and the statistics dealing with them are embraced in the records of Pennsylvania.

APPENDIX B

The following tables—relating to the ninety-five railways listed in Appendix A—are designed to throw some light on the relationship between the physical growth, capitalization, actual construction cost and net earnings of the American railroad system during the first thirty years of its existence. The figures used are also extracted from Poor's "History."

A study of the numerical statements here given shows a number of interesting conditions. The "total cost," as set forth for each year summarized, embraces the total cost of both construction and equipment for all railways in the state under consideration up to the year named. The "total capital" or "total liabilities" similarly represents the entire capital or liabilities of all the roads of the state up to the year in question. It will be observed that, as a general rule, the debts and construction expenditures of early American railways were substantially equal. In other words, their physical valuations, or costs of reproduction, were about equal to their liabilities. They had about a dollar's worth of tangible physical property for every dollar of indebtedness. The total capital or liabilities of all the railroads in the eleven states here reviewed was, in 1859, $506,486,841. At the same date the amount which had been expended in building and equipping those same roads was $484,991,861. More than 95.7 per cent. of the liabilities of those early roads was represented and balanced by physical property.

This favorable showing, moreover, was made in spite of the fact that in Pennsylvania and New York the aggregate liabilities of the railways in those states then exceeded their cost by about $23,000,000. In those two commonwealths, at the time, capital stock for some new enterprises had been issued, as usual, in advance of actual construction. If New York and Pennsylvania be omitted from the tabulation it will be found that in six of the nine remaining states—New Hampshire, Massachusetts, Rhode Island, New Jersey, Delaware and Maryland—the physical cost of the railways exceeded their liabilities in 1859, and if the figures for all nine states be combined it will be seen that $213,724,163 had been expended in railway construction and equipment, whereas the aggregate railroad liabilities or capital of the same nine states amounted to only $211,613,127.

It often happened, of necessity, that the railroad liabilities in some states exceeded the total amount expended for construction up to the same year, since building could not commence until the roads were au-

1389

thorized to borrow in order to undertake projected work. Perhaps the most noticeable instance of this sort is to be found in the Maryland conditions between 1835 and 1850. Between those years the tangible property of the new Maryland roads lagged behind their liabilities by millions of dollars, but by 1855 additional construction had almost balanced the account, and in 1859 the amount expended in the creation of physical property had passed the debt figures.

The inclusion of figures showing net earnings for each year named, and of others indicating the total mileage existing in each year named, will enable the student to calculate average costs per mile of equipped railway and the average percentage of net earnings. The tables follow:

MAINE:

Year.	Mileage.	Total Liabilities.	Total Cost.	Net Earnings.
1837	11	$354,000	$354,000	$5,848
1840	11	354,000	354,000	2,436
1845	62	1,650,000	1,615,286	86,049
1850	112	7,300,000	3,070,854	211,059
1855	386	15,605,000	14,141,629	575,018
1859	511	19,066,000	18,382,207	586,082

NEW HAMPSHIRE:

Year.	Mileage.	Total Liabilities.	Total Cost.	Net Earnings.
1842-3	34½	$725,000	$725,000	$43,728
1845-6	34½	800,000	800,000	93,424
1850-1	415	14,939,457	14,635,915	583,441
1855-6	547	18,192,932	17,910,093	709,465
1858-9	547	17,302,650	17,626,653	714,539

VERMONT:

Year.	Mileage.	Total Liabilities.	Total Cost.	Net Earnings.
1849	40	$800,000	$800,000	$33,560
1850	240¾	10,498,140	8,430,960	144,594
1855	487½	23,282,615	21,762,849	305,679
1859	511¾	23,429,004	23,133,231	451,471

MASSACHUSETTS:

Year.	Mileage.	Total Liabilities.	Total Cost.	Net Earnings.
1835	113½	$3,972,795	$3,972,795	$141,943
1840	318	11,727,299	11,775,595	560,313
1845	570¼	23,314,074	23,704,998	1,707,436
1850	1125	52,993,324	51,644,808	3,382,242
1855	1348½	63,531,113	61,835,726	3,436,695
1859	1393¼	61,230,417	62,527,333	4,218,177

RHODE ISLAND:

Year.	Mileage.	Total Liabilities.	Total Cost.	Net Earnings.
1844	50	$1,950,000	$1,950,000	$43,314
1850	50	2,045,946	2,045,946	95,313
1855	63½	2,336,800	2,363,860	107,922
1859	63½	2,254,892	2,258,567	121,155

CONNECTICUT:

Year.	Mileage.	Total Capital.	Total Cost.	Net Earnings.
1839	18	$729,606	$729,606	$20,433
1845	201¾	5,771,720	5,268,591	300,345
1850	408½	13,922,006	13,720,451	831,165
1855	649	24,451,223	23,993,028	1,265,247
1859	664½	24,757,052	24,747,869	1,281,888

NEW YORK:

Year.	Mileage.	Total Capital.	Total Cost.	Net Earnings.
1832	17	$795,303	$795,303	$20,152
1835	99¾	2,682,249	2,682,429	70,058
1840	394½	9,620,252	9,578,965	586,944
1845	722	21,413,500	21,269,126	1,002,702
1850	1452½	60,035,622	63,631,538	3,057,773
1855	2631½	145,835,217	129,147,518	8,487,689
1859	2643¾	143,770,938	131,538,580	7,356,672

1391

NEW JERSEY:

Year.	Mileage.	Total Capital.	Total Cost.	Net Earnings.
1833	51½	$1,374,327	$1,374,327	$181,050
1835	89½	3,654,527	3,613,917	407,891
1840	194¼	6,442,524	6,367,819	461,237
1845	197¼	7,260,959	7,731,212	698,708
1850	254½	10,702,786	11,192,817	887,191
1855	450¼	21,452,708	21,627,340	1,625,597
1859	502¾	26,574,803	27,398,853	2,594,367

PENNSYLVANIA:

Year.	Mileage.	Total Capital.	Total Cost.	Net Earnings.
1830	9	$186,042	$188,251	$13,145
1835	216¾	8,361,374	7,760,798	70,698
1840	474½	19,898,357	18,452,642	365,826
1845	502¾	30,271,685	26,478,108	1,221,227
1850	746¼	44,289,334	42,689,204	2,506,922
1855	1580	104,999,506	97,725,285	7,290,067
1859	2349¾	151,102,776	139,729,118	7,782,382

DELAWARE:

Year.	Mileage.	Total Capital.	Total Cost.	Net Earnings.
1850	16¼	$1,042,548	$908,927	$18,564
1855	16¼	999,404	853,405	—28,278
1859	16¼	749,171	723,551	—387

MARYLAND:

Year.	Mileage.	Total Capital.	Total Cost.	Net Earnings.
1830	14	$1,356,619	$1,178,165	$2,726
1835	101	8,260,239	3,911,251	116,881
1840	178½	15,253,028	8,722,917	280,853
1845	296	17,492,270	12,534,410	509,276
1850	296	20,697,843	14,397,256	980,119
1855	523	31,099,561	30,124,572	1,977,644
1859	572½	34,779,070	35,228,071	2,470,594

APPENDIX C

It is stated in the text that no less than twelve different railway gauges were in use in the United States until as late a date as 1866. In the following table are cited thirty railroads, located from Maine to Missouri and Texas, indicating the condition named. The figures given are taken from "Ashcroft's Railway Directory for 1867."

Road.	State.	Length in Miles.	Gauge.
Albany & Susquehanna R.R.	N. Y.	103	6 feet
Alabama & Florida R.R.	Ala.	114	5 feet
Atlantic & Great Western R.R.	N. Y., Pa., O.	507	6 feet
Belvidere & Delaware R.R.	N. J., Pa.	67	4 feet 10 inches
Bellefontaine R.R.	O., Ind.	202	4 feet 10 inches
Central Ohio R.R.	O.	137	4 feet 10 inches
Cincinnati, Hamilton & Dayton R.R.	O.	60	4 feet 10 inches / 6 feet (used 4 r'ls.)
Cumberland Valley R.R.	Pa., Md.	74	4 feet 8 inches
Delaware & Hudson R.R.	Pa.	32	4 feet 3 inches
Delaware, Lackawanna & Western R.R.	Pa., N. Y., N. J.	251	6 feet
Erie R.R.	N. Y.	460	6 feet
Galveston, Houston & Henderson R.R.	Tex.	50	5 feet 6 inches
Hackensack & New York R.R.	N. J.	13	6 feet
Houston & Texas Central R.R.	Tex.	80	5 feet 6 inches
Illinois Central R.R.	Ill.	365	4 feet 8½ inches
Kentucky Central R.R.	Ky.	99	5 feet
Lackawanna & Bloomsburg R.R.	Pa.	80	4 feet 8½ inches / 6 feet (used 3 r'ls.)
Lake Erie & Louisville R.R.	O., Ind.	175	4 feet 9¼ inches
Maine Central R.R.	Me.	110	5 feet 6 inches
Portsmouth Branch R.R.	O.	56	5 feet 4 inches
North Missouri R.R.	Mo.	170	5 feet 6 inches
Northern Railroad of New Jersey	N. Y., N. J.	35	6 feet
Ohio and Mississippi R.R.	O., Ind., Ill.	340	6 feet
Pacific and Missouri River R.R.	Mo., Kan.	283	5 feet 6 inches
Pittsburgh, Ft. Wayne & Chicago R.R.	Pa.,O.,Ind.,Ills.	468	4 feet 10 inches
Sandusky, Mansfield & Newark R.R.	O.	117	4 feet 9½ inches
Sycamore & Cortland R.R.	Ill.	4½	4 feet 8 inches
Tyrone & Clearfield R.R.	Pa.	23½	4 feet 5½ inches
Virginia & Tennessee R.R.	Va., Tenn.	204	5 feet
Wilton R.R.	N. H.	15	4 feet 7 inches

APPENDIX D

On July 2, 1873, James A. Garfield delivered before the student body of Hudson College an address on "The Future of the Republic: Its Dangers and Hopes." A considerable part of the speech dealt with the railway problem and the economic relationship between the railroad and the corporation. Garfield's speech was printed in pamphlet form, and a portion of it relating to the subject matter of these volumes is here reproduced. The quoted parts of the utterance will be found [pages 15 to 33] in a pamphlet bearing the title of the address, and published in Cleveland in 1873. The speaker said:

"There is another class of dangers, unlike any we have yet considered—dangers engendered by civilization itself, and made formidable by the very forces which man is employing as the most effective means of bettering his condition and advancing civilization. I select the railway problem as an example of this class. I can do but little more than to state the question, and call your attention to its daily increasing magnitude.

"We are so involved in the events and movements of society that we do not stop to realize—what is undeniably true—that during the last forty years all modern societies have entered upon a period of change, more marked, more pervading, more radical than any that has occurred during the last three hundred years. . . The changes now taking place have been wrought and are being wrought, mainly, almost wholly, by a single mechanical contrivance, the steam locomotive. . . . .

"I have noticed briefly what society has done for the locomotive, and what it has done for society. Let us now inquire what it is doing and is likely to do *to* society.

"The national constitution and the constitutions of most of the States were formed before the locomotive existed; and of course no special provisions were made for its control. Are our institutions strong enough to stand the shock and strain of this new force? A government made for the kingdom of Lilliput might fail to handle the forces of Brobdignag. . .

"It cannot have escaped your attention that all the forces of society, new and old, are now acting with unusual vigor in all departments of life. . . May it not be true that the new forces are also over-weighting the strength of our social and political institutions? The editor of 'The Nation' declares the simple truth when in a recent issue he says:

" 'The locomotive is coming in contact with the framework of our institutions. In this country of simple government, the most powerful centralizing force which civilization has yet produced must, within the next score years, assume its relations to that political machinery which is to control and regulate it.'

"The railway problem would have been much easier of solution if its difficulties had been understood in the beginning. But we have waited until the child has become a giant. We attempted to mount a columbiad on a carriage whose strength was only sufficient to stand the recoil of a twelve-pound shot.

"The danger to be apprehended does not arise from the railroad, merely, but from its combination with a piece of legal machinery known as the private corporation. . .

"Under the name of private corporations, organizations have grown up, not for the perpetuation of great charity, like a college or hospital, nor to enable a company of citizens more conveniently to carry on a private industry; but a class of corporations unknown to the early law writers has arisen; and to them have been committed the vast powers of the railroad and the telegraph, the great instruments by which modern communities live, move and have their being.

"Since the dawn of history the great thoroughfares have belonged to the people—have been known as the king's highways or the public highways, and have been open to the free use of all on payment of a small, uniform tax or toll to keep them in repair. But now the most perfect, and by far the most important roads known to mankind, are owned and managed as private property, by a comparatively small number of private citizens.

"In all its uses the railroad is the most public of all our roads; and in all the objects to which its work relates, the railway corporation is as public as any organization can be. But, in the start, it was labeled a private corporation; and so far as its legal status is concerned it is now grouped with eleemosynary institutions and private charities, and enjoys similar immunities and exemptions. It remains to be seen how long the community will suffer itself to be the victim of an abstract definition.

"It will be readily conceded that a corporation is strictly and really private when it is authorized to carry on such a business as a private citizen may carry on. But when the State has delegated to a corporation the sovereign right of eminent domain, the right to take from the private citizen, without his consent, a portion of his real estate; to build its structure across farm, garden and lawn; into and through, over or under, the blocks, squares, streets, churches and dwellings of incorporated cities and towns; across navigable rivers, and over and along public highways, it requires a stretch of the common imagination and much refinement and subtlety of the law to maintain the old fiction that such an organization is not a public corporation.

"In the famous Dartmouth College Case of 1819 it was decided, by the Supreme Court of the United States, that the charter of Dartmouth College is a contract between the State and the Corporation, which the legislature cannot alter without the consent of the corporation; and that any such alteration is void, being in conflict with that clause of the constitution of the United States which forbids a State to make any law impairing the obligation of contracts.

"This decision has stood for more than half a century as a monument of judicial learning and the great safeguard of vested rights. But chief justice Marshall pronounced this opinion ten years before the steam railway was born; and it is clear he did not contemplate the class of corporations that have since come into being. But, year by year, the doctrine of that case has been extended to the whole class of private corporations, including Railroad and Telegraph Companies. But few of the States, in their early charters to railroads, reserved any effectual control of the operations of the corporations they created. In many instances, like that of the Illinois Central charter, the right to amend was not reserved. In most States each legislature has narrowed and abridged the powers of its successors, and enlarged the powers of the corporations; and these by the strong grip of the law, and in the name of private property and vested rights, hold fast all they have received. By these means not only the corporations but the vast railroad and telegraph systems have virtually passed from the control of the State. It is painfully evident from the experience of the last few years, that the efforts of the States to regulate their railroads have amounted to but little more than feeble annoyance. In many cases the corporations have treated such efforts as impertinent intermeddling, and have brushed away legislative restrictions as easily as Gulliver broke the cords with which the Lilliputians attempted to bind him.

"In these contests the corporations have become conscious of their strength, and have entered upon the work of controlling the States. Already they have captured several of the oldest and strongest of them; and these discrowned sovereigns now follow in chains the triumphal chariot of their conquerors. And this does not imply that merely the officers and representatives of States have been subjected to the railways, but that the corporations have grasped the sources and fountains of power, and control the choice of both officers and representatives.

"The private corporation has another great advantage over the municipal corporation. The jurisdiction of the latter is confined to its own territory; but by the recent constructions and devices of the law a private corporation, though it has no soul, no conscience, and can commit no crime, yet it is a citizen of the State that creates it, and can make and execute contracts with individuals and corporations of other States.

"Thus the way has been opened to those vast consolidations which have placed the control of the whole system in the hands of a few, and have developed the Charlemagnes and the Cæsars of our internal commerce.

1396

A HISTORY OF TRAVEL IN AMERICA

"In addition to these external conquests, the great managers have in many cases grasped the private property of the corporations themselves; and the stocks which represent the investment have become mere counters in the great gambling houses of Wall street, where the daily ebb and flow of the stock market sweeps and tosses the business and trade of the Continent.

"If these corporations were in reality private corporations, transacting only private business, the community might perhaps stand by in wonder and amazement at their achievements; but a great and vital public interest is involved in the system, an interest which affects the social and political organization in a thousand ways. Prominent among these is the public necessity for means of transportation. . .

"In view of the facts already set forth the question returns: What is likely to be the effect of railway and other similar combinations upon our community and our political institutions? Is it true, as asserted by the British writer quoted above,[1] that the State must soon recapture and control the railroads or be captured and subjugated by them? Or do the phenomena we are witnessing indicate that general breaking up of the social and political order of modern nations, so confidently predicted by a class of philosophers whose opinions have hitherto made but little impression on the public mind? . . .

"The consolidation of our great industrial and commercial companies, the power they wield and the relations they sustain to the State and to the industry of the people do not fall far short of Fourier's definition of Commercial or Industrial Feudalism. The modern barons, more powerful than their military prototypes, own our greatest highways and levy tribute at will upon all our vast industries. And, as the old Feudalism was finally controlled and subordinated only by the combined efforts of the kings and the people of the free cities and towns, so our modern Feudalism can be subordinated to the public good only by the great body of the people, acting through their governments by wise and just laws.

"My theme does not include, nor will this occasion permit, the discussion of methods by which this great work of adjustment may be accomplished. But I refuse to believe that the genius and energy that have developed these new and tremendous forces will fail to make them not the masters but the faithful servants of society. It will be a disgrace to our age and to us if we do not discover some method by which the public functions of these organizations may be brought into full subordination to the public, and that too without violence, and without unjust interference with the rights of private individuals. It will be unworthy of our age and of us, if we make the discussion of this subject a mere warfare against men. For in these great industrial enterprises have been and still are engaged, some of the noblest and worthi-

[1] Reference is made to an article in the "London Quarterly Review" of April, 1873, quoted by Garfield in his address.

est men of our time. It is the system—its tendencies and its dangers—which society itself has produced, that we are now to confront. And these industries must not be crippled, but promoted. The evils complained of are mainly of our own making. States and communities have willingly and thoughtlessly conferred these great powers upon railways; and they must seek to rectify their own errors without injury to the industries they have encouraged.

"Already methods are being suggested. Massachusetts is discussing the proposal to purchase and operate a portion of her railroad system, and thus bring the rest into competition with the State as the representative of the people. It is claimed that the success of this plan has been proved by the experience of Belgium.

"Another proposition is that the State purchase the roads and open them like other highways to the free use of the public, subject to such regulations and toll as the safety of transportation and the maintenance of the system may require. This, it is claimed, would remove the stocks and bonds from the gambling operations of the markets, and place the levying of the transportation tax in the hands of the State, and under the control of those who pay.

"Others, again, insist that the system has overgrown the limits and the powers of the separate States, and must be taken in hand by the national government under that provision of the national constitution which empowers Congress 'to regulate commerce among the several States.' When it is objected that this would be a great and dangerous step towards political centralization—which many think has already been pushed too far—it is responded that as the railway is the greatest centralizing force of modern times, nothing but a kindred force can control it; and it is better to rule it than to be ruled by it. Other solutions have been proposed; but these are sufficient to show how strongly the current of public thought is setting towards the subject. Indications are not wanting that the discussion will be attended by passion, and by a full exhibition of that low political cunning which plays with the passions and prejudices of men, and measures success by results and not by the character of the means employed. I have ventured to criticise the judicial application of the Dartmouth College case; and I venture the further opinion that some features of that decision, as applied to the railway and similar corporations, must give way under the new elements which time has added to the problem. But this must be done, not by denouncing judges who faithfully administer the law, but by such prudent changes in the law, and perhaps in our constitutions, as will guide the courts in future adjudications.

"It depends upon the wisdom, the culture, the self-control of our people, to determine how wisely and how well this question shall be settled. But that it will be solved, and solved in the interest of liberty and justice, I do not doubt. . . ."

1398

APPENDIX E

A list of the principal canals in the United States in 1850.
From "Disturnell's American and European Railway and Steamship
Guide, etc., etc., New York, 1851." Pages 7-8.

Name.	State.	From	To	Miles.
Cumberland & Oxford...	Maine	Portland	Long Pond	50½
Middlesex...............	Mass.	Boston	Lowell	27
Champlain	N. Y.	Junction Erie	Whitehall	64
Erie	"	Albany	Buffalo	364
Chenango	"	Utica	Binghamton	97
Black River............	"	Rome	Boonville	35
Cayuga & Seneca........	"	Montezuma	Geneva	21
Oswego	"	Syracuse	Oswego	38
Oneida Lake............	"	Erie Canal	Oneida Lake	6
Chemung	"	Jefferson	Elmira	23
Feeder do.............	"	Horseheads	Corning	16
Crooked Lake...........	"	Dresden	Penn Yan	8
Genesee Valley..........	"	Rochester	Olean	108
Dansville Branch.......	"	Near Mt. Morris	Dansville	11
Delaware & Hudson....	N. Y. & Pa.	Rondout, N. Y.	Honesdale, Pa.	109
Morris	New Jersey	Jersey City	Easton, Pa.	102
Delaware & Raritan....	"	New Brunswick	Bordentown	43
Feeder do..............	"	Trenton	Saxtonsville	23
Pennsylvania Canal				
Central Division......	Penn.	Columbia	Hollydaysburg	173
Western do...........	"	Johnstown	Pittsburgh	104
Susquehanna do.......	"	Duncan's Island	Northumberland	40
North Branch........	"	Northumberland	Farrandsville	75
West Branch..........	"	Northumberland	Lock Haven	72
Delaware Division....	"	Bristol	Easton	60
Beaver	"	Beaver	Erie	136
Franklin	"	Franklin	Meadville	45
Schuylkill Nav..........	"	Philadelphia	Port Carbon	108
Lehigh do..............	"	Easton	Stoddartsville	84
Union	"	Reading	Middletown	82
Susquehanna	Pa. & Md.	Wrightsville, Pa.	Havre de Grace	45
Chesapeake & Delaware..	Del. & Md.	Delaware City	Back Creek, Md.	14
Chesapeake & Ohio......	Md. & Va.	Alexandria, Va.	Cumberland, Md.	191
James River............	Virginia	Richmond	Lynchburg	146
Dismal Swamp..........	"	Deep Creek	Joyce's Creek	23

A HISTORY OF TRAVEL IN AMERICA

Name.	State.	From	To	Miles.
Weldon	N. Carolina	Weldon	Blakeley	12
Santee	S. Carolina	Charleston	Santee River	22
Savannah	Georgia	Savannah	Alatamaha River	16
Brunswick	"	Brunswick	Alatamaha River	12
Muscle Shoals...........	Alabama	Tennessee River	Florence	36
Huntsville	"	Huntsville	Triana	16
Barataria	Louisiana	New Orleans	Bayou Terre Bonne	21
Orleans	"	New Orleans	L. Pontchartrain	6
Louisville	Kentucky	Louisville	Portland	2½
Ohio and Erie..........	Ohio	Cleveland	Portsmouth	309
Walhonding	"	Roscoe	Rochester	25
Hocking	"	Carroll	Athens	56
Miami	"	Cincinnati	Dayton	65
Extension do...........	"	Dayton	Junction	115
Warren	"	Lebanon	Middletown	19
Muskingum Nav........	"	Dresden	Marietta	91
Whitewater	Indiana	Laurensburg	Cambridge	68
Wabash & Erie.........	O. & Ind.	Mahattan, O.	Evansville, Ind.	467
Illinois & Michigan......	Illinois	Chicago	Peru	100

	Total miles	4,002

APPENDIX F

An extract from the "Address delivered by Wm. H. Seward, at the commencement of the Auburn and Owasco Canal, October 14, 1835, with the proceedings of the celebration. Auburn, 1835." [1]

"It is moreover necessary to cherish a liberal spirit in regard to public improvements in other parts of the state and of the country. And such a spirit is no less enlightened and just, than it is expedient for us to indulge it. I regret to say that on this subject there has been, in my judgment, much error prevailing among us and throughout the state. The eastern counties, while they have found the value of their land enhanced nearly twofold, and their towns increased in nearly the same proportion, by means of the great increase of commerce effected by the construction of the Erie Canal, have not yet altogether surmounted the jealousy with which they regarded the accomplishment of that great work. Finding that they are not, as they at first anticipated they would be, oppressed with taxation to defray the cost of its construction, many of their citizens now deem it just to impose on the canal the expense of the support of the government, at the hazard of driving into other channels that very trade which makes it productive and invites their cupidity. The denial of the applications, at the last session of the legislature, for charters for constructing railroads from Utica to Syracuse, and from Auburn to Rochester, was a part of the same policy, and proceeded upon the grounds that railroads, parallel to the Erie Canal, would have the effect, by diminishing the canal tolls, to reduce the revenue of the state. . . . So, also, a portion of our citizens have been opposed to the construction of the New York and Erie Railroad, through the southern counties, owing to the apprehension that it would depreciate the property in the northern counties; and in retaliation, 'the sequestered counties,' as those are called which are on the route of the southern railroad, unite with the eastern counties to prevent the improvements required by us.

"Plausible pretexts are never wanting to cover the real odiousness of these sectional jealousies; and these may generally be resolved into a great and anxious concern for the safety of the state treasury. Now in my humble opinion, the state can no more wisely conduct its affairs than by contributing to the internal improvement of the territory within its limits a large proportion of its revenues and credits. . . . Where individual enterprise and capital are sufficient to accomplish a desirable

---

[1] The text as here given varies in unimportant particulars from that later included in "The Works of William H. Seward, as edited by George E. Baker"; vol. iii, pages 128 to 134.

work, they ought to be at once called into exercise. Where they are incompetent, the state ought in justice and sound policy to contribute. And yet the very opposite of this is the doctrine maintained by many of our statesmen, who hold that the state ought to embark only in those improvements which will be immediately productive. But as such works will be met by citizens with private funds, it follows according to this principle that the state ought never to make any improvements. With such men there is an everlasting apprehension of an eternal public debt and eternal taxation. And yet if all the internal improvements required to cross this state in every direction, at such intervals as to leave not a single sequestered county or town within its limits, were to be made at once, the debt which would be created would not impair the public credit or retard the public prosperity a single year. The expenses of a single year of war would exceed the whole sum of such cost. Every year after their construction would show the resources of the state so much increased that a nominal tax would be sufficient to establish a sinking fund ample for the redemption of the debt within one generation—if indeed it were just that one generation should bear the entire expense of improvements destined to become more and more productive while the government shall exist. To compare such appropriations to the heavy national debts incurred by monarchical governments in desolating and exterminating wars, is as unsound in politics as to assimilate in agriculture the effects of invigorating rains to the sterility produced by the burning sun.

"The popular error on this subject unquestionably arises from an inability to understand the extent of the resources of this great country. It is forgotten that besides the lands we cultivate there is a territory of almost inconceivable dimensions lying on our borders, with an annual increase of strong and willing hands to reclaim and bring it into a productive condition. It is forgotten that every five or six years brings a new state into this confederacy, with its fresh and fertile soil yielding most luxuriant burthens, while the older states are all the time increasing in wealth and prosperity. It is forgotten that this is a government made for the reign of peace and humanity. It is forgotten that we have not, and with the favor of God never will have, any aristocracy, pensioners and placemen in Church or State to consume the substance of the people. It is forgotten that we are daily demonstrating by our experience the new and gratifying theory that national poverty, as well as individual destitution, are not the decree of a harsh and offended deity, but the fault of men. . . . It is time, fellow citizens, that we explode these prejudices and rise to the sublime conviction that Providence has spread around us an immense territory to improve—to cultivate it and make it the abode of peace, of science, and of liberty. When we shall have impressed this truth, and become imbued with its influence, we shall rejoice in every work which will improve the condition of any portion of the people, and which will add to the prosperity of any part of the country. . . .

"Splendid as will be the results of the work we this day commence, and bright as are the visions of national prosperity dawning upon us, it ought to be borne in mind that those results and those prospects are not, and ought not to be, the chief end of our exertions. While it is true that individual wealth and national prosperity tend to increase and to multiply domestic enjoyments, and elevate and refine the social condition, it is equally true that the perpetuity of this Union under its existing form of government is, and ought to be, the object of the most persevering and watchful solicitude on the part of every American citizen. And it is as certainly true that neither the happiness of our people, nor the stability of our government, depends on the length and number of our canals and railroads or the individual or collective wealth of our citizens. On the other hand, wealth and prosperity have always served as elements which introduce vice, luxury and corruption into republics. And luxury, vice and corruption have subverted every republic which has preceded us, that had force enough in its uncorrupted state to resist foreign invasion. So closely are moral good and moral evil, political good and political evil, associated in this probationary state. But in addition to the other eminent blessings by which we are distinguished, our lot has been cast in an age and situation when we can change this tendency of wealth and prosperity and convert them into agents for the preservation and maintenance of the liberty we enjoy. We are under a fearful responsibility to posterity and to the friends of free government throughout the world that the institutions established here, dearer to them than all the wealth of the ancient East and the modern West, shall not be subverted through our fault.

"That responsibility can be discharged, faithfully, successfully, triumphantly, by the education of the people. This great work it is practicable for us to accomplish. . . . There is only one obstacle to the work—and that is, the prevailing belief that it is already accomplished. Our orators and some of our statesmen point boastingly to the catalogues which show that almost every citizen can read and write, and thereupon unhesitatingly pronounce us the wisest and most enlightened of all the nations of the earth. We lay this flattering unction to our souls and rest content. But it is a dangerous, it is a universal— God grant it does not prove a fatal—delusion. That the most of the American people have been instructed to read and write and that they make profitable use of these precious acquirements, I am as proud to declare as any citizen. But does the acquirement of reading and writing constitute knowledge? No, fellow citizens, they are only the means of acquiring it; and without some higher cultivation of the mind, the ability to read and write has a tendency almost as strong to acquire and disseminate error as truth. It prepares us to become the support of

1403

demagogues, and the slaves of popular passion, caprice and excitement. Something more is wanted. . . . But let it be always remembered that to elevate the standard of general education, and to extend its benefits, is the most important duty of the age in which we live. Better would it be for our successors that the waters of Erie and Hudson had pursued their ancient passage to the ocean strangers to each other, as they were before the towering intellect of Clinton compelled them to be united; better for them would it be that the Atlantic cities were a forest, and the valley of the Mississippi had remained an inhospitable prairie, than that we should transmit to them, with the mighty improvements of this age, a subtle poison which should undermine their social condition. We must make our improvements in the minds of the people keep progress with those of our territory, if we would preserve those institutions without which all the wealth and prosperity we can secure will only invite more rigorous and avaricious oppression. . . .

"Perhaps at some distant day the curious searcher of antiquities may find, in the ruins which sooner or later must cover this work, like all other human inventions, the corner-stone we are now to deposit in the earth, and studiously decipher the inscription it bears, as a memorial of a people whose career will have terminated, and over whose memory oblivion will have begun to draw her dark mantle. Then, when all the notoriety given to the proceedings of this day by an ephemeral press shall have passed away, we shall be judged not by the improvements we make in our lakes or our rivers, our mountains or our valleys, nor yet by the wealth we accumulated or the monuments we reared—but we shall be judged by the indelible impression we shall have left upon the moral condition of our country. So far as our influence may go in forming the character of the age in which we live, let not the discovery of these works recall the memory of a people who acquired wealth without wisdom, and enjoyed the luxury that it brought, reckless of their responsibility to posterity and mankind. . . ."

APPENDIX G

The following tables, giving information concerning the public lands of the United States in 1826, and concerning the relationship of the Indians to those lands, are quoted from "Laws of the United States, Resolutions of Congress Under the Confederation, Treaties, Proclamations, Spanish Regulations and Other Documents Respecting the Public Lands. Compiled [1] in Obedience to a Resolution of the House of Representatives of the United States, Etc. Washington, 1828."

"Synopsis of the public lands within the boundaries of the several States and Territories of the United States":

TABLE I

Quantity of land purchased by the United States.................	258,377,667
Quantity of land not yet ceded by the Indians..................	55,947,453
Acres	314,325,120
Quantity of public land surveyed to Jan. 1, 1826................	138,988,244
Quantity of public land sold to same date......................	19,239,412
Amount paid by purchasers of public lands at the several land offices to Jan. 1, 1826.......................................	$31,345,968.73
Amount due from purchasers on same date....................	7,955,831.03
	$39,301,799.76
Add sales to the Ohio Company, to John Cleves Symmes and associates. Also, sales at New York and Pittsburg prior to the opening of the land offices................................	1,050,080.43
	$40,351,880.19
Quantity of land sold at the United States land offices. Sales to John Cleves Symmes and associates; sales to the Ohio Company; and sales at New York and Pittsburg.................. Acres	19,239,412
Amount of the one thirty-sixth part of the public lands appropriated to support schools, and special donations for colleges....	7,708,066
Quantity of land appropriated for military bounties, private claims and donations	21,156,889
Quantity of land remaining unsold on Jan. 1, 1826..............	210,273,300
Making the total quantity of land purchased by the United States to Jan. 1, 1826.......................................Acres	258,377,667
Extent of land lying within the limits of the United States, but not embraced in the boundaries of States and Territories.....Acres	750,000,000

[1] By Matthew St. Clair Clarke, Clerk of the House of Representatives.

1405

TABLE II

Total expenditures on account of public lands:

Purchase of Louisiana	$15,000,000
Paid State of Georgia and Yazoo script	6,200,000
Paid on account of Indian cessions, to Jan. 1, 1826	3,392,494
Paid for surveying 138,988,224 acres of public lands	2,164,368
Expenses incidental to sale of 19,239,412 acres of public lands	1,154,951
	$27,911,813
Due on account of the Florida loan	5,000,000
	$32,911,813

The public lands, excluding Louisiana and Florida purchase money, cost, per acre, less than	5 cents
Including Louisiana and Florida, about	12½ "
Indian lands alone, cost, per acre	3-147/1,000 "

TABLE III

From a statement politely furnished by the General Land Office it appears that the United States have acquired lands from the Indians as follows:

In Ohio	24,854,888	acres
In Indiana	16,243,685	"
In Illinois	29,384,744	"
In Louisiana	2,492,000	"
In Alabama	19,586,560	"
In Mississippi	12,475,231	"
In Missouri	36,169,383	"
In Michigan Territory	17,561,470	"
In Arkansas Territory and West	55,451,904	"
Total	214,219,865	"

Exclusive of the lands acquired, under various treaties with the Creeks and Cherokees, for the States of Georgia, Tennessee, North Carolina and South Carolina.

1406

TABLE IV

	Number of Indians.	Quantity of Land Claimed.
Maine	956	92,260 acres
Massachusetts	750	....
Rhode Island	420	3,000 "
Connecticut	400	4,300 "
New York	5,143	246,675 "
Virginia	47	27,000 "
South Carolina	450	144,000 "
Ohio	2,350	409,501 "
Michigan Territory	28,316	7,057,920 "
Indiana	} 11,679	{ 10,104,000 "
Illinois		5,314,560 "
Georgia		{ 9,537,920 "
Alabama	} 53,625	7,272,576 "
Tennessee		1,055,680 "
Mississippi		15,705,000 "
Florida Territory	5,000	4,032,640 "
Louisiana	1,313	....
Missouri	} 18,917	{ 2,782,726 "
Arkansas Territory		13,612,560 "
	129,366	77,402,318 acres

["Table I" on page 1052 of work quoted; "Table II" on page 1062; "Tables III and IV" on page 1067.]

Note by S. D.—An apparent contradiction will be observed in these governmental statements concerning the lands, in organized states and territories, which had not yet been ceded by the Indians. Table I gives the amount as 55,947,453 acres, and Table IV names the quantity so claimed as 77,402,318 acres. A large proportion of the additional 750,000,000 acres mentioned in the last paragraph of Table 1 was afterward bought from the Indians by the white government, although native ownership of the areas in question is not directly asserted in the official report here quoted.

Up to the year 1826, as shown by the tables, the United States had acquired 214,219,865 acres from the Indians at a total cost of $3,392,494, the average price paid to the red men per acre being stated as 3.147 cents. For the 19,239,412 acres of these lands already sold by the government it had received $40,351,880.19.

Another apparent discrepancy is contained in the figures relating to the cost of lands already obtained from the natives. If the average price had been 3.147 cents per acre, the cost of the 214,219,865 acres would have been about $6,735,000, instead of the smaller sum specified in Table II. Perhaps the $3,392,494 "paid on account of Indian cessions to Jan. 1, 1826," represented only partial payment on the purchases, leaving the remainder still due. If we were compelled to accept without qualification the statement that 214,219,865 acres had already been acquired from the Indians in 1826—as recited in Table III—and if we were likewise forced to accept without qualification the figures of Table II—wherein it is said that "Indian lands, alone, cost 3 147/1000 cents an acre"—then the 214,000,000 acres had been acquired at an average expense of about 1.580 cents an acre.

APPENDIX H

Reference was made in Chapter V of the text to statements by early white chroniclers concerning the character of the Indians and their relations with the Caucasian race. The following discussions of the subject, written at various times between 1643 and 1847, by American historians or contemporary commentators, are examples of the statements referred to:

I

From Roger Williams' "A Key into the Language of America: London, 1643." Text as here quoted taken from the reprint contained in volume one of the "Collections of the Rhode Island Historical Society. Providence, 1827."

"If any stranger come in, they presently give him to eate of what they have; many a time, and at all times of the night (as I have fallen in travell upon their houses) when nothing hath been ready, have themselves and their wives, risen to prepare me some refreshing. It is a strange truth, that a man shall generally finde more free entertainment and refreshing amongst these Barbarians, than amongst thousands that call themselves Christians." [pp. 36-37.]

"In Summer-time I have knowne them lye abroad often themselves, to make roome for Strangers, English, or others." [p. 38.]

"There are no beggars amongst them, nor fatherlesse children unprovided for." [p. 45.]

"The poore amongst them will say, they want nothing." [p. 53.]

"I have heard of many English lost, and have oft been lost my selfe, and my selfe and others have often been found, and succoured by the Indians." [p. 73.]

"I have heard them say to an Englishman (who being hindred, broke a promise to them) you know God, will you lie Englishman." [p. 116.]

"I could never discerne that excesse of scandalous sins amongst them, which Europe aboundeth with. Drunkennesse and gluttony, generally they know not what sinnes they be; and although they have not so much to restraine them (both in respect of knowledge of God and lawes of Men) as the English have, yet a man shall never heare of such crimes amongst them of robberies, murthers, adulteries, &c., as amongst the English." [p. 121.]

II

From Benjamin Trumbull's "A Complete History of Connecticut, etc., 1818."

1408

"The Indians, at their [the Englishmen's] first settlement, performed many acts of kindness towards them. They instructed them in the manner of planting and dressing the Indian corn. They carried them upon their backs, through rivers and waters; and, as occasion required, served them instead of boats and bridges. They gave them much useful information respecting the country, and when the English or their children were lost in the woods, and were in danger of perishing with hunger, or cold, they conducted them to their wigwams, fed them, and restored them to their families and parents. By selling them corn, when pinched with famine, they relieved their distresses and prevented their perishing in a strange land and uncultivated wilderness." [p. 57.]

"In this distressful situation a committee was sent to an Indian settlement called Pocomtock, since Deerfield, where they purchased such quantities, that the Indians came down to Windsor and Hartford, with fifty canoes at one time, laden with Indian corn." [pp. 94-95.]

III

From Jedediah Morse's "A Report to the Secretary of War of the United States on Indian Affairs, Comprising a Narrative of a Tour Performed in the Summer of 1820, Under a Commission from the President of the United States, for the Purpose of Ascertaining, for the Use of the Government, the Actual State of the Indian Tribes in Our Country, Etc., Etc. New Haven, 1822."

". . . We should scarcely have supposed, that any man, acquainted with history, or making any pretensions to candor, would be found among the objectors to attempts to civilize our Indians, and thus to save them from perishing. Yet, painful as is the fact, objections have been made to the present course of procedure with Indians, and from men too, whose standing and office in society are such, as it would be deemed disrespectful to pass unnoticed. 'The project,' it has been said, 'is visionary and impracticable. Indians can never be tamed; they are incapable of receiving, or of enjoying, the blessings proposed to be offered to them.' Some, I will hope, for the honor of our country, that the number is small, have proceeded farther, and said: 'Indians are not worth saving. They are perishing—let them perish. The sooner they are gone, the better. . .'

"It is too late to say that Indians cannot be civilized. The facts referred to, beyond all question, prove the contrary. The evidence of actual experiment in every case, is paramount to all objections founded in mere theory, or, as in the present case, in naked and unsupported assertions. . . To look down upon them, therefore, as an inferior race, as untameable, and to profit by their ignorance and weakness; to take their property from them for a small part of its real value, and in other ways to oppress them; is undoubtedly wrong. . . To remove these Indians far away from their present homes . . . into a wilderness, among strangers possibly hostile, to live as their new neighbors live, by hunting, a state to which they have not lately been accustomed, and which is incompatible with civilization, can hardly be reconciled with the professed views and objects of the Government in civilizing them. This would not be deemed by the world a wise course, nor one which would very probably lead to the desired end." [pp. 81-83.]

"There is evidently a great and important revolution in the state of our Indian population already commenced, and now rapidly going forward, affecting immediately the tribes among us and on our borders, and which will ultimately and speedily be felt by those at the remotest distance. . . . Honor, justice, humanity, all that makes man respectable in the sight of God and men, imperiously require us to go forward, in full faith, till this work, so auspiciously commenced, shall be accomplished. This new state of things requires corresponding measures on the part of the government, to whom we look to take the lead in carrying on this revolution, which, if rightly directed and conducted, will save the Indians from ruin, and raise them to respectability and happiness, and reflect high and lasting honor on the Administration which shall accomplish it. . . .

"Another evil equally destructive of the Indians, and equally necessary to be provided against by proper laws and regulations, is, intercourse with unprincipled white people. Indians complain, and justly too, that their morals are corrupted by bad white men. This is well known to be the fact, and the cause of incalculable injury to the Indians, as well as of national disgrace." [pp. 84-85.]

"The Table which accompanies this Report, compiled from official documents, shows, that more than two hundred millions of acres of some of the best lands in our country, have been purchased, after our manner, and at our own prices, of the Indian tribes. Of these lands, previously to October, 1819, there had been sold by the government about eighteen and a half millions of acres, for more than forty-four millions of dollars. The remainder of these lands, if sold at the same rate, and the sums paid to the Indians for them deducted, would yield to the government a net profit of more than five hundred millions of dollars! . . ." [p. 94.]

"The character of the Cherokees for courage, fidelity, hospitality, and cleanliness, stands high. They are generally of a fine figure, as to their persons, polite in their manners, and fond of learning and improvement in the arts. . . ." [p. 153.]

"The attempts of the Cherokees to institute civil government for themselves, adapted to their improved condition, succeed quite as well as could be expected. Their incipient jurisprudence appears to secure the respect of the people. The distribution of the legislative, judicial, and executive powers of government, is made with considerable skill and judgment. . . . " [p. 180.]

1410

"The Choctaws have strong tendencies towards a civilized state. They are friendly to travellers, for whose accommodation they have established a number of public inns, which for neatness and accommodations, actually excel many among the whites. . . Within a few years they have made great advances in agriculture, and other arts of civilized life. They raise corn and different kinds of pulse, melons, and cotton. In one year they spun and wove ten thousand yards. . . The Choctaws raise a great many cattle. They have laid aside hunting, as a business, though they sometimes engage in it for amusement. . . . " [pp. 182-183.]

"The Chickasaws have always been warm friends of the United States, and are distinguished for their hospitality. Some of the chiefs are half breed, men of sense, possess numerous negro slaves, and annually sell several hundred cattle and hogs. The nation resides in eight towns, and like their neighbors, are considerably advanced in civilization. The American Board of Commissioners for Foreign Missions, have in contemplation the speedy establishment of a mission among these Indians, preparations for which are already made. This is done at the earnest solicitation of the nation."

Morse included in his report a synopsis of the civil and criminal code of the Cherokees. The following Indian laws, indicating the social condition and practises of that nation, are cited by him: [pp. 172-176.]

There shall be one Judge and one Marshal in each district,[1] and one Circuit Judge, who shall have jurisdiction over two districts, to associate with the district judges in determining all causes agreeable to the laws of the nation.

The head of each family shall pay a poll tax of fifty cents per annum into the national treasury, and each single man under the age of sixty years shall also pay fifty cents per annum.

Single white men are admitted to be employed as clerks in any of the stores that shall be established in the nation by natives, on condition that the employer obtains a permit and becomes responsible for the good behavior of such clerks.

Any person who shall bring into the nation, without permission from the National Committee and Council, a white family, and rent land to the same, proof being satisfactorily shown before any of the Judges in the District Councils, for every offense shall forfeit the sum of five hundred dollars and receive one hundred stripes on the bare back.

Parents who permit their children to play truant from schools or seminaries shall be compelled thereafter to pay all expenses incurred by their children while in the schools.

The nation shall procure at the public expense a set of tools for every apprentice who shall have faithfully served his time and learned a trade.

---

[1] The nation was divided, in 1820, into eight judicial and administrative districts.

Schoolmasters, blacksmiths, millers, saltpeter and gunpowder manufacturers, ferrymen, turnpike keepers and unmarried mechanics are privileged to reside in the nation on condition that their employers procure permits for their residence and become responsible for their good conduct and behavior. Such persons are subject to expulsion for misdemeanor. They may, while resident in the nation, improve and cultivate twelve acres of ground for their own benefit.[1]

Retail storekeepers shall obtain licenses for vending merchandise, said licenses costing twenty dollars per annum.

None but citizens of the nation shall be allowed to establish permanent stores.

No person not a citizen of the nation shall be allowed to bring into the nation any spirituous liquors, on pain of their confiscation.

Any white man who takes a Cherokee woman to wife shall be married to her by a minister of the Gospel or other authorized official, after procuring a marriage license from the National Clerk.

The property of a Cherokee woman so married to a white man shall not be subject to the disposal of her husband contrary to her consent.

There shall be companies of light horse or mounted constabulary in each district, to suppress crime, take those who transgress the law, and protect property and fatherless children.

No private feuds or vengeance shall be allowed.

Murder shall be punished by death.

IV

From Edwin James's introductory chapter to "A Narrative of the Captivity and Adventures of John Tanner, Etc., Etc. New York, 1830." [James was also editor of Major Long's account of his Expedition to the West.]

". . . Have we in our collective character, as a people, any disposition to interpose the least check to the downward career of the Indians? The last inquiry will be unhesitatingly answered in the negative, by all who are acquainted with the established policy of our government in our intercourse with them. The determination evinced by a great part of the people, and their representatives, to extinguish the Indian title to all lands on this side the Mississippi—to push the remnants of these tribes into regions already filled to the utmost extent their means of subsistence will allow—manifests, more clearly than volumes of idle and empty professions, our intentions toward them. The vain mockery of treaties, in which it is understood, that the negotiation, and the reciprocity, and the benefits, are all on one side; the feeble and misdirected efforts we make for their civilization and instruction, should not, and do not, deceive us into the belief that we have either a regard

[1] This and the following six laws were enacted in 1819.

for their rights, where they happen to come in competition with our interests, or a sincere desire to promote the cause of moral instruction among them. . . More than two hundred years have passed, during all which time it has been believed that systematic and thorough exertions were making to promote the civilization and conversion of the Indians. The entire failure of all these attempts ought to convince us, not that the Indians are irreclaimable, but that we ourselves, while we have built up with one hand, have pulled down with the other. Our professions have been loud, our philanthropic exertions may have been great, but our selfish regard to our own interest and convenience has been greater, and to this we ought to attribute the steady decline, the rapid deterioration of the Indians. . . We ought not to forget that injustice and oppression have been most active among the causes which have brought them down to their present deplorable state. . .

"That there exists, in the moral or physical constitution of the Indians, any insuperable obstacle to their civilization, no one will now seriously assert. . . The first labor of the philanthropist, who would exert himself in this cause, should be to allay or suppress that exterminating spirit so common among us, which, kept alive by the exertions of unprincipled land jobbers, and worthless squatters, is now incessantly calling for the removal of the Indians west of the Mississippi. . . Is it absolutely necessary, that while we invite to our shores, and to a participation in all the advantages of our boasted institutions, the dissatisfied and the needy of all foreign countries, not stopping to inquire whether their own crimes, or the influence of an oppressive government, may have made the change desirable for them, we should, at the same time, persist in the determination to root out the last remnants of a race who were the original proprietors of the soil, many of whom are better qualified to become useful citizens of our republic, than those foreigners we are so eager to naturalize? . . . It is believed by many, that national as well as individual crimes, are sure to be visited, sooner or later, by just and merited punishments." [pp. 14-20.]

V

From Benjamin Drake's "The Great Indian Chief of the West: or, Life and Adventures of Black Hawk: 1848."

". . . Fraud, oppression and violence, have characterized our intercourse with the Indians, and it is in vain to hope for any amelioration of their savage condition, so long as an intercourse of this kind is permitted. . . It is to this intercourse that the Indian wars, which have so frequently caused the blood of the white and the red man to flow in torrents, upon our frontier, are mainly to be attributed. . . If kindness, good faith and honesty of dealing, had marked our social, political and commercial intercourse with the Indians, few, if any of these bloody wars would have occurred; and these people, instead of being debased by our intercourse with them, would have been improved and elevated in the scale of civilization. . .

"If the laws enacted by Congress for the protection and civilization of the aborigines of this country, had been regularly and rigidly enforced, and a more impartial interpretation of the treaties made with them, had been observed, their condition would have been far better than it now is — they would have passed from the hunter to the pastoral state, and have grown in numbers, virtue and intelligence. But these laws and these treaties, have been year after year violated by our own people, and the result has been a constant deterioration of the Indians. This is especially true of those laws intended to prevent our citizens from hunting on the Indian lands, residing in their country, and trading with them without a license from the United States. These have generally been a dead letter upon the national statute book, and the encroachments of the lawless frontiersmen, the trader, the land speculator, and the vender of spirituous liquors, have impoverished, degraded, and vitiated, more or less, every tribe within the limits of the United States. It is to this intercourse, with these classes of persons, that the bad faith, the savage barbarities and border-wars, of which so much complaint is made against the Indians, are to be mainly attributed. The rapacity of our people, for their peltries and their land, the feeble execution of laws made for their protection, and the loose morality which has governed our general intercourse with them, have wasted their numbers, debased their character, and tarnished the honor of that nation, which, from the very organization of its government, has claimed to be their benevolent protector."

VI

From Jacob Burnet's "Notes on the Early Settlement of the North-Western Territory: 1847."

"The imaginary physical difference, pretended to exist between the Europeans and the natives of this continent, vanishes at once, on an unprejudiced comparison between the civilized white man and the civilized, educated Indian. . . .

"As soon as the Cherokees, and the Wyandotes, were surrounded by a white population, and their territory was so contracted as to cut off their dependence on hunting and fishing, they became farmers, and manifested a strong desire to till the earth and cultivate the arts; and this would have been the choice of the whole Indian race, if the policy of government had permitted it.

"It is not just, to consider the natives of this country, as a distinct, and inferior race because they do not generally imitate us, when we not only remove every consideration that could induce them to do so; but in fact, render it impossible. . . .

"As soon as they were brought to a situation in which necessity

1414

prompted them to industry, and induced them to begin to adopt our manners and habits of life, the covetous eye of the white man was fixed on their incipient improvements, and they received the chilling notice that they must look elsewhere for permanent homes. . .

"At the time our settlements were commencing, northwest of the Ohio, that hardy race was its acknowledged owners and sovereigns. The government claimed no right, either of occupancy or soil, but as they obtained it by purchase. . . .

"Unconscious of the ruinous consequences that were to follow their intimacy with white men, they ceded to the American Government large and valuable portions of their country at nominal prices. Those lands were rapidly settled by Americans, in whose purity and friendship the unsuspecting natives had great confidence; nor did they awake from that delusion, till their habits of sobriety and morality had been undermined. . .

"Their subsistence became precarious; . . . their health declined; . . . their self-respect, their dignity of character, and the heroism inherited from their ancestors were lost. . . . They became, in their own estimation, a degraded, dependent race. The Government, availing itself of their weakness and want of energy, succeeded, by bribes and menaces, in obtaining the best portions of their country, and eventually in driving them from the land of their birth, to a distant home, in an unknown region.

"This distressing chapter of aboriginal history began at the treaty of Greenville, in 1795, and terminated in less than fifty years. The writer of these notes witnessed its commencement, progress, and close." [pp. 387-391.]

APPENDIX I

The appended letter was published in the "Indiana [Vincennes] Centinel," of December 2, 1820, and signed "An Indianian." The author of the communication is unknown. It related to the selection of a name for the new state capital, the site of which had recently been chosen. The letter in part read:

"The legislators of Indiana have now an opportunity of showing their own greatness of mind by a display of their magnanimity. . . . By honoring manly worth in the memory of an enemy in whom manly worth was unrivalled. . . .

"I mean Tecumseh. It is true he was our enemy; but he was born on his own soil, reared with his own kindred. He saw his soil alienating, and his kindred perishing, and we, intrusive strangers, cannot charge him with his hatred. His enmity was love of country. His hostility was the brightest patriotism; such patriotism as we are all proud of; such patriotism as has immortalized the name of Washington. . . His was no partisan contest; no mercenary quarrel. What Washington and a thousand others were to us, so was Tecumseh to his countrymen.

"Every schoolboy in the Union now knows that Tecumseh was a great man. He was truly great—great in every accepted sense of the word; and his greatness was his own, unassisted by science or the aids of education. As a statesman, a warrior and a patriot, 'Take him for all in all, we shall not look upon his like again.'

"If such a man had lived in the Roman or Spartan Republic, what honors would have been paid to his memory! But, alas, Tecumseh was an Indian and a savage.

"Tecumseh was probably endowed with more native genius than any other of our red American brothers. It is true that the whites were his natural enemies, as he had a mind above becoming a slave to the vices of civilized society. He early saw, and felt, that to preserve his tribe they must be detached from and independent of the whites. . . . It was reserved for a mind as capacious and strong as Tecumseh's to bring about this herculean task. He formed a plan upon a grand scale to unite all the Indian tribes from the Floridas to the Lakes in one firm band to resist the encroachments of the whites. . .

"He was no barbarian, with brutish passions and with appetites merely animal:—it is true his mind had not the culture of civilization, but it was strong in its native excellence, and was admiraby fitted to the station which was assigned to him by his Maker. He had all the virtues, without one of the vices, which are conspicuous in our societies. His name, when pronounced by future generations, will bring to remembrance all that is great, all that is glorious, and all that is worthy of the imitation of posterity. . ."

1416

APPENDIX J

The following document is an executive message written by the heads of the Cherokee Nation in October of 1828, and by them addressed to a joint sitting of the two chambers of the National Congress, whose members held their seats by virtue of popular suffrage. The text as here quoted was published in the *Cherokee Phœnix,* Volume I, number 34, on October 22, 1828; page 1, columns 1 to 5.

To the Members of the Committee and Council, in General Council Convened:

Fellow citizens, in addressing you on this momentous occasion, we cannot, in justice to our feeling, forbear a solemn pause, and, with grateful feelings, meditate on so many blessings which a kind Providence has conferred on us as a people. Although we have had trials and tribulations to encounter, and in some instances the sad effects of intemperance have been experienced within the circle of our citizens, yet there is every reason to further us in the hope that, under wise and wholesome laws, the preponderating influences of civilization, morality, and religion will secure to us and our posterity an ample share of prosperity and happiness.

Occupying your seats by the free suffrage of the people, under the privileges guaranteed by the constitution, the various subjects requiring your deliberation the present session will necessarily be met. The organization of the new government, and refining and amendment of old laws, so as to make them in unison with the principles of the constitution, will require your attention; and it cannot escape your wisdom that the laws should be short, plain, and suitable to the condition of the people, and to be well executed. The judiciary system demands your serious deliberation, and the mode for conducting suits in courts should be free from all complicated formalities, and no other form should be required than to let both parties know distinctly what is alleged, that a fair trial may be had.

A law should be passed requiring managers and clerks of all public elections to register the names of the persons voting, as well as the names of the candidates to whom the votes are given. By observing such a course, illegal voters will be deducted, and the laws conducted with more regularity, harmony and satisfaction.

The public press deserves the patronage of the people, and should be cherished as an immediate vehicle for the diffusion of general information, and as a no less powerful auxiliary in asserting and supporting our political rights. Under this impression, we cannot doubt that you will continue to foster it by public support. The only legislative provision necessary for conducting the press, in our opinion, is to guard

1417

against the admission of scurrilous productions of a personal character, also against cherishing sectarian principles on religious subjects. The press being the public property of the nation, it would ill become its character if such infringements upon the feelings of the people should be tolerated. In other respects the liberty of the press should be as free as the breeze that glides upon the surface.

From the accompanying memorial, signed by several of our respectable citizens, together with the public treasurer, you will discover that further indulgence is called for in behalf of the public debtors, and it is for your wisdom to determine whether it would be just and proper that the law requiring the treasurer to call in all the money loaned out should be amended so as to give further indulgence to the borrowers, that the payments may be made with two installments. Owing to the extreme scarcity of money, from the general pressure in business, such indulgence would, no doubt, be a great relief; and the probable distress and confusion from the sacrifice of property, consequent from public sales, may be avoided.

After receiving the treasurer's report and ascertaining the true condition of the public funds, it will also be your province to determine the expediency of making suitable provisions for the erection of a national Academy of New-Echota. This subject, for some time past, has been agitated, and is anticipated with the utmost zeal by the reflecting part of our citizens, and it should receive your particular attention. By the treaty of 1819 four tracts of land, equal to fifteen miles square, were reserved for the purpose of creating a revenue for a school fund to be applied under the direction of the president of the United States for the education of the youth of this nation. The lands were to have been sold under the direction of the president, in the same manner as the public lands of the United States; and notwithstanding repeated and urgent requests which have been made for the sale of these lands, and the no less repeated promise on the part of the general government to attend to it, for reasons unknown, they are not yet sold. We would recommend you to memorialize the president on this important subject, and respectfully to request that the available funds may be applied to the contemplated national academy.

Several charity schools in this country, under the immediate patronage of benevolent societies of the several states, should not escape your notice. Although the superintendents of these schools, under the direction of respective societies, have the right of conducting them according to the dictates of their own discretion and judgment, yet, without presuming any disparagement to their regulations, we would suggest the expediency of selecting a visiting committeee on the part of the nation, for the purpose of inspecting their public examinations, and at such other times as said committee may deem it proper, and that they should be required to make a general report on the state of improvement, etc.,

1418

to be laid before the session of each general council. Such a course, pursued by the authorities of the nation, in relation to these institutions, would no doubt excite an interest among the peoples, and add to the vigilance of their preceptors, and at the same time produce a general satisfaction. An indifferent course, perhaps, might eventually produce relaxation and apathy in their operations; and we should endeavor to avoid the dishonor of any circumstances which might possibly take place that would defeat the fondest expectations of those upon whose benefaction they are founded.

The circumstances of our government assuming a new character, under a constitutional form, and on the principles of republicanism, has in some degree excited the sensation of the public characters of Georgia, and it is sincerely to be regretted that this excitement should have been manifested by such glaring expressions of hostility to our true interests. By the adoption of the constitution our relation to the United States, as recognized by existing treaties, is not in the least degree affected; but, on the contrary, this important change in our government is strictly in accordance with the recommendation, views, and wishes of the great Washington, under whose auspicious administration our treaties of peace, friendship, and protection, were made, and whose policy, in regard to Indian civilization, has been strictly pursued by the subsequent administrations.

The pretended claim of Georgia to a portion of our lands is alleged on the following principles: First, by discovery; secondly, by conquest; thirdly, by compact.

We shall endeavor briefly to illustrate the character of this claim. In the first place, Europeans, by the skill and enterprise of their navigators, discovered this vast continent, and found it inhabited exclusively by Indians of various tribes; and by a pacific courtesy and designing strategems the aboriginal proprietors were induced to permit a people from a foreign clime to plant colonies; and, without the consent or knowledge of the native lords, a potentate of England, whose eyes never saw, whose purse never purchased, and whose sword never conquered the soil we inhabit, presumed to issue a parchment, called a "charter," to the Colony of Georgia, in which its boundary was set forth, including a great extent of country inhabited by the Cherokees and other Indian nations.

Secondly, after a lapse of many years, when the population of their colonies had become strong, they revolted against their sovereign, and by success of arms established an independent government, under the name of "the United States." It is further alleged that the Cherokee nation prosecuted a war at the same time against the colonies.

Thirdly, several years after the treaties of peace and friendship and protection, which took place between the United States and the Cherokee nation, and by which the faith of the United States was sol-

1419

emnly pledged to guarantee to the Cherokee nation forever, a title to their lands, a compact was entered into between the United States and the state of Georgia by which the United States promised to purchase for the use of Georgia certain lands belonging to the Cherokee nation, so soon as it could be done on reasonable and peaceable terms.

Thus stands the native claim of Georgia to a portion of our lands. The claim advanced under the plea of discovery is preposterous. Our ancestors, from time immemorial, possessed this country, not by a "charter" from the hand of mortal king, who had no right to grant it, but by the will of the King of Kings, who created all things, and liveth for ever and ever.

The claim advanced under the second head, on the ground of conquest, is no less futile than the first, even admitting that the Cherokees waged a war with the colonies at the time they fought for their independence. The Cherokees took a part in the war only as the allies of Great Britain, and not as her subjects, being an independent nation, over whose lands she exercised no rights of jurisdiction; therefore nothing could be claimed from them, in regard to their lands, by the conqueror, over the rights of Great Britain. At the termination of the war the United States negotiated with the Cherokees on the terms of peace as an independent nation, and, since the close of that war, other wars took place, and at their terminations other treaties were made; and in no one stipulation can there be found a single idea that our title to the soil has ever been affected or claimed as the terms of peace; but, to the contrary, we discover that the United States solemnly pledged their faith that our title should be guaranteed to our nation forever.

The third pretension is extremely lame. The United States enters into a compact with Georgia that they will purchase certain lands, which belong to us, for Georgia, so soon as they can do it on peaceable and reasonable terms. This promise was made on the part of the United States without knowing whether this nation would even consent to dispose of these lands on any terms whatever; and the Cherokees not being a party in the compact, their title could not be affected in the slightest degree. It appears astonishingly unreasonable that all those hard denunciations, which have been unsparingly lavished against our sacred rights and institutions by interested politicians, have arose from no other circumstances than our refusal to sell to the United States lands for the fulfillment of their compact with Georgia. Although our views and condition may be misrepresented—although we may be stigmatized with the appellation of "nabobs," and should be represented as ruling with an "iron rod," and "grinding down into dust the wretched and abject mass" of our citizens; and although we may be called avaricious for refusing to sell our lands, we should not be diverted from the path of rectitude. In all our intercourse with our neighboring white brethren, we should endeavor to cultivate the utmost harmony and good understanding by strictly observing the relations which we sustain to the United States.

Owing to the various misrepresentations respecting us, we have been frequently called upon to make a treaty of concession; and, under the hope of succeeding with us, a treaty has been entered into by the United States with that portion of the Cherokees who have absolved themselves from all connection with us by removing west of the Mississippi and establishing themselves there as a distinct community, stipulating that all those Cherokees residing east of the Mississippi, who will consent to emigrate west of that river, shall receive a bounty consisting of a rifle gun, and blanket, and steel trap, and brass kettle, and five pounds of tobacco. Such are the temptations offered to induce us to leave our friends, our relatives, our houses, our cultivated farms, our country, and everything endeared to us by the progress of civilization—for what? To tread the barren wilds and dreary waste on the confines of the Rocky Mountains, with those necessary accoutrements and appendages of the hunter on our backs, in pursuit of the buffalo and other wild animals. With a view of carrying this burlesque on our happiness into effect, the United States agent for this nation has been instructed, by the secretary of war, to visit us at our firesides, accompanied by James Rogers and Thomas Maw, two of the Cherokees residing west of the Mississippi, and who composed a part of the chiefs that negotiated the late treaty. This extraordinary movement has been made, though without any effect; and we are happy to state that our citizens generally have treated the agent and associates with civility, and have with great propriety restrained their indignant feelings from committing any violence on the persons of the two Arkansas chiefs for the indignity offered by the design of their visit. We would recommend you, as the immediate representatives of the people, to submit a respectful memorial to the Congress of the United States expressive of the true sentiments of the people respecting their situation, and praying that measures may be adopted on the part of the United States for the adjustment of their compact with the state of Georgia otherwise than to anticipate any further concession of land from this nation.

WILLIAM HICKS,
JOHN ROSS.

New-Echota, C. N., Oct. 13, 1828.

APPENDIX K

A catechism for overland travellers. From J. E. Sherwood's "Pocket Guide to California. New York: 1849."

First Question—The Route.—Which route by land is best for the emigrant:

Answer.—The route via Independence or St. Joseph, Mo., to Fort Laramie, South Pass, Fort Hall, the Sink of Mary's River, &c., &c., the old route. Let no emigrant, carrying his family with him, deviate from it or imagine that he can find a better road. This road is the best that has yet been discovered, and to the Bay of San Francisco and the Gold Region it is much the shortest. The Indians, moreover, on this route, have, up to the present time, been so friendly as to commit no acts of hostility on the emigrants. The trail is plain and good where there are no physical obstructions, and the emigrant by taking this route, will certainly reach his destination in good season and without disaster. From our information we would most earnestly advise all emigrants to take this trail, without deviation, if they would avoid the fatal calamities which almost invariably have attended those who have undertaken to explore new routes.

Second—Wagon and Team.—What kind of wagon and team is preferable?

Answer.—The lightest wagon that can be constructed of sufficient strength to carry 2,500 pounds weight, is the vehicle most desirable. No wagon should be loaded over this weight, or if it is, it will be certain to stall in the muddy sloughs and crossings on the prairie in the first part of the journey. This wagon can be hauled by 3 or 4 yokes of oxen or six mules. Oxen are usually employed by the emigrants for hauling their wagons. They travel about 15 miles per day, and all things considered, are perhaps equal to mules for this service, although they cannot travel so fast. They are, however, less expensive, and there is not so much danger of their straying and of being stolen by the Indians.

Pack-mules can only be employed by parties of men. It would be very difficult to transport a party of women and children on pack-mules, with the provisions, clothing, and other baggage necessary to their comfort. A party of men, however, with pack mules, can make the journey in less time by one month than it can be done in wagons,—carrying with them, however, nothing more than their provisions, clothing and ammunition.

For parties of men going out, it would be well to haul their wagons, provisions, &c., as far as Fort Laramie, or Fort Hall, by mules, carry-

1422

ing with them pack-saddles and atforjases, or large saddle-bags, adapted to the pack-saddle, with ropes for packing, &c., when, if they saw proper they could dispose of their wagons for Indian ponies, and pack into California, gaining perhaps two or three weeks' time.

Third.—What provisions are necessary to a man?

Answer.—The provisions actually necessary per man, are as follows: 150 lbs. of Flour, 150 lbs. Bacon, 25 lbs. Coffee, 30 lbs. Sugar.

Added to these, the main items, there should be a small quantity of rice, 50 or 75 lbs. of crackers, dried peaches, &c., and a keg of lard, with salt, pepper, &c., and such other luxuries of light weight as the person outfitting chooses to purchase. He will think of them before he starts.

Fourth.—What arms and ammunition are necessary?

Answer.—Every man should be provided with a good rifle, and, if convenient, with a pair of pistols, five pounds of powder and ten pounds of lead. A revolving belt pistol may be found useful.

With the wagon, there should be carried such carpenters' tools as a handsaw, auger, gimlet, chisel, shaving-knife, &c., an axe, hammer, and hatchet. This last weapon every man should have in his belt, with a hunter's or bowie knife.

Fifth.—What is the length of the journey?

Answer.—From Independence to the first settlement in California, which is near the gold region, it is about 2,050 miles—to San Francisco, 2,290 miles.

Sixth.—What are the facts in regard to the statements respecting the gold mines?

Answer.—The accounts that have been received and published in regard to the wealth and productiveness of the gold mines, and other mines in California, are undoubtedly true. They are derived from the most reliable and authentic sources, and from individuals whose veracity may be undoubtingly believed.

Seventh.—What could a young man, or a man with a family, with or without profession, do, should he emigrate to California?

Answer.—When he arrives there, he must turn his attention to whatever seems to promise the largest recompense for his labor. It is impossible in the new state of things produced by the late discoveries, and the influx of population, to foresee what this might be. The country is rich in agricultural resources, as well as in the precious metals, and with proper enterprise and industry, he could scarcely fail to do well.

Families, as well as parties going out, should carry with them good tents, to be used after their arrival as houses. The influx of population will probably be so great that it will be difficult, if not impossible, to obtain other shelter for some time after their arrival. The climate of the country, however, even in winter, is so mild that with good tents, comfort is attainable. They should be careful, also, to carry as much subsistence into the country as they can; as what they purchase there after their arrival, they will be compelled to pay a high price for.

Eighth.—What is the time of starting?

Answer.—Emigrants should be at Independence, St. Joseph, Mo., or the point of starting, by the 20th of April, and start as soon thereafter as the grass on the prairies will permit. This is sometimes by the 1st of May, and sometimes ten days later, according to the season.

Emigrants should not take the route via the South end of the Great Salt Lake, but continue on by Fort Hall, when they will again intersect Mr. B.'s route on Mary's River, about sixty miles from its head waters. On this route they will always, except in two instances, find water and grass within short distances.

Table of distances as given by Bryant in his route overland from Independence, Missouri, to Sutter's Fort on the Sacramento river, Upper California.

From Independence to Fort Laramie	672	miles
From Fort Laramie to Pacific Springs (South Pass)	311	"
From the South Pass (Pacific Springs) to Fort Bridger	123	"
From Fort Bridger to Salt Lake	106	"
From Salt Lake to Mary's river	315	"
From Mary's river to the Sink	274	"
From the Sink to Truckee Lake	124	"
From Truckee Lake to Johnson's	111	"
From Johnson's to Sutter's Fort	35	"

Total distance from Independence, Missouri, to Sutter's Fort, in California.............................2,071 "

The distance from Sutter's Fort by land, to the town of San Francisco (via the Pueblo of San Jose) near the mouth of the Bay of San Francisco, and five miles from the Pacific Ocean, is............................... 200 "

Total to the sea........................2,271 miles

APPENDIX L

A list of the principal overland travel routes between the Mississippi valley and the Pacific Ocean, as used by caravans from about 1849 to 1868. Based on the itineraries given, from page 181 to page 251, in Burton's edition of Marcy's "The Prairie Traveler," London, 1863. The routes here listed may be traced on the accompanying map of western roads, although the numbers used on the map are not here followed.

1.—From Fort Smith, Arkansas, westward along the Canadian River and thirty-fifth degree of north latitude, through Indian Territory,[1] Texas and New Mexico, to Santa Fé (819 miles) and Albuquerque (814¾ miles). Captain Marcy's route of 1849.

2.—From Fort Leavenworth, Kansas, southwestward through Kansas, Colorado and New Mexico to Santa Fé.

3.—From Fort Smith, Arkansas, southwestward through Indian Territory and Texas to El Paso. A route discovered and marked by Marcy in 1849. Distance, 860 miles.

4.—From St. Joseph, Missouri, through Kansas, along the North Fork of the Platte in Nebraska, and thence through Wyoming and Utah to Salt Lake City. Distance, 1,136 miles. A principal route for overland emigrants. Average length of time on the road in good weather, 75 days.

5.—From Salt Lake City, southwest through Utah, Nevada and California to Sacramento and Benicia. Distance, 973 miles. Total distance from St. Joseph to Sacramento, 2,109 miles.

6.—From Salt Lake City, southwest through Utah, Nevada and California to Los Angeles. Distance, 773 miles.

7.—From Los Angeles northward through California to San Francisco. Distance, 465 miles.

8.—From Soda Springs, Idaho, northwest through Idaho, Washington and Oregon to Oregon City and Salem. Distance, 964 miles.

9.—From New Orleans to Fort Yuma, California. By steamboat from New Orleans to Powder Horn, on the Texas coast. Thence by wagon road northwest to San Antonio. Distance, 144 miles. Thence by wagon road 654 miles to El Paso. Thence by wagon road 644 miles to Fort Yuma. Total overland distance from Powder Horn to Yuma, 1,442 miles.

10.—From Fort Yuma northward to Benicia, California, 800 miles.

11.—From Fort Yuma westward to San Diego, California. Distance, 217 miles.

[1] Now Oklahoma.

1425

12.—From El Paso to Fort Yuma, via Santa Cruz. Distance, 756 miles.

13.—From Westport, Missouri, to the Pike's Peak gold diggings and Denver. Westward through Kansas and Colorado. Distance, 685¼ miles.

14.—From St. Paul, Minnesota, westward through Minnesota, Dakota, Montana and Washington to Fort Wallah Wallah. Distance, 1,685¾ miles.

15.—From Albuquerque, New Mexico, westward through New Mexico, Arizona and California to Los Angeles. Distance, 1,010 miles.

16.—From Fort Thorne, New Mexico, westward through New Mexico and California to Fort Yuma. Distance, 571 miles.

17.—From the Laramie Crossing of the South Platte River, Nebraska, to Fort Bridger, Wyoming, via Bridger's Pass. Distance, 520½ miles. By the Fort Laramie Road the distance was 569 miles.

18.—From Denver, Colorado, to Fort Bridger. Distance, 372 miles.

19.—From Camp Floyd, Utah, southwest through Utah, Colorado and New Mexico to Fort Union. Distance, 712 miles.

APPENDIX M

The heretofore unpublished narrative of an overland journey to California in 1849 from which the following passages are transcribed is a manuscript diary written by Stanislaus Lasselle, of Logansport, Indiana, and now among the Lasselle Papers of the Indiana State Library. He and the party with him travelled along or near the Santa Fé trail, and his account of the expedition is an excellent portrayal of the experiences and conditions encountered while journeying to California through that part of the continent crossed by him. Lasselle and his companions departed from Logansport on February 6, and reached their destination late in August. Their real overland trip began early in March, and from that time onward the writer tells his story thus:

March 2. Travelled eleven miles. James Dale burnt his whiskers by pouring cold water on hot grass. First time we cook by messes.

Saturday 3d.
Travelled fourteen miles. Enquired of a young farmer why he lived in such a country, his answer was because he was born there.

Monday 5th.
Travelled six miles. Teams half a mile and stalled. Boys scattered all along the road.

Tuesday 6.
Travelled two miles. Teams six miles behind.

Wednesday 7th.
Laid by all day. Teams came up.

Friday 9th.
Travelled sixteen miles. Beautiful views. The boys all delighted with the country and road.

Sunday 25th.
Travelled five miles. Camped near Fort Smith at Sulphur Spring. Found a company from New York as well as other states encamped.

Monday 26
Encamped all day. Singing in camp.

1427

Tuesday 27

Encamped all day. Pistols stolen by mess No. 1. Persons should be cautious who they take for messmates.

Wednesday 28

Encamped all day. Lectures, speeches and singing in camp.

Thursday 29th.

Encamped all day. Impossible for mechanics at Fort Smith to do the work of emigrants.

Friday 30

Travelled six miles. Camped in the Choctaw territory.

Saturday 31

Past the Pateau river in ferry. Runaway match between a Choctaw and a Chickasaw girl. Married in the State of Arkansas. The mother of the girl took her home. Met a wandering Choctaw fidler. Played for us. Beautiful prairie and spurs of hills.

Sunday 1st April

Setting prairie on fire by the emigration to the great annoyance of the party. Last night a party of Choctaws from the wedding stop at Camp and dance and sang until two o'clock in the morning. Nearly all could speak English and seemed well contented with their wild and primitive life. They are fond of liquor. Most of them were dressed like the whites, but the turban is still common among them.

Tuesday 3

Saw in the prairie eleven Kickapoos taking some forty mules to Fort Smith to sell. They were all painted and had bows and arrows.

Wednesday 4

The Creek Indian country begins after crossing the Canadian [river]. Saw five young buffaloes in a field. Travelled ten miles.

Thursday 5

Making preparatory steps to organization. Various suggestions and propositions by various persons. Invited by Rev. Mr. Hay (a missionary among the Creek) to attend his school. An Indian prayed in his language and seemed eloquent.

Friday 6

I was solicited to run for captain but declined. A board of five was selected, selecting one from Indiana, Tennessee, Arkansas, Mississippi, Louisiana.

Saturday 7

There were several young Indians in camp with bows and arrows. To see their expertness with the bow and arrow some of the company place on the end of a twig stuck in the ground a dime and the one that hit it was entitled to it. They had hit the dime and also knocked it off before they were entitled to it. The company tried to encamp for the first time in order, but instead of camping in order as a military camping in two parallel lines, one line was formed in a semi-circle and the other a right angle, while some were entirely out of line. Some of the tents were fronting one way and some another. A deputation of five Comanches visited one of the chief of the Creek nation to know the motives of emigrants passing to California through their country. The Creek Chief informed them and reconciled them and gave them a letter.

Sunday 8th.

Went to church to hear Gen. McIntosh. He is a very popular, as well as a very talented Indian. A prejudice existing between the company among western and southern emigrants. Advantages taken by southerners because they have the powers. After they had formed a constitution requiring two-thirds to amend it, a resolution was introduced and passed that no one should leave the company or pack through until they reached Santa Fe. This resolution was passed to bind us to help some large wagons from other states. First time I stood guard on the trip. In the meantime, I dryed my socks and becoming very hungry, I fried some bacon and eat it without bred.

Monday 9

In travelling in the fore part of the day the company stalled several times and became disheartened, and came very near, some of them, of turning back. One mess from ———— sold their waggon and camp'd with the intention of packing. In the afternoon we past one of the most beautiful prairies I ever saw. The company was better satisfied and again cried ho! for California. The sun also which was hidden in the fore part of the day made his appearance and seemed to cheer up the dampened spirits. Travel'd six miles.

Sunday 15th.

Traveled eight miles. Snow fell three inches thick. Night and morning very cold. Prairie all covered with snow. Mules and horses could not pick grass. A person would have perished without tent or fire.

Monday 16.

Preparation for packing. All new hands at it. A great Ball by the Indians in honor of the Firemaker.

Wednesday 18

Crossed Little river with waggons. River very high. Emigrants delayed in consequence of it. We had to tie a cable to our waggons and draw them across half loaded, the balance of the load was taken across on horses. Several persons in crossing the river were either thrown off of their horses or got entirely wet. As we had concluded to pack we disposed of a great many articles at sacrifice. Went about one mile from the village [of Indians] and camp'd for the purpose of preparing to pack. All new hands at it.

Friday 20

Having all packs ready we left in the forenoon. Difficulty in putting packs on horses. Got some Indians to put them on for us. Several stampedes of mules in camp. Laughable to see the mules scatter the packs through the woods. A bag of crackers belonging to Dale broke open and scattered the crackers for two or three hundred yards. The Indians that were in camp discovered it was bread and broke for it. Traveled ten miles.

Saturday 21

Traveled twenty miles. Took the wrong trail and went to a Delaware settlement. Hired a Delaware to put us on the right trail.

Sunday, 22nd.

Pass Choteau's Trading House. Struck the plain at the Canadian. No road from there.

Wednesday 25th.

Overtook the Knickerbockers [emigrants from New York], part with waggons and part packing. Also a few packers from Tennessee and Arkansas. Buffalo signs.

Thursday 26th.

Traveled twenty-five miles. Past through a city of prairie wolves covering some three or four hundred acres. Looked like a deserted town, being so much tramped by them. Fine spring water all day.

Saturday 28th.

Laid by all day to rest the teams. A Knickerbocker washing in the creek. He was boiling all of the color out of his shirt. First Buffalo seen and killed.

Sunday 29th.

Traveled fifteen miles. Saw three or four droves of Buffalo. The train stopped that all who wanted a chase after Buffalo might have one. The meat was very tough and two or three meals of buffalo meat seemed to satisfy all who was so anxious to eat buffalo meat. The Knickerbockers in the chase had double-barrel shotguns, which created a good deal of laughter and sport to the rest of the company. The black-bird are very tame and often light on the horses as they were going along. The buffalo all seemed to be going north.[1]

Monday 30th.

Traveled about fifteen or twenty miles. Saw some fifty thousand buffalos during the day. From morning until night they were seen on either side of us, indeed, it seemed as if we had to cut our way through them. As far as the eye could reach they were seen and I believe we could see fifteen or twenty miles on all sides.[2] Grass all eaten up and stamped by buffalos.

Tuesday May 1st.

A great many complaining of being sick. Some believed it was the buffalo meat and others thought it was the brackish water. A fight between A. Searight and Jo. Rheins.

Wednesday 2nd.

The company killed a buffalo near the train. The Knickerbockers opened it to get the heart and liver. They got the heart but could not find the liver and left the carcass. The country became more broken and seemed to change.

Thursday 3rd.

Saw antelope. Water brakish. Country broken. Soil red. Camped at night without water.

Saturday 5th.

The boys while scouting came across a party of Indians. I, with some others, immediately plaited [contemplated?] to overtake them but they were gone, which the Captain thought was rather a bad sign. That night we increased our guard. We also thought we could get information about the way we had to go, as we had a very little idea where we were. Killed several snakes. They can be heard rattling 100 feet. Buchanan saw a bear.

Sunday 6th.

An Indian, to the great surprise, as well as the gratification of some of our party came in camp, being one of those that had been seen the day before. The Indian's face was painted all over with yellow clay— around his eyes was red paint. He had on a buffalo robe, with [feath-

---

[1] As they always did at that season of the year.
[2] The party had evidently encountered one of the five or six main bodies of migrating bison, in each of which there were many hundreds of thousands of the animals.

ers?] from the back of his head reaching to the ground. His risks [1] were covered with brass wire, rather large. He had a rifle covered over with white cow hide and at the mussle of the gun was ten or twelve strings of white cow hide twisted, which gave it the appearance of a pennant at a distance. At the brigg of the gun was a bunch of turkey feathers cut short. He had a pouch also strung with white beads as was the strap. He also had a small bag where he kept his looking glass, and he seemed to take as much care of it as a lady would of her toilet. His features were rather feminine and did not indicate that he was much of a warrior. He was invited to get off his horse, which he done, and was taken into one of the tents where a breakfast was brought to him when he commenced eating. Seeing there was no knife or fork he by signs gave us to understand that he was somewhat acquainted with the use of them. His errant, as he said, was to informed us that there were some Pawmenahom [Pawnee?] lurking around our camp for the purpose of stealing our horses.

Monday 7th.

Country broken and very sandy having change from red clay to yellow sand. A bear and cub killed by Dale and Buchanan. A Knickerbocker shot at the bear after it was dead. Saw dwarf oak trees from 6 to 18 inches high which bears acorns. We stopt at noon to rest our horses and to dine under a very beautiful cotton tree. It was very large and its limbs spread every direction which made a very good shade.

Tuesday 8

Traveled about twelve miles. Did not start so soon as usual. had to mend a wagon. A general quarreling among the messes. Knats [gnats] bad. A Knickerbocker knocked off his horse by fighting two others. Stuned.

Thursday 10

We dined in a cottonwood grove. In the grove the dove, martin, mocking bird &c were heard singing which reminded me of home. Hearing the dove in the wilderness singing was rather unexpected. Pack company wanted to leave the waggons. Some of company who were bitten by knats this morning had the faces and hands very much swollen. About sun down we had a terrible hail storm and strong wind, blowing down some of the tents of the Knickerbockers. After the storm two or three of the K's crawled out of their tents to the sport of the company. I stood guard. Mocking birds singing at night.

Friday 11

A Knickerbocker kicked by a mule. He was walking leasurely along with a green veil over his face to keep the knats from biting him, and

[1] Wrists.

happening to get too close to the mule's heels, the mule lambed away and struck him on the shin bone. It was a severe kick, much worse than a knat bit. Several of the K's today have their faces tied up with eyes so swollen that they as some say cannot see ten feet. What accounts for the mule kicking. A K. thought that jurk meat was called so because it was jurked off of the skeleton. Saw for the first time the wild rose. The river becoming so small and the valley narrowing so much made me believe that the Guadalope mountains so long looked for was close at hand.

Saturday 12

After traveling about 4 miles in the bottom of the river [the Canadian] we left it and took on top of the hill where we took a south west course, believing that we had left the Canadian. but toward evening when it was time to camp to our great surprise we found ourselves again on the banks of the Canadian, and as we could not find either wood or water we endeavored to get in the river bottom but it was impossible the bluffs were too steep and rocky. Late at night some of the boys getting very thirsty myself among them we ventured down the mountain in search of water. We all felt that we were lost and instead of wishing to go the right course we began to want to get to settlements that we might get on the right course. The waggon horses were about to give out and those who had waggons felt anxious to have others [other horses]. A fight between two Knickerbockers. A Knickerbocker lost his coat. Toward evening as we pushed ahead rapidly some of the waggons did not come up until late at night while others did not come up at all. Heretofore we generally formed in order but tonight there was no order.

Sunday 13

Laid by all day. In the morning we found ourselves camped in great disorder entirely surrounded by deep ravines with the exception of the side that we came.

Monday 14

In leaving camp in the morning we went back the same road. There was difference of opinion to what course to take. While I and some others were some two or three miles in advance of the train we saw an Indian making towards us on horse full speed. We shook hands with him which seemed to please him very much. We learned from him that we were five days travel from Mexican settlements. He told us he was an Apache and motioned to the south.

Tuesday 15

Travel'd twenty miles. Passed over a country rolling and very much broken. The company very much discourage. No sight of the mountains yet. Two fights by the company. One of them by two Knickerbockers.

Wednesday 16

It was my turn to stand guard. As the night was extremely cold we got our blankets an rapt around us. I had a pair of mackinaw blankets around me but the cold piercing wind seemed to strike through them.

Friday 18

Traveled about twelve miles. As the afternoon was very stormy we did not travel. As the company had been pestered by hail they became very cautious of the black looking clouds. They all contrived some way or other to shelter from hail. I saw three Hoosiers in a cave that they had dug in the side of a ravine. They were snugly secured from the hail. They had used a spade to make the hole.

Saturday 19

Still had the bluffs all day on our right. In the evening we found water but it was in small basin and it was all used up, having none for morning. We saw a Comanche who told us of this water and I believe if it had not been for him we would not have got the water.

Sunday 20

In the morning the oxen were missing and it was supposed they had been stolen. After going some four or five miles met a train of Mexicans and also got from them the distances of different places. This was gratifying to us after being so long in suspense. We were eight days travel from Santa Fee. A Knickerbocker took a young jack the Mexicans had packing for a young buffalo which was considered a good joke and created a good deal of laughter. We had not left the Mexican train long before we saw on rising ground ahead of us a large body of Indians. We all halted immediately and examined whether our arms were in order and as the waggon train was some ten miles behind, we consulted each other whether to go ahead or not. In the mean time there were two or three of the Comanches riding toward us. They soon came up and seemed to be very friendly. After informing them that we were waiting for the waggon train and that as soon as it came up we would go on, he seemed to be reconciled, but after some time waiting they became uneasy and insisted very strong that some of us should go up immediately. Myself and Jackson concluded to go with them. One was a chief. When we got within half a mile I saw many more than I thought was there. As soon as we got within a hundred yards of them, they all mounted their horses and made a great deal of noise by talking loud and hollering. Once and awhile I could hear among [them] voices giving command coming no doubt from the

Chiefs. We were immediately surrounded by some fifty young men who came galloping towards us through curiosity I suppose. They were not long around us before they were ordered to leave. We were led up to several chiefs ten or twelve in number who were seated on blankets and invited to dismount and set down by them. I got off my horse handed him to an Indian to hold, set down by the side of them. I had not been seated long before a very old Indian dressed in a white blanket coat and cap came up before me and the chiefs and knealed on the grass also putting his elbows on the grass and placing his hands together. He muttered as I thought a prayer and then talked to the chiefs. He done this several times. It struck me that he was either priest, prophet or medicine man among them and that it depended on his decision what our fate was to be. The main chief after a while unrapt a paper carefully wrapped up and handed it to me. I read it and found that it was from the Indian Agent for the Platte and Arkansas country stating that they had visited him and that it was their intention to be friendly to the Americans passing through their country. While I was seated with the chiefs all the Indians some eight hundred or a thousand made a circle around us. . . . Believing there was no danger we went on without the waggons and travelled some five miles farther when we came up to their encampment numbering at least two hundred lodges. Here we encamped for the night. The Indians generally had nothing on them but buffalo robes, beads and paint. They came to our camp unarmed. They had about their camp some three thousand horses and mules. A few of them noble animals.

Tuesday 22

Traveled thirty miles. Saw several beautiful landscape views. Some of the Knickerbockers entirely out of provisions.

Wednesday 23

Saw mountains on right covered with snow. I was riding behind a chief and his squaw. The chief droped some ornament the squaw got off her horse and picked it up and handed it to the chief. This is Comanche politeness. Water is beginning to get scarce.

Thursday 24

Traveled twenty miles. Country very broken. The captain (Ebbetts) declined acting as captain any more.

Friday 25

Country very broken. It was nothing but down and uphill all day. This day expecting to pass the first signs of civilization. About two o'clock we came to a ranch called Bernae, having some twenty-five persons. Here is the Independence road that leads to Santa Fee. It has been worked by the government and much used.

Monday 28

Traveled twenty-five miles. Reach'd Sante Fe. The town built of mud. Very dusty. Extortion by Mexicans and Americans for corn and hay. Fandangos every night.

Tuesday 29

Laid in Sante Fe all day. New preparations for outfitting. Many of the Knickerbockers preparing to pack. Gambling among Mexicans and Americans. Five churches. Officers gave a fandango.

Wednesday 30

Many of the emigrants got to gambling. Gambling on the increase as the Americans came. One of the Knickerbockers had his pistol stolen at a gambling table.

Thursday 31

Left Santa Fee on the Spanish trail. Traveled 30 miles. A battle was fought this day eight miles from us and immediately on our road between the U. S. troops and Apaches. Twenty Apaches killed. No Americans killed. Two Mexicans killed was the cause of the fight. The road all day hilly and barren.

Friday June 1st

Laid by all day. Difference of opinion as to the route. Some discouraged. Another battle between the troops and Apaches.

Saturday 2

Laid by all day. Arranging packs. Footmen discouraged. They conclude to go back. The Indians in St. John have schuttle holes from the tops of their houses and no lower doors. Report that there were eight tribes of Indians collecting for the purpose of fighting the emigrants.

Monday 4th.

Traveled sixteen miles. Camped two miles above Abuquerte [Albuquerque]. Abuquerte is an Indian village. A company of volunteers stationed in it.

Thursday 7

Traveled eight miles and camp'd on the Chames river not being [able] to ford it. Preparations for crossing in building rafts. Unsuccessful with rafts. Commence building a canoe. Work on it until twelve o'clock at night. River water cold as ice. Good grass and wood.

Friday 8

Laid by all day. Crossed four or five loads in canoe. Lost two loads of packs in crossing river. One mess lost five hundred dollars in silver in one of his packs. The upsetting of canoe frightened the rest. No more crossing during the day. Dissention of part. Some wanted to go the northern route some the southern route.

Saturday 9

Not being able to cross after using great exertion all concluded to return back.

Sunday 10

Traveled twenty-five miles. Coming down the mountain was very hard on the mules.

Monday 11

Traveled thirty miles. Past Albuqu. Procured at Albuku. Larue, who had been with Kerney [General Kearney] and Cook as our guide. Horse shoes and nails wanted bad by the company.

Wednesday 13

Company again divided, part left to accompany Day, who concluded to await a few days before leaving. Elected Miller captain. The guide did not know the road on the south side of the river, and as we did not wish to cross the river we concluded to continue on the south side.....
Hearing that there was a road going to [Horner ?] we concluded to take that road. The moment we left the river we entered a pass in the mountain and traveled along a path some ten miles when the road run out. We continued the pass until we could not get any farther. The pass entirely closed up. Seeing it impossible to go any farther we return the same road some eight miles when we camped for the night. Dissention again among the party. Day tried to get our guide.

Thursday 14

Returned back to the Rio Grande thinking it best not to venture any other path without a guide who had traveled the road. We procured an Indian. It seemed that we had taken the wrong road about eight miles up the pass. Taking the left instead of the right. For my part I did not see any right hand road. The left hand road was made by herding stock. Strangers should never travel without a guide. Water and grass is always scarce.

Friday 15

Traveled fifteen miles. Nearly all day in going up and down a mountain.

Saturday 16

Traveled twenty-five miles. The road very mountainous. Most of the day down hill. Saw bear in the morning. Knickerbocker mules mired.

Sunday 17

Past two Pueblo villages. In the first as we past it we saw in the plaza a number of Indians at, as I thought, some kind of game. They were naked and painted with white clay with the exception of two who were painted black and had horns on their heads. Those dressed or painted white had animals painted on their backs with black paint. They all formed in a line except the black ones who it seems were privileged to go where they pleased. The black ones would go to the white ones and rub against them as well as embraced them. The black ones had greese on them which made them shine. Around the plaza on tops of houses as well as in the plaza were a great many females chiefly very neat and who seemed to take a delight as onlookers. Reached the Rio Grande river and camped on its bank.

Monday 18

Traveled twenty miles down the valley of the Rio Grande.

Tuesday 19

Traveled down the valley twelve miles and camped opposite albeque. Saw two Navaho Indians.

Wednesday 20

Laid by all day. Made another outfit. A person never gets done making outfits.

[From the 21st to the 25th, inclusive, the emigrants traveled along the Rio Grande about 110 miles.]

Tuesday 26

Traveled thirty miles. Past St. Antoine, the last Mexican settlement. Past waggons for California.

Thursday 28

After traveling twelve miles we left the Rio Grande and took Gen. Kearney's trail. We past over beautiful table land, with the exception of three or four deep ravines. From the river to where we camped some twenty miles there was no water.

Saturday 30

Beautiful little valley with plenty of cottonwood, ash, walnut, &c. Eat and stewed fine currents. Fish'd in the river. Country mountainous.

A HISTORY OF TRAVEL IN AMERICA

Sunday July 1st.

Camped at the copper mine, once considerable of a town but now destroyed by the Apaches. An alarm at night. Guard herd as he thought an Indian yell on the mountain. As had rain the two preceeding days there was not many of the arms in order.

Monday 2

One of the company lost his mule and pack.

Tuesday 3

Camped on the Hula [Gila] river where Gen. Kearney had camped and where Emory says he camped. Was amidst mountains that looked like huge hay stacks.

Wednesday 4

Did not travel today. It being the 4th in the morning w: fire a salute. Had for my dinner grizly bear soup with rice. Some parties went a fishing some hunting and some a gambling. Emory says that the fish in the Gila river have no scales. He is mistaken.

Saturday 7

Traveled ten miles. Saw Apache Indians (three) for the first time. Disappointed in getting horse shoes and nails left by Kearney.

Sunday 8

Took a cut-off over the mountains and avoided the Devil's turnpike spoken off by Emery. We save three or four days travel by doing so. After ascending the mountains about fifteen miles we reached the summit of the mountains and to our great surprise saw the Gila river on the other side......After reaching the top of the mountains and seeing the river we became careless of the water not supposing the river to be over eight miles. Some thought it not over three miles but to our great distress it was some twenty miles. For my part I suffered very much for water and it was with much difficulty that I succeeded in reaching the river. Men and horses both gave out. I was the only person who walked the distance without giving out. I was so dry for water that could not swaller or utter a sound. I drank about 3 quarts of water and 1 quart of coffee.

Monday 9th.

Traveled ten miles only for the reason that we had to rest our horses.

Thursday 12

Today we traveled about a mile from camp, but David C. Buchanan meeting a serious accident we return to where we had camp. While

Buchanan was riding by the side of White off White's rifle went and struck Buchanan in the thigh. Doctor Bush tried to extract the bullet but he could not succeed. Several plans were suggested to carry Buchanan on. The plan adopted was to send some thirty men on this evening nine miles down the river and make canoes, there being no timber here suited for that purpose.

Friday 13

Built a raft for Buchanan but it was impracticable. The river was too low and too many rapids. They brought Buchanan on a litter nine miles to where timber could be had. He was carried by men.

Saturday 14

Capt. Miller resign his office. Ridley elected in his place. A litter was prepared for Buchanan partly carried by men and partly by mules. While traveling today we overtook several Indians by surprise. They had no sooner seen us than they broke and run leaving their packs behind of muscal[1] and parched corn. We hailed them. They were all naked and had bows and arrows. We bought their muscal by paying them powder, bullets, buttons, needles, thread, tobacco, &c. A Mexican along pulled off his shirt to trade for muscal.

Sunday 15

Traveled twelve miles through ᴜɪe canon. The men found much trouble in carrying Buchanan up and down the mountains as well as crossing the river several times. We camped in the canon.

Monday 16

In the afternoon another mule was hitched to the litter, which made it easier on the men. We camped at night where there was an Indian encampment. They had a kind of jelly made of the apple of the cactus. It eats very good and makes drinkable wine. As soon as they saw us they all broke and ran but as soon as they saw we were friendly they came back to us and presented us with muscal &c in abundance. They were all naked when we saw them but as soon as they traded for a shirt or a handkerchief they would put it on. The squaws could do no trading and had to remain naked.

Wednesday 18

We nooned where there was a large quantity of prickly pears. The company eated to excess and many were made sick. At night after camping it was [found] that an Irishman was left behind who complained of being sick by eating the prickly pears. He laid out all night.

[1] Meaning a very strong intoxicating drink of Mexico and the southwestern border.

Sunday 22

Laid by all day. Buchanan was taken to the Head Chief of the Pinos who seemed to be hospitable toward him as well as kind.

Monday 23

The chief was down in our camp and one of the company showed him his likeness in Emorv's work. His wife was by and recognized the likeness. It greatly tickled other Indians who was standing by at the time.

Tuesday 24

Camped near the Maracopees [Maricopi]. We were informed by them that the Apaches had killed five American emigrants and also two Maracopees and that they had sent out four hundred warriors to fight them. They had many worn out horses they had got from the whites that was ahead of us. We had plenty of roasting ears and watermelons. The Pinos and Maracopees will steal. They were caught at it.

Wednesday 25

Party again divided. A party of some thirty men left about four o'clock in the afternoon expecting to travel all night. The rest, some fifty-four concluded to leave in the morning. The Knickerbockers again divided. I believe a husband and wife divided.

[From Thursday, July 26 to Tuesday, July 31st, inclusive, the party proceeded without noteworthy incident through the Gila River valley, covering about 120 miles during the six days.]

Wednesday August 1st.

The company divided and scattered for twenty miles up and down the river.

Thursday 2

Adopted the plan of traveling in the night and in the morning.[1]

Friday 3

Saw Indian tracks. Did not know what to think about them. I was satisfied their intention was not to trouble us as they kept the main trail, and which was thronged from the Pinos' villages to the Colorado with emigrants. A great many of the company destitute of shoes and clothing.

Saturday 4

Traveled twenty miles. One third of the company is now afoot having lost or broken down their horses and mules.

[1] Owing to the heat of the other hours.

Sunday 5

Two miles after leaving camp we past poor Buchanan. He was in good spirits. He looked very thin and pale. While stoped at noon, Buchanan and waggon past us. At night we past him again.

Tuesday 7

Crossing the Colorado river all day. We hired the Indians to make us rafts to cross us over. We put on our baggage and the Indians and ourselves swam and pulled them over. We did not discover until too late that they had concocted a premeditated plan to rob us until it was too late. They in landing us were careful that we were scattered along the river for two miles. Some of the rafts were robbed, our raft, being too many whites, was unmolested. The Indians also were very particular to land our horses far apart and sometimes turn[ed] them down the stream and land them on the same side when they would get on them and ride off. This is the way our mess lost two horses.

Wednesday 8

Today we crossed the balance of our horses and were more successful not losing any of them, however it was owing to the plan we had adopted. We got a lot of mules on a sand bar and walked them around and around while the [other] mules were swimming over. The mules coming over would as soon as they saw those on the sand bar make for them, and it was impossible for the Indians, with all their expertness in swimming to get them. We also had men stationed along both banks of the river. Yesterday we rushed our animals over in too great a hurry .....Some of the company were in favor of making the Indians returning the mules or routing the Indians from this point, but other[s] oppose it believing it to be a bad policy, as it might have a bad tendency on others who may travel the road.

Thursday 9

Laid by all day making preparations for crossing the desart.

Saturday 11

Part of the company lost taking another road, but I think it came into the waggon road. Came to wells made by Gen. Kearney. Saw today a great many mules and horses dead on the road. Saw a part of a skeleton being the arm of a human. A great many packs empty strewed the road. The skeleton might have perished for want of water.

Monday 13

The party suffered much for water. Many were not able to go through. Those reaching water went back with water to relieve those suffering.

Wednesday 14

Traveled sixteen miles. Camped at Citron pool where Kearney camped. It came upon our view unexpectedly. It really was a green spot in a barren country. A great many Mexicans leaving California. They report gold at San Felippe, twelve miles from us. Accounts prove the gold region favorable. Saw specimens of the gold dust.

Thursday 16

Traveled ten miles. Came to Aqua Caliente. (warm ranch.) Really the first settlement we reach in California.

Friday 17

Travelled eight miles [nothing more set down].

Saturday 18

Traveled thirty miles [no other entry].

Sunday 19

Traveled twenty miles [no other entry].

Monday 20

Traveled twenty miles [no other entry].

Tuesday 21

Traveled ten miles. Camped at William's ranch. [no other entry].

There is one more page to the journal, but the writing on it is very faint because it was also the outer page of the volume and was rubbed much by handling. Doubtless the few words thus lost were not of importance, for after the entry of August 14th, which tells of beholding actual gold, the entries were bare records of distances traversed.

Thus ends the narrative of a journey which began in Logansport, Indiana, on Tuesday, February 6, 1849. The man who wrote it spent six months and two weeks of time and ceaseless personal toil in getting from that town to California.

BIBLIOGRAPHY

A CONTRIBUTION TO A BIBLIOGRAPHY OF THE HISTORY OF TRAVEL IN AMERICA

The following titles have been transcribed from certain of the books, pamphlets, broadsides and maps gathered for use in the preparation of these volumes. Nearly all of them—and the exceptions will not be difficult of recognition—are primary accounts for all or part of the narratives or information contained in them.

The list almost wholly excludes earlier works dealing solely with technical, engineering, financial, economic and commercial phases of American transportation history. The profuse modern writings on those phases of the subject have already been catalogued in numerous bibliographies issued by the Congressional Library and other similar institutions. There is not, on the other hand—so far as the author of these pages is aware—any comprehensive published list of material which deals with the early, personal experiences of the American people while devising, arguing over, building and using the various travel facilities by which they have overrun the country. These titles are offered as a contribution to such a list. The subject matter of the books described constitutes a partial record of the early ideas of the people in relation to travel facilities; their wrangles and disputes over the question at different periods; their efforts to create various and ever more pretentious methods of travel; and their experiences while using the conveyances and travel systems thus brought into being.

An unexpectedly large number of the titles here given are not usually found in library catalogues or those other lists of Americana to which the public refers when in search of material dealing with the earlier conditions of the country. One of the reasons for the preparation of this list is to be found in the hope that its publication will be of measurable value to librarians, historical societies, universities, colleges, and students of the subject, and that it will add, in a certain measure, to a knowledge of the historical material relating to America which still exists. None of the items is an excerpt from other or unnamed works. All are individual publications unless otherwise stated.

Owing to limitations of space certain long titles have been abbreviated, as indicated, but in all cases a sufficient transcript has been made to render identification sure. Nor has it been possible, within reasonable space, to follow scientific catalogue practise to its last detail in this bibliography. The author believed it was more desirable to describe

1447

many items in the manner adopted, and to outline the nature and contents of a book when necessary, rather than to curtail the list of titles for the sake of giving the size, pagination, collation and publisher's imprint of only two-thirds the number. Nor have certain numerous and important works been included. Books such as Gregg's "Commerce of the Prairies," Inman's "Great Salt Lake Trail," Colden's "Erie Canal Celebration of 1825," the exploration narratives of Lewis and Clark, Pike, and Long, Parkman's "Oregon Trail," and the various editions of Zadoc Cramer's "Navigator"—for example—are too well known to make mention of them necessary. The titles of various state and local histories and other similar works mentioned in foot-notes have also been omitted, since they do not treat exclusively of the subject in hand. Following is the list prepared:

(Abbott, Jacob.)—Marco Paul's Travels and Adventures in the Pursuit of Knowledge. On the Erie Canal. Boston, 1848.

Abbott, Jacob.—Marco Paul on the Erie Canal, n.p., n.d. (New York, 1852.) [The preceding book, with a new introduction.]

Abbott, Jacob.—The same, n. p., n. d. [An 1880, New York, reprint of preceding title.]

(Abbott, Jacob.)—Marco Paul's Travels and Adventures in the Pursuit of Knowledge. City of New York. Boston, 1848.

Abdy, E. S.—Journal of a Residence and Tour in the United States of America, from April, 1833, to October, 1834. In three volumes. London, MDCCCXXXV.

Abert, John J., Lieut. Col., U. S. A.—Report to Hon. Lewis Cass, Secretary of War, Washington, 1835. [Reviewing the work then being performed by Army Engineers in planning or constructing roads, canals and railroads throughout the country. Contained in Report No. 95, Ho. of Reps., 24th Congress, 1st Session.]

Abert, John J., Col., Engineer Corps, U. S. A.—Reports of the Secretary of War, with Reconnaissances of Routes from San Antonio to El Paso, by Brevet Lt. Col. J. E. Johnston, Lieut. W. F. Smith, Lieut. F. T. Bryan, Lieut. N. H. Michler and Capt. S. G. French; . . . Also, The Report of Capt. R. B. Marcy's Route from Fort Smith to Santa Fé; and the Report of Lieut. J. H. Simpson of an Expedition into the Navajo Country; and the Report of Lieut. W. H. C. Whiting's Reconnaissances of the Western Frontier of Texas. Washington, 1854 [The volume is Senate Ex. Doc. No. 64, 31st Congress, 1st Session. Has 250 pages of text, 2 folding maps of the routes and 75 plates. Few copies contain every plate, owing to omissions or duplications in binding.]

Abstracts of Bills reported by the Committee on Roads and Canals and Internal Improvements of the House of Representatives, and of the Committee on Roads and Canals of the Senate from the year 1815 to 1834, inclusive: With the estimates, etc., etc., and a statement in regard to the Cumberland Road, from its commencement in 1806 to the close of 1834. Washington, 1836. Contained in Rep. No. 850, Ho. of Reps., 24th Congress, 1st Session. [This document, of 91 closely printed pages, is apparently the only collected record of the Federal government's early activity and work during the period in which the need of better transportation facilities became acute.]

Adams, Charles Francis, Jr.—Notes on Railroad Accidents. New York, 1879.

Adams, Charles Francis, Jr.—Railroads: Their Origin and Problems. New York, 1879.

A Full and Particular Account of all the Circumstances Attending the Loss of the Steamboat Lexington, in Long Island Sound, on the night of January 13, 1840; as elicited in the evidences of the witnesses examined . . . immediately after the lamentable event. Providence, 1840.

Alderson, M. A.—An Essay on the Nature and Application of Steam, with an Historical Notice of the Rise and Progressive Improvement of the Steam Engine. London, 1834.

Allen, Ebenezer.—Galveston and Red River Railroad. To the People of Eastern and Northern Texas. (Galveston, 1852.)

Alspach, S.—Schuylkill Canal Navigator. Philadelphia, 1827. [Giving directions to the captains of canal boats by the aid of which they might avoid accident or wreck on the canal in question. Title reproduced in the text.]

American Rail-Road Journal. Volume 1, New York, Jan. 1 to Dec. 22, 1832. Published weekly. [The magazine was continued for many years.]

(Anbury, Thomas.)—Travel through the Interior Parts of America, etc. In Two Volumes. London, MDCCXCI.

Anderson, Alex. D.—The Mississippi and its Forty-four Navigable Tributaries, etc. Washington, 1890.

Anecdotes for the Steamboat and Railroad, etc. By an Old Traveller. Philadelphia, 1853.

(Armroyd, George.)—A Connected View of the Whole Internal Navigation of the United States, Natural and Artificial; Present and Prospective. [192 pages and folding maps.] Philadelphia, 1826.

(Armroyd, George.)—The same. "Corrected and Improved from the edition of 1826." Philadelphia, 1830. [This edition has 617 pages, a large folding map and folding profiles.]

Arnold, Edmond S. F., M.D.—On Medical Provision for Railroads, as a Humanitarian Measure, as well as a Source of Economy to the Companies, etc. New York, 1862.

Ashcroft, John.—Ashcroft's Railway Directory for 1867, Containing an Official List of the Officers and Directors of the Railroads in the

United States and Canadas, Together with their Financial Condition and Amount of Rolling Stock. New York (1867).

A True Picture of Emigration; or Fourteen Years in the Interior of North America; Being a Full and Impartial Account of the Various Difficulties, etc., of an English Family who emigrated . . . in the year 1831. London, n.d. (1845.)

(Bagby Resolutions.)—Resolved, That the Constitution of the United States, etc., etc. (Washington) 1848. [Being Miscellaneous No. 32, Senate, 30th Congress, 1st Session. Bagby contended that "the power to construct roads, cut canals, . . . etc., in any one or more of the States or Territories of this Union is not among the powers expressly granted to the general government by the constitution, nor is the exercise of such a power necessary and proper," etc., etc.]

(Baltimore and Ohio Railroad.)—Proceedings of Sundry Citizens of Baltimore convened for the Purpose of Devising the most Efficient Means of Improving the Intercourse between that City and the Western States. Baltimore, 1827.

(Baltimore and Ohio Railroad.)—Report of the Engineers of the Reconnaissance and Surveys, made in Reference to the Baltimore and Ohio Railroad. Baltimore, 1828.

Barnes, Demas.—From the Atlantic to the Pacific, Overland . . . Describing a Trip from New York, via Chicago, Atchison, the Great Plains . . . Bridger's Pass, etc., etc. New York, 1866.

Barton, James L.—Lake Commerce: Letter to the Hon. Robert M'Clelland, Chairman of the Committee on Commerce in the U. S. House of Representatives, in relation to the Value and Importance of the Commerce of the Great Western Lakes. Buffalo, 1846. Folding table.

Beggs, S. R.—Pages from the Early History of the West and North-West: Embracing Reminiscences and Incidents of Settlement, etc., etc. Cincinnati, 1868.

Bennett, Emerson.—Mike Fink: A Legend of the Ohio. Cincinnati, n.d. (1852).

Birkbeck, Morris.—Notes on a Journey in America, from the Coast of Virginia to the Territory of Illinois, etc. Folding map. Dublin, 1818.

Bloodgood, S. De Witt.—A Treatise on Roads, their History, Character and Utility. Albany, 1838.

Bly, Myron T.—Legal Hints for Travellers. A Compilation of Judicial Decisions Pertaining to the Rights of Travellers upon Passenger Transportation Lines. Boston, 1887.

Bogart, W. H.—Daniel Boone, and the Hunters of Kentucky. Philadelphia, 1876.

(Boston and Albany Railroad.)—Report of the Select Committee of the House of Representatives of Massachusetts on the Practicability and Expediency of Constructing a Railway from Boston to the Hudson

River, at or near Albany. (Boston, 1827.) [H. R. No. 13, January 19, 1827.]

Bowen, Ele.—Rambles in the Path of the Steam Horse. . . . Embracing . . . Prominent Features of the Travelled Route from Baltimore to Harper's Ferry, Cumberland, Cincinnati, etc., etc. Philadelphia, 1855.

Bowen, Eli.—The Pictorial Sketch-Book of Pennsylvania. . . . Its Scenery, Internal Improvements, etc., Popularly Described. Philadelphia, 1852.

Boyce, J. R., Sr.—Facts About Montana Territory and the Way to Get There. (Helena) 1872.

(Bromwell, William.)—Off-Hand Sketches; A Companion for the Tourist and Traveller over the Philadelphia, Pottsville and Reading Railroad, etc. Philadelphia, 1854.

Brown, Samuel R.—The Western Gazeteer; or Emigrants' Directory, containing a Geographical Description of the Western States and Territories, viz., the States of Kentucky, Indiana, Louisiana, Ohio, Tennessee and Mississippi: And the Territories of Illinois, Missouri, Alabama, Michigan, and North-Western. With an Appendix containing Sketches . . . and Directions to Emigrants. Auburn, N. Y., 1817. [Has 360 pages of text.]

Brown, William H.—The History of the First Locomotives in America. From Original Documents and the Testimony of Living Witnesses. [Folding and other illustrations.] New York, 1871.

Buckingham, J. S.—The Eastern and Western States of America. In three volumes. London, n.d. (1843.)

Bunn, Alfred.—Old England and New England, in a Series of Views Taken on the Spot. In two volumes. London, 1853.

Burbanks, Chester.—A Brief Autobiography of My Life. . . . By Chester Burbanks, One of the Oldest of Surviving Boatmen of the Hudson and Other Rivers, with Connecting Canals and Lakes. Albany, 1888.

Burn, Robert Scott.—The Steam Engine: Its History and Mechanism. London, 1857.

Campbell, Albert H.—Report upon the Pacific Wagon Roads, constructed under the direction of the Hon. Jacob Thompson, Secretary of the Interior, in 1857-'58-'59. Washington, 1859. [Contains 125 pages of text and six extremely large folding maps (from six to nine square feet each) of the western country and overland roads herein described. The book is Ho. Rep. Executive Document No. 108 of the 35th Congress, 2nd Session. Campbell was in charge of the expeditions.

The new routes discussed are

    1.—Fort Ridgeley and South Pass Road.

    2.—Fort Kearney, South Pass and Honey Lake Road.

    3.—El Paso and Fort Yuma Road.

    4.—Nebraska Road.]

Canals.—An Historical Account of the Rise, Progress and Present State of the Canal Navigation in Pennsylvania, etc., etc. Large Folding Map. Philadelphia, MDCCXCV. Published by direction of the Schuylkill and Susquehanna, and the Delaware and Schuylkill Navigation Companies. [Title reproduced in the text.]

Canals.—Circular of the Commissioners of the Ohio Canal Fund, to the Stockholders of the State. New York, 1843.

Canals.—[Documents praying that the National Congress enlarge the powers of the Chesapeake and Ohio Canal. Contained in] Doc. No. 143, Ho. of Reps., 24th Congress, 1st Session.

Canals.—Engravings of Plans, Profiles and maps illustrating the Standard Models from which are built the Important Structures on the New York State Canals: [Accompanying the Annual Report of the State Engineer (van R. Richmond) on the Canals for 1859. The volume contains a large folding map and 15 large folding plates and diagrams.] Albany, 1860.

Canals.—Harper, Claudius. Schuylkill Navigation. Premiums to Canal Boatmen. The Board of Managers of the Schuylkill Navigation Company offer the following Premiums to the Captains of all Boats trading on their Canal . . . for quick trips to Philadelphia . . . for quick trips to New York . . . etc., etc. (Philadelphia) April 12, 1847. [Large folio broadside. Harper was secretary of the Company, and signed the announcement.]

Canals.—Report of the Committee on Roads and Canals [of the House of Representatives] in reply to the memorials of the Chesapeake and Ohio Canal, the Baltimore and Ohio Railroad and the inhabitants of Virginia, Maryland and Pennsylvania, praying for an additional subscription by the United States to the Capital Stock of the Chesapeake and Ohio Canal. 378 pages, diagrams and folding plate. Washington, 1834. [Contained in Rep. No. 414, Ho. of Reps., 23d Congress, 1st Session. An elaborate review of all phases of the canal question at the commencement of the railroad era.]

Canals.—Rules for the Collection of Toll on the Schuylkill Navigation, and Rates of Toll for 1829, n.p., n.d. (Philadelphia, 1828.) [Folio Broadside. Closely printed in two wide columns separated by a vertical rule composed of small typographical ornaments. The "Rules" occupy the first column; the "Rates of Toll" are in the second.]

Canals.—The Erie Canal. Its National Character: Its Through and Local Trade Compared. An Argument in Favor of Making it a National Work. By George S. Hazard. Published by order of the Board of Trade of Buffalo, N. Y. n.p., n.d. (1873.)

Carvalho, S. N.—Incidents of Travel and Adventure in the Far West; with Col. Fremont's Last Expedition Across the Rocky Mountains: Including Three Months' Residence in Utah, and a Perilous Trip Across the Great American Desert to the Pacific, New York, 1859.

Chapin, William.—A Complete Reference Gazeteer of the United States of North America; Containing a General View . . . and a Notice of the Various Canals, Railroads and Internal Improvements, etc., etc. New York, 1839.

Chapman, William.—Observations on the various systems of canal navigation . . . in which Mr. Fulton's plan of wheel-boats and the utility of subterraneous and of small canals are particularly investigated. London, 1797. [Quarto. This work is a discussion of the ideas set forth by Fulton in his "Treatise" on canal navigation published in London during the previous year.]

Charter of the Morris Canal and Banking Company, and the Several Acts of the Legislature in Relation Thereto. Jersey City, 1832.

Chicago.—Eighth Annual Review of the Trade and Commerce, and of the Condition and Traffic of the Railways Centering in the City of Chicago, for the year 1859, etc., etc. Chicago, 1860.

Chittenden, Hiram Martin.—History of Early Steamboat Navigation on the Missouri River: Life and Adventures of Joseph La Barge, Pioneer Navigator and Indian trader, for Fifty Years Identified with the Commerce of the Missouri Valley. In two volumes. New York, 1903. [Published in an edition of 950 copies by Francis P. Harper.]

Cincinnati Almanac (The), for the year 1846: Being a Complete Picture of Cincinnati, etc., etc. First Edition. Cincinnati, 1846. Folding map.

Cincinnati Excursion to California (The): Its Origin, Progress, Incidents and Results. History of a Railway Journey of Six Thousand Miles, etc., etc. Cincinnati, 1870.

Clark, Peter.—A Letter to the Honorable James Clark, on the Use of Railroads. (Nashua, N. H., 1842.) [Deals with the Massachusetts, New Hampshire and Connecticut roads.]

Colburn, Zerah.—The Locomotive Engine. Philadelphia, 1853.

Colden, Cadwallader D.—A Vindication of the Steam Boat Right granted by the State of New York; in the form of an Answer to the Letter of Mr. Duer, addressed to Mr. Colden. Albany, 1818. [A 178-page argument, by Fulton's first biographer, defending the travel monopoly given to Fulton and Livingston.]

Collections on the History of Albany, from its Discovery to the Present Time, etc., etc. Vol. II; 507 pages. Albany, New York; J. Munsell, 1867. [The "Collections" were a continuation of Munsell's earlier "Annals of Albany." Each volume complete in itself. Has material relating to early stage coach travel and canals.]

Collins, George.—A Strange Railroad Wreck. New York, 1904.

Colton, J. H.—Traveler and Tourist's Route-Book through the United States of America and the Canadas: Containing the Routes and Distances on the Great Lines of Travel by Railroads, Stage-roads, Canals, Lakes and Rivers. New York, 1851.

Colton.—See also Fisher, Richard S.

Conclin, George.—A Book for all Travellers. Conclin's New River Guide, or a Gazeteer of All the Towns on the Western Waters: Containing Sketches of the Cities . . . and Many Interesting Events of History, etc. Cincinnati, 1855.

Cottman, George S.—Canals of Indiana. Indianapolis, n.d. (1907.)

Cottman, George S.—Early Railroads of Indiana. Indianapolis, n.d. (1907.)

Cottman, George S.—The First Thoroughfares of Indiana: The National Road. Indianapolis, n.d. [Cottman's three pamphlets are private reissues of his monographs in the Indiana Magazine of History.]

(Courtenay, William A.)—Charleston, S. C. The Centennial of Incorporation, 1783-1883. n.p., n.d. (Charleston, 1884.) [An elaborate history of the city, from official records, covering the period from 1670. With numerous folding maps, facsimiles of early plans, documents, etc., etc.]

Crawford, Lucy.—The History of the White Mountains from the First Settlement of Upper Coos and Pequaket. Portland, Maine, 1883. [A reprint of the edition of 1845.]

(Crofutt, Geo. A.)—Crofutt's Trans-Continental Tourist's Guide. containing a full and authentic description . . . while passing over the Union Pacific Railroad, Central Pacific Railroad of Cal., their Branches and Connections by Stage and Water, etc., etc. Third vol., Second Annual revise, n.p., n.d. (New York, 1871.)

Crofutt, George A.—New Overland Tourist and Pacific Coast Guide, Chicago, 1878.

Cuming, F.—Sketches of a Tour to the Western Country; . . . A Voyage down the Ohio and Mississippi rivers . . . commenced at Philadelphia in the Winter of 1807, and concluded in 1809. Pittsburgh, 1810.

Cummings, Samuel.—The Western Pilot; containing charts of the Ohio River and of the Mississippi, etc., accompanied with Directions for Navigating the Same, and a Gazeteer; or Description of the Towns on their banks, etc., also a variety of matter interesting to Travellers, etc., etc. Cincinnati, 1843. [Published in annually revised editions from 1838. Also describes the Missouri River and its tributaries.]

Currier, John J.—Historical Sketch of Ship Building on the Merrimac River. Newburyport, 1877.

Dare, Charles P.—Philadelphia, Wilmington and Baltimore Railroad Guide. . . . Including Historical Sketches, Legends, etc. Philadelphia (1856).

Daring (The) Adventures of Kit Carson and Frémont. . . . Being a Spirited Diary of the Most Difficult and Wonderful Explorations ever made, Opening through yawning Chasms and over Perilous Peaks, the Great Pathway to the Pacific. New York, n.d.

Davis, Emerson.—The Half Century; or, A History of Changes that have taken place, and events that have transpired, chiefly in the United States, between 1800 and 1850. Boston, 1851.

Davis, John P.—The Union Pacific Railway. A Study in Railway Politics, History and Economics. Chicago, 1894.

Delano, A.—Life on the Plains and Among the Diggings; Being Scenes and Adventures of an Overland Journey to California: With Particular Incidents of the Route, Mistakes and Sufferings of the Emigrants, etc., etc. Auburn and Buffalo, 1854.

Dillon, John B.—Oddities of Colonial Legislation in America, as Applied to the Public Lands, Primitive Education, Religion, Morals, Indians, etc., etc., with Authentic Records of the Origin and Growth of Pioneer Settlements, etc. Indianapolis, 1879.

Disturnell, J.—A Guide Between Washington, Baltimore, Philadelphia, New York and Boston: Containing . . . Railroad and Steamboat Routes; Tables of Distances, etc. Also, Routes of Travel from Boston to Buffalo, and from New York to Montreal. New York, June, 1846.

Disturnell, J.—American and European Railway and Steamship Guide; Giving the arrangements on all the Great Lines of Travel through the United States, etc., etc. Three large folding maps. New York, 1851.

Disturnell, J.—Disturnell's Hudson River Guide Steamboat Arrangement—1850. Passage Boats Running between New York, Albany, and Troy. [Large folio broadside, printed in seven columns, the central of which is a map of the Hudson River and its neighborhood, in colors. The other six columns contain a description of the country along the river. (Third edition) New York, 1850. Copyrighted and first issued in 1848. The Steamboat schedule is given in a large square on lower right corner of the sheet.]

(Disturnell, J.)—The New-York State Guide; Containing an Alphabetical List of . . . Canals and Railroads, Lakes and Rivers, Steamboat Routes, Canal Routes, Railroad Routes, Stage Routes and Tables of Distances, etc. Albany, 1842. Large Folding map.

(Disturnell, J.)—The Northern Traveller; Containing the Hudson River Guide, and Tour to the Springs, Lake George and Canada, etc., etc. New-York, 1844. Folding map.

Disturnell, J.—The Traveller's Guide through the State of New York, Canada, etc. . . The Hudson River Guide, . . . with Steam-Boat, Rail-Road and Stage Routes. Accompanied by correct maps. New York, MDCCCXXXVI.

Dodge, Richard Irving.—The Black Hills. A Minute description of the Routes, Scenery, Soil, Climate, Gold, etc., etc. Large folding map and plates. New York, 1876.

Domestic (The) Manners of the Americans; or, Characteristic Sketches of the People of the United States. Glasgow, MDCCCXXX-VI. [This is not Mrs. Trollope's work, as its title might suggest, but a little book of 60 pages. Title reproduced in the text.]

Dorsey, Edward Bates.—English and American Railroads Compared. New York, 1887.

Drake, Samuel Adams.—The Old Boston Taverns and Tavern Clubs. Boston, 1886.

Duane, William.—A View of the Law of Roads, Highways, Bridges, and Ferries in Pennsylvania. Philadelphia, 1848.

Duncan, John M.—Travels through Part of the United States and Canada in 1818 and 1819. In two volumes. New York, 1823.

Earle, Thomas.—A Treatise on Rail-Roads and Internal Communications, etc. Folding plates: Philadelphia, 1830. [Title reproduced in the text.]

Easton, Alexander A.—A Practical Treatise on Street or Horse-Power Railways. . . Together with their Comparative Advantages over the Omnibus System, Etc. Philadelphia, 1859. Plates.

Ellet, Charles, Jr.—An Essay on the Laws of Trade, in reference to the Works of Internal Improvement in the United States. Richmond, 1839.

Ellet, Mrs. E.—Summer Rambles in the West. New York, MDCCCLIII.

Elliott, Richard Smith.—Notes Taken in Sixty Years. Boston, 1884.

Erie Canal.—The Advantages of the Proposed Canal from Lake Erie, to Hudson's River, fully illustrated in a correspondence between the Hon. Gouverneur Morris, and Robert Fulton, Esq., n. p., 1814.

Everett, Edward.—The Mount Vernon Papers. New York, MDCCLX.

Fairbairn, William.—Remarks on Canal Navigation, illustrative of the Advantage of the Use of Steam as a Moving-Power on Canals. . . Also, Plans and Descriptions of Certain Classes of Steam Boats, etc. Large folding plates. London, MDCCCXXXI.

Fairchild, C. B.—Street Railways; their Construction, Operation and Maintenance. New York, 1892.

Far West: (The) or, A Tour Beyond the Mountains. Embracing Outlines of Western Life and Scenery, Sketches of the Prairies, etc., etc. In two volumes. New York, 1838.

Fish, Hamilton.—Report of the Select Committee of the Senate of the United States on the Sickness and Mortality on Board Emigrant Ships. Washington, 1854. [Being Rep. Com. No. 386, of the 33rd Congress, 1st Session.]

Fisher, Richard S., Compiled by.—Colton's Traveler and Tourist's Guide-Book through the New England and Middle States. . . . Containing the Routes and Distances on the Great Lines of Travel, by Railroads, Stage-Roads, Canals, Lake and Rivers; etc., etc. New York, 1856. Folding map. [Previously issued in 1852, under same title, without Fisher's name.]

Fitch, John.—The Original Steam-Boat Supported; or, a Reply to Mr. James Rumsey's pamphlet. Shewing the True Priority of John Fitch, and the False Datings, etc., of James Rumsey. Philadelphia, MDCCLXXXVIII. [A reprint may be found in O'Callaghan's "Documentary History of the State of New York; Vol. 2, Albany, 1849.]

Fitch-Rumsey Controversy.—Remarks on Mr. John Fitch's reply to Mr. James Rumsey's pamphlet, by Joseph Barnes, formerly assistant, and now attorney in fact to James Rumsey. Philadelphia, 1788.

Fleming, Sandford, Engineer-in-Chief.—Canadian Pacific Railways: Report of Progress on the Explorations and Surveys up to January, 1874. With 286 pages and 10 large folding maps. Ottawa, 1874.

Flint, Henry M.—The Railroads of the United States; Their History and Statistics. . . Their Earnings and Expenses. . . A Synopsis of the Railroad Laws of the United States, etc., etc. Philadelphia, 1868.

Forman, Major Samuel S.—Narrative of a Journey Down the Ohio and Mississippi in 1789-90. Cincinnati, 1888. [First published in the year named, by Robert Clarke, from the original manuscript of Forman.]

(Forney, M. N.)—Locomotives and Locomotive Building; Being a Brief Sketch of the Growth of the Railroad System and of the Various Improvements in Locomotive Building in America, together with a History of the Origin and Growth of the Rogers Locomotive Works. Plates. New York, 1886.

Fossett, Frank.—Colorado: Its Gold and Silver Mines . . . and Health and Pleasure Resorts. Tourist's Guide to the Rocky Mountains. New York, 1879.

Fulton, Robert.—A Treatise on the improvement of Canal Navigation, etc. By R. Fulton. London, 1796.

Gale, George.—Upper Mississippi: or, Historical sketches of the Mound Builders, the Indian Tribes and the Progress of Civilization in the North-West, etc. Chicago, 1867.

Genesee Country.—A View of the Present Situation of the Western Parts of the State of New York, called the Genesee Country, etc., etc. Frederick-Town, Printed for the Author, 1804. [Reprinted in an edition of 300 copies by George Humphrey of Rochester, in 1892.]

George's Emigrant's Guide to the United States and the Canadas: Containing Advice to Emigrants; . . . Voyage down the Ohio . . . Various Routes by Canals, Rail Roads, and Turnpikes to the Ohio and Western Country, etc., etc. With maps of the Ohio, Indiana, and Illinois States. London; Printed for the Author, n.d. [about 1835.]

Gerhard, Fred.—Illinois As It Is; Its History, Geography, Statistics. . . . Lands and Land Prices . . . Commerce . . . Railroads, Public Institutions, . . . etc., etc. Chicago and Philadelphia, 1857.

Gilman, Caroline.—The Poetry of Travelling in the United States. New York, 1838.

Goode, Rev. William H.—Outposts of Zion, with Limnings of Mission Life. 464 pages, Cincinnati, 1863. [This title conceals an important narrative of life, travels and conditions in the West and Southwest during the period between 1842 and 1859.]

(Goodrich, A. T.)—The New York State Tourist. Descriptive of the Scenery of the Mohawk and Hudson Rivers . . . Rail Roads and Canals, etc. New York, 1840.

(Goodrich, A. T.)—The North American Tourist. Folding maps. New York. (1839.)

(Goodrich, A. T.)—The Northern Traveller: Containing the Routes to Niagara, Quebec and the Springs, with the Tour of New England and the Route to the Coal Mines of Pennsylvania. Second Edition. New York, 1826.

Gordon, Alexander.—A treatise upon Elemental Locomotion and Interior Communication, wherein are Explained . . . the History, Practice and Prospects of Steam Carriages; and the Comparative Value of Turnpike Roads, Railways and Canals. Plates. London, MDCCCXXXIV.

Guide-Book of the Central Railroad of New Jersey and its Connections, etc. New York, 1864.

Guild, William.—A Chart and Description of the Boston and Worcester and Western Railroads; In which is noted the Towns . . . Bridges, Viaducts, Tunnels . . . and other Objects passed by this Line of Railway . . . Constituting a Novel and Complete Companion for the Railway Carriage. Boston. (1847.)

Guild, William.—A Chart and Description of the Rail-Road from Boston to New York, via Worcester, Springfield, Hartford, and New Haven, in which are noted the Towns . . . Bridges, Viaducts, Tunnels . . . and other objects passed by this Line of Railway, etc., etc. Boston, 1850.

Guthrie, Alfred.—Memorial of Alfred Guthrie, a Practical Engineer, Submitting the Results of an Investigation made by him into the Causes of the explosion of steam-boilers, n.p., n.d. (Washington, 1852). [Being Miscellaneous Doc. No. 32, of the 32nd Congress, 1st Session. Folding plates. Deals with the danger of steamboat travel.]

Hale, Edward E.—Kansas and Nebraska: The History . . . and Political Position of Those Territories; An Account of the Emigrant Aid Companies, and Directions to Emigrants. Boston, 1854.

Hall, Edward H.—The Great West: Railroad, Steamboat and Stage Guide and Hand-Book for Travellers, Miners and Emigrants to the Western, Northwestern and Pacific States and Territories. Folding map. New York, 1866.

Hall, James.—Statistics of the West, at the Close of the year 1836. Cincinnati, 1836.

Hall, James.—The West: Its Commerce and Navigation. Cincinnati, 1848.

Hall, Major Samuel S.—Arizona Jack; or, Giant George's Tender-Foot Pard. New York, 1882. [One of the Beadle Library publications. A story of stage-coach days on the western plains and in Arizona. "Arizona Jack" was Burke, a celebrated character in the West. Within recent years it has come to be realized that the once despised Beadle Library stories of the frontier, instead of being fanciful descriptions are substantially accurate portrayals of the life, times, localities and characters discussed. They were written by men who knew the country intimately.]

Hammond, S. H.—Hunting Adventures in the Northern Wilds; or, a Tramp in the Chateaugay Woods, etc. New York, 1860. [In which are quoted the observations of a backwoodsman on the travel-progress he had beheld.]

Harrison, Joseph, Jr.—The Locomotive Engine, and Philadelphia's Share in its Early Improvements. Philadelphia, 1872.

Hartley, Cecil B.—Life and Times of Colonel Daniel Boone, Comprising History of the Early Settlement of Kentucky, etc. Philadelphia, 1860.

Hayes, A. A., Jr.—New Colorado and the Santa Fe Trail. New York, 1880.

Hayward, John.—The New England Gazeteer, etc., etc. Fourteenth edition. Boston, 1841.

(Hazard, W. P.)—The American Guide Book; Being a Hand-Book for Tourists and Travellers through Every Part of the United States, . . . the whole preceded with Short Directions to Travellers, etc., etc. Philadelphia, 1846.

Heap, Gwinn Harris.—Central Route to the Pacific, from the Valley of Mississippi to California: Journal of the Expedition . . . from Missouri to California, in 1853. Folding map and colored plates, Philadelphia, 1854.

Hebard, Grace Raymond.—The Pathbreakers from River to Ocean. Chicago, 1911. [A review of western exploration and travel from the time of Coronado until 1870. With a bibliography of 110 titles for further reading and study.]

(Henderson, Charles G.)—A Hand-Book for the Stranger in Philadelphia. Philadelphia, 1846.

Hewett, D.—The Universal Traveller. Published and Delivered every month in Philadelphia and New York in a Book form, and from Time to Time in a Chart form. Arranged in Three Departments: I. Department of Geography, etc. II. Department of Roads, Stages, and Steam Boats in all Directions thro the Union, etc. III. Advertisements containing objects of Interest to the Traveller and Man of Business, n. p., 1826. [The above title transcribed from issue Number 9 of the Universal Traveller, dated April, 1826.]

Hewett, A. M.—The American Traveller; or, National Directory, containing an Account of all the Great Post Roads and Most Important Cross Roads . . . to the Several Extremities of the Union . . . Some of the Principal Lines of Stages, Steam-boats and Packets . . . A Geographical and Statistical View of the United States; with information on other subjects Interesting to Travellers. Washington, 1825. [A volume of 440 pages. Title reproduced in the text.]

Hewitt, Girart.—Minnesota: Its Advantages to Settlers. 1869. Being a brief synopsis of its History and Progress, . . . Its Lakes, Rivers and Railroads, etc., etc. St. Paul, 1869.

Hickenlooper, Frank.—An Illustrated History of Monroe County, Iowa . . . Including Sketches of Pioneer Life, Anecdotes, Biography, etc., etc. Map and 360 pages. Albia, Iowa, 1906.

Hillyer, John.—Hillyer's American Railroad Magazine. New York, 1859-1861. [Volume I No. 1 was issued in March, 1859.]

History (A) of the Lehigh Coal and Navigation Company. Published by order of the Board of Managers. Philadelphia, 1840. Folding maps.

Hogg, Alexander, M. A.—The Railroad as an Element in Education. Louisville, 1887.

Holditch, Robert.—The Emigrant's Guide to the United States of America, containing the Best Advice and Directions, etc., etc. London, 1818.

Holley, O. L., Edited by.—The Picturesque Tourist; Being a Guide through the Northern and Eastern States and Canada, etc., etc. New York, 1844.

Holloway, W. R.—Indianapolis: A Historical and Statistical Sketch of the Railroad City, etc. Indianapolis, 1870.

Holmes, H.—Brief History of Belleville. (New Jersey.) Reminiscences of Belleville: From the Old Stage Coach to the Iron Horse . . . Different Steamboats on the River: Inducements offered the Last Proprietor: . . . Newark's First Horse Railroad, etc., etc. n.p., n.d. [Apparently printed locally about 1875-1880. Has 96 pages of text.]

Hopkins, W. R.—Report relative to the Rail Road Line from the west end of the Harrisburg (Pa.) Bridge . . . to the Borough of Chambersburg, together with an Estimate of the Cost, and from Chambersburg . . . to the Borough of York. Harrisburg, 1829.

Hoyt, J. K.—Pen and Pencil Pictures on the Delaware, Lackawanna and Western Railroad. New York (1874).

Humason, W. L.—From the Atlantic Surf to the Golden Gate. First Trip on the Great Pacific Rail Road . . . with Scenes and Incidents. Hartford, 1869.

Hurlbut, Henry H.—The Walk-in-the-Water, the First Steamboat on Lake Erie. Chicago, Printed for the Compiler, 1890.

Improved Railway Connections in Philadelphia. Philadelphia, MDCCCLXIII.

Incidents of Travel by River and Rail, n.p., n.d. [A volume of 238 pages, printed about 1860.]

Internal Navigation.—A Great Continental as well as National Enterprise: Continuous water and steam navigation from the Valley of the Mississippi to the Atlantic Ocean. Des Moines, 1871.

Internal Navigation.—Improvements at Mouths of Mississippi River. Remarks by Prof. Forshay before the Senate Committee on Transportation, etc., etc. n.p., n.d.

Internal Navigation.—Memorial to Congress of the Commissioners for the Improvement of the Ohio River and Its Tributaries. Cincinnati, 1872. [The Commissioners were appointed by Pennsylvania, West Virginia, Indiana, Illinois, Ohio, Kentucky and Tennessee, under resolution of the Cincinnati Convention of Feb., 1872.]

Internal Navigation.—The Levees of the Mississippi River: Speech of Hon. Frank Morey, of Louisiana, in the H. of R., April 21, 1874. Wash., 1874.

Interstate Commerce.—The Constitutional Power of Congress to Regulate Commerce among the States. Speech of Hon. Julius C. Burrows, of Michigan in the H. of R., March 14, 1874. Wash., 1874.

James, Edmund J.—The Canal and the Railway, with a note on the Development of Railway Passenger Traffic [and also] II. Canals and their Economic Relation to Transportation. By Lewis M. Haupt, Baltimore, 1890. [Being Vol. V, Nos. 3 and 4 (printed together) of the Publications of the American Economic Association.]

Janson, Charles William.—The Stranger in America, containing Observations made during a long Residence in that Country on the Genius, Manners and Customs of the People, etc., etc. Plates. London, 1807.

Jefferson, Thomas.—Message from the President of the United States communicating an additional Report . . . Under an act entitled "An Act to regulate the laying out and making a road from Cumberland, in the State of Maryland, to the State of Ohio." Washington, 1808.

Jervis, John B.—Report on the Hudson River Railroad. New York, 1846. [Jervis was Engineer in charge of construction.]

Johnson, Emory A.—American Railway Transportation. New York, 1903.

Johnson, William.—Reports of Cases Adjusted in the Court of Chancery of New York. Second edition. Philadelphia, 1834. [Contains the litigation resulting from the steamboat monopoly granted by New York to Fulton and Livingston.]

Jones, Alexander.—Historical Sketch of the Electric Telegraph: Including its Rise and Progress in the United States. New York, MDCCCLII.

Kennedy, John P.—Memoirs of the Life of William Wirt, Attorney-General of the United States. A New and Revised Edition. In Two Volumes. Philadelphia, 1850.

Kennedy, Wm. Sloane.—Wonders and Curiosities of the Railway: or Stories of the Locomotive in Every Land. 2nd Edition. Chicago, 1884.

Kimball, James.—The Exploration of the Merrimac River, in 1638, by order of the General Court of Massachusetts, with a Plan of the same. Folding plate, n.p., n.d. Reprinted from Essex Institute Historical Collections, Vol. XIV, No. III.

(Knauer, J., Civil Engineer.)—Minnesota Territory: An Account of its Geography, Resources and Settlement. Together with the Census of 1850. [Accompaniment to Knauer's map of U. S. Survey. New York, 1853. With a large folding map containing the first U. S. Topographical Survey of the Territory.]

Knox, Thomas W.—How to Travel. Hints, Advice and Suggestions to Travelers by Land and Sea, all over the Globe. New York, 1881. [Contains, also, "The Past and Present of a Great Railroad." Meaning the Erie.]

Lardner, Dionysius.—Railway Economy; A Tréatise on the New Art of Transport, its Management, Prospects and Relations, Commercial, Financial and Social, etc., etc. New York, 1850.

Latrobe, J. H. B.—A Lost Chapter in the History of the Steamboat. Baltimore, March, 1871.

Latrobe, John H. B.—The Baltimore and Ohio Railroad: Personal Recollections. Baltimore, n.d. (1868.)

Lecount, Lieut. Peter, R. N.—A Practical Treatise on Railways, etc. Folding plates. Edinburgh, MDCCCXXXIX.

Leverich, G.—The Cable Railway on the New York and Brooklyn Bridge. New York, 1888. Folding plates.

Leverich, G.—The Traffic Capacity of the New York and Brooklyn Bridge Railway. Brooklyn, 1889. Folding plates.

Life and Death of Jay Gould and How He Made His Millions. 208 pages. New York, n.d. (1892.)

Life in the West; or, the Moreton Family. Philadelphia (1851).

(Link, William F.)—The Hudson by Daylight. Map showing the . . . Historic Landmarks. Indian Names, etc., with Descriptive Pages. New York. (1878.) Long folding map.

Linn, John Blair. [Published under the direction of].—Charter to William Penn, and Laws of the Province of Pennsylvania, Passed between the years 1682 and 1700, etc., etc. Edited by Staughton George, Benjamin M. Nead and Thomas McCamant. Harrisburg, 1879.

Lloyd, James T.—Lloyd's Steamboat Directory, and Disasters on the Western Waters: Containing . . . History of the early Steamboat Navigation on Western Waters . . . A Complete List of Steamboats and all other vessels now afloat on the Western Rivers and Lakes, etc., etc. Cincinnati, 1856.

Lloyd, W. Alvin.—Steamboat and Railroad Guide, Containing the Sinking, Explosion and Collisions of all the Steamboats on the Southern and Western Rivers, the number of Human Lives Lost by these Terrible Accidents within the Last Forty-four years: Also, many of the Principal Railroads in the United States, etc., etc. New Orleans, 1857.

Loomis, J. V. & Co.—The United States Statistical Directory, or Merchants' and Travellers' Guide; with a Wholesale Business Directory of New York. New York, 1847.

Loree, L. F.—The Grade Crossing Problem, n.p. (1900.)

Luce, Robert.—Electric Railways and the Electric Transmission of Power. Boston, 1886.

Lyford, W. G.—The Western Address Directory: Containing the Cards, etc., of Business Men in Pittsburgh, Wheeling, Zanesville, Portsmouth, Dayton, Cincinnati, Madison, Louisville, St. Louis; Together with Historical, Topographical and Statistical Sketches for the year 1837, etc. Intended as a Guide to Travellers. To which is added a list of the Steam-Boats on the Western Waters. [468 pages.] Baltimore, 1837.

Macfarlane, Robert.—History of Propellers and Steam Navigation. New York, 1851.

Maclean and Lawrence.—Sectional Map of Kansas Territory. [A large map, 40¾ by 41¼ inches, drawn by C. P. Wiggin, certified by Maclean of the Surveyor General's Office at Lecompton, and published in Pittsburgh in 1857. It shows the overland routes leading westward from the Mississippi River.]

Macleod, William—Harper's New York and Erie Rail-Road Guide Book. Seventh edition, New York, 1852.

Manly, William Lewis.—Death Valley in '49. Important Chapter of California Pioneer History . . . And Particularly reciting the Sufferings of the Band of Men, Women and Children who gave "Death Valley" its Name. San Jose, 1894.

Mann, William.—A Description of a New Method of Propelling Locomotive Machines, etc., etc. Colored folding plate. London, 1830.

Mapes, James J., Editor.—The American [monthly] Repertory of Arts, Sciences and Manufactures. Vols. 1 and 2. New York, Feb., 1840 to Jan., 1841, inclusive.

March, Daniel.—The Iron Horse. Hartford, 1840. [March's poem was written and delivered as a literature exercise while he was a junior at Yale College, in 1839. It is usually found bound up with his "Yankee Land."]

Marconi, G.—The Trans-Atlantic Times. Volume 1. Number 1.

T. W. Bradfield, Editor-in-Chief. "Published on board the St. Paul, at Sea, en route for England. November 15, 1899." [Small folding broadside, printed on writing paper bearing the engraved heading "U. S. M. S. St. Paul." Paper water-marked "Joynson's Parchment," with a water-mark shield bearing three griffin's heads. First and fourth pages blank; second and third occupied by printed news received by wireless telegraphy, with the title extending across both pages. A few copies printed and sold on the vessel at $1.00 a copy. First printing of a wireless newspaper at sea. Marconi operated.]

Marcy, Capt. Randolph B., U. S. A.—The Prairie Traveller. A Hand-Book for Overland Expeditions, etc., etc. New York, 1859. [Contains folding map of the western overland trails and travellers' itinerary for each.]

Marcy, Captain Randolph B.—The same. London, 1863. [Edited, with notes, by Richard Burton, and with a better map. The map of the English edition is reproduced in these volumes.]

Marestier, M.—Memoire sur Les Bateaux a Vapeur des Etats-Unis D'Amerique, avec un appendice sur diverses Machines Relatives a la Marine; Par M. Marestier, etc., etc. Paris, 1824.

Marvin, Henry.—A Complete History of Lake George: Embracing a Great Variety of Information . . . with an especial reference to meet the wants of the Traveling Community, etc., etc. New York, 1853. Folding map.

Mason, Otis Tufton.—Primitive Travel and Transportation. (Washington, 1894.) [Being a monograph of 593 pages, with plates and illustrations, contained in the Report of the National Museum for 1894. Deals with the methods of American Indians and other aboriginal peoples.]

McAfee, Robert B.—History of the Late War in the Western Country, etc., etc. Lexington, Ky., 1816.

McConnel, J. L.—Western Characters, or Types of Border Life in the Western States. Redfield, 1853.

McDonald, Wm. L.—Southern Carriage Repository. Epitome of the Various Styles of Coaches, Carriages, etc., manufactured expressly for Southern Consumption. New York. (1858.)

McNeill, William Gibbs, Capt. U. S. Topographical Engineers.—Report on the Condition of the Chesapeake and Ohio Canal. Washington, 1834. Contained in Doc. No. 38, Ho. of Reps., 23d Congress, 1st session.

Melish, John.—Map of the United States, with the contiguous British and Spanish possessions. Compiled from the latest and best authorities. Engraved by Wallace and Tanner. Philadelphia, 1820. [Perhaps the best map of the country made up to that time. Published on 50 sheets, each about 5⅝ by 8½ inches, which, when mounted, form a map 43¾ inches high and 58 inches wide. It shows the turnpike system of the East; the government road from the Ohio Country to New Orleans; General Jackson's road through Alabama, Mississippi and Louisiana; Lewis and Clark's route, Pike's route and other existing links of the travel system of the time. Reproduced in these volumes.]

Memoirs of the Long Island Historical Society. Volume 1. Brooklyn, N. Y., 1867. [Contains the account, by Jaspar Dankers and Peter Schluter, of their journey from New York to the Delaware River during the winter of 1679-1680. Translated from the original manuscript discovered by Henry C. Murphy in Amsterdam.]

Memorial (A) to Congress to Secure an Adequate Appropriation for a Prompt and Thorough Improvement of the Mississippi River. With an appendix by Sylvester Waterhouse of Washington University. St. Louis, 1877. [Contains the action of the River Improvement Convention held at St. Paul in October, 1877, and a paper on the subject of river navigation prepared by Waterhouse for the St. Louis Board of Trade.]

Memorial of the Chicago Convention in favor of the improvement of harbors and rivers by the general government. (Washington) 1848. [Being Miscellaneous No. 146, Senate, 30th Congress, 1st Session. The Chicago Convention of July, 1847, was an important one, and was attended by delegates from Massachusetts, New York, Kentucky, Indiana, Missouri, Rhode Island, Iowa, Ohio, Connecticut, Pennsylvania, Wisconsin, Georgia, Florida, Michigan, Maine, Illinois, New Jersey and New Hampshire.]

Memorial of the Citizens of Cincinnati, to the Congress of the United States, Relative to the Navigation of the Ohio and Mississippi Rivers. Cincinnati, 1844.

Merrill, D. D.—The Northern Route to Idaho: And the Pacific Ocean. St. Paul. (1864.) [With a folding map, 20¼ by 45 inches. The map was drawn by C. A. F. Morris, and lithographed in colors in St. Paul in 1864. It shows the land routes from the Mississippi to the Pacific Ocean, north of central Kansas. The "Rubber Stamp" map of the Northwest. Reproduced in these volumes.]

Michaux, F. A.—Travels to the Westward of the Allegany Mountains, in the States of Ohio, Kentucky and Tennessee, in the year 1802. Translated from the French. London, 1805. Large folding map.

Milburn, William Henry—The Pioneers, Preachers and People of the Mississippi Valley. New York, 1860.

Minnesota: Its Resources and Progress; . . . And Its Attractions and Advantages as a Home for Immigrants. Compiled by the Commissioner of Statistics and Published by Direction of Horace Austin, Governor. St. Paul, 1870.

Mitchell.—An Accompaniment to Mitchell's Reference and Distance Map of the United States; . . . An Index of the Rivers . . . With an Account of the Actual and Prospective Internal Improvements throughout the Union, etc., etc. [324 pages.] Philadelphia, 1835.

Mitchell's Compendium of the Internal Improvements of the United States; Comprising General Notices of all the Most Important Canals and Rail-Roads, etc., etc. Large folding map. Philadelphia, 1835.

Mitchell's Travellers' Guide through the United States. With folding map. Philadelphia, 1835. [The text is contained, in the shape of tables, on a large, closely printed, folding broadside.]

Monroe, James.—Message from the President of the United States, transmitting a Report of the Examination which has been made by the Board of Engineers, with a View to Internal Improvement, etc. Washington, 1825.

Moore, Henry Charles.—Omnibuses and Cabs: Their Origin and History. London, 1902.

Moreau, P., and Notre, A.—Description of the Rail-Road from Liverpool to Manchester; Together with a History of Railroads, etc. [Lithographic plates by Pendleton.] Boston, 1833.

Morrison, Thomas.—The Traveller's Companion . . . Containing a map of the Hudson or North River . . . the Lengths of the Principal Rail-Roads and Canals, finished or in Progress, in the United States. Philadelphia, n.d. About 1830. Both text and map are contained on a large, closely printed folding broadside, enclosed in covers.]

Mott, Edward Harold.—The Story of Erie. New York, 1901.

Municipal Ownership and Municipal Franchises. Philadelphia, 1906. Being Vol. XXVII, No. 1 of the Annals of the American Academy of Political and Social Science. [Contains Walter S. Allen's historical monograph on street railways in Massachusetts.]

(Nelson, T., and Sons, Publishers.)—The Central Pacific Railroad: A Trip across the North American Continent from Ogden to San Francisco. New York, n.d. (1870.) Colored plates.

O'Hanlon, Rev. J.—The Irish Emigrant's Guide for the United States. Boston, 1851. [Folding map; 221 pages of text.]

Olden Time in New York. (The). By a Member of the New York Genealogical and Biographical Society. New York, MDCCCLXXII.

O'Rielly, Henry, Editor.—Practical Statesmanship in Connection with the American Railway System. New York, 1867. [Being Document V, Sept., 1867, of a series of monthly pamphlets in which were gathered serious current discussions relating to the railroad problem. This number contains 28 speeches, letters, newspaper editorials, etc.]

The Same.—Issue No. 6; October, 1867.

Orr, J. W.—Pictorial Guide to the Falls of Niagara: A Manual for Visitors, Giving an Account . . . with every Historical Incident, etc., etc. Buffalo, 1842.

Page, Herbert W., M. A.—Railway Injuries: with Special Reference to Those of the Back and Nervous System, in their Medico-Legal and Clinical Aspects. London, 1891. [The author was Examiner in Surgery at the University of Cambridge.]

Pambour, Chevalier F. M. G. de.—A Practical Treatise on Locomotive Engines upon Railways, etc., etc. Folding plates. Philadelphia, 1836.

Pangborn, J. G.—Picturesque B. and O. Historical and Descriptive. Chicago, 1883.

Parker, Nathan H.—Iowa as It is in 1856; A Gazetteer for Citizens and a Hand-book for Emigrants, embracing a full description of the State . . . The Various Railroad Lines Being Built and those Projected . . . Information for the Immigrant, etc., etc. Chicago, 1856.

Parker, Nathan H.—The Minnesota Handbook for 1856-7. With a new and accurate map. Boston, MDCCCLVII.

Parker, Rev. Samuel.—Journal of an Exploring Tour beyond the Rocky Mountains . . . Containing a Description of the Geography . . . with a map of Oregon Territory. Fifth Edition. Auburn, (N. Y.) 1846.

Parsons, Horatio.—Book of Niagara Falls. Third Edition. Buffalo, 1836. Folding map.

Peck, J. M.—A New Guide for Emigrants to the West, etc., etc. Boston, 1836.

Penniman, Edward A.—The Stourbridge Lion. A Compilation of authorities proving the Claim made for the Stourbridge Lion as having been the First Locomotive to turn a wheel on the Western Hemisphere, together with a brief Biographical Sketch of Horatio Allen, the First Locomotive Engineer in America. Honesdale, Pa., 1903.

Phelps and Ensign.—Traveller's Guide through the United States: Containing Stage, Steamboat, Canal and Rail-road Routes with Distances from Place to Place, etc. New York, 1841. Large folding map.

Piercy, Frederick.—Route from Liverpool to Great Salt Lake Valley: Illustrated with Steel Engravings and wood cuts from Sketches made by Frederick Piercy, . . . together with a Geographical and Historical Description of Utah, and a Map of the Overland Routes to that Territory from the Missouri River. Also, an authentic History of the Latter-Day Saints Emigration from Europe from the Commencement. With Statistics. Edited by James Linforth. Liverpool and London, MDCCCLV. [Folding map and 29 full-page plates, 22 of the plates being travel-scenes in the Mississippi valley and far West, engraved after sketches from nature made by the English artist Piercy, in 1853, at the direction of the authorities of the Church of Latter Day Saints. Published by the Mormon Church.]

Pierson, Rev. Hamilton W.—In the Brush: or, Old-Time Social, Political and Religious Life in the Southwest. New York: 1881.

Pittsburgh: Its Industry and Commerce, etc. Pittsburgh, 1870. Copyrighted by David Lowry, James Mills and E. A. Myers. [A historical chronicle and review, from about 1795.]

Poor, Henry V.—History of the Railroads and Canals of the United States of America, Exhibiting their Progress, Cost, Revenues, Expenditures and Present Condition. In two volumes. New York, 1860. [The contemplated second volume was never published. Volume one— of 612 pages—deals with the six New England states, and with New York, New Jersey, Pennsylvania, Delaware and Maryland.]

Poor, John Alfred.—The First International Railway and the Colonization of New England. Life and Writings of John Alfred Poor. Edited by Laura Elizabeth Poor. New York, 1892.

Pope, Thomas.—A Treatise on Bridge Architecture . . . With an Historical Account and Description of Different Bridges Erected in Various Parts of the World, etc., etc. Plates. New-York, 1811. [Contains the first proposal to bridge the Hudson River.]

Potter, Isaac B.—The Gospel of Good Roads. New York, 1891.

Preble, Rear-Admiral George Henry, U. S. N.—A Chronological History of the Origin and Development of Steam Navigation. Philadelphia, 1883.

Railroads.—Albany, Troy and Lebanon Springs. The Cars of the New York and Harlem Rail Road Leave the City Hall Station, New York, Daily, . . . M. Sloat, Supt. Small folio broadside. New York, Sept. 21, 1852.

Railroads.—Baldwin Locomotive Works. Illustrated Catalogue of Locomotives. Second Edition. Philadelphia, 1881. [With historical account.]

Railroads.—Drawings of Maps, Bridges, Profiles, Coal Burning Locomotives, . . . etc., accompanying the Report of the (New York) Board of Railroad Commissioners for 1856. Albany, 1856. [Large folding plates show the railroad building practise of the period.]

Railroads.—Erie Rail Road, n.p., n.d. (New York, 1851.) [Being a special number issued under the heading "Supplement to the Illustrated American News. Third Edition. T. W. Strong, Publisher. Price Ten cents." Folio, containing 14 pages printed in 3 columns each, and with 25 illustrations, a map, and a table showing the time schedule of the five daily trains on the road, with distances and rates of fare.]

Railroads.—Garfield, James A. The Future of the Republic: Its Dangers and Its Hopes. An Address delivered before the Literary Societies of Hudson College, July 2, 1873. Cleveland, Ohio, 1873. [Chiefly an analysis of the results of railway domination of political and industrial affairs.]

Railroads.—Hudson River Railroad. Reduction of Fares. New York to and from Albany & Troy . . . On and after Monday, July 12, the Trains will run as follows, etc., etc. Folio broadside, printed in two wide columns on blue paper. New York, July 10, 1852. [Reproduced in the text.]

Railroads.—Instructions for the Running of Trains, etc., on the Atlantic and Great Western Railway. To go into effect January 1, 1863. Cleveland, 1863.

Railroads.—Instructions for the Running of Trains, etc., on the New York and Erie Railroad. To go into effect on Saturday, August 1, 1857. New York, 1857.

Railroads.—Lands for the People; not Monopolies. Speech of Hon. Jackson Orr of Iowa in the H. of R., March 23, 1872. Wash., 1872. [On the governmental aid given to railroads.]

Railroads.—Miniature Illustrated Railway Guide of the Lake Shore and Michigan Southern Railway, etc. Buffalo, 1874.

Railroads.—New-York & Albany Rail-Road. New York, March 24, 1842. [A printed circular letter, calling the attention of the public to the report of certain proceedings—which are also given—in advocacy of a railroad between New York City and Albany. Signed by A. G. Thompson, Peter Cooper, Peter Schermerhorn and ten others. This pamphlet is the documentary corner-stone of the Hudson River Railroad, now a part of the New York Central. Title page reproduced in the text.]

Railroads.—New York & Harlem Rail Road Company. Summer Arrangement. On and after Thursday, June 10th, 1847; the Cars will run as follows, until further notice. Up trains will Leave the City Hall . . . Extra trains on Sundays to Harlem and Morristown in fine weather . . . etc., etc. Small broadside. (New York, 1847.) [Reproduced in the text.]

Railroads.—New York Supreme Court. The Farmers' Loan and Trust Company, Trustee, against the Erie Railway Company and others. (New York) 1876-1877. [A collection of the printed briefs, complaints, arguments, appeals, and other legal papers relating to the operation and finances of the road and the litigation resulting therefrom. Comprising 1180 pages.]

Railroads.—Northern Pacific Railroad: Speech of Hon. William Windom, of Minnesota, delivered in the H. of R., Jan. 5, 1869. Wash., 1869. [Advocating its support.]

Railroads.—Ohio Railroad Guide, Illustrated, The.—Cincinnati to Erie, via Columbus and Cleveland. Columbus, 1854.

Railroads.—Pennsylvania Railroad, Its Necessity and Advantages to Philadelphia. Folio broadside, printed in two wide columns. (Philadelphia, 1847.) [An appeal to the Citizens of Philadelphia urging the building of a railway between Philadelphia and Pittsburgh. Signed, "By order of the Commissioners. T. B. Cope, Chairman."]

Railroads.—Points for Consideration by the Investigating Committee of the Pennsylvania Railroad Company, n. p., 1867.

Railroads.—Proceedings of the National Railroad Convention Which Assembled in the City of St. Louis, on the Fifteenth of October, 1849. To which is prefixed the Proceedings of the Primary Meetings of the Citizens of St. Louis, held previous to the Meeting of Said Convention. St. Louis, 1850.

Railroads.—Proceedings of the Railroad Convention, assembled at Harrisburg (Pa.), March 6, 1838. Philadelphia, 1838. [Delegates came from Pittsburgh, Cleveland, Philadelphia and elsewhere.]

Railroads.—Rail Road March. For the Fourth of July. Dedicated to the Directors of the Baltimore & Ohio Rail Road. Composed & arranged for the Piano Forte. C. Meineke. Baltimore. [And at bottom] Entered according to act of Congress the 3d day of July, 1828, etc. [A piece of sheet music, folio in size, of ten pages, three of which are occupied by the music score. The score itself is printed, but the title is engraved, and contains a picture of a locomotive, tender, and three cars. The music was sold in Baltimore on July 4, 1828, as part of the celebration attending the commencement of the Baltimore and Ohio Railway on that day. Title page reproduced in the text.]

Railroads.—Railroads Fifty-Six Years Ago. n.p., n.d. (1867.) [A small broadside containing the letter written by R. R. Livingston to Stevens in 1811 regarding railroads and their future.]

Railroads.—Railroads in the States: Speech of Hon. James R. Doolittle, of Wisconsin, delivered in the Senate of the U. S., Jan. 22, 1869. Wash., 1869. [Opposing the building of interstate railways by Federal charter.]

Railroads.—Railroads to the Pacific. Speech of Mr. Dodge, of Iowa, on the Bill . . . for the Construction of a Railroad and Telegraph line from the Mississippi Valley to the Pacific Ocean. (Washington, 1853.)

Railroads.—Rapid Transit Assured: A Feast of Thanksgiving. (New York, 1878.) [An account of the meeting of Dec. 26, 1877, in celebration of the success of the New York Elevated Railroad.]

Railroads.—Report of Senator Bright, of the Committee on Roads and Canals, to whom were referred the memorials of Asa Whitney, Thomas Allen, Winslow Lanier & Company, the Chamber of Commerce of New York, and others, praying for the Construction of a national railroad and electric telegraph from the Mississippi river to the Pacific Ocean. Washington, 1850. [Being Rep. Com. No. 194, of the 31st Congress, 1st Session.]

Railroads.—Report of the Committee on Roads and Canals, to whom were referred the memorial . . . of a meeting of delegates for several states held in St. Louis the 16th of October last, praying for the location and construction of a national railroad and electric telegraph from the Mississippi river to the Pacific ocean; also . . . various and numerous resolutions . . . from State Legislatures, . . . large public meetings in several different cities of the Union . . . in favor of the plan of Mr. Asa Whitney, etc., etc. (Washington) 1850. [Being Rep. Com. No. 194, Senate, 31st congress, 1st session. The committee recommends the South Pass route.]

Railroads.—Report of the Committee . . . to whom was referred the memorial of Asa Whitney, relative to the Construction of a railroad from Lake Michigan to the Pacific Ocean, etc. (Washington) 1848. [Being Rep. Com. No. 191, Senate, 30th Congress, 1st Session.]

Railroads.—Report of the Committee . . . to whom were referred a memorial of Sundry citizens of Indiana, praying the construction of a national railroad from the Mississippi to the Columbia river, and the memorial of Asa Whitney, suggesting the means, and submitting a proposition, for the construction of such roads, etc., etc. (Washington) 1846. [Being Senate, 466; 29th Congress, 1st Session. A general review of transcontinental travel and transportation as it then existed, and a discussion of the possibility and desirability of building the railway.]

Railroads.—Resolutions of the Legislature of Connecticut, in favor of a Railroad from Lake Michigan to the Pacific, on the plan proposed by Mr. Whitney. (Washington) 1847. [Being Miscellaneous No. 18, Senate, 30th Congress, 1st Session.]

Railroads.—Salt Lake and Colorado Railroad: Remarks of Hon Wm. H. Claggett, of Montana, in the H. of R., April 18, 1872. (1872.) [A debate revealing travel conditions in the West, particularly the peculiar situation in Utah, which territory granted private monopolies in roads, bridges and ferries to Brigham Young and other prominent members of the Mormon Church.]

Railroads.—Speech of Hon. Truman Smith, of Conn., in support of the Bill . . . for the Construction of a Railroad and telegraph line from the Mississippi Valley to the Pacific Ocean. (Washington) 1853.

Railroads.—Speech of Mr. Bell, on the Foreign Relations of the United States. (Washington) 1853. [Deals with the effect, upon world affairs, of transcontinental American railroads.]

Railroads.—Speech of Mr. Dodge, of Iowa, on the Bill reported from the Select Committee for the Construction of a Railroad and Telegraph Line from the Mississippi Valley to the Pacific Ocean. Delivered in the Senate, Feb. 18, 1853. Washington, 1853.

Railroads.—Standard Gauge Locomotives Manufactured by the Rhode Island Locomotive Works, Providence, R. I., With Weights, Dimensions, etc., n.p., n.d.

Railroads.—The Official History of the Great Strike of 1886 on the Southwestern Railway System. Compiled by the Bureau of Labor Statistics and Inspection of Missouri. Jefferson City, 1887.

Railroads.—The Reading Railroad. The History of a Great Trunk Line. (Philadelphia) n.d.

Railroads.—The Union Pacific Railroad Company, Chartered by the

United States. Progress of their Road west from Omaha, Nebraska, Across the Continent. Making, with its connections, an unbroken Line from the Atlantic to the Pacific Oceans. Five Hundred miles completed October 25, 1867. New York, 1868.

Railroads.—To Southern Travellers. Fall and Winter Arrangement of the Great Southern Mail Line direct from New York, Philadelphia and Baltimore, via Washington . . . to New Orleans. Baltimore, September, 1857. [Folio broadside with woodcut of railroad train in title. Signed by Stockton & Falls; E. F. Krebs, Agent.]

Railroads.—Uniform Rates of Transportation. Speech of Hon. Charles W. Kendall of Nevada in the H. of R., May 24, 1872. Wash., 1872. [Reviewing the amount of public lands and other governmental aid given to the railways.]

Railroads.—See also, "Resolutions" and "Whitney."

Read, John M.—Opinion of, Against the Right of the City Councils [of Philadelphia] to Subscribe for Stock in the Pennsylvania Railroad Company, etc., etc. Philadelphia, 1846.

Redpath, James; and Hinton, Richard J.—Hand-Book to Kansas Territory and the Rocky Mountains' Gold Region, etc. Two large folding maps. New York, 1859.

Reigart, J. Franklin.—The Life of Robert Fulton, one of the most distinguished Inventors the World has ever produced. With interesting Incidents indicating the Character of the Man in his Youthful Days, the Dawnings of Genius then displayed; until he embarked in the Voyage of Life, and, by untiring Industry Raised Himself above the buffeting Storms, Erected his own Illustrious Name, and Secured the Highest Distinction that Mortal Man can attain—the Admiration, Honor, and Gratitude of Nations and Posterity. This volume contains a simple record of facts, etc. Philadelphia, 1856.

Remarks on the Practicability and Expediency of Establishing a Railroad on one or more Routes from Boston to the Connecticut River. By the Editor of the Boston Daily Advertiser. Boston, 1827.

Renwick, James.—Treatise on the Steam Engine. Second edition, revised and enlarged. Plates. New York, 1839.

Report of the Committee on Roads [of the New York City Board of Assistant Aldermen] relative to the New York and Harlem Railroad Company rendering accommodations to the inhabitants on the line of their road, etc. New York, March 3, 1852.

Resolution of the Legislature of Indiana in relation to the improvement of the Iroquois and Kankakee rivers. (Washington) 1848. [Being Miscellaneous No. 109, Senate, 30th Congress, 1st Session. In advocacy of slack-water navigation.]

Resolution of the Legislature of Indiana relative to the National Road. (Washington) 1848. [Being Miscellaneous No. 111, Senate, 30th Congress, 1st Session. Complaining that the Federal government had not finished that part of the National Road located in Indiana, and asking its relinquishment to the state in order that it might be completed.]

Resolutions of the Legislature of Georgia in favor of Whitney's plan for the Construction of a Railroad from Lake Michigan to the Pacific (Wash.) 1848. Miscellaneous No. 58. Senate, 30th Congress, 1st Session.

Resolutions of the Legislature of Illinois, in favor of a Railroad from Lake Michigan to the Pacific, on the plan proposed by Mr. Whitney. (Wash.) 1848. Miscellaneous No. 76, Senate, 30th Congress, 1st Session.

Resolutions of the Legislature of Maine, in favor of a Railroad from Lake Michigan to the Pacific, on the Plan proposed by Mr. Whitney. (Wash.) 1847. Miscellaneous No. 5, Senate, 30th Congress, 1st Session.

Resolutions of the Legislature of New Jersey in favor of the construction of a railroad from Lake Michigan to the Pacific, on the plan proposed by Mr. Whitney. (Washington) 1848. Miscellaneous No. 77, Senate, 30th Congress, 1st Session.

Resolutions of the Legislature of New Jersey in relation to internal improvements. (Washington) 1848. [Being Miscellaneous No. 78, Senate, 30th Congress, 1st Session. Advocating the conclusions of the Chicago Convention of 1847 relating to river navigation.]

Resolutions of the Legislature of Ohio, in favor of the Construction of a Railroad from Lake Michigan to the Pacific Ocean, on the plan of Asa Whitney. (Wash.) 1848. Miscellaneous No. 124, Senate, 30th Congress, 1st Session.

Resolutions of the Legislature of Rhode Island, in favor of Whitney's plan for a railroad from Lake Michigan to the Pacific (Wash.) 1847. Miscellaneous No. 4, Senate, 30th Congress, 1st Session.

Resolutions of the Legislature of Tennessee, in favor of the construction of a railroad from Lake Michigan to the Pacific Ocean, on the plan proposed by Mr. Asa Whitney. (Wash.) 1848. Miscellaneous No. 29, Senate, 30th Congress, 1st Session.

Resolves Concerning Steamboats. (Boston) One Thousand Eight Hundred and Forty. [Being Senate Document No. 31 of the Common wealth of Massachusetts; legislature of 1840. Report of a committee appointed to consider the constant disasters to steamboats and propose remedies.]

Richards, T. Addison.—The Fulton Folly, or, the First Steamboat: A Romance of American Biography. [Printed serially in the Orion, a monthly magazine of Literature and Art which was published in Athens and Penfield, Georgia, by William C. Richards in 1842-3-4. The tale begins in Vol. III, No. 1, Sept., 1843.]

Ritter, Abraham.—Philadelphia and her Merchants as Constituted

Fifty @ Seventy years ago . . . and incidents and anecdotes of the Day. Maps and diagrams. Philadelphia, 1860.

Roads (The) and Railroads, Vehicles, and Modes of Travelling, of Ancient and Modern Countries; with Accounts of Bridges, Tunnels and Canals in Various Parts of the World. London, MDCCCXXXIX.

Root, Frank A., and Connelley, William Elsey.—The Overland Stage to California. Personal Reminiscences and Authentic History of the Great Overland Stage Line and Pony Express from the Missouri River to the Pacific Ocean. Topeka, Kansas, 1901. [Published by the Authors.]

Rumsey, James.—A Short Treatise on the Application of Steam, whereby it is Clearly Shown . . . that Steam may be applied to propel Boats or Vessels, etc., etc. Philadelphia. MDCCLXXVIII. [Title reproduced in the text. A reprint may be found in O'Callaghan's "Documentary History of the State of New York," Vol. 2, Albany, 1849.]

Saladee, C. W.—The Coach Makers Illustrated Monthly Magazine. Volume II. Columbus, Ohio, 1856. [Saladee was editor and proprietor.]

Searight, Thomas B.—The Old Pike. A History of the National Road, with Incidents, Accidents and Anecdotes Thereon. Uniontown, Pa. Published by the Author, 1894.

Sennett, A. R.—Carriages Without Horses Shall Go. London, 1896.

Seward, William H.—Address delivered by, at the Commencement of the Auburn and Owasco Canal, October 14, 1835: With the Proceedings of the Celebration. Auburn, 1835.

Shaw, R. C.—Across the Plains in Forty-Nine. Farmland, Indiana, 1896. [A 200 page narrative of an overland journey from Boston to California.]

Shaw, William.—Golden Dreams and Waking Realities; Being the Adventures of a Gold Seeker in California, etc. London, 1851.

Shea, George.—City Railway Fares. Argument of Mr. George Shea in the case of Newman versus Second Avenue Railroad Company. n.p, n.d. [Dealing with conditions arising out of the Civil War legislation which put a tax on public passenger-carrying vehicles.]

Sherwood, J. E.—The Pocket Guide to California; A Sea and Land Route Book, Containing a full description of the El Dorado . . . and the various Routes and Distances to the Gold Regions. Large folding map. New York, 1849. [Title reproduced in the text.]

Shortfield, Luke.—The Western Merchant. A Narrative Containing Useful Instruction for the Western Man of Business Who Makes His Purchases in the East; also, Information for the Eastern man whose Customers are in the West; Likewise, Hints for those who

Design Emigrating to the West. Deduced from Actual Experience. Philadelphia, 1849.

Sinclair, Angus.—Development of the Locomotive Engine. New York, 1907.

Sipes, William B.—The Pennsylvania Railroad: Its Origin, Construction, Condition and Connections. Embracing Historical, Descriptive and Statistical Notices, etc. Philadelphia, 1875.

Smith, J. Calvin.—Smith's Hand-Book for Travellers through the United States of America: Containing . . . the Railroad, Steamboat, and Stage Routes, and the Distance from Place to Place on all the Great Travelling Routes, etc., etc. New York, 1856. Folding map.

Smith, Truman, U. S. Senator.—Speech of, in Support of the Bill reported by the Hon. Mr. Rusk, of Texas, from a Select Committee, for the Construction of a Railroad and Telegraph Line from the Mississippi Valley to the Pacific Ocean. Delivered in the United States Senate, Feb. 17, 1853. Washington, 1853.

Smith, Wm. Prescott.—The Book of the Great Railway Celebrations of 1857, embracing a full account of the Opening of the Ohio & Mississippi, and the Marietta & Cincinnati Railroads . . . With Histories and Descriptions of the Same, etc., etc. New York, 1858. Map and 264+178+40 pages.

Speed, Thomas.—The Wilderness Road, a Description of the Routes of Travel by which the Pioneers and Early Settlers First Came to Kentucky. Louisville, 1886. [Number Two of the Filson Club monographs.]

Spooner, C. E.—Narrow Gauge Railways. Folding maps and plates. London, 1871.

Spooner, Lysander.—The Unconstitutionality of the Laws of Congress Prohibiting Private Mails. New York, 1844.

Stage Coaches.—Great United States Mail Lines to the South & West, via Baltimore & Ohio R. R. to Cumberland, and National Road to Wheeling. Six Daily Lines of Mail and Passenger Coaches leave Cumberland every evening, after the arrival of the Cars at that place, for Wheeling, Cincinnati, Louisville, St. Louis and New Orleans. Through to Pittsburgh or Wheeling in forty-four hours, etc., etc. [Small folio broadside, printed in green ink. n.p., n.d. Enclosed in a wide border of printer's ornaments, with a picture of a railroad train at top, and a stage-coach in center. Reproduced in the text.]

Stage Coaches.—Johnson's Reports, in the Congress of the United States, on the Sunday Mail Question. [Large folio broadside, New York n.d. (1830.) Printed in five columns of small type, the whole surrounded by a large, heavy border of printer's ornaments. The title is enclosed in a small border of printer's ornaments, and has the picture of an open stage wagon with six passengers, drawn by four galloping horses. Contains the text of the reports of 1829 and 1830 which determined Congress not to legislate against Sunday travelling.]

Stage Coaches.—Philadelphia and Baltimore regular land stages. The Proprietors having supplied the line with good and comfortable carriages and able horses, respectfully inform the public, etc., etc. Small broadside, Philadelphia, July 26, 1788. [Contains, also, an announcement of "The Philadelphia, Charleston and Baltimore New Line of Stages and the Chestertown mail stage."]

Stansbury, Howard, U. S. Ass't. Civil Engineer.—A Report of the Survey of the Cumberland River. With 16 large folding maps. Washington, 1835. [Continued in Doc. No. 171, Ho. of Reps., 23d Congress, 2nd Session.]

Stansbury, P.—A Pedestrian Tour of Two Thousand Three Hundred Miles, in North America . . . Performed in the Autumn of 1821. New York, 1822.

Steamboat Disasters and Railroad Accidents in the United States, etc., etc. Revised and improved, Worcester, 1846. [Copyrighted and first issued in 1842.]

Steamboat Monopoly.—The Opinion of the Supreme Court of the United States in the case of Gibbons vs. Ogden, delivered by Chief Justice Marshall, March 2, 1824, with a preface, containing an Historical Sketch of the Steamboat Controversy. Albany, 1824.

Steamboat Monopoly.—The Right of a State to Grant exclusive Privileges, in Roads, Bridges, Canals, Navigable Waters, etc., Vindicated by a Candid examination of the grant from the State of New York to, and contract with, Robert R. Livingston and Robert Fulton, for the Exclusive Navigation of Vessels, by Steam or Fire, for a limited time, on the waters of said State, and within the Jurisdiction thereof. Printed by E. Conrad. (New York), 1811. [Livingston's argument in favor of a state's right to control the use of steam for the purposes of travel and navigation, and to bestow such use as a monopoly if it so desired.]

Steamboats.—Hilliard, Chester. Awful Conflagration of the Steamboat Lexington in Long Island Sound on Monday Eve., Jan. 13th, 1840, by which melancholy occurrence over 120 passengers Perished. Captain Hilliard's Testimony. New York. (1840.) [Large folio broadside. Upper half of sheet occupied by a lithographic view (colored) of the burning boat drawn by W. K. Hewitt and engraved by N. Currier. Below, in 4 columns, is a list of the lost, and at bottom, in two wide columns, is Hilliard's account of the disaster. He was the only passenger saved of the eighty-seven on board. Three of the crew of 40 were also saved. Hewitt's drawing reproduced in the text.]

Steele, Mrs. E.—A Summer Journey in the West. New York, 1841.

Sterne, Simon.—Closing Argument on Behalf of the Chamber of Commerce and Board of Trade and Transportation of New York, . . .

before the Special Assembly Committee on Railroads appointed under a Resolution of the Assembly to Investigate Alleged Abuses in the Management of Railroads. New York, 1880.

Stevens, Francis B.—The First Steam Screw Propeller Boats to Navigate the Waters of any Country. n.p., n.d.

(Stevens, John.)—Documents Tending to Prove the Superior Advantages of Railways and Steam-Carriages over Canal Navigation. [Written by John Stevens of Hoboken and published by T. & J. Swords of New York City in 1812. The earliest known American printed work on railroads.]

Stevenson, David.—Sketch of Civil Engineering in North America: Comprising remarks on the . . . Steam Navigation, . . . Canals. Roads, Railways, etc., in that Country. London, MDCCCXXXVIII.

Stimson, A. L.—History of the Express Business: Including the Origin of the Railway System of America. New York, 1881. [Privately printed.]

Stimson, H. K.—From the Stage Coach to the Pulpit. Saint Louis, 1874.

Stone, Roy.—New Roads and Road Laws in the United States. New York, 1894.

Stranger's (The) Guide to Baltimore, etc., etc. By a Baltimorean. Baltimore, 1852.

Stratton, Ezra M.—The World on Wheels; or, Carriages, with their Historical Associations from the Earliest to the Present Time, etc. 489 pages. New York, Published by the Author, 1878.

Street Railways.—Cable Traction Systems of the Rapid Transit Cable Company, New York. New York (1889.)

Strickland, William.—Reports on Canals, Railways, Roads, and other Subjects, made to the Pennsylvania Society for the Promotion of Internal Improvement. Plates. Philadelphia, 1826.

Strickland, W. P.—The Pioneers of the West; or, Life in the Woods. New York. (1856.)

Stuart, Charles B.—Lives and Works of Civil and Military Engineers of America. Plates. New York, 1871.

St. Vrain, Major E. L.—Brimstone Bob, and his Lightning Horse Quartette; or, Major Bragg's Ride to Tombstone. New York, 1886. [One of the Beadle Library publications. A story of stage-coach life and experiences in Arizona during the days soon after the Civil War.]

Sunday Mails.—An Account of Memorials Presented to Congress During its Last Session, by numerous Friends of their Country and its Institutions; praying that the mails may not be Transported, nor Post-Office kept open, on the Sabbath. New York, 1829.

Tanner, H. S.—A Description of the Canals and Rail Roads of the United States, comprehending notices of all the Works of Internal Improvement throughout the Several States. New York, 1840.

1477

Tanner, H. S.—Memoir on the Recent Surveys, Observations and Internal Improvements in the United States. With brief notices of . . . Canals and Rail Roads never before Delineated. Philadelphia, 1829.

Tanner, H. S.—The American Traveller, or Tourists' and Emigrants' Guide through the United States. Containing brief notices of the several States, Cities, Principal Towns, Canals, Railroads, etc., etc. Maps. New York, 1846.

Tanner, H. S.—The Traveller's Hand Book for the State of New York and the Province of Canada: Containing . . . Modes of Conveyance, Tables of Distances by Railroad, Canal, Stage, and River Routes in Every direction, etc., etc. New York, 1844. Folding map.

Tavernier, M. H.—Les Tramways aux Etats-Unis. (Paris, 1896.) [370 pages of text and 20 large folding plates. Tavernier was one of the French delegates to the Engineering Congress held in Chicago in 1893, and this is his report on American street railway systems.]

Taylor, Benj. H.—The World on Wheels, and other Sketches. Chicago, 1874.

Taylor, Joseph.—A Fast Life on the Modern Highway; Being a Glance into the Railroad World from a New Point of View. New York, 1874.

Telegraphs.—Report of the Committee on Post-Office and Post Roads on bills for governmental telegraph lines. H. of R. Report No. 32, Fortieth Cong., 3d session, Feb. 24, 1869. [Adverse report.]

Thayer, Eli.—The New England Emigrant Aid Company and Its Influence, through the Kansas Contest, upon National History. Worcester, MDCCCLXXXVII.

Thornton, W.—Short Account of the Origin of Steam Boats, written in 1810, and now Committed to the Press. Albany: 1818. [Title reproduced in the text.]

Thurston, Robert H.—A History of the Growth of the Steam-Engine. New York, 1878.

Tourist (The), or Pocket Manual for Travellers on the Hudson River, the Western and Northern Canals and Railroads: the Stage Routes to Niagara Falls, etc., etc. New York, 1841. Folding map.

(Touzalin, A. E.)—How to go West. A Guide to Southern Iowa, Nebraska, Kansas, California, and the Great West. Folding maps. Chicago, 1872.

Trans-Continental, The.—[A daily newspaper published on the special train of the Boston Board of Trade during its trip between Boston and San Francisco, and return, in 1870. Complete file is twelve numbers. The editor of the paper was W. R. Steele. All contents of the paper were written, put into type and printed on board the moving train, one car being equipped as a printing shop.]

Tredgold, Thomas.—A Practical Treatise on Railroads and Carriages, Showing the Principles of Estimating their Strength, Proportions, Expense, and Annual Produce, and the Conditions which Render them Effective, Economical and Durable, etc., etc. (New York) MDCCCXXXV. [Reprinted from the London edition of the same year.]

Trego, Charles B.—A Geography of Pennsylvania: Containing an Account of the Railroads, Canals, etc., of the State. . . . To which is appended a Travellers' Guide, or Table of Distances on the Principal Rail Road, Canal and Stage Routes in the State. Philadelphia, 1843.

Trips in the Life of a Locomotive Engineer. New York, 1863.

Tucker, T. W.—Waifs from the Way-Bills of an Old Expressman. Boston, 1872.

Valentine, David T.—A Compilation of the Existing Ferry Leases. and Railroad Grants made by the Corporation of the City of New York, together with the Grants from the Legislature of the State to use the Streets of the City for Railroad Purposes, etc., etc. New York, 1866.

(Van Cleve, J.)—The Ontario and St. Lawrence Steamboat Company's Hand-Book for Travellers to Niagara Falls, Montreal and Quebec, and through Lake Champlain to Saratoga Springs. Buffalo, 1852.

(Vandewater, R. J.)—The Tourist, or Pocket Manual for Travellers on the Hudson River, the Western Canal, and Stage Road, etc., etc. Large folding map. New York, 1830.

(Vandewater, R. J.)—The Same; Third Edition, enlarged and improved, New York, 1834.

Varnum, Joseph B., Jr.—The Seat of Government of the United States. A Review of the Discussions, in Congress and Elsewhere, on the Site and Plans of the Federal City. Second edition. Washington, 1854. [Not a government publication. First issued in 1848.]

View of the Valley of the Mississippi, or the Emigrant's and Traveller's Guide to the West. Containing a General Description of that Entire Country; and also notices of the . . . Rivers and other Channels of Intercourse and Trade, etc., etc. Second edition, Philadelphia, 1834. [Contains 372 pages of text and folding maps. By R. Baird.]

Walker, James Scott.—An accurate Description of the Liverpool and Manchester Rail-Way. . . . An Account of the Opening of the Railway, and the Melancholy Accident which Occurred, with a map of the Line, etc., etc. Liverpool, MDCCCXXX.

Walker, W. M., Commander, U. S. N.—Notes on Screw Propulsion: Its Rise and Progress. New York, 1861.

Warner, I. W.—The Immigrant's Guide and Citizen's Manual: A Work for Immigrants of all classes . . . with directions and valuable information for travellers. New York, 1848.

Waters, Thomas Franklin.—A History of the Old Argilla Road in Ipswich, Massachusetts. Salem, Mass., 1900.

Watkins, J. Elfreth.—The Development of the American Rail and

Track, as illustrated by the Collection in the U. S. National Museum. [Being a monograph included in the Report of the Museum for 1889. Also printed in Transactions of the American Society of Civil Engineers, April, 1890.]

Watson, Elkanah.—History of the Rise, Progress and Existing Condition of the Western Canals in the State of New York, from September 1788, to the Completion of the Middle Section of the Grand Canal in 1819. Albany, 1820.

Watson, John F.—Annals of Philadelphia; Being a Collection of Memoirs, Anecdotes, and Incidents . . . from the Days of the Pilgrim Founders, etc., etc. Philadelphia, 1830.

Watson, Winslow C.—Men and Times of the Revolution; or, Memoirs of Elkanah Watson, etc. New York, 1856.

Westcott, Thompson.—Life of John Fitch, the Inventor of the Steam-Boat. Philadelphia, 1857.

Wheeler, A. C.—The Iron Trail: A Sketch. New York, 1876. [Conditions of travel from the East to Colorado at that time.]

Whitney, Asa.—Memorial of, praying for a grant of Land to enable him to Construct a Railroad from Lake Michigan to the Pacific Ocean. Washington, 1845. Senate, Doc. 69; 28th Congress, 2nd Session.

Whitney, Asa.—Memorial of, praying for a grant of land to enable him to construct a railroad from Lake Michigan to the Pacific Ocean. (Washington) 1848. Miscellaneous No. 28, Senate, 30th Congress, 1st Session. [Gives his plan in detail.]

Whittemore, Henry.—The Past and the Present of Steam Navigation on Long Island Sound, n. p. (1893.)

Willey, Benjamin G.—Incidents in White Mountain History. . . . Together with Numerous Anecdotes Illustrating Life in the Back Woods. . . . To which is added an Accurate Guide from New York and Boston to the White Mountains. Boston, 1856.

Williams, Edwin.—The New York Annual Register for the Year of Our Lord 1837. New York, 1837.

Williams, Frederick S.—Our Iron Roads: Their History, Constuction and Social Influences. London, 1852.

Williams, W.—Appleton's Northern and Eastern Traveller's Guide: With new and authentic maps, etc., etc. New York, MDCCCL.

Williams, W.—The Traveller's and Tourist's Guide through the United States of America, etc., containing the Routes of Travel by Railroad, Steamboat, Stage and Canal, etc., etc. Large folding map. Philadelphia, MDCCCLIV.

Williams, W. G., Capt. U. S. Topographical Engineers.—Report of the plan and estimates for constructing a ship canal to connect Lakes Erie and Ontario, with a review of the effect of such a waterway on the travel and transportation conditions of the country. Washington,

1836. [Contained in Doc. No. 214, Ho. of Reps., 24th Congress, 1st Session.]

(Wilson, H.)—Wilson's Illustrated Guide to the Hudson River. Twelfth Edition. New York, March 15, 1851.

(Wilson, H.)—The same. New York, 1854.

Wilson, Hon. Jeremiah M., of Indiana.—Speech of, in the H. of R., Feb. 10, 1872, on the Two Per Cent Funds of Ohio, Indiana and Illinois. (1872.)

Wilson, W. Hasell.—A brief Review of Railroad History from the Earliest Period to the Year 1894. Philadelphia, 1895.

With, Emil.—Railroad Accidents: Their Causes and the Means of Preventing Them. Boston, 1856.

Wood, Nicholas.—A Practical Treatise on Railroads, etc., etc. Folding plates. London, 1831.

Wood, Nicholas.—The Same. American edition. Philadelphia, 1832. Folding plates.

Wootton, W. T.—Report of the Joint Committee [of the Maryland legislature] Appointed to Inquire into the Expenditures of the State in Works of Internal Improvement, n.p., n.d. [1835?]

Wright, A. E.—Boston, New York, Philadelphia and Baltimore Commercial Directory . . . together with a list of the Principal Public Institutions. Rail Road and Steamboat Routes, Rates of Fare, etc. New York and Philadelphia, 1840.

Wrongs and Rights of a Traveller: By Boat—By Stage—By Rail. By a Barrister at Law. Toronto, 1875. [The cases, comment and anecdote relate mainly to United States conditions.]

Young, Charles Frederick T.—The Economy of Steam Power on Common Roads . . . with its History and Practice in Great Britain . . . and [by Alexander Holley and J. K. Fisher] Its Progress in the United States. London (1861).

Young, Egerton Ryerson.—By Canoe and Dog Train Among the Cree and Salteaux Indians. N. Y., n. d.

Zeigler, Wilbur G., and Grosscup, Benj. S.—The Heart of the Alleghanies, or Western North Carolina: Comprising its Topography, History . . . Incidents and Pictures of Travel, etc., etc. Raleigh, N. C., n. d. (1883.)

INDEX

INDEX

1485

INDEX

Arkansas River, 1133.
Arnold, Benedict, knowledge spread by campaign of, 312.
Ashcroft's Railway Directory, figures taken from, 1393.
Ashland, 1095.
Ashley, William H., fur trader, 1192, 1194, 1214.
Ashley River, 36, 94, 95.
Ashtabula, 1109.
Assiniboin, grant travel privileges, 1176.
Assiniboine, career of, 1147, 1148, 1159.
Astor, John Jacob, fur trader, 1188.
Astoria, 1190.
Atkinson, General, in Black Hawk's War, 459-466.
Atlanta, 1122, 1124.
Atlantic and Great Western Railroad, gauge of, 1348.
Auburn, N. Y., 1109.
Audubon, J. J., trip of on Missouri River, 1154, 1157, 1158.
Auglaize River, 428.
Augusta, Ga., 95, 1085, 1119, 1122.
Awandoe Creek, 76.
Ayres, Captain, railroad conductor, 1026, 1027.

Backwoodsmen, *see "Pioneer Life."*
Bailes, Congressman, advocate of Oregon settlement, 1190.
Baldwin, Matthias, locomotive builder, 977, 978, 980, 982, 992, 1016, 1073, 1077, 1079, 1369.
Baldwin's Model, early locomotive, 977.
Balloons, popular interest in mentioned by Fitch, 243.
Baltimore: the early city, 88; traffic between and Philadelphia, 191; first steamboat at, 398; fare from to Frederick, 739; wagon traffic from, 753; meetings at to further railroad building, 943, 944; road begun at, 945, 946; trial of Cooper's locomotive at, 947; railway car built at, 949; second trial of Cooper's locomotive at, 952; passenger traffic to and from increased by railroads, 1009; celebration at, 1090, 1094, 1095; fare from to Pittsburgh, 1118; mentioned, 160, 190, 199, 201, 317, 318, 792, 759, 810, 878, 888, 903, 1044, 1088, 1097, 1112, 1113, 1114, 1119, 1122, 1123, 1335.
Baltimore *American,* 1016.
Baltimore and Ohio Railroad: origin of, 943 et seq.; number of passengers carried by in 1835, 1009; first passenger car on, 1113-1115; progress westward, 1088-1090; in operation to Cumberland, 1113; born of broad vision, 1379.
Baltimore *Chronicle,* 1045.
Baltimore *Gazette,* 952.
Barbour, Secretary of War, report to on Cherokees, 524.
Barge: construction, use, 286, 302, 307; passenger accommodations on, 287; Ohio packet boat, 287, 302; starting signal, 1008; mentioned by Cass, 1092.
Barlow, Joel, gets letter from Fulton, 369.
Barlow, Samuel B., urges Pacific railroad, 1321, 1322.
Batteau, character, use, 281, 312.
Bayard, N., describes wilderness, 14.
Bear Creek, 880.
Bear River, 1213, 1291.
Bellevue, 1156, 1157, 1158, 1159.
Belton, Major, permits use of field piece at a celebration, 962.

INDEX

Bergen Neck, 186.

Bermuda, Va., 88.

Berry, Captain John, pioneer tavern keeper, 651, 675-677, 1369.

Berry Trace, location of, 651.

Best Friend, early locomotive, 960, 962, 966, 1050.

Beste, J. Richard, describes travel on interior canals, 868-871.

Beste, Lucy, daughter of J. Richard, 869, 870.

Big Elk, assists Mormons, 1261.

Bison Streets, *see sub-caption under "Roads."*

Bisonette, ——, Indian trader, 1169.

Blackfeet, mentioned, 1167.

Black Hawk: war of, 459 et seq.; overturned, 768; mentioned, 444, 653.

Black Hills, 1322, 1352.

Black River, 1109.

Black Rock, 334, 336.

Blessing of the Bay, launched, 28.

Bloomfield, Joseph, rides on Fitch's boat, 256.

Bloomington, Iowa, 1204, 1206.

Blue River, 431.

Bluffton, Mo., 1137.

Boats: pioneer vehicles, 12; water routes preferred, 16, 159, 275, 1139; ferries established, 27; in mass migrations, 30 et seq.; permitted on Ohio, 78; economic value of, in South, 85; built by Bullitt, 132; relation of to settlement of Kentucky, 155, 159; up-stream trips avoided, 163; in connection with stage wagons, 182 et seq., 991; competition between, 183; competition with wagons, 190; water route to interior, 224; small change in, 228; use in occupying Mississippi valley, 268, 279, 288, 456; duration of voyages, 307; end of timber boat era, 308; river transportation insufficient, 415; use of Tennessee River, 496; claiming lost boats, 640; official pilots, 642; *see also, "Ark," "Barge," "Batteau," "Canoe," "Flatboat," "Keel-Boat," "Pole-Boat," "Skiff," "Steamboat," "Missouri River."*

Boggs, Lalburn, Governor of Missouri, 1241, 1324.

Boileau, Nathaniel, aids Fitch, 235.

Bonneville, Captain, fur trader, 1206, 1216, 1218.

Boone, Daniel: appears, 117; fitness for task, 120; first trip to Kentucky, 121; leads party, 126, 155; attacked, 130; postpones advance, 131; rescues Bullitt, 133; negotiates with natives, 134; makes first road to interior, 136 et seq.; advises Henderson, 141, 145; effects of work, 159, 648; life of west of Kentucky, 1135 et seq., 1141; mentioned, 674, 803, 1094, 1208, 1247, 1369.

Boone, Daniel, son of Daniel, 1136.

Boone, James, killed, 130.

Boone, Nathan, son of Daniel, 1136.

Boone, Squire: meets Daniel in the forest, 123; accompanies Daniel, 126.

Boonesborough, 140, 142, 152, 154, 162.

Boone's Lick, 1136.

Boone's Lick Road, 1136, 1208.

Borden, Joseph, advertises his boats, 183.

Bordentown, 182, 256, 352, 397, 990, 992, 994.

Boston: shipbuilding established at, 28; road built to Plymouth from, 29; ship carries settlers from to Connecticut, 30; establishes ferries, 42, 43; roads built from, 53; periodic travel to and from established, 186; stage-coach travel to New York from, 187, 188, 201; wheeled vehicles in, 205; numerous taverns in, 208; cost of a meal in, 209; fare to New

1487

INDEX

INDEX

California: the finding of gold and its effect, 1270; national conditions prior to gold discovery, 1271; conditions in just preceding discovery, 1276.
Calk, William: diary of, 142; road followed by, 152; influence of, 159, 1299.
Calvert, Lord, catalogues his party, 90.
Cambridge, Ohio, 332.
Camden and Amboy Railroad: opening of, 976, 978, 990; character of cars on, 1016; T rails used on, 1041.
Camden, N. J., 924, 928, 976, 978, 990, 991, 992, 994, 995, 1016, 1042.
Canal Boats: construction, appearance, 780, 781, 797, 800, 848 et seq., 864; different sorts of, 850, 864, 1108, 1111; internal arrangements, 852, 864, 868; locks, inclined planes, 787, 794, 799, 802; travel on, in general, 798, 799, 801, 822, 847 et seq., 859 et seq., 1009, 1108; family boats, 864; poles used in navigation of, 867; Beste's trip, 868; seating on, 800, 841, 850, 851, 854, 858, 861, 870, 871, 1111, 1118; sleeping on, 850, 851, 854, 868, 870, 871, 1111, 1118; speed of, 799, 800, 824, 841, 850, 851, 861, 871, 1111, 1118, 1120; crew, 801, 852, 854, 858, 862; no serious accidents to, 859, 865; guidebook for prevention of accidents to, 865; cost of travel on, 800, 842, 851, 861, 871, 1108, 1110, 1118, 1119, 1120; *Chief Engineer,* 779; *Pittsburgh,* 800; *Indiana,* 841, 868, 871; list of, 841 note; sleeping bunk of copied by railroads, 1044.
Canals: demanded by West, 630; as possible Federal enterprises, 700, 708, 714; cause of canal period, 770; first suggested, 771; Franklin's ideas, 772; first American, 772 et seq.; Watson's influence, 775; New York's procedure, 778, 819, 846, 881, 886; Pennsylvania's system, 802, 846; affected by state jealousies, 805, 806, 808, 810, 811, 829, 1401; national system of, 816, 824, 839, 845, 846, 1399; Ohio's activity, 818 et seq., 845, 846; Indiana's work, 825 et seq., 846; popular discussion, 830, 836, 900, 916; arguments in favor of, 834, 896, 938; arguments against, 921; financial troubles of states, 840; Illinois' plan, 840; junction basins, 870; control of by railroads, 995, 1104; used in conjunction with stagecoaches, steamboats, railroads, 1105, 1108, 1110, 1118, 1120; modern use of, 1368; Seward's address on, 1401; *see also names of specific canals.*
Canasagi River, 525.
Canida, Joseph, boat captain, 183.
Canoe, Bark: construction, use, 20; unpracticed management, 27; feared by traveller, 56; at Boonesborough, 146; on Susquehanna, 226; model for Durham boats, 282.
Canoe, Log: construction, use, 21, 280, 281; suitable trees for protected by authority, 28; as coach ferries, 46; in Virginia, 87; Oglethorpe's, 95; dug-outs, 104; increase of, 223; on Susquehanna, 227; pirogues, 281, 1141; mentioned by Chase, 1091; of Missouri River, 1136, 1140.
Cape Fear River, 35.
Captivity of John Tanner, 1412.
Car of Neptune, built by Fulton, 379.
Carbondale, 926, 955, 956.
Carbondale and Honesdale Railroad, building of, 955.
Carlisle, 200.
Carroll, Charles, lays cornerstone, 945.
Cars, *see sub-caption under "Railroads."*
Carson River, 1314.
Carthage, Mo., 1244.
Carts, *see sub-caption under "Wagons."*
Cartwright, Peter, English inventor, 359.
Carver, Hartwell, urges Pacific railroad, 1324.
Cascade Mountains, 1235, 1236.

INDEX

INDEX

Chicago: native path to from Galena, 653; description of in 1822, 663; muddy streets of in 1833, 756; first railway of built, 1079, 1082; railway communication from New York to, 1082, 1088, 1109, 1120; smaller than Nauvoo, 1242; convention at to promote a transcontinental, 1334; favors Oregon route, 1335; mentioned, 12, 13, 1336, 1348, 1349, 1355, 1365.

Chicago and Galena Railroad, buys the *Alert*, 1080.

Chicago River, 429, 1580.

Chickasaws: Tecumseh's appeal to, 442; strength of, 444; possessions of, 488; unwilling to cede all their lands, 511; development of, 528; pressure of whites upon, 552 et seq.; cede lands and remove to West, 601; grant right to build railroads, 1178, 1182; mentioned, 486, 515, 520, 619, 1172, 1411.

Chillicothe, 331, 1091.

Chinook, Indian tribe, mentioned, 1236.

Chippewa, reaches Fort Benton, 1159.

Chippewas, treaties with, 444, 449.

Chittenden, Hiram M., writer, 1156.

Choctaws: Tecumseh's appeal to, 442; strength of, 444; possessions of, 488; permit establishment of inns, 502; propose to cede lands, 504; unwilling to give up all their lands, 511; development of, 528; pressure of whites upon leading to removal to the West, 552 et seq.; grant right to build railroads, 1178; mentioned, 486, 513, 520, 601, 619, 1165, 1172, 1411.

Chowan River, 35.

Cincinnati: in a remote region, 12; regular packets ply to, 287; advertisement of such a packet, 303, 304; trips to of first steamer on the Ohio, 391; steamer line to Louisville from, 396; terminus of a canal, 821, 824; canal conference at between representatives of Ohio and Indiana, 829, 830; principal city of Middle West, 1083; views growing importance of route from New York to Chicago with concern, 1087, 1088; railroad opened to St. Louis, 1090-1094; fare by river from Pittsburgh to, 1118, fare and routes to various cities from, 1119, 1120, 1121, 1124; keel-boats built at, 1141; mentioned, 13, 307, 338, 625, 639, 659, 692, 756, 759, 800, 839, 841, 842, 870, 1355.

Claiborne, Governor, discusses steamboat monopoly with Fulton, 388, 389.

Clark, George Rogers: campaign of, 149, 427; mentioned, 667.

Clark, Marston G., pioneer judge, 667, 668.

Clark, William, explorer, 1132, 1133, 1170, 1188, 1189, 1196, 1197.

Clarke, Louis Gaylord, urges Pacific railroad, 1324.

Clarke, William, of Northwest Territory oligarchy, 642.

Clay, Henry: advocates National Road, 709, 710, 756, 1091; plays joke, 732; accident to, 767.

Clearwater River, 1199, 1200.

Cleaver, Charles, describes early Chicago, 756.

Cleaver's *History of Chicago,* 756.

Clermont: Schulz uses, 334, 335; early career of, 342; first trip of, 344; rebuilt, 347; evolution of, 347 et seq., 358 et seq.; appearance of, 369; historical importance of, 371.

Cleveland: first steamer on Lake Erie runs to, 403, 404; terminus of a canal, 821, 822; in time tables, 1119, 1120, 1124; mentioned, 70, 1109.

Clinch River, 114, 131, 138, 141.

Clinton, De Witt, interest of in canals, 819, 821, 822, 826, 1369, 1404.

Clinton, General, knowledge spread by campaigns of, 312.

Coachmakers' Journal, 978.

Coffee, General John, confers with Chickasaws, 578.

Colden, Cadwallader, considers future traffic routes, 224.

INDEX

INDEX

INDEX

Dodge, Colonel G. M., explorer, 1218.
Donner, George: California immigrant, 1276, 1294, 1295, 1369; *for various members of Donner party, see* 1286, 1287, 1288, 1290.
Donner, Jacob, California immigrant, 1276, 1287, 1294.
Donner, Tamsen, 1294, 1295.
Donner (Truckee) Lake, 1284, 1291, 1360.
Dorchester, 28, 32.
Douglas, Stephen A., work of for public improvements, 1075.
Dover, Del., 239.
Dover, N. H., 33.
Drake, Benjamin, discusses race troubles, 1413.
Dripps, Isaac, locomotive builder, 992, 1042, 1043, 1068.
Dubuque, 1120, 1324.
Dunmore, Lord: war with natives, 76, 133; investigates reports about Kentucky, 131; sends Boone after Bullitt, 133, 155.
Durham, Robert, pioneer boat builder, 282.

Eagle, at Baltimore, 398.
Eaton, Secretary of War, 1215.
Edinburg, 351.
Education, Popular, Seward's address on importance of, 1403.
Edwards, Aaron, boat captain, 183.
Elgin, 1080.
Elijah, Indian preacher, 1231.
Elizabethport, 52, 402, 412, 414, 995, 1115.
Ellicott's Mills, 946, 947, 952.
Ellsworth, Oliver: rides on Fitch's boat, 250; steamboat named for, 407.
El Paso, passes mouth of Milk River, 1159.
Emigrant, Ann Arbor newspaper, transcontinental proposed by, 1320, 1321.
Enterprise, fourth steamboat in the West, 393.
Erie, 752, 1109.
Erie and Kalamazoo Railroad, first Michigan railroad, 1083.
Erie Canal: origin, 777, 881; celebrations at opening, 778 et seq.; dimensions, 783; cost, 783, 787; effect of success, 829, 831; travel on, 871, 1063, 1108, 1118, 1119, 1120; tickets for, 1037, 1108; locomotives and rails carried on, 1065, 1079.
Erie, Lake: time required to go from Ohio River to, 339; first steamer upon, 403; free passage to granted by Indians, 428; completion of Erie Canal to, 783, 787; proposals to connect the Potomac and Ohio with, 806, 811, 820, 821, 830; Indiana obtains outlet to, 839, 840; passenger traffic by canal to and from, 848, 864, 1063; proposed railway to, 882; telegraph line from New York to, 1045; Mad River Railroad to extend to, 1066; mentioned, 58, 70, 315, 335, 427, 513, 654, 696, 816, 819, 824, 836, 1065, 1088, 1321, 1335, 1348.
Erie Railroad: first train on, 863; use of bell rope originates on, 1026-1028; telegraph follows line of, 1045; accident on, 1056; travelling on, 1115, 1116; gauge of, 1348; born of broad vision, 1379; construction of opposed, 1401.
European Influences and Activities: Spanish and French explorations, 24; colonizing contests, 25; Dutch and English competition, 30, 33; Swedes on Delaware River, 35; Dutch abandon Jersey, 52; struggle for a continent, 69; Champlain's expedition, 71; Britain limits colonial growth, 73; the Revolution, 78; early immigrations from Europe, 94 et seq.; British reprove Pennsylvania lawmakers, 192; wars retard progress,

1494

INDEX

1495

INDEX

INDEX

Fulton, Robert: steamboat builder, 335, 342 et seq., 357 et seq., 375 et seq., 393, 395 et seq., 402, 412, 413, 771, 1092. *See also "Steamboats—Steamboat Travel," sub-caption "Fulton and His Work."*
Fulton, career of, 407, 408, 410.

Galena, 653, 654, 1079, 1080.
Galenian, 461.
Gallatin, Albert, proposes Cumberland Road, 708.
Gallatin, Tenn., 157.
Galloway, Jim, Indian, mentioned by Harrison, 432.
Garden Grove, 1248.
Gaston, 1085.
Gauges, *see sub-caption under "Railroads."*
General Pike, Cincinnati's first steamboat, 396.
Genesee River, 316, 317, 318, 781.
George, Lake, 70, 71, 402.
Georgetown, 805, 810, 812, 815.
Georgia Railroad, building of, 1085.
Germantown, 976, 978, 980, 982, 984, 1016, 1017, 1018.
Gerstner, Chevalier von, civil engineer, 951.
Gibbons, Thomas, overthrows monopoly in steam navigation, 414.
Gilmer, Governor, Cherokee message of, 588.
Gist, Christopher, mentioned, 1094.
Gloucester, 28.
Gnadenhutten, 1269.

GOVERNMENTAL CREATION, OWNERSHIP OR CONTROL OF TRAVEL, TRANSPORTATION AND COMMUNICATION ROUTES

In General: attitude toward introduction of steam, 234, 374, 384, 386, 412 et seq., 1047; creation of wagon roads, 304, 811, 826; early Federal policy, 700 et seq., 712 et seq., 806, 810, 811, 826, 886, 890, 892; cause of state initiative, 826; opposition to, 827; political and economic thought during period in which national and state governments built traffic routes, 1344 et seq.; Seward's address, 1401; *see also "Indians," sub-caption "Travel Privileges Granted by."*
Federal Actions and Attitudes: National Road, 691 et seq., 826, 1330, 1342. Canals: in general, 700, 811; refusal to build, 778, 819, 826; aid given in building, 805, 810, 812, 828; refusal to aid, 815; surveys made, 816, 1083; involved in failure, 842. Railroads: tests refused, 882, 886, 888, 889, 1047; surveys, 1083, 1338; control of assumed, 1102; transcontinental railroad considered, 1328 et seq.; Pacific railroad undertaken, 1341; gauge of Pacific road established, 1349; Alaskan railroad undertaken, 1356 note. Telegraphs: 1047, 1050. During Western Migrations: in general, 1175; *see also "Indians," sub-caption "Travel Privileges Granted by."*
State Actions and Attitudes: Wilderness Trails: by Virginia, 162; Kentucky, 162. Wagon Roads: by Kentucky, 162, 163; New York, 319; Pennsylvania, 785, 827. National Road: consent of states, 697; state opposition, 710. Canals: by New York, 777 et seq., 819, 826, 827, 846, 1110; Pennsylvania, 784 et seq., 810, 826, 827, 829, 846; Virginia, 804, 805, 810, 815; Maryland, 805, 810, 815; Ohio, 819, 827, 829, 830, 839, 846; Indiana, 826 et seq., 832, 834, 845, 846. Railroads: by Connecticut, 1328; Illinois, 1075, 1076, 1079; Indiana, 836, 1070, 1072, 1074, 1075, 1328; Kentucky, 1328; Maine, 1328; Maryland, 1328; Michigan, 1082, 1328; New Hampshire, 1328; New Jersey, 1328; New York, 881, 886, 888, 1059,

INDEX

Governmental Creation, etc.—*Continued.*
    1328; Ohio, 1066, 1067, 1328; Pennsylvania, 789 et seq., 888, 1328; Rhode Island, 1328; Tennessee, 1328; Vermont, 1328.
    Territorial Actions and Attitudes, joint agreements with Federal government regarding lands, roads and finance, 696, 698, 700.
Grafton, Mass., 32.
Grafton, Va., 1089, 1090.
Grand Island, 1266.
Granville, Mass., 1321.
Greathouse, ——, Indian trader, 77.
Great Lakes: small early importance of, 25; a native travel route, 60; America's political boundaries reach, 81; use of in attaining interior, 159; Washington's project of a canal to, 776; New York authorizes canal to, 777; use of in conjunction with canals, 846; Stevens advocates railway to, 881; Governor Ray suggests union of with Ohio River, 1070; mentioned, 427, 441, 776, 777, 785, 817, 1096, 1118.
Great Miami River, 428, 816, 821, 1094.
Great Ogeechee River, 1085.
Great Salt Lake: Mormon migration to, 1247, 1250, 1267; Donner party reach, 1280; Abbey mentions and visits, 1305, 1306, 1308.
Greeley, Horace: describes canal trip, 871; meets Whitman, 1219; discusses Oregon migration, 1221.
Green Bay, 663.
Green River, 1213, 1216, 1266, 1305.
Greensville Railroad, length of, 1084.
Greenwich, Conn., 361.
Griffith, William, legal representative of Nicholas Roosevelt, 400.
Grosventres, grant travel privileges, 1176.
Groton, 765, 766.
Guess, George, mentioned, 526 note.
Guide Books: for navigating the Ohio, 1064; innumerable, 1105; warnings contained in, 1106; information in, 1111.
Guilford, 35.
Gunnison, Lieutenant, explorer, 1253.

Hagerstown, 199, 739.
Hall, Captain Basil, draws picture of stage-coach, 722.
Hamburg, S. C., terminus of an early railroad, 829, 924, 958, 1009, 1085.
Hammil, Abraham, locomotive engineer, 1026, 1027.
Harlan, Joshua, Indiana pioneer, 670.
Harmar, General, mentioned, 674.
Harpe, ——, bandit, 650.
Harrisburg, Pa., 1114.
Harrisburg and Lancaster Railroad, mentioned, 1114.
Harrison, Daniel, boat captain, 183.
Harrison, William Henry: describes conditions in interior, 430 et seq., 437, 440, 455, 469, 476, 631; issues traders' licenses, 471, 472; member of oligarchy, 642, 643, 644, 646, 647; travels in stage-coach, 738.
Harrod, James, settlement established by, 155.
Harrod's Town, 142.
Hartford, 32, 351, 750.
Harvard College: president of, 187; mistaken for a tavern, 212 note.
Harvey, Henry, historian of Shawnees, 452, 454.
Haskell, ——, describes locomotive *Old Ironsides*, 978.

1498

INDEX

INDEX

1500

INDEX

Caucasian Attitude Toward: Governmental: colonial diplomacy, 67; desire for territory, 70; apology, 73; natives sought as allies, 79; death of Cornstalk, 80; problem created by success of Revolution, 81; methods in Northwest Territory, 82; travel privileges and land sought, 418, 424, 426, 540; citizenship for natives discussed, 425, 504, 506, 512, 529, 570, 574, 604; white civil war feared because of Indian problem, 426, 532, 555, 580, 602, 611; Harrison's recommendations, 436; inviolability of native possessions pledged, 449, 456, 512, 540, 562, 570, 575, 577, 601, 604; Shawnees, 452 et seq.; Sacs and Foxes, 458 et seq.; licensed trading system, 469 et seq., 517; Indian agents, 478; Jefferson's position, 503; extradition, 495, 504; inconsistencies in, 512, 514, 544; Monroe's position and statements, 513 et seq.; new policy adopted, 515 et seq.; acts of Adams, 531 et seq., 542; bribery, 531; migration urged, 539; approval of native progress stops, 545; Jackson's program, 555 et seq.; Jackson defines Federal position to Chickasaws, 575; relief at success of, 579; fear of judicial attitude, 587; Georgia's acts, 588 et seq.; native sovereignty denied, 590; native sovereignty conceded, 594; use of army, 605 et seq.; official reports on, 610; summary of, 611; relations maintained by treaties, 1161, 1163 et seq., 1185; travel privileges for whites bought from natives, 1162 et seq.; use of military force, 1166 et seq., 1172, 1192; native rights respected, 1173; opinions of white commentators concerning, 1409 et seq.; *see also "Indians," sub-captions "Sovereignty" and "Treaties."*

Caucasian Attitude Toward: Popular: lands coveted, 60, 69, 468; manner of land purchase, 61; comparative hospitality, 63; contemporary Caucasian accounts of, 64, 1409 et seq.; beliefs regarding race relations, 68; death of Logan's family, 77; fear of attack, 159; effect of missionary reports, 224; importance of Iroquois territory, 311; ill treatment, 431, 450, 456, 458, 462, 466 note, 530; use of liquor, 62, 431, 435, 436, 457, 469, 471, 473, 481; white traders' practices, 450, 454, 469 et seq., 474, 477 et seq., 504, 551; misconception of native character, 548; arrogance, 549; growth of interest in, 1195 et seq.; result of Caucasian contact with, 1235; agreement of Mormons with, 1261; during construction of transcontinental railroad, 1351; statements of white commentators regarding, 1409 et seq.; native aspirations defended, 1416.

Character, Aboriginal Customs: water travel preferred, 18; overland paths, 19, 20; speed of runners, 20; canoe making, 21; manner of fishing, 40; dog-sleds, 51; abhorrence of deceit, 62; personal accountability, 62; native qualities, 64 et seq., 469, 485, 543, 547; frugal of game, 434; voting in council, 442; tribal obligations, 474, 504; attitude toward traitors, 531, 605; effect of early Spanish cruelties, 547, 551; mental processes, 549; communal kindness, 550, 568; absence of crime, 551, 1408.

Civilization: new order of life adopted, 418, 506, 514, 1410; helped by white contact, 436, 453, 503, 504, 506, 512, 514, 518 et seq., 524 et seq., 536, 544, 570, 572, 574, 604, 1417 et seq.; hurt by white contact, 425, 430, 431 et seq., 454, 481, 517 et seq., 524, 543, 572, 601, 608, 1410, 1412 et seq.; Caucasian religion adopted, 436, 438, 522, 525, 551, 566, 567, 570, 574, 605, 1411; religion a cause of race misunderstanding, 546; military compulsion by whites not useful in advancing, 551; artizans, farmers, manufacturers, 436, 452, 453, 454, 459, 506, 513, 522, 525, 526, 528, 537, 545, 570, 572, 574, 1411; education sought, 482, 520, 525, 528, 570, 572, 1411, 1418; race contact in South, 485; natives live in houses, 536, 572, 574, 608; advancement mentioned in treaty, 570, 604; effect of native progress on later Caucasian interest in western Indians and Oregon question, 1195.

1501

INDEX

Indians—*Continued.*

Laws, Resolutions, Memorials, Concerning: for removal to West, 437, 562; forbidding advice to, 440, 495; asking consent for road, 445; on liquor trade, 472, 473; defining native society, 496, 498 et seq.; regulating race association, travel, extradition, 495, 510; claiming sovereignty over and lands of, 534, 537, 538; against native movement, 537; against native government, 538, 553, 554; removing legal rights, 538; admitting white encroachments, 553; characterized by Jackson, 576.

Sovereignty: Federal acknowledgment of, 81, 419 et seq., 426 et seq., 486, 492, 495, 503, 513, 514, 517, 533, 542, 562, 569, 594; Federal opposition to, 518 et seq., 555, 558, 565, 582; state acknowledgment of, 508, 510, 552, 594; state hostility toward, 532, 534, 552, 555, 564, 566, 575, 586, 588, 594; geographical extent of, 424, 427, 429, 485 et seq.; government, 80, 525, 526, 528, 534, 536, 537, 546, 559, 563, 566, 572, 574, 590, 594, 604, 1417; native jurisdiction over Caucasians, 427, 429, 491, 525, 1412; Caucasian problems created by, 486 et seq., 491, 511, 539, 556, 593, 602; white violation of, 491, 510, 553, 558, 593, 605; Wirt's opinion on, 559; *see also, "Indians," sub-captions "Treaties" and "Caucasian Attitude Toward: Governmental."*

Travel Privileges Granted by: In General: on Ohio River, 78; native consent necessary, 419, 422, 424, 500; in Ohio and Indiana, 444; white use of, 456; consistently sought, 513. Specific Routes or Privileges: in Northwest Territory, 428; Michigan Road, 446; in Tennessee, 491; on Tennessee River, 491; Kentucky Road, 492; Natchez Road, 494; in Tennessee and Alabama, 500; for Federal postal service, 502; for horse path, 502; for roads, by Choctaws, 503; Unicoy Road, 507; on roads and rivers in Georgia, Tennessee and Mississippi, 511; for canal in Indiana, 835. In West: in general, 1175; telegraph lines permitted by natives, 1178, 1180; ferries and inns established by native consent, 1180; Indians paid to remove from travel routes, 1181; Santa Fé Trail, 445, 1137, 1165, 1166, 1171, 1172, 1229. Specific Privileges Gained by Treaty: from Apache, 1176; Arapaho, 1176, 1184; Arikara, 1176; Assiniboin, 1176; Blackfeet, 1178; Cherokees, 1165, 1184; Cheyenne, 1176, 1184; Chickasaws, 1178, 1182; Choctaws, 1165, 1178, 1182; Comanche, 1165, 1176, 1182, 1184; Crows, 1176; Delawares, 1184; Flatheads, 1178; Grosventres, 1176; Kickapoo, 1178; Kiowa, 1165, 1176, 1182, 1184; Mandans, 1176; Navahos, 1176; Omaha, 1178; Osage, 1165, 1181; Pawnees, 1164; Quapaw, 1165; Senecas, 1165; Shawnees, 1178; Shoshoni, 1180; Shoshoni-Goship, 1181; Sioux, 1164, 1176, 1180, 1184; Utes, 1176; Wichita, 1165.

Treaties: In General: Fort Pitt, 73; Fort Stanwix, 76; Dunmore's, 78; Greenville, 83, 422, 426, 428, 431, 437, 456, 1415; with Wautaga, 116; with Henderson, 135; how negotiated, 420, 488; Fort Wayne, 437; only method of race compact, 486, 503; violated by whites, 491, 532; violated by natives, 605; Caucasian instructions concerning, 495, 558; fraudulent, 531; Holstein, 594. Specific Treaties: with Cherokees, 491, 492, 500, 502, 507, 510, 511, 540, 604; Chickasaws, 494, 601; Chippewas, 444, 449; Choctaws, 494, 502, 505, 512, 569; Creeks, 502, 511, 531, 532, 533, 601; Delawares, 73, 437; Iroquois, 72, 73; Kansa, 445; Kaskaskias, 438; Menomonies, 449; Miamis, 449, 835; Osage, 445; Ottawas, 444; Potawatomi, 444, 446, 449, 477; Sacs and Foxes, 449, 455, 468; Seminoles, 601; Senecas, 444; Shawnees, 73, 449 et seq.; Winnebagos, 449; Wyandots, 444, 454; Kansa, 1165; Sioux, 1167, 1181; Cheyennes, 1167.

Wars and Warfare: inter-tribal, for territory, 59; with whites, 66 et seq.; under European flags, 70; Iroquois aid English, 70; French and Indian,

INDEX

73; Pontiac's, 73, 195; Dunmore's, 76 et seq., 133; Revolution, 78 et seq., 151; Fallen Timbers, 83, 418; with Wautaga, 116; inter-tribal, 138; Braddock's defeat, 196; Tippecanoe, 444; Thames, 444; Black Hawk's, 444, 446, 455, 458 et seq.; Bad Axe, 462; abandoned against Caucasian advance, 488; self-defense permitted by treaty, 570; Georgia's attitude equivalent to, 593.

See also names of tribes and of individual Indians.

Inns, *see "Taverns."*

Insurance, on Ohio River packet boats, 304.

Iowa City, 1204, 1206.

Iowas: deliver up murderers, 504; mentioned, 1173.

Iroquois: clearings of, 18; well organized, 60; hold deceit in abhorrence, 62; position of toward French and English, 70, 72; treaties with, 72, 73; mentioned, 311.

Jackson, Andrew: on Shawnee treaty, 452; on Black Hawk campaign, 466; appeal to by Potawatomi, 478; frames Choctaw treaty, 512, 517; defines position on Indian problem, 539; enters presidency, 552; utterances of on Indian problem, 555, 562, 568, 579; southern natives fight under, 568; urges Chickasaw migration, 572, 575; attitude of in Tassel case, 590; attitude in Worcester case, 596; attitude toward South Carolina, 597; secures treaties, 601; uses army against Cherokees, 605; character of, 611; attitude toward National Road, 712-715; declines free coach, 737; speed attained by message of, 754; interested in far West, 1200, 1214, 1215.

Jackson, David, fur trader, 1214.

Jacksonville, Ill., 1077.

Jamaica, L. I., 35.

James, Edwin, discusses race troubles, 1412.

James River, 144, 773.

Jefferson, Thomas: writes Declaration in tavern, 214; on Indian sovereignty, 492; letter to Cherokees, 503, 514, 601; message, 504; effect of his policy on natives, 506; attitude toward National Road, 692, 697, 708.

Jeffersonville, 838.

Jennings, Governor, on canals, 826.

Jersey City, 383, 994, 1115.

John Bull, early locomotive, 978, 992, 1042.

Johnson, Justice, opinion of in Cherokee case, 592.

Johnson, Overton, Oregon emigrant, 1167, 1169, 1230, 1231, 1232, 1234, 1235.

Johnson, Thomas, visited by Fitch, 237, 238.

Johnstown, Pa., 788, 794, 798, 799.

Jouffroy, M. de, French steamboat inventor, 349, 363.

Julesburg, 1352.

Juliana, Hudson River ferry boat, 882.

Junction, 870.

Juniata River, 786.

Kalamazoo, 1083.

Kalm, Peter, mentions frauds on natives, 62.

Kane, Elisha, 1253.

Kane, Thomas, accompanies Mormons, 1253, 1254, 1256, 1257, 1258, 1260, 1264, 1268, 1269.

Kansa, treaty with, 445.

Kaskaskia, 149, 653.

Kaskaskias: desire half of annuity spent for farming implements and stock, 436; treaty with, 438.

1503

INDEX

Kearny, Colonel Philip, 1168, 1169.
Keel-Boat: construction, 281; origin, use, 282, 301, 307; modifications of, 282; migrations by, 288; first sleeping bunks, 302; used by Schultz, 334, 337; method of navigating shallow streams by, 336; customs of passengers, 338; cost, 338; on rivers of Ohio, 338; ancestor of canal boat, 848; on Missouri River, 1141.
Kellogg, ——, Illinois pioneer, 653.
Kellogg's Trail, opening of, 653, 654.
Kensington, 260.
Kent, Chief Justice, of New York, decision of in steamboat case, 385.
Kenton, Simon, mentioned, 674.
Kentucky *Gazette,* 164.
Kentucky River, 134, 140, 432.
Key West, reaches Fort Benton, 1159.
Kickapoos: grant right of way to railroad, 1178; mentioned, 436, 1173.
Kiowas: in Texas, 1172; grant travel privileges, 1165, 1176, 1182, 1184.
Kirtland, Ohio, 1240.
Kiskiminitas River, 786, 880.
Kittanning River, 76.
Knight, John, Boston ferryman, 43.
Knight, Jonathan, civil engineer, 952.
Knight, Mistress, trip of, 55, 1359.
Knox, General Henry: on race relations, 491; Jefferson's letter to, 492.
Knoxville, 496, 502, 1119.
Krudener, Baron, Russian Minister, 949.

La Barge, Joseph, pioneer steamboatman, 1147, 1150, 1156, 1157, 1158, 1369.
Lackawanna River, 798.
Lafayette, 840, 841, 842, 843, 1120, 1124, 1230.
Lancashire, 352.
Lancaster, Ohio, 321.
Lancaster, Pa., 746, 1114.

LAND: LAND PROBLEMS

In General: relation of to national affairs, 419, 425; how bought, 420; Caucasian purposes in relation to, 518 et seq.; price paid for native, 615, 1406, 1407; attitude of South toward use of governmental, 1340; early transactions of Federal government in, 1405 et seq.
Disputes: Among Federal and State governments over boundaries, 72; between whites and natives, 432, 508, 564; among natives, 478; over Georgia's land cession, 500, 520, 534; over cessions to states or corporations, 827; over Northwest as common property of all states, 827, 1094.
Encroachments: In General: native alarm over, 73; deductions drawn by natives from character of white caravans, 131; condemned by Harrison, 432; described by Knox, 491; admitted by Georgia, 510; threatened by Georgia, 534; mentioned by Jackson, 576; in Georgia, 587 et seq.; natives recompensed for in treaty, 605; in far West, 1153, 1173, 1175, 1186, 1194. Specific: on territory of Cherokees by Boone's party, 130; on Cherokee land, by settlers, 491; on Cherokee land by gold seekers, 559; on Creeks by Georgia, 532; on Chickasaws in Mississippi, 553, 572; on Choctaws in Mississippi, 553; on Sacs and Foxes, 455, 466 note.
Native Proprietorship: character of, 58; considered at Fort Pitt, 73; acknowledged west of Alleghanies, 73; in South, 486 et seq., 500; law regarding, 496; discussed by Adams, 542; maintained by Cherokees,

INDEX

INDEX

INDEX

INDEX

Miami and Erie Canal: begun, 822; dimensions, 824; effect of, 828; travel on, 870, 1064.
Miamis: hunt in Kentucky, 138; mentioned by Harrison, 434, 435; treaty with, 449; endeavor to become civilized, 482; their town of Ke-ki-on-ga, 651; grant permission to build a canal, 835.
Michaux, F. A., travels in interior, 324.
Michigan Central Railroad, opened, 1082.
Michigan, Lake: roadway from to Wabash River ceded by Indians, 448; native path from Rock River to, 653; Pacific Railroad from proposed, 1324, 1327; mentioned, 427, 446, 448, 1321.
Michigan Road: importance of, 448; relation of to Indian problems, 468; right to use granted by natives, 477, 492; mentioned, 494, 1074.
Middleton, Conn., 722.
Middleton, N. Y., 1116.
Middleton, Ohio, 822.
Middleton, Pa., 774, 802.
Mifflin, Thomas: Fitch's letter to, 243; rides on steamboat, 254.
Migrations: early population movements, 33 et seq.; see also "Mormons," "Overland Emigrants," "West" and "White Americans," sub-caption "Early Population Movements."
Milford, Conn., 722.
Military and Naval Magazine, 465.
Milk River, 1159.
Mill Creek, 1267.
Millar, Patrick, steamboat inventor, 350, 363.
Miller, Joseph, Indian agent, 1158.
Mills, John, stage driver, 764.
Milwaukee, 1109, 1120.
Minneapolis, 1365.
Mississinewa, 446.
Mississippi River: a gateway for travel, 25; not a factor in development of American travel system during its European control, 96; Virginia claims territory to, 131, 247; Fitch thinks his steamboat adapted to navigation of, 234, 260; Fitch plans to put boats upon under patronage of Spain, 258; arks popular upon, 284; navigation of dangerous to flatboats, 296; banks of often undermined, 300; boats upon, 308; Fulton suggests use of steamboats upon, 366; first steamboats upon, 386, 387, 388, 389, 394, 396; National Road to, 692, 700, 704; first steamboat on upper waters of, 758; proposal to join Great Lakes with, 826, 846; reached by railroad, 871; linked by rail with Atlantic coast, 1090, 1093, 1095; number of steamers plying upon, 1097; Mormons cross, 1243, 1244, 1246, 1250; encamped on its banks, 1252; mentioned, 17, 26, 58, 84, 224, 266, 286, 291, 307, 323, 339, 416, 419, 425, 427, 429, 430, 432, 437, 438, 449, 455, 458, 459, 462, 465, 468, 470, 478, 481, 486, 498, 504, 512, 513, 514, 520, 522, 524, 525, 532, 550, 556, 557, 651, 677, 803, 832, 1074, 1076, 1079, 1089, 1123, 1124, 1125, 1126, 1128, 1130, 1133, 1135, 1136, 1137, 1138, 1141, 1144, 1149, 1162, 1170, 1172, 1173, 1195, 1197, 1215, 1237, 1240, 1242, 1252, 1257, 1261, 1270, 1321, 1334, 1335, 1338.
Mississippi Valley, *see sub-caption under "Pioneer Life of Caucasians."*
Missouri River: early steam navigation of, 1126, 1133, 1146 et seq.; timber and skin boats of, 1136, 1139, 1140, 1141, 1143, 1144, 1150; as an early route to far West, 1139 et seq., 1171; erratic course and habits of, 1149; relation of to Oregon question and affairs, 1195; Mormons live in bottoms of, 1263, 1267; Samuel Parker follows, 1322; mentioned, 1125, 1166, 1190, 1192, 1194, 1218, 1253, 1261, 1271, 1321.

INDEX

Mitchell, Gusty, tavern character, 730.
Mitchell, Israel, Indiana pioneer, 758.
Mobile, 96, 1086, 1087, 1119, 1123.
Mobile River, 502, 514.
Mohawk and Hudson Railroad: building of, 965 et seq.; departure of first train on announced by blast on horn, 1008.
Mohawk River, 70, 71, 282, 311, 312, 315, 335, 696, 776, 777.
Mohegans, fate of mentioned, 556.
Monongahela River, 160, 806.
Monopoly: first in transportation facilities, 176; *see also "Companies," "Rail-roads," "Steamboats."*
Monroe, James: appealed to by Fulton, 366; 367; on Indian problem, 513 et seq., 528, 532, 546; attitude toward National Road, 701, 702, 704, 705, 706, 710, 712, 811, 891; on Federal aid to canals, 810, 811; mentioned, 1163.
Monroe, Ohio, 1109.
Monterey, 1277.
Montgomery, Ala., 1119, 1122, 1123.
Monthly Magazine (of England), 352, 354.
Montreal, 1116.
Moore, James, introduces periodicity in travel and transportation, 180 et seq.
Morey, Samuel, steamboat inventor, 351, 352, 361, 363, 369.
Morgantown, N. C., 328.
Mormons: migration of did not disturb natives, 1170, 1171; origin of, 1238; early history of, 1240; flight of from Nauvoo, 1243, 1256; pilgrimage of, 1247 et seq.; Kane's description of march, 1253 et seq.; treatment of by Indians, 1261; the Mormon Trail, 1266; reach Great Salt Lake, 1267; reception of California emigrants by, 1268, 1269.
Mormon Station, 1314.
Morris, Robert, work of for public improvements, 785.
Morrison, W. W., military commander, 633.
Morrow, Governor, inaugurates canal, 822.
Morse, Jedediah, report of on Indians, 1409.
Morse, Samuel F. B., electrician, 1047.
Motor Cars, effect of on highway building, 277, 1364.
Mount Carbon, Pa., 773, 867.
Mount Pisgah, 1248.
Mount Vernon, 273, 776.
Mountain Meadow, 1269.
Munden, 349.
Muskingum River, 816.
Mystic, 28.

Napoleon, sells Louisiana, 1136.
Narragansetts, fate of mentioned, 556.
Nashua, N. H., 880.
Nashville, 156, 157, 328, 609, 800, 1119, 1124.
Natchez, 392, 393, 431, 494, 650, 1087.
Natchez Road, origin of, 494.
National Road, *see sub-caption under "Roads," also "On National Road," under caption "Stage-Coaches."*
Nauvoo, Mormons at, 1242, 1243, 1244, 1247, 1248, 1250, 1252, 1253, 1254, 1256, 1263, 1268.
Navahos, grant travel privileges, 1176.
Needham, 1001, 1002.

1509

INDEX

Neponset, 880.
New Albany, Ind., 1301, 1308.
New Amsterdam, *see "New York."*
Newark, N. J., 35, 995, 1115.
New Brunswick, N. J., 52, 182, 888, 995, 1115.
New Brunswick and Trenton Railroad, length of, 1115.
New Buffalo, Mich., 1082.
Newbury, Mass., 36.
Newcastle, Pa., 1028.
Newcastle and Frenchtown Railroad, how trains were stopped on, 1028.
New Echota, 551, 605, 1418.
New England: early conditions in, 28 et seq., 172; mass migrations from, 34
    et seq., 94, 97; severity of theocratic rule in, 45; compared with South,
    84 et seq., 104, 220 et seq.; route to interior from, 159; land travel to
    northern, 186; early laws of, 208 et seq.; movement from to Susque-
    hanna region, 222 et seq., 312, 313; steam engines in, 241; first steam-
    boats in, 404 et seq.; angered at New York's steamboat laws, 407; early
    progress of compared, 526, 650; canals of, 846; travel facilities from,
    1097; interest of in Oregon affairs, 1200, 1219; *see also "Railroads."*
New Haven, 28, 34, 35, 250, 407, 408, 753.
New Jersey, at Baltimore, 398.
New Jersey Railroad, mentioned, 1115.
New London, 28, 407, 408.
New Orleans: a prize of European warfare, 96; time required to make round
    trip to from Ohio, 307; cost of trip from Pittsburgh to, 338; first
    steamboat reaches, 392, 393; other early steamboats at, 394, 395; time
    required to reach by steamboat from Cincinnati, 625; first railroads at,
    1086, 1087; mentioned, 300, 431, 502, 525, 1092, 1097, 1119, 1122, 1123,
    1355.
New Orleans: first steamboat on the Mississippi, 389; construction and
    speed of, 392, 393.
Newport, R. I., 28, 404, 405, 407, 408, 410, 1016.
Newton, Mass., 999, 1000, 1001.
New Town, 32.
New Town, Cherokee Nation, 525.
New York City, *including New Amsterdam:* travel from to Boston and
    Philadelphia common by 1783, 42; has a number of wheeled vehicles in
    1797, 48; one of chief centers of activity in the North, 52; trip of Mis-
    tress Knight to, 55, 1359; aeroplane flight from to Philadelphia, 53;
    wheeled traffic between and Philadelphia, 177, 179; stage-boat to Am-
    boy, 182; stage-coaches to Philadelphia, 184, 187; stage-coaches to Bos-
    ton from, 188; prices of certain commodities in, 219; Fitch in, 234, 252,
    261, 352; time required to go to and from various other cities, 324, 329,
    334; hardships of trip from to western settlements, 339; *Clermont's* voy-
    age from, 341, 344, 367, 368, 369; other early steamboats at, 351, 355, 356,
    361, 383, 397, 398, 402, 405, 407, 408, 414; early canals and, 777, 778, 783;
    early railroads and, 903, 948, 956, 960, 976, 984, 985, 987, 990, 995, 996,
    1005, 1015, 1016, 1036, 1037, 1045, 1082, 1087, 1108, 1110, 1113, 1115, 1116,
    1119, 1120; Marcus Whitman visits, 1219; transcontinental and, 1321,
    1324, 1325, 1335, 1355; mentioned, 9, 30, 35, 175, 201, 335, 360, 368, 388,
    396, 412, 677, 746, 750, 751, 753, 756, 759, 800, 888, 952, 994, 1026, 1097,
    1188.
New York *American,* 916.
New York and Harlem: opening of, 976, 984; an early car on, 1015, 1016.
New York Bay, 25, 59, 176, 412, 783, 991, 992.

PIONEER LIFE OF CAUCASIANS

INDEX

INDEX

York and Philadelphia, 52, 175, 182; in the South, 85, 103, 220; on Boone's Wilderness Road, 137, 142 et seq.; to Tennessee, 157; relation of land and water routes, 158 et seq.; from interior to East, 163; to Susquehanna region, 222, 226, 227, 312, 319; to Northwest Territory, 269; by timber boats, 280, 288, 296; to interior from East before age of steam, 339; through Indian possessions, 419, 421, 424, 427 et seq., 491, 492, 494, 500, 510, 604; due to native sovereignty, 485; passports necessary, 495, 496, 497, 510; *see also "West."*

Mississippi Valley Conditions: In General: popular attention directed toward, 322; investigated, 323 et seq.; big trees, 327; cotton and paroquets in Ohio, 330; the region linked to East, 427, 429; race antagonism, 431 et seq., 633; acquirement of title to country, 437 et seq.; white immigration, 456, 648; natives outmatched, 468; fur trade, 469 et seq.; development of region, 621 et seq., 656 et seq.; better transportation facilities demanded, 630, 826; economic importance of horse, 647, 663; improved security for travellers, 648; political feeling, 670; social conditions, 678; inhabitants confronted by new needs, 684 et seq. Contemporary Accounts of: Michaux's, 324 et seq.; Cuming's, 329 et seq.; Smith's, 657 et seq. Early Government: an oligarchy, 631 et seq.; first elections, 639; Indiana Territory decrees, 642 et seq.; relation of Federal Congress to, 646; District of Louisiana, 647; Michigan created, 647; taxation methods, 657; campaigning for office, 660. Character and Qualities of People: fond of music, 332; careless of native rights, 456, 471, 1192; intolerant of authority, 459, 501; outspoken, 478, 501; self-estimation, 621 et seq.; ignorant of outside world, 627, 661, 677, 682, 689; rough, cruel, 637, 677; fond of liquor, 641, 677, 822; ostentation disliked, 661; knowledge of near-by regions desired, 663; enjoyment of practical joking, 675; character formation, 681 et seq. Popular Customs, Methods, Habits: highway acquaintanceship, 326, 331; wasteful of game, 434, 476; obtaining homesteads, 639; amusements, 659; court scenes and judicial procedure, 667 et seq. Outward Personality of Pioneers: masculine costume of cloth fabrics, 664, 666; costume of skins, 667. Speech and Writings of Pioneers: examples of, 431, 633, 657, 659, 660, 661, 663, 664, 667, 668, 669, 670, 672, 677, 834. Inter-Relations of Whites: farmers hospitable, 331; need of oligarchy recognized, 633; bandits suppressed, 649; *see also "Laws in General," subcaption "Of Northwest Territory."* Popular Attitude Toward Natives: unfriendly, unfair, 431 et seq., 633, 643, 672, 674; friendly, just, 660, 674, 675. Pioneer Travel Routes: French Creek, 338; Scioto and Sandusky Rivers, 338; granted by natives, 428; Michigan Road, 446; Indiana system of, 651; Illinois system of, 653; *see also "Roads."* Difficulty of Travel: descriptions of extensive trips, 324 et seq., 329 et seq., 660; utility of freshets, 336; infrequency of communication with East, 646; hewing a trace, 652. Horseback Travel: instances of, 325, 327, 331, 660, 662; necessity of, 647, 657. Pedestrian Travel: through Kentucky, 327; through Ohio, 331; knapsack, 331. Canoe Travel: down the Ohio, 326; from St. Louis to Pittsburgh, 330; crossing a river, 660. Wheeled Vehicles: chaises appear, 657; *for other phases of life or travel in Mississippi valley see "Boats," "Canals," "Flatboatmen," "Indians," "Land," "Packmen," "Railroads," "Stage-Coach Drivers," "Steamboats," "Wagonmen."*

Planters: character of southern development, 87; social cleavage, 89; leadership of in society, 90; work and diversions of, 91; Washington as a type of, 92; entertainment of travellers and strangers by, 220.

Pittsburgh: Pioneer Fast Line, 13; Bullitt leads his men to, 132; early trail

INDEX

INDEX

1517

INDEX

INDEX

state for use of, 792, 1072; theories regarding construction of, 920, 921;
theories regarding use of, 931, 932, 933, 1395; first for steam power,
960; unequal to traffic demands, 1054; how built, 792, 795, 878, 880, 923,
926, 927, 928, 946, 947, 998, 999, 1003, 1067, 1072; inclined planes as part
of, 791, 795, 876, 878, 955, 965, 1070; trestlework, 878, 926, 955.
Springs, 985, 1013, 1014, 1021.
Tickets, Passes, 1001, 1036 et seq., 1108.
Time Tables, Schedules, 932, 950, 1001, 1005, 1033, 1034, 1039, 1059, 1060,
1067, 1077, 1078, 1112 et seq.
Train Crews: engineer, 968, 970, 1024, 1025, 1026, 1027, 1030, 1060, 1069;
captain, master of the cars, superintendent, conductor, 969, 1001, 1006,
1016, 1024, 1025, 1039, 1046, 1059, 1060; authority of captain estab-
lished, 1026, 1028; brakemen, firemen, station agents, other employees,
1028, 1030, 1031, 1032, 1034, 1037, 1045, 1059, 1060.
Wheels, 791, 878, 933, 952, 956, 980, 985, 1012, 1013, 1014, 1015, 1018, 1028,
1077.
*See also names of specific roads and tabular lists of early roads, 1382 et
seq. and 1393.*
Railroad Journal, 985, 988.
Rails, *see sub-caption under "Railroads."*
Raisin River, 479.
Raleigh, 1084, 1085.
Raleigh and Gaston Railroad, origin of, 1085.
Rapidan River, 144.
Raritan, built by Fulton, 379.
Raritan River, 35, 36, 186, 995.
Ray, Governor, of Indiana, favors railroads, 1070.
Read, Nathan, American inventor, 363.
Reading, 774, 802, 866, 867.
Red Clay, 605.
Redhawk, accompanies Cornstalk, 80.
Redstone, 160, 270.
Reno, 1282.
Report to the Secretary of War, by Morse, quoted, 1409.
Revolution, effects of on public thought and action, 3, 78, 228, 310, 312.
Reynolds, Governor, of Illinois, acts against Black Hawk, 460.
Richmond, 160, 220, 238, 753, 772, 878, 1084, 1119, 1122.
Richmond, Fredericksburg and Potomac Railroad, description of, 1084.
Rio Grande River, 1133.
Rittenhouse, David, writes about Fitch's boat, 250.

Roads, Paths, Tote-Roads, Traces, Trails

In General: native trails the basis of Caucasian overland routes, 19; result of northern habits on road creation, 172; establishment of periodicity in commercial traffic on, 173, 175, 179, 180, 186, 190; poor condition of, 177, 191, 192, 193, 657, 746, 752, 1112; effective construction
methods unknown, 193; opposition to improvement of, 194; early
American, compared with European, 334; more needed in South, 492,
506; how made, 718, 720, 752; insufficient to interior, 825; controlled
by railroad, 995; no widespread improvement in modern, 1368; *see also*
"*Laws.*"
Bison Streets: observed by Bullitt, 132; adopted by white men, 133, 1091;
followed in Kentucky by Boone, 140; used by Henderson, 155.
Indian Trails: nature of, 19; prevalence, 20; used by whites, 21, 651, 653,
659, 1091; improvement of, 29; Old Connecticut Path, 32, 159; link

1519

INDEX

Roads, Paths, etc.—*Continued.*

principal towns, 42; across New Jersey, 52, 991, 994, 1367 caption; used by backwoodsmen, 103; changed to roads, 120; Warriors' Path, 139, 152, 156; Logan's Kentucky route, 155; along Cumberland River, 156; Catskill Turnpike an illustration of growth from, 320; in Indiana, 651; in Illinois, 653.

Made by Caucasians: *not including National Road:* first, 29; need of more, 42; between Delaware River towns, 53; from Boston to Philadelphia, 53; in South, 89; to Pittsburgh, 132, 696; Boone's Wilderness Road, 136 et seq.; political effect of Wilderness Road, 149; travel over Boone's road, 151, 152, 155, 156, 159, 162, 163, 166; highways joining Boone's road, 151; junction point on Boone's road, 153; into Tennessee, 154, 156, 496, 694; from Boone's road to Louisville, Vincennes and St. Louis, 154; through Pennsylvania, 160, 316; from Baltimore to Redstone, 160, 696; through Virginia, 160; corduroy, 195; Braddock's, 196, 198, 200; from New England to Susquehanna River, 224, 313, 316, 319; from east to Northwest Territory, 270; turnpikes, 277; in interior New York, 314; Zane's Trace, 331; from Presque Isle, 336; Santa Fé Trail, 445, 1137, 1165, 1166, 1171, 1172, 1229; Michigan Road, 448, 477, 494, 1074; relation of to Indian problem, 468; travel over permitted by natives, 492; Natchez Road, 494; Unicoy Road, 507; in Georgia, Tennessee and Mississippi, 511; first in Northwest Territory, 641, 648; Berry Trace, 651; Whetzel Trace, 651; Kellogg's Trail, 653, 654; in Ohio, 654; in Pennsylvania, 786; improving in South, 1120; Boone's Lick road, 1136, 1208; made by Mormons, 1248, 1267; Hastings' Cut-off, 1280; Sublette's Cut-off, 1305.

Made by Consent of Indians, *see "Indians," sub-caption "Travel Privileges Granted by."*

National Road: importance of, 449, 494; needed by West, 630; economic, legal, financial and political review of, 691 et seq., 1091, 1113, 1330; relation of to Federal railroad policy, 704 et seq., 890; effect of on public opinion, 828; used by emigrants to interior, 1064; monument to Clay on, 1091, 1094; *see also "Laws" and "Stage-coaches."*

Of Middle West: Schultz' comment on, 755; in Chicago, 756; in Indiana, 756; regular communication with East over, 758 et seq.; effect of travel on, 762.

Pack-Train Trails: from South to Philadelphia, 153; improvement of opposed, 193, 277; pack-horse transportation an organized business, 194; importance of pack-trains to outlying regions, 198; nature and appearance of, 199, 200; reason for Pennsylvania's extensive system of, 202; to Northwest Territory, 270; course of adopted by railroad, 1067.

Roanoke, 1086.

Roanoke River, 1084, 1085.

Robb, Alexander, early engraver, 1013.

Robertson, Chief Justice, of Kentucky, describes Wilderness Road, 166.

Rochester, 744, 781, 1109, 1324.

Rockcastle River, 140, 162.

Rocket, early locomotive, 904, 999, 1016.

Rock River, 653.

Rocky Mountains: Lewis and Clark cross, 1133; J. S. Smith travels from to California, 1194; deemed by many to be impassable, 1215; Mormons pass beyond, 1237, 1246; Parker crosses, 1322, 1323; transcontinental railroad passes through, 1328, 1352, 1353; mentioned, 550, 1095, 1138, 1141, 1167, 1172, 1189, 1206, 1221, 1234, 1271, 1321.

Rogers, James, mentioned, 1421.

INDEX

Rogues River, 1235.
Rome, N. Y., 778, 779, 780.
Roosevelt, Nicholas J., steamboat inventor and builder, 359, 360, 361, 363, 369, 386, 390, 399, 400, 402, 1369.
Ross, John, a leader of the Cherokees, 559, 563, 1421.
Route Across the Rocky Mountains, quoted, 1230 et seq.
Rumsey, James, steamboat inventor, 250, 349, 357, 359, 362.
Rumseyian Society, purpose and activities of, 252.
Runcorn, England, 352.
Rush, Richard, letter of on Chesapeake and Ohio Canal, 814.
Rushville, Ill., 1310.
Russell, David, Indian negotiator for Georgia, 507.

Sacramento, 1313, 1318, 1350, 1353, 1355.
Sacs and Foxes: mentioned by Harrison, 436; treaties with, 449, 455, 468; in Black Hawk War, 460 et seq.; surrender criminals, 504; mentioned, 619, 653.
Sailing Craft: introduction of, 28; varieties, 28; use, 29; fortified against attack, 87; preferred to stage wagons, 187; few in Pennsylvania, 202; on Hudson, 312; from South to North by, 324, 752, 753, 1119; used by Schultz, 334, 335; fight introduction of steamboats, 345, 396, 405, 408, 410; popular on Atlantic coast, 405.
St. Augustine, 1119.
St. Charles, Mo., 1137, 1150.
St. Clair, Arthur: member Northwest Territory oligarchy, 634, 639; mentioned, 674.
St. Francisville, Miss., 1087.
St. Joseph, Mich., 1082.
St. Joseph, Mo., 1301.
St. Joseph River, 1082.
St. Lawrence River, 25.
St. Louis: a little settlement in the far interior, 96; path prolonged to, 156; arrival of boats at from upper Mississippi, 308; National Road and, 692, 717; stage lines to, 759, 762; packet-boat travel to, 799, 800; early railroads to, 1087-1095; four days from Pittsburgh by boat, 1097; fares to from various points, 1118, 1119, 1120, 1124; sale of salt to early inhabitants of, 1136; steamboat between and Leavenworth, 1146; connection with Oregon travel, 1190, 1192, 1195, 1196, 1215, 1216, 1229; Overland Mail to San Francisco, 1319; transcontinental railroad and, 1322, 1334, 1335, 1336, 1355, 1365; mentioned, 12, 262, 330, 756, 758, 1133, 1150, 1153, 1268.
St. Louis *Times,* 465.
St. Peter River, 550.
Salem, Mass., 28, 404.
Salt Lake City, 1268, 1306, 1318.
San Antonio, 677.
San Diego, 1194.
Sandusky, early locomotive, 1065, 1070.
Sandusky, 404, 654, 1064, 1065, 1067, 1083, 1109.
Sandusky River, 339, 428.
San Francisco: prophecy of rapid transit to, 1095; United States covets bay of, 1200, 1333; words of alcalde of quoted, 1272; Overland Mail to, 1319; celebration of transcontinental at, 1355, 1359; mentioned, 1229.
San Francisco, Bay of, 1112, 1200.
Sangamon, 1079.

INDEX

1522

INDEX

Smith, John, English steamboat inventor, 352, 363.
Smith, Joseph, founder of Mormon church, 1240, 1244.
Smith, Oliver H., Indiana pioneer, 660, 661, 666, 667, 669, 670, 672, 674, 675, 676, 1048, 1050, 1369.
Smith, Provost, of Princeton College, writes a letter for Fitch, 234.
Smith, Solomon, introduces periodicity in travel and transportation, 180 et seq.
Snag, Joe, Mississippi boatman, 677.
Snow, Erastus, Mormon leader, 1267.
Snow, Lorenzo, Mormon leader, 1264.
Snyder, Colonel, pioneer blacksmith, 200.
Social Conditions, *see "Pioneer Life of Caucasians."*
Society for Promoting the Improvement of Roads and Inland Navigation, work of, 784.
Sonoma, 1277, 1278.
Southampton, L. I., 35.
Spalding, H. H., missionary, 1199, 1230, 1232.
Spotswood, N. J., 994.
Springfield, Ill., 1076, 1077, 1124, 1276.
Springfield, Mass., 30, 32, 1116.
Springfield, Ohio, 654, 1065, 1091.

STAGE-COACHES

In General: last used in far West, 8; a pioneer vehicle, 12; symptoms presaging first appearance of, 185, 196, 223; everywhere subsequent to the Conestoga wagon, 202; effect on road improvement, 277; reach interior, 304, 321; of small use in interior, 329; from New England to South, 329; in Ohio, 334; from East through Wheeling to the South, 338; in opposition to steamboats, 396, 404; used in conjunction with steamboats, canals or railroads, 397, 398, 788, 790, 1005, 1097, 1105, 1110 et seq., 1122 et seq.; culminating period of, 624, 1097; grow in popularity, 662; competition between, 743; retire before railroad competition, 768, 1005; contest between coach and steam locomotive, 953; copied in building railroad cars, 955, 986, 1012, 1013, 1016, 1018, 1020, 1028, 1043; starting signal for, 1008; travel by compared with railroad travel, 1009, 1011; for use to interior, 1063, 1065, 1088; established through far West, 1318.

Cost of Travel by, 321, 322, 324, 329, 398, 739, 743, 750, 751, 760, 1110 et seq., 1119, 1122 et seq., 1319.

On National Road: first to Wheeling, 717; prominent drivers and stage tavern keepers, 718, 726, 727, 764; physical obstacles to use of, 719; extent of travel by, 720, 735; rapid movement of, 721, 726, 735; appearance and construction of, 722, 737; comfort of travel by, 724, 726, 736; Concord coaches, 724; names bestowed on, 726, 737, 738; operating companies, 727, 734; presidential trips by, 735 et seq.; accidents to, 739, 767, 768; free travel in, 739.

On Other Roads: hardships of travel by, 742; speed of, 742, 743, 749, 750, 752, 756, 759, 761, 762; in conjunction with steamboats, 743; competing for passengers, 743; use of in winter, 750, 751; accidents to, 752, 765, 1112; through Middle West and South, 758, 1119; passengers pay according to their weight, 760.

Particular trips by: New York to Philadelphia, 324; Boston to Savannah, 329; Providence to Boston, 742; Washington to Baltimore, 742; Philadelphia to Pittsburgh, 749; Boston to New York, 750; Pittsburgh to

1523

INDEX

1524

INDEX

INDEX

1526

INDEX

Ustanula River, 525.
Utes, grant travel privileges, 1176.
Utica, 334, 778, 779, 780, 781, 1010, 1080, 1109, 1120.

Vail, Aaron, interest of in steamboats, 260-262.
Van Buren, President: message of carried at high speed, 726; travels in stage-coach, 738.
Vance, Congressman, advocates aid for Shawnees, 453.
Vandalia, 715, 716.
Vanderbilt, Cornelius, steamboat proprietor, 1005.
Vanderburgh, Henry, member of Northwest Territory oligarchy, 642.
Van Twiller, Governor, advises Pilgrims, 30, 33.
Varnum, John Mitchell, member Northwest Territory oligarchy, 634.
Vermont, on Lake Champlain, 382.
Vernon, 1072.
Vesuvius, career of, 393.
Vicksburg, 1087.
Vincennes, also Fort St. Vincent, and Post Vincent: Clark's march to, 149; distance from Philadelphia to, 153; early trails to, 155, 156, 651, 759; Harrison's letter from, 430; treaty of, 438; Indian affray in, 469; government of Indiana Territory meets at, 642, 647; tax upon wheeled vehicles in, 657; horse thief whipped at, 666-668; stage lines to, 761, 762, 1088, 1089, 1119; mentioned, 479, 639, 654, 692.
Virginia, goes far up the Mississippi, 758.
Voight, Henry, assistant to Fitch, 236, 241, 253, 254.

Wabash and Erie Canal: origin, 828; begun, 830; opened, 835; failure of Indiana's plans, 836; joined to Ohio system, 839; travel on, 840, 843, 868, 1120; longest, 842; paralleled by railroad, 842; attacked by mobs, 844; abandoned, 845; family boats on, 865; scenery on, 870.
Wabash River: early canals joining, 816, 828, 829, 830, 834, 840; improvement of proposed, 1075; mentioned, 58, 149, 429, 436, 446, 449, 477, 654, 660, 1064.
Wabesepinnecon River, 465.
Wagonmen: pride of in their vehicles, 204; methods on a journey, 205; appearance of wagons, 727; life of on National Road, 728 et seq.; cigars made especially for, 740; anger of at railroads, 769.

WAGONS: WHEELED VEHICLES

Exclusive of Stage-Coaches

In General: pioneer vehicles, 12; no travel by, 29; private coaches appear, 42; method of crossing streams, 46; introduced in Delaware River towns, 53; in South, 89; Boone's road not intended for, 137; reach Tennessee, 157; on forest roads of East, 160; on Boone's road, 162, 163; first across New Jersey, 176; character and appearance of, 176, 184, 185, 186, 746; not mentioned in first ferry laws, 178; mentioned in ferry laws, 179; first periodic, 180; conditions of travel by, 182, 184; increase in use of, 182, 192; the *Flying Machine,* 184, 991; the *Flying Diligence,* 186; in New England, 186; compete with rail boats, 190; scarcity of, 196, 205, 214; place of in travel history, 275, 1063; invade Ohio, 331; troubles of on bad road, 336; appear in Indiana, 65, 659, 661; use of on Sunday, 942; railroads cause horse panics, 972.

INDEX

Wagons—*Continued*.
    Carts: introduction of, 48, 192; appearance of, 53; development from, 179; ferry charge for, 179.
    Chair: introduction, appearance of, 46; the caleche, 46.
    Chaise: introduction, appearance of, 46 et seq.; Governor Trumbull's, 48, 390; ferry charge for, 179; number of in Philadelphia, 205; in interior, 657.
    Conestoga Wagon: a pioneer vehicle, 9; evolved in Pennsylvania, 196, 201; origin of name, 202; construction and appearance of, 203, 727, 852; general use of, 204, 223; reaches interior, 304, 331; manner of travelling by, 332, 1063; on Santa Fé trail, 446; pulled by oxen, 659; on National Road, 720, 721, 727, 734, 740; between North and South, 752; across Indiana and Illinois, 763; early railroad cars resemble, 1012; used by showman, 1070; *for relation of large, canvas-covered wagons to Western overland migrations, see "Overland Emigrants."*
    Family Coach: introduction and appearance of, 46; in Connecticut, 48; ferry charge for, 179; number of in Philadelphia, 205.
Waiilatpu, 1200, 1227, 1232.
Walker, Felix, joins Boone, 138.
Walk-in-Water, first steamboat on Lake Erie, 403.
Walla Walla, mentioned, 1170, 1230.
Walla Walla River, 1199.
Wapakonetta, 450.
War of 1812: effect of on progress in travel and transportation, 752, 778, 802, 819, 825, 885.
Warrior, part of in Black Hawk War, 462.
Warriors' Path, used by Boone and other pioneers, 139, 152, 156.
Warville, Brissot de, writes of Fitch's boat, 257.
Washington, George: character of, 92; suppresses Whisky Rebellion, 198; listens to Fitch, 237; studies transportation question, 311; name considered for steamboat, 317; opinion of on Indian treaties, 613; interested in canals, 775, 776, 803; Cherokees esteem, 1419.
Washington: Shawnee delegation at, 452; Cherokee ambassadors visit, 510; stage-coach travel to and from, 739, 742, 746, 751, 756; conventions to promote Chesapeake and Ohio Canal meets in, 805, 806, 812; early railroads and, 888, 1009, 1112; mentioned, 9, 572, 662, 732, 754, 758, 759, 767, 768, 810, 949, 1091, 1092, 1094, 1150, 1175, 1228, 1355.
Washington, Pa., 768.
Washington, built by Shreve, 394, 395.
Washington Branch Railroad, mentioned, 1380.
Washington District, 491, 496.
Watertown, Mass., 32.
Watson, Elkanah, canal advocate, 775, 776, 777, 1369.
Watson's *Journal,* 775, 776.
Wautaga: a backwoods republic, 116; a settlement resembling, 289; situation of Oregon pioneers similar to that of, 1224.
Wautaga River, 115.
Wayne, Gen. Anthony: defeats Indians, 83; treaty following victory of, 426, 651, 1094; southern natives fight under, 568.
Weas, mentioned by Harrison, 434, 435.
Weaversville, Cal., 1316.
Weber River, 1308.
Webster, Daniel, argues against steamboat monopoly, 414.
Weed, Thurlow, makes stage-coach trip, 744.
Weiser, Conrad, records native opinion, 63.
Weldon, 1086.

INDEX

White Americans—*Continued.*

national preparation for future needs, 372; influence of jealousies, 374; enthusiasm over, 828, 829, 914; serious discussion of, 830, 836, 886, 900 ; telegraphic messages, 1047; patience under imposition, 1361.

Governmental Road Building, favored, 709.

Indians: *see "Indians: Caucasian Attitude Toward."*

Motor Cars, whole economic value of demanded, 1364.

Primitive Conditions and Travel Facilities: vehicles devised for personal use, 1; desire for speed, 2, 3, 184, 228, 912, 938; effects of national traits, 10; scant early records, 15, 56, 469; causes of progress, 24; spirit of restlessness, 36, 72, 172, 490, 1202; opinion regarding water travel, 40, 227; spirit of conquest, 74; result of Revolutionary outbreak, 78; lack of geographical knowledge, 118, 224, 268, 291; caution on journeys, 164; general westward advance begins, 167, 268 et seq.; sense of unity lacking, 174; sectional influences dominant, 175; effect of wars, poverty, political turmoil, 195, 229, 490; no conception of future, 228; interest regarding interior, 322 et seq.; self-admiration, 344, 626 et seq.; national character formation, 416; public needs and purposes, 418 et seq.; frontier opinion of natives, 471; Indian problem of South, 544 et seq.; Indian problem as a whole, 543, 546, 563, 598, 612 et seq.; irritation over adverse criticism, 628; social basis of modern conditions, 678 et seq.; Sunday travel, 748, 941; relations of East and interior, 803.

Railroads: importance not realized, 5; use retarded by jealousy, 9; prediction of creates laughter, 661; war diverts attention from, 886; foreseen, 908 et seq.; discussed, 914 et seq., 935; horse-power expected on, 933; sermons preached about, 939; enthusiasm over, 944, 977, 1062; steam power wanted for, 947; co-operation between desired, 975, 1101; supremacy of acknowledged, 1007, 1098; serious accidents not expected on, 1052; public pride in, 1067.

Social Change: historic landmarks, 7; situation prior to modern epoch, 12; opposition to luxury, 45, 118; color ornamentation, 47, 203, 206, 370, 405, 852; taverns and hotels, 208.

Steam and Steamboats: value not seen, 5; early monopolies and their effect, 240; Fitch's boat jeered, 241; importance recognized, 341 et seq., 371; clamor for, 347, 383; monopoly opposed, 382, 388, 407, 408; relation of steam to national unity, 384; impression produced by a steamboat, 391.

Transcontinental Railroad: favored, 1328; considered certain, 1331; Mexican War and gold discovery influence, 1332; on day of completion, 1355, 1356.

West: migrations to, 1126 et seq.; Indians and race troubles of, 1192, 1195; Oregon question, 1195, 1200, 1202; territorial conquest as expressed by Pilcher, 1215; discovery of gold, 1271 et seq.

Wheeled Vehicles; Stage-Coaches: introduction opposed, 46; curiosity over, 48; need of betterment seen, 191; use of considered a sign of pride, 661; more rapid conveyances not expected, 741.

See also "Pioneer Life of Caucasians."

White Raccoon, mentioned, 835.

Whitesborough, N. Y., 780, 781.

White River, 436, 651.

White Water River, 651.

Whitman, Marcus, missionary, 1199, 1216, 1218, 1219, 1226, 1227, 1229, 1230, 1231, 1232.

Whitney, Asa, advocate of Pacific railroad, 1325, 1328, 1329, 1331, 1333, 1335, 1336, 1369.

INDEX